SOUTH CAROLINA
DEED ABSTRACTS 1719-1772

VOL. II

1740 - 1755, Books V — P-P

Abstracted by

Clara A. Langley

Southern Historical Press, Inc.
Greenville, South Carolina

SOUTHERN HISTORICAL PRESS, INC.
PO BOX 1267
Greenville, SC   29601

ISBN #0-89308-272-4

Printed in the United States of America

To

AGNES LELAND BALDWIN

whose dedicated efforts have made the
sources for South Carolina History and
Genealogy widely available to persons doing
South Carolina Research

SOUTH CAROLINA
COUNTY OUTLINE MAP

GAFFNEY
PICKENS
SPARTANBURG
YORK
WALHALLA
GREENVILLE
UNION
CHESTER
LANCASTER
CHESTERFIELD
BENNETTSVILLE
ANDERSON
LAURENS
WINNSBORO
DILLON
NEWBERRY
CAMDEN
DARLINGTON
MARION
ABBEVILLE
GREENWOOD
SALUDA
COLUMBIA
BISHOPVILLE
FLORENCE
McCORMICK
LEXINGTON
SUMTER
CONWAY
EDGEFIELD
ST. MATTHEWS
MANNING
KINGSTREE
AIKEN
ORANGEBURG
GEORGETOWN
BARNWELL
BAMBERG
MONCKS CORNER
ALLENDALE
ST. GEORGE
WALTERBORO
HAMPTON
CHARLESTON
RIDGELAND
BEAUFORT

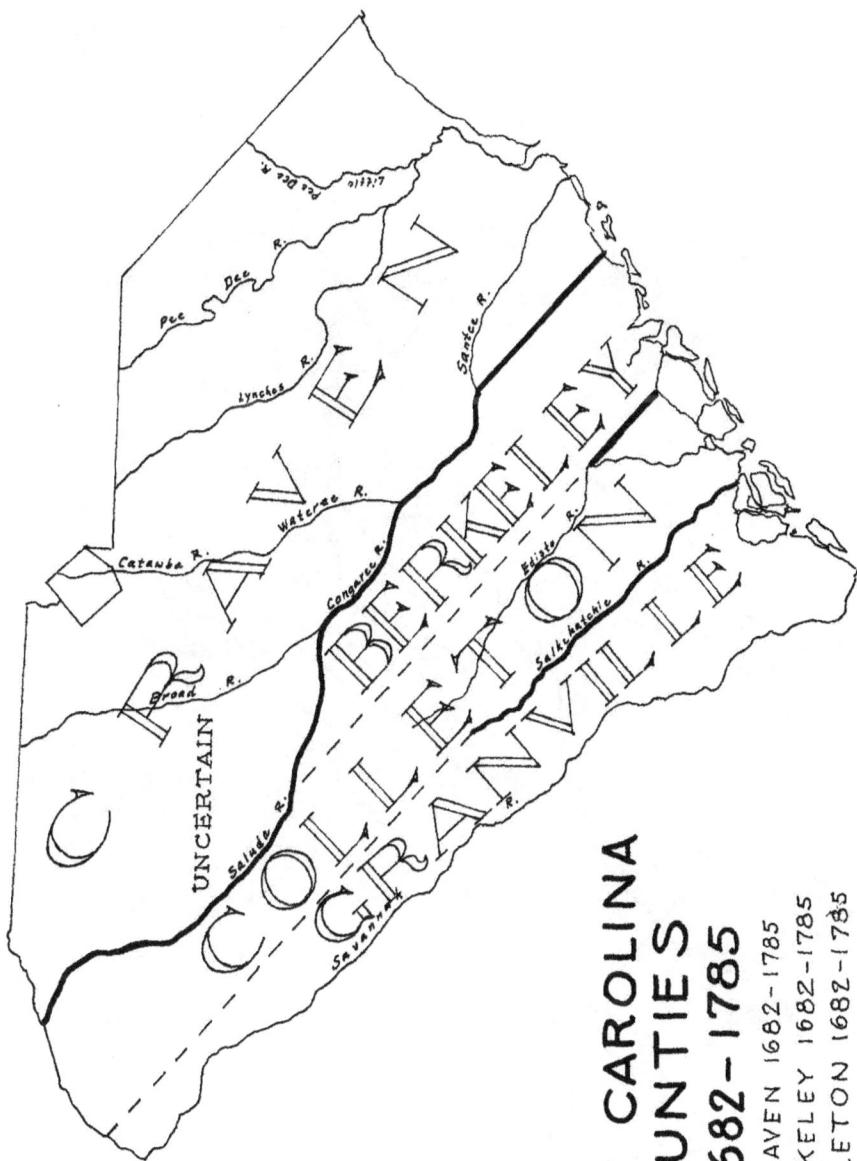

SOUTH CAROLINA
COUNTIES
1682-1785

CRAVEN 1682-1785
BERKELEY 1682-1785
COLLETON 1682-1785
GRANVILLE 1710-1785

SOUTH CAROLINA
PARISHES

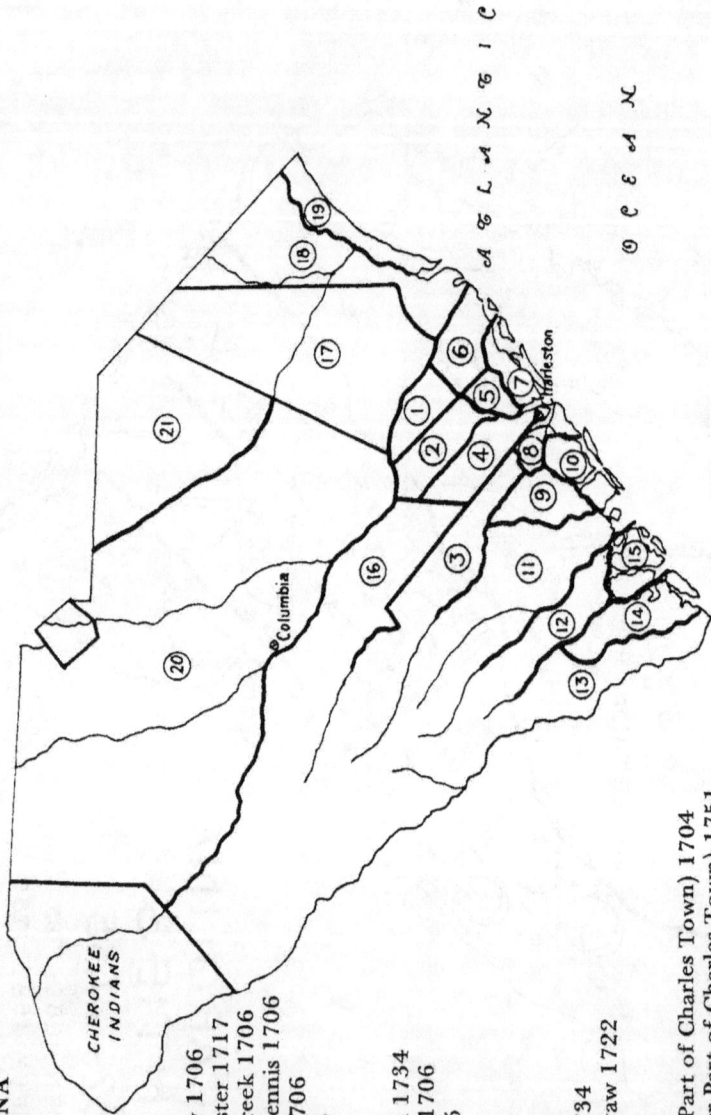

KEY

1. St. Stephen's 1754
2. St. John's, Berkeley 1706
3. St. George, Dorchester 1717
4. St. James, Goose Creek 1706
5. St. Thomas & St. Dennis 1706
6. St. James, Santee 1706
7. Christ Church 1706
8. St. Andrews 1706
9. St. Paul 1706
10. St. John's, Colleton 1734
11. St. Bartholomew's 1706
12. Prince William 1745
13. St. Peter's 1747
14. St. Luke's 1767
15. St. Helena 1712
16. St. Matthew's 1768
17. Prince Frederick 1734
18. Prince George Winyaw 1722
19. All Saints 1767
20. St. Mark's 1757

St. Philip's (Upper Part of Charles Town) 1704
St. Michael's (Lower Part of Charles Town) 1751

BY ELMER ORIS PARKER

CHEROKEE INDIANS

Columbia

Charleston

ATLANTIC

OCEAN

INTRODUCTION

Before 1790, land transactions for the entire State of South Carolina were recorded in Charleston. Many of these records are now in the custody of the Charleston County Register of Mesne Conveyance. Between 1936 and 1938 the Works Progress Administration employed Miss Clara A. Langley to prepare abstracts of the earliest seventy-four volumes of conveyances and miscellaneous records that remained in Charleston, and these abstracts are being published here for the first time. Proprietary land records and all Royal grants had earlier been transferred to Columbia, and were not abstracted.

These four volumes of deeds consist largely of abstracts of conveyances or transfers of title to land that had earlier been granted. Conveyances during the Royal period ususally took the form of a "lease and release." Under English law, for an unrestricted conveyance to be made, a buyer had to have possession of a piece of land as a lessor. A separate "lease" for a nominal amount gave him tenancy rights for up to a year. He became eligible to claim possession one day following execution of the lease and thus became entitled to obtain a "release" that gave him absolute and unqualified ownership. These "L. & R." documents contain essentially the same information, and each set was accordingly abstracted as though it were a single record.

Volumes of conveyances were ordinarily used to record only "mesne" or intermediate conveyances. The volumes of "miscellaneous records" that are intermixed in series with them contain any document that a colonist was willing to pay to have registered. Most commonly, these are mortgages and assignments of mortgages, bonds and counterbonds, bills of sale, powers of attorney and revocations of powers of attorney, and apprenticeship agreements. Some other types include bills of exchange, judgments, receipts, petitions, contracts, and purchases of freedom.

The abstracts of all of these records attempt to give every name, relationship, profession, and place mentioned. Only the wording common to every record type was intentionally omitted. Most of this information is accessible only through the indexes prepared for this publication. The names of lessors and lessees was published in 1977 by the Southern Historical Press in *Index to*

Deeds of the Province and State of South Carolina, 1719-1785, and Charleston District, 1785-1800, but this volume did not include the names of adjacent property owners, plantations, and creeks or other information such as professions and Indian names. All of this information has been conscientiously indexed by the indexing staff of Southern Historical Press, and it will be of great assistance in the preparation of local histories and family histories.

Each volume of the records abstracted carries a separate letter designation. The first set was lettered A through Z. The letter B was used twice and so was made B and B-2 (or Ba and Bb). Next, the double letters AA-ZZ were used, and afterwards the letters A through Z again with a 3 added (A3-Z3). The letters U and JJ appear to have been omitted.

Deeds were recorded in roughly chronological order, but some were recorded many years after they were written. For nearly all of the period covered, Charleston was the only place in the Province where deeds could be recorded, and colonists who lived elsewhere had to apply for registration there. Some deeds were never recorded, particularly during the transition from Proprietary to Royal government (1719-1731) and during the period of the American Revolution.

The great majority of conveyances were recorded, though, and they are a tremendously important source of information about most of the 18th Century residents of South Carolina. With no Pre-Revolutionary census and with nearly all early tax records missing, these deeds are the most inclusive set of records available, and they contain the only mention of many individuals in the surviving public records. Only grants and wills are of comparable importance. Very often, a place of residence can be ascertained for an individual and with this knowledge a researcher can turn to local records such as church registers for additional information.

Title searchers who need to exhaust every possibility should consult not only conveyances, grants, and wills, but also collections of plats and memorials in the State Archives. Other significant collections of land records are in the South Caroliniana Library in Columbia and in the Register of Mesne Conveyance and the South Carolina Historical Society in Charleston. For legal purposes, the earliest surviving copies of all of these records should be consulted to minimize the possibility of a transcription error. In the case of the W.P.A. abstracts, Miss Langley first made notes; these were neatly copied in longhand (the second generation copy of the names); the longhand copy was typed with a cloth ribbon and was too indistinct to be reproduced (the third generation copy). All of the information had to be retyped for this publication, which is four generations removed from the certified copies, which themselves were not originals. The typist who prepared the final typescript, Mrs. Pearl Baker, consulted Miss Langley's initial notes whenever questions arose and typed from the handwritten abstracts for the final volumes of deeds that had not previously been typed. She did everything feasible to ensure the accuracy of each entry.

Ideally, the final typescript should have been compared with the copies given to each property owner, but most of these originals have not survived, and even the ones in public collections are widely scattered. The certified copies in the Register of Mesne Conveyance would have been an adequate substitute, but many of them have deteriorated greatly in nearly a half century, and a careful comparison would have required thousands of hours and would have had to be done by a volunteer experienced in reading 18th Century handwriting and knowledgeable of South Carolina names. This too proved unfeasible. As a whole, the present publication is an amazingly accurate version that is far more useful than the official records themselves because they are much less thoroughly indexed.

Moreover, the publication of these records fills a major gap for genealogists and historians. Even individuals of the Proprietary Period were better known because of Agnes Leland Baldwin's *First Settlers of South Carolina, 1670-1680* and A.S. Sally, Jr.'s *Warrants for Land in South Carolina, 1672-1711*. Mrs. Baldwin's work has been expanded to include every known reference to every individual who settled in South Carolina before 1700, and the publication of this research will be forthcoming. After the Revolution, the Census of 1790 and subsequent national censuses have most Americans represented. It was for the period of Royal Government that we knew the least about South Carolinians, and now Mrs. Baldwin has helped to fill this gap by initiating this publication and by seeing it through.

Gene Waddell,
Director
South Carolina Historical Society

CONTENTS

Book V, p. 1   JOHN PAGE, planter, to CHARLES PERONNEAU & Co.,
23 & 24 May 1740   merchants, all of Colleton Co., for Ł 500 cur-
L & R by Mortgage   rency, 432 a. in Colleton Co., bounding E on a
                      creek out of Tooboodoo Creek; N on Tooboodoo
Creek; S & W on WILLIAM EDINGS. Date of redemption: 1 Jan. 1740. Wit-
nesses: SAMUEL PERONNEAU, SAMUEL WENBORN. Before JACOB MOTTE, J.P. ROB-
ERT AUSTIN, Register.

Book V, p. 4   CHARLES PINCKNEY, ESQ., & ELIZABETH his wife,
20 & 21 June 1740   of Charleston, to the Rev. MR. TIMOTHY MILLE-
L & R   CHAMP, Rector of Parish of St. James, Goose
                      Creek, in trust for the Parish, for Ł 1200
currency, 300 a., being the N part of 548 a.; bounding W on Goose Creek;
SW on the Parish Glebe land & churchyard; N on ARTHUR MIDDLETON, ESQ. &
the parsonage land; E on other part of 548 a. Whereas CHARLES PINCKNEY
by L & R dated 5 & 6 May 1735; 548 a. in Parish of St. James Goose Creek,
bounding W on Goose Creek; SW on Glebe land & 2 a. containing the Church
& churchyard; S on COL. JOHN HERBERT; N on ARTHUR MIDDLETON, ESQ.; E on
JAMES GOODBEE & other lands; & whereas several of the principal inhabitants desired to purchase land to make an addition to the Glebe & for the
use of a school to be erected & established, & contributed several large
sums of money, the land so purchased to be conveyed to the Rector & his
successors; now they purchase 300 a. from PINCKNEY. Witnesses: SUSANNA
GREGORY, HENRY GIBBES, DAVID STOUT (clerk to CHARLES PINCKNEY). Before
WILLIAM TREWIN, J.P. ROBERT AUSTIN, Pub. Reg.

Book V, p. 10   ULISSE ANTHONY ALBERGOTTI (ULESE ANTHONY ALBER-
28 & 29 Jan. 1739   GOTTY), gentleman, to RICHARD HAZZARD, planter,
L & R   both of Granville Co., for Ł 1600 SC money, 3
                      tracts, total 800 a.; 2 tracts having grants,
1 laid out by warrant. Whereas by 2 letters patent, 1 dated 13 Mar. 1735,
the other 3 Feb. 1737/8, 1 signed by the Hon. THOMAS BROUGHTON, ESQ., the
other by Lt. Gov. WILLIAM BULL, 2 tracts of land in Granville Co. were
granted to said ALBERGOTTI; 1 tract being 550 a. (part of land reserved
for Town of Purysburgh) bounding N on WILLIAM ROBERTS; the other being
50 a. bounding W on ALBERGOTTI & JOHN ROBERTS; N on vacant land; other
sides on marshes of Oketty Creek; also 200 a. (not yet granted) laid out
by warrant dated 23 Sept. 1736 from Lt. Gov. THOMAS BROUGHTON, to JAMES
ST. JOHN, Sur. Gen. (plat dated 15 June 1737), bounding E on Oketty Creek
& vacant land; N on vacant land; W on WILLIAM ROBERTS: S & N lines of
lands of Purysburgh. Witnesses: JOSEPH EDWARD FLOWER, EDWARD WIGG, HILL
WIGG. Before THOMAS WIGG, J.P. ROBERT AUSTIN, Register. ALBERGOTTI
also sells to HAZZARD 4 Negro men, 4 Negro women, 1 clock, 4 axes, 8 hoes,
1 grindstone, 2 mills, 4 mortars, 13 head cattle, 36 hogs.

Book V, p. 15   RICHARD MALONE, planter, of Winyaw, Prince
29 & 30 Nov. 1737   George Parish, Craven Co., to ALEIMUS GAILLARD,
L & R   planter, of Craven Co., for Ł 2000 currency,
                      500 a. in Craven Co., an inland tract, granted
6 Aug. 1735 to JOHN GOUGH, JR.; bounding W on WILLIAM SHACKELFORD; S on
JOHN LANE; E & N on vacant land. Witnesses: WILLIAM SHACKELFORD, ESTER
SHACKELFORD, THOMAS WISE. Before WILLIAM WHITESIDE, J.P. ROBERT AUSTIN,
Register.

Book V, p. 18   ALCIMUS GAILLARD, planter, & SARAH his wife,
20 June 1740   to CHARLES BENOIST, planter, all of Craven Co.,
L & R   for Ł 1050 SC money, 500 a. in Craven Co.,
                      bounding W on WILLIAM SHACKELFORD; S on JOHN
LANE; E & N on vacant land. Witnesses: JAMES BELIN, WILLIAM BELIN, ALL-
ARD BELIN. Before THOMAS HENNING, J.P. ROBERT AUSTIN, Register.

Book V, p. 22   DAVID HEXT, gentleman, & ANNE his wife, of
17 & 18 July 1740   Charleston, to DAVID ALLAN, planter, of Craven
L & R   Co., for Ł 75 SC money, 750 a. in Craven Co.,
                      granted to HEXT by letters patent dated 5 July
1740, signed by Lt. Gov. WILLIAM BULL; bounding SE on PHINEAS SPRY; NW on

1

vacant land; NE on vacant land & an impassable swamp. Witnesses: HENRY
SHERIFF, JOSEPH MURRAY. Before HENRY GIBBES, J.P. ROBERT AUSTIN, Register.

Book V, p. 26   ANNIBEL BAGEN, (formerly ANNIBEL STEVENSON)
12 & 13 Aug. 1740   widow, to ROYAL SPRY, planter, both of St.
L & R   Paul's Parish, Colleton Co., for L 1000 cur-
                                rency, 300 a. in St. Paul's Parish, bounding S
on JAMES BASFORD; N, E, & W on BRYAN BYLEY & heirs of WILLIAM WILLIAMSON.
Witnesses: JAMES GREEME, JAMES DRUMMOND. Before ROBERT AUSTIN, J.P. &
Register.

Book V, p. 29   JOHN (his mark) ROBERTSON to ALEXANDER NISBETT,
26 & 27 May 1740   for L 1000 currency, 400 a. in Williamsburgh
L & R by Mortgage   Township, Craven Co., granted to ROBERTSON 10
                                April 1730 by the Hon. WILLIAM BULL, Pres.;
bounding NE & SE on MARY MUCKLE ROY (MCELROY?); SW on the Rev. MR. STUART;
NW on vacant land. Date of redemption: 17 July 1741. Witnesses: WILLIAM
OSWALD, CHARLES LYON. Before JAMES MICHIE, J.P. ROBERT AUSTIN, Register.

Book V, p. 31   WILLIAM PARTRIDGE, planter, (1 of the sons of
2 Sept. 1740   NATHANIEL PARTRIDGE, gentleman, & of ANN PAR-
Deed of Sale   TRIDGE, widow of NATHANIEL) & SUSANNA his wife,
                                of Berkeley Co., to BENJAMIN SAVAGE, merchant,
of Charleston, for L 1469 SC money; part of lot #73 measuring 52 ft. 4 in.
on S side of Tradd Street, Charleston, bounding W 100 ft. on JOHN FRASER;
S 52 ft. 4 in. on THOMAS CAPERS; E 99 ft. on GARRET VAN VELSEN. Whereas
NATHANIEL PARTRIDGE owned the above part of lot #73 which by will dated
28 Apr. 1722, he devised to his son, WILLIAM, provided his wife ANNE
should have full & free use of 1/3 part for her natural life; & whereas
WILLIAM has come of age, & ANNE by deed of assignment dated 30 Aug. 1740
renounced her dower; now WILLIAM sells to SAVAGE. Witnesses: BENJAMIN
SINGLETON, ROBERT ADAMS. Before THOMAS LAMBOLL, J.P. ROBERT AUSTIN,
Register.

Book V, p. 35   JOHN DUBOSE, planter, & MARY his wife, to
30 & 31 Aug. 1738   ELIAS JAUDON, planter, all of Winyaw, Craven
L & R   Co., for L 1100 currency, 500 a. in Prince
                                Fredericks Parish, Winyaw, Craven Co., on Daho
Lake, on N side Santee River; bounding S on vacant land; E & N on land
purchased by SAMUEL PRIOLEAU, ESQ., of Charleston; W on Glebe land of St.
James Santee Parish, opposite to DASSENS. Witnesses: JAMES ROBERTS,
JAMES HAWKINS, JOHN LEGER. Before THOMAS LAROCHE, J.P. ROBERT AUSTIN,
Register.

Book V, p. 38   THOMAS FERGUSON, planter, & ANN his wife, to
5 & 6 Feb. 1734   ALEXANDER MCKELVEY, planter, all of Berkeley
L & R   Co., for L 400 currency, 330 a. in Berkeley
                                Co., within land, bounding N on RICHARD BALL;
E on ARTHUR MIDDLETON, ESQ.; S on JAMES LEBAS, ESQ.; W on MICHAEL CLENCH.
Witnesses: PAUL DE ST. JULIEN, SAMSON BALL. Before JAMES LEBAS, J.P.
ROBERT AUSTIN, Register.

Book V, p. 42   JAMES ROBERT, planter, of Craven Co., to ISAAC
31 Aug. & 1 Sept. 1737   MAZYCK, merchant, of Charleston, for L 865 SC
L & R by Mortgage   money, 600 a. in Craven Co. originally granted
                                to JOHN BROWN who conveyed to JAMES ROBERT; on
Peedee River, which runs through the middle of the tract; bounding SE on
CAPT. THOMAS HENNING; NW on WILLIAM BROWN; SW & NE on vacant land. Date
of redemption 1 Sept. 1738. Witnesses: EDWARD HORN FORREST, DAVID DELE-
SCURE, BENJAMIN MAZYCK. Before PETER DE ST. JULIEN, J.P. ROBERT AUSTIN,
Register.

Book V, p. 46   JOHN (his mark) WESTCOAT, (WASCOAT), planter,
1 & 2 Sept. 1739   of Craven Co., to WILLIAM RUMSEY (ROMSEY),
L & R   merchant, of Georgetown, for L 813 currency,
                                500 a. in Craven Co., bounding SE on MR. SMITH;
NW on vacant & other land; NE on Peedee River; which tract was granted
WESTCOAT on 4 Dec. 1735 by Lt. Gov. THOMAS BROUGHTON. Witnesses: WILLIAM
POOLE, JOSEPH (his mark) WESTCOAT, ABIGAIL (her mark) MILLER. Before

2

THOMAS HENNING, J.P. ROBERT AUSTIN, Register.

Book V, p. 49   WILLIAM WILKINS, planter, & SARAH his wife, of
1 Mar. 1738   St. Andrews Parish, James Island, Berkeley Co.,
Deed of Sale   to HENRY BEDON, shopkeeper, of Charleston, for
                             Ł 200 currency, 6 a. of marsh & land called
Fogg Island, adjacent to James Island bounding N S & W on marsh belonging
to WILLIAM & SARAH WILKLNS; E on Ashley River; which Fogg Island was purchased from ROBERT GUY. Witnesses: SARAH STONE, GEORGE BEDON. Before
ROBERT AUSTIN, J.P. & Register.

Book V, p. 52   JOHN DEXTER & SUSANNAH his wife, to THOMAS
27 Aug. 1740   HENNING, merchant, all of Georgetown, Winyaw,
Deed of Sale   Craven Co., for Ł 605 currency, lot #62 front-
                             ing NE 100 ft. on Prince Street; SE 217.9 ft.
on lot #63; SW on lots 27 & 28; NW on lot #61. Whereas by L & R dated 14
& 15 Jan. 1734 ELISHA SCRIVEN & HANNAH, his wife, sold GEORGE PAWLEY,
WILLIAM SEINTON, & DANIEL LAROCHE, trustees, 274-1/2 a. at Sampit, Prince
George Parish, Winyaw, bounding SW on Georgetown River; other sides on
ELISHA SCRIVEN; & whereas said trustees on 29 June 1736 conveyed to THOM-
AS BOLEM, vintner, lot #62; & whereas BOLEM, by will dated 2 July 1737
bequeathed to his loving wife, SUSANNA BOLEM (now SUSANNAH DEXTER) the
lot·#62; now, in pursuance of BOLEM'S will, they sell the lot to HENNING.
Witnesses: JOHN BARKSDALE, JOHN DAVIS. Before WILLIAM ROMSEY (RUMSEY),
J.P. ROBERT AUSTIN, Register.

Book V, p. 54   JAMES ROBERT, planter, & SARAH his wife, of
23 & 24 Jan. 1738   Prince Fredericks Parish, to NOAH SERRE, ESQ.,
L & R   of St. James Santee, Craven Co., for Ł 232 cur-
                             rency; 230 a. on N side Santee River, Craven
Co., part of 1400 a. granted on 24 May 1734 to ANDREW REMBERT planter, of
St. James Santee; bounding S on River Swamp; W on vacant land; N on JAMES
ROBERT; E on DAVID BALDY. Witnesses: DANIEL HORRY, JAMES SAVINEAU, JOHN
HOLMES. Before ANTHONY BONNEAU, J.P. ROBERT AUSTIN, Register.

Book V, p. 58   ANDREW REMBERT, planter, to JAMES ROBERT,
23 & 24 Dec. 1734   planter, both of Craven Co., for Ł 1000 SC mon-
L & R   ey, 1400 a. in Craven Co., on N side Santee
                             River, bounding W partly on JAMES KINLOCH; &
partly on PAUL MAZYCK, then intended for ANDREW DE LAVILLETTE which is
the reason why it was so called in the plat & grant; S on PAUL BRUNEAU &
JAMES KINLOCH; E on JOHN BARNET; N on vacant land. Witnesses: JOSEPH
BUGNION, ARCHIBALD HAMILTON, PETER LIEUBREY (LEUEBREY). NOAH SERRE, J.P.
"The 28 June 1735 I sold 500 a. of land part of the within mentioned
1400 a. to MR. DAVID BALDY by lease & release pr. JAMES ROBERT." "The
15th Feb. 1737/8 I sold 230 a. of land to MR. NOAH SERRE being part of
the remaining 900 a. within mentioned & sold at publick vandue pr. JAMES
ROBERT." ROBERT AUSTIN, Register.

Book V, p. 61   JAMES ROBERT, gentleman, & SARAH his wife, to
18 & 19 Aug. 1740   PETER LIEUBREY, planter, all of Craven Co.,
L & R   Winyaw, for Ł 500 SC money, 310 a. in Prince
                             George Parish, bounding NE on HENRY DURANT,
all other sides on JAMES ROBERT, as by grant dated 18 July 1740. LEWIS
PALMARIN, D. BALDY ALRAN. Before WILLIAM ROMSEY, J.P. ROBERT AUSTIN,
Register.

Book V, p. 64   JAMES ROBERT, gentleman, & SARAH his wife, to
14 & 15 May 1740   PETER LEIUBREY, vintner, all of Craven Co.,
L & R   for Ł 1500 SC money, 670 a. in Craven Co.,
                             bounding S on NOAH BALDY; E on DAVID BALDY; W
on ABRAHAM MICHAUX; other sides on vacant land; which tract was granted
to ANDREW REMBERT, who sold to JAMES ROBERT. Witnesses: LEWIS PALMARIN,
D. BALDY, & ALRAN. Before WILLIAM ROMSEY, J.P. ROBERT AUSTIN, Register.

Book V, p. 67   SOLOMON LEGAREE, SR., goldsmith, of Charleston,
27 Aug. 1740   to his beloved son, SOLOMON LEGAREE, JR., tan-
Deed of Gift   ner & currier, also of Charleston, for natural
                             love & affection, 2 lots in Charleston #224 &
264 bounding N on Tradd Street; W on a street leading from Tradd Street

3

to the White Point; E on widow HOLMES & estate of THOMAS HOLTON; S on
PETER SHAW. Lot #264 is that of which the said SOLOMON LEGAREE nos pos-
sesses the 1/2 where his dwelling house & garden are & fronts N on Tradd
Street; E on widow HOLMES; W on street leading from Tradd Street to White
Point; S on lot #224. SOLOMON LEGAREE, SR., during his natural life, to
occupy the W half of lot #264 where his dwelling house, garden, etc., are.
Witnesses: RICHARD MASON, JOHN LAURENS (saddler). Before HENRY GIBBES,
J.P. ROBERT AUSTIN, Register.

Book V, p. 69   WILLIAM COLT, planter & REBECCA ANN his wife,
28 & 29 Aug. 1740   of Craven Co., to JOHN CLELAND & WILLIAM WAL-
L & R by Mortgage   LACE, merchants, of Charleston, as security on
                       bond of even date in penal sum of Ł 2167:15:4
for payment of Ł 1083:17:8 currency, with interest, on 1 Jan. 1740; 900 a.
on Black River in Craven Co., bounding N on THOMAS MORITT & the river; E
on JOHN WHITE; S on CALEB AVANT & Green's Creek; which tract was granted
on 24 May 1734 to COLT by Gov. ROBERT JOHNSON (recorded 8 July 1734).
Witnesses: ALEXANDER MURRAY, ARCHIBALD BAIRD. Before JACOB MOTTE, J.P.
ROBERT AUSTIN, Register.

Book V, p. 73   PETER LANE, planter, of Craven Co., to ISAAC
7 & 8 Feb. 1737   MAZYCK, merchant, of Charleston, for Ł 1000 SC
L & R by Mortgage   money, 482 a. on Black River in Craven Co.,
                       bounding W on DANIEL & THOMAS LAROCHE & vacant
land; S on vacant land; E & N on NOAH SERRÉ & the Barony. Date of redemption, 8 Feb. 1739. Witnesses: ALEXANDER GRAMAHEE, PAUL MAZYCK, BENJAMIN
MAZYCK. Before JOHN DART, J.P. ROBERT AUSTIN, Register.

Book V, p. 76   SAMUEL SMITH, carpenter, to ROBERT HARVEY,
20 Dec. 1739   carpenter, both of Charleston, for Ł 275 cur-
Bill of Sale   rency, part of lot #222 in Charleston, bound-
                       ing E 35 ft. on King Street; W on Widow HOLMES;
N 140 ft. on JOHN DANIELS; S on MR. ROBERTS. Witnesses: DAVID BURNEY,
ANN DEXTER, ANNA MIDDLETON, WILLIAM SMITH. Before ROBERT AUSTIN, J.P. &
Pub. Reg.

Book V, p. 77   ROBERT HARVEY, carpenter, & MARY his wife, of
22 & 23 Oct. 1740   St. Philip's Parish, Charleston, to WILLIAM
L & R   HARRIS, of same place, for Ł 230, part of lot
                       #222 in Charleston on "the green," fronting E
17-1/2 ft. on King Street; bounding S 140 ft. on SAMUEL SMITH, JR., carpenter; W on Widow HOLMES'S garden; N on JOHN DANIEL'S tenement. Witnesses: BENJAMIN ROBERTS, JAMES HILLIARD. Before ROBERT AUSTIN, J.P. &
Pub. Reg.

Book V, p. 81   GEORGE LUCAS, gentleman, formerly of Island of
29 Aug. 1739   Antigua, now of SC, to OTHNIEL BEALE, merchant,
Bond & Mortgage   of Charleston, as security on bond of even
                       date in penal sum of Ł 9740 for payment of
Ł 4870 currency, with interest, on 1 Nov. 1739; (1 Aug. 1741?); 1500 a.
in Colleton Co., bounding SW on Saltcatcher River; NW on OTHNIEL BEALE;
NE on land which was vacant in Sept. 1733; SW on WILLIAM RHETT, JR. Wit-
nesses: WILLIAM SCOTT, THOMAS COOPER. Before JACOB MOTTE, Register.
ROBERT AUSTIN, Register.

Book V, p. 84   SAMUEL BACON, planter, of St. George Parish,
21 & 22 Jan. 1735   Berkeley Co., to ISAAC HOLMES, merchant, of
L & R   Charleston, for Ł 80 SC money, a 1/2 a. lot
                       English measure in Dorchester Township, part
of a 50 a. lot, near STEVENS or Bacons Bridge over Ashley River, bounding
from an old oak stump W on the High Road; S about 1 chain from Ashley
River & the bridge, & N & E on other lands of SAMUEL BACON; HOLMES &
others to have free ingress & egress to river for loading & unloading.
Witnesses: THOMAS MILES, SR., PETER GOULDING. Before ROBERT WRIGHT, J.P.
ROBERT AUSTIN, Register.

Book V, p. 87   JOHN ABBOT, merchant, formerly of Georgetown,
6 & 7 July 1739   SC, by his attorneys DANIEL & THOMAS LAROCHE,
L & R   merchants of Georgetown, to JOSEPH SHUTE, mer-
                       chant, of Charleston, for Ł 900 SC money,

4

430 a. in Craven Co., bounding E on the sea; S (?) on Little River; W on
NICHOLAS TRINK. On 20 Mar. 1737 ABBOT appointed DANIEL & THOMAS LAROCHE
his attorneys to dispose of all his real estate in SC. Witnesses: JAMES
CRADDOCK, NATHANIEL TREGAGLE. Before THOMAS HENNING, J.P. ROBERT AUSTIN,
Register.

Book V, p. 90   DAVID ARNETT, planter, of Christ Church Parish,
24 & 25 May 1740   Berkeley Co., to ROBERT AUSTIN, ESQ., for
L & R by Mortgage   Ⴑ 707:15 currency, 400 a. in Christ Church Par-
                                   ish, bounding N on JAMES PAINE; E on the sea;
S on THOMAS BARKSDALE; W on RICHARD FOWLER. Date of redemption: 1 Nov.
next. Witnesses: WILLIAM BANBURY, RICHARD PHILLIPS. Before HENRY GIBBES,
J.P. ROBERT AUSTIN, Register. AUSTIN declared mortgage satisfied. No
date given.

Book V, p. 94   JOHN GOODBE, planter, & HANNAH his wife, to
12 & 13 Sept. 1740   GEORGE MARSHALL & Co., merchants, all of Berke-
L & R   ley Co., for Ⴑ 600 SC money, 450 a. on N side
                                   Edisto River, St. Georges Parish, in Berkeley
Co., granted 5 Feb. 1739 by letters patent signed by the Hon. WILLIAM
BULL, Pres., to JOHN GOODBE; bounding NW on MRS. FRANCIS LONGUEMAR; NE &
S on land laid out & vacant land; SW on vacant land. Witnesses: NATHAN-
IEL SNOW, CAPT. JAMES MOORE. Before WILLIAM SANDERS, J.P. ROBERT AUSTIN,
Register.

Book V, p. 97   WILLIAM SNOW, planter, of Craven Co., to ALEX-
15 & 16 Feb. 1737   ANDER NISBETT, as security on bond of even
L & R by Mortgage   date in penal sum of Ⴑ 548 for payment of
                                   Ⴑ 274 sterling British on 1 Dec. 1730; 1800 a.
in Craven Co., bounding SW on JAMES MOORE; NW on Widow HILL; SE on vacant
land; E on ALEXANDER NISBETT & vacant land. Witnesses: JAMES MCCLELLAN,
THOMAS MCCLELLAN, JAMES DRUMMOND. Before JAMES GREEME, J.P. ROBERT AUS-
TIN, Register.

Book V, p. 100   ALEXANDER (his mark) SMITH, tailor, to JOHN
7 & 8 May 1740   FRASER, gentleman, both of Charleston. Where-
L & R by Mortgage   as SMITH gave FRASER a bond dated 20 Sept.
                                   1735 in penal sum of Ⴑ 6000 for payment of
Ⴑ 3000 currency on 20 Sept. 1736; & whereas SMITH, with ROBERT DUCATT &
JOHN SMITH, gentlemen, of Charleston gave FRASER a bond dated 8 Aug. 1738
in penal sum of Ⴑ 200 for payment of Ⴑ 100 currency on 8 Feb. next; &
whereas SMITH, with JOHN SEABROOK, gentleman, gave FRASER a bond dated 5
May 1740 in penal sum of Ⴑ 800 for payment of Ⴑ 400 currency on 3 May
next; now, for security, SMITH conveys to FRASER lot #190 bounding N on
RICHARD MASON; S 60 ft. on Tradd Street; W 170 ft. on RICHARD MASON; E on
WILLIAM FAIRCHILD (son of RICHARD FAIRCHILD). Witnesses: JOHN RATTRAY,
JOHN JOHNSON. Before ROBERT AUSTIN, J.P. & Register. On 10 Sept. 1744
FRASER assigned mortgage to THOMAS FARR.

Book V, p. 104   DAVID BALDY, planter, to DANIEL LAROCHE &
5 & 6 Nov. 1740   THOMAS LAROCHE, merchants, all of Craven Co.,
L & R   for Ⴑ 250 currency, 500 a. in Craven Co., part
                                   of 1400 a. which JAMES ROBERTS purchased from
ANDREW REMBERT, on Cedar Creek; the 500 a. taken from the E side of the
original tract, from the S line down to the N line containing 143 chains
60 links in length & 34 chains 50 links in breadth from MR. BARNETT'S W
line goine W in said tract of 1400 a.; bounding E on land sold to MOSES
DUTARTRE by JOHN BARNETT; S on JAMES KINLOCH; W on remainder of 1400 a.
tract (formerly JAMES ROBERT); N on vacant land; E on LEWIS PALMERIN.
Witnesses: ANDREW DELAVILLETTE, WILLIAM SMITH. Before THOMAS HENNING,
J.P. ROBERT AUSTIN, Register.

Book V, p. 107   ABRAHAM SANDERS, planter, & MARGARET his wife,
20 & 21 Oct. 1740   of Berkeley Co., to ADAM LEWIS, chapman, for
L & R   Ⴑ 850 SC money, 576 a. in Berkeley Co., grant-
                                   ed LAMBERT SANDERS by the Lords Proprs. by
letters patent, dated 5 Feb. 1704, signed by the Hon. NATHANIEL JOHNSON,
JAMES MOORE, NICHOLAS TROTT & JOB HOWE; bounding E on HENRY RUSSELL,
other sides on vacant land. Witnesses: JAMES RICHEBOURG, ABRAHAM SANDERS,
JR., THEODORE CHASTAIGNIER. Before WILLIAM SANDERS, J.P. ROBERT AUSTIN,

Register.

Book V, p. 110 JONATHAN SKRINE, vintner, of Georgetown, Win-
21 & 22 Nov. 1740 yaw, to THOMAS HENNING, merchant, as security
L & R by Mortgage for 3 bonds in penal sum of Ł 1120 for payment
of Ł 560 currency, with interest; lot #23,
containing 1/2 a., bounding SW on Front Street; SE on lot #24; NE on lot
#60; NW on lot #22. Witnesses: JOHN BARKSDALE, NATHANIEL TREGAGLE. Be-
fore WILLIAM ROMSEY, J.P. ROBERT AUSTIN, Register.

Book V, p. 112 JALE (her mark) ATTERBURY to WILLIAM M. GILLIV-
2 Aug. 1738 RAY, for good considerations, & for 5 shil-
Lease lings per year, per a., for 6 years, from date,
40 a. adjoining lands of JOHN STANYARNE & SAM-
UEL UNDERWOOD. Witnesses: ROBERT SAMS, GABRIEL NORRIS. Recepit dated 12
Aug. 1738 for Ł 5, 1 year's rent, signed by WILLIAM (his mark) DEAN, "for
use of my mother." Before ROBERT AUSTIN, J.P. & Register.

Book V, p. 113 JOHN DANIELL, planter, & SARAH his wife, of
21 & 22 Mar. 1739 Parish of St. Thomas & St. Dennis, Berkeley
L & R by Mortgage Co., to ELIZABETH JENYS, widow, of Charleston,
for Ł 6000 currency, 700 a. known as Thomas's
Island or Daniell's Island, whereon JOHN & SARAH dwell, bo-nding S & W on
WILLIAM TREWIN & CHARLES CODNER (formerly MRS. SARAH DANIEL & RICHARD
CODNER); N & W on ISAAC LESESNE & the creek back of the island; E on Wan-
do River. Date of redemption: 22 Mar. 1740. Witnesses: THOMAS JENYS,
CHARLES PINCKNEY. Before JOHN DART, J.P. ROBERT AUSTIN, Register.

Book V, p. 117 ISAAC CORDES, to FRANCIS CORDES, both of St.
6 & 7 Mar. 1738 John's Parish, Berkeley Co., for Ł 100 curren-
L & R cy, 651 a. in St. John's Parish, granted ISAAC
CORDES on 10 Apr. 1738; bounding N on CAPT.
PETER PORCHER; W on FRANCIS CORDES; SW on vacant land & THEODORE VERDITTY;
S N E & E on vacant land; S & E on JAMES LEBAS. Witnesses: CHARLES LYON,
ISAAC PORCHER, JOHN CORDES. Before ISAAC PORCHER, J.P. ROBERT AUSTIN,
Register.

Book V, p. 120 MARTHA BOOTH, widow, of ROBERT BOOTH, planter,
24 & 25 Oct. 1740 of Berkeley Co., to WILLIAM ELLIOTT, planter,
L & R of Berkeley Co., for Ł 2000 currency, 2 tracts
in St. Paul's Parish, Colleton Co., 200 a.
bounding N on THOMAS FITCH; S & W on WILLIAM WILLIAMSON; E on WILLIAM
HARVEY (formerly MANLY WILLIAMSON); also 401 a. granted ROBERT BOOTH in
1732, bounding N & NW on BRYAN RAYLY; S & SW on WILLIAM WILLIAMSON "that
was to the SE & NE on the said BOOTH'S land." Witnesses: SARAH CART-
WRIGHT, JOSHUA PEART, THOMAS ELLIOTT. Before ROBERT AUSTIN, Register.

Book V, p. 123 THOMAS ROSE, planter, & BEULAH his wife (with
15 & 16 Dec. 1740 her free consent), to THOMAS GADSDEN, ESQ.,
L & R all of Berkeley Co., for Ł 2000 currency, 2
eighth parts of a lot or lots in Charleston
bequeathed to THOMAS ROSE by his father THOMAS ROSE, planter; lying between S side of Broad Street & ELLIOTT ALLEY, bounding W on WILLIAM MC-
KENSIE, merchant & ALBERT MULLER, merchant, being 37-1/2 ft. from E to W.
Witnesses: ANNE (her mark) DAVISON, ROBERT RAPER. Before THOMAS LAMBOLL,
J.P. ROBERT AUSTIN, Register.

Book V, p. 128 THOMAS INNS, of Granville Co., to WILLIAM BULL,
10 & 11 Oct. 1735 JR., gentleman, of Charleston, for Ł 300 cur-
L & R rency, 300 a. in Granville Co., granted to
INNS on 7 June 1735, by Lt. Gov. THOMAS BROUGH-
TON, bounding NW on COL. WILLIAM BULL; other sides on marshes & creeks of
Port Royall River. Witnesses: JOSEPH BRYAN, STEPHEN BULL, JAMES GIRAR-
DEAU. Before THOMAS DRAYTON, J.P. ROBERT AUSTIN, Register.

Book V, p. 131 JOHN THORPE, gentleman, of London, by his at-
24 & 25 May 1737 orney ROBERT THORPE, ESQ., of Granville Co.,
L & R SC, to WILLIAM BULL, JR., ESQ., of Charleston,
for Ł 784 SC money, 126 a. English measure,
part of a Barony of 12,000 a. in Granville Co., commonly called the

6

Yamasees Lands; the 126 a. bounding N on COL. WILLIAM BULL; SW on COL.
WILLIAM BULL (formerly CAPT. THOMAS INNS); S & E on marsh belonging to
COL. WILLIAM BULL. Witnesses: JOHN BULL, NASSAW HASTIE, WILLIAM BULL, B.
GODIN. Before ARTHUR MIDDLETON, J.P. Plat of 126 a. on Haspaw Neck,
Granville Co., part of 12,000 a. laid out to THOMAS LOWNDES & WILLIAM
BULL by grant from Lords Proprs. dated 25 Oct. 1726. ROBERT AUSTIN, Reg-
ister.

Book V, p. 135   LAWRENCE WITHERS, peruke-maker, of St. Philips
19 & 20 Sept. 1737   Parish, Charleston, to MARY OWEN, widow, of
L & R by Mortgage   same place, for ₺ 1124:18:6 SC money, due on
                        his bond, part of lot #49 in Charleston.
Whereas on 1 Mar. 1735 JOHN BRETON, merchant, of Charleston, conveyed to
his granddaughter, ELIZABETH WITHERS, wife of LAWRENCE WITHERS, part of
lot #49 in Charleston on 2 tenements are built, 1 occupied by SUSANNA
EDDLESTONE, the other by DUNCAN CAMPBELL & ANNE his wife; fronting W on
Church Street, & bounding E on rails or fence of part of said lot occupied by THOMAS BAKER; N on PAUL DOUXSAINT; S on the alley leading from
Church Street to Union Street with the "2 tenements & all other buildings
thereon;" BRETON to hold the premises during his natural life; & whereas
LAWRENCE WITHERS, by right of his wife, owned the premises for his natural life (after BRETON'S death); & whereas WITHERS gave MARY OWEN a bond
dated 21 June 1736 in penal sum of ₺ 2000 for payment of ₺ 1000 SC money,
with interest, on a certain date; now WITHERS gives the 2 houses & lot as
security. Witnesses: JOHN JOHNSON, CLEMENT SACKVILLE. Before THOMAS
DALE, J.P. ROBERT AUSTIN, Register.

Book V, p. 138   FRANCIS LEBRASSEUR, merchant, & KATHERIN his
28 Oct. 1708   wife, to DOMINICK ARTHUR, merchant, all of
Conveyance   Charleston, for good causes & valuable consid-
                        erations, a lot on the Bay. Whereas JOHN BUCK-
LEY, merchant, of Charleston, former husband of said KATHERINE, bought
from BENJAMIN SCHENCKINGH & MARGARET, his wife, a piece of ground fronting E 56 ft. on the Bay, measuring 116 ft. S on a neighborhood alley; &
bounding W 72 ft. on DR. JOHN THOMAS; N on ISAAC MAZYCK & Landgrave JOHN
COLLETON; & whereas BUCKLEY, by will dated 27 Nov. 1706 bequeathed to his
loving wife KATHERIN the piece of ground; now KATHERINE & her present
husband convey to ARTHUR. Witnesses: JOHN GOUGH, MICHAEL MAHON. Before
the Hon. ROBERT GIBBES, C.J. of Ct. of C.P. Before JOHN WRIGHT, J.P.
ROBERT AUSTIN, Register.

Book V, p. 140   DOMINICKE ARTHUR, merchant, of Charleston, to
29 Feb. 1710   FRANCIS LEBRASSEUR, & KATHERINE his wife, for
Conveyance   good causes & valuable considerations, the lot
                        & buildings conveyed to him (p. 138) by LE-
BRASSEUR. Witnesses: JOHN GOUGH, MICHAEL MAHON. Before the Hon. SAMUEL
EVELEIGH. ROBERT AUSTIN, Register.

Book V, p. 142   ANNE LEBRASSEUR, widow of FRANCIS LEBRASSEUR,
22 & 23 Dec. 1740   gentleman, to JOHN WATSON, merchant, all of
L & R   Charleston, for ₺ 5000 SC money, paid or secur-
                        ed to be paid, part of lot #13 fronting E 56
ft. on the Bay of Charleston, bounding S 100 ft. on Elliotts Alley; W 71
ft. on lot reserved to ANNE LEBRASSEUR; N 112 ft. on JOHN COLLETON.
Whereas BARNARD SCHENCKINGH of SC owned several lots in Charleston, particularly lot #13 on the Bay; & whereas BENJAMIN SCHENCKINGH, son of said
BARNARD after his father's death, petitioned the General Assembly to confirm his title to certain lots & lands which he claimed as son & heir
(the original papers being lost, burned, wornout, or obliterated in such
manner as to be of little use to him); & whereas the General Assembly
confirmed his title to several plantations & town lots; & whereas BENJA-
MIN SCHENCKINGH & MARGARET his wife on 14 Feb. 1705 sold to JOHN BUCKLEY,
merchant, of Charleston, said part of lot #13; & whereas BUCKLEY, by will
proved before Gov. NATHANIEL JOHNSON on 28 Jan. 1706, bequeathed the
premises to his wife KATHERINE; & whereas she afterwards married FRANCIS
LEBRASSEUR & on 28 Oct. 1708 they sold to DOMINICK ARTHUR, who, on 29
Feb. 1710 reconveyed to FRANCIS & KATHERINE LEBRASSEUR; & whereas KATH-
ERINE died soon afterwards & FRANCIS LEBRASSEUR became sole owner; &
whereas, by L & R Tripartite 28 & 29 Jan. 1730 between FRANCIS LEBRASSEUR
of 1st part; THOMAS GADSDEN & JOHN KING, of Charleston, of 2nd part; &

ANNE SPLATT, widow of RICHARD SPLATT, of Charleston, of 3rd part; reciting that a marriage was contemplated between LEBRASSEUR & ANNE SPLATT &
LEBRASSEUR conveyed the premises to GADSDEN & KING, as trustees for ANNE;
& whereas the marriage took place & shortly after (on 3 Dec. 1736) LE-
BRASSEUR died at Charleston & ANNE became sole owner; now she sells the
property to JOHN WATSON. Witnesses: GABRIEL MANIGAULT, JAMES WRIGHT.
Before ROBERT AUSTIN, J.P. & Pub. Reg.

Book V, p. 149   JOHN ALLEN, gentleman, & ANN his wife, of
8 & 9 Dec. 1740   Charleston, with ANN'S free consent, to ALEX-
L & R   ANDER HEXT, planter, of Colleton Co., for
                    ₺ 2200 currency, the E end of JOHN ALLEN'S
part of lot #6 in Charleston measuring N from East Bay W along Tradd
Street 120 ft. 8 in.; bounding E 21 ft. 9 in. on East Bay; S on JAMES
MATHEWS; W on W end of ALLEN'S lot; also the shoal or water lot lying E
of the Bay & opposite the E part of lot #6; which shoal was granted AN-
DREW ALLEN, merchant, father of JOHN, on 17 Dec. 1714; the shoal measur-
ing 21 ft. x 300 ft., bounding N on land at front of said street; E on
Cooper River; S on SAMUEL HARTLEY; W on the front wall of the town. Wit-
nesses: THOMAS LAMBOLL, BENJAMIN SAVAGE, JAMES MATHEWS. Before ROBERT
AUSTIN, J.P. & Pub. Reg.

Book V, p. 159   WILLIAM SWINTON, planter, of Craven Co., to
6 Jan. 1740   ALEXANDER NISBETT, ESQ., of Berkeley Co., as
Mortgage   security on bond dated 1 Jan. 1740 in penal
                    sum of ₺ 1000 for Payment of ₺ 100 British to
NISBETT yearly & every year during the natural life of NISBETT by 2 equal
half-year payments, to wit, 1 Jan. & 1 July every year beginning 1 July
1741; several plantations; in Craven Co.; 400 a. bounding SE on Peedee
River; SW on DANIEL LAROCHE; NW on JOHN GREEN; NE on HUGH SWINTON (form-
erly STEPHEN PROCTOR); which 400 a. is part of 900 a. granted by Gov.
ROBERT JOHNSON to JAMES PAINE on 6 Apr. 1733 & conveyed by him to WILLIAM
SWINTON by L & R dated 24 & 25 July 1733; also 125 a., part of 325 a.
granted by Gov. ROBERT JOHNSON to WILLIAM SWINTON on 6 Dec. 1733, bound-
ing SE on a thoroughfare leading to Waccamaw River; NE on HUGH SWINTON;
NW on Peedee River; SW on DANIEL LAROCHE; also 500 a. bounding N on
Georgetown River; E on land not laid out; SE on ROBERT SCREVEN; W on
CAPT. GEORGE SMITH; which land was granted by Gov. ROBERT JOHNSON to WIL-
LIAM SWINTON on 23 May 1734; also 130 a. granted by THOMAS BROUGHTON,
ESQ., to WILLIAM SWINTON on 14 Feb. 1735, bounding NE on ELIAS FOISSIN;
NW on Peedee River; also 160 a. granted by THOMAS BROUGHTON, ESQ., to
DANIEL CRAWFORD on 14 Feb. 1735, & by him conveyed to WILLIAM SWINTON on
21 Feb. 1735, bounding SE on Peedee River; NW on vacant land; NE on JOHN
GLEN; SW on JOSEPH WRAGG, ESQ. Witnesses: JOHN MOULTRIE, JAMES DRUMMOND.
Before JAMES GRAME, J.P. ROBERT AUSTIN, Register.

Book V, p. 163   SARAH MCKENSIE, widow, & JOHN MCKENSIE, mer-
29 & 30 Jan. 1740   chant, of Charleston, executrix & executor of
L & R   will of WILLIAM MCKENSIE, merchant, to THOMAS
                    GADSDEN, ESQ., of Berkeley Co., for ₺ 2000 cur-
rency, part of lot #12 in Charleston, 34 ft. x 80 ft., bounding W on JAM-
ES FOWLER (formerly CHARLES HILL); S on Poinsett Street or Alley; N on
ALBERT MULLER; E on THOMAS ROSE. Whereas THOMAS CARY, ESQ., of Berkeley
Co., by deed of feoffment dated 26 Aug. 1740 (reciting that he, CARY,
owned part of lot #12, 30 ft. x 80 ft., formerly laid out to RICHARD
SEARL as it was formerly belonging to WALTER FRANCIS & afterwards es-
cheated & reverted to the Lords Proprs. by Act of Assembly), for ₺ 60
currency, conveyed to FRANCIS FIDLING part of lot #12, bounding S on an
alley leading from the Bay W by the houses of PETER POINSETT & FRANCIS
FIDLING; W on JOSEPH CROSSKEYS & CAPT. JOHN FLAVEL; N on CHARLES BURNHAM;
E on THOMAS ROSE, planter; & whereas FRANCIS FIDLING, by deed of feoffment dated 25 Apr. 1706, for ₺ 55 currency, sold to LEWIS LANSAC, merchant, that part of lot #12; & whereas JOHN GUERARD on 11 Dec. 1707, for
₺ 200 currency purchased the part of the lot & messuage standing thereon
from LEWIS LANSAC: & whereas JOHN GUERARD by will dated 21 June 1714 devised that part of lot #12 to his beloved son BENJAMIN GUERARD "as well
all that my part of the houses & part of a town lot in Charleston situate
in a street or lane leading from Cooper River W by the houses on FRANCIS
LEBRASSEUR, DR. JOHN HUTCHINSON, CAPT. THOMAS HEPWORTH" & directed that
should any of his children (BENJAMIN, DAVID, JOHN, MARTHA) die in infancy

8

that child's part should be sold, the other children being given prefer-
ence, & proceeds divided equally amongst the survivors; & whereas BENJA-
MIN died in infancy & DAVID refused to purchase, BENJAMIN GODIN, merchant,
only surviving executor of JOHN GUERARD, by L & R dated 1 & 2 Jan. 1725,
sold the part of lot for Ł 800 to BENJAMIN DELA CONSEILLERE, bounding W
on CHARLES HILL; S on the lane; N on CAPT. EDMUND PORTER; E on THOMAS
ROSE; DAVID GUERARD confifming DELA CONSEILLERE in his possession; &
whereas by L & R dated 3 & 4 Jan. 1723 DELA CONSEILLERE sold the property
to BENJAMIN GODIN for Ł 800 currency; & whereas the deeds & titles from
LANSAC to GUERARD were lost or mislaid & not to be found, SUSANNAH LANSAC,
daughter & heir of LEWIS LANSAC, on 5 Jan. 1723, confirmed GODIN in his
possession; & whereas by L & R dated 7 & 8 July 1730, BENJAMIN GODIN, for
Ł 1800 currency, sold the property to WILLIAM MCKENSIE, bounding W on
CHARLES HILL; S on lane; N on ALBERT MULLER; E on ROSE; & whereas by will
dated 4 Aug. 1738 MCKENSIE appointed his wife SARAH MCKENZIE, JOHN MC-
KENSIE & GABRIEL MANIGAULT (who refused to act) his executrix & executor,
& ordered that his lands, houses, & slaves sold to beat advantage (except
4 Negroes for his wife & children, & the house & garden on Church Street
which he bequeathed to his son THOMAS; reserving to SARAH the right to
live in it during her lifetime); now the executors sell to THOMAS GADSDEN.
Witnesses: ELIZABETH DONEN, JAMES MICHIE. Before JAMES WRIGHT, J.P.
ROBERT AUSTIN, Pub. Reg.

Book V, p. 171   WILLIAM DRY, ESQ., & REBECCA his wife, of St.
14 & 15 Mar. 1734   James Goose Creek, Berkeley Co., to WILLIAM
Confirmation of L & R   MCKENSIE, merchant, of Charleston. Whereas
                          WILLIAM & REBECCA DRY, by L & R dated 12 & 13
Mar. last, for Ł 5700 currency sold WILLIAM MCKENSIE 975 a. in St. James
Goose Creek, bounding N on estate of JOHN LLOYD (formerly ROBERT STEPHENS,
later JOHN VICARIDGE) & on COL. JAMES MOORE; S on ARTHUR MIDDLETON, ESQ.;
E on BENJAMIN SCHENCKINGH & COL. THOMAS SMITH; W on heirs of THOMAS MOORE
& PETER TAYLOR, ESQ. (formerly BENJAMIN GIBBES) as by a plat made on
parchment by JOHN BAILEY with an addition of 4 pricked lines on NE part;
2 with ink, 2 with block lead; & whereas doubts may arise in regard to
the title to 430 a. part of the 975 that is, to 300 a. within the pricked
lines on NE part which DRY purchased from JOHN MOORE, planter, & 130 a.
within the pricked lines, marked CCCC on N part, which DRY purchased from
the Lords Proprs.; now WILLIAM & REBECCA DRY confirm MCKENSIE in his possession of the 430 a. near the Quarter-House, in St. James Goose Creek,
on which WILLIAM & REBECCA DRY live, bounding N on JOSEPH HURST; W on
WILLIAM DRY; S on a creek & marsh of estate of CHARLES BURNHAM; E on a
creek & marsh fronting Cooper River. Condition: DRY to procure from
JAMES MOORE, son & heir of JOHN MOORE, planter, within 6 months after
JAMES MOORE reaches age of 21, a good title & conveyance of the 300 a.,
being the NE part of the 975 a.; & within 3 years to procure a title to
the 130 a. Witnesses: THOMAS CLIFFORD, ROBERT BREWTON, JR., CHARLES
PINCKNEY. Before ROBERT AUSTIN, J.P. & Register.

Book V, p. 178   WILLIAM DRY, ESQ., & REBECCA his wife, (lately
12 & 13 Mar. 1734   REBECCA BARKER), of St. James Goose Creek,
L & R   Berkeley Co., to WILLIAM MCKENSIE, merchant,
                         of Charleston, for Ł 5700 currency, 975 a. in
St. James Goose Creek, bounding N on estate of JOHN LLOYD, ESQ., (formerly of ROBERT STEPHENS, later of JOHN VICARIDGE) & on COL. JAMES MOORE; S
on ARTHUR MIDDLETON, ESQ.; E on BENJAMIN SCHENCKINGH, ESQ. & on COL.
THOMAS SMITH; W on THOMAS MOORE & PETER TAYLOR (formerly BENJAMIN GIBBES);
as by plat on parchment made by JOHN BAILEY with an addition of 4 pricked
lines, 2 with ink, 1 with black lead. Witnesses: THOMAS CLIFFORD, ROBERT
BREWTON, JR., CHARLES PINCKNEY. Before ROBERT AUSTIN, J.P. & Pub. Reg.
Plat represents 200 a. from BENJAMIN GIBBES; 30 a. BENJAMIN SCHENCKINGH;
130 a. formerly vacant; & part of Boochaw tract.

Book V, p. 183   THOMAS ELLIOTT, JR., planter, of St. Pauls Par-
14 Aug. 1727   ish, Colleton Co., to LUKE STOUTENBURGH, sil-
Bill of Sale   versmith, of Charleston, for Ł 265 currency,
                         the W half of lot #205. Whereas the Hon. WIL-
LIAM, Earl of Craven, Palatine, & the Lords Proprs., on 9 May 1694 granted JANE FLOWER, widow, of Berkeley Co., town lot #205 in Berkeley Co.,
containing half an a., English measure, bounding according to certificate;
& whereas she, by will dated 23 Nov. 1703, devised the lot to THOMAS

ELLIOTT, JR., party hereto; & whereas before her death JANE FLOWER sold part of the lot but it being uncertain how much or from what part of the lot the share was taken, & ELLIOTT having agreed to sell his right & title to the rest of lot, to be divided equally between LUKE STOUTENBURGH & JOHN RAVEN, gentleman, of John Island, Colleton Co., now ELLIOTT sells the W half to STOUTENBURGH. A piece of turf cut up therefrom & delivered in presence of HENRY HARGRAVE, HUGH GRANGE, MILES BREWTON. Before THOMAS COOPER, J.P. ROBERT AUSTIN, Register.

Book V, p. 185   JOHN TIPPER (TAIPOR, TIRPE), sailmaker, to
4 & 5 Feb. 1740   JOHN BEEKMAN, block maker, both of Charleston,
L & R   for ₺ 350 currency, lot #210 in Charleston,
                        fronting E 25 ft. on King Street, & bounding W
on THOMAS BLUNDELL; N 125 ft. on JOHN TIPPER; S on a 6 ft. alley left by
TIPPER for BLUNDELL'S use & joins S on MILES BREWTON. Signed JOHN TAIPOR,
S'USA TIRPE. Witnesses: JOSIAH CLAYPOOLE, PETER LAURENS, JOHN CARION.
Before ROBERT AUSTIN, J.P. & Pub. Reg. On 6 May 1742 JOHN BEEKMAN ex-
changed this lot & received full satisfaction from JOHN TIPPER. Witness:
ROBERT AUSTIN, Register.

Book V, p. 187   RALPH JERMAN, planter, to NOAH SERRÉ, ESQ.,
23 & 24 Dec. 1740   both of St. James Santee, Craven Co., for
L & R by Mortgage   ₺ 500 SC money, 250 a. in St. James Santee,
                        bounding NE on Wahaw Creek; SW on vacant land;
SE on ISAAC MAZYCK, ESQ.; NW on ANTHONY BONNEAU; also 100 a. on al island
in Santee River, opposite the above 250 a., bounding NE on Santee River;
SE & SW on Wahaw Creek; NW on ANTHONY BONNEAU. Date of redemption: 24
Dec. 1741. Witnesses: JAMES WRIGHT, JAMES MICHIE. Before ISAAC MAZYCK,
J.P. ROBERT AUSTIN, Register. JOHN DUTARQUE, executor of NOAH SERRÉ,
declared mortgage satisfied 3 Oct. 1755. Witness: PETER MONCLAR.

Book V, p. 190   SAMUEL STONE, & ELIZABETH (her mark) his wife,
13 & 14 Dec. 1736   to JAMES AKIN, ESQ., all of Berkeley Co., for
L & R   ₺ 66 SC money, 648 a., in Craven Co., granted
                        to SAMUEL STONE by letters patent date 9 Apr.
1736, signed by Lt. Gov. THOMAS BROUGHTON, bounding E on MR. NESMITH; N
on MR. GIBBS; W on CAPT. BROCKINGTON; S on MR. MCKICKAN. Witnesses: WIL-
LIAM RUSSELL, JOHN LEPPER. Before JOSEPH BLAKE, J.P. Witnesses to receipt: CHARLES SHEPHEARD, THOMAS HEPWORTH. Before ROBERT AUSTIN, J.P. &
Pub. Reg.

Book V, p. 193   SAMUEL EVELEIGH, merchant, & ELIZABETH his
21 & 22 Sept. 1736   wife, of Charleston, to JAMES AKIN, planter,
L & R   of St. Thomas & St. Dennis Parish, for ₺ 170
                        currency, 550 a. in Craven Co., bounding W on
Gov. NATHANIEL JOHNSON; N on THOMAS AKIN. Witnesses: NATHAN BASSETT,
THOMAS DALE. Before THOMAS DALE, J.P. ROBERT AUSTIN, Register.

Book V, p. 196   ALEXANDER CRAMAHE, gentleman, of Charleston.,
13 & 14 Dec. 1736   to JAMES AKIN, planter, of St. Thomas & St.
L & R   Dennis Parish, for ₺ 400 currency, 900 a. in
                        Kingston Township, Craven Co., bounding on all
sides on vacant land; also a half-a. lot #4 in town of Kingston. Witnesses: EDMUND BELLINGER, ROBERT BREWTON, JR. Before HENRY GIBBES, J.P.
ROBERT AUSTIN, Register.

Book V, p. 199   The Church Wardens & Vestry of the Parish
5 June 1738   Church of St. Georges in Dorchester (by virtue
Pew Grant   of law passed 9 Apr. 1734) to JOHN DORSEY, for
                        ₺ 125 currency, pew #7, provided he shall not
alter its present uniformity. Signed: RICHARD WARING, N. WICKHAM, RICH-
ARD BAKER, JONATHAN (?) PORTELL, THOMAS WARING, JOSEPH BLAKE, A. SKENE,
W. IZARD. On 23 Aug. 1739 JOHN DORSEY assigned above per #7 to HUGH BUT-
LER, JR. for the use of MARY DORSEY. Witnesses: GEORGE COLLETON, JOHN
LEPPER. Before JOHN COLLETON, J.P. ROBERT AUSTIN, Register.

Book V, p. 200   THOMAS DISTON, gentleman, to JOHN DORSEY, both
6 & 7 Nov. 1737   of Berkeley Co., for ₺ 500 currency, 500 a. on
L & R   E side Edisto River part of a larger tract,
                        bounding N on GEORGE SOMMERS (formerly THOMAS

10

DISTON); E & S on THOMAS DISTON. SARAH, wife of THOMAS DISTON, to renounce her dower when requested. Before THOMAS BARNES, JOHN LEPPER. Before MALACHI GLAZE, J.P. ROBERT AUSTIN, Register.

Book V, p. 203   THOMAS BUER, planter, of Colleton Co., to his
22 Sept. 1735   loving brother WILLIAM MELVIN, for love & af-
Deed of Gift   fection, 100 a. purchased from the Lords
                        Proprs., bounding E on THOMAS BUER; N on JOHN
PENNEY; S on JAMES BUER; W on BOON. Witnesses: MOSES MARTIN, JOHN ANDREW,
WILLIAM WESBERY. Before JAMES SKIRVING, J.P. ROBERT AUSTIN, Register.

Book V, p. 204   THOMAS ELLIOTT, (formerly called THOMAS ELLI-
20 Feb. 1740   OTT, JR.), planter, of St. Pauls Parish, Col-
Confirmation of Title   leton Co., to JOHN RAVEN, planter, son & heir
                        of JOHN RAVEN, of Johns Island, Colleton Co.,
the E half of lot #205, or the half of the part that THOMAS ELLIOTT was
entitled to by will of JANE FLOWER. Whereas the Lords Proprs. on 9 May
1694 granted JANE FLOWER lot #205 in Charleston; & whereas by will dated
23 Nov. 1703 she devised the lot to THOMAS ELLIOTT, JR., who took possession & on 14 Aug. 1727, for a valuable consideration, sold it to JOHN
RAVEN, (father of JOHN RAVEN, party hereto) & to LUKE STOUTENBOURGH, silversmith, of Charleston; i.e. the E half to RAVEN, the W half to STOUTEN-
BOURGH; & whereas JOHN RAVEN, the father, took possession & made several
improvements & built several houses thereon; & whereas RAVEN died on 21
Nov. 1733 & the property descended to his eldest son & heir at law, JOHN,
party hereto subject to the right of dower of ELIZABETH, widow of JOHN
RAVEN, since called ELIZABETH JENYS; & whereas by the dreadful fire on
Tuesday, 18 Nov. last, in which the greater part of Charleston was in a
very short time "consumed to ashes," among others the house in which ELIZ-
ABETH JENYS lived, the conveyances from ELLIOTT to RAVEN were destroyed;
now ELLIOTT confirms RAVEN in his title to the E half of lot #205. Witnesses: CHARLES PINCKNEY, DAVID STOUT. Before ROBERT AUSTIN, J.P. & Pub.
Reg.

Book V, p. 206   WILLIAM CATTELL, ESQ., to JANE MONGER, widow,
14 & 15 Mar. 1736   both of Berkeley Co., for Ł 800 currency, a
L & R   1/2 a. lot, #2, in St. Andrews town, & the
                        tenement thereon. Whereas JOHN, Earl of Bath,
Palatine, & the Lords Proprs. on 12 Oct. 1701 granted FRANCIS FIDLING
38 a., English measure, in Berkeley Co., on S side Ashley River, bounding
E on a marsh & creek; S on FRANCIS FIDLING; W on EDMUND BELLINGER (formerly SHEM BUTLER); & whereas FRANCIS FIDLING & MARY his wife by deed of
feoffment dated 24 Feb. 1701 conveyed the 38 a. to THOMAS ROSE, planter,
of Berkeley Co.; & whereas the land by several conveyances became vested
in THOMAS DYMES, merchant, who at the time of his death owned a certain
messuage or tenement at Ashley River Ferry, commonly called Ashley Ferry
Store, adjoining the 38 a. which DYMES purchased from SAMUEL DEANE, ESQ.
(formerly belonging to THOMAS ROSE) & also owned 2 or 3 a. of marsh land
adjoining the store; & whereas DYMES, by will dated 27 Dec. 1729 directed
his executors (JOSEPH WRAGG & ROBERT HUME) to sell his real estate & they,
by L & R dated 21 & 22 May 1734, for Ł 2000 SC money sold the 38 a., the
store & the marsh land, to WILLIAM CATTELL; & whereas CATTELL has laid
out the 38 a. in town lots, called St. Andrews Town; now CATTELL sells 1
lot to JANE MONGER. Witnesses: The Rev. MR. WILLIAM GUY, EDWARD ORD,
WILLIAM FULLER, JAMES SCARLETT. Before HENRY GIBBES, J.P. ROBERT AUSTIN,
Register.

Book V, p. 211   CHARLES KING, planter, of Craven Co., to HENRY
6 & 7 Mar. 1740   IZARD, planter, of Berkeley Co., as security
L & R by Mortgage   on bond of even date in penal sum of Ł 200 for
                        payment of Ł 100 British, with interest, on 7
Mar. 1743; 750 a. in Craven Co., bounding SE on JOHN SCOTT; other sides
on vacant land. Witnesses: EDWARD KNIGHT, WILLIAM SMITH. Before WILLIAM
GEORGE FREEMAN, J.P. ROBERT AUSTIN, Register.

Book V, p. 215   CHARLES CODNER, planter, & ANN his wife, to
1 & 2 May 1736   JAMES AKIN, ESQ., all of Berkeley Co., for
L & R   Ł 500 SC money, 500 a. in Craven Co., granted
                        by Lt. Gov. THOMAS BROUGHTON on 9 Apr. last to
CODNER; bounding NE on JAMES AKIN; other sides on vacant land. Witnesses:

11

WILLIAM BRUCE, JOHN STEWART. Before WILLIAM TREWIN, J.P. Before ROBERT
AUSTIN, Register.

Book V, p. 218   BENJAMIN STANYARNE, planter, son & heir of
12 & 13 Nov. 1740   JANE MONGER, widow; of Berkeley Co.; to FRAN-
L & R   CIS GODDARD, vintner, of Charleston, for ₺ 400
                        currency, lot #2 in St. Andrews Town, contain-
ing half an a., & the tenement on the lot. Witnesses: NATHANIEL DEAN,
THOMAS DEAN, THOMAS GREENE. Before HENRY GIBBES, J.P. ROBERT AUSTIN,
Register.

Book V, p. 222   ANNE LEBRASSEUR, widow of FRANCIS LEBRASSEUR,
10 & 11 Mar. 1740   gentleman, to PETER CALVET, shopkeeper, all of
L & R   Charleston, for ₺ 740 SC money, lot #13 in
                        Charleston, fronting S 18 ft. on Elliott's
Alley or Middle Street; bounding N on ISAAC MAZYCK, ESQ.; E 71-1/3 ft. on
JOHN WATSON; W on JOSEPH WRAGG. Witnesses: DR. JOHN MARTIN, JOHN YON.
Before ROBERT AUSTIN, J.P. & Pub. Reg.

Book V, p. 228   MARTHA (her mark) NICHOLS, of Granville Co.,
2 Feb. 1740   to BENJAMIN STONE, planter, of James Island,
Quit claim   Berkeley Co., for ₺ 400 currency, releases all
                        her claim to the tracts of land on James Is-
land which she recently conveyed to JOHN MCKAY, because several controversies have arisen concerning the titles owing to the fact that she was
under age when she conveyed the land to MCKAY. Witnesses: ANDREW WALKER,
JONATHAN TUBB. Before ISAAC MAZYCK, J.P. ROBERT AUSTIN, Register.

Book V, p. 229   JOHN FRASER, merchant, of Charleston, surviv-
7 & 8 Mar. 1740   ing executor of JOHN MACKAY, shopkeeper, of
L & R   Charleston, to BENJAMIN STONE, planter, of
                        James Island, Berkeley Co., for ₺ 581 currency,
83 a. on James Island, bounding N on JOHN BEE; S on a marsh; E on BENJA-
MIN STONE; W on WILLIAM RIVERS, THOMAS DIXON, & JOSEPH SPENCER. Whereas
JOHN MACKAY by will dated 14 Aug. 1739 ordered his plantation of 170 a.
on James Island & part of a tenement on Broad Street, Charleston, be sold
as soon as convenient, & appointed JOHN FRASER & JAMES FISHER his executors; now they sell a part to STONE. Witnesses: ROBERT RIVERS, JOSEPH
SPENCER. Before ROBERT AUSTIN, J.P. & Pub. Reg.

Book V, p. 233   WILLIAM BROCKINTON, planter, of Craven Co.,
3 & 4 Nov. 1740   Winyaw, to JOHN DUTARQUE, planter, of Cainhoy,
L & R   Berkeley Co., for ₺ 180 currency, 500 a. in
                        Craven Co., on a place between Santee River &
Black River, called Oak Ridge, bounding on all sides on land not laid out;
& granted to BROCKINTON by Lt. Gov. THOMAS BROUGHTON on 29 Nov. 1735.
Witnesses: JOHN COOKE, JAMES ROBERT, PETER LANE. Before WILLIAM TREWIN,
J.P. ROBERT AUSTIN, Register.

Book V, p. 236   WILLIAM BROCKINTON, planter, of Craven Co.,
3 & 4 Nov. 1740   Winyaw, to JOHN DUTARQUE, planter, of Cainhoy,
L & R   Berkeley Co., for ₺ 220 currency, 300 a. in
                        Prince Frederick Parish, Craven Co., Winyaw,
on Oak Ridge Swamp, between the Santee & Black Rivers, bounding NE on
WILLIAM BORCKINTON; SW on GILES BOWERS; other sides on vacant land; which
300 a. was granted to BROCKINTON by Lt. Gov. THOMAS BROUGHTON on 29 Nov.
1735; also 350 a. on same swamp, bounding NW on BROCKINGTON, all other
sides on vacant land; which tract was granted to GILES BOWERS by Lt. Gov.
THOMAS BROUGHTON on 3 Dec. 1735 & sold by GILES BOWERS & MARTHA his wife,
by L & R dated 24 & 25 Aug. 1737, to BROCKINTON. Witnesses: JOHN COOKE,
JAMES ROBERT, PETER LANE. Before WILLIAM TREWIN, J.P. ROBERT AUSTIN,
Register.

Book V, p. 240   FRANCIS THOMPSON, planter, of St. Helena Is-
22 & 23 Mar. 1740   land, Granville Co., to JAMES MEGGETT, planter,
L & R   of same place, for ₺ 537:10 currency, 215 a.,
                        English measure, on St. Helena Island, bound-
ing NE on JOHN STANYARNE'S land beginning at a live oak tree by a small
creek; W on JAMES MEGGETT; S on creeks & marshes; N on land claimed by
RICHARD REYNOLDS. Witnesses: HUGH BRYAN, THOMAS FARR, AMARITTA FARR.

12

Before HENRY GIBBES, J.P. ROBERT AUSTIN, Register.

Book V, p. 243   FRANCIS THOMPSON, planter, of St. Helena Is-
22 & 23 Mar. 1740   land, Granville Co., to JOHN STANYARNE, plant-
L & R   er, of Johns Island, Colleton Co., for
                      Ł 2612:10 currency, 1045 a., English measure,
on St. Helena Island, bounding NE on the Sea bay; SE on creeks & marshes
separating it from the sea beach islands; SW on JAMES MEGGETT. Witnesses:
HUGH BRYAN, THOMAS FARR, AMARITTA FARR. Before HENRY GIBBES, J.P. ROB-
ERT AUSTIN, Register.

Book V, p. 246   JOHN STANYARNE, of Johns Island & JAMES MEG-
19 & 20 Mar. 1740   GETT, of Edisto Island, Colleton Co., planter,
L & R   executors of will of JOHN STEWART, planter, of
                      Granville Co., & MARY STEWART, widow & devisee
of said JOHN STEWART, to FRANCIS THOMPSON, planter, of St. Helena Island,
Granville Co., for Ł 3150 currency, 1260 a. bounding NE on the sea bay;
SE on creeks & marshes separating it from the sea beach islands; NW on
land claimed by RICHARD REYNOLDS & a small creek; SW on creeks & marshes
& land claimed by REYNOLDS. Whereas JOHN STEWART by will dated 19 Dec.
1739 ordered the rest of his land (of which the above 1260 a. was a part),
& all his slaves, be sold by his executors his friends ARCHIBALD CALDER,
JOHN STANYARNE & JAMES MEGGETT; & whereas CALDER refused to act; & whereas MARY, widow of JOHN STEWART, voluntarily consents to the sale of the
land & slaves, now she & the executors sell 1260 a. to THOMPSON. Witnesses: HUGH BRYAN, THOMAS FARR, AMARITTA FARR. Before HENRY GIBBES, J.P.
ROBERT AUSTIN, Register.

Book V, p. 250   THOMAS FORREST, vintner, to WILLIAM HARVEY,
21 & 22 Apr. 1740   merchant, both of Charleston, as security for
L & R by Mortgage   payment of a debt of Ł 100 SC money, 400 a. in
                      Queensborough Township, Craven Co., bounding
NE on vacant land; NW on JOHN HAYDON; SE on HENRY HALL; SW on Lynch's
Creek; also a 1/2 a. lot #49, in Town of Queensborough. Date of redemp-
tion: 1 Nov. next. Witnesses: JOHN RATTRAY, JOHN JOHNSON. Before ROBERT
AUSTIN, J.P. & Register.

Book V, p. 252   EDWARD BULLARD, merchant, to WILLIAM HARVEY,
22 & 23 Mar. 1740   merchant, both of Charleston, as security for
L & R by Mortgage   debt of Ł 500 currency, 1700 a. on Black River
                      in Craven Co., bounding NW on RICHARD WALKER &
WILLIAM BROCKINGTON; NE on ARTHUR FOSTER. Date of redemption: 20 Sept.
next. Witnesses: ROBERT COREAN (COWAN ?), JOHN RATTRAY. Before ROBERT
AUSTIN, J.P. & Register. WILLIAM HARVEY on 13 Feb. 1768 declared mort-
gage satisfied in full in MR. BULLARD'S lifetime. Witness: FENWICKE
BULL, Register.

Book V, p. 255   THOMAS ROSE, planter, of Ashley River, Berke-
26 & 27 Mar. 1741   ley Co., & BEULAH his wife (lately called BEU-
L & R   LAH ELLIOT, daughter & devisee of THOMAS
                      ELLIOT, planter, of Berkeley Co.), to BENJAMIN
SAVAGE, merchant, of Charleston, for Ł 1000 SC money, the N half of lot
#61 fronting E 50 ft. on New Church Street, bounding N 232 ft. on the
Baptist Congregation; W on the lot granted to ISAAC CALLIBEUF; S on the
other half of lot #61; which N half of the lot was by will dated 9 June
1731 devised by THOMAS ELLIOT to his daughter BEULAH, with the house
thereon in which CAPT. JOHN HEXT then lived. Witnesses: MARTHA BOOTH,
JOHN SAVAGE. Before JACOB MOTTE, J.P. ROBERT AUSTIN, Register.

Book V, p. 260   THOMAS HEPWORTH, planter, of St. Helena Parish,
2 & 3 Feb. 1740   Granville Co., to THOMAS BURTON, carpenter, of
L & R   Beaufort, for Ł 80 currency, lot #43 in Beau-
                      fort, bounding S on lot #44; W on Carteret
Street; N on Port Royal Street; E on lot #46; also lot #46 in Beaufort,
bounding S on lot #47; W on lot #43; N on Port Royal Street; E on New
Street. Witnesses: CHARLES RURRY, WILLIAM GOUGH. Before ROBERT AUSTIN,
J.P. & Pub. Reg.

Book V, p. 264   JACOB MOTTE, ESQ., of Charleston, & JOHN
4 & 5 Nov. 1740   GREENE, ESQ., (son of ELIZABETH GREENE, widow

L & R   & devisee of DANIEL GREENE, ESQ.), executors
                               of will of ELIZABETH GREENE, to MARY BRYAN,
widow, of Granville Co., for L 750 currency, that messuage or tenement on
part of lot #197 in Charleston, fronting E 31 ft. on a great street leading from Cooper River to the Market Place & old churchyard; bounding W on
JOHN RIVERS; S 230 ft., English measure, on JOHN RIVERS; N on other part
of the lot belonging to ALBERT DERTMAR; which house DANIEL GREENE, by
will dated 14 Nov. 1735, bequeathed to his wife ELIZABETH, who, by will
dated 14 Oct. 1737, devised all her real estate to her executor, JACOB
MOTTE, in trust, to be sold as soon as possible after her death. Whereas
by a codicil to her will dated 29 Feb. 1739 ELIZABETH appointed her son,
JOHN GREENE, an executor to act with JACOB MOTTE; now they sell the house
to MARY BRYON. Witnesses: EDWARD HEXT, JOSEPH PICKERING. Before ROBERT
AUSTIN, J.P. & Pub. Reg.

Book V, p. 268   ANTHONY MATHEWES, gentleman, & ANN his wife,
6 & 7 Feb. 1740   to JAMES VOULOUX, vintner, all of Charleston,
L & R   for L 800 currency, part of lot #104 fronting
                               N 32 ft. on Broad Street; bounding S on a lot
belonging to the French Church; E 200 ft. on MR. PAWLEY; W on part of lot
#104. Witnesses: WILLIAM LASSERS, PETER BOCQUET, LAWRENCE COULLIETTE.
Before ROBERT AUSTIN, J.P. & Pub. Reg.

Book V, p. 271   SAMUEL SIMONS, planter, & ELIZABETH his wife,
29 & 30 Mar. 1738   to JAMES BREMAR, planter, all of Berkeley Co.,
L & R   for L 600 currency, 300 a., English measure,
                               in Berkeley Co., bounding NE on the remaining
part of 700 a.; SW & NW on JAMES BREMAR; SE on MRS. ELIZABETH BREMAR;
which 300 a. is part of 700 a. on E side Cooper River given by ANTHONY
BONNEAU & JANE ELIZABETH his wife, to SAMUEL & ELIZABETH SIMONS. Witnesses: THOMAS ASHBY, PETER SIMONS, SAMUEL (his mark) KING. Before WILLIAM
TREWIN, J.P. ROBERT AUSTIN, Register.

Book V, p. 275   WILLIAM BRUCE, chirurgeon, to MATHURINE GUERIN,
12 & 13 Mar. 1740   planter, both of St. Thomas Parish, Berkeley
L & R by Mortgage   Co., for L 2750 SC money, 560 a., English mea-
                               sure, on NW side of N branch Wando River, late-
ly purchased by BRUCE from said GUERIN; bounding S on marsh of the river;
N on PETER PORTEVINE; W on ANDREW WARNOCK; E on JOHN SANDIFORD. Redeemable by payment of various sums on various dates. Witnesses: JOSEPH WAR-
NOCK, JANE MILLER. Before ROBERT AUSTIN, J.P. & Register. On 11 May
1748 MATHURINE declared mortgage satisfied. Witness: JOHN BEALE, Register.

Book V, p. 279   JOHN METHRINGHAM, carpenter, & MARY his wife,
25 Mar. 1741   to ANDREW DEVEAUX, planter, free from MARY'S
Bill of Sale   claim of dower, all of Berkeley Co., for L 500
                               currency, part of lot #11 fronting 27 ft. on S
side Broad Street, Charleston, 90 ft. deep, lately occupied by ABRAHAM
SKINNER, shop keeper; which part of a lot & premises were the inheritance
of JOHN BRETON, merchant, who devised the property in fee simple to MAG-
DALANE JUNEAU, then a widow of Charleston now the wife of ANDREW DEVEAUX;
the said ANDREW & MAGDALANE DEVEAUX conveying the property, by way of
settlement, to ISAAC MAZYCK, merchant, in trust for ANDREW DEVEAUX during
MAGDALENE'S life & afterwards for JOHN METHRINGHAM, son of MAGDALENE DE-
VEAUX. Witnesses: PENELOPE D'LESCURE, JAMES DRUMMOND. Before JAMES
GREENE, J.P. ROBERT AUSTIN, Register.

Book V, p. 281   DANIEL JAUDON, planter & MARIAN (MARY ANN) his
18 & 19 July 1738   wife, of St. James Santee, Craven Co., to
L & R   GEORGE CHICKEN, planter, of Berkeley Co., for
                               L 200 currency, 2 tracts of 200 a. each, total
400 a., in Prince Frederick Parish, bounding N on Black River, other
sides on land not laid out. Witnesses: ANDREW DELAVILLETTE, ELIAS JAUDON,
PHILIP NORMAND. Before ROBERT AUSTIN, J.P. & Pub. Reg.

Book V, p. 284   CHARLES REEVES to MARY MELLICHAMP, for L 250
4 Feb. 1740/1   SC money, a house & stable on lot # (?) at
Bill of Sale   Port Royal. Witnesses: JEMMIT COBLEY, THOMAS
                               HEPWORTH. Before ROBERT WRIGHT, J.P. of

Granville Co.   ROBERT AUSTIN, Register.

Book V, p. 284   WILLIAM ELLIOTT, planter, & FRANCES his wife,
17 Apr. 1741   of Berkeley Co., with the free consent of
Bill of Sale   FRANCES, to BENJAMIN SAVAGE, merchant, of
            Charleston, for ₤ 600 currency, part of lot
#61 in Charleston, on W side New Church Street, bounding N 232 ft. on
BENJAMIN SAVAGE; W 25 ft. on ISAAC CAILLIBEUF; S on JUDITH MILLER. Wit-
nesses: THOMAS LEE, JOHN SAVAGE. Before JACOB MOTTE, J.P. ROBERT AUSTIN,
Register.

Book V, p. 287   ELIZABETH BREMAR, widow, to FRANCIS BREMAN,
10 Mar. 1739   gentleman, for ₤ 450 SC currency, all her
Renunciation of Dower title to any of the land & houses in Berkeley
            Co. which belonged to her husband PETER BREMAR.
Witnesses: BENJAMIN ADDISON, HENRY LAURENS. Before ROBERT AUSTIN, J.P. &
Pub. Reg.

Book V, p. 288   ANTHONY BONNEAU, ESQ., & JANE ELIZABETH his
21 & 22 Apr. 1741   wife, of Berkeley Co., to DANIEL BOURGET, bak-
L & R   er, of Charleston, for ₤ 1600 currency the E
            part of lot #11 in Charleston fronting 36 ft.
on N side of Elliott Street; bounding N on MR. DEVEAUX, MR. COOPER; 86 ft.
on DANIEL BOURGET; W on BONNEAU'S other part of lot #11. Witnesses: ANN
MARTIN, JACOB MARTIN, THOMAS LAMBOLL. Before ROBERT AUSTIN, J.P. & Pub.
Reg.

Book V, p. 293   ISAAC HOLMES, gentleman, of Charleston; WIL-
8 & 9 Apr. 1741   LIAM SANDERS, planter, of Berkeley Co.; MAR-
L & R   GARET WILSON, widow of MOSES WILSON, planter,
            of Berkeley Co.; & ELIZABETH (her mark) FID-
LING, widow, of Charleston; executors & executrixes of will of MOSES WIL-
SON; to DANIEL BOURGET, baker of Charleston; for ₤ 1400 currency; 1/8 of
lot #11 in Charleston, lately belonging to MOSES WILSON; on N side of
Elliott Street; 28-1/2 ft. x 86 ft.; the houses lately standing thereon
having been destroyed by the dreadful fire; bounding N on CAPT. ISAAC
HOLMES; E on JAMES FOWLER; W on CAPT. ANTHONY BONNEAU. MARGARET WILSON
quit claims her dower to BOURGET. Whereas MOSES WILSON owned the above
mentioned 1/8 of lot #11 & by will dated 25 Feb. 1737 appointed ISAAC
HOLMES, WILLIAM SANDERS, his executors & MARGARET WILSON & ELIZABETH FID-
LING, his executrixes, with power to sell his part of the lot for ready
money, the money to be put out at interest until his daughters (ANNE &
MARGARET) should reach 16 years of age, or marry, then the money to be
divided equally between them; now they sell to BOURGET, the highest bidder. Witnesses: ANTHONY BONNEAU, J. MARTIN, THOMAS LAMBOLL. Before ROB-
ERT AUSTIN, J.P. & Pub. Reg.

Book V, p. 298   THOMAS WALKER, planter, of Berkeley Co., to
31 Mar. & 1 Apr. 1741 the vestry of the Parish of St. Thomas, Berke-
L & R by Mortgage   ley Co., for ₤ 400 SC money, 122-1/2 a., Eng-
            lish measure, on Thomas's Island, bounding NW
on Watcoe Creek; SW on JOHN DUHHAM; W on JOHN WALKER; being 1/2 of 245 a.
which THOMAS WALKER & JOHN WALKER lately purchased from JACOB WOOLFORD.
Date of redemption: 25 Mar. 1742. Witnesses: ROBERT SCOTT, ROBERT HOW.
Before HENRY GIBBES, J.P. ROBERT AUSTIN, Register.

Book V, p. 302   THOMAS ASHBY, planter, of Berkeley Co., to the
4 & 5 Feb. 1739   vestry of the Parish of St. Thomas, Berkeley
L & R by Mortgage   Co., for ₤ 500 currency, 500 a., English mea-
            sure, in Berkeley Co. where he lives; bounding
NW on JOHN ASHBY (father of THOMAS); NE on GABRIEL MANIGAULT, ESQ. & THOM-
AS JOHNSON. Whereas RICHARD BERESFORD of Berkeley Co., by will dated May
1715, bequeathed to THOMAS BROUGHTON, ESQ., all the residue of the yearly
profits & produce of his real & personal estate not already devised, until his son JOHN reaches 21 years of age upon trust that BROUGHTON pay
the same into the hands of the vestry to be disposed of as follows: 1/3
to the school master, 2/3 for the support & education of such of the
children of the poor of the Parish as should be sent there to school; &
in case there should be no school master, the money to be put out at interest; & whereas the vestry have loaned ASHLEY ₤ 500 at interest, to be

15

paid 25 Mar. 1740, now ASHBY gives the vestry 500 a. as security. Witnesses: JEAN BONNOIT, ROBERT HOW. Before HENRY GIBBES, J.P. ROBERT AUSTIN, Register.

Book V, p. 307　　　　　　ROBERT FLADGER of Berkeley Co., to JONAH COL-
5 July 1737　　　　　　　LINS, gentleman, of Craven Co., for ₺ 1464 SC
Mortgage　　　　　　　　money, 700 a., English measure, in Craven Co.,
　　　　　　　　　　　　on Little Peedee River, bounding NW on WILLIAM
BORLAND; as set down in grant dated 1730; also 10 Negro men. Date of redemption: 19 June next. Witnesses: PETER CUTTINO, JR., JAMES MCDONNELL, SAMUEL WOODGER. Before HENRY GIBBES, J.P. Recorded in Secretary's Book K.K. fol. 318-326 by JAMES MICHIE, Dec. Sec. ROBERT AUSTIN, Pub. Reg.

Book V, p. 310　　　　　　JOSHUA TOOMER, tanner, to BERNARD ELLIOTT,
6 Apr. 1741　　　　　　　planter, both of St. Andrews Parish, for the
Mortgage　　　　　　　　penal sum of ₺ 2600 currency, all the land
　　　　　　　　　　　　given JOSHUA TOOMER by the will of his father,
HENRY TOOMER, bounding E on JOSEPH ELLIOTT; W on JOHN TOOMER; N on BERNARD ELLIOTT; S on Stono River; to be redeemed within 1 year by payment of ₺ 1300 currency, with interest. Signed: JOSHUA TOOMER, MARY TOOMER (his wife). Witnesses: The Rev. MR. HENRY HEYWOOD, WILLIAM CHAPMAN, JOSEPH ELLICOTT. Before THOMAS DALE, J.P. ROBERT AUSTIN, Register.

Book V, p. 311　　　　　　GEORGE SMITH, merchant, & SARAH his wife, form-
9 Apr. 1741　　　　　　　erly of Charleston, SC, now of Philadelphia,
Letter of Attorney　　　appointed JAMES MATHEWES, merchant, ARCHER
　　　　　　　　　　　　SMITH, planter, & the Rev. MR. JOSIAH SMITH,
all of Berkeley Co., SC, their attorneys, to dispose of their real estate in SC, particularly a certain piece of land in Charleston facing E 27 ft. on Cooper River, bounding N on a small alley used by the persons who from time to time possessed the land on which (before the fire of 18 Nov. last) stood the house & stores of WILLIAM GIBBON, merchant; S on SAMUEL EVELEIGH, merchant; W on GEORGE SMITH (except the part conveyed to their adughter MARY on 6 Oct. 1732. Witnesses in Philadelphia: JOHN LEMON, WALTER MOODIE. Before SAMUEL HASSELL, Mayor of Philadelphia. SARAH signed voluntarily. LEMON & MOODIE appeared before ROBERT AUSTIN, J.P. & Pub. Reg. of SC.

Book V, p. 313　　　　　　GEORGE SMITH, merchant, & SARAH his wife, form-
8 May 1741　　　　　　　erly of Charleston, now of Philadelphia agree
Agreement　　　　　　　　that upon payment to them of ₺ 600 Pennsylva-
　　　　　　　　　　　　nia money (or security) by THOMAS JENYS & ELIZ-
BETH JENYS, of Charleston, they will convey to THOMAS & ELIZABETH JENYS, in fee simple, their lot in Charleston formerly in possession of STEAD EVANCE & Co., fronting E 27 ft. on Cooper River, bounding N on a alley used by the persons who, from time to time, possessed the land on which (before the fire of 18 Nov. last) stood the houses & stores lately belonging to WILLIAM GIBBON, merchant; also the right to use the alley; bounding S on SAMUEL EVELEIGH, merchant; W on (?); excepting such part' as they have given to their daughter MARY by deed dated 6 Oct. 1732; also the low water land lying before the lot. Witnesses: CHARLES PINCKNEY, DAVID STOUT. Before ROBERT AUSTIN, J.P. & Pub. Reg.

Book V, p. 314　　　　　　JOHN FENWICKE, ESQ., THOMAS LLOYD, & CHARLES
11 May 1741　　　　　　　PINCKNEY, of Charleston, agree upon the bonds
Agreement　　　　　　　　of their parts of lot #3 on the Bay as follows:
　　　　　　　　　　　　Whereas lot #3 was originally granted to THOM-
AS PINCKNEY, merchant, father of CHARLES PINCKNEY; & whereas THOMAS PINCKNEY in his lifetime sold & conveyed to CAPT. GEORGE SMITH 35 ft. in front on the Bay & so running the same breadth to the S or lower end of said lot, which part of a lot, by several conveyances has become the property of THOMAS LLOYD; & whereas CHARLES PINCKNEY sold JOHN FENWICKE 32 ft. in front on the Bay, being next adjoining part of the lot; & whereas since the "dreadful fire" on 18 Nov. last it appears that the back houses of THOMAS LLOYD at the upper end "were 7 in. on the part of the lot sold to FENWICKE at the lower end thereof the foundation of the said backhouses were laid 17 in. too far to the Northward" upon the part sold to FENWICKE; to remove all future disputes it was agreed that the line should be staked out beginning at the upper end of said outhouses where the same is 7 in. on FENWICKE'S land & running down to the lower end of

16

said houses where the foundation is 17 in. on FENWICKE'S land & so continuing to the W end of the lot, which was done by GEORGE HUNTER, survey-
or, on 8 this May & staked out in presence of FRANCIS GRACIA & JOHN BAL-
LANTINE; now they declare this the boundray. Witnesses: COL. MILES BREW-
TON, JOHN BALLANTINE. Before ROBERT AUSTIN, J.P. & Pub. Reg.

Book V, p. 315   WILLIAM & JOSEPH WHIPPEY, planters, to WILLIAM
11 Apr. 1741   BAYNARD, planter, all of Edisto Island, for
L & R   Ł 900 currency, 200 a. at Pon Pon, Colleton
                      Co., bounding S on JOHN ANDREWS; W on WILLIAM
GRAY; N on JOSEPH MACKEY; E on JOSEPH BOON'S Barony; which 200 a. was
granted by Gov. ROBERT GIBBES & the Lords Proprs. on 28 July 1711, for
Ł 4, to JOSEPH FARLEY, carpenter; who, for Ł 26 sold to EDWARD RIPPIN,
JR.; who, for Ł 200 sold to WILLIAM GRAY, SR.; who, for Ł 700 currency,
sold to TIMOTHY HENDRICKS; by whose death WILLIAM & JOSEPH WHIPPEY (sons
of WILLIAM WHIPPEY) became heirs to the plantation. They now sell to
BAYNARD. MARY, wife of WILLIAM WHIPPEY, freely surrenders her right of
dower. Witnesses: JOHN CALDER, JOSEPH SEABROOK, WILLIAM DAVIS. Before
HENRY GIBBES, J.P. ROBERT AUSTIN, Register.

Book V, p. 319   LOIS MATHEWS, widow, & JOHN MATHEWS, merchant,
10 & 11 Apr. 1741   of Charleston, to WILLIAM WILKINS, planter, of
L & R   Berkeley Co., for Ł 1000 currency, 617 a. on
                      James Island, Berkeley Co., bounding N on
Wappoe Creek & marsh of Ashley River; S on New Town Creek & GRIGORY SIS-
SON (formerly RICHARD SIMPSON); W on BELSHAZZER LAMBRIGHT (formerly ROB-
ERT GIBBES, heretofore of MR. SHABISHERE); E on marsh of New Town Creek &
Ashley River; as by plat certified 15 May 1701 by JAMES WITTER & annexed
to grant dated 18 Sept. 1703 from Gov. NATHANIEL JOHNSON & the Lords
Proprs. to DAVID DAVIS. Witnesses: DAVID STOUT, BENJAMIN MATHEWS. Be-
fore ROBERT AUSTIN, J.P. & Pub. Reg.

Book V, p. 323   WILLIAM WILKINS, planter, & SARAH his wife, to
13 & 14 Apr. 1741   SAMUEL PERONNEAU, planter, all of Berkeley Co.,
L & R   for Ł 5110 SC money, 617 a. on James Island,
                      bounding N on Wappoe Creek & marsh of Ashley
River; S on New Town Creek & GRIGORY SISSON (formerly RICHARD SIMPSON); W
on BELTESHAZER LAMBRIGHT (formerly ROBERT GIBBES, heretofore of MR. SHA-
BISHERE); E on marsh of New Town Creek & Ashley River; as by plat certified 15 May 1701 by JAMES WITTER & annexed to grant dated 18 Sept. 1703
from Gov. NATHANIEL JOHNSON & the Lords Proprs. to DAVID DAVIS. Witnesses: DAVID STOUT, BENJAMIN MATHEWS. Before ROBERT AUSTIN, J.P. & Pub.
Reg.

Book V, p. 327   THOMAS BONNY, planter, & RUTH his wife (free
21 & 22 Apr. 1739   from her claim of dower), to THOMAS WALKER,
L & R   planter, all of Berkeley Co., for Ł 1800 SC
                      money, 530 a., English measure, on E side Coop-
er River, bounding S on Simons's Creek; SE on lands of the vestry of Parish of St. Thomas for use of a free school; NE on PETER JOHNSON; NW on
LEWIS DUTARQUE; W on RICHARD GRIFFIN as by plat attached to grant to JOHN
WALBANK, father of RUTH BONNY, dated 27 June 1711. Witnesses: ANN BONNY,
DANIEL LEGER, ROBERT HOW. Before HENRY GIBBES, J.P. ROBERT AUSTIN, Register.

Book V, p. 332   EDWARD HOWARD, planter, of Craven Co., to
19 & 20 Apr. 1741   JAMES AKIN, ESQ., of Berkeley Co., for Ł 286:5
L & R by Mortgage   SC money, 618 a., English measure, in Craven
                      Co., bounding SE on Black River; SW on PETER
SANDERS; N on SAMUEL COMMANDER; E on JOHN SUMMERS & JOHN BONNELL; accord-
ing to plat attached to grant dated 12 Aug. 1737. Date of redemption: 1
Jan. 1741. Witnesses: PETER LANE, JOHN NAYLOR. Before ANTHONY BONNEAU,
J.P. ROBERT AUSTIN, Register.

Book V, p. 336   JAMES DALTON, to WILLIAM SHAW, both of Berke-
15 & 16 Jan. 1737   ley Co., for Ł 1300 currency, 500 a. on E side
L & R   of Edisto River, being part of lands surveyed
                      for THOMAS DISTON, SR., by his son THOMAS DIS-
TON, on 11 Nov. 1736 & conveyed by DISTON, SR. to JAMES DALTON on 11 Nov.
1736; JAMES DALTON to obtain, when requested, his wife"s (CATHERINE'S)

release of dower. Witnesses: JOHN DORSEY, WILLIAM CARWITHEN. Before
MALACHI GLAZE, J.P. ROBERT AUSTIN, Register.

Book V, p. 339   ELIZABETH GREENE, widow, of Charleston, to her
19 & 20 Feb. 1738   eldest son, JOHN GREENE, planter, of Berkeley
Deed of Gift   Co., for natural love & affection, the N half
                          of a quarter part of lot #19 at N end of the
Bay in Charleston, formerly occupied by FRANCIS SCAMPTON; bounding E 29
ft. on the Bay; S on HENRY PERONNEAU, JR. (formerly JOHN CUPPEL, late
JACOB LITTEN); W on RICHARD GRIMSTONE (formerly JOHN AHSBY, gentleman); N
on Queen Street. Witnesses: THOMAS GREENE, NATHANIEL GREENE. Before ROB-
ERT AUSTIN, J.P. & Pub. Reg.

Book V, p. 343   MARGARET GODFREY, widow, of Christ Church Par-
21 Jan. 1740   ish, farm lets to JOHN GARNIER, of St. Andrews
Lease   Parish, 47 a., known as Point Pleasant, on
                          Wampoe Creek, St. Andrews Parish, for Ł 40 SC
money a year, payable every 21 Jan.; with certain provisoes. Witnesses:
HENRY GIBBES, PETER GIRARDEAU. Before ROBERT AUSTIN, J.P. & Pub. Reg.

Book V, p. 344   THOMAS WRIGHT, planter, to ALEXANDER NISBETT,
26 & 27 May 1741   ESQ., both of Berkeley Co., as security on
L & R by Mortgage   bond of even date in penal sum of Ł 500 Brit-
                          ish for payment of Ł 50 British every year dur-
ing the natural life of NISBETT beginning 27 May 1742 in the Carolina
Coffee House in London; 1330 a. in St. Thomas Parish, at head of NE
branch of Cooper River, bounding NW on ROBERT QUASH; SE on JOHN HARLESTON;
NE on THOMAS AKIN; SW on GABRIEL MANIGAULT, ESQ. (formerly Gov. ROBERT
JOHNSON); which tract was conveyed by L & R dated 3 & 4 Mar. 1735 by ROB-
ERT BROWN, surgeon, of St. James Goose Creek to THOMAS WRIGHT. Witness-
es: JAMES MICHIE, KENNETH MICHIE. Before ROBERT AUSTIN, J.P. & Pub. Reg.

Book V, p. 348   THOEDORE GAILLARD, & LYDIA his wife, to MOSES
28 & 29 Aug. 1740   DUTART, all of Craven Co., for Ł 250 SC money,
L & R   100 a., being the full half part of 200 a. in
                          Craven Co., on Wadbaccon Island, on N side
Santee River, granted GAILLARD by Lt. Gov. THOMAS BROUGHTON; bounding E
on the half purchased lately by PETER REMBERT; N on RALPH IZARD, ESQ.; W
on NOAH SERRE. Witnesses: WILLIAM THOMAS, ANDREW REMBERT, JOHN REMBERT.
Before JAMES KINLOCH, J.Q. ROBERT AUSTIN, Register.

Book V, p. 352   THEODORE GAILLARD, & LYDIA his wife, to PETER
28 & 29 Aug. 1740   REMBERT; all of Craven Co.; for Ł 250 SC money,
L & R   100 a., being the full half part of 200 a. on
                          Wadbacon Island, Craven Co., on N side Santee
River, granted to GAILLARD by Lt. Gov. THOMAS BROUGHTON; bounding E on
ELIAS HORRY; W on other half of 200 a.; N on RALPH IZARD, ESQ. Witness-
es: WILLIAM THOMAS, ANDREW REMBERT, JOHN REMBERT. Before JAMES KINLOCH,
J.Q. ROBERT AUSTIN, Pub. Reg.

Book V, p. 355   JOHN (his mark) WANNEL, sawyer, of Colleton
14 Apr. 1731   Co., to his second son THOMAS WANNEL, planter,
Deed of Gift   for love & affection, 250 a. in Colleton Co.,
                          bounding NW on JOHN PAGE; NE on JAMES COCHRAN;
S on Folly Creek. Witnesses: HENRY HYRNE, JOHN BULL, THOMAS BOONE. Before JAMES SKIRVING, J.P. ROBERT AUSTIN, Register. A memorial entered
in Auditor's office 26 May 1733.

Book V, p. 356   JOHN WATSONE, merchant, of Charleston, & ABI-
3 & 4 June 1741   GAIL his wife, 1 of the daughters & devisees
L & R   of SHEM BUTLER, of Berkeley Co., to WILLIAM
                          BRANFORD, planter of Berkeley Co., for Ł 2817
currency, 313 a. on S side Ashley River, bounding NE on MRS. ESTHER
ELLIOTT; SE on the high road leading to & from Ashley River Ferry; SW on
CHAMPERNOON ELLIOTT; NW on BENJAMIN STANYARNE. Whereas SHEM BUTLER owned
sundry plantation, town lots, etc., particularly 313 a., & by will dated
9 Oct. 1718 bequeathed all his real & personal estate (after payment of
debts) to be divided equally amongst his wife & children, appointing his
loving brother RICHARD BUTLER, his brother-in-law SAMUEL WEST, & his son-
in-law EDMUND BELLINGER, his executors; & whereas the executors made an

equal division, allotting to ABIGAIL (1 of the daughters, wife of JOHN
WATSONE) by certificate dated 28 July 1738, signed by RICHARD BUTLER &
EDMUND BELLINGER, the 313 a., beside certain town lots, as her part; now
JOHN & ABIGAIL WATSON sell the 313 a. to BRANFORD. Witnesses: FRANCIS
HOLMES, WILLIAM BRANFORD, JR., WILLIAM RIND. Before JACOB MOTTE, J.P.
ROBERT AUSTIN, Pub. Reg.

Book V, p. 361   JOHN WATSONE, merchant, of Cahrleston, to WIL-
4 June 1741   LIAM BRANFORD, planter, of Berkeley Co., in
Bond   penal sum of Ⱡ 5000 currency, for keeping
                      terms of above conveyance (p. 356). Witness-
es: FRANCIS HOLMES, WILLIAM BRANFORD, JR., WILLIAM RIND. Before JACOB
MOTTE, J.P. ROBERT AUSTIN, Register.

Book V, p. 361   JOHN (his mark) COWEN, planter, & SARAH (her
17 & 18 May 1741   mark) his wife, to JOHN OPHIN, planter; all
L & R   of Granville Co.; for Ⱡ 1610 currency, 402-1/2
                      a. on St. Helena Island, Granville Co., bound-
ing SE on marshes & a creek; NE on COWEN; W on ARTHUR DICKS; S on JOHN
CHAPLIN. Witnesses: HILL WIGG, WILLIAM HAZZARD, JR., THOMAS WIGG. Before HUGH BRYAN, J.P. ROBERT AUSTIN, Register.

Book V, p. 364   JOSEPH SHUTE, & ANNA his wife, of Charleston,
3 June 1741   to JOHN MCKINZIE, merchant, of Charleston, for
Deed of Sale   Ⱡ 4000 SC money, that part of lot #10 in
                      Charleston fronting 20 ft. on Callibeufs Lane,
bounding W 87 ft. on WILLIAM ELLIOTT; E on the part belonging to THOMAS
ELLIOTT; S back home to end of other part of WILLIAM ELLIOTT'S part of
the lot; also that part of lot #10 fronting 5 ft. on Callibeufs Lane;
bounding W 87 ft. on WILLIAM ELLIOTT; E on THOMAS KEMBERLY. Whereas WIL-
LIAM ELLIOTT, planter, of Berkeley Co., & KATHERINE his wife, on 5 May
1722 conveyed to THOMAS KEMBERLY, charimaker of Charleston, that part of
lot #10 fronting 20 ft. on Callibeufs Lane, bounding W 87 ft. on WILLIAM
ELLIOTT; E on another part of lot #10; for the term of the natural lives
of THOMAS KEMBERLY & ISABEL, his wife, & after their death to their daughter ANNA GOOLL; & whereas WILLIAM ELLIOTT, by another conveyance dated
15 Nov. 1722, sold THOMAS KEMBERLY 5 ft. of lot #10, fronting 5 ft. on
Callibeufs Lane, 87 ft. deep, bounding as abovesaid; & whereas THOMAS &
ISABEL KEMBERLY died & ANNA GOOLL (now ANNA SHUTE, wife of JOSEPH) came
into possession; now she & JOSEPH sell to MCKINZIE. Witnesses: JOHN RAT-
TRAY, MATTHEW ROCHE. Before ROBERT AUSTIN, J.P. & Pub. Reg.

Book V, p. 367   JOHN MOORE & JEHU MOORE, planters, of Berkeley
16 & 17 Apr. 1741   Co., to ALEXANDER NISBETT, of Berkeley Co., as
L & R by Mortgage   security on their bond of even date in penal
                      sum of Ⱡ 8400 for payment of Ⱡ 4200 currency
with interest on 25 Mar. 1754; 600 a. in Craven Co., on S side Peedee River, bounding W on MARY FORD; S & E on vacant land; being the tract which
ALEXANDER NISBETT purchased from JOSIAS GAR. DUPREE; also 500 a. on N
side Peedee River, bounding SE on JOHN COIT; NW on HUGH SWINTON; NE on vacant land; being the tract NISBETT purchased from JOHN SNOW; also all of
NISBETTS title to lot #10 in Georgetown (sold by NISBETT to JOHN & JEHU
MOORE). Witnesses: JOHN MAN, JOHN SIMSON. Before JAMES MICHIE, J.P.
ROBERT AUSTIN, Register.

Book V, p. 371   (L. on p. 387 of original). JAMES SAVINEAU, &
19 Sept. 1739   JANE his wife, to JAMES GUERRY; all of Craven
Release   Co., for Ⱡ 1000 SC money, 500 a., part of
                      1000 a. in St. James Santee, Craven Co., pur-
chased by SAVINEAU from DANIEL HUGER; the 500 a. bounding NW on LEWIS
GODIN; N on Wambaw Creek; NE on JAMES SAVINEAU. Witnesses: ANDREW REM-
BERT, NATHANIEL SAVINEAU, LOUIS GOURDIN. Before NOAH SERRE, J.P. Plat
of 500 a. as surveyed by JOHN HENTIE on 11 Apr. 1740. ROBERT AUSTIN,
Register.

Book V, p. 374   RICHARD (his mark) GODWIN, carpenter, & ANN
22 Sept. 1731   his wife, to ALBERT DETMAR, victualer; all of
Bill of Sale   Charleston; for Ⱡ 90 currency, 1/2 of lot
                      #197 in Charleston, bounding E 16 ft. on the
great street leading from Ashley River to the Market Place; S 23 ft. on

RICHARD GODWIN; W 16 ft. on MR. RIVERS; N on ALBERT DETMAR'S lot where he now lives. Witnesses: DAVID DAVIES, JACOB ASHTON, WILLIAM HALES. Before ROBERT AUSTIN, J.P. & Pub. Reg.

Book V, p. 375
4 & 5 Sept. 1734
L & R

JOHN BRAND, innholder, to PHILIP MASSEY, gun-smith; both of Charleston; for ₤ 620 SC money, part of lot #164 in Charleston, bounding E 60 ft. on a street leading up to the broad road out of town (heretofore called a little street leading from Ashley River by MR. JONES'S lot); W on JOHN RYNOLDS; S 142 ft. on JOHN LEWIS; N on JOHN BRAND. Witnesses: LEWIS TIMOTHY, THOMAS BEEKITT. Before ROBERT AUSTIN, J.P. & Pub. Reg.

Book V, p. 379
4 & 5 May 1741
L & R by Mortgage

GEORGE LIVINGSTON, planter, of Port Royal Is-land, Granville Co., to JORDAN ROCHE, gentle-man, of Charleston, as security on bond of even date in penal sum of ₤ 1833 British for payment of ₤ 916:13:4 British on 1 Mar. 1741; 770 a. on Port Royal Island, part of several tracts devised to GEORGE LIVINGSTON by the will of his father, the Rev. MR. WILLIAM LIVINGSTON; bounding W on Port Royal River; N on EPHRAIM MIKELL (formerly GEORGE LIVINGSTON); E on NICHOLAS HATCHER; S on JOHN HENDRICK. Witnesses: JOHN HOPE, WILLIAM SMITH. Before ROBERT AUSTIN, J.P. & Pub. Reg.

Book V, p. 383
11 & 12 Mar. 1740
L & R

JOHN CLELAND, ESQ., of Charleston, & MARY his wife, daughter & devisee of JOHN PERRY, mer-chant, of St. James Parish, Westminster, Co. of Middlesex, Great Britain, & formerly of the Island of Antigua; to CAPT. GEORGE BENISON, of Christ Church Parish, Berkeley Co.; for ₤ 4910 SC money, paid or secured; 982 a. in Christ Church Parish, called Yeoghall, being the remaining part of 1300 a. owned by JOHN PERRY; bounding SE on a great marsh & on CAPT. BENISON; SW on MR. HAMLIN & CAPT. THOMAS BOONE; NW on MR. BARTON & CAPT THOMAS BOONE'S land. Whereas Gov. JOHN ARCHDALE & the Lords Proprs. on 14 May 1696 granted CAPT. GEORGE DEARSLEY 1300 a. on SE side She-a-wee Sound, in Berkeley Co., bounding NE on WILLIAM CROSBY & lands not laid out; NW on MR. PATY & other lands not laid out; which 1300 a. afterwards became vested in THOM-AS HAMLIN, planter, of Berkeley Co., part of which he conveyed in fee to WILLIAM CAPERS, & the remaining part, 982 a. by deed of feoffment dated 1 Jan. 1704 he conveyed in fee to JOHN PERRY of Antigua; & whereas PERRY bequeathed the land to his daughter MARY, now wife of JOHN CLELAND (See record of Prerogative Court of Canterbury); now CLELAND sells to BENISON. Witnesses: DANIEL LAROCHE, WILLIAM FLEMING. Before ANDREW RUTLEDGE, J.P. ROBERT AUSTIN, Register.

Book V, p. 388
2 & 3 Feb. 1740
L & R

JOHN FRASER, merchant, of Charleston, surving executor of will of JOHN MCKAY, shopkeeper, of Charleston, to BENJAMIN MAVERICK, mariner, for ₤ 300 currency, 37-1/2 a. on James Island, Berkeley Co., bounding W on GABRIEL MANIGAULT, ESQ.; N on marsh; S on JER-EMIAH LEAYCROFT & JOHN BEE; SW on JOHN BEE; E on JOHN BEE. Whereas JOHN MCKAY, by will dated 14 Aug. 1739, ordered that his plantation of 170 a. on James Island & part of a tenement on Broad Street, Charleston, be sold, & appointed JAMES FISHER & JOHN FISHER his attorneys; now JOHN FISHER sells a part of the plantation to MAVERICK. Witnesses: ISAAC MAZYCK, JAMES MICHIE. Before ROBERT AUSTIN, J.P. & Pub. Reg.

Book V, p. 392
1 & 2 Feb. 1737
L & R

ANDREW RUTLEDGE, ESQ., of Charleston, to ED-WARD HAZLEWOOD, victualler, of Berkeley Co., for ₤ 500 currency, 10 a. on which JOHN METH-RINGHAM lived & laterly purchased from METH-RINGHAM by RUTLEDGE; also 40 a. (adjoining the 10 a.) also lately pur-chased from METHRINGHAM; total 50 a.; being part of a larger tract grant-ed to PHILIP JONES; bounding N & E on CAPT. BOND; W & S on RICHARD FOWLER & MR. LAWES. Witnesses: EDWARD FENWICKE, ROBERT BREWTON. Before ROBERT AUSTIN, J.P. & Pub. Reg.

Book V, p. 394
7 & 8 May 1741
L & R

HENRY PERONNEAU, JR., & JAMES OSMOND, mer-chants, of Charleston, surviving executors & devises of will of ARTHUR HALL, ESQ., of

Berkeley Co., to WILLIAM STEWART & JAMES MICHIC, ESQRS., of Charleston,
(1/2 to each), for Ł 4000 currency, 3 tracts of 1354 a. Whereas the
ords Proprs. on 13 July 1694 granted JAMES MARTEL GOULARD DEVERVANT, ESQ.,
1000 a. in Colleton Co., between Ashepoo River & S Edisto, bounding N &
SW on Ashepoo River & marsh; NE on marsh: SE on marsh & lands not laid
out; & whereas DEVERVANT on 12 Sept. 1694 sold the 1000 a. to ROBERT SEA-
BROOK, planter, of Colleton Co., & whereas Gov. JOHN ARCHDALE & the Lords
Proprs. on 9 Sept. 1696 granted ROBERT SEABROOK 244 a. in Colleon Co.,
bounding N on marsh of S Edisto River; NW on DEVERVANT; W on Ashepoo River, S & E on marsh; & whereas Gov. JAMES MOORE, & the Lords Proprs. on 11
Jan. 1700, granted ROBERT SEABROOK 110 a. in Colleton Co., being 3 islands on W side S Edisto River, which 3 tracts are adjoining, making 1
tract of 1354 a.; & whereas by will dated 20 Sept. 1710 SEABROOK bequeathed the 1354 a. (called Seabrooks Island) & the adjoining lands to his son
ROBERT SEABROOK (& for want of heirs then to JOSEPH & BENJAMIN SEABROOK);
& whereas ROBERT, JR., died an infant in the lifetime of his father; &
whereas ROBERT, SR. died, leaving the will in full force, & the 1354 a.
became vested in JOSEPH & BENJAMIN SEABROOK in jointenancy; & whereas at
BENJAMIN'S death the jointenancy had not been altered, & the land became
the property of JOSEPH SEABROOK; & whereas by L & R dated 1 & 2 Nov. 1726
he sold to ARTHUR HALL; & whereas on 26 Nov. 1726 JOSEPH SEABROOK & AR-
THUR HALL agreed that should SEABROOK pay HALL Ł 4439 SC money on 1 Feb.
1728 at the house of COL. MILES BREWTON in Charleston, then within 6
months after payment HALL would reconvey the land to SEABROOK; & whereas
that sum was not paid, ARTHUR HALL, by will dated 27 June 1732 devised
his title in Seabrooks Island to his executors in trust for his brother-
in-law JOSEPH SEABROOK if JOSEPH should pay the executors Ł 4600 on 10
Mar. next; failing that, the land to be sold & the money used to pay his
debts; appointing as his executors, HENRY PERONNEAU, JAMES OSMOND, JOHN
RAVEN, & MARTHA HALL; & whereas on 20 Sept. 1732 HALL died, leaving the
will in full force; & whereas by release dated 19 Feb. 1734 from JOSEPH
SEABROOK to HENRY PERONNEAU & JAMES OSMOND, executors, reciting that SEA-
BROOK had not paid the Ł 4439 or the Ł 4600 as agreed, & the 1343 a. re-
verted to PERONNEAU & OSMOND, as executors; & reciting also that at a
Court of Common Pleas held 2nd Tuesday in Oct. 1734 before ROBERT WRIGHT,
C. J. a judgment was obtained against SEABROOK, the sum of Ł 5495 now be-
ing due & to avoid controversies SEABROOK quit claimed to PERONNEAU & OS-
MOND his title to the 3 tracts; now the executors sell to STEWART & MICH-
IE. Witnesses: ALEXANDER PERONNEAU, SAMUEL PRIOLEAU, JR. Before ROBERT
AUSTIN, J.P. & Pub. Reg.

Book V, p. 404   Whereas their dearly beloved brother, JOSEPH
24 Apr. 1740   ELLIOTT, after signing & sealing his will,
Agreement   ordered them (WILLIAM ELLIOTT, THOMAS FARR, &
                        BERNARD ELLIOTT, his heirs) to give the follow-
ing legacies; viz; to sister AMMIRENTIA FARR a snuff box, some rings,
earrings, etc., to his 2 nephews SAMUEL & JOSEPH ELLIOTT, all the marsh
land lying between his upland & Stono River; & believing he meant them to
have part of the land purchased from SAMUEL JONES, adjoining the land he
lived on, though not particularly mentioned by him to his sister-in-law
MRS. FRANCES ELLIOTT Ł 1000 currency as some gratuity for the loss of her
land sustained by attendance on his wife; to his niece, KATHERINE BOOTH,
Ł 500; to his friend, WILLIAM CHAMPIAN, 1 horse named Florick; which legacies they confirm in consideration of their love, good will, & affection
for their relatives; & should this instrument not give them sufficient
title to the legacies they bind themselves under the penalty of double
the value of each legacy to make other sufficient titles. Witnesses:
JOHN CLIFFORD, SARAH TURNER. Before ROBERT AUSTIN, J.P. & Pub. Reg.

Book V, p. 405   MARY NISBETT, widow, of Berkeley Co., daughter
19 & 20 June 1741   & devisee of THOMAS HEPWORTH, ESQ., of Charles-
L & R Tripartite   ton, of 1st part; MARY PORTALL, widow, of
                        Charleston, of 2nd part; ALEXANDER VANDERDUS-
SEN, ESQ., of Berkeley Co., of 3rd part. Whereas THOMAS HEPWORTH owned
part of lot #26 in Charleston, fronting 29 ft. S on ELLIOTTS (or POIN-
SETT'S) lane or alley, running from Cooper River W by the houses of DR.
JOHN THOMAS, MOSES WILSON, & DR. JOHN HUTCHINSON; bounding E 90 ft. on
SHEM BUTLER; N ON (?); W on THOMAS HEPWORTH; & by will dated 11 Sept.
1727 bequeathed that piece of a lot to his daughter MARY (now MARY NIS-
BETT); & whereas THOMAS HEPWORTH bequeathed to his wife ANNE a consider-

able part of his real & personal estate in lieu of her title of dower; & whereas MARY his daughter married ROBERT NISBETT, merchant, of Charleston, & they, on 4 Aug. 1731, mortgaged the lot to ALEXANDER VANDERDUSSEN for L 1000 (date of redemption: 4 Feb. next); & whereas at NISBETT'S death the greater part had not been paid back; now MARY NISBETT & VANDERDUSSEN sell the piece of lot #26 to MARY PORTALL, free from ANNE HEPWORTH'S claim of dower for L 1300. Witnesses: SOPHIA HEPWORTH, JOHN HANCOCK. Witnesses to receipt: JOSEPH GAULTIER, GEORGE HUNTER, CHARLES PINCKNEY. Before ROBERT AUSTIN, J.P. & Pub. Reg.

Book V, p. 409   MOSES MARTIN, planter, of Colleton Co., to his
19 Feb. 1740   loving brother, ISAAC MARTIN; for love & af-
Deed of Gift   fection, & to promote his welfare & comfort-
                      able dwelling; 107-1/2 a. in Colleton Co., ac-
cording to plat. Witnesses: JOHN PERRIMAN, JOHN ANDREWS, JAMES DONOM.
Before JOSEPH WILKINSON, J.P. On 8 July 1741 JOHN ANDREW measured off
107-1/2 a. out of a plat of 530 a. A memorial entered in Auditor's office on 15 July 1741 by JAMES ST. JOHN, Dep. Aud. ROBERT AUSTIN, Pub.
Reg.

Book V, p. 410   JOHN (his mark) RICHARDS, mariner, of Winyaw
30 June & 1 July 1741   to DANIEL LAROCHE & THOMAS LAROCHE, merchants,
L & R by Mortgage   of Winyaw, as security on bond of even date in
                          penal sum of L 980 for payment of L 490 SC mon-
ey, with interest, on 1 Mar. next, (because the LAROCHES went on his bond
to WILLIAM SWINTON & MARY ALLEN, of Winyaw, in penal sum of L 1039 for
payment of L 519:10 currency with interest on 1 June next); 300 a. in
Craven Co., bounding W on Winyaw River; NE & S on a Barony laid out by
the Lords Proprs. Witnesses: WILLIAM WHITESIDE, THOMAS LEITH. Before
WILLIAM ROMSEY, J.P. ROBERT AUSTIN, Pub. Reg.

Book V, p. 415   JOHN TRIBOUDET, vintner, & LUCRETIA, his wife,
26 & 27 June 1741   to DR. JACOB MARTIN, all of Charleston, for
L & R by Mortgage   L 1200 currency, part of lot #17 in Charleston,
                          25 ft. x 160 ft. bounding E on part of same
lot fronting the Bay 7 70 ft. deep owned by JACOB WOOLFORD (heretofore of
JOHN RAPER & formerly purchased from DR. THOMAS COOPER & ELEANA his wife);
W on the street or lane leading from COL. MILES BREWTON'S saw-pit to
Union Street; S on CHARLES CODNER; N on a small alley running from the
Bay to Union Street. Should TRIBOUDET pay BENJAMIN WHITAKER, ESQ. (for
use of GEORGE ANSON, ESQ.) L 1200 currency, with interest, from 9 May
last to 9 May 1742, in full payment of a bond signed by MARTIN & TRIBOU-
DET & given to WHITAKER (for TRIBOUDET'S debt) in penal sum of L 2400 for
payment of L 1200 with interest dated 9 May last, this mortgage to be
void. Witnesses: MATHIEU VANALLE, LAWRENCE COULLIETTE. Before ROBERT
AUSTIN, J.P. & Pub. Reg. On 1 Mar. 1745/6 J. MARTIN declared mortgage
satisfied. Witness: JAMES HOWE, Pub. Reg.

Book V, p. 419   ROBERT SCRIVEN, planter, & MARTHA his wife, of
8 & 9 Oct. 1740   Berkeley Co., to WILLIAM FLEMING, merchant, of
L & R   Craven Co., for L 942:6:8 currency, 500 a. in
                          Craven Co., free from MARTHA'S claim of dower;
bounding E on WILLIAM FARBUSH; S on WILLIAM GARDNER; other sides on Black
River. Witnesses: JOHN ATCHISON, the Rev. MR. JOHN BAXTER. Before JAMES
MICHIE, J.P. ROBERT AUSTIN, Register.

Book V, p. 422   JOHN LLOYD, of Tarphley, St. James Goose Creek,
10 July 1733   Parish, leased to his brothers EDWARD & HUGH,
Lease   22 a. 3 roods, according to plat, for 50 years.
                          On 1 Feb. 1734 EDWARD LLOYD transferred his
title to his sister, SARAH LLOYD, widow, for signing his bond of even
date for L 100 & interest, given ROWLAND VAUGHAN, gentleman, of Charleston. Witnesses: HUGH EVANS, ROWLAND VAUGHAN. MAT. DRAKE, Dep. Sur., at
the request of JOHN LLOYD laid out 22 a. bounding S on land in dispute
between CAPT. DRY & MR. LLOYD; W on RALPH ISARD, ESQ.; N on LLOYD; E on
the Broad Path; certified 7 July 1733. ROBERT AUSTIN, Register.

Book V, p. 423   DANIEL CARTWRIGHT, planter, & SARAH his wife,
24 & 26 Nov. 1739   of Berkeley Co., to JOHN LEE, chairmaker, of
L & R   Charleston, for L 16:5 SC money, a 1/4 a. lot

22

#81 at Ashley River Ferry, bounding NW on lot #80; NE on lot #72; SE & SW
on 2 streets. Witnesses: HUGH CARTWRIGHT, CORNELIUS FENAGHTY, WILLIAM
SMITH. Before ROBERT AUSTIN, J.P. & Pub. Reg.

Book V, p. 427   JOHN BAGEN (BEGGON), planter, to THOMAS SACH-
28 & 29 May 1733   EVERELL, planter, both of Colleton Co., for
L & R   ₺ 750 SC money, 2 tracts of 450 a.; 100 a. be-
                        ing W of the freshes of Edisto River, within
land, near Horse Shoe Savanna, bounding N on BAGEN; E S & W on lands not
laid out; 350 a. being W of Horse Shoe Savanna, bounding N on JOHN COOK;
E & W on lands not laid out; S on BAGEN. Witnesses: WILLIAM PETER, MOSES
MARTIN, BELTESHAZZAR LAMBRIGHT. Before JAMES BULLOCH, J.P. Memorial entered in Auditor's office 27 Feb. 1735. ROBERT AUSTIN, Register.

Book V, p. 431   CHARLES PINCKNEY, gentleman, & ELIZABETH his
30 Apr. & 1 May 1731   wife, to MARTHA ROMSEY, widow, all of Charles-
L & R   ton, for ₺ 320 currency, a parcel of land
                        3-1/2 ft. wide fronting the Bay & laid out
from a cedar stake fixed as S boundray on front of lot #4 already belonging to MARTHA ROMSEY into the front of lot #3 of Charles PINCKNEY SW &
3-1/2 ft. wide all the way down the whole depth of the lot westwardly of
lots 3 & 4 in a straight line to the W end & all buildings thereon. Witnesses: JAMES ABERCROMBY, HENRY HARGRAVE. Before JOHN SKENE, J.P. ROB-
ERT AUSTIN, Register.

Book V, p. 434   JOSHUA SAUNDERS (SANDERS), planter, executor
1 & 2 June 1741   of will of WILSON SAUNDERS, planter, to WIL-
L & R   LIAM CATTELL, ESQ., for ₺ 500 currency, 320 a.
                        on Ashepoo or Cheechesay Creek, Colleton Co.,
bounding NE, E, & SE on an impassable swamp or marsh; W & S on said creek;
which tract was granted by the Lords Proprs. to JOHN DEAR, who, by L & R
dated 4 & 5 Jan. 1721 conveyed to JOHN SAUNDERS; & became vested in WIL-
SON SAUNDERS, brother & heir-at-law of JOHN; & devised by JOHN SAUNDERS
to JOSHUA SAUNDERS, executor, to be sold by him. Witnesses: WILLIAM CAT-
TELL, JR., WILLIAM GEORGE FREEMAN. ROBERT AUSTIN, J.P. & Pub. Reg.

Book V, p. 438   HUGH BRYAN, planter, of Granville Co., to
6 & 7 Aug. 1741   THOMAS JENYS, merchant, of Charleston, for 10
L & R   shillings currency, 640 a. in Granville Co.,
                        bounding S on Pocosaba Creek & marshes; W on
EDWARD CROFT; N on ISAAC MAZYCK, SR.; E on the Hon. FRANCIS YONGE; granted 5 Apr. 1734 to JEREMIAH MILNER, who by L & R dated 15 & 16 Apr. 1734
conveyed to HUGH BRYAN. Witnesses: DAVID STOUT, THOMAS SMITH. Before
ROBERT AUSTIN, J.P. & Pub. Reg.

Book V, p. 443   HUGH BRYAN, planter, of Granville Co., to THOM-
7 & 8 Aug. 1741   AS JENYS, merchant, of Charleston, for
L & R   ₺ 12,595:10 currency, several tracts of land
                        in Granville Co., namely; 939 a., 1269 a.;
270 a.; 78 a.; 30 a.; 700 a.; 300 a.; 1000 a.; 150 a.; & 222 a. Whereas
GEORGE II on 3 Apr. 1735 granted ANTHONY MATHEWS, SR., 939 a. on E side
of Whale Branch of Pocotaligo River, bounding W on the river, marsh & a
creek; N on a marsh, creek & JOSEPH BRYAN; E & S on HILL CROFT, marsh &
a creek; & he, by L & R dated 1 & 2 May 1735, conveyed to HUGH BRYAN; &
whereas GEORGE II on 8 Apr. 1733 granted ISAAC MAZYCK, SR., merchant, of
Charleston, 1269 a., bounding E on a branch of Port Royal River, small
creeks, & THOMAS GRAVE; S & W on MR. CROFT; N on JOSEPH BRYAN, HUGH BRYAN,
& JOSEPH MASSEY; & he, by L & R dated 5 & 6 Nov. 1733 conveyed to HUGH
BRYAN; & whereas GEORGE II on 5 Apr. 1734 granted JOHN TIPPER, sailmaker,
of Charleston, 270 a., bounding W on MR. LUDLAND & a branch of Pocotaligo
River; N & E on said land granted to MAZYCK; S on EDWARD CROFT; & TIPPER
by L & R dated 26 & 27 Apr. 1734 conveyed to HUGH BRYAN; & whereas GEORGE
II on 5 Apr. 1734 granted ROWLAND SERJANT, of Beaufort, 78 a. called
Roses Island, bounding S on creeks & marshes of Port Royal River; N on a
branch & marshes of Pocasaba Creek; & SERJANT conveyed to HUGH BRYAN; &
whereas GEORGE II on 11 July 1733 granted GARRAT VANVELSEN, cordwainer,
of Charleston, 1300 a., bounding W on marshes & a branch of Port Royal
River; NE on JAMES ST. JOHN; E on ISAAC MAZYCK; "& lyeth round a tract
of" ANDREW ALLEN; & VANVELSEN, by L & R dated L 7 2 Nov. 1733, conveyed
to HUGH BRYAN & whereas conveyed to PETER POSTELL 870 a. (part of the

1300 a.), & to WILLIAM SCOTT 400 a. (other part of the 1300 a.), leaving
HUGH BRYAN 30 a., being an island, bounding SW on a branch of Port Royal
River, other sides on marsh; & whereas GEORGE II on 16 Mar. 1732 granted
EDWARD CROFT, shopkeeper, of Charleston, 700 a., bounding E on CROFT'S
other lands; S & S on Pocasaba Creek; N on JOHN CROFT; & EDWARD CROFT by
L & R dated 1 & 2 Oct. 1733 conveyed to HYGY BRYAN; & whereas the Lords
Proprs. on 7 June 1717, granted HILL CROFT, gentleman, of Charleston,
300 a. on E side Coosa River, bounding E on CAPT. JOHN CROFT; N on JOSEPH
BRYAN; W on GEORGE PAWLEY; & HILL CROFT, by L & R dated 24 & 25 Feb. 1724
conveyed to RICHARD LUDLAM, clerk, late rector of St. James Goose Creek
Parish; & LUDLAM, by will dated 11 Oct. 1728 bequeathed all his real &
personal estate to the Society for Propagating the Gospel in foreign
parts in trust that they would erect a school for poor children in St.
James Goose creek Parish with the money arising from the sale of his real
& personal estate, appointing ARTHUR MIDDLETON, BENJAMIN GODIN, & THOMAS
CLIFFORD, his executors; & whereas the Society by letter of attorney dated 1 Oct. 1734 appointed the Rev. MR. ALEXANDER GARDEN & the Rev. MR.
WILLIAM GUY, clerks, of Charleston, their attorneys to dispose of LUD-
LAM'S estate; & they by L & R dated 1 & 2 Feb. 1736 sold the 300 a. to
HUGH BRYAN; & whereas ALEXANDER TRENCH, (merchant, of Charleston) attorney for JOHN BAILEY of Ballinaclough, Co. of Tipperary, Ireland, son &
heir of JOHN BAILEY of same place, by L & R dated 9 & 10 Feb. 1729 conveyed to FRANCIS YONGE, ESQ., of Berkeley Co., 1000 a. near Roses Island
on Port Royal River, being a point of Pocosaba Neck; & whereas FRANCIS
YONGE & LYDIA his wife by L & R dated 9 & 10 May 1733 sold the 1000 a. to
HUGH BRYAN; & whereas JOSEPH MASSEY, gunsmith, of Charleston, purchased
from the Lords Proprs. for Ł 0 currency, 300 a. on W side Tomatley Creek;
bounding N on JOHN STONE; S on CHARLES SHARPE; W on MAURICE HARVEY; & JO-
SEPH MASSEY & REBECCA his wife, in 1734 sold to HUGH BRYAN; & whereas
HUGH BRYAN conveyed the N half of the 300 a. to his niece ELIZABETH BULL;
retaining the S 150 a.; & whereas GEORGE II on 5 Apr. 1734 granted ANDREW
ALLEN, merchant, of Charleston, 222 a. on S side Combee River, bounding S
on COL. JOSEPH BLAKE & a branch of Combee River; N & E on the river; W on
another branch; & whereas JOHN ALLEN, son & devisee of ANDREW ALLEN, by
L & R dated 25 & 27 July 1741 conveyed the 222 a. to HUGH BRYAN; now BRY-
AN sell these various tracts to JENYS. Witnesses: DAVID STOUT, THOMAS
SMITH. Before ROBERT AUSTIN, J.P. & Pub. Reg.

Book V, p. 453   WILLIAM BAYNARD, planter, to JOSEPH WHIPPEY,
28 Apr. 1741   planter, both of Edisto Island, for Ł 900 SC
L & R   money, 200 a. at Pohon Pohon, Colleton Co.,
                         bounding S on JOHN ANDREW, SR.; W on WILLIAM
GRAY; N on JOSEPH MACKEY; E on JOSEPH BOON'S Barony; which tract was
granted by Gov. ROBERT GIBBES & the Lords Proprs. on 28 July 1711, for
Ł 4, to JOSEPH FARLEY, carpenter, of Colleton Co.; who, for Ł 26, sold to
EDWARD RIPPIN, JR.; who, for 200 currency, conveyed to WILLIAM GRAY, SR.;
who for Ł 700 currency, conveyed to TIMOTHY HENDRICKS; from whom it was
inherited by the sons of WILLIAM WHIPPEY (WILLIAM & JOSEPH); who, for
Ł 900 currency, sold to WILLIAM BAYNARD; who now sells to JOSEPH WHIPPEY.
MARY (her mark) BAYNARD, wife of WILLIAM, willingly surrenders her dowry.
Witnesses: JOHN CALDER, JOSEPH SEABROOK, WILLIAM DAVIS. Before JOSEPH
WILKINSON, J.P. ROBERT AUSTIN, Pub. Reg.

DEEDS BOOK "W"

Book W, p. 1   JOHN MIMMACK, planter, & ANNA his wife, of St.
13 & 14 Aug. 1741   James Goose Creek, to JOHN LAURENS, saddler,
L & R   of Charleston, for Ł 200 currency, 200 a. in
                         St. Thomas Parish, Berkeley Co., bounding E on
part of same tract belonging to JOHN MUSGROVE; W on JOHN GUERIN; S on
ALEXANDER VANDERDUSSEN; N on JOSEPH SINGLETARY. Witnesses: BENJAMIN ADDI-
SON, JOHN RATTRAY. Before ROBERT AUSTIN, J.P. & Pub. Reg.

Book W, p. 4   JOHN WALKER, planter, of Berkeley Co., appoint-
3 July 1741   ed his loving wife SUSANNAH his attorney to
Letter of Attorney   collect debts, etc. Witnesses: JOHN YERWORTH,
                         JOSEPH SPENCER. Before ROBERT AUSTIN, J.P. &

Pub. Reg.

Book W, p. 5   WALTER HOLMAN, planter, to THOMAS HOLMAN,
18 Dec. 1736   planter, both of Berkeley Co., 135 a. formerly
Bill of Dale   owned by THOMAS HOLMAN, planter, deceased; &
                     by several conveyances & devises now vested in
WALTER HOLMAN; bounding N on WILLIAM MILES; E on THOMAS HOLMAN; S on
THOMAS ELLIOTT; W on JOHN RIVERS. Witnesses: NATHANIEL BROWN, FRANCIS
THOMPSON, JOHN BROWN. Delivery by turf & twig. Before WILLIAM BULL, JR.,
J.P. ROBERT AUSTIN, Register.

Book W, p. 7   GEORGE ANSON, ESQ., captain of H.M.S. CENTUR-
25 & 26 June 1741   ION, by BENJAMIN WHITAKER, ESQ., of SC, his
L & R   attorney, to JOHN TRIBOUDET, vintner, of
                     Charleston, for Ł 1200 SC money, lot #17 in
Charleston; bounding E on part of the lot fronting 25 ft. on the Bay &
70 ft. deep, owned by JACOB WOOLFORD (formerly owned by DR. THOMAS COOP-
ER & ELEANA his wife; later by JOHN RAPER); W on the street now called
Union Street, leading from COL. MILES BREWTON'S sawpit to Broad Street; N
on an alley running from Union Street to the Bay; S on CHARLES CODNER.
Witnesses: WILLIAM LASSARRE, LAWRENCE COULLIETTE. Before ROBERT AUSTIN,
J.P. & Pub. Reg.

Book W, p. 12   WILLIAM WILKINS, planter, of Berkeley Co., to
16 Jan. 1739/40   his beloved son OBADIAH WILKINS, for love &
Deed of Gift   affection, 820 a. on John Island, Colleton Co.,
                     granted by the Lords Proprs. to CAPT. WILLIAM
DAVIS; bounding W on WILLIAM WHIPPEY; E on Stono River; N on A B Poolaw
Creek; S on a creek of Stono River; also 5 Negro men; reserving 200 a.
for himself during his (WILLIAM'S) life on which to build & plant. Wit-
nesses: WILLIAM WILKINS, JR., WILLIAM (his mark) FENDIN. Before ANTHONY
MATHEWES, J.P. ROBERT AUSTIN, Pub. Reg.

Book W, p. 13   THOMAS LOREY, carpenter, to MOSES JOY, cord-
3 & 4 Jan. 1736   winder & planter, both of Christ Church Parish,
L & R   Berkeley Co., for Ł 400 SC money, 75 a., part
                     of 237 a. formerly belonging to THOMAS LOREY,
father of THOMAS, party hereto; which 75 a. in Christ Church Parish is
bounding SE on marsh; SW on THOMAS LOREY; NW on MURREL & BROWN. Witnesses: WILLIAM HENDRICK, JOSEPH SAVERANCE, STEPHEN HARTLEY. Before DANIEL
CRAWFORD, J.P. ROBERT AUSTIN, Register.

Book W, p. 16   JOHN SNOW, planter, of Berkeley Co., to STE-
15 Apr. 1736   PHEN MILLER, merchant, of Charleston, for
Mortgage   Ł 215 SC money, 435 a., English measure, in
                     Berkeley Co., where SNOW lives bounding N on
vacant land; E on Gov. JOHNSON'S Barony; S on THOMAS THREADCRAFT; W on
JOHN CAREAH. Date of redemption, 15 Apr. 1737. Witnesses: JOHN GUERIN,
PETER GUERIN. Before MICHAEL DARBY, J.P. ROBERT AUSTIN, Register. Mortgage satisfied 11 June 1745. Witness: RICHARD HARRISON.

Book W, p. 19   JOHN JEFFERDS (JEFFORDS), planter, & MARGARET
22 Aug. 1741   (her mark) his wife, of St. Thomas Parish,
Deed of Gift   Berkeley Co., to their son JOHN, for natural
                     love & affection & other considerations, the
western half of 300 a. on Murrels Creek which PETER COWLEY deeded them 12
Sept. 1735, & on which half JOHN (the father) has settled a new planta-
tion; JOHN, JR. to take possession after the death of JOHN, SR. & MARGA-
RET his wife, or when he reaches 21 years. Witnesses: ROBERT HOW, ANDREW
GUERIN. Before ROBERT AUSTIN, J.P. & Pub. Reg.

Book W, p. 20   JOHN JEFFERDS, planter, & MARGARET (her mark)
22 Aug. 1741   his wife of St. Thomas Parish, Berkeley Co.,
Deed of Gift   to their son DANIEL, for love & affection &
                     other considerations, the eastern half of 300
a. on which their dwelling house now stands on Murrels Creek; which 300 a.
was given to them by PETER COWLEY on 12 Sept. 1735; DANIEL to take possession after the death of his parents, or when he reaches 21 years. Witnesses: ROBERT HOW, ANDREW GUERIN. Before ROBERT AUSTIN, J.P. & Pub. Reg.

Book W, p. 21   WILLIAM GUY, JR., gentleman, & HANNAH his wife,
3 & 4 Feb. 1740   of Berkeley Co., to CHARLES PINCKNEY, ESQ., of
L & R by Mortgage   Charleston, for Ł 1600 SC money, 488 a. on
                       Foster's Creek, St. James Parish Goose Creek,
bounding E on the creek & CAPT. JAMES GOODBEE; SE on JAMES GOODBEE; S on
COL. JOHN HERBERT; W on land lately sold by CHARLES PINCKNEY for a free
school in St. James Parish; N on JOB HOWES & ARTHUR MIDDLETON; which
488 a. consists of 2 tracts, the E tract of 240 a. having been purchased
by CHARLES PINCKNEY from ALEXANDER GOODBEE & ANNA his wife, & JOHN DANIEL,
ESQ.; the W tract of 248 a. being part of 548 a. which PINCKNEY purchased
from BENJAMIN GODIN, ESQ. To be redeemed by payment of certain sums on
certain dates. Witnesses: WILLIAM DAVY, ANN BLAKEWEY. Before ROBERT
AUSTIN, J.P. & Pub. Reg.

Book W, p. 26   JACOB MOTTE, ESQ. & JOHN GREENE, ESQ. (son of
22 & 23 May 1740   ELIZABETH GREENE, widow of DANIEL GREENE, ESQ.)
L & R   executors, of will of ELIZABETH GREENE, to WIL-
                       LIAM STONE, merchant, all of Charleston, for
Ł 3500 SC money a house & several lots. Whereas DANIEL GREENE owned the
tenement on part of lot #7, also part of the adjoining lot, 3 ft. in
breadth, part of an alley lying between the line of GABRIEL REBELLEAU'S
property & the line of DANIEL GREENE'S property, containing 33 ft. clear
front of the lot & running W 100 ft. from the E sill of DANIEL GREENE'S
dwelling house; which part of the lot lately belonging to DANIEL GREENE
is butting E on the street next to & parallel with Cooper River; N on MR.
KEYS; S on part of the alley belonging to JACOB MOTTE; W on JACOB MOTTE
(formerly ROBERT TRADD); & whereas DANIEL GREENE by will dated 14 Nov.
1735 bequeathed all his real & personal estate to his wife ELIZABETH, &
she by will dated 14 Oct. 1737 devised all her real estate in turst to
her executor JACOB MOTTE, directing him to sell the real estate, & by
codicil dated 29 Feb. 1739 appointed her son JOHN an executor, to act
with MOTTE; now MOTTE & GREENE sell to WILLIAM STONE. Witnesses: EDWARD
HEXT, JAMES OSMOND. Before ROBERT AUSTIN, J.P. & Pub. Reg.

Book W, p. 31   HUGH SWINTON, planter, of Craven Co., to JAMES
8 Jan. 1740   ABERCROMBY, ESQ., as security on several bonds,
Mortgage   in varying amounts, a tenement & 700 a. in
                       Craven Co., obunding SE on Peedee River; N on
WILLIAM WATIES; SW on WILLIAM SWINTON; shich tract was granted by Gov.
ROBERT JOHNSON to STEPHEN PROCTER on 16 Mar. 1732, & conveyed by PROCTER
to SWINTON; also 250 a. bounding NW on Peedee River; SE on a creek; SW on
WILLIAM SWINTON; which tract was granted by the Hon. THOMAS BROUGHTON on
4 June 1735 to SWINTON. Ł 280 sterling & Ł 4270 currency being the
amounts to be repaid. SWINTON reserves 70 a. sold to JAMES GORDON. Witnesses: ARCHIBALD BAIRD, JONATHAN SKRINE. Possession given with a key.
Before JOHN CLELAND, J.P. ROBERT AUSTIN, Pub. Reg.

Book W, p. 34   THOMAS DIXON, planter, of St. Andrews Parish,
15 Sept. 1741   Berkeley Co., leased to JOHN MEEK, bricklayer,
Agreement   of St. Philips, Charleston, for 18 years, at
                       Ł 80 yearly, payable quarterly; the lot front-
ing 29 ft. on N side Broad Street, bounding W 67 ft. on MRS. REBECCA FLA-
VELL; E on JOHN NEUFVILLE. MEEK agrees to build on the lot, at his own
cost, within 4 months, a 3 story brick house, the wall of the 1st story
2 bricks thick; 2nd &3rd stories 1-1/2 bricks thick; 29 ft. wide on
street side, 30 ft. deep; erect a balcony on 1st story across the whole
front; also build & furnish as many windows & lights as necessary & suitable; also build a brick kitchen & brick store of suitable dimensions &
as commodious & convenient as possible. Witnesses: WILLIAM MOVATT, JAMES
MICHIE. Before ROBERT AUSTIN, J.P. & Pub. Reg.

Book W, p. 37   MARY SMITH, widow of Landgrave THOMAS SMITH,
23 & 24 Mar. 1739   ESQ., of Berkeley Co., confirms to WILLIAM
L & R   PINCKNEY, ESQ., of Charleston, for Ł 250 cur-
                       rency, part of 2 low water lots. Whereas Land-
grave SMITH by will dated 6 May 1738 authorized his wife, MARY, to give
WILLIAM PINCKNEY a firm title to part of a low water lot on N side of
PINCKNEY'S wharf deducting 120 ft. from the front line E; 40 ft. of which,
adjoining PINCKNEY'S part, he gave to his wife MARY, the remaining 80 ft.
to his sons HENRY, THOMAS, GEORGE, & BENJAMIN, equally divided; now MARY,

confirms to WILLIAM PINCKNEY that piece of low water land E of the front
"wall or line" of Charleston, bounding E 25 ft. on Cooper River; bounding
N 225 ft. on low water land of CAPT. ANTHONY MATHEWES; W on the 40 ft.
given to MARY by her husband Landgrave SMITH; S on PINCKNEY'S wharf; also
her 40 ft. lot, bounding E on WILLIAM PINCKNEY; N on CAPT. MATHEWS; W on
the land of her sons, HENRY, THOMAS, GEORGE & BENJAMIN SMITH; S on PINCK-
NEY'S wharf, MARY quitclaims to PINCKNEY her title to "that Bridge Key or
Wharf" of PINCKNEY'S lying before the "great brick messuage in the Bay"
formerly belonging to Landgrave SMITH (lately to WILLIAM GIBBONO to which
she is entitled by virtue of any exception in the deeds of conveyance of
said "Bridge Key or Wharf" by Landgrave SMITH to THOMAS PINCKNEY, father
of said WILLIAM, PINCKNEY agrees to let sons HENRY, THOMAS, GEORGE & BEN-
JAMIN SMITH have a passage over the bridge to the houses & stores which
they may build on the remaining 80 ft. of low water land devised to them,
they paying PINCKNEY the usual wharfage; also agrees to build & maintain
a good slip or landing place on N side of wharf on MARY'S lot, suitable
for any tide. Witnesses: JAMES SCREVEN, MRS. MARY BASSETT (quaker). Before ROBERT AUSTIN, J.P. & Pub. Reg.

Book W, p. 42   WILLIAM PINCKNEY, gentleman, & RUTH his wife,
26 & 27 Aug. 1741   to ELIZABETH JENYS, widow, all of Charleston,
L & R   for Ł 7200 SC money, the N part of lot #5 E
                     23 ft. on the Bay, bounding N on ANTHONY MATH-
EWES, MR. HINSON, JEREMIAH MILNER, JOSEPH MOODY, HENRY SALTUS, & JAMES
MCCALL; W 21-1/2 ft. on THOMAS CAPERS; with free use of the alley between
the house heretofore standing on E end of said N part of lot #5 & the
great brick house of WILLIAM GIBBON (formerly Landgrave THOMAS SMITH);
also of that bridge key or wharf & land on which it is erected, lying before the brick house & running from "the bank before Charleston into
Cooper River, bounding E on Cooper River; S on other part of low water
lot before lot #5 lately belonging to CAPT. GEORGE SMITH; N on other part
of said low water lot lately belonging to Landgrave THOMAS SMITH; W on
said bank or wharf line; also the piece of low water land E of the front-
wall or line of Charleston, bounding E 25 ft. on Cooper River, N 225 ft.
on low water lot of Capt. ANTHONY MATHEWES; W on low water lot 40 ft.
long devised by Landgrave THOMAS SMITH to his wife MARY; S on WILLIAM
PINCKNEY'S wharf; also that part of low water lot 40 ft. deep, bounding E
on WILLIAM PINCKNEY; N on CAPT. ANTHONY MATHEWES; W on HENRY, THOMAS,
GEORGE & BENJAMIN SMITH; S on PINCKNEY'S wharf. Whereas THOMAS PINCKNEY,
merchant, owned the N part of lot #5, with use of the alley, also the
wharf; & whereas by Act of General Assembly the wharf became vested in
WILLIAM PINCKNEY, a son & devisee of THOMAS PINCKNEY; & whereas Landgrave
THOMAS SMITH by will dated 6 May 1738 authorized his wife, MARY, to give
WILLIAM PINCKNEY a firm title to a part of a low water lot on N side of
wharf, deducting from whole lot 120 ft. from front line E 40 ft. adjoining PINCKNEYS part which SMITH gave to his wife MARY, giving the remaining 80 ft. to his sons HENRY, THOMAS, GEORGE & BENJAMIN SMITH, equally; &
whereas MARY SMITH by L & R dated 23 & 24 Mar. 1739 conveyed to WILLIAM
PINCKNEY the 25 x 225 ft. lot E of MARY SMITH'S lot, & also her 40 ft.
lot; now PINCKNEY sells MRS. JENYS. Witnesses: STEPHEN BEDON, LEVI
DURAND, GEORGE LOGAN, JR. Before JACOB BOND, J.P. ROBERT AUSTIN, Register.

Book W, p. 51   HENRY CHRISTIE, carpenter, of St. Philips Par-
Undated   ish, Charleston, to JOHN LAURENS, saddler, for
Bill of Sale   Ł 100 currency, 300 a. in Kingstown Township,
                     Craven Co., bounding on all sides on vacant
land, also lot #35 in Kingstown, according to plat annexed to grant to
CHRISTIE from the Hon. THOMAS BROUGHTON. Witnesses: JOEL POINSETT, WIL-
LIAM HARVEY (merchant). Before WILLIAM TREWIN, 25 Sept. 1741. ROBERT
AUSTIN, Register.

Book W, p. 53   JOHN COOK (COOKE), planter, of St. Thomas Par-
22 & 23 Aug. 1741   ish, to FRANCIS VARAMBAUT, shopkeeper, of
L & R by Mortgage   Charleston, as security on bond of even date,
                     signed by JOHN COOK & GEORGE COOK, for JOHN'S
debt, in penal sum of Ł 1200 for payment of Ł 600 SC money, with interest,
on 1 Jan. 1744; 500 a. in Craven Co., bounding SW on JOHN COOK (formerly
EDWARD STANLEY); NW on WILLIAM WATIES; N & SE on vacant land. Witnesses:
MATHEW VANALL, ELIZABETH (her mark) VANALL, JOHN REMINGTON. Before

ROBERT AUSTIN, J.P. & Pub. Reg.

Book W, p. 57   Between ROBERT HOW, schoolmaster, of Berkeley
24 Sept. 1741   Co., & JOHN NAILOR (NAYLOR) planter, of Berke-
Agreement   ley Co. Whereas by L & R dated 6 & 7 June
                       1738 JOHN MOORE sold ROBERT HOW & JOHN NAILOR
700 a., English measure, in Craven Co., where MOORE formerly lived, bounding NE on RICHARD WALKER; SW on ROBERT HOW; SE on WILLIAM BROCKINGTON;
other sides on Black River; as by plat annexed to original grant dated 11
July 1733; now HOW & NAILOR agree that should either of them die before
division of the land, the survivor will permit the heirs of the other
partner to enjoy half the property, the whole to be divided into 2 equal
parts. Witnesses: THOMAS BONNY, JOHN SIMSON. Before ROBERT AUSTIN, J.P.
& Pub. Reg.

Book W, p. 60   RICHARD WOODWARD, gentleman, & ELIZABETH his
20 & 21 Aug. 1741   wife, of Beaufort, to CHARLES PURRY, gentleman,
L & R   of Granville Co., for Ł 250 currency, lot #8
                       in Beaufort, fronting S on the Bay; bounding W
on lot #7; N on lot #36; E on lot #9. Witnesses: ROBERT BRISBANE, ANDREW
BELL, JOHN DUNCAN. Before ROBERT AUSTIN, J.P. & Pub. Reg.

Book W, p. 64   THOMAS PARMETER, JR., to RICHARD HAZZARD, gen-
30 & 31 Mar. 1736   tleman, both of Port Royall Island, Granville
L & R   Co., for Ł 30 proclamation money, 100 a. on
                       Port Royall Island, bounding N on ROBERT ORR &
JOSEPH PARMETER; E on NISBETT; W on Port Royall River. Witnesses: WIL-
LIAM HAZZARD, RICHARD RICKETTS, ROBERT BRISBANE. On 30 May 1737 HAZZARD,
for Ł 300 currency, assigned the 100 a. to THOMAS BOWMAN, bill of sale
dated 25 May 1736. Witnesses: JAMES DUNLAPE, CHARLES REEVES, HENRY ORR.
Before THOMAS WIGG, J.P. Land resurveyed by WILLIAM STAPLES 13 Mar. 1735/
6. Witnesses: HENRY LANGDALE, WILLIAM HAZZARD. ROBERT AUSTIN, Register.

Book W, p. 70   RICHARD HAZZARD, JR., of Philadelphia, Penna.,
25 May 1736   to THOMAS BOWMAN, of Granville Co., SC, for
Bill of Sale   Ł 350 SC money, 100 a. Witnesses: ROBERT ORR,
                       HENRY ORR, CHARLES REEVES. Before HUGH BRYAN,
J.P. ROBERT AUSTIN, Pub. Reg.

Book W, p. 71   JOHN LAURENS, saddler, of Charleston, to LEWIS
7 Oct. 1741   MOUZON, planter, of St. Thomas Parish, for
L & R   Ł 300 currency, 200 a. in St. Thomas Parish,
                       bounding E on part of same tract belonging to
JOHN MUSGROVE; W on JOHN GUERIN; S on ALEXANDER VANDERDUSSEN; N on JOSEPH
SINGLETARY. Witnesses: FRANCIS DESCHAMPS, AUGUSTUS LAURENS. Before ROB-
ERT AUSTIN, J.P. & Pub. Reg.

Book W, p. 75   ROBERT BREWTON, ESQ., of Charleston, to THOMAS
11 & 12 Oct. 1741   BURTON, carpenter, of Beaufort, Granville Co.,
L & R   for Ł 60 currency, lot #97 in Beaufort, bound-
                       ing S on Port Royall Street; W on New Street;
N on lot #96; E on lot #102. Witnesses: BENJAMIN SMITH, THOMAS SMITH, AD.
LOYER, CHARLES PURRY. Before ROBERT AUSTIN, J.P. & Pub. Reg.

Book W, p. 80   ISABELLA (her mark) WATSON, widow of JOSEPH
4 & 5 Apr. 1740   WATSON, of Edisto Island, to JOHN DEVANT, car-
L & R   penter, of Edisto Island, for Ł 2000 SC money,
                       150 a. bequeathed to ISABELLA by her husband
JOSEPH WATSON; bounding N on Edisto Creek; E on WILLIAM ADAMS; W on WIL-
LIAM CONYERS; S on JOHN HAMBLETON; which 150 a. was purchased from MATHEW
MILLER, planter, & EAD his wife, of Edisto Island by deed of feoffment
dated 3 Jan. 1721/2. Witnesses: WILLIAM EDINGS, HENRY TOOMER, ALGERNOON
ASH. Before JOSEPH WILKINSON, J.P. ROBERT AUSTIN, Pub. Reg.

Book W, p. 86   JAMES KILPATRICK, practitioner in physic, &
12 & 13 Oct. 1741   ELIZABETH his wife, to PETER LAURENS, saddler,
L & R   all of Charleston, for Ł 2560 currency, the S
                       corner part of lot #26 in Charleston, bounding
E on THOMAS HEPWORTH; S 64 ft. on Elliott Street; W 56 ft. on Church
Street; N on part belonging to THOMAS HEPWORTH. Witnesses: GABRIEL

MANIGAULT, JAMES DRUMMOND, JOHN LAURENS. Before ROBERT AUSTIN, J.P. & Pub. Reg.

Book W, p. 92   JAMES NICHOLAS MAYRANT, planter, to PETER POTE-
22 Mar. 1725/6   VINE, planter, both of Berkeley Co., for 10
Deed of Sale   shillings, 20 a. bounding S & W on PETER POTE-
                       VINE; NE on said MAYRANT; being part of 600 a.
purchased from POTEVINE. Signed by JAMES NICHOLAS MAYRANT & SUSANNA MAY-
RANT. Witnesses: ROBERT HOW, PETER PERDRIAU. Before MICHAEL DARBY, J.P.
ROBERT AUSTIN, Pub. Reg.

Book W, p. 94   FRANCIS VARAMBAUT, apothecary, & MARTHA (her
23 Mar. 1738   mark) his wife, to ANTHONY PORTEVINE, planter,
Release   all of Berkeley Co., for Ł 250 SC money, 400 a.
                       in Berkeley Co., bounding W on LEWIS DUTARQUE;
N & S on vacant land; E on COL. ROBERT DANIEL. Whereas the Rt. Hon.
CHARLES CRAVEN & the Lords Proprs. on 29 Oct. 1728 granted SOLOMON BREMAR
400 a., which he bequeathed to his daughter MARTHA; & whereas MARTHA soon
afterwards married THOEDORE TREZEVANT, & he, shortly afterwards, sold to
PETER POITEVINE; but through the remissness of POITEVINE & partly because
he left the Province soon after, MARTHA TREZEVANT did not sign her right
of dower to POITEVINE; & whereas, after TREZEVANT'S death, MARTHA married
FRANCIS VARAMBOUT; now they confirm POITEVINE'S title. Witnesses: ROBERT
BREWTON, JR., LEWIS LORMIER. Before ROBERT AUSTIN, J.P. & Pub. Reg.

Book W, p. 99   JOHN HUNT & HANNAH his wife, of St. Bartholo-
22 Oct. 1741   mew's Parish, to their loving brother, JOSEPH
Deed of Gift   HUNT, 193 a. on NW side of high road leading
                       from Fish Pond Bridge to GODFREY SAVANNA "ex-
cepting my father JOHN HUNT doth think proper to interrupt me of the title of the said land". Witnesses: JOHN FIELD, JR., WILLIAM MILES, JR.
Before HENRY GIBBES, J.P. ROBERT AUSTIN, Pub. Reg.

Book W, p. 100   ANTHONY POITIVINE, planter, & MARY his wife,
31 Aug. 1741   to JOHN DUTARQUE, planter, all of Berkeley Co.,
Release   for Ł 1800 SC money, 400 a., English measure,
                       in Berkeley Co., where ANTHONY POITIVINE now
lives, bounding W on JOHN DUTARQUE; N on LEWIS DUTARQUE; E on heirs of
THOMAS LYNCH; S on JOHN DUTARQUE & THOMAS LYNCH; also 20 a., bounding S
on the 400 a.; NE on JAMES NICHOLAS MAYRANT; being part of 600 a. which
POITEVINE purchased from JAMES NICHOLAS MAYRANT. Whereas the Rt. Hon.
CHARLES CRAVEN & the Lords Proprs. on 29 Oct. 1708 granted SOLOMON BREMAR
400 a., which he bequeathed to his daughter MARTHA, who after her father's death married THEODORE TREZEVANT, who soon afterwards sold the
400 a. to PETER POITIVINE, father of ANTHONY POITIVINE; but through the
remissness of POITIVINE & his leaving the Province shortly afterwards
MARTHA TREZEVANT did not sign her right of dower over to POITIVINE; &
whereas TREZEVANT died & MARTHA married FRANCIS VARAMBAUT, & they confirmed the 400 a. to ANTHONY POITIVINE; now ANTHONY & MARY POITEVINE sell to
DUTARQUE. Witnesses: ROBERT HOW, ANTHONY BONNEAU, JR., PATRICK BIRD.
Before ROBERT AUSTIN, J.P. & Pub. Reg.

Book W, p. 105   JOHN BEEn, planter, of Colleton Co., executor
1 & 2 Oct. 1741   of will of JOHN BEE, gentleman, to WILLIAM
L & R   BRISBANE, practioner in Physic, for Ł 1400
                       currency, part of 2 lots, #24 & #25, in
Charleston, fronting W 67 ft. on a street running from Ashley River towards the New Brick Church; S 127 ft. 4 in., on parts formerly belonging
to CAPT. ANTHONY MATHEWS; N on JOHN CHAPMAN. Whereas by L & R dated 9 &
10 Oct. 1724 ROWLAND STORY, planter, & ELIZABETH his wife of Berkeley Co.,
sold to JOHN BEE, planter, for Ł 450 SC money parts of lots #24 & #25 in
Charleston; & whereas JOHN BEE, by will dated 7 Mar. 1739 appointed JOHN
BEE, party hereto, sole executor, authorizing him to dispose of the residue of his real estate (after payment of debts, etc.); now he sells to
BRISBANE. Witnesses: CHARLES SHEPHEARD, JAMES MICHIE. Before ROBERT
AUSTIN, J.P. & Pub. Reg.

Book W, p. 113   Between ROBERT QUASH, planter, & FRANCIS ROCHE,
25 Sept. 1740   planter (eldest son & heir of PATRICK ROCHE,
Agreement   planter), all of Berkeley Co. Whereas on

resurveying the lands of FRANCIS ROCHE & the lands lately belonging to BARTHOLOMEW ARTHUR (now to ROBERT QUASH) it appears that WUASH had 108 a. belonging to ROCHE, bounding N on FRANCIS ROCHE; W on DANIEL HUGER; S & E on ROBERT QUASH; & whereas ARTHUR made on allowance of Ł 566 currency in full satisfaction for the 108 a. & thereupon QUASH agreed to surrender the 108 a. to ROCHE; now QUASH renounces all title. Witnesses: JOHN GOUGH, SAMUEL PEYRE. Before FRANCIS LEJAU, J.P. ROBERT AUSTIN, Register.

Book W, p. 115
15 Oct. 1741
Assignment of Bond
JAMES KILPATRICK, practitioner in Physic, of Charleston, appoints GABRIEL MANIGAULT & JACOB MOTTE, ESQRS., his attorneys & transfers to them a certain bond in trust for his wife ELIZ-ABETH KILPATRICK. Witnesses: JOHN ROYER, GABRIEL BANBURY. Before ROBERT AUSTIN, J.P. & Pub. Reg. On 31 Mar. 1748 SAMUEL EVELEIGH received from HENRY LAURENS Ł 2094:9:6 in full of principal & interest on bond payable by JOHN LAURENS, of Charleston, to JAMES KILPATRICK, dated 13 Oct. 1741.

Book W, p. 116
27 May 1737
Bill of Sale
JOHN STUART, & MARY his wife, of Colleton Co., to JOSEPH ELLIOTT, SR., planter, for Ł 800 currency, 950 a. on St. Helena Island, bounding N on St. Helena River; W on Dawtau Creek; S & E on Nairns Creek. Witnesses: RICHARD CAPERS, JAMES MEGGET, MAGDALENE MAGGET. Before WILLIAM CATTELL, J.P. Memorial entered in Auditors office 11 Apr. 1733 by JAMES ST. JOHN, Dep. Aud. ROBERT AUSTIN, Pub. Reg.

Book W, p. 118
12 Apr. 1733
Bill of Sale
JOHN CHAPMAN, of Colleton Co., to JOSEPH ELLIOTT, son of WILLIAM ELLIOTT, of Berkeley Co., for Ł 1200, part of lot #25 in Charleston, granted to JOSEPH ELLICOTT (grandfather of JOHN CHAPMAN) on 9 May 1694 by Gov. THOMAS SMITH as recorded in Great Grant Book A.A. fol. 15; which part of lot #25 fronts 34 ft. 6 in. upon the broad street that fronts the New Church; & is 229 ft. through to Beadons Street & hath 32 ft. front on said street; S on JOHN CHAPMAN; N on JOHN LOYD & ANN SMITH. Witnesses: THOMAS SIMONDS, THOMAS FARR, BENJAMIN CHILD. Before ROBERT AUSTIN, J.P. & Pub. Reg.

Book W, p. 120
28 & 29 Aug. 1741
L & R
PETER SHAW, shopkeeper, & MARTHA his wife (only daughter & heri of JAMES CLEWES), to THOMAS FARR, gentleman, all of Charleston, for Ł 600 currency, lot #225 on E side of a certain back street now called Johnsons Street, granted by the Lords Proprs. on 9 May 1694 to JAMES CLEWES; bounding S 288 ft. on lot #240 belonging to JAMES STOBO; E 105 ft. on lot #221 belonging to MCKEWN; N 289-1/2 ft. on lot #224 belonging to SOLOMON LEGARE. Witnesses: JOHN WOODWARD, MATTHEW ROCHE, JOHN BLUNDELL. Before ROBERT AUSTIN, J.P. & Pub. Reg.

Book W, p. 127
22 & 23 Mar. 1739
L & R
THOMAS FARR, planter, & AMARENTIA his wife, of Colleton Co., to JOSEPH ELLICOTT, planter, of Berkeley Co., for Ł 1500 currency, 640 a. Whereas WILLIAM ELLIOTT, planter, of Berkeley Co., owned 640 a. on SW side of Ashley River; bounding NW on the Hon. WILLIAM BULL; NE & SE on WILLIAM ELLIOTT; SW on THOMAS WARING; & by will dated 15 June 1738 bequeathed to his beloved daughter AMARENTIA the 640 a. adjoining the land he gave to his son THOMAS, in Colleton Co., also his lands in Butlers Town, called Ashley River Town, now AMARENTIA & her husband THOMAS FARR sell the 640 a. to ELLICOTT, free from her claim of dower. Witnesses: CHARLES PINCKNEY, ROBERT BREWTON, JR. Before ROBERT AUSTIN, J.P. & Pub. Reg.

Book W, p. 133
17 & 18 Apr. 1740
L & R
JOSEPH ELLICOTT, planter, of St. Andrews Parish, Berkeley Co., to THOMAS FARR, planter, of Colleton Co., for Ł 1500 SC money, 640 a. on SW side Ashley River, bounding NW on the Hon. WILLIAM BULL; NE & SE on WILLIAM ELLIOTT; SW on THOMAS WARING. Witnesses: CHARLES PINCKNEY, ROBERT BREWTON, JR. Before ROBERT AUSTIN, J.P. & Pub. Reg.

Book W, p. 138
9 & 10 May 1740
L & R
WILLIAM ELLIOTT, THOMAS ELLIOTT, & THOMAS FARR, planters, executors of will of JOSEPH ELLIOTT, planter, to JOSEPH ELLICOTT, planter, all of

Berkeley Co., for ₤ 1500 currency, part of lot #25, except the part de-
vised to JOSEPH ELLICOTT. Whereas JOSEPH ELLIOTT owned part of lot #25
in Charleston, fronting W 69 ft. on New Church Street; E 64 ft. on Bedon
Street & runs 229 ft. from New Church Street to Bedon Street; S on JOHN
BEE & WILLIAM HARVEY; N on ANNE SMITH & MRS. LOIS MATHEWS, widow (formerly of JOHN LOYD); & by will dated 11 Feb. 1739 bequeathed to his friend
JOSEPH ELLICOTT the NW part of said lot, that is, 28 ft. on New Church
Street; 50 ft. deep on MRS. MATHEWS; directed the remainder sold, & ap-
pointed WILLIAM ELLIOTT, THOMAS ELLIOTT, & THOMAS FARR his executors; now
they sell to ELLICOTT. Witnesses: CHARLES PINCKNEY, DAVID STOUT. Before
ROBERT AUSTIN, J.P. & Pub. Reg.

Book W, p. 144   JOSEPH ELLICOTT, planter, to THOMAS FARR,
12 & 13 May 1740   planter, both of Berkeley Co., for ₤ 1500 cur-
L & R   rency, part of lot #25 in Charleston, except
                        the part devised to JOSEPH ELLICOTT. Whereas
JOSEPH ELLICOTT owned that part of lot #25 bounding W 69 ft. on New
Church Street; E 64 ft. on Bedon Street; & runns 229 ft. from New Church
Street to Bedon Street; S on JOHN BEE & WILLIAM HARVEY; N on ANNE SMITH &
MRS. LOIS MATTHEWS, widow (formerly JOHN LOYD); & by will dated 11 Feb.
1739 bequeathed to his friend JOSEPH ELLICOTT the NW corner of the lot,
i.e. fronting 28 ft. on New Church Street; & 50 ft. deep joining MRS.
MATHEWS land; ordered the rest of his real & personal estate sold, & ap-
pointed WILLIAM ELLIOTT, THOMAS ELLIOTT & THOMAS FARR his executors; &
whereas the executors by L & R dated 9 & 10 May 1740 conveyed to JOSEPH
ELLICOTT the "aforesaid part" of lot #25 (except the part devised to said
ELLICOTT); ELLICOTT sells to FARR "the aforesaid part of lot #25 except
the part devised to ELLICOTT. Witnesses: ROBERT BREWTON, JR., DAVID
STOUT. Before ROBERT AUSTIN, J.P. & Pub. Reg.

Book W, p. 150   RICHARD WOODWARD, gentleman, & ELIZABETH his
29 Oct. 1741   wife, of Beaufort, to ROBERT THORPE, gentleman,
Deed of Sale   for ₤ 2200 SC money, lot #3 in Beaufort front-
                        ing the Bay, originally granted by the Lords
Proprs. on 13 Aug. 1717 to the Hon. CHARLES HART; bounding W on lot #2; N
on lot #29; E on lot #4; with the stores, wharf, bridge, dwelling house,
scale house, etc., free from ELIZABETH'S claim of dower & all charges except the chief rent due the Lord of the fee in respect of his Seignory.
Witnesses to deed SUSANNAH SATUR, BENJAMIN GODIN, JR. Witnesses to recepit: CHARLES SHEPHEARD, JOHN THORPE. Before ROBERT AUSTIN, J.P. & Pub.
Reg.

Book W, p. 153   THOMAS STEWART, SUSANNAH STEWART, ARTHUR NASH,
16 & 17 Apr. 1741   & MARY ANN (her mark) NASH (his wife), to JOHN
L & R   STEEL (all of Charleston), for ₤ 500 currency,
                        the middle part of lot #218 in Charleston,
bounding N on part formerly belonging to THOMAS STEWART; S on part belonging partly to SUSANNAH STEWART (lately SUSANNAH MONROW) & partly to MARY
ANN NASH: & is bounded (the whole lot?) W by Church Street; E on JONATHAN
AMORY; S on JOSEPH PENDARVIS: N on MR. LEBOTT. Plat certified 17 Apr.
1741 by GEORGE HUNTER. Witnesses: HENRY WILLIAMS, ROBERT HARVEY, JOHN
RATTRAY. Before ROBERT AUSTIN, J.P. & Pub. Reg.

Book W, p. 160   GEORGE (his mark) ROBERTS of Wadmalaw Island,
10 Oct. 1741   Colleton Co., to HUGH CHRISTIE, planter, of
Lease for 19 yrs.   John's Island; for 19 years, for ₤ 16:18 shil-
                        lings yearly; 338 a. on Wadmalaw Island, bound-
ing on lands of JOHN STANYARNE, SAMUEL UNDERWOOD, ARTHUR HALL, JEAN THOMP-
SON, & WILLIAM STANYARNE. Some provisoes mentioned. Witnesses: ABRAHAM
WAIGHT, HENRY TOOMER. Before ANTHONY MATHEWES, J.P. ROBERT AUSTIN, Pub.
Reg.

Book W, p. 163   RICHARD ALLEIN, gentleman, & HESTER his wife,
27 July 1737   of St. James Santee Parish, Craven Co., to ED-
Bill of Sale   WARD THOMAS, gentleman, of St. Johns Parish,
                        Berkeley Co., for ₤ 1083:6:8 SC money, 650 a.
in St. James Santee, part of 1200 a. called Yaughan which ALLEIN purchased from WILLIAM WATIES, ESQ.; the 650 a. bounding SE on THOMAS ELLERY
(formerly JOHN MOORE); SW on EDWARD THOMAS; NW on RICHARD ALLEIN; N on
Santee River Swamp; reserving to ALLEIN the liberty of grinding grain

free of toll in any mill on the 650 a.; also reserving to the ALLEINS & their Negroes the right to hunt & fish on the 650 a. Witnesses: WILLIAM WATIES, ZENOBIA BILLING, SAMUEL THOMAS. Before ROBERT AUSTIN, J.P. & Pub. Reg. A memorial entered in Auditor's office 2 Dec. 1741 by JAMES ST. JOHN, Dep. Aud.

Book W, p. 166
8 & 9 May 1741
L & R by Mortgage

GIDEON NORTON, ship carpenter, of Charleston, to SAMUEL EVANS, planter, of St. Andrews Parish, Berkeley Co., for Ł 900 SC money, part of lot #92 fronting 60 ft. on N side Tradd Street, in Charleston, 102 or 103 ft. deep, bounding E on ROBERT COLLIS; W on ELIAS HANCOCK; N on THOMAS THOMPSON. To be redeemed by payment of certain dates. Witnesses: DAVID STOUT, JOHN COLEMAN, WILLIAM TRUEMAN. Before HENRY GIBBES, J.P. ROBERT AUSTIN, Pub. Reg.

Book W, p. 172
11 & 12 Dec. 1741
L & R

THOMAS CORDES, ESQ., to ROBERT AUSTIN, ESQ., both of Berkeley Co., for Ł 15 SC money, 400 a. in Craven Co. on S side Santee River Swamp, bounding SW on THOMAS CORDES; NW & S on CAPT. AUSTIN; NE on SAMUEL THOMAS; other side on vacant land; which 400 a. were granted by letters patent dated 13 (30?) June last by Lt. Gov. WILLIAM BULL to THOMAS CORDES. Witnesses: THOMAS SHUBRICK, ISAAC GODIN. Before THOMAS LAMBOLL, J.P. ROBERT AUSTIN, Pub. Reg.

Book W, p. 177
18 & 19 Dec. 1741
L & R

JOHN KAYS, planter, to JAMES OSMOND, merchant, of Charleston, for Ł 2400 SC money, part of the half part of lot #8 in Charleston, fronting E 24 ft. on the Bay; bounding 257 ft. on WILLIAM STONE (formerly DANIEL GREEN); W 24 ft. 3 in. on N 257 ft. on estate of JOHN WRIGHT; also that part of lot #326 extending to low water mark. Whereas the Rt. Hon. WILLIAM, Earl of Craven & the Lords Proprs. on 20 Apr. 1681 granted EDWARD MUSSON lot #8 in Charleston; & he on 29 Nov. 1681 sold to THOMAS GREATCATH, cordwainer, of Charleston, half the lot (or 1/4 a.) bounding E on Cooper River; W on PHILIP BURKELY; S on RICHARD TRADD; N on other half then belonging to JOHN MITCHELL; & whereas GREATCATH on 4 Oct. 1692 sold his half to WILLIAM WHALESBY, reserving for himself a piece 50 ft. square at the lower or E (W?) end; & whereas WHALESBY, by letter of attorney dated 2 Sept. 1696, authorized GEORGE RAYNOR, of Colleton Co., to dispose of his estate, & whereas GEORGE RAYNOR, attorney, & CATHERINE WHALESBY (wife of WILLIAM) on 20 Mar. 1697 sold the half part of lot #8 (except the 50 ft. sq.) bounding E on Cooper River; S on RICHARD TRADD, N on WILLIAM SMITH, vintner; W on a little street or lane; whereas the Lords Proprs. on 20 Dec. 1698 granted JOSEPH KAYS 1 front lot, #326, opposite lot #8 & fronting W on the wharf line laid out by the commissioners & running E to low water mark; & whereas KAYS bequeathed the S part of lot #8, on which was then standing a certain tenement occupied by JAMES KINLOCH, & that part of land in front of the tenement from the bank to low water mark, to his son JOHN KAYS (father of the party hereto) who died intestate in 1718 & the property descended to his son JOHN; now he sells to OSMOND. Witnesses: JAMES WRIGHT, GEORGE HUNTER. Before ROBERT AUSTIN, J.P. & Pub. Reg.

Book W, p. 186
17 Oct. 1738
Release

JOHN MCIVER (MCEVER), planter, & SARAH (her mark) his wife, to ELIZABETH BREMAR widow, all of Berkeley Co., for Ł 2000 SC money, 300 a., part of a grant of 640 a., English measure, in St. Thomas Parish, Berkeley Co., bounding NE on LEWIS DUTARQUE; NW on ROBERT HUME & STEPHEN FOGARTIE; S on JOHN MCEVER; also 75 a. bounding NE on LEWIS DUTARQUE; SE on the 300 a.; SW on STEPHEN FOGARTIE; according to plat attached to grant to JAMES ARMSTRONG dated 7 Aug. 1735. Whereas Gov. EDWARD TYNTE & the Lords Proprs. on 14 Apr. 1708 granted JOHN FOGARTIE 640 a.; & he sold LEWIS DUTARQUE 200 a. on the NE side of the 640 a. & gave his son STEPHEN FOGARTIE 140 a. in the SW part; & whereas JOHN FOGARTIE on 4 June 1728 sold to JOHN COLWELL, butcher, of Berkeley Co., the remaining part of the 640 a. (or 300 a.); & he, by will dated 1720 bequeathed to JUDITH SIMONS (now JUDITH SWINTON), after other legacies, the remainder of his real & personal estate; & whereas HUGH SWINTON & JUDITH, his wife, by L & R dated 8 & 9 Mar. 1732 sold the 300 a. to JAMES ARMSTRONG, planter, of Christ Church Paris, Berkeley Co.; who by will dated 29 Jan. 1734, ordered his real & personal estate sold by his executors:

for the benefit of his children; & whereas the executors, THOMAS LYNCH & ROBERT FLADGER, by L & R dated 16 & 17 July last sold to JOHN MCIVER; now he sells to MRS. BREMAR the 2 tracts of 375 a., free from SARAH MCIVER'S claim of dower. Witnesses: JAMES BREMAR, SOLOMON WHITHAM. Before ROBERT AUSTIN, J.P. & Pub. Reg.

Book W, p. 194
4 & 5 Mar. 1734
L & R

ISAAC MAZYCK, ESQ., to MARY ELLIAS, widow, both of Charleston, for Ł 1800 currency, part of lot #13 in Charleston, lately owned by MR. ESCOTT, carpenter; 80 ft. deep, bounding 16 ft. 3 in. on Broad Street; N (?) on ISAAC MAZYCK; W on DANIEL CRAWFORD'S lot; with use of alley between JOHN MACOIS (MCCOYS?) house & aforesaid lot, & also privilege of building & extending the rooms upstairs over 1/2 the alley. Witnesses: JOHN LAURENS, ROWLAND VAUGHAN. Before HENRY GIBBES, J.P. ROBERT AUSTIN, Pub. Reg.

Book W, p. 200
17 & 18 Oct. 1740
L & R

SOLOMON LEGARE, SR., silversmith, to MARY ELLIS, widow, both of Charleston, for Ł 1000 currency, the E half of lot #106 in Charleston, fronting S 45 ft. on Broad Street; E 216-1/2 ft. on JOHN LAURENS; N on RICHARD BERESFORD; W on SOLOMON LEGARE; which parcel of land was purchased by LEGARE from JOHN FRASER, DANIEL CRAWFORD & JOHN ALLEN, executors of will of JAMES PAINE. Witnesses: CAPT. WILLIAM SCOTT, JR. (a Quaker), GEORGE HESKETT. Before ROBERT AUSTIN, J.P. & Pub. Reg.

Book W, p. 206
23 & 24 July 1741
L & R

ISAAC MAZYCK & PAUL MAZYCK, executors of will of ISAAC MAZYCK, merchant, to MARY ELLIS, widow, all of Charleston, for Ł 700 SC money, part of lot #13 in Charleston, 52 ft. from E to W; breadth 27 ft. at E end; 21 ft. at W end; bounding N (that part 27 ft. broad) on parts of said lot belonging to GABRIEL GUIGNARD & PETER DELMESTRE (that part 21 ft. in breadth) "on other part of said lot belonging to said MARY ELLIS"; E on MR. COLLETON; S on JOHN WATSON & MR. CALVERT (formerly MRS. ANNE LEBRASSEUR); W on DANIEL CRAWFORD. Witnesses: ISAAC HOLMES (merchant), JOHN BAKER. Before ROBERT AUSTIN, J.P. & Pub. Reg.

Book W, p. 211
3 Jan. 1699
Grant

By warrant dated 1 Aug. 1699, signed by Gov. JOSEPH BLAKE, EDMUND BELLINGER, Sur. Gen., laid out for himself on 6 Aug. 1699, 1 lot on E side of Charleston at E end of Cooper Street (marked B on model); bounding N on the wharf before ELIZABETH CLAPP'S land; S on BENJAMIN SCHENCKINGH'S wharf; W on "the Front Street" parallel with Cooper River upon the line of wharfage laid out by commissioners; E on low water mark. Whereas JOHN, Earl of Bath, Palatine; GEORGE, Lord Carteret; SIR JOHN COLLETON, Baronet; THOMAS AMY, ESQ., & WILLIAM THORNBURY, ESQ., Lords Proprs., on 16 Aug. 1698 authorized Gov. JOSEPH BLAKE, Landgrave JOSEPH MORTON, ROBERT DANIEL, JAMES MOORE, EDMUND BELLINGER, & JOHN ELY, ESQRS., or any 3 of them, to sell & grant land; now they grant CAPT. EDMUND BELLINGER 1 front town lot (B); he to erect & keep in repair a sufficient part of stairs or common landing place 8-1/2 ft. wide, with bolts, rings & posts for common use. Signed by ROBERT DANIEL, JOSEPH (Great Seal) BLAKE, JOSEPH MORTON. ROBERT AUSTIN, Pub. Reg.

Book W, p. 214
24 & 25 July 1738
L & R

EDMUND BELLINGER, ESQ., & ELIZABETH his wife, of Ashley River, Berkeley Co., to EBENEZER SIMMONS, merchant, of Charleston, for Ł 800 currency, a front or low water lot (marked Bon Model), bounding N on the wharf or low water lot before ELIZABETH CLAPP'S land; S on BENJAMIN SCHENCKINGH'S wharf; W on the front street parallel with Cooper River upon the line of wharfage laid out by the commissioners; E on channel of Cooper River. Witnesses: JOHN BILLIALD, JAMES SCARLETT. Before WILLIAM BULL, JR., J.P. ROBERT AUSTIN, Pub. Reg.

Book W, p. 220
21 & 22 Nov. 1739
L & R

CHARLES LEWIS, planter, & MARTHA his wife, to EBENEZER SIMMONS, merchant, of Charleston, for Ł 1000 currency, the E half of lot #223, bounding W on MRS. SARAH MCKENSIE; S on WILLIAM CATTELL, ESQ.; E on ?; N on Tradd Street. Whereas on 26 Mar. 1694 THOMAS

33

SMITH, Gov. & Landgrave, directed the Sur. Gen. to lay out to PATRICK STEWART 1 town lot #223, bounding N on the street leading from Cooper River by GEORGE KEATING; S on JAMES FREEMAN (FROWMAN); E on JAMES FLOWERS; W on the street leading from Ashley River by MR. JONES: & whereas STEWART on 24 July 1694 sold the lot to WILLIAM BALLAUGH; who died intestate & the lot descended to JOHN BALLAUGH, his only son & heir; & whereas he died intestate the lot descended to his 2 daughters ELIZABETH & MARTHA; & whereas MARTHA, the younger, married CHARLES LEWIS; now CHARLES & MARTHA LEWIS sell their half (E half) to SIMMONS. Witnesses: DANIEL LAROCHE, JAMES CRADDOCK. Before THOMAS LAROCHE, J.P. ROBERT AUSTIN, Pub. Reg.

Book W, p. 227
17 & 18 July 1730
L & R

JOHN BRAND, carpenter, to EDWARD BULLARD, carpenter & joiner, both of Charleston, for ₤ 160 currency & part of lot #187 in Charleston, fronting E 43 ft. on a little street leading from Ashley River; S 200 ft. on JOHN STEVENSON; W on THOMAS BARTRAM (formerly ELIAS HANCOCK); N on JAMES WITHERS; which lot #187 was granted JOHN BRAND by L & R Tripartite dated 1 & 2 Mar. 1723 between MARY LAROCHE, widow & 1 of executors of will of JOHN LAROCHE, merchant, of Charleston, of 1st part; JOHN BRAND of 2nd part; ANTHONY MATTHEWS, merchant, of Charleston, of 3rd part. The part of lot to be free from claim of dower of ELIZABETH, wife of JOHN BRAND, for as much as the title deeds to this part of lot #187 also concern also the release of 1-1/2 other lots (164 & 186) BRAND retains the papers & agrees to produce them when requested. Witnesses: JAMES WITHERS, ADAM BATTIN. Before ROBERT AUSTIN, J.P. & PUB. REG.

Book W, p. 234
24 & 25 Dec. 1735
L & R

EDWARD BULLARD, carpenter, & ELIZABETH his wife, to EBENEZER SIMMONS, merchant, all of Charleston, for ₤ 600 currency, part of lot #187, fronting E 43 ft. on a little street leading from Ashley River; S 200 ft. on JOHN STEVENSON; W on JAMES KERR (formerly ELIAS HANCOCK); N on JAMES WITHERS. Witnesses: ABRAHAM CROFT, ROBERT STANBROUGH, THOMAS ELLERY. Before ROBERT AUSTIN, J.P. & Pub. Reg.

Book W, p. 239
16 & 17 Dec. 1741
L & R by Mortgage

WILLIAM (his mark) WAY, planter, to EDWARD WAY, planter, both of St. George's Parish, Berkeley Co., as security on various bonds amounting to ₤ 1062 currency, payable with interest at sundry times, 74 a., bounding SW on JOHN GIRARDEAU; SE on THOMAS DIXTON; NE on EDWARD WAY; NW on RICHARD BEDON; also 74 a. bounding SW on EDWARD WAY; SE on THOMAS DIXTON; NE on DANIEL WAY; NW on RICHARD BEDON; which 2 tracts are part of 408 a., partly in Berkeley Co., & partly in Colleton Co., granted to WILLIAM WAY; also 10 a. (1/5 of 50 a.) near Bacon's Bridge, Berkeley Co.; also 6 Negro slaves. Witnesses: THOMAS SACHEVERELL, BENJAMIN CHAPPELL, ANNE SACHEVERELL. Before RICHARD WARING, J.P. ROBERT AUSTIN, Pub. Reg.

Book W, p. 246
11 & 12 Jan. 1741
L & R

GABRIEL MANIGAULT, merchant, of Parish of St. Michael, Island of Barbados, to ELIZABETH CHEESMAN, widow, of St. Andrews Parish, Berkeley Co., SC, for ₤ 180 money of Island of Barbados, 2 tracts, 236 a. (150 a. & 86 a.), known as Lake Farm, on Ashley River. Whereas MARGARET GODFREY & JANE MONGER, widow, executrixes, of will of BENJAMIN GODFREY, planter, by L & R dated 17 & 18 Nov. 1735 conveyed to THOMAS LAKE 2 tracts of land formerly belonging to BENJAMIN GODFREY; 1 of 150 a., English measure, on Ashley River, Berkeley Co., bounding E on WILLIAM HARVEY (formerly BENJAMIN GODFREY); W & S on BENJAMIN WHITAKER (formerly JOHN WOODWARD); N on marsh of Ashley River; the other of 86 a. in Berkeley Co., bounding NE on CHARLES HILL; NW on ELIZABETH HILL, widow (formerly BENJAMIN GODFREY); SW on JOHN WOODWARD; SE on said 150 a.; & whereas THOMAS LAKE on 25 Feb. 1739, at Barbados, appointed GABRIEL MANIGAULT his attorney with authority to sell the 2 tracts (called THOMAS LAKE'S estate or LAKES Farm on Ashley River); now MANIGAULT sells to ELIZABETH CHEESMAN. Witnesses: The Hon. CHARLES PINCKNEY, DAVID STOUT. Before HENRY GIBBES, J.P.

Book W, p. 252
25 Feb. 1739
Letter of Attorney

THOMAS LAKE, merchant, of St. Michael's Parish, Island of Barbados, (as individual & as a partner of THOMAS CHEESMAN) appoints GABRIEL

MANIGAULT, merchant, of Charleston, his attorney to handle his affairs &
to dispose of his estate called Lake Farm or Ashley River; also to ship
his Negro slaves to Barbados. Witnesses: JOSHUA THOMAS, EDWARD LIGHTWOOD,
BENJAMIN LOMBERTS. Before HENRY GIBBES, J.P. ROBERT AUSTIN, Pub. Reg.

Book W, p. 253   THOMAS (his mark) BATES, planter, to JOHN WIN-
16 Dec. 1741   GOOD, planter, both of Christ Church Parish,
Mortgage   Berkeley Co., for ₤ 300 SC money, 33-1/3 a. on
                       which he lives, being 2/3 of a larger tract of
50 a. in Christ Church Parish, bounding E on JACOB OLIVARA; N on RICHARD
CAPERS; W on CAPT. GEORGE BENISON; S on CAPT. JOHN PARRIS; also 2 cows, 2
heifers, 1 calf, 1 young horse, 1 young mare, 2 Negro women, all household goods, furniture, & all things of value on the plantation. Date of
redemption: 1 Jan. 1742. Witnesses: ELINOR NELME, THOMAS WHITESIDE. Delivery by turf & twig, witnessed by THOMAS WHITESIDE, DANIEL LEWIS. Before DANIEL CRAWFORD, J.P. Recorded in Bk. P.P. fol. 385-387, by J. HAM-
MERTON. ROBERT AUSTIN, Pub. Reg.

Book W, p. 256   WILLIAM BULL, ESQ., & MARY his wife, of Berke-
30 Nov. & 1 Dec. 1733   ley Co., to STEPHEN BULL, gentleman, of Cane
L & R   Acres, Colleton Co., for ₤ 2000 currency, 4
                       tracts of 500, 500, 418, & 282 a. Whereas Gov.
CHARLES CRAVEN, & the Hon. ROBERT DANIEL, SAMUEL EVELEIGH, CHARLES HART,
& HUGH BUTLER, ESQRS., Lords Proprs., on 17 Dec. 1714 granted HENRY QUIN-
TYNE 500 a. in Colleton Co., bounding S on Combee River; E on a cypress
swamp belonging to HENRY QUINTYNE & on WILLIAM KIMBALL (now COL. JOSEPH
BLAKE); other sides then on land not laid out but now of COL. JOSEPH
BLAKE; & whereas SIR NATHANIEL JOHNSON & the Hon. NICHOLAS TROTT, HENRY
NOBLE, & THOMAS BROUGHTON, Lords Proprs., on 14 May 1707 granted HENRY
QUINTYNE 500 a., English measure, in Granville Co., bounding N on Coosaw
River; W on a creek; E on land not then laid out but late of HENRY QUIN-
TYNE & on head of creek; S on land not then laid out but now of COL. JO-
SEPH BLAKE; & whereas Gov. CHARLES CRAVEN & the Hon. ROBERT DANIEL, HUGH
BUTLER, & SAMUEL EVELEIGH, Lords Proprs. on 17 Dec. 1714 granted HENRY
QUINTYNE 418 a. on Port Royal Island, Granville Co., bounding NW on va-
cant land; NE on ROBERT WILKINSON; S on EVAN LEWIS & DAVID DUVAL; W on
ARTHUR DICKS, & whereas HENRY QUINTYNE owned 282 a. on S side of Coosaw
River in Granville Co., bounding W on HENRY QUINTYNE; S & E on CAPT. WAL-
TER IZARD; & whereas QUINTYNE died intestate in July 1716 leaving his
only sister MARY (wife of WILLIAM BULL) his heir at law; now MARY & her
husband sell the 4 tracts to STEPHEN BULL. Witnesses: ELIZABETH DRAYTON,
ROBERT WRIGHT, THOMAS DRAYTON. Before WILLIAM BULL, JR., J.P. ROBERT
AUSTIN, Pub. Reg.

Book W, p. 263   GEORGE CHICKEN & LYDIA his wife, to JOHN SIM-
15 & 16 July 1741   SON, for ₤ 500 currency, 4 tracts, or 1811 a.,
L & R   in Prince Frederick Parish, Winyaw, bounding
                       NE on RICHARD WALKER & on Black River; NW on
CAPT. THOMAS HENNING; SE on vacant land; the 4 tracts being 500 a. granted to MILES SWANY; 911 a. granted to GEORGE CHICKEN; 400 a. in 2 tracts
to DANIEL JAUDON, JR. Witnesses: PHILIP TOWLER, JOHN CLARKE. Before
JAMES KINLOCK, J.P. ROBERT AUSTIN, Pub. Reg.

Book W, p. 268   SAMUEL WILLIAMS, planter, to MATHEW HUNT,
4 & 5 Dec. 1741   planter, for ₤ 150 currency, 200 a. in Colle-
L & R   ton Co., on Saltketcher Swamp, granted to SAM-
                       UEL WILLIAMS; bounding on all sides on vacant
land. Signed by SAMUEL WILLIAMS & HANNAH (her mark) WILLIAMS. Witnesses: LEWIS BYNON, BENJAMIN CROSSWELL, WILLIAM FRANCKLYN. Before MAR. CAMP-
BELL, J.P., at New Windsor. ROBERT AUSTIN, Pub. Reg.

Book W, p. 273   ROBERT QUARTERMAN, planter, & JOHN SUMNER,
14 Feb. 1737   planter, of Colleton Co., executors of will of
Release   MOSES HAWKES, to BARNABY BRANFORD, planter, of
                       Berkeley Co., for ₤ 240 currency, 40 a. in St.
George Parish, Berkeley Co., bounding N on GEORGE HAMLIN; W on JOSEPH
BRUNSON; S on WILLIAM BRANFORD; E on BARNABY BRANFORD (formerly JOHN
HAWKES). Whereas MOSES HAWKES, by will, authorized his friends QUARTER-
MAN & SUMNER to sell his lands in Berkeley & Colleton Counties for the
payment of his debts, now the executors, sell 40 a. to BRANFORD.

Witnesses: JOHN DORSEY, THOMAS SUMNER (?). Before RICHARD WARING, J.P.
ROBERT AUSTIN, Pub. Reg.

Book W, p. 277   JOHN LUPTON, planter, of Craven Co., to BARNA-
2 May 1738   BY BRANFORD, planter, of Berkeley Co., for
Release   L 1605 currency, 321 a. in Berkeley Co., at
                   head of Ashley River (110 a. being part of a
tract granted to BENJAMIN SUMNER) on 20 Jan. 1710 & sold to JOHN LUPTON
by JOHANNA SUMNER on 16 Aug. 1736; 7 & 211 a. being part of 438 a. granted to ROGER SUMNER on 21 Apr. 1733 & conveyed to JOHN LUPTON on 21 Apr.
1738); the 321 a. bounding E on ALEXANDER LESSLY & BENJAMIN SUMNER; W on
WILLIAM CATOR & MAGDELENE BEDON; N on COL. JOSEPH BLAKE; S on BENJAMIN &
ROGER SUMNER. Signed by JOHN LUPTAN, MARY (her mark) LUPTAN (his wife).
Witnesses: GEORGE HAMLIN, THOMAS WAY, JR. Before THOMAS WARING, J.P.
ROBERT AUSTIN, Register.

Book W, p. 281   DAVID ALLEN (ALLAN), planter, & MARY his wife,
12 & 13 Dec. 1737   of Prince Frederick Parish, Craven Co., to
L & R   RYALL SPRY, planter, of St. Pauls Parish, Col-
                   leton Co., for L 400 SC money, 350 a. in St.
Bartholomews Parish, Colleton Co., bounding W on Horse Shoe Creek; N on
JOHN MARTIN; E on DANIEL MCEVANS; S on WILLIAM OSWEL & HENRY JACKSON.
Witnesses: ROBERT HERON, DAVID WITHERSPOON, ROBERT BYERS. Before JOHN
EDWARDS, J.P. of Craven Co. ROBERT AUSTIN, Pub. Reg.

Book W, p. 286   MARY ALLEIN, spinster, of Craven Co., to PETER
14 & 15 Oct. 1740   PORCHER, planter, of Berkeley Co., for L 1300
L & R   currency, 2 tracts in Craven Co., 1 of 500 a.
                   bounding E on MARY ALLEIN, & all other sides
on vacant land; the other of 150 a. bounding W on the 500 a.; SE on ROB-
ERT AUSTIN; other sides on vacant land. Witnesses: SAMUEL THOMAS, JAMES
RICHEBOURG. Before ISAAC PORCHER, J.P. ROBERT AUSTIN, Pub. Reg.

Book W, p. 293   JAMES SAVINEAU, planter, & JANE his wife, to
25 & 26 Jan. 1741/2   NATHANIEL SAVINEAU, planter, all of St. James
L & R   Santee Parish, Craven Co., for L 1800 currency,
                   2 tracts in St. James Santee, total 743 a.; 1
of 500 a. bounding SW on JAMES GUERRY; NE on PETER PERDRIAU; being part
of 1000 a. sold to SAVINEAU by DANIEL HUGER; the other being 243 a. granted to SAVINEAU & bounding N on JAMES SAVINEAU; E on PAUL BRUNEAU; S on vacant land; NE on ABRAHAM PERDRIAU & vacant land. Witnesses: WILLIAM THOM-
AS, AUGUSTUS LAURENS, ANDREW REMBERT. Before ROBERT AUSTIN, J.P. & Pub.
Reg.

Book W, p. 299   PETER VILLEPONTOUX, planter, & FRANCES his
19 & 20 Nov. 1741   wife, of Berkeley Co., to RACHEL RUSS, widow,
L & R   of Charleston, as security, on a bond dated 17
                   Oct. 1740 (signed by RACHEL RUSS & ZACHARIAH
VILLEPONTOUX, planter, of Berkeley Co., & PETER VILLEPONTOUX, for PETER'S
debt) given to WILLIAM HANCOCK, gentleman, formerly of Charleston, now of
City of Exon, England, in penal sum of L 3000 for payment of L 1500 SC
money, with interest, in certain amounts on certain dates; 300 a. in
Berkeley Co., on Ashley River; bounding SW on Hog Island Creek; NW on Ca-
pers Creek; NE on THOMAS BARKSDALE; E on CAPT. DANIEL GREEN (formerly
JAMES BASFORD); being part of a tract granted by the Lords Proprs on 6
July 1680 to FLORENTIA O'SULLIVAN; also 270 a. of marsh ground purchased
from COL. WILLIAM RHETT, at head of Capers Creek. PETER VILLEPONTOUX appoints RACHEL RUSS his attorney. Witnesses: JACOB MARTIN, WILLIAM MOVAT.
Before ROBERT AUSTIN, J.P. & Pub. Reg. On 17 Mar. 1747/8 RACHEL RUSS declared mortgage satisfied. Witness: JOHN BEALE.

Book W, p. 310   JOSEPH WARNOCK, planter, & MARY his wife, of
20 & 21 May 1740   St. Thomas Parish, to SAMUEL WELLS, carpenter,
L & R   of Berkeley Co., for L 500 currency, 150 a.,
                   English measure, in St. Thomas Parish, bound-
ing SE on Wando River; SW on JAMES FISHER; NW on JOHN RUSS; NE on JOSEPH
WARNOCK; being part of 400 a. purchased lately from JEREMIAH ROPER; the
400 a. being part of 1000 a. granted in 1709 to ABRAHAM WARNOCK (uncle of
JOSEPH); the land to be free from MARY'S claim of dower. Witnesses: JOHN
FOGARTIE, PATRICK BIRD, SAMUEL WARNOCK. Before ROBERT AUSTIN, J.P. &

Book W, p. 317   SAMUEL STOCKS, planter, to DOROTHY JONES, wid-
2 & 3 Aug. 1736   ow, both of St. Andrews Parish, Berkeley Co.,
L & R   for Ł 1100 SC money, 110 a. on E side Stono
                       River, bounding N & W on THOMAS STOCK; E on
SAMUEL JONES; S on Stono River; which 110 a. were part of a tract granted
by the Lords Proprs. to THOMAS STOCKS, father of SAMUEL, & purchased by
SAMUEL from THOMAS STOCKS, his brother, the eldest son & heir. Witness-
es: GEORGE HUNTER, ISAAC WAIGHT, THOMAS ELLERY. Before CULCHETH GOLIGHT-
LY, J.P. ROBERT AUSTIN, Pub. Reg.

Book W, p. 322   HENRY YONGE, planter, of Colleton Co., to
7 & 8 Apr. 1736   DOROTHY JONES, planter, of Berkeley Co., for
L & R   Ł 681:12 SC money, 426 a. in Colleton Co.,
                       bounding W on Combahe River; N on MR. BAT &
HENRY YONGE; the course of BAT'S plat adjoining said land being SW 39°,
continuing to Combahe River, including part of YONGE'S land lying W of
BAT'S Creek which is not included in the 1200 a. grant; E on DOROTHY
JONES; S on JEHU BARTON & the old ferry causeway; as specified in grant
to FRANCIS YONGE of 1200 a. signed by Gob. ROBERT JOHNSON dated 3 Mar.
1731. Witnesses: THOMAS ELLIOTT, JOSEPH ELLIOTT, FRANCIS THOMPSON. Before THOMAS DALE, J.P. ROBERT AUSTIN, Pub. Reg.

Book W, p. 330   ROBERT THORPE, ESQ., of Granville Co., to JOHN
25 & 26 Feb. 1741   THORPE, gentleman, of Charleston, for Ł 852 SC
L & R   money, 2 tracts; 1 of 84 a., part of 100 a.
                       marked No. 4 & described in survey by letter
G; bounding NE on road leading to Prioleaus ferry; NW on the great road;
W on marsh belonging to WILLIAM BULL & ROBERT THORPE; S on ROBERT THORPE;
also 200 a. marked H on the survey, being part of the 1000 a. marked No.
4, & bounding NW on the great road; NE on ROBERT THORPE; SW on remaining
part of 1000 a. Witnesses: ALEXANDER CRAMAKE (gentleman), GEORGE NICHO-
LAS (gentleman). Before WILLIAM GEORGE FREEMAN, J.P. Before ROBERT AUS-
TIN, Pub. Reg.

Book W, p. 335   ROBERT THORPE, ESQ., of Granville Co., to JOHN
25 & 26 Feb. 1741   THORPE, gentleman, of Charleston, for ₧ 852 SC
L & R   money, 284 a. in Granville Co., part of 1000 a.
                       marked No. 3 & described in survey by letter J;
bounding NW on 200 a. described by letter H in the survey; NE on JOHN
THORPE; SE on FRANCIS YONGE; SW on part of 1000 a. marked No. 3. Witnesses: ALEXANDER CRAMAKE, GEORGE NICHOLAS. Before WILLIAM GEORGE FREE-
MAN, J.P. ROBERT AUSTIN, Pub. Reg.

Book W, p. 340   JOHN GIBBES, planter, of St. Johns Parish, Col-
5 Mar. 1741   leton, to JOHN WOODWARD, planter, of Colleton
Bond   Co., in penal sum of Ł 5000 for payment of
                       Ł 200 British yearly during the natural life
of JOHN WOODWARD. Witnesses: CHARLES PINCKNEY, CULCHETH GOLIGHTLY, MI-
CHAEL JEANES, JOHN BAKER. Before ROBERT AUSTIN, J.P. & Pub. Reg.

Book W, p. 342   JAMES HUTCHINSON, surgeon of John's Island,
7 & 8 Mar. 1741   Colleton Co., to CULCHETH GOLIGHTLY, ESQ.,
L & R   both of Colleton Co., for Ł 750 currency, 370
                       a. Whereas on 16 Mar. 1732 (?) JOSEPH MACKEY
was granted 900 a. in Colleton Co., bounding SW on JOHN ANDREWS; SE on
FRANCIS HOLMES & HORSE SAVANNAH; other sides on vacant land; & he on 15
Apr. 1734 conveyed to JOHN MACKEY 470 a., part of the 900 a., bounding NW
on vacant land; NE on JOSEPH MACKEY; SE on said HOLMES; SW on JOHN AN-
DREWS; & whereas on 11 May 1740 JOHN MACKEY conveyed 370 a., part of the
470 a., to JAMES HUTCHINSON; now HUTCHINSON sells the 370 a. to GOLIGHTLY.
Witnesses: JOHN RUTLEDGE, RICHARD BODDICOTT, JAMES VAUGHAN. On 25 Feb.
1741, THOMAS CLIFFORD, Dep. Sur. surveyed the 370 a. bounding E on the
high road & CULCHETH GOLIGHTLY; SW on THOMAS CLIFFORD; NW on THOMAS CLIF-
FORD & EDWARD NORTH; NE on JOSIAH SULLIVAN (formerly JOSEPH MACKAY).
ROBERT AUSTIN, Pub. Reg.

Book W, p. 349   ZACHARIAH VILLEPONTOUX, planter, & SARAH his
8 & 9 Apr. 1736   wife, of St. John's Parish, Berkeley Co., to

L & R
GABRIEL MANIGAULT, ESQ., of Charleston, for
Ł 1615 SC money, 168 a. on N side James Island,
on S side Ashley River, bounding S on SAMUEL FRITH or WILLIAM CHAPMAN &
marsh; W on PETER VILLEPONTOUX; E on JAMES LESWERS & Kus-ke-waw Creek &
marsh. Witnesses: ROBERT WRIGHT, ROBERT BREWTON, JR. Before ROBERT AUS-
TIN, J.P. & Pub. Reg.

Book W, p. 355
8 & 9 Mar. 1741
L & R
JOHN TIPPER, sailmaker, & SUSANNAH his wife,
of Charleston, to HENRY SAMWAYS, planter, of
James Island, for Ł 400 SC money, part of lot
#210 in Charleston, bounding E 22 ft. on a
street leading from Ashley River to the Broad Path, now called King
Street; N 128 ft. on JOHN TIPPER; S on an alley adjoining MILES BREWTON'S
lot; W on JAMES STOBO; with the dwelling house, etc. Witnesses: JOHN
HODSDEN, WILLIAM COE, WILLIAM SMITH. Before ROBERT AUSTIN, J.P. & Pub.
Reg.

Book W, p. 362
22 & 23 Mar. 1739
L & R
ARTHUR FOSTER, planter, to ANTHONY ATKINSON &
MARY HUGHES, all of Craven Co., for Ł 716 SC
money, 775 a. on SE side Black River, Craven
Co., bounding NE on WILLIAM (alias GEORGE)
DICK; SE on WILLIAM WATSON; SW on CAPT. WILLIAM BROCKINTON; as by plat of
grant dated 7 Feb. 1735. Witnesses: JOHN EVANS, ELIZABETH ATKINSON, RICH-
ARD (his mark) FRYER. Before WILLIAM ROMSEY, J.P. ROBERT AUSTIN, Pub.
Reg.

Book W, p. 367
7 Aug. 1734
Deed of Gift
GEORGE FARLEY, planter, to his loving friend
ELIZABETH DIDCOTT, SR., both of Colleton Co.,
for love & affection, 136 a. in St. Bartholo-
mew's Parish, Colleton Co., bounding S on JO-
SEPH DIDCOTT; W on JOHN PETERS; N on JOHN BURNHAM; E on Horseshoe Creek.
Witnesses: JAMES MATHEWES, MARY (her mark) FARLEY. Before JACOB MOTTE,
J.P. ROBERT AUSTIN, Pub. Reg.

Book W, p. 368
16 & 17 Feb. 1741
L & R by Mortgage
JOHN RIVERS, & ELIZABETH his wife, to WILLIAM
MILES, all of Berkeley Co., lots #196, #142,
part of lot #216 as security on bond of even
date in sum of Ł 500 payable with interest on
17 Feb. 1742. Whereas the Lords Proprs. on 12 June 1694 granted WILLIAM
BAILEY a 1/2 a. lot, #196, in Charleston, bounding W on a little street
leading from Ashley River to MR. JONES; E on WILLIAM BAILEY; S on PETER
(?); N on CAPT. NOVVAMORE; & whereas after WILLIAM BAILEY'S death his son
& heir, JOHN BAILEY on 3 Aug. 1721 sold the lot to ANTHONY MATTHEWES, JR.;
who, on 3 May 1723, sold to JOHN RIVERS, SR.; & whereas the Lords Proprs.
on 15 June 1694 granted CHARLES CLARKE a 1/2 a. lot, #142, bounding S on
said CLARK; N on WILLIAM BAILEY; E on a great street leading from Cooper
River to the Market Place; W on MARY BENSON; & whereas CATHERINE TOOKER-
MAN by L & R dated 22 Mar. 1721 sold the lot to JOHN RIVERS, SR.; & where-
as the Lords Proprs. on 18 June 1694 granted FRANCIS FIDLING 2 lots, ·
1/2 a. each, #216 & #47; #216 bounding W on a little street running from
Ashley River to JOHN JONES; E on CAPT. CHARLES CLARK; N on WILLIAM BAILEY;
S on FRANCIS FIDLING; lot #47 bounding W & E & N on FRANCIS FIDLING; S on
Ashley River; & whereas, after FRANCIS FIDLING'S death, his son & heir,
DANIEL FIDLING, sold the 2 lots to WILLIAM LEVINGSTON CLARK (?) & whereas
WILLIAM LEVINGSTON CLARK & ANN his wife, on 6 Nov. 1717 sold the 2 lots
to JOHN RIVERS, SR.; who bequeathed them to his son, JOHN RIVERS, party
hereto; now he sells MILES the 2 lots 196 & 142 & part of lot #216 grant-
ed to FIDLING & adjoining #196, which is the whole of lot #216 except the
private street which JOHN RIVERS laid out from Meeting Street to King
Street & is bounding E on Meeting Street & MRS. BRYAN, widow of JOSEPH
BRYAN. Witnesses: THOMAS MILES, JOHN CHAMPNESS. Before WILLIAM BULL,
JR., J.P. ROBERT AUSTIN, Pub. Reg. On 16 Apr. 1744 WILLIAM MILES declared mortgage satisfied. Witness: JAMES MICHIE, D.P.R.

Book W, p. 376
8 & 9 Feb. 1741
L & R
ESTHER ELLIOTT, widow, to WILLIAM BRANFORD,
planter, both of Berkeley Co., for Ł 2520 currency, 280 a. in Berkeley Co. (part of her
share by will of SHEM BUTLER), bounding SE on
the ferry path & WILLIAM MILES; SW on WILLIAM BRANFORD (formerly JOHN
WATSON); NW on BENJAMIN STANYARNE; NE on WILLIAM MILES. Whereas Gov.

NATHANIEL JOHNSON, JAMES MOORE, & NICHOLAS TROTT, Lords Proprs. on July 16, 1703 granted SHEM BUTLER 1332 a., English measure, on SW side of Ashley River, bounding NW on a large creek & JONATHAN FITCH; SW on vacant land & JOSEPH & WILLIAM ELLIOTT; SE on SAMUEL JONES, CHARLES JONES & SHEM BUTLER; & whereas SHEM BUTLER by will dated 9 Oct. 1718 bequeathed all his real & personal estate (after paying his debts) to his wife & children, to be divided equally by his executors; & whereas RICHARD BUTLER & EDMUND BELLINGER, the executors on 1 May 1724 divided the property & apportioned to the widow (now ESTHER ELLIOTT) her share; now she sells to Branford. Witnesses: BARNABY BRANFORD, ELIZABETH BELLINGER. Before WILLIAM BULL, JR., J.P. ROBERT ASUTIN, Pub. Reg.

Book W, p. 384
15 & 16 Mar. 1741
L & R

CHARLES ARMSTRONG, bricklayer, to HENRY SHERIFF, planter, both of James Island, Berkeley Co., for ₤ 500 currency, 50 a. on S side Wappoo Creek, on James Island, bounding NE on a creek; E on ARCHIBALD HAMILTON; S on the broad path leading from Wappoo bridge to Johnson's Fort; W on CHARLES ARMSTRONG. Witnesses: ARCHIBALD HAMILTON, JAMES WALLACE, MARGARET (her mark) LESSLEY. Plat of 50 a., part of 379 a. granted to CHARLES ARMSTRONG, certified by THOMAS WITTER, Dep. Sur. on 11 Dec. 1741. Before ROBERT AUSTIN, J.P. & Pub. Reg.

Book W, p. 390
19 & 20 Mar. 1741
L & R

HENRY SHERIFF, planter, & MARGARET his wife, of James Island, Berkeley Co., to MICHAEL FINLYSON, of Charleston, for ₤ 350 currency, 350 a. in Craven Co., bounding NW on CAPT. SCOTT; other sides on vacant land. Witnesses: WILLIAM IRWIN, THOMAS RHODES, JOHN COWDEN. Before HENRY GIBBES, J.P. ROBERT AUSTIN, Pub. Reg.

Book W, p. 395
15 Jan. 1741
Bill of Sale

JOHN MULLRYNE, gentleman & CLAUDIA his wife, of Granville Co., to Lt. Gov. WILLIAM BULL, for (?), 58 a. in Granville Co. Witnesses: JOHN BILNEY, DANIEL BAYN. Plat by JOHN MULLRYNE, dated 15 Jan. 1741, showing 58 a. on SW side Cumbahee River, bounding NE on MR. MULLRYNE & a branch of Hawbauny (Habany) Creek; SE on MR. MULLRYNE, & WILLIAM BULL; NW on JOSEPH BRYAN. Before WILLIAM BULL, JR., J.P. ROBERT AUSTIN, Pub. Reg.

Book W, p. 397
16 Mar. 1741
Mortgage

HUGH SWINTON, planter, of Craven Co., to JAMES ABERCROMBY, ESQ., as security on bonds for ₤ 280 British, & ₤ 4270 SC money, with interest, dated Jan. 6. 1740 & 7 Mar. 1740; 1125 a. in Craven Co.; bounding SW on JOHN HADDRELL & JOHN BOGGS; E on HUGH SWINTON, CAPT. DICK & THOMAS LAROCHE; NE on MR. LAROCHE; NW on WILLIAM SWINTON; as by original grant to HUGH SWINTON. Witnesses: PAUL HAMILTON, LEO PAUL BOUDON, JAMES WEDDERBURN. Before JAMES WEDDERBURN, J.P.

Book W, p. 400
25 & 26 Mar. 1742
L & R

MARY SUTHERLAND, widow of Christ Church Parish, to JOHN MCKENSIE, merchant, of Charleston, for ₤ 1600 SC money, 190 a. in Christ Church Parish, on E side of Wando River, according to 2 grants from Lords Proprs. to FRANCES SIMMONDS dated 20 Mar. 1700. Witnesses: JOHN RATTRAY, WILLIAM MACKENSIE. Before ROBERT AUSTIN, J.P. & Pub. Reg.

Book W, p. 405
24 & 25 Dec. 1739
L & R

JOHN FRASER, merchant, of Charleston, executor of will of JOHN MCKAY, shopkeeper, formerly of Charleston lately, planter, of St. James Goose Creek, to BENJAMIN STONE, planter, of James Island, for ₤ 450 SC money, 50 a. on James Island, part of 170 a. formerly belonging to RICHARD RIVERS; bounding E on a creek; W & S on JOHN MCKAY; N on SAMUEL RIVERS. Witnesses: W. FRANKLIN, THOMAS JENKINS. Before ROBERT AUSTIN, J.P. & Pub. Reg.

Book W, p. 411
6 Mar. 1740
Bill of Sale

EDWARD THOMAS, planter, & ELIZABETH his wife, to his son, SAMUEL THOMAS, planter, all of St. James Santee, Craven Co., for ₤ 100 SC money, 650 a. in St. James Santee, being part of 1200 a. called Yaughn, now belonging to ROBERT AUSTIN & PETER PORCHER; the 650 a. bounding SE on THOMAS CORDEN (formerly JOHN MOORE); SW on

EDWARD THOMAS; NW on ROBERT AUSTIN & PETER PORCHER; N on Santee River
Swamp; reserving to EDWARD THOMAS & his heirs the liberty of grinding
grain for his family, only, toll free, on any mill on the 650 a., erected
or to be erected; & liberty for EDWARD THOMAS, his Negroes, & attendants,
of hunting, fishing, or fowling. Witnesses: THOMAS CORDES, PETER LEQUEUX,
JOHN CORDES. Before ROBERT AUSTIN, J.P. & Pub. Reg.

Book W, p. 414   JOHN DEXTOR, (DEXTER), of Craven Co., to PAUL
24 & 25 Jan. 1741   TRAPIER & CO., merchants, of Georgetown as se-
L & R by Mortgage   curity on bond of even date in penal sum of
                    Ł 2000 for payment of Ł 1000 currency with in-
terest on 1 Feb. 1742; 4 tracts in Prince George Parish; total 1500 a.; 1
of 500 a. bounding E on JOHN HODDY; SE on WILLIAM SHACKELFORD; SW on vacant land; 1 of 200 a. bounding on all sides on STEPHEN FORD; 1 of 500 a.
bounding E on vacant land; SE on JOHN HODDY; N on NICHOLAS MATTHISON; E
on DOMINICK ROCHE; 1 of 300 a. bounding S & W on STEPHEN FORD; N on vacant land; E on MRS. ELIZABETH SERRIE. Witnesses: THOMAS BLYTHE, PETER
DUBOURDIEU. Before WILLIAM WHITESIDE, J.P. ROBERT AUSTIN, Pub. Reg.

Book W, 419   JONATHAN SKRINE, of Georgetown, to COL. WIL-
30 Dec. 1741   LIAM WATIES, as security for several debts
Mortgage   amounting to Ł 375 currency, now due; & be-
                    cause WATIES & SKRINE have bought from CAPT.
JOSEPH HINCKSTON sundry goods amounting to Ł 798 currency, for which
WATIES gave a note & also to assure to WATIES payment of 1/2 the profits
from the sale of the goods; 2 lots, #23 & #60, in Georgetown, with the
houses, etc. Date of redemption: 1 Jan. 1742. Witnesses: JOHN WILLIAM
HINCHIE, NATHANIEL TREGAGLE. Before DANIEL LAROCHE, J.P. ROBERT AUSTIN,
Pub. Reg.

Book W, p. 421   STEPHEN RUSSELL, cordwainer, & JANE his wife,
6 & 7 Apr. 1742   to ROBERT RIVERS, JR., planter, all of James
L & R   Island, Berkeley Co., for Ł 704 currency,
                    105 a. on James Island, being the remainder of
a tract of 255 a.; bounding E & S on the Great Sound; W on JOSEPH SPENCER;
N on ROBERT RIVERS, SR. Whereas WILLIAM, Earl of Craven, Palatine, & the
Lords Proprs., & EDWARD TYNTE, ROBERT DANIEL, ROBERT GIBBE, THOMAS BROUGH-
TON, & FRANCIS TURBEVILLE, commissioners, on 14 Apr. 1710 granted WILLIAM
RUSSELL 255 a., English measure, in Berkeley Co.; & whereas he died in-
testate, the land was inherited by STEPHEN RUSSELL, who has been in quiet
possession of the 105 a. he now conveys to RIVERS. Witnesses: JAMES OS-
MOND, JAMES MICHIE. Before ROBERT AUSTIN, J.P. & Pub. Reg.

Book W, p. 431   Lt. Gov. WILLIAM BULL to his second son, the
9 & 10 Apr. 1742   Hon. WILLIAM BULL, the younger, Speaker of the
Deed of Gift   Hon. House of Assembly, for natural love & af-
                    fection & other considerations, 500 a. on S
side Ashley River, in St. Andrews Parish, being the NW part of 990 a.
granted by the Lords Proprs.; bounding SE on a marsh on S side of the orc-
hard, running towards the tan house & fish pond, inclusive, thence on a
road or avenue leading from the mansion or dwelling house on said 500 a.
tract towards the plantation called Little Berry as far as MR. NATHANIEL
BROWN'S line; SW on NATHANIEL BROWN; NW on JOHN CHAMPNESS & marsh land
granted WILLIAM BULL, SR.; NE on marsh land belonging to WILLIAM BULL,
SR.; also all the marsh land N of the 500 a.; also the mansion house or
capitol messuage on the 500 a.; also 20 slaves. Witnesses: The Hon.
JAMES HAMMERTON, The Hon. EDMUND ATKIN, RICHARD HILL, CHARLES PINCKNEY.
Before the Hon. JOSEPH WRAGG, J.Q. ROBERT AUSTIN, Pub. Reg.

Book W, p. 437   WILLIAM SPENCER, planter, & SARAH his wife, of
8 & 9 Apr. 1742   James Island, St. Andrews Parish, Berkeley Co.
L & R   to JOHN STANYARNE, planter, of Johns Island,
                    St. Johns Parish, Colleton Co., for Ł 298 cur-
rency 149 a. (part of 600 a.), bounding W on COL. ROBERT GIBBES; NW on
JOHN STANYARNE; N on BARWICK; E on EVANS; SW & SE on WILLIAM SPENCER.
Plat annexed. Whereas the Lords Proprs. on 15 Sept. 1705 granted HUGH
HEXT 600 a. in Colleton Co., which he on 10 Feb. 1705 conveyed to his 1
sons, EDWARD & HUGH; & whereas EDWARD & HUGH HEXT on 8 July 1728 conveyed
the 600 a. to HENRY NICHOLLS, who, by will bequeathed the tract to his
son ISAAC; & whereas ISAAC NICHOLLS, by L & R dated 5 & 6 Aug. 1733,

conveyed the 600 a. to WILLIAM SPENCER; now he sells to STANYARNE. Witnesses: RIBTON HUTCHINSON, WILLIAM SPENCER, JR., MIDDLETON EVANS. Before JACOB MOTTE, J.P. ROBERT AUSTIN, Pub. Reg.

Book W, p. 444   WILLIAM LEVINGSTON & ROYALL SPRY, executors of
20 Jan. 1740   will of DANIEL HENDRICK, dated 30 June 1738,
Bill of Sale   to GEORGE JACKSON, planter, all of Colleton
                       Co., for Ł 1000 currency 3 tracts of 100 a.
each, & 1 with unknown acreage. Whereas, Gov. CHARLES CRAVEN & the Lords
Proprs. on 21 Mar. 1715/6 granted DANIEL HENDRICK 100 a. in Colleton Co.,
according to plat; & whereas ROYALL SPRY, planter of Pon Pon, Colleton
Co., on 4 June 1723 sold DANIEL HENDRICK 100 a.; & whereas SAMUEL WIL-
LIAMS & HANNAH his wife, of Colleton Co.; by L & R, 14 & 15 Apr. 1737
sold DANIEL HENDRICK a plantation originally granted to JOHN PENNY; &
whereas SAMUEL WILLIAMS on 16 Apr. 1737 mortgaged 4 Negroes to HENDRICK
with the proviso that WILLIAMS should procure for HENDRICK of his (SAMUEL
WILLIAMS) & HANNAH'S (his wife) share in said plantation (number of a.
not known); & whereas WILLIAM FERGUSON, planter, of Colleton Co., on 25
Apr. 1739 sold HENDRICK 100 a. (part of 200 a. which he purchased from
ROYALL SPRY); now HENDRICKS'S executors sell to JACKSON RUTH WITHERSPOON,
JOHN HARRIS. Before JAMES BULLOCK, J.P. ROBERT AUSTIN, Pub. Reg.

Book W, p. 449   GEORGE JACKSON, to ROYALL SPRY, planter, for
20 Jan. 1740   Ł 1000 currency, 300 a. & a tract of uncertain
Bill of Sale   acreage; also 1 deed of mortgage for 1 Negro
                       woman & her 3 children being surety for the
uncertain acreage sold by SAMUEL WILLIAMS & HANNAH his wife; all in Colleton Co.; whereas WILLIAM LEVINGSTON & ROYALL SPRY, executors, of will
of DANIEL HENDRICK, sold GEORGE JACKSON several pieces of land, being
300 a. & 1 piece of uncertain size; now JACKSON sells to SPRY. Witnesses: RUTH WITHERSPOON, JOHN HARRIS. Before JAMES BULLOCK, J.P. ROBERT
AUSTIN, Pub. Reg.

Book W, p. 452   RICHARD WOODWARD, of Beaufort, Granville Co.,
13 May 1741   to ANDREW BELL, blacksmith, for Ł 200 curren-
Bill of Sale   cy, lot #7 in Beaufort. ELIZABETH WOODWARD
                       consents & signs. Witnesses: MACKEMSON, ROB-
ERT BRISBANE. Before ALEXANDER CRAMAHE, J.P. ROBERT AUSTIN, Pub. Reg.

Book W, p. 453   WILLIAM (his mark) KEMP, planter, & ELIZABETH
23 & 24 Feb. 1741   (her mark) his wife, to EDWARD HOWARD, plant-
L & R   er, all of Craven Co., for Ł 140 SC money,
                       300 a. in Williamsburgh Township, Craven Co.,
bounding S on FRANCIS GODDARD; E on FRANCIS TURBEVILLE; other sides on
vacant land. ELIZABETH to renounce her dower upon request. Witnesses:
JOHN SINKLER, THOMAS ASHBY, JR., JOSEPH WHITE. Before ROBERT FINLAY, J.P.
ROBERT AUSTIN, Pub. Reg.

Book W, p. 458   FRANCIS (FRANCOIS) VARAMBOUT, shopkeeper, &
19 & 20 June 1739   MARTHA (her mark) his wife, of Charleston, to
L & R   PETER PAGETT & JOHN PAGETT, planters, of St.
                       Thomas Parish, for Ł 245 currency, 1100 a. in
Craven Co., granted by GEORGE II on 18 Mar. 1735 to FRANCIS VARAMBOUT,
bounding N on Peedee River; E on MR. SANDERS; S on Geffers Creek; W on
JOHN BONNETHEAU. Witnesses: JOAN GARNIER, JAMES JORDAN. Before HENRY
GIBBES, J.P. ROBERT AUSTIN, Pub. Reg.

Book W, p. 464   DANIEL HORRY, planter, & MARY his wife, of St.
28 & 29 Jan. 1741   James Santee, to WILLIAM SHACKELFORD, planter,
L & R   of Craven Co., for Ł 249:11 currency, 825 a.
                       in Craven Co., in fork of Little Peedee River,
above NW branch to the NE; bounding on NOAH SERRÉ; other sides on vacant
land; according to grant to DANIEL HORRY dated 10 Apr. 1738 & signed by
Lt. Gov. WILLIAM BULL. MARY, wife of DANIEL HORRY, to renounce her dower
upon request. Witnesses: ELIAS HORRY, EDWARD JARMAN, SARAH FORD. Before
WILLIAM WHITESIDE, J.P. ROBERT AUSTIN, Pub. Reg.

Book W, p. 469   JOSHUA TOOMER, tanner, & MARY his wife, of St.
4 Aug. 1741   Andrews Parish, to BARNARD ELLIOTT, planter,
Mortgage   of same Parish, for Ł 227 currency, 22-1/4 a.

(part of a tract left him by his father HENRY TOOMER); bounding E & N on
BARNARD ELLIOTT; W on JOHN BONNEAU; S on JOSHUA TOOMER. Witnesses: HENRY
TOOMER, JACOB (his mark) BUTCHER, JOHN (his mark) MIRE. Before THOMAS
DRAYTON, J.P. ROBERT AUSTIN, Pub. Reg. On 4 Sept. 1744 BARNARD ELLIOTT
declared mortgage satisfied. Witness: MATTHEW GUERIN.

Book W, p. 471   WILLIAM (his mark) JONES, & ANSTY (her mark)
10 & 11 Apr. 1739   his wife, to JOSEPH TOBIAS, shopkeeper, all of
L & R   Christ Church Parish, for ℒ 430 currency, 30 a.
                        English measure, part of 50 a., on NW end of
the NE of the 50 a., on NW side of She-A-Wee Sound, on a place called
Boo-Watt Breach, & bounding SE on the Sound; SW on estate of JOHN EVANS;
NE on GEORGE BENTLEY & vacant land. Witnesses: PETER (PIERRO) COURT-
ENONNE, JOHN HARVEY. Before HENRY GIBBES, J.P. ROBERT AUSTIN, Pub. Reg.

Book W, p. 478   GEORGE HAYES, planter, of Winyaw, Craven Co.,
18 & 19 Nov.   to JOHN BONNOIT, storekeeper, of St. Thomas &
L & R   St. Dennis, Berkeley Co., for ℒ 1550 currency,
                        255 a. & the dwelling house on which CHARLES
HAYES, father of GEORGE lived, being 1/2 of 510 a. in Berkeley Co., the
510 a. consisting of 4 grants. Witnesses: JOHN WILLIAMS, ANTHONY BONNEAU,
ELIAS BONNEAU. Before ANTHONY BONNEAU, J.P. ROBERT AUSTIN, Pub. Reg.

Book W, p. 484   JORDAN ROCHE, gentleman, & REBECCA his wife,
26 & 27 Sept. 1740   to OTHNIEL BEALE, merchant, all of Charleston,
L & R   for ℒ 250 SC money, part of lot #169 in
                        Charleston which ROCHE purchased from DANIEL &
THOMAS LAROCHE 19 June 1735; which part of lot #169 bounds E 98 ft. on
OTHNIEL BEALE; N & S 51 ft. each on JORDAN ROCHE; W 98 ft. on BENJAMIN
WHITAKER. Witnesses: WILLIAM PINCKNEY, JAMES KILPATRICK, GEORGE MATTH-
EWES. Before ROBERT AUSTIN, J.P. & Pub. Reg.

Book W, p. 491   RICHARD HILL, ESQ., to OTHNIEL BEALE, merchant,
23 & 24 Mar. 1741   both of Charleston, for ℒ 2400 currency, part
L & R   of 2 several parts of a half town lot #9; part
                        of another lot; & a piece of shole or low wa-
ter lot. Whereas DANIEL LAROCHE, merchant, of Winyaw, son & devisee of
JOHN LAROCHE, merchant, of Charleston, owned part of 2 several parts of a
half town lot in Charleston known as lot #9, fronting E 25 ft. 4 in., on
the Bay, 217 ft. deep, 16-1/2 ft. at W end, as heretofore set out with
cedar stakes; bounding S on another part of the 2 parts of the half part
of lot #9; N on part of a lot belonging to the heirs of DANIEL GALE; W on
DANIEL LAROCHE (formerly belonging to heirs of CHARLES BASDEN); also that
piece of a lot adjoining the parcel first mentioned, 24 ft. 1 in. broad,
28 ft. 9 in. deep, bounding E on the land mentioned above; W & N on WIL-
LIAM ELLIOTT; S on CATHERINE IOOR; which 2 parts of lots were lately occupied by ISAAC CHARDON; also that piece of shole or low water land before the Bay, 25 ft. 4 in. broad, running E from the wharf line to low
water mark, & fronting the part of 2 several parts of lot #9; & whereas
DANIEL LAROCHE by L & R dated 21 & 22 Mar. 1731 conveyed the 2 parts of
lot #9 & the other adjoining part of RICHARD HILL & CHARLES HILL (father
of said RICHARD); & whereas the King on 6 Apr. 1733 granted CHARLES HILL
& RICHARD HILL the piece of shole land before the Bay, 25 ft. 4 in. running E from the wharf line to Cooper River, fronting the 2 parts of lot
#9; & whereas CHARLES HILL, by will dated 12 Apr. 1734 bequeathed his
half of the land to his son RICHARD: & whereas CHARLES HILL died on 26
July 1734 & the shole land became vested in RICHARD HILL as surviving
joint tenant; now he sells to OTHNIEL BEALE. Witnesses: THOMAS LAROCHE,
JOSEPH SHUTE, ANTHONY WHITE. Before ROBERT AUSTIN, J.P. & Pub. Reg.

Book W, p. 500   WILLIAM POOLE, THOMAS LAROCHE, & ALEXANDER
14 & 15 Jan. 1740   NISBETT, gentleman, executors, of will of ROB-
L & R   ERT BROWN, surgeon of Craven Co., to WILLIAM
                        ALSTON, for ℒ 1800 currency, 640 a. in Craven
Co. where ROBERT BROWN lived bounding E on a salt marsh; W on Waccamaw
River; N & S on WILLIAM ALSTON. Whereas by L & R dated 16 & 17 Apr. 1736
ROBERT BROWN purchased from ALEXANDER NISBETT 640 a. in Craven Co. & by
will dated 18 Apr. 1740 appointed WILLIAM POOLE, THOMAS LAROCHE, & ALEX-
ANDER NISBETT his executors with full power to sell all his real & per-
sonal estate for certain purposes; now they sell the 640 a. to ALLSTON;

Witnesses: JOHN OULDFIELD, JR., JAMES CRADDOCK. Before WILLIAM ROMSAY, J.P. ROBERT AUSTIN, Pub. Reg.

Book W, p. 506   HANNAH PROCTOR, widow, of Charleston, to her
30 Apr. & 1 May 1741   son JOHN ROYER, of Berkeley Co., for natural
Deed of Gift   love & affection, 300 a. on E branch of Cooper
                        River, bounding S on Ashby's Swamp; W on PETER
SIMONDS; which 300 a. was bequeathed by will of SAMUEL BURCHAM, dated 2
Sept. 1718, to HANNAH PROCTOR, by name of HANNAH ROYER, wife of JOHN ROY-
ER, cordwainer. Witnesses: JUDITH GIGNILLIAT, HENRY DEWICK, PETER SIMONS.
Before ANTHONY BONNEAU, J.P. ROBERT AUSTIN, Pub. Reg.

Book W, p. 510   JOHN ROYER, of Charleston, to HENRY VIDEAU,
1 & 2 May 1741   planter, of St. Thomas & St. Dennis Parish,
L & R   for Ł 300 currency, 300 a. in Berkeley Co.,
                        bounding NW on JOHN ASHBY; NE on SAMUEL KING;
SE on MR. SIMMONDS; SW on vacant land. Witnesses: HENRY DWEICK, DAVID
STOUT, PETER SIMONS. Before ANTHONY BONNEAU, J.P. ROBERT AUSTIN, J.P. &
Pub. Reg.

Book W, p. 515   SAMPSON BALL, planter, to JOHN COOK, carpenter,
22 & 23 Jan. 1741/2   both of Berkeley Co., for Ł 250 currency, 250
L & R   in Berkeley Co., bounding SE & SW on JOSEPH
                        MARY; other sides on vacant land; which 250 a.
were granted to SAMPSON BALL on 9 Oct. 1741. Witnesses: DAVID LAFONS,
GEORGE BURNET, JOHN (his mark) WEST. Before THOMAS MONCK, J.P. ROBERT
AUSTIN, Pub. Reg.

Book W, p. 518   BENJAMIN DIDCOTT, planter, of Tooboodoo, to
1 & 2 Sept. 1741   WILLIAM EDINGS, planter, of Edisto Island, for
L & R   Ł 1600 SC money, 332 a. at head of Tooboodoo
                        Creek, bounding E on a marsh & JOHN FABIAN &
JOHN DAVIS; S on WILLIAM EDINGS; W & N on JOHN DIDCOTT & AURELIA DIDCOTT,
wife of BENJAMIN, willingly surrender her right of dower. Whereas JOHN,
Lord Granville, Palatine; WILLIAM, Lord Craven; JOHN, Lord Carteret; MAU-
RICE ASHLEY; SIR JOHN COLLETON, & other Lords Proprs. on 18 June 1702
granted JOHN DIDCOTT 332 a. on Tooboodoo Creek, which was inherited by
his son BENJAMIN, now BENJAMIN sells to EDINGS. Witnesses: JOHN FREER,
JOSEPH WHIPPY. Before ROBERT YONGE, J.P. ROBERT AUSTIN, Register.

Book W, p. 524   JACOB BOND, ESQ., & SUSANNAH, his wife, of
16 & 17 Mar. 1741   Christ Church Parish, Berkeley Co., to NOAH
L & R   SERRÉ, ESQ., of St. James Santee, Craven Co.,
                        for Ł 727 SC money, 4 tracts, total 540 a.; 1
of 200 a. in St. James Santee, granted 5 Dec. 1696 to ARMAND BRUNEAU DE
CHABUSHIER; bounding N on Santee River; W on NOAH SERRÉ; S on heirs of
ISAAC LEGRAND; E on another tract; 1 of 40 a., part of 240 a. granted 19
Jan. 1688 to JOHN FRANCIS DE GIGNILLIATT; bounding N on Santee River; W
on above tract; S on heirs of ISAAC LEGRAND; E on heirs of ANDREW REMBERT;
1 of 50 a. in Prince Frederick Parish, granted 9 June 1714 to PETER ROB-
ERTS; bounding S on Santee River; W on NOAH SERRÉ; N on vacant land; E on
another tract; also 250 a., granted 1 June 1709 to HENRY BRUNEAU; bound-
ing S on Santee River; W on the 50 a. tract; N on vacant land; E on JAMES
KINLOCK. Witnesses: BENJAMIN SMITH, HENRY SAMWAYS. Before HENRY GIBBES,
J.P. ROBERT AUSTIN, Pub. Reg.

DEEDS BOOK "X"
MAY 1742 - FEB. 1743

Book X, p. 1   GEORGE BENISON, SR., of Christ Church Parish,
26 Dec. ....   Berkeley Co., to his son GEORGE BENISON, JR.,
Deed of Gift   for love & affection, 500 a., part of a larger
                        tract known as Youghall; bounding SW on part
of same tract; S on Copahee; NE on land purchased by BENISON from JACOB
MOTTE. Witnesses: ELIZABETH BREMAR, FRANCIS BREMAR?. Before ANTHONY
BONNEAU ?, J.P. JAMES HOME, Pub. Reg.

Book X, p. 5   JOSEPH SHUTE, merchant, of Charleston, & ANNE

14 & 15 May 1742   his wife to ANDREW BALFOUR, merchant, of Edin-
L & R   burgh, Great Britain, for Ⱡ 700 SC money, 1050
                                      a. on S side Georgetown Creek, Craven Co.,
bounding N on HENRY LAROCHE; W on CAPT. KING; E on MR. WOOLFORD; S on ?.
Witnesses: JOHN RATTRAY, JONATHAN SCOTT. Before ROBERT AUSTIN, J.P.
JAMES HOMES, Pub. Reg.

Book X, p. 19   WILLIAM POOLE, THOMAS LAROCHE, & ALEXANDER NIS-
2 & 3 Feb. 1741   BETT, gentleman, executors of will of ROBERT
L & R   BROWN, surgeon, of Craven Co., to WILLIAM THOM-
                                      AS, planter, of Craven Co., for Ⱡ 580 currency,
290 a. in Craven Co., bounding E on Wambaw Creek; N on MR. CARTER; W on
vacant land; S on MRS. DE RICHBOURGH. Whereas ROBERT BROWN purchased the
above said 290 a. from JOHN GENDRON & ELIZABETH his wife of Craven Co.,
by L & R dated 9 & 10 July 1739 (the original grant being to JOHN GEN-
DRON); & whereas BROWN, appointed WILLIAM POOLE, THOMAS LAROCHE & ALEXAN-
DER NISBETT, executors of his will; now the executors sell to WILLIAM
THOMAS. Before JAMES KINLOCH, J.P.

Book X, p. 28   STEPHEN MILLER, merchant, of Charleston for
9 Apr. 1742   divers causes & considerations, releases to
Quit Claim   WALTER DUNBAR, peruke-maker, & JEAN his wife,
                                      daughter of STEPHEN MILLER & MARY his wife,
all claim to that part of #115 fronting 66 ft. on Thread Street; 100 ft.
deep; bounding S on THOMAS HOLTON; E on LEWIS PATUREAU; W on JOHN SMITH.
Witnesses: ROBERT SCOTT, JOHN KINGSTON. Before ROBERT AUSTIN, J.P. JAM-
ES HOME, Pub. Reg. (See Bk. Z. p. 550).

Book X, p. 31   WILLIAM THOMAS, planter, & JUDITH his wife, to
1 & 2 May 1742   MICHAEL BINO, planter, all of St. James San-
L & R   tee Parish, Craven Co., for Ⱡ 300 currency, 4
                                      adjoining tracts of land containing 151 a. in
St. James Santee Parish; whereas BARNETT bequeathed to his wife JUDITH
(now wife of WILLIAM THOMAS) 4 tracts of land, vizt: 50 a. purchased by
BARNETT from ISAAC LEGRAND; sold by BARNETT to DANIEL DUTART; purchased
again by said BARNETT from MARY DUTART, widow of DANIEL, 50 a. purchased
by said BARNETT from ANDREW REMBERT; 23 a. purchased by said BARNETT from
said REMBERT; 28 a. purchased by _____ from ISAAC LEGRAND; the 4 tracts
bounding S on Santee High Road; W on CAPT. NOAH SERRÉ; N & E on ANDREW
REMBERT. However, THOMAS has leased part of the land to a MR. DUBOSE for
3 years. Witnesses: NATHANIEL SAVINEAU, ELIZABETH SEVINEAU, JUDITH BAR-
NETT. Before ROBERT AUSTIN, J.P. JAMES HOME, Pub. Reg.

Book X, p. 38   CAPT. JAMES MACPERSON, & RACHEL his wife, to
16 Jan. 1741/2   ANDREW MCCLELAND, planter, both of Granville
L & R   Co., for Ⱡ 900 currency, 500 a. in Granville
                                      Co., bounding NE on Combahee River; SE on pub-
lic land. Witnesses: JOHN GUINN, JOHN MACTEER, THOMAS SKEEN. Before
CHARLES WRIGHT, J.P. JAMES HOME, Pub. Reg.

Book X, p. 44   JOHN JACKSON, planter, & JANE his wife, to
21 May 1742   GEORGE JACKSON, planter, all of Pon Pon, Col-
L & R in Trust   leton Co., in trust, for Ⱡ 20 & other consid-
                                      erations; 113 lots or 400 a. laid out for a
village or town on Pon Pon River. Whereas the Lords Proprs. on 28 Aug.
_____ granted JOHN JACKSON (father of said JOHN JACKSON) 500 a. on Pon
Pon River, Colleton Co., bounding S on JOSEPH DIDCOTT; N on WILLIAM PETER;
other sides on vacant land; & whereas JOHN JACKSON, the father, bequeath-
ed the 500 a. to his son JOHN; now JOHN & his wife convey the land to
GEORGE JACKSON who is to deed the land to various persons. Witnesses:
ADAM MCDONALD, JAMES KERR. Before JACOB MOTTE, J.P. JAMES HOME, Pub.
Reg.

Book X, p. 54   ICHABOD WENBORN, planter, to ARCHIBALD CALDER,
30 & 31 May 1742   gentleman, both of St. John's Parish, for
L & R   Ⱡ 190 SC money, 100 a. on Edisto Island, bound-
                                      ing S on JOSHUA GRIMBELL, other sides on ICHA-
BOD WENBORN. Witnesses: ISAAC GODIN, JOHN RATTRAY. Before GEORGE SAXBY,
J.P. JAMES HOME, Pub. Reg.

Book X, p. 60   JOHN HAMMERTON, ESQ., of the Parish of St.
London   Martin in the Fields, in the Liberty of West-
18 June 1740   minster, Co. of Middlesex, appoints ALEXANDER
Deputation   GORDON of same place his deputy. Whereas KING
GEORGE the 2nd by letters patent dated at West-
minster 11 Feb. 1730 ? appointed EDWARD BERTIE & JOHN HAMMERTON to the
offices of Secretary & Register in SC, with authority to appoint deputies;
& whereas BERTIE died; now HAMMERTON appoints GORDON his deputy to act as
clerk of the Council, to be present at all meetings of the Gov. & Council
in General Assembly, to keep registers or journals of all their proceedings, acts & orders; granting GORDON all rights, fees, perquisites, & re-
wards of office, etc. Witnesses: ALEXANDER CALLENDER. Registered in SC
by SAMUEL GILLIBRAND, Dep. Sec. JAMES HOME, Pub. Reg.

Book X, p. 63   Between JOHN HAMMERTON, ESQ., & ALEXANDER GOR-
18 June 1740   DON, gentleman, both of the Parish of St. Mar-
Agreement   tin in the Fields, in the Liberty of Westminster, Co. of Middlesex, Great Britain. Where-
as GEORGE II by letters patent dated at Westminster 11 Feb. 1730 granted
EDWARD BERTIE & JOHN HAMMERTON the office of Secretary & Register of SC;
& whereas BERTIE died leaving HAMMERTON sole grantee; & whereas HAMMERTON
this date appointed GORDON his deputy, to execute the office of clerk of
the Council of SC & enjoy the rights, fees, perquisites, etc., of that
office, new, for Ł 200 British money, HAMMERTON agrees to let GORDON hold
the office of Secretary, & the whole profits & emoluments, etc., of that
office during HAMMERTON'S lifetime. Should HAMMERTON fail to keep his
agreements he shall pay GORDON Ł 500 British for trouble & expense of going to SC, etc. Witnesses: ALEXANDER CALLENDER, ALEXANDER MAINE, ROBERT
GARDEN, PETER DEQUIAU. JAMES HOME, Pub. Reg.

Book X, p. 72   EDWARD HAZELWOOD, victualler, of Berkeley Co.,
--- July 1741   to THOMAS BOLTON, merchant, of Charleston, as
Mortgage   security for going on HAZLEWOOD'S bond to HEN-
RY PERONNEAU, SR., of Charleston, dated 20 May
1740, in penal sum of Ł 1000 SC money, for payment of Ł 500 with interest
on 20 May 1742; 50 a. in Berkeley Co., part of a larger tract granted to
PHILIP JONES & lately purchased from ANDREW RUTLEDGE, ESQ., bounding N &
E on CAPT. BOND; W & S on RICHARD FOWLER & MR. LEWIS. Witnesses: WILLIAM
WILLIAMSON, JAMES WITHERS, ROBERT ROPER. Before ROBERT AUSTIN, J.P.
JAMES HOME, Pub. Reg. BOLTON declared mortgage satisfied. Witness: JAM-
ES HOME.

Book X, p. 79   ABRAHAM DUPONT, planter, & JANE his wife, of
20 Oct. 1736   St. James Goose Creek, Berkeley Co., for natu-
Deed of Gift   ral love & affection to (his brother ?) PETER
MAY, 200 a., part of 1000 a., English measure,
deeded to DUPONT by _____ ? in 1725/6; the 200 a. being on Wassumsaw
Swamp; bounding S on RICHARD BUTLER; W on ISAAC LEWIS; NE on GIDEON DU-
PONT; SE on DANIEL DEAN. JANE DUPONT voluntarily relinquishes her title
of dower. Witnesses: DANIEL DEAN, NATHANIEL DEAN, GIDEON DUPONT. Before
ISAAC PORCHER, J.P. JAMES HOME, Pub. Reg.

Book X, p. 87   PETER MAY, planter, & ESTHER his wife, to ROB-
21 & 22 Oct. 1736 ERT SANDERS, carpenter, all of Berkeley Co.,
L & R   for Ł 400 SC money, 200 a. on Wassumsaw Swamp,
bounding S on RICHARD BUTLER; W on ISAAC LEWIS;
NE on GIDEON DUPONT; SE on DANIEL DEAN. ESTHER MAY freely renounces her
dower. Witnesses: NATHANIEL DEAN, GIDEON DUPONT, WILLIAM SMITH. Before
ISAAC PORCHER, J.P. JAMES HOME, Pub. Reg.

Book X, p. 97   JAMES HOME, ESQ., appoints JAMES MICHIE, to be
Deputation   Deputy Public Register. Whereas GEORGE II by
letters patent dated 6 (26?) May 1742, signed
by Lt. Gov. WILLIAM BULL, appointed JAMES HOME to be Public Register of
SC with authority to appoint deputies to execute the office of Register;
now HOME appoints JAMES MICHIC his Dep. Pub. Reg. Witnesses: ALEXANDER
GORDON, WILLIAM MOUAL. Before OTHNIEL BEALE, J.P. JAMES MICHIE, Dep.
Reg.

Book X, p. 99   SAMUEL MORRIS, ESQ., of St. James Goose Creek

24 Mar. 1741 of 1st part; JANE MORRIS, wife of said SAMUEL
Deed in Trust. MORRIS (heretofore called JAKE PARKER, widow &
Tripartite administratrix of JOHN PARKER), of 2nd part;
the Hon. RALPH IZARD of 3rd part. Whereas it
was mutually agreed between SAMUEL & JANE MORRIS, before their marriage,
that JANE should have full authority to manage the estate of JOHN PARKER
with out interference from SAMUEL; now, to perfect the agreement, SAMUEL
MORRIS pronuses RALPH IZARD that JANE shall have absolute authority to
administer the estate of JOHN PARKER, her former husband, without SAM-
UEL'S interference; & SAMUEL & JANE convey to IZARD, all the real & personal estate, Negroes, furniture, bonds, mortgages & all goods & chattels
that belonged to JANE before her marriage, in trust, for the use of SAM-
UEL & JANE during their lives; with provisions as to the disposal of such
estate after the death of either of them; SAMUEL to make an inventory of
JANE'S property, SAMUEL MORRIS to convey to IZARD 400 a. on which his
(SAMUEL'S) dwelling house stands, in St. James Goose Creek, being part of
700 a. purchased from WILLIAM WATIES; also 13 slaves; also all cattle,
hogs, pettiaugers, tools, etc.; upon trust, for SAMUEL & JANE'S support.
Witnesses: THOMAS ELMES, HUGH FERGUSON, JOSIAH PENDARVIS. Before THOMAS
DALE, J.P. JAMES MICKIE, Pub. Reg.

Book X, p. 107 THOMAS ELLIOTT, planter, & SUSANNA his wife,
13 June 1742 to THOMAS BUTTLER, planter, all of Colleton
L & R Co., for L 1300 SC money, 759 a. in Colleton
Co., bounding N & NW on JONATHAN FITCH & ROGER
SAUNDERS; NE on unknown land; SE on COL. JOHN FENWICKE; S & SW on MR.
FAIRCHILD; which 759 a. was granted on 8 Aug. 1741 to THOMAS & SUSANNA
ELLIOTT. Witnesses: WILLIAM BUTLER, ELIZABETH SNOWDEN, THOMAS ELLIOTT,
JR. Before JAMES MICKIE, J.P. & Dep. Pub. Reg.

Book X, p. 113 FRANCIS LEJAU & ISAAC CHILD, gentleman, execu-
27 Aug. 1741 tors of will of MARGARET CHILD, widow, to WIL-
Bill of Sale LIAM HOPTON, gentleman, of Charleston, for
L 1479:7:8 SC money, part of lot #105 in
Charleston. Whereas WILLIAM LINTHWAITE, brasier, of Charleston, on 14
Jan. o735 gave bond to MARGARET CHILD in penal sum of L 1739:6:8 for payment of L 869:13:4 with interest on 14 Jan. 1736; & whereas by L & R dated 13 & 14 Jan. 1735 LINTHWAITE conveyed to MARGARET CHILD as security
for the said debt, part of lot #105 in Charleston, 60 ft. x 80 ft.; bounding N on JAMES PAINE; S on Broad Street, where the market is kept; E & W
on parts of same lot; & whereas there is now due on the bond & mortgage
the sum of L 1479:7:8 which the executors are legally entitled; now the
executors convey to HOPTON the part of a lot & the mortgage & papers.
Witnesses: ADAM LEWIS, HENRY GIGNILLIAT. Before JAMES MICKIE, J.P. &
Dep. Pub. Reg.

Book X, p. 118 SAMUEL UNDERWOOD, to PATRICK NORRIS, for L 760
29 & 30 Apr. 1742 510 (?) a. part of a tract granted by the
L & R Lords Proprs. & Gov. JOSEPH BLAKE, 8 Sept.
1697 to RICHARD UNDERWOOD (father of SAMUEL),
on S side Wadmalaw River, bounding N on 70 a. belonging to COL. BREWING-
TON; E on JOHN STANYARNE (formerly WILLIAM DENHAN); S by original line of
grant from W corner thereof along the original line formerly called BONUM
SAMS'S line to the S line of 100 a. sold to WILLIAM FREEMAN, now belonging to HUGH CHRISTEY; thence along said line to E line of CHRISTEY'S; a-
long said line to W end of first named N boundary line. BENJAMIN HARVEY,
THOMAS TATNELL, THOMAS MELLICHAMP, (_____) wife of SAMUEL UNDERWOOD renounced her dower before BENJAMIN WHITAKER, C.J. TATNELL appeared before
JAMES MICKIE, J.P. & Dep. Pub. Reg.

Book X, p. 125 JOHN MEEK, bricklayer ?, of Charleston, to
Date ? ANNE LEBRASSEUR, as security on a bond, 1
Mortgage large brick dwelling house, with a brick kit-
chen & storehouse (built by MEEK) fronting S
on Broad Street, bounding W on REBECCA FLAVEL; other sides on JOHN NEV-
ILLE. Witnesses: ALEXANDER VANDERDUSSEN, WILLIAM SMITH. Before THOMAS
LAMBOLL, J.P. JAMES MICKIE, Dep. Pub. Reg. On 14 Sept. 1742 THOMAS LAM-
BOLL acknowledged satisfaction of mortgage. JAMES MICKIE, Dep. Pub. Reg.
Mortgage satisfied 1 Sept. 1742. (See page 207).

Book X, p. 127   CHARLES JONES, planter, & RACHEL his wife, to
2 & 3 June 1737   ELIZABETH FULLER, widow, all of Berkeley Co.,
L & R   for Ŀ 150 SC money, the 3 lots #1, #14, & #15,
                        containing 3/4 a., in St. Andrews Town. Where-
as JOHN, Earl of Bath, Palatine, & the Lords Proprs. on 12 Oct. 1701
granted FRANCIS FIDLING 38 a., English measure, in Berkeley Co., on S
side Ashley River, bounding E on marsh & a creek; S on FRANCIS FIDLING; W
on EDMUND BELLINGER (formerly SHEM BUTLER); & whereas FRANCIS FIDLING &
MARY his wife, on 24 Feb. 1701 conveyed the 38 a. to THOMAS ROSE, planter,
of Berkeley Co., & whereas by several mesne conveyances & assignments the
land became the property of THOMAS DYMES, merchant; & whereas DYMES owned
a certain tenement (adjoining the 38 a.) at Ashley River Ferry, known as
Ashley Ferry Store, which he purchased from SAMUEL DEANE, also 2 or 3 a.
27 Dec. 1729 authorized his executors to sell his plantation lands, etc.,
appointing JOSEPH WRAGG & ROBERT HUME his executors; & whereas WRAGG &
HUME by L & R dated 21 & 22 May 1734, for Ŀ 1000 SC money, sold WILLIAM
CATTELL the 38 a., the Ashley Ferry Store, & the adjacent marsh land; &
whereas CATTELL laid out part of the land for a town called St. Andrews
Town, dividing it into lots; & whereas CHARLES JONES by an agreement with
CATTELL divided part of a pasture belonging to JONES into lots as part of
St. Andrews Town; now JONES sells ELIZABETH FULLER 3 lots, Nos. 1, 14, &
15. Witnesses: JAMES SCARLETT, RICHARD FULLER. Before WILLIAM BULL,
J.P. JAMES MICKIE, Dep. Pub. Reg.

Book X, p. 136   WILLIAM CATTELL, ESQ., of Berkeley Co., to
28 & 29 June 1738   ELIZABETH FULLER, widow, for Ŀ 50 currency,
L & R   lot # -, containing 1/4 a., English measure,
                        in St. Andrews Town. (See page 127). Witness-
es: JAMES SCARLETT, JOHN RAMSEY. Before WILLIAM BULL, JR., J.P. JAMES
MICKIE, Dep. Pub. Reg.

Book X, p. 147   JOSEPH WOOD, planter, son of HENRY WOOD, to
4 & 5 May 1742   WILLIAM WOOD, planter, son of ROBERT WOOD, all
L & R   of Berkeley Co., for Ŀ 230 SC money, 100 a.,
                        being the S part of 179 a. granted by ROBERT
DANIELL, Dep. Gov. & the Lords Proprs. to JOHN STOCKS in Dec. 1716; &
conveyed by WILLIAM STOCKS, son of JOHN STOCKS, to HENRY WOOD; who conveyed to his son JOSEPH; which 100 a. is on N side Ashley River, within
land, bounding E & SE on heirs of WILLIAM FULLER (formerly TOBIAS FITCH);
W on BENJAMIN WOOD; NW on THOMAS DRAYTON; N on remainder of 179 a. Witnesses: JOHN BURFORD, SAMUEL ELMES, BENJAMIN ELMES. Before HENRY GIBBES,
J.P. JAMES MICKIE, Dep. Pub. Reg.

Book X, p. 154   WILLIAM STEADS, JR. (son & heir of WILLIAM
19 June 1742   STEADS, SR.) & ANNE his wife, to RALPH IZARD,
Deed of Sale   silversmith, for Ŀ 450 currency, 400 a. (part
                        of 500 a.), at head of Ashley River, in Berke-
ley Co., within land, bounding W on WILLIAM STEADS, JR., & COL. BENJAMIN
WARING, & ROBERT SANDERS; S on JOHN _____; N on LAURENCE ? SANDERS (formerly BENJAMIN IZARD, GEORGE IZARD & WILLIAM SANDERS). From ISAAC PORCHER,
chirurgeon, & CLAUDE his wife, greetings. Whereas JOHN, Lord Granville,
Palatine, & the Lords Proprs. on 16 July 1703 granted ISAAC PROCHER 500 a.
in Berkeley Co., 400 a. of which they conveyed, for Ŀ 130 currency, to
WILLIAM STEADS, SR., planter, now WILLIAM STEADS, JR., conveys the 400 a.
to RALPH IZARD. ANNE STEADS renounces her dower. Witnesses: JOHN LACE,
SAMUEL ROBINSON, NATHANIEL DOAN. Before WILLIAM SANDERS, J.P. JAMES
MICKIE, Dep. Pub. Reg.

Book X, p. 160   NOAH SERRĖ, ESQ., & CATHERINE his wife, to
29 & 30 Sept. 1741   WILLIAM CHICKEN, planter, all of St. James San-
L & R   tee, Craven Co., for Ŀ 1000 currency, 1000 a.,
                        being 2 tracts of 500 a. each, in Prince Fred-
erick Parish, Craven Co., on S side Black River; 1 tract bounding W on
JACOB BOND; E on NOAH SERRĖ (being the 2nd tract); other sides on land
not laid out; the other bounding W on above tract; S on MR. MCINTOSH;
other sides on land not laid out; according to plats attached to 2 grants
from Gov. ROBERT JOHNSON dated May 1734. Witnesses: DAVID LINN, HENRY
NEWBERY, WILLIAM THOMAS. Receipt signed for Ŀ 800 in full. Before JAMES
KINLOCK, J.P. JAMES MICKIE, Dep. Pub. Reg.

Book X, p. 167   JOHN STEEL, & MARY his wife, to JOSEPH SPENCER,
14 Sept. 1742   for Ł 500 currency, a tract of land in Craven
Bill of Sale   Co., according to plat & grant recorded in
                        Book K.K. fol. 410. Witnesses: JOHN MCPHERSON,
_____ HAZARD, THOMAS COLSON. Before ROBERT AUSTIN, J.P. JAMES MICKIE,
Dep. Pub. Reg.

Book X, p. 169   ANDREW RUTLEDGE, ESQ., & SARAH his wife, (late-
2 & 3 Aug. 1739   ly widow & devisee of HUGH HEXT, ESQ., also de-
L & R   visee of SARAH FENWICKE, widow), all of Christ
                        Church Parish, to JOHN VANDERHORST of Christ
Church Parish & MICHAEL DARBY, ESQ., of St. Thomas & St. Dennis Parish,
for good causes & Ł 20 currency, 80 a., being the S part of 380 a. adjoining the plantation on which ANDREW & SARAH RUTLEDGE live, & on part of
which 80 a. stands a certain house; the 80 a. bounding S on JOHN SEVER-
ANCE; other sides on ANDREW RUTLEDGE; with the proviso that VANDERHORST &
DARBY at all times permit the dissenting paster or teacher of the Congregation of Christian People of the denomination of congregationalism to
assemble at the meeting place next adjoining the tract of 80 a. for the
public worship of God. Whereas SARAH FENWICKE owned 380 a. in Christ
Church Parish, bounding S on CAPT. ROBERT FENWICK (her husband) & on JOHN
SEVERANCE; E on JOHN HOLYBUSH; N on JOHN WHITE & JOHN CROSKEYS; W on JOHN
CROSKEYS & ROBERT FENWICKE; & by deed poll dated 18 Jan. 1726 for love of
her religion, & to carry out her husband's instructions, granted the 380
a. her husband purchased from JOHN HALES for that purpose, to VANDERHORST
& DARBY for a habitation of a dissenting pastor or teacher; & whereas
VANDERHORST & DARBY took possession of the 380 a. on 16 Jan. 1726 until
the 3rd of this Aug. & whereas VANDERHORST & DARBY (broken page) granted
ANDREW & SARAH RUTLEDGE (the 380 a.?); now RUTLEDGE reconveys 80 a. to
them. Witnesses: GEORGE OLIVER, JOHN SAVAGE, EDWARD FENWICK. Before
WILLIAM HENDRICKE, J.P. JAMES MICKIE, Dep. Pub. Reg.

Book X, p. 179   JONATHAN EVANS, planter, & ELIZABETH his wife,
10 & 11 Aug. 1742   to ARCHIBALD SCOTT, planter, all of James Is-
L & R   land, for Ł 700 SC money, 80 a. in Berkeley
                        Co., on NW side Newtown Creek, originally
granted to ROBERT DUTCH; bounding S & NW & NE on estate of COL. HALL
(formerly bounded S by JOSEPH ELLICOTT & NE by THOMAS DRAYTON). Witnesses: DANIEL CRAWFORD, JOHN RATTRAY. Before JAMES WEDDERBURN, J.P. JAMES
MICKIE, Dep. Pub. Reg.

Book X, p. 188   DANIEL CRAWFORD, planter, & SARAH his wife, of
23 Aug. 1742   Christ Church Parish, to ALEXANDER LEVIE, mer-
Deed of Feoffment   chant, of Charleston, for Ł 1000 SC money,
                        part of lot #12 in Charleston, fronting N 36
ft. on Broad Street; bounding on MARY ELLIS & ISAAC MAZYCK; W 100 ft. on
PETER BONOIST (formerly MRS. DILL); S 37 ft. 2 in. on JOSEPH WRAGG (form-
erly ISAAC CALLABEUF). Witnesses: JOHN RATTRAY, GEORGE PHILIP. Before
JAMES WEDDERBURN, J.P. Witnesses to livery & seizin: JOHN RATTRAY, HELEN
RATTRAY, GEORGE PHILP. JAMES MICKIE, Dep. Pub. Reg.

Book X, p. 191   JOHN MCKAY, of Charleston, & ELIZABETH his
9 June 1742   wife (lately ELIZABETH LEA, daughter of GEORGE
Deed of Feoffment   LEA, shipwright), to JOHN RATTRAY, gentleman,
                        all of Charleston, for Ł 600 SC money, the
house & lot in Charleston, being part of lot #18 on E side Union Street
opposite COL. CHARLES PINCKNEY; bounding N & S on parts of same lot; E on
JAMES CROKATT. Witnesses: THOMAS CHAPMAN, JOHN WILLIAM HINCHE, ROBERT
CORSAN. Before JAMES MICKIE, J.P. & Dep. Pub. Reg.

Book X, p. 195   Assignemtn of Lease for 18 years of a house in
25 Aug. 1742   Broad Street (See Book W. fol. 34-37; 18 Sept.
Assignment   1741). JOHN MEEK, to JAMES REID, merchants,
                        of Charleston, for Ł 3000 SC money, the messu-
ages & tenements on said lot now built by MEEK according to agreement,
with the cellar under the tenement already built, & several houses on the
premises, for unexpired term of years. CHARLES CALDER, JAMES WRIGHT.
Before JAMES MICKIE, J.P. & Dep. Pub. Reg.

Book X, p. 199   MARY ELLIS, widow, to GABRIEL GUIGNARD, cooper,

14 Jan. 1741   both of Charleston, for Ł 423:18 currency,
L & R   part of lot #12 in Charleston, containing
                      722-3/4 sq. ft., bounding E on JOHN COLLETON,
ESQ., S on JOHN WATSON & PETER CALVERT (formerly MRS. LE BRASSEUR); W on
MARY ELLIS; N on GABRIEL GUIGNARD & PETER DELMASTRE. Witnesses: JOHN
BECKMAN, JOHN MUNCREEF. Before HENRY GIBBES, J.P. JAMES MICKIE, Dep.
Pub. Reg.

Book X, p. 207   THOMAS LAMBOLL acknowledges receipt from JOHN
1 Sept. 1742   MEEK, by hand of CAPT. JAMES REED, of
Receipt   Ł 1051:15 currency in satisfaction of bond &
                      interest mentioned in mortgage (see page 125-
126). Witness: WILLIAM MOUET. Before JAMES MICKIE, J.P. & Pub. Reg.

Book X, p. 208   THOMAS SYLLAVANT, of Colleton Co., to RICHARD
25 Nov. 1739   WARING, of Berkeley Co., as security on bond
Mortgage   of even date in penal sum of Ł 4560 for pay-
                      ment of Ł 2280 SC money on 25 Mar. 1742; 484 a.
known as Pon Pon on W side S Edisto River, in Colleton Co., bounding N on
JOHN STOCKS; other sides on WILLIAM SINGLETON & vacant land. Witnesses:
ELIZABETH READ, THOMAS (his mark) READ, JEAN (her mark) READ. Before
JAMES SKIRVING. JAMES MACKIE, Dep. Pub. Reg.

Book X, p. 210   JAMES ATKIN, planter, & SARAH his wife, of Col-
9 & 10 June 1742   leton Co., to DANIEL LAROCHE, ESQ., of Craven
L & R   Co., for Ł 200 SC money, 110 a. in Craven Co.,
                      bounding S on Black River; E on _____?; W on
JOHN BOGGS; which 110 a. were granted to JAMES ATKINS by letters patent
dated 7 Aug. 1735 & signed by Lt. Gov. THOMAS BROUGHTON, as recorded in
Secretary's Book C.C., fol. 37. Witnesses: ISAAC MAZYCK, JAMES MICKIE.
Before JAMES MICKIE, J.P. & Dep. Pub. Reg.

Book X, p. 221   OBADIAH WILKINS, planter, & ELIZABETH his wife,
22 & 23 Oct. 1842   of St. John's Parish, Colleton Co., to WILLIAM
L & R   BOONE, ESQ., of Charleston, for Ł 2684 curren-
                      cy, 671 a., part of 820 a.; bounding S on Deep
Creek (out of Stono River) & OBADIAH WILKINS; N on A. B. Poolaw Creek; W
on JOHN WOODWARD. Whereas on 17 Aug. 1700 the Lords Proprs. granted CAPT.
WILLIAM DAVIS 820 a., English measure, on W side Stono River, in Colleton
Co., bounding E on marsh; S on a creek; W on JOHN WOODWARD; N on A. B.
Poolaw Creek; & whereas DAVIS died intestate, in 1710, leaving his only
daughter ELIZABETH his heir at law, & she married WILLIAM WILKINS, planter, of Berkeley Co., & whereas she died 14 June 1728 & her eldest son &
heir-at-law, OBADIAH, inherited, the father, WILLIAM WILKINS, having on
16 Jan. 1739, released the land to OBADIAH; now OBADIAH sells part of the
land to BOONE. Witnesses: CHARLES PINCKNEY, JAMES MATHEWS, THOMAS PINCK-
NEY. Before JACOB MOTTE, J.P. JAMES MICKIE, Dep. Pub. Reg.

Book X, p. 230   SUSANNA WIGGINTON, (formerly wife of EDWARD
15 & 16 Sept. 1719   RAWLINGS) of 1st part; THOMAS HEPWORTH, ESQ.,
L & R Tripartite   & ANNE his wife; MARY BLAMYER, widow; & EDWARD
                      RAWLINGS, joiner; ANNE, MARY & EDWARD being
children of EDWARD RALINGS, SR., of 2nd part; JOHN ROYER, cordwainer, of
3rd part; all of Charleston. Whereas EDWARD RAWLINGS, SR. by will dated
24 Sept. 1699 bequeathed to his loving wife SUSANNAH all his real & personal estate for her natural life, with power to dispose of the estate
for her maintenance & the bringing up of their children; & whereas she
has agreed to sell JOHN ROYER half of lot #30 for Ł 170 currency towards
her maintenance (to which THOMAS HEPWORTH & ANNE his wife, MARY BLAMYER,
& EDWARD RALINGS, JR. have consented); now SUSANNAH WIGGINTON sells to
ROYER, for Ł 170 currency, half of lot #30, fronting S 53 ft. on Broad
Street, bounding E 187 ft. on ISAAC MAZYCK; W on vacant land laid out for
a market. Witnesses: THOMAS BARTON, JOHN GARNIER. Before HENRY GIBBES,
J.P. JAMES MICKIE, Dep. Pub. Reg.

Book X, p. 238   DAVID (his mark) BLACK, planter, of Orangeburg
24 Mar. 1740   Township, to JAMES ROBERTSON, storekeeper, of
Mortgage   Pon Pon as security on bond of this date in
                      sum of Ł 800 SC money, with interest, 1/2 pay-
able 1 Aug., half on 1 Mar. next; 200 a. called Spring Gardens, in

Orangeburg Township; also 2 Negroes. Witnesses: JOHN MARTIN, ROBERT MC-
MURDY. Before JAMES SKIRVING, J.P. JAMES MICKIE, Dep. Pub. Reg.

Book X, p. 240   WILLIAM COOPER (COWPER), planter, of Edisto,
12 & 13 Nov. 1742   to JOHN HARN, planter, of Orangeburg Township,
L & R   for Ł 500 SC money, 400 a. in Berkeley Co., on
                          S side of Edisto River, in the fork, where
Orangeburg Township is laid out. Witnesses: WILLIAM TRUEMAN, SAMUEL WEST.
Before ANDREW RUTLEDGE, J.P. JAMES MICKIE, Dep. Pub. Reg.

Book X, p. 247   ELIZABETH JENKINS, widow, of Colleton Co., to
1 Jan. 1741   her sons DAVID ADAMS & NATHANIEL ADAMS, & to
Deed of Gift   her daughters MARY JENKINS & HANNAH CAPERS,
                          for maternal love & affection & other consid-
erations; 1/4 part, each, of part of lot #64 in Charleston fronting W 15
ft. on Church Street, bounding E 16 ft. on TWEEDIE SOMERVILLE; N 195 ft.
on her brother THOMAS CAPERS; S 195 ft. on a 5 ft. neighborhood alley;
each quarter lot being about 48 ft. 9 in. from E to W; lot #1, the W lot,
bounding on Church Street, granted to DAVID ADAMS; lot #2, adjoining #1,
to MARY JENKINS, lot #3, to HANNAH CAPERS; lot #4, to NATHANIEL ADAMS,
being the E quarter lot bounding on SOMERVILLE. Witnesses: GEORGE ASKEL,
ISAAC HOLMES, ROBERT PARKER. Witnesses to livery & seizin of lots #1 &
#2; THOMAS LAMBOLL, JOSEPH BAKER; of lots #3 & #4; EDWARD BROUGHTON, ROB-
ERT PARKER. Before HENRY GIBBES, J.P. JAMES HOME, Pub. Reg.

Book X, p. 251   WILLIAM HARRIS, butcher, to SAMUEL SMITH, SR.,
25 Aug. 1742   butcher, both of Charleston, as security on
Mortgage & Feoffment   bond of even date in penal sum of Ł 440 for
                          payment of Ł 220 SC money, on 25 Aug. 1743,
with interest, from 18 Mar. last; lot #220 in Charleston, fronting E 35
ft. on King Street; & bounding S 140 ft. on BENJAMIN ROBART; W on Widow
HOLMES'S garden; N on JOHN DANIEL'S tenement. Witnesses: JOHN RATTRAY,
THOMAS BECKET, SAMUEL SMITH, JR. Before HENRY GIBBES, J.P. JAMES HOME,
Pub. Reg.

Book X, p. 254   RICHARD WOODWARD, of Granville Co., & JOHN
11 Apr. 1739   WOODWARD, of Colleton Co., agree that RICHARD
Agreement   has sold JOHN his part of 2 tracts of 500 a.
                          each formerly belonging to RICHARD WOODWARD,
adjoining JOHN'S land on Ashepoo River for Ł 500 SC money, to be paid
RICHARD on 1 Apr. next; RICHARD giving bond of Ł 1800 to deliver the deed
to JOHN within 12 months. Witnesses: JOHN GIBBES, RIVERS STANYARNE. Before ALEXANDER CRAMAKE, M.C. JAMES HOME, Pub. Reg.

Book X, p. 255   JASPER (his mark) DUBOISE, planter, & SUSANNE
5 July 1738   his wife, of St. Thomas & St. Dennis Parish,
Bill of Sale   Berkeley Co., to WILLIAM NEWMAN, planter, of
                          Prince Frederick Parish, Craven Co., for Ł 50
currency, 500 a. in Craven Co., bounding SE on CAPT. COOPER; NE on JAMES
SINCLAIR; NW on Widow PALMER; SW on WILLIAM NEWMAN & vacant land; which
tract was granted on 30 Sept. 1736 by Lt. Gov. THOMAS BROUGHTON to JASPER
DUBOISE. Witnesses: PETER PAGETT, JOHN PAGETT. Before ANTHONY BONNEAU,
J.P. JAMES HOME, Pub. Reg.

Book X, p. 259   WILLIAM NEWMAN, planter, & DELIVERANCE (her
14 Dec. 1739   mark) his wife, to SAMUEL NEWMAN, planter, all
Bill of Sale   of Prince Frederick Parish, Craven Co., for
                          Ł 50 SC money, 2 tracts, total 800 a. in Fair-
forest, St. James Santee Parish, Craven Co., 1 tract of 300 a. purchased
by WILLIAM NEWMAN from JOHN CARRER, bounding S on CAPT. THOMAS COOPER; E
on land purchased by WILLIAM NEWMAN from JASPER DUBOISE & partly on vacant land; N on the Widow PALMER; W on DANIEL WILLIAMS; the other 500 a.
bounding SE on CAPT. THOMAS COOPER; NE on JAMES SINCLAIR; NW on the Widow
PALMER; SW on WILLIAM NEWMAN & vacant land; the 2 tracts together bounding S & SE on CAPT. COOPER; NE on JAMES SINCLAIR; NW & N on the Widow
PALMER; W on DANIEL WILLIAMS. Witnesses: FRANCIS (mis mark) PERRET, JOHN
NEWMAN, WILLIAM KEEFE, JOHN JUNE. Before JOHN BASSNETT, J.P. JAMES
HOME, Pub. Reg.

Book X, p. 263   The Hon. JOSEPH WRAGG, to HUGH ANDERSON,

17 & 18 Dec. 1742   master of the Free School, for ₤ 300 SC money,
L & R   part of 10 a., on Charleston Neck conveyed to
                            JOSEPH WRAGG by the heirs of BARTHOLOMEW GAIL-
LARD; being that portion bounding NE on the broad path leading to Charleston; SW on the parsonage & lands of the Free School; NW on the lane leading to the Free School; SE on JOSEPH WRAGG; extending 125 ft. from the
lane along the broad path. Witnesses: JOB ROTHMAHLER, JOHN RATTRAY. Before JAMES MICHIE, J.P. JAMES HOME, Pub. Reg.

Book X, p. 269   STEPHEN (his mark) MONK, ESQ., of Goose Creek,
2 Feb. 1727   Berkeley Co., son & heir of JOHN MONK, ESQ.,
Release   Cassigue; to JOHN MOORE, planter, of same Par-
                            ish; for ₤ 30:10 currency; 300 a. on Peedee
River, adjoining a cave that runs up from Second Bluff, or the bluff next
above Yauwarry; bounding on all sides on vacant land; being part of
24,000 a. granted by the Lords Proprs. to JOHN MONK, on 22 Feb. 1682.
Witnesses: WILLIAM WESTON, ROBERT JOHNSON, JOHN BAYLY. Plat certified 1
Feb. 1727 by JOHN BAYLY, surveyor. JAMES HOME, Pub. Reg.

Book X, p. 275   WILLIAM HARVEY, merchant, of Strawberry, to
30 & 31 Dec. 1742   MATTHEW ROCHE, merchant, of Charleston, for
L & R   ₤ 650 SC money, lot #176 in Charleston, bound-
                            ing E 97-1/2 on the Great Street leading from
Ashley River by the Market Place; W on the lot where the prison now
stands; S 232 ft. on MRS. HITCHINS (formerly CAPT. BASDEN); N on heirs of
JOHN CARMICHAEL (formerly MR. MIDDLECOTT); which lot was originally grant-
ed to CAPT. GEORGE REINER who bequeathed it to his daughter MARY as part
of her dividend & after her death was inherited by her son & heir, GEORGE
MOORE, who conveyed to said WILLIAM HARVEY. Witnesses: EDWARD SIMPSON,
JAMES DRUMMOND. JAMES HOME, Pub. Reg.

Book X, p. 284   RICHARD WOODWARD, planter, & ELIZABETH his
11 Dec. 1742   wife, of Berkeley Co., to the Hon. JOHN FEN-
Release   WICKE, ESQ., of Charleston, for ₤ 543 SC money,
                            181 a. in Colleton Co., bounding SW on JOHN
FENWICKE; NW on JOHN FENWICKE & land granted THOMAS WOODWARD & ELIZABETH
his wife; SE on EDWARD BELLINGER & THOMAS CORDES; NE on land claimed by
JOHN HAMMERTON & said RICHARD WOODWARD; being part of 1050 a. granted to
ELIZABETH WOODWARD, mother of RICHARD, party hereto, & inherited by him.
Witnesses: SAMUEL DAVID, JAMES DRUMMOND. Before JAMES GRAEME, J.P. Plat
given showing HAMMERTON line, WOODWARD'S old line, MRS. CHARDON'S corner,
E. BELLINGER'S line, COL. FENWICKE'S line, THOMAS & ELIZABETH WOODWARD'S
line. JAMES HOME, Pub. Reg.

Book X, p. 292   BENJAMIN STANYARNE, planter, son & devise of
12 & 13 Dec. 1742   JAMES STANYARNE, to JOHN DRAYTON, planter,
L & R   both of St. Andrews Parish, Berkeley Co., for
                            ₤ 1122 currency, 132 a., part of 1110 a., on S
side Ashley River, St. Andrews Parish, bounding NE on marsh; S & SE on
BENJAMIN STANYARNE; W on JOHN DRAYTON. Whereas the Lords Proprs. on 13
May 1696 granted (broken) 1110 a. on S side Ashley River, which by several mesne conveyances descended to JAMES STANYARNE, the father, who, by
will dated 23 Mar. 1716 devised the 1110 a. to his son BENJAMIN; now he
sells 132 a. to DRAYTON. Witnesses: JOHN PENNYMAN, JAMES JOLLITT. Before
THOMAS DRAYTON, J.P. Plat of 132 a. by JOHN MILES, surveyor, dated 26
Aug. 1742. JAMES HOME, Pub. Reg.

Book X, p. 303   ALEXANDER (his mark) SMITH, tailor, to EBENE-
21 & 22 Jan. 1742   ZER SIMMONS & BENJAMIN SMITH, merchant, all of
L & R by Mortgage   Charleston, as security of a bond in penal sum
                            of ₤ 2468 for payment of ₤ 1234 SC money, with
interest, on 22 July next, part of lot #39 in Charleston, bounding N on a
street paralled to Cooper River; W on tenement of MARY BULLOCK, widow of
JOHN BULLOCK; E 33 ft. on New Church Street; S 16 ft. on ?; also part of
lot #39 22 ft. x 104 ft., bounding E on Church Street, S & W on land formerly of JOHN BULLOCK; N on land formerly of WILLIAM CAPERS; the 2 pieces
of land together bounding E on Church Street; W on ROBERT BREWTON; S on
Tradd Street, N on JOSEPH MASSEY. Witnesses: JAMES WRIGHT, CHARLES CAL-
DER. Before JACOB MOTTE, J.P. JAMES HOME, Pub. Reg. On 9 June 1744
BENJAMIN SMITH acknowledged mortgage satisfied by ALEXANDER SMITH.

Witness: JOHN MILNER.

Book X, p. 314   JAMES AUBER, storekeeper, of Goose Creek, to
19 & 20 Jan. 1742   EBENEZER SIMMONS, BENJAMIN SMITH & JAMES CRO-
L & R by Mortgage   KATT, merchant, of Charleston as security on
                        bond of even date in penal sum of Ł 1740 for
payment of Ł 870 SC money with interest on 1 Aug. next; 400 a. in Berkeley Co., bounding E on Wassamsaw Swamp & ALEXANDER NISBETT; W on PAUL
MARION; S N & W on vacant land; also 400 a. on E side Wassamsaw Swamp, in
Berkeley Co., bounding NW & S on vacant land; E on PETER MARION; which
tract; which 2 tracts were lately granted to PETER MARION, who conveyed
them to JAMES AUBER. Witnesses: JAMES WRIGHT, GEORGE WARING. Before
JACOB MOTTE, J.P. JAMES HOME, Pub. Reg.

Book X, p. 323   HENRY VIDEAU, planter, of Parish of St. Thomas
10 & 11 May 1741   & St. Dennis, Berkeley Co., (son & heir of
L & R   PETER VIDEAU, of same place) & ANNE his wife,
                        to JOHN PAGETT, ESQ., of same parish, for
Ł 2300 SC money, 202 a. formerly owned by PETER VIDEAU, the father; being
part of 2 tracts of 250 a. & 100 a.; the 202 a. bounding SE on JAMES BRE-
MAR & part of said 2 tracts lately owned by JACOB BONNEAU; NW on WALTER
DALLAS & JOHN PAGETT & part of said 2 tracts; NE on JAMES BREMAR & part
on said 2 tracts; SW on Wisbee Creek, JOHN PAGETT, & part of said 2
tracts. Whereas PETER VIDEAU died 12 Oct. 1728 & the 202 a. were inherited by HENRY, now he conveys to PAGETT. Witnesses: PETER SIMMS, NICHO-
LAS BOCHET, ANTHONY BONNEAU. Before ANTHONY BONNEAU, J.P. JAMES HOME,
Pub. Reg. Plat given showing 102 a. sold to JACOB BONNEAU & JANE his
wife; 220 a. sold to JOHN PAGETT; piece sold to ANDREW RAMBERT now belonging to JAMES BREMAR; 16 a. belonging to ANTHONY BONNEAU, JR., & boundary
lines of WALTER DALLAS, JOHN PAGETT, & JAMES BREMAR.

Book X, p. 334   JOHN GEORGE DALLABAC, bricklayer, & JOANNA
26 & 27 Jan. 1742   ELIZABETH his wife, to JAMES VOULOUX, shop-
L & R by Mortgage   keeper, all of Charleston, as security on bond
                        of even date in penal sum of Ł 800 for payment
of Ł 400 SC money, with interest, on 25 Jan. 1744; that piece of land on
Charleston Neck conveyed by JOSEPH WRAGG by L & R dated 18 & 19 this Jan.
to DALLABAC, bounding NE on the broad path leading to Charleston; SW on
the parsonage & lands of the Free School; NW on HUGH ANDERSON; SE on JO-
SEPH WRAGG; being 60 ft. from HUGH ANDERSON along the Broad Path. Witnesses: JAMES LESSLEY, JAMES DRUMMOND. Before JAMES GRAEME, J.P. JAMES
HOME, Pub. Reg.

Book X, p. 343   JAMES MINOR, planter, late of Little River,
13 & 14 Oct. 1742   now of NC to JOHN ESHFIELD, innkeeper, of Lit-
L & R   tle River, Prince George Parish, SC, for Ł 300
                        SC money, the 375 a. granted by Lt. Gov. WIL-
LIAM BULL on 11 Aug. 1742 to JAMES MINOR, on N side of W branch of Little
River, bounding NE & NW on vacant land; SW on BRYAN ? GRANT. Witnesses:
JOHN IOOR, MARY IOOR. Before THOMAS BLYTHE, J.P. JAMES HOME, Pub. Reg.

Book X, p. 349   DANIEL (his mark) COUTURIERE, planter, & JOYCE
15 Dec. 1742   (her mark) his wife, to PETER COUTURIERE,
L & R   planter, all of Craven Co., for Ł 100 currency,
                        300 a. in Berkeley Co., granted COUTURIERE 12
Apr. 1739; bounding NW on DUNCAN MCGREGOR & vacant land; other sides on
vacant land. Witnesses: PETER BENOIST, DANIEL BENOIST, GIDEON COUTURIER.
Before THOMAS MONK, J.P. JAMES HOME, Pub. Reg.

Book X, p. 356   THOMAS (his mark) BRAND, & JOHN EYCOTT, gen-
20 Dec. 1742   tlemen, both of Charleston, agree as follows:
Agreement   BRAND to assign to EYCOTT all his real & per-
                        sonal estate inherited by him by will of his
father JOHN BRAND. EYCOTT agrees to pay BRAND Ł 100 SC money yearly during BRAND'S natural life; 1st payment to be made 25 Mar. next; & to provide BRAND with victuals, clothes lodging, etc. Witnesses: JOHN GORDON,
JAMES DRUMMOND. Before JAMES GRAEME, J.P. JAMES HOME, Pub. Reg.

Book X, p. 360   JOHN EYCOTT, gentleman, & MARY his wife, to
21 & 22 Dec. 1742   THOMAS BRAND, gentleman, all of Charleston, as

L & R by Mortgage   security on bond dated 20 Dec. 1742 in penal
sum of Ł 4000 currency for performance of
agreements mentioned in bond; 32 a., 2 rods, 26-1/2 perches, English measure, in St. Philip's Parish, Charleston, bounding N on marsh of a small
creek running into Ashley River & heirs of ROBERT HUME, ESQ.; E on the
broad path leading from Charleston to the Quarter House; S & W on DANIEL
CARTWRIGHT. Witnesses: JOHN GORDON, JAMES DRUMMOND. Before JAMES GRAEME,
J.P. JAMES HOME, Pub. Reg.

Book X, p. 367   JAMES RIPAULT, chirurgeon, & ELIZABETH his
3 & 4 July 1741   wife, of Berkeley Co., to JOHN CHAVINEAU,
L & R   planter, of Craven Co., for Ł 440 currency, 2
tracts of 200 a. & 215 a., total 415 a.; the
200 a. bounding W on PETER BENOIST; S & W on vacant land, NICHOLAS MAYHUM
& CHRISTOPHER BIRMAN; N on vacant land; which tract of 200 a. was granted
4 Sept. 1735 to ANN DONOVAN; the 215 a. bounding W on PETER BENOIST; E on
CHRISTOPHER BIRMAN; S on the 200 a.; N on vacant land; which tract of 215
a. was granted 4 Nov. 1740 to GEORGE COLLETON. Witnesses: PETER BENOIST,
GEORGE COLLETON, DAVID LAFONS. Before PETER DE ST. JULIEN, J.P. JAMES
HOME, Pub. Reg.

Book X, p. 376   THOMAS WRIGHT, ESQ., to ROBERT QUASH, planter,
23 & 24 Dec. 1742   for Ł 1872 SC money, 234 a. in Berkeley Co.,
L & R   part of the Cypress Barony devised by will of
CHRISTOPHER ARTHUR to PATRICK ROCHE & BARTHOL-
OMEW ARTHUR, & conveyed by BARTHOLOMEW ARTHUR to DR. ROBERT BROWN; who
conveyed to said THOMAS WRIGHT; bounding N on ROBERT QUASH; S on GABRIEL
MANIGAULT; E on Silk Hope Plantation; W on THOMAS WRIGHT. Witnesses:
FRANCIS ROCHE, PAUL LABILIERE. Before ROBERT AUSTIN, J.P. JAMES HOME,
Pub. Reg. Plat given.

Book X, p. 383   JOHN BENSTONE, planter, of Christ Church Par-
27 & 28 Jan. 1736   ish, Berkeley Co., to DANIEL CRAWFORD, mer-
L & R   chant, of Charleston, for Ł 2000 SC money the
remaining part of the 500 a. granted by WIL-
LIAM HARVEY, of Charleston, & PAUL CHERRON, executors of will of JOHN
BASSETT, of Charleston, to JOHN BENSTONE, 200 a. of which has since been
conveyed by JOHN BENSTONE to JONATHAN STOCKS & 100 a. to DANIEL LEGARE;
which remainder is in Christ Church Parish & bounding N on Wando River; E
on ROGER PLAYER; S on MR. COCKRAIN; W on JOHN SEVERANCE, JOHN HALE, & WIL-
LIAM WHITE; & any vacant land that may be remaining in said tract; the
land being free except for a mortgage to PAUL JENYS & JOHN BAKER, merchants, of Charleston & another mortgage to JOSEPH WRAGG, merchant, of
Charleston, which mortgage BENSTONE agrees to pay off out of the Ł 2000.
Witnesses: JAMES PAINE, WILLIAM GLEN. Before JACOB MOTTE, J.P. JAMES
HOME, Pub. Reg.

Book X, p. 393   STEPHEN BULL, ESQ., of Granville Co., to THOM-
6 & 7 Dec. 1742   AS JONES, planter, of St. Andrews Parish,
L & R   Berkeley Co., for Ł 1336 currency, 3 adjoining
tracts of 50 a., 14 a., & 103 a., total 157 a.,
bounding according to plat. Whereas Gov. NATHANIEL JOHNSON & the Lords
Proprs. on 3 Dec. 1709 granted WILLIAM BULL 50 a., English measure, in
Berkeley Co., bounding N & W on TIMOTHY SULLIVAN; E on CAPT. JOHN GODFREY
& a marsh; S on TIMOTHY SULLIVAN & Stono River; & whereas Dep. Gov. ROB-
ERT DANIELL & the Lords Proprs. on 22 June 1716 granted CAPT. WILLIAM
BULL 14 a. on N side Stono River, bounding NW on SAMUEL JONES; E on JOHN
BROWNE; S on WILLIAM BULL, & whereas WILLIAM BULL & MARY his wife by deed
poll dated 23 June 1730 conveyed the 2 tracts to STEPHEN BULL; & whereas
Lt. Gov. WILLIAM BULL on 17 Sept. 1742 granted STEPHEN BULL 103 a., bounding S & SW on THOMAS JONES & marsh of Stono River; N & NE on JOHN GOD-
frey; SE on JOHN GODFREY & marsh of Stono River; now STEPHEN BULL conveys
the 3 tracts to THOMAS JONES. Witnesses: WILLIAM BULL, MARY HENRIETTA
BULL, THOMAS INNS. Before WILLIAM BULL, JR. JAMES HOME, Pub. Reg. Plat
given.

Book X, p. 405   The Hon. JOSEPH WRAGG, ESQ., to JOHN GEORGE
18 & 19 Jan. 1742   DALLABAC, both of Charleston, for Ł 300 SC mon-
L & R   ey, the piece of land on Charleston Neck, being part of 10 a. conveyed to WRAGG by the

heirs of BARTHOLOMEW GAILLARD, bounding NE on the broad path leading to Charleston; SW on the parsonage & Free School land; NE on HUGH ANDERSON, ESQ., SE on JOSEPH WRAGG; extending 60 ft. on the broad path from HUGH ANDERSON'S land. Witnesses: JOSEPH WRAGG, JR. SAMUEL WRAGG. Before ROBERT AUSTIN, J.P. JAMES HOME, Pub. Reg.

Book X, p. 411
2 Jan. 1742
Bond
JOHN WRAGG, SAMUEL WRAGG.
Reg.

JOSEPH WRAGG, ESQ., to JOHN GEORGE DALLABAC, of Charleston, in penal sum of ₤ 1000 SC money, against claim of dower in above land (p. 405) by JUDITH, wife of JOSEPH WRAGG. Witnesses: Before ROBERT AUSTIN, J.P. JAMES HOME, Pub.

Book X, p. 412
26 Oct. 1742
Release

HENRY GIBBES, ESQ., formerly of Barbados now of SC, to LAWRENCE TRENT, ESQ., of Barbados, heir, sole executor & residuary legatee of will of the Rev. Mr. WILLIAM TRENT, of Biddenden, Co. of Kent, Great Britain. Whereas by mortgage dated 10 Jan. 1722 reciting that GIBBES owed TRENT, for principal & interest, ₤ 3373:10:4 Barbadan money, & reciting that by lease dated 24 May then last past between JOHN TRENT, ESQ., of Barbados, attorney to WILLIAM GIBBES certain lands & buildings for 5 years at ₤ 182 Barbadan money yearly, & reciting that to better enable GIBBES to convey the plantation, buildings, slaves, etc., to WILLIAM TRENT, GIBBES by indenture of bargain & sale leased the day before the date of the mortgage leased to TRENT 172 a. in St. James Parish, Island of Barbados, with 1 dwelling house, the moiety of 1 mill & boiling house with 3 coppers hung therein, 3/4 of 1 still house with 2 stills hung therein, with all the other buildings & utensils; also 67 Negro or Mulatto slaves; 40 head of cattle; the release stating that for ₤ 3373:10:4 GIBBES releaded the plantation, slaves, etc., to WILLIAM TRENT, with privilege of redemption on 24 May 1727 & pay the yearly rent for 5 years; & GIBBES convenanted with TRENT that the mortgage & several judgment should stand as security; & whereas the principal, the yearly rent & the interest have been paid; & whereas the mortgage was extended & amounted to ₤ 5552:5:6-1/2 Barbadan; & whereas JOHN TRENT while attorney for WILLIAM TRENT, paid several considerable debts due from HENRY GIBBES to sundry persons to which the mortgaged premises were liable, & there was due in 1727 from GIBBES the sum of ₤ 7662:7:0 Barbadan; now HENRY GIBBES for that debt & ₤ 50 British & other considerations quitclaims to LAWRENCE TRENT all the plantation, buildings, slaves, etc. Sealed & delivered in Carolina "where no treble 6 penny stamps are to be had". Witnesses: ROGER CLOAD, THOMAS SHUBRICK, (merchant), RICHARD SHUBRICK (merchant), CHARLES PINCKNEY. Before JOHN HAMMERTON, J.P. ROGER CLOAD being master of the ship _Minerva_, of London. JAMES HOME, Pub. Reg.

Book X, p. 421
2 Mar. 1741/2
Feoffment
THOMAS HODSON (formerly WILLIAM FULLER). Witnesses: JOHN BURFORD, WILLIAM (his mark) BOWMAN. Before THOMAS DRAYTON, J.P. JAMES HOME, Pub. Reg.

JOSEPH WOOD, cordwinder, of Berkeley Co., to THOMAS HODSON, for ₤ 210 currency, 79 a. on N side Ashley River, bounding E on PETER HASKINS; W on BENJAMIN WOOD, N on THOMAS MELL; S on ·

Book X, p. 424
12 & 13 Sept. 1740
L & R

JOHN GOODBE, planter, of Berkeley Co., & HANNAH (her mark) his wife, to JAMES MOORE, planter, for ₤ 600 SC money, 450 a. in St. George's Parish, Berkeley Co., on N side Edisto River; bounding NW on MRS. FRANCIS LONGUEMAR; NE & S on land laid out & vacant land; S on vacant land; which tract was granted to JOHN GOODBE by letters patent dated at Charleston 5 Feb. 1739, signed by the Hon. WILLIAM BULL. Witnesses: JEHU MOORE, JAMES POSTELL. Before WILLIAM SANDERS, J.P. JAMES HOME, Pub. Reg.

Book X, p. 430
10 Nov. 1741
L & R

JAMES MOORE, of Berkeley Co., to ROBERT STEEL, JOHN HUME, & GEORGE MARSHALL, of Charleston, for ₤ 600 SC money, the 450 a. on N side Edisto River, in St. George's Parish, Berkeley Co., granted 5 Feb. 1739 by Lt. Gov. WILLIAM BULL to JOHN GOODBE, SR., & conveyed by him in 1741 to said JAMES MOORE; bounding NW on MRS. FRANCIS LONGUEMAR; NE & S on land laid out & vacant land; S on vacant land; that

is to say; 1/3 to ROBERT STEEL; 1/3 to JOHN HUME; 1/3 to GEORGE MARSHALL.
Witnesses: JEHU MOORE, CHARLES MARSHALL. Before JAMES GRAEME, J.P.
JAMES HOME, Pub. Reg.

DEEDS BOOK "Y"
FEB. 1742 - OCT. 1743

Book Y, p. 1   HENRY JOSEPH VIDEAU, planter, only son & heir
28 & 29 Apr. 1742   of PETER VIDEAU, & ANNE his wife, to their sis-
Deed of Gift   ter, JANE BONNEAU, widow of JACOB BONNEAU,
                                planter, all of Berkeley Co., for tender love
& affection, 102 a. in Berkeley Co. Whereas PETER VIDEAU, planter, (fa-
ther of HENRY JOSEPH & JANE) soon after JACOB BONNEAU married daughter
JANE, in 1709, JACOB & JANE BONNEAU 102 a. in St. Thomas Parish, Berkeley
Co., bounding NE & SE on JAMES BREMAR; NW & SW on JOHN PAGETT; & JACOB &
JANE enjoyed the land until about 1734 when JACOB died intestate; then
JANE held the land but the deed was lost through accident; now HENRY &
ANNE VIDEAU confirm JANE BONNEAU in her possession. Witnesses: JOHN BON-
NIT, JOHN MIENSON. Before ANTHONY BONNEAU, J.P. JAMES HOME, Register.
Plat drawn by HENRY BRUNEAU, Dep. Sur.

Book Y, p. 7   WILLIAM LIVINGSTON, planter, of Colleton Co.,
1 & 2 July 1742   (only acting executor of will of ANNE LIVING-
L & R   STON, widow & devisee of will of HENRY LIVING-
                                STON, Planter), with the consent of DANIEL
BELL, carpenter, & GEORGE BELL, bricklayer, both of Charleston, sons &
residuary legatees & devises of said ANNE LIVINGSTON; to JACOB BRODWELL,
planter, of Colleton Co., for ℔ 1400 SC money; 500 a. Whereas WILLIAM
LIVINGSTON, the elder, owned (besides other lands) 500 a., & by will dated 17 July 1723, bequeathed to his eldest son WILLIAM (party hereto)
half the 3 tracts he purchased from JOHN KENNOWAY (to whom it was granted), within land, near Pon Pon River, making 1096 a., son WILLIAM to
choose his half; & gave his second son, HENRY, the other half; & whereas
by deed of partition dated 29 Oct. 1731, WILLIAM & HENRY agreed that HEN-
RY should have as his share, the 500 a. (conveyed by JOHN KENNEWAY) in
Colleton Co., W of freshes of Edisto River, bounding S on JOSEPH HOLLY &
JOSEPH DIDCOTT; W on an impassable swamp; N on a swamp & vacant land; E
on JOSEPH DIDCOTT; & whereas HENRY LIVINGSTON by will dated 31 Mar. 1737
bequeathed all his real estate to his wife ANNE; & she by will dated 15
Feb. 1738 desired all her real & personal sold for the payment of her
debts, the overplus (if any) to be divided equally between her 2 sons
DANIEL & GEORGE BELL, appointing WILLIAM LIVINGSTON & WILLIAM EDDINGS,
planter, her executors; & whereas EDDINGS refused to act; & whereas
ANNE'S debts were so great & the assets not being sufficient, it was
found necessary to sell the 500 a.; & whereas DANIEL BELL & GEORGE BELL
have attained 21 years & wish to satisfy her debts; & JACOB BRADWELL was
the highest bidder; now the sale is completed. Witnesses: JOHN BULL,
WILLIAM BULL. Before JAMES BULLOCH. JAMES HOME, Register.

Book Y, p. 18   CHARLES CANTEY, to BENJAMIN WOOD, both of St.
9 & 10 Feb. 1739   George Parish, Berkeley Co., for ℔ 410 curren-
L & R   cy, 250 a., part of 1000 a. granted 8 Feb.
                                1704 to GEORGE CANTEY; the 250 a. on N side
Ashley River, bounding N on JAMES BOSWOOD; E & S on JAMES DUNNAHO (Irish-
town) W on Widow FERGUSON; per re-survey 19 Dec. 1712 to CAPT. JOHN CAN-
TEY. Witnesses: THOMAS HODSON, DAVID RUSS. Before HENRY GIBBES, J.P.
JAMES HOME, Register.

Book Y, p. 24   JAMES BOSWOOD, planter, of St. George Parish,
9 & 10 Aug. 1742   Berkeley Co., to BENJAMIN WOOD, planter, of
L & R   St. James Parish, for ℔ 80 currency, 50 a. in
                                St. Andrews Parish, Berkeley Co., part of
1200 a. granted by the Lords Proprs. on 8 Feb. 1704 to THOMAS BARKER;
bounding E on THOMAS MELL; W on THOMAS DRAYTON; N on BENJAMIN WOOD; S on
THOMAS HUDSON. Witnesses: DAVID RUSS, JOSEPH RUSS. Before HENRY GIBBES,
J.P. JAMES HOME, Register.

Book Y, p. 29   WILLIAM HARVEY, merchant, of Strawberry, to

9 Feb. 1742   EDWARD SIMPSON, merchant, of Charleston, for
Deed of Feoffment   ₺ 1400 SC money, that messuage or tenement in
                     Charleston, lot #212, commonly called Charles-
ton Gaol, occupied by SAMUEL HURST, Provost Marshal, bounding W 97-1/2
ft. on the Broad Road leading from Charleston; N 237 ft. on JOHN CAR-
MICHAEL; E on MATHEW ROCHE; S on CAPT. BASDEN. Witnesses: MARY HURST,
MICHAEL JEANES, WILLIAM WILLIAMSON. Before JAMES WEDDERBURN, J.P. JAMES
HOME, Register.

Book Y, p. 32   WILLIAM WILKINS, planter, & ELIZABETH his wife,
11 Apr. 1713   heirs of CAPT. WILLIAM DAVIS, their father, to
Deed of Feoffment   TIMOTHY BELLAMY, felt-maker, for ₺ 150 curren-
                     cy, 600 a. in Colleton Co., granted by NATHAN-
IEL JOHNSON, JAMES MOORE, & NICHOLAS TROTT, commissioners for granting
lands, in 1703, to CAPT. WILLIAM DAVIS; bounding NW on Bohicket Creek; NE
on said DAVIS; other sides on vacant land; as by plat certified 8 Nov.
1702 by EDMUND BELLINGER, Sur. Gen. Witnesses: JOHN JONES, JONATHAN
STOCKS, ANTHONY LAMBRIGHT. Delivery by turf & twig. Memorial entered in
Auditor's office 30 Aug. 1732 in Old Grant Book, fol. 212, by DANIEL GIB-
SON, for JAMES ST. JOHN, Aud. Before ROBERT AUSTIN, J.P. JAMES HOME,
Register.

Book Y, p. 37   DANIEL CRAWFORD, planter, & SARAH his wife, of
14 May 1742   Christ Church Parish, to MATTHEW ROCHE, mer-
Release   chant, of Charleston, for ₺ 1700 SC money,
                     their proportionable & undivided part of a
town lot & 600 a. of land. Whereas TIMOTHY BELLAMY, merchant, of Charleston, owned a part of a lot in Charleston & "the messuage thereon" fronting 30 ft. on N side of Broad Street; 100 ft. deep; bounding E & N on
JAMES CROKATT (formerly JOSEPH WRAGG, ESQ.); W on a house & lot occupied
by MATTHEW ROCHE; & whereas BELLAMY by will dated 25 Feb. 1725 bequeathed
that part of a lot to his daughter MARY BELLAMY; but she died without issue & the property became vested in her sisters, SARAH (wife of DANIEL
CRAWFORD) & ANNE (wife of MATHEW ROCHE); as coparceners; & whereas TIM-
OTHY BELLAMY bequeathed to his daughters SARAY, MARY & ANNE, his tract of
600 a. in Colleton Co., bounding NW on Bohicket Creek; NE on WILLIAM DA-
VIS; which 600 a. became (after MARY'S death) the property of SARAH &
ANNE, as jointenants; now DANIEL & SARAH CRAWFORD sell their share to
ROCHE. Witnesses: CHARLES HAY, JAMES DRUMMOND. Before JAMES GREEME, J.P.
JAMES HOME, Register.

Book Y, p. 41   WILLOUGHBY WEST, planter, of Colleton Co., to
8 & 9 July 1742   JAMES MANNING, cordwainer, of Berkeley Co.,
L & R   for ₺ 700 SC money, 100 a., part of 250 a. in
                     Berkeley Co. Whereas FRANCIS LADSON, planter,
of Berkeley Co., by deed of feoffment dated 27 Mar. 1724 conveyed to SAM-
UEL WEST, planter, 250 a., bounding N on FRANCIS LADSON; E on CHARLES
WEST; S & W on STEPHEN DRAYTON; & whereas SAMUEL WEST (son & heir of said
SAMUEL WEST, & brother of WILLOUGHBY WEST) by deed of gift dated 8 Apr.
1734 given WILLOUGHBY WEST 100 a. (part of said 250 a.) bounding N on
FRANCIS LADSON; E on CHARLES WEST (part same tract); S & W on STEPHEN
DRAYTON. Witnesses: ROBERT COOPER, JAMES SCARLETT. Before WILLIAM BULL,
JR., J.P. Memorial entered in Auditor's office 6 Jan. 1742 by JAMES ST.
JOHN, Dep. Aud. JAMES HOME, Register.

Book Y, p. 48   THOMAS (his mark) DYEL, planter, & MARY (her
2 & 3 June 1740   mark) his wife, to NATHANIEL DREW, planter,
L & R   all of Craven Co., for ₺ 500 currency, 250 a.
                     on N side Black River, in Williamsburgh Town-
ship, Craven Co., also a lot bounding on all sides on vacant land; which
land was granted by letters patent dated 12 Apr. 1739 signed by Lt. Gov.
WILLIAM BULL to THOMAS DYEL. Witnesses: WILLIAM TURBEVILLE, JR., WILLIAM
(his mark) TURBEVILLE, SR., PATRICK PEIRCE. Before JOHN BASSNETT, J.P.
JAMES HOME, Register.

Book Y, p. 56   DAVID WEBSTER, planter, & JOSEPH NORMAN,
14 Jan. 1741   planter, both of St. James Goose Creek, Berke-
Agreement   ley Co., make this agreement: WEBSTER agrees
                     to convey on 1 Mar. next to NORMAN an inde-
feasibel estate 240 a. (according to plat) in said Parish, bounding N on

EDWARD KEATING; W on GEORGE CHICKEN (now DAVID WEBSTER); also 11 Negroes
now belonging to DAVID WEBSTER; also all the stock of horses, cattle,
hogs, poultry, etc., except a riding horse called Bacheldore, a saddle,
bridle, & household goods excepted. NORMAN agrees to pay WEBSTER Ł 557
sterling, or value in several payments & gives bond to secure payment.
Each binding himself in penal sum of Ł 1000 currency. Witnesses: THOMAS
HOOG, JAMES SMITH. Before PETER TAYLOR, J.P. JAMES HOME, Register.

Book Y, p. 58   STEPHEN BULL, gentleman, of Cane Acres, Colle-
15 & 16 Feb. 1733   ton Co., to WILLIAM BULL, ESQ., of Berkeley
L & R   Co., for Ł 2000 currency, 4 tracts (500, 500,
                       418, & 282 a.). Whereas Gov. CHARLES CRAVEN,
the Hon. ROBERT DANIEL, SAMUEL EVELEIGH, CHARLES HART, & HUGH BUTLER,
ESQRS., Lords Proprs., on 17 Dec. 1714 granted HENRY QUINTYNE 500 a. in
Colleton Co., bounding S on Cambee River; E on a cypress swamp then be-
longing to HENRY QUINTYNE & on WILLIAM KIMBALL (now of COL. JOSEPH BLAKE);
all other sides then vacant now of COL. JOSEPH BLAKE; & whereas the Hon.
SIR NATHANIEL JOHNSON, Knight, & the Hon. NICHOLAS TROTT, HENRY NOBLE &
THOMAS BROUGHTON, ESQRS., Lords Proprs. on 14 May 1707 granted HENRY QUIN-
TYNE 500 a., English measure, in Granville Co., bounding N on Coosaw Riv-
er; W on a creek out of Coosaw; E on land not then laid out but late of
HENRY QUINTYNE & head of creek; S on land not then laid out but now of
COL. JOSEPH BLAKE; & whereas Gov. CHARLES CRAVEN & the Hon. ROBERT DANIEL,
HUGH BUTLER & SAMUEL EVELEIGH, ESQRS., Lords Proprs. on 17 Dec. 1714
granted HENRY QUINTYNE 418 a. on Port Royal Island, Granville Co., bound-
ing NW on vacant land; NE on ROBERT WILKINSON; S on EVAN LEWIS & DAVID
DUVAL; W on ARTHUR DICK; & whereas HENRY QUINTYNE owned 282 a. on S side
Coosaw River, Granville Co., bounding W on HENRY QUINTYNE, deceased; S &
E on CAPT. WALTER IZARD; & whereas HENRY QUINTYNE July 1716 died intestate & without issue, leaving his only sister MARY (wife of WILLIAM BULL)
his heir at law; & whereas by L & R, 30 Nov. & 1 Dec. 1733 WILLIAM & MARY
BULL conveyed to STEPHEN BULL the 4 tracts with the understanding that
WILLIAM might buy back at same price if he so desired & dispose of it by
will or otherwise; now WILLIAM reposses himself of the 4 tracts. Witnesses: RICHARD ALLEIN, JOHN BULL, FREDERICK MEYER. Witnesses: 28 Jan.
1742: JOHN DART, JOHN PAGETT, RICHARD BEDON. Before DANIEL CRAWFORD,
J.P. JAMES HOME, Register.

Book Y, p. 66   ANTHONY ATKINSON & MARY HUGHES re-convey to
7 Jan. 1742   ARTHUR FOSTER, all of Craven Co., 775 a.
Deed of Feoffment   Whereas ARTHUR FOSTER, by L & R dated 21 & 22
                       Mar. 1739, for Ł 716 then due & owing from
FOSTER to ANTHONY ATKINSON & MARY HUGHES, as security conveyed to ATKIN-
SON & MARY HUGHES 775 a. on SE side Black River, in Craven Co., bounding
NE on WILLIAM alias GEORGE DICK SE on WILLIAM WATSON; SW on CAPT. WILLIAM
BROCKINTON; as by plat attached to original grant dated 7 Feb. 1735; now
FOSTER reimburses ATKINSON & MARY HUGHES Ł 716 currency & they reconvey
the land to him. Witnesses: JOHN PYATT, WILLIAM SANDERS, NATHANIEL MC-
CORMICK. Delivery by turf & twig witnessed by ANTHONY WHITE, THOMAS
POTTS, ELISHA SCREVEN. Before WILLIAM WHITESIDE, J.P. JAMES HOME, Reg-
ister.

Book Y, p. 69   ARTHUR FOSTER, planter, to ELISHA SCREVEN,
18 & 19 Feb. 1742/3   both of Craven Co., for Ł 1400 SC money, 700
L & R   a., part of 775 a.; bounding NE on DR. GEORGE
                       DICK (by mistake in original grant called DR.
WILLIAM DICK); SE on part of 775 a., (formerly WILLIAM WATSON) SW on
CAPT. WILLIAM BROCKINTON; NW on Black River. Whereas by letters patent
dated at Charleston 7 Feb. 1735, signed by Lt. Gov. THOMAS BROUGHTON,
ARTHUR FOSTER was granted 775 a. in Craven Co.; & whereas FOSTER by L & R
dated 21 & 22 Mar. 1739 conveyed the tract to ANTHONY ATKINSON & MARY
HUGHES; & whereas ATKINSON & MARY HUGHES on 7 Jan. 1742 reconveyed the
775 a. to FOSTER; now FOSTER sells to SCREVEN. Plat of re-survey certi-
fied by PETER LANE, Dep. Sur., 5 Feb. 1742/3. Witnesses: ANTHONY WHITE,
SAMUEL THEOPHILUS STUCORN, THOMAS POTTS. Before WILLIAM WHITESIDE, J.P.
JAMES HOME, Register.

Book Y, p. 74   THOMAS JENYS, merchant, of Charleston, to The
22 & 23 Feb. 1742   Society for the Propagation of the Gospel in
L & R by Mortgage   Foreign Parts, as security on bond of even

date in penal sum of ₤ 267:2 payment of ₤ 133:11 sterling British, with interest, on 23 Feb. 1743; 1269 a. in Granville Co., bounding E on a branch of Port Royal River, & a small creek, & THOMAS GRAVE; S & W on MR. CROFT; N on JOSEPH BRYAN, HUGH BRYAN, & JOSEPH MASSEY; as by plat attached to grant made to ISAAC MAZYCK, merchant, of Charleston, by Gov. ROBERT JOHNSON on 28 Apr. 1733; which tract MAZYCK conveyed to HUGH BRYAN, planter, who conveyed to THOMAS JENYS. Witnesses: JOHN OYSTON, JAMES DRUMMOND. Before JAMES GREEME, J.P. JAMES HOME, Register.

Book Y, p. 82　　　　　　　ARTHUR NASH, & MARY ANN (her mark) his wife;
7 Dec. 1741　　　　　　　　THOMAS (his mark) HEATHY & SUSANNAH, his wife;
Deed of Feoffment　　　　& THOMAS STEWART; to JOHN STEEL; all of
　　　　　　　　　　　　　　Charleston; for ₤ 250 SC money the S part of
lot #218 in Charleston, bounding N on part belonging to THOMAS STEWART & JOHN STEEL; S on part of lot #217 belonging to JOSEPH WRAGG; W 33 ft. on Church Street, E on THOMAS MIDDLETON. Witnesses: SAMUEL PERKINS, JOHN RATTRAY, BENJAMIN WARD. Before DANIEL CRAWFORD, J.P. JAMES HOME, Register.

Book Y, p. 85　　　　　　　JAMES MOORE, of Berkeley Co., by L & R dated
4 Mar. 1742　　　　　　　　10 Nov. 1741, conveyed to ROBERT STEILL, JOHN
Declaration　　　　　　　　HUME & GEORGE MARSHALL, 450 a. in Berkeley Co.,
　　　　　　　　　　　　　　formerly granted on 5 Feb. 1739 (signed by Lt.
Gov. WILLIAM BULL), to JOHN GOODBE, SR., who, by L & R dated 12 & 13 Sept. 1740 conveyed to JAMES MOORE (see Book X, p. 424-442). Whereas both the L & R from MOORE to STEILL, HUME & MARSHALL by mistake bear the date 10 Nov. 1741 & in the release a blank space was left for the dates of the L & R from GOODBE to MOORE; now MOORE declares that it was intended that the lease should have been dated 9 Nov. & that in the blank spaces should have been inserted the dates 12 & 13 Sept. 1740 (GOODBE to MOORE). Witnesses: CHARLES CALDER. Before JAMES WRIGHT, J.P. JAMES HOME, Register.

Book Y, p. 86　　　　　　　HENRY BOWER, planter, & ELIZABETH (her mark)
9 May 1717　　　　　　　　 his wife, & with her consent, of Colleton Co.,
Deed of Feoffment　　　　for six pence currency, convey to JOHN WHIT-
　　　　　　　　　　　　　　MARSH, JOHN HAYNE, PAUL HAMILTONE, JOSEPH RUS-
SEL, JAMES COCHRAN, ICHABOD WINGORN, JOHN KENNOWAY, for the benefit of a Presbyterian or Independent minister on Edisto Island duely called by the majority of the members of that church, as a perpetual inheritance to such pastors as shall be chosen; 300 a., English measure, on Edisto Island, Colleton Co., granted by JOHN, Lord Granville, Palatine & the Lords Proprs. (signed by Gov. NATHANIEL JOHNSON on 15 Sept. 1705 to HENRY BOWER; bounding S on Palmentier's Creek; W on WILLIAM BOWER & WILLIAM FRY; E on a creek & JOSEPH PALMENTER; N on BENJAMIN WILLMAN & WILLIAM FRY. "We are first to send to Old England & if faile of supply there, then we are to send to any other place". Witnesses: JOHN PARRY, BENJAMIN WILLMAN, THOMAS WENBORN. Before ROBERT YONGE, J.P. JAMES HOME, Register.

Book Y, p. 91　　　　　　　By warrent from Dep. Gov. ROBERT DANIELL, da-
　　　　　　　　　　　　　　ted 23 July 1717, FRANCIS YONGE, Sur. Gen. had
surveyed for JOSEPH PARMENTER, 1 lot #45 in Beaufort, Granville Co., bounding S on lot #15; W on Carteret Street; N on lot #44; E on lot #48. Certified 25 July.

Book Y, p. 92　　　　　　　The Hon. COL. ROBERT DANIELL, Dep. Gov., & the
8 Aug. 1717　　　　　　　　Lords Proprs. SAMUEL EVELEIGH, FRANCIS YONGE,
Grant　　　　　　　　　　　 CHARLES HART, & GEORGE CHICKEN to JOSEPH PAR-
　　　　　　　　　　　　　　MENTER, lot #45 in Beaufort, Granville Co.
Recorded in Secretary's office 9 Aug. 1717, fol. 413 by JOHN CROFT, Dep. Sec. JAMES HOME, Register.

Book Y, p. 93　　　　　　　BENJAMIN PARMENTER, planter, to his brother,
16 June 1738　　　　　　　 JOHN PARMENTER, planter, both of Granville Co.,
Deed of Gift　　　　　　　for natural love & affection & other considera-
　　　　　　　　　　　　　　tions, lot #45 in Beaufort, Port Royal Island,
which lot was granted to JOSEPH PARMENTER, SR., in 1717 & later purchased by BENJAMIN PARMENTER; bounding S on lot #15; W on Carteret Street; N on lot #44; E on lot #48. Witnesses: RICHARD RICKETTS, THOMAS GRIMBALL. Before THOMAS WIGG, J.P. JAMES HOME, Register.

Book Y, p. 95   JOHN PARMENTER, planter, & MARY (her mark) his
11 & 12 Jan. 1741   wife, of Port Royall Island, Granville Co., to
L & R   THOMAS BURTON, carpenter, of Beaufort, for
                       Ł 80 currency, lot #45 in Beaufort, bounding S
on lot #15; W on Carteret Street; N on lot #44; E on lot #48. Witnesses:
HILL WIGG, JAMES HOUSTON, BENJAMIN PARMENTER. Before THOMAS WILL, J.P.
JAMES HOME, Register.

Book Y, p. 100   HUGH DUFFEY, tanner, to JAMES AKIN, planter,
4 & 5 Dec. 1741   both of Berkeley Co., for Ł 1250 SC money, 150
L & R by Mortgage   a. in Berkeley Co., bounding NW on JAMES AKIN;
                       SE on SARAH TROTT; SW on THOMAS BONNY. Date
of redemption: 3 Dec. 1745. Witnesses: JOHN CUMING, THOMAS DEARINGTON.
Before ANTHONY BONNEAU, J.P. JAMES HOME, Register.

Book Y, p. 107   THOMAS LLOYD & SARAH his wife, of Charleston
13 & 14 May 1740   to WILLIAM CRASSKEYS, planter, of Port Royal,
L & R   for Ł 100 SC money, 300 a. in Craven Co., on N
                       side Cousa River, bounding W on vacant land; S
on MR. FRASER'S plantation commonly called the Bonagust Plantation; E on
Bull's Creek. Witnesses: JOHN BALLANTINE, JR., GEORGE HOGG, WILLIAM
SMITH. Before THOMAS LAMBOLL, J.P. JAMES HOME, Register.

Book Y, p. 114   HUGH SWINTON, surgeon, of Craven Co., to ALEX-
9 & 10 Sept. 1740   ANDER DICK, mariner, of Charleston, for Ł 75
L & R   sterling British, 80 a. in Craven Co., being
                       the N part of 250 a. granted to SWINTON; bound-
ing NW on Peedee River; SE on SWINTON'S Creek; SW on WILLIAM SWINTON.
The land to be free from claim of dower by JUDITH, wife of HUGH SWINTON.
Witnesses: WILLIAM ROSE, JAMES DRUMMOND. Before JAMES GREEME, J.P. JAM-
ES HOME, Register.

Book Y, p. 121   JOHN MACKENZIE & MATTHEW ROCHE, merchants, (as
1 & 2 Feb. 1742   attorneys for JANET DICK), to JOSEPH SHUTE,
L & R   merchant, all of Charleston; for Ł 3250 SC mon-
                       ey, several tracts; 300 a., bounding NW on
SWINTON'S Creek; NE on Peedee River & Gordon's Thoroughfare; S on Glen's
Thoroughfare; SE on GEORGE PAWLEY; 100 a. (1/2 of 200 a.), bounding E on
WILLIAM ALSTON & Pawley's Creek; N on WILLIAM SWINTON; SW on Peedee River
& Gordon's Thoroughfare; 500 a. commonly called Wehaw, bounding SW on the
Duke of Beaufort's Barony; E on Peedee River, 150 a. in Craven Co., bound-
ing SW on HUGH SWINTON; N on last 500 a.; SE on Peedee River; all of
which tracts formerly belonged to JAMES GORDON, planter, of Prince George
Parish, & were sold by his executors (JOHN CLELAND, WILLIAM WALLACE, WIL-
LIAM SWINTON, & GEORGE PAWLEY, named in his will) for a valuable consideration to ALEXANDER DICK; also 80 a. being the N part of 450 a., bounding NW on Peedee River; SE on Swinton's Creek; SW on WILLIAM SWINTON;
which 80 a., for a valuable consideration, were conveyed to ALEXANDER
DICK by HUGH SWINTON, surgeon, by L & R dated 9 & 10 Sept. 1740. Whereas
JANET DICK, only sister & heir-at-law of ALEXANDER DICK, mariner, of City
of Bristol, by deed poll dated 5 Feb. 1741 appointed GEORGE MACKENZIE,
merchant, of West Cowes, Isle of Wight, Southampton, her attorney, with
authority to dispose of all real estate that belonged to her brother &
whereas MACKENZIE on 22 Feb. 1741 appointed JOHN MACKENZIE & MATTHEW RO-
CHE, his substitutes, to sell such real estate in SC; now they sell several tracts in Craven Co. to SHUTE. Witnesses: MAURICE HARVEY, JAMES
DRUMMOND. Before JAMES GREEME, J.P. JAMES HOME, Register.

Book Y, p. 132   JOSEPH SHUTE, merchant, & HANNAH (ANNA) his
16 & 17 Feb. 1742   wife, to JOHN MACKENZIE, merchant; all of
L & R   Charleston; for Ł 3250 SC money; several
                       tracts in Craven Co.; 300 a. bounding NW on
Swinton's Creek; NE on Peedee River & Gordon's Thorofare; S on Glen's
Thorofare; SE on GEORGE PAWLEY; also 100 a. (1/2 of 200) bounding E on
WILLIAM ALSTON & Pawley's Creek; N on WILLIAM SWINTON; SW on Peedee River
& Gordon's Thorofare; also 500 a. called Wehaw, bounding SW on the Duke
of Beaufort's Barony; E on Peedee River; also 150 a. bounding SW on HUGH
SWINTON; N on said 500 a., SE on Peedee River; also 80 a. being the N
part of 250 a., bounding NW on Peedee River; SE on Swinton's Creek; SW on
WILLIAM SWINTON. Witnesses: JAMES DRUMMOND, MAURICE HARVEY. Before

JAMES GREEME, J.P.   JAMES HOME, Register.

Book Y, p. 140   THEODORE GAILLARD, planter, & LYDIA his wife,
30 Apr. 1741   to CHARLES BENOIST, planter, all of Craven Co.,
L & R   for Ł 112 SC money, 550 a. on S side of Black
                                 River, bounding W on STEPHEN FORD; S on MR.
GOUGH & MR. MAZYCK; E on CAPT. WHITE; N on ____. Witnesses: ANNE LE-
GRAND, TACITUS GAILLARD, RALPH BUGNIAN. Before HENRY GIBBES, J.P. JAMES
HOME, Register.

Book Y, p. 147   SARAH (her mark) PRINGLE, of James Island, to
17 & 18 May 1742   ARTHUR BAXTER, planter, of Kingston Township,
L & R   on Waccamaw River, for Ł 400 currency, 3
                                 tracts in Kingston Township. (1) 100 a. & lot
#9, bounding NE on MR. SHEPPERD; SE on MRS. WHITE; SW on COL. LUCAS; NW
on COL. WATES; (2) 214 a. bounding NE on vacant land; NW on THOMAS JEN-
KINS; SW & SE on ADAM MCLEDOOSE, which 2 tracts were granted to SARAH
PRINGLE 7 Aug. 1741 by the Hon. WILLIAM BULL; (3) 36 a. bounding NW on
JOHN MORRALL; SW on WILLIAM GAW; E on ALEXANDER CAMPBELL; which tract was
granted to SARAH PRINGLE 8 Aug. 1741 by the Hon. WILLIAM BULL. Witness-
es: JAMES MAITLAND, JAMES ADLAM, GEORGE (his mark) HAMILTON. Before HEN-
RY GIBBES, J.P. JAMES HOME, Register.

Book Y, p. 154   DANIEL (his mark) MCDONALD, planter, & MARY
26 & 27 Aug. 1742   (her mark) his wife, to THOMAS BURTIN, JR.,
L & R   planter, both of Craven Co., for Ł 525 curren-
                                 cy, 550 a. in Craven Co., granted 4 Dec. 1735
by Lt. Gov. THOMAS BROUGHTON to MCDONALD; bounding N on THOMAS POTT;
other sides on land not laid out. Witnesses: JOHN SINKLAR, JOHN MCDONALD.
Before JOHN BASSNETT, J.P. JAMES HOME, Register.

Book Y, p. 161   SAMUEL MASTARS, planter, of Little River, Cra-
17 & 18 Jan. 1737   ven Co., to JOHN RICHARDS, planter, of Winyaw,
L & R   Craven Co., for Ł 1100 SC money, 200 a. in
                                 Craven Co., bounding W on Winyaw River; NE & S
on a Barony. Witnesses: JONATHAN SKRINE, JOHN BONNELL. Before DANIEL LA-
ROCHE, J.P. JAMES HOWE, Register.

Book Y, p. 166   ISAAC SECARE, planter, to BENJAMIN WHITAKER,
25 & 26 Mar. 1740   ESQ., for Ł 750, all his undivided 1/3 part of
L & R   2 town lots. Whereas STEPHEN TAVERON, cooper,
                                 by will dated 19 July 1729 bequeathed to his
grandsons PETER SECARE & ISAAC SECARE & to his granddaughter MARY LAROCHE
(now wife of ELIAS FOISSIN) that lot in Charleston fronting S 41 ft. on
Broad Street, & bounding E on the lot given by said will to DANIEL LA-
ROCHE & THOMAS LAROCHE; W on another of his town lots; N on a street; to
be equally divided among them; & also bequeathed to them, equally, the
lot fronting S 42 ft. on Broad Street, bounding E on above lot; W on another of his lots; N on a street; now ISAAC SECARE sells his third part
to WHITAKER. Witnesses: ROBERT PLADGER, THOMAS (his mark) EVENS. Before
DANIEL LAROCHE, J.P. JAMES HOME, Register.

Book Y, p. 174   GEORGE VINSON (VINCENT) son & heir of GEORGE
24 & 25 Jan. 1737   VINCENT, planter, to CULCHETH GOLIGHTLY, gen-
L & R   tleman, of Colleton Co., for Ł 60 currency,
                                 200 a., English measure, in Collton Co., with-
in land on Horse Shoe Savannah, granted by Gov. NATHANIEL JOHNSON & NICH-
OLAS TROTT & JAMES MOORE, Lords Proprs. (by a commission from JOHN, Lord
Granville, Palatine) on 10 Feb. 1704 to GEORGE VINCENT, father of GEORGE
VINSON, party hereto; bounding SW on WILLIAM WILLIAMSON; other parts on
vacant land. Witnesses: ROGER SAUNDERS, NATHANIEL PAYNE. Before JAMES
BULLOCK, J.P. JAMES HOME, Register.

Book Y, p. 182   GEORGE MOORE, gentleman, of Cape Fear, NC, to
26 July 1737   JOHN STANYARN, planter, of Colleton Co. Where-
Confirmation & Release   as E. MARY MOORE (whose maiden name was E.
                                 MARY RAYNOR) mother of GEORGE MOORE, owned sev-
eral tracts of land in SC, & several lots in Chalreston; & whereas she
married ROGER MOORE, ESQ., then of Berkeley Co., SC, now of Cape Fear, NC;
& whereas she died, leaving GEORGE her only child & heir, but ROGER MOORE

the father, took possession of the property as tenant for life by "the Curtesie of England" & on 30 Oct. 1717 conveyed to JOHN STANYARN 1350 a. in Colleton Co., half of what is commonly called Kiawah Island; & whereas ROGER MOORE did not have the power to convey; & whereas GEORGE MOORE hereby acknowledges that he received from his father full value & more than the value for his right & inheritance in the tract; now GEORGE MOORE approves & confirms the conveyance to STANYARN. Witnesses: THOMAS AKIN, REBECCA COKE, SARAH SMITH. Before FRANCIS LEJAU, J.P. JAMES HOME, Register.

Book Y, p. 187   RICHARD WRIGHT, ESQ., & MARY his wife, of St.
11 & 12 Apr. 1743   Paul's Parish, Colleton Co., to FRANCIS MILES,
L & R by Mortgage   widow, of London, Great Britain, as security
                        on bond of even date in penal sum of Ł 2000
for payment of Ł 1000 British with interest on 1 Apr. o745; 688 a. on
which RICHARD WRIGHT now dwells, on NW branch Stono River; in St. Paul's
Parish, consisting of 3 smaller adjoining tracts, 350 a., 100 a., & 238
a.; bounding N on MR. ELLIOTT & MR. WILLIAMSON; W on WILLIAMSON; SW on
WILLIAM HARVEY & JONATHAN FITCH; NE on MESHEW; E on ALEXANDER HEXT; also
50 Negro & other slaves. A gold watch delivered in name of the whole.
Witnesses: NICHOLAS MAETTEYSEN, CHARLES PINCKNEY. Before JAMES WRIGHT,
J.P. JAMES HOME, Register.

Book Y, p. 198   JOHN TIPPER to WILLIAM RANDALL & wife. See
Probate   Book O, p. 253 for L & R. Witnesses: WILLIAM
                        SMITH, THOMAS WEAVER, JOHN PANTON. Before
JAMES GREEME, J.P. JAMES HOME, Register.

Book Y, p. 199   ELISHA SCREVEN, gentleman, to THOMAS IRETON
26 Feb. 1742   CROMWELL, schoolmaster, both of Craven Co.,
Deed of Feoffment   for Ł 100 currency, 500 a., in Craven Co.,
                        bounding E on JAMES BREMAR & JOHN GARDINER; SW
on vacant land; N on vacant land & JAMES BREMAR; as by grant to BENTLEY
COKE dated 7 Aug. 1735; also as by release dated 21 Jan. 1735 from COKE
to SCREVEN. HANNAH SCREVEN, wife of ELISHA, willingly surrenders her
right of dower. Witnesses: SAMSON LALO, JOSEPH SCREVEN, LETTICE (her
mark) MCNEALE (MCNEALLEE). Before WILLIAM WHITESIDE, J.P. JAMES HOME,
Register.

Book Y, p. 202   EPHRAIM MIKELL, planter, & ELIZABETH his wife,
4 & 5 Mar. 1742   of Granville Co., to JAMES SKIRVING, ESQ., of
L & R   Colleton Co., for Ł 600 SC money, 407 a. on W
                        side Pon Pon River, St. Bartholomew's Parish,
Colleton Co., bounding according to release dated 10 Aug. 1729 from ALEX-
ANDER TRENCH to JOHN BAILEY of Goose Creek. Whereas WILLIAM TENNANT &
JOHN MCGILLIVRAY, Indian traders, by L & R dated 29 & 30 Oct. 1731 (de-
rived from & under BAILEY'S patent) owned, in jointenancy, 407 a. (as
above) bounding N on JOHN BAILEY (BAYLY) of Goose Creek; E on COL.
CHARLESWORTH GLOVER; S & W on BRYAN KELLY & vacant land; & whereas WIL-
LIAM TENANT on 22 July 1732 died leaving MCGILLIVRAY sole owner; & he by
will dated 1 Apr. 1736 bequeathed to his loving wife ELIZABETH (who, in
June 1736 married EPHRAIM MIKELL) the rest of his real & personal estate
(after other bequests), including the 407 a.; (MCGILLIVRAY dying in Apr.
1736); now they sell to SKIRVING. Witnesses: CHARLES PINCKNEY, THOMAS
PINCKNEY. Before HENRY GIBBES, J.P. JAMES HOME, Register.

Book Y, p. 212   JOHN BROWN, planter, & CHRISTIANNA his wife,
11 & 12 July 1738   of St. John's Parish, to NATHANIEL BROWN,
L & R   planter, of St. Andrews Parish, Berkeley Co.,
                        for Ł 500 currency, 53 a. in St. Andrews
Berkeley Co., bounding S on JOHN BROWN, JR.; SW on NATHANIEL BROWN. Wit-
nesses: NICHOLAS MAHAM (MAYHAM), MOSES BUTLER. Before THOMAS FERGUSON,
J.P. JAMES HOME, Register.

Book Y, p. 218   JOHN BROWN, JR., planter, & JUDITH his wife,
22 Feb. 1739   to NATHANIEL BROWN, planter, for Ł 1100 SC
L & R   money, 100 a. in Berkeley Co., bounding SW on
                        estate of THOMAS ELLIOTT, STEPHEN BULL & THOM-
AS JONES; N on SYLIAS WELLS & JOHN CHAMPNEYS; NE on COL. WILLIAM BULL &
NATHANIEL BROWN. Whereas Gov. NATHANIEL JOHNSON & the Lords Proprs. on

on 5 May 1705 granted CHARLES JONES 220 a., English measure, in Berkeley Co., bounding N & E on STEPHEN BULL, ESQ., S on JOHN BROWN; W on TIMOTHY SULLIVAN & whereas the Lords Proprs. on 26 Jan. 1714/15 granted JOHN BROWN 33 a. in Berkeley Co., bounding N on JOHN BROWN; SE on JOHN GODFREY; SW on WILLIAM BULL; & whereas CHARLES JONES & PRISCILLA his wife, on 10 May 1705 conveyed the 220 a. to ROBERT WILKINSON for a valuable consideration & whereas ROBERT WILKINSON, & MARY his wife, on 30 May 1711, conveyed the tract to JOHN BROWN, who, by 2 deeds of gift, gave the 2 tracts (253 a.) to his 2 sons NATHANIEL & JOHN; 1 gift dated 17 Aug. 1736, giving son JOHN 100 a.; now JOHN, JR. sells his 100 a. to NATHANIEL. Witnesses: JOSEPH SULLIVAN, RICHARD WOOD, MOSES BUTLER. Before WILLIAM BULL, JR., J.P. JAMES HOME, Register.

Book Y, p. 228　　　　　　RALPH HOLMES, planter, & ANNE his wife, to SOL-
21 & 22 Sept. 1740　　　　OMON FREER, planter, all of Colleton Co., for
L & R　　　　　　　　　　£ 400 SC money, 100 a. on Johns Island, Colle-
　　　　　　　　　　　　　ton Co., bounding E & W & N on THOMAS ROBARTS;
S on WILLIAM HOLMES. Witnesses: OBADIAH WILLIAMS, JONATHAN WILKINS, SOL-
OMON FREER, JR. Before ANTHONY MATHEWS, J.P. JAMES HOME, Register.

Book Y, p. 235　　　　　　ANNE SMITH, spinster, of Charleston, conveys
24 & 25 Nov. 1738　　　　 to WILLIAM SMITH & PETER TAYLOR, as trustees
L & R in Trust　　　　　　for ANNE SMITH because of her intended mar-
　　　　　　　　　　　　　riage to THOMAS DALE, ESQ., of Charleston, &
to secure her real estate to her own use; a lot on Bedon's Street,
Charleston, bounding E on Bedon Street, S on JOSEPH ELLIOT; W on estate
of ANTHONY MATHEWS & WILLIAM MCKENZY & MRS. ELIZABETH SMITH; N on STEPHEN
BEDON. THOMAS DALE assents to this deed of settlement. Witnesses: JOHN
MILNER, BENJAMIN SMITH, THOMAS DALE. Before HENRY GIBBES, J.P. Recorded
in Secretary's office in Book Q.Q. fol. 201-204 on 9 Mar. 1742 by J. HAM-
MERTON. JAMES HOME, Register.

Book Y, p. 242　　　　　　THOMAS DALE, ESQ., of Charleston, to WILLIAM
25 Nov. 1738　　　　　　　SMITH & PETER TAYLOR, of Berkeley Co., trus-
Declaration　　　　　　　tees for ANNE SMITH of Charleston. Whereas a
　　　　　　　　　　　　　marriage is shortly to be solemnized between
THOMAS DALE & ANNE SMITH; & whereas ANNE by L & R dated 24 & 25 Nov. 1738
conveyed to SMITH & TAYLOR, her trustees, a lot in Charleston on W side
Bedon's Street; (see p. 235); now DALE promises that ANNE may bequeath
the lot as she sees fit. Witnesses: JOHN MILNER, BENJAMIN SMITH. Before
HENRY GIBBES, J.P. Recorded in Secretary's Book Q.Q. fol. 206-207 on 11
Mar. 1742 by J. HAMMERTON. JAMES HOME, Register.

Book Y, p. 244　　　　　　JOHN LLOYD, planter, of St. James Parish,
31 Mar. & 1 Apr. 1743　　Berkeley Co., to JOHN CLELAND, ESQ., of
L & R　　　　　　　　　　Charleston, for £ 1145:11 currency, 300 a. in
　　　　　　　　　　　　　Berkeley Co., on W side Four-Hole Swamp, con-
veyed by JOHN OULDFIELD to JOHN LLOYD; bounding S on tract laid out to
executors of WILLIAM ADAMS; N on JOHN LLOYD; other sides on vacant land;
also 500 a. on W side Four-Hole Swamp conveyed by RICHARD SINGLETON to
LLOYD; bounding SE & NE on JOHN LLOYD & vacant land; NE on WILLIAM ADAMS;
SW on JAMES COACHMAN; other sides on vacant land; also 90 a. (granted to
JOHN BERRINGER & by several conveyances come to LLOYD) known as My Lady's
Bluff, on W side Four-Hole-Swamp; bounding W on Edisto River. Witnesses:
CHARLES CALDER, JAMES DRUMMOND. Before JAMES HOME, J.P. & Register.

Book Y, p. 252　　　　　　JOHN CLELAND & WILLIAM WALLACE, merchants, of
18 & 19 July 1740　　　　 Charleston, & WILLIAM SWINTON, & GEORGE PAW-
L & R　　　　　　　　　　LEY, planters, of Winyaw, to ALEXANDER DICK,
　　　　　　　　　　　　　mariner, of Charleston, for £ 3850 currency,
several tracts formerly belonging to JAMES GORDON. Whereas JAMES GORDON,
planter, of Prince George Winyaw owned several tracts & by will dated 12
June authorized his executors, CLELAND, WALLACE, SWINTON & PAWLEY, to
sell his plantation in Craven Co., now they sell DICK 300 a. granted to
PETER BENOIST & conveyed to GORDON; bounding NW on Swinton's Creek; NE on
Peedee River & Gordon's Thoroughfare; S on Glen's Thoroughfare; SE on
GEORGE PAWLEY; also 100 a. (part of 200 a. granted to BENOIST & conveyed
to GORDON) bounding E on WILLIAM ALSTON & Pawley's Creek; N on WILLIAM
SWINTON; SW on Peedee River & Gordon's Thoroughfare; also 500 a. commonly
called Wehaw, bounding SW on the Duke of Beaufort's Barony; E on Peedee

River; which 500 a. were granted by the Lords Proprs. to WILLIAM KITCHEN
& by sundry conveyances came to GORDON; also 150 a. bounding SW on HUGH
SWINTON; N on said 500 a.; SW on Peedee River; which 150 a. were conveyed
by HUGH SWINTON & JUDITH his wife, to WILLIAM WATIES, who conveyed to
GORDON. Witnesses: ALEXANDER MURRAY, JAMES DRUMMOND. Before JAMES HOME,
J.P. & Pub. Reg.

Book Y, p. 262   ELISHA SCREVEN, planter, & HANNAH his wife, of
13 & 14 June 1737   Winyaw, Craven Co., WILLIAM SCREVEN, planter,
L & R   & ELEANOR his wife, of James Island, Berkeley
                                Co.; JAMES SCREVEN, planter, & MARY his wife,
of James Island; & FRANCIS GRACIA, planter, & MARY his wife, of James Island; to JOHN CLELAND, merchant, & MARY his wife, of Charleston, for
Ł 4000 currency; 500 a. in Craven Co., granted by Lords Proprs. to JOHN
PERRY, bounding N on Wahaw River; E on Wineau River; S on EDWARD PERRY; W
on ELIZABETH ELLIOT; also 200 a. granted by Lords Proprs. to JOHN PERRY,
bounding S on Sampeet Creek, E & W on EDWARD PERRY; also 100 a. granted
by Lords Proprs. to JOHN PERRY, bounding S on Sampeet Creek; W on JOHN
ABRAHAM MOTTE; N on ELIZABETH ELLIOT; E on EDWARD PERRY; also 500 a.
granted to EDWARD PERRY, bounding N on JOHN PERRY; E on Wineau River; W
on JOHN PERRY; also 100 a. granted to EDWARD PERRY, bounding S on Sampeet
Creek; E & W on JOHN PERRY; N on ELIZABETH ELLIOT; also 1900 a. granted
to ELIZABETH ELLIOT; bounding S on JOHN & EDWARD PERRY & JOHN ABRAHAM
MOTTE; E on EDWARD PERRY; N on JOHN ABRAHAM MOTTE; W on vacant land; this
conveyance not to include any part of the several tracts lying within the
bounds of the Town & Common of Georgetown, Prince George Parish, Wineau
as granted by ELISHA SCREVEN to GEORGE PAWLEY, WILLIAM SWINTON & DANIEL
LAROCHE by L & R, 14 & 15 Jan. 1734; & not to include 200 a. now belong-
ing to JOHN FORBES, bounding S on JOHN ABRAHAM MOTTE; N on ARTHUR FORSTER;
which 200 a. are a part of said 1900 a. granted to ELIZABETH ELLIOT.
Witnesses to ELISHA SCREVEN'S signature: RICHARD ALLEIN, JAMES WEDDERBURN,
GEORGE DICK, CHARLES HOPE. Witnesses to HANNAH SCREVEN'S signature: JOHN
SMITH, JOHN ASKOEW, CHARLES HOPE. Witnesses to signatures of WILLIAM &
ELINOR SCREVENS, JAMES & MARY SCREVEN, FRANCIS & MARY GRACIA: JAMES WED-
DERBURN, ALEXANDER MURRAY. Before JOHN HAMMERTON, J.P. JAMES HOME, Reg-
ister.

Book Y, p. 275   WILLIAM WOOD, merchant, in Frederica, Colony
25 Aug. 1740   of Georgia, promises before God to make his
Bond   dear & well-beloved friend ANN BAX, widow, his
                                true & lawful wife, & no other woman. Should
he not marry ANN he binds himself to pay to ANN on the marriage date
Ł 500 sterling British. He also promises to make over to ANN by bond before marriage & by will after marriage "all that is & may be mine after
my death if she doth a wife's part by me, at her disposal forever". Witnesses: ARCHIBALD SINCLAIR, ISOBALL MCNEAL (?) SINEATH (?). JAMES HOME,
Register.

Book Y, p. 276   WILLIAM WOOD, of Town of Frederica, Colony of
18 Nov. 1740   Georgia, promises to make over to his well-be-
Obligation   loved friend ANN BAX, after she becomes his
                                wife, his worldly estate after his death, un-
der penalty of Ł 1000 sterling of England to be paid her if she lives
with him as a wife ought to live with a husband; he also makes over to
her Ł 100 sterling with all her clothes & wearing apparel "that she has
at present at her own disposal & all that may be hers in England to dispose of as she pleases". Witnesses: WILLIAM ABBOTT, ARCHIBALD SINCLAIR.
JAMES HOME, Register.

Book Y, p. 276   WILLIAM (his mark) PRICE, & ANNA his wife, of
10 & 11 Oct. 1729   Cape Fear, to WILLIAM WATIES, of Craven Co.,
L & R   for Ł 120 SC money, 500 a. in Craven Co., on W
                                side Peedee River, commonly called Wehaw,
bounding SW on the Duke of Beaufort's Barony. Witnesses: WILLIAM FARRIS,
RACHEL FARRIS. Memorial recorded in Auditor's office in Old Grant Bk.
No. 1, fol. 423 on 29 Jan. 1732 by JAMES ST. JOHN, Dep. Aud. JAMES HOME,
Register.

Book Y, p. 279   HUGH SWINTON, & JUDITH his wife, of Prince
22 Nov. 1733   George Parish, to WILLIAM WATIES of St. James

Deed of Feoffment   Santee, for £ 100 SC money, 150 a. on Peedee
                                  River, in Prince George Parish, Craven Co.,
bounding SW on HUGH SWINTON; N on WILLIAM WATIES. Witnesses: JOHN SELL-
ERY, ESTHER SIMONS. 150 a. curveyed 6 Jan. 1734/5 by ALEXANDER ROBERTSON,
Dep. Sur. Witnesses to delivery of possession: HUGH ROSE, ALEXANDER ROB-
ERTONSON. Before THOMAS LAROCHE, J.P. JAMES HOME, Register.

Book Y, p. 281   WILLIAM WATIES, & DOROTHY his wife, of St.
7 Jan. 1734   James Santee, to JAMES GORDON, of Prince
Deed of Feoffment   George Parish, for £ 800 SC money, 2 tracts on
                                  NW side Peedee River, in Prince George Parish;
500 a. & 150 a., making 650 a., commonly called Wehaw, bounding according
to plats & grants. Witnesses: HUGH SWINTON, ALEXANDER ROBERTSON. Before
WILLIAM SWINTON, J.P. JAMES HOME, Register.

Book Y, p. 283   MOSES NORMAN, planter, of Beech Hill, Colleton
12 Aug. 1740   Co., to JAMES MARTIN, planter; of Colleton Co.,
Deed of Feoffment   for £ 100; 735 a. in Colleton Co.; bounding W
                                  on Salcacha River; S on THOMAS MILES; other
sides on vacant land. Witnesses: JOSEPH NORMAN, WILLIAM CHAMBERLINE,
SAMUEL STEVENS. Before CULCHETH GOLIGHTLY, J.P. JAMES HOME, Register.

Book Y, p. 286   JAMES COFING (COFFING), planter, of Berkeley
23 & 24 Mar. 1741   Co., to ELIHU BAKER, planter, son of SUSANNAH
L & R   BAKER, for £ 500 SC money, 100 a. in Berkeley
                                  Co., bounding S on JOSEPH HASFORT'S land pur-
chased by him from HUGH FERGUSON; W on HANNAH BURNLEY; N on RICHARD CART-
WRIGHT'S land which he purchased from JOSEPH CANTY. Witnesses: JOSEPH
BOSWOOD, WILLIAM BOSWOOD. JAMES HOME, Register.

Book Y, p. 291   WILLIAM BOSWOOD, planter, of Berkeley Co., to
23 & 24 Mar. 1741   ELIHU BAKER, planter, son of SUSANNAH BAKER,
L & R   also of Berkeley Co., for £ 600 SC money, 65 a.
                                  on N side Ashley River, bounding N on JOSIAH
CANTY & RICHARD CARTWRIGHT; S on JAMES COFING (formerly JAMES BOSWOOD).
Witnesses: JAMES BOSWOOD, JOSIAH BAKER. Before HENRY GIBBES, J.P. JAMES
HOME, Register.

Book Y, p. 296   MICHAEL (his mark) SCULLY, of Charleston, as-
13 May 1743   signs to SAMUEL HURST, ESQ., subject to pay-
Assignment   ment of the ground rent, for £ 50 currency.
                                  Whereas ISAAC HOLMES, merchant, of Charleston,
on 10 Oct. 1741, "farm let" to ELIZABETH SCULLY, wife of MICHAEL SCULLY,
for 5 years, commencing 1 Apr. 1741 (?) for £ 25 a year in quarterly payments a house & lot in Charleston 16 ft. by 60 ft., bounding E on Church
Street; other sides on ISAAC HOLMES; & whereas MICHAEL SCULLY, by virtue
of his marriage to ELIZABETH SCULLY, is entitled to the lot & premises
for the remainder of the term, with power to transfer the same; now he
sub-lets to HURST. Witnesses: SAMUEL WAINWRIGHT, JOHN WHEELER. JAMES
HOME, J.P. & Pub. Reg.

Book Y, p. 299   WILLIAM HARRIS, butcher, & SARAH his wife, of
9 May 1743   St. Philip's Parish, Charleston, to SAMUEL
L & R   WAINWRIGHT, of same Parish, for £ 600 currency,
                                  part of lot #222 on the Green in Charleston,
fronting 17-1/2 ft. E on King Street, 140 ft. ddep; S on SAMUEL SMITH,
JR., carpenter; W on a garden belonging to widow HOLMES; N on tenement of
JOHN DANIEL. Witnesses: JOSEPH BARRY, WILLIAM ELLIS, THOMAS COLSON. Before HENRY GIBBES, J.P. JAMES HOMES, Register.

Book Y, p. 306   EDWARD FORTH, planter, to THOMAS SNIPES, plant-
17 & 18 May 1743   er, for £ 1090 SC money, 500 a. in Colleton
L & R   Co., bounding NW on THOMAS ELLIOTT; NE on COL.
                                  JOHN FENWICKE; SE on MR. MCKAY; SW on MR. FAIR-
CHILD & MR. CLIFFORD. Witnesses: JOHN JOHNSON, RICE PRICE, JAMES THOMSON.
Before ROBERT AUSTIN, J.P. JAMES HOME, Register.

Book Y, p. 313   JOHN BULL, planter, executor of will of JAMES
20 & 21 May 1741   WRIXHAM, planter, to JAMES BERRIE, planter,
L & R   all of Colleton Co., for £ 1020 currency;

340 a. Whereas JAMES WRIXHAM owned 500 a. in Colleton Co., & by will dated 14 Oct. 1739 directed that 340 a. on the head of this tract should be sold, & appointed JOHN BULL, sole executor; now BULL sells the 350 a., bounding E on THOMAS ELLIOTT; S on JOHN BULL; W on other part of 500 a.; N on JACOB BRADWELL & JANE MCCORD. Witnesses: JACOB BRADWELL, ROBERT MC-MURDY, WILLIAM BULL. Before CHARLES WRIGHT, J.P. JAMES HOME, Register.

Book Y, p. 320
16 & 17 May 1743
L & R

NOAH SERRÉ, ESQ., of St. James Santee, Craven Co., & CATHERINE his wife, to GEORGE CHICKEN, planter, of St. James Goose Creek, Berkeley Co., for Ł 1350 SC money, 270 a., part of 48,000 a., in St. James Goose Creek, near head of Back River, bounding S on heirs of Landgrave THOMAS SMITH; N on LYDIA DURHAM, widow. Whereas the Rt. Hon. JOHN, Earl of Bath, & the Lords Proprs. by letters patent dated 16 Aug. 1698 created JOHN BAYLY; of Ballinaclough, Co. of Tipperary, Kingdom of Ireland, a Landgrave & Cassique of SC, giving him 48,000 a. in SC; & whereas JOHN BAYLY, his son & heir, by deed poll dated 9 Nov. 1722 appointed ALEXANDER TRENCH, ESQ., of SC his attorney, with power to set aside 8000 a. for the use of JOHN BAYLY & dispose of the 40,000 a.; & whereas TRENCH yb L & R dated 11 & 12 Aug. 1730 convey 270 a. to EDWARD THOMAS, planter, of St. Johns Parish, Berkeley Co., who by L & R dated 19 & 20 Nov. 1731 conveyed to NOAH SERRÉ; now SERRÉ conveys to CHICKEN. Witnesses: ABRAHAM CROFT, GEORGE HUNTER. Before OTHNIEL BEALE, J.P. JAMES HOME, Register.

Book Y, p. 321
16 & 17 May 1743
L & R by Mortgage

JOHN JOHNSTON, planter, of Granville Co., to MAJ. WILLIAM STEWART, of Island of New Providence, as security on bond of even date in penal sum of Ł 4000 for payment of Ł 2000 SC money, with interest, on certain dates; 500 a. in Granville Co., according to plat of grant; also 344 a. in Granville Co., total 844 a., known as Pocosabo Island in Port Royall River. Witnesses: JOHN JOHNSTON, JOHN NEUFVILLE, JR. Before JAMES MICKIE, J.P. JAMES HOME, Register. Mortgage satisfied 7 Jan. 1746.

Book Y, p. 327
19 Apr. 1743
Affidavit

CATHARINE (her mark) UMBLE, testifies to the good character & behaviour of ANNE WOOD, wife of WILLIAM WOOD; having known ANNE for 5 years & having been her constant companion on their passage from Frederica, Georgia, into SC; & that there was no familiarity, no light or indecent behavior between ANNE WOOD & ADAM MCDONNALD or any other man whatever. Before THOMAS DALE, J.P. JAMES HOME, Register.

Book Y, p. 328
19 Apr. 1743
Affidavit

JAMES WATTS testifies he has been employed almost 2 years by WILLIAM WOOD as patrone of the pettiagua called the WILLIAM & ANNE, & before that of a long-boat named the Priscilla, & he generally went in these boats to Fredarica, Georgia, & back again with goods & merchandise, & that ANNE WOOD, wife of WILLIAM WOOD, most commonly went with him, this patrone, to Frederica, a-trading, & he never did see any familiarity or indecent behavior pass between ANNE WOOD & ADAM MCDONNALD, or any other man whatever but always demeaned herself as became a prudent & vertuous woman. Before THOMAS DALE, J.P. JAMES HOME, Register.

Book Y, p. 329
19 Apr. 1743
Affidavit

JANE (her mark) BREZ testified she was a passenger in same pettiagua with ADAM MCDONNALD & ANNE WOOD from Frederica to Charleston & never saw any familiarity or light & wanton behavior pass between said ADAM & ANNE but they demeaned themselves with utmost prudence & civility. Before THOMAS DALE, J.P. JAMES HOME, Register.

Book Y, p. 329
20 Apr. 1743
Affidavit

JAMES WATTS testified that some time in Dec. last as he was going from the pettiagua of which he was patrone to the house of WILLIAM WOOD, his employer, he found MRS. ANNE WOOD, wife of WILLIAM, standing near the house in the dark & rain & asking why she stood there she replied that her husband had turned her out of doors. Deponant fetched a candle & lantern & ANNE went with him to the pettiague. Sometime after, ADAM MCDONNALD came on board & finding MRS. WOOD there immediately sent his boy to tell CAPT. WOOD his wife was safe on board. WOOD shortly after came on board with a naked sword under his night gown. Lying down on the gangway with 1 hand, with the other he made a pass by deponant's breast at his wife as she lay in the cabin so that the sword went through her clothes & in all probability would have killed her had not MCDONALD struck his arm back. WOOD afterwards went into the cabin to his wife. WATTS & CAPT. MCDONALD retired & walker the deck, unwilling to interrupt or interfere in conversation between husband & wife. ANNE soon after cried out "murder". Deponant returned to cabin, found ANNE'S mouth bloody, lips much swelled. Going ashore next day with a message from MR. GRANT & CAPT. MCDONNALD to WOOD, advising him to come in a canoe & receive his wife as became a husband, WOOD replied to deponant he would have nothing to say to her. Before THOMAS DALE, J.P.

Book Y, p. 338
20 & 21 May 1743
L & R
SOLOMON FREER, planter, of Johns Island, Colleton Co., to JOHN HEARN, hat maker, of James Island, Berkeley Co., for Ł 450 SC money, 100 a. on Johns Island, bounding NE & W on THOMAS ROBERTS; S on WILLIAM HOLMES. Witnesses: THOMAS WITTER, PETER HEARNE, JOSEPH SPENCER. Before JACOB MOTTE, J.P. JAMES HOME, Register.

Book Y, p. 345
31 Mar. & 1 Apr. 1743
L & R
JOHN SHEPPARD & FRANCIS SHEPPARD, executors of will of their father JOHN SHEPPARD, of Charleston, to FREDERICK GRIMKE, merchant, of Charleston, for Ł 1650 SC money, that house & lot or part of a lot formerly belonging to & occupied by JOHN SHEPPARD, fronting 50 ft. on N side Tradd Street, bounding E on 154 ft. on CAPT. FRANCIS BAKER; N & W on heirs of ELIAS HANCOCK; which lot, by will dated 15 Jan. 1737, JOHN SHEPPARD authorized his executors to sell; his wife to have the use of the house during her life & the money from the sale to go to his sons JOHN & FRANCIS. HANNAH SHEPPARD, wife of JOHN, died during his lifetime, & now they sell to GRIMKE. Witnesses: JACOB BRADWELL, JUSTINUS STOLL. Before JACOB MOTTE, J.P. JAMES HOME, Register.

Book Y, p. 352
1 Apr. 1743
Quitclaim
FRANCIS BAKER, gentleman, of Charleston, for Ł 5 paid by JOHN SHEPPARD & FRANCIS SHEPPARD, executors of will of their father JOHN SHEPPARD, releases to FREDERICK GRIMKE all claim to the W half of a quarter-part of a lot in Charleston. Whereas MARTHA GORING, widow, of Berkeley Co., by L & R dated 10 & 11 Jan. 1732 sold to JOHN SHEPPARD & FRANCIS BAKER, 1/4 of a lot in Charleston bounding S on JOHN SHEPPARD'S & FRANCIS BAKER'S lots; NE & W on ELIAS HANCOCK; being 98 ft. from E to W & 54 ft. from N to S; & whereas a clear division was afterwards made by SHEPPARD & BAKER, the E half, 49 ft. x 54 ft. & buildings thereon, bounding S on BAKER'S land, being allotted to BAKER; the W half, 49 ft. x 54 ft. with the buildings thereon, bounding S on SHEPPARD'S land, being allotted to SHEPPARD; & whereas JOHN SHEPPARD, by will dated 15 Jan. 1737 authorized his executors (after the death of his wife HANNAH) to sell the house & lot in which he dwelt, (the W half of the quarter-part being the N end), the money from the sale to go to his sons JOHN & FRANCIS; & whereas HANNAH, wife of JOHN SHEPPARD died in his lifetime; & the executors, by L & R dated 31 Mar. & 1 Apr. 1743, sold the house & lot on N side Tradd Street to GRIMKE; now, to remove all possible doubts or defects, BAKER renounces all claim to the W half o the 1/4 part of the lot. Witnesses: JACOB BRADWELL, JUSTINUS STOLL. Before JACOB MOTTE, J.P. JAMES HOME, Register.

Book Y, p. 359
14 & 15 Feb. 1739
L & R
JOHN ATCHISON, planter, to JOHN LINING, "pratitioner in Physick", for Ł 500 SC money, 440 a. in Craven Co., bounding NW on Washaw Creek; N on Santee River & marsh; E & S on Alligator Marsh; W on JOHN BENNETT; which land was tranted by his majesty to RICHARD ASH & WILLIAM LIVINGSTON, executors of will of SAMUEL ASH, & conveyed by them to JOHN ATTCHISON; also 795 a. of adjoining marsh land N of the 440 a.; bounding W on JOHN ATCHINSON'S marsh; SE on Alligator Creek; which tract was lately granted to ATCHISON. Witnesses: WILLIAM FREEMAN, CHARLES SHEPPARD. Before JAMES HOME, J.P. & Pub. Reg. Plat given.

Book Y, p. 364
JAMES SAVINEAU, planter, & JANE his wife, to

26 & 27 Apr. 1743   JOHN PERDRIAU, all of Craven Co., for Ł 1000
L & R   SC money, 2 plantations in Craven Co., 500 a.
                       bounding SW on JAMES GUERRY; NE on PETER PER-
DRIAU; & 243 a. bounding N on JAMES SAVINEAU; E on PAUL BRUNEAU; SW on
vacant land; NE on ABRAHAM PERDRIEU & vacant land. Witnesses: WILLIAM
BUCHANAN, JOHN FITCH, JR. Before WILLIAM WHITESIDE, J.P. JAMES HOME,
Register.

Book Y, p. 371   JOSHUA (JOSIAH) SANDERS, of Colleton Co., to
14 & 15 Apr. 1742   JERMYN WRIGHT, gentleman, for Ł 2200 currency,
L & R   480 a. in Colleton Co., bounding E on Pon Pon
                       River; W on BENJAMIN UEAP (?); N on ELIZABETH
CLIFT & JOHN HUNT; S on JOSEPH BOONS Barony. Witnesses: JAMES SKIRVING,
JOHN LAND. Before CULCHETH GOLIGHTLY, J.P. JAMES HOME, Register.

Book Y, p. 378   Whereas King GEORGE II by letters patent dated
13 June 1743   26 May. 1742, signed by Lt. Gov. WILLIAM BULL,
Deputation   appointed JAMES HOME, ESQ., of Berkeley Co.,
                       Public Register of SC; & whereas HOME with the
permission of the Lt. Gov. is going to leave SC for some time; now he appoints JAMES MICKIE, ESQ., of Charleston his deputy. Witnesses: JOHN
HUME, WILLIAM PLAYTERS. Before HECTOR BERENGER DE BEAUFAIN, J.P. JAMES
MICKIE, Dep. Pub. Reg.

Book Y, p. 379   MRS. ANNE WATKINSON, widow, residuary legatee
30 June 1742   & sole executrix of will of JOHN WATKINSON,
Letter of Attorney   mariner, of Parish of St. Anne, Co. of Middle-
                       sex, appeared before SAMUEL MARTYN, notary &
tabellion public, in London, & appointed JOHN NICKLESON, RICHARD SHUBRICK,
& THOMAS SHUBRICK, merchants, of Charleston, SC her attorneys to take
possession of & dispose of the estate of JOHN WATKINSON in SC. Witnesses: HENRY HARRAMOND, ROYER CLOAD. CLOAD appeared before ROBERT AUSTIN,
J.P. of Charleston. JAMES MICKIE, D.P.R.

Book Y, p. 383   ANNE WATKINSON, widow, residuary legatee, &
8 & 9 Mar. 1742   sole executrix of will of JOHN WATKINSON, mar-
L & R   iner, of St. Anne's Parish, Co. of Middlesex,
                       Great Britain, through her attorneys RICHARD
SHUBRICK & THOMAS SHUBRICK, merchants, of Charleston; to MOSES MITCHELL,
cordwainer, & MARY his wife, of Charleston; for Ł 1800 SC money, 1/2 of
the S half of lot #18 fronting 46-10/12 ft. on Union Street; bounding
114-1/2 ft. on Unity Alley. Whereas JOHN WATKINSON by L & R dated 12 &
13 Aug. 1726 purchased from JOHN SUMMERS, planter, & SUSANNAH his wife,
of Berkeley Co., a half of the S half of lot #18 in Charleston, bounding
N on a part of lot #18 belonging to GEORGE LEA; S on lot #17 called COD-
NER'S lot; fronting W 46-10/12 ft. on the street leading from Broad
Street, by MR. LOUGHTON'S house, to MR. AMORY, commonly called Union
Street; E on JAMES CROCKATT; & measuring 114-1/2 S along Unity Alley; &
whereas WATKINSON, by will dated 26 June 1740 & proved in Preogative
Court of Canterbury, bequeathed the residue of his real & personal estate
to his wife ANNE; now she sells to MITCHELL. Witnesses: CHARLES PINCKNEY,
THOMAS PINCKNEY. Before HENRY GIBBES, J.P. JAMES MICKIE, D.P. Reg.

Book Y, p. 392   (See Bk. R. p. 281). BENJAMIN WHITAKER, ESQ.,
14 June 1743   for Ł 1936 SC money, being principal & inter-
Assignment   est, assigns mortgage to ROBERT LADSON, execu-
                       tor of SAMUEL STOCK. Witnesses: THOMAS LEGARE,
JOHN HODSDEN. Before JAMES MICKIE, J.P. & D.P.R. On 8 May 1753 ANDREW
LETCH, administrator of ROBERT LADSON for himself & THOMAS & JAMES LADSON
declared mortgage paid off. Witness: WILLIAM HOPTON.

Book y, p. 393   CRAFTON HERWON, vintner, of Craven Co., to
19 May 1743   ELIAS HORRY & DANIEL HORRY, planters, as secu-
L & R by Mortgage   rity on bond of even date in penal sum of
                       Ł 1365:11-1/2 for payment of Ł 682:10:5:3 cur-
rency on 19 May 1743; lot #109, containing 1/2 a., in Georgetown, Craven
Co., bounding NW on Broad Street; NE on lot #110; N on High Street; S on
lot #85. Witnesses: ALEXANDER BROWN, JOSEPH DUBOURDIEU. Before WILLIAM
WHITESIDE, J.P. JAMES MICKIE, Dep. Pub. Reg.

Book Y, p. 398   JOHN PERDRIAU, saddler, to GEORGE SIMONETT,
8 & 9 June 1743   planter, both of Berkeley Co., for ₤ 1200 SC
L & R   money, 2 plantations in Craven Co., 500 a.
                        bounding SW on JAMES GUERRY; NE on PETER PER-
DRIAU; 243 a. bounding N on JAMES SAVINEAU; E on PAUL BRUNEAU; SW on va-
cant land; NE on ABRAHAM PERDRIAU & vacant land. Witnesses: THOMAS COOP-
ER, JOHN RAMSAY, DAVID CHRISTINA. Before HENRY GIBBES, J.P. JAMES MICK-
IE, D.P.R.

Book Y, p. 404   JOHN MEEK, bricklayer, & SARAH his wife, to
10 & 11 June 1743   HUGH CARTWRIGHT, bricklayer, all of Charleston,
L & R by Mortgage   as security on bond dated 10 June 1743 in pe-
                        nal sum of ₤ 3000 for payment of ₤ 1500 SC
money with interest on 10 June 1747; that parcel of land in Charleston
occupied by SAMUEL PERKINS, cocah-maker; bounding S 130 ft. 9 in. on
THOMAS ELLERY; N on land occupied by PETER SHAW; E on the garden fence of
THOMAS COOPER; W 50 ft. on the great street leading from Ashley River, by
the Market Place & Presbyterian Meeting House. Witnesses: MARY HURST,
JAMES DRUMMOND. Before JAMES GREEME, J.P. JAMES MICKIE, D.P.R. On 26
Nov. 1748 HUGH CARTWRIGHT acknowledged to have received full satisfaction
of mortgage from JAMES HUNTER.

Book Y, p. 410   Rec'd. June 11, 1743 from ROBERT WRIGHT, ESQ.,
                        & others possessors of 2500 a. of land, part
of Ashley Barony, formerly sold to MR. JACOB SATUR ₤ 26:11:8 sterling on
account of rent due thereon. SAMUEL WRAGG. Witnesses: WILLIAM OSWALD,
ADAM BEAUCHAMP. Before JAMES MICKIE, J.P. & D.P. Reg.

Book Y, p. 411   WILLIAM EDDINGS, SR., planter, & THEODORA his
7 July 1742   wife, of Colleton Co., of 1st part; WILLIAM
L & R Tripartite in   EDDINGS, JR. eldest son of said WILLIAM, plant-
Trust   er, of 2nd part; ABRAHAM EDDINGS, only son &
                        heir of ABRAHAM EDDINGS, planter, of 3rd part.
Whereas WILLIAM EDDINGS, planter, father of WILLIAM, JR. owned 210 a. on
Edisto Island, originally granted to JOHN FRAMPTON on 15 Sept. 1704, then
bounding N & W on THOMAS DAWS; E on vacant land; S on Old Edisto Creek; &
by deed of feoffment dated 25 Feb. 1707 conveyed to EDDINGS; also 290 a.
in Colleton Co., bounding NW on Toobedoe Creek; E on JOSEPH TOWNSEND; S
on other land of WILLIAM EDDINGS; W & SW on WILLIAM DONHOLME; which 290 a.
was originally granted to EDDINGS on 12 Jan. 1705; & whereas said EDDINGS
by will dated 28 Mar. 1712 bequeathed to his son ABRAHAM (since deceased)
2 tracts of 210 & 290 a.; & to son WILLIAM (after several other legacies)
the remaining part of his estate; & whereas WILLIAM EDDINGS, the testator,
died without altering his will & the reversion was in the said WILLIAM
EDDINGS, & ABRAHAM EDDINGS (deceased) was only tenant for life; & after
the death of ABRAHAM the fee-simple became vested in WILLIAM EDDINGS, eldest son & heir; & whereas ABRAHAM EDDINGS (deceased) had a son ABRAHAM,
his only son & child, party hereto; now WILLIAM EDDINGS, for natural love
& affection for his nephew & for valuable considerations, & with the consent of his wife THEODORA, & of WILLIAM EDDINGS, JR., his son, grants
WILLIAM EDDINGS, JR. the 2 tracts of 210 & 290 a., for the use & behoof
of ABRAHAM EDDINGS during his natural life. Witnesses: RICHARD ASH, MAR-
THA ASH, JOSEPH ASH. Before JOSEPH WILKINSON, J.P. JAMES MICKIE, Dep.
Pub. Reg.

Book Y, p. 418   The Hon. JOHN COLLETON, ESQ., of Fairlawn Bar-
15 & 16 Mar. 1742   ony, St. John's Parish, Berkeley Co., to NA-
                        THANIEL BROUGHTON, ESQ., of St. Johns Parish,
for ₤ 1266 currency, 211 a., being the front of 300 a. & part of Fairlawn
Barony; bounding S on other land of NATHANIEL BROUGHTON, called the Mul-
berry Tract; SW on the 300 a. tract; E & NE on W branch of the T of Cooper River; N on part of Fairlawn Barony & said branch of Cooper River.
Whereas JOHN COLLETON (by virtue of & under the patent or grant from the
Lords Proprs. to SIR JOHN COLLETON, Baronet, for 12,000 a. on the W
branch of the T of Cooper River, commonly called Fairlawn Barony) owns
the 211 a., being the "front" of 300 a., a part of the Barony conveyed by
SIR JOHN COLLETON to the Hon. THOMAS BROUGHTON, ESQ., father of said NA-
THANIEL BROUGHTON; now COLLETON sells to NATHANIEL BROUGHTON. Witnesses:
JOHN HENTIE, ANN LEBAS, THOMAS SABB. Before THOMAS MONCK, J.P. JAMES
MICKIE, D.P.R. At the request of the Hon. JOHN COLLETON & of NATHANIEL

BROUGHTON, JOHN GOUGH, surv. on 14 Mar. 1742/3 re-surveyed the 300 a. formerly purchased by the Hon. THOMAS BROUGHTON from SIR PETER COLLETON & the other part contains 211 a. sold to CAPT. BROUGHTON by the Hon. JOHN COLLETON, ESQ., butting E on the W branch of Cooper River; W on said BROUGHTON; N on said COLLETON; it being all river swamp. (Plat).

Book Y, p. 425
2 & 3 July 1743
L & R

HENRY FERGUSON, planter, & SARAH (her mark) his wife, to JOHN MCKEWN, weaver, all of St. Bartholomew's Parish, Colleton Co., for Ł 200 SC money, 200 a. in Colleton Co., bounding N on HUGH CAMPBEL; NW & SW on JOB ROTHMAHLER; NE on vacant land. Witnesses: ALEXANDER MCLROY, JACOB PFFISTER (FISTER). Before CULCHETH GOLIGHTLY, J.P. JAMES MICKIE, D.P.R.

Book Y, p. 431
12 Mar. 1742
Mortgage

ARTHUR FOSTER, planter, to SAMUEL EVELEIGH, executor of estate of SAMUEL EVELEIGH, as security on bond of even date in penal sum of Ł 402:12:6 for payment of Ł 201:6:3 SC money on 12 Mar. 1734; 54 a. within a short mile of Georgetown, Winyaw, bounding E on the Broad Path frome Georgetown to Santee; W on JOHN DEXTER; S on CAPT. JOHN WHITE; also a corner lot #56 in Georgetown, fronting Prince & Orange Streets. Witnesses: WILLIAM WHITESIDE, THOMAS LAROCHE. Before JACOB MOTTE, J.P. JAMES MICKIE, Dep. Pub. Reg.

Book Y, p. 433
23 & 24 Mar. 1736
L & R

EDMUND BELLINGER, ESQ., & ELIZABETH his wife, of Berkeley Co., to JOHN BEE, JR., planter, of Colleton Co., for Ł 1400 SC money, 770 a., English measure, in Colleton Co., bounding N on JAMES COCKRAN; E on JOHN BEE; W & S on Pon Pon River. Witnesses: HENRY LIVINGSTON, JAMES SCARLETTE. Before THOMAS DRAYTON, J.P. JAMES MICKIE, D.P.R.

Book Y, p. 442
4 July 1743
Renunciation of Dower

ELIZABETH BELLINGER, widow of EDMUND BELLINGER, releases to JOHN BEE, all her right & title of dower to the above mentioned 770 a. Before THOMAS DRAYTON, J.P. JAMES MICKIE, D.P.R.

Book Y, p, 443
12 Feb. 1742
Deed of Gift

ROBERT JOHNSON (JOHNSTON), planter, & SARAH his wife, to JOHN NAILOR, & MARY his wife; all of Berkeley Co., for love & affection for their daughter MARY & for other considerations; that part of lot #73 in Charleston, which JONATHAN COLLINGS (husband of said SARAH) purchased jointly from their sister MRS. MARY BASDEN; fronting N 20 ft. on Tradd Street; bounding S on WILLIAM PINCKNEY; E on the Rev. MR. GEEY; W on part same lot. Witnesses: FRANCIS BREMAR, ROBERT HOW. Before HENRY GIBBES, J.P. JAMES MICKIE, D.P.R.

Book Y, p. 445
20 & 21 June 1743
L & R

WILLIAM FORBES, planter, & CHARITY his wife, to WILLIAM FLEMING, merchant; all of Craven Co., for Ł 840 currency, 500 a. in Craven Co., on S side Black River, bounding E on Rice Bryer; W on ROBERT SCREVEN; S on vacant land. Witnesses: ANDREW JOHNSTON, ARCHIBALD KNOX. Before JOHN CLELAND, J.P. JAMES MICKIE, D.P.R.

Book Y, p. 452
15 & 16 May 1743
L & R

WILLIAM STEWART & ANN, his wife, of the Island of New Providence, by their attorneys JAMES OSMOND, GEORGE SEAMAN & JAMES MICKIE, of Charleston, to JOHN JOHNSTON, planter, of Granville Co., for Ł 2000 SC money. 2 tracts of land; 500 a. & 344 a., (844 a.), in Granville Co., known as Pocosabo Island, in Port Royall River. Whereas JOHN, Lord Carteret, Palatine, & the Lords Proprs. on 13 June 1717 by grant signed by COL. ROBERT DANIELL, Dep. Gov.; CHARLES HART, FRANCIS YONGE, COL. GEORGE CHICKEN & SAMUEL EVELEIGH, ESQRS., gave GEORGE LEVINGSTON 500 a. in Granville Co., & whereas, on 13 June 1716, JOHN, Lord Carteret, by COL. ROBERT DANIELL, Dep. Gov., & NICHOLAS TROTT, FRANCIS YONGE, SAMUEL EVELEIGH & THOMAS SMITH, ESQRS., granted GEORGE LEVINGSTON 344 a. in Granville Co., & whereas by L & R dated 2 & 3 Dec. 1717 GEORGE LEVINGSTON, merchant, of Berkeley Co., & MARY his wife, for Ł 633 currency sold the 2 tracts (Potosabo Island) to ARTHUR HALL, gentleman, of Colleton Co.; & whereas ARTHUR HALL by will dated 27 June 1732 devised

to his executors the 844 a. & another tract of 450 a. called Bowers Point
in trust for the use of his daughter ANN HALL & appointed his dear wife
MARTHA HALL, his beloved cousin (Law?) HENRY PERONNEAU, JAMES OSMOND &
JOHN RAVEN, ESQRS., his executors & executrix; & whereas ANN married WIL-
LIAM STEWART & they, by letter of attorney, 27 Dec. 1717 appointed OSMOND,
SEAMAN & MICKIE, their attorneys, to dispose of the 3 tracts (500, 344, &
450 a.); & whereas letters testamentary were granted by ROBERT JOHNSON,
Ordinary of the Province, to PERONNEAU, OSMOND & RAVEN, on 8 June 1733;
now WILLIAM & ANN STEWART (through their attorneys) sell Pocosabo Island
to JOHN JOHNSTON. Witnesses: JOHN JOHNSTON, JOHN NEUFVILLE, JR. Before
ROBERT AUSTIN, J.P. JAMES MICKIE, D.P.R.

Book Y, p. 467   HENRY FLETCHER, gentleman, to JAMES ROUSHAM,
21 Jan. 1742   carpenter, both of Dorchester, Berkeley Co.,
Mortgage   for Ł 375 currency, lot #9 in Dorchester bound-
                       ing SW on WILLIAM CATTELL; NW on Market Square;
NE on a kitchen on lot #8 belonging to CAPT. RICHARD BAKER; as by L & R
dated 21 Jan. 1742 from ROUSHAM to FLETCHER. Date of redemption not giv-
en. Witnesses: JOSEPH ARDEN, EDWARD (his mark) VANVELSON. Before J.
SKENE, J.P. JAMES MICKIE, D.P.R.

Book Y, p. 470   ROBERT MINORS, shipwright, of Craven Co., to
24 & 25 Nov. 1742   JOSEPH HUGGINS, planter, as security on bond
L & R by Mortgage   of even date in penal sum of Ł 850 for payment
                       of Ł 425 currency on 24 Nov. 1744; lot #116
(1/2 a.) in Georgetown, Craven Co., bounding NE on High Street; SE on
Queen Street; SW on lot #92; NW on lot #115. Date of redemption 25 Nov.
1744. Witnesses: JOHN SKRINE, THOMAS MCKEITHEN, WILLIAM BUCHANAN. Before THOMAS BLYTHE, J.P. JAMES MICKIE, D.P.R.

Book Y, p. 475   ISAAC PERONNEAU, silver-smith, & MARY his wife,
16 & 17 Aug. 1743   of Berkeley Co., to SARAH STOUTENBURGH & JOHN
L & R by Mortgage   MCKENZIE, merchant, of Charleston, executor &
                       executrix of will of WILLIAM MCKENZIE, mer-
chant, as security on bond of even date in penal sum of Ł 481:12:8 for
payment of Ł 240:16:4 currency, with interest, on 1 Mar. next; 315 a. in
Berkeley Co., bounding NE on part of tract sold to WILLIAM MIDDLETON,
ESQ., SE on CAPT. JAMES MOORE; NW on JOHN BOISSAN; being part of 500 a.
granted ABRAHAM DELAPLAN. Whereas the Lords Proprs. on 9 Sept. 1696
granted ABRAHAM DELAPLAN 500 a. in Berkeley Co., bounding SE on CAPT.
JAMES MOORE; NW on JOHN BOISSAN & ABRAHAM DELAPLAN; SW & NE on land not
laid out; & whereas DELAPLAN (by the name of ABRAHAM FLOREE DELAPLAN,
gentleman) by will 2 Aug. 1721 devised to his loving brother ISAAC FLOREE
833 a. for his natural life; & after his (ISAAC'S) death to his granddaughter MARIAN (wife of TOBIAS FITCH) for her natural life; & after her
death, to his great-grandson STEPHEN FITCH; & by default of his heirs, to
great-granddaughter MARY FITCH; & by default, to said MARIAN for disposition, etc.; & whereas said MARIAN is "daughter of aforesaid MARION" & is,
together with ISAAC, legally possessed of the land by said will; & whereas MARY Married ISAAC PERONNEAU & has become party hereto; & whereas
ISAAC PERONNEAU is under bond to SARAH STOUTENBOURGH & JOHN MCKENZIE; now
he conveys 315 a. to them as security. Witnesses: JAMES MICKIE, WILLIAM
PLAYTERS. Before ALEXANDER STEWART, J.P. JAMES MICKIE, D.P.R. Witness:
FENWICKE BULL.

Book Y, p. 484   WILLIAM RHETT, ESQ., the elder, & SARAH his
3 & 4 Aug. 1716   wife, to WILLIAM RHETT the younger, gentleman,
L & R by Gift   only son of WILLIAM RHETT the elder & SARAH;
                       all of Charleston; for 5 shillings, & for nat-
ural love & affection & other considerations; half of lot #15 in Charleston, bounding E on the wharf on Cooper River; N on heirs of MARY NARY,
widow (formerly belonging to MARY CROSS, widow); S on other half of lot
#15; extending W 134 ft. & joining "unto the W unto the end that is part-
ed by a brick wall from the other part of said lot" & the buildings of
said half-lot, i.e., 1 large brick tenement fronting the Bay of Cooper
River, the kitchen, & several large storehouses built with brick & all
other buildings standing on the same; together with the bridge or wharf
fronting the brick tenement & extending into Charleston Harbour, being
lot #333. Witnesses: NICHOLAS TROTT, JAMES KINLOCH, MICHAEL COLE, JOHN
WALLIS, RICHARD ROWE. Before RICHARD ALLEIN, J.P. JAMES MICKIE, D.O.R.

Book Y, p. 495   WILLIAM RHETT, the younger, gentleman, to NICH-
4 & 5 Oct. 1717   OLAS TROTT, ESQ., & WILLIAM RHETT, the elder,
L & R in Trust   ESQ., all of Charleston, in consideration of a
                        marriage to be solemnized between WILLIAM
RHETT & MARY TROTT, daughter of NICHOLAS TROTT; & for love & affection
for MARY & to provide an estate for her should she survive him; that half
of lot #15 in Charleston bounding E on the wharf on Cooper River; N on
heirs of MARY NARY, widow (formerly belonging MARY CROSS, widow); S on
other half of lot; & extending W 134 ft. & joining at the W to the end
that is parted by a brick wall from the other half of said lot; & the
buildings thereon; i.e., 1 large brick tenement fronting the Bay, the
kitchen & several large storehouses built with brick, & all other buildings; also the bridge or wharf fronting the brick tenement & extending
into Cooper River, being lot #333. Witnesses: JOHN BEE, NEVILL KIDWELL,
JOHN WALLIS, TIFFORD ATTWELL. RICHARD ROWE. Before RICHARD ALLEIN, J.P.
JAMES MICKIE, D.P.R.

Book Y, p. 506   SARAH TROTT (lately SARAH RHETT0 sole execu-
10 & 11 June 1743   trix, & devisee of will of NICHOLAS TROTT,
L & R by Gift   ESQ., of Charleston, to THOMAS FRANKLAND
                        (FRANKLIN), ESQ., & SARAH his wife, (lately
SARAH RHETT, granddaughter of said SARAH TROTT) & MARY JANE RHETT (also
granddaughter of said SARAH TROTT, & sister of said SARAH FRANKLAND); in
consideration of her natural love & affection for her grand-children
(SARAH FRANKLAND & MARY JANE RHETT); lot #113 fronting E 60 ft. on Church
Street; 60 ft. deep; bounding N on part said lot belonging formerly to
DR. GEORGE FRANKLIN, lately to ANNE LEBRASSEUR; S on BARNARD SCHENCKINGH;
W on RICHARD BERESFORD (formerly BARNARD SCHENCKINGH); to be divided
equally between them. Whereas the Lords Proprs. on 14 Sept. 1693 granted
NICHOLAS BARLEYCORN lot #113 in Charleston, bounding N on little street
leading from Cooper River by the lot then belonging to DAVID MAYBANK into
the country; S on the lot of MR. SCHENCKINGH; E on a street leading by
the lots then belonging to WILLIAM CHAPMAN, BURTELAH BARTELL & others to
CAPT. DANIEL'S swamp; W on a lot belonging to MR. SCHENCKINGH; & whereas
part of lot #113 (i.e., 60 ft. on the street leading by the lots of CHAP-
MAN, BARTELL & others to CAPT. DANIEL'S swamp; & running back from said
street to W side of said lot 60 ft.) by several mesne conveyances became
vested in COL. WILLIAM RHETT, which part is bounding N on the part belonging to DR. GEORGE FRANKLIN (lately to ANNE LEBRASSEUR); S on BARNARD
SCHENCKINGH; E on the street that leads to St. Philip's Church; W on RICH-
ARD BERESFORD (formerly BERNARD SCHENCKINGH; & whereas WILLIAM RHETT, by
will dated 6 July 1722, appointed his then wife SARAH RHETT (now SARAH
TROTT) sole executrix to dispose of all his real estate, except as excepted; & whereas SARAH RHETT, during her widowhood, by L & R dated 1 & 2 Mar.
1725 conveyed to NICHOLAS TROTT that part of lot #113; & whereas she later married NICHOLAS TROTT; & he, by will dated 14 Aug. 1739, bequeathed
the residue of his estate (after paying debts) to his loving wife, SARAH,
party hereto; now she gives the lot to her 2 granddaughters, to be divided equally. SARAH TROTT, however, to enjoy the rents & profits during
her natural life. Witnesses: CATHERINE MOORE, SARAH COKE, MARY CLARK.
Before JAMES WRIGHT, J.P. JAMES MICKIE, D.P.R.

Book Y, p. 517   BENJAMIN WHITAKER, ESQ., to JOHN HUTCHINSON,
2 & 3 June 1736   gentleman, for ₺ 2600 SC money (paid or accur-
L & R   ed to be paid), 950 a. in Colleton Co., grant-
                        ed him 7 Aug. 1735; bounding N on part of JOHN
SEABROOK'S Island; E on Ashepoo River; S on CAPT. THOMAS FLEMING & JOHN
DEARE. Witnesses: JOHN GUERARD, WILLIAM FREEMAN. Before ALEXANDER CRA-
MAHE, J.P. Memorial entered in Auditor's office 29 Aug. 1740 by JAMES
ST. JOHN, Dep. Aud. JAMES MICKIE, D.P.R.

Book Y, p. 524   JOHN WHITE, planter, of Craven Co., to SABINA
31 Aug. & 1 Sept. 1743 LYNCH, of Berkeley Co., widow & administratrix
L & R by Mortgage   of rights & credits of COL. THOMAS LYNCH; as
                        security on bond of even date in penal sum of
₺ 10,111 for payment of ₺ 5055:11:6 currency with interest on 1 Sept.
1744; 500 a. in Craven Co., on W side NW branch of Black River, bounding
W on JOHN WHITE; S on JOSIAS GAR. DUPRÉ; N on JOHN WHITE (originally
granted CHRISTOPHER BUTTLER); also 289 a. in Craven Co., bounding E on N
branch of Black River; W on DOUGAL MCKEITHEN; N on WILLIAM FORBES; S on

71

JOHN WHITE (formerly granted RICHARD WIGG); also 1000 a. in Craven Co.,
near Horse Savanna, bounding N on HENRY SHERRIFF, other sides on vacant
land. Witnesses: COL. ANTHONY WHITE, ELIZABETH FLEMING. Before WILLIAM
FLEMING, J.P. JAMES MICKIE, D.P.R.

Book Y, p. 533   JOHN BASSNETT, planter, of Williamsburgh, SC
16 Nov. 1739   to ROBERT PRINGLE, merchant, of Charleston, as
Mortgage   security on bond of even date in penal sum of
                       L 8000 for payment of L 4000 currency, with
interest, on 1 Mar. next, 1/2 a. town lot #5 near the Kings Tree in Williamsburgh, with the dwelling house, etc. Witnesses: WILLIAM SMITH, WIL-
LIAM ALLEN. Before ALEXANDER STEWART, J.P. JAMES MICKIE, D.P.R.

Book Y, p. 535   WILLIAM WILKINS, planter, & SARAH his wife;
23 & 24 Sept. 1743   OBADIAH WILKINS, planter, & ELIZABETH his wife;
L & R   BETHEL DEWES & MARGARET his wife, all of SC;
                       to SAMUEL ADAMS, merchant, of Kingstown, Ja-
maican money, that piece of ground in Kingstown, 30 ft. from E to W; 90
ft. from N to S, bounding E on Prince Street; W on JAMES STEWART; N on
Water Lane; S on Harbour Street, which lot formerly belonged to JOHN
CROSKEYS, of Charleston, SC & by his will dated 15 Mar. 1722 bequeathed
(equally) to SARAH CROSKEY'S (then his wife, now SARAH WILKINS) & his 2
daughters, ELIZABETH & MARGARET, parties hereto. Witnesses: JAMES HAMIL-
TON, GEORGE MATHEWES. Before JACOB MOTTE, J.P. JAMES MICKIE, D.P.R.

Book Y, p. 542   ELISHA BUTLER, & WILLIAM BUTLER, of Berkeley
1 & 2 June 1739   Co., executors of will of RICHARD BUTLER, to
L & R   JOSEPH CANTEY, of Craven Co., for L 62 curren-
                       cy, Mount Hope Plantation, on N side Santee
River, Craven Co., bounding S on a Savannah, other sides on land not laid
out; being 560 a. granted 24 Dec. 1730 to Landgrave EDMUND BELLINGER (son
& heir of Landgrave EDMUND BELLINGER); & sold by EDMUND BELLINGER & ELIZ-
ABETH his wife, on 22 Feb. 1730 to RICHARD BUTLER; who, by will, authoriz-
ed his executrix to sell. Witnesses: RIBTON HUTCHINSON, FREDERICK GRIMKE,
CHARLES CANTEY. Before ROBERT AUSTIN, J.P. JAMES MICKIE, D.P.R.

DEEDS BOOK "Z"
NOV. 1743 - OCT. 1744

Book Z, p. 1   WILLIAM POOLE, gentleman, & HANNAH his wife,
15 Oct. 1743   of Craven Co., SC to CAPT. DAVID ROSE, ship-
L & R   master, of Inverness, North Britain, now from
                       London, for L 500 SC money, 500 a., English
measure, in Craven Co., bounding NW on JONAH COLLINS; SW on Little PeeDee
River; other sides on vacant land; according to plat attached to grant
dated 13 July 1737; free from HANNAH"S claim of dower. Witnesses: THOMAS
MITCHELL, ABRAHAM WARNOCK, JOHN HITCHCOCK. Before WILLIAM WHITESIDE,
J.P. JAMES MICKIE, D.P.R.

Book Z, p. 8   SARAH BLAKEWEY, widow of Charleston, appointed
10 Oct. 1741   her loving friend CHARLES PINCKNEY, ESQ., of
Power of Attorney   Charleston, her attorney, with authority to
                       dispose of her real estate in SC. Witnesses:
SUSANNA GREGORY, ROBERT AUSTIN. Before HENRY GIBBES, J.P. JAMES MICKIE,
D.P.R.

Book Z, p. 10   SARAH BLAKEWEY, lately of Charleston, widow,
27 & 28 Jan. 1742   devisee, residuary legatee, & sole executrix
L & R   of will of WILLIAM BLAKEWEY, ESQ., by her at-
                       torney, CHARLES PINCKNEY, to NOAH SERRÉ,
planter, of Craven Co., for L 400 British, the S part of a part of lot
#33 fronting E 50 ft. on the Bay of Charleston, formerly occupied by the
Hon. JOHN HAMMERTON; bounding S 206-1/2 ft. on ISAAC HOLMES; W on JOHN
SIMMONS; N on the part sold by WILLIAM BLAKEWEY to the Hon. JOSEPH WRAGG;
also the shole land before the same, down to low water mark. Whereas
WILLIAM BLAKEWEY owned the S part of lot #33, fronting E 78 ft. on the
Bay & running the full depth of the lot, & also owned the shole land in
front; & whereas by will dated 1 July 1727 he ordered the land sold & the

money applied to payment of his debts; making his wife SARAH residuary legatee & appointing SARAH, his wife, & JOHN DANIELL, executrix & executor; & whereas SARAH paid off the debts; now she sells part of the lot to NOAH SERRE. Witnesses: FRANCIS GUICHARD, THOMAS PINCKNEY. Before HENRY GIBBES, J.P. JAMES MICKIE, D.P.R.

Book Z, p. 19
16 & 17 May 1743
L & R

GEORGE CHICKEN, planter, & LYDIA his wife, of St. James Goose Creek Parish, Berkeley Co., to NOAH SERRE, ESQ., of St. James Santee Parish, Craven Co., for ₺ 3100 currency, 2 tracts of land; 1 of 100 a., the other containing 797 a., or 1050 a. less 253 a. sold to JAMES KINLOCK. Whereas the Lords Proprs. on 12 Jan. 1705 granted THOMAS BELLAMY 100 a. in Berkeley Co., bounding NE on DANIEL DEAN; other sides on THOMAS BELLAMY; & he devised the 100 a. to his wife CATHERINE, who later married COL. CHICKEN by whom she had several children; & whereas she died intestate the 100 a. were inherited by her eldest son & heir-at-law, GEORGE CHICKEN; & whereas the Lords Proprs. on 12 Jan. 1706 granted CATHERINE BELLAMY, then a widow, 1050 a. in Berkeley Co., bounding N on said 100 a. & on THOMAS BAKER, DANIEL DEAN, WILLIAM NORMAN, DANIEL MCDANIEL & THOMAS JONES; W on CAPT. WILLIAM HEWITT & JOHN STROUD; S on ROGER GOFF; E on WILLIAM MOORE & land not laid out; which tract descended to her son GEORGE CHICKEN; & whereas he sold the Hon. JAMES KINLOCK, ESQ., 253 a. of that tract; now he sells the 100 a. tract & the 797 a. to NOAH SERRE; the 797 a. now bounding N on the 100 a. & on DEWARD KEATING, estate of JOB ROTHMAHLER, RAGBY, RICHARD SINGLETON & JAMES KINLOCK; S on ROBERT HUME; E on JOSEPH NORMAN. Witnesses to deed: PETER HUME, ANN HUME, THOMAS ELING; to receipt, ABRAHAM CROFT, GEORGE HUNTER. Before HENRY GIBBES, J.P. JAMES MICKIE, D.P.R.

Book Z, p. 27
4 Aug. 1743
Bill of Sale

THOMAS LOOPE (LOUP), wheelmaker & freeholder of town of Frederica, St. Simon's Island, Colony only of Georgia, to CAPT. ADAM MCDONALD, for ₺ 8 British money, leased for 21 years, his lot on N side of Frederica between the lots of DANIEL CARNELL & ERNEST AMBROSIUS DETZNER, in which street FRANCES MOORE'S lot (formerly DR. LAPELL) begins "that side of the street from the W end thereof", being the 2nd lot down, from FRANCIS MOORE'S lot where CAPT. HORTON now lives; after all out-lots, lands, or tenements in the Colony granted to LOOPE; after the 21 years LOOPE bequeaths such property to CAPT. MCDONALD. Witnesses: ROBERT PATERSON, naval officer; THOMAS WALKER, ALEXANDER MACCAULAY; THOMAS HIRDE ?, constable, WILLIAM ABBOTT. JAMES MICKIE, D.P.R.

Book Z, p. 29
24 Jan. 1742
Bill of Sale

RENE (his mark) MERCHAND, planter, to GABRIEL GUIGNARD, cooper, of Charleston, for ₺ 1000 currency, 810 a. in Berkeley Co., in 3 tracts; 210 a., bounding N on JAMES TILLER; E on HENRY RUSSELL; S & W on vacant land; also 500 a. bounding N on THOMAS COX, JAMES TILLY, SR., & LAMBERT SAUNDERS: S on JOHN MILLS; E on HENRY RUSSELL; W on vacant land; also 100 a. bounding N on MAJ. CHARLES COLLETON; S on WILLIAM BETTISON; E on MR. LEBOS; W on THOMAS COX. Witnesses: ROBERT BLYTH, JEAN LOUIS POYAS. Before JAMES MICKIE, D.P.R.

Book Z, p. 32
24 Jan. 1743
Bill of Sale

RENE MERCHAND to GABRIEL GUIGNARD. Same as above except year 1743 given instead of 1742.

Book Z, p. 35
28 June 1719
Bill of Sale

RICHARD (his mark) HEATLEY, planter, & MARY (her mark) his wife, to his daughter, RACHEL HEATLEY (with MARY'S consent), for ₺ 10 SC money, 60 a., English measure, in Berkeley Co., bounding NE on heirs of BENJAMIN SIMONS (formerly MARY ANNANT?); SW on THOMAS LYNE. Witnesses: JOSEPH (his mark) SPENCER, WILLIAM MOORE. On 2 Sept. 1742 MRS. MARY RUSSELL (formerly said MARY HEATLEY wife of said RICHARD HEATLEY) acknowledged before GEORGE HAIG, J.P. & acknowledged above sale. JAMES MICKIE, D.P.R.

Book Z, p. 37
1 Aug. 1743
L & R

CAPT. HUGH HEXT, & SUSANNAH his wife, to JOHN FENDIN, of St. Helena, Granville Co., for ₺ 640 currency, 320 a. on St. Helena Island, bounding N on JOSEPH CELIA; W on Port Royall

the Less; S on JOHN CHAPLIN; E on other half of original 640 a. granted
by Gov. ROBERT GIBBES & the Lords Proprs. to EDWARD & HUGH HEXT & bequeathed to his nephew HUGH HEXT, party hereto, by said EDWARD. Witnesses: JOHN HILL, JACOB WAIGHT, JOHN FENDIN, JR. Before HENRY GIBBES, J.P.
JAMES MICKIE, D.P.R.

Book Z, p. 44   RALPH IZARD, ESQ., to his oldest son, HENRY
4 & 5 Sept. 1739   IZARD, gentleman, (& his male heirs), both of
Deed of Gift   St. James Goose Creek, Berkeley Co., for natu-
                       ral love & affection & other considerations,
for 6 plantations in St. Andrews Parish, Berkeley Co., 1000 a. b unding
NE on Landgrave THOMAS SMITH; E & SE on EDWARD WEEKLY & WILLIAM DRY; S &
SW on WILLIAM WILLIAMS & THOMAS PINCKNEY; N & W on vacant land; 100 a.
bounding W on WILLIAM DRY; NW on CHRISTOPHER SMITH; E on WILLIAM WILLIAMS,
ESQ.; S on ARTHUR LAUGHARNE; 70 a. bounding SE & NE on RALPH IZARD; NW on
Landgrave THOMAS SMITH; SW on the Rev. MR. EBENEZER TAYLOR; 120 a. bounding W on JOHN & BENJAMIN CATTELL; S on MANLEY WILLIAMS; other sides on
RALPH IZARD; 30 a. bounding S on the 120 a., other sides on vacant land;
160 a. bounding N on Landgrave THOMAS SMITH'S land known as "Jeoffords";
E on RALPH IZARD (bought from Hinsoydah-English); S on RALPH IZARD
(bought from THOMAS PINCKNEY); W on JONATHAN FITCH; making 1 tract of
1480 a. now commonly called "Camp Plantation"; free from claim of dower
by MAGDELENE ELIZABETH, wife of RALPH IZARD. Proviso: whenever RALPH
IZARD shall by sufficient conveyance or by will conveys to said HENRY
IZARD the capital messuage, houses, etc., together with the plantation on
which it stands, on which RALPH IZARD usually lives, near Goose Creek
Bridge, that HENRY IZARD shall convey the 6 plantations to CHARLES IZARD,
second son of RALPH, or to such person named by RALPH IZARD. HENRY assents. Witnesses: SUSANNAH LANSAC, SAMUEL GODIN, JR., ALEXANDER CRAMAHE.
Before JAMES MICKIE, J.P. & D.P.R.

Book Z, p. 53   HENRY IZARD, gentleman, eldest son & heir ap-
25 Sept. 1739   parent of RALPH IZARD, both of St. James Goose
Lease in Trust   Creek Parish, to NATHANIEL BROUGHTON, ANDREW
                       BROUGHTON, & GABRIEL MANIGAULT, ESQRS., of
Berkeley Co., the "Camp Plantation" in St. Andrews Parish consisting of 6
plantations, total 1100 a. bounding E on Landgrave THOMAS SMITH, EDWARD
WEEKLEY & WILLIAM DRY; S on WILLIAM BULL, W on EDMUND BELLINGER, PETER
CATTELL & ROGER SAUNDERS; N on the "Jeoffards" tracts; under conditions
mentioned in release following. Witnesses: DANIEL (?) DWIGHT, THOMAS
BROUGHTON. Before ALEXANDER CRAMAHE, J.P.

Book Z, p. 55   HENRY IZARD, gentleman, eldest son & heir ap-
26 Sept. 1739   parent of RALPH IZARD, of St. James Goose
Marriage Settlement   Creek Parish, of 1st part; MARGARET JOHNSON,
                       eldest daughter & devisee of Gov. ROBERT JOHN-
SON, of 2nd part; NATHANIEL BROUGHTON, ANDREW BROUGHTON & GABRIEL MANI-
GAULT, ESQRS., of 3rd part. Whereas a marriage is intended between HENRY
IZARD & MARGARET JOHNSON; & HENRY will be entitled to, & will receive
from MARGARET Ł 1500 British, 4 slaves, certain jewels & personal ornaments formerly belonging to her mother & devised to MARGARET by her father; & whereas all parties have agreed that HENRY during his natural
life shall have the use of the Ł 1500 & the 4 slaves; & that the Ł 1500
the 4 slaves & the jewels & personal ornaments should be secured by HENRY
to MARGARET in case she should survive him & she should have immediate
possession on HENRY'S death; should MARGARET die before HENRY, leaving
issue, she to have power to make a will & bequeath the Ł 1500, the 4
slaves, the jewels & her fortune amoung such issue as she may desire, not
to take effect, however, until after HENRY'S death; in default of her
will her property to be equally divided amongst her children; should MAR-
GARET die, without issue, in HENRY'S lifetime, the property to be HENRY'S.
Now to carry out this agreement, & in consideration of the intended marriage portion, & for making provisions for MARGARETS support should she
survive HENRY, he agrees with the 2 BROUGHTONS & MANIGAULT that should
the marriage take place & MARGARET die before HENRY, leaving issue, she
may by her will bequeath or charge HENRY'S estate with, said Ł 1500, 4
slaves & their increase, the jewels ornaments & fortune of MARGARET (ef-
fective after HENRY'S death) to her children as she deems fit; HENRY to
fulfil the will; should she leave no will, HENRY to divide her fortune
equally amongst such children; should MARGARET outlive HENRY to bequeath

MARGARET'S fortune to her; should MARGARET die, without issue, before HEN-
RY then HENRY to have her property; as security for keeping the agreements HENRY conveys to the 2 BROUGHTONS & MANIGAULT, the Camp Plantation
of 1100 a., bounding E on Landgrave THOMAS SMITH, EDWARD WEEKLEY & WIL-
LIAM DRY; S on WILLIAM BULL, W on EDMUND BELLINGER, PETER CATTELL & ROGER
SAUNDERS; N on "Jeoffards"; & delivers to them 30 Negro slaves, in trust,
according to agreements. Should HENRY'S executors after his death, not
give MARGARET her fortune they shall sell Camp Plantation & as many of
the slaves as necessary to obtain Ł 1500, etc. Should HENRY, after marriage, dispose of the plantation or any of the 30 slaves he shall give
the trustees notice & shall convey to them others of equal value. Witnesses: DANIEL DWIGHT, THOMAS BROUGHTON. Before ALEXANDER CRAMAHE, J.P.
JAMES MICKIE, D.P.R.

Book Z, p. 68
2 Dec. 1743
Notice to Change
Conveyance

HENRY IZARD (see p. 55) notifies NATHANIEL
BROUGHTON & GABRIEL MANIGAULT to convey the
Goose Creek Plantation instead of Camp Plantation. Whereas in the marriage settlement referred to it was provided that should IZARD
decide (after marriage) to dispose of Camp Plantation or any of the 30
Negroes he would convey other land or slaves of equal value to the trustees; & whereas the marriage took place & HENRY & MARGARET had 1 daughter,
MARGARET, & 1 son, RALPH, & MARGARET (HENRY'S wife) died; now HENRY IZARD
wants the 1100 a. Camp Plantation conveyed to him so that he may convey
it to his brother CHARLES IZARD, in accordance with the will of their father, RALPH IZARD; & wants to dispose of the slave AESOP because of stub-
borness & rebellion (1 of the 30); & HENRY conveys to the trustees his
capital messuage, tec., on his plantation, also the plantation on which
his father (RALPH) lived, & Negro slave "JULY". Witnesses: THOMAS BROUGH-
TON, CHARLES PINCKNEY. Before ALEXANDER CRAMAHE, J.P. JAMES MICKIE,
D.P.R.

Book Z, p. 73
7 & 8 Dec. 1743
L & R

NATHANIEL BROUGHTON & GABRIEL MANIGAULT, (AN-
DREW BROUGHTON being dead) trustees, release
to HENRY IZARD (see foregoing papers, page 55-
73) the Camp Plantation & the slave AESOP.
Witnesses: HENRY MIDDLETON, MORGAN SABB, CHARLES PINCKNEY, THOMAS BROUGH-
TON, JR. Before ALEXANDER CRAMAHE, J.P. JAMES MICKIE, D.P.R.

Book Z, p. 83
5 & 6 Dec. 1743
Settlement of Goose
Creek Plantation

See foregoing pages. HENRY IZARD to NATHANIEL
BROUGHTON & GABRIEL MANIGAULT, trustees. HEN-
RY'S mansion house on his St. James Goose
Creek Plantation where his father RALPH IZARD
lived & died; also the 950 a. on which the
mansion stands; also his tracts of 500 a., & 115 a. adjoining the 950 a.
Witnesses: HENRY MIDDLETON, MORGAN SABB, CHARLES PINCKNEY. Before ALEX-
ANDER CRAMAHE, J.P. JAMES MICKIE, D.P.R.

Book Z, p. 94
7 & 8 Dec. 1743
L & R

See foregoing pages. HENRY IZARD, ESQ., of
St. James Goose Creek, to his brother CHARLES
IZARD, for natural love & affection & to carry
out their father's will (RALPH IZARD'S) 6
plantations (p. 44). Witnesses: HENRY MIDDLETON, MORGAN SABB, CHARLES
PINCKNEY. Before ALEXANDER CRAMAHE, J.P. JAMES MICKIE, D.P.R.

Book Z, p. 101
17 June 1743
Release

DAVID LEWIS, planter, & SIDNEY (her mark) LEW-
IS, to SAMUEL WILDS, both of Craven Co., for
Ł 60 proclamation money, 250 a. granted to
LEWIS by letters patent dated 29 Jan. 1742,
signed by Lt. Gov. WILLIAM BULL, lying in the welch tract, Craven Co.,
bounding SW on Peedee River; other sides on vacant land. Witnesses: WIL-
LIAM HUGHES, WILLIAM JAMES. Before JAMES MICKIE, J.P. & D.P.R.

Book Z, p. 105
24 & 25 Nov. 1741
L & R

WILLIAM (his mark) STEVENS, SR., planter, to
PETER LAND, planter, both of Prince Frederick
Parish, Craven Co., for Ł 600 currency, 450 a.
in Craven Co., granted by Lt. Gov. 12 Aug.
1737; bounding NW on JOSIAH GAR. DUPRE; NE on Peedee River; other sides
on vacant land. Witnesses: WILLIAM STEVENS, JR., JOHN (his mark) DAVIS,
JOSEPH WHITE. Before JOHN BASSNETT, J.P. JAMES MICKIE, D.P.R.

Book Z, p. 109
25 & 26 Jan. 1741
L & R

PETER LANE, planter, & SARAH his wife, to JO-
SEPH PORT, planter, all of Prince Frederick
Parish, Craven Co., for L 680 currency, 450 a.
in Craven Co., bounding NW on JOHN MOORE (form-
erly JOSIAS GARNER ? DUPRE); NE on Peedee River; other sides on vacant
land; as granted 12 Aug. 1737 by Lt. Gov. THOMAS BROUGHTON to WILLIAM
STEVENS & by him sold to PETER LANE; SARAH to renounce her dower when requested. Witnesses: WILLIAM CLARK, JAMES LANE, JAMES SUMMERS. Before
WILLIAM WHITESIDE, J.P. JAMES MICKIE, D.P.R.

Book Z, p. 113
17 Jan. 1743/4
Mortgage

HUGH SWINTON, to JAMES ABERCROMBY. Whereas
ABERCROMBY has become security for payment of
L 441:2:1-1/2 SC money with interest, due by
SWINTON on a bond dated 17 Jan. 1743/4 payable
to ROBERT STEIL & JOHN HUME, the premises mentioned (see Bk. W. fol. 31-
34) shall be further security for above sum. Witness: THOMAS YOUNG. Before JAMES WEDDERBURN, J.P. JAMES MICKIE, D.P.R.

Book Z, p. 114
15 & 16 Jan. 1743
L & R by Mortgage

ANTHONY WHITE, planter, of Craven Co., to SA-
BINA LYNCH, widow, of Berkeley Co., as security for L 2780:14:9 SC money, payable with interest on 9 Mar. 1743, according to bond of
even date; 500 a. purchased by WHITE from ALEXANDER TRENCH, attorney for
JOHN BAYLY, son & heir of JOHN BAYLEY, Cassique, of Co. of Middlesex, Ireland; bounding NW, SW, & SE on ANTHONY WHITE; also 1150 a., part of 1400
a. which WHITE purchased from ALICE GIBBS, widow, of Berkeley Co., bounding NW on JOHN THOMPSON, SR., & WILLIAM BROCKINGTON; N on land granted to
THOMAS WRIGHT & to be conveyed to JASPER KING; S on ANTHONY WHITE. In
case of default, MARY, wife of ANTHONY WHITE, to renounce her dower. Witnesses: WILLIAM FLEMMING, JOHN RATTRAY. Before DANIEL CRAWFORD, J.P.
JAMES MICKIE, D.P.R.

Book Z, p. 120
30 Jan. 1743/4
Deed of Gift

JAMES BOSWOOD, & MARTHA his wife, of Berkeley
Co., to his cousin JOSEPH WELLS, for love &
affection & other considerations, 45 a. in
Berkeley Co., bounding W on ELIHU BAKER; N on
JOSIAH CANTEY; S on DAVID RUSS. MARY renounces her dower. Witnesses:
JOHN BURFORD, HENRY WOOD, of St. Andrews Parish, DAVID RUSS. Before THOM-
AS DRAYTON, J.P. JAMES MICKIE, D.P.R.

Book Z, p. 123
12 Dec. 1718
Deed of Gift

DOROTHY OGLE, widow of THOMAS OGLE, planter,
of Edisto Island, Colleton Co., to her daugh-
ter, HANNAH, wife of JOHN SAM, 200 a. being
1/2 of 400 a. granted by WILLIAM, Lord Craven,
Palatine, & the Lords Proprs., signed by Gov. ROBERT GIBBS, to DOROTHY
OGLE; bounding N on ECHABOD WANBUN & THOMAS GRIMBALL; E on THOMAS GRIM-
BALL; S on other half; W on JONAS WAIT. Witnesses: ROBERT WYATT, JOHN
JENKINS, LUD GRANT. Before HENRY GIBBES, J.P. JAMES MICKIE, D.P.R.

Book Z, p. 125
31 Jan. & 1 Feb. 1735
L & R

JEREMIAH ROPER, planter, to SAMUEL DRAKE, for
L 1000 SC money, 400 a. on N side Wando River,
bounding W on JOSEPH WARNOCK; N on THOMAS RUSS;
S on SAMUEL WARNOCK. Witnesses: WILLIAM
GEORGE FREEMAN, WILLIAM SMITH. Before JACOB MOTTE, J.P. JAMES MICKIE,
D.P.R.

Book Z, p. 132
30 Sept. & 1 Oct. 1743
L & R

SAMUEL DRAKE, planter, & MARY (her mark) his
wife, TO ANTHONY BONNEAU, JR., planter, all of
Berkeley Co., for L 730 SC money, 2 adjoining
tracts of land & marsh, total 400 a., in Berke-
ley Co., being 250 a., 100 a., & 50 a. of marshland; bounding S on Wando
River; W on JOSEPH WARNOCK; N on THOMAS RUSS; E on SAMUEL WARNOCK. Whereas the Lords Proprs. granted ANDREW WARNOCK, planter, of Berkeley Co.,
500 a. on N side Wando River; & whereas ANDREW WARNOCK & MARY his wife by
deed of feoffment dated 24 Jan. 1714/5 conveyed to JEREMIAH ROPER, turner,
250 a. being the W part of the 500 a., bounding on ABRAHAM WARNOCK & AN-
DREW WARNOCK, fronting on N side Wando River; & whereas the Lords Proprs.
granted ABRAHAM WARNOCK 1000 a.; & whereas after said ABRAHAM'S death his
son ABRAHAM WARNOCK, & THOMASON ? his wife, on 3 Mar. 1725 conveyed to
JEREMIAH ROPER, planter, of Berkeley Co., 500 a. being 1/2 the E part of

said 1000 a., bounding S on marsh & creeks of Wando River; W on ABRAHAM
WARNOCK; N on THOMAS RUSS; E on JEREMIAH ROPER; & whereas JEREMIAH ROPER
has sold to JOSEPH WARNOCK, 400 a., being the W part of the 500 a. he
bought from ABRAHAM WARNOCK, reserving 100 a. on the E side; & by L & R
dated 1 Feb. 1735/6 JEREMIAH ROPER sold to SAMUEL DRAKE 250 a. purchased
from ANDREW WARNOCK & 100 a. purchased from ABRAHAM WARNOCK, & about 50 a.
of marsh land fronting the 2 tracts; total 400 a.; now DRAKE sells to
BONNEAU. Witnesses: JOSEPH WARNOCK, SAMUEL WARNOCK, STEPHEN MILLER, JR.
Before JACOB MOTTE, J.P. JAMES MICKIE, D.P.R.

Book Z, p. 139   WILLIAM MELVIN (MELVEN), planter, to SAMUEL
1 & 2 Feb. 1741/2   CLARK, both of Colleton Co., for ₺ 400 SC mon-
L & R   ey, 100 a. in Colleton Co., bounding N on JOHN
                        PENNY; S on JAMES BUER; W on BOON. Whereas
the Lords Proprs. granted 300 a. to MOSES MARTIN, which he conveyed to
THOMAS BUER; & whereas he by deed of gift, gave WILLIAM MELVIN 100 a. of
the W part of the 300 a.; now MELVIN sells his 100 a. to CLARK. Witnesses: JOHN PAGE, JOSEPH OSWILL. Before CHARLES WRIGHT, J.P. JAMES MICKIE,
E.P.R.

Book Z, p. 148   JOHN GEORGE (his mark) DALLABAC, bricklayer, &
8 Feb. 1743   JOANNA ELIZABETH (her mark) his wife, of St.
Mortgage   Philips Parish, to JAMES VOULOUX, shopkeeper,
                        of Charleston, as security on bond dated 1 Feb.
inst., in penal sum of ₺ 2200 for payment of ₺ 1100 SC money with interest on 6 Feb. 1744; that piece of land on Charleston Neck, bounding NE on
the Broad Path leading to Charleston; SW on the parsonage & land belonging to the Free School; NW on HUGH ANDERSON; SE on JOSEPH WRAGG; being
60 ft. on the Broad Path from HUGH ANDERSON'S; as conveyed by L & R dated
18 & 19 Jan. 1742 by JOSEPH WRAGG to DELLABAC; also the new brick house
lately built thereon by DELLABAC. Witnesses: PETER BOCQUET, JAMES DRUM-
MOND. Before THOMAS DALE, J.P. JAMES MICKIE, D.P.R. JACQUES VOULOUX declared mortgage satisfied 17 July 1747. JOHN BEALE, Register.

Book Z, p. 153   THOMAS BROWN, planter, to WILLIAM ALSTON,
1 & 2 Oct. 1736   planter, both of Craven Co., for ₺ 400 SC mon-
L & R   ey, 3 tracts in Craven Co., total 300 a., on
                        upper thoroughfare of Peedee River; 100 a.
bounding S on Peedee River; other sides on vacant land; as by grant dated
28 Nov. 1735; 129 a. bounding NE on vacant land; S on upper thoroughfare
of Peedee River; other sides on main river; as by grant dated 29 Nov.
1735; 71 a. bounding W on PERCIVAL PAWLEY; S on COL. WATIES; other sides
on upper thoroughfare of Peedee River; as by grant dated 29 Nov. 1735
from Lt. Gov. THOMAS BROUGHTON. ANN BROWN, wife of THOMAS, willingly
surrenders her title. Witnesses: JOHN LUPTON, CHARLES HAY (now gone of
this Province 6 June 1742). Before THOMAS BLYTHE, J.P. JAMES MICKIE,
D.P.R.

Book Z, p. 161   ALEXANDER MOON, storekeeper, of Colleton Co.,
2 & 3 Sept. 1743   to WILLIAM YEOMANS, merchant, of Charleston,
L & R by Mortgage   as security on bond of even date in penal sum
                        of ₺ 9788:10:3 for payment of ₺ 1500 SC money,
with interest, on 1 Mar. next; & ₺ 3392:13:1-1/2, with interest, on 1
Mar. 1744; (debt being ₺ 4892:13:1-1/2); 1000 a. on Combahee River, com-
monely called Mount Alexander, where ALEXANDER MOON now dwells; bounding
E on JAMES HARTLIE; W on JOSHUA SANDERS; NW on JOSEPH BUTTLER; & all
houses thereon. Witnesses: JAMES GRINDLAY, THOMAS HOLMES, JOSEPH BROWN.
Before WILLIAM GEORGE FREEMAN, J.P. JAMES MICKIE, D.P.R.

Book Z, p. 167   JAMES RATTERY (RATTRAY), planter, to WILLIAM
1 Jan. 1743   DAVIDSON, practitioner in physic, both of
Mortgage   Berkeley Co., as security on bond of even date
                        in penal sum of ₺ 3000 for payment of ₺ 1500
currency on 1 Jan. next; 436 a. in Parish of St. George, formerly owned
by CAPT. WILLIAM DEWS; according to plat; also 9 Negroes. Witnesses: JO-
SEPH CREIGHTON, ALEXANDER DAVIDSON. Before JAMES MICKIE, J.P. & D.P.R.
One bay mare delivered in name of whole. Recorded in Secretary's Book
Q.Q. fol. 456-457 by JOHN CHAMPNEYS, Dep. Sec.

Book Z, p. 169   THOMAS DISTON, ESQ., & ELIZABETH his wife, to

3 June 1711   THOMAS HEPWORTH, ESQ., of Charleston, for
Release   Ŀ 350 currency, his half of half a lot, bound-
                        ing W on a street parallel with Cooper River;
N on Madam PIPIN (alias CHEVALIER); S on a neighborhood street; E on MOS-
ES JOY, cordwainer. ELIZABETH renounces her dower. Whereas JOHN, Lord
Berkeley, Palatin, & the Lords Propors. on 3 Oct. 1679 granted ANTHONY
SHORY lot #26 in Charleston, & he on 6 Oct. 1687 appointed MARTINE COOK,
planter, of SC his attorney, with power to sell all of SHORY'S lands,
goods & chattels in SC & whereas COCK, on 8 May 1688, sold to JOHN GIVIN,
cordwainer, of Charleston, 1/2 of lot #26, 1/2 of which half lot GIVEN,
on 5 Dec. 1688 sold to MARY CROSS, widow, the quarter lot bounding E on
JOHN GIVIN; W on a street parallel to Cooper River; N on JOHN GIVIN or
MR. PEPIN; N on LAURANCE SANDERS, planter; & whereas MARY CROSS on 1 Dec.
1692 sold the quarter lot to JOHN MOORE, gentleman, of Berkeley Co., & he
on 6 May 1693 sold to GEORGE RAYNOR, planter, of Colleton Co.; who, on 10
May 1698 sold to THOMAS CARY; who on 23 Jan. 1698/9, for Ŀ 200 currency
sold to GEORGE LOGAN, ESQ., who, on 13 Dec. 1709, for Ŀ 330 currency,
sold to THOMAS DISTON; now he sells to HEPWORTH. Witnesses: WILLIAM GIB-
BON, MILES BREWTON, JOHN COCK, JR., JOSEPH MORTON. Before THOMAS DALE,
J.P. JAMES MICKIE, D.P.R.

Book Z, p. 178   MARTHA DISTON, MARY CANTEY, & JOHN STEVENS,
2 Oct. 1736   husband of ELIZABETH CANTEY (MARTHA, MARY &
L & R   ELIZATETH being daughters of JOHN CANTEY & co-
                        heirs to the estate of their brother EPAPHRO-
DITUS); to CHARLES CANTEY; all of Berkeley Co.; for Ŀ 900 currency, 200 a.
or half the 400 a. granted 25 Dec. 1696 by the Lords Proprs., to JOHN CAN-
TEY; always reserving 1/4 a. for a burying place. Witnesses: JOSEPH CAN-
TEY, JR., ANN (her mark) BRUNSON. Before ALEXANDER SKENE, J.P. JAMES
MICKIE, D.P.R.

Book Z, p. 184   GEORGE JACKSON, of Colleton Co., to JERMYN
1 & 2 June 1742   WRIGHT, gentleman, for Ŀ 800 currency, 8 lots
L & R   in Colleton Co., Nos. 1, 2, 3, 4, 18, 19, 20,
                        28 (4 a.) in Town of Jacksonburgh; that is, in
the Old Field adjacent to Pon Pon bridge; 7 of the lots (1, 2, 3, 4, 18,
19, & 20) bounding E on the High Road, or King Street; NW on Union Street,
or lots of JOHN JACKSON; SW on Market Street, or lots of JOHN COCK & JOHN
ANDREW; SE towards the Bay & lot of JOSEPH ANDREW, lot #28 bounding NW on
Union Street; NE on Market Street; SE on JOHN ANDREW. Witnesses: GREGORY
FAGAN, JOSEPH ANDREW, JR. Before ROBERT WRIGHT, J.P. JAMES MICKIE, D.P.
R.

Book Z, p. 191   CAPT. JOHN JACKSON, of Colleton Co., to JERMYN
19 July 1742   WRIGHT, gentleman, for Ŀ 800 currency, 8 1/2 a.
L & R   lots, Nos. 1, 2, 3, 4, 18, 19, 20, & 28 in the
                        Old Field adjacent to Pon Pon bridge, on Pon
Pon River, as by moded of a certain town lately laid out; being 4 a. own-
ed by JOHN JACKSON, formerly by JOHN AUGUST, & since in possession of
JERMYN WRIGHT & CHARLES WRIGHT; bounding E on the High Road, or King
Street; NW on Union Street; NE on Market Street; SE on lot of JOSEPH AN-
DREW; lot #28, bounding NE on Market Street; SE on JOHN ANDREWS. Witness-
es: JOHN GWYN, JOHN LAIRD. Before ROBERT WRIGHT, J.P. JAMES MICKIE, D.
P.R.

Book Z, p. 197   JACOB DONNOM, planter, & MARGETT his wife, of
14 & 15 June 1742   Colleton Co., to JOSEPH SCOTT, planter, of St.
L & R   Helena, Parish, Granville Co., for Ŀ 130 cur-
                        rency, 750 a. in Granville Co., at head of
Conbahee River, bounding SE on JOSEPH BUTLER; other sides on vacant land.
Witnesses: MOSES MARTIN, GEORGE JACKSON. Before CHARLES WRIGHT, J.P.
JAMES MICKIE, D.P.R.

Book Z, p. 201   RICHARD FREEMAN, planter, to JOHN HOGG, plant-
28 & 29 July 1738   er, both of Colleton Co., for Ŀ 5 currency,
L & R   50 a. on Wadmalaw Island, Colleton Co., bound-
                        ing N on RICHARD FREEMAN; S on WILLIAM MCGIL-
LIVRAY & of JOHN STANYARNE; E on SAMUEL UNDERWOOD; W on heirs of JOHN
SAMS. Witnesses: SAMUEL UNDERWOOD, JAMES (his mark) WHITE, ZEBULON GUY.
Before ROBERT YONGE, J.P. JAMES MICKIE, D.P.R.

Book Z, p. 207   JOHN BAKER, planter, & SARAH (her mark) his
27 Mar. 1741   wife, of Craven Co., to ROBERT MURRELL, of
Release   Christ Church Parish, Berkeley Co., for Ⱡ 300
             currency, 300 a. in Craven Co., granted to
BAKER 14 Dec. 1739; bounding SE on a great marsh; SW on JOHN BAKER (form-
erly THOMAS JOANS); other sides on vacant land. Witnesses: ROBERT SCRE-
VEN, JONATHAN (his mark) MURRELL. Before JACOB BOND, J.P. JAMES MICKIE,
D.P.R.

Book Z, p. 212   ROBERT QUASH, & ELIZABETH his wife, of Berke-
20 & 21 Mar. 1743   ley Co., to JANE FULTON, of Craven Co., for
L & R   Ⱡ 800 currency, 275 a. in Craven Co., on S
             side of Peedee River, bounding E on THOMAS CON;
SW on vacant land; NW on SAMUEL FULTON. ELIZABETH to renounce her title.
Witnesses: PATRICK WELCH, SUSANNA JUNE, NATHANIEL DREW. Before HENRY
GIBBES, J.P. JAMES MICKIE, D.P.R.

Book Z, p. 217   ROBERT QUASH, & ELIZABETH his wife, of Berke-
20 & 21 Mar. 1743   ley Co., to SAMUEL FULTON, of Craven Co., for
L & R   Ⱡ 800 currency, 275 a. in Craven Co., on S
             side Peedee River; bounding SE on JANE FULTON;
NW on vacant land. ELIZABETH to renounce her title. Witnesses: PATRICK
WELCH, SUSANNA JUNE, NATHANIEL DREW.

Book Z, p. 222   WILLIAM (his mark) WESTBURY, planter, now of
14 Mar. 1716/7   Berkeley Co., with the free consent of his
Release   wife, MARY (her mark) to JOHN GIVIN, planter,
             of Colleton Co., for Ⱡ 70 currency, 398 a. in
2 tracts, near Horse Shoe Savanna, Colleton Co., bounding N on JAMES SAD-
LER; E on THOMAS BUR; S & W on vacant land. Whereas Dep. Gov. ROBERT
DANIEL & the Lords Proprs. on 23 Jan. 1716 granted WILLIAM WESTBURY 198 a.
on S side Pon Pon River, back land; & whereas Gov. CHARLES CRAVEN & the
Lords Proprs. on 17 Aug. 1714 granted THOMAS HOWARD 200 a. which he, on 4
Oct. 1714, sold to WILLIAM WESTBURY; now WESTBURY sells the 2 tracts to
GIVIN. Witnesses: JOHN GODFREY, THOMAS BIGGS, WILLIAM CATTELL. Before
THOMAS DRAYTON, J.P. JAMES MICKIE, D.P.R.

Book Z, p. 227   JOHN PHIPPS, mason, formerly of Kingston, Ja-
22 Sept. 1743   maica, now in Santee, SC, & MARGARET his wife,
Release   (formerly widow of DANIEL HACKETT) now in
             Kingston, Jamaica, to LETTICE HACKETT, spin-
ster daughter & heiress of DANIEL HACKETT, butcher, of Kingston; for natural love & affection & Ⱡ 30 Jamaican currency, 2 lots of land & all edi-
fices thereon. Whereas CHARLES II by letters patent dated 4 May, 17 yr.
of his reign, granted SAMUEL BARRY, ESQ., of Jamaica, 530 a. in St. Andrews Parish, Jamaica commonly called The Crawle, bounding SW on the harbor; NW on Savannah; E on MAJ. RICHARD HOPE; W on Lt. HENRY ARCHBOLD; &
whereas BARRY on 22 Feb. (22 yr. of King CHARLES II) sold to WILLIAM BEES-
TON, ESQ. (afterwards SIR WILLIAM BEESTON, knight) the 330 a., on which,
or part of which, the Town of Kingston has since been built & now stands;
& whereas several of these lots, besides those called front lots over
which there was formerly a controversy between SIR CHARLES ORBY, baronet,
& DAME ANN HOPEGOOD, his wife, widow of SIR WILLIAM BEESTON, & the inhabitants of Kingston, the fee simple & inheritance of them since the
death of DAME JANE MODDIFORD (alias LONG) only daughter of said SIR WIL-
LIAM BEESTON, knight, being legally vested in CHARLES LONG, son & heir of
said DAME JANE; & whereas CHARLES LONG by letter of attorney dated 15 May
(4th year of King GEORGE) appointed his brother, SAMUEL LONG, ESQ., COL.
GEORGE BENNET, & JAMES KNIGHT his attorneys, to sell his unsold lots in
Kingston; & whereas CHARLES LONG on 4 Oct. 1730 conveyed to JOHN PHIPPS
2 lots laid out in 1 parcel, each lot 150 ft. from E to W & 50 ft. from
N to S; bounding N on Tower Street; S on unsold land; E on CHARLES LONG,
next the hospital land; W on ROSEMARY LANE; being the 283rd & 284th lots
from the Court House in Kingston, neither being part of the land lately
in controversy, nor any part of the land excluded from being sold in said
letter of attorney; now PHIPPS gives the 2 lots to LETTICE HACKETT. Witnesses: JOHN FRY, JOHN DART, GEORGE SMITH. Before JACOB MOTTE, J.P.
JAMES MICKIE, D.P.R.

Book Z, p. 232   JOHN POSTELL, JR., planter, to JERMYN WRIGHT,

1 & 2 Mar. 1735   gentleman, both of Berkeley Co., for £ 1200
L & R   currency, 550 a. in Berkeley Co., bounding N
                        on WILLIAM SANDERS, ISAAC PORCHER, & JOHN
BOISSEAU; E on THEODORE VERDITTY; W on ELIAS HORRY & JOHN BOISSEAU; also
200 a., bounding N & NE on ISAAC PORCHER; SE & NW on JOHN BOISSEAU; SW on
BENJAMIN WARING. Witnesses: ROBERT WRIGHT, JOHN POSTELL, SR. Before
ROBERT WRIGHT, J.P. JAMES MICKIE, D.P.R.

Book Z, p. 239   EDWARD CROFT, & LYDIA his wife, of Christ
12 & 13 Apr. 1744   Church Parish, to HENRY WARD, ESQ., for £ 1700
L & R   currency, part of lot #177 in Charleston, &
                        the house in which JAMES GREENE now lives,
fronting N 62 ft. on Broad Street; bounding E on part of same lot; S on
HENRY BEDON; W on WILLIAM ELLICOTT. Witnesses: JOSEPH HAMAR, EDWARD
CROFT, JR., ALLEN SIMONS. Witnesses to receipt: ANDREW RUTLEDGE, THOMAS
COOPER, ROBERT MITCHELL. Before ANDREW RUTLEDGE, J.P.

Book Z, p. 246   JOHN WHITE, gentleman, of Prince Frederick
19 Apr. 1744   Parish, Craven Co., to his son ANTHONY WHITE,
Deed of Gift   JR., planter, of same place, for love & affec-
                        tion, 500 a. in Craven Co., on S side Black
River, bounding W & S on WILLIAM COLT; SE on CAPT. HINCKLEY; according to
original grant dated 12 Dec. 1735. Witnesses: WILLIAM FORD, DAVID JOHN-
STON. Before THOMAS DALE, J.P. JAMES MICKIE, D.P.R.

Book Z, p. 247   EDWARD CROFT, & LYDIA his wife, of Christ
9 & 10 Apr. 1744   Church Parish, to CAPT. THOMAS COOPER, mer-
L & R   chant, of Charleston, for £ 1200 SC money,
                        part of lot #177 in Charleston & the house in
which THOMAS CORBET now lives, fronting N 38 ft. on Broad Street, &
bounding E on heirs of WILLIAM LOUGHTON; W on part same lot; S on WILLIAM
HANCOCK. Witnesses: JAMES MATHEWES, PETER SEGAR. Before ROBERT AUSTIN,
J.P. JAMES MICKIE, D.P.R.

Book Z, p. 254   ANNE ELLERY, widow & devisee of THOMAS ELLERY,
25 Jan. 1743   gentleman, of St. John's Parish, Berkeley Co.,
L & R   to THOMAS DALE, doctor in medicine, of Charles-
                        ton, for £ 500 SC money, 66 a. Whereas Land-
grave THOMAS SMITH, & MARY his wife, on 16 Dec. 1726 sold to JAMES FER-
GUSON, planter, of Pon Pon, Colleton Co., 66 a. of his patent, lying in
Berkeley Co., & bounding E, N & S on heirs of CHARLES BURNHAM; W & N on
heirs of WILLIAM SKIPPER; W & S on Broad Path leading from Goose Creek to
the Quarter House & on RALPH IZARD; & whereas FERGUSON by L & R dated 10
& 11 Apr. 1732, for £ 350 currency, sold the 66 a. to THOMAS ELLERY, who,
by will dated 2 Oct. 1738 bequeathed the residue of his real & personal
estate (including the 66 a.) to his wife, ANNE; except the front lot in
Charleston & his pew in St. Philip's Church, devised to her for live only;
now she sells the 66 a. to DR. DALE. Witnesses: JORDAN ROCHE, WILLIAM
JOHNSON. Before HENRY GIBBES, J.P. JAMES MICKIE, D.P.R. By virtue of a
warrant from Dep. Gov. ROBERT DANIEL, dated 29 Sept. 1716, JOHN BAYLY,
surveyor, laid out for Landgrave THOMAS SMITH, 66 a. in Berkeley Co.,
part of the land granted him 13 May 1691, as by plat certified 21 Oct.
1726. Plat copied by GEORGE HUNTER, Sur. Gen., 11 Feb. 1743. Adjacent
lands belonging to CHARLES BURNHAM, RALPH IZARD, WILLIAM HEPWORTH.

Book Z, p. 263   JAMES DALTON, planter, of N Edisto, Colleton
13 & 14 Apr. 1744   Co., & KATHARINE his wife, to KATHARINE DAL-
L & R   BIAC, widow, of Charleston; for £ 360 curren-
                        cy, part of lot #37 in Charleston, fronting N
18 ft. on the street sometimes called Middle Street, leading from WILLIAM
ELLIOTT'S wharf, & bounding E 40 ft. S 18 ft. on WILLIAM YEOMANS, mer-
chant; W 40 ft. on DALTON'S other part of lot. Witnesses: JOSEPH MOODY,
WILLIAM THOMAS, JAMES EDES. Before ROBERT AUSTIN, J.P. JAMES MICKIE,
D.P.R.

Book Z, p. 271   JOHN TOOMER, planter, of Stono, Colleton Co.,
2 & 3 Apr. 1744   (son & devisee of CALEB TOOMER, cordwainer) &
L & R   ELIZABETH his wife, to WILLIAM BRADLEY, plant-
                        er, of Stono, for £ 1350 SC money, 546 a.,
called the Point. Whereas CALEB TOOMER, owned 3 adjacent tracts; being

180 a. granted by Lords Proprs. to JAMES STANYARNE; 216 a. granted JOHN
STEVENS; & 150 a. granted JAMES LAROCH; which 3 tracts by several mesne
conveyances descended to CALEB TOOMER & were made 1 tract of 546 a. on W
side S branch of Stono River, St. Pauls Parish, Colleton Co., bounding N
on Middle branch Stono River; W on land formerly belonging to RICHARD
WAKEFIELD; & whereas TOOMER, by will dated 2 July 1710 bequeathed to his
wife, PHEBE TOOMER, his plantation, stock, goods & chattels until his son
JOHN should come of age, should she remain a widow so long, afterwards to
have only her thirds; should she remarry, the estate, except her thirds,
to son JOHN; now JOHN sells to BRADLEY, free from PHEBE'S claim of thirds.
Witnesses: CHARLES CARROLL, ROBERT SCOTT. Before HENRY GIBBES, J.P.
JAMES MICKIE, D.P.R.

Book Z, p. 279   WILLIAM BRADLEY, of Stono, Colleton Co., to
1 & 2 May 1744   ALEXANDER RANTOWLE, of same place for Ł 2500
L & R   currency, 546 a. on SW side Stono River in St.
                        Paul's Parish, Colleton Co., bounding W on
RICHARD WAKEFIELD; being the 546 a. conveyed on page 271; also 466 a. of
marsh land, lying between the 546 a. & the S & SW branches & NW branches
of Stono, & lately laid out to WILLIAM BRADLEY. Witnesses: JONATHAN
THOMPSON, JOHN RATTRAY. Before HENRY GIBBES, J.P. JAMES MICKIE, D.P.R.

Book Z, p. 286   GEORGE HUNTER, gentleman, to JOHN DANIEL, ship-
9 & 10 July 1741   wright, both of Charleston, for Ł 600 currency,
L & R   part of lot #A in Charleston bounding E on
                        Cooper River; N on the part occupied by the
Public Fortifications, Granville, Bastion, & a brick wall & by a wooden
bridge over part of the marsh of said lot; S on part of the lot; W on a
creek now filed up but nearly represented by the straight line marked SE
06-1/2 in plat; as by lines colored yellow in plat of part of Lot A.
Whereas the Lords Proprs. on 5 Mar. 1680 granted SIR PETER COLLETON, baronet; THOMAS COLLETON, ESQ.; & Landgrave JAMES COLLETON, lot #A in
Charleston with all the marsh belonging thereto, bounding N on lot #1; S
on a little creek running out of Cooper River; W tending N; E on Cooper
River; W on part of said creek; original grant recorded in Book G fol.
130; which lot A by several mesne conveyances came to JOHN COLLETON, of
Fairlawn Barony, St. Johns Parish, Berkeley Co., who, by L & R dated 13 &
14 July 1736 conveyed to GEORGE HUNTER; now HUNTER sells to DANIEL. Witnesses: GEORGE SAXBY, JOHN WRAGG, JOHN RATTRAY. Before JACOB MOTTE, J.P.
JAMES MICKIE, D.P.R.

Book Z, p. 294   JOSHUA WILKS, planter, (son & heir of JOSHUA
30 Apr. & 1 May 1744   WILKS) & JOAN his wife, of Christ Church Par-
L & R   ish to JOHN DANIEL, merchant, of Charleston,
                        for Ł 2400 SC money, 600 a., bounding E on
JAMES ALLEN; W on COL. ROBERT BREWTON, SR., & ROBERT BREWTON, JR.; S on
JOSHUA WILKS & Rowser's Creek; N on a great marsh of Wando River; also
170 a. in Berkeley Co., bounding S on JACOB BOND; W & N on the 600 a.; E
on JACOB BOND & Wando Church. Whereas the Lords Proprs. on 22 Mar. 1682
granted JOHN STEPHENSON 600 a. on Wando River; bounding E on MARTHA
SMALLWOOD & MARY MCMERVIL; S on Rowsers Creek, MARTHA SMALLWOOD & WILLIAM
WILKINSON; W on CLEMENT BROWNE; N on marsh; & whereas, after JOHN STEPHEN-
SON'S death, his wife, MARY (?), inherited the land & afterwards married
JOHN BELL, bricklayer, of Berkeley Co., & whereas said JOHN BELL, & ANN
(?) his wife (formerly wife of JOHN STEPHENSON) on 27 June 1692 sold 200
a., part of the 600 a., to JOSHUA WILKS, father of JOSHUA, party hereto;
& whereas said JOHN BELL & ANN his wife, on 29 Oct. 1698 conveyed to
JOSHUA WILKS, the father, 400 a. (the other part of said 600 a.); & whereas the Lords Proprs. by SIR NATHANIEL JOHNSON conveyed the 600 a. to
JOSHUA WILKS, son & heir; & whereas the Lords Proprs. on 11 Aug. 1677
granted MARY MCMERVIL 170 a., English measure, at head of Rowsers Creek,
bounding S on marsh; N on land not taken up; W on JOHN STEPHENSON &
PRISCILLA SULLIVAN, & land not taken up; & she on 19 May 1688 conveyed
the 170 a. to NATHANIEL LAW, gentleman, of said Co.; who, on 14 June 1692
conveyed to JOSHUA WILKS; & whereas on 5 May 1704 the Lords Proprs. by
SIR NATHANIEL JOHNSON conveyed the 170 a. to JOSHUA WILKS, son & heir;
now he conveys the 2 tracts to JOHN DANIEL. Witnesses: JOHN RATTRAY,
JAMES GRINDLEY. Before JACOB MOTTE, J.P. JAMES MICKIE, D.P.R.

Book Z, p. 306   ELIZABETH CHEESMAN, widow, to "her brother of

81

31 Dec. 1742 &   the whole blood", RICHARD LAKE, ESQ., both of
1 Jan. 1743   St. Andrews Parish, Berkeley Co., for natural
Deed of Gift   love & affection, 2 tracts of 150 a. & 86 a.
                        making 1 tract of 236 a., commonly called Lake
Farm; also 4 slaves; & whereas ELIZABETH CHEESMAN "expects" 15 other
slaves, she agrees to convey them also to RICHARD LAKE so soon as they
become her property. Whereas MARGARET GODFREY & JANE MONGER, widows,
acting executrixes of will of BENJAMIN GODFREY, planter, by L & R dated
17 & 18 Nov. 1735 conveyed to THOMAS LAKE, merchant, of St. Michael's
Parish, Island of Barbados, 2 tracts formerly owned by BENJAMIN GODFREY,
1 of 150 a., English measure, on Ashley River, bounding E on WILLIAM HAR-
VEY (formerly BENJAMIN GODFREY); W & S on BENJAMIN WHITAKER (formerly
JOHN WOODWARD); N on marsh; the other of 86 a. bounding NE on CHARLES
HILL; NW on ELIZABETH HILL, widow, (formerly BENJAMIN GODFREY); SW on
JOHN WOODWARD; SE on said 150 a.; the 2 tracts making 1 tract of 236 a.;
& whereas THOMAS LAKE, by his attorney, GABRIEL MANIGAULT, by L & R dated
11 & 12 Jan. 1741 conveyed the 2 tracts, called Lake Farm to ELIZABETH
CHEESMAN, widow, now she gives them to her brother RICHARD LAKE. Wit-
nesses: SAMUEL PERKINS, WILLIAM SMITH. Before HENRY GIBBES, J.P. JAMES
MICKIE, D.P.R.

Book Z, p. 315   JOHN PAGE, planter, of Colleton Co., to ISAAC
8 & 9 July 1743   HOLMES, merchant, of Chare-ston for Ŀ 578 cur-
L & R   rency, 432 a. in Colleton Co., purchased from
                        ROBERT YONGE & HANNAH his wife; bounding E on
a branch of Tooboodoo Creek; N on Tooboodoo Creek; W & S on WILLIAM ED-
INGS. Whereas the Lords Proprs. on 20 Apr. 1698 granted NATHANIEL PRICH-
ARD 100 a. on W side Tooboodoo Creek, bounding W on WILLIAM EDINGS; S on
a creek; N on vacant land; & whereas the Lords Proprs on 15 Sept. 1705
granted ROBERT COCKRAN 120 a. on W side Tooboodoo Creek, bounding W on
WILLIAM EDINGS; N & S on vacant land; & whereas the Lords Proprs. on 12
Jan. 1705 granted ABRAHAM EVE 112 a. bounding S & E on Tooboodoo Creek; N
on said EVE; W on WILLIAM EDINGS; & whereas NATHANIEL PRICHARD on 27 Jan.
1704 sold his 100 a. to ABRAHAM EVE; & whereas ROBERT COCKRAN on 16 Feb.
1705 sold his 120 a. to ABRAHAM EVE; & whereas ABRAHAM EVE now owned several contiguous tracts making 1 tract of 432, & by will dated 22 Mar.
1722 bequeathed his plantations to his wife HANNAH; & whereas, after
ABRAHAM'S death, HANNAH married ROBERT YONGE, ESQ., of Colleton Co., &
they, on 19 May 1733 sold the 432 a. to JOHN PAGE, planter, of Colleton
Co., now PAGE sells to HOLMES. Witnesses: JAMES MATHEWES, EDWARD JENKINS,
JR. Before JAMES WRIGHT, J.P. JAMES MICKIE, D.P.R.

Book Z, p. 326   ISAAC HOLMES, merchant, of Charleston, to JOHN
4 & 5 May 1744   PAGE, the younger, planter, both of Colleton
L & R   Co., for Ŀ 845:5 currency, 432 a. in Colleton
                        Co., purchased from JOHN PAGE (see p. 315);
bounding E on a branch of Tooboodoo Creek; N on Tooboodoo Creek; S & W on
WILLIAM EDINGS. Witnesses: JAMES MATHEWES, CHARLES CALDER. Before JAMES
WRIGHT, J.P. JAMES MICKIE, D.P.R.

Book Z, p. 333   RICHARD LAKE, ESQ., of Berkeley Co., to JOSHUA
10 & 11 May 1744   SANDERS, planter, of Colleton Co., for Ŀ 1000
L & R   SC money, 1266 a. in Colleton Co., bounding
                        according to plat attached to grant dated 11
July 1733 from Gov. ROBERT JOHNSON to CAPT. JAMES LLOYD; & conveyed by
LLOYD by L & R dated 11 & 12 Mar. last. Witnesses: JAMES GREEME, JAMES
DRUMMOND. Before HENRY GIBBES, J.P. JAMES MICKIE, D.P.R.

Book Z, p. 340   PETER HUME, gentleman, of St. James Goose
26 & 27 Mar. 1744   Creek, as attorney (by letter dated 22 Feb.
L & R   1742) for JOHN BARKSDALE, merchant, & ANNE,
                        wife of JOHN BARKSDALE, of Georgetown, Craven
Co., to DANIEL HUGER, planter, of Berkeley Co.; for Ŀ 900 currency, part
of lot #26 in Charleston, fronting 38 ft. on Church Street; bounding N
63 ft. on said DANIEL HUGER; S on DANIEL HUGER (formerly DR. JAMES KIL-
PATRICK); which lot #26 was granted to ANTHONY SHORY by JOHN, Lord Berkeley, Palatine, & the Lords Proprs. on 3 Oct. 1679; 1/2 of which was conveyed by MARTIN COCK, planter, (attorney for SHORY, by letter dated 6
Oct. 1687) to JOHN GWIN, of Charleston, on 8 May 1688; 1/2 of said half
being afterwards conveyed by GWIN to MARY CROSS, widow, on 5 Dec. 1688;

82

& conveyed, on 1 Dec. 1692, by MARY CROSS to JOHN MOORE, gentleman, of
Berkeley Co., who, on 6 May 1693 conveyed to GEORGE RAYNOR, planter, of
Colleton Co.; who, on 10 May 1698 conveyed to THOMAS CARY; who, on 23
Jan. 1698 or 99 conveyed to GEORGE LOGAN, ESQ.; who on 13 Dec. 1709 conveyed to THOMAS DISTON; who, with his wife, ELIZABETH, on 3 June 1711 conveyed to THOMAS HEPWORTH, ESQ., of Charleston; who conveyed 1/2 of the
quarter part of lot #26 to JAMES KILPATRICK because of the marriage between said JAMES KILPATRICK & ELIZABETH, daughter of THOMAS HEPWORTH; who
conveyed the 1/8 part to PETER LAURENS, saddler, of Charleston; who, with
his wife LYDIA soon afterwards conveyed to DANIEL HUGER. The other half
part of the quarter part (the part hereby conveyed) was bequeathed by
THOMAS HEPWORTH to his wife ANNE for her natural life & afterwards to
daughter ANNE (now ANNE BARKSDALE, party hereto). ANNE HEPWORTH, in consideration of daughter ANNE'S marriage with JOHN BARKSDALE, & other considerations, conveyed the 1/8 part to JOHN BARKSDALE by L & R dated 16 &
17 Dec. 1736. Now BARKSDALE, by his attorney HUME, conveyed to HUGER.
Witnesses: ANDREW RUTLEDGE, JAMES DRUMMOND. Before JAMES GREEME, J.P.
JAMES MICKIE, D.P.R.

Book Z, p. 349   ANNE HEPWORTH, widow, to DANIEL HUGER. Where-
27 Mar. 1744   as THOMAS HEPWORTH, ESQ. of Charleston, by
Quitclaim   will dated 11 Sept. 1727 devised to his wife,
                       ANNE, that new messuage or tenement in
Charleston with the piece of ground adjoining, being part of a lot #26
purchased from MR. DISTON, fronting 38 ft. on E side Church Street; 63
ft. deep; & she by L & R dated 16 & 17 Dec. 1736, conveyed her title to
her daughter ANNE & ANNE'S husband JOHN BARKSDALE, reserving to herself
the use of 1 or more apartments in the house then standing on the premises; & whereas PETER HUME, gentleman, of St. James Goose Creek, as attorney for JOHN & ANNE BARKSDALE, by L & R this date has conveyed said part
of a lot to DANIEL HUGER, planter, of Berkeley Co.; now ANNE HEPWORTH relinquishes her title. Witnesses: ANDREW RUTLEDGE, JAMES DRUMMOND. Before JAMES GREEME, J.P. JAMES MICKIE, D.P.R.

Book Z, p. 351   JOSHUA SANDERS, planter, & ELIZABETH CLARK
14 & 15 May 1744   SANDERS, his wife, of Colleton Co., to RICHARD
L & R by Mortgage   LAKE, ESQ., of Berkeley Co., as security on
                       bond dated 11 this may, in penal sum of ₺ 2000
for payment of ₺ 1000 currency, with interest, on 11 May 1745; 1266 a. in
Colleton Co., bounding according to plat attached to grant dated 11 July
1733 from Gov. ROBERT JOHNSON to CAPT. JAMES LLOYD. Witnesses: JAMES
GREEME, JAMES DRUMMOND. Before HENRY GIBBES, J.P. JAMES MICKIE, D.P.R.

Book Z, p. 358   RICHARD WOODWARD, ESQ., to AMBROSE REEVES,
19 Nov. 1743   doctor of Physic, for ₺ 24 currency, 4-1/2 a.
Sale   English measure on Port Royall Island, bound-
                       ing on the Broad Road; E on the Common of
Beaufort; W on Parmenter's Creek; S on AMBROSE REEVES; surveyed by JAMES
HOUSTON. Witnesses: BENJAMIN LLOYD, JOHN THORPE. Before JOHN MULRYNE,
J.P. JAMES MICKIE, D.P.R.

Book Z, p. 361   DANIEL TOWNSEND, merchant, & ABIGAIL TOWNSEND,
24 Mar. 1741   of Charleston, to WILLIAM WHIPPEY, planter, of
L & R   Edisto Island, for ₺ 162 currency, 500 a. in
                       Granville Co., granted 11 May 1739 to TOWNSEND,
bounding E on JOHN WHIPPEY; W on ROBERT SAMPLE; N & S on unknown land.
Witnesses: JONATHAN TUBB, THOMAS FULLFORD, BENJAMIN COX. Before HENRY
GIBBES, J.P. JAMES MICKIE, D.P.R.

Book Z, p. 368   JERMYN WRIGHT, to WILLIAM WHIPPEY, for ₺ 750
3 & 4 Mar. 1743   currency, 500 a. in Granville Co., bounding NW
L & R   on public land; NE on Combahee River; SE on
                       WILLIAM BUCHANAN (formerly WILLIAM MCPHERSON);
which 500 a. were granted by Gov. ROBERT JOHNSON on 28 Apr. 1733 to ANNE
HERGRAVE, widow; & by L & R dated 23 & 24 Dec. 1736 conveyed by her to
JERMYN WRIGHT. Witnesses: RICHARD WOODWARD, JOSEPH BUTLER. Before ROB-
ERT YONGE, J.P. JAMES MICKIE, D.P.R.

Book Z, p. 375   WILSON SANDERS, planter, of Berkeley Co., to
23 & 24 May 1735   THOMAS FLEMING, gentleman, of Charleston, for

L & R   Ł 1000 SC money, 500 a., called Deers Island,
                                   in Colleton Co., bounding NE & NW on Sale
Creek; SW & S on impassable swamp; SE on EDWARD DREPEN. Witnesses: JOSH-
UA SANDERS, RICHARD WOOD, WILLIAM BROWN. Before WILLIAM SANDERS, J.P.
JAMES MICKIE, D.P.R.

Book Z, p. 380   DAVID ROBERTS, tailor, of Granville Co., to
24 Feb. 1743/4   EDWARD WIGG, storekeeper, for Ł 643 currency,
Sale   lot #115 in Beaufort, Port Royal Island, where
                                   ROBERTS lives. Witnesses: THOMAS WIGG, WIL-
LIAM HARVY. Before JOHN MULLRYNE, J.P. JAMES MICKIE, D.P.R.

Book Z, p. 383   ALCIMUS GAILLARD, planter, of Prince George
21 & 22 Feb. 1743   Parish, Craven Co., to TACITUS GAILLARD, plant-
L & R   er, of St. James Santee, Craven Co., for
                                   Ł 1000 currency, 300 a. on S side Winyaw Bay,
Prince George Parish, Craven Co., bounding S & E on Landgrave SMITH; W on
land given by Landgrave SMITH for a town; which 300 a. was the part ALCI-
MUS received of the land left by his father's (BARTHOLOMEW GAILLARD'S)
will, dated 15 July 1718, to his sons, THEODORE, ALCIMUS, & TACITUS.
Deed of partition dated 3 Aug. 1741. Witnesses: THEODORE GAILLARD, JAMES
GUERRY, ISAAC DUBOSE. Before HENRY GIBBES, J.P. JAMES MICKIE, D.P.R.

Book Z, p. 387   RICHARD GODFREY, planter, of Berkeley Co., eld-
9 & 10 Apr. 1742   est son & heir-at-law of RICHARD GODFREY, eld-
L & R   est uncle of the whole blood to JOHN GODFREY
                                   who was only son & child surviving of JOHN GOD-
FREY; to FRANCIS HOLMES, merchant, of Charleston. Whereas RICHARD GOD-
FREY gave bond dated 24 Mar. 1742 to FRANCIS HOLMES, in penal sum of
Ł 1169 for payment of Ł 584:4 SC money, with interest, on 24 Mar. 1742; &
whereas FRANCIS HOLMES, with RICHARD GODFREY (for RICHARD'S debt) gave
bond dated 25 Mar. last to ELIZABETH HILL, widow, of St. Andrew's Parish,
in penal sum of Ł 1182 for payment of Ł 591 SC money, with interest, on
25 Mar. 1743; now, as security on the first bond & to indemnify FRANCIS
HOLMES on second bond, RICHARD GODFREY gives HOLMES a mortgage on the
224 a., part of a larger tract, which RICHARD had received as heir-at-law
to JOHN GODFREY (who dies intestate), to whom it was bequeathed by his
father, JOHN GODFREY; which 224 a. is an inland plantation on S side Ashley River, bounding N on ANDREW DEVEAUX; E on ELIZABETH HILL; S on MR.
LUCAS; W on RICHARD GODFREY. Witnesses: WILLIAM WOODDROP, WILLIAM GLAZE.
Before HENRY GIBBES, J.P. JAMES MICKIE, D.P.R.

Book Z, p. 400   JOHN RUBERRY, planter, of Berkeley Co., gave
6 Dec. 1718   ANTHONY DEBURDEAUX (DUBOURDIEU?), joiner, a
Bond   bond in penal sum of Ł 1190 SC money, for keep-
                                   ing agreements in sale this date of 587 a.,
bounding NW on MR. AKIN; S on WILLIAM NORTH; SE on JOHN FOGARTIE; NE on
DONOMON. Witnesses: VINCENT GUERIN, PETER JOHNSON, THOMAS JENKINS, ISAAC
TREZEVANT, ROBERT CLYATT. Before DANIEL BREBANT, J.P. JAMES MICKIE,
D.P.R.

Book Z, p. 401   JOHN RUBERRY, planter, & ELIZABETH (her mark)
6 Dec. 1718   his wife, of Berkeley Co., to ANTHONY DEBUR-
Sale   DEAUX (DUBOURDIEU?), joiner & planter, of
                                   Berkeley Co., for 2 Negro women, 40 bushels of
corn, Ł 20 currency, & 65 barrels merchantable pitch; convey 587 a.,
bounding NW on MR. AKIN; S on WILLIAM NORTH; SE on JOHN FOGARTIE; NE on
DONOMON. Whereas Gov. CHARLES CRAVEN, SAMUEL EVELEIGH, RALPH IZARD,
CHARLES HART, NICHOLAS TROTT, & ROBERT DANIEL, Lords Proprs., on 10 Mar.
1714 granted JASPER BARSKERFIELD 587 a. in Berkeley Co., as recorded in
Secretary's Office 18 Mar. fol. 401 by JOHN CROFT, Dep. Sec.; & whereas
BARSKERFIELD, for Ł 8 currency, sold JOHN RUBERRY the 587 a.; now RU-
BERRY sells to DEBURDEAUX. Witnesses: VINCENT GUERIN, PETER JOHNSON,
THOMAS JENKINS, ISAAC TREZEVANT, ROBERT CLYATT. Before DANIEL BREBANT,
J.P. JAMES MICKIE, D.P.R.

Book Z, p. 406   JOSEPH WHIPPY, planter, of Edisto Island, to
5 & 6 Jan. 1743   SIBELLAH GRAY, widow, of Pon Pon, for Ł 900
L & R   currency, 200 a. at Pon Pon, Colleton Co.,
                                   bounding S on JOHN ANDREWS, SR.; W on ISAAC

HAYNES (formerly WILLIAM GRAY); N on JOHN ST. JOHN (formerly JOSEPH
MACKY); E on the Barony of JOSEPH BOON. Whereas Gov. ROBERT GIBBES & the
Lords Proprs. on 28 July 1711, for Ь 4, granted JOSEPH TURLEY, carpenter,
of Colleton Co., 200 a.; which he for Ь 26 sold to EDWARD RIPPIN, JR.;
who, for Ь 200 currency conveyed to WILLIAM GRAY, SR., who, for Ь 700 currency conveyed to TIMOTHY HENDRICK; & whereas WILLIAM & JOSEPH WHIPPY,
sons of WILLIAM WHIPPY, became heirs at TIMOTHY HENDRICK'S death; & whereas WILLIAM & JOSEPH WHIPPY, for Ь 900 currency, conveyed to WILLIAM BAY-
NARD, of Edisto Island; who, for Ь 900 currency conveyed to JOSEPH WHIPPY;
now he sells to SIBELLAH GRAY. ANN WHIPPY, wife of JOSEPH, willingly
surrenders her dower. Witnesses: JAMES AUCHENLECK, JOHN FREER, THOMAS
WILSON. Before JAMES BULLOCK, J.P. JAMES MICKIE, D.P.R.

Book Z, p. 413   The Hon. JOHN HAMMERTON, ESQ., & ELIZABETH
26 July 1743   HAMMERTON, widow, to COL. SAMUEL PRIOLEAU,
Release   ESQ., all of Charleston, for Ь 100 currency, 2
                        lots, #60 & #55, in Beaufort, on Port Royal
Island, Granville Co. Whereas by letters patent dated 8 May 1735 ELIZA-
BETH HAMMERTON was granted 2 lots in Beaufort, #60 & #55, in trust for
HOLLIER HAMMERTON, son of ELIZABETH; & whereas HOLLIER died intestate &
unmarried, & JOHN HAMMERTON, his uncle of the whole blood, & heir-at-law,
inherited; now he sells to PRIOLEAU. Witnesses: RAWLINGS LOWNDES, JANE
JENKINS. Before JOHN CHAMPNEYS, J.P. JAMES MICKIE, D.P.R.

Book Z, p. 418   JOHN (his mark) MACOY, planter, to THOMAS DAW-
12 Dec. 1743   SON, both of Colleton Co., for Ь 200 currency,
Sale   200 a. near Horse Shoe Savannah, Colleton Co.,
                        bounding SE on MR. MASH _____; SW on JOHN COOK;
other sides on vacant land. Witnesses: JOHN SALSBE BARTON, RICHARD DAW-
SON, GEORGE MILLER, ALEXANDER CLAIN. Before CULCHETH GOLIGHTLY, J.P.
JAMES MICKIE, D.P.R.

Book Z, p. 420   WILLIAM SINGELTON, of St. Bartholomew Parish,
16 Nov. 1742   Colleton Co., to his brother, DANIEL SINGELTON,
Deed of Gift   for natural love & affection & other considera-
                        tions, 274 a., part of 822 a. laid out to WIL-
LIAM SINGELTON on 27 Nov. 1731; the 274 a. being on the W end of the
tract willed to DANIEL SINGELTON by his father WILLIAM SINGELTON. Witnesses: JAMES PERRIMAN, GEORGE JACKSON. Before CHARLES WRIGHT, J.P.
JAMES MICKIE, D.P.R.

Book Z, p. 422   WILLIAM SINGELTON, of St. Bartholomew Parish,
16 Nov. 1742   Colleton Co., to his brother SAMUEL SINGELTON,
Deed of Gift   for natural love & affection & other considera-
                        tions, 274 a., part of 822 a. laid out to WIL-
LIAM SINGELTON on 27 Nov. 1734; being the E end of the tract willed to
SAMUEL SINGELTON by his father WILLIAM SINGELTON. Witnesses: JAMES PERRI-
MAN, GEORGE JACKSON. Before CHARLES WRIGHT, J.P. JAMES MICKIE, D.P.R.

Book Z, p. 423   COL. ALEXANDER HEXT, to THOMAS HEXT, both of
29 & 30 Apr. 1728   Colleton Co., for Ь 1200 currency, 620 a., on
L & R   Johns Island, Colleton Co., being part of 640
                        a. granted by the Lords Proprs. to MRS. ELIZA-
BETH GODFREY on 17 Apr. 1710; bounding N on vacant land; E on HENRY WOOD-
WARD; W on a creek out of Kayanay River; W on ELIZABETH GODFREY. Wit-
nesses: RICHARD TIMMONS, MARY SEABROOK, JAMES WILLIAMS. Before ANTHONY
MATHEWES, J.P. JAMES MICKIE, D.P.R.

Book Z, p. 428   ANTHONY BONNEAU, planter, & MARGARET HENRIETTA,
18 & 19 June 1744   his wife, of Berkeley Co., to DANIEL HORRY,
L & R   planter, of Craven Co., for Ь 1500 SC money,
                        3 tracts, total 600 a., which BONNEAU had pur-
chased from JOHN SPENCER & DOROTHY his wife, by L & R dated 16 & 18 July
1737, as recorded in Bk. R. fols. 428-435; 2 of the tracts being adjacent
& containing 250 a. each; bounding N on Santee River; E on RALPH JERMAN:
S on vacant land; W on DANIEL HORRY; also 100 a. being the middle part of
an island in Santee Vier, bounding E on RALPH JERMAN; W on DANIEL HORRY.
Witnesses: ELIAS HORRY, HENRY BONNEAU. Before JACOB MOTTE, J.P. JAMES
MICKIE, D.P.R.

Book Z, p. 435   WILLIAM MCPHERSON, to WILLIAM BUCHANAN, for
1 & 2 Feb. 1741   Ł 1200 currency, 200 a. in Colleton Co., bound-
L & R   ing SW on marsh of Combahee River; SE on NA-
                        THANIEL NICHOLLS; NW on ISAAC STEWART; NE on
EMANUEL SMITH & vacant land. Witnesses: WILLIAM ROSE, WILLIAM MILES, JR.,
THOMAS KING. Before HENRY HYRNE, J.P. JAMES MICKIE, D.P.R.

Book Z, p. 442   WILLIAM MIDDLETON & HENRY MIDDLETON, ESQRS.,
9 June 1741   of Berkeley Co., to THOMAS MIDDLETON, ESQ.,
Sale   for 5 shillings part of lot #199 in Charleston,
                        being the N third part marked C as by plat cer-
tified by JAMES ST. JOHN, Sur. Gen. on 7 Aug. 1735 annexed to grant to
ARTHUR MIDDLETON, ESQ., who devised lot #199 to his sons WILLIAM & HENRY
MIDDLETON; bounding E on JOSEPH WRAGG; N on land marked on plat as belong-
ing to JOSEPH WRAGG but since found to be land formerly granted to CAPT.
JONATHAN ADDICE (?); W on DAVID HEXT & heirs of MR. STEWART; S on part of
same lot marked B. Witnesses: JAMES MIDDLETON, ELIZABETH BRAILSFORD,
ELIZABETH CHAMBERLIN. (This lease brought to be recorded by mistake).

Book Z, p. 444   GRACE WAINWRIGHT, widow, to RICHARD WAINWRIGHT,
6 & 7 July 1743   both of St. Philip's Parish, Charleston, for
L & R   Ł 80 currency, 600 a. in Craven Co., bounding
                        SE on the 8 miles swash on the seashore on
Long Bay; other sides on vacant land. Witnesses: BENJAMIN WAINWRIGHT,
THOMAS COLSON. Before JOHN CHAMPNEYS, J.P. JAMES MICKIE, D.P.R.

Book Z, p. 451   STEPHEN (his mark) CAILLABEUF, chairmaker, to
23 & 24 July 1744   MILES BREWTON, ESQ., both of Charleston, for
L & R   Ł 1050 SC money, 3 lots, #308, #309, & #310,
                        in Charleston, bounding S on a marsh; W on Old
Church Street; N on lot #60; E on lots #57, 62, 61, & 77. Whereas ISAAC
CAILLABEUF the elder owned the 3 lots, #308, #309, & #310 by 3 grants
dated 14 Mar. 1694/5 as recorded in Secretary's Book A. fol. 35, & by
will dated 18 Sept. 1699 devised the 3 lots to his 3 children, ISAAC,
STEPHEN, & MARY, the will being recorded in Secretary's Book C. fols. 123,
124, & 125; & whereas STEPHEN & MARY died intestate & without issue; &
whereas son ISAAC died, leaving his son STEPHEN, party hereto, only surviving male heir of ISAAC the younger, & heir at law to STEPHEN & MARY
(his father's brother & sister); now STEPHEN sells the 3 lots to BREWTON.
Witnesses: EDWARD SEULL, JOHN REMINGTON. Before THOMAS DALE, J.P. JAMES
MICKIE, D.P.R.

Book Z, p. 456   HENRY PERONNEAU, JR., merchant, to HENRY
17 & 18 May 1743   CHRISTIE, carpenter, both of Charleston, for
L & R   Ł 800 currency, part of a quarter part of lot
                        #19 in Charleston, fronting E 25 ft. on the
Bay; bounding W on GEORGE LEA, carpenter; S on GEORGE HESKETT; N 112 ft.
on JOSEPH BLAKE. Witnesses: ALEXANDER PERONNEAU, SAMUEL PERONNEAU. Before JACOB MOTTE, J.P. JAMES MICKIE, D.P.R.

Book Z, p. 461   HENRY CHRISTIE, carpenter, & SARAH his wife,
1 & 2 June 1743   to RICE PRICE, vintner, all of Charleston, for
L & R   Ł 800 SC money, part of a quarter part of lot
                        #19 in Charleston, fronting E 25 ft. on the
Bay; bounding S 112 ft. on GEORGE HESKETT; N on JOSEPH BLAKE; W on GEORGE
LEA, carpenter. Witnesses: JAMES HOLDITCH, JOHN REMINGTON. Before JACOB
MOTTE, J.P. JAMES MICKIE, D.P.R.

Book Z, p. 466   JOHN VANN, carpenter, to WILLIAM HOPTON &
2 Apr. 1744   THOMAS SMITH, merchant, all of Charleston, as
Assignment by Mortgage security on bond of even date in penal sum of
                        Ł 1000, reciting that whereas said HOPTON &
SMITH gave bond, with VANN, this date, to JOHN RATTRAY, JAMES WITHERS, &
MOSES AUDIBERT, officers of the SC Society, in penal sum of Ł 1000 for
payment of Ł 500 & interest on 2 Apr. next; also reciting that whereas
the bond was entered into by HOPTON & SMITH for VANN'S debt only & not
for their debt; with the condition that should VANN pay the officers of
the SC Society the Ł 500 & interest & keep HOPTON & SMITH indemnified,
the bond should be void; & whereas by lease dated 1 Oct. 1742 the Rev.
MR. FRANCIS GUICHARD, GABRIEL MANIGAULT, ISAAC MAZYCK, PAUL MAZYCK, JACOB

MARTIN, JOHN NEUFVILLE, BENJAMIN D'HARRIETTE & GIDEON FAUCHERAUD, of
Charleston, conveyed to JOHN VANN part of lot #93 fronting W 30 ft. on
King Street; bounding S on JAMES HILLIARD; E on MRS. BOUSHAR; N on part
of same lot; for 50 years at Ŀ 3:4 per year; now as security VANN assigns
to HOPTON & SMITH the lease, the part of a lot with the buildings on it &
all his interest. Witnesses: WILLIAM SCOTT, WILLIAM GEORGE FREEMAN. Before THOMAS DALE, J.P. JAMES MICKIE, D.P.R.

Book Z, p. 474   MARTHA GODFREY, executrix of will of BENJAMIN
24 & 25 Jan. 1743   GODFREY, planter, & WILLIAM GODFREY, eldest
L & R   son & heir at law of BENJAMIN GODFREY, to NA-
                      THANIEL BROWNE, of Berkeley Co., for Ŀ 512
currency, 64 a. in Berkeley Co., bounding SW on COL. WILLIAM BULL; NW on
JOHN BROWN; N on MR. GIRARDEAUX; SE & S on RICHARD GODFREY; which 64 a.
is part of a tract of 672 a. in 3 lots formerly belonging to CAPT. RICH-
ARD GODFREY, deceased, afterwards to SAMUEL JONES, & lately conveyed to
BENJAMIN GODFREY by ISAAC WAIGHT & DOROTHY JONES. Whereas WILLIAM GOD-
FREY by deed poll dated 9 Feb. 1740 reciting that whereas BENJAMIN GOD-
FREY on 17 Apr. then last past made his will; & the will has since been
lost or mislaid; & whereas WILLIAM GODFREY, heir-at-law to BENJAMIN, & 1
of the executors named in the will, had agreed with MARTHA GODFREY that
he would abide by the will; & would, within 3 months after the date of
the deed poll, convey BENJAMIN'S lands, tenements, etc., in trust; &
whereas BENJAMIN in his will had directed in his will that in case his
creditors were uneasy his real & personal estate should be sold to discharge his debts; now MARTHA & WILLIAM sell 64 a. to BROWNE. Witnesses:
SAMUEL CARNE, WILLIAM GEORGE FREEMAN. Before HENRY GIBBES, J.P. JAMES
MICKIE, D.P.R.

Book Z, p. 482   PETER LANE, planter, & SARAH his wife, to MAR-
27 & 28 Mar. 1743   MADUKE BELL, planter, all of Craven Co., for
L & R   Ŀ 51:9:8 currency, 100 a. in Craven Co.,
                      bounding NE on JOHN BROWN & JOHN WALLIS; SE on
WILLIAM SWINTON; SW on MRS. MARTHA BELL; which 100 a. by letters patent
dated 15 Feb. 1736/7 were granted by Lt. Gov. THOMAS BROUGHTON to MRS.
SARAH JOHNSON (now wife of PETER LANE). Witnesses: JOHN MCCANTS, WILLIAM
BROCKINGTON, JAMES LANE. Before WILLIAM WHITESIDE, J.P. JAMES MICKIE,
D.P.R.

Book Z, p. 488   LIONEL CHALMERS, practitioner in physic, of
15 & 16 July 1743   Berkeley Co., to SARAH STOUTENBURGH (late
L & R by Mortgage   SARAH MCKENZIE) & JOHN MCKENZIE, merchant, of
                      Charleston, executrix & executor of will of
WILLIAM MCKENZIE, merchant, of Charleston, as security on a debt, 460 a.
on SW side Wando River. Whereas the Lords Proprs. on 11 May 1699 granted
FRANCIS GRACIA 460 a. on SE side Wando River, in Berkeley Co., bounding
NE & SE on a creek; W & SW on vacant land; which by deed of feoffment
dated 18 Oct. 1708 FRANCIS GRACIA, joiner, & ELIZABETH his wife, conveyed
to GEORGE LOGAN, ESQ., of Charleston; & he, by will dated 18 Mar. 1719
devised the 460 a. to his son, PATRICK LOGAN, or, by default of heirs, to
his daughter HELEN; & whereas PATRICK died without heirs & HELEN interi-
ted; & she married ROBERT DANIEL, ESQ., & by L & R dated 31 Jan. & Feb.
1727 they conveyed the tract to THOMAS COOPER, ESQ., of Charleston; who
by L & R dated 1 & 2 Mar. 1727 conveyed to MARTHA LOGAN, spinster, of
Berkeley Co., eldest daughter of GEORGE LOGAN; & whereas she married LI-
ONEL CHALMERS, & by L & R dated 29 & 30 July 1743 they conveyed the land
to WILLIAM CARR, Pettiagua man; who by L & R dated 31 July & 1 Aug. 1743
conveyed to LIONEL CHALMERS, surgeon, who, this date gave bond to SARAH
STOUTENBURGH & JOHN MCKENZIE in penal sum of Ŀ 3304:3 for payment of
Ŀ 1652:1:6 currency, with interest, on 3 July next; now he conveys the
land to them as security. Witnesses: JAMES MICKIE, WILLIAM PLAYTERS.
Before GEORGE HAIG, J.P. JAMES MICKIE, D.P.R. On 14 Feb. 1748/9 SARAH
STOUTENBURGH acknowledged full satisfaction of mortgage. Witness: WIL-
LIAM HOPTON.

Book Z, p. 500   GEORGE FERGUSON, planter, of Berkeley Co., to
25 & 26 May 1743   SARAH STOUTENBURGH & JOHN MACKENZIE, of
L & R by Mortgage   Charleston, executrix & executor of will of
                      WILLIAM MACKENZIE, merchant, as security on
bond of even date in penal sum of Ŀ 2191:9:10 for payment of Ŀ 1095:14:11

SC money with interest at house of SARAH STOUTENBURGH on 26 May 1744; 325 a. in Colleton Co., bounding NE on WILLIAM MACKENZIE; NW on THOMAS MILES; SW on the Hon. JOSEPH WRAGG; SE on vacant land, which tract King GEORGE II by letters patent dated 12 Apr. 1739, signed by Lt. Gov. WILLIAM BULL, granted to GEORGE FERGUSON with the usual provisoes. Witnesses: LUKE STOUTENBURGH, JR., JAMES MICKIE.

Book Z, p. 510
26 May 1744
Bond

GEORGE FERGUSON, to SARAH STOUTENBURGH & JOHN MCKENZIE, in penal sum of Ł 482:10 for payment of Ł 241:5 SC money with interest on 25 May 1745. Witnesses: ELIZABETH DONEN, JAMES MICKIE. Before GEORGE HAIG, J.P. JAMES MICKIE, D.P.R.

Book Z, p. 512
1 May 1744
Release

GEORGE LEA, carpenter, & ELIZABETH his wife, to JOHN MACKAY, mariner, all of Charleston, for Ł 370 SC money, part of lot #18 on E side of Union Street, bounding N on part belonging to JOHN RATTRAY; S on MOSES MITCHELL; E on JAMES CROKATT. Whereas GEORGE LEA, shipwright, by will dated 22 Nov. 1739 bequeathed to his son, GEORGE LEA, his dwelling house with 1/3 of the land (the whole divided into 3 parts) backwards from the whole depth of the house; & gave his daughter, ELIZABETH LEA, the house next adjoining, with the land backwards belonging to the same; & to his daughter LYDIA LEA the house adjoining the 1 given to ELIZABETH, with the land backward belonging to the same; & directed that should LYDIA die before the age of 16 her share to be equally divided between the survivors; & whereas LYDIA died before reaching 16 years of age, her share was divided between GEORGE & ELIZABETH (now wife of JOHN MACKAY) now GEORGE sells his share of LYDIA'S lot to MACKAY. Witnesses: ROBERT ALLEN, JOHN BULL, JR. Before ROBERT AUSTIN, J.P. JAMES MICKIE, D.P.R.

Book Z, p. 517
1 May 1744
Bond

GEORGE LEA, carpenter, of St. Philip's Parish, Charleston, to JOHN MACKAY, mariner, of same Parish, in penal sum of Ł 500 currency, for performance of agreements in above release (p. 512). Witnesses: ROBERT ALLAN, JOHN BULL, JR. Before ROBERT AUSTIN, J.P. JAMES MICKIE, D.P.R.

Book Z, p. 519
6 Aug. 1744
Sale

JOHN MACKAY, mariner, & ELIZABETH his wife, to MOSES MITCHELL, cordwainer, & MARY his wife, all of Charleston, for Ł 700 SC money, all that messuage or tenement or part of lot #18 on E side Union Street, bounding N on part same lot belonging to JOHN RATTRAY; S on MOSES MITCHELL & MARY his wife; E on JAMES CROKATT. Witnesses: JOHN ROBERSON, JOHN REMINGTON, RICHARD HOWARD. Before ROBERT AUSTIN, J.P. JAMES MICKIE, D.P.R.

Book Z, p. 523
4 & 5 July 1744
L & R by Mortgage

BENJAMIN STANYARNE, planter, of Berkeley Co., to WILLIAM CATTELL, ESQ., & ELIZABETH HILL, widow, as security on bond dated 15 July 1743, given WILLIAM CATTELL by STANYARNE, in penal sum of Ł 12,580 for payment of Ł 6,290 SC money, with interest, on 15 July next; & another bond to ELIZABETH HILL, dated 25 June 1744, in penal sum of Ł 1429 for payment of Ł 714:10 SC money, with interest, on 25 June 1745; & another bond dated 20 June 1744, to ELIZABETH HILL, in penal sum of Ł 412 for payment of Ł 206:11:6 SC money, with interest, on 20 June 1745; 983 a. on S side Ashley River, Berkeley Co., bounding SW on UMPHREY ELLIOTT; SE on THOMAS BUTLER & WILLIAM BRADFORD; NW on ROBERT LADSON; also 26 Negro slaves; 23 Negro women slaves. Witnesses: SUSANNA BARLOW, WILLIAM GEORGE FREEMAN. Before JAMES WRIGHT, J.P. JAMES MICKIE, D.P.R.

Book Z, p. 531
30 & 31 Aug. 1744
L & R

CHARLES PINCKNEY, ESQ., to GABRIEL GUIGNARD, cooper, both of Charleston, for Ł 1450 currency, 3 adjacent lots or divisions of lot #80, known in the plat as L.M.M.; bounding E on a street 33 ft. wide, laid out in said lot #80, & called Charles Street; S on a small street laid out in same lot; N on Pinckney Street running E into Cooper River; W on WILLIAM WATIES (formerly GERRARD). Whereas the Lords Proprs. on 5 Mar. 1680 granted SIR PETER COLLETON a lot in Charleston containing 9 a., 2 roods, 21 perches, English measure of dry land &

marsh land with a small creek in the marsh land which lot is known as #80; bounding E on Cooper River & lots of THOMAS COLLETON, & Landgrave JAMES COLLETON, W on a small unnamed street; S on CAPT. WILLIAM WALLEY'S lot & 2 lots belonging to CAPT. JAMES ADIE; N on THOMAS COLLETON & another small unnamed street; & whereas by several mesne conveyances lot #80 became vested in JOHN COLLETON of Fairlawn Barony, St. John's Parish, Berkeley Co., & whereas JOHN COLLETON & SUSANNA his wife, by L & R dated 13 & 14 July 1736, for ₺ 500 currency, conveyed lot #80 to GEORGE HUNTER; & whereas CHARLES PINCKNEY &1 THOMAS ELLERY, gentleman, of Charleston were equally concerned with HUNTER in the purchase & paid their equal parts of the purchase money, HUNTER'S name being used in trust for himself, PINCKNEY & ELLERY; & whereas ELLERY died & an agreement was made by HUNTER, PINCKNEY & ANNE ELLERY (devisee of THOMAS) to lay out lot #80 in several lots, streets, lanes, docks, & water passage, convenient for disposing of them; & whereas the division was made & lots C.F.L.M.C.C.F.F. I. M.M. were conveyed to CHARLES PINCKNEY as his share; & whereas GEORGE HUNTER by L & R dated 21 & 22 Mar. 1742 sold CHARLES PINCKNEY lots C.F.L.M.C.C. f.f. I. M & M; now PINCKNEY sells 3 divisions to GUIGNARD. Witnesses: RICHARD CURR, PETER TIMOTHY, CHARLES PINCKNEY, JR. Before JAMES GREEME, J.P. JAMES MICKIE, D.P.R.

Book Z, p. 540
9 & 10 July 1744
L & R

BETHEL DEWES, planter, & MARGARET his wife, of St. George's Parish, Berkeley Co., to GEORGE SUMMERS, planter, of Berkeley Co., for ₺ 1000 currency, 425 a. in Berkeley Co., free from MARGARET'S claim of dower; bounding E on COL. JOSEPH BLAKE & JOHN PORTALL; NE on BENJAMIN WARING; N on JEREMIAH KNOTT; W on THOMAS DISTON; S on JAMES RATTRAY; 250 a. were purchased from the Lords Proprs. sometime before; the rest of the tract, back of the 250 a., was run out by the King's warrant to BETHEL & his brother WILLIAM. Witnesses: WILLIAM WEBB, JOHN GWYN. Before ROBERT AUSTIN, J.P. JAMES MICKIE, D.P.R.

Book Z, p. 547
29 Aug. 1744
Feoffment

JOHN RATTRAY, gentleman, to MOSES MITCHELL, shoemaker, & MARY his wife; all of Charleston; for ₺ 830 currency, that house, & land backwards, being part of lot #18, on E side Union Street; opposite to COL. CHARLES PINCKNEY; bounding S & N on other parts same lot; E on JAMES CROKATT. Witnesses: JOHN WATSON, JOHN GODMENT, JOHN ROBERSON. Before HENRY GIBBES, J.P. JAMES MICKIE, D.P.R.

Book Z, p. 550
6 June 1744
Further Confirmation
of Sale

See Book X, p. 28. STEPHEN MILLER, having executed a deed of gift to WALTER DUNBAR, & JEAN his wife, for love & affection & for JEAN'S support & maintenance; on this date delivers to them possession of the tenement & lot by delivering the key of the door, & a clod of earth from said lot, in name of the whole. Witnesses: ROBERT SCOTT, HENRY BONNEAU. Before JAMES MICKIE, J.P. & D.P.R.

DEEDS BOOK "A-A"
SEPT. 1744 - MAY 1745

Book A-A, p. 1
1 & 2 June 1742
L & R

JAMES MICKIE, ESQ., & MARTHA his wife, of Charleston, to JOSEPH MURRAY, planter, of Craven, Co., for ₺ 500 SC money, 900 a. in Craven Co., known as Mount Hope, bounding NW on MR. BUTLER; SW on Santee River; SE on MR. TOOMER; NE on vacant land. Whereas King GEORGE II by letters patent dated 30 Sept. 1736, signed by Lt. Gov. THOMAS BROUGHTON, granted WILLIAM CLELAND 900 a. known as Mount Hope (as above) with the usual provisoes; & whereas by L & R dated 4 & 5 Mar. 1736 WILLIAM CLELAND, chirurgeon, of Charleston, & MARGARET his wife sold the tract to JAMES MICKIE, gentleman, of Charleston; now MICKIE sells to MURRAY. Witnesses: (SCARPMORE BRX.?), DAVID CAW. Before JAMES WRIGHT, J.P. JAMES MICKIE, D.P.

Book A-A, p. 10
25 & 26 Sept. 1744
L & R

ELIZABETH BELLINGER, widow & executrix of will of Landgrave EDMOND BELLINGER, of Berkeley Co., to MAJ. WILLIAM BOONE, planter, of St.

John's Parish, Colleton Co., for ₤ 1250 currency, 500 a., being the E end of 2000 a.; bounding SE on JAMES BROZETT (BROZET) (formerly WILLIAM SCOTT); E (NE) JOHN SMILIE (formerly JOSEPH SCOTT); NW on CAPT. THOMAS FLEMING & COL. ALEXANDER HEXT (formerly HENRY COWEN & JAMES COCHRAN); W on other part of 2000 a.; as by plat certified by WILLIAM MCPHERSON, Dep. Sur. on 17 Mar. 1744. Whereas EDMOND BELLINGER on 21 May 1734 by grant signed by Gov. ROBERT JOHNSON, was granted 2000 a. in St. Bartholomew's Parish, Colleton Co., between Chehaw & Ashepoo Rivers, at or near the Bay of Honduras Swamp, bounding E on JOSEPH SCOTT & WILLIAM SCOTT; S on JAMES SMITH; W & NW on WILLIAM COCHRAN; N on JAMES COCHRAN & WILLIAM COWEN; & whereas BELLINGER, by will, ordered his wife ELIZABETH (& in case of her death, his son EDMOND) to sell the 2000 a. & divers other lands in SC; now she sells 500 a. to BOONE. Witnesses: HENRY HYRNE, WILLIAM BACKSHALL. Before ANTHONY MATHERS, J.P. JAMES MICKIE, D.P.R.

Book A-A, p. 18
5 & 6 Jan. 1743
L & R
ULISSE ANTHONY ALBERGOTTE, planter, to RICHARD HAZZARD, planter, both of Granville Co., for ₤ 20 currency, 200 a. in Granville Co. on Okety Creek, bounding E on the creek & vacant land; N on vacant land; W on WILLIAM ROBERTS & to the N & S lines of Purrysburgh lands; NE on Gov. JOHNSON; S on ALBERGOTTE'S land which he formerly sold to said HAZZARD. Witnesses: THOMAS WIGG, EDWARD WIGG. Before JOHN MULLRYNE, J.P. JAMES MICKIE, D.P.R.

Book A-A, p. 27
11 & 12 Apr. 1744
L & R by Mortgage
SAMUEL COMMANDER, planter, of Craven Co., to JAMES MICKIE, ESQ., of Berkeley Co. Whereas MICKIE, by L & R dated 13 & 14 Aug. 1737, for ₤ 430 currency, sold COMMANDER 500 a. in Craven Co., bounding W on CAPT. BROCKINGTON; S & N on Black River; N on SAMUEL COMMANDER; E on WILLIAM SWINTON; which 500 a. was part of 1000 a. granted to WILLIAM SWINTON; & whereas COMMANDER gave bond, this date to MICKIE, in penal sum of ₤ 1789:6 for payment of ₤ 894:13 SC money on 12 Aug. 1744; now, as security COMMANDER conveys to MICKIE the said 500 a. Witnesses: GEORGE DICK, NATHANIEL MCCULLOUGH. Before WILLIAM WHITESIDE, J.P. JAMES MICKIE, D.P.R.

Book A-A, p. 35
17 & 18 Apr. 1744
L & R
PAUL WILKINS, planter, of Edisto, to JOHN SPENCER, planter, of Johns Island, Colleton Co., for ₤ 1100 SC money, 162-1/2 a. on W side Stono River, bounding S on part of same tract belonging to ARCHIBALD WILKINS; E on 2 parts same tract belonging to JONATHAN WILKINS & SAMUEL WILKINS; W on THOMAS FLEMMING; N on BENJAMIN DARRIATT (D'HARIETTE?) & on a creek of Stono River. Witnesses: WILLIAM WILKINS, THOMAS HEYWARD, JOSEPH BURCHALL. Before ROBERT AUSTIN, J.P. JAMES MICKIE, D.P.R.

Book A-A, p. 42
22 & 23 Nov. 1744
L & R
ELIZABETH BELLINGER, widow & executrix of EDMOND BELLINGER, the second Landgrave, to WILLIAM BUCHANAN, merchant, of St. Helena Parish, Granville Co., for ₤ 180 SC money (& rent of 4 pence sterling forever for each lot), 2 lots in town of Edmundsbury on Ashepoo River #3 & #13, containing 1/2 a., each 105 ft. square, fronting the Bay & Bridge Street, #3 now occupied by DAVID JONES (formerly by WILLIAM BUCHANAN); #13 fronting Bridge Street & Edmund Street & adjoining lot #3 first sold to RICHARD WEBB & by bill of sale cum als made over to WILLIAM BUCHANAN by WEBB. Witnesses: JANE HILL, WILLIAM BACKSHALL. Before JAMES MICKIE, J.P. & D.P.R.

Book A-A, p. 51
27 Nov. 1744
Agreement
THOMAS SACHEVERELL, planter, of Pon Pon, Colleton Co., grandson & heir-at-law of MATHEW BEE, of Charleston, (who was eldest brother & heir-at-law to MARY FRANKLIN, widow) of the 1 part; JOHN COLEMAN, hatter, & MARTHA his wife, of Charleston, of other part. Whereas MARY FRANKLIN owned a half-acre lot, English measure, on S side Dock Street (now Queen Street), bounding E on JOHN BEE; S on ANDREW DUPY; W on ROBERT HUME; & by will bequeathed the lot & the rent due for her house there to be equally divided among her brothers THOMAS BEE & JOHN BEE & her sister MARTHA DUCAT, which devise for want of proper legal words did not convey the fee simple & inheritance of the lot to the devisees & they were only tenants in common for life, the fee simple

remaining in MARY FRANKLIN & her heirs; & whereas THOMAS SACHEVERELL is
the heir-at-law of MARY FRANKLIN, being only grandson of MATHEW BEE, her
eldest brother, & should have possession after the death of THOMAS, JOHN
& MARTHA, but notwithstanding his right to the property JOHN BEE, carpenter, of Charleston, (son of THOMAS BEE) did for divers years keep possession & built several tenements thereon; & whereas said JOHN BEE (son of
THOMAS) purchased in fee simple from JOHN BERRISFORD, ESQ., a piece of
ground adjoining the lot, fronting 32-1/2 ft. on Dock Street & built a
house thereon & died seized thereof; & whereas on the death of JOHN BEE
the piece of land descended to THOMAS SACHEVERELL as heir-at-law (as
grandson of MATHEW BEE, eldest brother of THOMAS BEE, father of said JOHN
BEE); & whereas MARTHA (late wife of JOHN BEE, now wife of JOHN COLEMAN)
is entitled to dower; now to settle & remove all disputes regarding their
several claims, they agree as follows: IN consideration of MARTHA & JOHN
COLEMAN immediately putting SACHEVERELL as heir in full possession of the
2 lots, SACHEVERELL assigns the second lot (purchased from BERRISFORD)
with its houses to MARTHA COLEMAN put SACHEVERELL in possession of first
lot. Witnesses: PETER POINTSETT, WILLIAM SMYTH. Before HENRY GIBBES,
J.P. JAMES MICKIE, D.P.R.

Book A-A, p. 54   COL. MILES BREWTON & MARY his wife, to EBENE-
21 & 22 Sept. 1744   ZER SIMMONS, merchant, all of Charleston, for
L & R   Ł 600 SC money, 2 lots, #309 & #310, in
                              Charleston, bounding S on marsh; W on Old
Church Street; N on lot #308; E on lots 62, 61, & 77. Witnesses: DANIEL
BADGER, JOHN REMINGTON. Before ROBERT AUSTIN, J.P. JAMES MICKIE, D.P.R.

Book A-A, p. 60   HENRY YONGE, storekeeper, of Wadmalaw Island,
19 & 20 Sept. 1744   Colleton Co., to JOHN WATSON, merchant, of
L & R by Mortgage   Charleston, as further security on debt of
                              Ł 1768:2:3 & interest, 500 a. in Colleton Co.;
also 200 a. on John's Island; also lots #10 & #138 in town of Beaufort.
Whereas FRANCIS YONGE by deed poll dated 29 Feb. 1743 sold HENRY YONGE
500 a. at Tooboodoo, adjoining the lands of ROBERT YONGE & HENRY HYRNE; &
whereas WILLIAM CHAMBERS, & ISABELLA his wife, by L & R dated 27 & 28
Feb. 1743, sold HENRY YONGE 200 a. on John's Island as by plat & grant
from Gov. JAMES MOORE to COL. ROBERT GIBBES dated 29 May 1702; & whereas
HENRY YONGE owns 2 lots, #10 & 138 in Beaufort, Granville Co.; & whereas
HENRY YONGE gave bond dated 19 May 1743, together with JOSEPH WILKINSON,
to JOHN WATSON in penal sum of Ł 3178:9:10 for payment of Ł 1589:4:11 SC
money, with interest, on 15 Jan. next; & whereas there is now due
Ł 1768:2:3 now YONGE gives the above named properties as security; re-
deemable 1 Mar. next. Witnesses: THOMAS BROUGHTON, JR., HUGH ANDERSON.
Before JAMES WRIGHT, J.P. JAMES MICKIE, D.P.R.

Book A-A, p. 71   ELIZABETH BELLINGER, of Berkeley Co., widow,
3 & 4 Jan. 1743   devisee & executrix of will of Landgrave ED-
L & R   MUND BELLINGER, & devisee of HESTER ELLIOTT,
                              widow; to CHARLES PINCKNEY, ESQ., of Charles-
ton; in consideration of council & advice frequently given by said PINCK-
NEY to said Landgrave BELLINGER, & for Ł 100 currency, 500 a. at head of
fork of Pogotalligo River, in St. Helena Parish, Granville Co.; also lot
#20 in town of Edmundsburg; also lot #4 in Shem Town (alias Butler's
Town) near Ashley River Ferry. Whereas Landgrave BELLINGER owned 500 a.
under patent from Lords Proprs. granted to EDMOND BELLINGER, his father,
at the forks of the head of Pogotalligo River, St. Helena Parish, Granville Co., bounding SW & W on the River; NW on estate of EDMUND BELLING-
ER; NE on lands of said estate intended for WILLIAM ELLIOTT; SE on lands
of said estate run out as a legacy to GEORGE BELLINGER & lately occupied
by ARTHUR BULL, planter; & whereas BELLINGER also owned 6000 a. on S side
Ashepoo River, in St. Bartholomew's Parish, called Occatee, being part of
his father's patent; & whereas EDMOND BELLINGER by will dated 21 Feb.
1739 directed that a town should be laid out on part of the Occatee tract
near the bridge over Ashepoo River (which was done & the town called Edmundsbury); & directed all lands, not devised, to be sold by his wife (or
in case of her death, by his son EDMOND) & whereas ELIZABETH by will of
her mother HESTER ELLIOTT, owned lot #4 in Shem Town (alias Butler's
Town) at Ashley River Ferry, in St. Andrews Parish, Berkeley Co., (HESTER
ELLIOTT having title by will of her husband SHEM BUTLER, father of ELIZA-
BETH BELLINGER); now ELIZABETH BELLINGER conveys the 500 a., lot #4, &

91

lot #20 to PINCKNEY. Plat showing 500 a. on fork between Stoney Creek &
Pocotalligo River laid out by ELISHA BUTLER, surveyor, for CHARLES PINCK-
NEY, at request of ELIZABETH BELLINGER bounding SW on JONATHAN BRYAN; NW
on land (called DALL SAVANNAH) belonging to estate of BELLINGER sold but
not conveyed to THOMAS BUTLER; NE on land of said estate intended for
WILLIAM PALMER; the 500 a. being part of 13,000 a. conveyed to Landgrave
BELLINGER, the son, in 1728, under the patent granted by the Lords Proprs.
to the father as part of 48,000 a. in patent. Plat certified 21 Nov.
1741. Witnesses: JANE HILL, WILLIAM BACKSHALL. Before THOMAS DRAYTON,
J.P. JAMES MICKIE, D.P.R.

Book A-A, p. 79   JOHN MCMECHAN, planter, to ALEXANDER NISBETT,
9 & 10 Dec. 1743   ESQ., late of Charleston, by JAMES MICKIE &
L & R by Mortgage   JAMES AKIN, his lawful attorneys in this be-
                         half, as security on bond of even date in pe-
nal sum of Ŀ 2517:10 for payment of Ŀ 1258:15 SC money, with interest, on
10 Dec. 1747; 3 Negro men, 1 Negro boy; & 440 a., part of 900 a. lately
sold by NISBETT to MCMECHAN & ANTHONY WHITE, JR.; bounding NW on land
sold by NISBETT to ANTHONY WHITE; other sides on vacant land. Witnesses:
WILLIAM SNOW, VELSON GREIMS (GRIMES), JOSEPH CHAMBERLIN. A clasp knife
delivered. Before JAMES MICKIE, J.P. & D.P.R.

Book A-A, p. 87   ELIZABETH HILL, of Berkeley Co., widow & ex-
11 Dec. 1744   ecutrix, of CHARLES HILL, ESQ., to THOMAS
Release   DEARINGTON, planter, for Ŀ 300 currency, 400
                         a., English measure, in Berkeley Co., bounding
S on head of Simmons's Creek, out of Cooper River; N on said creek; W on
SAMUEL COMMANDER; E on RICHARD BERESFORD. Witnesses: JAMES MCKELVEY,
WILLIAM SMITH, CHARLES HILL. Before THOMAS DALE, J.P. JAMES MICKIE,
D.P.R.

Book A-A, p. 92   JOHN (his mark) HUBURT, tailor, of Saxe Gotha
2 May 1738   Township, Berkeley Co., & JACOB SPEAR (SPEARS),
Sale   laborer, to THOMAS BROWN, Indian trader, of
                         Craven Co., for Ŀ 52 SC money, 50 a. in Saxa
Gotha Township, on SW side Santee River, Berkeley Co., bounding SW on
JOHN WELDRICK MILLER (now to HANNAH MILLER, widow); SW on JACOB SPEAR; NW
on land reserved for a town; being the front half of 100 a. laid out to
HUBERT & SPEAR. Witnesses: STEPHEN MARET, CHARLES O'NEAL. Before GEORGE
HAIG, J.P. Delivery by turf & twig. JAMES MICKIE, D.P.R.

Book A-A, p. 95   MATTHEW ROCHE; merchant, & ANNE his wife, to
26 & 27 Nov. 1744   JAMES MATTHEWS, merchant, all of Charleston,
L & R   for Ŀ 6000 SC money, part of lot #28 fronting
                         20 ft. on N side Broad Street, 100 ft. deep,
where GEORGE PHILIP & ALEXANDER LEVIE now keep store; also that half of
part of a lot fronting 30 ft. on N side Broad Street, 100 ft. deep, occupied by JOHN RATTRAY. Whereas TIMOTHY BELLAMY, merchant, of Charleston,
by will dated 25 Feb. 1725 bequeathed to his daughter, ANNE, now wife of
MATTHEW ROCHE, that part of lot #28 fronting 20 ft. on N side Broad
Street, 100 ft. deep, with house in which he then lived & other buildings
thereon, now occupied by GEORGE PHILIP & ALEXANDER LEVY, where they keep
store; & bequeathed to his daughter MARY part of a lot fronting 50 ft. on
N side Broad Street, 100 ft. deep, with the messuage & other houses thereon, now occupied by JOHN RATTRAY, & whereas MARY died & her part of a lot
descended to her 2 sisters, SARAH the wife of DANIEL CRAWFORD & said ANN
ROCHE, as coparceners; & whereas DANIEL & SARAH CRAWFORD on 14 May 1742
sold their share to MATTHEW ROCHE & he became owner of 1/2 of the part of
said lot in his own right & on the other half by right of his wife; &
whereas TIMOTHY BELLAMY gave his wife MARY the remaining part of lot #28,
fronting 34 ft., 100 ft. deep, with the messuage & tenements, for her
natural life; after her death to daughter ANNE; which messuage is at
present also occupied by GEORGE PHILIP & ALEXANDER LEVY; now ROCHE sells
MATTHEWS 2 parts of lot #28 on N side Broad Street. Witnesses: JAMES
DRUMMOND, ISAAC FOSTER. Before JAMES GREEME, J.P. JAMES MICKIE, D.P.R.

Book A-A, p. 104   JOHN DUBOSE to JAMES ALLEN, planter, for Ŀ 300
15 Nov. 1744   (paid by JAMES MCDANNIELL for ALLEN), all &
Sale   every of his lands in Christ Church Parish,
                         Berkeley Co. Signed by JOHN DUBOSE, MARY

DUBOSE. Witnesses: JOHN HOPE, SAMUEL NEILSON, JAMES MCDANNELL. Before
WILLIAM HENDRICK, J.P. JAMES MICKIE, D.P.R.

Book A-A, p. 106   WILLIAM GODFREY, planter, & ANN his wife, of
16 & 17 Mar. 1743   Berkeley Co., to MARTHA GODFREY, widow, for
L & R   Ł 50 SC money, 24 a. in Berkeley Co., bounding
                          W on RICHARD GODFREY; NE on PETER LESADE; S on
JOHN GODFREY. Witnesses: ROBERT D'ARQUES, JAMES SCARLETT. Before JOHN
CHAMPNEYS, J.P. JAMES MICKIE, D.P.R.

Book A-A, p. 112   RICHARD (his mark) MYRICK (MYZICK), planter,
7 & 8 Aug. 1744   & ELIZABETH (her mark) his wife, to WILLIAM
L & R   BAKER, shoemaker, all of Saxe Gotha Township,
                          Berkeley Co., for Ł 95 SC money, 350 a. in
Saxe Gotha Township & lot #91 containing 1/2 a. Whereas GEORGE II by
letters patent dated 12 Apr. 1744, signed by Gov. JAMES GLEN, granted
RICHARD MYZICK 350 a. in the limits of Saxe Gotha Township on SW side
Santee River, now bounding SE on CHRISTIAN RHETELSPERG; NW on GEORGE
HAIG; also a 1/2 a. town lot, #91. Witnesses: THOMAS WALLEXALLSON, JAMES
DENLEY. Before GEORGE HAIG, J.P. JAMES MICKIE, D.P.R.

Book A-A, p. 119   RICHARD GODFREY, gentlemen, of St. Andrews
4 Dec. 1744   Parish, to RICHARD LAKE, of same place, for 5
Lease   years from 25 Mar. next; for Ł 3 currency
                          yearly per a. cleared during said term; 100 a.
part of 224 a. known as Tyger Swamp in Berkeley Co., bounding N on ANDREW
DEVEAUX; E on MRS. ELIZABETH HILL; S on COL. GEORGE LUCAS; W on RICHARD
GODFREY. Witnesses: WILLIAM HARE, ELIZABETH CHEESEMAN, WILLIAM SMITH.
Before JACOB MOTTE, J.P. JAMES MICKIE, D.P.R.

Book A-A, p. 123   JOSEPH SPENCER, planter, to JOSEPH RIVERS,
25 Feb. 1743/4   cordwainer, for Ł 50 currency, 7 a. on James
Release   Island, Berkeley Co., bounding NE on THOMAS
                          DICKSON; S on dividing line; W on WILLIAM
CHAPMAN; E on part same tract; which land formerly belonged to ALEXANDER
SPENCER; was inherited by his son ALEXANDER SPENCER; then by his brother,
said JOSEPH SPENCER. REZIA (her mark) COZIAH, wife of JOSEPH SPENCER,
freely surrenders her dower. Witnesses: JOSEPH RIVERS, ROBERT RIVERS.
Before HENRY GIBBES, J.P. JAMES MICKIE, D.P.R.

Book A-A, p. 126   Vestry of Parish of St. Thomas, Berkeley Co.,
4 Dec. 1744   to ELIZABETH GIBBES, wife of COL. JOHN GIBBES
Assignment of Mortgage   (formerly ELIZABETH JENYS, widow, of Charles-
                          ton), for Ł 658:13:10 currency, the mortgage &
all deeds & papers relating to said mortgage. See Book G, p. 281. Signed: WILLIAM BRUCE, THOMAS HASELL, ISAAC LESESNE, PETER SIMONS, JAMES
LESESNE. Witnesses: EDWARD BULLARD (a Quaker), THOMAS WEAVER, J. HARTLEY.
Before JOHN DART, J.P. JAMES MICKIE, D.P.R.

Book A-A, p. 128   ROBERT BREWTON, SR., & ROBERT BREWTON, JR., to
12 & 13 Apr. 1743   DANIEL BADGER, painter, all of Charleston, for
L & R   Ł 300 currency, part of lot #39 in Charleston.
                          Whereas JOHN BULLOCH, bricklayer, by several
mesne conveyances, owned part of lot #39 on N side Tradd Street, which he
bequeathed (with the rest of his estate) to his wife, MARY, for her natural life, then to his daughter MILLICENT BREWTON, wife of ROBERT BREWTON,
SR.; which lot is bounding E & NE on JOHN FRASER; W on MR. DUCKATT; &
whereas MARY BULLOCK died soon after her husband's death, & MILLICENT inherited the property; & she dying soon after, her husband, ROBERT BREW-
TON, SR., became tenant for life by courtesy of England; & after his
death ROBERT BREWTON, JR. will inherit; now father & son convey to BADGER.
Witnesses: JOSEPH MOODY, MOSES AUDEBERT. Before THOMAS DALE, J.P. JAMES
MICKIE, D.P.R.

Book A-A, p. 136   JOHN LAURENS, saddler, to RICHARD BODICOTT,
7 & 8 Dec. 1744   vintner, both of Charleston, for Ł 1100 SC
L & R   money, 40 a. in Berkeley Co., with the tene-
                          ment commonly called the Quarter House, form-
erly belonging to JOSEPH HAWKINS; bounding W & S on RALPH IZARD; E on
JOHN BIRD; N on PAUL GRIMBALL. Witnesses: THOMAS BOLTON, JOHN FITCHETT.

Book A-A, p. 141   RICHARD GRIMSTONE, gentleman, to THOMAS HARDEN,
12 Jan. 1744   mariner, both of Charleston, for Ł 540 SC mon-
Feoffment   ey, tenement & part of lot #18 in Charleston,
                         bounding W 43 ft. on Union Street; S 136 ft.
on EDMOND HAWKINS; E on RICE PRICE & JAMES WITHERS; N on Queen Street.
Witnesses: RICE PRICE, JOHN REMINGTON, EDWARD BULLARD. Before HENRY GIB-
BES, J.P. JAMES MICKIE, D.P.R.

Book A-A, p. 146   RICHARD GRIMSTONE, gentleman, of Charleston,
12 Jan. 1744   declares he is lawful owner of tenement & part
Affidavit   of lot #18 bounding W 43 ft. on Union Street;
                         S 136 ft. on EDMUND HAWKINS; E on RICE PRICE &
JAMES WITHERS; N on Queen Street. Before HENRY GIBBES, J.P. JAMES
MICKIE, D.P.R.

Book A-A, p. 147   FREDERICK GAILLARD, planter, to JONATHAN
20 Apr. 1736   SKRINE, gentleman, both of St. James Santee,
Release of Inheritance   Craven Co. Whereas BARTHOLOMEW GAILLARD, of
                         St. James Santee bequeathed to his wife ELIZA-
BETH a plantation of 4 adjacent tracts, total 500 a., on Santee River,
commonly called Skrines Ferry, bounding S on vacant land & on BARTHOLOMEW
GAILLARD; E on MARY ESTHER KINLOCK; W on JOHN GENDRON; & whereas BARTHOL-
OMEW GAILLARD bequeathed to his wife, ELIZABETH, 2 other tracts in St.
James Santee, reputed to belong to the 4 before mentioned tracts as part
of the plantation on which BARTHOLOMEW GAILLARD lived until his death; 1
of 100 a., bounding N on BARTHOLOMEW GAILLARD & JOHN GENDRON; S & E on
vacant land; W on JOHN GENDRON; the other, 150 a., bounding E on BARTHOLO-
MEW GAILLARD; W on JOHN GENDRON; N & S on vacant lands; the 2, with the
4, making 850 a.; & whereas BARTHOLOMEW GAILLARD bequeathed the said
lands to FREDERICK GAILLARD, his eldest son (immediately after the death
of ELIZABETH his wife); now, for Ł 500 SC money, FREDERICK GAILLARD quit
claims to JONATHAN SKRINE, (SKRINE being in possession by right of his
wife, the said ELIZABETH) for his natural life, then to JOHN SKRINE &
MARY SKRINE, son & daughter (1/2 to each). Witnesses: JOHN HENTIE, JOHN
BARKSDALE. Before NOAH SERRE, J.P. JAMES MICKIE, D.P.R.

Book A-A, p. 153   MARGARET DUPLESSES (DUPLESSIS) widow of the
3 Dec. 1740 (44?)   Rev. MR. PETER DUPLESSES, Rector of the Parish,
Deed of Gift   for natural love & affection, to her children,
                         ELIZABETH, ANNE, ELISHA, MARGARET, (now MAR-
GARET CHICKEN), ANDRE, PETER, LYDIA, MADELAIN GUERRY, to be equally divided, according to value, her interest for her natural life in the real
& personal estate in Craven Co. of her father, except 1 Negro woman, 1
horse, 1 bed, & furniture of her own choosing. Whereas ANDRE REMBERT,
father of MARGARET DUPLESSES, by will dated 14 Mar. 1704 (old style) bequeathed divers legacies to his eldest daughter, ANN, & among his grandchildren, & later bequeathed to his daughter, said MARGARET, (then widow
of PETER GUERRY) for her natural life & afterwards to her children all
his real & personal estate not before devised; now MARGARET relinquishes
her title. Witness: ALEXANDER DUPONT. Before JOHN GENDRON, J.P. JAMES
MICKIE, D.P.R.

Book A-A, p. 155   WILLIAM WHIPPEY, planter, eldest son of WIL-
6 & 7 Oct. 1740   LIAM WHIPPEY, to JOSEPH WHIPPEY, planter, both
L & R   of Edisto Island, for Ł 1200 SC money, 230 a.
                         on Edisto Island, bounding W on said JOSEPH
WHIPPEY; N on marsh of THOMAS RAKE; other sides on vacant land. MARY
WHIPPEY, wife of WILLIAM, willingly surrenders her dower. Whereas WIL-
LIAM, Earl of Craven, Palatine; JOHN, Earl of Bath; ANTHONY, Lord Ashley;
GEORGE, Lord Carteret; SIR JOHN COLLETON, Baronet; & THOMAS AMY, ESQ.;
Lords Proprs.; on 31 Aug. 1694 granted WILLIAM WHIPPEY, 430 a., part of a
tract on Edisto Island formerly laid out for SIR PETER COLLETON, & where-
as his eldest son, WILLIAM, inherited; now the son sells part to JOSEPH
WHIPPEY. Witnesses: HENRY BAILEY, THOMAS RAKE, SAMUEL EATON, JOHN CAL-
DER. Before HENRY GIBBES, J.P. JAMES MICKIE, D.P.R.

Book A-A, p. 168   JOSEPH STANYARNE, planter, & ELIZABETH his
18 & 19 Dec. 1744   wife, of Johns Island, St. Johns Parish, Col-
L & R   leton Co., to HENRY SAMWAYS, planter, of James
                         Island, Berkeley Co., for Ł 1650 currency,

94

700 a. called Folly Island, bounding SE on the sea; NW on marsh & a creek; S on James Island; NE on a creek of S channel of Ashley River; SW on a creek. Whereas the Lords Proprs. on 9 Sept. 1696 granted WILLIAM RIVERS 700 a. in Berkeley Co. called Folly Island; which by his will dated 3 Oct. 1717 he gave to JOSEPH STANYARNE & RIVERS STANYARNE; & whereas on 7 July 1732 RIVERS STANYARNE conveyed half the island to JOSEPH STANYARNE; now JOSEPH sells to SAMWAYS. Witnesses: JOSEPH PHIPPS, THOMAS HUNSCOMB, JOHN JORDINE. Before ANTHONY MATHEWS, J.P. JAMES MICKIE, D.P.R.

Book A-A, p. 174   ELIZABETH BELLINGER, widow, devisee & execu-
24 & 25 July 1744   trix of will of Landgrave EDMOND BELLINGER, of
L & R   St. Andrews Parish to JAMES DEVEAUX, planter,
                        of Granville Co., for Ł 1812 currency, 906 a.,
part of 13,000 a., on TOMOTLEY SAVANNAH, Granville Co., bounding SW on JOSEPH BRYAN; NW on part of the 13,000 a. laid off to COL. JOHN PALMER; NE on CAPT. JOHN BULL & on the high road leading from the Huspa Neck to Salkeehas, also on the part resurveyed under THOMAS BULLINE'S warrant. Whereas EDMOND BELLINGER under his Landgrave's patent for 48,000 a. owned 13,000 a. in Granville Co., at the head of the N branch of Port Royal River, bounding E on COL. WILLIAM BULL & all other sides on land not laid out; & whereas by will dated 21 Feb. 1739 he directed all his land not otherwise disposed of to be sold by his wife (or in case of her death by his son EDMOND), & the money used to pay his debts; now she sells a piece of land to DEVEAUX. Witnesses: HENRY BYRNE, WILLIAM BACKSHELL. Before JOHN DRAYTON, J.P. JAMES MICKIE, D.P.R. Plat of 906 a. certified 10 May 1744 by HUGH BRYAN, Dep. Sur.

Book A-A, p. 179   CHARLES PINCKNEY, ESQ., of Charleston, to AN-
19 & 20 Oct. 1744   DREW DEVEAUX, JR., planter, of St. Helena Par-
L & R   ish, Granville Co., for Ł 1125 currency, 500 a.
                        Whereas Landgrave EDMUND BELLINGER, besides
other lands, granted by the Lords Proprs. to his father Landgrave EDMOND BELLINGER, owned 500 a. near the forks of the head of Pogotalligo River, St. Helena Parish, Granville Co., bounding SSW & W on branches of said river; NW on estate of EDMOND BELLINGER; NE part of said estate intended for WILLIAM ELLIOTT; SE on part of the estate run out as a legacy for GEORGE BELLINGER & lately occupied by ARTHUR BULL, planter; & whereas by will dated 21 Feb. 1739 Landgrave BELLINGER directed the residue of his real estate sold by his wife, ELIZABETH (or in case of her death, by his son EDMOND); & whereas ELIZABETH BELLINGER by L & R dated 3 & 4 Jan. 1743 sold the 500 a. to CHARLES PINCKNEY; now PINCKNEY sells to DEVEAUX. Witnesses: WILLIAM BULL, JR., CHARLES PINCKNEY, JR. Before HENRY GIBBES, J.P. JAMES MICKIE, D.P.R.

Book A-A, p. 185   ISAAC DUBOSE, son of SUSANNAH COOK, & heir-at-
12 June 1742   law to her real estate, to ELIZABETH WHILDEN,
Deed of Gift   for divers considerations, 150 a., part of his
                        mother's tract; to his brother, DANIEL DUBOSE,
150 a.; to his brother, STEPHEN DUBOSE, 150 a.; to his brother, JOHN DU-BOSE, 186 a. on which his mother lived; to his brother, ANDREW DUBOSE, 186 a. in the Pine Barren, adjoining the land given to JOHN; ELIZABETH WHILDEN, DANIEL DUBOSE, & STEPHEN DUBOSE to pay equal shares of Ł 100 to PETER DUBOSE. Witnesses: LEWIS GOURDIN, PAUL BRUNNEAU, JOHN LEGER. Before JOHN GENDRON, J.P. JAMES MICKIE, D.P.R.

Book A-A, p. 187   MATHEWRINE GUERIN, planter, & his wife, to
5 & 10 Sept. 1744   BERNARD ELLIOTT, planter, both of Berkeley Co.,
L & R by Mortgage   for Ł 2300 currency, 305 a., English measure,
                        in St. Andrews Parish, Berkeley Co., bounding
S on Stono River; E on JOSHUA TOOMER; W on JOHN TOOMER; N on BERNARD ELLIOTT & JOHN BONNEAU; which 305 a. GUERIN purchased from JOSHUA TOOMER; to be redeemed 10 Sept. 1745 by payment of Ł 2300 with interest. Witnesses: WILLIAM GLEN, JAMES SMITH, EDWARD FOWLER. Before ROBERT AUSTIN, J.P. JAMES MICKIE, D.P.R. Plat of 305 a. & 100 a. of marsh, part of a tract granted to HENRY TOOMER, on N side Stono River, bounding N on MR. BONNEAU, BERNARD ELLIOTT, & JOHN TOOMER; E on BERNARD ELLIOTT & JOSHUA TOOMER'S land & marsh; S on JUSHUA TOOMER'S marsh; W & NW on JOHN TOOM-ER'S land & marsh; certified 9 May 1741 by THOMAS WHITTER, Dep. Surv. Mortgage delcared satisfied 17 May 1748. JOHN BEALE, Register.

Book A-A, p. 195   ROWLAND PRITCHETT, planter, of New Windsor,
2 & 3 Jan. 1743   SC, to JAMES PARIS, saddler, of Charleston, &
L & R   WILLIAM MCCARTY, planter, of St. Johns, Berke-
                          ley Co., for Ł 400 SC money, 250 a. in New
Windsor Township, Granville Co., bounding E on vacant land; S on ROBERT
MCMURDY; W on Savannah River; N on EDMOND COUSIN; also lot #48 in said
town; also 200 a. in New Windsor Township, bounding S on ROBERT MCMURDY;
W on Savannah River; N on land laid out for use of the fort; E on the
town; also a town lot formerly granted to ROBERT VAUGHAN. Witnesses:
JOHN BAPTIST BARONES, SARAH SMITH, GEORGE (his mark) MCNICKLE. JAMES
MICKIE, D.P.R.

Book A-A, p. 201   ROWLAND PRITCHETT, planter, of Granville Co.,
27 & 29 June 1744   to WILLIAM MCCARTY & JAMES PARIS, Indian trad-
L & R   er & saddler, for Ł 600 currency, 300 a. in
                          New Windsor Township, bounding SE on MARTHA
MCGILLVEY, afterwards sold to WILLIAM HAMILTON; N on town line & ROBERT
VAUGHAN; SW on Savannah River; as by plat dated 12 Sept. 1741 belonging
to ROBERT MCMURDY. Witnesses: ROBERT MCMURDY, JOHN YOU, CHRISTIAN FOL-
BRIGHT. Before HENRY GIBBES, J.P. JAMES MICKIE, D.P.R.

Book A-A, p. 213   ANTHONY MATTHEWS, & ANN his wife, to JAMES
16 Sept. 1744   VOULOUX, of Charleston, for Ł 325; 13 ft. in
Deed of Sale   Broad St., bounding E on the part sold by
                          MATTHEWS to VOULOUX; W on ANTHONY MATTHEWS; N
on Broad Street; S on the French Church or Meeting House. Witnesses:
PETER BOCQUET, JAMES BALLANTINE. Before THOMAS DALE, J.P. JAMES MICKIE,
D.P.R.

Book A-A, p. 215   WILLIAM SNOW, & MARY his wife, to JOHN HEND-
15 & 16 Dec. 1742   LEN, planter, all of Craven Co., for Ł 295
L & R   currency, 500 a. part of 1800 a. in Williams-
                          burgh Township, Craven Co., on head of Black
Mingo Swamp, bounding SE on 400 a. laid out for DAVID ALLEN; NE on WIL-
LIAM SNOW; NW on vacant land; SW on MADAM MARY HILL. Whereas GEORGE II
by grant, dated 5 July 1737, signed by Lt. Gov. THOMAS BROUGHTON, granted
WILLIAM SNOW 1800 a. in Craven Co., now he sells 500 a. to HENDLEN, free
from MARY'S claim of dower. Witnesses: PAUL TRAPIER, JOHN MCIVER,
CHARLES KING, DENNIS O'BRYAN (school master). Before WILLIAM WHITESIDE,
J.P. JAMES MICKIE, D.P.R. Plat certified 15 Dec. 1742 by PETER LANE,
Dep. Surv.

Book A-A, p. 222   JOHN TIPPER, sail maker, of Charleston, to
7 & 8 Feb. 1744   JAMES HAWKINS, mariner, of H.M.S. The Rose,
L & R   for Ł 400 SC money part of lot #210 in
                          Charleston, bounding E 21 ft. on King Street;
W on WIDOW SHAW; S 130 ft. on MR. THEUS; N on MR. BECKMAN. Witnesses:
CHARLES RICHMOND GASCOIGNE, WILLIAM SMITH, ANN SMITH. Before JOHN CHAMP-
NEYS, J.P. JAMES MICKIE, D.P.R.

Book A-A, p. 228   WILLIAM SNOW, & MARY his wife, to WILLIAM JAM-
15 & 16 Dec. 1742   ES, all of Craven Co., for Ł 300 currency,
L & R   400 a., being the upper part of the 1800 a.
                          granted WILLIAM SNOW by GEORGE II, signed by
Lt. Gov. THOMAS BROUGHTON, on 5 July 1737; the 400 a. being in Williams-
burgh Township, on the head of Black Mingo Swamp, Craven Co., bounding SW
& SE on WILLIAM GRAHAM; SE & NE on JAMES MCNEALLY; NW on the 1800 a.
tract; the land being free from MARY'S claim of dower. Witnesses: PAUL
TRAPIER, CHARLES KING, DENNIS O'BRYAN (schoolmaster). Before JOHN BASS-
NETT, J.P. JAMES MICKIE, D.P.R. Plat of 400 a. certified 15 Dec. 1742
by PETER LANE, Dep. Surv.

Book A-A, p. 236   JACOB JEANNERET, & MARGARET his wife, of St.
15 & 16 Feb. 1744   James Santee Parish, Craven Co., to DANIEL
L & R by Mortgage   HUGER, planter, of St. John's Berkeley, for
                          Ł 1065 SC money, 3 plantations, total 850 a.,
in St. James Santee; 50 a. purchased from DANIEL JAUDON bounding N on
Echau Creek; E on ABRAHAM MICHEAU; W on PAUL BRUNNEAU; 400 a. purchased
from JOHN BARNETT, bounding N on Santee River; other sides on vacant land;
400 a. granted JEANNERET by Gov. ROBERT JOHNSON, bounding N on Santee

96

River; E & S on Watoohon Creek; W on above 400 a. & on Manigault's Island; upon condition that JEANNERET pay HUGER a Ł 900 bond dated 13 June 1739, with interest. Witnesses: WILLIAM THOMAS, DANIEL HORRY, DUKE BELL, ANDREW REMBERT, JR. Before FRANCIS LEJAU, J.P. JAMES MICKIE, D.P.R.

Book A-A, p. 243
15 & 16 Feb. 1744
L & R by Mortgage

JACOB JENNERETT, planter, & MARGARET his wife, of St. James Santee, Craven Co., to DANIEL HUGER, planter, of St. Johns, Berkeley Co., for Ł 1065 currency, part of lot #105 in Charleston, bounding N on part of same lot; S on REBECCA FLAVELL; E on JAMES PAIN; W 13-1/2 ft. on a street leading from White Point to the Quakers Meeting House; as security for the payment of a bond dated 13 June 1739 for Ł 900 currency, with interest. Witnesses: DANIEL HORRY, WILLIAM THOMAS, DUKE BELL, ANDREW REMBERT, JR. Before FRANCIS LEJAU, J.P. JAMES MICKIE, D.P.R.

Book A-A, p. 250
14 & 15 June 1742
L & R

JAMES (JACQUE) YOU, barber & MARY his wife, of Charleston, to THOMAS CONN, tailor, of Craven Co., for Ł 200 currency, 450 a. in Craven Co., on S side Peedee River, bounding SW on THOMAS CONN; SE on JOHN CONN; NW on MR. QUASH. Witnesses: HENRY SHERIFF, RICHARD WAINWRIGHT, WILLIAM SMITH. Before HENRY GIBBES, J.P. JAMES MICKIE, D.P.R.

Book A-A, p. 257
6 & 7 Feb. 1744/5
L & R by Mortgage

WILLIAM WHIPPEY, planter, & MARY his wife, of Colleton Co., to WILLIAM EDDINGS, JOSEPH RUSSELL, WILLIAM BURD, WILLIAM JENKINS, & JAMES CUTHBERT, as trustees for the Presbyterian Meeting House on Edisto Island; for Ł 1020:2:9 currency, 2 tracts, total 282 a., on Edisto Island; 212 a. bounding E on CHRISTIAN LINELY; NW on Daho Creek; S on WILLIAM WHIPPEY; 70 a. bounding E on WILLIAM WHIPPEY; other sides on creeks & marshes; as security for payment by WHIPPEY of the above amount, with interest, on 1 Mar. 1748/9. Witnesses: WILLIAM RUSSELL, PAUL HAMILTON, CATO ASH. Before ROBERT AUSTIN, J.P.

Book A-A, p. 265
22 Dec. 1740
Deed of Gift

FRANCIS HEXT, SR., planter, of St. John's Parish, Colleton Co., to his beloved son FRANCIS HEXT, JR., planter, of same place, for love & affection, 9 Negroes & 6 shares out of 30 of the produce of the plantation & barrels equivalent, all the cattle & hogs "in his mark", all the horses he calls his; a bed & furniture for same; his arms & ammunition; 380 a. formerly belonging to THOMAS HEXT, bounding N on WILLIAM STEVENS; E on JOHN STANYARNE; S on HUGH HEXT. Witnesses: WILLIAM GUY, CAPT. HUGH HEXT, JOHN LADSON. Before ANTHONY MATHEWS, J.P. JAMES MICKIE, D.P.R.

Book A-A, p. 267
23 Mar. 1743
Deed of Gift

MERIAM (her mark) OWEN, of Charleston, to her loving husband, JOHN OWEN, & to her children, for love & affection, part of lot #115, 67 ft. square, bounding N on Tradd Street; W on LEWIS PACQUEREAU; S on JOHN DANIEL (formerly THOMAS HOLTON); E on King Street leading to the Broad Path; which lot MERIAM OWEN purchased from THOMAS DIXON & EDWARD VANVELSON; JOHN OWEN, the husband, to have possession during his lifetime & after his death the land to be sold & the money divided equally amongst the children then living; the names of the present children being: ROBERT HAWKS, WILLIAM HAWKS, MARY HAWKS, SARAH HAWKS, JANE OWEN, & ELIZABETH OWEN. Witnesses: THOMAS BUSH, JAMES BALLANTINE, WILLIAM SMITH. Before HENRY GIBBES, J.P. JAMES MICKIE, D.P.R.

Book A-A, p. 270
20 & 21 Feb. 1744
L & R

JOHN STEEL, tavern keeper, & MARY his wife, to the Hon. JOSEPH WRAGG, ESQ., all of Charleston, for Ł 2500; part of lots #218 & 199 in Charleston, bounding W on Church Street; E on MR. SCOTT & JOSEPH WRAGG; S on HENRY MIDDLETON, JOHN CART, JAMES KINLOCK, & JOSEPH WRAGG; N on MR. NASH & land claimed by JOSEPH BEE. Witnesses: WILLIAM POLETRAMPTON, JOHN RATTRAY. Before ROBERT AUSTIN, J.P. JAMES MICKIE, D.P.R. Plat showing southern 2/3 parts of lot #218 bounding N on the third part belonging to ARTHUR NASH; E on part of lot #199 belonging to said STEEL; S on lot #217 belonging to the Hon. JOSEPH WRAGG, the Hon. JAMES KINLOCK, & JOHN CART; W on Church Street; also part of the northern

third part of lot #199 belonging to JOHN STEEL, bounding N on other third
part claimed by JOSEPH BEE; E on JOSEPH WRAGG & CAPT. WILLIAM SCOTT; S by
middle third part of lot #199 belonging to HENRY MIDDLETON; W on part of
said CART'S land & lot #218 belonging to JOHN STEEL & ARTHUR NASH. Certified 20 Feb. 1744 by GEORGE HUNTER, Sur. Gen. #76 granted CAPT. JOHN
ADDIE Mar. 5 1680 since surveyed for JOHN LADSON, May 11 1697.

Book A-A, p. 277   JOHN SELLENS, staymaker, of Winyaw, to WILLIAM
2 & 3 Mar. 1736   POOLE, planter, for Ł 250 currency, lot #29 in
L & R   Georgetown, containing 1/4 a., English meas-
                          ure, which SELLENS purchased on 25 Feb. 1734
from GEORGE PAWLEY, WILLIAM SWINTON & DANIEL LAROCHE, all of Prince
George Parish, Winyaw, Craven Co.; which lot #29 is bounding SW on Front
Street; SE on lot #30; NE on lot #63; NW on lot #28. Witnesses: CHARLES
HOPE, THOMAS LAROCHE, JOSEPH ALLEN, HENRY WARNER. Before PAUL TRAPIER,
J.P. JAMES MICKIE, D.P.R.

Book A-A, p. 281   WILLIAM POOLE, planter, of Winyaw, to JOHN
13 & 14 Sept. 1743   OYSTON, merchant, of Charleston, for Ł 300
L & R   currency, lot #29 in Georgetown containing
                          1/4 a., English measure, bounding SW on Front
Street; SE on lot #30; NE on lot #63; NW on lot #28. Whereas on 25 Feb.
1734 GEORGE PAWLEY, WILLIAM SWINTON & DANIEL LAROCHE, all of Prince
George Parish, Winyaw, Craven Co., sold the above lot #29 to JOHN SELLENS;
& whereas SELLENS conveyed the lot on 3 Mar. 1736 to WILLIAM POOLE; now
POOLE conveys to OYSTON. Witnesses: HENRY WARNER, ROBERT PIERCE HENDER-
SON. Before JOHN BASSNETT, J.P. JAMES MICKIE, D.P.R.

Book A-A, p. 287   WILLIAM GUY, JR. to THOMAS LAMBOLL & GEORGE
12 & 13 Mar. 1744   SEAMAN, merchants, as tenants in common & not
L & R by Mortgage   as joint tenants, as security on bond of even
                          date in penal sum of Ł 347:2:10 for payment of
Ł 173:11:5 SC money with interest on 13 Mar. next; & as security on bond
of even date given GEORGE SEAMAN in penal sum of Ł 207:4:6 for payment of
Ł 103:12:3 currency, with interest, on 13 Mar. next; 1/3 part of a part
of lot #73 in Charleston, bounding N 20 ft. on Tradd Street; W on the
part belonging to JONATHAN COLINGS & SARAH his wife; E on GEORGE DUCATT;
S on THOMAS ROSE. Witnesses: JOHN ALLEN, CHARLES CALDER. Before JAMES
WRIGHT, J.P. JAMES MICKIE, D.P.R. THOMAS LAMBOLL acknowledged receipt
of Ł 176:11:5 currency from WILLIAM GUY, JR. & declared mortgage discharged of all claim by him. GEORGE SEAMAN acknowledged receipt of
Ł 105:5:9 currency, in full of all claim by him.

Book A-A, p. 294   WILLIAM (his mark) PRICE, planter, & ANN his
9 & 10 Aug. 1743   wife, of Prince Frederick's Parish, Craven
L & R   Co., to EDWARD CLEMENTS, planter, of Prince
                          George's Parish, for Ł 300 currency, 300 a. on
SE side Waccamaw River, Craven Co., bounding NE on MR. FRANK; SW on MI-
CHAEL JEAN; SE on vacant land. Witnesses: WILLIAM WATIES, JOHN HENTIE.
Before JOHN GENDRON, J.P. JAMES MICKIE, D.P.R.

Book A-A, p. 300   DANIEL LAROCHE, ESQ., of Prince George Parish,
11 Feb. 1744   Craven Co., to JOHN HENTIE, gentleman, of
Deed of Sale   Georgetown; for Ł 10 currency, 500 a. in Cra-
                          ven Co., orginally granted to WILLIAM HINCKLEY,
bounding NE on Black River; SW on JOHN WHITE; SE on Green's Creek & WIL-
LIAM CRIPPS; NW on JOHN WHITE; as by plat signed by DANIEL LAROCHE; to
hold the tract for 10 years. Should HENTIE, himself, within the 10 years,
pay LAROCHE Ł 71:10 sterling British, or value, the land to be his; but
if paid by executors or administrators, then the land to next heir at law;
if paid by assigns, then they to hold the land. Witnesses: WILLIAM COLT,
JOHN BEAN. Before PAUL TRAPIER, J.P. JAMES MICKIE, D.P.R. On 2 Jan.
1750 JOHN HENTIE, for valuable considerations, surrendered to DANIEL LA-
ROCHE, as in his former estate, all his claim to above land. Witness:
DAVID MONTAIGUT (?). Not proved but recorded 9 Feb. 1764 by WILLIAM HOP-
TON, Pub. Reg.

Book A-A, p. 304   THOMAS BOWEN, weaver, & CHRISTIAN (her mark)
4 Mar. 1744   his wife, to SAMUEL D'SAURENEY, yeoman, both
Release   of Craven Co., for Ł 150 currency, 100 a. in

Welch tract, Craven Co., bounding SE on PeeDee River; SW on vacant land; NE on WILLIAM CAREY; as by grant dated 29 Jan. 1742. Witnesses: JOHN EVANS, JOB EDWARDS. Before WILLIAM JAMES, J.P. JAMES MICKIE, D.P.R.

Book A-A, p. 306   JAMES DIXEY (DIXSEE), planter, of Granville
24 May 1744   Co., to his son, JAMES DIXEY, JR., for love &
Deed of Gift   affection, 60 a. on Stony Creek, bounding E &
                         N on said creek; S & W on JONATHAN BRYAN,
planter. Witnesses: WILLIAM GRICKSON, DAVID RICE. Before HENRY GIBBES,
J.P. JAMES MICKIE, D.P.R.

Book A-A, p. 308   THOMAS STEWART & THOMAS (his mark) HEATLEY &
2 Apr. 1741   SUSANNAH HEATLEY (wife of THOMAS), to ARTHUR
Deed of Feoffment   NASH, all of Charleston, for ₤ 500 SC money,
                        the northern part of lot #218 in Charleston,
fronting W 41 ft. 4 in. on Church Street; bounding S 239-1/4 ft. on JOHN
STEEL; E on THOMAS MIDDLETON; N on JAMES JORDAN. Witnesses: WILLIAM HAR-
RIS, ROBERT HARVEY, JR., JAMES HILLIARD. Before JACOB MOTTE, J.P. JAMES
MICKIE, D.P.R.

Book A-A, p. 311   The Rev. MR. FRANCIS GUICHARD, pastor of
1 Oct. 1742   French Protestant Church of Charleston, GAB-
Lease   RIEL MANIGAULT, ISAAC MAZYCK, PAUL MAZYCK, JA-
                        COB MARTIN, JOHN NEUFVILLE, BENJAMIN D'HAR-
RIETTE, & GIDEON FAUCHERAUD, to JAMES HILLIARD, watchmaker, of Charleston,
for 50 years, for ₤ 2:13:7 sterling, or value, per annum in 2 half yearly
payments; part of lot #93 fronting W 25 ft. on King Street; bounding S on
ROBERT HARVEY; E on MR. BOUGUARD; N on part same lot; HILLIARD to pay all
taxes & assessments & at his own expense build a substantial brick house
15 ft. front, 27 ft. deep, with 2 chimneys therein, at least 1 story high,
with garrets in roof, & keep same in good repair. The lot & houses to be
returned in good order to parties of first part, or their survivors, at
expiration of term. Witnesses: THOMAS PINCKNEY, CHARLES PINCKNEY. Before THOMAS DALE, J.P. JAMES MICKIE, D.P.R.

Book A-A, p. 317   CATHERINE TAYLOR, widow, of St. John's Parish,
4 & 5 Jan. 1741   Berkeley Co., heretofore called CATHERINE LE-
L & R   NOBLE (daughter & devisee of HENRY LENOBLE,
                        merchant, of Charleston), RENE RAVENEL, plant-
er of St. John's Parish, & SUSANNAH his wife (sister of CATHERINE TAYLOR
& daughter & devisee of CATHERINE LENOBLE the elder late the widow & devisee of said HENRY LENOBLE), & RENE RAVENEL, the younger, planter (son &
heir apparent of said SUSANNAH RAVENEL & grandson & 1 of the devisees of
said CATHERINE LENOBLE), to the Rev. MR. FRANCIS GUICHARD, pastor of the
church of French Protestants in Charleston, GABRIEL MANIGAULT, ISAAC MAZ-
YCK, PAUL MAZYCK, JACOB MARTIN, PAUL NEUFVILLE, PAUL DOUXSAINT, BENJAMIN
D'HARRIETTE, & GIDEON FAUCHERAUD, of Charleston; for ₤ 100 currency; 2
lots #92 & 93, in Charleston, for the use of the French Protestants.
Whereas the Lords Proprs. on 14 Nov. 1701 granted HENRY LENOBLE & PETER
BURTELL for the use of the French Protestants 2 lots, #92 & 93 in Charleston, bounding S on JAMES TOMSON, butcher, (formerly JOHN BROWN); N on
PETER UNDERWOOD'S lots; E on MR. DEARSLEY & others; W on King Street running from Ashley River between the lots of JOHN STEVENS & MARY BENSON; &
whereas HENRY LENOBLE, as owner of the 2 lots, by will dated 18 July 1715,
bequeathed the residue of his estate (including said 2 lots) equally to
his wife, CATHERINE LENOBLE, & his daughter CATHERINE (now CATHERINE TAY-
LOR); & whereas CATHERINE, the mother, & CATHERINE the daughter, owned
the lots as tenants in common; & whereas CATHERINE, the mother, by will
dated 25 Feb. 1725, (after several devises to & among her grandsons,
children of said SUSANNA RAVENEL), bequeathed the residuum of her estate
(including her half of said 2 lots), equally to her 2 daughters, said
SUSANNAH RAVENEL & CATHERINE LENOBLE (now TAYLOR); by which the half of
said 2 lots became vested in CATHERINE TAYLOR, SUSANNAH RAVENEL & RENE
RAVENEL the younger; now they, & RENE RAVENEL the elder, convey the land,
as above; for the use of the French Protestants of the Province. Witnesses: STEPHEN MAZYCK, JOHN RICHBOURG, SAMUEL EDGAR. Before JACOB MOTTE,
J.P. JAMES MICKIE, D.P.R.

Book A-A, p. 327   GEORGE II, to JAMES ST. JULIEN & JAMES STEWART,
5 Jan. 1741   ESQRS. Whereas by L & R dated 4 & 5 Jan. 1741,

Writ of Dedimus Postatem   (see p. 317) CATHERINE TAYLOR, widow; SUSANNAH, wife of RENE RAVENEL the elder; & RENE RAVENEL the younger; of St. John Parish, Berkeley Co., of the 1 part; conveyed to the Rev. MR. FRANCIS GUICHARD, pastor of church of French Protestants of Charleston, GABRIEL MANIGAULT, ISAAC MAZYCK, PAUL MAZYCK, JACOB MARTIN, JOHN NEUFVILLE, PAUL DOUXSAINT, BENJAMIN D'HARRIETTE, GIDEON FAUCHERAUD, of the other part, lots #92 & 93 in Charleston; & whereas SUSANNAH RAVE-NEL by reason of certain indispositions cannot come before our Chief Justice to make her acknowledgment & recognition for releasing her title & interest without great inconvenience & prejudice of her health, we command you to go to said SUSANNAH & personally receive her acknowledgements & recognitions & cause them to be returned before our Chief Justice of Court of C.P. at Charleston. Witness: BENJAMIN WHITAKER, C.J.   JAMES MICKIE, D.P.R.

Book A-A, p. 329   SUSANNAH RAVENEL, wife of RENE RAVENEL, being
10 Mar. 1741   privately & separately examined by JAMES ST.
Release & Renunciation   JULIEN & JAMES STEWART, commissioners named in
                         annexed Writ of Dedimus Potestatem, acknowl-
edged that she freely & voluntarily consented & joined with her husband in L & R dated 4 & 5 Jan. 1741 (see p. 317) made between CATHERINE TAYLOR, widow; said SUSANNAH RAVENEL; said RENE RAVENEL the elder; & RENE RAVENEL the younger, of the 1 part; & the Rev. MR. FRANCIS GUICHARD, pastor of the church of French Protestants, GABRIEL MANIGAULT, ISAAC MAZYCK, PAUL MAZYCK, JACOB MARTIN, JOHN NEUFVILLE, PAUL DOUXSAINT, BENJAMIN D'HAR-RIETTE, & GIDEON FAUCHERAUD; conveying lots #92 & #93 as a gift for the use of the French Protestants of the Province. JAMES MICKIE, D.P.R.

Book A-A, p. 332   JOHN (his mark) GREEN, planter, of Craven Co.,
9 Aug. 1742   to his loving son, WILLIAM SMITH, cordwainer,
Deed of Gift   for love & affection, 300 a. in Craven Co., at
                         Winyaw, bounding S on MR. LLOYD & on MOREAU
SARRAZIN; N on said JOHN GREEN; E on Black River. Witnesses: WILLIAM GREEN, OLIVER UPSALL. Before PAUL TRAPIER, J.P. JAMES MICKIE, D.P.R.

Book A-A, p. 333   FRANCIS DESCHAMPS, planter, of Berkeley Co.,
1 Dec. 1744   to STEPHEN MILLER (or MOUMIER), merchant, as
Release by Mortgage   security on bond of even date in penal sum of
                        ᴸ 1400 for payment of ᴸ 700 SC money, with in-
terest, on 1 Dec. 1748; 3 Negro men, 3 Negro women, & 170 a.; purchased from THOMAS JOHNSON, in Christ Church Parish, Berkeley Co.; bounding NW on THOMAS JOHNSON; NE on Winyaw Creek; SE on the sea shore. Witnesses: SAMUEL DRAKE (a Quaker), BENJAMIN SINGLETARY. A couple of lancets delivered in the name of the whole. Before ROBERT AUSTIN, J.P. JAMES MICKIE, D.P.R. On 25 July 1750 STEPHEN MILLER declared mortgage satisfied. Witness: LACHᴺ MCKINTOSH.

Book A-A, p. 340   GENEROUS GRIMSTON, gentleman, son of RICHARD
26 Mar. 1745   GRIMSTON, formerly of London, now of Charles-
Renunciation of Right ton, SC, for divers considerations, releases
                        to THOMAS HARDEN, mariner, of Charleston, all
his right, title & interest in that part of lot #18 in Charleston bounding W 43 ft. on Union Street; S on a messuage & piece of ground occupied by EDMUND HAWKINS; E on RICE PRICE & JAMES WITHERS; N 136 ft. on Queen Street. Witnesses: WILLIAM SAXBY, JOHN REMINGTON. Before ROBERT AUSTIN, J.P. JAMES MICKIE, D.P.R.

Book A-A, p. 342   JOSHUA WILKS (WILKESY), planter, of Christ
16 Nov. 1744   Church Parish, Berkeley Co., to SAMUEL JONES,
Deed of Sale   planter, of Sampeet, St. George's Parish, for
                        ᴸ 600 SC money, 768 a. at head of Sampit Creek,
Winyaw, Craven Co., bounding N on MR. HODDY; E on CAPT. BONNIE; W on JO-SIAH SMITH & HODDY; S on land granted NATHANIEL FORD. JOHANNA, wife of JOSHUA WILKS, freely gives up her title of dower. Witnesses: JAMES OUS-LEY, JOHN HOLMES. Before JCO. BOND, J.P. JAMES MICKIE, D.P.R.

Book A-A, p. 345   SUSANNAH HEXT, widow, & FRANCIS HEXT the young-
28 & 29 Mar. 1745   er, of St. John's Parish, Colleton, (executrix
L & R   & executor of will of HUGH HEXT, planter), to
                        Lt. of Marines HECTOR VAUGHAN, of COL.

COTTERILLS Regiment, for Ⱡ 1080 SC money, 350 a. on Johns Island, Colle-
ton Co., on SE side Stono River, bounding SW on THOMAS TATNELL; SE on
ISAAC WAIGHT (formerly HUGH HEXT & ABRAHAM WAIGHT); NE on JOHN STANYARNE,
JR. Whereas HUGH HEXT was seized in his demesne as of fee in 350 a. on
Johns Island which he had purchased from THOMAS TAINALL, & by will dated
9 Nov. 1744 directed that the tract be sold & the money applied to pay-
ment of his just debts, now the executrix & executor sell to VAUGHAN.
Witnesses: GEORGE NICHOLAS, MUMFORD MILNER, THOMAS TATNALL. Before JAMES
WEDDERBURN, J.P. JAMES MICKIE, D.P.R.

Book A-A, p. 352   SUSANNAH HEXT, widow of HUGH HEXT, planter, of
29 Mar. 1745   St. Johns Parish, Colleton Co., for Ⱡ 10 cur-
Renunciation of Dower   rency, to Lt. of Marines HECTOR VAUGHAN, of
                        COL. COTTERELL'S Regiment, her title of dower
in the 350 a. purchased by HUGH HEXT from THOMAS TATNALL. (See p. 345).
Witnesses: MUMFORD MILNER, GEORGE NICHOLAS. Before JAMES WEDDERBURN, J.P.
JAMES MICKIE, D.P.R.

Book A-A, p. 355   WILLIAM THOMAS, planter, & JUDITH his wife, to
3 & 4 Feb. 1744   MAJ. ELIAS HORRY, of St. James Santee, Craven
L & R by Mortgage   Co., for Ⱡ 3000 currency, 290 a. in St. James
                        Santee, bounding E on Wambaw Creek; N on MR.
CARTER; W on vacant land; S on MR. RICHBURGH. Bond given for full amount
& interest. Witnesses: DANIEL HORRY, ANDREW DELAVILLETTE. Before JOHN
GENDRON, J.P. JAMES MICKIE, D.P.R. On 21 May 1752 ELIAS HORRY declared
mortgage paid in full. Witness: WILLIAM HOPTON.

Book A-A, p. 360   TACITUS GAILLARD, planter, of St. James Santee,
28 & 29 Mar. 1745   Craven Co., to ELIAS HORRY, of Prince George
L & R   Parish, for Ⱡ 650 currency, 300 a. in Craven
                        Co., bounding SE on Santee River; NW on BAR-
THOLOMEW GAILLARD; NE on vacant land; E on ELIAS HORRY (formerly JOHN
BELL). Witnesses: THEODORE GAILLARD, ALCIMUS GAILLARD, DUKE BELL. Be-
fore JOHN GENDRON, J.P. JAMES MICKIE, D.P.R.

Book A-A, p. 365   WILLIAM BROWN, planter, to WILLIAM FLEMING,
20 & 21 Feb. 1744   planter, both of Craven Co., as security on
L & R by Mortgage   bond of even date in penal sum of Ⱡ 3020 con-
                        ditioned for payment of Ⱡ 1512:11 SC money on
1 Mar. next, 700 a. in Craven Co., bounding NW on PETER CREEK; SW on
Black River; SE on THOMAS BOGGS; SE on vacant land. Witnesses: SAMUEL
HUNTER, EDMUND ROBINSON. Before PAUL TRAPIER, J.P. JAMES MICKIE, D.P.R.

Book A-A, p. 371   The Rev. MR. FRANCIS GUICHARD, pastor of
1 Oct. 1742   church of French Protestants, GABRIEL MANI-
Lease for 50 Years   GAULT, ISAAC MAZYCK, PAUL MAZYCK, JACOB MARTIN,
                        JOHN NEUFVILLE, BENJAMIN D'HARRIETTE, & GIDEON
FAUCHERAUD, to JOHN VAUN (VAUGHAN), carpenter, all of Charleston, for 50
years, at yearly rent of Ⱡ 3:4 sterling, or value, in 2 half-yearly payments, that part of lot #93 fronting W 30 ft. on King Street; bounding S
on JAMES HILLIARD; E on MR. BOUGHAR; N on other part same lot; VAUN to
pay all taxes & at his own cost build & keep in good repair a substantial
brick house, at least 15 ft. front & 27 ft. deep, with 2 chimneys; at
lease 1 story high with garrets in roof. Witnesses: CHARLES PINCKNEY,
JOHN BONNETHEAU. Before THOMAS DALE, J.P. JAMES MICKIE, D.P.R.

Book A-A, p. 377   The Rev. MR. FRANCIS GUICHARD, pastor of
1 Oct. 1742   church of French Protestants, GABRIEL MANI-
Lease for 50 Years   GAULT, ISAAC MAZYCK, PAUL MAZYCK, JACOB MARTIN,
                        JOHN NEUFVILLE, BENJAMIN D'HARRIETTE, & GIDEON
FAUCHERAUD, to ROBERT HARVEY, carpenter, all of Charleston, for 50 years,
at yearly rent of Ⱡ 2:13:7 sterling, payable semi-annually, that part of
lot #93 fronting W 25 ft. on King Street; bounding S on WILLIAM FARROW
(PHARROW); E on DANIEL BOURGETT; N on other part same lot; HARVEY to pay
all taxes & build at his own cost & keep in good repair a substantial
brick house at least 15 ft. front & 27 ft. deep, with 2 chimneys; at
lease 1 story high, with garrets in roof. Witnesses: THOMAS PINCKNEY,
CHARLES PINCKNEY. Before THOMAS DALE, J.P. JAMES MICKIE, D.P.R.

Book A-A, p. 383   The Rev. MR. FRANCIS GUICHARD, pastor of the

1 Oct. 1742   church of French Protestants, GABRIEL MANI-
Lease for 50 Years   GAULT, ISAAC MAZYCK, PAUL MAZYCK, JACOB MARTIN,
                              JOHN NEUFVILLE, BENJAMIN D'HARRIETTE & GIDEON
FAUCHERAUD, to EDWARD SCULL, vintner, all of Charleston, for 50 years at
yearly rent of Ł 2:13:7 sterling, payable semi-annually, that part of lot
#92 fronting W 25 ft. on King Street; bounding S on MATHEW VANALL; E on
DANIEL BOURGETT; N on WILLIAM THARROW; SCULL to pay all taxes & to build
at his own expense, & keep in good repair, a substantial brick house at
least 15 ft. front, 27 ft. deep, at least 1 story high, with 2 chimneys,
& garrets in roof. Witnesses: THOMAS PINCKNEY, CHARLES PINCKNEY. Before
THOMAS DALE, J.P. JAMES MICKIE, D.P.R.

Book A-A, p. 388   The Rev. MR. FRANCIS GUICHARD, pastor of
1 Oct. 1742   church of French Protestants, GABRIEL MANI-
Lease for 50 Years   GAULT, ISAAC MAZYCK, PAUL MAZYCK, JACOB MARTIN,
                              JOHN NEUFVILLE, BENJAMIN D'HARRIETTE, & GIDEON
FAUCHERAUD, to MATHEW VANALL, carpenter, all of Charleston, for 50 years
at yearly rent of Ł 4:5 sterling, payable semi-annually, part of lot #92
fronting W 40 ft. on King Street; bounding S on JAMES TOMSON; E on DANIEL
BOURGATT; N on EDWARD SCULL; VANALL to pay all taxes & to build at his
own expense, & keep in good repair, a substantial brick house at least
30 ft. long & 16 ft. deep, at least 1 story high, with 2 chimneys, & garrets in roof. Witness: THOMAS PINCKNEY. Before THOMAS DALE, J.P. JAMES
MICKIE, D.P.R.

Book A-A, p. 394   The Rev. MR. FRANCIS GUICHARD, pastor of
1 Oct. 1742   church of French Protestants, GABRIEL MANI-
Lease for 50 Years   GAULT, ISAAC MAZYCK, PAUL MAZYCK, JACOB MARTIN,
                              JOHN NEUFVILLE, BENJAMIN D'HARRIETTE, & GIDEON
FAUCHERAUD, to DAVID MONGIN (MUNGIN), watch-maker, all of Charleston, for
50 years, at yearly rent of Ł 3:5 sterling, payable semi-annually, that
part of lot #93 fronting W 30 ft. 6 in. on King Street; bounding S on
JOHN VAUGHAN; E on MR. MCKENZIE; N on MARY POSTELL; MONGIN to pay all
taxes & to build at his own expense, & keep in good repair, a substantial
brick house at least 15 ft. front, 27 ft. deep, at least 1 story high,
with 2 chimneys, & garrets in roof. Witnesses: THOMAS PINCKNEY, CHARLES
PINCKNEY. Before THOMAS DALE, J.P. JAMES MICKIE, D.P.R.

Book A-A, p. 400   The Rev. MR. FRANCIS GUICHARD, pastor of
1 Oct. 1742   church of French Protestants, GABRIEL MANI-
Lease for 50 Years   GAULT, ISAAC MAZYCK, PAUL MAZYCK, JACOB MARTIN,
                              JOHN NEUFVILLE, BENJAMIN D'HARRIETTE, & GIDEON
FAUCHERAUD, to WILLIAM PHARROW (FARROW), mariner, all of Charleston, for
50 years, at a yearly rent of Ł2:13:7 sterling, payable semi-annually,
part of lot #92, fronting W 25 ft. on King Street; bounding S on EDWARD
SCULL; E on DANIEL BOURGETT; N on ROBERT HARVEY; FARROW to pay all taxes,
& at his own expense to build, & keep in good repair, a substantial brick
house, at least 15 ft. front & 27 ft. deep, at least 1 story high, with 2
chimneys, & with garrets in roof. Witnesses: CHARLES PINCKNEY, THOMAS
PINCKNEY. Before THOMAS DALE, J.P. JAMES MICKIE, D.P.R.

Book A-A, p. 406   GEORGE JACKSON, planter, to JOHN ANDREW, plant-
16 & 17 Feb. 1742/3   er, both of St. Bartholomew's Parish, Colleton
L & R   Co., for Ł 125 currency, lot #27 in Jackson's
                              Borough, fronting 100 ft. on Market Street;
218 ft. deep. Witnesses: THOMAS SIMMONS, WILLIAM SIMMONS. Before JAMES
BULLOCK, J.P. JAMES MICKIE, D.P.R.

Book A-A, p. 411   JOHN ANDREWS, planter, of St. Bartholomew's
1 & 2 Feb. 1744/5   Parish, Colleton Co., to ELIZAH BREBANT, pe-
L & R   ruke-maker, for Ł 100 currency, lot #27 in
                              Jackson's Borough, fronting 100 ft. on Market
Street; 218 ft. deep. Witnesses: JONATHAN WITTER, JOHN LAIRD. Before
CHARLES WRIGHT, J.P. JAMES MICKIE, D.P.R.

Book A-A, p. 417   JAMES LUBBOCK & THOMAS LUBBOCK, millwrights,
15 & 16 Apr. 1745   to JOHN PERDRIAU, planter, all of Craven Co.,
L & R by Mortgage   as security on bond of even date in penal sum
                              of Ł 1200 for payment of Ł 600 SC money, with
interest, on 15 Oct. 1747, 463 a., part of a tract of 900 a. Whereas by

grant dated 27 Nov. 1735, signed by Lt. Gov. THOMAS BROUGHTON, PAUL BRU-
NEAU, gentleman, was granted 900 a. in St. James Santee, Craven Co.,
bounding SE on Wambaw Creek; SE on PETER DE ST. JULIAN; N on ABRAHAM PER-
DRIAU; S on PAUL MAZYCK; W on vacant land; & whereas on 4 Sept. 1736 he
granted ANDREW REMBERT, planter, 483 a., part of the 900 a., bounding SE
on Wambaw Creek; E on PETER DE ST. JULIEN; N on ABRAHAM PERDRIAU; W & S
on PAUL BRUNEAU; & whereas REMBERT, by L & R dated 13 & 14 June 1744 sold
the 483 a. to JOHN PERDRIAU; & he, by L & R dated 12 & 13 Apr. 1745, sold
the 483 a. to JAMES LUBBOCK & THOMAS LUBBOCK; now they mortgage the tract
to JOHN PERDRIAU. Witnesses: JAMES ROBERT, THEODORE GAILLARD, MARY
SKRINE. Before JOHN GENDRON, J.P. JAMES MICKIE, D.P.R.

Book A-A, p. 428   AUGUSTUS LAURENS, planter, to JOHN PERDRIAU,
24 Apr. 1745   planter, both of St. James Santee, Craven Co.,
L & R   for Ł 430 SC money, 770 a. on Wambaw, Craven
                          Co., bounding NE on PAUL MAZYCK; NW on AUGUS-
TUS LAURENS; SE on vacant land; also 186-1/2 a. on Wambaw, bounding SE on
the 770 a.; other sides on vacant land; also 93-1/2 a. on Wambaw, bound-
ing NE on the 770 a.; SW on vacant land. Witnesses: FRANCIS DESCHAMPS,
PHILIP NORMAND, LOUIS MOUZON, JR. Before WILLIAM HENDRICK, J.P. JAMES
MICKIE, D.P.R.

Book A-A, p. 435   JOHN SANDIFORD, SR., feltmaker, of St. Andrews
27 July 1744   Parish, Berkeley Co., to his loving son JOHN
Deed of Gift   SANDIFORD, JR., for love & affection, 400 a.
                         in Parish of St. Thomas & St. Dennis, on N
side of NE branch of Wando River; bounding E on VINCENT GUERIN; N on MR.
BURDOC; W on ROBERT KING & a marsh. Witnesses: WILLIAM SCREVEN, ELENOR
SCREVEN, SARAH WESTBURY. Before THOMAS DALE, J.P. JAMES MICKIE, D.P.R.

Book A-A, p. 436   THOMAS (his mark) SIMMONS, cooper, & MARY (her
24 & 25 Mar. 1745   mark) his wife, to JOHN DELAGAYE, gentleman,
L & R   all of Granville Co., for Ł 500 currency,
                         250 a. in Granville Co., bounding NE on JOHN
GRAYTON; SW & NW on a creek; SE on PETER PALMETER. Witnesses: EDWARD
WIGG, RICHARD WIGG'. Before JOHN MULLRYNE, J.P. JAMES MICKIE, D.P.R.

Book A-A, p. 442   JOSEPH BRYAN, to STEPHEN BULL, both of Gran-
1 & 2 Feb. 1743   ville Co., for 5 shillings, 217 a. of marsh
L & R   land on SE side Combahee Causeway, part of
                         411 a. in Colleton Co., granted BRYAN 23 Apr.
1735, grant signed by Gov. ROBERT JOHNSON; the 411 a. bounding N on FRAN-
CIS YONGE; W on vacant land; all other sides on Combahee River. Witnesses: THOMAS DRAYTON, JOHN DRAKE, STEPHEN BULL, JR. Before WILLIAM
BULL, JR., J.P. JAMES MICKIE, D.P.R.

Book A-A, p. 449   PETER VILLEPONTOUX, planter, of Berkeley Co.,
6 & 7 May 1745   to HENRY GRAY, master's mate of H.M.S. Rose,
L & R by Mortgage   now lying at anchor near Charleston, as secu-
                         rity on bond of even date in penal sum of
Ł 4600 for payment of Ł 2300 currency, with interest, on 7 May 1746,
300 a. in Berkeley Co., on NE side Ashley River; bounding SW on Hog Island Creek; NW on Capers Creek; NE on THOMAS BARKSDALE; E on land formerly belonging to JAMES BASHFORD, afterwards to FLORENTIA O'SULLIVAN,
grant dated 6 July 1680; also, 270 a. of marsh land in Berkeley Co., purchased from COL. WILLIAM RHETT, bounding NW on Ashley River & reaching to
head of Capers Creek; also 4 Negro slaves. Witnesses: ALEXANDER WARREN,
JOHN RATTRAY. Before JACOB MOTTE, J.P. JAMES MICKIE, D.P.R.

Book A-A, p. 457   WILLIAM HANCOCK, merchant, formerly of
17 & 18 Nov. 1741   Charleston, SC, now of City of Exon, England,
L & R   by his attorney, JAMES OSMOND, merchant, of
                         Charleston; to PETER VILLEPONTOUX, planter, of
Berkeley Co.; for Ł 1500 currency, 300 a. on NE side Ashley River, bound-
ing SW on Hogg Island Creek; NW on Capers Creek; NE on THOMAS BARKSDALE;
SE on land formerly belonging to JAMES BASFORD, afterwards to DANIEL
GREEN; part of a larger tract granted by the Lords Proprs. to FLORENTIA
O'SULLIVAN on 6 July 1680; also the 270 a. of marsh ground purchased from
COL. WILLIAM RHETT, bounding on NW of Ashley River reaching to head of
Capers Creek. Whereas by L & R dated 9 & 10 Feb. 1727, SARAH BARKSDALE

(widow of JOHN BARKSDALE, & sole executrix of his will), & THOMAS BARKS-
DALE, planter, of Berkeley Co., conveyed to ELIAS HANCOCK, victualler,
for Ł 800 currency, the 300 a. (as above), & whereas SARAH BARKSDALE by
deed poll dated 2 Mar. 1727, for Ł 25 currency, paid by HANCOCK renounced
her title to the 270 a. of marsh land purchased from COL. WILLIAM RHETT
on 12 Sept. 1711; & whereas by will dated 20 Nov. 1729 HANCOCK bequeathed
to his eldest son, WILLIAM, the 300 a. but made no conveyance of the
270 a. of marsh land which descended to son WILLIAM as heir at law; &
whereas WILLIAM HANCOCK, now in Exon, England, stated "whereas I am seized & possessed of a messuage or dwelling house...in Charleston, & of a
plantation in Christ Church Parish...several Negroes & household goods...
& several debts are due me...in particular 1 account unadjusted between
me & JAMES KERR my father-in-law as he was 1 of my guardians, during my
minority...& an agreement made by PETER VILLEPONTOUX of Charleston, planter, with said JAMES KERR & JAMES OSMOND, of Charleston, merchant, also a
guardian for me...which contract is not yet brought into execution", & on
14 Aug. 1741 appointed OSMOND his attorney to handle all his affairs in
SC; now OSMOND sells to VILLEPONTOUX. Witnesses: JACOB MARTIN, WILLIAM
MOUATT. Before JACOB MOTTE, J.P. JAMES MICKIE, D.P.R.

Book A-A, p. 472   JAMES THOMPSON (THOMSON), butcher, of Charles-
7 May 1745   ton, to THOMAS DRAYTON, planter, as security
Mortgage   on bond of even date in penal sum of Ł 1462
                       for payment of Ł 730:12 currency, with inter-
est, on 1 May next, the dwelling house, etc., & 6 a. on which THOMPSON
now lives, commonly called The Summer House, near Charleston, bounding E
on the Broad Path. Witness: THOMAS SMITH, merchant, of Charleston. Before STEPHEN BULL, J.P. Silver watch delivered. JAMES MICKIE, D.P.R.
On 10 Aug. 1745 DRAYTON declared mortgage satisfied.

Book A-A, p. 474   HENRY LIVINGSTON, planter, of Colleton Co., &
19 & 20 Oct. 1744   WILLIAM LIVINGSTON, planter, of Craven Co., to
L & R   GEORGE MITCHELL, practiser of physick, of Col-
                       leton Co., for Ł 1092 SC money, 520 a. in Col-
leton Co., part of 1000 a. granted 25 Feb. 1714 by Gov. CHARLES CRAVEN &
the Lords Proprs. to WILLIAM LIVINGSTON, planter, deceased, who by will
dated 17 July 1723 bequeathed the 1000 a. to said HENRY & WILLIAM LIVING-
STON. Witnesses: ALEXANDER STEWART, JAMES DRUMMOND. Before JAMES GREEME,
J.P. JAMES MICKIE, D.P.R.

Book A-A, p. 481   JOSEPH BRYAN, planter, gives bond to STEPHEN
2 Feb. 1743   BULL, ESQ., both of Granville Co., in penal
Bond   sum of Ł 1000 currency, as security that MARY,
                       wife of JOSEPH BRYAN, shall not claim her dow-
er in 217 a. of marsh land on NE side Combahee River, Colleton Co., bounding NW on Combahee Causeway; NE on marsh; other sides on Combahee River;
conveyed this date by BRYAN to STEPHEN BULL. Witnesses: THOMAS DRAYTON,
JOHN DRAKE, STEPHEN BULL, JR. Before WILLIAM BULL, JR., J.P. JAMES
MICKIE, D.P.R.

Book A-A, p. 483   ROBERT GLASS, planter, to ISAAC NICHOLS, plant-
13 & 14 Mar. 1744   er, both of St. Pauls Parish, Colleton Co., as
L & R by Mortgage   security on bond of even date in penal sum of
                       Ł 2572:5 for payment of Ł 1286:2 currency with
interest on 14 Mar. 1747; 350 a. in Colleton Co., bounding E & S on MEL-
CHER GARNER; N on JOSEPH HASFORT; NW on JAMES MCLAUGHLIN; as by release
dated 12 Mar. 1744 from NICHOLAS to GLASS. In case of default, NICHOLAS
to sell the land at public sale. Witnesses: PHILLIP EVANS, ANDREW LETCH,
WILLIAM MAINE. Before JACOB MOTTE, J.P. JAMES MICKIE, D.P.R. On 5 June
1752 NICHOLAS declared mortgage satisfied. Witness: WILLIAM HOPTON.

Book A-A, p. 491   MELCHER GARNER, planter, to ISAAC NICHOLAS,
13 & 14 Mar. 1744   planter, both of St. Pauls Parish, Colleton
L & R by Mortgage   Co., as security on bond of even date in penal
                       sum of Ł 1770:2 for payment of Ł 888:11 cur-
rency, with interest, on 14 Mar. 1749; 350 a., part of 2 tracts, at BOB
SAVANNAH, St. Pauls Parish Colleton Co., bounding S on CHARLES FILBEAN,
JOHN FILBEAN, & SILAS WELLS; W on JAMES MCLAUGHLIN & ROBERT GLASS; N on
JOSEPH HASFORT & ROBERT GLASS; E on ANDREW LIDDLE & JOHN DRAYTON; as by
plat to release dated 12 Mar. 1744 to MELCHER GARNER. Witnesses: PHILLIP

EVANS, WILLIAM MAINE, ANDREW LETCH. Before JACOB MOTTE, J.P. JAMES
MICKIE, D.P.R. On 5 June 1752 ISAAC NICHOLAS declared mortgage satisfied.
Witness: WILLIAM HOPTON.

Book A-A, p. 499   ISAAC HOLMES, gentleman, & SUSANNAH his wife,
22 Apr. 1735   with her full consent, to HENRY BEDON, shop
Release   keeper, both of Charleston, for ₺ 1100 SC mon-
                         ey, 1/2 of lot #228 in Charleston, bounding E
on heirs of ELIAS HANCOCK; W on ISAAC HOLMES; S on Tradd Street; N on
CAPT. EDWARD CROFT. Witnesses: RICHARD BEDON, SR., LAWRENCE WITHERS.
Before JAMES WRIGHT, J.P. JAMES MICKIE, D.P.R.

Book A-A, p. 503   HENRY BEDON, gentleman, & MARY ANN his wife,
8 & 9 May 1745   of Charleston, to JOSEPH WATSON, gunner of
L & R   H.M.S. Rose, for ₺ 1600 currency, 1/2 of lot
                         #228 in Charleston, bounding W on part same
lot (formerly WILLIAM SMITH); E on heirs of ELIAS HANCOCK (formerly JOHN
ELLIOTT); S on Tradd Street; N on CAPT. EDWARD CROFT (formerly MR. DUQUE).
Whereas the Lords Proprs. on 12 June 1694 granted THOMAS ROSE, gentleman,
lot #228 in Charleston containing 1/2 a.; & whereas THOMAS ROSE, cordwainer, son & heir of said THOMAS ROSE, on 8 Aug. 1710, sold the lot to
HENRY SAMWAYS, planter, who bequeathed it to his 2 sons, HENRY & RICHARD;
& whereas by L & R dated 8 & 9 Feb. 1731 RICHARD SAMWAYS sold his share
to his brother HENRY; who with MARY his wife, by L & R dated 25 & 26 Oct.
1734 sold to ISAAC HOLMES 1/2 the lot, bounding E on heirs of ELIAS HAN-
COCK; W on a lot formerly granted to WILLIAM SMITH later belonging to his
daughter CATHERINE SMITH; N on CAPT. EDWARD CROFT (formerly DUQUE); &
whereas ISAAC HOLMES & SUSANNA his wife by L & R dated 21 & 22 Apr. 1735,
sold the half lot to HENRY BEDON, bounding W on part of lot #228 belonging to ISAAC HOLMES; now BEDON sells to WATSON. Witnesses: CHARLES PINCK-
NEY, THOMAS DOUGHTY, JAMES MICKIE, D.P.R.

Book A-A, p. 512   WILLIAM GUY, JR., gentleman, of Charleston, to
9 & 10 May 1745   JOSEPH WATSON, gunner of H.M.S. Rose, for
L & R   ₺ 600 currency, 1/3 of a piece of lot #73 in
                         Charleston. Whereas the Lords Proprs. on 16
Mar. 1693 granted CAPT. CHARLES BASDEN, lot #73 on Tradd Street in
Charleston, & he died intestate, leaving 3 daughters, SARAH, REBECCA, &
MARY, co-heiresses-at-law; & whereas SARAH married JONATHAN COLLINGS,
REBECCA married the Rev. MR. WILLIAM GUY (father of WILLIAM, party here-
to); & whereas JONATHAN & SARAH COLLINGS, WILLIAM & REBECCA GUY, & MARY
BASDEN by deed of partition, divided the lot amongst themselves, by which
WILLIAM GUY & REBECCA his wife were allotted that part fronting N 20 ft.
on Tradd Street; bounding W on the part allotted to JONATHAN & SARAH
COLLINGS; E on GEORGE DUCATT; S on THOMAS ROSE; & whereas REBECCA GUY
(mother of WILLIAM party hereto) died & WILLIAM became her heir-at-law;
the father, however, being entitled to hold the property during his natural life; & whereas the father, by deed of surrender dated 12 Mar. last,
gave up his interest to son WILLIAM; now he conveys to WATSON. Witnesses: THOMAS DOUGHTY, CHARLES CALDER. Before JAMES WRIGHT, J.P. JAMES
MICKIE, D.P.R.

Book A-A, p. 520   DAVID HEXT, merchant, & ANN his wife, of
1 & 2 Feb. 1742   Charleston, to JOHN SEABROOK, planter, of Col-
L & R   leton Co., for ₺ 2500 currency, 303 a. in Col-
                         leton Co., bounding W on BENJAMIN D'HARRIETTE;
E & S on Stono River; N & NW on JOHN SEABROOK; free from ANN'S claim of
dower. Witnesses: JOHN MCCALL, BENJAMIN DART, JONATHAN FITCH. Before
JACOB MOTTE, J.P. JAMES MICKIE, D.P.R.

Book A-A, p. 526   JOHN SEABROOK, planter, & MARY his wife, of
24 & 25 Apr. 1745   Colleton Co., to Lt. JOHN PAYNE, of H.M.S. The
L & R   Rose, now in Charleston harbor, for ₺ 2600
                         currency, 303 a. in Colleton Co., bounding W
on BENJAMIN D'HARRIETTE; E & S on Stono River; N & NW on JOHN SEABROOK;
free from MARY'S claim of dower. Witnesses: JOHN GODFREY, JOHN LADSON,
JOHN WILKINS. Before JACOB MOTTE, J.P. JAMES MICKIE, D.P.R.

Book A-A, p. 533   SARAH (her mark) LANNING, widow of JAMES LAN-
5 & 6 Oct. 1744   NING, of John's Island, Colleton Co., to ISAAC

LYM; for ₺ 500 currency, 175 a. on John's Island, bounding W on Bohicket Creek; S & E on THOMAS ROBERTS & JAMES MATHEWS; N on GEORGE GOUGH. Witnesses: JOSEPH STANYARNE, WILLIAM WALSBY, HUGH WILSON. Before ANTHONY MATHEWS, J.P. JAMES MICKIE, D.P.R.

Book A-A, p. 540
13 & 14 May 1745
L & R
ELISHA POINSETTE, victualler, to JACOB MARTIN, physician, both of Charleston, for ₺ 3000 SC money, the tenement & part of lot #27 in Charleston. Whereas JOEL POINSETTE, victualler, was seized in his demesne as of fee, a tenement & part of lot #27, bounding S 43 ft. on Middle Street; E 88 ft. on land occupied by JOHN PAGET; W on MR. ATKINS; N on ISAAC HOLMES & Heirs of SAMUEL HEY; & by will dated 6 Jan. 1743/4 appointed his son, ELISHA POINSETTE, & his son-in-law, ISAAC HOLMES, executors, with instructions to sell all his rent & personal estate & pay his debts; now son ELISHA, as executor, sells to MARTIN. Witnesses: WILLIAM GLEN, JOHN REMINGTON. Before ROBERT AUSTIN, J.P. JAMES MICKIE, D.P.R.

Book A-A, p. 546
15 & 16 May 1745
L & R
JACOB MARTIN, physician, & ANN his wife, to ELISHA POINSETTE, victualler, all of Charleston, for ₺ 3000 SC money, that tenement & part of lot #27, fronting S 43 ft. on Middle Street, bounding E 88 ft. on lot occupied by JOHN PAGET; W on ATKINS; N on ISAAC HOLMES & heirs of SAMUEL HEY. Witnesses: WILLIAM GLEN, JOHN REMINGTON. Before ROBERT AUSTIN, J.P. JAMES MICKIE, D.P.R.

DEEDS BOOK "B-B"
MAY 1745 - APRIL 1746

Book B-B, p. 1
17 & 18 May 1745
L & R by Mortgage
ELISHA POINSETT, victualler, & CATHERINE his wife, to JACOB MARTIN, physician, both of Charleston, as security on bond of even date in penal sum of ₺ 6600 for payment of ₺ 3300 SC money, with interest, on 18 May 1748; the tenement & part of lot #27 fronting S 43 ft. on Middle Street; E 88 ft. on JOHN PAGET; W on ATKINS; N on ISAAC HOLMES & heirs of SAMUEL HEY; & delivers 1 Negro man & 1 Mulatto girl whose indenture is for 12 years. Witnesses: WILLIAM GLEN, JOHN REMMINGTON. Before ROBERT AUSTIN, J.P. JAMES MICKIE, D.P.R. On 17 Dec. 1755 JACOB MARTIN declared mortgage satisfied. Witness: WILLIAM HOPTON.

Book B-B, p. 7
27 Apr. 1745
Bond
NATHANIEL WICKHAM, ESQ., of SC to the Society for the Propagation of the Gospel in Foreign Parts, in full sum of ₺ 234 British, with interest, to be paid 27 Apr. 1746. Witnesses: JOHN HUTCHINS, JAMES DRUMMOND. Before JAMES GREEME. JAMES MICKIE, D.P.R.

Book B-B, p. 8
26 & 27 Apr. 1745
L & R by Mortgage
NATHANIEL WICKHAM, ESQ., to the Society for the Propagation of the Gospel in Foreign Parts, as security on bond of even date in the penal sum of ₺ 468 for payment of ₺ 234 British, with interest, on 24 Apr. next; 657 a., part being known as Cow Savannah, in Ashley Barony, on S side Ashley River, Berkeley Co., bounding NW on High Road leading from Bacons Bridge to Stono Chapel; S on ROBERT JOHNSON (alias BLACK ROBIN); E on WILLIAM WALLACE & ALEXANDER SKENE. Witnesses: JOHN HUTCHINS, JAMES DRUMMOND. Before JAMES GREEME. JAMES MICKIE, D.P.R.

Book B-B, p. 14
1 Mar. 1743
Release by Mortgage
HUGH SWINTON, planter, to WILLIAM FLEMING, merchant, both of Craven Co., as security for payment of ₺ 6000, with interest; 9 tracts of land in Craven Co., total 7575 a., being 700 a., 500 a., 250 a., 400 a., 400 a., 200 a., 1000 a., 3000 a., & 1125 a. Whereas GEORGE II on 16 Mar. 1732, by Gov. ROBERT JOHNSON, granted STEPHEN PROCTOR 700 a. bounding SE on PeeDee River; N on WILLIAM WATIES; SW on WILLIAM SWINTON; & whereas GEORGE II on 11 July 1733, by Gov. ROBERT JOHNSON, granted THOMAS ELLERY 500 a. bounding NE on PeeDee River;

SE on ROBERT MCNOTT; SW on vacant land; NW on JAMES PAINE; & whereas
GEORGE II, by Lt. Gov. THOMAS BROUGHTON, on 4 June 1735 granted HUGH SWIN-
TON (party hereto) 250 a., bounding NW on Peedee River; SE on a creek; SW
on WILLIAM SWINTON; & whereas GEORGE II, by Lt. Gov. THOMAS BROUGHTON, on
25 June 1736 granted JAMES ABERCROMBY 400 a. in Queensborough Township,
on S side PeeDee River; bounding SE on JAMES ABERCROMBY; SW & NW on vacant lands; & whereas GEORGE II, by Lt. Gov. THOMAS BROUGHTON, on 25 June
1736, granted JAMES ABERCROMBY 400 a. in Queensborough Township, on S
side PeeDee River, bounding SE on ABRAHAM STAPLES; SW on vacant land; NW
on JAMES ABERCROMBY; & whereas GEORGE II , by Lt. Gov. THOMAS BROUGHTON,
on 25 June 1736 granted JAMES ABERCROMBY 200 a. in PeeDee Township, bounding NW on LYNCH & vacant land; other sides on vacant land; & whereas
GEORGE II, by Lt. Gov. THOMAS BROUGHTON, on 30 Sept. 1736 granted JAMES
ABERCROMBY 1000 a. in Queensborough Township, bounding SW on PeeDee Riv-
er; NW on JOHN SKENE; other sides on vacant land; & whereas GEORGE II, by
Lt. Gov. WILLIAM BULL, on 11 May 1739, granted JAMES ABERCROMBY 3000 a.,
bounding NW on ALEXANDER SKENE; SW on vacant land; SE on JAMES MATHEWS;
NE on PeeDee River; & whereas GEORGE II, by Lt. Gov. WILLIAM BULL, on 30
June 1741, granted HUGH SWINTON (party hereto) 1125 a., bounding SW on
GEORGE HADDRELL & JOHN BOGGS; E on HUGH SWINTON, CAPT. DICK, & THOMAS LA-
ROCHE; NE on MR. LAROCHE; NW on WILLIAM SWINTON; & whereas STEPHEN PROC-
TOR by L & R dated 12 & 13 Apr. 1733 conveyed his 700 a. to HUGH SWINTON;
& whereas THOMAS ELLERY, by L & R dated 1 & 2 Dec. 1735 conveyed his
500 a. to HUGH SWINTON; & whereas JAMES ABERCROMBY, by L & R dated 24 &
25 Feb. 1740 conveyed to HUGH SWINTON the tracts of 400 a., 400 a., 200
a., 1000 a., & 3000 a., (total 5000 a.); & whereas HUGH SWINTON gave bond
of even date to WILLIAM FLEMING in penal sum of L 12,000 for payment of
L 6000 SC money on 1 Mar. next; now as security he conveys 9 tracts, total 7575 a., to FLEMING. Witnesses: EDWARD ROBINSON, ARCHIBALD JOHNSTON.
Before WILLIAM WHITESIDE.

Book B-B, p. 27   Whereas WILLIAM FLEMING has become security
1 May 1744   for L 978, with interest, due by HUGH SWINTON
Further Mortgage   on bond dated 1 Mar. 1743, payable to ANDREW
                         JOHNSTON, the within premises shall extend as
further security on said bond. Witnesses: WILLIAM HUGHES, EDWARD ROBIN-
SON.

Book B-B, p. 27   HUGH SWINTON, to WILLIAM STEWART, ESQ., of New
16 May 1745   Providence, as security on 2 bonds dated 20
Mortgage   Apr. 1741 & 16 May 1745, for L 73:14:11 Brit-
                         ish, with interest, further extends the pre-
mises (p. 14) after the payment & satisfaction of the sum mentioned, & of
the further sum due ANDREW JOHNSON on back of within deed unto said WIL-
LIAM STEWART. Witnesses: JAMES MICKIE, WILLIAM PLAYTERS.

Book B-B, p. 28   HUGH SWINTON, to ALEXANDER NISBETT, ESQ., as
16 May 1745   security on bond dated 2 Oct. 1743 in penal
Mortgage   sum of L 129:10 British, for payment of
                         L 64:16 British, with interest, also on bond
of equal date in penal sum of L 22:7 for payment of L 11:3:6 British; ex-
tends the premises mentioned in first mortgage (p. 14) after satisfaction
of previous mortgages. Witnesses: JAMES MICKIE, WILLIAM PLAYTERS. Before JOHN LINING, J.P. JAMES MICKIE, D.P.R.

Book B-B, p. 29   THOMAS COOPER, gentleman, & MARY his wife, to
5 & 6 June 1745   ISAAC HOLMES, gentleman, both of Charleston,
L & R   for L 685:15 SC money, part of lot #26 in
                         Charleston, fronting N 20 ft. on Broad Street;
bounding E 97 ft. on ISAAC HOLMES; S on DANIEL BOURGET; (formerly CHARLES
HILL); W on unoccupied same lot. Whereas by L & R dated 23 & 24
Dec. 1728 JOHN BRETON, merchant, of Charleston, conveyed to THOMAS COOP-
ER & MARGARET MAGDALEN his then wife (granddaughter of said JOHN BRETON)
the tenement lately destroyed by the great fire in Charleston (formerly
the property of THOMAS FLEMING) with the land, being part of lot #26; &
whereas MARGARET MAGDALEN COOPER died & THOMAS COOPER became owner; now
he sells to ISAAC HOLMES. Witnesses: JOHN BALLANTINE, JR., JAMES GRIND-
LEY. Before OTHNIEL BEALE, J.P. JAMES MICKIE, D.P.R.

Book B-B, p. 35   JAMES HOPKINS, of Congarees, Craven Co., to

15 June 1737   THOMAS BROWN, Indian trader, of same place,
Deed of Sale   for Ł 1000 currency, 3 tracts; 2 at the Conga-
                    rees opposite the Township of Saxe Gatha, 1 of
which was purchased from DR. DANIEL GIBSON, the other from HENRY GIGNIL-
LIAT; the other at Eighteen Mile Branch from the Congrees. Witnesses:
GEORGE HAIG, WILLIAM LYTHERLAND. Before STEPHEN CRELL, J.P. JAMES
MICKIE, D.P.R.

Book B-B, p. 36   JOHN WATSON, mariner, & SARAH his wife, in
3 & 4 June 1745   trust to JOHN REMINGTON, all of Charleston,
L & R in Trust   for Ł 20 SC money & other considerations, that
                    tenement & piece of ground on Charleston Neck,
called Bowling Green, bounding W on the Broad Road or Path, beginning at
a line at MRS. TROTT'S fence, then running N along the Broad Path 138 ft.,
then E 600 ft., then S 138 ft. then W 600 ft. to the Broad Path; containing 2 a.; that is to the use of JOHN WATSON during his natural life; then
to the use of said SARAH WATSON during her natural life; then to WILLIAM
WATSON, son of JOHN, forever. Should SARAH die before her husband, then
he may change or revoke this conveyance. Witnesses: ALEXANDER MAINE,
JOHN REMINGTON, JR. Before JACOB MOTTE, J.P. JAMES MICKIE, D.P.R.

Book B-B, p. 41   ANTHONY WHITE, JR., planter, of Craven Co., to
14 & 15 Dec. 1744   ALEXANDER NISBETT, ESQ., formerly of Charles-
L & R by Mortgage   ton, as security for payment debt of
                    Ł 1956:17:6, with interest, 500 a., part of
940 a. at head of Black Mingo Swamp, Craven Co., also 500 a. in Prince
Frederick Parish, Craven Co., on S side Black River. Whereas ALEXANDER
NISBETT, by L & R dated 14 & 15 Dec. 1743, through his attorneys JAMES
MICKIE & JAMES AKIN, for Ł 500 SC money, conveyed to ANTHONY WHITE, JR.,
500 a., part of 940 a., on head of Black Mingo Swamp, bounding according
to plat; & whereas JOHN WHITE, planter, of Prince Frederick Parish by
deed poll dated 19 inst. Apr. recorded in Book Z. fol. 246, 247 on 24
inst. Apr. conveyed to ANTHONY WHITE 500 a. in Prince Frederick Parish on
S side Black River, bounding W & S on WILLIAM COLT; SE on CAPT. HINCKLEY;
which tract was on 12 Dec. 1735 granted by Lt. Gov. THOMAS BROUGHTON to
said JOHN WHITE; & whereas ANTHONY WHITE, JR. gave bond of even date to
ALEXANDER NISBETT in the penal sum of Ł 3913:15 for payment of
Ł 1956:17:6 currency, with interest, on 15 Dec. 1750; now WHITE gives 2
plantations as security. Witnesses: JAMES MICKIE, WILLIAM PLAYTERS. Before JAMES WRIGHT, J.P. JAMES MICKIE, D.P.R. Plat of 500 a. upper part
of 940 a., made by P. LANE 10 Dec. 1743, showing boundary lines NE & SW
on vacant land; NW on WILLIAM SNOW; SE on JOHN MCMOCHAN.

Book B-B, p. 49   COL. JOHN BEE, of Colleton Co., residuary leg-
1 & 2 June 1745   atee & devise of JOHN BEE, late of Charleston
L & R   & executor of his will, to JOHN MACKENZIE,
                    merchant, of Charleston, for Ł 3000 currency,
lot #42 in Charleston. Whereas JOHN BEE, the elder, owned lot #42 in
Charleston, bounding S 65-1/3 ft. on Broad Street; E 88-1/2 ft. on Church
Street; N 67-1/2 ft. on MARY WATSON (formerly JOHN GARMER); W 89 ft. on
ROBERT HUME; & by will dated 7 Mar. 1739 appointed JOHN BEE (party hereto) sole executor with power to sell his real & personal estate, not
otherwise devise, & pay his (the elder's) debts; after which the residue
was devised to JOHN BEE, party hereto; now BEE sells lot #42 to MACKENZIE.
Witnesses: WILLIAM PLAYTERS, JAMES MICKIE. Before JOHN LINING, J.P.
JAMES MICKIE, D.P.R. Plat of E part of lot #42 in Charleston, granted
originally on 3 Mar. 1681 to ARTHUR MIDDLETON, ESQ., certified 12 June
1745 by GEORGE HUNTER, SUR. GEN.

Book B-B, p. 56   SAMUEL BACOT, planter, & REBECCA his wife, to
22 Mar. 1744   GIDEON FAUCHERAUD, planter, both of Berkeley
Deed of Sale   Co., for Ł 700 currency, 150 a., English mea-
                    sure, being part of 160 a. on N side Goose
Creek Branch, Berkeley Co., bounding S on ABRAHAM DELAPLAINE; E on JOHN
GIBBES; N on GIDEON FAUCHERAUD; W on JONATHAN FITCH. Witnesses: MATHEW
BEAIRD, PETER BACOT, CHARLES FAUCHERAUD. Before THOMAS DALE, J.P. JAMES
MICKIE, D.P.R.

Book B-B, p. 60   WILLIAM CHAPMAN, of Berkeley Co., to THOMAS
19 Aug. 1741   ELLIOTT, of Colleton Co., for Ł 550 currency,

Deed of Sale   100 a. bequeathed to WILLIAM CHAPMAN by JOSEPH
                                ELLIOTT whose will stated that the 100 a. to
be laid off with a N & S course at the upper part of JOSEPH ELLIOTT'S
land where it joins JAMES SCREVEN'S land; bounding S on THOMAS ELLIOTT; W
& S on JAMES SCREVEN; E on said ELLIOTT. Witnesses: THOMAS BULLINE,
JAMES BOLTON, ELIHU BAKER. Before HENRY HYRNE, J.P.   JAMES MICKIE, D.P.R.

Book B-B, p. 62   GABRIEL MARION, planter, of Craven Co., to JO-
21 & 22 Feb. 1744   SEPH DUBOURDIEU, of Georgetown for Ł 2250 SC
L & R   money, 2 tracts total 500 a. ESTHER MARION,
                                wife of GABRIEL, willingly surrenders her ti-
tle. Whereas Gov. ROBERT GIBBES & the Lords Proprs. on 23 July 1711
granted to PERCIVAL PAWLEY 200 a. in Craven Co., bounding NE on Sampit
Creek; S & W on vacant land; which PAWLEY, bequeathed to his daughter
SUSANNAH, who married MATHEW DRAKE, whose property it became; & whereas
on 30 Mar. 1742 MATHEW & SUSANNAH DRAKE sold the 200 a. to GABRIEL MARION;
& whereas Lt. Gov. THOMAS BROUGHTON on 14 Feb. 1733 granted CAPT. THOMAS
CORDES 300 a. on Georgetown River in Craven Co., bounding _____ on GEORGE
LAYAN; W on GEORGE PAWLEY; & on NW branch Turkey Creek; & whereas THOMAS
CORDES on 21 Jan. 1740 sold the 300 a. to GABRIEL MARION; now MARION
sells both tracts to DUBOURDIEU. Witnesses: SUSANNAH GIGNILLIAT, SAMUEL
HENDERSON, ISAAC TRAPIER. Before PAUL TRAPIER, J.P. JAMES MICKIE, D.P.
R.

Book B-B, p. 69   ROBERT LADSON, planter & SABINA his wife, to
18 Jan. 1738/9   ISAAC LADSON, planter, for Ł 450 currency,
Feoffment   60 a., part of 440 a., except the burying
                                place 10 ft. square. Whereas Gov. CHARLES
CRAVEN & the Lords Proprs. on 17 Aug. 1741 granted FRANCIS LADSON, plant-
er, 440 a. in Berkeley Co., on S side Ashley River, bounding N on said
FRANCIS LADSON & WILLIAM FULLAR; E on RALPH EMMS, WILLIAM FULLAR & JOHN
AGER; S on THOMAS DRAYTON & said FRANCIS LADSON & JOHN CATTELL; & whereas
FRANCIS LADSON & SARAH his wife, for Ł 95 currency, conveyed to ROBERT
LADSON, planter, 60 a., part of the 440 a., on S side Ashley River,
bounding N & S on the 440 a.; E on WILLIAM FULLAR & JOHN AGER; W on FRAN-
CIS LADSON; & whereas ROBERT LADSON, SR., by will dated 19 Dec. 1732, be-
queathed to his son ROBERT the 60 a.; now ROBERT LADSON, the son with
consent of SABINA, his wife, sells the 60 a. to ISAAC LADSON. Witnesses:
WILLIAM LADSON, JR., WILLIAM WELLS. Before J. SKENE, J.P. JAMES MICKIE,
D.P.R.

Book B-B, p. 73   JOHN BESWICKE, merchant, of Charleston, to
4 Nov. 1742   WILLIAM PALMER, planter, of Granville Co., for
Deed of Sale   Ł 1000 SC money, 300 a. called Grapnall Plan-
                                tation, alias Ekotarrgo Neck; also the stock
of cattle, hogs, crop of corn & peas, & plantation tools & utensils.
Witnesses: ROBERT RAPER, JOHN PICKERING. Before W. BERINGER DEBEAUFINE,
J.P. JAMES MICKIE, D.P.R.

Book B-B, p. 74   ANNE ROTHMAHLER, widow & executrix of will of
26 & 27 June 1743   JOB ROTHMAHLER, ESQ., of Charleston to ROBERT
L & R   THORPE, ESQ., for Ł 500 currency, lot # ___ in
                                Beaufort. Whereas the Lords Proprs. by Dep.
Gov. ROBERT DANIEL in 1717 granted SAMUEL EVELEIGH lot #4 in Beaufort
fronting S on the Bay & bounding W on lot #3; N on lot #29; E on lot #5;
& whereas by L & R dated 12 & 13 June 1721 ROTHMAHLER sold the lot to JOB
ROTHMAHLER who, by will dated 17 Jan. 1729 directed his executors to sell
his lands, not otherwise devised, for payment of his debts; now his widow
sells the lot to THORPE. Witnesses: ROBERT BRISBANE, JOSEPH WRAGG, JR.
Before JOHN DART, J.P. JAMES MICKIE, D.P.R.

Book B-B, p. 82   THOMAS COOPER, merchant, & MARY his wife, to
9 & 10 May 1745   HENRY PERONNEAU, merchant, all of Charleston,
L & R   for Ł 4200 currency, 3 contiguous lots in
                                Charleston, #188, #189, & #79, making 1 lot
72 ft. in rear & front, 226 ft. deep, fronting S on Queen Street (form-
erly Dock Street), W on JOHN CHAMPNEYS (formerly JAMES OSMOND); N on
Presbyterian burying ground; E on CAPT. WILLIAM WARDEN. Whereas FRANCIS
SIMMONS in her lifetime was seized in her demesne as of fee in 3 lots in
Charleston, #188, #189, & #79, & by will dated 6 Dec. 1707 bequeathed to

her kins-woman. FRANCES NORTHALL her dwelling house & all land not otherwise devised of which the 3 lots were a part, except a small part before
settled in trust for the Presbyterian church; & whereas FRANCES NORTHALL
married THOMAS ALLIN, planter, of Berkeley Co., & they, on 20 June 1713
conveyed the 3 lots to WILLIAM GIBBON & ANDREW ALLEN, merchants, of
Charleston (except as excepted), the lots then bounding S on the street;
W on COL. ROBERT DANIEL, JONATHAN AMORY, JOHN HUTCHINSON, & GEORGE FRANK-
LIN; W on a back street next the entrenchments leading to the Presbyterian Meeting House; E on JOHN HUTCHINSON; N on land of Presbyterian Meeting
House & other land; & whereas, by Articles of Agreement, dated 1 May 1722,
reciting that GIBBON & ALLEN were joint purchasers & joint tenants of
sundry houses & lots in Charleston, it was agreed that the survivor
should hold the share of the deceased in trust for the heirs of the 1 dying without benefit of survivorship; & whereas WILLIAM GIBBON died, without having made a will, leaving ELIZABETH CAWOOD, wife of JOHN CAWOOD,
merchant, of Charleston, his only sister & heir-at-law; & whereas JOHN
CAWOOD died at Charleston & his widow, ELIZABETH, in 1720 married TWEEDIE
SOMERVILLE, merchant, of Charleston; & whereas ANDREW ALLEN & SARAH his
wife, & TWEEDIE SOMERVILLE & ELIZABETH his wife, on 19 Jan. 1729, by deed
of partition agreed to make a division of the real estate which GIBBON &
ALLEN had purchased in jointenancy, & that SOMERVILLE should have the 3
lots; & whereas SOMERVILLE & his wife on 16 Mar. 1729 sold to ANDREW AL-
LEN, to THOMAS that part of the 3 lots fronting S 190-1/2 ft. on the
street as far back as the Presbyterian Meeting House; & whereas ANDREW
ALLEN, by L & R dated 1 & 2 Dec. 1730 sold to THOMAS ELLERY, gentleman,
of Charleston, that part of the 3 lots, bounding W on TWEEDIE SOMERVILLE
& the little house & lands of the dissenting congregation; 72 ft. from E
to W, 26 ft. from N to S, bounding E on CAPT. WARDEN; W on THOMAS ELLERY;
S on THOMAS COOPER; N on meeting burial ground; whereby THOMAS COOPER &
his wife became lawfully seized in their demesne as of fee in jointenancy
of all those pieces of the 3 lots (#188, #189, & #79) making 1 lot 72 ft.
front & rear, 226 ft. deep, bounding S on Dock Street, (now Queen Street),
W on JAMES OSMOND (formerly THOMAS ELLERY); N on Meeting House Burial
Ground; E on WILLIAM WARDEN; & whereas MARGARET MAGDALENE died & THOMAS
COOPER became sole owner; now he & MARY, his present wife, sells to HENRY
PERONNEAU as first stated. Witnesses: JAMES DRUMMOND, JOHN ROBERSON.
Before JAMES GREEME, J.P. JAMES MICKIE, D.P.R.

Book B-B, p. 101   JOHN FENDIN, SR., & MARTHA his wife, of St.
5 Feb. 1744/5   Helena Parish, Granville Co., to their beloved
Deed of Gift   son JOHN FENDIN, JR., for love & affection,
                         160 a. on St. Helena Island fronting W on Port
Royall River the Less; bounding N on JOSEPH SEALE; E on JOHN TOOMER; S on
JOHN FENDIN, SR. Witnesses: WILLIAM CHAPLIN, WILLIAM ADAMS. Before
ROBERT THORPE, J.P. JAMES HOME, Pub. Reg.

Book B-B, p. 102   ALEXANDER BENNETT, ESQ., of London, by his at-
      1743   torney BENJAMIN WHITAKER, ESQ., of Charleston,
L & R   to JOHN HUME, merchant, of Charleston, for
                         Ł 1400 currency, 46 a. in St. Philips Parish,
Charleston, bounding E on JOSEPH BLAKE, ESQ., S on THOMAS GADSDEN, ESQ.;
W & N on RICHARD CARTWRIGHT. Witnesses: WILLIAM GEORGE FREEMAN, WILLIAM
BURROWS. Before JAMES WRIGHT, J.P. JAMES HOME, Pub. Reg.

Book B-B, p. 107   ELIZABETH COLLETON, widow, of Charleston, to
5 Aug. 1745   RICHARD POWERS, tallow chandler & soap boiler,
Bond   of Charleston, in full sum of Ł 2000 SC money
                         to perform the agreements in a lease of even
date. Witnesses: PETER BENOIST, JOHN REMMINGTON. Before JOHN CHAMPNEYS,
J.P. JAMES HOME, Pub. Reg.

Book B-B, p. 108   ELIZABETH COLLETON, widow, of Charleston, to
5 Aug. 1745   RICHARD POWERS, tallow chandler & soap boiler,
Lease   of Charleston, during natural life of ELIZA-
                         BETH, that brick house & piece of ground
fronting S 17 ft. on Broad Street, 107 ft. deep, at a yearly rent of
Ł 150 SC money payable quarterly. Witnesses: PETER BENOIST, JOHN REMMING-
TON. Before JOHN CHAMPNEYS, J.P. JAMES HOME, Pub. Reg.

Book B-B, p. 112   WILLIAM READ (REED), planter, of St. George's

1 & 2 Aug. 1745   Parish, Berkeley Co., to ROBERT PAISLEY, of
L & R   St. Paul's Parish, Colleton Co., & THOMAS SIMP-
                       SON, of St. George's Parish, Berkeley Co., for
Ł 500 currency, 502 a. in Craven Co., bounding SE on THOMAS SNOW; NW on
JAMES SINGELLTON; NE on vacant land; SW on Williamsburgh Township line &
unknown land; which 502 a. were originally granted to JOHN REED, father
of WILLIAM & inherited by WILLIAM. CATHERINE (her mark) READ voluntarily
renounces her claim. Witnesses: BENJAMIN SHERROD, WILLIAM MAINE. Before
ROBERT WRIGHT, J.P. JAMES HOME, Pub. Reg.

Book B-B, p. 118   SAMUEL MCQUOID, planter, & ABIGAIL his wife,
31 May & 1 June 1745   of St. Johns Parish, Colleton Co., to EBENEZER
L & R by Mortgage   SIMMONS, BENJAMIN SMITH & JAMES CROKATT, mer-
                        chants, in Company, of Charleston, as security
on bond of even date in penal sum of Ł 3726:11:6 for payment of
Ł 1863:5:9 SC money, with interest, on 1 Sept. next, 100 a. on Wadmalaw
Island, Colleton Co., bounding S on THOMAS GLOBE; N on JAMES YOUNG; E on
SAMUEL JONES; W on WILLIAM HECKNOW (formerly HENRY WALKER). Witnesses:
JOHN PALMER, JOHN REMMINGTON. Before JOHN CHAMPNEYS, J.P. JAMES HOME,
Pub. Reg.

Book B-B, p. 125   ELIZABETH VICARDIGE, widow & executrix of will
29 & 30 Dec. 1737   JOHN VICARIDGE, ESQ., to ROBERT AUSTIN, mer-
L & R   chant, both of Charleston, for Ł 1000 currency,
                        part of lot #82 in Charleston. Whereas JOHN
VICARIDGE by L & R dated 3 & 4 Sept. 1730 conveyed to ROBERT AUSTIN part
of lot #82 in Charleston lately belonging to JOHN HOGG, fronting W 60 ft.
on the street leading from ASHLEY RIVER by the Quakers Meeting House; N
225 ft. on other part same lot; S on MR. WELLS; as security on bond for
payment to JOHN FENWICKE, JOSEPH WRAGG, PAUL JENYS, OTHNIEL BEALE & THOM-
AS LAMBOLL the sum of Ł 853:6:8 currency, with interest, on 23 Mar. 1730;
but neither VICARIDGE nor any of his heirs paid the bond; & whereas VIC-
ARIDGE by will dated 11 May 1737 directed his executors to sell the residue of his estate not otherwise devised for payment of his debts & appointed his wife, ELIZABETH, & GEORGE AUSTIN executrix & executor; &
whereas on 15 June 1737 VICARIDGE died, leaving his will in full force; &
whereas GEORGE AUSTIN refused to act & ELIZABETH VICARIDGE became sole
executrix; now she sells to ROBERT AUSTIN for Ł 1000 currency towards
satisfaction of debt due FENWICKE, WRAGG, JENYS, BEALE & LAMBOLL. Witnesses: GEORGE AUSTIN, SAMUEL BRAILSFORD. Before JOHN DART, J.P. JAMES
HOME, Pub. Reg.

Book B-B, p. 131   GEORGE WARING, storekeeper, of Dorchester, St.
31 July 1745   George's Parish, to JOHN MORTON, planter, of
L & R   St. James Goose Creek, for Ł 1400 SC money,
                        496-1/2 a. in Berkeley Co., bounding N on THOM-
AS WARING; E on JOHN WALTERS; S on BENJAMIN WARING; W on MR. DEWS. Whereas Gov. NATHANIEL JOHNSON, JAMES MOOR, & NICHOLAS TROTT, on 14 Mar. 1704
granted BENJAMIN WARING, father of said GEORGE WARING, 600 a., English
measure, in Berkeley Co., & whereas Gov. NATHANIEL JOHNSON, JAMES MOOR, &
JOB HOWES, on 10 Dec. 1705 granted MOSES WAY 300 a., English measure, in
Berkeley Co., & whereas MOSES WAY conveyed his tract to BENJAMIN WARING;
& whereas Gov. CHARLES CRAVEN & the Lords Proprs. on 12 Nov. 1714 granted
BENJAMIN WARING 360 a. in Berkeley Co., & whereas on 24 Nov. 1732 (see
Secretary's Bk. A.A. fol. 6) Gov. ROBERT JOHNSON granted BENJAMIN WARING
129 a. in Berkeley Co., bounding N on WILLIAM STEED; W on vacant land &
land for use of children of ROBERT DEWS; S on JOSEPH BLAKE; E on BENJAMIN
WARING'S old tract; the 4 tracts containing 1389 a.; & whereas by will
dated 3 Apr. 1736 bequeathed to his son GEORGE, party hereto, when 21
years old, the full half "at the cypruss"; & the executors laid out
694-1/a a. for him; now GEORGE WARING conveys the tract to MORTON. Witnesses: MRS. SARAH MIDDLETON, JOSEPH WARING, JR., ANDREW SHAPLEY. Before
WILLIAM MIDDLETON, J.P. JAMES HOME, Pub. Reg.

Book B-B, p. 137   GEORGE ANSON, ESQ., by his attorney, BENJAMIN
25 May 1745   WHITAKER, ESQ., to DANIEL CRAWFORD, ESQ., for
Deed of Sale   Ł 506:5 currency, 2 contiguous lots of 2 a. 4
                        perches marked V & W on plan of Ansonborough,
bounding S on lot X; W on lot U; N on GEORGE Street; E on Anson Street,
as recorded in Sur. Gen's office on 14 Feb. 1744; also right of passage

through the most convenient street to & from landing place on a creek of
Cooper River. Witnesses: HUGH ANDERSON, WILLIAM HUNT. Before JOHN LIN-
ING, J.P. JAMES HOME, Pub. Reg.

Book B-B, p. 139   EDWARD CROFT, of Craven Co., to GEORGE HAMIL-
18 & 19 Aug. 1745   TON, of Charleston, for Ł 550 currency, part
L & R   of the lot in Charleston, fronting W 16 ft.
                          8 in. on Union Street; bounding E on EDWARD
CROFT'S storehouse; S 70 ft. on JOHN DANIELL; N on the part belonging to
HENRY PERRINEAU. Witnesses: WILLIAM SAXBY, JAMES MCKELVEY. Before JOHN
CHAMPNEYS, J.P. JAMES HOME, Pub. Reg.

Book B-B, p. 145   ALEXANDER CHOVIN, planter, to NOAH SERRÈ, ESQ.,
11 & 12 June 1745   both of St. James Santee, Craven Co., as secur-
L & R by Mortgage   ity for payment a bond of even date or Ł 880
                          SC money, on 12 June 1746; 2 tracts, total
400 a., in said Parish, bounding E & W on NOAH SERRE; S on ALEXANDER CHO-
VIN; N on Santee River; also 2 tracts, total 263 a.; 63 a. of which were
purchased from NOAH SERRÈ, being part of a larger tract; the 263 a. being
on Wadbaccan Island in Santee River, bo-nding E & W on NOAH SERRÈ; N on
Wadbaccan Creek. Witnesses: PAUL BRUNNEAU, JOHN HENTIE. Before JOHN
GENDRON, J.P. JAMES HOME, Pub. Reg.

Book B-B, p. 150   The Hon. CHARLES PINCKNEY, late Speaker of the
21 & 22 Aug. 1745   Hon. Commons House of Assembly of SC, & GAB-
L & R   RIEL MANIGAULT, ESQ., late Pub. Treas. & Rec-
                          eiver of SC, as trustees for the public, ap-
pointed by the General Assembly 25 Mar. 1738; to GEORGE SEAMAN, merchant,
of Charleston, for Ł 9828:9 (being Ł 6700 plus Ł 3128:9 interest from 14
Dec. 1740 to this date) 1/2 of lot #8 (formerly belonging to JOHN PARRIS);
bounding N on THOMAS ELLIOTT (formerly ANDREW PERCEVALL); W on JOSEPH
ELLIOTT (formerly HENRY SIMMONDS); S on other half belonging to heirs of
JOHN WRIGHT (formerly JOSEPH KEYS); E on Bay Street. Whereas by L & R
dated 23 & 24 Mar. 1737 JOHN PARRIS, ESQ., of Charleston, eldest son &
heir of ALEXANDER PARRIS, ESQ., (late Pub. Treas. & Receiver of SC) also
devise & executor of will of his father, conveyed to the Hon. CHARLES
PINCKNEY & GABRIEL MANIGAULT (reciting that whereas said ALEXANDER PARRIS
was indebted to the public for divers large sums of money, & certain commissioners had been appointed to settle his accounts & reports to the
Assembly on 2nd day of that inst. March & it was resolved that said AL-
EXANDER PARRIS was indebted to the public in sums of Ł 22,931 on account
of outstanding "appropriation orders"; Ł 800 allowed for crossing & filing of orders which appeared not to have been duly performed;
Ł 1930:18:8:3 as balance of tax accounts in 1727, 1731, 1732, 1733;
Ł 1509:5:8-1/2 on account of fortifications; total Ł 27,171:4:5:1 currency; which JOHN PARRIS agreed to be the total; & further reciting that it
was agreed that over & above said amount the estate should be charged
with what sums should thereafter appear to have been paid by any persons
mentioned as defaulters in payment of any part of the Ł 3171:5:6; & whereas it was agreed that as several sums amounting to Ł 8587:3:9 had been
put in the account of said commissioners, dated 23 Jan. last, for which
no vouchers had been produced, but that such vouchers (as ?) were lying
in the hands of persons who had accounts with the treasurer should be indemnified against future demands; now JOHN PARRIS, to raise the necessary
amounts, conveys to PINCKNEY & MANIGAULT); the following: the lot on the
Bay on which stood ALEXANDER PARRIS'S dwelling house (later to JOHN PAR-
RIS, then in possession of SEAMAN & CROKATTO; Three Pines Island, behind
JOHNSON'S Fort, lately owned by JOHN PARRIS; 552 a. in Craven Co., granted to ALEXANDER PARRIS, bounding W on NOAH SERRÈ; N on vacant land &
Black River; S on vacant land; 500 a. on Winyaw River, in Craven Co.,
bounding E on PeeDee River; S on MR. DITTON; W & N on vacant land; 9 town
lots in Beaufort, Granville Co., Nos. 5, 27, 30, 63, 64, 66, 82, 86, &
301, lately belonging to JOHN PARRIS; half of ARTHUR'S Island, near Port
Royall, Granville Co., formerly owned by ALEXANDER PARRIS, now in possession of JOHN DELAZON, ESQ., & as further security, JOHN PARRIS delivers 60 slaves; PINCKNEY & MANIGAULT to sell the above property & discharge said debts; the overplus, if any, to be conveyed to JOHN PARRIS;
JOHN PARRIS to have the use of the estate for 12 months. Whereas the
trustees were directed to execute their trust within 18 months after the
expiration of said 12 months; & whereas JOHN PARRIS neither paid his

father's debt nor procured purchasers for any of the estate; & whereas the trustees on 23 Sept. 1740, at public sale, sold the dwelling house & lot on the Bay (them in possession of SEAMAN & CROKETT) to GEORGE SEAMAN, for ₤ 6700 currency; now they sell half of lot #8 to SEAMAN. Witnesses: JACOB MOTTE, JAMES LENNOS, CHARLES CALDER. Before JAMES WRIGHT, J.P. JAMES HOME, Pub. Reg.

Book B-B, p. 168   ELIZABETH COLLETON, widow, to RICHARD POWERS,
5 Aug. 1745   tallow chandler & soap boiler, both of
Lease   Charleston, during her natural life, for ₤ 150
                      currency a year, payable quarterly, that brick
house fronting 17 ft. on N side Broad Street; 107 ft. deep; now occupied
by POWERS. Witnesses: PETER BENOIST, JOHN REMMINGTON. Before JAMES
MICKIE, J.P. HAMES MOME, Pub. Reg.

Book B-B, p. 171   MRS. MARY SMITH, widow of Landgrave THOMAS
2 & 3 Aug. 1745   SMITH, to JOHN DANIEL, ship carpenter, of
L & R   Charleston, for ₤ 1400 SC money part of lot
                      #1 at S end of the Bay, fronting E on the Bay;
bounding S on the brick wall that joins GRANVILLE BASTION, & on the piles
of a small bridge; W on marsh; N on part same lot belonging to heirs of
GEORGE SMITH. Witnesses: JAMES REID, JOHN RATTRAY. Before ROBERT AUSTIN,
J.P. JAMES HOME, Pub. Reg.

Book B-B, p. 177   JOHN (his mark) IMDORFF, & MAGDALENE (her
5 June 1742   mark) his wife, of Orangeburgh Township, Berke-
Gift   ley Co., (after their decease) to GEORGE GIES-
                      SENDANNER, the elder, of same place, for nat-
ural love & affection & other considerations, the tenements where they
dwell & 150 a., formerly belonging to JACOB PIERAN, in Orangeburgh Township, bounding NE on MELLCHIOR SACKWEILLER; NW on Orangeburgh; SW on Pon
Pon River; SE on JOHN SIMMONS & PETER ROTE. Witnesses: WILLIAM SIDDALL,
MICHAEL CHRISTOPHER ROW, JAMES PENDARVIS, JOHN DIETREILS, BRAND PENDARVIS,
SETH HATCHER. Before JOHN CHEVILLETTE, J.P. JAMES HOME, Pub. Reg.

Book B-B, p. 179   PETER HOOK (HUGG) to JOHN GIESSENDANNER, both
7 June 1745   of Orangeburgh Township, Berkeley Co., for nat-
Gift   ural love & affection & other considerations,
                      50 a. in said Township bounding NE on HANS
SPRING; SE on HENRY HOYM; SW on PETER HOOK; NW on JACOB KAMMETER. Wit-
nesses: JOHN DANNER, PETER HUBER. Before JOHN CHEVILLETTE, J.P. JAMES
HOME, Pub. Reg.

Book B-B, p. 181   RICHARD (his mark) HEATHLEY (HEATHY) planter,
15 Apr. 1721   to JOHN CUMYNG, planter, for ₤ 80 currency,
Sale   60 a. on which HEATLY now lives. Witnesses:
                      JOHN (his mark) STRAND (STRAEHAN), ROBERT (his
mark) BEA. Before ANTHONY BONNEAU, J.P. JAMES HOME, Pub. Reg.

Book B-B, p. 183   CHRISTOPHER BEECH, carpenter & joiner, to JOHN
3 May 1722   CUMING, both of Berkeley Co., for ₤ 200 cur-
Sale   rency, 121 a. bequeathed to BEECH by his fa-
                      ther, CHRISTOPHER BEECH, SR., shipwright, of
St. Thomas Parish; bounding NW on E branch of T of Cooper River; NE on
BENJAMIN SIMONS or remars Creek; SE & SW on JOHN CUMING. Witnesses: JOHN
ELDERS, MRS. ANN (her mark) THULIS. Before DANIEL HUGER, J.P. Enrolled
in Auditors Office in Old Grant Book #2, fols. 521-522. JAMES HOME, Pub.
Reg.

Book B-B, p. 186   HENRY PERONNEAU & ALEXANDER PERONNEAU, mer-
26 & 27 Aug. 1745   chant, to WILLIAM GARNES, shopkeeper, all of
L & R   Charleston, for ₤ 1400 SC money, part of the
                      half of lot #15 & buildings thereon, bounding
N on JOHN BONNITHEAU; E on the part owned by HENRY & ALEXANDER PERONNEAU;
S 70 ft. on EDWARD CROFTS; W 33 ft. 4 in. on Union Street. GARNES agrees
to permit the eaves dropping of the PERONNEAU'S stores, with liberty of
opening the back windows of said stores on the E end of released premis-
es; & that GARNES shall not, in any way, obstruct the same. Witnesses:
BENJAMIN D'HARRIETTE, JOHN REMMINGTON. Before ALEXANDER CRAMAHÉ, J.P.
JAMES HOME, Pub. Reg.

Book B-B, p. 191   JOHN PAGE, planter, of Colleton Co., gives
10 & 11 Sept. 1745   AUSTIN ROBERT LOCKTON, mariner, of Charleston,
L & R by Mortgage   a bond of even date in penal sum of Ł 2200 for
                          payment of Ł 1100 currency, contingent on a
particular happening; & as security mortgages 432 a. in Colleton Co.,
bounding E on a creek out of Tuboodoo Creek; N on Tuboodoo Creek; S & S
on WILLIAM EDINGS; also 4 Negro slaves as further security. Page also
gives LOCKTON a bond dated 4 Sept. 1745 (signed by JOSEPH PAGE & SARAH
PAGE) for payment of Ł 304:12:6 currency on 4 Sept. following; appointing
LOCKTON his attorney to receive payment, with interest. If at any time
after this date, a certain schooner or vessel The Charming Peggy now hir-
ed & set to freight by LOCKTON to said PAGE, should happen to be taken by
enemies or detained by any foreign power, or seized or condemned for un-
lawful trade while in the service of JOHN PAGE, PAGE shall pay LOCKTON
Ł 1100 currency, this being the condition mentioned in first bond. Witnesses: CHARLES CALDER, ROBERT SCOTT. Before JAMES WRIGHT, J.P. Recorded in Secretary's Book R.R. fols. 209, 210, & 211 by JOHN CHAMPNEYS, Dep.
JAMES HOME, Pub. Reg.

Book B-B, p. 198   JAMES (his mark) HAWKINS, mariner, lately of
2 Nov. 1743   H.M.S. Rose, now of Charleston, & REBECKAH
L & R   (her mark) HAWKINS, to TALBERT BROWN, vintner,
                          of Charleston, for Ł 440 currency, lot #210 in
Charleston, bounding S 130 ft. on part same lot; N on MR. BECKMAN; E
21 ft. on King Street; W on Widow SHAW. Witnesses: JAMES ROBERTSON, AL-
EXANDER MARSHALL. Before JOHN CHAMPNEYS, J.P. JAMES HOME, Pub. Reg.

Book B-B, p. 203   GEORGE LEA, carpenter, & ELIZABETH his wife,
11 & 12 July 1744   to GEORGE HESKETT, shipwright, all of Charles-
L & R   ton, for Ł 1005 currency, part of lot #18 in
                          Charleston, bounding N 126-1/2 ft. on HENRY
FINCH; E on JAMES CROKATT & GOERGE HESKETT; S on JOHN RATTRAY; W 18-1/2
ft. on Union Street; which lot was part of the estate of GEORGE LEA, the
elder, shipwright, who, by will dated 22 Nov. 1739 devised the part of
the lot to his son GEORGE, party hereto. The land conveyed free from
ELIZABETH'S claim of dower. Witnesses: ALEXANDER PERONNEAU, JOHN HODSDEN.
Before ROBERT AUSTIN, J.P. JAMES HOME, Pub. Reg.

Book B-B, p. 212   ROBERT BREWTON, gentleman, & MARY his wife, of
10 & 11 Aug. 1744   Berkeley Co., to GEORGE HESKETT, shipwright,
L & R   of Charleston, for Ł 2000 SC money, part of
                          half the lot #14 fronting S 20 ft. on Broad
Street; bounding W 110 ft. on JOHN DANIEL'S house & lot; N on EDWARD
CROFT; E on house & lot belonging to estate of JOHN KING. Whereas the
Lords Proprs. on 1 Feb. 1678 granted JOHN BULL lot #14 in Charleston;
which he in Feb. 1678 sold to LAURENCE READ, merchant, who, on 6 Feb.
1679, sold to EDWARD MIDDLETON, gentleman; & whereas when EDWARD MIDDLE-
TON died intestate at Charleston he was seized in his demesne as of fee
in the S half of lot #14 which descended to HENRY MIDDLETON, "oyleman"
(oil-man?), then of London, as eldest son & heir-at-law; & whereas on 10
Oct. 1696 he sold the S half to JOSEPH CROSSKEYS, of Charleston; who, on
11 Dec. 1696, sold to EDWARD LOUGHTON, of Charleston, that piece of the
said moiety fronting 40 ft. 7 in. S on Broad (alias Cooper) Street;
bounding N 42 ft. on WILLIAM DRY (formerly MR. HORNE); W on a small
neighborhood street laid out by CROSSKEYS & LOUGHTON between said moiety
& a lot owned by the heirs of GEORGE PAWLEY; E on the other half of lot
#14 belonging to JOSEPH CROSSKEYS; & whereas EDWARD LOUGHTON'S piece of
lot became vested in his son, WILLIAM LOUGHTON who, also owning several
other lots in Charleston, by will dated 7 Dec. 1727, bequeathed all his
real estate to his loving wife, MARY LOUGHTON (now MARY BREWTON, party
hereto) & to his 2 daughters MARY (now wife of WILLIAM MATTHEWS) & ANNE
(wife of BENJAMIN SMITH) as joint tenants; & whereas ROBERT BREWTON &
MARY his wife, WILLIAM MATTHEWS & MARY his wife, & BENJAMIN SMITH & ANNE
his wife, by deeds of partition dated 28 Nov. 1740, made an absolute partition so that each might hold his own part in certainty; & whereas it
was agreed that ROBERT BREWTON & MARY his wife, in the right of MARY,
should have all that part of a lot, with the buildings thereon, occupied
by JOHN BESWICK, fronting S 20 ft. on Broad Street; & bounding as first
mentioned; now BREWTON & his wife sell that part of the lot #14 to HES-
KETT. Witnesses: JAMES WRIGHT, ALEXANDER PERONNEAU. Before ROBERT

AUSTIN, J.P. JAMES HOME, Pub. Reg.

Book B-B, p. 219   WILLIAM HARE, merchant, of Charleston, only
15 & 16 Apr. 1745   executor of will of REBECCA FLAVELL, widow, of
L & R   Charleston, to GEORGE HESKETT, shipwright, of
                        Charleston, for Ł 1425 currency, the eastern-
most of 2 brick houses & its lot, as occupied by WILLIAM HARE, bounding S
16 ft. on Broad Street; W 90 ft. on the other house & lot devised to
ELIZABETH COLLETON; N on THOMAS DICKSON; E on THOMAS DICKSON & JOHN NEU-
FUILE. Whereas REBECCA FLAVELL owned 2 brick houses on N side Broad
Street, the house to the E bounding E on the houses of THOMAS DICKSON &
JOHN NEUFUILE, the house to the W bounding W on MRS. MIDDLETON'S house in
which DR. CAW dwells; & by will dated 18 Jan. 1743 bequeathed 1 of the
houses to her daughter ELIZABETH COLLETON & ordered the other house sold
to enable her executors to pay her debts & legacies, appointing WILLIAM
HARE, ISAAC MAZYCK & PAUL MAZYCK her executors; & whereas ISAAC & PAUL
MAZYCK refused to act; & whereas ELIZABETH COLLETON chose the house to
the W; now HARE sells the 1 to the E to HESKETT. Witnesses: ALEXANDER
PERONNEAU, WILLIAM GLEN. Before ROBERT AUSTIN, J.P. JAMES HOME, Pub.
Reg.

Book B-B, p. 224   JOSEPH BUTLER, ESQ., of Granville Co., 1 of
13 & 14 June 1745   the sons & devisees of SHEM BUTLER, EST., &
L & R   MARY his wife, to BENJAMIN WHITAKER, ESQ., for
                        Ł 1900 currency, 313 a., part of 340 a. which
SHEM BUTLER had purchased in several tracts; that is, 100 a. from heirs
of THOMAS GRUDGER FIELD; 30 a. from PATRICK SCOTT & SARAH his wife; 90 a.
from HINROYDAH ENGLISH; 120 a. from Lords Proprs.; the 313 a. being on N
side Ashley River, in St. Andrews Parish, bounding SE on CAPT. BARNABY
BULL & SHEM BUTLER; NE on SHEM BUTLER & BARNABY BULL; NW on CAPT. WILLIAM
BULL & JOHN MELL; S on JOHN MELL & SHEM BUTLER; BUTLER also sells WHIT-
AKER 11 lots in Butlers Town on S side Ashley River, Nos. 8, 9, 21, 73,
74, 75, 83, 84, 85, 87, & 88. Whereas SHEM BUTLER, the father, owned
several tracts of land, total 340 a., English measure, on N side Ashley
River, & by will dated 17 Oct. 1718 bequeathed all his real & personal
estate to be divided equally amongst his wife & children, the executors
to divide & allot the shares, & appointed his brother, RICHARD BUTLER,
his brother-in-law, SAMUEL WEST, & his son-in-law, EDMUND BELLINGER, his
executors; & whereas they allotted to son JOSEPH 313 a.; now he sells
this land to WHITAKER. Witnesses: THOMAS COOPER, WILLIAM BURROWN (gentleman). Before JAMES WEDDERBURN, J.P. JAMES HOME, Pub. Reg.

Book B-B, p. 233   ALEXANDER VANDERDUSSEN, ESQ., to JOHN CARRUTH-
31 Mar. & 1 Apr. 1741   ERS, gentleman, of Bramley, Co. of Middlesex,
L & R by Mortgage   Great Britain, but now residing in SC, as se-
                        curity on bond of even date in penal sum of
Ł 1000 sterling British, for payment of Ł 500 British, with interest, on
1 Apr. 1744; 500 a. in Goose Creek Parish, bounding SW on Goose Creek; SE
on Cooper River; NE on 200 a. granted WILLIAM WATIES & on BENJAMIN
SCHENCKINGH; NW on ROBERT HOWES; which 500 a. was granted by the Lords
Proprs. to LEWIS PASQUEREAU & by various mesne conveyances became vested
in ALEXANDER VANDERDUSSEN. VANDERDUSSEN also delivers to CARRUTHERS 20
Negro men. Witnesses: WILLIAM GEORGE FREEMAN, WILLIAM FRANKLIN. Before
JAMES WRIGHT, J.P. Recorded in Secretary's book R.R. fols. 181-184 by
JOHN CHAMPNEYS, Dep. Sec. JAMES HOME, Pub. Reg. On 15 Feb. 1745 WILLIAM
GEORGE FREEMAN, as attorney, for JOHN CARRUTHERS, declared mortgage sat-
isfied. JAMES HOME, Pub. Reg.

Book B-B, p. 239   ANDREW SLANN, THOMAS WARING & RICHARD WARING,
10 & 11 July 1745   JR., executors of will of JOSIAH WARING,
L & R   planter, of Berkeley Co., to JAMES SKIRVING,
                        gentleman, of Pon Pon, for Ł 1610 currency,
483 a., part of 500 a., in Berkeley Co., bounding N on RICHARD WARING; E
on HENRY IZARD, ESQ.; S on WILLIAM ELLIOTT; W on RICHARD WARING. Whereas
the Lords Proprs. on 28 June 1711, by Gov. ROBERT GIBBES, granted THOMAS
WARING 500 a. in Berkeley Co., bounding NE on PETER SLANN; NW on THOMAS
WARING; other sides on vacant land; & whereas THOMAS WARING on 1 Apr.
1714 sold the 500 a. to JOSIAH WARING, who, by will dated 19 Jan. 1744,
authorized his executors to sell all his real & personal estate not otherwise devised; now they sell 483 a. to SKIRVING. Plat shows SE line

115

bounding on HENRY PARD (formerly MR. KETTLES). Witnesses: JOSEPH BRAILS-
FORD, REGINALD JACKSON. Before RICHARD WARING, J.P. JAMES HOME, Pub.
Reg.

Book B-B, p. 247   ANTHONY DEBOURDEAUX, now of Craven Co., to
22 & 23 Mar. 1735   JAMES DEBOURDEAUX, shoemaker, of Berkeley Co.,
L & R   for Ł 500 currency, 505 a. near N part of Bull-
                          head Swamp, in St. Thomas Parish, Berkeley Co.,
bounding N on ROBERT JOHNSON, planter (formerly MR. DONOVAN); W on ISAAC
TREZVANT (formerly JAMES AKIN); E on MR. FERGORTY; S on MARY WATTS & on
JOHN RUBERRY'S land (which JOHN RUBERRY, SR., reserved for himself ouf of
the original tract & now owned by his son JOHN RUBERRY); the 505 a. being
part of a tract formerly belonging to JOHN RUBERRY, SR. & sold by him to
ANTHONY DEBOURDEAUX, joiner, & now vested in his son ANTHONY. Witnesses:
JAMES ROBERT, JOHN DUBOSE, ANDREW GRAY. Before JOHN GENDRON, J.P. JAMES
HOME, Pub. Reg.

Book B-B, p. 251   JOB ROTHMAHLER, merchant, & ANNE his wife, to
24 & 25 May 1725   JOSEPH WRAGG, merchant, all of Charleston, for
L & R   Ł 2750 SC money, all their 1/3 part of all the
                          real estate to which said JOB is entitled in
the right of his wife ANNE. Whereas JOHN THOMAS by will dated 22 July
1710 devised to his loving wife MARY THOMAS 1/3 part of all his real estate during her natural life & after her death equally to her 3 daughters,
MARY WRAGG (wife of SAMUEL WRAGG, merchant, of London), JUDITH DUBOSE
(now wife of JOSEPH WRAGG, merchant, of Charleston), & ANNE DUBOSE; &
further gave the remainder of his real estate to be equally divided among
MARY, JUDITH & ANNE; & whereas MARY THOMAS on 21st of this inst. released
her claim to SAMUEL & MARY WRAGG, JOSEPH & JUDITH WRAGG & JOB & ANNE ROTH-
MAHLER; now JOB & ANNE ROTHMAHLER convey their 1/3 part to JOSEPH WRAGG.
Witnesses: RICHARD LAMBTON, JOHN COLCOCK, ROBERT HUME. Before ROBERT
AUSTIN, J.P. A memorial entered in Auditor's office 15 May 1733. JAMES
HOME, Pub. Reg.

Book B-B, p. 256   HUGH DUFFEY, tanner, & ANSTIS (ANSTIES) his
4 & 5 Dec. 1744   wife, to CAPT. JAMES AKIN, planter, all of
L & R   Berkeley Co., for Ł 1250 currency, 150 a. in
                          Berkeley Co., bounding NW on JAMES AKIN; SE on
SARAH TROTT; SW on THOMAS BONNY; which 150 a. DUFFY purchased from AKIN
on 3 Dec. 1741 & which DUFFEY on 5 Dec. 1741 mortgaged to AKIN as securi-
ty for payment of Ł 1250 currency, with interest, to AKIN, as recorded 15
Mar. 1742. Witnesses: JEANE (her mark) DYER, EDWARD HARLESTON. Before
FRANCIS LEJAU, J.P. JAMES HOME, Pub. Reg.

Book B-B, p. 261   WILLIAM PORTER, nonconformist pastor & teacher,
24 Jan. 1744/5   of Christ Church Parish, to SAMUEL GRIER, weav-
Deed of Gift   er, & planter, living in the Township of Wac-
                          chamaw, Prince George Parish, Craven Co., for
good will & affection, 350 a. in Craven Co., purchased by the family warrant of SARAH HOOKER, widow, & conveyed by SARAH HOOKER by L & R to WIL-
LIAM PORTER; bounding SW on Wacchamaw Township, as by grant from Lt. Gov.
THOMAS BROUGHTON dated 17 Mar. 1735. SARAH, wife of WILLIAM PORTER, will-
ingly surrenders her title of dower & thirds. Witnesses: JAMES EDEN,
SARAH HUGGINS. Before OTHNIEL BEALE, J.P. JAMES HOME, Pub. Reg.

Book B-B, p. 263   WILLIAM PORTER, nonconformist pastor & teacher,
30 Nov. 1745   of Christ Church Parish, & SARAH his wife, to
Deed of Gift   JOSEPH MOODY, merchant, of Charleston, for
                          love & affection, 200 a. laid out as part of
PORTER'S family warrant given by Lt. Gov. THOMAS BROUGHTON, the 200 a.
being in Craven Co., near Wacchamar River, between land run out for JONAS
BONHOSTE & the 400 a. PORTER gave to THOMAS TODD; bounding according to
plat of grant from Lt. Gov. WILLIAM BULL dated 14 Dec. 1739. SARAH willingly renounces her right of dower. Witnesses: GEORGE HUGGINS, SARAH
HUGGINS, JAMES EDEN. Before OTHNIEL BEALE, J.P. JAMES HOME, Pub. Reg.

Book B-B, p. 264   ISAAC MARION, of Craven Co., to PAUL TRAPIER,
15 & 16 Dec. 1745   BENJAMIN ROMSEY & GABRIEL MARION, merchants,
L & R by Mortgage   of Georgetown, as security on bond of even
                          date in penal sum of Ł 3074:5:7 for payment of

L 1537:2:9-1/2 currency, with interest, on 1 Sept. 1746; 500 a. in Craven
Co., on Waccamaw River; bounding S on JOHN LOYD; E & N on WILLIAM WATIES.
Witnesses: JOHN BROWN, GABRIEL MARION, JR. Before WILLIAM WHITESIDE, J.P.
JAMES HOME, Pub. Reg.

Book B-B, p. 269   SARAH WILKINS, OBADIAH WILKINS, WILLIAM WIL-
2 Nov. 1744   KINS & BENJAMIN HALL, executrix & executors of
Bond   will of WILLIAM WILKINS, of James Island, &
                         EBENEZER SIMMONS & BENJAMIN SMITH, attorneys
for JAMES CROKATT, merchant, of London to SOLOMON LEGARE, JR., of Charleston, in penal sum of L 4000 currency as security that whereas SOLOMAN LE-
GARE has paid them L 2000 currency they will, by 1 Nov. next, at the
house of BENJAMIN SMITH in Charleston convey to him a sufficient title in
law to the 540 a. on SW side Stono River, in Colleton Co., lately belonging to WILLIAM WILKINS, & by his will subjected to the payment of his
debts; bounding N on JOHN PRESCOTT & ROBERT COLES; E on said PRIESCOTT
(formerly ELIZABETH GODFREY); S on JOHN GODFREY & PAUL TORQUET; W on TOR-
QUET; LEGARE to take immediate possession. Witness: JOHN MILNER. Before
ANTHONY MATHEWES, J.P. JAMES HOME, Pub. Reg. On 23 July 1747 SOLOMON LE-
GARE, JR. declared bond satisfied by delivery of L & R. Witness: JOHN
BEALE, Register.

Book B-B, p. 271   THOMAS WRIGHT, ELISHA BUTLER, & WILLIAM ROPER,
2 & 3 Apr. 1745   executors, & MARY WRIGHT, executrix, of will
L & R   of RICHARD WRIGHT, gentleman, of Colleton Co.,
                         to RICHARD LAKE, ESQ., of St. Andrews Parish,
Berkeley Co., for L 1265 currency, 193-1/2 a., commonly called Wappo
Plantation. Whereas RICHARD WOODWARD of James Island, St. Andrews Parish,
Berkeley Co., was seized in his demesne as of fee in the above plantation
on N side Wappoe Creek, bounding E on Mill Creek, BENJAMIN WHITAKER & BEN-
JAMIN GODFREY; W & N on GEORGE LUCAS; & by will dated 13 Apr. 1725 bequeathed to his beloved wife, SARAH, the use of 1/3 of his real estate
during her life, & to his daughter ELIZABETH 1/3 forever; & to daughter
MARY 1/3 forever; & whereas ELIZABETH, the eldest daughter, married RICH-
ARD WRIGHT; & WHEREAS certain lands & plantations, part of WOODWARD'S estate, were allotted by the executors to ELIZABETH; & the 193-1/2 a. with
several other plantations were allotted to MARY, the younger daughter,
who afterwards married ISAAC CHARDON, merchant, of Charleston; & whereas
MARY CHARDON & RICHARD WRIGHT, by release & exchange dated 21 June 1742,
exchanged their holdings so that WRIGHT received the 193-1/2 a. & MARY
obtained the James Island tract; & whereas by will dated 2 Jan. 1744 RICH-
ARD WRIGHT devised some part of his personal estates & directed his executors to dispose of the rest of his real & personal estate, & appointed
his wife MARY executrix, & THOMAS ELLIOTT, his brother THOMAS WRIGHT,
ELISHA BUTLER, & THOMAS ROPER, executors, but ELLIOTT would not act; now
the executors sell Wappoo Plantation to LAKE. Witnesses: CHARLES PINCK-
NEY, CHARLES CALDER. Before JAMES WRIGHT, J.P. JAMES HOME, Pub. Reg.

Book B-B, p. 280   BENJAMIN STONE, carpenter, to WILLIAM RIVERS,
27 Jan. 1744   planter, for L 231 currency, 33 a. on James
Sale   Island, Berkeley Co., bounding N on MRS. BEE;
                         S on BENJAMIN STONE; W on WILLIAM RIVERS; E on
part same tract; which land formerly belonged to JOHN MACKAY, at whose
death it came to JOHN FRASER, who sold it to BENJAMIN STONE. ELIZABETH
STONE, wife of BENJAMIN, willingly surrenders her dower. Witnesses: ROB-
ERT RIVERS, BENJAMIN MAVERICK. Before ROBERT AUSTIN, J.P. JAMES HOME,
Pub. Reg.

Book B-B, p. 282   THOMAS RADCLIFFE, tanner, of St. Andrews Par-
20 & 21 Dec. 1743   ish, at Ashley Ferry, Berkeley Co., to BENJA-
L & R by Mortgage   MIN MAZYCK, planter, of St. James Goose Creek,
                         Berkeley Co., as security on bond of even date
in penal sum of L 4000 for payment of L 2000 currency, by 1 Apr. 1747;
25 a. on Charleston Neck, bounding E on the Broad Path; N on WILLIAM EL-
LIOT (formerly CAPT. SCHENCKINGH); W on a small creek; S on SAMUEL WRAGG;
which tract was granted by the Lords Proprs. on 21 Mar. 1715 to CATHERINE
LAPOSTRE; who, by deed of feoffment dated 26 Mar. 1719 conveyed to THOMAS
FAIRCHILD & RICHARD FAIRCHILD his brother; & whereas THOMAS FAIRCHILD by
will dated 26 June 1733 authorized his executors ELIZABETH FAIRCHILD &
WILLIAM FAIRCHILD to sell any part of his real or personal estate & pay

his debts; & they on 15 Feb. 1736 conveyed 25 a. on Charleston Neck to
BENJAMIN MAZYCK, of Charleston; & whereas BENJAMIN MAZYCK & DAMARIS his
wife on 20 Dec. 1743 to THOMAS RADCLIFFE; now he mortgages the tract to
MAZYCK. Witnesses: PAUL MAZYCK, DANIEL HOY. Before JAMES MICKIE, J.P.
JAMES HOME, Pub. Reg. On 25 June 1765 BENJAMIN MAZYCK declared mortgage
satisfied. Witness: FENWICKE BULL.

Book B-B, p. 289   FRANCIS WILKINSON, planter, of Colleton Co.,
17 July 1745   brother, heir-at-law, & devise of JOSEPH WIL-
Release   KINSON, planter, to SARAH MIDDLETON, widow, of
                          St. James Goose Creek, Berkeley Co., as a re-
compense & satisfaction of JOSEPH WILKINSON'S debt; several tracts of
land. Whereas JOSEPH WILKINSON owned 160 a. originally granted by the
Lords Proprs. to COL. ABRAHAM EVE, being an island on W side of S Edisto
River, in Colleton Co., the lower part of the island fronting Willtown,
the upper part fronting MOSES PINGRY; also 2 other plantations of 500 a.
each, in Colleton Co., originally granted by the Lords Proprs. to PETER
MANN, bounding N on THOMAS DISTON, ESQ., E on WILLIAM CATER & JOHN SIM-
MONDS; S on vacant land; W on S Edisto (Pon Pon) River; also lot #6 in
New London, commonly called Willtown, granted by the Lords Proprs. to JAM-
ES COCKRAN, ESQ., bounding N on Beaufort Street; E on lot #23; S on lot
#7; W on Tower Stairs; & whereas JOSEPH WILKINSON was indebted to SARAH
MIDDLETON by bonds in the sum of Ł 8870:13:2 currency, with interest, payable 25 Mar. 1742, & for security on 25 Mar. 1741 mortgaged all the above
real estate & his personal estate to SARAH MIDDLETON; & by will directed
that all his debts be paid & bequeathed the remainder of his estate to
his brother FRANCIS, party hereto, appointing FRANCIS his sole executor;
& whereas JOSEPH died before discharging his debt & the mortgaged property is not of the value of the debt & interest owing to MRS. MIDDLETON;
now FRANCIS WILKINSON conveys to MRS. MIDDLETON the 160 a., 500 a., & the
town lot #6. Witnesses: ANDREW SLANN, THOMAS MIDDLETON, RICHARD WARING,
JR. Before WILLIAM MIDDLETON, J.P. JAMES HOME, PUB. Reg.

Book B-B, p. 293   GEORGE HESKETT, shipwright, to his son-in-law
10 Jan. 1745   JOHN DANIELL, shipwright, both of Charleston,
Deed of Feoffment   for love & affection, Ł 5 currency, & other
                          considerations, part of a lot in Charleston,
bounding E 26 ft. on part of same lot belonging to CAPT. KING; N 22-1/2
ft. on GEORGE HAMILTON; W on JOHN DANIELL; S on GEORGE HESKETT. Witnesses: GEORGE (his mark) HAMILTON; JOHN REMINGTON. Witnesses to possession
& seizin: ADRIAN LOYER, JOHN COWDEN, GEORGE HAMILTON & JOHN REMINGTON.
Before JAMES HOME, J.P. & Pub. Reg.

Book B-B, p. 296   JOHN ANDREW, SR., planter, of Colleton Co., to
9 May 1733   his loving & obedient son, JOHN ANDREW, JR.,
Deed of Gift   for love & affection, 150 a., English measure,
                          in St. Bartholomews Parish, bounding E on JOHN
HAINS; S on GEORGE BADGER & JOHN MITCHELL; W on GEORGE MITCHELL, SR.; N
on the plantation on which JOHN ANDREW, SR., lives. Witnesses: JOSEPH
ANDREW, JOSEPH MITCHELL. Before CULCHETH GOLIGHTLY, J.P. JAMES HOME,
Pub. Reg.

Book B-B, p. 297   ELIZABETH BELLINGER ELLIOTT, lately widow &
1 & 2 Nov. 1745   executrix of will of Landgrave EDMUND BELLING-
L & R   ER the 2nd; to the Hon. WILLIAM BULL, Lt. Gov.;
                          STEPHEN BULL, ESQ.; ROBERT THORP, ESQ.; JAMES
DEVEAUX, gentleman, & JOHN GREEN, gentleman & to the rector of the Parish;
all of Prince William Parish for Ł 10 currency & other considerations;
50 a. in Granville Co., bounding SE on Lt. Gov. BULL; other sides on BEL-
LINGER'S Landgravate. Whereas ELIZABETH ELLIOTT, by virtue of her husband's will & be deeds of settlement made when she married THOMAS ELLIOTT,
had full power to dispose of her late husband's lands; & whereas by Act
of Assembly passed 25 May last to divide the Parish of St. Hellens &
create a new one by the name of Prince William Parish & appointed WILLIAM
BULL, STEPHEN BULL, ROBERT THORP, JAMES DEVEAUX & JOHN GREEN commissioners for building the Parish Church & parsonage house for the new Parish &
to receive & purchase lands for the use of the rector; & whereas ELIZA-
BETH ELLIOTT was willing for herself & her family to contribute towards
the building of a church & the maintenance of its rector; now she conveys
50 a. for that purpose. Plat dated 1 Nov. 1745. Witnesses: JAMES

JOLLIFF, WILLIAM BACKSHELL. Before WILLIAM BULL, JR., J.P. JAMES HOME,
Pub. Reg.

Book B-B, p. 302   ROBERT ELLIS, merchant, of Philadelphia, to
8 Dec. 1742   ELIZABETH CHEESEMAN, executrix of will of
Sale   THOMAS CHEESEMAN, for Ł 300 SC money, 4 lots
                          in Wilmington, New Hanover Co., NC, bounding
as follows: 1 water lot #31 & 1 front lot #32, both bounded N on lot on
which CALEB GRAINGER'S dwelling house now stands; S on SAMUEL HASELL;
lots #33 & #34 bounded N by WILLIAM FARRIS; S on JOSHUA GRAINGER; paying
the crown rents as expressed in JOHN WATSON'S patent. Witnesses: ROBERT
WALKER, JAMES SMALLWOOD, JAMES CAMPBELL. Proved in Wilmington Dec. Court
1742. Recorded in New Hanover Co. Register's office, in Bk. C. fol 1. on
21 Feb. 1742/3 by JAMES SMALLWOOD, C.C. & Register. JAMES HOME, Pub. Reg.
Charleston.

Book B-B, p. 304   ELIZABETH CHEESMAN, widow, to RICHARD LAKE,
5 & 6 Aug. 1745   ESQ., both of Berkeley Co., for Ł 100 SC money,
L & R   4 lots in Wilmington, NC, Nos. 31, 32, 33 & 34;
                          water lot #31 & front lot #32 bounding N on
lot where CALEB GRAINGER'S dwelling house stands; S on SAMUEL HASELL;
lots 33 & 34 bounding N on WILLIAM FARIS, ESQ.; S on JOSHUA GRAINGER.
Witnesses: JOHN HARVEY, RICHARD GODFREY. Before JAMES GREEME, J.P. JAM-
ES HOME, Pub. Reg.

Book B-B, p. 308   THOMAS COOPER, merchant, to WILLIAM HOPTON,
4 & 5 Feb. 1745   merchant, of Charleston, for Ł 6000 currency,
L & R   part of lot #177 in Charleston, with the house
                          where THOMAS CORBET lived, fronting N 38 ft.
on Broad Street; bounding E on heirs of WILLIAM LOUGHTON; S on WILLIAM
HANCOCK; W on part same lot; & also 15 Negro slaves. Witnesses: JOSEPH
WILLIAMS, JOHN SMITH. Before JOHN LINING, J.P. JAMES HOME, Pub. Reg.

Book B-B, p. 312   JAMES MICKIE, ESQ., & MARTHA his wife, of
3 & 4 Feb. 1743   Charleston, to WILLIAM CHAMBERS, tailor, of
L & R   Colleton Co., for Ł 2800 SC money, 600 a.
                          known as Bugbys Hole, on Wadmalaw Island, Col-
leton Co., bounding E on WILLIAM CHAMBERS & ABRAHAM WEIGHT; W on MR.
JONES; S on JOHN LADSON & land belonging to the Presbyterian Meeting
House on Johns Island. Witnesses: EDWARD FENWICKE, JOHN COOPER. Before
JAMES HOME, J.P. & Pub. Reg.

Book B-B, p. 317   THOMAS COOPER, & MARY his wife, of St. Johns
5 & 6 Feb. 1745   Island, Colleton Co., to JOHN CHAMPNEYS, of
L & R by Mortgage   Charleston, as security for payment of Ł 3000
                          SC money, with interest, on 6 Feb. 1746;
325 a. on Johns Island, on N side A. B. Poolaw Creek, bounding E on CAPT.
THOMAS FLEMING; W on AARON HUNSCOMB & THOMAS LADSON; N on LADSON & D'HAR-
RIETTE. Witnesses: LUCY HANSON, WILLIAM COWELL. Before WILLIAM BOONE,
J.P. JAMES HOME, Pub. Reg.

Book B-B, p. 323   MATTHEW & THOMAS BURNLEY, cordwinder, & car-
27 Sept. 1745   penter, to PETER HASKIN (HAWSKIN) planter, all
Sale   of Berkeley Co., for Ł 100 SC money, 136 a.
                          purchased from the Lords Proprs. by their fa-
ther WILLIAM BURNLEY & bequeathed to MATTHEW & THOMAS. Witnesses: HUGH
FERGUSON, SARAH FERGUSON, MARY BURNLEY. Before JOHN LINING, J.P. JAMES
HOME, Pub. Reg.

Book B-B, p. 324   HENRY YONGE, storekeeper, of Morton Town, SC
13 & 14 Feb. 1745/6   to FRANCIS WILKINSON, planter, of Colleton Co.,
L & R by Mortgage   as security on several bonds amounting to
                          Ł 4810 currency; 2 lots #7 & #8, of 1/2 a.
each, English measure, in Morton Town on E side Wadmalaw River; also lot
#3, containing 1/2 a., in town of New Chelsea, on N side Stono River;
also 103 a. on Wadmalaw Island, bounding S on marsh of Boarded Bridge
Creek; W on Landgrave MORTON; N on PETER BROWN; E on WILLIAM NASH; as by
L & R, dated 20 June 1745 from JOHN FREER; also 300 a., on Wadmalaw Is-
land, part of 700 a., granted by Gov. JAMES GLEN on 24 May 1745 to HENRY
YONGE, bounding SE & W on marshes & creeks of Lednewa; N & NW on HENRY

YONGE. Whereas FRANCIS WILKINSON, at the special instance & request & for the debt of HENRY YONGE & his late partner, JOSEPH WILKINSON, stands bound with HENRY YONGE & JOSEPH WILKINSON, to ISAAC HOLMES, merchant, & to WILLIAM WEBB, merchant, both of Charleston, & to SAMUEL PERONNEAU, planter, & to MARTHA PERONNEAU, for 4 bonds in the penal sum of Ⱡ 2405 each, for payment of Ⱡ 1202:10, with interest, on 20 Mar. 1743/4; but the sums remain unpaid; now YONGE mortgages the above property as security. Witnesses: THOMAS CORBETT, JOHN BULL, JR. Before WILLIAM GEORGE FREEMAN, J.P. JAMES HOME, Pub. Reg.

Book B-B, p. 330   JOHN GUERRARD, merchant, of Charleston, to
29 Jan. 1744   THOMAS ELLIOTT, planter, for Ⱡ 450 currency,
L & R   that lot in Charleston fronting E 45 ft. on
                         Friend Street; bounding N 140 ft. on JAMES MC-
KEWN; S on the heirs of THOMAS FAIRCHILD, butcher, W on RICHARD MASON;
which lot formerly belonged to THOMAS FAIRCHILD & was conveyed by him in
fee to MRS. CATHERINE BETTESON, who was afterwards the wife of DANIEL
WELLSHUYSON, ESQ., of Craven Co.; & by them conveyed to RICHARD HILL; who
conveyed to JOHN GUERARD; who now conveys to ELLIOTT. Witnesses: RICHARD
HILL, FREDERICK GRIMKE. Before JAMES HOME, J.P. & Pub. Reg.

Book B-B, p. 334   ALEXANDER CHOUIN (CHOUXVINE), planter, & HES-
1 & 2 Nov. 1745   TER, (ESTHER) his wife, to CATHERINE SERRE,
L & R   widow, all of St. James Santee Parish, Craven
                         Co., for Ⱡ 1100 currency, 3 tracts of 200 a.,
200 a., & 350 a., total 750 a.; on S side Santee River; being the planta-
tion on which CHOUIN now resides; bounding NW & SE on estate of NOAH
SERRÉ; SW on vacant land; also 2 adjoining tracts on Wadbauan Island in
Santee River, opposite the others; 1 being 200 a., the other 63 a.; with
the others making 1013 a.; the last 2 bounding SE & NW on estate of NOAH
SERRÉ; NE on Wadbauan Creek; SW on Santee River. Witnesses: JOHN HENTIE,
DANIEL JAUDON. Before JOHN GENDRON, J.P. JAMES HOME, Pub. Reg.

Book B-B, p. 340   ANN PARTRIDGE, widow, to WILLIAM SMITH, plant-
1 & 2 July 1732   er, both of Berkeley Co., for Ⱡ 600 SC money,
L & R   640 a. in Berkeley Co., bounding N on CORNEL-
                         IUS DUPREE; W on MR. KAYDON & SAMUEL MELLER; S
on MELLER & MR. SANDERS; E on MR. ADAMS. Witnesses: WILLIAM ROPER, ED-
WARD JENKINS, JR. Before JAMES HOME, J.P. & Pub. Reg.

Book B-B, p. 343   WILLIAM SMITH, planter, of Berkeley Co., to
21 & 22 July 1743   THOMAS JENYS & GEORGE SEAMAN, merchants, of
L & R   Charleston, for Ⱡ 814:6 SC money, 640 a. in
                         Berkeley Co., bounding N on CORNELIUS DUPREE;
W on MR. KAYDON & SAMUEL MELLER; S on MELLER & MR. SANDERS; E on MR.
ADAMS. Witnesses: JAMES LENNOX, SAMUEL HURST. Before JAMES HOME, J.P. &
Pub. Reg.

Book B-B, p. 347   ELIZABETH BELLINGER ELLIOTT, (lately widow &
14 & 15 Feb. 1745   executrix of will of Landgrave EDMUND BELLIN-
L & R   GER the 2nd) & GEORGE BELLINGER, ESQ., of St.
                         Andrews Parish, to WILLIAM PALMER, ESQ., of
Prince William Parish, for Ⱡ 2500 currency paid to said GEORGE BELLINGER,
1000 a. in Granville Co., bounding SE on WILLIAM PALMER; SW on JONATHAN
BRYAN; NE on JOHN BULL; NW on BELLINGER'S Landgravate. Whereas ELIZABETH
ELLIOTT by deed of settlement on her marriage to THOMAS ELLIOTT of Stono
is impowered to act as if unmarried, & impowered by will of her late husband to dispose of his lands & lay out the legacies therein mentioned; &
whereas 1000 a. had been left to GEORGE BELLINGER; now he & MRS. ELLIOTT
sell the tract to PALMER. Witnesses: JAMES JOLLIFF, WILLIAM BACKSHELL.
Before JAMES HOME, J.P. & Pub. Reg.

Book B-B, p. 352   ELISHA SCREVEN, planter, to JOHN SMITH, plant-
26 & 27 Mar. 1745   er, both of Craven Co., for Ⱡ 400 SC money, 2
L & R   tracts, total 1750 a., in Craven Co., being
                         850 a. on Peedee River originally granted to
said ELISHA SCREVEN, bounding SW on JOHN OWENS; other sides on vacant
land; & 900 a. originally granted to JOHN OWEN, & CONVEYED by L & R dated
25 & 26 Oct. 1738 to SCREVEN; bounding NE on ELISHA SCREVEN; other sides
on vacant land. Witnesses: JAMES HEPBURN, THOMAS IRETON CROMWELL.

Before WILLIAM FLEMING, J.P.   JAMES HOME, Pub. Reg.

Book B-B, p. 358   CRAFTON KARWON, vintner, of Craven Co., to
19 & 20 Feb. 1745   PAUL TRAPIER, BENJAMIN ROMSEY, JAMES WRIGHT,
L & R by Mortgage   ANDREW JOHNSTON, JOHN CLELAND, & WILLIAM FLEM-
                                ING; all of Georgetown; as security on bond of
even date in penal sum of Ł 800 for payment of Ł 400 currency, with interest, on 1 Apr. ensuing; & as secutiry on bond to JAMES WRIGHT in penal sum of Ł 600 for payment of Ł 300 currency, with interest, on 1 Apr.
ensuing; as also to ANDREW JOHNSTON in penal sum of Ł 440 for payment of
Ł 220, with interest, on said 1st Apr., as also to JOHN CLELAND & WILLIAM
FLEMING in penal sum of Ł 800 for payment of Ł 400 currency on 1st Apr.;
4 plantations in Craven Co.; 550 a. in Williamsburgh Township, on SW side
Black River, bounding SE on JOHN ROBERTSON; other sides on vacant land;
500 a. in said Township, on SW side Black River, bounding NW on vacant
land & CAPT. JOHN WHITFIELD; NE on JOHN WHITFIELD & DANIEL MOONEY; SE &
SW on vacant land; 200 a. granted to DANIEL MOONEY, now belonging to KAR-
WON, in said Township, bounding NW on MARY MUCKLERY; NE on Black River;
other sides on vacant land; 1000 a. on PeeDee River, near the WELCH
tract. Witnesses: ARCHIBALD JOHNSTON, WILLIAM DICKSON. Before JOHN LIN-
NING, J.P. JAMES HOME, Pub. Reg.

Book B-B, p, 365   ALEXANDER BROWN, planter, to WILLIAM FLEMING,
31 Jan. & 1 Feb. 1745   planter, both of Craven Co., as security on
L & R by Mortgage   bond of even date given by said ALEXANDER
                                BROWN & LEONARD WHITE, planter, of Craven Co.,
in penal sum of Ł 3366:16:6 for payment of Ł 1683:8:3 SC money, with in-
terest, on 1 Mar. 1746; 650 a. in Craven Co., bounding N on RALPH GERMAN;
S on N branch of Black River; SE on MARY KELLY; also 600 a. in Craven
Co., bounding SW on Black River; NW on MARY KELLY; other sides on BENJA-
MIN SAVAGE. Witnesses: WILLIAM BROWN, WILLIAM DICKSON. Before JOHN CLE-
LAND, J.P. JAMES HOME, Pub. Reg.

Book B-B, p. 370   Received of MATHEW ROCHE & ANN ROCHE, his
28 Feb. 1744   wife, L & R of the house wherein JOHN RATTRAY
Receipt   now lives; also of the store wherein MESSRS.
                                PHILP & LEVIE live; also the reversion of the
dwelling house where MESSRS. PHILP & LEVIS live, all of which are in 1
deed dated 14 Dec. 1744; for Ł 6000 currency; also a bond dated 17 Nov.
1744, payable with interest in 12 months, signed JAMES MATHEWS & JAMES
TOURQUETT to MATT. ROCHE; which deeds & bonds I have received as security
for payment of Ł 1000 sterling I this day guaranteed the payment of to
JAMES CROKATT in London in behalf of MATHEW ROCHE. I further promise
that when ROCHE frees me from the engagement to CROKATT I will reconvey
the above premises to him & return the bond to ROCHE. Signed: JAMES
MATHEWES. Witness: CHARLES STEVENSON. Before THOMAS LAMBOLL, J.P. JAM-
ES HOME, Pub. Reg.

Book B-B, p. 371   ELIZABETH MATHEWES, executrix, & ANTHONY MATH-
28 Dec. 1745   EWES, JOHN MATHEWES, WILLIAM MATHEWES, BENJA-
Reconveyance   MIN MATHEWES & THOMAS LAMBOLL, executors, of
                                will of JAMES MATHEWES, merchant, of Charles-
ton, to MATHEW ROCHE, merchant, of Charleston & ANN his wife. Whereas
MATHEW ROCHE & ANN his wife, by L & R dated 26 & 27 Nov. 1744, & ANN by
her acknowledgment made 14 Dec. 1744 before the Chief Justice, conveyed
to JAMES MATHEWES that house & messuage in Broad Street, where JOHN RAT-
TRAY then & now lives; also that store or shop then in possession of
MESSRS. PHILP & LIVIE; also the reversion of that dwelling house in Broad
Street, inhabited by MESSRS. PHILP & LIVIE; for Ł 6000 currency; & whereas by deed poll signed by JAMES MATHEWES 28 Feb. 1744 it appears that the
conveyance executed by MATHEW & ANN ROCHE was intended to be a mortgage
to secure payment of Ł 1000 sterling to JAMES CROKATT, merchant, of London, for the making good whereof to said CROKATT the said JAMES MATHEWES
stood bound on behalf of ROCHE; & whereas the Ł 1000 dur CROKATT was paid
by ROCHE & the other conditions of the mortgage complied with; now ELIZA-
BETH, ANTHONY, JOHN, WILLIAM & BENJAMIN MATHEWES & THOMAS LAMBOLL, for
the said Ł 1000 paid to CROKATT & for Ł 100 currency paid them by ROCHE,
they reconvey to MATHEW & ANN ROCHE the houses, messuages, stores, shops,
etc., in Broad Street, Charleston, that had been conveyed to JAMES MATH-
EWES, also the reversion of the dwelling house where PHILP & LIVIE live.

Witnesses: CHARLES STEVENSON, JOHN PRATT. Before JACOB MOTTE, J.P. JAM-
ES HOME, Pub. Reg.

Book B-B, p. 374   WILLIAM POWER, schoolmaster, of Wadmalaw Is-
23 Mar. 1744/5   land, & SARAH (her mark) his wife, to HENRY
Mortgage   YONGE, surviving partner of YONGE & WILKINSON,
                         of Morton Town, storekeeper; as security on
bond of even date for payment of Ł 555:4:6 currency, with interest, on 1
Mar. ensuing; 100 a. on Wadmalaw Island as by deed of gift dated 30 Apr.
1733 from ROBERT COLE & MARY his wife to their son MICAJAH COLE (see Bk.
T. p. 163-164) & as bequeathed by COLE to SARAH SPENCER, now wife of WIL-
LIAM POWER. POWER also mortgages to YONGE 2 Negro men, 1 Negro woman,
about 12 head neat cattle branded   & all his horses. Witnesses: WIL-
LIAM BOULD (BOULD), ALEXANDER MCGILLIVRAY. Before THOMAS CHARNOCK, J.P.
Recorded in Secretary's Book R.R. fol. 83, 84, 85 by JOHN CHAMPNEYS, Dep.
Sec. JAMES HOME, Pub. Reg.

Book B-B, p. 377   NATHANIEL FORD, shipwright, to THOMAS BEZELEY,
10 & 11 Apr. 1745   shipwright, both of Berkeley Co., for Ł 600
L & R   currency, 2 plantations of 25 a. each, making
                         1 tract of 50 a. on N side Wakindaw Creek,
bounding N on EDWARD CROFT; W on CROFT & ANDREW QUELCH; E on marsh & WIL-
LIAM VIZER (VISSER?). Whereas by L & R dated 23 & 24 Oct. 1732 the Rev.
MR. WILLIAM GUY, minister of St. Andrews Parish, Berkeley Co., & REBECCA
his wife; ROBERT JOHNSON, gentleman & SARAH his wife; & MARY BASDEN of
St. Philips Parish, Charleston, conveyed to NATHANIEL FORD, 25 a. in
Christ Church Parish, Berkeley Co., bounding S on NICHOLAS FORD; N on
WILLIAM AXTON; E on Wakendaw Creek; & whereas by L & R dated 15 & 16 Nov.
1732 JONATHAN STOCKS, cordwainer, of Christ Church Parish, & ELENOR his
wife conveyed to NATHANIEL FORD 25 a. in Christ Church Parish, bounding S
on ROBERT SESSIONS Creek; W on WILLIAM AXTON; N on JOHN HALL; E on WIL-
LIAM VIZIOR (VISSER?). Witnesses: JAMES HILLIARD, WILLIAM PLAYTERS. Before THOMAS DALE, J.P. JAMES HOME, Pub. Reg. Plat of 50 a., part of
larger tract granted to RICHARD ROUSOUR, & by several conveyances now in
possession of NATHANIEL FORD, on N side Wackinaw Creek, Berkeley Co.,
bounding N on EDWARD CROFT; W on CROFT & ANDREW QUELCH; E on marsh & WIL-
LIAM VISER. Certified 12 June 1733 by THOMAS WITTER, Dep. Ser.

Book B-B, p. 383   Between JAMES MATHEWES, merchant, of Charles-
27 Dec. 1734   ton, & SAMUEL RIVERS, planter, of James Island,
Agreement   St. Andrews Parish, Berkeley Co. Whereas JAM-
                         ES MATHEWS & ELIZABETH his wife by deed poll
dated 24 this Dec. sold 100 a. on James Island for Ł 1400 SC money, &
"although the receipt money therein is duly signed (though not paid) as
plainly appears by the said SAMUEL RIVERS & ELIZABETH his wife by their
deed poll bearing date" 26 inst. Dec. "sheweth & sets forth (for the well
& true payment of the said sum" of Ł 1400 "with the interest growing due
& what other charge may arise from the same) by them given to the said
JAMES MATHEWES...if the same be not paid within 1 year from the date.
thereof"; & whereas much waste & damage may be done to the 100 a. in
clearing the ground & selling the timber, RIVERS being in peaceable possession; therefore SAMUEL RIVERS & ELIZABETH his wife, for the payment of
Ł 1400, with interest, & other charges if any, have sold 6 slaves to MATH-
EWES. It is further agreed that RIVERS may pay MATHEWES for 7 years,
i.e. until 27 Dec. 1735, Ł 200 with the interest on Ł 1400 (Ł 340 for 1st
year, & every year) until the whole is paid. MATHEWES & RIVERS bind themselves in penal sum of Ł 2000 currency. Witnesses: MARY ODINGSELLS, NI-
COLAS SMITH. Before JACOB MOTTE, J.P. JAMES HOME, Pub. Reg.

Book B-B, p. 386   MARY BREWTON, widow of MILES BREWTON, gentle-
5 Mar. 1745   man, of Charleston (lately MARY BELLAMY), to
Feoffment   MATHEW ROCHE, merchant, of Charleston, for
                         Ł 2000 SC money, & other considerations, all
her claim to that part of lot #28 with the tenement thereon, adjoining
the dwelling house where TIMOTHY BELLAMY, her late husband, lived; bounding E 100 ft. on said dwelling house now owned by MATHEW ROCHE; W on JOHN
CROKATT'S house (formerly MRS. CATHERINE LEPORTER, then of DR. JOHN DE-
LAUNE); N on the heirs of MR. JENYS (formerly MADAM BRETELL); S 34 ft. on
Broad Street. Whereas TIMOTHY BELLAMY, merchant, of Charleston, by will
dated 25 Feb. 1725 devised to his wife, MARY, during her natural life,

that part of lot #28 adjoining his dwelling house, with the tenement then to be built on the lot, & after her death to his daughter ANN BELLAMY, now wife of MATHEW ROCHE: now she releases her claim to ROCHE. Witnesses: JOHN RATTRAY, JAMES GRINDLAY. Witnesses to livery & seizin: ALEXANDER LIVIE, JOHN RATTRAY, JAMES GRINDLAY. Before JACOB MOTTE, J.P. JAMES HOME, Pub. Reg.

Book B-B, p. 389
19 & 21 Oct. 1732
L & R by Mortgage

ROBERT HUME, attorney-at-law, of St. Philip's Parish, Charleston, to ALEXANDER HUME, gentleman, of London, as security on bond dated 1 May last, in penal sum of Ł 1000 British for payment of Ł 575 British as follows: Ł 25 on 1 May 1733; Ł 25 on 1 May 1734; Ł 525 on 1 May 1735; & on another bond of even date in penal sum of Ł 2200 British for payment of Ł 1265 British as follows: Ł 55 on 21 Oct. 1733; Ł 55 on 21 Oct. 1734; Ł 1155 on 21 Oct. 1735; that brick tenement in Charleston wherein SUSANNAH WIGINGTON now lives & the "timber messuage or tenement thereto adjoining" which ROBERT HUME now uses for his office, with the land on which it stands & adjoining the same, being part of lot #42; being 31 ft. in front; & bounding N on JOHN GARNIER; S on Broad Street; E on JAMES MAZYCK (alias DUPOIDS D'OR, now of JOHN BEE); W on ST. JULIEN; with the kitchens & buildings behind the same; which tenement & part of a lot HUME purchased from CAPT. JONATHAN SKRINE; also 284-1/2 a. on Charleston Neck, St. Philips Parish, where ROBERT HUME now lives, consisting of 3 adjoining tracts; being 174-1/2 a. purchased from GILSON CLAPP; 10 a. purchased from CHARLES HART, ESQ.; & 100 a. of marsh purchased from ALEXANDER TRENCH (out of Landgrave BAILEY'S patent); the 284-1/2 a. bounding N on Gov. ROBERT JOHNSON; S on CHARLES HART; E on marsh & creek of Cooper River; W on the high road leading from Charleston; also 84 a. which HUME bought from ROBERT DANIELL, ESQ., & HELEN his wife; on Charleston Neck; bounding N on MR. COLLINGS (formerly JOHN WATKINS); E on the high road leading to Charleston; S on DANIEL CARTWRIGHT; W on marsh of Ashley River & MR. CARTWRIGHT; also 890 a. purchased by HUME from ROGER MOORE, ESQ., in St. James Goose Creek Parish, bounding SW on land called Thorowgoods belonging to ANDREW ALLEN; E on MR. WEBSTER & JAMES MOORE; N on COL. GEORGE CHICKEN. Witnesses: JOHN ALLEN, JOHN BLAMYER. Before JACOB MOTTE, J.P. JAMES HOME, Pub. Reg.

Book B-B, p. 398
18 & 19 Mar. 1745
L & R by Mortgage

ANN (her mark) SCULL, widow, to SARAH STOUTENBROUGH, widow, & JOHN MACKENZIE, merchant, all of Charleston, as security on bond of even date in penal sum of Ł 1600 for payment of Ł 800 SC money, with interest, on 19 Mar. 1746; part of lot #82 in Charleston, formerly occupied by EDWARD SCULL, fronting W 60 ft. on the street leading from Ashley River by the Quaker Meeting House; N 225 ft. on other part same lot; S on MR. WELLS. Witnesses: THOMAS POOLE, JOHN REMINGTON. Before JACOB MOTTE, J.P. JAMES HOME, Pub. Reg.

Book B-B, p. 403
29 & 30 Aug. 1745
L & R

ROBERT AUSTIN, merchant, to THOMAS BOLTON & JOHN REMINGTON, executors of will of EDWARD SCULL, joiner, all of Charleston. Whereas ROBERT AUSTIN & EDWARD SCULL in 1741 reciprocally agreed that for Ł 1200 to be paid by SCULL, AUSTIN would convey to SCULL in fee, part of a lot then occupied by SCULL; & whereas at that time WRAGG & LAMBTON held a bond dated 23 July 1730 from JOHN VICARIDGE & ROBERT AUSTIN to JOHN FENWICKE, JOSEPH WRAGG, PAUL JENYS, OTHNIEL BEALE & THOMAS LAMBOLL, in penal sum of Ł 1706:13:4 for payment of Ł 853:6:8 currency on which there remained unpaid Ł 840:2:6, which bond at the request of AUSTIN, SCULL assumed; & on 30 Sept. 1741 paid WRAGG & LAMBTON Ł 530:15 & afterwards, in 3 payments, paid Ł 194; & whereas SCULL by will dated 11 Oct. last past appointed THOMAS BOLTON & JOHN REMINGTON his executors, & died without completing the payment, & without receiving title; & whereas on 20 Oct. last the will was proved & the executors paid the balance to JOSEPH WRAGG; & whereas BOLTON & REMINGTON were in doubt as to the amount paid & the amount due; wherefore for settling any disputes between AUSTIN & SCULL'S estate, AUSTIN & the executors on 11 July last agreed to stand by the award & judgment of RICHARD HILL, THOMAS LAMBOLL, OTHNIEL BEALE, & GEORGE AUSTIN; the arbitrators on 5 Aug. inst. ordering AUSTIN on 1 Sept. next to execute a conveyance to the executors in trust for discharging SCULL'S debts & performing his will & upon execution the executors to pay AUSTIN Ł 289:18:4 SC money; now BOLTON & REMINGTON pay

that sum to AUSTIN who conveys to them that part of lot #82 in Charleston
formerly belonging to JOHN HOOG & lately occupied by EDWARD SCULL, fronting W 60 ft. on the street leading from Ashley River by the Quakers Meeting House; N on other part same lot; S 225 ft. on MR. WELLS. Witnesses:
JEMIT COBLEY, HENRY GIBBES. Before JOHN DART, J.P. On 17 Mar. 1745 BOL-
TON & REMINGTON received from ANN SCULL, widow, & residuary legatee of
will of EDWARD SCULL Ł 800 SC money towards discharging SCULL'S debts &
they transfer to her the title in above land & premises. Witnesses: THOM-
AS POOLE, SUSANNAH STOUTENBROUGH. Before ROBERT AUSTIN, J.P. JAMES
MICKIE, Dep. Pub. Reg.

Book B-B, p. 410   MATHEW ROCHE, merchant, & ANN his wife, to
5 & 6 Mar. 1745   JOHN WATSON, JR., merchant, all of Charleston,
L & R   for Ł 4500 SC money, lot #28 in Charleston
                     with the messuage thereon now occupied by
PHILP & LEVIE, fronting 54 ft. on N side Broad Street; bounding W 100 ft.
on JOHN CROKATT'S house (formerly DR. JOHN DELAUNE); N on heirs of MR.
JENYS (formerly MADAM BRETELL); E on a lot belonging to MATHEW ROCHE.
Witnesses: JOHN RATTRAY, JAMES GRINDLAY. Before JACOB MOTTE, J.P. JAMES
MICKIE, Dep. Pub. Reg.

Book B-B, p. 415   MATHEW ROCHE, merchant, to JOHN WATSON, JR.,
6 Mar. 1745   merchant, both of Charleston, in sum of Ł 4500
Bond   currency, to keep agreements in above L & R.
                     Witnesses: JOHN RATTRAY, JAMES GRINDLAY. JAM-
ES MICKIE, Dep. Pub. Reg.

Book B-B, p. 416   THOMAS WEAVER, carpenter, & MARTHA his wife,
10 & 11 Mar. 1745   to MATHEW ROCHE, merchant, all of Charleston,
L & R   for Ł 700 currency, part of lot #280 in
                     Charleston, fronting S 25 ft. on Moores Street,
leading from Old Church Street, to King Street; W 80 ft. on BRYANT ROYLE;
N & E on MATHEW ROCHE. Whereas EDWARD VANVELAIN, cordwainer, & CATHERINE
his wife, of Charleston, on 5 July 1728 sold to THOMAS WEAVER & RUTH his
late wife, part of lot #280, as above; now WEAVER sells to ROCHE. Witnesses: JOHN PRATT, JAMES GRINDLAY. Before JACOB MOTTE, J.P. JAMES
MICKIE, Dep. Pub. Reg.

Book B-B, p. 422   MATHEW ROCHE, merchant, & ANN his wife, to
14 & 15 Mar. 1745   JOHN RATTRAY, gentleman, all of Charleston,
L & R   for Ł 2700 currency, part of a lot, with the
                     house thereon fronting 30 ft. on N side Broad
Street, bounding E & N on JAMES CROKATT (formerly occupied by JOSEPH
WRAGG); W 100 ft. on a house & lot of JOHN WATSON, JR. Witnesses: JOHN
PRATT, JAMES GRINDLAY. Before JACOB MOTTE, J.P. JAMES MICKIE, Dep. Pub.
Reg.

DEEDS BOOK "C-C"
APRIL 1746 - DEC. 1747

Book C-C, p. 1   THOMAS ROSE, planter, of St. Paul's Parish,
17 & 18 Apr. 1746   Colleton Co., & BEULAH his wife (lately called
L & R by Mortgage   BEULAH ELLIOTT, daughter & devisee of THOMAS
                     ELLIOTT, planter), to the Rev. MR. ALEXANDER
GARDEN, rector of St. Philip's Parish, Charleston, for certain considerations & as further security on money due on bond; 60 a. Whereas THOMAS
ELLIOTT was seized in his demesne as of fee in a plantation on Charleston
Neck, St. Philips Parish, known as Ladsons, which he had purchased from
MR. LADSON, & by will dated 9 June 1731 bequeathed the plantation to his
grandson WILLIAM ELLIOTT, son of his son WILLIAM ELLIOTT (except 60 a.
adjoining MR. PENDARVIS, being the part on which the schoolhouse was
built); & bequeathed the said 60 a. to his daughter BEULAH ELLIOTT who
later married THOMAS ROSE; & whereas THOMAS ROSE gave ALEXANDER GARDEN a
bond dated 7 Apr. 1743 in penal sum of Ł 2155 for payment of Ł 1051:13:4
currency, with interest, on 7 Apr. 1744; & whereas all the principal money & a great part of the interest money is due & ROSE has asked GARDEN
for more time (till 7 Apr. 1747), giving more security; now ROSE conveys
the 60 a. to GARDEN. Witnesses: CHARLES PINCKNEY, CHARLES CALDER.

Before JAMES WRIGHT, J.P. JAMES MICKIE, Dep. Pub. Reg. At the request
of THOMAS ELLIOTT, executor to his sister BEULAH ROSE, 60 a. bequeathed
to BEULAH by her father, were laid out, on Charleston Neck, Berkeley Co.,
bounding S on JOSEPH PENDARVIS; W on Ashley River; N on WILLIAM ELLIOTT;
E on the Broad Path leading from Charleston to Goose Creek. Plat certified 19 May 1735 by JOSEPH ELLIOTT, Dep. Sur.

Book C-C, p. 8   WILLIAM SIMPSON, planter, of Craven Co., to
31 Dec. 1745 & 1 Jan.   PAUL TRAPIER, merchant, of Georgetown, as se-
1745/6   curity on bond of even date in penal sum of
L & R by Mortgage   Ł 1454:9 for payment of Ł 725:14:6 currency,
                        with interest, on 1 Mar. 1745; 500 a. commonly
called Wincaw, in Prince George Parish, Craven Co., on Waccamaw River.
Witnesses: THOMAS BLYTHE, SIMON STEAD. Before ROBERT AUSTIN, J.P. JAMES
MICKIE, Dep. Pub. Reg.

Book C-C, p. 13   WILLIAM DAY (DEA), Sergt. of Independent Com-
1 May 1746   pany COL. ALEXANDER VANDERDUSEN, CAPT. & form-
Sale   erly of N. Windsor, innkeeper; to SAMUEL SMART,
                        for Ł 80 currency; his house in N Windsor with
all the out-houses, shades, fences & shuffle board. Witnesses: JEREMIAH
KNOTT, DAVID DOUGLASS. Before JOHN FALLOWFIELD. JAMES MICKIE, Dep. Pub.
Reg.

Book C-C, p. 14   THOMAS GREEN & NATHANIEL GREEN, gentlemen, of
28 & 29 June 1745   SC, EDWARD JENKINS of Charleston & ELIZABETH
L & R   his wife; to WILLIAM STONE, merchant, of SC,
                        for Ł 500 currency; part of lot #7 on the Bay
of Charleston; also part of the adjoining lot, 3 ft. in breadth & part of
the alley between the line formerly of GABRIEL RABELLEAU & the line of
DANIEL GREEN, ESQ., father of THOMAS & NATHANIEL; the part of lot #7
fronting E 33 ft. on the Bay; bounding N 100 ft. on part of same lot, belonging to JAMES OSMOND; S on the part of the alley owned by JACOB MOTTE;
W on JACOB MOTTE. Witnesses: JOHN RATTRAY, JOHN YARWORTH. Before JACOB
MOTTE, J.P. JAMES MICKIE, Dep. Pub. Reg.

Book C-C, p. 20   JOHN DUVAL, planter, of Granville Co., to ED-
25 & 26 Mar. 1746   WARD WIGG, merchant, of Beaufort, as security
L & R by Mortgage   on bond of even date in penal sum of Ł 629:13
                        for payment of Ł 314:16:5 currency, with in-
terest, on 25 Mar. 1748; 226 a. in Granville Co., on Port Royal Island,
bounding E on JAMES WATSON; S on THOMAS GRIMBALL; N on RICHARD HAZZARD; W
on Port Royall River; which tract was purchased by his mother, CATHERINE
DUVAL from THOMAS PARMENTER, in 1730. Witnesses: THOMAS WIGG, HILL (HIL-
DERSON?) WIGG, WILLIAM HARVEY. Before JOHN MULLRYNE, J.P. JAMES HOME,
Pub. Reg.

Book C-C, p. 26   RICHARD HILL, ESQ., upon trust to JACOB MOTTE,
7 & 8 May 1746   merchant, for Ł 100 currency, part of lot #7
L & R   in Charleston, fronting E 30 ft. 4 in. on Coop-
                        er River, bounding N 100 ft. on WILLIAM STONE
(formerly EDMOND MEDLICOT); S & W on part same lot; which part of a lot
was devised to ELIZABETH, wife of JACOB MOTTE by PATRICK MARTIN & conveyed by JACOB & ELIZABETH MOTTE to RICHARD HILL; upon trust that JACOB
MOTTE shall by some deed executed in his lifetime, or by will convey said
part of a lot & buildings thereon to ELIZABETH MOTTE for her natural life;
& after her death to all of the younger children of JACOB & ELIZABETH
MOTTE. Witnesses: ROBERT HILL, WILLIAM HOVEL HILL. Before ROBERT AUSTIN,
J.P. JAMES HOME, Pub. Reg.

Book C-C, p. 31   JACOB MOTTE, merchant, & ELIZABETH his wife,
2 & 3 May 1746   to RICHARD HILL, ESQ., for Ł 100 currency,
L & R   part of lot #7 in Charleston, fronting 30 ft.
                        4 in. on Cooper River, bounding N 100 ft. on
WILLIAM STONE (formerly EDMUND MEDLICOT); S & W on part of same lot de-
vised to ELIZABETH MOTTE by PATRICK MARTIN. Witnesses: WILLIAM GEORGE
FREEMAN, JAMES LAURENS. Before ROBERT AUSTIN, J.P. JAMES HOME, Pub.
Reg.

Book C-C, p. 36   JOHN ALEXANDER PARRIS, nephew of JOHN PARRIS,

20 May 1746   merchant, formerly of Kingston Jamaica, & de-
Redemption of Mortgage   vise of certain lands & tenements that belong-
             ed to JOHN PARRIS, of 1st part; & PHILIP PRIO-
LEAU, JOHN BELL & GEORGE PAPLEY, merchants, of Kingston, Jamaica, of 2nd
part. Whereas by L & R dated 9 & 10 Jan. 1729 JAMES WOODCOCK, merchant,
of Kingston, sold to JOHN PARRIS, merchant, of same place, 3 lots in the
town & parish of Kingston, each 90 ft. from N to S, & 30 ft. from E to W,
bounding S on Harbour Street, N on Water Lane; W on JOHN MOORE, ESQ.,
also a lot in Kingston 90 ft. from N to S, 30 ft. from E to W on the W
side of a gully, bounding W on the 3 lots; S on Harbour Street, N on Water Lane; & whereas JOHN PARRIS on 30 June 1732 mortgage the 4 lots to
ISAAC FEURTADO, merchant, of Kingston, as security for the payment of
Ł 300, Jamaican, with interest, on 31 Dec. ensuing; & whereas JOHN PARRIS
gave FEURTADO a bond of same date as mortgage, in penal sum of Ł 600 for
payment of Ł 300 Jamaican, with interest, on said 31 Dec. ensuing; &
whereas PARRIS gave another bond of same date to FEURTADO in penal sum of
Ł 600 Jamaican, for the performance of the several agreements; & whereas
by deeds of bargain & sale & assignment, dated 1 Nov. 1744, ISAAC FEURTA-
DO assigned to PHILIP PRIOLEAU, JOHN BELL & GEORGE PAPLEY, the 4 lots,
with the L & R & mortgage, & the 2 bonds; & whereas JOHN PARRIS, by will
dated 6 May 1736 after several bequests gave the remainder of his real &
personal estate to his beloved son JOHN ALEXANDER PARRIS, & in case of
his death before reaching 18 years, to his beloved nephew JOHN ALEXANDER
PARRIS, party hereto; & whereas JOHN PARRIS died soon afterwards, & his
son JOHN ALEXANDER PARRIS died shortly after his father & before reaching
18 years, so that the nephw JOHN ALEXANDER PARRIS inherited; & whereas
neither the principal nor the interest have been paid & the amount due is
greater than the mortgaged premises are worth; now JOHN ALEXANDER PARRIS
releases all his equity of redemption in the mortgaged premises to PRIO-
LEAU, BELL & PAPLEY. Witnesses: ELEAZER PHILLIPS, DANIEL DONOVAN. Before JAMES MICHIE, J.P. JAMES HOME, Pub. Reg.

Book C-C, p. 44   GEORGE JACKSON & REGINALD JACKSON, planters,
6 & 7 Dec. 1745   executors of will of JOHN LEVI, planter, to
L & R   ROBERT OSWELL, planter, all of Colleton Co.,
             for Ł 732 currency, at public auction, 400 a.
in Colleton Co., W of the freshes of Edisto River, bounding N on SAMUEL
FARLEY; S on JOHN JACKSON; E on WILLIAM PETERS; W on a tupelow swamp; according to plat certified by THOMAS BROUGHTON, Sur. Gen. dated 6 July
1705. Whereas JOHN LEVI by will dated 4 Sept. 1745, recorded in Secretary's book C, p. 34, directed that all his real & personal estate, that
is, the plantation on which he lived, his negroes, horses & cattle, be
sold at public auction & his debts paid, & appointed GEORGE & REGINALD
JACKSON his executors; now they sell 400 a. to OSWELL. Witnesses: THOMAS
SIMMONS, THOMAS DEAN, KENNETH MACKENZIE. Before JAMES SKIRVING, J.P. of
Colleton Co. JAMES HOME, Pub. Reg.

Book C-C, p. 51   JOHN JACKSON, planter, of St. Bartholomews
5 & 6 Feb. 1743/4 Parish, to JOHN SPLATT, planter, of St. Pauls
L & R   Parish, both in Colleton Co., for Ł 35 curren-
             cy, a lot of land in the town or village of
Jacksonburgh, bounding N 100 ft. on lot #12, & 109 ft. deep. Witnesses:
GEORGE JACKSON, JONATHAN WITTER, THOMAS MELVEN. Before JAMES BULLOCK,
J.P. JAMES HOME, Pub. Reg.

Book C-C, p. 56   GEORGE JACKSON, planter, of St. Bartholomews
16 & 17 Jan. 1742 Parish, to JOHN SPLATT, planter, of St. Pauls
L & R   Parish, both in Colleton Co., for Ł 100 cur-
             rency, lot #12 in Jacksonborough, Colleton
Co., on N side of Pon Pon River, fronting 100 ft. on King Street, 218 ft.
deep. Witnesses: ISAAC HAYNE, WILLIAM GLAZE, REGINALD JACKSON. Before
JAMES SKIRVING, J.P. JAMES HOME, Pub. Reg.

Book C-C, p. 62   JOHN CONNERY, gentleman, of Caharally, Co. of
15 Jan. 1736 (1746?) Limerick, & ANNA MARIA CONNERY, alias MOTTE,
Power of Attorney his wife, appoint JACOB MOTTE, merchant, of
             Charleston, SC, their attorney. Whereas JOHN
ABRAHAM MOTTE, merchant, of Charleston, owned 462 a. in Christ Church
Parish; 500 a. in Santee Parish; the island called MOTTE'S Island; & part
of a lot on the Bay in Charleston; all in SC; & by will bequeathed 1/3

part to his wife, 1/3 to his son JACOB MOTTE, merchant, of Charleston,
1/3 to be equally divided between his 2 daughters; & whereas on the death
of JOHN ABRAHAM MOTTE'S widow, son JACOB MOTTE, inherited her third; & on
the death of 1 of the daughters became owner of 1/6 part as her heir-at-
law; & whereas ANNA MARIA, daughter of JOHN ABRAHAM, was entitled to the
other sixth by her father's will; & whereas JACOB MOTTE has contracted
with GEORGE BENNISON for the absolute sale of the 462 a. in Christ Church
Parish for Ł 700 Carolina currency; & has contracted with FRANCIS BRITTON
for the absolute sale of 500 a. in Santee Parish for Ł 500 currency; &
with JOHN BRUCE for the sale of MOTTE'S Island for Ł 1400 currency; &
with DANIEL GREEN for the sale of said part of a lot on the Bay in
Charleston for Ł 500 currency; now JOHN CONNERY & ANNA MARIA his wife,
authorize JACOB MOTTE to convey the lands. Sealed & delivered in 1746.
Witnesses: BOURK FURNELL, RICHARD HILL. HILL appeared before JOHN DART,
J.P. JAMES HOME, Pub. Reg.

Book C-C, p. 65   WILLIAM LIVINGSTON, planter, upon trust to
20 & 21 June 1746   JOHN SMELIE & WILLIAM SMELIE, planter, all of
L & R in Trust   Colleton Co. Whereas MARY LIVINGSTON, wife of
                         WILLIAM, daughter & devisee of HUGH COCHRAN,
of Colleton Co., at the time of her marriage owned 1173 a. on the Chehaw
River, & 480 a. at the head of Chehas marsh (?), also 250 a. on Cuekilds
Creek out of Combahee River, & 9 lots in the town of New London, alias
Wiltown, Nos. 43, 44, 65, 66, 67, 81, 82, 83 & 84; all in Colleton Co., &
whereas at the time of her marriage she owned 15 slaves, all except 3 being grown, & several being this country born slaves, valued then at about
Ł 3000 currency; & also owned several beds, household stuff, & furniture
valued at Ł 200 currency; & whereas MARY after her marriage, relying upon
the faith & honor of WILLIAM that he would settle upon her an estate
equal in value to her land estate, which he faithfully promised to do,
joined her husband, L & R dated 20 & 21 Sept. 1734, in the sale of all
her lands & lots to ALGERNON ASH for Ł 3000 currency, & renounced all her
title before ROBERT WRIGHT, C.J.; & whereas WILLIAM failed to make settlement on her, but owned 200 a., called Pingerys, E of the freshes of Edisto River, in Colleton Co., bounding NE & S on a swamp, granted 23 July
1711 to MOSES PINGRY, & by deed of feoffment dated 22 Dec. 1714 conveyed
to WILLIAM LIVINGSTON, father of WILLIAM, party hereto; & by will of WIL-
LIAM, the father, dated 17 July 1743, devised to his son THOMAS, & by L &
R dated 15 & 16 Dec. 1735 conveyed to WILLIAM LIVINGSTON, party hereto,
now he, towards fulfilling his marriage agreement & to provide for MARY &
for the considerations, conveys to JOHN & WILLIAM SMELIE, the 200 a. in
trust, they to clear & cultivate, plant & improve the 200 a., rent part,
& apply the money to MARY'S use without interference from WILLIAM & after
WILLIAM'S death to convey the tract to MARY or her heirs. Witnesses:
JOHN MILNER, JR., HENRY LIVINGSTON. Before JOHN HUTCHINSON, J.P. JAMES
HOME, Pub. Reg.

Book C-C, p. 76   ANN WAIGHT, widow of Johns Island, to JONATHAN
9 & 10 May 1746   BADGER, cabinet-maker, of Charleston, for
L & R   Ł 1000 currency, the E half of a lot in
                         Charleston, bounding N 44 ft. on Tradd Street,
E 98 ft. on COL. BREWTON; S on JORDAN ROCHE; W on the half occupied by
THOMAS CORBET. Whereas THOMAS ELLIOTT, planter, of Berkeley Co., was
seized in his demesne as of fee in a lot on Tradd Street near COL. BREW-
TON'S, & by will dated 9 June 1731 bequeathed all the lot to his daughter
ANN (then the wife of RODGER SAUNDERS) & to his daughter ELIZABETH BUTLER,
directing that ANN should have that part nearest the Bay; now she sells
her part to BADGER. Witnesses: GEORGE BODDINGTON, JOHN CLARK, ELIZABETH
BUTLER. Before ROBERT AUSTIN, J.P. JAMES HOME, Pub. Reg.

Book C-C, p. 85   RICHARD JACKSON, planter, & MARY (her mark)
17 & 18 June 1746   his wife, of Craven Co., to DANIEL MORPHEW,
L & R   Indian trader, for Ł 100 currency, 200 a.,
                         part of 400 a. in Craven Co., bounding NW on
PATRICK'S Creek; NE on THOMAS BROWN & HUGH MURPHY; SE on vacant land &
HENRY SNELLING; SW on HENRY SNELLING'S part of the 400 a. Whereas King
GEORGE II by letters patent dated 14 Feb. 1735, signed by Lt. Gov. THOMAS
BROUGHTON, granted JAMES ST. JOHN 400 a. in Craven Co., bounding N on the
heirs of THOMAS STIT SMITH & THOMAS BROWN; E on THOMAS BROWN & vacant
land; S & W on vacant land; & whereas JAMES ST. JOHN, of Charleston, on

14 May 1736 for Ł 40 currency, conveyed the 400 a. to RICHARD JACKSON; & whereas RICHARD JACKSON has given WILLIAM JANEWAY, his son-in-law, 100 a. lying NW of PATRICK'S Creek, & has given HENRY SNELLING, his son-in-law, 100 a. lying SW of a line beginning on PATRICK'S Creek from a white oak marked with 3 cuts & running S 60° E 23 chains 40 links to a gum tree marked with 3 cuts, & from thence running S 20° E 29 chains 30 ft. to a stake marked with 3 cuts in 1 of the original lines of the 400 a. tract; now JACKSON sells the remaining 200 a. to MORPHEW. Witnesses: JAMES LESS-LEY, HUGH (his mark) MORPHY. Before STEPHEN CRELL, J.P. JAMES HOMES, Pub. Reg.

Book C-C, p. 94   RICHARD JACKSON, planter, & MARY (her mark)
17 May 1744   his wife, of Craven Co., to his well beloved
Deed of Gift in Trust   friend HUGH MORPHEY, for love & affection &
                         other considerations in trust for the use of
JACKSON'S daughter SARAH, now married to HENRY SNELLING; 100 a. part of a tract on which JACKSON lately lived, on S side of the creek running through the tract, the N part being owned by son-in-law WILLIAM JANEWAY; the original 400 a. having been granted by Lt. Gov. THOMAS BROUGHTON to JAMES ST. JOHN on 14 Feb. 1735/6. Witnesses: WILLIAM JANEWAY, JAMES (his mark) JENKINS, HANNAH (her mark) JACKSON, EDWARD WILLINGHAM. Before STEPHEN CRELL, J.P. JAMES HOME, Pub. Reg.

Book C-C, p. 95   JOHN RUTLEDGE & SARAH his wife, of Charleston,
16 & 17 July 1746   to JOHN TOOMER, planter, of St. Helena Island,
L & R   Granville Co., for Ł 640 currency, 320 a. on
                         St. Helena's Island, Granville Co., bounding S
on JOHN CHAPLIN & marsh; NE by a line running N 47° W from the marsh 82 chains to the corner tree of JOSEPH GEELIAS E line; N on part of CHAP-LIN'S E line; W on JOHN FENDIN; being half of 640 a. granted to EDWARD & HUGH HEXT, descending by defect of mall issue to SARAH RUTLEDGE, daughter of HUGH HEXT. Witnesses: JOHN CART, ROBERT PIERCE HENDERSON. Before ROBERT AUSTIN, J.P. JAMES HOME, Pub. Reg.

Book C-C, p. 102   JAMES STOBO, planter, & ELIZABETH his wife, of
15 & 16 Mar. 1733   Colleton Co., to JAMES ABERCROMBY, Attorney
L & R   Gen.; JOHN ALLEN, DANIEL CRAWFORD, JOHN BEE,
                         JOHN FRASER, GEORGE DUCATT & JAMES PAINE, mer-
chants of Charleston, trustees of the Presbyterian Meeting House in Charleston; for Ł 1200 currency, that part of a lot fronting E 50 ft. on the great street leading from the Oyster Point to the market place & Pres-byterian Meeting House; bounding N 237 ft. on JOHN RAVEN & LUKE STOUTEN-BURG; S on part same lot granted by WILLIAM DONNING to SAMUEL JONES; W on JOHN FROWMAN; upon trust, for building & erecting a Presbyterian church or meeting house thereon for divine worship according to the doctrine & discipline used by the church of Scotland; & for a place for christian burial; & after erection in trust for the Rev. MR. HUGH STEWART, minister of the gospel in Charleston & for a Presbyterian minister professing & using the doctrine, discipline & worship now used in the church of Scot-land & subscribing the Westminster confession of faith, to be chosen by the majority of said trustees & by the majority of the congregation be-longing to same church. Whereas the Rt. Hon. WILLIAM, Earl of Craven, Palatine; ANTHONY, Lord Ashley; GEORGE, Lord Carteret; SIR PETER COLLE-TON, Baronet SETH SOTHELL, THOMAS ARCHDALE & THOMAS AMY, Lords Proprs.; & the Hon. Landgrave THOMAS SMITH, Gov. & principal trustee for granting lands, on 15 June 1694 conveyed to ANDREW PERCIVAL, a lot #241 in Charles-ton containing 1/2 a., English measure, bounding E on the Great Street leading from Oyster Point to the market place; W on JOHN FROWMAN; N on JEAN FLOWERS; S on ANDREW PERCIVAL; as recorded in Secretary's Book A. fol. 3; & whereas JAMES PERCIVAL, son of said ANDREW PERCIVAL, gentleman, of Hammersmith, Middlesex Co., Great Britain, by will dated 5 Aug. 1708 bequeathed all his real & personal estate in Carolina, or elsewhere, to which he was entitled by his father's will, to his brother ANDREW PERCI-VAL, subject to the payment of Ł 100 per annum to his mother ESSEX PERCI-VAL during her natural life & liable to the charge of the purchase of an annuity of Ł 20 per annum out of the annuities granted by Parliament for 99 years for the use of his sister MARY PERCIVAL (will registered in Prerogative Court of Archbishop of Canterbury); & whereas by L & R dated 25 & 26 Apr. 1723 ANDREW PERCIVAL, the son, of Middlesex Temple, London, the said ESSEX PERCIVAL, widow, of St. Ann's Parish, Middlesex Co., &

MARY PERCIVAL, spinster, of same place, conveyed to WILLIAM DONNING, all
those plantations in SC commonly called PERCIVAL'S Upper & Lower Plantations, the Ponds (or WESTON HALL, or PAUL PARKER'S Plantation); & whereas
by L & R dated 29 & 30 Mar. 1732 WILLIAM DONNING, formerly of Purton, Co.
of Gloucester, Great Britain, lately of Berkeley Co., SC, for Ł 1000 SC
money, sold to JAMES STOBO part of said lot #241 in Charleston 50 ft. x
237 ft., bounding as first mentioned except that lot on S was granted by
DOWNING to SAMUEL JONES; now STOBO sells his part of the lot to the trustees of the Presbyterian Meeting House; ELIZABETH STOBO, wife of JAMES,
to renounce her dower before 16 Sept. Witnesses: RICHARD ALLEIN, FRED-
ERICK MEYER. Witnesses to execution: GEORGE PHILIP, JOHN RATTRAY. Before JAMES HOME, J.P. & Pub. Reg.

Book C-C, p. 116   RICHARD GODFREY, planter, to ELIZABETH HILL,
7 & 8 July 1746   widow, as security on bond dated 25 Jan. 1745
L & R by Mortgage   in penal sum of Ł 3220 for payment of
                          Ł 1610:4:10 currency, with interest, on 25 Jan.
1746; 234 a. on S side Ashley River, bounding N on ANDREW DEVEAUX; E on
ELIZABETH HILL; S on COL. GEORGE LUCAS; W on RICHARD GODFREY; also 106 a.
on S side Ashley River, bounding N on NATHANIEL BROWN; E on TYGAR Swamp;
S on JOHN RIVERS; W on JOHN GODFREY. Witnesses: WILLIAM GEORGE FREEMAN,
WILLIAM BURROWS. Before BENJAMIN WHITAKER, C.J. JAMES HOME, Pub. Reg.

Book C-C, p. 123   JAMES BULLOCK, planter, of Colleton Co., &
26 & 27 May 1746   ANNE his wife (lately ANNE FERGUSON, widow),
L & R   to THOMAS DALE, Doctor of Physick, of Charles-
                          ton, for Ł 182 currency, 104 a., part of 280 a.
Whereas the Lords Proprs. on 11 Jan. 1700 granted WILLIAM SCREVEN 260 a.
(formerly laid out to CAPT. ADDIE & reverted by escheat to the Lords
Proprs.) on S side Cooper River, bounding NW on MR. DRY; E & SE on CAPT.
WILLIAM HAWIT; SW on CHRISTOPHER SMITH & WILLIAM ELLIOTT; & whereas the
260 a. by several mesne conveyances became vested in WILLIAM SKIPPER,
planter, of Berkeley Co., who by will dated 2 Jan. 1724 bequeathed to his
3 sons WILLIAM, JOHN & BENNING, 280 a. to be equally divided among them;
& whereas after the father's death, both sons, WILLIAM & JOHN died before
coming of age, & the 280 a. was inherited by son BENNING SKIPPER; who by
will dated 29 Nov. 1743 bequeathed to his mother ANNE FERGUSON (party
hereto) the residue of his real & personal estate, she paying his just
debts; now she & her present husband JAMES BULLOCK, sell 104 a. to DR.
DALE. Witnesses: THOMAS SIMMONDS, ROBERT WILLIS. Before THOMAS LAMBOLL,
J.P. JAMES HOME, Pub. Reg.

Book C-C, p. 132   DAVID GODET, of Purisburgh, SC, to FRANCIS
29 June 1745   HENRY, as security on 3 notes dated 22 June
Mortgage   1742, 25 July 1744, & 22 Feb. 1744/5 in the
                         sum of Ł 343:3 SC money with interest; his
town lot in Purisburgh, his house & other buildings, his cattle, household goods, jewels, plate; & all his possessions. Date of redemption: 1
July 1746. Witnesses: JOHN PYE, recorder, STEPHEN (his mark) TARRYAN.
Before WILLIAM SPENCER, bailiff of Savannah. JAMES HOME, Pub. Reg.

Book C-C, p. 133   THOMAS BONNY, planter, of Berkeley Co., to
16 & 17 May 1740   JONAH COLLINS, planter, of Craven Co., for
L & R by Mortgage   Ł 2000 currency, 1300 a., English measure, in
                         Prince George Parish, Craven Co., bounding N
on JOSEPH PORTE; W on JOSHUA WILKS; S on THOMAS MORRETT & WILLIAM WHITE-
SIDES; NE on WILLIAM RAE. Date of redemption: 17 May 1741. Witnesses:
COL. OTHNIEL BEALE, MARY WATSON. Before JOHN DART, J.P. JAMES HOME,
Pub. Reg.

Book C-C, p. 140   WILLIAM COOPER, planter, & SARAH his wife, of
27 Feb. 1744   Colleton Co., to BRAND PENDARVIS, yeoman, of
Sale   Orangeburg, Berkeley Co., for Ł 200 currency,
                         400 a. in Colleton Co., where WILLIAM & SARAH
COOPER dwell, bounding E on Pon Pon River; other sides on vacant land; as
by plat & grant dated 4 June 1735. Witnesses: DAVID (his mark) BLACK,
WILLIAM SIDDALL, JACOB RUMPF (shoemaker). Before JOHN CHEVILLETTE, J.P.
JAMES HOME, Pub. Reg.

Book C-C, p. 142   JOHN MULLRYNE, planter, & CLAUDIA his wife, of

19 & 20 Sept. 1746   Granville Co., to JOHN MACKENZIE & MATHEW
L & R   ROCHE, merchants, of Charleston, for Ł 2000
                            British sterling, 850 a. on Combahee River,
bounding NE on the river; SW on Gov. BULL; SE on the road leading to Port
Royal; NW on JOHN GREENE; also 900 a. on Port Royal Island, bounding E on
RICHARD WOODWARD; SE & NW on creeks; W on THOMAS WIGG & THOMAS PALMENTER;
N on RODGER HOGG; also 3 lots in Beaufort, Nos. 319, 320 & (?). Witness-
es: JEMMET COBLEY, JAMES GRINDLAY. Before JACOB MOTTE, J.P. JAMES HOME,
Pub. Reg.

Book C-C, p. 148   THOMAS BUTLER, planter, & CONSTANTIA his wife,
1 & 27 Sept. 1746   to CULCHETH GOLIGHTLY, planter, all of St.
L & R by Mortgage   Bartholomew's Parish, as security on bond of
                           even date in penal sum of Ł 1860 for payment
of Ł 930 currency, with interest, on 1 Oct. next; 759 a. on a tupelow
swamp at N end of Horseshoe Savannah, Colleton Co., bounding N on CHARLES
JONES; E on CULCHETH GOLIGHTLY; S on THOMAS SNIPES; also 47 Negro & other
slaves; also all his horses, colts, cattle (about 50) branded thus   his
hogs & sheep, his household goods & furniture. A Negro boy delivered in
lieu of the whole. Witnesses: GEORGE BELLINGER, SAMUEL WEST. Before JA-
COB MOTTE, J.P. JAMES HOME, Pub. Reg.

Book C-C, p. 154   CAPT. JAMES COACHMAN, & REBEKAH ANN, his wife,
23 & 24 Sept. 1746   (with her full consent) to CAPT. ABRAHAM DU-
L & R   PONT, all of Berkeley Co., to Ł 250 SC money,
                           610 a. Whereas King GEORGE II by letters pat-
ent dated 11 July 1733, signed by Gov. THOMAS BROUGHTON, granted WILLIAM
SANDERS 710 a. in Berkeley Co., on Indian Field Swamp, bounding NW on
widow ELIZABETH MORRIS & on vacant lands; NE on land laid out; SE on SAM-
UEL MILLER & vacant land; SW on vacant land; now COACHMAN sells 610 a. of
the tract to DUPONT. Witnesses: GEORGE SNOW, ELIZABETH HAYES, ANN DUPONT.
Before PETER TAYLOR, J.P. JAMES HOME, Pub. Reg.

Book C-C, p. 161   GEORGE ANSON, ESQ., by his attorney BENJAMIN
28 Mar. 1746   WHITAKER, to ALEXANDER GORDON, ESQ., for Ł 250
Feoffment   currency, a piece of land containing 1 a., 2
                           roods, 20 perches, marked H on the plat of
GEORGE ANSON'S land, now called Ansonborough; also right of passage
through the most convenient streets to & from the landing place on a
creek of Cooper River. Witnesses: WILLIAM BURROWS, LEOPOLD BOUDON. Witnesses to possession & seizin: GEORGE HUNTER, WILLIAM BURROWS. Before
JOHN LINING, J.P. JAMES HOME, Pub. Reg.

Book C-C, p. 163   GEORGE ANSON, ESQ., by his attorney, BENJAMIN
20 Feb. 1745   WHITAKER, to THOMAS NIGHTINGALE, for Ł 300 SC
Feoffment   money, a tract of 1 a., 2 roods, marked G in
                           the plat of GEORGE ANSON'S lands, now called
Ansonborough; also right of passage through the most convenient streets
to & from the landing place on a creek of Cooper River. Witnesses: WIL-
LIAM GLEN, WILLIAM BURROWS. Witnesses to possession & seizin: WILLIAM
BURROWS, DAVID MONGIN. Before OTHNIEL BEALE, J.P. JOHN BEALE, Recorder.

Book C-C, p. 164   GEORGE ANSON, ESQ., by his attorney, BENJAMIN
20 Feb. 1745   WHITAKER, to DAVID MONGIN, of Charleston, for
Feoffment   Ł 250 currency, 1 a. of land marked O in the
                           plat of GEORGE ANSON'S lands, now called Anson-
borough; also right of passage through the most convenient streets to &
from the landing place on a creek of Cooper River. Witnesses: WILLIAM
BURROWS, THOMAS NIGHTINGALE. Before OTHNIEL BEALE, J.P. JOHN BEALE,
Recorder.

Book C-C, p. 166   GEORGE ANSON, ESQ., by his attorney BENJAMIN
8 Apr. 1745   WHITAKER, to DAVID MONGIN, watchmaker, of
Feoffment   Charleston, for Ł 300 currency, a tract of 1 a.
                           2 roods, marked C in the plat of GEORGE AN-
SON'S land, part of a plantation. Witnesses: EDWARD LLOYD, JACOB AXSON.
Before THOMAS DALE, J.P. JOHN BEALE, Recorder.

Book C-C, p. 167   GEORGE ANSON, ESQ., by his attorney, BENJAMIN
25 May 1745   WHITAKER, to JOHN PADGET, ESQ., for Ł 250

Foeffment   currency, a lot of 1 a., marked S in the plat
of GEORGE ANSON'S land, now called Ansonbor-
ough; also right of passage through the most convenient streets to & from
the landing place on the creek of Cooper River. Witnesses: WILLIAM BUR-
ROWS, WILLIAM BORLAND. Witnesses to possession & seizin: WILLIAM BURROWS,
DAVID MONGIN. Before JAMES WRIGHT, J.P. JOHN BEALE, Recorder.

Book C-C, p. 169   MARY BASSETT, widow, to PETER LAURENS, saddler,
17 Aug. 1743   both of Charelston, for Ł 40 currency, part of
Feoffment   lot #315 in Charleston, bounding S 3 ft. on
                                 Broad Street, E 105 ft. on PETER LAURENS; W on
MARY BASSETT; which land was sold to MARY BASSETT by JOHN LAURENS, sad-
dler, & ELIZABETH his wife, on 20 Aug. 1742. Witnesses: JOHN LAURENS,
BENJAMIN ADDISON. JOHN BEALE, Recorder.

Book C-C, p. 170   JOHN LAURENS, saddler, to PETER LAURENS, sad-
8 & 9 Mar. 1741   dler, both of Charleston, for Ł 3000 currency,
L & R   part of lot #315 in Charleston, fronting S 41
                                 ft. on Broad Street, bounding E 105-1/2 ft. on
Market Square; W on the part owned by JOHN LAURENS; N on an alley which
is part of said lot & also belongs to JOHN LAURENS; which part of a lot
has a large house on it known as White Hall. Witnesses: JOHN WARWICK,
BENJAMIN ADDISON. Before JACOB MOTTE, J.P. JOHN BEALE, Recorder.

Book C-C, p. 175   The Hon. CHARLES DUNBAR, ESQ., of Island of
23 Aug. 1746   Antigua, to Lt. Gov. GEORGE LUCAS, of Island
Release of Mortgage   of Antigua, for Ł 518 British sterling, paid
                                 by the hand of CHARLES ALEXANDER, ESQ., quit
claim to all the plantation, tenements, slaves, cattle, horses, & all the
premises recited in certain indentures dated 5 July 1708. Whereas on 5
July 1708 GEORGE LUCAS, for Ł 350 sterling, British, sold to CHARLES DUN-
BAR 600 a. on Wappoo Creek, near Charleston, bounding E on MRS. WOODWARD
& BENJAMIN GODFREY; N, S & W on MRS. HILL, widow; also all buildings on
the plantation; also 12 Negro men, 8 Negro women, all cattle & horses,
plantations utensils, etc.; conditioned for the payment of Ł 350 sterling,
with interest, from date of indenture to date of actual payment; & whereas Ł 518 sterling is now due; now the mortgage is canceled upon payment
of that amount to DUNBAR. CHARLES DUNBAR appoints the Hon. CHARLES PINCK-
NEY & COL. OTHNIEL BEALE, of SC, his attorneys, to acknowledge & deliver
these presents. Witnesses: CAPT. THOMAS VAVASOR, CAPT. EDWARD STILES.
Before ROBERT AUSTIN, J.P. JOHN BEALE, Dep. Pub. Reg.

Book C-C, p. 179   The Hon. GEORGE LUCAS, Lt. Gov. of Island of
25 Aug. 1746   Antigua, to CHARLES ALEXANDER, ESQ., of same
Mortgage   Island, for Ł 2595 British, 5 plantations, to-
                                 tal 4500 a., in SC on several small rivers;
being 600 on Wappoo Creek near Charleston, now in the possession of MR.
HARVEY, bounding E on MRS. WOODWARD & BENJAMIN GODFREY; N, S & W on MRS.
HILL; 1500 a. on Combahee River, bounding E on (?); W on COL. OTHNIEL
BEALE; N on vacant land; S on the river; 1150 a. on Wancama River, in
Craven Co., near Kingstown, formerly settled by MR. STARRAT; also an unsettled tract of 1300 a. on Wancama River, in Craven Co., in Kingstown
Township, bounding NW on MR. CAMPBELL; NE on MR. SHEPPARD; SE on the river; SW on MR. MASH; also an unsettled tract of 500 a. on said river,
bounding SE on JAMES SMITH; other sides on vacant land; also the mansion
houses, dwelling houses, works, & all buildings, etc.; also the Negro &
other slaves named in schedule No. 1; also all the cattle, horses, mares,
all other stock, plantation utensils & implements; also the dwelling
house in Negate Street, Town of St. John, Island of Antigua, now occupied
by JOHN HUSBAND, surgeon; also all the slaves named in schedule #2.
Should GEORGE LUCAS pay CHARLES ALEXANDER the full sum of Ł 155:13 British being a years interest on every 25 Aug. beginning 1747 until 1750 &
Ł 2750:13 in Town of St. John, on 25 Aug. 1751 this deed shall be void.
GEORGE LUCAS & CHARLES ALEXANDER appointed the Hon. CHARLES PINCKNEY &
COL. OTHNIEL BEALE their attorneys to appear before the register of deeds
& acknowledge & deliver these presents. Schedule #1 listing slaves at
Garden Hill, SC, & in Charleston; & Schedule #2 listing slaves in Antigua,
given in full. Witnesses: THOMAS VAVASOR, JONATHAN SKRINE, HARRY WEBB.
Acknowledged before JOHN WATKINS, register, in Antigua, 25 Aug. 1746.
CAPT. THOMAS VAVASOR appeared before ROBERT AUSTIN, J.P., Berkeley Co.,

SC, 18 Oct. 1746. JOHN BEALE, Dep. Pub. Reg.

Book C-C, p. 188   CHARLES PINCKNEY, ESQ., of Charleston, of 1st
30 Sept. 1746   part; THOMAS PINCKNEY, eldest son of MAJ. WIL-
Covenant   LIAM PINCKNEY of Charleston, the youngest
                         brother of said CHARLES PINCKNEY, of 2nd part;
MARY PINCKNEY, eldest daughter of said WILLIAM PINCKNEY, of 3rd part;
SARAH PINCKNEY, second daughter of said WILLIAM PINCKNEY, of 4th part.
Whereas MARY BETSON, widow of Charleston, mother of said CHARLES & WIL-
LIAM PINCKNEY, at the time of her death was seized in her demesne as of
fee in parts of 2 lots in Charleston on Queen Street, (formerly called
Dock Street) Nos. 20 & 73 measuring in front on Queen Street from the
corner of Union Street to the lot of NOAH SERRE 192 ft.; & on Union
Street from the corner of Union Street to the other part of said 2 lots,
lately belonging to CHARLES PINCKNEY & now to MOSES MITCHELL, 80 ft.; &
in depth from N to S on W end, adjoining NOAH SERRE'S lot, 137 ft. for
about 62 ft. in breadth; the parts of the 2 lots bounding E partly on
Union Street & partly on other part of the 2 lots now belonging to MOSES
MITCHELL; W on NOAH SERRE; N on Queen Street; S on parts of the 2 lots
belonging to MOSES MITCHELL & to CAPT. ADAM BEAUCHAMP, & whereas CHARLES
PINCKNEY in his mother's lifetime, & with her consent, expended divers
sums of money, amounting to upwards of L 1200 currency, in repairing &
building new & convenient apartments on said lot; & whereas MARY BETSON
died on 6 Oct. last past, possessed of the lands & without making a will
whereby the parts of the 2 lots descended to CHARLES PINCKNEY, her eldest
son & heir-at-law; but whereas he believes it was his mother's intention
to bequeath the property to her grandchildren (children of MAJ. WILLIAM
PINCKNEY) after said CHARLES should have the use of the property for so
long as the value thereof should amount to the amount spent by him on improvements; now to carry out his mother's intentions, & to emulate the
pious & laudable example of his eldest brother, THOMAS PINCKNEY, to whom
the very lands now intended to be settled & all the rest of his father's
real estate, consisting of several town lots & plantations, descended, as
heir-at-law to his father by reason of a defect in the execution of the
will, yet THOMAS PINCKNEY on coming of age generously consented to the
estate being equally divided amongst his mother, MARY BETSON, himself
(THOMAS PINCKNEY), & his younger brothers, CHARLES & WILLIAM PINCKNEY;
now CHARLES PINCKNEY, for the above motives, & for natural love & affection for his nephew & nieces, agrees to stand seized of the parts of the
2 lots, #20 & #73, for several purposes; that is, the NE part of the 2
lots, marked A on the plat, fronting 50 ft. on Union Street, & 130 ft. on
Queen Street, an oblong; for the use of THOMAS PINCKNEY; the W part marked B, with the houses & buildings thereon, in which CHARLES PINCKNEY now
dwells, fronting 62 ft. on Queen Street, 137 ft. deep, an oblong, to the
use of MARY PINCKNEY; the SE part, marked C, fronting 30 ft. on Union
Street, 130 ft. deep, an oblong, to the use of SARAH PINCKNEY; provided,
that, in case MARY BETSON was indebted to any person in Great Britain &
CHARLES PINCKNEY should pay such debt, he may retain possession until re-
imbursed by rents & profits; & that, as satisfaction for money paid out
for improvements he, CHARLES PINCKNEY, may remain on the premises until
24 Mar. 1747, when he expects the dwelling house he is now erecting to be
completed; provided, also, that should THOMAS, MARY or SARAH die before
coming of age, CHARLES PINCKNEY may convey that one's property to the
others as he shall think fit; CHARLES to give proper conveyances as they
come of age. Witnesses: GEORGE HUTNER, CHARLES CALDER. Before ROBERT
AUSTIN, J.P. JOHN BEALE, Dep. Pub. Reg. Memo. The number of 1 of the
lots, copied from an incorrect plat, is called 74 instead of 73; the cor-
rect number 73 is shown in the record of the Sur. Gen's. certificate & in
original grant to NICHOLAS TOWNSEND in Book B. fol. 26. The lot 73 is
the easternmost of the 2 lots. Signed: CHARLES PINCKNEY 14 Nov. 1746.

Book C-C, p. 193   JAMES SKIRVING, ESQ., & MARY his wife, to JO-
22 & 23 Sept. 1746   SEPH GLOVER, planter, all of Colleton Co., for
L & R   L 1300 currency, 407 a. on W side Pon Pon Riv-
                         er, in St. Bartholomew's Parish, bounding N on
JOHN BAILEY of Goose Creek; E on COL. CHARLESWORTH GLOVER; S & W on BRIAN
KELLY & vacant land; as by plat attached to release dated 10 Aug. 1729
from ALEXANDER TRENCH (attorney for ?) to JOHN BAILEY; which tract by con-
veyances & alterations in property became vested in EPHRAIM MIKELL & ELIZ-
BETH his wife (widow & devisee of JOHN MCGILLIVRAY), who by L & R dated 4

132

& 5 Mar. 1742 conveyed to JAMES SKRIVING in fee; also the NW half part of
397 a. (being 198-1/2 a.) in Colleton Co., bounding SW on Madam BOONE; NW
on JAMES KELLY; N on JOHN MUSGROVE; NE on PAUL JENYS; E on MR. JENYS &
MOSES MARTIN; SE on SAMUEL SLEIGH; according to plat of grant to SAMUEL
SLEIGH by Lt. Gov. THOMAS BROUGHTON dated 11 Dec. 1736, & conveyed by
SLEIGH to JAMES SKIRVING & MOSES MARTIN by L & R dated 1 & 2 Apr. 1737,
who divided the tract on 14 Jan. 1743 so that the NW half became JAMES
SKIRVING'S share. Witnesses: JONATHAN THOMPSON, MARY CAMPBELL. Before
HENRY HYRNE, J.P. JOHN BEALE, Dep. Pub. Reg.

Book C-C, p. 201 GEORGE ANSON, ESQ., by his attorney, BENJAMIN
3 May 1745 WHITAKER, to WILLIAM YEOMANS & THOMAS HOYLAND,
Feoffment for Ł 708:15 currency, 2 lots containing 3 a.,
2 roods, 7 perches, marked K L on the plan of
GEORGE ANSON'S lands, now called Ansonborough; also richt of passage
through the most convenient streets to & from the landing place on a
creek of Cooper River. Witnesses: WILLIAM BURROWS, LEOPOLD BOUDON. Witnesses to livery & seizin: WILLIAM BURROWS, GEORGE HUNTER. Before WIL-
LIAM GEORGE FREEMAN, J.P. JOHN BEALE, Dep. Pub. Reg.

Book C-C, p. 202 Whereas in pursuance of H.M. Writ of Fiere
10 Mar. 1744 Facias, signed on 1 Jan. last by BENJAMIN WHIT-
Sale on a Judgement AKER, C.J. & directed to Provost Marshall SAM-
UEL HURST commanding HURST to levy
Ł 11,920:16:10-1/2 currency on the goods & chattles, houses, Negroes,
real estate, etc., which belonged to THOMAS HENNING, merchant, deceased,
which JOHN SIMPSON, JR. had recovered by judgement of the Court of C.P.
against BENJAMIN SMITH, JOSEPH SHUTE, ROBERT THORPE, & ALEXANDER WOOD,
administrators of THOMAS HENNING; now HURST, for Ł 105 currency, sells to
BENJAMIN D'HARRIETT, ESQ., of Charleston, at public ourcray, a piece of
land fronting part of lot #16 on the Bay of Charleston, 25 ft. in breadth
fronting Cooper River as far as low water mark; bounding N on BENJAMIN
D'HARRIETTE; S on the part belonging to STEPHEN MILLER. Witnesses: JO-
SEPH TOBIAS, FRANCIS HOLMES. Before ROBERT AUSTIN, J.P. JOHN BEALE, Dep.
Pub. Reg.

Book C-C, p. 204 ALEXANDER HUME, ESQ., of London (brother & de-
23 & 24 Oct. 1746 vise named in will of ROBERT HUME, attorney-at-
L & R law, of St. Philips Parish, SC) by his attorney JOHN GUERARD, merchant, of Charleston, to
BENJAMIN D'HARRIETTE, merchant of Charleston; for Ł 2200 SC money, the N
part of 3 lots in Charleston, fronting 150 ft. on Queen Street; & 194-1/2
ft. on Meeting House Street (formerly old Church Street), bounding E on
JOHN BEE & backwards S from Queen Street, upon that E line 197 ft.; S on
ANTHONY BONNEAU & backwards upon that S line from Meeting House Street,
153 ft. Whereas MARY CROSS, widow, of Charleston, owned 3 lots near the
market place of Charleston by virtue of certain grants from the Lords
Proprs. & of a deed of feoffment with livery & seizin to her from JOHN
BIRD, planter, dated 1 June 1688; & by her will dated 28 Aug. 1698 directed that the lots be divided into 3 equal parts by straight N & S lines,
fronting Broad Street to theS, & that little street which then ran by DR.
FRANKLIN & MR. SIMMONDS (now called Queen Street), to the N; the western-
most of which lots she left to her son WILLIAM BAILEY for his lifetime &
afterwards equally to her 2 daughters MARY BASDEN & SUSANNAH RAWLINGS;
giving the E lot to her daughter SUSANNAH RAWLINGS; & the middle, or 3rd
lot to her daughter MARY BASDEN; & whereas after the death of MARY CROSS
& of her son WILLIAM BAYLEY, the lots were divided by a line running from
E to W into 6 lots, 3 fronting Broad Street, 3 fronting Queen Street, the
E & W lots of the N division becoming the property of SUSANNAH RAWLINGS
(afterwards SUSANNAH WIGGINTON); the E lot of which, fronting Queen
street, she by deed poll dated 30 June 1720, conveyed to EDWARD RAWLINS,
joiner, of Charleston, & MARY his wife; & whereas PETER MANIGAULT, vinter,
of Charleston, & MARY his wife, & whereas PETER MANIGAULT, vintner, of
Charleston, became owner of the middle of the N lots (half the lot bequeathed by MARY CROSS to her daughter MARY BASDEN); & EDWARD RAWLINGS
owned the middle third part of the S division (being the other half bequeathed to MARY BASDEN); & whereas MANIGAULT & RAWLINGS agreed to exchange their holdings with each other, so that on 4 May 1721 MANIGAULT
sold his half to RAWLINGS: & whereas EDWARD & MARY RAWLINGS, now already
owning the E third of the N division (by conveyance from SUSANNAH

WIGGINTON) & obtaining the middle third of the N division by exchange
with MANIGAULT, by L & R dated 7 & 8 Mar. 1721 sold to ROBERT HUME 2/3 of
the whole front of said 3 lots on the street running E from Cooper River
by the lots of GIBBON & ALLEN, now Queen Street, & backwards from that
street to the land fenced in & owned by PETER MANIGAULT & the land formerly of TOBIAS FITCH, bounding E on MR. JACKSON; W on a part of the 3
lots; & whereas SUSANNAH WIGGINTON owned 1/3 of the N division & EDWARD
RAWLINGS owned 2/3, they agreed that the western most third part of the N
division, fronting Old Church Street, should be conveyed to said ROBERT
HUME & the E third part of N division be conveyed to SUSANNAH WIGGINTON,
in consequence of which agreement, containing more fully in an indenture
dated 16 Mar. 1721, SUSANNAH granted ROBERT HUME all the W third part of
the N half of the 3 lots, which deed also contained a conveyance of the E
third part of the N division from ROBERT HUME to SUSANNAH WIGGINGTON; &
whereas SUSANNAH WIGGINTON, claiming certain title to said third part of
the N division devised to MARY BASDEN by MARY CROSS, for the better settling there of & of the W third part, by deed poll dated 11 Jan. 1723
confirmed to ROBERT HUME that part of the 3 lots fronting 100 ft. on
Queen Street, & backwards as far as MR. MANIGAULT'S fence, bounding E on
the part belonging to SUSANNAH WIGGINTON; W on the street running towards
the Presbyterian Meeting House; & whereas SUSANNAH WIGGINTON by L & R dated 15 & 16 Dec. 1731 sold to ROBERT HUME the E third lot in the N division being the same conveyed to HUME by EDWARD RAWLINGS & MARY his wife,
& by HUME to SUSANNAH WIGGINTON in exchange for the W third of the N division; & whereas ROBERT HUME, owning the whole N division, by will dated
16 Dec. 1736 bequeathed to ALEXANDER HUME, his brother, party hereto that
part whereon HUME'S coachhouse & stable stood, being 1-1/2 lots, with
certain other lands mentioned in the will (HUME dying in 1737); whereas
ALEXANDER HUME by letter of attorney dated at London, 5 Aug. 1743, appointed JAMES ABERCROMBY, RICHARD HILL & JOHN GUERARD his attorneys, to
dispose of all the real estate left by ROBERT HUME for him; & by another
letter of attorney in 1744 authorized HILL & GUERARD to act in ABERCROM-
BY'S absence; & whereas ABERCROMBIE & HILL have been absent from SC for
some time; now GUERARD, in their absence; conveys to D'HARRIETTE the N
half of the 3 lots. Witnesses: RIBTON HUTCHINSON, JOHN RATTRAY. Before
ROBERT AUSTIN, J.P. JOHN BEALE, Dep. Pub. Reg.

Book C-C, p. 215   WILLIAM HANCOCK, merchant, to ALEXANDER
5 & 6 Aug. 1746   CHISOLME, vintner, both of Charleston, for
L & R   Ł 4400 SC money, lot #229 in Charleston, con-
                          taining 1/2 a., English measure, bounding S on
the little street leading from Cooper River by RICHARD TRADD to GEORGE
KEELING; N on MR. DUGUE; E on JOHN HILL; W on THOMAS ROSE; formerly purchased from RICHARD GRINSTON, gentleman, of Berkeley Co., & ELLINOR his
wife, by ELIAS HANCOCK on 28 Feb. 1726. Witnesses: CHARLES WRIGHT, JAMES
MICKIE. Before JAMES HOME, J.P. JOHN BEALE, Dep. Pub. Reg.

Book C-C, p. 219   WILLIAM HANCOCK, merchant, of Charleston, to
30 Aug. 1746   ALEXANDER CHISOLME, vintner, of Charleston, in
Bond   penal sum of Ł 4000 SC money, as security that
                          he, HANCOCK, shall procure his wife's (MARY'S)
renunciation of dower to the lot #229 sold in L & R on 5 & 6 Aug. Witnesses: THOMAS NEWTON, DAVID DONOVAN. Before JAMES HOME, J.P. JOHN
BEALE, Dep. Pub. Reg.

Book C-C, p. 221   JAMES WATSON, JR., planter, to JOHN BARNWELL,
18 & 19 Jan. 1744/5   planter, both of Granville Co., for Ł 612 cur-
L & R   rency, 222 a. in Granville Co., bounding E on
                          flats & marshes; S on EDWARD HEXT; W on DANIEL
DIX; N on NICHOLAS HATCHER. Witnesses: MARY WIGG, EDWARD WIGG. Before
HUGH BRYAN, J.P. JOHN BEALE, Dep. Pub. Reg.

Book C-C, p. 224   KANNAWAY NORTON, planter, & SARAH (her mark)
9 & 10 Aug. 1746   his wife, to JOHN BARNWELL, planter, for
L & R   Ł 1200 SC money, an isalnd of 560 a. commonly
                          called Washua Island (its original Indian
name) in Granville Co., divided on the S by a creek from JOHN COWEN &
JOHN NORTON; E by a creek from Data Island; bounding N & NW by a river
between Combahee Island & St. Helena Island; SARAH NORTON to renounce her
dower within 12 months. Witnesses: JONATHAN NORTON, ISAAC WAIGHT,

WILLIAM DAVIS. Before OTHNIEL BEALE, J.P. JOHN BEALE, Dep. Pub. Reg.

Book C-C, p. 226
10 Aug. 1746
Bond

KANNAWAY NORTON, planter, to JOHN BARNWELL, planter, in penal sum of Ł 2400 SC money, to keep the agreements in L & R of this date covering sale of Washua Island. Witnesses: JONATHAN NORTON, ISAAC WAIGHT, WILLIAM DAVIS. JOHN BEALE, Dep. Pub. Reg.

Book C-C, p. 230
9 & 10 Sept. 1746
L & R

JOHN HASELL, planter, of Berkeley Co., to CAPT. THOMAS ASHBY, SR., planter, for Ł 1050 currency, 4 adjoining plantations, total 1000 a., bounding SE on CAPT. THOMAS ASHBY; NW on THOMAS HASELL & RICHARD SHUBRICK; SW on THOMAS HASELL & THOMAS ASHBY; NE on GABRIEL MANIGAULT. Witnesses: DANIEL LESESNE, PETER SIMONS. Before FRANCIS LEJAU, J.P. JOHN BEALE, Dep. Pub. Reg.

Book C-C, p. 233
10 & 11 Jan. 1746
L & R by Mortgage

JOHN HUTCHINS, warden, & ELIZABETH (her mark) his wife, of St. Philip's Parish, Charleston, to JAMES SCREVEN, & MARY his wife, of Colleton Co., for Ł 1600 currency, 524 a. in St. Pauls Parish, Colleton Co., bounding E on THOMAS ELLIOTT; S on EDMUND BELLINGER; N on JOHN GODFREY. Date of redemption: 11 Jan. 1751. Witnesses: FRANCIS GRACIA, WILLIAM SCREVEN. Before OTHNIEL BEALE, J.P. JOHN BEALE, Dep. Pub. Reg. On 9 Mar. 1751 JAMES SCREVEN declared mortgage satisfied. Witness: WILLIAM HOPTON.

Book C-C, p. 237
15 & 16 Dec. 1746
L & R

THOMAS HUTCHINSON, gentleman, of Granville Co., (son & heir-at-law of JOHN HUTCHINSON), & ANN his wife (heretofore ANN HOLLAN); to ALEXANDER PERONNEAU, gentleman, of Charleston for Ł 4000 SC money, lot #83 in Charleston, bounding N on the churchyard; E 120 ft. on Church Street; S 262-1/2 ft. on Queen Street; W on WILLIAM WARDEN. Whereas the Lords Proprs. & Gov. THOMAS SMITH on 12 June 1694 granted JOHN WILLIAMSON, planter, of Colleton Co., lot #83 in Charleston containing 1/2 a., English Measure; & he on 7 Apr. 1699, sold to WILLIAM RUBERRY, on 26 Mar. 1710, sold the lot & buildings to ABRAHAM EVE, ESQ., of Colleton Co., who, with SARAH his wife, on 6 Jan. 1710 (11?) conveyed to ANNE HOLLAND; who afterwards married said JOHN HUTCHINSON, then practitioner in physic, in Charleston; & whereas JOHN & ANNE HUTCHINSON died without making any disposition of the property, which was inherited by their son THOMAS; now he sells to PERONNEAU. Witnesses: JAMES WRIGHT, CHARLES CALDER. Before JAMES MICKIE, J.P. JOHN BEALE, Dep. Pub. Reg.

Book C-C, p. 243
12 Nov. 1746
Sale on Judgment

Provost Marshall RAWLINS LOWNDES, to JOHN DANIEL, ship carpenter, of Charleston. Whereas ROBERT HUME, gentleman, of Charleston owned part of lot #42 fronting S 31 ft. on Broad Street, bounding W on MR. DE ST. JULIEN; N on MRS. WATSON; E on JOHN MACKENZIE; & by will dated 16 Dec. 1736 appointed his brother PETER his executor; & whereas ROBERT HUME gave bond dated 31 Oct. 1735 to his brother ALEXANDER HUME, merchant, of Londong, in penal sum of Ł 5000 British for payment of Ł 2572:10 British, & whereas by act of Parliment by divers Prorogations held at Westminster, Co. of Middlesex, on 13 Jan. 1731, it was enacted that after the 29 Sept. 1732, the houses, Negroes, real estate, etc., within the plantations of a debtor should be liable for the satisfaction of debts due H.M. subjects; & whereas ALEXANDER HUME, after ROBERTS death, impleaded PETER as executor in an action for recovery of said Ł 5000 sterling & obtained a judgment for that amount, & costs; & in consequence a writ of freri facias dated 12 Aug. 1746 was issued; now Provost Marshall RAWLINS LOWNDES, for Ł 1800 currency, conveys to JOHN DANIEL, the highest bidder at public auction, the part of lot #42 & the houses thereon, fronting 31 ft. on Broad Street. Witnesses: JOHN RATTRAY, JAMES GRINDLAY. Before OTHNIEL BEALE, J.P.

Book C-C, p. 246
9 & 10 Jan. 1746
L & R by Mortgage

JOHN HUTCHINS, warden of the workhouse, Charelston, & ELIZABETH (her mark) his wife, to JOHN TRIBOUDET, vintner, of Charleston, as security on a bond of even date in penal sum of Ł 623:1:8 for pyament of Ł 311:10:10 currency, with interest, on 10 Jan. 1748; that lot in Ansonsburgh fronting 160 ft. on the Broad Path

leading from Charleston; & fronting 100 ft. on the 30 ft. street; being
part of a lot containing 1 a., 2 roods, English measure, marked D on the
plan of GEORGE ANSON'S lands & lately purchased fy JOHN HUTCHINS from
BENJAMIN WHITAKER as attorney for GEORGE ANSON; also the brick house or
houses thereon. Witnesses: DANIEL ROULAIN, WILLIAM MOUAT. Before JAMES
MICKIE, J.P. JOHN BEALE, Pub. Reg. On 2 Mar. 1762, JOHN TRIBOUDET declared mortgage, satisfied. Witness: WILLIAM HOPTON.

Book C-C, p. 250   SAMUEL MAVERICK & BENJAMIN STONE, shipwrights,
Sale   as administrators of the estate of BENJAMIN
                          MAVERICK, to CAPT. ROBERT RIVERS, planter, of
Berkeley Co. MAVERICK & STONE, administrators, at public auction, for
Ⱡ 603 currency on 16 Dec. 1746, conveyed to ROBERT RIVERS 37-1/2 a. with
a wooden dwelling house & other buildings on James Island, bounding E & S
on MARTHA BEE & SAMUEL STENT; N on BENJAMIN STYLES; N on marsh & a small
creek; being real estate of BENJAMIN MAVERICK sold for debts; which property ROBERT RIVERS on 20 Jan. 1746 for Ⱡ 605 currency conveyed to SAMUEL
MAVERICK. Witnesses: WILLIAM RIVERS, SAMUEL STENT (a Quaker, according
to his profession). Before THOMAS LAMBOLL, J.P. JOHN BEALE, Register.

Book C-C, p. 252   WILLIAM FORD, bricklayer, to RICHARD WAIN-
14 Feb. 1746/7   WRIGHT, butcher, both of Charleston, as secur-
Mortgage   ity on a bond of even date in penal sum of
                          Ⱡ 200 for payment of Ⱡ 100 currency, with in-
terest, on 14 Feb. 1747 a lot in Charleston on White Point adjoining RICH-
ARD MORTIMORE; also 350 a. on the forks of Little Peedee, adjoining JO-
SEPH ALLEN; which lot & 350 a. were bequeathed to FORD by his father NA-
THANIEL FORD; also 2 tables, 2 feather beds, 6 chairs, 13 silver spoons,
4 large china bowls, 12 china cups & saucers; 1 small chestnut colored
horse branded on the near buttock   4 cows marked with a crop in the
off ear & 2 slits in the near ear. Witnesses: JAMES BRADLEY, WILLIAM
MOUAT. Before JACOB MOTTE, J.P. JOHN BEALE, Register.

Book C-C, p. 253   WILLIAM (his mark) ASHMAN, planter, to DANIEL
19 Apr. 1745   DALY, planter, both of Granville Co., as se-
Mortgage   curity on bond of even date in penal sum of
                          Ⱡ 798:4 for payment of Ⱡ 399.:2 SC money, with
interest, on 26 Mar. 1749; 305 a. in Granville Co., bounding NW on ALEX-
ANDER HEXT; S & W on DANIEL DALY; E on a creek & marsh. Possession of
the grant of 305 given DALY. Witnesses: JOHN MIKELL, JOSEPH MIKELL. Before JOHN MULLRYNE, J.P. JOHN BEALE, Register.

Book C-C, p. 254   ALEXANDER HUME, ESQ., now of London, late of
19 & 20 Nov. 1746   St. Philips Parish, Charleston, (brother & de-
L & R   vise of ROBERT HUME of SC), by JOHN GUERARD,
                          of Charleston, his attorney; to JOHN DUTARQUE,
planter, of St. Thomas Parish, Berkeley Co., for Ⱡ 200 currency; 360 a.
whereas ROBERT HUME owned 360 a. in the Parish of St. Thomas & St. Dennis,
Berkeley Co., which he had purchased from JOHN FOGARTIE & which on 23
July 1711 had been granted by the Lords Proprs. to JONATHAN RUSS, bounding SE on LEWIS DUTARQUE & JOHN FOGARTIE; SE on MARY WARNOCK; NE on JAS-
PER BASKERFIELD; & by will dated 16 Dec. 1736 bequeathed the 260 a. to
his brother ALEXANDER HUME; & whereas ROBERT HUME died in 1737 without
altering his will; & whereas ALEXANDER HUME, attorney-at-law, in London,
on 5 Aug. 1743 appointed JAMES ABERCROMBY, RICHARD HILL & JOHN GUERARD,
his attorneys to dispose of the estate left by ROBERT HUME; & whereas
HILL died & ABERCROMBY absent from the Province; now GUERARD, as attorney, conveys to DUTARQUE. Witnesses: JAMES SHARP, JOHN RATTRAY. Before
OTHNIEL BEALE, J.P. JOHN BEALE, Register.

Book C-C, p. 260   The Hon. WILLIAM BULL to JOHN DRAYTON, ESQ.,
10 Dec. 1746   for Ⱡ 10 currency, the back part of a lot in
Feoffment   Charleston, bounding N on WILLIAM YEOMANS; W
                          on MR. TOWNSEND; E on the front or other half
of said lot belonging to THOMAS DRAYTON & DR. BULL; S on a lane leading
from the street westerly the length of the lot; being 90 ft. from YEO-
MAN'S land to the lane & 117-1/4 ft. deep. Witnesses: MARY H. BULL, JOHN
RATTRAY. Before OTHNIEL BEALE, J.P. JOHN BEALE, Register.

Book C-C, p, 262   WILLIAM FORBES, planter, & CHARITY his wife,

136

27 & 28 Dec. 1744   of Prince Frederick Parish, Craven Co., to
L & R   PAUL TRAPIER, merchant, of Georgetown, for
                           Ł 1500 currency, 482 a. near the mouth of Sam-
pit Creek, on same side as Georgetown, bounding S & E on Sampit Creek; W
on ARTHUR FOSTER; N on the Hon. JOHN CLELAND; E on JOHN CLELAND & Georgetown Common; plat signed by WILLIAM FORBES 28 Dec. 1744. Witnesses: MARY
KARWON, JOHN BASSNETT, JASPER KING. Before JACOB MOTTE, J.P. JOHN BEALE,
Register.

Book C-C, p. 266   DAVID CUTLER BRADDOCK, mariner, to EDWARD WIGG,
1 & 2 July 1746   merchant, both of Beaufort, Granville Co., as
L & R by Mortgage   security on bond dated 22 May 1746 given by
                           BRADDOCK to JOSHUA MORGAN, of St. Helena Is-
land, in penal sum of Ł 1050 for payment of Ł 525 currency on 22 Nov.
1746, for which bond EDWARD WIGG became security; lot #314 in Beaufort,
bounding N on North Street; E on Newcastle Street; S on lot #309 & on
half of the breadth of lot #308 granted to ROBERT WILLIAMS; W on lot #313.
Witnesses: HILL WIGG, RICHARD WIGG. Before JOHN MULLRYNE, J.P. JOHN
BEALE, Register.

Book C-C, p. 269   WILLIAM SEALY, JR., of Granville Co., to his
30 Oct. 1746   brother MIKELL SEALY, the 300 a. on Yawhaw
Gift   Creek bequeathed to WILLIAM SEALY by his fa-
                          ther, JOHN SEALY. Witnesses: WILLIAM SEALY,
SR., WILLIAM ELBERT, FRANCIS PELOT. Before HUGH BRYAN, J.P. JOHN BEALE,
Register.

Book C-C, p. 271   WILLIAM OSWILL (eldest son & heir-at-law) &
10 Feb. 1746   JOSEPH OSWILL (2nd son), planters, only sur-
L & R   viving sons & devises of WILLIAM OSWILL, the
                         elder; to SAMUEL DAVIDSON, planter, all of
Colleton Co., for Ł 500 currency, their undivided plantation of 340 a.,
English measure, originally granted by the Lords Proprs. in 3 adjoining
parcels to several persons; now bounding N on Sewanchehooe (commonly
called Toobadoe) Creek & marsh; E on the creek & marsh & WILLIAM EDDINGS;
S on a marsh & WILLIAM EDDINGS; W on ABRAHAM WALCUTT, (formerly ALEXANDER
CLARKE). Whereas by sundry mesne conveyances & other assignments WILLIAM
OSWILL, the elder, became owner of 340 a. & by will dated 22 July 1730
directed that his lands be equally divided amongst his 3 sons, WILLIAM,
JOSEPH, JOSEPH & BENJAMIN when JOSEPH reached 18 years of age; & whereas
BENJAMIN died a minor before JOSEPH reached 18, & WILLIAM & JOSEPH have
since reached the age of 21; now they sell the undivided 340 a. to DAVID-
SON. Witnesses: REGINALD JACKSON & WILLIAM LITTLE (according to their
profession) & JOHN BEE. Before CHARLES WRIGHT, J.P. JOHN BEALE, Register.

Book C-C, p. 276   JOHN SEABROOK, planter, to GEORGE SAXBY, gen-
17 & 18 Mar. 1746   tleman, to indemnify SAXBY & his estate from
L & R   the payment of several debts & sums of money
                         (SAXBY having given bond to CHARLES PINCKNEY,
OTHNIEL BEALE & BENJAMIN D'HARRIETTE, THOMAS FRANKLAND, THOMAS WRIGHT,
ELISHA BUTLER & WILLIAM ROPER & WILLIAM MCCLUER, in divers sums, amount-
ing to the whole, exclusive of interest, to Ł 11,998 SC money, all for
the sole debt of said JOHN SEABROOK); the plantation on which JOHN SEA-
BROOK lives, on Johns Island, devised to him by will of COL. ALEXANDER
HEXT. Should SEABROOK pay the various amounts, with interest, on the
dates named, this mortgage to be void. Witnesses: JOHN GIBBES, JOHN RAT-
TRAY. Before JOHN LINING, J.P. JOHN BEALE, Register.

Book C-C, p. 279   JOHN SEABROOK, planter, of Johns Island, to
17 & 18 Mar. 1746   GEORGE SAXBY, gentleman, of Charleston, as
L & R by Mortgage   further security for the payment of several
                          sums, with interest, already due, & to indem-
nify GEORGE SAXBY; 3 adjoining tracts in Colleton Co., 100 a. purchased
from THOMAS ELLIOTT, SR., planter; 72 a. purchased from WILLIAM FAIRCHILD,
planter; 340 a.; making 1 tract of 512 a., bounding N on THOMAS ELLIOTT &
WILLIAM FAIRCHILD; S on SARAH WOODWARD & MARTHA EMMS; E on WILLIAM TRED-
WELL BULL; W on THOMAS ELLIOTT; also 200 a. adjoining the 512 a., purchased by JOHN SEABROOK from THOMAS ELLIOTT. Whereas JOHN SEABROOK gave
bond dated 17 May 1744 to JAMES MATHEWS & GEORGE SAXBY in the penal sum

of Ꮮ 6477 currency reciting that whereas on 16 Feb. 1743 JOHN SEABROOK, JAMES MATHEWS & GEORGE SAXBY gave bond to CHARLES PINCKNEY, OTHNIEL BEALE & BENJAMIN D'HARRIETTE, of Charleston, in the penal sum of Ꮮ 6477 for payment of Ꮮ 3238 currency on 16 Feb. 1744 for the debt of JOHN SEABROOK; & whereas JOHN SEABROOK gave GEORGE SAXBY a bond dated 23 Feb. 1744/5 in penal sum of Ꮮ 2000 British sterling reciting that whereas SAXBY gave bond (jointly with SEABROOK for SEABROOKS debt) dated 21 Feb. 1744/5 to THOMAS FRANKLAND, commander of H.M.S. Rose in penal sum of Ꮮ 2000 British for payment of Ꮮ 1000 sterling British, with interest, on 20 Feb. 1745; & whereas SEABROOK gave SAXBY another bond dated 2 July 1745 in penal sum of Ꮮ 3570 SC money reciting that whereas SAXBY, for JOHN SEABROOKS debt, gave bond, with SEABROOK, to THOMAS WRIGHT, ELISHA BUTLER & WILLIAM ROPER, executors, of will of RICHARD WRIGHT, dated 2 Apr. 1745, in penal sum of Ꮮ 1520 for payment of Ꮮ 760, with interest, on 2 Apr. 1746; & also reciting that whereas SAXBY, at SEABROOK'S request, gave another bond dated 16 May 1745 to WILLIAM MCCLURER, of John's Island, in penal sum of Ꮮ 2000 for payment of Ꮮ 1000 currency, with interest, on 16 May 1746; now for further security SEABROOK conveys several tracts of land to SAXBY. Witnesses: JOHN GIBBES, JOHN RATTRAY. Before JOHN LINING, J.P. JOHN BEALE, Register.

Book C-C, p. 285
19 & 20 Aug. 1745
L & R

GEORGE LIVINGSTON, planter, & ELINOR his wife, of St. Helena Parish, Port Royal, Granville Co., to HILLERSDON WIGG; gentleman, of Granville Co., for Ꮮ 160 currency, lot #311 in Beaufort, fronting S on Craven Street, bounding N on equal parts of lots #315 & 316; E on lot #312; W on lot #310. Witnesses: THOMAS WIGG, EDWARD WIGG. Before HUGH BRYAN, J.P. JOHN BEALE, Register.

Book C-C, p. 289
9 Dec. 1746
Release of Inheritance

CATHERINE WRIGHT, late CATHERINE CRAIGIE, wife of WILLIAM WRIGHT, silversmith of Charleston, declared before JOHN LINING, Justice, that she voluntarily joined with her husband in L & R dated this Dec. by which WILLIAM & CATHERINE WRIGHT conveyed to BENJAMIN SAVAGE & JOHN SAVAGE, merchants, of Charleston, all their interest in lot #179 in Charleston fronting 17 ft. on W side Old Church Street, bounding N on GABRIEL ESCOTT; W on JOHN RIVERS; S on MARY BRYAN; also their interest in lot #80 in Ashley Ferry Town, bounding NW on lot #79; SW on Broad Street, SE on lot #81, the agreement being that the lots were a gift from WILLIAM & CATHERINE WRIGHT to BENJAMIN & JOHN SAVAGE. Before JOHN LINING, commander in writ of dedimus potestatum from BENJAMIN WHITAKER dated 25 Sept. 1746. JOHN BEALE, Register.

Book C-C, p. 290
8 & 9 Dec. 1746
L & R by Mortgage

WILLIAM WRIGHT, silversmith & CATHERINE his wife (lately CATHERINE CRAIGIE) of Charleston, to BENJAMIN SAVAGE & JOHN SAVAGE, merchants, of Charleston, as security for the payment of Ꮮ 600 currency, with interest; part of lot #179 in Charleston, fronting 17 ft. on W side of Old Church Street & bounding N on GABRIEL ESCOTT; W on JOHN RIVERS; S on MARY BRYAN; also lot #80 in middle of Ashley Ferry Town. Whereas ALBERT DETMAR, gentleman, of Charleston, owned part of lot #179 in Charleston with 1 tenement thereon; also lot #80 in Ashley Ferry Town; which 2 tracts of land on 15 Oct. 1745 became legally vested in CATHERINE CRAIGIE; & whereas on 15 Mar. last she married WILLIAM WRIGHT; & whereas WILLIAM WRIGHT gave bond of even date to BENJAMIN & JOHN SAVAGE, in penal sum of Ꮮ 1200 for payment of Ꮮ 600 currency, with interest, on 8 Dec. next; now WILLIAM & CATHERINE WRIGHT convey the 2 lots to secure payment. Witnesses: SARAH MARSHALL, CHARLES CALDER. Before JAMES WRIGHT, J.P. JOHN BEALE, Register.

Book C-C, p. 295
24 & 25 Mar. 1747
L & R by Mortgage

GEORGE DICK, gentleman, & MARY his wife, of Georgetown, Winyaw, to ALEXANDER HUME, ESQ., of London, as security on bond of even date given by GEORGE DICK & DANIEL LAROCHE, gentleman, of Winyaw, to ALEXANDER HUME, in penal sum of Ꮮ 2600 for payment of Ꮮ 1300 currency, with interest, on 6 Dec. next; 1000 a. in Craven Co., bounding NW on Black River; SE on DANIEL & THOMAS LAROCHE; SW on ARTHUR FOSTER; NE on GEORGE DICK & on DANIEL & THOMAS LAROCHE; which tracts was originally granted to EDWARD VANVELSIN; also 1600 a. in Craven Co., bounding NW on Black River; NE on WILLIAM SWINTON; SE on MR. FOSTER & on

GEORGE DICK (formerly CAPT. MEREDITH HUGHES); E on JOHN LEAN; originally
granted to DANIEL LAROCHE; also 200 a. in Craven Co., originally granted
to GEORGE DICK; bounding SE & NE on Black River; SE on DANIEL & THOMAS
LAROCHE; SW on vacant land; NW on MEREDITH HUGHES. Witnesses: ELIZABETH
BROCKINGTON, HESTER BILLING. Before WILLIAM WHITESIDE, J.P. JOHN BEALE,
Register. Reference: on 5 Jan. 1788 JOSEPH BLYTHE appeared before SAMUEL
SMITH, J.P. & made oath he heard PAUL TRAPIER acknowledge the (following)
to be his handwriting. "I do hereby certify that GEORGE DICK & DAN'L LA-
ROCHE joint bond to ALEXANDER HUME, ESQ., of Great Britain for Ł 1300
principal (which) is mentioned in the within letter from MR. WM. PARKER
was paid to the said WM. PARKER attorney to said ALEXANDER HUME & said
bond (with) a mortgage of 3 tracts of land to secure the payment of the
debt on said bond to the said ALEXANDER HUME, ESQ., were sent to me by
the said WM. PARKER the whole demands thereon being fully satisfied &
paid, which bond & mortgage I delivered to MISS MARY DICK, daughter, of
the above named GEORGE DICK who was solely concerned in them. Witness my
hand the 20th Nov. 1786. PAUL TRAPIER. Witness: JOS. BLYTH. N.B. satisfaction made this 9th day of Jan. 1788 by P. HORRY, register, who is
fully acquainted with & knows the same to be the handwriting of PAUL
TRAPIER."

Book C-C, p. 300   RICHARD CAPERS, planter, of Granville Co., to
6 & 7 Mar. 1746   JAMES DAWKINS, ESQ., of Island of Jamaica, for
L & R   Ł 707 currency, 1500 a. in Granville Co., on
                          Port Royal River, granted by Lt. Gov. THOMAS
BROUGHTON, on 12 May 1735 to RICHARD CAPERS; bounding N on marsh & creeks;
E on first inlet from Port Royal River; S on Sea Bay; W on Port Royal Riv-
er. Witnesses: JAMES MICKIE, DANIEL DONOVAN. Before JOHN LINING, J.P.
JOHN BEALE, Register.

Book C-C, p, 305   JOHN TRIBOUDET, vintner, to JACOB MARTIN, phy-
19 & 20 Mar. 1746   sician, both of Charleston, as security on
L & R by Mortgage   bond of even date in penal sum of Ł 2000 for
                           payment of Ł 1000 currency, with interest, on
20 Mar. 1747; that brick house & part of lot #17 bounding W 25 ft. on
Union Street; E on JOHN TRIBOUDET; S on the house & lot of JAMES WITHERS;
N 60 ft. on an alley leading from Union Street, to the Bay. Witnesses:
E. POINSETT, JOHN REMINGTON. Before OTHNIEL BEALE, J.P. JOHN BEALE, Reg-
ister.

Book C-C, p. 310   ARTIMAS ELLIOTT, planter, to HUMPHREY ELLIOTT,
4 Apr. 1745   for 5 shillings, 125 a. in Berkeley Co., bound-
Sale   ing N on BENJAMIN STANYARN; NW on MRS. LADSON;
                           SW on THOMAS DRAYTON; S on WILLIAM ELLIOTT; E
on BENJAMIN WILLIAMSON. Signed by: ARTIMUS ELLIOTT & MARY ELLIOTT (his
wife). Witnesses: WILLIAM BRANFORD, JR., BORNABY COCKFIELD, BENJAMIN LAD-
SON. Possession delivered by turf & twig. Before CULCHETH GOLIGHTLY,
J.P. JOHN BEALE, Register.

Book C-C, p. 311   BENJAMIN WILLIAMSON & ELIZABETH his wife, to
30 Nov. & 1 Oct. 1746   HUMPHREY ELLIOTT, all of Colleton Co., for
L & R   Ł 1000 currency, half the plantation of 378 a.
                           in St. Andrews Parish, Berkeley Co., bounding
NW on JONATHAN FITTS; NE on CHARLES JONES & SHEM BUTLER; SE on SAMUEL
JONES; SW on WILLIAM ELLIOTT. Witnesses: SAMUEL WOODBERY, PENELOPE WOOD-
BERY, MARY WILLIAMS. Before CULCHETH GOLIGHTLY, J.P. JOHN BEALE, Regis-
ter.

Book C-C, p. 314   WILLIAM HARTMAN, to MAJ. GEORGE BENISON, both
14 Aug. 1746   of Christ Church Parish, as security on bond
Mortgage   of even date in penal sum of Ł 1560 for pay-
                           ment of Ł 780 currency on 15 Aug. next; 150 a.
in Christ Church Parish, bounding S on RICHARD ROWSER; N on GEORGE BENI-
SON; also 3 Negro men. Witnesses: WILLIAM GIBBES, JOHN HOLLYBUSH. Before ROBERT AUSTIN, J.P. JOHN BEALE. Register.

Book C-C, p. 315   JOHN ATCHISON, planter, to SABINA LYNCH, widow,
10 & 11 Feb. 1746   both of Craven Co., for Ł 8694:15:3 SC money,
L & R by Mortgage   100 a. on Wadmalaw River; on JOHN ATCHISON
                           (formerly JAMES GILBERTSON); & on JOSEPH BLAKE;

139

also 3 tracts, total 996 a., on Wadmalaw River; bounding on JOSEPH BLAKE
& on JOHN ATCHISON; also 650 a., being half an island in Santee River;
bounding on the part owned by KENNETH MICKIE; E on 4 mile creek; also
452 a. in Santee River, bounding W on 4 mile creek; E on vacant marsh;
also 623 a., part of 1400 a. granted to JOHN ATCHISON, bounding W on
Wassoe Creek & CHARLES HILL; S on vacant land; E on Alligator Creek; N on
JOHN LINING; as security on bond of even date in penal sum of
Ł 17,389:10:6 currency. MARY, wife of JOHN ATCHISON, to renounce her
dower within 3 months after default. Witnesses: WILLIAM FLEMING, DAVID
CHENEY. Before DANIEL CRAWFORD, J.P. JOHN BEALE, Register.

Book C-C, p. 321   JOHN NEWBERY, yeoman, to ROBERT WILLIAMS, yeo-
19 & 20 Aug. 1746   man, both of Craven Co., for Ł 120 currency,
L & R   100 a. in the WELCH tract on great PeeDee Riv-
                      er, Craven Co., granted 6 Dec. 1744 by Gov.
JAMES GLEN to said JOHN NEWBERY. Witnesses: THOMAS EVANS, JOHN JONES.
Before WILLIAM JAMES, J.P. JOHN BEALE, Register.

Book C-C, p. 325   JOHN EVANS, planter, of the WELCH tract, Cra-
20 & 21 Aug. 1746   en Co., to ROBERT WILLIAMS, yeoman, of Craven
L & R   Co., for Ł 120 currency, 100 a. in the WELCH
                      tract, in Craven Co., granted by Gov. JAMES
GLEN on 6 Dec. 1744 to JOHN EVANS. Witnesses: THOMAS EVANS, JOHN JONES.
Before WILLIAM JAMES, J.P. JOHN BEALE, Register.

Book C-C, p. 328   HILLERSDON WIGG, gentleman, & ELIZABETH his
9 & 10 Mar. 1746   wife to JOHN DELAGAYNE, gentleman, all of St.
L & R   Helena Parish, Granville Co., for Ł 1100 SC
                      money, lot #305 in Beaufort fronting E on
Charles Street, bounding N on lots #303 & #304; S on lots #300 & #301.
Witnesses: JOSEPH EDWARD FLOWER, JOHN CHAPMAN. Before HUGH BRYAN, J.P.
JOHN BEALE, Register.

Book C-C, p. 332   ESAIE BRUNET, carpenter & SUSANNAH MARY, his
28 & 29 Sept. 1743   wife to WILLIAM COMMER, pettiaugerman, all of
L & R   Charleston, for Ł 275 SC money the W part of
                      lot #171 in Charleston, fronting N 25 ft. on
Queen Street, (alias Dock Street), bounding W 150-3/4 ft. on lot #169 be-
longing to WILSON WILSON; S 25 ft. on JOHN MOORE; E 155-1/4 ft. on MR.
BRAND. Witnesses: WILLIAM GUY, JR., WILLIAM AMEY. Before OTHNIEL BEALE,
J.P. JOHN BEALE, Register.

Book C-C, p. 335   ALEXANDER HUME, of London, (brother & devisee
15 & 16 June 1744   in will of ROBERT HUME, attorney-at-law, of
L & R   St. Philip's Parish, Charleston, SC) by his
                      attorneys JAMES ABERCROMBY, RICHARD HILL, &
JOHN GUERARD, merchants, of Charleston; to GEORGE SAXBY, ESQ., of
Charleston; for Ł 500 British, 184-1/2 a. in Berkeley Co., SC, on
Charleston Neck; & 100 a. of adjoining marsh land; marked A on the plat;
also 84 a. on Charleston Neck, adjoining the 284-1/2 a., marked B on the
plat; making 368-1/2 a. Whereas GILSON CLAPP, merchant, & MARGARET his
wife, of Berkeley Co., by L & R dated 1 & 2 Sept. 1726 (reciting that
GILSON then owned 4 adjoining tracts, 1 tract of 112 a.; 1 of 13 a.; 1 of
39-1/2 a.; & 1 of 10 a.; total 174-1/2 a., on Charleston Neck, bounding N
on COL. ROBERT JOHNSON; S on CHARLES HART; W on the highway leading from
Charleston; E on marsh of Cooper River; which 174-1/2 a. he conveyed to
ROBERT HUME & whereas CHARLES HART, ESQ., of Berkeley Co., by L & R dated
21 & 22 _____ 1728 sold to ROBERT HUME 10 a. on Charleston Neck, bounding
N on the Broad Road; all other sides on ROBERT HUME; whereas ALEXANDER
TRENCH, gentleman, Granville Co., sold to ROBERT HUME 100 a. of marsh
land on Charleston Neck adjoining the 174-1/2 a., thus making 1 tract of
284-1/2 a., according to Plat A attached to a lease dated 15 June 1744
between the attorneys of ALEXANDER HUME & GEORGE SAXBY; & whereas Landgrave ROBERT DANIEL, ESQ., & HELEN his wife, of Berkeley Co., by L & R
dated 1 & 2 Sept. 1726 sold to ROBERT HUME 84 a. on Charleston Neck,
bounding N on JONATHAN CONDON (formerly JOHN WATKINS); E on the Broad
Path; S on CARTWRIGHT; W on marsh & CARTWRIGHT; according to plat B,
attached to said lease; & whereas ROBERT HUME who died in 1737 by will
dated 16 Dec. 1736 bequeathed to ALEXANDER HUME, his brother party hereto, all the land he had bought from GILSON CLAPP, CHARLES HART & the

100 a. of marsh purchased from TRENCH out of BAYLY'S patent, also the
84 a.; & whereas said ALEXANDER HUME, of London, by letter of attorney
dated at London 5 Aug. 1743 appointed JAMES ABERCROMBY, RICHARD HILL &
JOHN GUERARD his attorneys to dispose of all the lands formerly owned by
ROBERT HUME; now they sell the 368-1/2 a. to SAXBY. Witnesses: ROBERT
HILL, JAMES WRIGHT. Before OTHNIEL BEALE, J.P. JOHN BEALE, Register.

Book C-C, p. 345   CHARLES WEST, planter, to JOHN DRAYTON, ESQ.,
9 & 10 Apr. 1747   as security on bond of even date in penal sum
L & R by Mortgage   of Ł 1055:7 for payment of Ł 527:13:6 curren-
                          cy, with interest, on 10 Apr. next; 100 a. in
Berkeley Co., bounding E on RICHARD BUTLER; W on WILLOUGHBY WEST; N on
FRANCIS LADSON; which 100 a. was conveyed by CHARLES WEST to SAMUEL WEST
& is part of 250 a. belonging to SAMUEL WEST. Witnesses: WILLIAM GEORGE
FREEMAN, WILLIAM BURROWS. Before JOHN LINGING, J.P. JOHN BEALE, Regis-
ter.

Book C-C, p. 349   ROBERT HANCOCK, planter & MARY his wife, to
6 & 7 Mar. 1746   SAMUEL WAINWRIGHT, butcher, of Charleston, for
L & R   Ł 1000 SC money, part of lot #92 in Charleston,
                          bound S on Tradd Street; N on HESTER SIMMONS
(formerly CORNELIUS BATTOON); E on ROBERT HANCOCK & WILLIAM HANCOCK, his
brother; W on King Street, being 50 ft. & 123 ft. Witnesses: RICHARD
WAINWRIGHT, WILLIAM MOUAT. Before JAMES MICKIE, J.P. JOHN BEALE, Register.

Book C-C, p. 353   WILLIAM PINCKNEY, ESQ., to CHARLES PINCKNEY,
18 & 19 Nov. 1746   ESQ., both of Charleston. Whereas CHARLES &
L & R by Mortgage   WILLIAM PINCKNEY (for WILLIAM'S debt) gave
                          HENRY & ALEXANDER PERONNEAU, merchants, of
Charleston, a bond dated 20 July 1743 in penal sum of Ł 2000 for payment
of Ł 1000 currency, with interest, on 20 July 1744; & (for WILLIAM'S
debt) a bond to HENRY PERONNEAU, dated 1 Sept. 1743 in penal sum of
Ł 2200 for payment of Ł 1100, with interest, on 1 Sept. 1744 & (for WIL-
LIAM'S debt) a bond to ALEXANDER PERONNEAU dated 1 Sept. in penal sum of
Ł 2560 for payment of Ł 1280 with interest on 1 Sept. 1744 & whereas WIL-
LIAM has not paid any part of the said sums; & whereas WILLIAM on the 28
Aug. 1739 ave CHARLES PINCKNEY a bond in penal sum of Ł 1310 for payment
of Ł 665:10 currency on 1 Mar. next & whereas on 3 Sept. 1743 Ł 500 remained due, with interest; & whereas on the settlement this day of a running account between said WILLIAM & CHARLES PINCKNEY a balance of Ł 207:7
currency is due from WILLIAM to CHARLES for which WILLIAM has given
CHARLES a bond in penal sum of Ł 415 for payment of Ł 207:7 currency,
with interest, on 1 Jan. 1747; now, as security on said bond & the other
bonds; WILLIAM conveys to CHARLES 200 a. on S end of Horse Shoe Savannah,
in Colleton Co., bounding NE & SE on said Savannah; SW & SE on STEPHEN &
BENJAMIN MAZYCK; which 200 a. WILLIAM PINCKNEY purchased from JOHN &
RICHARD WOODWARD; WILLIAM also conveys to CHARLES his open pettyauger,
capacity 70 bbls.; with all her equipment, which he now employs on Ashepoo River; also 30 slaves (men, women & children). WILLIAM to pay off
all the above debts before 29 Jan, 1747. Witnesses: GEORGE HUNTER,
CHARLES CALDER. Before JAMES WRIGHT, J.P. JOHN BEALE, Reigster.

Book C-C, p. 359   JOHN BRAND, gentleman, to WILLIAM COMMER, mar-
21 Aug. 1739   iner, both of Charleston, for Ł 250 currency,
Release   part of lot #171 in Charleston, bounding N 25
                          ft. on Dock Street, (alias Queen Street), W on
HUGH EVANS; S 25 ft. on JOHN MOORE; E 154-1/2 ft. on MRS. NIART. Wit-
nesses: JOHN THOMPSON, WILLIAM CRAY, WILLIAM SMITH. Before OTHNIEL BEALE,
J.P. JOHN BEALE, Register.

Book C-C, p. 361   MARGARET BROWN, widow, executrix & sole lega-
20 Mar. 1746   tee of will of TALBOT BROWN, mariner, to
Feoffment   GEORGE AUSTIN, merchant, all of Charleston,
                          for Ł 381:11 SC money, part of lot #210 in
Charleston, bounding S 130 ft. on JEREMIAH THEUS; N on JOHN BECKMAN; E
21 ft. on King Street; W on MARTHA SHAW. Whereas JOHN TIPPER, sailmaker,
of Charleston, owned part of lot #210, which by L & R dated 7 & 8 Feb.
1744 he conveyed to JAMES HAWKINS, mariner, of H.M.S. Rose, a certain
piece of said lot as recorded in Bk. A.A. p.p. 222-228; & whereas by L &

R dated 2 Nov. 1745 JAMES HAWKINS & REBECCA sold that part of lot #210 to TALBOT BROWN (see Secretary's Bk. B.B. p. 198-203) & whereas by will dated 25 Apr. 1746 appointed his wife, MARGARET, executrix & sole heir to his real & personal estate; now she sells to AUSTIN. Witnesses: THOMAS BOLTON, JOHN REMINGTON, JEREMIAH THEUS. Before OTHNIEL BEALE, J.P. JOHN BEALE, Register.

Book C-C, p. 365
6 & 7 May 1747
L & R by Mortgage

ROBERT THORPE, merchant, to RICHARD STEVENS, both of Granville Co., as security on bond for Ŀ 551:15 currency, payable with interest, on 14 May 1748; lot #4 in Beaufort, bounding E on lot #5; W on lot #3; S on the Bay. Witnesses: SAMUEL PRIOLEAU, OTHNIEL BEALE. Before JACOB MOTTE, J.P. JOHN BEALE, Register.

Book C-C, p. 368
25 & 26 Mar. 1747
L & R

BENJAMIN STANYARNE, planter, to JOHN GORDON, planter, for Ŀ 1250 currency, 200 a. in St. Andrews Parish, bounding N on WILLIAM CATTELL, SR.; E on WILLIAM BRANFORD; S on BENJAMIN STAN-YARNE; W on estate of ROBERT LADSON. Witnesses: JAMES SCARLETT, WILLIAM HULL. Before CHARLES PINCKNEY, J.P. JOHN BEALE, Register.

Book C-C, p. 371
31 July & 1 Aug. 1746
L & R by Mortgage

THOMAS JONES, planter, of Berkeley Co., to ABRAHAM WAIGHT, JR., ISAAC WAIGHT, JOSEPH WAIGHT & WILLIAM WAIGHT, executors of will of ISAAC WAIGHT, planter, as security for the payment of several debts; the 560 a., in St. Andrews Parish, Berkeley Co., on which THOMAS JONES lives; bounding E of STEPHEN BULL; N on NATHANIEL BROWN; W on THOMAS ELLIS; S on Stono River; also 1181 a. at Combahee, St. Bartholomews Parish, Colleton Co., bounding NW on BENJAMIN GODIN; E on DANIEL WELSHUYSEN; SW on Batts Creek; S on MRS. JACKSON. Whereas THOMAS JONES gave bond of even date to ABRAHAM WAIGHT, JR., ISAAC WAIGHT, JOSEPH WAIGHT, & WILLIAM WAIGHT in penal sum of Ŀ 2158 for payment of Ŀ 1079 currency, with interest, on Apr. next; & another bond of even date in penal sum of Ŀ 580 (reciting that whereas ISAAC WAIGHT, at request of JONES, & for JONES'S debt, joined JONES in a bond dated 18 Sept. 1744 to JOHN HODGSDEN, merchant, of Charleston, in penal sum of Ŀ 580 for payment of Ŀ 290 currency, with interest, on 1 May 1745 which bond is still unpaid) conditioned for payment by JONES to HODGSDEN of Ŀ 290 currency, with interest, on 1 Apr. next & indemnify (?) the executors & the estate of ISAAC WAIGHT; the principal & interest being still owing; now JONES gives 2 tracts as security for the payment of the debts. Witnesses: BENJAMIN MICKIE, DANIEL DONOVAN, JOHN CHAMPNEYS, J.P. JOHN BEALE, Register. Satisfaction of mortgage acknowledged on 28 Feb. 1748 by ABRAHAM WAIGHT & ISAAC WAIGHT, executors. JOHN BEALE, Register.

Book C-C, p, 377
9 & 10 Jan. 1746
L & R

PETER LAURENS, saddler, to JOHN LAURENS, saddler, both of Charleston, for Ŀ 2000 currency, part of lot #315, with the tenement thereon known as White Hall; bounding S 44 ft. on Broad Street; W 105 ft. on the part sold by JOHN LAURENS to MARY BASSETT; N on an alley; E on Market Square; which part of a lot was conveyed by JOHN LAURENS to PETER LAURENS by L & R dated 8 & 9 Mar. 1741 except the western slip of the premises fronting 3 ft. on Broad Street; which was conveyed to PETER LAURENS by MARY BASSETT by feoffment dated 17 Aug. 1743. Witnesses: BENJAMIN ADDISON, JOHN BULL, JR. Before WILLIAM GEORGE FREEMAN, J.P. JOHN BEALE, Register.

Book C-C, p. 382
24 & 25 Feb. 1746
L & R by Mortgage

ALEXANDER MCGRIGOR, victualler, & HANNAH his wife, to JOHN LAURENS, merchant, all of Charleston, as security on bond of even date in penal sum of Ŀ 2000 for payment of Ŀ 1000 currency, with interest, on 25 Feb. 1748 that house & lot bounding E on JAMES ROLLIN & JANE DUPUY; W 43-1/2 ft. on Meeting Street; S 135 ft. on JOHN LAURENS, STEPHEN MILLER & JAMES ROLLIN; N on JAMES EADES. Witnesses: FRANCIS LEJAU, DAVID GREENE. Before OTHNIEL BEALE, J.P. JOHN BEALE, Register.

Book C-C, p. 386
10 & 11 Apr. 1747
L & R by Mortgage

CHARLES WEST, planter, to JOHN GUERARD, merchant, (surviving partner of RICHARD HILL), as security on bond dated 12 Mar. 1744 given by

CHARLES & SAMUEL WEST to GUERARD & HILL, in penal sum of Ł 3286 for payment of Ł 1692:17:8 currency, with interest, on 25 Mar. 1745; 500 a. on E side S Edisto River, in Colleton Co., bounding N on CAPT. PETER SLANN; E on JOHN SIMMONS & JOHN BRANFORD; S on RICHARD BUTLER; W on the River; also 100 a. given CHARLES WEST by his brother SAMUEL WEST, being part of 250 a. in Berkeley Co., purchased by their father, SAMUEL WEST, from FRANCIS LADSON; the 100 a. bounding E on RICHARD BUTLER; W & S on WILLOUGHBY WEST; N on FRANCIS LADSON; also 25 a. devised to CHARLES WEST by will of SARAH WEST, his mother, dated 24 Oct. 1734. Witnesses: WILLIAM HOVEL HILL, JOHN RATTRAY. Before OTHENIEL BEALE, J.P. JOHN BEALE, Register.

Book C-C, p. 391
18 & 19 June 1747
L & R by Mortgage

JOHN WHITE, planter, to SABINA LYNCH, widow, both of Craven Co., for Ł 5794:16:3 SC money, 640 a., bounding S on Georgetown River; E on ARTHUR FOSTER; N on ANTHONY WHITE; W on COL. GEORGE PAWLEY; also the tract on Black River, bounding E on MR. HUNTER; W on MR. SOMERVILLE; N on ANTHONY WHITE; also lot #19 in Georgetown, bounding SW 50 ft. on Front Street; SE 217.9 ft. on lot #20; NE on lot #58; NW on lot #18; also lot #93 in Georgetown, bounding SW 100 ft. on Prince Street; SE 217.9 ft. on lot #94; NE on lot #117; NW on Queen Street. Date of redemption: 1 Sept. next; 2 bonds having been given. MARY, wife of JOHN WHITE, to renounce her dower within 3 months after default. Witnesses: JOHN JENNER, WILLIAM FLEMING. Before JOHN CLELAND, J.P. JOHN BEALE, Register. On 25 May 1749, THOMAS LYNCH, administrator of estate of SABINA LYNCH, declared mortgage satisfied. Witness: JOHN LOGAN.

Book C-C, p. 396
27 & 28 Mar. 1747
L & R by Mortgage

THOMAS JEWNING, to WILLIAM FLEMING, both of Craven Co., as security on bond dated 1 Mar. 1747 in penal sum of Ł 1319:15:8 for payment of Ł 659:17:10 SC money, with interest, on 1 Mar. 1747; lot #21 in Georgetown, containing 1/4 a.; bounding SW 50 ft. on the Bay or Front Street; SE 217.9 ft. on lot #22; NE on lot #59; NW on lot #20; which lot #21, was conveyed to ALLAN WELLS & by sundry mesne conveyances has become vested in THOMAS JEWNING. MARY, wife of THOMAS JEWNING to renounce her dower within 3 months after default. Witnesses: CRAFTON KARWON, JAMES AXFORD. Before JOHN CLELAND, J.P. JOHN BEALE, Register.

Book C-C, p. 400
25 & 26 Mar. 1747
L & R by Mortgage

PETER JOHNSON, planter, to WILLIAM FLEMING, JOHN CLELAND, & WILLIAM FLEMING & ANDREW JOHNSTON, all of Craven Co., 750 a. in Craven Co., bounding SW on JAMES JOHNSON; other sides on vacant land; also 500 a., bounding SE on THOMAS JENKINS; NW on ISAAC DAVIS; other sides on vacant land; as security to WILLIAM FLEMING for payment Ł 949:19; to JOHN CLELAND & WILLIAM FLEMING for Ł 716 & to ANDREW JOHNSON for Ł 634:1; total Ł 2300 currency, with interest, for which sums bonds were given. Witnesses: PETER JOHNSON, JR., NATHANIEL MCCULLOUGH. Before JOHN MAN, J.P. JOHN BEALE, Register.

Book C-C, p. 404
6 & 7 Jan. 1744
L & R

WILLIAM WHIPPY, planter, & MARY his wife, & with her free consent, to THOMAS SACHEVERELL, planter, all of Colleton Co., for Ł 650 currency, 150 a. on E side of Pon Pon River in Colleton Co., bounding N on JAMES FULTON & Landgrave JOSEPH MORTON; E on SAMUEL TOWLES (LOWLES?); S on JOHN WILLIAMSON; W on MOSES MARTIN. Whereas the Lords Proprs. granted SAMUEL LOWLE (TOWLE?) a tract of land in St. Pauls Parish, Colleton Co.; & whereas he conveyed to TIMOTHY HENDRICK 150 a., part of the above grant, which part was measured beginning at the N corner adjoining JAMES FULTON & run S halfway the line joining MOSES MARTIN, then run E till the 150 a. be measured; & whereas HENDRICK bequeathed the 150 a. to ROBERT WHIPPY, who died intestate & the land became vested in WILLIAM WHIPPY, ROBERTS eldest brother; now WILLIAM conveys to SACHEVERELL. Witnesses: PAUL WILKINS, PAUL HAMILTON, JOSEPH SEALY. Before THOMAS DALE, J.P. JOHN BEALE, Register.

Book C-C, p. 409
17 & 18 Apr. 1744
L & R

ALEXANDER (his mark) SMITH, tailor to JOHN REDMAN, bricklayer, both of Charleston, for Ł 225 currency, part of lot #39, fronting S 23 ft. on Tradd Street, bounding N & E on ALEXANDER SMITH; W 33 ft. on DANIEL BADGER. Witnesses: WILLIAM RANDELL, JOHN

REMINGTON. Before JACOB MOTTE, J.P. JOHN BEALE, Register.

Book C-C, p. 413   RICHARD CAPERS, planter, to THOMAS PALMER,
1 & 2 Jan. 1741   planter, both of Christ Church Parish, Berke-
L & R   ley Co., for Ł 650 currency, 115 a., English
measure, in Christ Church Parish, bounding SW
on MAJ. BENISON; NW on ANDREW RUTLEDGE; E on JOHN BENNET & MESSRS. JONES
& WHITESIDES. Witnesses: WILLIAM HENDRICK, WILLIAM GIBBES, DAVID BLAIR.
Before JOHN RUTLEDGE, J.P. JOHN BEALE, Register. Plat dated 14 Aug.
1715 also shows boundary on JOHN WINGWOOD.

Book C-C, p. 416   ROBERT BREWTON, SR., of Berkeley Co., & ROBERT
22 & 23 Apr. 1743   BREWTON, JR., gentleman, of Charleston, to
L & R   ALEXANDER SMITH, tailor, of Charleston, for
Ł 225 currency, & for other considerations on
the part of ROBERT BREWTON, SR.,; part of lot #39 bounding S 23 ft. on
Tradd Street; NE on ALEXANDER SMITH; W 33 ft. on DANIEL BADGER. Witness-
es: RICHARD MASON, JAMES PORTER. Before JACOB MOTTE, J.P. JOHN BEALE,
Register.

Book C-C, p. 420   PAUL GRIMBALL, planter, of St. John's Parish,
6 Oct. 1746   Colleton Co., to his son JOHN PAUL GRIMKE
Gift   (husband of daughter ANN) for love & affection,
1 Negro man, 1 Negro girl, bought at MRS. LARD-
ANT'S sale; Ł other Negro girl, 1 boy gelding; also 500 a. on Edisto Island surveyed by HENRY YONGE, Dep. Sur. Witnesses: JAMES REID, EDWARD
NEUFVILLE. Before OTHNIEL BEALE, J.P. JOHN BEALE, Register.

Book C-C, p. 421   EDWARD DEARSLEY (DARSLEY), Indian trader, to
26 June 1741   SARAH BLAKEWEY, widow, of Charleston, for Ł 60
Sale   currency, lot #158 in Charleston, bounding W
on a street leading to the parsonage; S on
SARAH BLAKEWEY; E on GEORGE LOGAN. Witnesses: WILLIAM HAMILTON, ANN
BALKEWEY. On 26 June 1741, for Ł 60 currency, SARAH BLAKEWEY assigned
the above lot to GEORGE LOGAN. On 25 May 1747 ELIZABETH LOGAN identified
ANN BLAKEWEY'S handwriting before JOHN RUTLEDGE, J.P. JOHN BEALE, Register.

Book C-C, p. 422   JOHN CUMING, student in divinity, to JAMES
2 & 3 Feb. 1746/7   AKIN, planter, both of the Parish of St. Thom-
L & R by Mortgage   as & St. Dennis, for Ł 140 currency, 928 a. in
Berkeley Co., bounding NW on the E branch of
the T of Cooper River; SE on BENJAMIN SIMONS; THOMAS DEARINGTON, etc., NE
on Languemare's Creek; SW on PETER BONNEAU. Date of redemption: 2 Aug.
1747. Witnesses: HUGH DURFFEY, RICHARD SIMMONS. Before JACOB MOTTE,
J.P. JOHN BEALE, Register.

Book C-C, p. 427   JOSEPH SHUTE, merchant, & ANNA his wife, to
13 Apr. 1747   MATHEW ROCHE, merchant, both of Charleston,.
Feoffment   for Ł 500 currency, 100 a. in Berkeley Co.,
bounding SW on Ashley River; NE on WILLIAM
BULL & DANIEL CARTWRIGHT; NW on THOMAS HOLTON (now EDMUND BELLINGER); SE
on JOHN DONOHOE (now JOSEPH BUTLER). Witnesses: CHARLES MCNAIRE, JOHN
RATTRAY. Before THOMAS DALE, J.P. JOHN BEALE, Register.

Book C-C, p. 429   JOHN ROYER, storekeeper, & ANNE his wife, to
14 & 15 Apr. 1747   WILLIAM HOPTON, merchant, all of Charleston,
L & R   for Ł 3250 SC money, the W half of lot #30 in
Charleston, bounding E 187 ft. on PAUL MAZYCK
(formerly ISAAC MAZYCK); S 53 ft. on Broad Street; W on vacant land since
laid for & called the New Market. Whereas by L & R Tripartite dated 15 &
16 Sept. 1719 between SUSANNAH WIGGINTON (formerly wife of RICHARD RAW-
LINGS) of 1st part; THOMAS HEPWORTH & ANNE his wife; MARY BLAMYER, widow;
& EDWARD RAWLINGS; joiner (ANNE, MARY & EDWARD being children of said ED-
WARD RAWLINGS), of 2nd part; & JOHN ROYER, cordwainer, of Charleston
(father of JOHN ROYER, party hereto, of 3rd part; reciting that SUSANNAH
WIGGINTON sold to JOHN ROYER the W half of lot #30; which he bequeathed
to his wife, HANNAH, for her lifetime all his houses & lands not otherwise devised provided she remained his widow, but should she re-marry
then only until his youngest son SAMUEL ROPER should come of age then the

estate to be divided between his sons JOHN & SAMUEL; & whereas said JOHN
ROYER died in 1722 & HANNAH afterwards married STEPHEN PROCTOR; & whereas
SAMUEL died under age, the half lot became vested in JOHN ROYER, party
hereto; now he conveys to WILLIAM HOPTON. Witnesses: LEOPOLD BOUDON,
CHARLES PRYCE. Before THOMAS DALE, J.P. JOHN BEALE, Register.

Book C-C, p. 435   HANNAH PROCTOR, widow, formerly the widow of
28 Apr. 1747   JOHN ROYER, cordwainer, of Charleston, to WIL-
Quit claim   LIAM HOPTON, merchant, of Charleston, all her
                        title of dower & interest in the W half of lot
#30 in Charleston, formerly the estate of her former husband, JOHN ROYER,
& now purchased by WILLIAM HOPTON, from JOHN ROYER, the son by L & R dated 14 & 15 this Apr. (p. 429). Witnesses: LEOPOLD BOUDON, CHARLES PRYCE.
Before THOMAS DALE, J.P. JOHN BEALE, Register.

Book C-C, p. 437   MARY TOOMER of Stono, widow & executrix of
8 Aug. 1747   HENRY TOOMER, to JOHN TOOMER, JR., for Ł 50
Sale   currency, all her right to JOHN TOOMER, JR.'s.
                        plantation in St. Andrews Parish, & the dwel-
ling-house & kitchen left her by his father, HENRY TOOMER. Witnesses:
WILLIAM CHAPMAN, DAVID TOOMER. Before JACOB MOTTE, J.P. JOHN BEALE, Register.

Book C-C, p. 437   JOHN ALEXANDER PARRIS, gentleman, to JOSEPH
27 & 28 May 1746   SHUTE, merchant, of Charleston, for Ł 300 cur-
L & R   rency, 224 a. of marsh land in Berkeley Co.
                        Whereas Gov. ROBERT GIBBES & the Lords Proprs.
on Aug. 1711 granted COL. ALEXANDER PARRIS 224 a. of marsh land in Berkeley Co., bounding E & S on Ashley River; W on Cooper River; N on Hogg Island Creek; which he, by will dated 6 Feb. 1735 bequeathed to his son,
JOHN PARRIS; & which he, by will dated 6 Aug. 1736, bequeathed to his son,
JOHN ALEXANDER PARRIS, with the proviso that in case of his son's death
his nephew, of same name, should inherit; & whereas son JOHN ALEXANDER
died soon after his father's death, & nephew JOHN ALEXANDER PARRIS inherited; now he sells the marsh land to SHUTE. Witnesses: JOHN CHAMPNEYS,
THOMAS LANKESTER. Before ALEXANDER STEWART, J.P. JOHN BEALE, Register.

Book C-C, p. 443   DAVID MUNGIN (MONGIN), watchmaker, to JOHN
3 Aug. 1747   GORSSER, bar maker, both of Charleston, for
Feoffment   Ł 130 currency (payment being secured by a
                       bond); a lot in Ansonsburgh, bounding N 137 ft.
on JOSEPH MEXIE; S on DAVID MUNGIN; E on JOHN DART; W 30 ft. on a street
newly laid out; being part of a lot purchased by MUNGIN from BENJAMIN
WHITAKER, attorney to GEORGE ANSON & marked O on the plan of ANSON'S land.
Witnesses: STEPHEN TONSSIGER, WILLIAM MOUAT. Before JAMES MICKIE, J.P.
JOHN BEALE, Register.

Book C-C, p. 445   JOSHUA TOOMER, of St. Pauls Parish, Colleton
10 & 11 July 1747   Co., to JOHN WATSON, merchant, of Charleston,
L & R by Mortgage   as security on bond dated 29 Nov. 1746 in pe-
                       nal sum of Ł 317:3:8 for payment of
Ł 158:11:10 currency, with interest, on 1 May 1747; 400 a. in Colleton
Co., bounding E on JAMES HARTLEY; N on THOMAS ELLIOTT; W on THOMAS SAN-
DERS; S on ROBERT MCKEWN. Witnesses: WILLIAM MOULTRIE, WILLIAM DANDY.
Before OTHNIEL BEALE, J.P. JOHN BEALE, Register.

Book C-C, p. 450   MARY (her mark) ALLEN (ALINE, ALEINE), widow,
7 Sept. 1746   of St. Andrews Parish, Berkeley Co., to her
Gift   loving son, JOHN STARLING, & her daughter MARY
                       STARLING, for love & affection, her interest
(at her death), in a lease of 10 a. on James Island which said JOHN STAR-
LING & MARY his wife, gave to BENJAMIN STILES on 15 Dec. 1726; which
lease STILES, sometime after, made over to ZEBULON GUY; & GUY, on 15 May
last, made over to MARY ALLEN. Witnesses: ELSWORTH DARVELL, WILLIAM LAN-
CASTER. Before THOMAS LAMBOLL, J.P. JOHN BEALE, Register.

Book C-C, p. 451   MARMADUKE AISH, saddler, to SAMUEL SMART, mer-
11 & 12 Aug. 1747   chant, & CATHARINE, his wife, all of Charles-
L & R by Mortgage   ton, as security on bond of even date in penal
                       sum of Ł 2400 for Ł 1200 currency, with

145

interest, on 12 Aug. 1749; the E part of lot #26 & the brick house there-
on where SAMUEL SMART now lives; bounding E on ISAAC HOLMES; S on DANIEL
BOURGET; W on part of same lot; N on Broad Street. Witnesses: JOHN RAT-
TRAY, JAMES GRINDLAY. Before DANIEL CRAWFORD, J.P. JOHN BEALE, Regis-
ter. On 14 June 1748 CATHERINE SMART declared mortgage satisfied. JOHN
BEALE, Register.

Book C-C, p. 456   JOHN HUTCHINS, of Charleston, to BENJAMIN GOD-
16 & 17 Mar. 1746   FREY, of Berkeley Co., as security on bond of
L & R by Mortgage   even date in penal sum of Ł 600 for payment of
                          Ł 300 currency on 26 Mar. 1748; 34 a. in St.
Andrews Parish, part of the land devised by RICHARD GODFREY (father of
said BENJAMIN) to his children & the part allotted to BENJAMIN by partition; bounding N on BENJAMIN GODFREY; E on JOHN RIVERS; S on marsh of
Stono River; W on BENJAMIN HEAPE; also so much of a Pine Island adjacent
to said tract as lies W of the W line of JOHN RIVERS'S land is continued
across the island; also the small island W of said island; also his interest in the marsh land. Witnesses: WILLIAM BURROWS, JOHN SCOTT. Before JOHN LINING, J.P. JOHN BEALE, Register. On 27 July 1753 BENJAMIN
GODFREY declared mortgage satisfied. Witness: THOMAS LINTHWAITE.

Book C-C, p. 462   THOMAS BURTIN, planter, & ELIZABETH his wife,
30 & 31 Jan. 1746/7   to JOSEPH WHITE, planter, both of Craven Co.,
L & R   for Ł 55 currency, 300 a. in Craven Co., on a
                          small branch of Black Mingo Swamp, bounding on
all sides on vacant land. Witnesses: EDWARD HOWARD, GEORGE (his mark)
HOWARD, SARAH BRITTON. Before WILLIAM FLEMING, J.P. JOHN BEALE, Register.

Book C-C, p. 465   STEPHEN BULL, of Newbury near Radnor, Gran-
7 July 1747   ville Co., to WILLIAM BULL, JR., of St. An-
Mortgage   drew's Parish, Berkeley Co., as security for
                          going on STEPHEN'S bond, dated 1 May last,
given HENRY PERONNEAU, of St. Philip's Parish, Charleston, in penal sum
of Ł 4800 for payment of Ł 2400 on 26 Mar. 1749; all his 31 slaves. Witnesses: WILLIAM BULL, MARY H. BULL. Before OTHNIEL BEALE, J.P. JOHN
BEALE, Register. On 28 Nov. 1759 WILLIAM BULL declared mortgage satisfied. Witness: WILLIAM HOPTON.

Book C-C, p. 469   CULCHETH GIBBES, planter, of St. Bartholomew's
29 & 30 Dec. 1746   Parish, to EDWARD FENWICKE, ESQ., of Charles-
L & R by Mortgage   ton, for Ł 673 currency, 500 a. in Colleton
                          Co., on N & S sides of Fish Ponds Creek com-
monly called Ashepoo River, bounding S & W on JOHN WOODWARD; N on THOMAS
CORD; E on vacant land; which tract was granted on 28 Apr. 1733 by Gov.
ROBERT JOHNSON to JOHN GIBBES; also 5 Negro slaves. Date of redemption:
1 Jan. 1747. A pocketbook delivered in leiu of the Negroes. Witnesses:
JOHN GIBBES, JOHN BASSNETT. Before JOHN CHAMPNEYS, J.P. JOHN BEALE,
Register.

Book C-C, p. 474   MAGDALENE ELIZABETH IZARD, widow, of the Hon.
8 Aug. 1745   RALPH IZARD, of St. James Goose Creek Parish,
Deed of Partition   Berkeley Co., & granddaughter & devisee of
                          PETER BURTELL, merchant, of Charleston, of 1st
part; NATHANIEL BROUGHTON, ESQ., of St. John's, Berkeley Co., & CHARLOTTE
HENRIETTA, his wife, another granddaughter & devisee of PETER BURTELL, of
2nd part; PAUL MAZYCK, planter, of St. James Goose Creek, & CATHARINE his
wife, great-granddaughter of PETER BURTELL & granddaughter & heir-at-law
of ALEXANDER JESSE CHAILAIGNER, ESQ., of 3rd part. Whereas PETER BURTELL
was seized in his demesne as of fee in 5 lots in Charleston, Nos. 165,
166, 167, 179, & 180, & by will dated 22 Jan. 1701 bequeathed all his estate, after the death of his wife, ELIZABETH BURTELL equally to his
grandchildren, ALEXANDER CHAILAIGNER, (father of said CATHARINE MAZYCK);
MAGDALENE ELIZABETH CHALAIGNER (now MAGDALENE ELIZABETH IZARD); & CHAR-
LOTTE HENRIETTA CHAILAIGNER (now CHARLOTTE HENRIETTA BROUGHTON); & whereas ALEXANDER died, leaving said CATHERINE his only daughter & heir-at-law;
& whereas MAGDALENE ELIZABETH IZARD, NATHANIEL & CHARLOTTA HENRIETTA
BROUGHTON & PAUL & CAHTARINE MAZYCK have agreed to an equal partition &
allotment of the 5 lots & have allotted to MAGDALENE ELIZABETH IZARD lot
#180; to NATHANIEL & CHARLOTTE HENRIETTA BROUGHTON lots #165 & #167; & to

146

PAUL & CATHARINE MAZYCK lots #166 & 179; now each of them agrees to accept the allotment given them. Witnesses: ALEXANDER CRAMAHE, HENRY IZARD. Before OTHNIEL BEALE, J.P. JOHN BEALE, Reigster.

Book C-C, p. 478   JOHN CUMING, of the Parish of St. Thomas & St.
15 Aug. 1747   Dennis, Berkeley Co., for natural love & pa-
Gift   ternal affection, to his son BENJAMIN CUMING,
                         & to _____ CUMING, his unborn child; all his
real & personal estate, except 135 a. (which he had by right of his wife,
& by purchase from JOSEPH BEECH) which he gave to his daughter ANNE CUM-
ING. Whereas JOHN BLAKE, of said Parish, sold 100 a. which he had purchased from JOHNSON LYNCH & MARGARET his wife; & whereas PETER TAMPLET
sold to said JOHN CUMING 135 a. in said Parish (but the title being pre-
carious, CUMING purchased it again from JOSEPH BEECH, a memorial being
entered in Auditor's Office); & whereas CUMING HAD 135 a. in right of his
wife, GRACE BEECH, & her right being disputable he again purchased it
from JOSEPH BEECH (see conveyance of all the lands on Cooper River in St.
Thomas's Parish belonging to JOSEPH BEECH); & whereas JOSEPH BEECH sold
to JOHN CUMING a tract of 170 a., & another of 100 a., on E branch of the
T of Cooper River (memorials entered in Auditor's office); & whereas
CHRISTOPHER BEECH sold to JOHN CUMING 121 a. on E branch of the T of
Cooper River, bounding SW on CUMING'S other lands; NE on Languemare's
Creek; & whereas RICHARD HEATLY of said Parish sold CUMING 60 a. on the W
branch of the T of Cooper River; & whereas WILLIAM NICHOLAS & MARY his
wife sold CUMING 100 a. on the E branch, being a third part of 300 a.
which CHRISTOPHER BEECH bequeathed to his son JOHN BEECH (THOMAS DEARING-
TON having purchased the other 200 a.); & whereas JOHN CUMING owned a
small personal or movable estate, viz: a Negro man, several horses, mares,
cattle, household furniture, books, bonds, leases, etc., etc.; now JOHN
CUMING gives his property (except as excepted) equally to his son BENJA-
MIN & to his unborn child. Witnesses: GUILLAUME GALLATIN, JOHN COYTE.
Livery & seizin delivered to son BENJAMIN & to NAOMI CUMING (wife of
JOHN). JOHN CUMING reserves (1) right to fill in blank spaces with the
name of the now unborn child after it is baptized; (2) the donees not to
sell any part of the property until they are 25 years old; but (3) when
BENJAMIN is 21 years old each may choose 2 or 3 men to divide the estate
(except ANNE'S share) into equal parts; (4) the estate is indebted to
JAMES AKIN in sum of ₺ 255, which JOHN CUMING is to pay partly out of the
real estate & partly out of the personal estate. Before HENRY GIBBES,
J.P. JOHN BEALE, Register.

Book C-C, p. 483   RAWLINS LOWNDES, Provost Marshall of SC, by
15 Oct. 1747   writ of fieri facias dated 7 Oct. 1746 from
Sale   JOHN LINING, Ass't. J. of Ct. of C.P., in ab-
                         sence of BENJAMIN WHITAKER, C.J. commanding
him to levy a debt of ₺ 1082:18 currency on the houses, lands, Negroes,
real estate, etc., formerly belonging to THOMAS STOCK, planter, of Chehaw,
which amount JOHN WATSONE, merchant, of Charleston, had recovered by
judgement against RACHAEL STOCK, widow & executrix of will of THOMAS
STOCK; at public auction, to said RACHEL STOCK, widow; for ₺ 632 currency, 432 a. in Colleton Co., bounding E on Cheraw River; S on ISAAC SMART;
W on vacant land; N on the Glebe land. Witness: CHARLES PRYCE (gentleman). Before HENRY GIBBES, J.P. JOHN BEALE, Register.

Book C-C, p. 484   WILLIAM HULL, tailor, & ANN his wife, of Col-
31 July & 1 Aug. 1747   leton Co., to ELIZABETH SNIPES, executrix of
L & R by Mortgage   will of ABRAHAM MESHEW, as security on a bond
                         of even date in penal sum of ₺ 800 for payment
of ₺ 400 SC money, with interest, on 1 Aug. 1748; 200 a. in Colleton Co.,
bounding S on CAPT. JOHN COCK & JOHN WILLIAMSON; all other sides on Horse
Shoe Savannah & its swamp; as by plat & grant dated 21 June 1709; also
71 a. in Colleton Co., in Horse Shoe Savannah, as by grant dated 28 Apr.
1733. Witnesses: WILLIAM SMYES, WILLIAM HARDEN, JACOB (his mark) SPICER.
Before HENRY HYRNE, J.P. JOHN BEALE, Register.

Book C-C, p. 488   WILLIAM CHAMBERS, planter & tailor, of Wadma-
3 Nov. 1747   law Island, St. Johns Parish, Colleton Co., to
Mortgage   HENRY SHIRRIF, planter, of James Island,
                         Berkeley Co., as security on bond of even date
in penal sum of ₺ 7062 for payment of ₺ 3531 SC money, on 1 Feb. next;

17 slaves; also 300 a. on Wadmalaw Island, called Bugby's Hole, with the
buildings; also 10 horses & mares, his neat cattle, hogs, sheep, 1 canoe,
household goods, & chattles of every kind. Witnesses: RICHARD KENT,
ARCHIBALD HAMILTON. One Negro boy delivered in name of whole. Before
DANIEL PEPPER, J.P. JOHN BEALE, Register.

Book C-C, p. 489   HENRY IZARD, ESQ., of Charleston, of 1st. part;
30 Apr. 1747   PAUL MAZYCK, gentleman, & CATHERINE his wife,
Agreement   of St. James Goose Creek Parish, Berkeley Co.,
                    of 2nd part; CATHERINE (her mark) TAYLOR, wid-
ow, of St. Johns Parish, Berkeley Co., of 3rd part; RENE RAVENEL, gentle-
man, of St. John's Parish, Berkeley Co., (in behalf of his sons, HENRY,
DANIEL & JAMES RAVENEL) of 4th part. Whereas HENRY IZARD owns lot #180
in Charleston, bounding E on New Church Street, & whereas PAUL & CATHER-
INE MAZYCK own lot #179 bounding W on Old Church Street & whereas CATHER-
INE TAYLOR owns lot #175 bounding on New Church Street, & whereas RENE
RAVENEL (in behalf of his 3 sons) owns lot #174, bounding on Old Church
Street, & whereas, for the ease, improvement & conveniency of their lots,
& the public use & utility of the town, they have mutually consented &
agreed to leave a street, 22 ft. wide, through their lots, running from
New Church Street, to Old Church Street, that is, 11 ft. on the S sides
of lots #174 & #175, & 11 ft. on the N sides of lots #180 & #179; now, to
confirm the agreement & make it effectual they severally & respectively
consent, grant & agree, each with the other, that 11 ft. shall be taken
from each of the lots on the N side & 11 ft. from each of the lots on the
S side making a street 22 ft. wide, to remain forever an open & public
street in Charleston. Witnesses: DAVID LAFONS, RENE RAVENEL, JR., ISAAC
MAZYCK. Before JACOB MOTTE, J.P. JOHN BEALE, Register.

Book C-C, p. 491   HENRY WILLIAMSON, planter, of St. Pauls Parish,
20 June 1742   Colleton Co., to BENJAMIN WILLIAMSON, of same
Bond   Parish, in penal sum of Ł 4000 for payment of
                    Ł 2000 currency. Should he (HNERY) at any
time, by course of law or otherwise, recover certain tracts of land; namely: (1) 640 a. which BENJAMIN WILLIAMSON now plants, near Spoons Savannah,
bounding N & E on WILLIAM WILLIAMSON, deceased; W on JAMES RIXAM; S on MR.
SPRY; (2) 100 a. adjoining Spoons Savannah, bounding on all sides on WIL-
LIAM WILLIAMSON, deceased; (3) the land lying between the Broad Path &
the middle of Stono River, being a part of 1000 a. between the middle & S
branch Stono River, bounding N on the middle branch; E on MRS. ANN WAKE-
FIELD; S on JACOB BEAMOR; W on land not laid out; & being part of the
tract he (HENRY WILLIAMSON) sold to HENRY HAYWOOD. Witnesses: GEORGE
WILLIAMSON, DAVID CRAWFORD, JOHN SMITH. Before HENRY GIBBES, J.P. JOHN
BEALE, Register.

Book C-C, p. 493   SAMUEL JONES, planter, of Jones Island, Colle-
21 & 22 May 1747   ton Co., to BENJAMIN D'HARRIETTE, merchant, of
L & R by Mortgage   Charleston, as security on bond dated 20 May
                    1747 in penal sum of Ł 7000 for payment of
Ł 3500 currency, with interest, on 20 May 1748; 2500 a. at head of Cayaw,
Colleton Co., part being an island commonly called Jones Island, the remainder adjoining thereto, which tract was devised to him by will of his
father, SAMUEL JONES, dated 5 Aug. 1736; & delivers (subject to proviso)
27 slaves. REBECCA JONES, wife of SAMUEL to renounce her dower after default. One Negro delivered. Witnesses: RIBTON HUTCHINSON, PROVIDENCE
HUTCHINSON, (gentlewoman). Before HENRY GIBBES, J.P. JOHN BEALE, Register. On 6 May 1755 BENJAMIN D'HARRIETTE declared mortgage satisfied.
Witness: PETER MONCLAR.

Book C-C, p. 499   NATHANIEL BRANCHHURST WICKHAM (eldest son &
8 Jan. 1746   heir-at-law of NATHANIEL WICKHAM, ESQ., of
Release & Confirmation Berkeley Co.), & JAMES HARTLEY, the only act-
                    ing executors of will of NATHANIEL WICKHAM;
for 20 shillings currency, release & confirm to WILLIAM RIND, 133 a. of
land. Whereas NATHANIEL WICKHAM & MARY his wife, on 20 July 1739 conveyed to JOSIAH BAKER, of St. George's Parish, Berkele- Co., 133 a. (part of
1790 a.) bounding NW on JOHN GOLDING & the estate of SAMUEL CLARK; NE on
ROBERT WRIGHT; SE on the public road from Stevens Bridge to Stono Chapel;
SW on JOHN GOLDING & DR. WILLIAM RIND (formerly MRS. SUSANNAH BAKER); &
whereas the 133 a. by divers mesne conveyances became vested in WILLIAM

RIND in fee simple; now the executors of NATHANIEL WICKHAM confirm RIND'S
title. Witnesses: JOHN FOQUET (FOUQUET), CHARLES CALDER. Before JAMES
WRIGHT, J.P. JOHN BEALE, Register.

Book C-C, p. 501   THOMAS BUTLER, planter, & ELIZABETH his wife,
2 & 3 June 1746   of Prince William Parish, Granville Co., to
L & R   WILLIAM RIND, gentleman, of Charleston, for
                          ₺ 1100 currency, 2 contiguous plantations of
100 & 128 a.; also certain lots at Ashley River Ferry Town. Whereas JO-
SIAH BAKER owned 2 adjoining plantations, 1 of 100 a. devised to him by
his mother SUSANNAH BAKER, the other of 128 a., which he purchased from
NATHANIEL WICKHAM; making 1 tract of 228 a. at Cow Savannah, Berkeley Co.,
bounding according to play by JOHN STEVENS annexed to lease; & whereas
JOSIAH BAKER by will dated 9 Nov. 1742 bequeathed to his wife REBECCA the
above property; & whereas REBECCA BAKER also owned sundry lots at Ashley
River Ferry Town; & whereas she later married WILLIAM RIND & soon after,
in July 1745, died intestate & without issue & the land descended to
THOMAS BUTLER, party hereto, as her eldest brother & heir-at-law; now he
conveys to RIND. Witnesses: ELISHA BUTLER, JOHN WATSONE, WILLIAM MOUL-
TRIE. Before JAMES WRIGHT, J.P. JOHN BEALE, Register.

Book C-C, p. 503   Plat dated 23 Apr. 1745 by JOHN STEVENS of
                          228 a. on S side Ashley River in St. George's
Parish, 128 a. of which were purchased from MAJ. WICKHAM by JOSIAH BAKER;
the other 100 a. being part of a tract left to JOSIAH BAKER by his mother,
SUSANNAH BAKER; which 228 a. were left by JOSIAH BAKER to his wife REBEC-
CA, & now in possession of DR. WILLIAM RIND who married said REBECCA
BAKER; bounding NW on HENRY IZARD, JOHN GOULDING & estate of SAMUEL
CLARKE; NE on ROBERT WRIGHT; SE on the public road & JOHN GOULDING; SW on
land left by JOSIAH BAKER to the children of RICHARD BAKER.

Book C-C, p. 507   JAMES CROKATT, merchant, formerly of Charles-
22 & 23 July 1747   ton, SC, now of London, by his attorneys, EB-
L & R   ENEZER SIMMONS & BENJAMIN SMITH, merchants, of
                          Charleston; to SOLOMON LEGARE, JR., of Charles-
ton; for ₺ 2000 currency, 540 a. in SC. Whereas WILLIAM WILKINS, planter,
of James Island owned 540 a., part of 640 a. on SW side Stono River, in
Colleton Co., bounding N on JOHN PRESCOTT & ROBERT COLE; E on said PRES-
COTT & ELIZABETH GODFREY; S on JOHN GODFREY & PAUL TORQUET; W on other
part of said 640 a. adjoining PAUL TORQUET; & whereas WILLIAM WILKINS &
SARAH his wife, by L & R dated 1 & 2 June 1739 mortgaged the 540 a. to
JAMES CROKATT for ₺ 763:5 British payable 1 Jan. 1740; & whereas on 9
Oct. 1744, after the death of WILKINS, CROKATT filed his bill in the
Court of Chancery against the heir-at-law & executors of WILKINS to com-
pel them to redeem the mortgaged premises, to which bill the defendants
answered & on 28 May last CROKATT obtained final decree foreclosing the
estate; & whereas JAMES CROKATT now of London, on 23 Aug. 1744 appointed
EBENEZER SIMMONS, BENJAMIN SMITH, GEORGE SEAMAN, GEORGE AUSTIN, & ROBERT
RAPER, merchants, of Charleston, his attorneys, to foreclose & dispose of
the property; now SIMMONS & SMITH sell the 540 a. to LEGARE. Witnesses:
JOHN MILNER, JOHN REMINGTON. Before JACOB MOTTE, J.P. JOHN BEALE, Register.

Book C-C, p. 514   JOSEPH MOODY, to SOLOMON LEGARE, gentleman,
10 Aug. 1742   both of Charleston, as security on bond of
Mortgage   even date in penal sum of ₺ 1600 for payment
                          of ₺ 800 currency, with interest, on 10 Aug.
1743, part of a lot in Charleston fronting 18 ft. on Tradd Street, 92 ft.
deep; with all the buildings thereon, known as "By the sign of the Griffin". Witnesses: JOHN SAVAGE, BENJAMIN SAVAGE. Before THOMAS LAMBOLL,
J.P. JOHN BEALE, Register.

Book C-C, p. 515   ESTHER ELLIOTT, widow & devisee of SHEM BUTLER,
7 & 8 Oct. 1741   planter, of St. Andrews Parish, Berkeley Co.,
L & R   to ELIZABETH BELLINGER, widow of Landgrave ED-
                          MOND BELLINGER, of same place; for ₺ 330 cur-
rency, 33 a. Whereas RICHARD BUTLER & EDMOND BELLINGER, executors, of
will of SHEM BUTLER, allotted to ESTHER ELLIOT as her share of SHEM BUT-
LER'S estate, 280 a. on NW side of the Ferry Path on high road leading
from Ashley River Ferry to Stono, in St. Andrews Parish, Berkeley Co.

Also, 33 a. on the SE side of said Ferry Path, bounding SE on CHARLES JONES; SW & NE on the land allotted to ELIZABETH BELLINGER by the executors; now ESTHER ELLIOTT conveys to ELIZABETH BELLINGER. Witnesses: JOHN WATSONE, WILLIAM BRANFORD, JR., WILLIAM BUCHANAN. Before OTHNIEL BEALE, J.P. JOHN BEALE, Register.

Book C-C, p. 521　　　　　WILLIAM ELLIOTT, ESQ., & FRANCIS his wife, of
5 & 6 May 1743　　　　　　Berkeley Co., to ELIZABETH BELLINGER, widow of
L & R & Assignment　　　　Landgrave EDMUND BELLINGER, of Butlers, Berke-
　　　　　　　　　　　　　ley Co., for Ꝉ 100 currency, 1/2 a lot at Ashley Ferry adjoining Butler Town, bounding NW on the Broad Street, of the
town; SE on the other half sold by WILLIAM ELLIOTT to WILLIAM CATTLE
(CATTELL), ESQ.; NE on Ashley River. Whereas the half lot came to WIL-
LIAM ELLIOTT by deed of gift dated 11 Mar. 1722 from SHEM BUTLER in part
of dower with WILLIAM'S then wife ESTHER; & whereas WILLIAM & FRANCES
ELLIOTT on 19 Feb. 1733 sold to WILLIAM CATTLE a half lot which CATTLE on
5 July 1740 sold to ELIZABETH & made over by indorsement on back of said
deed; now WILLIAM ELLIOTT promises that all deeds & writings shall at all
times be produced to confirm the title. Witnesses: JOHN SNELLING, ANDREW
BROUGHTON. Before OTHNIEL BEALE, J.P. JOHN BEALE, Register.

Book C-C, p. 525　　　　　JAMES MANNING, shoemaker, of St. Andrews Par-
3 & 4 Aug. 1747　　　　　　ish, to ELIZABETH BELLINGER ELLIOTT (lately
L & R　　　　　　　　　　　widow & executrix of will of EDMUND BELLINGER,
　　　　　　　　　　　　　the 2nd Landgrave) for Ꝉ 613 currency, 100 a.,
part of 250 a., in Berkeley Co. Whereas FRANCIS LADSON, planter, of
Berkeley Co., by deed of feoffment dated 27 Mar. 1724, conveyed to SAMUEL
WEST 250 a., bounding N on FRANCIS LADSON; E on CHARLES WEST; S & S on
STEPHEN DRAYTON; & whereas SAMUEL WEST son & heir of said SAMUEL WEST &
brother of WILLOBY (WILLOUGHBY) WEST, by deed of gift dated 8 Apr. 1734
gave WILLOBY WEST 100 a., part of the 250 a.; & whereas said WILLOUGHBY
WEST by L & R dated 8 & 9 July 1742, for Ꝉ 700 currency, conveyed the
100 a. to JAMES MANNING; now MANNING sells to ELIZABETH ELLIOTT. Witnesses: JANE HILL, WILLIAM BACKSHALL. Before OTHNIEL BEALE, J.P. JOHN BEALE,
Register.

Book C-C, p.　　　　　　　HENRY WILLIAMSON, planter, to HENRY HEYWOOD,
16 Mar. 1742　　　　　　　 clerk (cleric?) both of Colleton Co., for good
Sale　　　　　　　　　　　 causes & considerations & for Ꝉ 370; 200 a. on
　　　　　　　　　　　　　 Log Bridge Creek, part of 1000 a. on W side of
middle branch of Stono River, formerly purchased from the Lords Proprs.
by JOHN WILLIAMSON, cordwainer. Witnesses: BENJAMIN WILLIAMSON, BENJAMIN
HARVEY, WILLIAM BUTLER. Delivery by turf & twig. Before THOMAS DALE,
J.P. JOHN BEALE, Register.

Book C-C, p. 530　　　　　JOHN TERRY, late recorder of Frederica, in
7 Aug. 1746　　　　　　　　Colony of Georgia, to MARY DAVIS, of Charles-
Sale　　　　　　　　　　　 ton, for Ꝉ 500 currency, his plantation near
　　　　　　　　　　　　　 Frederica, with his share of household goods,
& the remaining period of his apprentice's (JOHN RAGNOUS) time of indenture. Witnesses: MARK ANTHONY BESSELLEN, FRANCIS (his mark) DELGRASS.
Before DANIEL CRAWFORD, J.P. JOHN BEALE, Register.

Book C-C, p. 530　　　　　PETER TAMPLET, & ISABELLA his wife, of Prince
12 June 1736　　　　　　　 Frederick Parish, Winyaw, to THOMAS DEARINGTON,
Release　　　　　　　　　　planter, of St. Thomas Parish, for Ꝉ 300 cur-
　　　　　　　　　　　　　 rency, 200 a. in Berkeley Co., on E side of T
of Cooper River, bounding S on WILLIAM NICHOLS; E on JOHN ASHBY; W on
JOHN CUMING; being part of 300 a. granted by the Lords Proprs., their
commission dated 8 July 1704. Witnesses: PHILLIP LAKE, DAVID MEKANE,
JOHN BLAKE. Before JOHN WALLIS, J.P. JOHN BEALE, Register.

DEEDS BOOK "D-D"
DEC. 1747 - JULY 1748

Book D-D, p. 1　　　　　　FRANCIS CLARK, bricklayer of Charleston, to
10 Nov. 1747　　　　　　　 ROBERT SCOTT, vintner, of Charleston, as se-
Mortgage　　　　　　　　　 curity on bond of even date in penal sum of

150

Ŀ 296:16:6 for payment of Ŀ 148:8:3 SC money, with interest, on 1 Feb.
next; a lot in Ansonburgh on which he is now building, fronting S 27 ft.
on a street newly laid out; bounding E 110 ft. on a lot laid out by DAVID
MONGIN to WILLIAM HARRIS; other sides on DAVID MONGIN. Witness: WILLIAM
MORGAN. Before OTHNIEL BEALE, J.P. JOHN BEALE, Register.

Book D-D, p. 2   JOHN GEORGE DALLABACH, bricklayer, & JOANNA
4 & 5 Dec. 1747   ELIZABETH his wife, of St. Philips Parish,
L & R by Mortgage   Charleston, to FRANCIS VARAMBAUT, physician,
                        of Charleston, as security on bond dated 4
this Dec. in penal sum of Ŀ 460 for payment of Ŀ 230 SC money, with interest, on 4 Dec. 1750; that piece of land on Charleston Neck bounding NE
on the Broad Path leading to Charleston; SW on the parsonage or lands belonging to the Free School; NW on JAMES VOUBOUX (lately granted him by
said DALLABACH); SE on JOSEPH WRAGG; being 25 ft. in breadth from JAMES
VOULOUX along the Broad Path; & 416 ft. in depth from the Broad Path; being part of the land conveyed by JOSEPH WRAGG to DALLABACH. Witnesses:
ABRAHAM SNELLING, JOHN REMINGTON. Before JACOB MOTTE, J.P. JOHN BEALE,
Register. On 19 Feb. 1752 FRANCIS VARAMBAUT declared mortgage satisfied.
Witness: WILLIAM HOPTON.

Book D-D, p. 6   RAWLINS LOWNDES, Provost Marshall of SC, to
24 Nov. 1747   JAMES MARION, planter, of Berkeley Co., at
Sale on Execution   public outcry, for Ŀ 220 currency; 220 a.,
                        English measure, on W branch of Goose Creek,
formerly bounding E & N on RALPH IZARD; S on JOHN MOORE; W on ROBERT
ADAMS; according to original grant from the Lords Proprs. to ISAAC FLEURY.
Whereas PETER MARION, planter, of Berkeley Co., owned 220 a. on Goose
Creek, &, dying intestate, his brother JAMES MARION, as brother & next of
kin, obtained from Gov. JAMES GLEN letters of administration of the estate; & whereas PETER MARION gave bond dated 9 Oct. 1744 to BENJAMIN GO-
DON, gentleman, of Berkeley Co., in penal sum of Ŀ 90 for payment of Ŀ 45
currency, & gave a bond dated 22 Dec. 1744 to WILLIAM YEOMANS, merchant,
in penal sum of Ŀ 511:15 for payment of Ŀ 255:17:6 currency; & whereas,
after the death of PETER MARION, GODIN & YEOMANS brought 2 actions
against JAMES MARION, administrator of the estate, for recovery of the 2
sums & obtained judgments & costs; & whereas it had been enacted by Parliment that after 29 Sept. 1732, the lands, Negroes, real estate, etc.,
of a debtor would be chargeable with all debts owing by such person; &
whereas 2 suits of fieri facias were issued; now the land is sold to
JAMES MARION, the highest bidder. Witnesses: CHARLES LOWNDES, LEOPOLD
BOUDON. Before CHARLES PINCKNEY, J.P. JOHN BEALE, Register.

Book D-D, p. 10   JOSHUA TOOMER, planter, of St. Andrews Parish,
29 Nov. 1746   Berkeley Co., to MATHURINE GUERINE; ELISHA
Mortgage   BUTLER & WILLIAM BUTLER, trustees of the Bap-
                        tist Church at Stono, as security on bond of
even date in penal sum of Ŀ 513:18:6 for payment of Ŀ 256:19:3 currency,
with interest, on 25 Mar. next; 150 a. on which TOOMER lives, with marsh
land, buildings & tan yards; bounding N & E on marsh & JOSEPH ELLIOTT; W
on MATHURINE GUERINE; S on Stono River. Penknife delivered to WILLIAM
BUTLER in lieu of premises. Witnesses: STEPHEN ELLIOTT, BENJAMIN BUTLER,
DAVID TOOMER. Before JOHN CHAMPNEYS, J.P. JOHN BEALE, Register.

Book D-D, p. 12   DANIEL CRAWFORD, planter, of Christ Church
26 & 27 May 1747   Parish, to the Society for the Propagation of
L & R by Mortgage   the Gospel in Foreign Parts, as security on
                        bond of even date in penal sum of Ŀ 2400 for
payment of Ŀ 1200 SC money, with interest, on 27 May 1748; part of lot
#12 in Charleston, bounding E 100 ft. on MARY ELLIS; W on PETER BENOIST
(formerly MRS. DILL); N 30 ft. on Broad Street; S 37 ft. 2 in. on JOSEPH
WRAGG (formerly ISAAC CALLEFEUFF). Witnesses: JOHN RATTRAY, JAMES GRIND-
LAY. Before JOHN LINING, J.P. JOHN BEALE, Register. On 14 July 1749
ALEXANDER GARDEN declared mortgage satisfied.

Book D-D, p. 15   JAMES MARION, planter, of Goose Creek, son &
29 & 30 Nov. 1747   devisee of BENJAMIN MARION, planter, to the
L & R by Mortgage   Rev. MR. ALEXANDER GARDEN, Rector of St.
                        Philip's Parish, Charleston; HENRY IZARD of
St. James Goose Creek; attorneys for the Society for the Propagation of

the Gospel in Foreign Parts; as security on bond of even date for payment
of ₺ 1000 currency, with interest, on 30 Nov. 1748; 3 tracts of 220 a.,
100 a., & 105 a., total 425 a. Whereas BENJAMIN MARION owned 220 a. at
head of Yeoman's Creek, now called Goose Creek, in Berkeley Co., bounding
S on JOHN MOORE; W on ROBERT ADAMS; E on RALPH IZARD; N on vacant land at
time of original grant from Lords Proprs. on 28 Mar. 1694 to ISAAC FLEURY;
which 220 a. were conveyed by FLEURY by deed of feofment dated 22 Feb.
1712 to BENJAMIN MARION; & whereas BENJAMIN MARION owned 100 a. at head
of Yeoman's Creek (now Goose Creek), bounding E on RALPH IZARD; N on
RALPH IZARD & JOHN BERRINGES; W on BENJAMIN MARION & FRANCIS GARING;
which 100 a. was granted by the Lords Proprs. on 5 May 1704 in 2 parts
(90 & 10 a.) to BENJAMIN MARION; & whereas BENJAMIN MARION owned the 105
a., part of 230 a., at head of Goose Creek, formerly belonging to JOHN
BERRINGER & by several mesne conveyances vested in JOHN GIBBES, gentleman,
who by L & R on 4 & 5 Apr. 1720 sold to BENJAMIN MARION; the 230 a.,
bounding N on JOHN GIBBES; NW on PETER BACOT; SW on BENJAMIN MARION; SE
on RALPH IZARD; being 125 a. of the N end of 1230 a. sold by BENJAMIN
MARION to RALPH IZARD, leaving only 105 a. with MARION; & whereas MARION
owned the 3 adjoining tracts of 220, 100 & 105 a., total 425 a., & by
will in French dated 13 Jan. 1734 devised all his lands at Goose Creek to
his 2 sons, PETER MARION & JAMES MARION, PETER to have his choice in the
division, with this proviso, that either of them dying without issue, his
share to go to survivor; & whereas each of them married & they became
tenants in common & they agreed to divide the 425 a.; & whereas the tract
of 220 a. was allotted to PETER & the 2 tracts of 100 & 105 a. to JAMES;
& whereas PETER died intestate & several actions were brought against the
administrator & the 220 a. seized for debts & sold on 25 inst Nov. by the
Provost Marshall to JAMES MARION for ₺ 220 currency, by which purchase
JAMES became owner of the 425 a.; & whereas JAMES has borrowed ₺ 1000
from ALEXANDER GARDEN & HENRY IZARD, attorneys for the Society for the
Propagation of the Gospel in Foreign Parts, for which he has given bond;
now he conveys the 425 a. to them as security. Witnesses: CHARLES PINCK-
NEY, ELIZABETH PINCKNEY. Before OTHNIEL BEALE, J.P. JOHN BEALE, Regis-
ter.

Book D-D, p. 23   RICHARD WIGG, merchant, to JORDON ROCHE, gen-
21 & 27 Feb. 1738   tleman, both of Charleston, as counter securi-
L & R by Mortgage   ty on several bonds, 500 a. on Port Royal Is-
                         land, Granville Co., bounding W on DANIEL CAL-
AHAM; N on Dicks Creek; other sides on vacant land. Whereas ROCHE, at
WIGGS request, gave a bond dated 5 Nov. 1734 to OWEN OWEN, merchant, of
London, in penal sum of ₺ 4555 SC money for remitting to OWEN in merchantable produce of SC of the value of ₺ 700 currency at prime cost on 5
May next & ensuing; also for remitting to OWEN the value of ₺ 1577:7:3
currency at prime cost on 5 Nov. 1735; & whereas ROCHE, at WIGG'S request,
gave a bond dated 8 Apr. 1737 to WILLIAM YEOMANS & GABRIEL ESCOTT in penal sum of ₺ 1463:16:3 for payment of ₺ 739:8:1-1/2 SC money, with interest, on 1 Jan. next ensuing; now to secure ROCHE from payment of said
bonds, WIGG conveys to him 500 a. in Granville Co. Witnesses: JOHN MAR-
TINI, JOHN BURFORD. Before JOHN DART, J.P. JOHN BEALE, Register.
ARNOLDUS VANDERHORST as heir to MRS. ELIZABETH JENYS, to whom the mortgage was given as a counter security with another mortgage of same tract
not recorded here, declared mortgage discharged in full. Witness: GEORGE
DAVIDSON. No date.

Book D-D, p. 27   JACOB JEANNERET, planter, & MARGARET his wife,
27 & 28 Nov. 1747   of St. James Santee, Craven Co., to DAVID CAW,
L & R   practitioner in physic, of Charleston, for
                         ₺ 2000 currency, 800 a. in 2 tracts. Whereas
the Lords Proprs. on 27 July 1711 granted LEWIS GOURDIN 400 a. in St.
James Santee Parish, bounding NW on Santee River; other sides on vacant
land; now said to be partly on Manigault's Island & partly on the main-
land & bounding N on the river; W on NOAH SERRÉ; E on JOHN MARANT; S on
_____; which 400 a. after several mesne conveyance, became vested in JOHN
BARNET; & whereas JOHN BARNET & JUDITH his wife, on 10 June 1729 sold the
tract to JACOB JEANNERET; & whereas the King on 24 May 1734 granted JEAN-
NERET another 400 a. on Manigaults Island, to the W of first tract,
bounding N & E on Santee River; S on Manigault's Creek; the 2 tracts making 800 a. on which JEANNERETTE lived. Witnesses: DANIEL JAUDON, ELIAS
JOUDON. Before JOHN GENDRON, J.P. JOHN BEALE, Register.

Book D-D, p. 33   JACOB JEANNERET, planter, of St. James Santee,
28 Nov. 1747   Craven Co., to DR. DAVID CAW, of Charleston,
Bond for Ren. of Dower   in penal sum of Ł 1000 currency, conditioned
                         on MARGARET, wife of JACOB JEANNERETT, renounc-
ing her dower in above 800 a. (p. 27) in Charleston within 6 months, she
not being able to make the journey at this time. Witnesses: DANIEL JOU-
DON, ELIAS JOUDON. JOHN BEALE, Register.

Book D-D, p. 33   ABRAHAM WALCUTT, cordwainer, of Colleton Co.,
19 Sept. 1747   to JAMES SOMMERS, cordwainer, of Charleston,
Mortgage   as security on bond of even date in penal sum
                         of Ł 1000 for payment of Ł 500 SC money on 19
Sept. 1751; 3 tracts of land in Colleton Co., total 450 a. Witnesses:
JOHN CORSER, JOHN GITTENS. Before HENRY GIBBES, J.P. JOHN BEALE, Regis-
ter.

Book D-D, p. 35   ROBERT HOW, schoolmaster, of St. Thomas Parish,
10 & 11 Mar. 1745   Berkeley Co., to JOHN NICKLESON, RICHARD SHU-
L & R by Mortgage   BRICK & Co., merchants, of Charleston, as se-
                         curity on bond of even date in penal sum of
Ł 5200:16:10 for payment of Ł 2600:8:5 currency, with interest, on 25
Mar. 1748; 4 tracts of 200, 400, 350 & 300 a.; the 200 a., English measure, lying in St. Thomas Parish, Berkeley Co., bounding S on Wando River;
E on ALEXANDER PERONNEAU; N on _____; W on a creek & lands of Presbyterian Meeting House; the 400 a., English measure, in Craven Co., bounding
NE & NW on ROBERT HOW; SE on RICHARD WALKER; as by grant dated 23 Apr.
1735; the 350 a., English measure, in Craven Co., bounding SW on the 400
a.; NW on Black River; NE on JOHN NAYLOR; SE on MR. BROCKINGTON; being
part of 700 a. which ROBERT HOW & JOHN NAYLOR purchased from JOHN MOORE;
the 300 a., English measure, being in Craven Co., bounding N & SW on JOHN
DELESSLINE; NW & SE on vacant land; as by grant dated 8 July 1736; the 4
tracts being free of all debt except for 1 mortgage on the 200 a. to the
vestry of the Parish of St. Thomas for Ł 440. Witnesses: ROBERT BRISBANE,
JAMES HEYWARD. Before JACOB MOTTE, J.P. JOHN BEALE, Register.

Book D-D, p. 41   JAMES EDES, & PENELOPE his wife, to ADRIAN
7 Dec. 1747   LOYER & CATHARINE his wife, as security on
Mortgage   bond given to JOHN MARTINEY (?) surgeon, on
                         this date, in penal sum of Ł 2000 for payment
of Ł 1000 SC money, with interest, on 7 Dec. 1750, part of lots on Old
Church Street, bounding S on ALEXANDER MCGREGOR; N on JAMES EDES; 21 ft.
front; 131 ft. deep; with the dwelling house & all improvements. Witnesses: JOSEPH MOODY, JAMES FISHER. Before THOMAS DALE, J.P. JOHN BEALE,
Register. On 13 July 1754, CATHERINE LOYER, widow of ADRIEN LOYER declared bond paid & mortgage void.

Book D-D, p. 42   STEPHEN FOGARTIE, planter, to ANDREW WARNOCK,
6 & 7 Sept. 1747   planter, both of St. Thoams Parish, Berkeley
L & R by Mortgage   Co., as security on bond dated 7 Sept. last
                         past, given for FORGARTIES debt to JOHN DUTAR-
QUE, planter, of Berkeley Co., executor of will of NOAH SERRE, in penal
sum of Ł 350 for payment of Ł 350 SC money, with interest; & on another
bond of same date to ISAAC LESESNE, planter, of Berkeley Co., executor of
will of WILLIAM SANDERS, in penal sum of Ł 227 for payment of Ł 227 SC
money, with interest, on 7 Sept. 1748; 140 a., English measure, in St.
Thomas Parish, on which STEPHEN FOGARTIE lives (which he owns by 2 deeds
of gift from his father JOHN FOGARTIE); bounding NE & NW on DANIEL LE-
SESNE; SW on MR. BERESFORD. Witnesses: SAMUEL WARNOCK, SAMUEL SMITH, JO-
SEPH BURGES. Before OTHNIEL BEALE, J.P. JOHN BEALE, Register.

Book D-D, p. 47   DAVID HEXT, gentleman, & ANN his wife, to SAM-
23 & 24 Mar. 1746   UEL PRIOLEAU, JR., & PROVIDENCE his wife,
Gift   daughter of DAVID & ANN HEXT, all of Charles-
                         ton, for natural love & affection for their
daughter in consideration of her marriage & for other considerations; the
S part of lot #54 in Charleston fronting W 32 ft. on the great street
leading northward from Ashley River by the old churchyard & Market Place;
bounding N on the part belonging to WILLIAM ROPER; E on BENJAMIN GODIN; S
on THOMAS WITTER. Whereas the Lords Proprs. on 12 Mar. 1682 granted WIL-
LIAM JONES lot #54 in Charleston, & whereas his son & heir, WILLIAM

JONES, on 5 Apr. 1700 sold the lot to JOHN WERE; & whereas by several mesne conveyances the lot became vested in DAVID HEXT; now HEXT conveys the S part of the lot to his daughter. Witnesses: SARAH JOHNSTON, MARTHA MCCALL, JOHN MCCALL. Before OTHNIEL BEALE, J.P. JOHN BEALE, Register.

Book D-D, p. 52
21 & 22 Dec. 1747
L & R

JOSEPH BRYAN, planter, & MARY his wife, to the Rev. MR. GEORGE WHITEFIELD, all of Granville Co., for Ł 1200 currency, 640 a. (part of 740 a. purchased from HUGH BRYAN, being part of 3140 a. granted to JOSEPH & HUGH BRYAN in joint tenancy), bounding N on Landgrave EDMUND BELLINGER; E on the part of the 740 a. sold to JOSEPH BOWRY; S on the part of the 3140 a. now belonging to ELIZABETH BULL; W on the part of the 3140 a. now owned by JONATHAN BRYAN. Whereas GEORGE II on Nov. 1732 granted JOSEPH BRYAN & HUGH BRYAN, in fee, 3140 a. on E side of Whale Branch or Pocotalago River, Granville Co., bounding N on CAPT. EDMUND BELLINGER; E on Hoospa Creek; S on HILL CROFT & GEORGE PAWLEY; & whereas on 9 Feb. 1735 JOSEPH BRYAN died intestate & HUGH inherited; & whereas by L & R dated 25 & 26 Mar. 1743 HUGH BRYAN sold 740 a. to JOSEPH BRYAN; now JOSEPH sells 640 a. to WHITEFIELD. Witnesses: WILLIAM PARKER, ELIJAH PRIOLEAU. Before HUGH BRYAN, J.P. JOHN BEALE, Register.

Book D-D, p. 57
22 Dec. 1747
Bond

JOSEPH BRYAN, planter, of Prince William Parish, to the Rev. MR. GEORGE WHITEFIELD, in penal sum of Ł 2400 currency for performance of agreements in above conveyance (p. 52); MARY renouncing her dower. JOHN BEALE, Register.

Book D-D, p. 58
11 Aug. 1747
Sale

RAWLINS LOWNDES, Provost Marshall, to BENJAMIN SAVAGE, merchant, of Charleston, for Ł 1395 currency, part of a lot fronting 33 ft. 6 in. on Tradd Street, 100 ft. deep; bounding E on JOSEPH MOODY; S on Gov. THOMAS SMITH; W on JOSEPH WATSONE. Whereas LOWNDES, by 2 writs of fieri facias dated 7 July last, by JOHN LINING, Ass't. J in absence of BENJAMIN WHITAKER, C.J. was commanded to levy a debt of Ł 800 currency, & a debt of Ł 54:16:8 durrency on the real & personal estate of HENRY SALTUS, planter, which amounts HENRY PERONNEAU & ALEXANDER PERONNEAU, executors of will of HENRY PERONNEAU, gentleman, had recovered by judgment against RICHARD BEDON, administrator, & THOMAS PORTER & ELIZABETH his wife (lately ELIZABETH SALTUS, administratrix of HENRY SALTUS); & another debt of Ł 204 currency & Ł 53:3:1-1/2 which LAWRENCE SANDERS had recovered by judgment against THOMAS & ELIZABETH PORTER, administrators; now LOWNDES sells part of a lot at public auction. Witnesses: MOSES AUDEBERT, JACOB MOTTE, JR. Before JACOB MOTTE, J.P. JOHN BEALE, Register.

Book D-D, p. 60
17 Feb. 1747
Release

JOHN ALLEN, gentleman, (son, heir-at-law, residuary legatee, & devisee of will of ANDREW ALLEN, merchant) dated 29. Mar. 1735 & ANN his wife, to BENJAMIN SAVAGE, merchant; all of. Charleston; for Ł 2000 currency, his part of 2 lots on W side of Old Church Street, & on N side of Tradd Street, Nos. 87 & 88; 73 ft. x 195 ft.; bounding N on DANIEL BOURGET; W on ROBERT PRINGLE. Witnesses: GEORGE DUCAT, JAMES BOONE. Before JACOB MOTTE, J.P. JOHN BEALE, Register.

Book D-D, p. 64
20 Dec. 1737
Sale

ABRAHAM CHARDONET, planter, of Purisburg, Granville Co., to BENEDICT BOURQUIN, planter, for Ł 100 currency, 300 a. bounding S on May River; N & W on vacant land; E & S on PETER MASON & JOHN HENRY DE ROCKE. Witnesses: ELIE BORNAU, JIVAN DOMINICO ODDETS (ADDETS) MARY LAFON, on 13 Jan. 1747, testified as to CHARDONETS handwriting. Before HENRY GIBBES, J.P. JOHN BEALE, Register.

Book D-D, p. 66
19 & 20 Nov. 1747
L & R

FRANCIS ROSE, planter, & MARY ANN his wife, of Berkeley Co., to WILLIAM BRANFORD, planter, in St. Andrews Parish, for Ł 700 currency, 73-1/4 a. in Berkeley Co., on S side Ashley River, bounding NE on FRANCIS ROSE; other sides on WILLIAM BRANFORD; being part of 3 tracts; viz.; 11 a., part of 100 a. granted 8 July 1696 to THOMAS CLARKE; 19 a., part of 36 a. granted ANTHONY CHURNE on 21 Apr. 1677;

43-1/4 a., part of 156 a. granted JAMES BRYAN on 9 June 1709. Whereas THOMAS ROSE, planter, of St. Andrews Parish, owned several tracts of land which he bequeathed to his son, FRANCIS ROSE; now FRANCIS sells part of the land to BRANFORD. Witnesses: ROY SAUNDERS, SARAH CHAMPNEYS. Before JOHN CHAMPNEYS, J.P. JOHN BEALE, Register.

Book D-D, p. 72   RICHARD CAPERS, planter, of St. Helena Island,
17 Nov. 1743   Granville Co., to NATHANIEL ADAMS, planter, of
Lease for Life   same place, for the term of NATHANIEL'S life,
                         under certain conditions & agreements; 100 a.
on St. Helena Island, bounding W on a creek; S on WILLIAM CHAPMAN; E on RICHARD CAPERS; N on the path going to the Kings High Road. Witnesses: JAMES MEGGETT, FRANCIS THOMPSON. Before THOMAS DALE, J.P. JOHN BEALE, Register.

Book D-D, p. 73   PETER COMMET & HANNAH his wife, of St. Philips
15 & 16 Sept. 1747   Parish, Charleston, to KENNETH MICHIE, mer-
L & R by Mortgage   chant, of Charleston, for Ⱡ 3410 currency,
                         184-1/2 a. on Charleston Neck, Berkeley Co.,
bounding W on the Broad Path; N on Gov. GLEN; S on JOHN COLLETON; E on marsh of Cooper River. Date of redemption: 10 Sept. 1748. Witness: BEN-JAMIN MICHIE. Before JAMES MICHIE, J.P. JOHN BEALE, Register.

Book D-D, p. 79   JOSEPH MIKALL (MIKELL) planter, & MARY his
8 & 9 Jan. 1747   wife, to THOMAS BOWMAN, planter, for Ⱡ 1000
L & R   currency, 532 a., English measure, in Gran-
                         ville Co., bounding W on marsh & creeks of
Port Royal River; N on MR. HYDE & MAJ. QUINTYNE; E on EVANS SERVIS; S on GEORGE LIVINGSTON. MARY MIKELL to renounce her dower within 12 months. Witnesses: ANDREW BELL, DAVID FERGUSON. Before ROBERT WILLIAMS, J.P.

Book D-D, p. 84   JEREMIAH ROPER, planter, & LILLEY his wife, to
23 & 24 Nov. 1737   ELISHA SCREVEN, planter, all of Craven Co.,
L & R   for Ⱡ 150 SC money, 77 a., part of 500 a. on
                         which JEREMIAH ROPER now lives, in Craven Co.,
bounding SE on THOMAS POTTS & JOSEPH COMMANDER; SW on ELISHA SCREVEN; NW on ELISHA SCREVEN; NE on JEREMIAH ROPER. Whereas GEORGE II on 1 Sept. 1736, by Lt. Gov. THOMAS BROUGHTON, granted WILLIAM BROCKINTON 2140 a. in Craven Co., bounding S on Black River; N on vacant land; E on WILLIAM SWINTON & SAMUEL COMMANDER; W on THOMAS HENNING, JOHN BONNELL, JOSEPH ROPER & ELISHA SCREVEN; & whereas WILLIAM BROCKINTON by L & R dated 28 & 29 July 1737 sold to JEREMIAH ROPER 500 a., bounding N on said ROPER; E on SAMUEL COMMANDER; S on SAMUEL COMMANDER & THOMAS POTTS; W on ELISHA SCREVEN; now ROPER sells a part to SCREVEN. Witnesses: JOHN SMITH, JOHN ASKEW. Before ROBERT FINLAY, J.P. of Craven Co. JOHN BEALE, Register.

Book D-D, p. 90   RICHARD PALMER, to JAMES DEVEAUX, both of
23 Jan. 1747   Granville Co., as security on 2 bonds, 1 for
Mortgage   Ⱡ 140 & Ⱡ 550, & interest, 4 tracts of about
                         1350 a.; being 250 a. purchased by COL. JOHN
PALMER'S father from JAMES ADKINS, on W side Combee River, known as Green Point, 370 a. on SW side Combee River, purchased from WHITESIDES WHITE-HEAD; 2 tracts containing 730 a. adjoining first 2 tracts; on W side Com-bee River, bounding S on ROBERT THORPE; W & NW on STEPHEN BULL. Wit-nesses: WILLIAM KENNEDY, WALTER ORD, EDWARD (his mark) HONEYHORN. Before STEPHEN BULL, J.P. JOHN BEALE, Register.

Book D-D, p. 92   MARTHA (her mark) LEOPARD, WILLIAM CHAPMAN &
27 & 28 Dec. 1745   MARGARET his wife, to WILLIAM CATTELL & JOHN
L & R in Trust   DRAYTON, ESQ., & WILLIAM BACKSHELL, all of St.
                         Andrews Parish, in trust for HENRIETTA BACK-
SHELL, spinster, of Antigua, for Ⱡ 150 currency, 37-1/2 a., or 1/4 of 150 a., on SW side Ashley River, Berkeley Co., bounding SE on Cuppain Creek; SW on WILLIAM CLEAY; NW on ELIZABETH BELLINGER ELLIOTT; NE on SAM-UEL JONES. Whereas the Lords Proprs. on 10 June 1704 granted MANLEY WIL-LAIMSON 150 a. on SW side Ashley River; which he, on 8 Nov. 1714 conveyed to RICHARD VINCENT; who by will dated 23 Jan. 1718 bequeathed 1/4 part (150 a.) to MARTHA, his wife; who by deed of gift dated 8 Dec. 1729 (by the name of MARTHA PARSONS, being then again a widow), conveyed the 150 a. to her daughter, MARGARET PARSONS (now wife of WILLIAM CHAPMAN, shoemaker,

of St. Pauls Parish), now they convey, as above. Witnesses: JAMES HART-
LEY, JACOB GOSS. Witnesses to MARTHA'S signature: JOHN (his mark) MC-
NEALE, JANE HILL, at Ashley Ferry. Before CHARLES HILL, J.P. 13 July
1747. Before OTHNIEL BEALE, J.P. 21 Oct. 1747. JOHN BEALE, Register.

Book D-D, p. 99   ANNE ELLERY, widow, executrix, & devisee of
3 & 4 Mar. 1746   THOMAS ELLERY, gentleman, to JOHN MCKENZIE,
L & R   merchant, all of Charleston, for Ŀ 500 curren-
                         cy, part of lot #80 in Charleston, marked # in
a general plat, 35 ft. x 150 ft., bounding N on a street from Cooper River; E on lots G belonging to ANNE ELLERY, & E & F belonging to GEORGE
HUNTER; S on a street; W on lot I belonging to GEORGE HUNTER; also part
of the lot marked K, 35 ft. x 150 ft., bounding N & S on 2 streets; E on
lot I; W on a neighborhood street. Whereas the Lords Proprs. on 5 Mar.
1680 granted SIR PETER COLLETON a lot in Charleston containing 9 a. 2
roods, 21 perches, English measure, of dry land & marsh & a small creek
in the marsh, known in the model at lot #80, bounding E on Cooper River,
JAMES COLLETON & Landgrave THOMAS COLLETON; W on a small unnamed street;
S on CAPT. WILLIAM WALLEY & 2 lots belonging to CAPT. JAMES ADIE; N on
THOMAS COLLETON & another small unnamed street; & whereas the lot by various mesne conveyances became vested in JOHN COLLETON of Fairlawn Barony,
in St. Johns Parish, Berkeley Co., & whereas JOHN COLLETON & SUSANNAH his
wife, by L & R dated 13 & 14 July 1736, for Ŀ 5000 currency, sold the lot
to GEORGE HUNTER, gentleman, of Charleston; & whereas the title was made
out to GEORGE HUNTER alone, but the purchase money was paid by GEORGE
HUNTER & CHARLES PINCKNEY & THOMAS ELLERY, jointly; & whereas THOMAS
ELLERY by will dated 2 Oct. _____ bequeathed to his wife ANNE certain
property; & whereas by an agreement between GEORGE HUNTER, CHARLES PINCK-
NEY & ANNE ELLERY (widow of THOMAS), the land was laid out in small lots,
streets, & lanes, according to a general plat; & whereas GEORGE HUNTER,
by L & R dated 9 & 10 Feb. last, conveyed to ANNE ELLERY several parcels
of land marked on the plat as H, K, & O; now she sells that part shown as
to MACKENZIE. Witnesses: JAMES WRIGHT, ALEXANDER MACAULY. Before
OTHNIEL BEALE, J.P. JOHN BEALE, Register.

Book D-D, p. 105   WILLIAM SPENCER, JR., house carpenter, to
10 & 11 Aug. 1746   GEORGE RIVERS, JR., son of ROBERT, planter,
L & R   all of James Island, Berkeley Co., for
                         Ŀ 960:10 currency, 113 a. (part of 150 a.)
bounding E on STEPHEN RUSSELL; S on the great Sound; W on JOSEPH RIVERS;
N on THOMAS DIXON. Whereas WILLIAM, Earl of Craven, Palatine, & the
Lords Proprs., by grant dated 14 Apr. 1710, signed by EDWARD TYNTE, ROB-
ERT DANIEL, ROBERT GIBBS, THOMAS BROUGHTON & FRANCIS TURBEVILLE, granted
EDWARD WESBURY 400 a., English measure, in Berkeley Co., & whereas WES-
BURY died intestate & all his real estate descended to his heir-at-law,
THOMAS WESTBURY; & whereas he sold 150 a. (part of the 400 a.) to ALEXAN-
DER SPENCER; at whose death it was inherited by his son ALEXANDER SPENCER;
at whose death it descended to his brother JOSEPH SPENCER; who bequeathed
the 150 a. to his brother WILLIAM SPENCER, JR., now he sells part (113
a.) to GEORGE RIVERS. Witnesses: CAPT. ROBERT RIVERS, DANIEL STENT, WIL-
LIAM RIVERS. Before THOMAS LAMBOLL, J.P. JOHN BEALE, Register.

Book D-D, p. 112   JOHN (his mark) ELLIS, SR., planter, & JUDITH
25 & 26 Feb. 1746   his wife, to THOMAS RIVERS, weaver, all of
L & R by Mortgage   James Island, as security on bond (signed by
                         RIVERS at request of ELLIS) to WILLIAM SCRE-
VEN, JAMES SCREVEN, & SAMUEL EVANS, executors of will of JONATHAN EVANS,
in penal sum of Ŀ 842 for payment of Ŀ 421 currency, with interest, on a
certain date; 100 a. on SW part of James Island; part of 170 a. granted
by the Lords Proprs. to his father, JOHN ELLIS; bounding NE on GEORGE
GANTLETT; SE on WILLIAM SPENCER, SR.; other side on marsh. Witnesses:
STEPHEN BEDON, WILLIAM GOUGH. Before THOMAS LAMBOLL, J.P. JOHN BEALE,
Register.

Book D-D, p. 118   CHARLES ALEXANDER, ESQ., of Antigua, appoints
19 Mar. 1747   WILLIAM BOONE, ESQ., & ANDREW RUTLEDGE, ESQ.,
Letter of Attorney   of SC, his attorneys to manage 5 plantations
                         in SC, sell the produce thereof, & remit to
SLINGSBY BETHEL, merchant, of London, on ALEXANDER'S account, or to
CHARLES ALEXANDER, in Antigua; & also gives his attorneys authority to

sell the plantations, slaves, & a certain mortgage for the principle sum
of Ł 2595 British. Whereas on 25 Aug. 1746, the Hon. GEORGE LUCAS, Lt.
Gov. of Antigua, mortgaged to CHARLES ALEXANDER, for Ł 2595 British 5
plantations in SC containing 4500 a., with the slaves named in certain
schedule, also all the cattle, horses & mares, plantation utensils, etc.,
conditioned for the payment of Ł 155:13 British in St. John, Antiqua, on
25 Aug. 1747, & the same sum annually until 1751; & in dafault of which
payments ALEXANDER might take possession of the premises except for 1
mortgage to RICHARD BODICOT, merchant, of London; & whereas LUCAS died
leaving a will devising the remainder of his real & personal estate
(after some legacies) to his 2 sons, GEORGE & THOMAS, appointing GEORGE
LUCAS, the son, & THOMAS WARNER, ESQ., of Antigua, & the Hon. CHARLES
PINCKNEY, of SC & ELIZABETH his wife, his executors & executrix; & whereas CHARLES ALEXANDER has demanded payment of GEORGE LUCAS, the son, who
refused to pay, claiming he has no assets of testator with which to pay;
& whereas WARNER refused to act; & ALEXANDER has claimed the property;
now he appoints attorneys with authority to sell. Witnesses: THOMAS OS-
BORN & CONNOR BOOTH, of St. John, Antigua. OSBORN testified before JACOB
MOTTE, J.P. of SC. JOHN BEALE, Register.

Book D-D, p. 121   GRIFFITH BULLARD, hat maker, to RICHARD BODDI-
20 & 21 May 1747   COT, vinter, both of St. Philip's Parish,
L & R by Mortgate   Charleston, as security on a loan of Ł 700 SC
                          money, 2 plantations on N side Ashley River,
in St. Andrews Parish; 20 (?) a.; bounding N on CHARLES CANTEY; NW on
JOHN BURFORD; S on HENRY WOOD & WILLIAM FULLER; SW on marsh; NE on WIL-
LIAM FULLER; which tract was conveyed to GRIFFITH BULLARD by DAVID WEB-
STER & HANNAH BURNLEY by L & R dated 3 & 4 Mar. 1739; also 181 a., (part
of 25 a.) on N side Ashley River (167 a. land, 14 a. marsh) bounding W on
Ashley River, N on above tract; E on heirs of WILLIAM FULLER; S on
HENRY WOOD & heirs of WILLIAM FULLER; which tract was conveyed to BULLARD
by HENRY WOOD, & ANNE his wife, by L & R dated 28 & 29 Jan. 1740. Wit-
nesses: MARMADUEK AISH, CHARLES PRYCE. Before THOMAS DALE, J.P. JOHN
BEALE, Register.

Book D-D, p. 127   From the fragments available it would appear
30 Aprl. & j June 1747   that the General Assembly appointed the Hon.
L & R   WILLIAM BULL, ISAAC HOLMES, OTHNELE BEALE,
                          ISAAC MAZYCK, & DAVID HEXT, trustees, to sell
at public auction certain surplus land in Schenckingh Square & with the
money obtained pay the owners & proprietors of certain lots, including
lot #249, "taken up by the ditch & ramparts"; the surplus money to be
placed in the public treasury; & accordingly they sold a lot (#4?) to
HENRY PERONNEAU for Ł 500 plus, being the NE part (?), fronting 49 ft. on
Old Church Street, apparently bounding on Queen Street; N on DR. JACOB
_____; S on WILLIAM WEBB'S lot #3 (?). Witnesses: WILLIAM WEBB, MOREAU
SARRAZIN. Before JAMES WRIGHT, J.P. JOHN BEALE, Register.

Book D-D, p. 132   JOHN GEORGE DALLIBACH, bricklayer, & JOHANNA
_____ July 1747   ELIZABETH his wife, of Berkeley Co., to JAMES
Release   VOULOUX, gentleman, for Ł 350 (Ł 1350 ?) cur-
                          rency, the NW part of DALLIBACH'S land, pur-
chased from JOSEPH WRAGG by L & R dated 18 & 19 Jan. 174?, being on
Charleston Neck, St. Philip's Parish, Berkeley Co., bounding on the High
Road, HUGH ANDERSON & the Parish Glebe. Witnesses: FREDERICK STRUBELL,
THOMAS LAMBOLL. Before THOMAS LAMBOLL, J.P. JOHN BEALE, Register.

Book D-D, p. 135   RICHARD GODFREY, planter, to WILLIAM CATTELL,
14 & 15 Aug. 1745   SR., both of Berkeley Co., as security on bond
L & R by Mortgage   of even date in sum of Ł 2060 currency, to be
                          paid, with interest, on 15 Aug. 1746; 224 a.
in Berkeley Co., marked #7 on the general plat, known as Silk Hope Plantation, bounding SW on Stono River; NE on RICHARD GODFREY. Witnesses:
JAMES SCARLETT, CHARLES GUY. Before JOHN DRAYTON, J.P. JOHN BEALE, Register.

Book D-D, p. 139   THOMAS GOREING, tailor, to WILLIAM CATTELL,
27 & 28 Feb. 1746   SR., ESQ., both of Berkeley Co., for Ł 325 SC
L & R by Mortgage   money, lot #14 in Butler Town. Date of re-
                          demption: 28 Feb. 1747. Witnesses: JAMES

SCARLETT, HENRY LADSON. Before CHARLES HILL, J.P. JOHN BEALE, Register.

Book D-D, p. 142   JOSEPH (his mark) HASFORD, planter, to WILLIAM
5 & 6 June 1747   CATTELL, ESQ., both of Berkeley Co., as se-
L & R by Mortgage   curity on bond of even date in penal sum of
                          ₺ 3080 for payment of ₺ 1540:5:6 currency,
with interest, on 6 June, 1748; 160 a. on Charleston Neck, in Berkeley
Co., bounding E on the broad path; W on Ashley River; S on THOMAS ELLIOTT;
N on CHILDERMAS CROFT. Witnesses: THOMAS ELMES, RICHARD BUTLER. Before
WILLIAM GEORGE FREEMAN, J.P. JOHN BEALE, Register.

Book D-D, p. 146   WILLIAM WATIES, SR., of Prince George Parish,
_____ Nov. 1741   to ABRAHAM JERDON, for ₺ 600 currency, 350 a.
Mortgage   known as Cold Bear Swamp, in Kings Township,
                          granted to WILLIAM PRICE, who sold to WILLIAM
WATIES. Witnesses: ROBERT _____; JOSEPH HON _____. Before PAUL TRAPIER,
J.P. JOHN BEALE, Register.

Book D-D, p. 147   HENRY (his mark) RIGBY, carpenter, of St.
_____ Mar. 1747   James Goose Creek, to MARY SMITH, widow of
Mortgage   Landgrave THOMAS SMITH, for ₺ 425:10 currency,
                          189 a. in said Parish, known as Halfway House;
bounding of WILLIAM FLUD, Goose Creek high road, & _____ HURST. Date of
redemption: 25 Mar. 1753. Witnesses: HENRY SMITH, JAMES COLLETON. Before HENRY HYRNE, J.P. JOHN BEALE, Register.

Book D-D, p. 148   CHARLES JONES, planter, of Colleton Co., to
10 & 11 June 1747   ELIZABETH FULLER, widow, of Berkeley Co., for
L & R   ₺ 100 SC money, 3 a., English measure, in St.
                          Andrews Town, bounding E on CHARLES JONES; W
on High Street; N on ELIZABETH FULLER; S on Kings High Road. Witnesses:
JAMES SCARLETT, JOHN CLARK, Before JOHN WALTER, J.P. JOHN BEALE, Register.

Book D-D, p. 151   JACOB BONNEAU, planter, & MARY his wife, to
25 & 26 Apr. 1748   ANTHONY BONNEAU, planter, both of Berkeley Co.,
L & R   for ₺ 150 (?) currency, 102 a. in St. Thomas
                          Parish, Berkeley Co., bounding NE & SE on
JAMES BREMER; NW & SW on the widow PAGETT. Whereas PETER VIDEAU, planter (grandfather of JACOB BONNEAU, party hereto, in 1709 gave to JACOB
BONNEAU & JANE his wife (father & mother of JACOB BONNEAU party hereto),
102 a. in Berkeley Co., & whereas PETER VIDEAU'S deed of gift to JACOB
BONNEAU & JANE his wife, has been accidentally lost; & whereas it appears
that since that time, HENRY VIDEAU (?) & ANN his wife, have by L & R dated 28 & 29 Apr. 174? given JANE BONNEAU (what?); now JACOB & MARY BONNEAU
convey the 102 a. to ANTHONY BONNEAU. Witnesses: JOHN COMBE, MOSES MIL-
LER, WALTER DALLAS. Before JAMES AKIN, J.P. JOHN BEALE, Register.

Book D-D, p. 155   JOHN HUME, merchant, & SUSANNAH his wife; &
13 & 14 Nov. 1747   GEORGE MARSHALL, shopkeeper, & ELIZABETH MARY
L & R   ANN, his wife, to ROBERT STIELL, merchant, all
                          of Charleston; for ₺ 800 currency, 300 a., be-
ing 2 undivided third parts of 450 a. in St. George Parish, Berkeley Co.,
on N side Edisto. Whereas JAMES MOORE owned 450 a. in St. George's Parish which he conveyed to STIELL, HUME & MARSHALL as tenants in common &
not as joint tenants; 1/3 to each; bounding NW on MRS. FRANCES LONGUEMARE;
other sides on vacant land; now HUME & MARSHALL sell to STIELL. Witnesses: JOHN NEUFVILLE, JR., JOHN STANYARNE. Before OTHNIEL BEALE, J.P.
JOHN BEALE, Register.

Book D-D, p. 159   JOHN HUTCHINS, to BENJAMIN WHITAKER, ESQ.,
7 & 8 Apr. 1747   both of Charleston, as security on bond of
L & R by Mortgage   even date in penal sum of ₺ 1089 for payment
                          of ₺ 554:10 currency, with interest, on Jan. 1
next; 1 a., 2 roods, English measure, marked D in the general plan of
GEORGE ANSON'S land, known as Ansonsburgh. Witnesses: SARAH HUTCHINS,
WILLIAM BURROWS. Before WILLIAM GEORGE FREEMAN, J.P. JOHN BEALE, Reg-
ister. On 12 July 1748 BENJAMIN WHITAKER declared mortgage satisfied.
Witness: JOHN BEALE.

Book D-D, p. 163   COL. LAWRENCE SANDERS, & SARAH his wife, to
24 & 25 Sept. 1736   WILLIAM SANDERS, planter, both of Colleton Co.,
L & R   for ₺ 350 currency, 147-1/2 a. in St. Bartholomew's Parish, Colleton Co., bounding S on
land purchased by COL. SANDERS from the King; W on MRS. BOON; N on estate
of MOSES MARTIN; E on unknown land. Witnesses: DANIEL CLEMENT, ABRAHAM
ROBERT, MARY FINLEY. Before CULCHETH GOLIGHTLY, J.P. JOHN BEALE, Register.

Book D-D, p. 167   CORNELIUS SOLMS, mariner, of Charleston, to
24 May 1746   GABRIEL GIGNIARD, cooper, of St. Philip's Par-
Mortgage   ish, Charleston, as security on bond of even
date in penal sum of ₺ 240 for payment of
₺ 120 currency, with interest, on 24 May 1749; a lot 30 x 75 ft. bounding
N on MADAM TROTT; E & S on GABRIEL GIGNIARD; W on 12 ft. of land belonging to said GIGNIARD. Witnesses: MARK ANTHONY BESSELLEN, JOHN RODOLPH
LIFENOR. Before OTHNIEL BEALE, J.P. JOHN BEALE, Register.

Book D-D, p. 168   WILLIAM DICKS, bricklayer, to GABRIEL GUIGNARD,
14 June 1746   cooper, of St. Philip's Parish, Charleston, as
Mortgage   security on bond of even date in penal sum of
₺ 240 for payment of ₺ 120 currency, with in-
terest, on 14 June 1749; a lot 30 x 75 ft. formerly belonging to GABRIEL
GUIGNARD & bounding on all sides on said GUIGNARD. Witnesses: MARK AN-
THONY BESSELLEU, FRANCIS (his mark) DELGRASS. Before OTHNIEL BEALE, J.P.
JOHN BEALE, Register. On 12 Dec. 1749 mortgage declared satisfied. Witness: WILLIAM HOPTON.

Book D-D, p. 169   JAMES MCRELLESS, planter, of Christ Church
29 May 1747   Parish, to GABRIEL GUIGNARD, cooper, of
Bond   Charleston, in penal sum of ₺ 800 currency, to
keeping good repair a certain floodgate.
Whereas by deed of feoffment of even date GUIGNARD conveyed to MORELLESS
part of lot #80 in Charleston, in which it was covenanted that MCRELLES
would keep a certain floodgate in good repair; now MCRELLESS gives a bond
of performance. Witnesses: JOHN HOLMES, JOHN REMINGTON. Before ROBERT
AUSTIN, J.P. JOHN BEALE, Register.

Book D-D, p. 170   JAMES MCRELLES, planter, of Christ Church Par-
30 & 31 July 1747   ish, to GABRIEL GUIGNARD, cooper, of Charles-
L & R by Mortgage   ton, as security on bond dated 29 May last in
penal sum of ₺ 800 currency for payment of
₺ 300 in merchantable lime at 2 shillings per bushel & ₺ 100 currency to
be paid on 29 May 1748; part of lot #80 in Charleston bounding E 46 ft.
on an alley 12 ft. wide called French Alley; S 65 ft. on Ellery Street; W
& N on GABRIEL GUIGNARD. Witnesses: ALEXANDER GOODBE, ROBERT HAMILTON.
Before ROBERT AUSTIN, J.P. JOHN BEALE, Register. On 18 Nov. 1749 GUIG-
NARD declared mortgage satisfied. Witness: JOHN LOGAN.

Book D-D, p. 173   DAVID CHRISTINA, carpenter, to GABRIEL GUIG-
16 Apr. 1748   NARD, cooper, both of Charelston, as security
Mortgage   on a certain bond, the SW part of a lot in
Ansonborough; marked F on the plan of Anson-
borough, 41-1/9 ft. x 200 ft., bounding N by a common Avenue dividing the
2 parts of lot F; E & S on HUGH ANDERSON; W on the Broad Path leading to
Charleston. Two slaves delivered. Whereas CHRISTINA borrowed ₺ 600 from
the SC Society ₺ 600 SC money & at his request JAMES VOULOUX, of Charleston, became bound with CHRISTINA in a bond of even date given MOREAU SAR-
AZIN, THOMAS WEAVER & JEREMIAH THEUS, officers of SC Society, in penal
sum of ₺ 1200 for payment of ₺ 600 currency, with interest, on 16 Apr.
1749; & whereas GABRIEL GUIGNARD, at the request of CHRISTINA, signed his
bond to JAMES VOULOUX in penal sum of ₺ 2400 SC; now to secure GUIGNARD,
CHRISTINA mortgages a part of a lot. Witnesses: JOHN NEUFVILLE, SAMUEL
PRIOLEAU, JR. Before OTHNIEL BEALE, J.P. JOHN BEALE, Register. On 2
Nov. 1750 GUIGNARD declared mortgage satisfied. Witness: WILLIAM HOPTON.

Book D-D, p. 176   MATTHEW BEARD, planter, & ELIZABETH his wife,
14 & 15 May 1747   of St. James Goose Creek, Berkeley Co., to ANN
L & R   BAKER, widow of WILLIAM BAKER, planter, of St.
George Parish, for ₺ 1600 SC money, 2

plantations, total 360 a., formerly owned by his father, MATTHEW BEARD; 168 a. bounding NE on WILLIAM BRANFORD & BARNABY BRANFORD; NW & SW on MARY WALTERS; SE on JOHN BRUNSON; 200 a. bounding NW on ROBERT MILLER & JOHN SHUTE; SW on a range of 50 a. lots belonging to inhabitants of Dorchester; SE & NE on JOHN BRUNSON & MARY WALTERS. ELIZABETH BEARD voluntarily renounces her dower. Witnesses: AMERENTIA TAYLOR, GEORGE FREDERICK GEIGER. Before PETER TAYLOR, J.P. JOHN BEALE, Register.

Book D-D, p. 182   GABRIEL MANIGAULT, merchant, of Charleston, &
16 & 17 Nov. 1745   CHARLES PURRY, merchant, of Beaufort, as exe-
L & R   cutors of will of the Rev. MR. LEWIS JONES, of
                    St. Helena's Parish, Granville Co., to JOHN
CARVEY, mariner, of Granville Co., for ₤ 850 currency, lot #335 in Beaufort, fronting S on the bay; bounding W on lot #336; N on lot #344; E on lot #334. Witnesses: WILLIAM BANBURY, ELIZABETH BANBURY, WILLIAM ELLIS. Before HENRY GIBBES, J.P. JOHN BEALE, Register.

Book D-D, p. 186   JOHN GARVEY, mariner, of Granville Co., to
23 & 24 Sept. 1747 CHARLES PURRY, storekeeper, of Beaufort, for
L & R   ₤ 850 currency, lot #335 in Beaufort fronting
                    S on the Bay; bounding W on lot #336; N on lot
#344; E on lot #334. Witnesses: GABRIEL MANIGAULT, WILLIAM ELLIS, WILLIAM BANBURY. Before HENRY GIBBES, J.P. JOHN BEALE, Register.

Book D-D, p. 190   FRANCIS BREMAR, merchant, & MARTHA his wife,
27 & 28 Jan. 1747   of Charleston, to JAMES BREMAR, planter, of
L & R   St. Thomas Parish, Berkeley Co., for ₤ 1500 SC
                    money, all those plantations formerly owned by
PETER BREMAR, on St. Thomas Parish, total 1025 a.; bounding N on JAMES BREMAR, SAMUEL SIMONS, ANDREW DEVEAUX, & JOHN DANIEL; E on JOHN MCCALL; S on PETER BOCHETT, HENRY BOCHETT, JAMES BILBOA & THEODORE TREZEVANT; W on THEODORE TREZAVANT. Whereas the Lords Proprs. on 15 Sept. 1705 granted SOLOMON BREMAR (grandfather of said FRANCIS) 365 a. in Berkeley Co., & on 13 Jan. 1710 granted SOLOMON BREMAR 640 a.; & whereas SOLOMON BREMAR by will dated 13 Sept. 1720 directed that his 2 sons JAMES & PETER BREMAR should cast lots for dividing between them certain lands belonging to SOLOMON; & whereas on 18 Dec. 1722, JAMES & PETER made certain agreement, giving bonds for performances, & the 365 a. known as the Midway tract & 640 a. known as Bullhead Plantation became vested in PETER BREMAR, father of FRANCIS, party hereto; & whereas said PETER afterwards conveyed 78 a., part of Midway, & 302 a. (part of Bullhead) to DANIEL TREZEVANT; & whereas DANIEL TREZEVANT, & SUSANNAH his wife, on 31 Jan. 1722 conveyed to PETER BREMAR 400 a. (part of 530 a.) purchased from the Lords Proprs. by DANIEL TREZEVANT on 17 Dec. 1703, & also 100 a. (purchased from JONATHAN RUSS in 1711) within land, on E side Cooper River, bounding S on PETER POITEVANT; N on LAMONIER DAUGHTER; NE on JAMES BREMAR; & whereas PETER BREMAR owned 287 a., 338 a., & 400 a. (1025 a.) & died intestate in 1732; & the 3 tracts descended to FRANCIS, party hereto, as eldest son & heir-at-law; now he sells to JAMES BREMAR. Witnesses: GEORGE BARKSDALE, JOHN REMINGTON. Before JACOB MOTTE, J.P. JOHN BEALE, Register.

Book D-D, p. 196   PAUL SMYSER, shopkeeper, & RACHAEL (her mark)
24 May 1748   his wife, to JAMES VOULOUX, gentleman, all of
Mortgage   Charleston, as security on bond of even date
                    in penal sum of ₤ 1400 for payment of ₤ 700
currency, with interest, on 24 May 1751; part of a lot fronting 25 ft. 10 in. on S side of Broad Street, bounding W 200 ft. on JAMES VOULOUX; S on the French Church; E on MATHURIN GUERIN. Witnesses: MATHIEU VANALL, JOHN REMINGTON. Before OTHNIEL BEALE, J.P. JOHN BEALE, Register. On 1 Nov. 1751 FRANCIS GUICHARD, executor of will of JAMES VOULOUX declared mortgage satisfied. Witness: WILLIAM HOPTON.

Book D-D, p. 199   THOMAS HASELL, planter, of Prince George Par-
10 & 11 June 1747   ish, to JOHN HASELL, planter, of St. Thomas
L & R   Parish, for ₤ 1627 currency, 1127 a. in St.
                    Thomas Parish, Berkeley Co., bounding NW on
E branch of Cooper River; NE on RICHARD SHUBRICK; SE on THOMAS ASHBY; SW by chapel glebe. Witnesses: WILLIAM BRUCE, MRS. ELIZABETH HASELL. Before FRANCIS LEJAU, J.P. JOHN BEALE, Register.

Book D-D, p. 201   JOSEPH (his mark) PORTE, planter, Sampit, Cra-
    Mar. 17   ven Co., & ANN his wife, to JOHN SUMMERS, of
L & R   Craven Co., for Ⱡ 1520 currency, 760 a. in
Craven Co., granted him in Apr. 1736 by Lt.
Gov. THOMAS BROUGHTON, on the N of Georgetown River & head of Deep Gully
Creek, bounding N on WILLIAM SHACKELFORD & DANIEL & THOMAS LAROCHE; S on
CAPT. BONNY. ANN renounces her claim. Witnesses: RICHARD MALONE, WIL-
LIAM SHACKELFORD. Before PAUL TRAPIER, J.P. JOHN BEALE, Register.

Book D-D, p. 206   ARCHIBALD CROLL, to EDMUND KELLY, both of Col-
1 & 2 Aug. 1747   leton Co., for Ⱡ 300 currency, 650 a. in Col-
L & R   leton Co., bounding N on vacant land & on
JAMES ____; to S on THOMAS CROLL & vacant
land; E on vacant land; which 650 a. was granted by Lt. Gov. THOMAS
BROUGHTON on 12 Aug. 1737 to MRS. (?) CROLL. Witnesses: JUDITH BULL,
ROBERT RUNYAN. Before STEPHEN BULL, J.P. JOHN BEALE, Register.

Book D-D, p. 210   Fragments of deed of partition between NICHO-
LAS HARLESTON of Berkeley Co., & SARAH his
wife, of 1st part; JOHN HARLESTON of St. Thomas Parish & HANNAH his wife,
of 2nd part; ELIAS BALL, of St. Johns Parish, & LYDIA his wife (formerly
LYDIA CHICKEN) of 3rd part; & SAMUEL THOMAS, of Craven Co., in behalf of
his son (EDWARD ?) of 4th part. Whereas JAMES CHILDS, father of ISAAC
CHILDS, of the town of Childsbury bequeathed all ____ whatsoever to his
sisters; & whereas NICHOLAS HARLESTON & SAMUEL THOMAS married 2 of the
sisters; & whereas they now wish to divide the land (adjoining the town
of Childsbury); they agree that HANNAH wife of JOHN HARLESTON, shall have
760 (?) a.; LYDIA, wife of ELIAS BALL, to have a certain tract, etc. etc.,
(Pages too broken). Witnesses: EDWARD HARLESTON, JOHN COMINGS BALL. Before HENRY GIBBES, J.P. JOHN BEALE, Register. (Other names occuring in
deed: MARY, mother's brother; DURHAM tract; MEPSHEW; ALEXANDER NISBETT;
FRANCIS WILLIAMS; NICHOLAS MAHIM; JOSEPH BYRMONT; DANIEL WELCH).

Book D-D, p. 215   RICHARD GOUGH, planter of Berkeley Co., to
22 Mar. 1740 (?)   JOHN BALL, for Ⱡ 3000, currency, 705 a. in St.
Release   John's Parish, Berkeley Co. Witnesses: NICHO-
LAS HARLESTON, EDWARD GOUGH, NATHANIEL DEAN.
Before JOHN GOUGH, J.P. JOHN BEALE, Register.

Book D-D, p. 218   EDWARD GOUGH, O'NEALE GOUGH, & FRANCIS GOUGH,
13 Feb. 1747   (3 sons of JOHN GOUGH, planter), & MARY, wife
Release   of O'NEALE GOUGH, of 1 part; to JOHN COMINGS
BALL, planter, of 2nd part; for Ⱡ 3000 curren-
cy, 1910 a. part of 3500 a. on E branch of Cooper River, granted by his
4 sons (JOHN, EDWARD, O'NEALE, & FRANCIS) equally; the 19 a. bounding E
on Cooper River; S on JOHN COMINGS BALL & estate of JOHN GOUGH; W on
lands of several persons. Witnesses: JOHN HENTIE, NICHOLAS HARLESTON.
Before HENRY GIBBES, J.P. JOHN BEALE, Register.

Book D-D, p. 223   ROBERT MACKEWN, planter, of Colleton Co., &
25 & 26 Feb. 1747   ROBERT MACKEWN, JR. (son of said ROBERT MAC-
L & R   KEWN & eldest son & heir-at-law of SUSANNAH
MACKEWN, his wife, formerly SUSANNAH PLAYER,
daughter & devisee of ROGER PLAYER), to FREDERIC GRIMKÉ, gentleman, of
Charleston, for Ⱡ 450 currency, the N half of lot #221 on King Street,
Charleston, originally granted by the Lords Proprs. on 9 May 1694 to WIL-
LIAM NOWELL; bounding N on heirs of SOLOMON MIDDLETON; W on THOMAS FARR;
E on King Street; S 202 ft. on S half of lot. Whereas by several mesne
conveyances the title to the N half of lot #221 became vested in ROGER
PLAYER, who, by deed poll dated 24 Jan. 1711, gave his daughter SUSANNAH,
on the day of her marriage said half lot; & whereas SUSANNAH married ROB-
ERT MACKEWN & had 1 son ROBERT, JR., who has attained his majority; &
whereas ROBERT, the father, is tenant for life, by the Courtesy of England; now father & son convey to GRIMKÉ. Witnesses: ALEXANDER RIGG,
STEPHEN ELLIOTT. Before OTHNIEL BEALE, J.P. JOHN BEALE, D.P.R.

Book D-D, p. 230   FRANCIS BAKER, merchant, of Charleston, & MARY
18 & 19 June 1747   his wife, to FREDERIC GRIMKÉ, gentleman, of
L & R   Charleston, for Ⱡ 166:13:4 currency, part of a
lot on the E side of land formerly sold by

WILLIAM HANCOCK to ALEXANDER CHISOLME; bounding E 61 ft. on land sold by
WILLIAM HANCOCK to said FRANCIS BAKER; N 50 ft. on JOHN LEAY; S on FRED-
ERIC GRIMKÉ. Witnesses: THOMAS BULLINE, SR., PETER MAY. OTHNIEL BEALE,
J.P. JOHN BEALE, D.P.R.

Book D-D, p. 236   PAUL TRAPIER, merchant, of Georgetown, & MAG-
9 & 10 Mar. 1746   DALEN his wife, to JOHN PAUL GRIMKÉ, jeweler,
L & R   of Charleston, for Ł 1400 currency, part of a
                         lot in Charleston now occupied by GRIFFITH
BULLARD, fronting S 27 ft. on Broad Street; N on PAUL TENNY; W 103 ft. on
MESSRS. HOPTON & SMITH (formerly PAUL TENNY); E on JOHN CROCKATT. Wit-
nesses: JOHN HORRY, ISAAC TRAPIER. Before WILLIAM WHITESIDES, J.P. JOHN
BEALE, D.P.R.

Book D-D, p. 241   WILLIAM WILLIAMS, tailor, of Stono, Colleton
1 & 2 July 1747   Co., to ALEXANDER RANTOWLES, store-keeper, as
L & R by Mortgage   security on bond of even date in penal sum of
                         Ł 800 for payment on Ł 400 currency, with in-
terest, on 2 Sept. next; 200 a. on Stono Island, bequeathed to WILLIAMS
by MICHAEL REYNOLDS; bounding on RICHARD FLOYD, JAMES WILLIAMS, Bohicket
Creek & vacant lands. Witnesses: CHARLES MELLICHAMP, HANS GEORGE SHILL-
ING. Before JAMES BULLOCK, J.P. JOHN BEALE, D.P.R.

Book D-D, p. 247   JOHN SKENE, gentleman, of Berkeley Co., to
9 & 10 Mar. 1747   CHARLES PURRY, gentleman, of Granville Co.,
L & R   for Ł 300 currency, lot #35 in Beaufort, bound-
                         ing S on lot #36; W on lot #34; N on Port
Royal Street; E on Scott Street. Whereas the Lords Proprs. on 8 Aug.
1717, by the Hon. COL. ROBERT DANIELL & other trustees, granted LILIA
HAIG in free & common soccage lot #35 in Beaufort Town, Granville Co.,
which she, by will dated 1 June 1742, gave to her nephew JOHN SKENE; &
whereas GEORGE II, by Gov. JAMES GLEN, on 5 Mar. inst., granted JOHN
SKENE, in free & common soccage, lot #36 in Beaufort, bounding N on lots
32, 33, 34, & 35; E on Scott Street; S on lots 7, 8, 9, & 10; W on part
of lot #31 belonging to COL. PRIOLEAU; now SKENE sells both lots 35 & 36,
to CHARLES PURRY. Witnesses: HENRY DEWICK, JOHN BLAMYER. Before ROBERT
WRIGHT, J.P. JOHN BEALE, D.P.R.

Book D-D, p. 253   MARY WINGWOOD, widow of CHARVIL WINGWOOD, &
4 & 5 May 1741   daughter & devisee of JOHN SAUSEAU (?); with
L & R   the consent of CHARLES BARKSDALE, cabinet
                         maker, who is "upon a treaty of marriage with
her"; to JOHN HOLLYBUSH, planter; all of Christ Church Parish, Berkeley
Co., 250 a. in said Parish on which MARY lives & devised to her by her
father; in trust for MARY for her natural life; then for CHARVIL WINGOOD,
her eldest son & heir; then to JOHN SAUSEAU (?) WINGWOOD, her 2nd son; &
so on. Witnesses: GEORGE BENISON, CHARLES BARKSDALE, ANDREW RUTLEDGE.
Before ANDREW RUTLEDGE, J.P. JOHN BEALE, D.P.R.

Book D-D, p. 258   ROBERT PRINGLE, merchant, of Charleston, to
19 & 20 June 1747   JOHN JAMISON, planter, of Williamsburgh, Cra-
L & R   ven Co., for Ł 200 currency, lot #5, with the
                         dwelling house thereon, "near the Kings Tree"
in Williamsburg, containing half an a. Witnesses: JOHN NELSON, JOHN
HOLMES. OTHNIEL BEALE, J.P. JOHN BEALE, D.P.R.

Book D-D, p. 262   ANNE OLIVER, widow of THOMAS OLIVER, merchant,
16 & 17 Oct. 1745   to FRANCIS HOLMES, merchant, of Charleston,
L & R   for Ł 3000 SC money, part of lot #73 on S side
                         Tradd Street, 32 ft. x 100 ft.; bounding E on
GARRET VANVELSIN; S on THOMAS CAPERS; W on BENJAMIN SAVAGE. Witnesses:
RICE PRICE, EBENEZAR SIMMONS. Before THOMAS DALE, J.P. JOHN BEALE, D.
P.R.

Book D-D, p. 267   FRANCIS HOLMES, merchant, & ELIZABETH his wife,
16 & 17 June 1748   of Charleston, to WILLIAM BOONE, ESQ., of Col-
L & R   leton Co., for Ł 500 sterling British, part of
                         lot #73 on S side of Tradd Street, 32 x 100 ft.
bounding E on FRANCIS HOLMES; S on THOMAS CAPERS; W on BENJAMIN SAVAGE.
Whereas GARRET VANVELSON & REBECCA his wife by L & R dated 7 & 8 Apr.

1741 sold part of lot #73 in Charleston to THOMAS OLIVER & ANN his wife; & whereas THOMAS OLIVER died & ANNE, as sole owner by L & R dated 16 & 17 Oct. 1745 sold the part of the lot to FRANCIS HOLMES; now HOLMES conveys to BOONE. Witnesses: JOHN HANSON, ABRAHAM LADSON. Before THOMAS DALE, J.P. JOHN BEALE, D.P.R.

Book D-D, p. 275   JOSEPH ELLIOTT, planter, of St. Andrews Parish,
4 & 5 May 1748   Berkeley Co., to JOSEPH SHUTE, merchant, of
L & R   Charleston, for Ь 1700 currency, part of a lot
                    fronting 25 ft. on S side of Elliott Street;
bounding E 91 ft. on an alley belonging to ELIZABETH HOLMES; S on COL. OTHNIEL BEALE (formerly RICHARD HILL); W on other part of same lot devised by JOSEPH ELLIOTT to his son THOMAS. Whereas THOMAS ELLIOTT, planter, by various mesne conveyances, became owner of part of a lot fronting 50 ft. on S side of Elliott Street; & 91 ft. deep; & by will dated 9 June 1731 bequeathed the lot to his son JOSEPH; who on 17 Dec. 1738 bequeathed the lot to his 2 sons JOSEPH & THOMAS ELLIOTT; the tenement then rented by WILLIAM ROPER being given to son JOSEPH ELLIOTT, party hereto; now JOSEPH sells to SHUTE. Witnesses: THOMAS ELLIOTT, ELISHA POINSETT. Before JOHN CHAMPNEYS, J.P. JOHN BEALE, D.P.R.

Book D-D, p. 281   JOSEPH SHUTE, merchant, & ANN his wife, of
7 & 8 June 1748   Charleston, to ISABELLA SHUTE, daughter of
L & R   said JOSEPH & ANN SHUTE. Whereas ISABELLA
                    KIMBERLY, widow, of Charleston, by will dated
23 Nov. 1739 bequeathed to her granddaughter, ISABELLA SHUTE, party hereto, Ь 1500 SC money, & appointed said JOSEPH SHUTE, her executor, which will was proved 1 Apr. 1741; now to discharge the legacy, & for natural love & affection, & other considerations, JOSEPH & ANN SHUTE convey to their daughter, ISABELLE, part of a lot fronting 25 ft. on S side of Elliott Street, 91 ft. deep; bounding E on alley belonging to ELIZABETH HOLMES; S on COL. OTHNIEL BEALE (formerly RICHARD HILL); W on THOMAS ELLIOTT (son of JOSEPH ELLIOTT, deceased); being the same piece of a lot which JOSEPH ELLIOTT, planter, of St. Andrews Parish by L & R dated 4 & 5 May last sold to JOSEPH SHUTE for Ь 1700, with all buildings & improvements. Witnesses: FREDERICK MERCKLEY, JOHN REMINGTON. Before ALEXANDER STEWART, J.P. JOHN BEALE, D.P.R.

Book D-D, p. 287   MARY COOPER, widow of THOMAS COOPER, of
20 May 1748   Charleston, having, during the lifetime of her
Renunciation of Dower   husband, voluntarily signed a release, dated 6
                        Feb. 1745, to JOHN CHAMPNEYS, of 325 a. in NS
of A.B. Poolaw Creek, on Johns Island, Colleton Co., bounding E on CAPT. THOMAS FLEMING; W on AARON HUNSCOMB & THOMAS LADSON; N on said LADSON & BENJAMIN D'HARRIETTE, now for Ь 5 she renounces all claim of dower. Witness: THOMAS EVANCE. Before WILLIAM BOON. JOHN BEALE, D.P.R.

Book D-D, p. 289   JOHN CHAMPNEYS, ESQ., & SARAH his wife, of
21 & 22 May 1748   Charleston, to CONNOR BOOTH, merchant, form-
L & R   erly of Island of Antiguq, now of Charleston,
                    for Ь 1500 currency, 325 a. according to plat
made by THOMAS WALTER, surveyor, said to contain 358 a. Whereas the Lords Proprs. on 11 Jan. 1700 for Ь 4 currency, granted WILLIAM BRACKHAS 200 a., English measure, in Colleton Co., & whereas on 17 Aug. 1700, the Lords Proprs. for Ь 9 currency granted WILLIAM BRACKHAS 450 a., English measure, in Colleton Co., & whereas BRACKHAS died intestate, leaving 1 child, his daughter SARAH BRACKHAS, his heir-at-law to the 650 a.; & whereas SARAH married JOHN WILKINS, planter, & had 2 daughters, SARAH & ELIZABETH, co-heirs; & whereas ELIZABETH died intestate & SARAH became sole owner; & whereas said SARAH WILKINS married a MR. HALL, whom she survived, & by L & R dated 22 & 23 Feb. 1733 conveyed a part to CRAFTON CARWON (KARWON), planter, of Johns Island, for Ь 2000 currency, being 325 a. on N side A.B. Poolaw Creek, St. Pauls Parish, bounding E on CAPT. THOMAS FLEMING; & whereas KARWON by L & R dated 3 & 4 June 1736 for Ь 1950 currency, conveyed the 325 a. to THOMAS COOPER, merchant, & MARGARET MAGDALENE, his wife, of Charleston; & whereas she died & he (with MARY COOPER, his second wife) by L & R dated 5 & 6 Feb. 1745 mortgaged the 325 a. to JOHN CHAMPNEYS (date of redemption being 6 Feb. 1746), for Ь 3000 currency & interest; & whereas COOPER did not pay CHAMPNEYS; now CHAMPNEYS conveys to BOOTH subject to the equity of redemption of

COOPER'S heirs; there now being due Ł 3687:10 shillings. Witnesses: JOHN HANSON, WILLIAM BACKSHELL. Before WILLIAM BOONE, J.P. JOHN BEALE, D.P.R.

Book D-D, p. 300   HENRY SIMONDS, gentleman, of Bladen Co., NC,
14 June 1748   son & heir-at-law of JUDITY SIMONDS (daughter
Deed of Feoffment   & heir-at-law of PETER GIRARD, merchant, of
                         Berkeley Co.), by his brother (& his attorney
on this behalf) PETER SIMONDS, of 1st part; to CHARLES PINCKNEY, of
Charleston, of 2nd part; for Ł 210 currency, lot #200 in Charleston.
Whereas the Lords Proprs. on 17 May 1694 granted PETER GIRARD, merchant,
of Charleston, (grandfather of said HENRY SIMONDS), lot #200 in Charles-
ton, bounding E on a marsh at the head of MAJ. DANIEL'S Creek; W on the
Great Street leading from Oyster Point to the Market Place by CAPT. SY-
MOND'S lot; S on the marsh; N on another lot belonging to said PETER
GIRARD; & whereas PETER GIRARD by will dated 3 Aug. 1707 devised all the
residue of his estate (including lot #200) to his beloved daughter JUDITH
GIRARD (mother of said HENRY SIMONDS) who married HENRY SIMONDS, planter,
of St. Johns Parish, Berkeley Co., & whereas HENRY SIMONDS (her eldest
son & heir-at-law) by letter dated 2 May 1748 appointed his beloved
brother, PETER, his attorney; to take possession of the 2 lots, #200 &
#207, & dispose of them; now PETER SIMONDS, as attorney for HENRY, sells
lot #200 to CHARLES PINCKNEY. Witnesses: THOMAS WALKER, JAMES CLARK.
Before WILLIAM PINCKNEY, J.P. JOHN BEALE, D.P.R.

Book D-D, p. 304   JOHN HANDYSIDE, planter, of the Congarees, to
21 & 22 June   CHARLES PINCKNEY, ESQ., of Charleston, for
L & R   Ł 60 currency, 400 a., part of 840 a. Whereas
                         on 8 Dec. 1744, ELIZABETH VERDITY was granted
840 a. on Four Hole Swamp, St. James Goose Creek Parish, Berkeley Co.,
bounding W on vacant land & on GEORGE HAIG; N on GEORGE HAIG & JOHN HAM-
ILTON; E on MRS. ANNE GOODBEE & JAMES GOODBEE; S on JAMES GOODBEE & CAPT.
ABRAHAM DUPONT; & whereas ELIZABETH VERDITY by L & R dated 1 & 2 July
1745 sold the S part (400 a.) to JOHN HANDYSIDE, bounding W on vacant
land & GEORGE HAIG; N on GEORGE HAIG & JOHN HAMILTON; E on ANNE GOODBEE &
JAMES GOODBEE; S on JAMES GOODBEE & CAPT. ABRAHAM DUPONT; now HANDYSIDE
sells the 400 a. to CHARLES PINCKNEY. Witnesses: JOSEPH OARUM, ELIZABETH
CORNISH. Before WILLIAM PINCKNEY, J.P. JOHN BEALE, D.P.R.

Book D-D, p. 309   STEPHEN BULL, gentleman, of Granville Co., &
14 & 15 Dec. 1747   JUDITH his wife (lately JUDITH MAYRANT), to
L & R   JOHN DRAYTON, gentleman, of Berkeley Co., for
                         Ł 5000 currency, several tracts of 520 a.,
620 a., 500 a., 533 a., 631 a., (being the undivided half of 1262 a.).
Whereas Gov. ROBERT GIBBES & the Lords Proprs. on 7 June 1710 granted
WILLIAM BULL, ESQ., 520 a. on W side Ashley River, bounding NE on MR.
WARRIN; SE on WILLIAM ELLIOTT; SW on WILLIAM BULL; NW on vacant land; &
whereas Gov. ROBERT GIBBES on 27 June 1710 granted WILLIAM BULL 620 a. on
W side Ashley River, bounding NE on WILLIAM BULL; SE on WILLIAM ELLIOTT;
SW & NW on vacant land; & whereas Gov. CHARLES CRAVEN on 12 May 1714
granted WILLIAM BULL 500 a., on SW side Ashley River, bounding S on WIL-
LIAM BULL; N & E on WILLIAM ELLIOTT, MOSES WAY, STEPHEN DOWSE & THOMAS
OSGOOD; & whereas WILLIAM BULL & MARY his wife, by deed poll dated 23
June 1730 granted STEPHEN BULL, 1120 a. (the 500 a. & 620 a. first men-
tioned, being contiguous); & whereas WILLIAM BULL by L & R dated 9 & 10
Jan. 1733 conveyed to STEPHEN BULL 520 a. (part of the second mentioned
620 a.) bounding NE on STEPHEN BULL; SE on WILLIAM ELLIOTT; SW on PETER
TAYLOR; NW on WILLIAM BULL; & whereas Lt. Gov. THOMAS BROUGHTON on 29 May
1736 granted SUSANNAH MAYRANT 1262 a. in Craven Co., bounding N & S on
ELIAS HORRY; W on MRS. MAYRANT; E on the Great Swamp; & whereas she bequeathed the land (called 1240 a. on N side Santee River) equally to her
2 daughters, ELIZABETH MAYRANT & JUDITH MAYRANT; & whereas STEPHEN BULL
married JUDITH MAYRANT & became entitled to 631 a. (1/2 of 1262 a.); &
whereas to avoid any disputes that may arise between JOHN MAYRANT (heir-
at-law to SUSANNAH MAYRANT) & STEPHEN BULL & JUDITH his wife, concerning
the validity of SUSANNAH'S will, said JOHN MAYRANT by deed of release &
confirmation dated 15 this inst. Dec. released all his title thereto &
confirmed the estate & devise of the premises according to the true intent of his will; & whereas Lt. Gov. THOMAS BROUGHTON on 13 July
1737 granted STEPHEN BULL 533 a. in Colleton Co., bounding NE & SE on
STEPHEN BULL; SW on STEPHEN DOWSE; NW on THOMAS OSGOOD; so that STEPHEN

BULL became owner of several tracts of 520 a., 620 a., 500 a., 631 a., &
533 a., all of which he now sells to JOHN DRAYTON. Witnesses: THOMAS
DRAYTON, ELIZABETH DRAYTON. Before HENRY MIDDLETON, J.P. JOHN BEALE,
D.P.R.

Book D-D, p. 319   JOHN MAYRANT, of Craven Co., only son & heir-
15 Dec. 1747   at-law of SUSANNAH MAYRANT, widow; of 1st part;
Release & Confirmation   STEPHEN BULL & JUDITH his wife, of 2nd part.
                           Whereas SUSANNAH MAYRANT by will dated 16 Sept.
1735 bequeathed equally to her 2 daughters, ELIZABETH & JUDITH, a tract
supposed to contain 1240 a. on N side Santee River, bounding on PETER
HORRY, to be divided when the 1st came of age or married; & whereas
said SUSANNAH had at the time of making her will only a survey & did not
obtain a grant until 29 May 1736 (tract supposed to be 1240 being granted
for 1262 a.); & whereas some doubts may arise as to the validity of said
will (because the will was dated prior to grant); now to remove such
doubts & for natural affection for his sister JUDITH, now wife of STEPHEN
BULL of Granville Co., & for his nieces SUSANNAH ST. JULIEN & JUDITH ST.
JULIEN (daughters of ELIZABETH MAYRANT who married JOSEPH ST. JULIEN),
JOHN MAYRANT confirms to STEPHEN BULL & JUDITH his wife, & to said SU-
SANNAH ST. JULIEN & JUDITH ST. JULIEN the tract of 1262 a. Witnesses:
JAMES WRIGHT, CHARLES CALVER. Before JOHN LINING, J.P. JOHN BEALE, D.
P.R.

Book D-D, p. 321   FRANCIS CLARKE, bricklayer, to WILLIAM HARRIS,
7 June 1748   butcher, both of Charleston, as security on
Mortgage   bond of even date in penal sum of Ł 395:15 for
                           payment of Ł 197:17:6 currency, with interest,
on 22 June inst.; part of lot marked O in the plan of Ansonborough, St.
Philip's Parish, Berkeley Co., bounding E on WILLIAM HARRIS (formerly
DAVID MONGIN); S 27 ft. on a new street; other sides on DAVID MONGIN;
110 ft. deep; subject only to the payment of a mortgage of Ł 160 currency
to OTHNIEL BEALE, merchant, of Charleston. Witnesses: MARTHA (?) REMING-
TON, JOHN REMINGTON. Before OTHNIEL BEALE, J.P. JOHN BEALE, D.P.R.

Book D-D, p. 324   JOHN MARTINI, surgeon, & MARY his wife, to
7 & 8 Mar. 1743   WILLIAM CLIFFORD, planter, all of St. James
L & R   Goose Creek Parish, for Ł 2500 currency,
                           96-1/4 a. in St. James Goose Creek, bounding N
on DR. MARTINI; W on "Jefferys" Plantation; SW on RALPH IZARD; E on the
Broad Path; also 27-1/2 a. in same Parish, bounding W on RALPH IZARD; SE
on CAPT. WILLIAM DRY; NE on the Broad Road; also 19-1/2 a. in same Parish,
bounding N & S on Landgrave THOMAS SMITH; E on the Broad Path or Road
from Charleston to Goose Creek; W on "Jefferys". Witnesses: ISAAC CHAND-
LER, JAMES ELDERTON. Before HENRY GIBBES, J.P. JOHN BEALE, D.P.R.

Book D-D, p. 330   JOHN MOULTRIE, surgeon, of Charleston, to THOM-
19 & 20 Nov. 1747   AS CARTER, planter, of St. John's Parish,
L & R   Berkeley Co., for Ł 300 SC money, 400 a. in
                           Berkeley Co., bounding SW & SE on vacant land;
N on JOHN NELSON; NW on PETER DE ST. JULIEN. Witnesses: RICHARD BUTLER,
LEOPOLD BOUDON. Before JAMES MICKIE, J.P. JOHN BEALE, D.P.R.

Book D-D, p. 335   JOHN TRIBOUDET, merchant, to ROBERT ROPER, gen-
21 & 22 Mar. 1747   tleman, both of Charleston, as security on
L & R by Mortgage   bond of even date in penal sum of Ł 2949:7 for
                           payment of Ł 1474:13:6 SC money, with interest,
on 22 Mar. 1748; part of lot #17 in Charleston 25 x 100 ft.; bounding E
on a part of said lot fronting the Bay 75 ft. deep formerly possessed by
JOHN ROPER, then by JACOB WOOLFORD, now by JOHN SCOTT, gunsmith; W on
JOHN TRIBOUDET; N on a small alley leading from the Bay to Union Street,
S on CHARLES CODNER. Witnesses: WILLIAM GEORGE FREEMAN, WILLIAM BURROWS.
Before JAMES MICKIE, J.P. JOHN BEALE, D.P.R.

Book D-D, p. 341   STEPHEN BEDON, JR., merchant, of Charleston,
2 Dec. 1747   to ISAAC NICHOLAS, planter, of Stono, as secur-
Mortgage   ity on bond of even date in penal sum of
                           Ł 4000 currency, with interest, on 1 Jan. 1748;
549 a. & marsh on Daniell's Island, formerly belonging to ROBERT DANIELL,
ESQ., now to STEPHEN BEDON, JR.; also all cattle, horses, sheep, hogs,

plantation tools, boats, etc. Witnesses: HENRY BEDON, GEORGE BEDON. Before THOMAS DALE, J.P. JOHN BEALE, D.P.R.

Book D-D, p. 344   WILLIAM BROWN, planter, & MARGARET his wife,
18 & 19 Jan. 1747   of Colleton Co., to SAMUEL EDGAR, planter, of
L & R   Craven Co., for Ł 200 SC money, 205 a. on SE
                      side Santee River, in Berkeley Co., bounding
on all sides on heirs of BENJAMIN SCHENCKINGH & EMANUEL MARQUESS; which
205 a. (part of 24,000 a. granted by letters patent dated 22 Feb. 1682 to
JOHN MONK, Cassique) were sold by STEPHEN MONK (son & heir of JOHN MONK)
by L & R dated 7 & 8 Mar. 1725 to JOHN HERBERT. Whereas by deed of par-
tition quadripartite dated 30 Jan. 1747 between WILLIAM WOOD, planter, of
St. James Goose Creek, & WILLOUGHBY his wife (a daughter of JOHN HERBERT)
of 1st part; WILLIAM BROWN & MARGARET his wife (another daughter of JOHN
HERBERT) of 2nd part; HENRY WOOD, planter, of St. Andrews Parish, & ELIZ-
ABETH his wife (another daughter of JOHN HERBERT), of 3rd part; & THOMAS
HODSON, planter, of Berkeley Co., & MARY his wife (another daughter of
JOHN HERBERT) of 4th part; for dividing amongst the 4 daughters the 7
plantations that belonged to their father (their only brother SAMUEL hav-
ing died, & they being his heirs also); it was agreed that MARGARET BROWN
(party hereto) should have said 205 a.; now she & her husband convey to
SAMUEL EDGAR. Witnesses: JOSEPH GLOVER, WILLIAM OSWALD, WILLIAM CORAN.
Before THOMAS DALE, J.P. JOHN BEALE, D.P.R.

Book D-D, p. 352   MARMADUKE AISH, saddler, to ARENONT (?) SCHER-
10 & 11 June 1748   MERHORNE, merchant, & CATHERINE SMART; all of
L & R by Mortgage   Charleston; as security on bond of even date
                      in penal sum of Ł 3000 for payment of Ł 1500
currency, with interest, on 11 June 1750; lot #26 on S side Broad Street;
the brick house thereon now occupied by JOHN PAUL GRIMKË & LEO CHALMERS;
bounding E on ISAAC HOLMES; S on DANIEL BOURGET; W on ANDREW DEVEAUX.
Witnesses: JOHN BONNEAHEAU, JOHN RIVIERE. Before HENRY GIBBES, J.P.
JOHN BEALE, D.P.R. On 15 Apr. 1751 ARNONT SCHERMERHORNE & CATHERINE
SCURLOCK (formerly CATHERINE SMART), declared mortgage satisfied. Witness: WILLIAM HOPTON.

Book D-D, p. 357   HILLERSDON WIGG, merchant, & ELIZABETH his
24 & 25 July   wife, to MARGRITT CATTELL, gentlewoman, all of
L & R   Beaufort; for Ł 300 SC money; lot #304 in Beau-
                      fort, bounding N on Craven Street; E on
Charles Street; S on lot #305 belonging to JOHN DELIGEA; W on lot #303;
ELIZABETH to renounce her dower within 12 months. Witnesses: JOHN GREEN,
EDWARD WIGG. Before JOHN MULLRYNE, J.P. JOHN BEALE, D.P.R.

Book D-D, p. 363   JOHN WESTFIELD, blacksmith, & SARAH his wife,
10 & 11 June 1745   to SAMUEL DESAURENCY, yeoman, all of Craven
L & R   Co., for Ł 380 currency; 300 a. in the Welch
                      tract, Craven Co., on which the WESTFIELDS
live; bounding N on Peedee River; other sides on vacant land; as by plat
dated 17 Dec. 1741, certified 1 Nov. 1743; & grant dated 11 Nov. 1743.
Witnesses: JOHN EVANS, JOHN GOODWYNN. Before WILLIAM JAMES, J.P. JOHN
BEALE, D.P.R.

Book D-D, p. 369   RICHARD (his mark) BARRON, planter, to JACOB
8 & 9 Feb. 1747   SAURENCY, planter, both of the WELCH tract,
L & R   Craven Co., for Ł 150 SC money, 150 a. in the
                      WELCH tract, granted by Gov. JAMES GLEN on 24
May 1745 to RICHARD BARRON; bounding N on SAMUEL DE SAURENCY; other sides
on vacant land. Witnesses: PHILLIP DOUGLAS, DANIEL DEVONALD. Before
WILLIAM JAMES, J.P. JOHN BEALE, D.P.R.

Book D-D, p. 373   JAMES MARSH, to JAMES FOWLER, gentleman; both
25 Mar. 1748   of Charleston; as security on 5 bonds of even
Mortgage   date for Ł 2000, Ł 2000, Ł 400, Ł 600, &
                      Ł 1000 for payment of Ł 1000, Ł 1000, Ł 200,
Ł 300, & Ł 500 currency, with interest, on 25 Mar. next; part of lot #12
in Charleston; 34 x 80 ft., bounding W on JAMES FOWLER; S on Poinsett
Street or alley; N on ALBERT MULLAR; E on THOMAS ROSE. Witnesses: JAMES
FOWLER, JR., WILLIAM BRISBANE. Before JAMES SKERVING, J.P. JOHN BEALE,
D.P.R.

Book D-D, p. 377   JOHN MCKENZIE, JR., of Charleston Neck, to
7 & 8 1748   JOHN MCKENZIE, SR., & JOHN RATTRAY, gentleman,
L & R by Mortgage   of Charleston, as security on bond of even
                          date in penal sum of Ł 7120 for payment of
Ł 3560 SC money, with interest, on 1 Jan. 1748; 81 a. on Charleston Neck,
bounding N on heirs of JOHN PENDARVIS; S on BRANFIL EVANCE (formerly
CHILDERMAS CROFT); E on JAMES MCLOTHLIN; W on marsh; except half an a.
adjoining a dam or causeway crossing the marsh between the land of BRAN-
FIL EVANCE & that hereby conveyed. Witnesses: GEORGE HUNTER, HUGH CART-
WRIGHT. Before WILLIAM GEORGE FREEMAN, J.P. JOHN BEALE, D.P.R.

Book D-D, p. 382   ANDREW QUELCH, planter, of Hobkaw, Christ
11 & 12 July 1748   Church Parish, to THOMAS BOLTON, merchant, of
L & R by Mortgage   Charleston, as security on bond dated 4 this
                          July in penal sum of Ł 10,300 for payment of
Ł 5150 currency, with interest, on 4 July 1749; 340 a.; & delivers 34
slaves. Whereas the Lords Proprs. on 11 May 1709 granted BENJAMIN QUELCH
(father of said ANDREW QUELCH) 340 a., English measure, on SE side Wando
River, bounding N on Wackindaw Creek; E on DAVID MAYBANK; S on Molassa
Creek; & whereas by will dated 17 July 1716 BENJAMIN QUELCH bequeathed
the 340 a., on which he then dwelt, to his beloved wife ELIZABETH for her
lifetime, & afterwards to his son GEORGE QUELCH; or by default to son AN-
DREW; or to son BENJAMIN; & whereas sons GEORGE & BENJAMIN died, also
said ELIZABETH, & ANDREW inherited; now he mortgages to BOLTON. A penknife delivered. Witnesses: The Hon. CHARLES PINCKNEY, ELIZABETH PINCK-
NEY. Before WILLIAM PINCKNEY, J.P. JOHN BEALE, D.P.R.

Book D-D, p. 391   JOHN (his mark) FRYERSON, SR., to WILLIAM NEIL-
4 Jan. 1747   SON, both of Craven Co., for Ł 125 currency,
Release   in note & bond, paid by NEILSON to FRYERSON,
                          300 a. in Williamsburg Township, Craven Co.,
on Black River granted by the Kings & Lord Carteret to JOHN FRYERSON, SR.,
bounding E on JOHN JONES & vacant land. Witnesses: MATHEW NEILSON, ALEX-
ANDER FLEMING, ROBERT FRIERSON. Before ROGER GIBSON, J.P. JOHN BEALE,
D.P.R.

Book D-D, p. 396   JOSEPH (his mark) RODOSS, & ANN (her mark) his
30 Mar. 1747/8   wife, of Craven Co., to WILLIAM NEILSON, for
Mortgage   Ł 200 currency, which RODOSS acknowledged as
                          his debt to NEILSON, 300 a. in Williamsburgh
Township, Craven Co., on Black River, bounding on all sides on vacant
land; granted by Lord Carteret to JOSEPH & ANN RODESS. Witnesses: WIL-
LIAM YOUNG, SAMUEL MOUNTGOMERY. Before ROGER GIBSON, J.P. JOHN BEALE,
D.P.R.

Book D-D, p. 400   JOHN EVANS, planter, of St. Helena Parish,
11 & 12 Apr. 1743   Granville Co., to JOSEPH ELLICOT CAPERS, plant-
L & R   er, of same place, for Ł 1500 currency, 3
                          tracts of land, total 820 a. Whereas Gov.
ROBERT GIBBES, & the Lords Proprs. on 23 July 1711 granted RANDOLPH EVANS
500 a. on St. Helena Island, Granville Co., bounding NE on WALTER MELVIN
& JOHN COWAN; SE on THOMAS NAYRNES; SW on vacant land; W on THOMAS
NAYRNES; NW on vacant land; & whereas the King on 28 Apr. 1733 granted
RANDOLPH EVANS 166 a. on St. Helena Island, bounding N, S & E on COL. WIL-
LIAM BULL; W on JONATHAN NORTON; & on 11 July 1733 granted said EVANS
154 a. on St. Helena Island, bounding NE & SE on RANDOLPH EVANS; NW & SW
on COL. WILLIAM BULL; & whereas, on the death of RANDOLPH EVANS, JOHN
EVANS become owner of the 3 tracts; now he conveys them to CAPERS. Wit-
nesses: FRANCIS THOMPSON, NATHANIEL ADAMS, WILLIAM REYNOLDS. Before
OTHNIEL BEALE, J.P. JOHN BEALE, D.P.R.

Book D-D, p. 404   WILLIAM HART, ship carpenter, of Charleston,
19 Mar. 1746   to DAVID MUNGIN, watchmaker, of Charleston, as
Mortgage   security on bond of even date in penal sum of
                          Ł 260 for payment of Ł 130 currency, with in-
terest, on 19 Mar. 1747; that lot in Ansonburgh, near Charleston; 30 x
137 ft., with houses thereon; bounding W on a new street; SE & N on JOHN
DART, ESQ.; S on DAVID MUNGIN; also 1 mahogany table, 3 common tables, 1
corner cupboard, 6 burnt china saucers & 5 cups, 6 blue & white china
cups & saucers, 4 coffee cups, 1 milk pot, 1 small china bowl, 1 tray, 6

silver teaspoons, 1 large Delft dish, 6 plates, 1 Japanned mug, 1 punch bowl, 2 pewter dishes, 1 dozen plates, 1 teakettle, 1 pot, 1 large brass kettle, 1 pair dogs, 1 spit, 1 gridiron, 1 frying pan, 1 pot rack, 10 chairs, 6 pictures, 2 cases, 1 chest, 2 trunks, 1 looking glass, 1 gun, 1 cartouche box, 12 patty pans, 3 pair sheets, 2 blankets, 2 pillows, 1 bolster, 1 mattress, 1 calico coverlet, 1 pair curtains, a bedstead, 3 wash tubs & 1 pail. Witnesses: JOSEPH MAXEY, STEPHEN TOUSSIGER. Before OTHNIEL BEALE, J.P. JOHN BEALE, D.P.R. On 22 July 1749 DAVID MONGIN declared satisfied. Witness: WILLIAM HOPTON, P.R.

DEEDS BOOK "E-E"
JULY 1748 - APRIL 1749

Book E-E, p. 1   JOHN TOWNSEND, cooper, to WILLIAM TURNER, bar-
18 Oct. 1745   ber & peruke-maker, both of Charleston, for
Lease for 30 years   Ł 30 a year, for 30 years; part of 2 lots #24
                        & #25 in Charleston, bounding N 74 ft. on
PETER LEGER, cooper; S on a small tenement occupied by ELIZABETH SERGEANT;
W on buildings erected on part of said lots owned by JOHN TOWNSEND; E 30
ft. on Bedon's Alley; with the fences. TURNER, at his own expense, to
build thereon a good substantial brick dwelling-house, 16 x 30 ft. covered with slate or tile, & keep it in good repair; but shall not erect
any buildings at the W end nearer than 2 feet to the windows in TOWN-
SEND'S buildings so that the windows may be opened freely & TOWNSEND have
benefit of light. TOWNSEND agrees to furnish TURNER at end of every year,
for first 5 years, a good large fat turkey cock & a good large chine of
bacon, with sufficient quantity of good wine punch & other liquors to
make a complete treat for 8 men or women. Witnesses: JOHN RICE, EDWARD
EDGAR, WILLIAM SMITH. Before THOMAS LAMBOLL, J.P. JOHN BEALE, Dep. Pub.
Reg.

Book E-E, p. 3   JONATHAN FITCH, planter, & FRANCES his wife,
13 & 14 May 1735   to ROGER SAUNDERS, ESQ., both of Berkeley Co.,
L & R   for Ł 2700 SC money, 202-1/2 a., English mea-
                        sure, on N side Ashley River, Berkeley Co.,
                        bounding SE on RALPH IZARD (formerly THOMAS PINCKNEY, gentleman); NW on
_____ (formerly JOSEPH OLDYS); also 90 a. part of 250 a.; bounding on
RALPH IZARD. Whereas Gov. NATHANIEL JOHNSON, JOB HOWES & JAMES MOORE,
Lords Proprs. on 3 Nov. 1703 granted WILLIAM CANTY, JR.; yeoman, 202-1/2
a. on N side Ashley River; which CANTY & ARABELLA his wife, by deed of
feoffment dated 8 Apr. 1704 conveyed to ANDREW RUSS, yeoman, of Berkeley
Co.; who, by deed of feoffment dated 20 May 1709 conveyed to JONATHAN
FITCH, grandfather of JONATHAN, party hereto; & whereas Gov. NATHANIEL
JOHNSON, THOMAS BROUGHTON & NICHOLAS TROTT, Lords Proprs. on 1 May 1708
granted WILLIAM WILLIAMS 250 a., English measure, in Berkeley Co., bounding N on Landgrave THOMAS SMITH; E on RALPH IZARD (formerly CHRISTOPHER
SMITH); S on RALPH IZARD (formerly THOMAS PINCKNEY); W on THOMAS FITCH
(formerly MR. CHAPMAN) & on ANDREW RUSS (now JONATHAN FITCH); & whereas
WILLIAM WILLIAMS by will dated 2 Nov. 1710 bequeathed all his real estate
to HINROYDA ENGLISH; gentleman; who, by deed of feoffment dated 17 Sept.
1712, conveyed the 250 a. to EBENEZER TAYLOR, gentleman, of Berkeley Co.;
who, on 12 Oct. 1714 conveyed to JONATHAN FITCH, grandfather of JONATHAN,
party hereto; so that JONATHAN FITCH, the grandfather, became owner of
the 2 tracts of 202-1/2 a. & 250 a. & by will dated 4 Nov. 1715 bequeathed the residue of his whole estate real & personal, including the 2
tracts, equally between SUSANNAH FITCH & his son JOSEPH FITC H; & whereas
JOSEPH FITCH, & CONSTANT, his wife, on 16 Oct. 1724 conveyed their half
of the 2 tracts to JONATHAN FITCH, party hereto; & whereas SUSANNAH FITCH,
the grandmother of JONATHAN, party hereto, by deed of gift dated 21 Mar.
1725 conveyed to JONATHAN FITCH, party hereto, the plantation on which
she lived, which was left to her by her husband, JONATHAN the grandfather
(her half of the 2 tracts); & whereas JONATHAN FITCH, the grandson, now
owner of the entire 2 tracts, by L & R dated 17 & 18 Apr. 1734, conveyed
to RALPH IZARD 160 a., part of the 250 a., so that 90 a. remained; now he
sells the 202-1/2 a. & the 90 a. to SAUNDERS. Witnesses: THOMAS FITCH,
CONSTANT FITCH, MARY NEILSON. CONSTANT BUTLER (formerly CONSTANT FITCH)
testified as witness before WILLIAM GEORGE FREEMAN, J.P. on 29 Aug. 1747.
JOHN BEALE, Register.

Book E-E, p. 11   WILLIAM TWEEDY, & MARY his wife, to DAVID BET-
12 Dec. 1741   TISON, planter, both of Colleton Co.; for
Sale   Ŀ 100 currency; 200 a. in Colleton Co., near
head of Ashepoo River; bounding NW on CAPT.
LLOYD; other sides on vacant land. Witnesses: JOHN FIELD, JR., WILLIAM
DALTON, RICHARD DAWSON. Before CULCHETH GOLIGHTLY, J.P. JOHN BEALE,
Register.

Book E-E, p. 13   RICHARD DAWSON, planter, to DAVID BETTISON,
20 Apr. 1746   planter, both of Colleton Co., for Ŀ 200 cur-
Sale   rency, 200 a. in Colleton Co., near Horse Shoe
Savannah, bounding N on WILLIAM EBERSON; SW on
JOHN COOK; SE on MR. BETTISON; other sides on vacant land. Witnesses:
THOMAS DAWSON, THOMAS BATTOON. Before HENRY HYRNE, J.P. JOHN BEALE,
Register.

Book E-E, p. 15   FRANCIS CLARK, bricklayer, & MARY his wife, to
25 & 26 July 1748   HUGH CARTWRIGHT, bricklayer, all of Charleston;
L & R by Mortgage   as security on bond of even date in penal sum
of Ŀ 1376:3:8 for payment of Ŀ 688:1:10 cur-
rency, with interest, on 5 Aug. 1748; part of a lot marked O in the plan
of GEORGE ANSON'S land known as Ansonsborough, near Charleston, sold by
BENJAMIN WHITAKER as attorney for GEORGE ANSON to DAVID MONGIN; bounding
E 110 ft. on WILLIAM HARRIS (formerly DAVID MONGIN); S 27 ft. on a new
street; other sides on DAVID MONGIN; with all houses & improvements thereon, with right of passage through the most convenient street to & from
the landing place on a creek of Cooper River. Witnesses: HENRY DONGWORTH
(LONGWORTH?), JAMES GRINDLAY. Before JOHN RATTRAY, J.P. JOHN BEALE,
Register.

Book E-E, p. 19   THOMAS HEPWORTH, gentleman, of Charleston, to
22 & 23 Mar. 1737   JOSEPH ALLEN, shipwright, of Winyaw, Craven
L & R   Co., for Ŀ 1173 SC money, 391 a., on which
ALLEN lives, in Craven Co., bounding E on WIL-
LIAM ALSTON (formerly THOMAS HEPWORTH); S on PERCIVAL PAWLEY (formerly
DR. JOHN HUTCHINSON); W on Hepworth Creek; N on WILLIAM ALSTON (formerly
THOMAS HEPWORTH); which 391 a. is part of 500 a. granted by the Lords
Proprs. & Gov. ROBERT GIBBES on 28 June 1711 to THOMAS HEPWORTH; the
original plat & grant being in the hands of PERCIVAL PAWLEY. Witnesses:
WILLIAM ALLSTON, JOHN LUPTON. HENRY WARNER recognized the handwriting of
witnesses before WILLIAM POOLE, J.P. JOHN BEALE, Register.

Book E-E, p. 23   ALEXANDER GOODBE, shop keeper, to GABRIEL
2 Feb. 1747   GUIGNARD, cooper, both of Charelston, as se-
Mortgage   curity on 2 bonds, 1 dated 30 Jan. last in penal sum of Ŀ 400 for payment of Ŀ 200 curren-
cy, with interest, on 25 Mar. 1749; the other of same date in penal sum
of Ŀ 350 for payment of Ŀ 175 currency, with interest, on 30 Jan. 1750;
that part of Colleton Square which GOODBE recently purchased from
GUIGNARD, bounding N 75 ft. on Guignard Street; W on GABRIEL GUIGNARD; S
on THOMAS BURNHAM; E 50 ft. on a 12 ft. alley called French Alley. Witnesses: MARGARET REMINGTON, JOHN REMINGTON. Before WILLIAM PINCKNEY,
J.P. JOHN BEALE, Register.

Book E-E, p. 28   OLIVER SPENCER, cordwinder, & REBECCA (her
10 & 11 Feb. 1738/9   mark) his wife, to JOHN MITHRINGHAM, house
L & R   carpenter, both of Christ Church Parish, Berkeley Co., for Ŀ 200 currency; 25 a., English
measure, part of 50 a. in Christ Church Parish; bounding E on OLIVER
SPENCER; S on JOSEPH LAW; W on RICHARD ROUSER; N on Quelch's Creek; also
priviledge of a landing, with passage thereto in order to transport any
goods or produce by water, but not so as to damage said SPENCER. Witnesses: JOHN BURDELL, STEPHEN HARTLEY, JOHN (his mark) STEEL. Before
ROBERT AUSTIN, J.P. JOHN BEALE, Register.

Book E-E, p. 32   JOHN METHRINGHAM, house carpenter; of Christ
4 & 5 Apr. 1748   Church Parish, Berkeley Co., to THOMAS BOLTON,
L & R by Mortgage   shopkeeper, of Charleston, as security on bond
of even date in penal sum of Ŀ 619:6 for pay-
ment of Ŀ 309:13 currency, with interest, on 5 Apr. 1749; 25 a., part of

169

50 a., formerly belonging to EDMUND MORRAINE, in Christ Church Parish, bounding E on OLIVER SPENCER; S on JOSEPH LAW; W on RICHARD ROUSIN; N on Quelch's Creek. Witnesses: PETER DAVID, JOHN REMINGTON. Before ROBERT AUSTIN, J.P. JOHN BEALE, Register. On 24 Feb. 1749 BOLTON acknowledged full satisfaction of mortgage from JOHN CHAMPNEYS & WILLIAM GEORGE FREEMAN, trustees for ELIZABETH BEAUCHAMP, now ELIZABETH METHRINGHAM. Witness: WILLIAM HOPTON.

Book E-E, p. 38
1 & 2 Jan. 1747
L & R

CHARLES DEVON, gentleman, of London, (son & heir of RICHARD DEVON, of London), by his attorney, JOHN CALCOCK, merchant, of Charleston, to DANIEL WELSHUYSEN, ESQ., of Charleston; for Ł 1250 currency, 500 a., English measure, on the High Road between Ashepoo & Combahee Rivers, Colleton Co., bounding at the time of the original grant, W & NW on JAMES BATTS. Whereas CHARLES CRAVEN & the Lords Proprs. on 25 Feb. 1714 granted JOHN HILL 500 a. in Colleton Co., which he & his wife ELIZABETH on 5 Sept. 1716 conveyed to RICHARD DEVON; & whereas on his death the 500 a. descended to his son & heir CHARLES DEVON; who, by letter dated 16 Sept. 1741 appointed JOHN CALCOCK his attorney with authority to sell the plantation; now CALCOCK sells it to WELSHUYSEN. Witnesses: JOHN CORBETT, JOB MILNER. Before OTHNIEL BEALE, J.P. JOHN BEALE, Register.

Book E-E, p. 45
10 & 11 July 1744
L & R

Landgrave EDMUND BELLINGER, 2nd, & MARY LUCIA his wife, to WILLIAM HUTSON, (cleric?), of St. Helena Parish, Granville Co., for Ł 2000 currency, 500 a., the NE half of 1000 a. on Head of Pocotallago River, bounding SW on the river & on EDMUND BELLINGER; NW on ELIZABETH BELLINGER; NE on JOHN BULL; SE on estate of EDMUND BELLINGER the father. Whereas Landgrave EDMUND BELLINGER, 1st, father of EDMUND, 2nd, under his Landgrave's patent for 48,000 a. had 13,000 a. set aside for him at the head of Pocotalligo River in Granville Co., bounding E on COL. WILLIAM BULL & all other sides on vacant land; & whereas the father by will dated 21 Feb. 1739 bequeathed to his son EDMUND 1000 a. of his patent land, to be assigned to the son by testator's wife ELIZABETH; & whereas she assigned to EDMUND the son 1000 a., part of the 13,000 a., bounding S & SW on the High Road & part of the 13,000 a.; NW on ELIZABETH BELLINGER; N on JOHN BULL; E on part of 13,000 a.; now EDMUND BELLINGER, 2nd, sells half his tract to HUTSON. Witnesses to EDMUND'S signature: JAMES DEVEAUX, WILLIAM BACKSHELL. Witnesses to MARY LUCIA BELLINGER'S signature: ELIZABETH BULL, WILLIAM BACKSHELL. Before OTHNIEL BEALE, J.P. JOHN BEALE, Dep. Pub. Reg.

Book E-E, p. 51
5 & 6 Aug. 1747
L & R by Mortgage

ROBERT THORPE, ESQ., to ELIZABETH WOODWARD, widow, executrix of will of RICHARD WOODWARD, as security on bond of even date in penal sum of Ł 2659:15:7 for payment of Ł 1329:17:9-1/2 currency, with interest, on 6 Aug. next; that lot #3 in Beaufort Town, Granville Co., originally granted by the Lords Proprs. on 13 Aug. 1717 to the Hon. Charles Hart fronting S on the Bay; bounding W on lot #2; N on lot #29; E on lot #4; together with the stores, wharf, bridge, dwelling house, scale house, & other improvements. Witnesses: THOMAS BESWICKE, JOHN GREENE. Before JOHN MULLRYNE, J.P.

Book E-E, p. 55
17 & 18 Dec. 1747
L & R by Mortgage

THOMAS ELMES, planter, & ANN his wife, of Charleston Neck, Berkeley Co., to RICHARD BAKER, planter, of St. George's Parish, as security on bond of even date in penal sum of Ł 1224 for payment of Ł 612 currency, with interest, on 18 Dec. 1748; 226 a. in Berkeley Co., bounding N on WILLIAM HASFORT; E on Madam BARKER; S on THOMAS ELMES; SW on MRS. PARKER; also 250 a. in Berkeley Co., bounding N on THOMAS ELMES; S on WILLIAM CANTEY; E on THOMAS BARKER; W on GEORGE CANTEY; also 8 slaves. ANN ELMES voluntarily renounces her dower. Witnesses: ELIZABETH PENDARVIS, JOSIAH PENDARVIS, WILLIAM MAINE. Before CHARLES HILL, J.P. JOHN BEALE, Register.

Book E-E, p. 60
21 Nov. 1747
Feoffment

WILLIAM HARRIS, butcher, & SARAH his wife, of Charleston, to MATHEW NEILSON, planter, for Ł 140 currency, part of an a. lot marked O on general plan of GEORGE ANSON'S land near

Charleston, 35 x 110 ft., bounding S on a new street; E on JOHN DART; W on FRANCIS CLARK (formerly DAVID MUNGIN). SARAH voluntarily renounces her dower. Witnesses: THOMAS DOUGHTY, RICHARD BUTLER. Before OTHNIEL BEALE, J.P. JOHN BEALE, Register.

Book E-E, p. 62
1 & 2 June 1747
L & R

ROBERT HANCOCK, planter, of Colleton Co., son & devisee of ELIAS HANCOCK, victualer of Charleston; & MARY, ROBERT'S wife; & WILLIAM HANCOCK, son, devisee, & heir of ELIAS HANCOCK, & MARY, WILLIAM'S wife; all of the 1st part; to SAMUEL WAINWRIGHT, butcher, of Charleston; for Ł 1000 currency, half of lot #92 in Charleston bequeathed by ELIAS HANCOCK to his son ROBERT, party hereto; fronting W 100 ft. on King Street; formerly called Benson Street, bounding E on other part of lot; N on HESTHER SIMMONS (formerly CORNELIUS BATTOON); S 61-1/2 ft. on Tradd Street. Witnesses: FRANCIS BAKER, CHARLES CALDER. Before JAMES WRIGHT, J.P. JOHN BEALE, Register.

Book E-E, p. 69
3 June 1747
Renunciation of Dowers

MARY HANCOCK, wife of ROBERT HANCOCK, planter, of Colleton Co., son & devisee of ELIAS HANCOCK, victualer, of Charleston; & MARY HANCOCK, wife of WILLIAM HANCOCK, devisee, son & heir of said ELIAS HANCOCK; appeared before JOHN LINING (of Ct. of C.P. appointed by writ of dedimus potestatum signed by the Hon. BENJAMIN WHITAKER, C.J., now absent from the Province) & voluntarily renounced their claim of dower in the half of lot #92 in Charleston conveyed by their husbands to SAMUEL WAINWRIGHT (see p. 62). JOHN BEALE, Dep. Pub. Reg.

Book E-E, p. 70
3 & 4 Oct. 1748
L & R by Mortgage

JAMES SMITH, blacksmith, of Charleston, to SAMUEL WAINWRIGHT, butcher, as security on bond of even date in penal sum of Ł 5000 for payment of Ł 2500 currency, with interest, on 3 Oct. 1749; that brick house & lot of land 40 x 75 ft. which SMITH purchased from GABRIEL GUIGNARD, at Trott's Point, St. Philip's Parish, Charleston, bounding E on a new street called Charles Street; S on Guignard Street; other sides on GABRIEL GUIGNARD. Witnesses: JOHN FRYER, JOHN BALLENTINE, JR. Before THOMAS LAMBOLL, J.P. JOHN BEALE, D.P.R.

Book E-E, p. 76
20 Oct. 1748
Release

JOHN SANDIFORD, JR., hatter, of James Island, Berkeley Co., to JOHN MILLER, planter, of Parish of St. Thomas & St. Dennis Berkeley Co., for Ł 1600 currency, 400 a., English measure, in St. Thomas & St. Dennis Parish, bounding E on ISAAC GUERIN & STEPHEN MILLER, SR.; S on NE branch of Wando River; W on HENRY GRAY; N on DANIEL LESESNE. Whereas the Lords Proprs. granted WILLIAM NORTH 500 a. in Berkeley Co., then bounding N on vacant land; W on ROBERT KING; E on THOMAS BASKERFIELD; S on NE branch Wando River; & whereas WILLIAM NORTH on 21 July 1712 sold to WILLIAM DANFORTH 350 a. (part of 500 a.); on 16 Apr. 1716 sold DANFORTH 50 a. (another part of the 500); & whereas DANFORTH by will dated 19 Dec. 1717 bequeathed to his grandson WILLIAM DANFORTH BELIN, the 400 a.; & he, on 1 July 1736 sold the 400 a. to JOHN SANDIFORD, SR., the father, who by deed of gift dated 17 July 1744 gave the tract to his son JOHN, party hereto; who now sells to MILELR. Witnesses: WILLIAM ELLIS, ROBERT HOW. Before WILLIAM PINCKNEY, J.P. JOHN BEALE, D.P.R.

Book E-E, p. 81
28 May 1748
Mortgage

THOMAS NISBETT, planter, to ALEXANDER RANTOWLE, store keeper, both of St. Paul's Parish, Colleton Co., as security on bond of even date in penal sum of Ł 300 for payment of Ł 150 currency, with interest, on 1 July 1748; all his household goods, horses, cattle, 2 tracts & all his possessions; namely 1 bed & furniture, 1 table, 5 chairs, plates & dishes, 1 tea kettle, his present year's wages when due from FREDERICK GRIMKÉ, 1 large bay mare branded A on off shoulder, 1 sorrel mare branded N on mounting shoulder & her colt, 1 sorrell stallion branded F, 500 a. on Peedee & 500 a. on Jefferses Creek. Witnesses: SAMUEL O'HEAR, CHARLES MELLICHAMP. Before JOHN RUTLEDGE, J.P. JOHN BEALE, D.P.R.

Book E-E, p. 83
13 & 14 Oct. 1748

CONNOR BOOTH, planter, of John's Island, Colleton Co., to WILLIAM BOONE, JR., of

Assignment of Mortgage   Charleston, for Ł 1620 currency, subject to
                          THOMAS COOPER'S equity of redemption; 325 a.
according to plat made by THOMAS WITTER & thereby said to contain 358 a.
Whereas the Lords Proprs. on 11 Jan. 1700 for Ł 4 currency, granted WIL-
LIAM BROCKHAS 200 a., English measure, in Colleton Co.; & whereas the
Lords Proprs. on 17 Aug. 1700, for Ł 9 currency, granted said BROCKHAS
450 a., English measure, in Colleton Co.; & whereas BROCKHAS died testate, leaving only 1 child, his daughter SARAH, who inherited at the
death of their mother; & whereas ELIZABETH WILKINS died intestate & her
sister, SARAH WILKINS, inherited; & whereas SARAH married a MR. HALL,
whom she survived; & afterwards by L & R dated 22 & 23 Feb. 1733 sold to
CRAFTON KARWEN, planter, of Johns Island, Colleton Co., for Ł 2000 currency, 325 a. on N side "A.B. Poolow" Creek bounding E on CAPT. THOMAS
FLEMING; & whereas KARWEN by L & R dated 3 & 4 June 1736, for Ł 1950 currency, sold to THOMAS COOPER, merchant, & MARGARET MAGDALENE, his wife,
of Charleston, the 325 a.; & whereas MARGARET MAGDALENE COOPER died &
THOMAS COOPER as surviving jointenant inherited; & whereas THOMAS COOPER
& his second wife, MARY, on 6 Feb. 1745 mortgaged the 325 a. to JOHN
CHAMPNEYS, of Charleston, for Ł 3000 currency, redeemable on 6 Feb. 1746;
the 325 a. bounding S on A.B. Poolaw Creek; E on CAPT. THOMAS FLEMING; W
on AARON HUNSCOMB & THOMAS LADSON; N on LADSON & D'HARRIETTE; & whereas
COOPER did not pay the mortgage at the appointed time, so that on 22 May
1748 the principal & interest due was Ł 3687:10 currency, & JOHN CHAMP-
NEYS & SARAH his wife by L & R dated 21 & 22 May 1748 for Ł 1500 currency,
assigned the mortgage to CONNOR BOOTH; now BOOTH assigns the mortgage to
BOONE. Witnesses: DAVID OLIPHANT, JOHN HANSON. Before JOHN CHAMPNEYS,
J.P. JOHN BEALE, Register.

Book E-E, p. 91   WILLIAM MCCORMICK, planter, to THOMAS CARSON,
21 & 22 Sept. 1747   planter, both of Williamsburgh Township, Cra-
L & R   ven Co., for Ł 100 SC money, 500 a. on which
                         MCCORMICK lives, bounding SE on GEORGE HUNTER,
Sur. Gen.; NE on an impassable swamp & vacant land; SW on vacant land; NW
on WILLIAM MCCORMICK. Witnesses: JOHN LIVISTON, JOHN DICK, JR. Before
ROGER GIBSON, J.P. JOHN BEALE, Register.

Book E-E, p. 95   BENJAMIN DINSLEY, planter, to DAVID BETTISON,
19 Sept. 1748   planter, both of Colleton Co.; for Ł 80 cur-
L & R   rency, 220 a. in Colleton Co., granted by Lt.
                         Gov. WILLIAM BULL to said BENJAMIN DINSLEY,
bounding on the plantations of JOHN WOODWARD, WILLIAM PINCKNEY, & DAVID
BETTISON. Witnesses: SAMUEL NICHOLLS, ROBERT TODD. Before HENRY HYRNE,
J.P. JOHN BEALE, Register.

Book E-E, p. 98   SARAH MEEK, widow (lately SARAH BRICKLES), to
26 Nov. 1748   JAMES HUNTER, shopkeeper, & FRANCIS his wife,
Feoffment   all of Charleston, for Ł 2300 SC money, part
                         of 3 lots in Charleston, #188, #189, & #79.
Whereas THOMAS ELLERY, gentleman, & ANN his wife, of Charleston, by L & R
dated 1 & 2 Nov. 1736, sold RICHARD BRICKLES, house carpenter, of Charleston & SARAH his wife, part of 3 lots, #188, #189, & #79, bounding E 50
ft. on the garden fence of THOMAS COOPER; W 50 ft. on the Great Street
leading from Ashley River by the Market Place & Presbyterian Meeting
House; S 130 ft. 9 in. on THOMAS ELLERY; N on DAVID MONGIN; now SARAH, as
surviving jointenant, conveys to HUNTER. Witnesses: JOHN RATTRAY, JAMES
GRINDLAY, CHARLES HALSON. Before OTHNIEL BEALE, J.P. JOHN BEALE, Register.

Book E-E, p. 102   MATHEW BEAIRD, planter, son of MATHEW BAIRD,
28 & 29 Nov. 1748   planter, of St. James Goose Creek, & ELIZABETH
L & R   his wife, to MELLER ST. JOHN, gentleman, of
                         Berkeley Co., for Ł 1500 SC money, 2 tracts of
300 a. & 260 a., total 560 a. on Johns Island. Whereas JOHN, Lord Granville, Palatine, & the Lords Proprs. on 15 Dec. 1705, by Gov. NATHANIEL
JOHNSON, granted AMBROSE HILL 300 a., English measure, in Colleton Co.,
bounding SW on RICHARD FLOYD; NW on Bohicut Creek; other sides on vacant
land; & whereas Gov. NATHANIEL JOHNSON & the Lords Proprs. on 1 Sept.
1706 granted AMBROSE HILL 260 a., English measure, in Colleton Co.,
bounding E & NE on WILLIAM ALLEN; W on AMBROSE HILL; & whereas AMBROSE
HILL by will dated 5 Dec. 1705 bequeathed to his only daughter & heiress

ELIZABETH the tract on which he lived, on Stono (?) Island; & whereas
ELIZABETH married JOHN CROSKEYS, planter, of Berkeley Co., & they, by L &
R dated 15 & 16 Oct. 1723 sold the 2 adjoining tracts to JOHN BAILEY,
cordwainer; who by L & R dated 27 & 28 Dec. 1723 sold them to MATHEW
BEAIRD; who, by will dated 25 Sept. 1743 bequeathed them to his son,
party hereto; now he sells to MELLER ST. JOHN. Witnesses: LAMBERT LANCE,
CHARLES FAUCHERAUD. Before ROBERT AUSTIN, J.P. JOHN BEALE, Register.

Book E-E, p. 110   HUGH ANDERSON, gentleman, to JOHN MCKENZIE,
29 & 30 July 1747   merchant, both of Charleston, as security on
L & R by Mortgage   bond of even date in penal sum of Ł 1200 for
                      payment of Ł 600 currency, with interest, on
30 July 1748; that part of 10 a. on Charleston Neck formerly conveyed by
the representatives of BARTHOLOMEW GAILLARD to JOSEPH WRAGG; bounding NE
on the Broad Path; SW on the parsonage & lands of the Free School; NW
125 ft. on lane to Free School; SE on DALLIBACK (formerly JOSEPH WRAGG).
Witnesses: JOHN RATTRAY, MAURICE HARVEY. Before OTHNIEL BEALE, J.P.
JOHN BEALE, Register.

Book E-E, p. 113   WILLIAM WILKINS, planter, of Johns Island,
19 & 20 Apr. 1748   Parish of St. Johns, Colleton Co., to THOMAS
L & R   JINKS, cordwainer of same place, for Ł 400
                      currency, 100 a. on Johns Island, bounding NW
on JOSEPH STANYARNE; E on SOLOMON LEGREE, JR. Witnesses: JOSEPH PHIPPS,
MARTHA PHILLIPS. Before THOMAS LAMBOLL, J.P. JOHN BEALE, Register.

Book E-E, p. 118   ROBERT HOW, schoolmaster, & ELIZABETH his wife,
1 & 2 Dec. 1736   of St. Thomas Parish, Berkeley Co.; to the Rev.
L & R by Mortgage   MR. THOMAS HASELL, rector; JOHN BERESFORD,
                      JAMES AKIN, WILLIAM TREWIN, ISAAC LESESNE,
JOHN DANIEL, & THOMAS WALKER, vestrymen of said Parish as security on
bond of even date in penal sum of Ł 451:8 for payment of Ł 251:8:9 cur-
rency, with interest, in the vestry room on 25 Mar. 1737; 200 a. in St.
Thomas Parish, bounding E on ALEXANDER PERONNEAU; S on Wando River; W on
JONATHAN RUSS & Cainhoi Meeting land; N on _____; according to grant from
Lords Proprs. to CHARLES KING on 15 July 1697. Witnesses: JOHN VICARIDGE,
WILLIAM POOLE. Before PAUL TRAPIER, J.P. JOHN BEALE, Register.

Book E-E, p. 124   JOSEPH LABRUCE, planter, of Waccamaw, Craven
9 Apr. 1746   Co., to JOHN LABRUCE, planter, for 10 shil-
Gift   lings, 600 a. between another tract belonging
                      to JOSEPH LABRUCE & lands of PERCIVAL PAWLEY;
formerly conveyed by THOMAS PAGETT to JOSEPH LABRUCE; also 3 Negro men, 1
Negro woman, 3 Negro boys. Witnesses: JOHN PYATT, JOHN WARNER. Before
PAUL TRAPIER, J.P. JOHN BEALE, Register.

Book E-E, p. 124   PETER DUMAY, planter, of St. James Santee, Cra-
14 Jan. 1747   ven Co., to DANIEL HORRY, PAUL BRUNEAU, RALPH
Gift in Trust   JERMAN, PETER ROBERT, & JOHN GENDRON, JR.,
                      commissioners appointed by an Act of Assembly
for building a Chapel of Esse at Itchaw for use of the inhabitants of the
Parish; for a chapel & burying place; 2 a. not far from Itchaw Creek, be-
ing part of 200 a. granted to JOHN FRANCIS GIGNILLIOT on 11 Feb. 1696/7.
Witnesses: ELIAS HORRY, JACOB JEANNERET, WILLIAM THOMAS. Before PAUL
TRAPIER, J.P. JOHN BEALE, Register.

Book E-E, p. 126   JACOB JEANNERET, planter, of St. James Santee
7 Apr. 1748   Parish, Craven Co., to DANIEL HORRY, PAUL
Gift in Trust   BRANNEAU, RALPH JERMAN, PETER ROBERT, & JOHN
                      GENDRON, JR., commissioners appointed by Act
of Assembly for building a Chapel of Ease at Itchaw for the use of the
inhabitants of the Parish; as an addition to the land given by PETER DU-
MAY for a chapel & burial place; 1/2 a. in Itchaw Old Field. Witnesses:
ELIAS HORRY, MARGARETT JEANNERET. Before PAUL TRAPIER, J.P. JOHN BEALE,
Register.

Book E-E, p. 127   ANN LEBAS, widow, of Berkeley Co., to THOMAS
16 Dec. 1748   SABB, planter, as security for payment of
Mortgage   Ł 3000 SC money, on 1 Jan. 1748/9; 2 tracts; 1
                      of 500 a. called Beeth (?) hall, bounding S on

Watboo Barony; N on EDWARD THOMAS; 1 of 445 a., bounding N on vacant land;
E on Watboo Swamp; S on Watboo Barony; W on HENRY SIMMONS. Witnesses:
DEBORAH SABB, WILLIAM SABB, DAVID LAFONS. Before NATHANIEL BROUGHTON,
J.P. JOHN BEALE, Register.

Book E-E, p. 129   HUGH ANDERSON, gentleman, to ESAIE BRUNET, for
27 Apr. 1747   Ł 250 currency, that piece of land in Anson-
Sale   borough, 50 ft. x 410 ft., bounding S on Lot E;
                         E on LUKE STOUTENBOROUGH; N on part of Lot E
belonging to BENJAMIN BATES & on HUGH ANDERSON; W on the highway leading
to Charleston. Witnesses: WILLIAM HUNT, WILLIAM JORDAN. ALEXANDER TAY-
LOR testified before OTHNIEL BEALE, J.P. JOHN BEALE, Register.

Book E-E, p. 130   HUGH ANDERSON, gentleman, to ALEXANDER TAYLOR,
27 Apr. 1747   tailor, of Charleston, for Ł 250 SC money, a
Sale   lot in Ansonborough, 50 ft. x 410 ft., bound-
                         ing W on the road leading to Charleston; S on
lot D belonging to MR. HUTCHENS; E on LUKE STOUTENBOROUGH; N on part of
lot # belonging to HUGH ANDERSON. Witnesses: WILLIAM HUNT, WILLIAM JOR-
DAN. ESAIE BURNET testified before OTHNIEL BEALE, J.P. JOHN BEALE, Register.

Book E-E, p. 131   RAWLINS LOWNDES, Provost Marshal, to JOHN
1 Oct. 1748   STANYARNE, at public outcry for Ł 360 SC money,
Sale   380 a. in St. Johns Parish, Colleton Co.,
                         bounding N of WILLIAM STEVENS; S on HUGH HEXT;
E on JOHN STANYARNE; W on ABRAHAM WEIGHT. Whereas EBENEZER SIMMONS, BEN-
JAMIN SMITH & JAMES CROKATT recovered against ELIZABETH HEXT, JOHN STAN-
YARNE & WILLIAM HEXT, executrix & executors of will of FRANCIS HEXT,
planter, a judgement for Ł 217:13:6 currency & Ł 67:11:3 costs, & a writ
of fieri facias was issued on 5 Apr. last by JOHN LINING, in absence of
BENJAMIN WHITAKER, C.J., whereby LOWNDES was commanded levy said sums on
the real & personal estate of FRANCIS HEXT; now LOWNDES sells to STAN-
YARNE exclusive of the widows dowry. Witnesses: MILES BREWTON, JOHN
JONES. Before ROBERT AUSTIN, J.P. JOHN BEALE, Register.

Book E-E, p. 133   WILLIAM PALMER, planter, & ANN his wife, of
26 Jan. 1748   Granville Co., to ANDREW DEVEAUX, planter, of
Release   Berkeley Co., for Ł 2460:10 currency, 935 a.
                         in Granville Co., bounding N on CAPT. PETER
GIRARDEAU & estate of JOSEPH IZARD; S on JONATHAN BRYAN; E on JAMES DE-
VEAUX; W on estate of Landgrave EDMUND BELLINGER; according to plat certified by WILLIAM MACPHERSON, Dep. Sur. Whereas EDMUND BELLINGER owned
several large tracts of land & by will dated 21 Feb. 1739 devised to his
nephew WILLIAM PALMER, 1000 a. of his patent land & devised to his son
GEORGE BELLINGER 1000 a. of his patent land, & appointed his wife, ELIZA-
BETH BELLINGER, sole executrix; & whereas by L & R dated 14 & 15 Feb.
1735 ELIZABETH BELLINGER & GEORGE BELLINGER sold WILLIAM PALMER the
1000 a in Granville Co., devised to GEORGE BELLINGER; bounding E on WIL-
LIAM PALMER; SW on JONATHAN BRYAN; NE on JOHN BULL; NW on estate of ED-
MUND BELLINGER; now PALMER sells part of the 2000 a. to DEVEAUX. Wit-
nesses: GEORGE CUSSINGS, (COSSINGS), gentleman, of Prince William Parish;
JAMES GIRARDEAU; HENRI JEANNERET, FRANCIS CHRISTIAN, WILLIAM SCOTT, WIL-
LIAM SMELIE. Before ROBERT THORPE, J.P. JOHN BEALE, Register.

Book E-E, p. 138   Between MOSES (his mark) MITCHELL, cordwainer,
8 Apr. 1748   of Charleston, & MARY MARRINER (sole trader),
Covenant   wife of EDWARD MARRINER. Whereas in 1727 a
                         separation occurred between EDWARD MARRINER &
MARY MARRINER, EDWARD being at Boston or in some Northern Colony, & MARY
being in Charleston, SC, with her mother, MRS. MARY HARRIS, midwife; &
whereas after 7 years' absence during which time MARY did not hear from
EDWARD or had any notice that he was alive, & supposing EDWARD was dead
MARY married MOSES MITCHELL in 1735; & whereas MOSES & MARY lived as man
& wife for 12 years & by their labor, frugality & industry acquired a
competent livelihood & fortune & thereby & with what they received from
MARY HARRIS have been able to purchase several houses, lands & tenements
in Union Street & on Unity Alley, in the name of MOSES MITCHELL & MARY
his wife in jointenancy, & have also purchased several slaves, plate,
household furniture & other goods & chattels which are now in their

possession; & whereas EDWARD MARRINER after an absence of 20 years recently returned to SC; & whereas during his absence EDWARD did not contribute
anything to the support or maintenance of MARY, by a proper instrument
dated 26 Mar. last EDWARD agreed with a trustee appointed in behalf of
MARY that all the estate, real & personal, which MARY had acquired during
the separation or afterwards should be to the sole use of MARY & free of
EDWARD'S claim, power, or control; & whereas doubts may arise as to the
validity of MARY'S claim to the property purchased by MOSES & MARY in
jointenancy because in the conveyances MARY is called the wife of MOSES,
& the legality of MARY'S marriage to MOSES is subject to dispute, because
EDWARD was living; & whereas other differences & disputes may arise between MOSES & MARY touching their rights & interests in the slaves, good
& chattles, now in their possession; in order to settle such disputes
MOSES agrees with MARY that MOSES & his heirs shall stand seized of the
houses, lands, etc., which they purchased from the attorneys of ANN WAT-
KINSON, widow, & from JOHN RATTRAY, situated on E side Union Street & N
side Unity Alley, & from CHARLES PINCKNEY situated on W side Union Street;
also certain 8 slaves (named); the plate, the houshold stuff & furniture
mentioned in attached schedule; & all other real & personal estate to
which MOSES might be entitled on this date as jointenant; the future
rents, profits, etc., to the joint use of MOSES & MARY, then to the longest liver, & his or her heirs; the rents, issues & profits of the premises & the earnings of the slaves, to be used jointly to discharge debts;
the surplus to be used in purchasing other property; should either be
minded to sell any of the real or personal estate they must first sign an
agreement, the money to be used in other purchases of real or personal
estate, in jointenancy. MOSES binds himself in penal sum of Ⱡ 10,000 currency for performance of agreement. Schedule given of plate, household
stuff & furniture. Witnesses: CHARLES PINCKNEY, DANIEL BOURGET. Before
WILLIAM PINCKNEY, J.P. JOHN BEALE, Register.

Book E-E, p. 142   ULYSSES ANTHONY ALBERGOTTI, vintner, & PRU-
4 & 5 Nov. 1748   DENCE (her mark) his wife, to JOHN DELAGAYE,
L & R   storekeeper, both of Port Royal Island, Gran-
                      ville Co., for Ⱡ 1600 currency, 630 a. on Wam-
bee Island, Granville Co., bounding W on WILLIAM BULL; N on WILLIAM LES-
LEY; S on Bull's Creek; E on small marshes & creeks of Little Port Royal
River; being part of 689 a., 500 a. of which were granted by the Lords
Proprs. to WILLIAM LESLEY, the other 189 a. granted to ALEXANDER VANDER-
DUSSEN; & by sundry mesne conveyances now vested in ALBERGOTTI. Witness-
es: EDWARD WIGG, WILLIAM GOUGH. Before ROBERT WILLIAMS, J.P. JOHN BEALE,
Register.

Book E-E, p. 146   WILLIAM WATIES, ESQ., to THOMAS LYNCH, planter,
10 & 11 Nov. 1748   both of Prince George Parish, Craven Co., for
L & R   Ⱡ 600 currency, lot #60 in Georgetown, bound-
                      ing SE on Broad Street, 167.9 ft., English
measure, from corner of Broad & Prince Streets to the front street; NE
100 ft. on Prince Street; NW on lot #59; SW on part of said lot of WIL-
LIAM WATIES; forming a long square. Witnesses: ANDREW (ARCHIBALD?) JOHN-
STON, JOHN JOHNSTON. Before WILLIAM FLEMING, J.P. JOHN BEALE, Register.

Book E-E, p. 149   JONATHAN WHILDEN, planter, of Christ Church
22 & 23 Jan. 1745   Parish, Berkeley Co., to JOHN BOLLOW, cord-
L & R   winder, of Seewee, same Parish, for Ⱡ 250 cur-
                      rency, 141 a., English measure, in Christ
Church Parish, as specified in a plat of 148 a. Witnesses: WILLIAM YOUNG,
JAMES ALLEN, JOHN BASKERFIELD. Before JOHN RUTLEDGE, J.P. JOHN BEALE,
Register.

Book E-E, p. 153   JOHN STEWART, of Combehe, for good causes &
7 July 1746   valuable considerations, to his cousin, WIL-
Gift in Trust   LIAM DALTON, son of THOMAS DALTON, & to his
                      (JOHN'S) sister MARTHA DALTON, 140 a. fronting
on Chehaw River, in Colleton Co., bounding on PETER GIRARDEAU; to THOMAS
for his lifetime, & to his sister MARTHA for her life; then to cousin
WILLIAM. Witnesses: JAMES KID, DANIEL DALTON. Before JAMES BULLOCK,
J.P. JOHN BEALE, Register.

Book E-E, p. 154   LIONEL CHALMERS, surgeon, of Christ Church

21 & 22 Jan. 1747   Parish, Berkeley Co., & MARTHA his wife (late-
L & R   ly MARTHA LOGAN, niece & devisee of PATRICK
                           LOGAN, gentleman, son & devisee of COL. GEORGE
LOGAN, ESQ., all of same place), to ALEXANDER PERONNEAU, merchant, of
Charleston, for Ł 2250 currency, 460 a. on SE side Wando River. Whereas
WILLIAM, Earl of Craven, Palatine, & the Lords Proprs. on 11 May 1699, by
the Hon. JOSEPH BLAKE & other trustees, granted FRANCIS GRACIA 460 a.,
English measure, in Berkeley Co., bounding NNW on Wando River; NE on a
creek; SE on the creek; W & SW on GEORGE LOGAN; & whereas FRANCIS GRACIA
& ELIZABETH his wife by deed of feoffment dated 18 Oct. 1708 conveyed the
460 a. to GEORGE LOGAN; who, by will dated 18 Mar. 1719 bequeathed the
tract to his son PATRICK LOGAN with the proviso that should PATRICK die
without issue then daughter HELEN to inherit; & whereas PATRICK died
without heirs but by will dated 18 Oct. 1726 bequeathed to his niece
MARTHA LOGAN, JR. (daughter of MARTHA LOGAN); now MARTHA CHALMERS, party
hereto, the residue of his real & personal estate; & whereas after PAT-
RICK'S death doubts arose as to the validity of the devise in GEORGE LO-
GAN'S will; to remove such doubts HELEN & her husband, ROBERT DANIEL, by
L & R dated 31 Jan. 7 1 Feb. 1727 conveyed the 460 a. to THOMAS COOPER,
ESQ., of Charleston, who, by L & R dated 1 & 2 Mar. 1727, for Ł 500 cur-
rency, conveyed to MARTHA LOGAN, spinster, eldest daughter of GEORGE LO-
GAN; now she & her husband sell to PERONNEAU. Witnesses: ELIZABETH PINCK-
NEY, The Hon. CHARLES PINCKNEY. Before WILLIAM PINCKNEY, J.P. JOHN
BEALE, Register.

Book E-E, p. 160   JOSEPH SHUTE, merchant, & ANNA his wife, to
10 Sept. 1748   OTHNIEL BEALE, merchant, both of Charleston;
Feoffment   for Ł 100 currency, part of a Bay lot #9,
                          bounding N 123 ft. on OTHNIEL BEALE; W 8 ft.
on OTHNIEL BEALE; S on part of JOSEPH SHUTE'S land by a straight line E
8° N 122-1/2 ft. from SC corner of OTHNIEL BEALE'S new brick store to SW
corner of OTHNIEL BEALE'S new brick kitchen, both now occupied by MESSRS.
STIEL & HUME, where it terminates in the point by intersecting the first
mentioned boundary line forming an acute angle. Witnesses: JOHN RATTRAY,
SAMPSON NEYLE. Before JACOB MOTTE, J.P. JOHN BEALE, Register.

Book E-E, p. 162   WILLIAM SHACKELFORD, to PAUL TRAPIER & BENJA-
19 & 20 Sept. 1748   MIN ROMSEY, merchants; all of Georgetown; as
L & R by Mortgage   security on bond of even date in penal sum of
                          Ł 3543:10:6 for payment of Ł 1807:1:6 currency,
with interest, on 1 July 1750; lot #26 in Georgetown, bounding SW 50 ft.
on the Bay Street; SE 217.9 ft. on lot #27; NW on lot #25. Witnesses:
JOHN DAVIS, WILLIAM PARKER. Before WILLIAM POOLE, J.P. JOHN BEALE, Register.

Book E-E, p. 165   WILLIAM YEOMANS, merchant, in trust to ISAAC
9 & 10 Feb. 1748   MAZYCK, GABRIEL MANIGAULT, BENJAMIN D'HAR-
L & R by Mortgage   HIETTE, SAMUEL EVELEIGH, THOMAS SMITH, SR., &
                          LUKE STOUTENBURGH, merchants, all of Charles-
ton; as security for the payment of various debts (names & amounts listed
in schedule); lot #278 in Charleston, on W side Great Street leading from
White Point to Old Church Yard & running thence by the Presbyterian Meeting House; bounding W on DANIEL TOWNSEND; S on the Hon. WILLIAM BULL; N
on lot #195; which lot #278 YEOMANS purchased from JOSEPH BUTLER, planter,
of St. Andrews Parish, & MARY his wife, daughter & devisee of JAMES LA-
ROACH; also 376 a. in Berkeley Co., bounding E & NE on CAPT. WILLIAM
SAUNDERS; NW on MAJ. TOBIAS FITCH; W on WILSON SAUNDERS; S on JOHN BROWN
(messenger of Lower House of Assembly); which 376 a. YEOMANS purchased
from JAMES DALTON & CATHERINE his wife; also 250 a. being 1/2 of 500 a.
in St. James Goose Creek, purchased from JAMES ST. JOHN & BENJAMIN WARING,
attorneys for EDWARD SMITH of New Hanover, NC, bounding NW on MR. POURCH-
ER; SW on RALPH IZARD; E & NE on JAMES GIGNILLIAT; also YEOMAN'S interest
in a mortgage from ALEXANDER Moon of 1000 a. commonly called Mount Alexander, on Combee River, bounding E on JAMES HEARTLY; also YEOMAN'S title
to the lands & tenements in Charleston which descended to his wife, MARY,
from her father ABRAHAM LESUR, vintner, of Charleston. List of creditors
named in schedule; estate of WILLIAM MCKENZIE, the widow STOUTENBURGH,
SAMUEL & GEORGE EVELEIGH, SMITH & COSSENS, ISAAC MAZYCK, estate of PAUL
MAZYCK, WILLIAM ELLIOTT, estate of HENRY IZARD, NICHOLAS HARLESTON, GA-
BRIEL MANIGAULT, JONATHAN SCOTT, WILLIAM WEBB, JOHN SAVAGE & CO., GEORGE

AUSTIN, STEAD & EVANCE, JOHN SCOTT on the Bay, SHUBRICK & Co., JACOB
MOTTE, estate of JOHN DANIEL, JOHN MARTINI, RICHARD BEDON, HENRY BEDON,
COLCOCK & WRAGG, JURDAN ROCHE, JOHN SCOTT (carpenter) JOHN RATTRAY, WIL-
GEORGE FREEMAN, GEORGE JACKSON, ELIAS BALL, CATHERINE IOOR, WILLIAM WOOD-
ROPE, LENOX & DEAS, DR. MURRAY, EDWARD FOWLER, JOHN TRIBEAUDET, ALEXANDER
PATRE, DANIEL WELCHUSEN, THOMAS HOLMANS, WILLIAM GLEN, MILLER (gunsmith),
JOHN COLCOCK, JOHN MCCALL, COL. BREWTON, RAE & BARKSDALE, WILLIAM HARVEY,
estate of MOSES BENNETT, JAMES STOBO, THOMAS DRAYTON. List of creditors
in England: Rev. MR. JOSEPH CHILLINGWORTH, SAMUEL WRAGG, THOMAS BINFORD,
estate of GABRIEL ESCOTT, MORGAN THOMAS. In London: WILLIAM WILLY, ROD-
RIGO PACHACO, JACOB BERNALL, FRANCIS DALBY, estate of JOHN BELL, JACOB
BELL, THOMAS FORSTER. Witnesses: CHARLES PINCKNEY, JOSEPH BROWN, WILLIAM
GEORGE FREEMAN. Before OTHNIEL BEALE, J.P. JOHN BEALE, J.P. JOHN
BEALE, Register.

Book E-E, p. 174   SAMUEL (his mark) WIGGEN, planter, to ROBERT
4 & 5 June 1747   WILLIAMS, yeoman, both of the WELCH tract, in
L & R   Craven Co., for L 150 currency, bounding S on
                          HENRY ROACH & MR. CUNNINGHAM; E on JOHN EVANS
& a creek; NW on JAMES BAKER (?). Witnesses: MATTHEW CREED, THOMAS
JAMES. Before WILLIAM JAMES, J.P. JOHN BEALE, Register.

Book E-E, p. 178   CORNELIUS (his mark) REINE, planter, to ROBERT
4 & 5 June 1747   WILLIAMS, yeoman, both of the WELCH tract,
L & R   Craven Co., for L 200 currency, 200 a. in the
                          WELCH tract, bounding NW on PeeDee River; E on
NATHANIEL EVANS; S on GILES BOWERS; W on JOHN EVANS. Witnesses: BARTHOL-
OMEW BALL, JAMES MISKIMEN. Before WILLIAM JAMES, J.P. JOHN BEALE, Reg-
ister.

Book E-E, p. 183   PETER FAURE, of Berkeley Co., to WILLIAM BAR-
7 Jan. 1748/9   RIE, for 5 shillings, 200 a. in Orangeburgh
Sale   Township, Berkeley Co., bounding SW on Pon Pon
                          River; other sides on the Township. Witness-
es: BENJAMIN PAYTON, JOHN (his mark) FERREE, CATHERINE (her mark) PUCK-
RIDGE. SARAH (her mark) FAURE renounced her dower. Before ROBERT AUS-
TIN, J.P. JOHN BEALE, Register.

Book E-E, p. 185   HUGH CARTWRIGHT, bricklayer, to JOHN RATTRAY,
8 & 9 Feb. 1748   gentleman; both of Charleston; as security for
L & R by Mortgage   payment of several debts; 3 adjoining tracts,
                          total 1354 a. in Colleton Co., called Sea-
brooks Island, between Ashepoo & south Edisto Rivers; which 3 tracts were
granted by the Lords Proprs. separately to JAMES MARTEL GENLARD DE VER-
VANT, ESQ., & ROBERT SEABROOK, planter, of Colleton Co., & bounding according to L & R dated 30 Nov. & 1 Dec. 1744, between JAMES MICHIE &
MARTHA his wife, of Charleston, of 1st part; WILLIAM STEWART, ESQ., of
Island of New Providence, by his attorney, GEORGE SEAMAN, merchant, of
Charleston, of 2nd part; & HUGH CARTWRIGHT, of 3rd part. Whereas JOHN
RATTRAY became security for HUGH CARTWRIGHT, on a bond dated 24 Feb. 1747
to MARTHA WITHERSTONE, widow, of Charleston, in penal sum of L 3000 for
payment of L 1500 currency, with interest, on 24 Feb. 1748; & on another
bond to ISAAC HOLMES, of Charleston, dated 4 Mar. 1747 in penal sum of
L 1601 for payment of L 800:10 currency, with interest, on 4 Mar. 1748; &
on another bond to ISAAC HOLMES dated 19 Mar. 1747 in penal sum of L 3000
for payment of L 1000, with interest, on 19 Mar. 1748; & another bond to
THOMAS LAMBOLL, of Charleston, dated 2 Aug. 1748, in penal sum of
L 1469:2 for payment of L 734:11 currency, with interest, on 2 Aug. 1749
& another bond to THOMAS LAMBOLL, HENRY PERONNEAU, ALEXANDER PERONNEAU &
GEORGE EVELEIGH, of Charleston, dated 13 Nov. 1748 in penal sum of L 2000
for payment of L 1000 currency, with interest, on 30 Nov. 1749; & another
bond to WILLIAM STEWART dated 1 Sept. 1748 in penal sum of L 2337:19:10
for payment of L 1168:19:11 currency, with interest, on 1 Sept. 1749; now
CARTWRIGHT gives 3 tracts as security. Witnesses: PETER MANIGAULT, ROB-
ERT WILLIAMS, JR. Before WILLIAM GEORGE FREEMAN, J.P. JOHN BEALE, Register.

Book E-E, p. 192   ARNOLDUS VANDERHORST, planter, of Berkeley
23 & 24 Feb. 1743   Co., to ESAIE BRUNET, carpenter, of Charles-
L & R   ton, for L 850 currency, that lot in

Charleston bounding S on the heirs of JOHN VANDERHORST, JR.; W on Meeting House Street; N on a canal or creek running NW out of Ashley River; E on Church Street & the Great Bridge lately built in said street & crossing said canal in a NNE course; with all the adjoining marsh land; which lot & marsh land (marked B) is part of several lots at White Point devised by JOHN VANDERHORST, planter, of Berkeley Co., father of ARNOLDUS VANDER-HORST, to his sons, & divided into lots according to plat certified by GEORGE HUNTER, surveyor, & recorded in Great Grant Book begun in 1694, fol. 273-274. Witnesses: ANTHONY FURNIS, ALEXANDER PERONNEAU. Before OTHNIEL BEALE, J.P. JOHN BEALE, Register.

Book E-E, p. 198
22 Feb. 1748
Feoffment

MATHEW ROCHE, merchant, & ANN his wife, to SAMUEL PERKINS, coachmaker; both of Charleston; for L 750 currency, 100 a. in Berkeley Co., bounding SW on Ashley River; NE on vacant land (now WILLIAM BULL & DANIEL CARTWRIGHT); NW on THOMAS HOLTON (now EDMOND BELLINGER); SE on JOHN DONOHOE (now JOSEPH BUTLER). Witnesses: GEORGE SAXBY, JOSEPH SHUTE. Before JACOB MOTTE, J.P. WILLIAM HOPTON, Register.

Book E-E, p. 201
14 Feb. 1748
Conditional Assignment
of Lease

WILLIAM TURNER, peruke-maker, of Charleston, to ROBERT TOD (TODD), planter, for L 105:16:8 SC money, the unexpired term of the lease of 2 lots, #24 & #24, with tenements; leased 18 Oct. 1745 for 30 years by JOHN TOWNSEND, cooper, of Charleston, to WILLIAM TURNER, for L 30 a year; (the two lots) bounding N 74 ft., English measure, on PETER LEGER, cooper; S on a small benement occupied by ELIZABETH SERJEANT; W on buildings erected on part of said lots erected by JOHN TOWNSEND; E 30 ft. on Bedon's Alley; TURNER to redeem the lease by returning the amount to TODD by 7 Aug. 1749. Witnesses: JAMES GRINDLAY, ROBERT WILLIAMS, JR. Before JOHN RATTRAY, J.P. WILLIAM HOPTON, Register. On 15 Feb. 1750 TODD acknowledged receipt of payment in full. Witness: WILLIAM HOPTON.

Book E-E, p. 206
24 & 25 Mar. 1742
L & R by Mortgage

FRANCIS ROCHE, planter, to the vestry of Parish of St. Thomas, Berkeley Co., as security on bond of even date in penal sum of L 1400 for payment of L 700 currency, with interest, on 25 Mar. 1742 at the vestry room of St. Thomas; 907 a., English measure, in Berkeley Co., on head of E branch of Cooper River, where ROCHE now lives, being part of 5000 a. granted by the Lords Proprs. to DOMINICK ARTHUR; which 5000 a. was part of Colleton's Barony; the 907 a. bounding S & N on DANIEL HUGER; NE on the Rev. MR. THOMAS HASELL; SE on ROBERT QUASH. Witnesses: MATTHEW QUASH, ROBERT HOW. Before LIONEL CHALMERS, J.P. WILLIAM HOPTON, Register.

Book E-E, p. 212
15 & 16 June 1744
L & R by Mortgage

BENJAMIN SIMONS, planter, to the Parish of St. Thomas, Berkeley Co., as security for payment of L 700 currency, with interest, on 25 Mar. 1745; 1083 a. in St. Thomas Parish, bounding NE on Glebe land; SE on THOMAS HASELL; SW on POPLAR'S land; NW on E branch of Cooper River; being several tracts granted by the Lords Proprs.; 1 grant to BENJAMIN SIMONS dated 15 Sept. 1705; 1 to JOHN AUNANT dated 12 May 1703; 1 to BENJAMIN SIMONS dated 5 May 1704; 1 to NICHOLAS DELONGUEMARE dated 14 Mar. 1693/4. Witnesses: WALTER DUNBAR, MOSES MILLER, WILLIAM CONNOR. Before JAMES AKIN, J.P. WILLIAM HOPTON, Register. On 5 Oct. 1752 ALEXANDER GARDEN, JR., Rector of St. Thomas Parish, declared mortgage satisfied. Witness: WILLIAM HOPTON.

Book E-E, p. 217
22 & 23 Feb. 1748
L & R

ROBERT HANCOCK, planter, of St. Bartholomews Parish, with the consent of his wife MARY, to THOMAS POOLE, pilot, of Charleston, for L 1550 currency, the E half of lot #92 in Charleston with the houses, offices, buildings, etc. Whereas ELIAS HANCOCK, vintner, of Charleston, father of said ROBERT, by will dated 20 Nov. 1729 bequeathed the E half of lot #92 to his second son, ELIAS, & the W half to his third son, ROBERT, party hereto, but should any son die without issue his fortune should go to the surviving children; & whereas ELIAS the second son, & all the other children of ELIAS, except ROBERT, died without issue & ROBERT became heir-at-law; & whereas ROBERT had agreed to give POOLE a

good title to the E half of lot #92; ROBERT having sold the W half to
SAMUEL WAINWRIGHT; now ROBERT conveys the E half to POOLE. Witnesses:
ISAAC HUMPHREYS, ANDREW RUTLEDGE. Before OTHNIEL BEALE, J.P. WILLIAM
HOPTON, Register.

Book E-E, p. 221   EDMUND (his mark) E. KELLY, tanner, of St.
10 Aug. 1748   Bartholomews Parish, to ALEXANDER RANTOWLE,
Mortgage   storekeeper, of St. Pauls Parish, Colleon Co.,
                         as security on bond of even date in penal sum
of Ł 224:5 for payment of Ł 112:2:6 SC money, with interest, on 1 Oct.
1748; 650 a. in St. Bartholomews Parish, adjoining JAMES BOGGS & bounding
according to grant from MR. ARCHIBALD (?). Witnesses: JOHN GAVIN, ANDREW
AGNEW. Before JAMES BULLOCK, J.P. WILLIAM HOPTON, Register. On 31 Oct.
1768 ALEXANDER RANTOWLE declared mortgage paid. Witness: FENWICKE BULL,
Register.

Book E-E, p. 223   ROBERT HANCOCK, planter, & MARY his wife, of
1 & 2 Mar. 1748   St. Bartholomews Parish, Colleton Co., to
L & R   ZACHARIAH VILLEPONTOUX, JONATHAN DRAKE, & JOHN
                         MOORE, planters, of Berkeley Co., executors of
will of PETER VILLEPONTOUX, planter, of Berkeley Co., for Ł 1200 currency,
300 a. & premises formerly owned by ELIAS HANCOCK, situate on the NE of
Ashley River; SW on Hog Island Creek; SE on DANIEL GREEN. Whereas ELIAS
HANCOCK, the elder, vintner, of Charleston, owned the above named 300 a.
by will dated 20 Nov. 1729 bequeathed the 300 a. to his well beloved eldest son, WILLIAM, when 21; but should WILLIAM die without issue his fortune to be divided among the surviving children of ELIAS; & whereas WIL-
LIAM, after his father's death, reached 21, & by his attorney, JAMES OS-
MOND, merchant, of Charleston (appointed 14 Aug. 1741), by L & R dated 17
& 18 Nov. 1741 sold the 300 a.; & whereas said VILLEPONTOUX died, having
appointed ZACHARIAH VILLEPONTOUX, DRAKE & MOORE his executors; to whom
ROBERT agreed to sell the 300 a.; now ROBERT HANCOCK carries out his
agreement & conveys to the executors. Witnesses: THOMAS LAMBOLL, JACOB
MOTTE. Before JAMES WEDDERBURN, J.P. WILLIAM HOPTON, Register.

Book E-E, p. 230   DEBORAH FISHER, spinster, to SAMUEL WELLS,
17 & 18 Jan. 1748   planter, both of St. Thomas Parish, Berkeley
L & R   Co.; for Ł 700 currency, 500 a. on N side Wan-
                         do River, bounding W on PETER ALSTON & RICHARD
BERESFORD; N on ROBERT DANIELL; E on SAMUEL WELLS. Whereas JAMES FISHER,
merchant, of Charleston, on 1 Mar. 1736 purchased from ABRAHAM WARNOCK,
planter, of Prince George Parish, for Ł 1050 currency, 500 a. in St.
Thomas Parish; & by will dated 28 Mar. 1734 bequeathed to his wife DEB-
ORAH, party hereto, the residue of his real & personal estate, appointing
her sole executrix (letters testamentary granted by Lt. Gov. WILLIAM BULL
on 7 Dec. 1739); now DEBORAH sells the 500 a. to WELLS. Witnesses: JOHN
SANDERS, SAMUEL SMITH, STEPHEN HARTLEY. Before ROBERT AUSTIN, J.P. WIL-
LIAM HOPTON, Register.

Book E-E, p. 235   THOMAS JONES, & HANNAH his wife, of Charles-
24 & 25 Feb. 1748/9   ton, to WILLIAM BRANFORD, SR., planter, of St.
L & R   Andrews Parish, Berkeley Co., for Ł 3000 cur-
                         rency, 628 a. Whereas the Lords Proprs. on 20
Jan. 1710 granted GEORGE KNIGHT & ELIZABETH his wife (formerly ELIZABETH
SULLIVANT) 200 a. in Berkeley Co., which they sold on 24 Sept. 1711 to
SAMUEL JONES for Ł 90 & whereas the Lords Proprs. on 21 May 1717 granted
SAMUEL JONES 100 a. in Berkeley Co.; making 1 tract of 300 a.; which by
will dated 7 Jan. 1727 JONES bequeathed to his son THOMAS JONES, party
hereto, in these words "I give to my well beloved son THOMAS JONES the
house & tract of land I now live on, with all my slaves & all other my
moveables whatever after the decease of his mother"; & whereas after the
death of his mother THOMAS JONES married MARY, daughter of JOHN EDWARDS,
& they had 1 child; & whereas MARY died & THOMAS married HANNAH & they
had 1 child; & whereas DOROTHY JONES mother of THOMAS, had owned 110 a.
which she, by L & R dated 2 & 3 Aug. 1736 had purchased from SAMUEL
STOCKS for Ł 1100, which 110 a. was on E side Stono River, in Berkeley
Co., was granted by the Lords Proprs. to THOMAS STOCKS, father of SAMUEL
& purchased by SAMUEL from his brother THOMAS, eldest son & heir; boung-
ing N on THOMAS STOCKS; E on SAMUEL JONES; W on SAMUEL STOCKS; & whereas
GEORGE II on 14 Dec. 1739, by Lt. Gov. WILLIAM BULL, granted DOROTHY

JONES 51 a. of marsh land, bounding N & E on marsh of said JONES; S on
Stono River; W on marsh of said JONES; S on Stono River; W on marsh of
THOMAS ELLIOTT; making a tract of 161 a., which by will dated 20 Dec.
1739 she bequeathed to her son THOMAS "until he have an heir or heirs,"
otherwise to the eldest son of her daughter MARY WAITS; & whereas THOMAS
became owner; & whereas by L & R dated 6 & 7 Dec. 1742 THOMAS JONES pur-
chased from STEPHEN BULL an adjoining tract of 167 a. of land & marsh in
St. Andrews Parish, Berkeley Co.; making 1 tract of 628 a., English mea-
sure, bounding S on Stono River & marsh; W on THOMAS & BENJAMIN ELLIOTT;
N on NATHANIEL BROWN, STEPHEN BULL, & RICHARD GODFREY; E on marsh of
Stono River; now THOMAS JONES sells to BRANFORD. Witnesses: WILLIAM
GEORGE FREEMAN, WILLIAM WEBB, JR. Before J. COLLETON, J.P. WILLIAM HOP-
TON, Register.

Book E-E, p. 244   ALEXANDER LIVIE, merchant, of Charleston, to
28 Aug. 1742   DANIEL CRAWFORD, planter, for ₤ 1000 SC money,
Feoffment   part of lot #12 in Charleston, bounding E 100
                         ft. on MARY ELLIS; W on PETER BENOIST (former-
ly MRS. DILL); N 36 ft. on Broad Street; S 37 ft. 2 in. on JOSEPH WRAGG
(formerly ISAAC GALLEBEUF). Witnesses: GEORGE PHILIP, JOHN RATTRAY, HEL-
EN RATTRAY. Before JAMES WEDDERBURN, J.P. WILLIAM HOPTON, Register.

Book E-E, p. 246   ABRAHAM WALLCUT, cordwainer, of St. Bartholo-
21 Jan. 1748/9   mew Parish, Colleton Co., to SAMUEL SPRY, ex-
Mortgage   ecutor of ROYAL SPRY; planter, of St. Pauls
                         Parish, as security on bond of even date in
penal sum of ₤ 244 for payment of ₤ 122 currency, on 1 Jan. next; 200 a.
on Penny's or Bees Creek, in St. Pauls Parish, bounding S on ISAAC TAY-
LOR. Witnesses: ROBERT ALLEN, WILLIAM CATHCART. Before ROBERT AUSTIN,
J.P. WILLIAM HOPTON, Register. On 6 Sept. 1749 SAMUEL SPRY declared
mortgage satisfied. Witness: WILLIAM HOPTON.

Book E-E, p. 247   SARAH LLOYD, widow, to JOHN MARTINI, chirur-
12 & 14 Nov. 1748   geon; as security for payment of ₤ 2000 cur-
L & R by Mortgage   rency, with interest, on 14 Nov. next; part of
                         lot #3 in Charleston, fronting E 35 ft. on the
Bay; bounding W on marsh of WILLIAM CHAPMAN. Whereas THOMAS LLOYD, gentleman, owned part of a lot fronting E 35 ft. on the Bay of Charleston;
bounding W on marsh of WILLIAM CHAPMAN; S on JOSEPH BOONE, ESQ.; N on
JOHN FENWICKE, ESQ.; & by will dated 2 Aug. 1742 authorized his executors
& executrix to sell his real & personal estate; & whereas THOMAS LAMBOLL
refused to act as executor & SARAH LLOYD, executrix, on 2 July 1748 exposed the lands of THOMAS LLOYD to sale at public auction by DANIEL CRAW-
FORD, Public Vendue Master, & she, as highest bidder, became owner of the
part of the town lot #3; now she mortgages it to DR. MARTINI. Witnesses:
JOHN CHAMPNEYS, JOHN TIMOTHY. Before THOMAS DALE, J.P. WILLIAM HOPTON,
Register.

Book E-E, p. 254   ANDREW ALLEN, merchant, to WILLIAM WARDEN,
26 & 27 Oct. 1730   mariner, both of Charleston; for ₤ 700 SC mon-
L & R   ey; free from claim of dower by SARAH, wife of
                         ANDREW ALLEN; the E part of 3 lots in Charles-
ton, Nos. 188, 189, & 79; bounding N on part of lot #188; E on lots 83,
84, & 191; S 63 ft. 8 in. on Dock Street; in depth from S to N "down to
the pailes of the burying place belonging to the Meeting House" 237 ft.;
& in breadth at the corner end, from E to W, 60 ft. Witnesses: GABRIEL
MANIGAULT, ROBERT HUME. Before ROBERT AUSTIN, J.P. Description of plat:
From a cedar post in fence on Dock Street, the corner of #79 & #83, along
said street W 63 ft. 8 in. to a cedar stake; from said corner post along
pales of #83, #84, & #192, 237 ft. to the pales of the Meeting House yard
in #188; along said pales 60 ft. to a cedar stake. Certified 26 June
1730 by G. HUNTER, Surveyor. WILLIAM HOPTON, Register. Plat given.

Book E-E, p. 260   JOHN BAYLEY, ESQ., of Ballinaclough, Co. of
24 Nov. 1726   Tipperary, Ireland, son & heir of JOHN BAYLY,
Lease for 1 Year   ESQ., by his attorney ALEXANDER TRENCH, mer-
                         chant, of Charleston; to WILLIAM PRICE, plant-
er, of Craven Co., for 10 shillings a year, 330 a. in Craven Co., bounding NE on WILLIAM WATIES; N & NW on vacant land. Witnesses: JOHN BEN-
STONE, SAMUEL MASTERS, WILLIAM WATIES. WILLIAM HOPTON, Register. Not

proved. No release recorded.

Book E-E, p. 260   JONATHAN COLKINS, carpenter, & MARGARET (her
5 Mar. 1747   mark) his reputed wife, of Prince George Par-
Sale   ish, Craven Co., to JACOB ROYALL, ESQ., of
                          Boston, Suffolk Co., Mass. Bay Province, New
England, for ₤ 300 SC money, 330 a. in Prince George Parish, part of
BAYLY'S patent purchased through his attorney, ALEXANDER TRENCH; bounding
NE on WILLIAM WATES; N & NW on vacant land; SE on Little River. Witness-
es: JOHN IOOR, HENRY (his mark) BRADLEY, SARAH WALLACE. Before PAUL
TRAPIER, J.P. WILLIAM HOPTON, Register.

Book E-E, p. 262   JACOB ROYALL, ESQ., of Boston, Suffolk Co.,
10 Apr. 1747   Mass. Bay Province, New England, only acting
Letter of Attorney   executor of will of ISAAC ROYALL, formerly of
                          Charleston, Middlesex Co., Mass. (?), later of
Island of Antigua; appoints JOHN IOOR, gentleman, of NC, his attorney,
with authority to receive from JONATHAN CAULKINS, yeoman, formerly of
Norwich, Co. of New London, Colony of Connecticut, New England, now re-
siding in NC, due estate of ISAAC ROYALL on bond dated 14 July 1730, etc.
Witnesses: JOHN FOYE, JOSEPH MARION. Before EDWARD HUTCHINSON, J.P. of
Suffolk Co. On 27 June 1747 JOSEPH MARION, Notary & Tabellion Public, of
Boston, certified that EDWARD HUTCHINSON was J.P. as noted. WILLIAM HOP-
TON, Register.

Book E-E, p. 264   JOHN BONNOIT, planter, & MAGDALENE his wife,
28 & 29 Mar. 1749   to WALTER DOLLAS, planter; both of Parish of
L & R   St. Thomas & St. Dennis, Berkeley Co.; for
                          ₤ 1700 currency; 255 a., being 1/2 of 4 tracts
of 510 a., on which CHARLES HAYES, father of GEORGE HAYES, lived, which
210 a., by L & R dated 18 & 19 Nov. 1741, GEORGE HAYES sold to JOHN BON-
NOIT (see Registers Office, Book W. fol. 478-484). Witnesses: JASPER DU-
BOIS, JOHN REMINGTON, WILLIAM GLEN. Before ROBERT AUSTIN, J.P. WILLIAM
HOPTON, Register.

Book E-E, p. 268   GEORGE II appoints WILLIAM HOPTON to office of
7 Mar. 1748   Public Register. Signed by JAMES GLEN. WIL-
                          LIAM HOPTON, Register.

DEEDS BOOK "F-F"
APRIL 1749 - FEBRUARY 1749

Book F-F, p. 1   JOSEPH SEALEY, planter, of Pon Pon, nephew &
31 Mar. & 1 Apr. 1749   heir of JOSEPH BAGGEN, to JOHN SPLATT, plant-
L & R   er, of same place, for ₤ 2400 currency, 4 ad-
                          joining tracts in Colleton Co., total 963 a.;
bounding E on JOHN BEE & on Bees Creek; W on BULLOCK & SACHEVERELL (formerly JOHN PETERS); N on PETERS & HAYNE; S on PETER TAYLOR. Whereas the
Lords Proprs. on 1 May 1701 granted JOHN PECKUM 200 a. in Colleton Co.; &
on 1 May 1704 granted him 400 a.; & whereas JOHN PECKUM & DOROTHY his
wife by deed poll dated 13 Dec. 1710 sold the 600 a. to OWIN BAGGIN; &
whereas the Lords Proprs. on 23 July 1711 granted OWIN BAGGIN 296 a.; &
whereas BAGGIN died, leaving an only son, JOHN, who inherited the 3
tracts; & whereas GEORGE II, by Gov. THOMAS BROUGHTON, granted JOHN BAG-
GIN 67 a., bounding S & W on JOHN BAGGIN; N on JOHN HAYNE & MR. PETER; E
on JOHN HAYNES & vacant land; & whereas JOHN BAGGIN died & the 4 tracts
descended to his nephew & heir at law, JOSEPH SEALY; now SEALEY sells the
4 tracts to SPLATT. Witnesses: JOHN RATTRAY, ROBERT WILLIAMS, JR. Before DANIEL CRAWFORD, J.P. WILLIAM HOPTON, Register.

Book F-F, p. 6   ULYSSES ANTHONY ALBERGOTTI, shopkeeper, & PRU-
3 & 4 Apr. 1749   DENCE (her mark) his wife, to THOMAS BURTON,
L & R   carpenter; both of Beaufort, on Port Royal Is-
                          land, Granville Co.; for ₤ 600 currency, 250
a., part of 500 a. granted by the Lords Proprs. in 1705 to MARK MATHEW;
which 250 a. by several mesne conveyances became vested in JOHN DELAGAYE,
who, by L & R dated 2 & 3 Nov. 1748 sold the 250 a. to ALBERGOTTI; bounding NE on Wilkinsons Creek; NW on Salt Water Creek & SOMERFIELD'S land;

181

SW on JOHN HOGG; S & SE on other part of 500 a. Witnesses: SAMUEL HARD-
ALL, WILLIAM GOUGH. Before ROBERT WILLIAMS, J.P. WILLIAM HOPTON, Register.

Book F-F, p. 10   MARTHA BEE, widow, formerly of Berkeley Co.,
30 & 31 Dec. 1748   now of Colleton Co., to BENJAMIN STONE, ship-
L & R   wright, of James Island, St. Andrews Parish,
                            Berkeley Co., for Ł 3600 currency, 215 a.,
English measure, on James Island, bounding E on Witpencho Creek & marsh &
on FRANCIS GRACIA & THOMAS LAMBOLL; S on ELIZABETH RIVERS, widow, & on
BENJAMIN STONE; W on WILLIAM RIVERS, SAMUEL STENT, SAMUEL MAVERICK, &
Kuskewah Creek & marsh; N on Kuskewah Creek & marsh & Ashley River; which
215 a. consists of 2 tracts 170 a. & 45 a.; the 170 a. granted by the
Lords Proprs. on 14 Feb. 1706 to MARTHA PATEY; the 45 a. (N of the 170
a.), being the NE pàrt of 2 tracts of 70 & 5 a.; which 75 a. were granted
by the Lords Proprs. on 3 Sept. 1709 to WILLIAM RIVERS the elder & by
several wills & mesne conveyances became vested in MARTHA BEE. MARTHA
BEE sold 25 a., the W part of the 75 a., to WILLIAM RIVERS. Witnesses:
WILLIAM BOWER, PAUL HAMILTON, a Quaker. Before THOMAS LAMBOLL, J.P.
WILLIAM HOPTON, Register.

Book F-F, p. 18   The Rev. MR. SAMUEL HUNTER, cleric, of Prince
16 & 17 Mar. 1748   Frederick Parish, Craven Co., to PAUL TRAPIER,
L & R with Condition   ESQ., of Georgetown. Whereas TRAPIER at HUNT-
                            ER'S request became security on HUNTER'S bond
dated 1748 to JOHN DUTARQUE, executor of will of NOAH SERRÉ, in penal sum
of Ł 2000 for payment of Ł 1000 currency, with interest, on a certain
date in 1749; & whereas HUNTER gave TRAPIER a bond dated 18 Mar. 1748 in
penal sum of Ł 2000 for payment to DUTARQUE of said Ł 1000 currency; now
to assure TRAPIER & protect him, HUNTER conveys to TRAPIER, as security,
559 a., in Prince Frederick's Parish, bounding E on WILLIAM GARDNER,
other sides on Black River, granted to HUNTER on 22 Feb. 1745. Witnesses: WILLIAM POOLE, JR., WILLIAM PARKER. Before WILLIAM POOLE, J.P.
WILLIAM HOPTON, Register.

Book F-F, p. 22   WILLIAM BRANFORD, JR., planter, & MARY his
26 & 27 Feb. 1747   wife, of St. Andrews Parish, Berkeley Co., to
L & R   JOHN ALLSTON, planter, of Craven Co., for
                            Ł 900 currency, 640 a. in Craven Co., on Wac-
camaw River, bounding E on creeks & salt marsh on Seaside; N on GEORGE
PAWLEY; S & W on JOHN ALSTON. Whereas JOHN, Earl of Bath, & the Lords
Proprs. on 7 Mar. 1698 granted Landgrave ROBERT DANIELL a certain number
of a. in SC & whereas DANIELL ran out 1280 a. in Craven Co., part of his
patent, which parcel of land was granted to him by the Lords Proprs. on
18 June 1711; & on 19 June 1711 sold the 1280 a. to THOMAS SMITH, ESQ.; &
whereas SMITH on 10 Sept. 1711 sold the tract to JOHN CROFTS; who, on 20
Dec. 1714 sold to WILLIAM BRANFORD, who, by will dated 17 May 1717 bequeathed the tract to his son, BARNABY, & his daughter, MARTHA, to be divided according to the will; which was done; & whereas the N part, or
640 a. fell to MARTHA (afterwards MARTHA BRYAN) who died intestate, leaving 1 daughter, MARY, now MARY BRANFORD, party hereto; now she & her husband sell the tract to ALLSTON. Witnesses: EBENEZER SIMMONS, FRANCIS
HOLMES. Before JACOB MOTTE, J.P. WILLIAM HOPTON, Register.

Book F-F, p. 27   SARAH BELIN, widow, of JAMES BELIN, planter,
24 Feb. 1747   of Prince George Parish, to her son, ALLARD
Gift   BELIN, for natural love & affection, all her
                            claim to the 1000 a. in Prince George Parish,
bounding N on Landgrave THOMAS SMITH'S Barony; E & S on THOMAS LYNCH; to
which she was entitled during her lifetime, the reversion belonging to
her son. Witnesses: WILLIAM BELIN, ELIZABETH LABRUCE, JOHN LABRUCE. Before PAUL TRAPIER, J.P. WILLIAM HOPTON, Register.

Book F-F, p. 28   JOHN GENDRON, ESQ., to DANIEL HORRY, ESQ.,
20 & 21 Feb. 1748   both of St. James Santee Parish, Craven Co.;
L & R   for Ł 1000 currency, 3 tracts of 500, 250, &
                            182 a.; the 500 a. bounding N on Wambaw Creek;
E on the 2nd tract of 250 a.; the 250 a. bounding N on Wambaw Creek; W on
the 500 a.; E on DANIEL HORRY; the 182 a. bounding S on Wambaw Creek; N &
W on DANIEL HORRY; which 2 tracts of 500 & 250 a. were granted to MICHAEL

CLYNCH on 29 Mar. 1715. Witnesses: JOHN HENTIE, EDWARD JERMAN, SUSANNAH LEGANDRE. Before SAMUEL THOMAS, J.P. WILLIAM HOPTON, Register.

Book F-F, p. 34   THOMAS STEPHENS, gentleman, to WILLIAM CHAM-
8 Sept. 1745   BERS, tailor; both of Wadmalaw Island; as se-
Mortgage   curity on bond of even date in penal sum of
                       L 2652 for payment of L 1826 currency, with
interest, on 8 Feb. 1746; 394 a. on Wadmalaw Island, part of the plantation called Bugby's Hole lately sold by JAMES MICHIE to WILLIAM CHAMBERS;
bounding N on Wadmalaw Creek; E on ABRAHAM _____; S & SE on _____; W on
SAMUEL JONES. Witnesses: SAMUEL QUINCY, JOHN BEATTY. Before JOHN LINING,
J.P. WILLIAM HOPTON, Register.

Book F-F, p. 36   THOMAS BEAZLEY, shipwright, of Charleston, to
25 Mar. 1749   JOHN BRUCE, planter, of Berkeley Co., in penal
Bond   sum of L 2000 for payment of L 1000 SC money,
                       on 6 Aug. 1749. Witnesses: JOHN GREEN, JOHN
BRUCE, SUSANNE NICKLESS. Before ROBERT AUSTIN, J.P. WILLIAM HOPTON, Register.

Book F-F, p. 37   THOMAS BEAZLEY, shipwright, of Charleston, to
25 Mar. 1749   JOHN BRUCE, planter, of Berkeley Co., as se-
Mortgage   curity on above bond (p. 36), conveys 2 tracts
                       of 50 & 200 a. Witnesses: JOHN GREEN, JOHN
BRUCE, MRS. SUSANNA NICKLESS. Before ROBERT AUSTIN, J.P. WILLIAM HOPTON,
Register,

Book F-F, p. 38   REGINALD JACKSON, planter, of Pon Pon, to
23 & 24 June 1748   JAMES SKIRVING, gentleman, of Berkeley Co.,
L & R   for L 1200 currency, 3 tracts of 376 a., 100
                       a., & 55 a. Whereas the Lords Proprs. on 16
Aug. 1698 created JOHN BAYLY, ESQ., of Ballinaclough, Co. of Tipperary,
Ireland, a Landgrave & Cassick of SC, granting him 48,000 a. of land in
SC; & whereas he died intestate & his son JOHN inherited the title & land;
& he on 9 Nov. 1722 appointed ALEXANDER TRENCH, merchant, of Charleston,
his attorney, with authority to lay out & sell the land; & whereas TRENCH,
by L & R dated 26 & 27 Jan. 1725, sold to ROBERT COX, 376 a., in Colleton
Co., bounding N on JOHN WHITMARSH; E on WILLIAM OSWELL; S on Pocotaligo
Swamp; W on Horse Shoe Creek; & whereas COX died intestate & his eldest
son, JOHN COX, cordwainer, of Colleton Co., inherited; & he, by deed poll
dated 12 Jan. 1730 sold the 376 a. to HENRY JACKSON, planter, who, on 22
Dec. 1733 gave the tract in jointenancy to his 2 sons, SAMUEL & WILLIAM;
& whereas SAMUEL JACKSON, on (Jan. 1734 died & WILLIAM became sole owner;
& he died intestate in Oct. 1739 & the 376 a. descended to his only son &
heir, REGINALL JACKSON, party hereto; & whereas the Lords Proprs. on 20
Mar. 17__ granted JOHN WHITMARSH 100 a. on the marshes of Edisto River,
bounding on lands belonging to WILLIAM JACKSON, HENRY JACKSON & DAVID
ALLEN; which 100 a. is now the property of REGINALD JACKSON, party hereto;
& whereas GEORGE II, by Lt. Gov. THOMAS BROUGHTON, on 7 Aug. 1735 granted
HENRY JACKSON 55 a. in Colleton Co., bounding S on WILLIAM JACKSON; W on
Horse Shoe Creek; & whereas HENRY JACKSON by deed poll dated 27 Oct. 1735
sold the 55 a. to WILLIAM JACKSON, after whose death it descended to his
son REGINALL JACKSON; now he sells the 3 tracts to SKIRVING. Witnesses:
ELEANOR SANDWELL, THOMAS BROUGHTON. Before HENRY IZARD, J.P. WILLIAM
HOPTON, Register.

Book F-F, p. 46   RICHARD BAKER, planter, of Berkeley Co., to
13 & 14 Mar. 1748   EDWARD LIGHTWOOD, gentleman, of Charleston,
L & R   for L 1400 currency, part of lot #7 in Charles-
                       ton, bounding N on estate of JAMES OSMOND; E
94 ft. on THOMAS LAMBOLL; S 28 ft. 9 in. on Tradd Street; W on MRS. ANN
BOONE; which piece of land was sold to WILLIAM BAKER, father of RICHARD,
by ROBERT TRADD by deed of feoffment dated 27 Feb. 1702/3 & inherited by
RICHARD as eldest son & heir. Witnesses: HENRY MIDDLETON, STEPHEN CATER.
Before JACOB MOTTE, J.P. WILLIAM HOPTON, Register.

Book F-F, p. 51   RICHARD GOUGH, to ELIAS BALL, for L 3400 cur-
(10 May 1749?)   rency, 600 a. (the part RICHARD inherited from
Release   his brother) on head of E branch of Cooper Riv-
                       er, in St. Johns Parish, Berkeley Co.,

183

bounding S on JOHN BALL (brother of ELIAS); N & W on the part of 3500 a. sold to JOHN BALL by EDWARD GOUGH, O'NEALE GOUGH, & FRANCIS GOUGH. Whereas JOHN GOUGH, planter, of St. Johns Parish, Berkeley Co., bequeathed to his 4 sons, JOHN, EDWARD, O'NEALE, & FRANCIS equal portions of all his land, but willed that JOHN should have as his share the part where the house was; & whereas JOHN died intestate & RICHARD, his eldest brother inherited, & RICHARD Has asked his brothers for a plat showing his portion, now they sign their names to the plat dated 27 Feb. 1747. Witnesses: JOHN HENTIE, NICHOLAS HARLESTON. Before FRANCIS LEJAU, J.P. WILLIAM HOPTON, Register.

Book F-F, p. 55
5 & 6 Aug. 1746
L & R by Mortgage

ALEXANDER CHISOLME, vintner, & JUDITH his wife, to SARAH STOUTENBURGH, widow; both of Charleston; as security on bond of even date in penal sum of Ł 4000 for payment of Ł 2000, with interest, on 5 Aug. 1747; lot #229, containing 1/2 a., English measure, in Charleston, bounding S on the little street leading from Cooper River by RICHARD TRADD'S to GEORGE KEELING; N on MR. DUGU; E on JOHN HILL; W on THOMAS ROSE; which lot was purchased by ELIAS HANCOCK from RICHARD GUNSTON, gentleman, & ELLINOR his wife, of Berkeley Co., on 28 Feb. 1726. Witnesses: THOMAS NEWTON, WILLIAM HANCOCK, DANIEL DONOVAN. On same date ALEXANDER & JUDITH CHISOLME also borrowed from SARAH STOUTENBURGH Ł 800 for which they gave bond in penalty of Ł 1600 for payment, with interest, on 20 Aug. 1748, conveying lot #229 & premises as further security. Witnesses: DANIEL DONOVAN, JOHN CATTELL. Before ROBERT AUSTIN, J.P. WILLIAM HOPTON, Register.

Book F-F, p. 60
16 & 17 May 1745
L & R of Reversion

HUGH BRYAN, planter, & MARY his wife, of Granville Co., of 1st part; & MARY BRYAN, widow (mother of ANNE BRYAN, infant daughter of JOSEPH BRYAN, brother of HUGH BRYAN), of 2nd part. For natural love & affection which HUGH BRYAN bears for his niece, ANNE, & his brother JOSEPH'S children, HUGH & his wife grant MARY (ANNE'S mother) 500 a., English measure, part of 3140 a. granted by the King to JOSEPH BRYAN & HUGH BRYAN in jointenancy; the 500 a. bounding E on a tract of 900 a. owned by STEPHEN BULL & ELIZABETH his wife (1 of JOSEPH BRYAN'S daughters); S on HILL CROFT & ANTHONY MATTHEWES; W on Pocotalago River; N on JONATHAN BRYAN; to hold till ANNE reached 18 years of age; in case ANNE dies without heirs then ELIZABETH BULL'S heirs; in case ELIZABETH leaves no heirs, then to heirs of JOSEPH BRYAN. Witnesses: WILLIAM HUTSON, JONATHAN BRYAN. Before THOMAS LAMBOLL, J.P. WILLIAM HOPTON, Register.

Book F-F, p. 67
14 & 15 June 1742
L & R

WILLIAM BULL, ESQ., of Berkeley Co., to EDWARD PERRY, planter, of Colleton Co., for Ł 2705 currency, 2 tracts, total 722 a., English measure, on SW side Ashley River, in Berkeley & Colleton Cos. Whereas the Lords Proprs. on 27 June 1710 granted WILLIAM ** BULL 572 a. in Berkeley Co., bounding NW on JOHN COOPER; NE on Gov. EDWARD TYNTE; SE on WILLIAM SAUNDERS; SW on WILLIAM ELLIOTT; & on 15 Feb. 1716/17 granted WILLIAM BULL147 a. in Berkeley Co., bounding NE on WILLIAM BULL; SE on CAPT. RICHARD DEVON; SW on WILLIAM ELLIOTT; NW on ABEL KETTLEBEE; now BULL sells to PERRY. Witnesses: WILLIAM MILES, FRANCIS THOMPSON. Before WILLIAM BULL, JR., J.P. WILLIAM HOPTON, Register.

Book F-F, p. 73
15 Dec. 1748
Gift

EDWARD PERRY, SR., planter, to EDWARD PERRY, JR., planter, both of Colleton Co., of his free will & for good causes, 400 a., partly in Berkeley, partly in Colleton Co., bounding SE on PHILIP EVANS; NE on RICHARD BAKER; NW on HENRY IZARD; SW on EDWARD PERRY, SR. Witnesses: SAMUEL DRAYTON, WILLIAM MAINE. Before J. SKENE, J.P. WILLIAM HOPTON, Register.

Book F-F, p. 75
21 Feb. 1748/9
Sale

SAMUEL WOOD, tailor, to JOHN CLARK, cordwainer, both of Berkeley Co., for Ł 15 currency, lot #96, containing 1/2 a., in Ashley Ferry Town, called Butlers Town, bounding NE on lot #95; SW on a street leading to Ferry Path; SE on lot #87; NW on a street leading to Ashley River. Witnesses: THOMAS GOREING, PETER CATTELL, JOHN SMITH. Before CHARLES HILL, J.P. WILLIAM HOPTON, Register.

Book F-F, p. 76   WALTER IZARD, JR., RALPH IZARD, & THOMAS
26 May 1749   BROUGHTON, executors of will of HENRY IZARD,
Lease   ESQ., of Charleston, to BENJAMIN SMITH, mer-
                        chant, of Charleston. Whereas HENRY IZARD, a
few days before his death, sold BARNARD ELLIOTT 10 or 12 a., part of HEN-
RY IZARD'S tract, opposite the Quarter House & adjoining ELLIOTT'S land;
& at the same time HENRY IZARD sold BENJAMIN SMITH 50 or 60 a., part of
same tract & adjoining BARNARD ELLIOTT'S piece; & fixed the bounds of the
2 pieces to be on Ashley River; but HENRY IZARD died before titles were
made; with which agreement & sale the executors are well acquainted &
satisfied; & whereas a survey was made & BENJAMIN SMITH agreed to accept
the whole of the survey, being 71-1/2 a.; now the executors lease the
71-1/2 a. to SMITH, until HENRY IZARD'S heir comes of age, when the heir
shall make proper conveyance, SMITH promising to pay Ł 892 currency, with
interest, at 8% from date hereof. Witnesses: JOHN PALMER, MILES BREWTON.
Before JAMES WRIGHT, J.P. WILLIAM HOPTON, Register. Plat certified by
THOMAS BLYTHE, Dep. Sur., 20 May 1749, shows 71-1/2 a. bounding W on BAR-
NARD ELLIOTT; S on Ashley River; E & N on HENRY IZARD.

Book F-F, p. 78   JOHN RATTRAY, gentleman, & HELEN his wife, to
9 & 10 Mar. 1747   HENRY KENNAN, merchant; both of Charleston;
L & R   for Ł 3500 SC money, part of a lot with the
                        messuage thereon, bounding S 30 ft. on Broad
Street; E & N on THOMAS SMITH, JR. (formerly JOSEPH WRAGG); W 100 ft. on
a house & lot belonging to JOHN WATSON, JR. Witnesses: JOHN WATSON, JR.,
JAMES GRINDLAY. Before JOHN LINING, J.P. WILLIAM HOPTON, Register.

Book F-F, p. 83   SARAH CLIFFORD, widow, of Charleston (formerly
29 & 30 Nov. 1748   called SARAH SMITH, daughter of WILLIAM SMITH,
L & R   the elder gentleman, of Berkeley Co.), to HEN-
                        RY KENNAN, merchant, of Charleston, for Ł 800
SC money, lot #306 bounding N on Broad Street; W & S on a marsh; E on
JAMES GRAEME, ESQ., (formerly MARTIN COOK) containing 1/2 an a., English
measure. Whereas the Lords Proprs. on 19 Mar. 1694/5 granted WILLIAM
SMITH lot #306 in Charleston containing 1/2 a., bounding N on the Great
Street leading from Cooper River by the Market Place; which, by deed of
feoffment dated 30 July 1712, for natural love & affection, conveyed to
his daughter, SARAH SMITH; now she sells to KENNAN. Witnesses: JOSEPH
LLOYD, CHARLES PRYCE. Before ROBERT AUSTIN, J.P. WILLIAM HOPTON, Register.

Book F-F, p. 89   ANDREW SLANN, planter, & ANN his wife, to
8 & 9 Aug. 1748   RALPH IZARD, planter, both of Berkeley Co.;
L & R   for Ł 200 currency, 197 a. of pine land, part
                        of tract of pine land run out for MAJ. BENJA-
MIN WARING; in St. George Parish, Dorchester, Berkeley Co., bounding N on
the Broad Road; W on THOMAS WARING. Witnesses: JOSEPH ARDEN, JOHN ED-
WARDS, THOMAS WARING. Before RICHARD WARING, J.P. WILLIAM HOPTON, Register.

Book F-F, p. 94   HENRY BEDON, shopkeeper, & MARY ANN his wife,
7 & 8 Mar. 1748   to GEORGE SEAMAN, merchant, both of Charleston;
L & R of Reversion   for Ł 800 currency; part of lot #8 in Charles-
                        ton, given to HENRY BEDON by FRANCES SIMMONS,
widow, by her will dated 6 Dec. 1707; bounding E 40 ft. & S 40 ft. on
GEORGE SEAMAN; W 40 ft. on BEDON'S Alley; N 40 ft. on THOMAS ELLIOTT.
Witnesses: PHILIP BOX, JOHN REMINGTON. Before JOHN DART, J.P. WILLIAM
HOPTON, Register.

Book F-F, p. 100   GABRIEL GUIGNARD, of Charleston, to TIMOTHY
29 May 1747   CROSBEY, bricklayer, for Ł 240 currency, part
Conditional Feoffment   of lot #80 in Charleston, bounding N 30 ft. on
                        Pinckney Street; E 75 ft. on JOHN LEA; W on
JOSEPH BLACK; S on RICHMOND GASCOIGNE; as laid out by GEORGE HUNTER, Sur.
Gen. Date of redemption, 29 May 1749. Witnesses: WILLIAM BEE, JOHN
REMINGTON. Witnesses to livery & seizen: REBEKAH GOODBE, JANE RIEN. Be-
fore ALEXANDER HUME, J.P. WILLIAM HOPTON, Register.

Book F-F, p. 102   TIMOTHY CROSBY, bricklayer, of Charleston, to
8 & 9 May 1749   WILLIAM HENDRICK, planter, of Christ Church

L & R by Mortgage   Parish, as security on bond of even date in
                          penal sum of Ł 800 for payment of Ł 400 SC
money, with interest, on 9 May 1750; part of lot #80 in Charleston,
bounding N 30 ft. on Pinckney Street; E 75 ft. on JOHN LEA; W on JOSEPH
BLACK; S on RICHMOND GASCOIGNE. Witnesses: JOHN REMINGTON, WILLIAM ED-
WARDS. Before ROBERT AUSTIN, J.P. WILLIAM HOPTON, Register. On 11 Nov.
1751 DANIEL LEGARE, executor of will of WILLIAM HENDRICK declared mortgage paid in full. Witness: WILLIAM HOPTON.

Book F-F, p. 106   NEWEL EDWARDS, planter, son & heir of EDWARD
18 & 19 May 1749   EDWARDS, to HERCULES COYTE, dyer; both of St.
L & R   Thomas Parish; for Ł 120 SC money, 25 a., part
                          of 100 a. formerly belonging to NATHANIEL WIL-
LIAMS, on Davis Point Island; bounding N on Widow BUCKLEY; S & E on a
creek of Cooper River running around THOMAS ISLAND; W on marsh. Whereas
NATHANIEL WILLIAMS owned 100 a. on Davis Point Island, bounding N on Widow BUCKLEY; S & E on a creek of Cooper River that runs around Thomas Island; W on marsh; & by will dated 16 Nov. 1729 gave his Negro boy, JO-
SEPH, his freedom from all slavery; & bequeathed to said JOSEPH 25 a. at
the SE part of the tract; & whereas JOSEPH, by L & R dated 28 & 29 Sept.
1731, by name of JOSEPH WILLIAMS, planter, sold the 25 a. to EDWARD ED-
WARDS, father of NEWEL; now NEWELL as son & heir, conveys to COYTE. Witnesses: JAMES GRINDLAY, RICHARD PROCTOR. Before JACOB MOTTE, J.P. WIL-
LIAM HOPTON, Register.

Book F-F, p. 110   ROBERT BREWTON, ESQ., to DANIEL BADGER, paint-
8 & 9 Jan. 1746   er; both of Charleston; for Ł 600 currency,
L & R   part of lot #39 in Charleston, bounding S 44
                          ft. on Tradd Street; W 100 ft. on GEORGE DUCK-
ET; N 15 ft. on DR. RUTLEDGE; E 67 ft. on MRS. OLIVER & JOHN MILLER; N
29 ft. on JOHN MILLER; E 33 ft. on ROBERT BREWTON. Witnesses: JORDAN
ROCHE, JOHN REMINGTON. Before THOMAS DALE, J.P. WILLIAM HOPTON, Register.

Book F-F, p. 114   WILLIAM LANCASTER, planter, to HENRY SHERRIFF,
19 & 20 June 1749   planter; both of James Island; for Ł 775 cur-
L & R   rency, 100 a. on James Island, Berkeley Co.,
                          bounding N on Wappoo Creek; S on MR. MICHIE; E
on MR. LAMBRIGHT; W on JAMES HAMILTON. Whereas the Lords Proprs. on 4
July 1717 granted ABIGAIL AYRES 100 a. on James Island, & she by will
dated 7 Aug. 1729 devised the tract to her daughter ANN AYRES, who took
possession & died intestate; & her nephew WILLIAM LANCASTER, grandson of
ABIGAIL AYRES, inherited; now he conveys to SHERRIFF. Witnesses: ROBERT
SCREVEN, WILLIAM CHAMBERS. Before WILLIAM PINCKNEY, J.P. WILLIAM HOP-
TON, Register. Plat certified 15 Apr. 1749 by ROBERT SCREVEN, Dep. Sur.

Book F-F, p. 117   WILLIAM LANCASTER, planter, of James Island,
20 June 1749   gives HENRY SHERRIFF, planter, bond in penal
Bond of Performance   sum of Ł 1500 SC money for keeping above
                          agreement (p. 114). Witnesses: ROBERT SCRE-
VEN, WILLIAM CHAMBERS. Before WILLIAM PINCKNEY, J.P. WILLIAM HOPTON,
Register.

Book F-F, p. 118   HENRY BEDON, wharfinger, to GEORGE SEAMAN,
6 Mar. 1748   merchant, both of Charleston, for 5 shillings,
Deed of Surrender   releases his claim to part of lot #8 bounding
                          E 10 ft. on the part belonging to GEORGE SEA-
MAN; S 40 ft. on JOHN REIN; W on BEDON ALLEY; N on HENRY BEDON. Witness-
es: PHILIP BOX, JOHN REMINGTON. Before JOHN DART, J.P. WILLIAM HOPTON,
Register.

Book F-F, p. 119   JOHN BALLENTINE, gentleman, of Charleston, to
23 & 24 June 1749   BURNABY BRANFORD, planter, of Berkeley Co., as
L & R by Mortgage   security on his bond dated 1 Apr. 1748 given
                          to FRANCIS HOLMES, merchant, of Charleston, in
penal sum of Ł 880 for payment of Ł 440 currency, with interest, on 1
Apr. 1749 (now past), which bond was assigned by HOLMES to BURNABY BRAN-
FORD; the Ł 440 & interest being due & unpaid; part of lot #297 in
Charleston, on E side Old Church Street, near a place called White Point,
bounding N 113 ft. on part of lot 397 sold by JOHN BALLANTINE to JOHN

186

ALLEN; E 94 ft. on heirs of KATHERINE HOLMES; S on a 12 ft. Alley between
JOHN BALLANTINE & heirs of THOMAS LYNCH; the land to be free from claim
of dower by ELIZABETH BALLANTINE, wife of JOHN. Witnesses: JOHN FRYER,
HENRY FENDIN. Before THOMAS LAMBOLL, J.P. WILLIAM HOPTON, Register.

Book F-F, p. 127   JOHN PAUL GRIMKÉ, silversmith, of Charleston,
19 & 20 June 1749   to JOSHUA GRIMBALL, planter, of Edisto Island,
L & R   Colleton Co., for Ł 1600 SC money, 500 a. on
                          Edisto Island as surveyed by HENRY YONGE, Dep.
Sur., on 29 Aug. 1746 at request of PAUL GRIMBALL, & conveyed by PAUL
GRIMBALL by deed poll dated 6 Oct. 1746 to JOHN PAUL GRIMKÉ. Witnesses:
JOHN JENKINS, JOHN REMINGTON. Before JACOB MOTTE, J.P. WILLIAM HOPTON,
Register. Plat of 500 a., part of 2 tracts, 1 granted by Gov. JOSEPH
BLAKE 12 May 1697 said to contain 1590 a., the other being surplus mea-
sure of said 1950 a. granted by Gov. _____ (broken).

Book F-F, p. 131   SAMUEL WEST, of Berkeley Co., to ISAAC LADSON,
1 June 1749   for Ł 100 currency, 25 a., part of 250 a. pur-
Sale   chased by his father, SAMUEL WEST, SR., from
                          FRANCIS LADSON; bounding W on JOHN CATTELL; S
on STEVEN FORD; E on RALPH ELMES; N on FRANCIS LADSON. Witnesses: ZACH-
ARIAH LADSON, GEORGE PURKIS, JOHN AINGER, JR. Before ROBERT AUSTIN, JR.
WILLIAM HOPTON, Register.

Book F-F, p. 133   WILLIAM HENDRICK, planter, of Christ Church
2 & 3 Oct. 1744   Parish, Berkeley Co., to STEPHEN CALLABOUF,
L & R   chairmaker, of Berkeley Co., for Ł 250 curren-
                          cy, 25 a., English measure, in Christ Church
Parish, bounding NW & S on WILLIAM ELLIOTT; SE on JOSEPH LAW; N on RICH-
ARD ROUSER. Witnesses: HENRY VARNOR, THOMAS HILDORSLEY SHERRETT, STEPHEN
HARTLEY. Before WILLIAM PINCKNEY, J.P. WILLIAM HOPTON, Register.

Book F-F, p. 136   THOMAS HOYLAND, tanner, & ANNA MARIA his wife,
19 July 1749   of Ansonborough, to WILLIAM HOPTON, merchant,
Feoffment   of Charleston, for Ł 2400 SC money, their
                          equal half shares of 2 lots containing 3 a.,
2 roods, 7 perches, marked K on plat of land of GEORGE ANSON called AN-
SONBOROUGH. Witnesses: JOHN MARTINI, JOHN LOGAN, WILLIAM VANDERHORST.
Before JOHN LINING, J.P. WILLIAM HOPTON, Register.

Book F-F, p. 138   ROBERT LUCAS, tavern keeper, of Craven Co., to
27 Aug. 1748   WILLIAM WAITIES, planter, of same Co., as se-
Mortgage   curity on bond of even date in penal sum of
                          Ł 3000 for payment of Ł 1500 currency, with
interest, on 27 Aug. 1749; 3 lots & houses in Georgetown, 2 of them being
adjoining front lots on the Bay, 1/4 a. each, #41 & #42; the other of 1/2
a., #69, lying back of other 2. Witness: ARCHIBALD BAIRD. Before WIL-
LIAM POOLE, J.P. WILLIAM HOPTON, Register.

Book F-F, p. 139   DANIEL CRAWFORD, of Charleston, to the Society
14 & 15 July 1749   for the Propagation of the Gospel in Foreign
L & R by Mortgage   Parts, as security on bond of even date in
                          penal sum of Ł 2400 for payment of Ł 1200 cur-
rency, with interest, on 15 July 1750; part of lot #12 in Charleston,
bounding E 100 ft. on MARY ELLIS; W on PETER BENOIST (formerly MRS. DILL);
N 36 ft. on Broad Street; S 37 ft. 2 in. on JOSEPH WRAGG (formerly ISAAC
CAILLEBEAUF). Witnesses: JAMES GRINDLAY, ROBERT WILLIAMS, JR. Before
JOHN RATTRAY, J.P. WILLIAM HOPTON, Register.

Book F-F, p. 143   JOHN LAURENS, merchant, & ELIZABETH his wife,
23 & 24 Feb. 1746   to ALEXANDER MCGRIGOR, victualler, both of
L & R   Charleston, for Ł 1800 currency, that lot in
                          Charleston bounding E on JAMES ROLLIN & JANE
DUPREY; W 43-1/2 ft. on Meeting Street; S 63-1/2 ft. on JOHN LAURENS &
71-1/2 ft. on STEPHEN MILLER & JAMES ROLLIN; N 135 ft. on JAMES EADE;
with the dwelling house thereon. Plat given. Witnesses: FRANCIS LEJAU,
DAVID GRAEME. Before JAMES GRAEME, J.P. WILLIAM HOPTON, Register.

Book F-F, p. 148   WILLIAM SPOODE, to WILLIAM HAZZARD, both of
10 July 1749   Granville Co., as security on bond of even

Mortgage   date in penal sum of Ŀ 1000 for payment of
                                  Ŀ 500 currency, on 25 Mar. 1750 & 1751; 2
tracts, 600 a., granted SPOODE in 2 grants dated 18 Mar. 1735 & 3 Feb.
1737. Witnesses: THOMAS WIGG, EDWARD WIGG. Before ROBERT WILLIAMS, J.P.
WILLIAM HOPTON, Register.

Book F-F, p. 149   RICHARD HAZZARD, planter, to COL. WILLIAM HAZ-
16 Feb. 1747/8   ZARD, both of Granville Co., as security for
Mortgage   payment of Ŀ 1200 SC money, with interest, on
                                  25 Mar. 1749; 3 tracts, 550 a., in Township of
Purysburg, 200 a. without the Township; & 50 a. leased for a year; all
purchased from ANTHONY ULYSSES ALBERGOTY; all fronting on Ockety Creek;
also 40 heads of cattle, a bay mare & colt, a grey mare & colt, a brown
horse, a roan horse, & a young grey horse. Witnesses: LAWRENCE COOK,
WILLIAM TWEEDY. Before ROBERT WILLIAMS, J.P. WILLIAM HOPTON, Register.

Book F-F, p. 150   THOMAS STEPHENS, gentleman, of Colleton Co.,
19 & 20 July 1749   to WILLIAM HOPTON, merchant, of Charleston, as
L & R by Mortgage   security for payment of several sums of money
                                  covered by 3 bonds; 2 tenements & 100 a. of
meadow & pasture, adjoining, called Spanne, in the Manor of Barton, Isle
of Wight, Co. of Hants, England; which premises THOMAS STEPHENS holds of
Winchester College during his natural life by virtue of a copy of Court
Roll dated 23 Aug. 1721, & whereof said THOMAS STEPHENS after the death
of his brother RICHARD SETPHENS was admitted tenant for life at a Court
of said Manor held 26 May 1743; upon trust that HOPTON shall apply the
rents & profits to payment of said bonds; then in trust for use of THOMAS
STEPHENS. STEPHENS gives HOPTON an inventory of goods & chattles in
trust that HOPTON shall apply the money obtained from their sale to the
payment of STEPHENS'S bonds, debts, etc. Whereas THOMAS STEPHENS gave
BENJAMIN WHITAKER a bond dated 25 Jan. 1743 for payment of Ŀ 320 currency
with interest within a year; & gave LILIAS MOWBRAY, executrix of ARTHUR
MOWBRAY, a bond dated 24 Feb. 1746 for payment of Ŀ 502 currency with
interest within 1 year; & gave WILLIAM HOPTON a bond dated 5 Feb. last
for payment of Ŀ 150 sterling of Great Britain on 10th of same inst. Feb.;
now STEPHENS conveys to HOPTON, as security, certain lands, goods &
chattles. Witnesses: JOHN LOGAN, WILLIAM VANDERHORST. Before JAMES
WRIGHT, J.P. WILLIAM HOPTON, Register. On 19 Apr. 1757 LILIAS MOWBRAY,
executrix, declared mortgage satisfied as it relates to her. Witness:
PETER MONCLAR (?).

Book F-F, p. 156   STEPHEN (his mark) CAILLABEUF, chairmaker, &
9 & 10 Jan. 1748   MARY (her mark) his wife, of Christ Church
L & R   Parish, to THOMAS BOLTON, merchant, of Charles-
                                  ton, for Ŀ 300 SC money, 60-1/2 a. in Christ
Church Parish, Berkeley Co., on S side Wackendaw Creek; bounding NE on
OLIVER SPENCER; SW on MR. ELLIOTT; SE on MR. EDINGS; NW on Wackindaw
Creek. Witnesses: PETER DAVID, JOHN REMINGTON. Before WILLIAM PINCKNEY,
J.P. WILLIAM HOPTON, Register.

Book F-F, p. 161   WILLIAM GEORGE FREEMAN, ESQ., to CHARLES SHEP-
10 May 1746   HEARD, vintner, of Charleston, for Ŀ 149; 4 a.,
Feoffment   31 perches, the NW part of FREEMAN'S farm
                                  called Pickpocket, in St. Philips Parish,
Berkeley Co. Should SHEPHEARD wish to re-sell he shall sell to FREEMAN
at same price, FREEMAN to pay for buildings as appraised by 2 indifferent
persons. Witnesses: GEORGE SAXBY, THOMAS BURNY. Before JACOB MOTTE,
J.P. WILLIAM HOPTON, Register. Plat of 4 a., 31 perches, bounding NW on
Road to Brampton Bryan Farm; NE on High Road; SE on Pickpocket Farm.
Certified 2 Dec. 1745 by GEORGE (HUNTER ?), Sur. Gen.

Book F-F, p. 163   MARY GAULTIER, widow of JOSEPH GAULTIER, sur-
18 & 19 Aug. 1749   geon, of Charleston (formerly MARY PORTALL,
L & R by Mortgage   widow of ANTHONY PORTALL, of Charleston), to
                                  ALEXANDER PERONNEAU, gentleman, of Charleston,
as security on bond of even date in penal sum of Ŀ 2000 for payment of
Ŀ 1000 SC money, with interest, on 19 Aug. next; part of lot #26 in
Charleston, bounding S 29 ft. on Elliotts or Poinsetts Lane running W
from Cooper River by the houses of DR. JOHN THOMAS, MOSES WILSON, & DR.
JOHN HUTCHINSON; E 90 ft. on SHEM BULTER; N on _____; W on THOMAS

HEPWORTH; which piece of land she, as MARY PORTILL purchased by L & R dated 19 & 20 June 1741 from MARY NISBETT & ALEXANDER VANDERDUSSEN. Witnesses: SAMUEL PERKINS, HENRY PERONNEAU. Before JAMES WRIGHT, J.P. WILLIAM HOPTON, Register. On 30 Nov. 1750 ALEXANDER PERONNEAU declared mortgage satisfied. Witness: WILLIAM HOPTON.

Book F-F, p. 170
5 Mar. 1745
Lease for Life

MATTHEW ROCHE, merchant, of Charleston, to MARY BREWTON, widow of COL. MILES BREWTON (formerly called MARY BELLAMY). Whereas MARY BREWTON by deed of feoffment of even date conveyed to MATTHEW ROCHE all her claim to that part of lot #28 adjoining the dwelling house where her late husband TIMOTHY BELLAMY lived bounding E on said house (now belonging to ROCHE); W 100 ft. on JOHN CROKATT (formerly DR. JOHN DELAINE); N on heirs of MR. JENYS (formerly Madam BRETELL); S 34 on Broad Street; now, in consideration of the sale, ROCHE agrees with MARY BREWTON that he will repair & finish the house he lately purchased from MARGARET HANBOROUGH, fronting Old Church Street, by adding another story in which ehre shall be 2 fire rooms, with sash windows & balcony, build a little house, repair the hen house, put pump in well, new fence around yard & garden, prepare garden for planting, & demised the same to MARY BREWTON for her lifetime; he to pay all repairs, taxes, etc., & pay MARY BREWTON Ł 120 SC money yearly in quarterly payments. Witnesses: JOHN RATTRAY, JAMES GRINDLAY. Before DANIEL CRAWFORD, J.P. WILLIAM HOPTON, Register.

Book F-F, p. 172
1 Aug. 1747
Feoffment by Mortgage

JAMES MACKRELLIS (MCKRELLIS), planter, of Berkeley Co., to CHARLES PINCKNEY, ESQ., of Charleston, as security on 2 bonds, of even date in total penal sum of Ł 600 for payment of Ł 300 currency, with interest, on certain dates; that lot of marsh land in Colleton Square, Charleston, marked ( ) on the plat, bounding W on a street 30 ft. wide laid across the marsh from the end of New Church Street; E on a street leading by CAPT. WALKER'S land to the canal in said marsh; S on the canal; N on Ellery Street. Witnesses: TIMOTHY CROSBY, MATTHEW FAGAN. Before WILLIAM PINCKNEY, J.P. WILLIAM HOPTON, Register.

Book F-F, p. 174
1 & 2 Sept. 1749
L & R by Mortgage

JAMES MACKRELLIS, planter, to THOMAS BOLTON & JOHN WRAGG, merchants, of Charleston (as tenants in common, not as jointenants) as security on bond of even date in penal sum of Ł 2400 for payment of Ł 1200 currency, with interest, on 1 Oct. 1749; that tenement & part of lot #80 in Charleston, bounding E 46 ft. on French Alley (10 ft. wide); S 85 ft. on Ellery Street; W & N on GABRIEL GUIGNARD; also 1000 a. in Craven Co., on S side Wateree River, bounding other sides on vacant land; also 1 Negro woman, 1 Negro girl, 8 working oxen with cart & gear, 9 horses & mares branded M. Witnesses: JOHN REMINGTON, JAMES BOLTON. Before JOHN DART, J.P. WILLIAM HOPTON, Register.

Book F-F, p. 180
21 & 22 June 1749
L & R

JACOB JEANNERET, planter, eldest son of JACOB JEANNERET of Winyaw, to JOHN TRIBOUDET, shopkeeper, of Charleston, for Ł 650 SC money, part of lot #105; that is 13-1/2 ft. fronting on King Street & the depth of the lot, bounding N on part of said lot belonging to estate of WILLIAM LINTHWAIT; S on REBEKAH FLAVELL (see Bk. S. fol. 149-151). Whereas DAVID CHRISTINAZ, carpenter, of Charleston, by L & R dated 5 & 6 Mar. 1737 sold to JACOB JEANNERET, father of JACOB party hereto, part of lot #105; & whereas JACOB, the father, died intestate & his eldest son & heir, party hereto, inherited; now the son sells a part of his lot to TRIBOUDET. Witnesses: JOHN REMBERT, JOHN REMINGTON. Before ROBERT AUSTIN, J.P. WILLIAM HOPTON, Register.

Book F-F, p. 185
1 & 2 May 1749
L & R

ANDREW RUTLEDGE, ESQ., of Charleston, to SAMUEL FULTON, planter, of Williamsburgh Township Craven Co., for Ł 400 currency, 1000 a. on Black River in Williamsburgh Township, granted 14 Feb. 1735 by Lt. Gov. THOMAS BROUGHTON to said ANDREW RUTLEDGE; bounding NE on CRAFTON KARWON; other sides on vacant land. Witnesses: JOSEPH BURGES, ALEXANDER GORDON, JR. Before JAMES MICHIE, J.P. WILLIAM HOPTON, Register.

Book F-F, p. 188   SETH HATCHER, planter, of Orangeburgh Township,
14 Sept. 1748   Berkeley Co.; to JOHN SIMMONS, carpenter, for
Feoffment   ₺ 25 currency, 100 a., part of 300 a. on which
                        HATCHER lives, in Orangeburgh Township, bound-
ing W & SW on JOHN CORNFELDER, NICHOLAS LORNE, & SIMON SYSE (?); N & NW
on SIMON PYSE (?); NE & E on SETH HATCHER; SE & S on JOHN ROBERSON. Witnesses: PETER FAURE, JOSEPH WOOD, JOHN (his mark) FARREE. ELIZABETH (her
mark) HATCHER, wife of SETH, renounces her dower. Before ROBERT AUSTIN,
J.P. WILLIAM HOPTON, Register.

Book F-F, p. 191   JOSEPH SHUTE, merchant, to JOHN MACKENZIE,
9 May 1747   merchant, both of Charleston; for ₺ 150 cur-
Feoffment   rency, half of 224 a. of marsh land (112 a.),
                        in Berkeley Co., bounding E & S on Ashley Riv-
er; W on Cooper River; N on Hogg Island Creek. Witnesses: JOHN RATTRAY,
GEORGE AVERY, JOSEPH FURNIS. Before DANIEL CRAWFORD, J.P. WILLIAM HOP-
TON, Register.

Book F-F, p. 193   ANNE ELLERY, widow, of St. Johns, & CHARLES
26 Feb. 1746   PINCKNEY, ESQ., of Charleston, agree that in
Agreement   consideration of PINCKNEY paying ₺ 120 curren-
                        cy to CAPT. EDWARD LIGHTWOOD on 1 Mar. 1747,
on account of ANNE ELLERY, she convey to PINCKNEY all her marsh or low
water land in Colleton Square on S side of the canal, known by letter "g"
in plan of Square, bounding E on the bridge; S on Landgrave DANIELL'S
lot; W on PINCKNEY'S marsh; PINCKNEY agrees to pay CAPT. LIGHTWOOD, on
ANNE'S account, ₺ 120 currency on 1 Mar. 1747 if ANNE will give him proper title to said land. (See Book I.I., p. 240-244). JAMES WRIGHT, ESQ.,
of Charleston, appeared before WILLIAM PINCKNCY, J.P. & recognized the
handwriting of ANNE ELLERY & of CHARLES CALDER, who had been his clerk
for several years. On 23 Feb. 1747 E. LIGHTWOOD acknowledged receipt of
₺ 120 currency from CHARLES PINCKNEY in payment of ANNE ELLERY'S proportion on bond from ELLERY, PINCKNEY, & HUNTER. On 16 Sept. 1749 LIGHTWOOD
acknowledged above receipt before JOHN DART, J.P. WILLIAM HOPTON, Register.

Book F-F, p. 194   WILLIAM ARNALL, planter, to ANTHONY MATHEWS,
10 Mar. 1726/7   JR., both of Berkeley Co., for ₺ 400 currency,
L & R   200 a. in Colleton Co., bounding S on JOHN
                        PRESKETT; N on Cypress Opening; E on JOSEPH
STANYARNE; W on vacant land. Witnesses: ARON HUNSCOMBE, MARK COLE, THOM-
AS (his mark) UMPHRIS (HUMPHRIS). Before WILLIAM BOONE, J.P. WILLIAM
HOPTON, Register.

Book F-F, p. 198   WILLIAM ELLIOTT, SR., planter, of St. Andrews
8 Sept. 1749   Parish, Berkeley Co., to his loving brother,
Gift   BARNARD ELLIOTT, planter, of Berkeley Co.,
                        227-1/2 a. bounding S on Ashley River; N on
JOHN CLIFFORD; E on MR. IZARD; W on WILLIAM ELLIOTT; with condition that
BARNARD shall not, during WILLIAM'S lifetime, give or hire the land to
anyone but BARNARD'S child or children. Witnesses: JOHN STONE, SAMUEL
ELLIOTT, SUSANNA STONE. Delivery by turf & twig. Before JOHN DART, J.P.
WILLIAM HOPTON, Register. Plat certified 4 July 1749, by ROBERT SCREVEN,
Dep. Sur.

Book F-F, p. 199   GEORGE ANSON, ESQ., by his attorney BENJAMIN
25 May 1745   WHITAKER, ESQ., to LUKE STOUTENBURGH, for
Feoffment   ₺ 250 currency, the 1 a. lot marked Q in the
                        plan of ANSON'S land called Ansonborough, &
right of passage through most convenient streets to & from the landing
place on a creek of Cooper River. Witnesses: JAMES WEDDERBURN, WILLIAM
BURROWS, WILLIAM DICKS. Before ROBERT AUSTIN, J.P. WILLING HOPTON, Register.

Book F-F, p. 200   GEORGE ANSON, ESQ., by his attorney BENJAMIN
2 Dec. 1745   WHITAKER, ESQ., to LUKE STOUTENBURGH, gentle-
Feoffment   man, all of Charleston; for ₺ 250 SC money,
                        the 1 a. lot marked P in the plan of ANSON'S
land called Ansonborough, & right of passage through the most convenient
streets to & from the landing place on a creek of Cooper River.

Witnesses: WILLIAM BURROWS, LEOPOLD BOUDON, WILLIAM DICKS. Before ROBERT
AUSTIN, J.P. WILLIAM HOPTON, Register.

Book F-F, p. 201   JAMES HILLIARD, watchmaker, to THOMAS BOLTON,
13 & 14 Oct. 1749   merchant, both of Charleston; as security on
L & R by Mortgage   bond of even date in penal sum of Ł 1041 for
                          payment of Ł 520:10 currency, with interest,
on 14 Apr. 1750; part of lot #80 in Charleston, bounding S 25 ft. on
Guignard Street; N on JOHN VAUN; E 100 ft. on JOHN MEEK; W on a 12 ft.
alley, called Goodbe's Alley. Witnesses: PETER DAVID, JOHN REMINGTON.
Before ALEXANDER STEWART, J.P. WILLIAM HOPTON, REgister. On 24 Feb.
1749 THOMAS BOLTON declared mortgage satisfied by JAMES HUNTER, baker, of
Charleston. Witness: WILLIAM HOPTON.

Book F-F, p. 205   WILLIAM CARWITHEN, cabinet maker, & MARY his
17 & 18 Mar. 1746   wife, of Berkeley Co., to ISAAC HOLMES, gen-
L & R of Reversion   tleman, of New Church Street, Charleston, for
                          Ł 750 currency, the E part of their part of
lot #37 in Charleston, on S side of the Middle Street leading W from WIL-
LIAM ELLIOTT'S wharf into New Church Street; which E part bounds N 26 ft.
on said Middle Street; E 80 ft. on JANE DALTON; S on JOHN ATKIN or EDMUND
ATKIN or both; W on CARWITHEN'S remaining part. Witnesses: JAMES BALLAN-
TINE, THOMAS LAMBOLL. Before THOMAS DALE, J.P. WILLIAM HOPTON, Register.

Book F-F, p. 209   JOHN DELAGAYE, storekeeper & CATHERINE his
24 & 25 Nov. 1748   wife, to MARY ALBERGOTTI, spinster, daughter
L & R   of ULYSSES ANTHONY ALBERGOTTI, vintner; both
                          of Beaufort; for Ł 1400 currency, lot #305 in
Beaufort, fronting E on Charles Street; bounding N on lots 303 & 304; S
on lots 300 & 301. Witnesses: EDWARD WIGG, JOHN SMITH. Witnesses to
receipt: WILLIAM GOUGH, CHARLES PURRY. Before ROBERT WILLIAM, J.P. WIL-
LIAM HOPTON, Register.

Book F-F, p. 212   THOMAS LOREY, carpenter, & MARY (her mark) his
30 Sept. & 1 Oct. 1736   wife, of Christ Church Parish, Berkeley Co.,
L & R   to ROBERT DARRELL, mariner, for Ł 500 curren-
                          cy, 119 a., English measure, bounding N on
MOSES JOY; NW on BROWN & MURRELL; SW on JOHN MITCHELL; SE on Coppahee
Sound, with the dwellings houses, buildings, etc., etc. Witnesses: JOHN
METHRINGHAM, JOHN SAVERANCE, NATHANIEL ARTHUR. Before JOHN RUTLEDGE,
J.P. WILLIAM HOPTON, Register.

Book F-F, p. 216   BENJAMIN BATES, cordwainer, to RICHARD RIPPIN,
21 Oct. 1749   carpenter; both of St. Philips Parish,
Mortgage   Charleston, as security on bond of even date
                          in penal sum of Ł 100 for payment of Ł 50 cur-
rency on 1 Mar. 1749; 250 a. in Williamsburgh Township, on Black River,
bounding 1 side on JAMES POLLAND; other sides on vacant land; also a lot
in Kingstree. Witnesses: JOHN READ, THOMAS (his mark) CLARKE. Before
ROBERT AUSTIN, J.P. WILLIAM HOPTON, Register.

Book F-F, p. 217   JAMES MAXWELL, planter, of St. Johns Parish,
31 Oct. & 1 Nov. 1749   Berkeley Co., to JORDON ROCHE, merchant, of
L & R by Mortgage   Charleston, as security on bond of even date
                          in penal sum of Ł 120,000 for payment of
Ł 60,000 currency, with interest, on 1 Jan. 1749; 1206 a. in St. Johns
Parish, in 4 adjoining tracts; 500 a. called Complement Hill or Bettisons
Plantation; 400 a. called Mount Pleasant; both purchased by MAXWELL from
MAJ. HUGH BUTLER; 206 a., & 100 a. purchased by MAXWELL from CAPT. ROBERT
TAYLOR; the 1206 a. bounding E on Wadboo Barony; S on DR. KEITH (bought
from MR. MONCK); W on JOHN PALMER; NW on heirs of the Rev. MR. DANIEL
DWIGHT; N on JOHN GIGNILLIAT (bought from DUBOURDIEU; also 2 tracts, to-
tal 40-0 a., within Amelia Township, on SW side Santee River; also lot
#73 in Amelia; the 2 tracts & lot according to grant to ROBERT WRIGHT,
ESQ., & conveyed by ISABELLA WRIGHT, widow & executrix of ROBERT, to
JAMES MAXWELL. Witnesses: JAMES GRINDLAY, ROBERT WILLIAMS, JR. Before
JOHN RATTRAY, J.P. WILLIAM HOPTON, Register.

Book F-F, p. 220   GATO ASH, a legatee named in will of JAMES

14 July 1749   COCKRAN, being now of age, demands his divi-
Allotment   dend from the executors, CAPT. RICHARD ASH,
                                SAMUEL PERONNEAU, & HUGH BRYAN. Therefore,
the executors divided the land & CATO ASH drew lot #2 & signed in presence of JOHATHAN BRYAN, CAPT. RICHARD ASH, & HUGH BRYAN, & MARY BRYAN
(wife of JONATHAN). Before HUGH BRYAN, J.P. of Granville Co. WILLIAM
HOPTON, Register. Following are divisions: #1; 1st lot on Cochrans Island, 350 a. taken off the SW part of said Island, by a line running
across it, in a due SE course, 1220 a. on DAWFUSKY, as by plat, a front
lot in Beaufort & _____ part of JACOB LOWNDENS land at Chehaw; #2; CATO
ASH, 2 tracts containing 816 a. on Cockran's Point; #3; 650 a. on Cock-
rans Island & the surplus land if any; #4; 600 a. on Toobadoo joining MR.
MORTON'S (broken page).

Book F-F, p. 221   GEORGE LOGAN, of Cape Fear, NC, to LIONEL
18 Mar. 1746   CHALMERS, of Berkeley Co., SC, as security on
Bond & Mortgage   bond of even date in penal sum of Ł 1500 for
                              payment of Ł 750 currency, with interest, on
18 Mar. 1745; 620 a. in Berkeley Co. Witnesses: SARAH DANIELL, JOHN
DANIELL. Before WILLIAM FORBES, J.P. for New Hanover Co. WILLIAM HOPTON,
Register.

Book F-F, p. 222   GEORGE LOGAN, gentleman, of Cape Fear, NC, to
17 & 18 Mar. 1746   LIONEL CHALMERS, surgeon, of Berkeley Co., as
L & R by Mortgage   security on above bond (p. 221); 620 a. in
                            Berkeley Co., on E side Wando River, bounding
E on LIONEL CHALMERS; S on COL. THOMAS LYNCH. Witnesses: SARAH DANIELL,
JOHN DANIELL. Before WILLIAM FORBES, J.P. for New Hanover Co. WILLIAM
HOPTON, Register. On 11 Jan. 1754 LIONEL CHALMERS declared mortgage paid
in full. Witness: WILLIAM HOPTON.

Book F-F, p. 226   ANTHONY MATTHEWES, ESQ., of 1st part; ELIZA-
9 Nov. 1749   BETH GIBBES, wife of JOHN GIBBES, ESQ. &
Agreement on Low   Guardian of her son GEORGE HENYS, of 2nd part;
Water Lots   GEORGE EVELEIGH, merchant, of 3rd part; JOHN
                             HODSDEN, merchant, of 4th part; CHARLES PINCK-
NEY, ESQ., of 5th part; EDWARD FENWICKE, ESQ., of 6th part, all of
Charleston; severally being seized in their demesnes as of fee in several
parcels of lots on the Bay of Charleston, known as Nos. 3, 4, 5, & 6, &
in several shole or low water lands fronting said lots & lying E on Bay
Street over the "curtain" line of Charleston & running from said "curtain" line E into Cooper River; & whereas several of said parties have
built wharves or bridges & made other improvements on their shole lands,
but because of the loss of the original plan of said shole lots, the certain course of their several shole lands cannot now be fixed or ascertained except by agreement; now each agrees with each of the others as follows: that the course of the several dividng lines of the shole lots
shall be deemed to run due E from the "curtain line" of Charleston, according to plat certified by ROBERT SCREVEN, Dep. Sur., on 19 Sept. 1749.
Witnesses: WILLIAM PINCKNEY, SAMUEL JONES. Before JACOB MOTTE, J.P.
WILLIAM HOPTON, Register. Plat represents shape of 6 parts of low water
land on N side MRS. LLOYD'S bridge.

Book F-F, p. 229   ANDREW JOHNSTON, gentleman, to FRANCIS YOUNG,
1 May 1748   planter; both of Craven Co.; for Ł 100 SC mon-
L & R   ey, 500 a. in Craven Co., on SW side PeeDee
                             River, granted by Gov. JAMES GLEN on 18 Nov.
1747 to ANDREW JOHNSON; bounding on all other sides on FRANCIS YOUNG.
Witnesses: BENJAMIN COACHMAN, PETER SECORE. Before JAMES GILLESPIE, J.P.
WILLIAM HOPTON, Register.

Book F-F, p. 231   GEORGE LOGAN, JR., of Christ Church Paris, hav-
4 Dec. 1749   ing purchased the mortgaged land, agrees to
Acceptance to Pay Bond   pay GEORGE LOGAN, SR.'S bond to LIONEL CHALM-
                             ERS, surgeon. Witnesses: HELEN TREWIN, JOHN
LOGAN. Before JACOB MOTTE, J.P. WILLIAM HOPTON, Register. (see p.
222).

Book F-F, p. 232   JOSEPH LABRUCE, planter, & ELIZABETH his wife,
25 & 26 Mar. 1745   of Craven Co., to DANIEL LESESNE, planter, of

L & R   Berkeley Co., for Ł 1000 currency, 375 a., Eng-
                             lish measure, in Berkeley Co., bounding NE on
LEWIS DUTARQUE; SE on RICHARD BERESFORD; SW on STEPHEN FOGARTIE; being 2
tracts of 300 a. & 75 a. conveyed by JOHN MCEVER & SARAH, his wife, to
ELIZABETH LABRUCE (then ELIZABETH BREMAR). Witnesses: THEODORE TRESVANT,
ROBERT HOW. Before ALEXANDER GORDON, J.P. WILLIAM HOPTON, Register.

Book F-F, p. 236   WILLIAM RIND, gentleman, of Charleston, to
12 & 13 Dec. 1749   RALPH IAZRD, ESQ., of Berkeley Co., for Ł 1600
L & R   currency, 2 adjoining tracts of 100 a. & 128
                            a., at a place called Cow Savannah, Berkeley
Co., which 228 a. were purchased by WILLIAM RIND from THOMAS BUTLER &
ELIZABETH his wife by L & R dated 2 & 3 June 1746; bounding according to
plat. Witnesses: WHITE OUTERBRIDGE, ALEXANDER FRASER. Before JAMES
WRIGHT, J.P. WILLIAM HOPTON, Register.

Book F-F, p. 240   ELIZABETH WOODWARD, widow & executrix, of
29 & 30 Nov. 1749   RICHARD WOODWARD, planter, to GEORGE AUSTIN,
L & R   merchant, of Charleston, for Ł 380 currency,
                            380 a. lying back from Ahsepoo River, in Col-
leton Co., granted by the Lords Proprs. on 15 Dec. 1703 to JOHN SEABROOK;
bounding NE on EDMOND BELLINGER; W on JAMES COCHRAN; S on MR. HEXT; E on
GEORGE AUSTIN. Whereas RICHARD WOODWARD owned the said 380 a. & by will
dated 14 Dec. 1742 directed his executors to sell his real estate to pay
his debts, appointing ELIZABETH his executrix; now she conveys to AUSTIN.
Witnesses: JOHN GUERARD, MARIANNE GUERARD. Before JACOB MOTTE, J.P.
WILLIAM HOPTON, Register.

Book F-F, p. 244   JONATHAN SKRINE, tavernkeeper, formerly of
20 Aug. 1744   Georgetown, SC, now of Brunswick, NC (by his
Feoffment   attorneys, WILLIAM FLEMING & ANDREW JOHNSTON,
                           merchants, of Georgetown, & ALEXANDER DUPONT,
tavernkeeper, of Prince Frederick Parish, Craven Co.) to WILLIAM WATIES,
planter, of Prince George Parish, Craven Co., SC; for Ł 1400 SC money, 2
lots in Georgetown, Nos. 23 & 60; lot #23 containing 1/4 a., fronting SW
50 ft. on Bay Street; & bounding NE on lot #60; SE 217.9 ft. on lot #24;
NW on #22; lot #60 containing 1/2 a., fronting SE 217.9 ft. on Broad
Street; NE 100 ft. on Princess Street; NW on lot #59; SW on #23 & #24;
with the "Right of Commoning" as originally designed for the inhabitants
of the town. Whereas JONATHAN SKRINE by letter of attorney dated 18 Feb.
1743 appointed FLEMING, JOHNSTON & DUPONT his attorneys, with authority
to sell his real & personal estate & discharge his debts; now they sell 2
town lots to WATIES. Witnesses: NATHANIEL TREGAGLE, THOMAS JEWNING.
Livery & seizin made with consent of DANIEL LAROCHE, tenant of lot #60.
Before ELISE FOISSIN, J.P. WILLIAM HOPTON, Register.

Book F-F, p. 247   CAPT. DAVID GODIN, of Parish of St. Bartholo-
3 July 1749   mew, Colleton Co., to JAMES SKIRVING, ESQ., of
Feoffment   same Parish, for Ł 16:10 currency, 8-1/2 a. in
                           Colleton Co., on N side "Pogotalligo Causey" &
on NE side Pogotalligo Creek; bounding S on the "Causey" & DAVID GODIN;
SW & W on the creek; other sides on JAMES SKIRVING. Witnesses: RICHARD
BEDON, JOHN NORMAN, WILLIAM (his mark) WEBB. Delivery by turf & twig.
Before HENRY HYRNE, J.P. WILLIAM HOPTON, Register.

Book F-F, p. 249   JAMES POSTELL, planter, to JAMES SKIRVING,
1 Dec. 1749   planter, both of Colleton Co., for Ł 70 curren-
Feoffment   cy, 30 a. in Colleton Co., bounding N on
                           JAMES POSTELL; all other sides on JAMES SKIRV-
ING; being part of a larger tract granted to ELEANOR OSWELL (? OSESELL?)
& by several conveyances came to POSTELL. Witnesses: ADAM CULLIATT, MARY
CAMPBELL. Delivery by turf & twig. Before HENRY HYRNE, J.P. WILLIAM
HOPTON, Register.

Book F-F, p. 250   JOHN COLLIER, shoemaker, to JOHN LAIRD, both
7 & 8 Aug. 1747   of Collton Co., for Ł 50 currency, 260 a. in
L & R   Colleton Co., bounding E on WILLIAM COLLIER.
                          Witnesses: JOHN MILNER, JR., BATHSHEBA BAT-
TOON, ALEXANDER (his mark) HENDERSON. Before THOMAS LAMBOLL, J.P. WIL-
LIAM HOPTON, Register.

Book F-F, p. 254   STEPHEN MILLER, planter, of Berkeley Co., to
16 & 17 Nov. 1749   PAUL TRAPIER, merchant, of Georgetown, Craven
L & R   Co., granted 30 Sept. 1736 by Lt. Gov. THOMAS
                          BROUGHTON to STEPHEN MILLER (Secretarys Book
G.G. fol. 223); bounding SW on PeeDee River; SE on STEPHEN MILLER, other
sides on vacant land. Witnesses: ANTHONY BONNEAU, STEPHEN ZOUSSIGER
(?TOUSSIGER). Before JAMES MICHIE, J.P. WILLIAM HOPTON, Register.

Book F-F, p. 259   RICHARD GODFREY, planter, & JANE his wife, to
19 Aug. 1728   ABRAHAM MESHEW, for Ł 600 currency, 300 a. in
Sale   Colleton Co., in several tracts granted by
                          JOHN, Earl of Bath, Palatine, & JOHN, Lord
Granville, Palatine to THOMAS ELLIOTT, SR., who bequeathed the 300 a. to
his son-in-law RICHARD GODFREY on 28 July 1718; bounding N on Keakea
Swamp; W on MANLY WILLIAMSON; S on WILLIAM TREDWELL BULL; E on said BULL.
Witnesses: ROBERT GODFREY, DANIEL CARTWRIGHT, ELIZABETH SNIPES. Before
HENRY HYRNE, J.P. WILLIAM HOPTON, Register.

Book F-F, p. 260   JOHN MACKENZIE, merchant, to LUKE STOUTEN-
8 & 9 Jan. 1749   BURGH, gentleman; both of Charleston; for
L & R   Ł 5250 currency several tracts in Craven Co.;
                          300 a., bounding NW on Swinton's Creek; NE on
PeeDee River & Gordon's Thoroughfare; also 100 a., half of 200 a., bound-
ing E on WILLIAM ALLSTON & Pawley's Creek; N on WILLIAM SWINTON; SW on
Peedee River & Gordon's Thoroughfare; also 500 a. called Wehaw, bounding
SW on Duke of Beaufort's Barony; E on Peedee River; also 150 a., bounding
SW on HUGH SWINTON; N on the 500 a.; SE on Peedee River; also 80 a., the
N part of 250 a., bounding NW on Peedee River; SE on Swinton's Creek; SW
on WILLIAM SWINTON. Witnesses: JOHN WATSONE, JOHN BUTLER. Before JOHN
RATTRAY, J.P. WILLIAM HOPTON, Register.

Book F-F, p. 266   ANN WATSON, widow, to the Rev. MR. ALEXANDER
23 & 24 Jan. 1749   GARDEN; both of Charleston; as security on
L & R by Mortgage   bond of even date in penal sum of Ł 5000 for
                          payment of Ł 2500 currency, with interest, on
24 Jan. 1750; part of lot #28 on N side of Broad Street, in Charleston,
with the messuage thereon; "presently possessed" by LIONEL CHALMERS;
bounding W on JOHN CROKATT (formerly DR. JOHN DELAUNE); N on heirs of MR.
JENYS (formerly Madam BRETALL); E on Cramahe & Co. Witnesses: JAMES
GRINDLAY, PETER MANIGAULT. Before JOHN RATTRAY, J.P. WILLIAM HOPTON,
Register. On 15 July 1752 ALEXANDER GARDEN declared mortgage satisfied.
Witness: WILLIAM HOPTON.

Book F-F, p. 270   JOHN GENDRON, ESQ., of St. James Santee, Cra-
17 & 18 July 1749   ven Co., to his son JOHN GENDRON, JR., & to
L & R   JOHN COMING BALL, planter, of St. Johns Parish,
                          Berkeley Co., for Ł 4000 currency, 1500 a. at
Wambaw, St. James Santee, bounding N on ISAAC MAZYCK & vacant land; S on
vacant land; E on vacant land & COL. THOMAS CORDES; W on PAUL DOUXSAINT &
the children of ISAAC LEGRAND DONERVILLE. Witnesses: TACITUS GAILLARD,
WILLIAM THOMAS, ISAAC LEGRAND DONERVILLE. Before JACOB MOTTE, J.P. WIL-
LIAM HOPTON, Register.

Book F-F, p. 274   FRANCIS YOUNG, ESQ., formerly of Charleston,
27 Feb. 1743   SC, now of the Parish of St. John the Evange-
Gift   list, City of Westminster, to his son HENRY
                          YOUNG, for love & affection, all his lands in
SC except 2000 a., mortgaged. Whereas FRANCIS YOUNG owns 2 town lots in
Beaufort, Granville Co.; 400 a. in Colleton Co., adjoining MR. HERNE,
which he purchased from _____; & 2000 a. which tract was mortgaged to
ROBERT JOHNSON, ESQ.; now he gives his son all his property in SC & the
equity of redemption in the 2000 a. if HENRY will satisfy the mortgage.
Witnesses: SARAH BLAKEWEY, RICHARD BERESFORD. Before ROBERT YONGE, J.P.
WILLIAM HOPTON, Register.

Book F-F, p. 275   KENNETH MICHIE, merchant, & MARY his wife, to
20 & 21 Mar. 1748   WILLIAM HOPTON, merchant, both of Charleston;
L & R   for Ł 350 currency, lots #10, 42, & 48, in
                          Dorchester, Berkeley Co.; also 1/5 of lots 87
& 89; also 9 a. near Dorchester, part of a tract called Miln land

bounding 1 side on WILLIAM WAY, SR.; 1 side on WILLIAM FISHBURN; 1 end on the common or undivided land adjoining Dorchester Town; which 3 lots, parts of lots, & 9 a. GILSON CLAPP purchased by L & R dated 4 & 5 June 1725 from JAMES CANTEY & ELIZABETH his wife; & which KENNETH MICHIE claims by right of his wife, MARY, surviving daughter & heir of GILSON CLAPP; also lot #59 in Dorchester purchased by GILSON CLAPP from RICHARD BAKER, & ELIZABETH his wife on 7 Dec. 1727; also lot #60 purchased by CLAPP from THOMAS WARING on 14 Sept. 1736; also 10 a. near Dorchester, bounding 35 rods S on the Broad Path; E on a 50 a. lot belonging to WIL-LIAM WAY; N & W on estate of MICHAEL BACON; which 10 a. by L & R dated 17 & 18 June 1726 was conveyed by JOHN JONES, & ANN his wife, to JOHN WRIGHT & GILSON CLAPP, in joint tenancy, & after the death of WRIGHT became the property of CLAPP. Witnesses: JOHN TROUP, TIMOTHY MORTGRIDGE. Before JACOB MOTTE, J.P. WILLIAM HOPTON, Register.

Book F-F, p. 284
26 & 27 Nov. 1739
L & R by Mortgage

GEORGE LOGAN, gentleman, to WILLIAM HOPTON, scribe, both of Charleston, as security on bond dated 5 inst. Nov. in penal sum of ₺ 600 for payment of ₺ 300 currency, with interest, on 5 Nov. 1740; lot #155 in Charleston, containing half an a., English measure, granted by the Lords Proprs. on 9 May 1695 to JOHN BARKSDALE, ESQ., then bounding E on a little street leading from Ashley River by MR. JONES & ____; N & W on JOHN BARKSDALE; S on MAJ. BOON; which lot BARKS-DALE sold to GEORGE DEARSLEY, who by will dated 20 June 1702, gave the lot to GEORGE LOGAN after the death of his brother PATRICK LOGAN, since deceased. Witnesses: JOHN ATKIN, GEORGE WARING. Before WILLIAM PINCKNEY, J.P. WILLIAM HOPTON, Register. On 28 Dec. 1753 WILLIAM HOPTON declared mortgage satisfied.

Book F-F, p. 290
21 June 1733
Feoffment

WILLIAM CATTELL & RICHARD FULLER, planter, of Berkeley Co., executors of will of WILLIAM FULLER, planter, of St. Andrews Parish, to JOSEPH FULLER & BENJAMIN FULLER, planters, for ₺ 7882:10 currency, 510 a., with the mansion house thereon. Whereas the Lords Proprs. & Gov. JOHN ARCHDALE on 14 Oct. 1696 granted to BENJAMIN PIERPOINT 510 a. on S side Ashley River, bounding S on MR. BODETT; E on Wappelaw Creek; W on JOHN MILES; N on SAMUEL JONES & THOMAS ROSE; which land became the property of ARTHUR LAUGHORNE, merchant, of Charleston; & on 7 Mar. 1712 LAUGHORNE mortgaged the land to FRANCIS HOLMES, merchant, of Charleston, for ₺ 330 currency, payable 7 Mar. 1713; & whereas LAUG-HORNE died in Aug. 1714 without having paid the mortgage & HOLMES obtain-ed a judgment & on 5 May 1716, for ₺ 371 currency, conveyed to WILLIAM FULLER; & whereas by decree of Ct. of Chancery dated 20 Sept. 1716 it was ordered that on payment of further sum of ₺ 629 currency by FULLER to SAMUEL DEAN, merchant, of Charleston, sole acting executor of will of LAUGHORNE, & guardian of REBECCA LANGHORNE, infant daughter & heir of ARTHUR; which, including the ₺ 371 due MILLER made ₺ 1000, the full value of the premises. REBECCA should stand foreclosed of all equity of redemp-tion; & whereas on 29 Sept. 1716 MILLER paid DEAN (DEANE) ₺ 629 & by Act of General Assembly was confirmed in his title on 15 Dec. 1716; & whereas FULLER, by will dated 30 Aug. 1731 authorized his executors, to sell the 510 a., on which he lived, & deivide the money as directed, appointing WILLIAM CATTELL & RICHARD FULLER his executors; now they sell to JOSEPH FULLER & BENJAMIN FULLER. Witnesses: WILLIAM GEORGE FREEMAN, HENRY YONGE, ZACHARIAH FULLER. Before THOMAS LAMBOLL, J.P. WILLIAM HOPTON, Register.

Book F-F, p. 298
20 & 21 June 1733
L & R of Reversion

WILLIAM CATTELL & RICHARD FULLER, planters, of Berkeley Co.; executors of will of WILLIAM FUL-LER, planter of St. Andrews Parish, to JOSEPH FULLER & BENJAMIN FULLER, planters, for ₺ 117:10 currency, 11-3/4 a., on S side of High Road adjoining the New "Causey" & bridge over Hooper's Creek, on S side Ashley River, bounding E on the 510 a. (p. 290); W on a marsh; being part of 20 a. granted 14 May 1707 by the Lords Proprs. to ISAAC STUART. Witnesses: WILLIAM GEORGE FREEMAN, ZACHARIAH FULLER, HENRY YONGE. Before THOMAS LAMBOLL, J.P. WILLIAM HOPTON, Register.

Book F-F, p. 304
20 & 21 June 1748
L & R of Reversion

BENJAMIN FULLER, planter, of Berkeley Co., to JOSEPH FULLER, planter, for ₺ 1900 currency, his undivided half of 510 a., on S side Ashley

River, in St. Andrews Parish, bounding S on WILLIAM MILES; E on THOMAS HOLMAN; Wapelawe Creek & marsh; W on 11-3/4 a. (p. 298); also all his half part of said 11-3/4 a. Whereas an Act of General Assembly dated 15 Dec. 1716 confirmed WILLIAM FULLER in his title to 510 a. originally granted to JAMES PIERPONT & later the property of ARTHUR LAUGHORNE; & whereas FULLER, by court decree dated 20 Sept. 1716 became owner of said 510 a. & by divers other mesne conveyances & assignments became owner of an adjoining tract of 11-3/4 a.; & by will dated 13 Aug. 1733 authorized his executors, WILLIAM CATTELL & RICHARD FULLER, to sell the 2 tracts; & they, on 21 June 1733 sold the 510 a. to JOSEPH FULLER & BENJAMIN FULLER half to each; & by L & R dated 20 & 21 June 1733 sold the 11-3/4 a. to JOSEPH & BENJAMIN FULLER (half to each); now BENJAMIN FULLER sells JOSEPH his half of the 510 a. & his half of the 11-3/4 a. Witnesses: ISAAC DU-MONS, RICHARD WATKINS. Before THOMAS LAMBOLL, J.P. WILLIAM HOPTON, Register.

Book F-F, p. 315
19 June 1749
Conveyance of Judgment

RAWLINS LOWNDES, Provost Marshall of SC, to ANN WATSON, widow, of Charleston, for Ł 5000 currency, lot #28 & house thereon. Whereas JOHN WATSON, JR., merchant, of Charleston, owned lot #28 with its buildings (formerly in possession of PHILIP & LEVIE, now of DR. LIONEL CHALMERS & CRAMAHE & Co.) fronting 54 ft. on N side Broad Street, bounding W 150 ft. on house of JOHN CROCKATT (formerly DR. JOHN DELAUNE); N on heirs of MR. JENYS (formerly Madam BRETELL); E on HENRY KENNAN (formerly MATTHEW ROCHE, later JOHN RATTRAY); & whereas by will dated 24 Oct. 1748, WATSON appointed CLAUD JOHNSON & SON, of London; JOHN RATTRAY, DAVID DEAS, & JAMES SHARP, of Charleston, his executors, & ANN WATSON, executrix; ANN being qualified as executrix by Gov. JAMES GLEN (RATTRAY, DEAS, & SHARP, refusing to act); & where JOHN WATSON gave 2 bonds dated 23 May 1747 to SAMUEL WILLSON & Son, hardwaremen, of Connon Street, London, 1 in penal sum of Ł 456 British for payment of Ł 228 British; the other in penal sum of Ł 386 for payment of Ł 193:8 British; & whereas after WATSON'S death SAMUEL WILLSON & Son obtained a judgment against ANN WATSON for the 2 sums; & whereas Parliament at Westminster on 13 Jan. 1731 passed an act for recovery of debts within the plantations after 29 Sept. 1732 from debtor's lands, Negroes, etc., & in consequence, a writ of fieri facias dated 9 May 1749 was directed to the Provost Marshall of SC, to levy a debt of Ł 842 British, against said ANN, also Ł 30:15:7-1/2 currency for costs, & have the money before the J. of Ct. of C.P. at Charleston the first Tuesday in July then next; & whereas RAWLINS LOWNDES exposed said lot #28 to sale at public auction & ANN WATSON was highest bidder; now the house & lot are conveyed to her. Witnesses: JOHN RATTRAY, JAMES GRINDLAY. Before DANIEL CRAWFORD, J.P. WILLIAM HOPTON, Register.

Book F-F, p. 320
1 Feb. 1749
Mortgage

ANN LEBAS, widow, to JAMES MAXWELL, planter, both of Berkeley Co., as security on bond of even date in penal sum of Ł 2402:7:10 for payment of Ł 1201:3:11 currency, with interest, on 1 Feb. 1754; 500 a. in Berkeley Co., commonly called Beeth Hall, bounding S on Watboo Barony; N on EDWARD THOMAS. Witnesses: THOMAS SABB, WILLIAM SABB, DEBORAH SABB. Before NATHANIEL BROUGHTON, J.P. WILLIAM HOPTON, Register.

Book F-F, p. 323
1 & 2 Feb. 1749
L & R by Mortgage

WILLIAM GREENLAND, gentleman, to THOMAS CROSTH-WAITE, gentleman, both of Charleston, as security on bond dated 18 Jan. 1748 in penal sum of Ł 3500 for payment of Ł 1700 currency, with interest, on 30 Aug. 1750; 222 a. in St. James Goose Creek, Berkeley Co., formerly belonging to STEPHEN CLIFFORD, who conveyed to ROBERT ELLIOTT; & conveyed by ARTEMAS ELLIOTT & MARY his wife, to WILLIAM GREENLAND; bounding NE on the Broad Path; SE on MR. SHEPWORTH; W on BENJAMIN WHITAKER; NW on WILLIAM DRY. Witnesses: JAMES GRINDLAY, ROBERT WILLIAMS, JR. Before JOHN RATTRAY, J.P. WILLIAM HOPTON, Register. On 24 Aug. 1750 MARY CROSTHWAITE, wife & attorney of THOMAS CROSTHWAITE, declared mortgage satisfied. Witnesses: JAMES JONES, WILLIAM HOPTON.

Book F-F, p. 327
18 & 19 Dec. 1749
L & R

RICHARD MALONE, planter, of St. George Parish, Island of Jamaica; & SAMUEL EVELEIGH & JOHN COLCOCK, merchants, of Charleston, attorneys for RICHARD MALONE; to COL. ELIAS HORRY, of Prince George Parish, Craven Co., for Ⱡ 600 SC money, 300 a. in Prince George Parish, Craven Co., on N side Santee River, bounding SE on land purchased by said ELIAS HORRY from TACTITUS GAILLARD (formerly BARTHOLOMEW GAILLARD); NW on FREDERICK GAILLARD; NE on ELIAS HORRY. Whereas the Lords Proprs. on 4 Feb. 1714/5 granted CAPT. BARTHOLOMEW GAILLARD 300 a. in Craven Co.; which with other tracts be devised equally to his 3 sons, THEODORE, ALCIMUS & TACITUS; & they be deed of partition wherein their older brother, FREDERICK, was made a party to confirm their titles by reason of some defect in their father's will, & said 300 a. was allotted to ALCIMUS; & he with SARAH, his wife, by L & R dated 30 Nov. & 30 Dec. 1737 conveyed the tract to RICHARD MALONE, father of RICHARD, party hereto; & RICHARD the son, inherited at the death of his father; now the son, through his attorneys, conveys to ELIAS HORRY. Witnesses: RICHARD LAMBTON, JOHN BAKER, BURCH EVANS. Before THOMAS MIDDLETON, J.P. WILLIAM HOPTON, Register.

Book F-F, p. 332   THOMAS MOONEY, planter, of the WELCH tract,
19 Sept. 1746   Craven Co., to JOHN BROWN, planter, of Craven
Mortgage   Co., as security for the payment of Ⱡ 120 currency on 27 Dec. 1747; 125 a. in the WELCH tract, on Peedee River, bounding S on PHILLIP DOUGLAS. Witnesses: SAMUEL POWERS, RICHARD (his mark) ROGERS, ABRAHAM KERSLAKE. Before WILLIAM JAMES, J.P. WILLIAM HOPTON, Register.

DEEDS BOOK "G-G"
FEB. 1749 - JULY 1750

Book G-G, p. 1   THOMAS DRAYTON, ESQ., & ELIZABETH his wife, of
5 & 6 Feb. 1749   Berkeley Co., to ROBERT STEPHENS, of Colleton
L & R   Co., for Ⱡ 900 currency, the 500 a., English measure, in Colleton Co., granted by Gov. NATHANIEL JOHNSON & the Lords Proprs. on 5 Nov. 1704 to THOMAS DRAYTON, father of THOMAS, party hereto, who devised the tract to his son, STEPHEN DRAYTON, who died while a minor, & THOMAS, his eldest brother & heir, inherited; now he conveys to STEPHENS. Witnesses: MARY H. BULL, SARAH YEOMAN. Before ALEXANDER STEWART, J.P. WILLIAM HOPTON, Register.

Book G-G, p. 5   JOHN MACKENZIE, merchant, to WILLIAM GEORGE
6 & 7 Feb. 1749   FREEMAN, gentleman, both of Charleston, as se-
L & R by Mortgage   curity on bond dated 19 Sept. 1748; signed by
                     JOSEPH SHUTE & MACKENZIE, in penal sum of
Ⱡ 600 for payment of Ⱡ 300 currency, with interest, on 1 Mar. 1749; & as security on MACKENZIE'S bond to FREEMAN, dated 3 Jan. 1749, in penal sum of Ⱡ 490:9:6 British for payment of Ⱡ 245:4:9 British, with interest, on 1 Mar. 1749; part of lot #10 in Charleston, fronting 20 ft. on Callibeuf's Lane; bounding W 87 ft. on WILLIAM ELLIOTT; E on THOMAS ELLIOTT; S on WILLIAM ELLIOTT; also that part of a part of lot #10 fronting 5 ft. on Callibeuf's Lane, & bounding W on WILLIAM ELLIOTT; E 87 ft. on part formerly belonging to THOMAS KIMBERLY. Witnesses: JOHN BUTLER, JAMES GRINDLAY. Before JOHN RATTRAY, J.P. WILLIAM HOPTON, Register.

Book G-G, p. 10   FRANCIS AVANT, planter, & SARAH his wife, to
20 July 1748   SAMUEL CLYATT, planter, both of Prince Fred-
L & R   ericks Parish, Craven Co., for Ⱡ 100 currency,
                  150 a., part of a tract granted by the Lords
Proprs. to FRANCIS AVANT, SR., on NE side Black River, Prince Fredericks Parish, bounding NW on Chappee Creek; other sides on FREDERICK AVANT. SARAH WIGFALL AVANT renounces her claim. Witnesses: CHARLES BAXTER, JAMES CLYATT, JONATHAN BROWN. Before JOHN MAN, J.P. WILLIAM HOPTON, Register.

Book G-G, p. 14   COL. GEORGE PAWLEY, gentleman, & ANN his wife,
24 & 25 May 1749   of Prince George Parish, to DOUGAL CAMPBELL,
L & R   merchant, of Georgetown, for Ⱡ 1700 currency,
                     2 adjoining lots in Georgetown, #31 & #32,
each 50 x 217.9 ft., #31 bounding NW on lots #30; lot #32 bounding SE on Scriven Street; NE on #60; SW on Front Street & down to low water mark; total frontage 100 ft. Witnesses: ANN PAWLEY, WILLIAM POOLE, JR. Before

WILLIAM POOLE, J.P. WILLIAM HOPTON, Register.

Book G-G, p. 18   JAMES MAXWELL, ESQ., of St. Johns Parish,
3 & 4 July 1749   Berkeley Co., to ROBERT PAWLEY, an infant of
L & R   Prince George Parish, Craven Co., for a cer-
                         tain sum previously paid by PERCIVAL PAWLEY,
father of said ROBERT, in behalf of his son; 510 a. on N side Peedee River, bounding NE on a creek; SE on a part of JOHN JORDAN'S land, which
tract was granted to JAMES MAXWELL on 12 Aug. 1737. Witnesses: BENJAMIN
SIMONS, JOHN HENTIE. Before FRANCIS LEJAU, J.P. WILLIAM HOPTON, Register.

Book G-G, p. 22   BENJAMIN SIMONS, ESQ., of St. Thomas Parish,
3 & 4 July 1749   Berkeley Co., to ROBERT PAWLEY, an infant, of
L & R   Prince George Parish, Craven Co., in consider-
                         ation of an agreement made by BENJAMIN SIMONS
with ANTHONY PAWLEY, uncle of said ROBERT PAWLEY (which ANTHONY PAWLEY
made his will in favor of his brother PERCIVAL, who made his will in favor of his son, said ROBERT), to convey certain lands to said ANTHONY,
which conveyance was never executed, & the right thereof has devolved on
said ROBERT; 350 a. on S side of Peedee River, Craven Co., bounding E & S
on MR. PAWLEY; W on WILLIAM WATSON & vacant land; which tract was granted
to BENJAMIN SIMONS on 11 Dec. 1736. Witnesses: FRANCIS SIMONS, JOHN HEN-
TIE. Before FRANCIS LEJAU, J.P. WILLIAM HOPTON, Register.

Book G-G, p. 25   The Hon. JAMES KINLOCK, ESQ., to MARGARET
25 & 26 Dec. 1749   O'NEAL, widow, of Berkeley Co., for Ł 200 cur-
L & R   rency, 200 a. in Berkeley Co., bounding SW & N
                         W on said KINLOCK; SE & NE on Landgrave FRENCH
(TRENCH?). Witnesses: GEORGE AUSTIN, WILLIAM WOODDROP. Before JACOB
MOTTE, J.P. WILLIAM HOPTON, Register.

Book G-G, p. 30   RAWLINS LOWNDES, Provost Marshal, to RACHEL
18 May 1749   STOCK, at public auction, for Ł 334 currency,
Sale   2 tracts of 286 a. & 48 a. Whereas JOHN WAT-
                         SON recovered a judgment against RACHEL STOCK,
executrix of will of THOMAS STOCK, planter, of Chehaw, for Ł 1082:18 currency & Ł 49:6:10-1/2 currency for costs, & a writ of testatum fieri facias signed 7 Oct. 1746 by JOHN LINING, Assistant J. of C.P. in absence
of BENJAMIN WHITAKER, C.J., was issued, commanding LOWNDES to levy the
sums on STOCK'S estate; & LOWNDES entered upon 1 tract of 286 a. on SW
side Chehaw River in Colleton Co., part of 550 a. granted to EMANUEL
SMITH; bounding S on MR. TOWNSHEND; W on MR. SNATCHPOLE, MR. NICHOLS, MR.
WILDBERRY & MR. SUMMERVEILD; N on MR. BOLTUS; E on Glebe land; also on a
tract of 48 a. in Colleton Co., bounding N on NOAH HURT BLANCOES land; SW
on SAMUEL SMITH; now LOWNDES conveys them to RACHEL STOCK the highest
bidder. Witness: ROBERT RAWLINS. Before JAMES WEDDERBURN, J.P. WILLIAM
HOPTON, Register.

Book G-G, p. 32   REGINALD JACKSON, JAMES JACKSON, & HENRY JACK-
22 Jan. 1748   SON, planters, of Colleton Co., to JAMES SKIRV-
Release   ING, gentleman, of Berkeley Co., for Ł 489 cur-
                         rency, 163-1/4 a., part of 400 a., in Colleton
Co., bounding W on Horse Shoe Creek; N & E on JAMES SKIRVING; S on Pogo-
talligo Creek & BENJAMIN GODIN. Whereas Landgrave EDMUND BELLINGER by L
& R dated 9 & 10 June 1731 sold HENRY JACKSON 400 a. on E side Ashepoo
River, in Colleton Co., bounding N on HENRY JACKSON; S on BENJAMIN GODIN;
& JACKSON by will dated 20 May 1738 devised the 400 a. to his 4 sons,
REGINALD, JAMES, JOHN & HENRY; & whereas JOHN died intestate 16 Aug. 1748
& his 3 brothers inherited his share; now they sell a part of the land to
SKIRVING. Witnesses: ANN JACKSON, LAMBERT LANCE. Before CULCHETH GO-
LIGHTLY, J.P. WILLIAM HOPTON, Register.

Book G-G, p. 35   JOSHUA TOOMER, planter, & MARY his wife, to
1 & 2 Oct. 1741   MATHURINE GUERIN, planter, both of Berkeley
L & R   Co., for Ł 2338 currency, 305 a., English mea-
                         sure, in Berkeley Co., on N side Stono River,
bounding N on MR. BONNEAU & BARNARD ELLIOTT & JOHN TOOMER; E on BARNARD
ELLIOTT & JOSHUA TOOMER & marsh; S on JOSHUA TOOMER'S marsh land; W & NW
on JOSHUA TOOMER & marsh; also 100 a. of marsh land bounding S on Stono

River; E & W on marsh; N on the 305 a. Witnesses: BARNARD ELLIOTT, WIL-
LIAM CHAPMAN, EDWARD WESTON. Before THOMAS DALE, J.P. WILLIAM ELLIOTT,
Register.

Book G-G, p. 42   DANIEL DEAN & ANN his wife, of St. James Goose
23 Apr. 1744   Creek, Berkeley Co., to GASPAR MORTINGER, of
Sale   Berkeley Co., for Ł 150 currency, 200 a. on
                         Wassamsaw Swamp; bounding NW on ABRAHAM DUPONT
& GIDEON DUPONT; NE on ABRAHAM DUPONT; SW on ARTHUR MIDDLETON; SE on EB-
ENEZER SINGELTON. ANN DEAN renounces her dower. Witnesses: ROBERT
ECALLES, RICHARD (his mark) CLARK, ROBERT ADAMS. Before THOMAS MIDDLETON,
J.P. WILLIAM HOPTON, Register.

Book G-G, p. 46   NEWELL EDWARDS, planter, to his God-daughter,
3 Mar. 1749   FRANCES ORAM, now an infant, for natural love
Gift in Trust   & affection, & for Ł 5 paid EDWARDS by JOSEPH
                         ORAM, carpenter, of Charleston, father & law-
full guardian of FRANCES, & for other considerations; 365 a. called Etiwan Island, on Cooper River; to be held by JOSEPH ORAM in trust for
FRANCES. Witnesses: WILLIAM PLAYTERS, WILLIAM HAWCKS. One steel buckle
delivered. Before ALEXANDER STEWART, J.P. WILLIAM HOPTON, Register.

Book G-G, p. 48   NEWEL EDWARDS, planter, agrees to deliver to
26 Sept. 1749   JOHN SCOTT, shipwright; both of Berkeley Co.;
Agreement   on EDWARD'S plantation where he dwells, 100
                         pine trees fit for sawing or splitting for
rails; 12 white oak trees, 12 red oak & all live oaks on the plantation.
SCOTT agrees to pay 5 shillings for each pine tree; 20 shillings for each
white oak; 10 shillings for each red oak; 2 shillings 6 d. for each live
oak. Each gives bond of Ł 50 currency. Witnesses: JOHN CROSTHWAITE,
BENJAMIN JONES. Before JACOB MOTTE, J.P. WILLIAM HOPTON, Register.

Book G-G, p. 49   RICHARD CAPERS, WILLIAM BENNISON, & RICHARD
22 & 23 Mar. 1748   BENNISON, executors of will of GEORGE BENNISON,
L & R   gentleman, of Christ Church Parish to CAPT.
                         RICHARD I'ON of same Parish, for Ł 1900 cur-
rency, the Swamp Plantation conveyed to GEORGE BENNISON by L & R dated 3
& 4 July 1722 by JOHN BONHOIST, planter, & then supposed to contain 500 a.
but later computed to be 492 a.; then bounding E on MR. DUBOIS; W on
ANTHONY BONNEAU; N on JONAS BONHOISE; S on JOHN WHITE. Whereas GEORGE
BENNISON by will dated 15 Sept. 1747 authorized his executors to sell a
tract of 400 a. known as White House Plantation & a tract of 492 a. called the Swamp Plantation, & use the money to pay his debts, & appointed
his brother RICHARD CAPERS, & his sons WILLIAM & RICHARD BENNISON, his
executors; & whereas GEORGE BENNISON died greatly in debt; now the executors sell the Swamp to I'ON, the highest bidder. Witnesses: DANIEL
YOU, THOMAS BONNY, JR., WILLIAM GIBBS. Before OTHNIEL BEALE, J.P. WIL-
LIAM HOPTON, Register.

Book G-G, p. 56   JOSEPH DUBOURDIEU, executor of will of ANTHONY
2 Mar. 1748   WHITE, of Prince Frederick Parish, Craven Co.,
Release   to WILLIAM SMITH, planter, of same Parish, for
                         Ł 130 currency, 400 a., part of 1620 a.; bound-
ing N on WILLIAM GREEN; E on MEREDITH HUGHES; S & W on ANTHONY WHITE.
Whereas Gov. THOMAS BROUGHTON on 12 Dec. 1735 granted ANTHONY WHITE 1620
a. in Craven Co., on S side Black River, bounding N on MEREDITH HUGHES;
W on JOHN GOUGH; S on JOHN LANE; SE & E on GEORGE HAMBLIN & STEPHEN LEAY-
CROFT (now ANTHONY WHITE); which land WHITE directed his executors to
sell to pay his debts; now they sell part to SMITH. Witnesses: WILLIAM
POOLE, JR., SAMUEL DUBOURDIEU. Before PAUL TRAPIER, J.P. WILLIAM HOP-
TON, Register.

Book G-G, p. 59   ABRAHAM WARNOCK, planter, of Waucamaw, Craven
20 & 21 Aug. 1736   Co., to PETER ALLSTON, for good causes & con-
L & R   siderations, 34 a. in Craven Co., bounding on
                         all sides on Waucamaw River. Witnesses: MARY
PAWLEY, MARY WAY, JOSEPH LABRUCE. Before GEORGE PAWLEY, J.P. WILLIAM
HOPTON, Register.

Book G-G, p. 63   DANIEL CONAWY, & ANN his wife (formerly ANN

5 & 6 May 1749   DANIEL, lately ANN GOODBEE, widow of ALEXANDER
L & R by Mortgage   GOODBEE), to JOHN CART, both of Charleston, as
                        security on bond dated 30 Apr. 1748 (signed
also by JAMES MACKRELLIS & PETER FISHER, of Charleston) in sum of Ł 540
for payment of Ł 270 SC money, with interest, on 30 Apr. 1749 (?); 380 a.
on E side Cooper River, in St. Thomas Parish, Berkeley Co., part of 2
tracts of 1005 a. granted by the Lords Proprs. to SOLOMON BREMAR & by
several mesne conveyances came to ALEXANDER GOODBE; according to plat of
380 a. attached to bill of sale dated 31 Jan. 1723 from PETER BREMAR to
DANIEL TREZEVANT. Witnesses: PETER MANIGAULT, ROBERT WILLIAMS, JR. Before JOHN RATTRAY, J.P. WILLIAM HOPTON, REgister. On 3 Sept. 1751 JOHN
CART declared mortgage satisfied. Witness: WILLIAM HOPTON, Register.

Book G-G, p. 68   HENRY PERONNEAU, ESQ., & ELIZABETH his wife;
22 & 23 Mar. 1749   JAMES MICKIE, ESQ., & MARTHA his wife; WILLIAM
L & R   STEWART, ESQ., & ANN his wife; & JOHN CATTELL,
                        son & heir of SARAH CATTELL; all of Charles-
ton; of 1st part; to DANIEL HOWARD, of Granville Co.; according to agreement, & for Ł 2840 currency; their respective interest & estate in 1420
a. Whereas Lt. Gov. THOMAS BROUGHTON on 7 Aug. 1735 granted HENRY PERON-
NEAU & JAMES OSMOND, as surviving executors of will of COL. ARTHUR HALL,
for the use of ROBERT HALL & CHRISTOPHER HALL, infants, 1420 a. in Granville Co., bounding N on CAPT. HAYWARD & vacant land; & whereas ROBERT &
CHRISTOPHER died in infancy (ROBERT dying first); & whereas ELIZABETH
(wife of HENRY PERONNEAU) & MARTHA (wife of JAMES MICHIE) & ANN (wife of
WILLIAM STEWART) & JOHN CATTELL, parties hereto, were co-heirs with
CHRISTOPℏER; & whereas JAMES OSMOND, joint granted, is dead; so that the
trust survived to HENRY PERONNEAU; now he, with the others, having agreed
to convey the tract to DANIEL HOWARD, keeps the agreement. Witnesses:
JOHN TROUP, HENRY PERONNEAU, JR. Before ROBERT AUSTIN, J.P. WILLIAM
HOPTON, Register.

Book G-G, p. 76   NEWEL EDWARDS, planter, of St. Thomas Parish,
27 & 28 Mar. 1750   Berkeley Co., to JOHN SCOTT, ship carpenter,
L & R   of Charleston, for Ł 170 currency, 65 a. in
                        St. Thomas Parish, bounding NW on a marsh of
Clousters Creek; NE on NEWEL EDWARDS & GEORGE LOGAN; SW on NEWELL EDWARDS;
being part of 365 a. granted by the Lords Proprs. on 23 July 1711 to
GRACE BUCKLEY. Witnesses: JOHN MACKAY, ROBERT HOW. Before ALEXANDER GOR-
DON, J.P. WILLIAM HOPTON, Register.

Book G-G, p. 81   GABRIEL GUIGNARD, cooper & FRANCES his wife,
23 & 24 Feb. 1749   of 1st part; THOMAS BOLTON, merchant, of 2nd
L & R   part; HALL RICHARDSON, watchmaker, executor of
                        of will of JAMES HILLIARD, of 3rd part; JAMES
HUNTER, baker, of 4th part; all of Charleston. Whereas by deed of feoffment dated 28 Feb. 1746 GABRIEL GUIGNARD, for Ł 250 currency mortgaged to
JAMES HILLIARD part of lot #80 in Charleston, which GUIGNARD had obtained
from the Hon. CHARLES PINCKNEY; to be redeemed 28 Feb. 1749; & whereas
HILLIARD put up a brick building of 28 ft. front, 3 ft. more than granted
him, & agreed to pay GUIGNARD Ł 30 currency for the 3 ft., for which
GUIGNARD agreed to give full conveyance for the whole when the mortgage
should be satisfied; & whereas HILLIARD on 14 Oct. last gave bond to BOL-
TON in penal sum of Ł 1041 for payment of Ł 520; 10 currency, with interest, on 14 Apr. then next & for security conveyed the above property; &
whereas HILLIARD by will dated 31 Oct. last commanded his executors to
dispose of his estate & pay his debts, appointing BOLTON & RICHARDSON his
executors; & whereas HILLIARD died leaving his debt to GUIGNARD unpaid; &
BOLTON refused to act; & RICHARDSON became executor; & RICHARDSON on 7
Jan. last published notice in SC Gazette that on Mon. 27 Jan. inst. would
be sold at public auction, under the New Market, for ready money, a brick
house & its lot, on N side Guignard Street, part of the estate of JAMES
HILLIARD; & whereas JAMES HUNTER was highest bidder; now, for Ł 190 SC
money, the balance due, GUIGNARD conveys to HUNTER that part of lot #80
bounding N on JOHN VAUN; E 100 ft. on JOHN MEEK; W on a 12 ft. alley called Goodbe's Alley; S 28 ft. on Guignard Street; & THOMAS BOLTON, for
Ł 559:15 SC money transfers to JAMES HUNTER the mortgaged premises. Witnesses: PETER DELEISSELINE, JOHN REMINGTON. Before ROBERT AUSTIN, J.P.
WILLIAM HOPTON, Register.

Book G-G, p. 89   (See p. 68). HENRY PERONNEAU, & ELIZABETH his
2 & 3 Apr. 1750   wife; JAMES MICHIE & MARTHA his wife; WILLIAM
L & R   STEWART, ESQ., formerly of New Providence, &
                          ANN his wife; & JOHN CATTELL, JR., eldest son
& heir of JOHN CATTELL & SARAH his wife; all of Charleston (ELIZABETH
PERONNEAU, MARTHA MICHIE, ANN STEWART, & SARAH CATTELL, were daughters of
COL. ARTHUR HALL, of Berkeley Co., & co-heirs with CHRISTOPHER HALL, son
& devisee of said ARTHUR HALL; all of 1st part; to WILLIAM BRANFORD, JR.,
planter, of St. Andrews Parish, Berkeley Co.; for £ 600 SC money; all of
lot #46 in Charleston, except that part on which by Act of General Assem-
bly a fort was to be erected, & 20 ft. reserved for a public street.
Whereas CHRISTOPHER HALL by his father's will owned lot #46 in Charleston,
bounding S on Ashley River; W on King Street; N on heirs of WILLIAM HAR-
VEY; E on a lot claimed by heirs of FRANCIS FIDLING & by the heirs of
JAMES COCHRAN; as by plat dated 15 Jan. 1745 certified by GEORGE HUNTER,
Sur. Gen.; which lot was granted by the Lords Proprs. on 18 June 1694 to
FRANCIS FIDLING, the plat of grant certified by STEPHEN BULL, Sur.; which
lot descended to JOHN FIDLING, eldest son & heir of FRANCIS; but he dying
intestate, the estate descended to DANIEL (a joiner), the 2nd son; &
whereas by deed of feoffment dated 4 July 1713, for £ 25 SC money, DANIEL
FIDLING & ELIZABETH his wife, sold the lot to ARTHUR HALL, planter, of
Colleton Co.; & whereas after the death of CHRISTOPHER HALL, HENRY PERON-
NEAU, took possession & by this lease demised the lot to WILLIAM BRANFORD
for 1 year; now all parties of 1st part release the premises to BRANFORD.
Witnesses: TIMOTHY MORGRIDGE, JOHN TROUP. Before JACOB MOTTE, J.P. WIL-
LIAM HOPTON, Register.

Book G-G, p. 96   SARAH COLLINS, widow of JONAH COLLINS, of Cra-
26 Feb. 1749/50   ven Co., having received the legacies & be-
Renunciation of Dower   quests to which she is entitled by the will of
                          her husband renounces to the executors all
claim she may have to the balance of her husband's real or personal estate. Whereas JONAH COLLINS by will dated 2 Apr. 1743 made sundry legacies & bequests to his wife, SARAH, & appointed JONAH COLLINS & WILLIAM
BUCHANON, planter, his executors; & the executors have delivered them to
SARAH; she acknowledges them to be in full satisfaction of dower. Witnesses: CLEMENT LAMPRIERE, GEORGE LOGAN, JR., JOHN MAYRANT. Before JACOB
MOTTE, J.P. WILLIAM HOPTON, Register.

Book G-G, p. 98   JOHN PARRIS to executors of JONAH COLLINS.
26 Feb. 1749/50   Whereas JONAH COLLINS, of Craven Co., by will
Quit Claim   dated 2 Apr. 1743 bequeathed to his daughter,
                          ELIZABETH COLLINS, various legacies, & appoint-
ed JONAH COLLINS & WILLIAM BUCHANAN, planters, his executors; & whereas
ELIZABETH married JOHN PARRIS, so that he became entitled to ELIZABETH'S
legacies; & whereas the executors have delivered said legacies to JOHN
PARRIS; now PARRIS renounces all claim to the real & personal estate of
JONAH COLLINS. Witnesses: CLEMENT LAMPRIERE, GEORGE LOGAN, JR., JOHN
MAYRANT. Before JACOB MOTTE, J.P. WILLIAM HOPTON, Register.

Book G-G, p. 100   SARAH COLLINS, widow of JOSEPH COLLINS, in ac-
26 Feb. 1749/50   cordance with her husband's will, renounces
Renunciation of Dower   all her claim to Bull's Island & a tract of
                          345 a. in St. James Santee Parish, now belong-
ing to JONAH COLLINS. Whereas JOSEPH COLLINS, husband of Sarah, owned
1580 a., in Berkeley Co., known as Bull's Island, & 345 a. in St. James
Santee Parish (which are now the property of 1 JONAH COLLINS, of Berkeley
Co.) & by will dated 2 Apr. 1743 bequeathed certain legacies to SARAH in
lieu of dower, now she formally renounces all claim to the 2 tracts.
Witnesses: CLEMENT LAMPRIERE, GEORGE LOGAN, JR., JOHN MAYRANT. Before
JACOB MOTTE, J.P. WILLIAM HOPTON, Register.

Book G-G, p. 103   BENJAMIN ELLIOTT, planter, to WILLIAM BRANFORD,
28 & 29 Sept. 1749   SR., planter, both of Stono, for £ 2000 cur-
L & R   rency, 326-1/2 a., on N side Stono River,
                          Berkeley Co., bounding E on WILLIAM BRANFORD;
S on WILLIAM BRANFORD & the River; W on THOMAS ELLIOTT; N on THOMAS HOL-
MAN; being part of 430 a. originally granted to THOMAS STOCK, who convey-
ed to THOMAS ELLIOTT the father, who devised the tract to his son BENJAM-
IN, party hereto. Whereas THOMAS ELLIOTT, by will dated 23 Oct. 1738

among other things devised to his 3 sons, THOMAS, BENJAMIN & SAMUEL, the
rest of his real & personal estate, to be equally divided as his executors saw fit, & appointed his brothers, WILLIAM, BARNARD, & JOSEPH, his
executors; & JOSEPH died, leaving WILLIAM & BARNARD surviving executors;
& whereas they allotted to BENJAMIN the said 326-1/2 a. in St. Andrews
Parish; now he sells to BRANFORD. Witnesses: BURNABY BRANFORD, NATHANIEL
BROWN. Before WILLIAM BULL, JR., J.P. WILLIAM HOPTON, Register.

Book G-G, p. 109   WILLIAM BRANFORD, JR., planter, & MARY his
4 & 5 Apr. 1750   wife, to FRANCIS ROSE, planter, both of St.
L & R   Andrews Parish, Berkeley Co., for ₺ 300 cur-
                          rency, the W half of lot #46 in Charleston,
bounding W on King Street; S on Ashley River; N on WILLIAM HARVEY; except
the part set aside by Act of General Assembly for the building of a fort
& a public street 20 ft. wide; according to plat certified by GEORGE HUN-
TER, Sur. Gen.; on 15 Jan. 1745. Whereas by L & R dated 2 & 3 Apr. 1750
HENRY PERONNEAU & ELIZABETH his wife; JAMES MICHIE, ESQ., & MARTHA his
wife; WILLIAM STEWART, formerly of New Providence but now of Charleston,
& ANN his wife; & JOHN CATTELL, JR., eldest son & heir of JOHN CATTELL &
SARAH his wife; which said ELIZABETH, MARTHA, ANN, & SARAH were daughters
of COL. ARTHUR HALL, of Berkeley Co., & co-heirs of CHRISTOPHER HALL, son
& devisee of said ARTHUR HALL; of the 1 part, & WILLIAM BRANFORD, JR.,
planter, of St. Andrews Parish, of the other part; reciting that whereas
CHRISTOPHER HALL, by will of his father, owned lot #46 in Charleston,
bounding S on Ashley River; W on King Street; N on heirs of WILLIAM HAR-
VEY; E on a lot claimed by heirs of FRANCIS FIDLING & Heirs of JAMES COCH-
RAN; which lot was granted by the Lords Proprs. on 18 June 1694 to FRAN-
CIS FIDLING, as by grant & certificate signed by STEPHEN BULL, surveyor;
& reciting that the lot so granted to FIDLING was inherited by eldest son
& devisee, JOHN FIDLING, who died intestate & was by deed of feoffment
dated 4 July 1713, for ₺ 25 currency, conveyed by DANIEL FIDLING, joiner,
(2nd son of said FRANCIS, & heir of his brother JOHN), & ELIZABETH his
wife, to ARTHUR HALL, planter, of Colleton Co.; & whereas HENRY PERONNEAU,
in right of the co-heirs of CHRISTOPHER HALL, after CHRISTOPHER'S death
took possession & by lease dated 4 Apr. 1750 demised the lot to WILLIAM
BRANFORD; now the conveyance is completed. Witnesses: JOHN MCKENZIE, JR.,
MARTHA WARING. Before THOMAS LAMBOLL, J.P. WILLIAM HOPTON, Register.

Book G-G, p. 118   JOHN ATCHESON, planter, of Berkeley Co., to
26 & 27 May 1743   DANIEL MCGRIGOR & WILLIAM BOHANNON, planters,
L & R in Trust   of Craven Co., for ₺ 2950 currency, 1580 a. in
                          Berkeley Co., known as Bull's Island; also
345 a. in Craven Co., both of which tracts were purchased by ATCHESON
from JONAH COLLINS, planter, of Craven Co.; both adjoining a tract of
500 a. where JONAH COLLINS now lives & land formerly belonging to MARK
SLOWAN; also 500 a. at Waccamaw (recently purchased by ACHESON from COL-
LINS) adjoining the half of another tract of 1000 a. sold by COLLINS to
ACHESON; also the other half of the 1000 a. (500 a.) at Waccamaw, also
purchased by ACHESON from COLLINS; the first 2 tracts for the use of said
JONAH COLLINS an infant, his lifetime, then to his heirs, with definite
instructions as to inheritance, including SARAH COLLINS & MARY COLLINS,
infants, sisters of said infant JONAH COLLINS. Witnesses: JAMES FOWLER,
THOMAS LAMBOLL. Before JACOB MOTTE, J.P. WILLIAM HOPTON, Register.

Book G-G, p. 128   ANDREW JOHNSTON, planter, of Winyaw, to JOHN
15 & 16 Oct. 1749   RATTRAY, gentleman, of Charleston, as security
L & R by Mortgage   on bond of even date in penal sum of ₺ 14,000
                          for payment of ₺ 7000 currency, with interest,
on 1 Sept. 1750; 1050 a. on Great Pedee, in Prince George Parish, Craven
Co., bounding N on COL. WILLIAM WATIES; E on Great Sand Island; S on JOHN
WATIES; W on JAMES MCKAY; also 1450 a. on Cypress Creek, in said Parish;
bounding E on JAMES MCKAY (MACKAY); S on JOHN WATIES; W on vacant land; N
on BENJAMIN COACHMAN; also 829 a. on Sampett Creek, same Parish, bounding
N on ISAAC MAZYCK; other sides on JAMES SUMMERS. Witnesses: JAMES GRIND-
LAY, ROBERT WILLIAMS, JR. Before DANIEL CRAWFORD, J.P. WILLIAM HOPTON,
Register.

Book G-G, p. 133   JOHN GANTLETT, house carpenter, to WILLIAM
10 May 1748   SPENCER the elder, planter, both of James Is-
Feoffment   land, for ₺ 33 currency, 16 a. known as MARION

GANTLETT'S Island, in St. Andrews Parish, Berkeley Co., bounding S on Folly River; E on Legare's Island; W on Dickson's Island. Witnesses: JOHN ELLIS, JR., WILLIAM SPENCER, JR., ANN SPENCER. Before ROBERT AUSTIN, J.P. WILLIAM HOPTON, Register.

Book G-G, p. 135　　　　　RAWLINS LOWNDES, Provost Marshal, to THOMAS
22 Mar. 1740　　　　　　 BOWMAN, planter, of Granville Co., for Ł 500
Sale on Execution　　　　currency, 532 a. on Port Royal Island, bound-
　　　　　　　　　　　　ing N on THOMAS BOWMAN; E on EVAN LEWIS & NICH-
OLAS HATCHER; S on JORDON ROCHE. Whereas COL. WILLIAM HAYWARD (HAZARD?),
COL. THOMAS WIGG, JOHN MIKELL & JOSEPH MIKELL, planters, of Granville Co.,
executors of will of EPRAIM MIKELL, by L & R dated 7 & 8 Aug. 1749 con-
veyed to EDWARD WIGG, merchant, of Beaufort, the said 532 a.; & EDWARD
WIGG mortgaged the tract to WILLIAM HOPTON & THOMAS SMITH, merchants, of
Charleston, as security on his bond dated 14 Feb. 1746 in penal sum of
Ł 330 sterling British for payment of Ł 167 like money; & whereas HOPTON
& SMITH obtained a judgment against WIGG for the amount of the debt &
costs, & a writ of fieri facias was issued directing the Provost Marshal
to levy against WIGG'S estate the sum of Ł 334 sterling & Ł 27:19:9-1/2
currency for costs, & at public auction BOWMAN was highest bidder; now
LOWNDES conveys the 532 a. to BOWMAN. Witnesses: GEORGE LODGE, WILLIAM
BAMPFIELD. Before WILLIAM PINCKNEY, J.P. WILLIAM HOPTON, Register.

Book G-G, p. 139　　　　　(See pp. 68 & 89). HENRY PERONNEAU, merchant,
9 & 10 Apr. 1750　　　　 & ELIZABETH his wife; JAMES MICHIE, & MARTHA
L & R　　　　　　　　　　his wife; WILLIAM STEWART, ESQ., & ANN his
　　　　　　　　　　　　wife; & JOHN CATTELL (eldest son & heir of
JOHN CATTELL & SARAH his wife); all of Charleston; ELIZABETH, MARTHA, ANN
& SARAH, being daughters of COL. ARTHUR AHLL, of Berkeley Co., & co-heirs
of CHRISTOPHER HALL, son & devisee of said ARTHUR HALL; of 1st part; to
ARCHIBALD SCOTT, planter, of James Island, for Ł 1374 currency, 99-1/2 a.
on NW side New Town Creek on James Island, Berkeley Co., bounding SW on a
small beach of said creek & RICHARD EDWARDS; NW on WILLIAM DAVIS; NE on
CHRISTOPHER GERARD; the 99-1/2 a., knwon as CARLISLE'S, being part of
100 a. granted on 18 Aug. 1697 to THOMAS DRAYTON & sold by WILLIAM CAR-
LISLE by deed of feoffment dated 8 Nov. 1720 to ARTHUR HALL; also 15 a.
on James Island, as by plat certified 4 Apr. 1750 by GEORGE HUNTER, Sur.
Gen.; being part of 21 a. conveyed by COL. ALEXANDER TRENCH to ARTHUR
HALL; the 2 tracts making 1 plantation of 114-1/2 a. Witnesses: TIMOTHY
MORGRIDGE, JOHN TROUP. Before ROBERT AUSTIN, J.P. WILLIAM HOPTON, Reg-
ister.

Book G-G, p. 146　　　　　GEORGE JACKSON, planter, & MARY his wife, of
18 & 19 Apr. 1750　　　　Colleton Co., to SARAH STOUTENBURGH (lately
L & R by Mortgage　　　 SARAH MACKENZIE) & JOHN MACKENZIE, merchant,
　　　　　　　　　　　　of Charleston, executrix & executor of will of
WILLIAM MACKENZIE, merchant, as security for payment of Ł 723:5:4 curren-
cy & interest due; 464 a. in Colleton Co., bounding W on THOMAS BURR; S
on BOON'S Barony; E on JOSHUA GREEN; N on JAMES FERGUSON. Whereas GEORGE
JACKSON & MATTHEW ROCHE gave bond dated 30 Aug. 1740 to SARAH STOUTEN-
BURGH & JOHN MACKENZIE (for estate of WILLIAM MACKENZIE) in penal sum of
Ł 1446:10:8 for payment of Ł 723:5:4 currency, with interest, on 30 Aug.
1746; & whereas SARAH STOUTENBURGH & GEORGE JACKSON have given GEORGE
JACKSON a further day for payment of said sum; now he gives security for
payment on 19 Apr. 1751. Witnesses: THOMAS SMITH, THOMAS DEAN, JAMES
GRINDLAY. Before JOHN RATTRAY, J.P. WILLIAM HOPTON, Register.

Book G-G, p. 152　　　　　JOHN (his mark) OPHIN (alias FINNY), planter,
8 & 9 Jan. 1749　　　　　to ELEANOR SCOTT, widow, both of Granville Co.,
L & R　　　　　　　　　　for Ł 1200 currency, 402-1/2 a. on St. Helena
　　　　　　　　　　　　Island, bounding SE on marsh & a creek; NE on
JOHN COWEN; W on ARTHUR DICK; S on JOHN CHAPLAIN; being part of 2 tracts
sold by JOHN BEAMOR to JOHN COWEN, who, with his wife, SARAH, conveyed
the 402-1/2 a. to JOHN OPHIN. Witnesses: WILLIAM HARVEY, WILLIAM GOUGH.
Before ROBERT WILLIAMS, J.P. WILLIAM HOPTON, Register.

Book G-G, p. 157　　　　　TACITUS GAILLARD, planter, to THEODORE GAIL-
15 Mar. 1739　　　　　　 LARD, planter, both of Craven Co., for Ł 250
Release　　　　　　　　　currency, 108 a. on Wambaw Swamp, Craven Co.,
　　　　　　　　　　　　according to plat signed by TACITUS GAILLARD,

& taken out of SE part of 300 a. granted to CAPT. BARTHOLOMEW GAILLARD. Witnesses: LOUIS GOURDIN, NATHANIEL SAVINEAU, RALPH BUGNION. Before SAMUEL THOMAS, J.P. WILLIAM HOPTON, Register.

Book G-G, p. 160
25 & 26 Apr. 1750
L & R

Landgrave EDMUND BELLINGER, the son & MARY LUCIA his wife, to FRANCIS PELOT, of Granville Co., for Ł 1050 currency, 600 a. Whereas Landgrave EDMUND BELLINGER, the father, under his patent for 48,000 a., owned 4,000 a. on W side of Uhaw Creek in Granville Co., bounding N on MR. WRAGG; E on creek & marshes; S & W on vacant land; & by will dated 21 Feb. 1739 bequeathed to his son, JOHN BELLINGER, 1000 a. to be allotted to him by testator's wife, ELIZABETH BELLINGER; & whereas JOHN died a minor & the 1000 a. descended to his brother, EDMUND; & whereas ELIZABETH assigned to EDMUND, the son, as part of the 1000 a., 600 a. (part of 4000 a.) at head of a branch of Uhaw Creek, bounding N on COL. HENRY HYRNE; E & W on estate of Landgrave EDMUND BELLINGER; now EDMUND, the son, conveys the 600 a. to PELOT. Witnesses: JOHN SHEPPHERD, ELIZABETH BULL, JOHN GARVIN. Before THOMAS LAMBOLL, J.P. WILLIAM HOPTON, Register. Plat by HUGH BRYAN, Dep. Sur. dated 7 Apr. 175_.

Book G-G, p. 166
3 & 4 Apr. 1749
L & R by Mortgage

MORGAN SABB, planter, of St. Johns Parish, Berkeley Co., to JOHN PALMER, merchant, of Charleston, as security on bond dated 31 May 1748 given by SABB to ALEXANDER PERONNEAU, merchant, of Charleston, on which bond PALMER stood security for SABB, in penal sum of Ł 1000 for payment of Ł 500 currency, with interest, on 31 May next; 1200 a. in St. Johns Parish, where SABB lives, bounding N on PHILIP PIROTT; E on vacant land; S on HENRY MIDDLETON; W on CAPT. HAIGE; 584 a. of which were conveyed to SABB by JAMES MAXWELL, & the remainder by BENJAMIN SMITH. Witnesses: JAMES KIRKWOOD, JOHN REMINGTON. Before ROBERT AUSTIN, J.P. WILLIAM HOPTON, Register.

Book G-G, p. 173
23 & 24 Feb. 1749
L & R in Trust

WILLIAM WOODDROP, JOHN MACKENZIE, & BENJAMIN STEED, merchants, of Charleston, who survived 1 KENNETH MICHIE, merchant, of Charleston; to DANIEL HORRY, planter, of Santee; for Ł 1005 currency, lot #29 in Georgetown, containing 1/4 a., English measure, bounding SW on Front Street; SE on #30; NE on #63; NW on #28. Whereas by L & R dated 10 & 11 Mar. 1746 JOHN BARKSDALE & JOHN OYSTON, merchants, of Winyaw, conveyed to WILLIAM WOODROP, JOHN MACKENZIE, BENJAMIN STEAD, & KENNETH MICHIE, 2 lots in Georgetown known as #86 & #29, with the agreement that they (of 2nd part) would sell the lots as soon as possible & distribute the money amongst themselves & the other creditors of said BARKSDALE & OYSTON; & whereas MICHIE died; now the surviving trustees sell lot #29 to HORRY. Witnesses: FRANCIS HOLMES, JOHN BUTLER. Before JACOB MOTTE, J.P. WILLIAM HOPTON, Register.

Book G-G, p. 178
28 & 29 Sept. 1748
L & R

JOSEPH WATSON, mariner, of Rotherhith, Surry Co., & ELIZABETH (her mark) his wife, to CHARLES WARHAM, joiner, of Charleston, for Ł 1000 SC money, part of lot #73 in Charleston, bounding N 20-1/2 ft. on Tradd Street; E 100 ft. on BENJAMIN SAVAGE; S 20-1/2 ft. on ELIZABETH GIBBS; W 100 ft. on JOHN MCCALL. Whereas the Lords Proprs. on 16 Mar. 1693 granted CAPT. CHARLES BASDEN, lot #73 on Tradd Street, Charleston, & he died intestate, leaving 3 daughters, SARAH, REBECCA & MARY, who inherited as co-heirs; & whereas SARAH married JONATHAN COLLINS, REBECCA married the Rev. MR. WILLIAM GUY; & whereas they, with MARY BASDEN, divided the lot amongst themselves, by which the part of lot #73 fronting N 20-1/2 ft. on Tradd Street; & bounding W on the part allotted to JONATHAN & SARAH COLLINS; E on GEORGE DUCAT; S on THOMAS ROSE; was allotted to WILLIAM & REBECCA GUY; & whereas REBECCA GUY died & her share descended to WILLIAM GUY the younger, son of said WILLIAM & REBECCA, as heir to his morther, the father holding the premises during his lifetime; & whereas the father, on 12 Mar. 1744, surrendered his title to his son, & WILLIAM GUY the younger, by L & R dated 9 & 10 May 1745 conveyed his share to JOSEPH WATSON, party hereto, gunner of H.M.S. Rose; now WATSON sells to WARHAM. Witnesses: THOMAS EASTON, JOHN SMITH, BIGG YORK. Before JACOB MOTTE, J.P. Proclamation of final agreement in Court at Westminster before JOHN WILLIS, THOMAS ABNEY, THOMAS BURNET & THOMAS BIRCH, justices present, between CHARLES WARHAM, plaintiff & JOSEPH

WATSON & ELIZABETH his wife, defendants, of 1/3 of a lot of 3 a. marked #73, lying in Tradd Street, Charleston, SC; at Islington; when JOSEPH & MARY acknowledged the third part belonged to CHARLES as a gift & that they had quitclaimed to CHARLES for which CHARLES had given them Ⱡ 60 sterling. First proclamation 28 Nov. in Michaelmas term of 22nd year of King; 2nd proclamation on 9 Feb. in Hillary term, 22nd year; 3rd proclamation 18 Apr., Easter term, 22nd year; 4th proclamation 3 June, Trinity term, 22nd year of King. Witness: T. B. LAKE, Dep. Rev. Examined with record in Chirographer's office in Inner Temple, London, 22 Nov. 1749 by THOMAS EASTON. At Custoo Brevium office No. 3 Brick Court Temple; GEORGE CHAMBERS. On 1 May 1750 EASTON appeared before JACOB MOTTE & declared above to be true copy. WILLIAM HOPTON, Register.

Book G-G, p. 189   RICHARD CAPERS, planter, & MARIAN his wife, of
9 & 10 Apr. 1750   Christ Church Parish, Berkeley Co., to DANIEL
L & R   HUGER, ESQ., of St. Johns Parish, Berkeley Co.,
                      for Ⱡ 775 currency, 190 a., part of 700 a.; in
Christ Church Parish; bounding N & W on DANIEL HUGER, ESQ., S & E on
RICHARD CAPERS. Whereas HANNAH WHITE, widow & executrix of JOHN WHITE,
mariner, was authorized by Act of Assembly dated 18 Dec. 1718 to sell 700
a., part of JOHN WHITE'S estate, in order to pay his debts, & on 9 Mar.
1714/15 sold the 700 a. to WILLIAM CAPERS, who devised the 700 a. to his
only son, RICHARD, party hereto; who now sells 100 a. to HUGER. Witnesses: WILLIAM YOUNG, JAMES ERWIN, WILLIAM CAPERS. Before FRANCIS LEJAU,
J.P. WILLIAM HOPTON, Register. Plat by JOHN HENTIE.

Book G-G, p. 195   JOHN MAYRANT, merchant, of Charleston, to DAN-
4 & 5 Jan. 1748   IEL HUGER, ESQ., of St. Johns Parish, Berkeley
L & R   Co., for Ⱡ 1970 currency, 580 a. on head of
                      Great Swamp on Wando River, in St. Thomas Par-
ish, Berkeley Co.; bounding S on JOHN DUTARQUE & DANIEL HUGER; W on JOHN
DUTARQUE; N & E on ANTHONY BONNEAU; also 140 a., part of 240 a. granted
to SUSANNAH MAYRANT on 7 Aug. 1735, on W side Wando River, in St. Thomas
Parish, bounding E on CAPT. HENRY BONNEAU. Whereas the Lords Proprs. on
6 May 1704 granted PETER POITEVINT 600 a. on said Great Swamp, bounded on
all sides by vacant land; & he by L & R dated 21 & 22 Oct. 1725 sold the
600 a. to JAMES NICHOLAS MAYRANT; & he after reconveying 20 a. in the SW
part to POITEVINT; died intestate & the remaining 580 a. with other lands,
descended to his only son & heir, JOHN MAYRANT; & whereas Lt. Gov. THOMAS
BROUGHTON on 7 Aug. 1735 granted SUSANNAH MAYRANT 240 a. on W side of
head of Wando River, & she devised the 240 a. to her son, said JOHN MAY-
RANT, but by a mistake in the original survey running into another's land,
said JOHN MAYRANT was entitled to only 140 a.; now he sells the 2 tracts,
580 a. & 140 a., to HUGER. Witnesses: JOHN HENTIE, JAMES ERWIN. Before
FRANCIS LEJAU, J.P. WILLIAM HOPTON, Register.

Book G-G, p. 202   WILLIAM MOORE, gentleman, of NC (devisee of
24 & 25 May 1748   MRS. SARAH TROTT, widow of NICHOLAS TROTT, Doc-
L & R   tor of Laws), to DANIEL HUGER, ESQ., of Berke-
                      ley Co., for Ⱡ 2500 SC money, 1000 a., English
measure, in Berkeley Co., bounding N on E branch of T of Cooper River; E
on ELIZABETH WILLIS & vacant land; S on vacant land; W on a Hagan Creek;
also 70 a., English measure, on said E branch of T of Cooper River, fronting on Wishboo Creek, bounding E on MARGARET DARNLEY (or DARNEE); other
sides on the HAGAN land; total 1070 a. Whereas WILLIAM, Earl of Craven,
Palatine; CHRISTOPHER, Duke of Albemarle; ANTHONY, Lord Ashley; GEORGE,
Lord Carteret; SIR PETER COLLETON, Baronet; SETH SOUTHILL, THOMAS ARCH-
DALE, & THOMAS AMY; Lords Proprs.; by their express order dated 18 Apr.
1684 & by their letters patent dated 24 Aug. 1688 granted SAMUEL WILSON,
gentleman, said 1000 a., English measure; & he by deed poll dated 28 Aug.
1690, for Ⱡ 41 sold the land to THOMAS GUNN, cooper, of Port Royal Parish,
Island of Jamaica; & whereas GUNN died intestate, leaving 3 nieces, ALICE
GUNN, ELIZABETH GUNN, & REBECCA GUNN, & the 1000 a., amongst other things,
became vested in them jointly; & whereas ALICE Married PETER MILLER,
planter, of Westmoreland Parish, Jamaica & ELIZABETH married 1 PARKER
whom she outlived; & whereas by L & R dated 23 & 24 May 1718, PETER &
ELIZABETH MILLER, ELIZABETH PARKER, widow, & REBECCA GUNN, spinster, sold
the 1000 a. to HENRY MILLER, mariner, of St. Andrews Parish, Island of
Jamaica, for Ⱡ 10 apiece, Jamaican currency; & MILLER, by the name of
CAPT. HENRY MILLER, merchant, & AGNES his wife, of Kingston, Jamaica by

205

L & R dated 20 & 21 Jan. 1720 sold the 1000 a. for Ⱡ 343 Jamaican currency to COL. WILLIAM RHETT, merchant, of Charleston, SC, & SARAH his wife;
& whereas by deed poll dated 3 Aug. 1697 PERCIVAL PAWLEY of SC, for Ⱡ 15
sterling, sold HUMPHREY TURQUETT, shipwright, of SC, 70 a. on E branch
fronting on Wishbow Creek; & whereas the Lords Proprs. on 11 Jan. 1700
granted HUMKRY TURQUET 320 a. in Berkeley Co., bounding N on E branch of
T. of Cooper River; E on Wishbow or Lynch's Creek & on MARGARET DARNLEY;
S on "a HAGAN" land (formerly SAMUEL WILSON); & is all that cedar swamp &
adjoining land between "a HAGAN" & Wishbow Creek; according to grant dated 10 May 1699; & whereas SARAH RHETT outlived her husband, COL. WILLIAM
RHETT, & later married NICHOLAS TROTT, ESQ., of St. Philips Parish,
Charleston; & whereas by L & R dated 27 * 27 Feb. 1729 JAMES BELIN, plant-
er, & SARAH his wife, & EBENEZER FORD, carpenter & JUDITH his wife; all
of Berkeley Co. (SARAH BELIN & JUDITH FORD being daughters & co-heirs of
HUMPHREY TURQUET), sold the 70 a. to NICHOLAS TROTT & SARAH his wife, for
Ⱡ 100, (the 70 a. being part of said 320 a. granted to TURQUET & with
said 1000 a. making the plantation called the HAGAN plantation); & whereas SARAH TROTT, who survived her husband NICHOLAS TROTT, by will dated 25
Nov. 1745 amongst other things bequeathed the Hagan Plantation to her
grandson, WILLIAM MOORE, son of her daughter, CATHERINE MOORE; now he
sells the 2 tracts of 1000 a. & 70 a. to DANIEL HUGER. Witnesses: THOMAS
AKIN, JOHN HENTIE, JAMES ERWIN. Before FRANCIS LEJAU, J.P. WILLIAM HOP-
TON, Register. Plat certified by JOHN HENTIE, Sur., 25 May 1748 accepted
by WILLIAM MOORE on same date.

Book G-G, p. 216 THOMAS BUTLER, planter, & ELIZABETH his wife,
15 & 16 Feb. 1725/6 to COL. ARTHUR HALL, both of Berkeley Co., for
L & R Ⱡ 1250 currency, that tract of land in Charleston fronting 45 ft. on Prince Street, reserv-
ing 27 ft. front from POINSETT'S land to COL. HALL'S land; bounding N on
CAPT. JOHN RAVEN & THOMAS HAYWARD; E on THOMAS BUTLER'S excepted land; S
on Prince Street leading from WILLIAM ELLIOTT'S bridge on Cooper River to
a street leading to New Church; W on MAJ. THOMAS HEPWORTH. Witnesses:
NICHOLAS SMITH, LAWRENCE COULLIETTE. Before THOMAS HEPWORTH, C.J. WIL-
LIAM HOPTON, Register.

Book G-G, p. 221 COL. GEORGE PAWLEY, & ANN his wife, to BENJA-
13 Mar. 1748 MIN TRAPIER, planter, both of Prince George
Sale Parish, Craven Co., for Ⱡ 800 currency, 500 a.
in Craven Co., bounding S on Georgetown River;
W on Three Mile Gully; N on vacant land; E on JOHN PETER SOMERHOOF. Witnesses: WILLIAM POOLE, ISAAC TRAPIER. Before PAUL TRAPIER, J.P. WILLIAM
HOPTON, Register.

Book G-G, p. 224 JOHN OSGOOD, clerk (cleric?), & HANNAH his
29 Mar. 1748 wife, & BENJAMIN BAKER, planter, & SUSANNAH
Release his wife, to BURNABY BRANFORD, planter, all of
St. George Parish, Berkeley Co., for Ⱡ 67:10
(?) currency, 45 a. in St. George Parish, bounding N & W on BURNABY BRAN-
FORD; S on WILLIAM BRANFORD; E on the Kings Highway. Witnesses: PARMENAS
WAY, BENJAMIN CHAPPELL, DANIEL SALDE. Memorial entered in Auditor's of-
fice 5 May 1750 in Bk. 5, fol. 244 by JAMES WEDDERBURN, Dep. Aud. Before
RICHARD WARING, J.P. WILLIAM HOPTON, Register.

Book G-G, p. 228 WILLIAM BRANFORD, planter, of Berkeley Co., to
13 Feb. 1749/50 BURNABY (BARNABY) BRANFORD, planter, of Dor-
Feoffment chester Parish, for Ⱡ 450 currency, 90 a. in
Dorchester, Berkeley Co., being 2 adjoining
lots, #23 & #24, sold with other lands by THOMAS WARING, attorney for
JOSEPH LORD, Minister of the Gospel, formerly of Dorchester, to JOSEPH
HAWKS, who sold to WILLIAM BRANFORD; the 90 a. bounding W on JOHN KITCHEN;
NE on SAMUEL WAY (now BURNABY BRANFORD); SE on land for a highway; SW on
JOSEPH BRUNSON, SR. Witnesses: NATHANIEL BROWN, THOMAS HOLMAN, WILLIAM
BRANFORD, JR. A memorial entered in Auditor's office 5 May 1750 in Bk.
5, fol. 244, by JAMES WEDDERBURN, Dep. Aud. Before JACOB MOTTE, J.P.
WILLIAM HOPTON, Register.

Book G-G, p. 231 CHRISTOPHER WILKINSON, to THOMAS FARR, ESQ.,
9 Dec. 1725 of Colleton Co., for Ⱡ 29 currency, 335 a.,
Sale part of 555 a. in Colleton Col., granted

WILKINSON by the Lords Proprs. on 12 Jan. 1705. Witnesses: HANNAH YONGE, FRANCIS SMITH, EDWARD BRAILSFORD, JR. Enrolled in Auditor's office in Grant Book No. 3, fol. 247 on 13 May 1737. Note: THOMAS FARR, SR. bequeathed the 335 a. to his son, WILLIAM FARR, & his daughters, CATHERINE FARR & MARY FARR, in joint tenancy. WILLIAM FARR is since dead. Before ROBERT YONGE, J.P. WILLIAM HOPTON, Register. On 11 Feb. 1741/2 ROBERT GODFREY appeared before ROBERT YONGE, J.P., & declared that on a late resurvey of 555 a. formerly belonging to CHRISTOPHER WILKINSON, bounding E on WILLIAMSON'S land; N on JACOB BEAMOR; he found his former division line & that FARR'S 335 a. were the southernmost part. WILLIAM HOPTON, Register.

Book G-G, p. 234　　　　　DAVID CRAWFORD, planter, & MARY his wife, of
26 May 1742　　　　　　　Colleton Co., to ANDREW JOHNSTON, merchant, of
Release　　　　　　　　　Charleston, for ₤ 1000 currency, 335 a., in
　　　　　　　　　　　　　Colleton Co., bounding E on THOMAS FARR; S on
JOHN HINDS; W on MR. JENYS. Whereas the Lords Proprs. on 12 Jan. 1705/6 granted CHRISTOPHER WILKINSON 555 a. in Colleton Co., bounding N & E on JACOB BEAMOR & JOHN WILLIAMSON; S & W on vacant land; & whereas on 9 Dec. 1725 WILKINSON sold THOMAS FARR, SR., 335 a. out of the S part of the 555 a.; & FARR by will dated 21 Oct. 1729 bequeathed the 335 a. to his daughters, MARY & CATHERINE, & his son, WILLIAM; & whereas CATHERINE & WILLIAM died & MARY (now MARY CRAWFORD) became sole owner; now she & her husband, sell the 335 a. to JOHNSTON; MARY to appear before BENJAMIN WHITAKER, C.J., to renounce her dower. Witnesses: JAMES KERR, DAVID STILES, GERTRUDE RANTOWLE. Before DANIEL CRAWFORD, J.P. WILLIAM HOPTON, Register.

Book G-G, p. 238　　　　　ANDREW JOHNSTON, merchant, to DAVID CRAWFORD,
28 May 1741/2　　　　　　planter, of Colleton Co., for ₤ 1000 currency,
Release　　　　　　　　　335 a. bounding E on THOMAS FARR; S on JOHN
　　　　　　　　　　　　　HINDS; W on MR. JENYS. (See p. 231, 234).
Witnesses: JAMES KERR, GERTRUDE RANTOWLE, DAVID STILES. Before DANIEL CRAWFORD, J.P. WILLIAM HOPTON, Register.

Book G-G, p. 242　　　　　JOHN MCCANTS, planter, & DOROTHY his wife, to
1 & 2 June 1748　　　　　ELISHA SCREVEN, gentleman, both of Winyaw,
L & R　　　　　　　　　　Craven Co., for ₤ 015 currency, 488 a. in Cra-
　　　　　　　　　　　　　ven Co., 228 a. thereof being part of 400 a.
granted 4 June 1735 to PAUL BRENEAU, & by L & R dated 20 & 21 Aug. 1736 conveyed to WILLIAM BROCKINTON; the other 200 a. of which were granted 14 Dec. 1739 to WILLIAM BROCKINTON; the 2 tracts having been conveyed by BROCKINTON to MCCANTS by L & R dated 21 & 22 Feb. 1739; bounding NW on the Rev. MR. JOHN BAXTER (formerly GEORGE HUNTER); NE on JOHN THOMPSON (formerly vacant land); SE on GEORGE CHICKEN & PAUL BRENEAU (BERNEAU) (now WILLIAM BROCKINTON); SW on BARTHOLOMEW BALL or JAMES CAMPBELL. Witnesses: JOHN SMITH, JAMES CAMPBELL. Memorial entered in Auditor's Office 19 May 1750 in Bk. No. 3, fol. 245, by JAMES WEDDERBURN, Dep. Aud. Before WILLIAM FLEMING, J.P. WILLIAM HOPTON, REgister. Plat of 288 a. surveyed 27 July 1733 for PAUL BERNEAU, being on N branch Black River, in Craven Co.; with addition of 200 a.; re-surveyed by JOHN SWINTON, Dep. Sur.; certified by him 28 May 1748.

Book G-G, p. 248　　　　　JOSEPH BLACK, bricklayer, & ANN (her mark) his
10 & 11 Nov. 1749　　　　wife, to ELIZABETH BAKER, widow, both of
L & R by Mortgage　　　　Charleston, as security on bond of even date
　　　　　　　　　　　　　in penal sum of ₤ 1000 for payment of ₤ 500 SC
money, with interest, on 11 Nov. 1750; part of lot #80 in Charleston, fronting N 40 ft. on Pinckney Street; bounding W & S on GABRIEL GUIGNARD; E 100 ft. on GRIFFITH TUBBS. Witnesses: RICHARD TAYLOR, JOHN REMINGTON. Before WILLIAM PINCKNEY, J.P. WILLIAM HOPTON, Register.

Book G-G, p. 253　　　　　THOMAS FARR, planter, & AMERINTIA, his wife,
21 & 22 Feb. 1744　　　　of Berkeley Co., to PETER LEGER, cooper, of
L & R　　　　　　　　　　Charleston, for ₤ 800 currency, part of lot
　　　　　　　　　　　　　#25 in Charleston, fronting W 34-1/2 ft. on
Church Street; bounding S 120 ft. on WILLIAM BRISBANE & JOHN TOWNSEND; N on part same lot; E on PETER LEGER. Witnesses: RICHARD MASON, ALEXANDER CHISOLME, ARTIMUS ELLIOTT. Before JOHN DART, J.P. WILLIAM HOPTON, Register.

Book G-G, 259   JOHN BOHANNON, planter, of Colleton Co., to
13 Feb. 1749   SAMUEL PERONNEAU, merchant, of Charleston, in
Bond   penal sum of Ł 2000 currency, to keep agree-
                      ment in L & R dated 12 & 13 Feb. 1749. Wit-
nesses: THOMAS LAMBOLL, JOSEPH CHILD. Before ROBERT AUSTIN, J.P. WIL-
LIAM HOPTON, Register.

Book G-G, p. 260   JOHN BOHANNON, planter, of Colleton Co., only
12 & 13 Feb. 1749   son & heir of JOHN BOHANNON the elder, tanner,
L & R   who died intestate; to SAMUEL PERONNEAU, mer-
                      chant, of Charleston, for Ł 450 currency, the
N half of lot #141 in Charleston, on W side of Old Church or Meeting
House Street, towards the S end of the street & near White Point; bound-
ing N 240 ft. on a lane called River Street running W from Old Church or
Meeting House Street; W 50 ft. on a brick wall & land of WILLIAM HARVEY;
S on the S half of lot #141. Whereas the Lords Proprs. on 15 June 1694
granted CHARLES CLARK lot #141 in Charleston which by several mesne conveyances became vested in KATHERINE ENGLISH (afterwards KATHERINE GRANT
afterwards KATHERINE TOOKERMAN, widow), who on 20 Feb. 1723 conveyed to
JOHN BOHANNON the elder. Witnesses: THOMAS LAMBOLL, JOSEPH CHILD. Before ROBERT AUSTIN, J.P. WILLIAM HOPTON, Register.

Book G-G, p. 270   CRAFTON KARWON, planter, of Prince George Par-
7 & 8 July 1747   ish, Craven Co., to JAMES GILLESPIE, planter,
L & R   of Prince Frederick Parish, for Ł 100 currency,
                      500 a. in Craven Co., bounding NW on JOSEPH
LAWS; SE on CRAFTON KARWON; NE & SW on vacnat land; being part of 1000 a.
granted by Gov. WILLIAM BULL to KARWON on 11 Nov. 1743, the 1000 a. bounding NW on JOSEPH LAWS; SE on JAMES TYLER; NE & SW on vacant land. Witnesses: JOHN WESTFIELD, SAMUEL KNOX. Memorial entered in Auditor's office 28 May 1750 in Book No. 3, fol. 246, by JAMES WEDDERBURN, Dep. Aud.
Before WILLIAM FLEMING, J.P. WILLIAM HOPTON, Register.

Book G-G, p. 275   THOMAS FARR, planter, & AMERINTIA his wife, of
24 & 25 Feb. 1740   Berkeley Co., to PETER LEGER, cooper, of
L & R   Charleston, for Ł 650 SC money, half of lot
                      #25 in Charleston, bounding S 100 ft. on JOHN
HARVEY; W on THOMAS FARR; N on THOMAS LEGER; E 32 ft. on Bedon Street.
Witnesses: DAVID STOUT, JOHN BEE. Before THOMAS LAMBOLL, J.P. WILLIAM
HOPTON, Register.

Book G-G, p. 281   JOHN JACKSON, planter, to GEORGE JACKSON, mer-
28 & 29 Jan. 1744   chant, both of St. Bartholomews Parish, Col-
L & R   leton Co., for Ł 250 currency, 2 lots, Nos. 5
                      & 7, in the Town or Village of Jacksonborough.
Witnesses: JONATHAN WITTERS, JOHN WILKINS. Before JAMES SKIRVING, J.P.
WILLIAM HOPTON, Register.

Book G-G, p. 285   WILLIAM WATIES, planter, of Winyaw, eldest son
30 & 31 Mar. 1747   & heir & executor of will of COL. WILLIAM
L & R   WATIES; & CAPT. JOHN COACHMAN, the other sur-
                      viving executor; to CHARLES PINCKNEY, ESQ., &
HENRY PERONNEAU, merchant, of Charleston, for Ł 1000 currency, 4 lots in
Charleston, Nos. 201, 202, 203, & 206. Whereas the Lords Proprs. on 17
May 1694 granted PETER GUERARD, merchant, of Berkeley Co., 4 lots in
Charelston, all bounding E on a marsh at head of COL. DANIEL'S Creek; & W
on the Great Street leading from Oyster Point to the Market Place by
CAPT. SIMMONDS'S lots; lot #201 bounding N on PETER GUERARD'S other lots;
also lot #203, bounding N & S on PETER GUERARD'S lots; also lot #206,
bounding S on PETER GUERARD'S lot; N on MAJ. DANIEL'S Creek & a vacant
lot; also lot #202 bounding N & S on GUERARD'S lots; each lot containing
half an a., English measure; & whereas PETER GUERARD (GIRARDO by will
dated 3 Aug. 1707 devised the residue of his estate, including the 4 lots,
to his beloved daughter JUDITH, who later married HENRY SIMMONDS, planter,
of St. John's Parish; & whereas HENRY SIMMONDS & JUDITH his wife, on 5
Mar. 1727 for Ł 150 currency, conveyed lot #202 to WILLIAM WATIES, planter, of Craven Co., father of WILLIAM, party hereto; & whereas on 11 Jan.
1731, HENRY & JUDITH SIMMONDS, for Ł 550 currency sold said WILLIAM
WATIES, the father, the other 3 lots, Nos. 201, 203, & 206; & he, by will
authorized his executors to sell any of his lots; & appointed his son,

WILLIAM, CAPT. JOHN COACHMAN, & DOROTHY (his wife) his executors & executrix, now WILLIAM WATIES, the son & JOHN COACHMAN, executor, sell the 4 lots to PINCKNEY & PERONNEAU. Witnesses: JOHN VANN, JOSEPH ORAM, EDMUND ATKIN. On 19 Sept. 1749 PINCKNEY & PERONNEAU agreed to divide the 4 lots between them as follows: PERONNEAU to have the NW part of the 4 lots, consisting of the 7 parts of the 4 lots numbered on the plan as 3, 4, 5, 6, 7, 8, & 9 & fronting W 150 ft. from N to S on Old Church Street; & 190 ft. deep, bounding N on Hunter Street laid out on N side said lots; E on CHARLES PINCKNEY'S parts; S on Ellery Street running through said lots; CHARLES PINCKNEY to have all the remaining parts of the 4 lots on S side Ellery Street, & E of HENRY PERONNEAU'S parts; the streets to remain free, public, & in common forever. Witnesses: WILLIAM PINCKNEY, ALEXANDER PERONNEAU. ATKIN appeared before WILLIAM PINCKNEY, J.P. WILLIAM HOPTON, Register.

Book G-G, p. 296   PETER (his mark) LAREY, blacksmith & ELIZABETH
11 Feb. 1747   his wife, to CHARLES PINCKNEY, ESQ., both of
Mortgage by Feoffment   Charleston, as security on bond dated 9 Feb.
                         1747 in penal sum of Ł 1100 for payment of
Ł 550 currency, by paying certain sums on certain dates; the S part of
lot #166 in Charleston lately purchased by LAREY from said PINCKNEY;
fronting 66 ft. from N to S on New Church Street measuring from fence of
present line of fortification; width from N to S at lower or W end 76 ft.
from said fence; depth on S side 178 ft. measured from New Church Street;
on N side along fortification fence, 120 ft.; also the marsh land lying W
of said lot, being part of marsh of Colleton Square sold by PINCKNEY to
LAREY, 82 ft. in depth W, measuring from W end on S side of lot #166; on
N side of said marsh, measuring 160 ft. W along said fortification fence
from end of said 120 ft.; so that the part of lot #166 & the marsh land
hereby sold make together an oblong figure 66 ft. on New Church Street;
width at W end 76 ft.; depth from E to W from New Church Street 260 ft.;
bounding E on said street; S on certain town lots; W on part of marsh of
Colleton Square; N on fortification fence. Witnesses: JAMES BOONE, WILLIAM PINCKNEY. Before JAMES MICHIE, J.P. WILLIAM HOPTON, Register. "I
believe this mortgage has been long ago satisfied, as I have no papers in
my hands respecting it. July 13th, 1820. CHARLES COTESWORTH PINCKNEY,
Executor. Witness: G. PARKER."

Book G-G, p. 300   CHARLES PINCKNEY, ESQ., & HENRY PERONNEAU, mer-
9 June 1750   chant, both of Charleston. Whereas PINCKNEY &
Severance of Joint   PERONNEAU on 31 Mar. 1747 purchased from WIL-
Tenancy   LIAM WATIES & JOHN COACHMAN, of Winyaw, Craven
                        Co., executors of will of COL. WILLIAM WATIES,
4 lots in Charleston, Nos. 201, 202, 203, & 206, on E side Old Church
Street, bounding W on said street leading from Oyster Point by the Market
Place & Place & old church yard; E on the marsh of DANIEL'S Creek; S on
lot #200; N on a vacant lot; & whereas PINCKNEY & PERONNEAU laid out the
4 lots into smaller lots & by agreement dated 19 Sept. 1749 decided to
separate the jointenancy; & PERONNEAU was allotted the NW part of the 4
lots marked 3, 4, 5, 6, 7, 8, & 9 on the plan, fronting W 150 ft. on Old
Church Street; 190 ft. deep; bounding N on Hunter Street on N side of the
4 lots; E on CHARLES PINCKNEY'S lots; S on Ellery Street running through
the 4 lots; CHARLES PINCKNEY being allotted the parts of the 4 lots lying
on S side Ellery Street, & also those parts lying E of PERONNEAU'S 7 lots;
now PINCKNEY releases all his claim to PERONNEAU'S 7 lots; & PERONNEAU
releases all his claim to PINCKNEY'S allotted share; they also agree that
the streets laid out by them shall be public streets. Witness: GEORGE
SEAMAN. Before WILLIAM PINCKNEY, J.P. WILLIAM HOPTON, Register.

Book G-G, p. 305   JANE DUPUY, widow to her granddaughter, JANE
18 & 19 June 1750   GROSSETT, spinster, both of Charleston, for
L & R by Gift   love & affection & for JANE GROSSETT'S care &
                        tenderness toward JANE DUPUY in her sickness &
old age, & for other considerations; 550 a. in Craven Co., bounding SW on
COL. WATIES; SE on JOSEPH MAYBANK; NE on MATTHEW DRAKE; NW on WILLIAM
WRIGHT; as by grant dated 26 June 1736 from LT. GOV. THOMAS BROUGHTON to
JANE DUPUY. Witnesses: JAMES GRINDLAY, GABRIEL GUIGNARD. Before WILLIAM
PINCKNEY, J.P. WILLIAM HOPTON, Register.

Book G-G, p. 311   THOMAS VALLEY, to JOHN HASELL, planter, both

26 & 27 Dec. 1749   of St. Thomas Parish, for Ł 1000 currency, 200
L & R   a., in St. Thomas Parish, Berkeley Co., bound-
                           ing N on SAMUEL KING; NE & SE on PETER SIMONS;
SW on HENRY VIDEAU. Witnesses: WILLIAM BRUCE, BENJAMIN SIMONS. Memorial
entered in Auditor's office 27 Mar. 1750 in Book #3, fol. 243, by JAMES
WEDDERBURN, J.P. Before JAMES AKIN, J.P. WILLIAM HOPTON, Register.

Book G-G, p. 315   SAMUEL SIMONS, SR., & GEORGE KING, executors
17 & 19 Mar. 1749   of will of SAMUEL KING, planter, of St. Thomas
L & R   Parish, Berkeley Co., to JOHN HASELL, planter,
                          of same Parish, at public sale, for Ł 1050 cur-
rency, 804 a. in St. Thomas Parish, bounding NW on GABRIEL MANIGAULT &
THOMAS JOHNSON; NE on MR. HARLESTON; SE on PETER SIMONS & THOMAS VALLEY;
SW on COL. THOMAS ASHBY & HENRY VIDEAU; which 804 a. SAMUEL KING in his
will dated 22 Nov. 1747 gave to his executors in trust to sell to highest
bidder & use the money as directed in said will. Witnesses: BENJAMIN
SIMONS, THOMAS WATTS. Memorial entered in Auditor's office 21 June 1750
in Book No. 3, fol. 247, by JAMES WEDDERBURN, Dep. Aud. Before FRANCIS
LEJAU, J.P. WILLIAM HOPTON, Register.

Book G-G, p. 320   JOHN MACKENZIE, merchant, to JOHN WATSON &
20 July 1749   KENNETH MICHIE, merchants, all of Charleston,
Release in Trust   SC, in trust, as counter security for payment
                          of several sums of money; lot #42 in Charles-
ton, conveyed to MCKENZIE by COL. JOHN BEE, planter, of Colleton Co.;
bounding S 65-1/3 ft. on Broad Street; E 88-1/2 ft. on Church Street; N
67-1/2 ft. on MRS. MARY WATSON; W 89 ft. on heirs of JOHN DANIEL (formerly ROBERT HUME); also part of lot #80, purchased from ANN ELLERY; bounding N 35 ft. on a street from Cooper River; E 150 ft. on ANN ELLERY &
GEORGE HUNTER; S on another street; & W on GEORGE HUNTER; also that piece
of lot bounding N 35 ft. on 2 _____; E 150 ft. on GEORGE HUNTER; W on a
neighborhood street; also purchased from ANN ELLERY; also 124 a. of marsh
land opposite Charleston, bounding E & S on Ashley River; W on Cooper River; N on Hogg Island Creek; also 190 a. in Christ Church Parish, Berkeley
Co., on E side Wando River; as by 2 original grants dated 20 Mar. 1700
from Lords Proprs. to FRANCES SIMMONS; which plantation MCKENZIE purchased from MARY SUTHERLAND (now MARY BISSETT); also part of lot #10 in
Charleston fronting N 20 ft. on CALLIBEUF'S lane (now Elliott Street);
bounding W on WILLIAM ELLIOTT; E 87 ft. on THOMAS ELLIOTT; S to part same
lot; also 5 ft. more fronting Elliott Street; bounding E on the 20 ft.;
87 ft. deep; purchased from JOSEPH SHUTE & ANN his late wife; also 300 a.
in Craven Co., bounding NW on Swinton's Creek; NE on Peedee River & Gordon's Thoroughfare; S on Glens Thoroughfare; SE on GEORGE PAWLEY; also
100 a., half of 200 a., in Craven Co., bounding E on _____ ALLSTON & PAW-
LEY'S Creek; N on WILLIAM SWINTON & _____; W on Peedee River & Gordon's
Thoroughfare; also 500 a., called Westons, in Craven Co., bounding SW on
heirs of HUGH SWINTON; N on said 500 a.; S on Peedee River; also 80 a.,
the N part of a tract of 250 a., in Craven Co., bounding NW on Peedee River; SE on Swinton's Creek; SW on WILLIAM SWINTON; also a piece of land on
Charleston Neck bounding NE on the Broad Path leading to Charleston; SW
on the parsonage & Free School lands; NW on lane leading to Free School;
SE on land formerly belonging to DALLIBACH; extending 125 ft. from the
lane 125 ft. along the Broad Path; being part of 10 a. conveyed by JOSEPH
WRAGG, merchant, of Charleston, to representatives of BARTHOLOMEW GAIL-
LARD. Whereas JOHN WATSON stood security on several of MCKENZIE'S bonds
in several large sums, now amounting with interest, to Ł 17,000 currency;
& whereas MICHIE stood security for MCKENZIE for Ł 4000; & whereas MC-
KENZIE owes large sums to various people, all of which are his personal
contracts; & whereas MCKENZIE wishes to secure his creditors by conveying
his real & personal estate in trust to WATSON & MICHIE, first to secure
them & afterwards to satisfy his other creditors; now MCKENZIE transfers
the above real estate. Witnesses: JAMES WRIGHT, JOHN RATTRAY. Before
WILLIAM PINCKNEY, J.P. WILLIAM HOPTON, Register. List of Creditors:
STEAD & EVANCE; OTHNIEL BEALE; AINSLIE & RAGG (WRAGG); Assigns WILLIAM
PINCKNEY; JOHN DART; SMITH & COSSENS; JOHN SAVAGE; STEPHEN NASH; GEORGE
MCKENZIE; ANDREW PRINGLE; THOMAS GLEN; WILLIAM DAVIDSON; DANIEL CRAWFORD;
MORTON & BRAILSFORD; ROBERT QUASH; STEWARD & REED; JOHN GUERARD; JAMES
KINLOCH; HENRY PATTY; JOSEPH & SAMUEL WRAGG; KENNON & CAMPBELL; CHARLES
BROCKENBURG; COLCOCK & WRAGG; LEWIS MATTHEWS; PATRICK BROWN; SMITH & PAL-
MER; WILLIAM WOODROP.

Book G-G, p. 328   SAMUEL PERKINS, coachmaker, & SARAH his wife,
8 May 1745   to JOHN WATSON, merchant, both of Charleston,
Counterpart of   for Ł 1525 currency, that part of a lot in
Conveyance in Trust   Charleston, bounding E 50 ft. on the street
                          leading by the Presbyterian Meeting House; N
235 ft. on MARY HEXT (formerly JONATHAN TUBB); S on DR. JACOB MARTIN; W
on MRS. MARTHA BOOTH (formerly SAMUEL WEST); in trust for said SARAH PER-
KINS; she to have full control. Whereas by L & R dated 10 & 11 Nov. 1735
from CATHERINE CHICKEN, widow of GEORGE CHICKEN, ESQ., of Berkeley Co.,
to GEORGE ELLERY, gentleman, of Charleston, reciting that whereas ABRAHAM
EVE, ESQ., & HANNAH his wife, by deed poll dated 15 Apr. 1719 sold GEORGE
CHICKEN a lot in Charleston, being the N lot of Schenckingh's Square; &
whereas GEORGE CHICKEN died intestate on 12 Mar. 1726 & the lot was inherited by his oldest son & heir, GEORGE CHICKEN; & that whereas by L & R
dated 8 & 9 June 1731, GEORGE CHICKEN & his wife LYDIA, sold the lot to
CATHERINE CHICKEN; & whereas by said L & R CATHERINE CHICKEN sold to
GEORGE ELLERY; who with his wife ANN, by L & R dated 23 & 24 Nov. 1735
sold the E half of the lot to THOMAS HENNING, merchant, of Charleston,
being the E half of the N lot of Schenckingh Square, bounding E 50 ft. on
the street leading from White Point by the old Presbyterian Meeting House;
W 235 ft. on other half belonging to CHILDERMAS CROFT; N on JONATHAN TUBB
& heirs of EDWARD WEEKLY; S on DR. JACOB MARTIN (formerly DANIEL GIBSON);
& whereas HENNING died intestate in 1741 & BENJAMIN SMITH, JOSEPH SHUTE,
ROBERT THORPE, & ALEXANDER WOOD were legally appointed administrators; &
whereas JOHN SIMPSON the younger, of London, on 29 Nov. last obtained a
judgment against the executors on HENNINGS bond dated in London 28 July
1735 payment of Ł 741:10 British on 20 July then next & obtained a writ
of fieri facias from BENJAMIN WHITAKER, C.J., on 1 Jan. last commanding
the Provost Marshal to collect Ł 11,856 SC & Ł 64:16:10-1/2 for costs; &
whereas SAMUEL HURST, P.M. on 10 Mar. last, at public auction, for Ł 1525
currency, sold to SAMUEL PERKINS, the said lot with its houses; now SAM-
UEL PERKINS & SARAH his wife, convey the lot to JOHN WATSON in trust for
SARAH; the Ł 1525 currency being the property of said SARAH, a part of
her estate before her marriage to SAMUEL, & secured to her by SAMUEL by
certain articles executed before their marriage. Witnesses: THOMAS
BROUGHTON, JR., ANDREW BROUGHTON. Before CHARLES PINCKNEY, J.P. WILLIAM
HOPTON, Register.

Book G-G, p. 336   SAMUEL HURST, Provost Marshal, to SAMUEL PER-
10 Mar. 1744   KINS, at public auction for Ł 1525 currency,
Feoffment   the above named lot (p. 328) which belonged to
                          THOMAS HENNING & which by writ of fieri facias
signed 1 Jan. 1744 by BENJAMIN WHITAKER, C.J., he was commanded to sell
at auction to satisfy a judgment obtained by JOHN SIMPSON, JR., of London.
Witnesses: JOHN REMINGTON, HUGH CARTWRIGHT. Delivery by turf & twig.
Witness: MICHAEL JEANES. Before ROBERT AUSTIN, J.P. WILLIAM HOPTON,
Register.

Book G-G, p. 337   THOMAS DOUGHTY, tavern keeper, of Charleston,
29 & 30 May 1750   & MARY his wife; to the vestry of the Parish
L & R by Mortgage   of St. Thomas, Berkeley Co., as security on a
                          bond (signed also by EDWARD BULLARD & JOHN
BEEKMAN) of even date in penal sum of Ł 2000 for payment of Ł 1000 currency, with interest, on 13 May 1751; the SE quarter part of lot #311 in
Charleston, which lot is part of that square taken up by JOHN ARCHDALE
known as #97, bounding W on WILLIAM SADLER'S part of the square; N on a
street leading from Cooper River by the lots of MAYBANK & PENDARVIS; E on
Broad (?) Street; S on THOMAS CARY, being part (#311) bounds S 120 ft. on
THOMAS CARY; E 50 ft. on a street leading from Market Place to Presbyterian House; N & W on other parts said lot. Witnesses: JAMES WRIGHT, JAMES
MOULTRIE. Before JAMES MICHIE, J.P. WILLIAM HOPTON, Register. On 27
Oct. 1777 ALEXANDER GARDEN, rector of St. Thomas Parish, declared mort-
gage satisfied. Witness: GEORGE SHEED.

Book G-G, p. 343   RAWLINS LOWNDES, Provost Marshal, at public
10 Apr. 1750   auction, to WILLIAM GEORGE FREEMAN, ESQ., of
Sale   Charleston, for Ł 100 SC money, 140 a., Eng-
                          lish measure, in Colleton Co., as granted by
Lords Proprs. 19 May 1699. Whereas BENJAMIN WHITAKER, in May 1746 obtained judgment against WILLIAM WHIPPY, planter, for Ł 2008:6:8 currency &

Ⱡ 31:3:11-1/2 for costs to be levied by the Provost Marshal on WHIPPY'S estate & whereas the P.M. in Oct. 1746 seized 140 a. which remained un - sold until 22 Mar. last for want of buyers, now LOWNDES sells to FREEMAN. Witnesses: WILLIAM BURROWS, WILLIAM WRIGHT. Before JACOB MOTTE, J.P. WILLIAM HOPTON, Register.

Book G-G, p. 344   GEORGE II to CAPT. JAMES LLOYD, 734 a. in Cra-
24 May 1734   ven Co., bounding N on Black River, E on JOHN
Grant & Sale   GREEN; W & S on vacant land; with the usual
                        provisoes. Recorded 19 June 1734 in Secre-
tary's Book B.B., fol. 7, by JAMES MICHIE, Dep. Sec. Memorial entered in
Auditor's office 9 Sept. 1736 by JAMES ST. JOHN, Dep. Aud. Signed by
Gov. ROBERT JOHNSON in Council; T. BADENHOP, C.C. WILLIAM HOPTON, Register. Plat dated 19 Mar. 1733 signed by JAMES ST. JOHN, Sur. Gen., 10
Apr. 1734. On plat is written "Received of THOMAS GADSDEN, ESQ., the sum
of 100 pounds currency in full for the within mentioned tract of 734 a.
of land to whom I make over all my right and title to him his heirs, executors, administrators, & assigns ever. Given under my hand & seal this
25 day of March 1735 at Charleston. JAMES LLOYD. Seal." Witnesses:
ALEXANDER MOORE; & _____. Before HENRY GIBBS, J.P. (broken).

DEEDS BOOK "H-H"
JULY 1750 - MAY 1751

Book H-H, p. 1   THOMAS TUCKER, mariner, of Charleston, to
26 & 27 Dec. 1749   ELIZABETH ROMSEY, widow, of Georgetown, for
L & R   Ⱡ 750 currency, lot #109 in Georgetown, con-
                        taining 1/2 a.; bounding NW on Broad Street; N
on High Street; S on lot #85; NE on lot #110. Witnesses: BENJAMIN ROM-
SEY, JOHN TUCKER. Before THOMAS LAMBOLL, J.P. WILLIAM HOPTON, Register.

Book H-H, p. 4   Sundry affidavits proving a marriage settle-
                        ment made between SAMUEL PERKINS, SARAH CART-
WRIGHT, & JOHN WATSONE whereby SARAH, before her marriage, conveyed all
her estate to JOHN WATSONE in trust for her sole use. JOHN REMINGTON, of
Charleston, testified before OTHNIEL BEALE, J.P., that sometime early in
Oct. 1744 HUGH CARTWRIGHT, bricklayer, of Charleston, delivered to him a
deed on a large skin of parchment the handwriting of which he recognized
as that of JOHN RATTRAY, attorney-at-law, the deed being dated 15 Apr.
1743 & between SARAH CARTWRIGHT, widow, of Charleston, of 1st part; JOHN
WATSONE, merchant, of Charleston, of 2nd part; & SAMUEL PERKINS, chairmaker, of Charleston, of 3rd part; reciting that a marriage was intended
between SARAH & SAMUEL & that it was agreed that all of SARAH'S real &
personal estate should be assigned to WATSONE in trust; & that to the
best of his remembrance the deed conveyed to WATSONE, in trust, 2 plantations, sundry lots in the town of Ashley River, sundry Negroes, plate,
jewels, rings & other things but the number, names & quantities he could
not remember but that the estates conveyed were for the distince use of
SARAH CARTWRIGHT & she reserved the right to change or make void the
trust; deponent further stated that at same time MR. CARTWRIGHT told him
he had agreed with MRS. PERKINS to purchase 216 a. & 11 town lots described in deed of settlement & deponent drew up a declaration to be executed by SARAH CARTWRIGHT (then called SARAH PERKINS) whereby she declared her mind & meaning altered & to make void the trust concerning the
216 a. in Berkeley Co., on S side Ashley River & 11 lots in Ashley River
Town & she ordered WATSONE to convey the 216 a. & 11 lots to HUGH CART-
WRIGHT for Ⱡ 1200 currency, to be paid WATSONE for the use of SARAH PER-
KINS; & deponent delivered the deed of settlement & the declaration to
WATSONE; & that when he persued the deed of settlement it appeared gen-
uine & regularly executed by aforesaid parties & he believed same was
signed by SARAH CARTWRIGHT, JOHN WATSONE & SAMUEL PERKINS; further that
afterwards he drew conveyances of L & R from JOHN WATSONE to HUGH CART-
WRIGHT for the 216 a. & 11 lots & that he well remember he advised HUGH
CARTWRIGHT to have the deed & declaration both proved & recorded to confirm his right to the land & lots. JOHN SNELLING, of Charleston, testified before OTHNIEL BEALE, J.P., that in 1743 he was clerk to JOHN WAT-
SONE, merchant, & well remembers that while he lived at MR. WATSONE'S
SAMUEL PERKINS & MRS. SARAH CARTWRIGHT were married on a Saturday evening

& that on the day of marriage, or the day before, he was asked to witness a paper & when he asked what it was MRS. CARTWRIGHT said it was a deed of settlement to make over everything she had to her own use & that JOHN WATSONE & SAMUEL PERKINS were then present. ABIGAIL WATSONE, wife of JOHN WATSONE, merchant, testified before WILLIAM BULL, JR., that she knows a deed of settlement was agreed upon by her sister SARAH CARTWRIGHT before her marriage with SAMUEL PERKINS; that, such deed was executed before the marriage whereby all SARAH'S estate before marriage, consisting of land, lots, Negroes, plate, jewels, rings & household furniture, were settled absolutely in the power of her sister to be disposed of as she thought proper by deed or by will; that her husband was trustee; that she is sure the deed was written on a large skin of parchment & signed by SARAH CARTWRIGHT, JOHN WATKINS (?) & SAMUEL PERKINS. WILLIAM HOPTON, Pub. Reg.

Book H-H, p. 7
2 & 3 Apr. 1750
L & R by Mortgage

JOHN HUTCHINS, Warden of the Workhouse, Charleston, to JOSEPH WRAGG, JR., & SAMUEL WRAGG, JR., merchants, of Charleston, as security on bond of even date in penal sum of Ł 857:15 for payment of Ł 428:17:6 currency, with interest, on 3 Apr. next; a lot of 1 a. 2 rods, English measure, marked D in plan of Ansonburgh, owned by GEORGE ANSON. Witnesses: PATIENCE CHAPPEL (DELA CHAPPELLE), RICHARD STOBO. Before ROBERT AUSTIN, J.P. WILLIAM HOPTON, Pub. Reg. On 2 Mar. 1752 SAMUEL WRAGG, survivor of WRAGG & WRAGG declared mortgage satisfied. Witness: WILLIAM HOPTON.

Book H-H, p. 11
19 Aug. 1734
Release

ALEXANDER (his mark) LESSLY, planter, of Berkeley Co., to JOHN LUPTON, planter, of Craven Co., for Ł 100 SC money, 650 a. granted LESSLY by GEORGE II on 17 May 1734; in Craven Co., bounding E on Peedee River; N & W on vacant lands; S on JOHN LUPTON. ELIZABETH, wife of ALEXANDER LESSLY, voluntarily renounces her title. Witnesses: RICHARD SINGLETON, MAGNUS BROOKS. Before THOMAS WARING, J.P. WILLIAM HOPTON, Register.

Book H-H, p. 13
14 & 15 Nov. 1749
L & R

WILLIAM SCREVEN, planter, of James Island, & SARAH his wife, to WILLIAM POOLE, planter, of Craven Co., for Ł 1800 SC money, 3 adjoining tracts of 200 a. each, (600 a.) in Craven Co., 1 bounding N on Waha Creek; NW on the middle tract; SE on ELIZABETH ELLIOTT, the middle tract bounding NE & S on the other 2 tracts; E on Weha Bluff; the other bounding SE on Black River; SW on middle tract; NW on JOHN GREEN. Whereas the Lords Proprs. on 14 Sept. 1705 granted JOHN ABRAHAM MOTTE 200 a. in Craven Co., which by several mesne conveyances became vested in WILLIAM SCREVEN in fee; & whereas Gov. ROBERT JOHNSON by 2 grants both dated 24 May 1734 granted WILLIAM SCREVEN as devisee, 2 tracts of 200 a. each which had been laid out to SAMUEL SCREVEN, father of WILLIAM, & devised to WILLIAM; now WILLIAM conveys to POOLE. Witnesses: ROBERT SCREVEN, JOHN REMINGTON. Before ROBERT AUSTIN, J.P. WILLIAM HOPTON, Register.

Book H-H, p. 18
16 & 17 July 1750
L & R

CHARLES PINCKNEY, ESQ., & ELIZABETH his wife, to the Rev. ALEXANDER GARDEN, rector of the Parish, in trust for JOHN WILLIAMS, joiner, & carpenter, of Charleston, for Ł 900 currency, paid by GARDEN on account of WILLIAMS; 2 subdivisions of 4 town lots, #13 & #14, to be held by WILLIAMS for 3 years & then to be sold by GARDEN at public auction if he wished, to pay the debt & costs; WILLIAMS giving GARDEN a bond of even date in penal sum of Ł 900, with interest, on 17 July 1753. Whereas said CHARLES PINCKNEY & HENRY PERONNEAU, merchant, of Charleston on 31 Mar. 1747 purchased from WILLIAM WATIES & JOHN COACHMAN, of Winyaw, Craven Co., executors of will of COL. WILLIAM WATIES, 4 lots in Charleston, #201, 202, 203, 206 on E side Old Church Street, bounding W on said street leading from Oyster Point by the Market Place & old churchyard; E on marsh of Daniel's Creek; S on lot #200; N on a vacant lot; & whereas PINCKNEY & PERONNEAU divided the 4 lots into smaller lots & by agreement dated 19 Sept. 1749, PERONNEAU received the NW part (marked 3, 4, 5, 6, 7, 8, & 9) fronting W 150 ft. on Old Church Street, 190 ft. deep; bounding N on Hunter Street (on N side of the 4 lots); E on the lots allotted to CHARLES PINCKNEY; S on Ellery Street (running through

the 4 lots); PINCKNEY receiving the lots on S side of Ellery Street &
those lying E of PERONNEAU'S 7 parts; & whereas PINCKNEY & PERONNEAU by
deed of partition dated 9 June 1750 divided the land (see G.G. fol. 300-
305); & whereas JOHN WILLIAMS has agreed to purchase 2 of the subdivisions (13 & 14) from CHARLES PINCKNEY; #14 bounding E 37-1/2 ft. on a
street running N & S; S 100 ft. on Ellery Street; W on division #10 sold
by PINCKNEY to CHRISTOPHER BLACK, bricklayer; N on #13; division #13
bounding E 37-1/2 ft. on a street; 100 ft. deep; S on #14; N on #12; W on
CHRISTOPHER BLACK; now GARDEN has advanced the Ł 900, for which WILLIAMS
has conveyed the 2 lots to GARDEN in trust for his (WILLIAMS'S) children;
AMY, MARY & SABINA; GARDEN agreeing to convey to WILLIAMS upon payment of
bond. Witnesses: GEORGE SEAMAN, THOMAS WALKER. Before JAMES WRIGHT,
J.P. WILLIAM HOPTON, Register.

Book H-H, p. 24   JOHN ALLEN, gentleman, to HENRY CHRISTIE, car-
25 May 1743   penter, both of Charleston, releases all claim
Release   to part of lot #268 in Charleston, bounding E
                        140-1/2 ft. on Allen Street; W on THOMAS BEN-
NET; N on an alley of JAMES ST. JOHN & ROBERT THORPE; S 36 ft. on Broad
Street, the part of the lot being part of Hawet's Square, since called
Gibbon's & Allen's Square, granted by the Lords Proprs. to WILLIAM HAWET
& by several mesne conveyances became vested in ANDREW ALLEN, merchant,
of Charleston who bequeathed to his son JOHN ALLEN, party hereto. Whereas on 28 Mar. 1736, for Ł 400, ALLEN conveyed the above lot to CHRISTIE
but the L & R were burned in the "late dreadful fire" on 18 Nov. 1740;
now ALLEN confirms CHRISTIE'S title. Witnesses: WILLIAM SCOTT, WILLIAM
DARROCOTT, SUSANNA SCOTT. Before ROBERT AUSTIN, J.P. WILLIAM HOPTON,
Register.

Book H-H, p. 26   HENRY CHRISTIE, carpenter, of Charleston, to
23 & 24 JULY 1750   the Rev. MR. ALEXANDER GARDEN, rector of St.
L & R by Mortgage   Philip's Parish, Charleston, as security on
                         bond of even date in penal sum of Ł 2000 for
payment of Ł 1000 currency, with interest, on 23 July 1751; part of lot
#268 in Charleston, bounding E 140-1/2 ft. on Allen Street; W on THOMAS
BENNET; N on an alley of JAMES ST. JOHN & ROBERT THORPE; S 36 ft. on
Broad Street; being part of Hawet's Square since called Gibbons & Allen's
Square. Witnesses: ALEXANDER BARON, JOHN REMINGTON. Before ROBERT AUS-
TIN, J.P. WILLIAM HOPTON, Register.

Book H-H, p. 30   JOHN ALLSTON, SR., planter, of Prince George
13 & 14 Feb. 1748   Parish, Craven Co., to JOHN ALLSTON, JR., for
L & R   Ł 5 SC money, 420 a. in Prince George Parish,
                         Craven Co., bounding E on Peedee River; S on
JAMES WALKER (formerly ANTHONY PAWLEY); N on JOHN ALSTON, SR. (formerly
PETER ALLSON); W on vacant land; also 100 a. bounding W on Peedee River;
S on JAMES WALKER; E on a thoroughfare from Peedee to Waccamaw Rivers; N
on JOHN ALLSTON, SR., also 150 a., part of 246 a., between Peedee & Wac-
camaw Rivers, bounding W on the 100 a. on JAMES WALKER; NE on the other
part of 246 a.; E on WILLIAM WATIES. Witnesses: SAMUEL DUPREE, BENJAMIN
MARION, ARCHIBALD JOHNSTON. Before PAUL TRAPIER, J.P. WILLIAM HOPTON,
Register.

Book H-H, p. 33   PAUL HAMILTON, planter, of Colleton Co., eld-
2 & 3 Feb. 1746   est son & heir of PAUL HAMILTON, to JOHN MC-
L & R   LEOD, gentleman, of Colleton Co., for Ł 3000
                         currency, 430 a., English measure, on N side
of Edisto Island granted by the Lords Proprs. on 10 May 1703 to THOMAS
SACHEVERILL; bounding N on Russell's Creek; S on THOMAS BOWER; W on LEWIS
PRICE; E on THOMAS SACHEVERILL & Russell's Creek; also 181 a. of marsh
land granted by letters patent dated 10 Apr. 1738 by Gov. THOMAS BROUGH-
TON to PAUL HAMILTON, bounding S & E on marsh of CAPT. WILLIAM BOWER; N
on PAUL HAMILTON the elder & va-ant marsh; W on HAMILTON & BOWER. Witnesses: WILLIAM JENKINS (a quaker), WILLIAM LAWTON, JEREMIAH CLARK. Before ROBERT AUSTIN, J.P. A memorial entered by the Rev. MR. JOHN MCLEOD
entered in Auditor's Book #3, fol. 220-224 on 29 June 1750 by J. WEDDER-
BURN, Dep. & WILLIAM HOPTON, Register.

Book H-H, p. 37   WILLIAM BOWER, planter, of Edisto Island, &
31 Jan. & 1 Feb. 1740   SARAH his wife, to the Rev. MR. JOHN MCLEOD,

L & R   of said Island, for Ł 1350 SC money, 300 a. on
                               Edisto, bounding S on a large creek & on JOHN
WHITMARSH; N & W on WILLIAM BOWER; E on parsonage land; the 300 a. being
part of 2 tradts of 600 & 270 a., both originally granted by Gov. JOSEPH
BLAKE on 1 Aug. & 2 Jan. 1697. Witnesses: JOHN RATTRAY, JAMES GRINDLAY.
Before ROBERT AUSTIN, J.P. WILLIAM HOPTON, Register.

Book H-H, p. 41   JOHN LUPTON, planter, of St. George's Parish,
22 & 23 Nov. 1749   Berkeley Co., & MARY (her mark) ALLEN (lately
L & R   widow of JOHN LUPTON), of Prince George Parish,
                              Craven Co., executor & executrix of will of
JOHN LUPTON, to WILLIAM POOLE, gentleman, of Georgetown, Craven Co., for
Ł 1411 SC money, 2 plantations of 650 & 171 a., total 821 a.; the 650 a.
granted to ALEXANDER LESSLEY & conveyed by him to JOHN LUPTON, bounding E
on Peedee River; N on vacant land; S on JOHN LUPTON; the 171 a. granted
to LUPTON, bounding E on Peedee River; S on MR. DRAKE; W on vacant land;
N on ALEXANDER LESSLEY. Witnesses: PAUL TRAPIER, JOSEPH ALLEN, JR. Before JOHN OULDFIELD, J.P. WILLIAM HOPTON, Register.

Book H-H, p. 44   DANIEL LAROCHE, merchant, of Prince George Par-
9 June 1744   ish, Craven Co., to JOHN MAN, surgeon, of
Feoffment   Prince Frederick Parish, Craven Co., for Ł 4
                              currency, 550 a. in Prince Frederick Parish,
bounding NW on Peters Creek; SW on WILLIAM BROWN; SE & NE on vacant land;
as by grant dated 12 Apr.   .

Book H-H, p. 46   ROBERT BREWTON, gentleman, of Town of St.
19 Feb. 1746/7   George, Bermuda Islands (alias Somer Islands)
Letter of Attorney   appoints his loving father, COL. ROBERT BREW-
                              TON, of Charleston, SC, his attorney, with
authority to convey to DANIEL BADGER, painter, of Charleston, for Ł 600
currency, the remainder of a certain lot in Charleston, fronting about
36 ft. on N side of Tradd Street, & to assure the title to the lot lying
to the W of the other part of said lot formerly conveyed to DANIEL BADGER
by his said attorney; & with part of the money to purchase a conveyance
from BADGER, to him, of the house & part of lot formerly sold to BADGER.
Witnesses: JOHN WADHAM, WILLIAM RENDALL. WADHAM appeared before JOHN
RUTLEDGE, J.P. WILLIAM HOPTON, Register.

Book H-H, p. 47   AGATHY MILNER, widow of JOHN MILNER; gunsmith,
29 June 1750   of Charleston, to JOHN MILNER & SOLOMON MILNER,
Renunciation of Dower   sons, devisees & executors of will of JOHN MIL-
                              NER, SR., for Ł 700 SC money, agrees to re-
nounce her title of dower in all or any of the real or personal estate of
her late husband. Witnesses: THOMAS LEGARE, FRANCIS HOLMES. Before JA-
COB MOTTE, J.P. WILLIAM HOPTON, Register.

Book H-H, p. 49   JOSEPH DUBOURDIEU, executor of will of ANTHONY
1 & 2 Mar. 1748   WHITE, of Prince Frederick Parish, Craven Co.,
L & R   to WILLIAM GREEN, planter, of Prince George
                              Parish, Craven Co., for Ł 75 currency, 400 a.,
part of 1620 a.; on W side of road between Georgetown & Prince Frederick's Church; bounding S on WILLIAM SMITH; N on CAPT. ANTHONY WHITE; E on
MEREDITH HUGHES. Whereas Lt. Gov. THOMAS BROUGHTON on 12 Dec. 1735 granted ANTHONY WHITE 1620 a. on S side Black River, in Craven Co., bounding N
on MEREDITH HUGHES, ESQ.; W on JOHN GOUGH; S on JOHN LANE; SE & E on
GEORGE HAMBLIN & STEPHEN LEAYCROFT (since in possession of ANTHONY WHITE);
& whereas ANTHONY WHITE in his will ordered his real & personal estate
sold to pay his debts; now DUBOURDIEU sells 1 tract to WILLIAM GREEN.
Plat 15 Nov. 1750 by P.V. (?) HASELL. Witnesses: WILLIAM POOLE, JR.,
SAMUEL DUBOURDIEU. Before PAUL TRAPIER, J.P. WILLIAM HOPTON, Register.

Book H-H, p. 53   RAWLINS LOWNDES, Provost Marshal of SC, to
16 Aug. 1750   ALEXANDER PERONNEAU, gentleman, of Charleston,
Sale on Execution   at public auction, lot #211 (by mistake called
                              #176) & part of adjoining lot #280. Whereas
JORDAN ROCHE, gentleman, of Charleston, on 3 Apr. 1750 recovered against
MATHEW ROCHE, merchant, of Charleston, a judgment for Ł 102,000 SC money,
& Ł 28:18:1-1/2 currency for costs (JAMES GRAME, C.J.) & RAWLINS LOWNDES,
as P.M., was commanded to levy those sums on the goods, chattles, lands,

215

& tenements of said MATTHEW ROCHE; now LOWNDES sells 2 lots at auction to
PERONNEAU; lot #211 (by mistake in some former conveyance called #176)
fronting 97-1/2 ft. on Meeting Street; 232-1/2 ft. deep; & part of adjoining lot #280; the 2 being marked A on the plat; & LOWNDES also entered
upon the residue of lot #280 (adjoining lot #211) fronting 75 ft. on Meeting Street & 232-1/2 ft. deep; as contained within the green lines of
plat marked B; which lot marked A said MATHEW ROCHE held in fee simple; &
which lot marked B he held in fee simple after the death of MARY BREWTON,
widow, who by deed dated 5 Mar. 1745 is tenant for life; now LOWNDES sells
sells the lot & buildings shown within lines of plat A to PERONNEAU for
Ł 6310 currency & for Ł 690 currency sells to said ALEXANDERPERONNEAU, at
public auction, the reversion of the part of lot represented as contained
within the green lines of plat B to hold immediately after MARY BREWTON'S
death. Witnesses: JAMES HUNTER, ROBERT COLLINS. Before JAMES WRIGHT,
J.P. Plat by GEORGE HUNTER, Sur. Gen., certified 6 Aug. 1750. WILLIAM
HOPTON, Register.

Book H-H, p. 55
18 Aug. 1750
Assignment of Lease

WILLIAM TURNER, peruke-maker, to THOMAS CORKER,
merchant, both of Charleston, for Ł 700 currency, his lease of 2 lots in Charleston, with
buildings & improvements. Whereas by lease
dated 18 Oct. 1745 JOHN TOWNSEND, cooper, of Charleston, leased to WIL-
LIAM TURNER for 30 years at Ł 30 a year, part of 2 lots #24 & #25, in
Charleston, bounding N 74 ft. on PETER LEGER, cooper; S on a small tenement occupied by ELIZABETH SERJEANT; W on buildings erected on part of
said lots by JOHN TOWNSEND; E 30 ft. on Bedon's Alley; now TURNER assigns
his leaseunexpired term to CORKER. Witnesses: JAMES GRINDLAY, RICHARD
PEAKE. Before JOHN DART, J.P. WILLIAM HOPTON, Register.

Book H-H, p. 58
16 Aug. 1750
Special Bond

JORDON ROCHE, gentleman, of Charleston, gives
ALEXANDER PERONNEAU, gentleman, of Charleston,
a bond in penal sum of Ł 4000 currency to protect PERONNEAU'S title to certain property
(see p. 53). Whereas JORDAN ROCHE recovered an judgment against MATHEW
ROCHE for Ł 102,000 currency, & Ł 29:18:1-1/2 currency for costs, & RAW-
LINS LOWNDES, P.M., was commanded to sell MATHEW ROCHE'S real estate, being part of lot #280 fronting 87-1/2 ft. on Meeting Street & 232-1/2 ft.
deep; marked A on the plat; also the remainder of lot #280, as contained
within the green lines on plat & marked B; & whereas sold the 2 parcels
of land to PERONNEAU (to have B after the death of MARY BREWTON, widow,
tenant for life); now ROCHE gives PERONNEAU a special bond of indemnity.
Witnesses: JAMES HUNTER, ROBERT COLLINS. Before JAMES WRIGHT, J.P. WIL-
LIAM HOPTON, Register.

Book H-H, p. 60
16 Aug. 1750
Bond

JORDAN ROCHE gives ALEXANDER PERONNEAU another
bond of the penalty of Ł 4000 currency to protect PERONNEAU'S title to lot #211 formerly
belonging to MATHEW ROCHE (see p. 53). Wit-
nesses: JAMES HUNTER, ROBERT COLLINS. Before JAMES WRIGHT, J.P. WILLIAM
HOPTON, Register.

Book H-H, p. 63
25 Mar. 1750
L & R by Mortgage

FRANCIS ROCHE, & ANN his wife, to EBENEZER
SIMMONS; all of Charleston; as security on
bond of even date in penal sum of Ł 20,000 for
payment of Ł 10,000 currency, with interest,
on 25 Mar. next; 907 a. on which FRANCIS ROCHE lately lived; in Berkeley
Co., at head of E branch of Cooper River; part of 5000 a. granted by the
Lords Proprs. to DOMINICK ROCHE, & commonly called COLLETON BARONY; bound-
ing S & N on DANIEL HUGER; NE on the Rev. MR. THOMAS HASELL; SE on ROBERT
QUASH; there being another mortgage to the vestry of St. Thomas Parish
for Ł 700 & interest, dated 24 & 25 Mar. 1742. Witnesses: AUSTIN ROBERT
LOCKTON, EBENEZER SUMMONS, JR. Before ALEXANDER GORDON, J.P. WILLIAM
HOPTON, Register.

Book H-H, p. 71
26 July 1737
Confirmation

GEORGE MOORE, gentleman, of New Hanover, Cape
Fear, NC to confirm conveyances from his father, ROGER MOORE, to MAURICE HARVEY, releases
to WILLIAM HARVEY, an infant, heir of said
MAURICE HARVEY, all claim to 2 town lots, with buildings thereon. Whereas MARY MOORE, whose maiden name was MARY RAYNER, mother of GEORGE MOORE,

owned as of fee in her own right, several tracts of land & several lots in Charleston; & whereas she married ROGER MOORE, then of Berkeley Co., SC, now of Cape Fear, NC, & on her death left said GEORGE her only child & heir; but ROGER MOORE the father held the property as tenant for life by Courtesy of England & by L & R dated 1 & 2 May 1732 sold to MAURICE HARVEY 2 of the town lots #176 & #212 bounding N on JOHN CARMICHAEL; S on BRYAN RHALY; E on a street; W on a street; but whereas the father did not have power to sell; but GEORGE MOORE acknowledges to have received full value for the lots & wished to confirm the title to the heirs of MAURICE HARVEY who died intestate, leaving his eldest son WILLIAM, an infant, now resident in Cape Fear, NC; now GEORGE MOORE confirms the title to the 2 lots to said infant. Witnesses: THOMAS AKIN, REBECCA COKE, SARAH SMITH. AKIN appeared before ROBERT BROWN, J.P. WILLIAM HOPTON, Register.

Book H-H, p. 74   CAPT. ABRAHAM EVE, ESQ., of Colleton Co., &
6 Jan. 1710   SARAH his wife, with her free consent, to Mad-
Feoffment   am ANN HOLLAND, spinster, of Charleston, for
                      Ł 200 currency, lot #83, bounding E on a
street parallel with Cooper River; N on JOHN WHITMARSH; S on a street running from Cooper River by JONATHAN AMORY, DR. GEORGE FRANKLIN, & MRS. FRANCIS SYMONS; W on FRANCIS SYMONS. Whereas WILLIAM, Earl of Craven, Palatine, & the Lords Proprs. by THOMAS SMITH trustee, on 12 June 1694, granted JOHN WILLIAMSON, planter, of Colleton Co., lot #83 in Charleston containing 1/2 a. English measure; & whereas JOHN WILLIAMSON on 7 Apr. 1699 conveyed the lot to WILLIAM RUBERRY, cooper, of Berkeley Co., who on 26 Mar. 1710 conveyed to ABRAHAM EVE, party hereto; now EVE conveys to ANN HOLLAND. Witnesses: JOHN CORK, JR., PERCIVAL PAWLEY, THOMAS HEPWORTH. On 15 June 1747 GEORGE PAWLEY of Craven Co., recognized PERCIVAL PAWLEY'S signature, PERCIVAL having been dead for several years. Before JAMES WRIGHT, J.P. WILLIAM HOPTON, Register.

Book H-H, p. 77   THOMAS LYNCH, planter, of Santee, & ELIZABETH
14 & 15 Sept. 1750   his wife, to THOMAS SMITH, SR., merchant, of
L & R   Charleston, for Ł 3880 SC money, 1817 a. in
                    Christ Church Parish, Berkeley Co., bounding W
on Wando River & GEORGE LOGAN; N on GEORGE LOGAN & vacant marsh; E on ARNOLDUS VANDERHORST; S on JOHN RUTLEDGE. Whereas JOHN, Earl of Bath, Palatine, & the Lords Proprs. granted THOMAS LYNCH, father of said THOMAS, party hereto, 400 a., English measure, in Berkeley Co., as by plat by ED-MUND BELLINGER, Sur. Gen. dated 2 Oct. 1702, bounding W on Wando River; S on a creek; E on FENWICKE'S marsh; N on vacant land; & whereas Gov. CHARLES CRAVEN on 19 Mar. 1715 granted THOMAS LYNCH, the father, 270 a. in Christ Church Parish, on S side Wando River; as by plat certified by THOMAS BROUGHTON, Sur. Gen., on 10 Mar. 1713, bounding N on Wilson Neck Creek; E on MR. VANDERHORST; S on CAPT. ROBERT FENWICKE; E & W on THOMAS LYNCH; as by plat certified by RICHARD BERESFORD, Sur. Gen., 18 Mar. 1713; which 3 adjoining tracts should have contained 990 a. but by a late survey certified by GEORGE HUNTER, Sur. Gen., dated 16 June 1750 is shown to only 817 a.; which 817 a. were inherited by THOMAS LYNCH, party hereto; now he conveys to THOMAS SMITH. Witnesses: MARY BONELL, WILLIAM WATIES. Before WILLIAM PINCKNEY, J.P. WILLIAM HOPTON, Register.

Book H-H, p. 84   JOSEPH RUSSELL, planter, of Berkeley Co., to
11 & 12 June 1750   ALEXANDER MCGRIGOR, innkeeper, of Charleston,
L & R   for Ł 173:5 SC money, 1000 a. in Colleton Co.,
                    granted by Lt. Gov. THOMAS BROUGHTON, on 12
Aug. 1737, to JEREMIAH RUSSELL, father of JOSEPH, party hereto, & conveyed by JEREMIAH to JOSEPH on 11 Feb. 1739; bounding SE on JOHN ELDERS; SW on Pon Pon River; other sides on vacant land. Witnesses: JAMES GRINDLAY, CHARLES LOWNDES. Before JAMES WEDDERBURN, J.P. WILLIAM HOPTON, Register.

Book H-H, p. 87   JOSEPH WRAGG, merchant, & JUDITH his wife, to
9 Feb. 1731   JAMES CROKATT, merchant, all of Charleston;
Release   for Ł 2450 SC money, part of 2 lots, #38 &
                    #81, fronting 41-1/2 ft. on N side of Broad
Street, in Charleston, bounding E 144 ft. on SAMUEL WRAGG; W on TIMOTHY BELLAMY & ELIZABETH BURETELL; N on WILLIAM BOLLARD; according to deed of feoffment dated 8 Apr. 1717 from the Rev. MR. WILLIAM GUY & REBECCA his wife, JAMES MCCALL & SARAH his wife, & MARY BASDEN, spinster, to JOSEPH WRAGG. Witnesses: RICHARD LAMBTON, ROBERT HUME. Before JAMES KINLOCH,

J.P.

Book H-H, p. 90   VIOLET (her mark) JINKS, widow & executrix of
19 & 20 July 1750   will of THOMAS JINKS; SAMUEL EVANS, JAMES SCRE-
L & R   VEN, & WILLIAM WILKINS, executors of will of
                          THOMAS JINKS, planter, of John's Island, St.
Johns Parish, Colleton Co., of 1st part; to SOLOMON LEGARE, JR., planter,
of Colleton Co., for ₺ 300 currency, 100 a. on John's Island, bounding
NW on JOSEPH STANYARNE; E on SOLOMON LEGARE, SR.; S on WILLIAM WILKINS; W
on SOLOMON LEGARE, JR. Whereas THOMAS JINKS owned certain lands & tenements, particularly the above 100 a., & by will dated 19 July 1749 ordered his real & personal estate not otherwise mentioned to be sold & the
proceeds equally divided; & appointed his wife VIOLET, executrix & SAMUEL
EVANS, JAMES SCREVEN, & WILLIAM WILKINS, executors, of his will; now they
sell 100 a. to LEGARE. Witnesses: JOHN OWEN, JOHN PRUE. Before THOMAS
LAMBOLL, J.P. WILLIAM HOPTON, Register.

Book H-H, p. 94   HENRY ROACH, planter, of the WELCH tract, Cra-
4 & 5 Dec. 1749   ven Co., to ROBERT WILLIAMS, yeoman, of same
L & R   place, for ₺ 200 currency, 150 a. in the WELCH
                          tract, bounding E on CUNNINGHAM; N on SAMUEL
WIGGINS; S & W on vacant land. Witnesses: ROBERT ROBINSON, HUGH DOYLE,
ELIZABETH (her mark) OFREEL. Before WILLIAM JAMES, J.P. WILLIAM HOPTON,
Register.

Book H-H, p. 98   JAMES ROGERS, planter, of Berkeley Co., to
18 Apr. 1746   SAMUEL WAINWRIGHT, butcher, as security on
Mortgage   bond of even date in penal sum of ₺ 800 for
                         payment of ₺ 400 currency, with interest, on
18 Apr. next; 65 a., part of 100 a. commonly called David's Point, in
Berkeley Co.; granted by Gov. ROBERT GIBBES & the Lords Proprs. to NATHAN-
IEL WILLIAMS, a Free Negro; & by his will dated 16 Nov. 1729 bequeathed
to ANN EDWARDS, present wife of JAMES ROGERS; the 65 a. bounding N on the
Widow BUCKLEY; S & E on a creek of Cooper River that runs around THOMAS
Island; W on a marsh; also to WAINWRIGHT 2 Negro slaves. Witnesses: JOHN
FOUQUET, JOHN WHEELER. Before ROBERT AUSTIN, J.P. Entered in Secre-
tary's Book R.R. fols. 387-389 by JOHN CHAMPNEYS, D.S. WILLIAM HOPTON,
Register.

Book H-H, p. 99   HENRY PERONNEAU, merchant, & ELIZABETH his
19 & 20 Apr. 1750   wife; JAMES MICHIE, ESQ., & MARTHA his wife;
L & R   WILLIAM STEWART, ESQ., & ANN his wife; JOHN
                         CATTELL, son & heir of SARAH CATTELL & co-heir
with said ELIZABETH, MARTH & ANN (daughters of ARTHUR HALL, ESQ., of
James Island); all of Charleston, of the 1st part; to GEORGE SEAMAN, merchant, of Charleston; for ₺ 5 & other considerations, 800 a., part of a
tract called Rattlesnake Neck, in Granville Co., bounding E on SAMUEL
SMALL; S & N on a branch of Port Royal River; NW on ARTHUR HALL; which
tract was granted 8 Aug. 1735 to HENRY PERONNEAU & JAMES OSMOND, then
surviving executors of will of ARTHUR HALL; also lot #26 in Beaufort,
bounding S on the Bay; W on lot #25; N on Port Royall Street; E on lot
#27; also lot #77 in Beaufort, bounding S on lot #78; W on Scott Street;
N on a public lot; E on lot #81; which 2 lots (26 & 77) were granted by
the Lords Proprs. on 8 Aug. 1717 to ARTHUR HALL. Witnesses: TIMOTHY
MORGRIDGE, JOHN TROUP. Before JOHN LINING, J.P. WILLIAM HOPTON, Register.

Book H-H, p. 104   SAMUEL SMITH, butcher, & MARY his wife, of 1st
29 Oct. 1750   part; DAVID MONGIN, watchmaker, & ELIZABETH
Deed of Partition   his wife of 2nd part; all of Charleston.
                         Whereas GEORGE ANSON, ESQ., by his attorney
BENJAMIN WHITAKER, by deed of feoffment dated 20 Feb. 1745 sold to SAMUEL
SMITH & DAVID MONGIN a 1 a. lot, marked R in the plan of Ansonburgh, with
right of passage through the most convenient street to & from the landing
place on a creek running through the marsh on Cooper River; & whereas
SMITH & MONGIN have agreed to divide the land into 2 equal parts, SMITH
to have the S half, MONGIN to have the N half; now, each being fully satisfied with said division, SAMUEL & MARY SMITH confirm DAVID & ELIZABETH
MONGINS title to the N half; bounding S on SAMUEL SMITH'S half; N on the
street called the Thirty Foot Street; E on JOHN PADGETT; W on a lot

fronting the Broad Path leading from Charleston belonging to DAVID MONGIN on which there is a brick house & other buildings; DAVID MONGIN, & ELIZA- BETH his wife, being pleased with the partition, confirm SAMUEL & MARY in their title to the S half of said lot, marked R in the plan of Anson- burgh, bounding N on DAVID MONGIN'S half; E on JOHN PAGETT; S & W on SAM- UEL SMITH'S lot. Witnesses: JOHN TROUP, EDWARD SMITH. Before JAMES WED- DERBURN, J.P. WILLIAM HOPTON, Register.

Book H-H, p. 108   DAVID MONGIN, watchmaker, & ELIZABETH his
2 & 3 Nov. 1750   wife, to HENRY PERONNEAU, merchant; all of
L & R by Mortgage   Charleston; as security on bond of even date
                       in penal sum of L 3200 for payment of L 1600
SC money, with interest, on 2 Nov. next; 800 a., part of a tract called
Rattlesnake Neck, in Granville Co., bounding E on SAMUEL SMALL; S on a
branch of Port Royal River; NW on ARTHUR HALL (late of James Island); N
on another branch of Port Royal River; which tract of 800 a. was sold by
said HENRY PERONNEAU & ELIZABETH his wife; JAMES MICHIE, ESQ., & MARTHA
his wife; WILLIAM STEWART, ESQ., & ANN his wife; & JOHN CATTELL (son &
heir of SARAH CATTELL & coheir with ELIZABETH, MARTHA & ANN, daughters of
said ARTHUR HALL) to GEORGE SEAMAN, merchant, of Charleston by L & R dated 19 & 20 Apr. 1750; & by L & R dated 1 & 2 Nov. 1750 sold by SEAMON to
MONGIN; also 1 a. 2 rods, English measure, in Ansonburgh, near Charleston,
marked with the letter C on plan of lands of GEORGE ANSON (now Lord AN-
SON); which piece of land by deed of feoffment dated 8 Apr. 1745 was sold
by ANSON, through his attorney BENJAMIN WHITAKER, to DAVID MONGIN; also
that half of a lot marked R on the plan sold by deed of feoffment dated
29 Feb. 1745 by ANSON to DAVID MONGIN & SAMUEL SMITH, SR., which by deed
of partition dated 29 Oct. 1750 was divided into 2 equal parts, SMITH
getting the S half & MONGIN the N half (see p. 104). Witnesses: TIMOTHY
MORGRIDGE, JOHN TROUP. Before JOHN LINING, J.P. WILLIAM HOPTON, Register. NB Note on P. 112. Part of this mortgage is discharged, that is,
the 1 a. & 2 roods in Ansonburgh marked C on plat, & the half of 1 a. in
Ansonburgh marked R, with all houses, see record in Bk. S.S. p. 183, but
remains in full force as to plantation & other premises. On 9 Feb. 1758
JAMES MICHIE for himself, & as attorney to COL. WILLIAM STEWART, acknow-
ledged full satisfaction of mortgage (assigned & transferred by HENRY
PERONNEAU to WILLIAM STEWART & JAMES MICHIE) by the hands of COL. DANIEL
HEYWARD. Witness: THOMAS BEE. Proved by THOMAS BEE before JOHN RATTRAY,
J.P. on 9 Feb. 1758.

Book H-H, p. 115   HERCULES HOYT, of St. Thomas Parish, to JAMES
29 & 30 July 1745   CROKATT, merchant, of London, as security for
L & R by Mortgage   payment of L 189:5, with interest, on 1 Feb.
                      next; 10 a., with a house thereon where COYTE
now lives, being part of 100 a. on Davis Point Island, bounding N on the
Widow BUCKLEY; S & E on a creek of Cooper River that runs round Thomas
Island; W on marsh. Witnesses: JOHN PALMER, JOHN BROWN. Before ALEXAN-
DER CRAMAHE, J.P. WILLIAM HOPTON, Register.

Book H-H, p. 119   SARAH JOHNSTON (formerly SARAH COLLINGS, widow
25 & 26 Oct. 1750   of JONATHAN COLLINGS the elder, mariner, of
L & R   Charleston, to JONATHAN COLLINGS, the younger,
                      planter, of Berkeley Co., for L 1900 currency,
4 tracts, total 150 a., English measure, in St. Philips Parish on W side
of High Road, including a small island SW of said plantation on W side of
a creek of Ashley River, bounding E near MR. CARTWRIGHT; the plantation
bounding N on 6-1/2 a. belonging to a Free Negro woman named JUDITH & on
The Rat Trap; W on marsh; S on marsh & creek & GEORGE MARSHALL; E on 2
pieces of marsh & on the High Road of Charleston Neck leading into the
country & on said 6-1/2 a. Witnesses: SAMUEL HURST, JOHN PAUL GRIMKE,
WILLIAM WRIGHT. Before THOMAS LAMBOLL, J.P. WILLIAM HOPTON, Register.

Book H-H, p. 123   JONATHAN COLLINGS, planter, & MARY his wife,
26 & 27 Oct. 1750   of Berkeley Co., to BENJAMIN D'HARRIETTE, mer-
L & R   chant, of Charleston, for L 2000 currency, 4
                      tracts, total 150 a., English measure, in St.
Philips Parish, including a small island on E side Ashley River, & SW of
said plantation & on W side of a certain creek, near Charleston Neck near
CARTWRIGHT'S land; bounding N on 6-1/2 a. now owned by a Free Negro woman
named JUDITH & on land called the Rat Trap; W on marsh; S on marsh, a

creek & GEORGE MARSHALL; E on 2 pieces of marsh & on High Road & on said 6-1/2 a.; according to plat certified 16 Oct. 1750 by THOMAS BLYTHE, Dep. Sur. Witnesses: JOHN MCCALL, JONATHAN BADGER. Before THOMAS LAMBOLL, J.P. Memorial registered in Auditor's office 1 Nov. 1750 in Book 3, fol. 253 by JAMES WEDDERBURN, Dep. Aud. WILLIAM HOPTON, Register.

Book H-H, p. 129
28 Sept. 1750
Release of Reversion
& Equity of Redemption

DAVID CHRISTINA to GABRIEL GUIGNARD for good causes & considerations, his claim to a piece of land in Ansonburgh, marked F in the general plan, 41-1/9 ft. x 200 ft., bounding N by a common avenue dividing lot F into 2 parts; E & S on HUGH ANDERSON; W on the Broad Road or Path leading to Charleston; the release being endorsed on a mortgage from CHRISTINA to GUIGNARD (see Book D.D., pages 173-176). Witnesses: CHARLES JACOB PICHARD, JOHN REMINGTON. Before ALEXANDER CRAMAHE, J.P. FRANCES CHRISTINA, wife of DAVID releaser her title of dower. WILLIAM HOPTON, Register.

Book H-H, p. 130
27 Sept. 1750
Feoffment

RICHARD COCHRAN ASH, planter, of Edisto Island, to RICHARD ASH, planter (father of RICHARD COCHRAN ASH), & MARTHA his wife, for dutiful respect, & natural love & affection, & L 100 SC money, for their natural lives, an entire island of 430 a. commonly called Dedcott's Island, bounding E on marsh; S on a large creek; N on Tooboodoo Creek; which island was granted by the Lords Proprs. on 11 May 1699 to JOHN DEDCOTT; who bequeathed half (215 a.) to his son JOHN DEDCOTT, & the other half (215 a.) to his son ABRAHAM DEDCOTT. JOHN DEDCOTT dying intestate, his eldest son & heir, JOHN, inherited & conveyed his half to RICHARD COCHRAN ASH; ABRAHAM DEDCOTT having sold his half to THOMAS CROLL, who bequeathed his half to his son JOHN CROLL, who sold to RICHARD COCHRAN ASH, who now became owner of both halves, & conveys the entire island to his parents & their children. Witnesses: SAMUEL DAVISON, JAMES LYNCH. Before JAMES BULLOCK, J.P. WILLIAM HOPTON, Register.

Book H-H, p. 133
1 & 2 Oct. 1750
L & R

PURCHASS BERRIE, planter, of Colleton Co., to WILLIAM ELLIOTT, planter, of St. Andrews Parish, for L 600 currency, 200 a. (commonly called Bear Island which her father purchased from JOHN FABIAN to whom it was granted) in St. Bartholomews Parish, Colleton Co., between Pon Pon & Ashepoo Rivers; bounding W on vacant land; N E & S on marsh & bay swamp laid out to JAMES BERRIE, her late husband; also 800 a. of marsh & bay land granted to her husband JAMES BERRIE, bounding NW & S on said 200 a. Witnesses: JOHN COCKFIELD, JOHN MORGIN. Before WILLIAM PINCKNEY, J.P. WILLIAM HOPTON, Register.

Book H-H, p. 137
3 & 4 Aug. 1722
Sale

DANIEL DONOVAN of Craven Co., to CHARLES BURNHAM, of Berkeley Co., for L 1100 currency, 500 a. in Craven Co., S on Santee River; also 500 head of neat cattle with earmarks & brands frequenting said land or cow-pen. Witnesses: PETER CATTELL, JOHN JONES. Memo of ear-marks & brands: 1st: a fork in right ear & crop & 3 slits in left; 2nd: upper keal & under keal in right & crop & 3 slits in ear left; 3rd: fork in left ear & upper keal & under in left; 4th: fork in left, hole in right, all branded DD/all the hogs. WILLIAM GREENLAND identified handwriting of CATTELL & JONES before ALEXANDER CRAMAHE, J.P. WILLIAM HOPTON, Register.

Book H-H, p. 139
25 & 26 Nov. 1750
L & R by Mortgage

BENJAMIN SINGELLTON, planter, & REBECCA his wife, to JAMES KINLOCH, ESQ., all of St. James Goose Creek Parish, Berkeley Co., as security on bond of even date in penal sum of L 1706 for payment of L 853 SC money on 26 Nov. 1751; 488 a. on E side Four Hole Swamp, bounding SE & NE on THOMAS SINGLETON & vacant land; SW & NW on Four Hole Swamp & vacant land; being part of 3 tracts laid out to STEPHEN MONCK, ESQ., son of JOHN MONCK, & RICHARD SINGELLTON severally. Witnesses: JAMES GRINDLAY, ROBERT WILLIAMS, JR. Before JAMES WEDDERBURN, J.P. WILLIAM HOPTON, Register.

Book H-H, p. 143
2 & 3 Mar. 1746
L & R in Trust

WILLIAM PINCKNEY, ESQ., & RUTH his wife, of Charleston, to JORDAN ROCHE, ESQ., JOHN MCKENZIE, & BRANFILL EVANCE, merchants of

Charleston, as trustees for themselves & other creditos, as security on
debts listed in a schedule attached to a certain deed poll or assignment
of even date of all the slaves & other personal estate belonging to WIL-
LIAM PINCKNEY; 2 tracts of 200 a. each on Horse She Savannah, in Colleton
Co., conveyed by L & R dated 23 & 24 Mar. 1737 to WILLIAM PINCKNEY by
JOHN WOODWARD & RICHARD WOODWARD, sons & devisees of JOHN WOODWARD, plant-
er; also 250 a. on Horse Shoe Savannah which PINCKNEY purchased from JOHN
REID & which formerly belonged to JOHN PAYCOM & was conveyed by him to
JONATHAN BETTISON (except such part as WILLIAM PINCKNEY conveyed to JOHN
PAYCOM); also 392 a. in Colleton Co. bounding NE on GEORGE ATWOOD; SE on
WILLIAM EBBERSON; S & SW on JAMES STANYARD & JOHN WOODWARD; other sides
on JOHN WOODWARD; also 181 a. in Colleton Co., bounding N on WILLIAM EB-
ERSON, S on WILLIAM PINCKNEY; E on GEORGE ATWOOD; W on JOSEPH DINGLE;
also 107 a. in Colleton Co., bounding E on THOMAS TUCKER; W & NW on
GEORGE ATWOOD & on OWEN BAGER; S & SE on WILLIAM EBERSON & EDWARD NORTH;
also 1700 a. & 1 lot #16 in Kingston Township, Craven Co., bounding S on
CAPT. SKEEN; W on ALEXANDER SKENE; E on MR. SIMPSON; NE on vacant land;
SE on Waccamaw River; also 494 a. on Pee Dee River, Craven Co., granted
to PINCKNEY, adjoining PAUL TRAPIER; also part of lot #270 in Charleston,
72 x 140 ft. bounding S on Broad Street; W on JAMES ST. JOHN; N & E on
other part said lot; also lot #128 in Beaufort, Granville Co., said real
estate to be sold & the money used first to pay PINCKNEY'S mortgages &
then to pay his debts listed in first schedule which are not secured by
mortgage. Witnesses: CHARLES STEPHENSON (STEVENSON), THOMAS PINCKNEY.
Before ALEXANDER CRAMAHE, J.P. WILLIAM HOPTON, Register.

Book H-H, p. 150   Gov. ROBERT JOHNSON & the Lords Proprs. to the
20 Oct. 1718   Hon. FRANCIS YONGE, Sur. Gen., lot #138 in
Grant   Beaufort, Granville Co., bounding S on the
                         Public Square; W on lot #132; N on lot #137; E
on Carteret Street, plat certified 24 Dec. 1717. Witnesses: J. SKENE,
THOMAS BROUGHTON, CHARLES HART, NICHOLAS TROTT, SAMUEL WRAGG. WILLIAM
HOPTON, Register.

Book H-H, p. 151   JOHN WATSONE, merchant, & ABIGAIL, his wife,
10 Apr. 1749   of Charleston, to ANNE REEVES, widow of Beau-
L & R   fort, for Ł 1320 currency, lot #10 in Beaufort,
                         as by plat certified 8 Aug. 1717; also lot
#132 in Beaufort as by plat certified 20 Oct. 1718; which lots were orig-
inally granted to FRANCIS YONGE & by several mesne conveyances became
vested in JOHN WATSONE. Witnesses: JONATHAN BRYAN, JOHN GIBBES, JR. Before WILLIAM PINCKNEY, J.P. WILLIAM HOPTON, Register.

Book H-H, p. 156   THOMAS BARKSDALE, of Christ Church Parish, to
1 June 1750   JACOB BOND, for Ł 1480 currency, principal &
Assignment of Mortgage   interest, all his claim to 492 a. & premises
                         mortgaged to BARKSDALE on 8 Mar. 1745 by
GEORGE BENISON, planter, of Christ Church Parish, bounding E on MR. DU-
BOIS; W on ANTHONY BONNEAU; N on JONAS BONHOIST; S on JOHN WHITE. Whereas BENISON gave bond to HENRY PERONNEAU (on which bond BARKSDALE was security), which debt BENISON did not pay; & whereas JACOB BOND has indemnified BARKSDALE & satisfied the obligation to PERONNEAU; now BARKSDALE
transfers the mortgage to JACOB BOND. Witnesses: CHARLES BARKSDALE, PAUL
VILLEPONTOUX, RICHARD TOOKERMAN. Recorded in Secretary's Book H.H. p.
341 on 30 Nov. 1750 by WILLIAM PINCKNEY, Dep. Sec. Before ROBERT AUSTIN,
J.P. WILLIAM HOPTON, Register.

Book H-H, p. 157   SAMUEL SHADDOCK, planter, of Edisto Island,
27 Dec. 1750   Colleton Co., to JOHN LAROCH, planter, of Wad-
L & R by Mortgage   malaw Island (because LAROCH signed SHADDOCK'S
                         bond to HENRY PERONNEAU, of Charleston, in
penal sum of Ł 484:3:6 for payment of Ł 242:1:9 currency, with interest,
on 5 May 1751); 166 a. on Wadmalaw Island, Colleton Co., according to
plat. Witnesses: BENJAMIN FREEMAN, JAMES LAROCH, ALEXANDER MCGILLORY.
Before ANTHONY MATTHEWS, J.P. WILLIAM HOPTON, Register.

Book H-H, p. 162   THOMAS JONES, planter, of St. Bartholomew's
26 Mar. 1749   Parish, Colleton Co., to SAMUEL BURGESS, boat-
Lease for 15 Years   man, of same Parish, for Ł 1 currency per year,
                         for 15 years, 50 a., bounding W on BENJAMIN

221

GODIN; E on DANIEL WELCHUYSEN; S & N on estate of THOMAS JONES. Witnesses: WILLIAM DALTON, CAROLUS FOLCHER. Before THOMAS LAMBOLL, J.P. WILLIAM HOPTON, Register.

Book H-H, p. 164   ISAAC LEGRAND DANNERVILLE, son, devisee & heir
9 June 1749   of ISAAC LEGRAND DANNERVILLE of St. James San-
L & R   tee, to CATHERINE WIGFALL, widow of SAMUEL
                        WIGFALL, ESQ., of Berkeley Co., in considera-
tion of certain agreements & for ₺ 1200 currency, 468 a., being the middle portion of 1406 a. (composed of 2 tracts) formerly owned by ISAAC LE-
GRAND DANNERVILLE, the father, & devised to his 3 children; which middle
portion was allotted to MARGARET, 1 of said children; & which descended
to her brother & heir, ISAAC LEGRAND, when she died intestate & without
issue. Whereas ISAAC LEGRAND DANNERVILLE, the father, owned in fee simple 2 tracts of land at Wambaw, Craven Co., 1 of 500 a. which by deed of
feoffment dated 10 May 1726 (livery & seizin delivered to said ISAAC 20
said May) was conveyed by Landgrave THOMAS SMITH & MARY his wife to said
ISAAC LEGRAND, the father, part of Landgrave SMITH'S patent of 48,000 a.
from the Lords Proprs.; the other of 906 a. conveyed to said ISAAC LE-
GRAND, the father, on 15 July 1722 by JOHN ASHBY, ESQ., eldest son & heir
of JOHN ASHBY, as part of his Cassigque's patent of 24,000 a. from the
Lords Proprs. (memorial entered in Auditors Office on 22 May 1735); the 2
tracts making 1406 a. which ISAAC LEGRAND DANNERVILL, the father, by will
dated 23 Feb. 1739 bequeathed equally to his 3 children; ISAAC LEGRAND,
ANN, & MARGARET; the land to be equally divided by his executors, to wit,
his wife ANN FRANCES LEGRAND DANNERVILLE & JAMES ST. JULIEN of St. Johns
Parish & PAUL BRUNEAU of St. James Santee; & whereas PAUL BRUNEAU, executor (ANN FRANCES LEGRAND DANNERVILLE & JAMES ST. JULIEN being then dead)
on 2 June 1746 divided the land into 3 parts & allotted to daughter ANN
(then wife of TACITUS GAILLARD) the NE part as her share; to MARGARET LE-
GRAND, the 2nd daughter, the middle part, bounding NE on ANN'S share; SW
on ISAAC'S share; & whereas MARGARET died intestate & without issue, so
that her share descended to ISAAC LEGRAND; & whereas said ISAAC LEGRAND
has agreed to sell to CATHERINE WIGFALL, for ₺ 1700 currency, the middle
tract of 468 a. formerly belonging to MARGARET; now the sale is completed.
The third part allotted to ISAAC LEGRAND DANNERVILLE, bounds SW on COL.
JOHN GENDRON. Plat dated 2 June 1746 by PAUL BRUNNEAU. Witnesses: AN-
DREW RUTLEDGE, ISAAC HUMPHRYS. Before ALEXANDER GORDON, J.P. WILLIAM
HOPTON, Register.

Book H-H, p. 169   CHARLES LEWIS, MARTH LEWIS (formerly of Christ
23 & 24 Feb. 1749   Church Parish, Berkeley Co., now of Prince
L & R   George Parish, Craven Co.), & STEPHEN PEMIL
                        (his mark) BULLOCK, of Christ Church Parish,
planters, of 1st. part; to SARAH HARTMAN, widow & spinster, of Christ
Church Parish, for ₺ 861 currency, 574 a. in said Parish, bounding NW on
GEORGE SMITH; SW on STEPHEN PEMIL BULLOCK (formerly JOHN HOLYBUSH); E on
JOHN HARTMAN & WATERS. Witnesses: WILLIAM BOLLOUGH, THOMAS BOONE, CAPERS
BOONE. Before WILLIAM PINCKNEY, J.P. WILLIAM HOPTON, Register. Plat by
JOHN GREEN, Sur., dated 15 Feb. 1749/50.

Book H-H, p. 175   DANIEL LAROCHE, merchant, of Georgetown, to
11 & 12 Jan. 1750   JOHN OULDFIELD, planter, of Craven Co., for
L & R   ₺ 354:6; 30 a. on W side Peedee River in
                        Prince George Parish, part of 1000 a. lately
belonging to THOMAS LAROCHE; bounding N on JOHN OULDFIELD; S on THOMAS
LAROCHE; also 25 a. on E side Peedee River, opposite the 30 a., being the
N part of 300 a. of river swamp lately belonging to THOMAS LAROCHE; bound-
ing N on part of the 300 a. originally granted to WILLIAM SWINTON now
owned by OULDFIELD; E on Squirrel Creek; S on part of said 300 a.; W on
Peedee River. Witnesses: STEPHEN PEAK, WILLIAM PEAK. Before PAUL TRAP-
IER, J.P. WILLIAM HOPTON, Register.

Book H-H, p. 179   JONATHAN WARD, planter, & ELIZABETH his wife,
11 Mar. 1729   to JOHN OULDFIELD, JR., both of Berkeley Co.,
Release   for ₺ 245 currency, 250 a. in St. Johns Par-
                        ish, Berkeley Co., bounding W on JOHN LAWSON;
N on STEPHEN MONK; E on JOHN WARD; S on JOHN GREENLAND; being part of 2
tracts of 558 a. & 545 a. granted by the Lords Proprs. to SAMUEL RUSCO,
planter, by 2 grants dated 23 July 1711, & conveyed on 14 Feb. 1712/13 by

him to JOHN WARD, father of said JONATHAN WARD. Witnesses: JOHN WARD, JOHN GREENALND. Memorial entered in Auditors office 23 May 1733. Before THOMAS FERGUSON, J.P. WILLIAM HOPTON, Register. Plat certified 11 Mar. 1729/30 by PETER DE ST. JULIEN, Dep. Sur.

Book H-H, p. 183
23 & 24 Nov. 1750
L & R by Mortgage

JOHN HARVEY, gentleman, to JORDAN ROCHE, gen-leman; both of Charleston; as security on bond of even date in penal sum of Ł 1772 for pay-ment of 786 SC money, with interest, on 24 Nov. 1751; part of 2 lots #162 & #169, or part of one of them, in Charles-ton, fronting S 51 ft. on Broad Street; bounding E 200 ft. on WILLIAM HAR-VEY; W on the Hon. BENJAMIN WHITAKER; N on COL. OTHNIEL BEALE. Witness-es: MARY DEANE, DANIEL CANNON. Before JOHN CHAMPNEYS, J.P. WILLIAM HOP-TON, Register. On 7 Oct. 1751 JORDAN ROCHE assigned this mortgage to FREDERICK GRIMKE. Witness: WILLIAM HOPTON, REgister.

Book H-H, p. 187
1 & 2 Aug. 1750
L & R

ROBERT LEWIS, planter, & SUSANNAH ELIZABETH, his wife, of Prince Frederick Parish, Craven Co., to JAMES AKIN, JR., a minor, of Parish of St. Thomas & St. Dennis, Berkeley Co., for Ł 2000 currency, 305 a. in Berkeley Co., bounding N & E on JAMES & MARY MARION (formerly JAMES BREMAR); NW on ANTHONY VIDEAU (formerly PETER VI-DEAU); W on EDWARD DONNELLY (formerly JOHN CARTOE); SW on ELIZABETH PAGET, minor (formerly FRANCIS PAGET); SE on heirs of JAMES BREMAR (formerly PETER BREMAR). Whereas JOHN, Lord Granville, Palatine, & the Lords Proprs. on 5 May 1704, granted PETER POITEVINT 400 a., English measure, S of E branch of Cooper River, bounding NW on JOHN CARTOE, DR. DANIEL BRE-BANT (formerly JAMES BORDEAUX, PETER VIDEAU, & SOLOMON BREMAR; NE on POTE-VIN, DANIEL TREZVANT, BREMAR & vacant land; SE on TREZVANT, POTEVIN, & vacant land; SW on TREZVANT, FRANCIS PAGIT, & PETER JOHNSON, SR., & where-as PETER POTEVIN in 1709 sold the 305 a. (part of the 400 a.) to JAMES AUMOMIER, carpenter, of Berkeley Co., bounding NW on JOHN CARTOE, & where-as JAMES AUMONIER bequeathed the tract to his son, JAMES, & daughter, SUSANNAH; & whereas JAMES, the son, died; & SUSANNAH married JOHN DUBOIS; & JOHN & SUSANNAH on 21 Sept. 1727, for Ł 800 currency, sold the 305 a. to JAMES BREMAR, of the Parish of St. Thomas & St. Dennis; & whereas JAM-ES BREMAR by will dated 16 Jan. 1732 bequeathed the 305 a. to his daugh-ter, SARAH BREMAR, who has since married JAMES AKIN; & whereas it is said that SUSANNAH DUBOISE was not 21 years old when she & her husband JOHN DUBOISE sold the land to BREMAR; & whereas SUSANNAH & JOHN had 1 daughter, SUSANNAH ELIZABETH DUBOISE, now wife of said ROBERT LEWIS; & whereas SAR-AH AKIN (daughter of JAMES BREMAR, & wife of JAMES AKIN, SR., & mother of JAMES AKIN, JR.) died on 5 June 1750, & JAMES AKIN, JR., became heir-at-law; now ROBERT & SUSANNAH ELIZABETH LEWIS convey the 305 a. to JAMES AKIN, JR. Witnesses: DAVID ANDERSON, JOSEPH PRINCE, CHARLES PINCKNEY, JR., JANE TRUSLER. Before FRANCIS LEJAU, J.P. On p. 240 an affidavit dated 29 Jan. 1750/1 shows that JUDITH THOMAS, wife of WILLIAM THOMAS; ESTER EMILE RAMBERT, wife of ANDREW RAMBERT, SR., both of St. James San-tee, Craven Co., testified before JOHN GENDRON, J.P. that SUSANNAH ELIZA-BETH, daughter of JOHN DUBOSE, now wife of ROBERT LEWIS, was born in said Parish & arrived at age of 21 years in August last. This affidavit was made & recorded to prove that SUSANNAH ELIZABETH LEWIS was of age when she re-executed a conveyance on 18 Jan. 1750 to JAMES AKIN. WILLIAM HOP-TON, Register.

Book H-H, p. 195
16 & 17 Jan. 1750
L & R by Mortgage

JOHN ALLEN, butcher, of Charleston, to JOSEPH CANTY, planter, of Craven Co., as security on bond of even date in penal sum of Ł 320, for payment of Ł 320, for payment of Ł 160 SC mon-ey, with interest, on 17 Apr. next; 300 a., part of 400 a. on a cedar swamp on Black Mingo Creek, Williamsburgh Township, granted by WILLIAM SNOW to DAVID ALLEN, who bequeathed to JOHN ALLEN; the 300 a. bounding on lands of WILLIAM JAMES, JOHN HENLING & JANE DICKSON. Witnesses: JAMES IRVING, JOHN REMINGTON. Before WILLIAM PINCKNEY, J.P. WILLIAM HOPTON, Register.

Book H-H, p. 200
4 & 5 Aug. 1748
L & R

JOHN HEXT, & HANNAH his wife, of Wadmelaw Is-land, St. Johns Parish, Colleton Co., to JO-SEPH PHIPPS, of Johns Island, Colleton Co., for Ł 500 currency, 200 a. on Wadmelaw Island bounding S & SE on a branch of Bohicket Creek; N & NE on Leadenwau Creek; other sides on WILLIAM ADAMS & THOMAS MANNING. Witnesses: OBADIAH WILKINS, EDWARD FISHER. Before ANTHONY MATTHEWS, J.P. WILLIAM HOPTON, Register.

Book H-H, p. 205
23 Feb. 1748
Feoffment

WILLIAM WATIES, of Winyaw, Prince George Parish, to THOMAS HASELL, of Georgetown, for Ł 1150 currency, the front part of 2 lots, 23 & 24, in Georgetown, bounding SW 100 ft. on Front Street; SE 74 ft. on Broad Street; NE by 2 lots; NW on lot #22; also all the ground lying between Front Street & low water mark opposite the front of said 2 lots, 100 ft. wide. Witnesses: WILLIAM FLEMING, WILLIAM POOLE, both of Winyaw, Craven Co. On 31 Jan. 1750 JOHN OULDFIELD, ESQ., & JAMES SUMMERS recognized the handwriting of FLEMING & POOLE. Before WILLIAM PINCKNEY, J.P. WILLIAM HOPTON, Register.

Book H-H, p. 208
15 Mar. 1734
Feoffment

WILLIAM ALSTON (ALLSTON), & ESTHER his wife, to JOHN HEARD; all of Craven Co.; for Ł 100 SC money, 235 a. on E side Waccamaw River, Craven Co., commonly called Heards Island; bounding E on Green's Creek; ESTHER to renounce her dower when required. Witnesses: JOHN MORRALL, JOHN ALLSTON, WILLIAM REAL, JOHN CAVENAUGH, TIMOTHY PENDER. Before THOMAS LAROCHE, J.P. WILLIAM HOPTON, Register.

Book H-H, p. 210
2 Feb. 1738
Sale

JOHN HEARD, planter, to JOSEPH PRINCE, tanner, both of Craven Co., for Ł 700 currency, 235 a. in Craven Co., bounding W on Waccamaw River; E on a creek. Witnesses: DAVID CHENEY, ANN (her mark) DONIFANT. Before WILLIAM WHITESIDE, J.P. WILLIAM HOPTON, Register.

Book H-H, p. 211
25 May 1745
Feoffment

JOSEPH PRINCE, planter, & ELIZABETH MARY his wife, of Prince George Parish, Craven Co., to EDWARD FREDERICK ROUSE, of Prince Frederick Parish, Craven Co., for Ł 450 currency, an island of 235 a. on E side Waccamaw River; bounding E on a creek; first granted 26 Feb. 1733 to WILLIAM ALLSTON, who conveyed to JOHN HARD, who conveyed to JOSEPH PRINCE; ELIZABETH MARY to renounce her dower when requested. Witnesses: WILLIAM MAY JOSIAH (his mark) HEWLETT, ROBERT OLIVER. Before PAUL TRAPIER, J.P. WILLIAM HOPTON, Register.

Book H-H, p. 214
18 & 19 Feb. 1749
L & R

EDWARD (his mark) ROUSE, planter, to ELIAS FOUSAINE, gentleman, for Ł 432 SC money, an island of 235 a. on E side Waccamaw River, bounding E on a creek. Witnesses: MATTHEW ROCHE, JOHN BUTLER. Before ROBERT AUSTIN, J.P. WILLIAM HOPTON, Register.

Book H-H, p. 218
10 Oct. 1749
Confirmation

WILLIAM & BARNARD ELLIOTT, executors of THOMAS ELLIOTT, to BENJAMIN ELLIOTT, his share of his fathers estate. Whereas THOMAS ELLIOTT (brother of WILLIAM & BARNARD ELLIOTT), of Berkeley Co., by will dated 23 Oct. 1738, gave his 3 sons, THOMAS, BENJAMIN & SAMUEL, all the residue of his real & personal estate, to be equally divided as the majority of his executors (WILLIAM ELLIOTT, BARNARD ELLIOTT & JOSEPH ELLIOTT, 3 brothers of said THOMAS ELLIOTT); & whereas JOSEPH died, leaving WILLIAM & BARNARD executors; & whereas they allotted to BENJAMIN (1 son) 2 tracts in St. Andrews Parish, Berkeley Co., 1 of 305 a. bounding E on WILLIAM BRANFORD; S on WILLIAM BRANFORD & Stono River; W on THOMAS ELLIOTT; N on THOMAS HOLMAN; the other of 325 a. bounding E on THOMAS HOLMAN; S on THOMAS ELLIOTT; W on SAMUEL ELLIOTT; N on MR. RIVERS; also 1/4 of ELLIOTT'S wharf in Charleston; & 1/4 of 10 a. at Bacon's Bridge, & 1/4 of a tract at Hobcaw which was purchased from JOSEPH LAW; also 38 Negroes, cattle, horses, silver, etc., all his share of his father's real & personal estate, but BENJAMIN is to allow his brother THOMAS Ł 900 out of the wharf & his brother SAMUEL Ł 550 to make their shares equal to his share. Witnesses: BENJAMIN SMITH, HENRY LAURENS, JOHN SCOTT. Before JACOB MOTTE, J.P. Recorded in Secretary's Book H.H. p. 387 on 5 Feb. 1750, by WILLIAM PINCKNEY, Dep. Sec. WILLIAM HOPTON, Register.

Book H-H, p. 220   GEORGE BENNISON (BENISON), & WILLIAM BENNISON,
23 Oct. 1750   planters, sons of CAPT. GEORGE BENNISON, of
Release   Christ Church Parish, Berkeley Co., to ARCHI-
                         BALD JOHNSTON, planter, of Craven Co., for
Ł 300 currency, 1504 a. in Craven Co., bounding SE on Long Bay; NE on MR.
RIVERS & STEPHEN PEAK; NW on MR. PEAK, MR. BOONE & vacant land; SW on
WILLIAM CATCHPOLE & GEORGE BENISON; also 1000 a. in Craven Co., bounding
S on above tract lately belonging to GEORGE BENISON; N on CAPT. LOGAN.
Whereas Lt. Gov. THOMAS BROUGHTON on 4 June 1735 granted CAPT. GEORGE
BENISON 1504 a. in Craven Co., (see Secretary's Book B.B., p. 400) of
which BENISON by will dated 15 Sept. 1747 authorized his executors, (WIL-
LIAM BENISON, RICHARD BENISON, & RICHARD CAPERS) to sell 1004 a. on Long
Bay (part of the 1504 a.) but made no provision in regard to the 500 a.,
which tract therefore was inherited by his eldest son & heir, GEORGE BEN-
ISON, party hereto; & whereas GEORGE BENISON, the father, owned another
1000 a. in Craven Co., bounding S on the 1504 a.; N on CAPT. LOGAN; for
which no provision was made in his will & therefore was inherited also by
son GEORGE; now GEORGE & WILLIAM BENISON sell the 2 tracts of 1504 a. &
1000 a. to JOHNSTON. Witnesses: JANE BONHOST, JONAH BONHOST, CHARLES
BENYSON. Before ROBERT AUSTIN, J.P. WILLIAM HOPTON, Register.

Book H-H, p. 224   JORDAN ROCHE, ESQ., JOHN MACKENZIE, & BRANFIL
25 & 26 Nov. 1750   EVANCE, merchants, of Charleston, as trustees,
L & R   to ROBERT QUASH, planter, of St. Johns Parish,
                         for Ł 1200 currency, part of lot #270 in
Charleston, bounding S 72 ft. on Broad Street; W 140 ft. on JAMES ST.
JOHN; N & E on parts same lot. Whereas by L & R dated 2 & 3 Mar. 1746
WILLIAM PINCKNEY, ESQ., & RUTH his wife, of Charleston, conveyed to JOR-
DAN ROCHE, JOHN MACKENZIE & BRANFIL EVANCE certain plantations, town lots,
etc., in trust, to dispose of said real estate & apply the money to cer-
tain uses; now they sell part of 1 lot to QUASH. Witnesses: JAMES GRIND-
LAY, ROBERT WILLIAMS, JR. Before JACOB MOTTE, J.P. WILLIAM HOPTON, Reg-
ister.

Book H-H, p. 230   ARTHUR NASH, mariner, & MARIA ANN (MARY ANN)
7 July 1750   his wife, to THOMAS HEATHY, shipwright; all of
Feoffment   Charleston; for Ł 800 SC money; the N part of
                         lot #218, bounding S 239-2/8 ft. on JOSEPH
WRAGG (formerly JOHN STEEL); W 41 ft. 4 in. on Church Street; E on JOSEPH
WRAGG (formerly THOMAS MIDDLETON); N on JAMES JORDAN; which N part was
granted by deed of feoffment dated 2 Apr. 1741 to ARTHUR NASH by THOMAS
STEWART, & THOMAS HEATHY & SUSANNAH his wife (THOMAS STEWART, SUSANNAH
HEATHY, & MARIA ANN NASH being children of THOMAS STEWART, the former
owner). Witnesses: JOHN SCOTT, JOHN REMINGTON. Witnesses to possession:
JOHN SCOTT, JOHN REMINGTON, ABRAHAM REMINGTON. Before WILLIAM PINCKNEY,
J.P. WILLIAM HOPTON, Register.

Book H-H, p. 234   THOMAS (his mark) HEADDY, shipwright, & SUSAN-
2 & 3 Oct. 1750   NAH his wife, to THOMAS BOLTON, shopkeeper;
L & R by Mortgage   all of Charleston; as security on bond dated
                         27 June last in penal sum of Ł 1000 for pay-
ment of Ł 500 currency, with interest, on 27 Feb. next; the N part of lot
#218, bounding S 239-2/8 ft. on JOSEPH WRAGG (formerly JOHN STEEL); W
41 ft. 4 in. on Church Street; E on JOSEPH WRAGG (formerly THOMAS MIDDLE-
TON); N on JAMES JORDAN. Witnesses: ABRAHAM REMINGTON, JOHN REMINGTON.
Before WILLIAM PINCKNEY, J.P. WILLIAM HOPTON, Register.

Book H-H, p. 241   JOSEPH (his mark) JOYNER, SR. to his loving
23 Aug. 1745   son NATHAN JOYNER, for love & affection, 300
Gift   a. on Santee River, in Amelia Township & his
                         half a. lot #171 in Amelia Town, as by plat
dated 6 Mar. 1735/6 signed by Gov. BULL 16 Sept. 1738. Witnesses: THOMAS
POWELL, EDWARD GIBSON, MARTIN (his mark) COONAR, ELIZABETH (her mark)
FRANSES. Before JOHN CHEVILLETTE, J.P. WILLIAM HOPTON, Register.

Book H-H, p. 242   GEORGE MCKENZIE, merchant, of West Cowes, Isle
22 Feb. 1741   of Wight, Co. of Southampton, attorney for
Power of Attorney   JANET DICK, substitutes & appoints JOHN MAC-
                         KENZIE & MATTHEW ROCHE, merchants, of
Charleston, SC, his attorneys. Whereas JANET DICK, only sister & heir of

ALEXANDER DICK, mariner, of Bristol, by deed poll dated 5 this inst. Feb. appointed GEORGE MCKENZIE her attorney, to collect money owing her brother, etc., & dispose of her brother's property; now MCKENZIE appoints MACKENZIE & ROCHE his substitutes. Witnesses: JEMMETT COBLEY, EDWARD SIMPSON. Before THOMAS MIDDLETON, J.P. WILLIAM HOPTON, Register.

Book H-H, p. 244   JOSEPH MACKEY, planter, & SARAH his wife, of
27 & 28 Feb. 1750   St. Bartholomew's Parish, Colleton, to CHARLES
L & R in Trust   PINCKNEY, EDWARD FENWICKE, EDMUND BELLINGER &
                      GEORGE AUSTIN, executors of will of CULCHETH
GOLIGHTLY, ESQ., of St. Bartholomew Parich, trustees for Ł 430 currency,
the NE part of 900 a. granted to JOSEPH MACKEY, the elder, being 430 a.
near Horse Shoe Savannah in St. Bartholomew Parish, bounding SW on the
remaining 470 a.; SE on estate of CULCHETH GOLIGHTLY (formerly HOLMES);
NE & NW on vacant land. Whereas on 16 Mar. 1732 the King granted JOSEPH
MACKEY, the elder, 900 a. in Colleton Co., bounding SW on JOHN ANDREWS;
SE on FRANCIS HOLMES & the Horse Shoe Savannah; other sides on vacant
land; & on 15 Apr. 1734 JOSEPH MACKEY sold the SW part, or 470 a., to
JOHN MACKEY, bounding NW on vacant land; NE on the remainder of JOSEPH
MACKEY'S land; SE on HOLMES; SW on JOHN ANDREW & whereas CULCHETH GOLIGHT-
LY on 8 Mar. 1741 purchased from DR. JAMES HUTCHESON 370 a. which JOHN
MACKEY had sold to DR. HUTCHESON, & wanted to purchase the NE part (430
a.) from JOSEPH MACKEY adjoining his land; & whereas JOSEPH MACKEY, the
elder, died & by his will his eldest son & devisee, JOSEPH MACKEY, party
herto, inherited; & whereas GOLIGHTLY by will appointed CHARLES PINCKNEY,
EDWARD FENWICKE, EDMUND BELLINGER, & GEORGE AUSTIN, his executors; with
power to improve his estate, sell lands or slaves, & lend the money out
at interest for the benefit of GOLIGHTLY'S children & devisees; & whereas
the executors have made considerable profits in the past year they decide
to purchase the 430 a. from JOSEPH MACKEY the younger, lying almost in
the center of GOLIGHTLY'S land; now the sale is made; the land being free
from claim of dower by CATHERINE SULLIVAN, mother of said JOSEPH MACKEY.
Witnesses: CHARLES PINCKNEY, JR., THOMAS BURRINGTON. Before WILLIAM
PINCKNEY, J.P. WILLIAM HOPTON, Register.

Book H-H, p. 253   DAVID STEPHENS, planter, & MARY his wife, of
5 & 6 Feb. 1750   St. Pauls Parish, Colleton Co., to JOHN MC-
L & R   QUEEN, storekeeper, of St. George's Parish,
                      Berkeley Co., for Ł 1000 currency, 2 extreme
corners of a tract of 230 a. in Colleton Co., originally granted by the
Lords Proprs. on 16 Jan. 1715 to JOHN PRESCOTT & after several mesne conveyances became vested in fee simple in ROBERT STEVENS, SR., planter,
father of DAVID, who devised the 230 a. equally to his 2 sons, ROBERT &
DAVID; 1 of the corners being 65 a. bounding S on JOHN MILES; W on JOHN
RAVEN; E on JOHN WARD; N on JOHN MCQUEEN; the other corner being 50 a.,
bounding NE on JOHN RAVEN; SE & SW on JOHN MILES; NW on JOHN MCQUEEN;
total 115 a., English measure; free from MARY'S claim of dower. Witnesses: ROBERT STEVENS, ISAAC BATTOON, BETHELL DEWES. Before RALPH IZARD,
J.P. WILLIAM HOPTON, Register.

Book H-H, p. 261   ROBERT STEVENS, planter, & ANN (her mark) his
12 & 13 Feb. 1749   wife, of St. Pauls Parish, Colleton Co., to
L & R   JOHN MCQUEEN, planter, of St. George Parish,
                      Berkeley Co., for Ł 2000 currency, the plan-
tation on which STEVENS lives, being 2 tracts in St. Pauls Parish; 1 of
130 a. (half of 260 a.) at NW end of Horse Savannah, bounding NE on FRAN-
CIS LADSON; SE on ROBERT STEVENS (formerly JOHN PRESCOTT); SW on JOHN RA-
VEN; NW on other half of 260 a. belonging to JACOB LADSON; which 260 a.
were granted by Gov. ROBERT JOHNSON & the Lords Proprs. on 9 July 1718 to
HENRY NICHOLES (NICHOLS) the other being 115 a. (half of 230 a.) in St.
Paul's Parish, at NW end of Horse Savannah, bounding NE on JOHN RAVEN; NW
on above 130 a.; W on JOHN RAVEN; S & E on DAVID STEVENS & JOHN MILES;
which 230 a. were ganted by Gov. CHARLES CRAVEN & the Lords Proprs. on 16
Jan. 1715 to JOHN PRESCOTT. For the better satisfaction of JOHN MCQUEEN
in regard to the right of ROBERT & ANN STEVENS to make over by L & R the
said 2 tracts, total 245 a., ROBERT STEVENS shows that whereas SAMUEL
EVANS, father of ANN STEVENS, died intestate, leaving only 2 daughters,
MARY & ANN EVANS (alias ANN STEVENS), ROBERT by his marriage with ANN is
now entitled to & invested with 1/2 part of the 260 a. first mentioned;
which 260 a. SAMUEL EVANS had purchased from HENRY NICHOLS. Whereas

226

ROBERT STEVENS, SR., bequeathed to his 2 sons, ROBERT & DAVID, the 230 a. to be equally divided, which a resurvey shows was done, now ROBERT owns the 2 adjoining tracts of 130 a. & 115 a., forming 1 tract of 245 a., which he conveys to MCQUEEN. Witnesses: ANDREW LETCH, BETHEL DEWES, JACOB STEVENS. Before RALPH IZARD, J.P. WILLIAM HOPTON, Register.

Book H-H, p. 271
14 & 15 Sept. 1750
L & R

JOHN DAVIS, planter, of Berkeley Co., to JAMES BENOIST, planter, of Craven Co., for L 400 currency, 314 a. in Craven Co., bounding SW on PETER COLLETON; NW on vacant land; NE on SAMUEL BENOIST; SE on vacant land; which 314 a. were granted on 12 Apr. 1739 to DAVID DAVIS. Witnesses: DAVID LAFONS, SAMUEL EDGAR, JOHN BENOIST. Before SAMUEL THOMAS, J.P. WILLIAM HOPTON, Register.

Book H-H, p. 276
10 Oct. 1749
Feoffment

BENJAMIN ELLIOTT, of St. Andrews Parish, Berkeley Co., to his Uncle WILLIAM ELLIOTT, of same Parish, for L 3500; 1/4 part of the great Wharf called Elliott's Wharf, on E side of Charleston on the Bay. Witnesses: BENJAMIN SMITH, HENRY LAURENS, JOHN SCOTT. Delivery by turf & twig. Before JACOB MOTTE, J.P. WILLIAM HOPTON, Register.

Book H-H, p. 277
15 July 1740
Grant

GEORGE II, by Lt. Gov. WILLIAM BULL, to PATRICK & JAMES DANNIELLE, 100 a. in Craven Co., Queensborough Township (50 a. to each), bounding NE on purchased land; NW on Lynch's Lake; SE & SW on vacant land; also lot #76. Witness: ALEXANDER CRAMAHE, C.C. Recorded in Secretary's Book E.E. fol 21. by WILLIAM GEORGE FREEMAN, Dep. Sec. WILLIAM HOPTON, Register. Plat certified 11 Nov. 1737 by JAMES ST. JOHN, Sur. Gen., according to warrant issued 15 Sept. 1736 by Lt. Gov. THOMAS BROUGHTON.

Book H-H, p. 279
6 & 7 Apr. 1749
L & R

JOSEPH SCOTT, planter, & ELIZABETH his wife, of Colleton Co., to JAMES JOURDAN, planter, of French Santee, for L 7 currency, 50 a. (part of 100 a.), & a quarter a. town lot (part of a half a. lot) in Queensborough Township. Witnesses: THOMAS SMITH, HUGH GRANT. Before JAMES SKIRVING, J.P. WILLIAM HOPTON, Register.

Book H-H, p. 282
9 & 10 Jan. 1750
L & R

WILLIAM THOMAS, schoolmaster & JUDITH his wife, to WILLIAM BOON (BOONE); all of St. James Santee; for L 600 currency, 290 a. in St. James Santee Parish, Craven Co., bounding N on CAPERS BOON (formerly STEPHEN CARTER); E on Wambaw Creek; S on MR. RICHBOURGH; W on vacant land. Whereas Brig. JOHN GENDRON owned 290 a. at Wambaw, which he sold to ROBERT BROWN, whose executors sold to WILLIAM THOMAS; now THOMAS sells to BOONE. Witnesses: JOHN BARNETT, ELISHA BARNETT, DANIEL DUBOSE. Before JOHN GENDRON, J.P. WILLIAM HOPTON, Register.

Book H-H, p. 287
13 June 1750
Release

ELIZABETH D'ARQUES, widow, of Berkeley Co., to ROBERT YONGE, planter, of Colleton Co., for L 3800 SC money, 313 a. in Berkeley Co., bounding NW on WILLIAM CATTELL; SE on HUGH CARTWRIGHT; NE on a marsh of Ashley River; SW on JOHN MILES; also part of lot #42 in Charleston, on S side Tradd Street, where DR. OLIPHANT lives; bounding N 44 ft. on Tradd Street; E 98 ft. on JONATHAN BADGER; S on MILES BREWTON; W on GEORGE CHICKEN. Witnesses: THOMAS LAMBOLL, JOSEPH LLOYD. Before JACOB MOTTE, J.P. WILLIAM HOPTON, Register.

Book H-H, p. 290
15 & 16 Mar. 1750
L & R
L & R

JOHN HUTCHINS, planter, & ELIZABETH (her mark) his wife, of Charleston, to ALEXANDER VANDERDUSSEN, ESQ., for 1700 currency, 529 a. in St. Paul's Parish, Colleton Co., bounding E on THOMAS ELLIOTT; S on EDMUND BELLINGER; N on JOHN GODFREY; which 529 a. JAMES SCRIVEN & MARY his wife by L & R dated 1 & 2 Jan. 1746 conveyed to JOHN HUTCHINS. Witnesses: TIMOTHY MORGRIDGE, JOHN TROUP. Before JAMES MICHIE, J.P. WILLIAM HOPTON, Register.

Book H-H, p. 297
21 Mar. 1751

JOHN HINDS, planter, of St. Pauls Parish, Colleton Co., to MICHAEL HINDS, planter, of same

227

place, for Ł 1500 currency, 2 plantations in St. Pauls Parish, total
600 a., bounding according to 2 plats. Witnesses: WILLIAM LITTLE, JOHN
CHANCY, PATRICK HINDS. Before THOMAS LAMBOLL, J.P. WILLIAM HOPTON, Register.

Book H-H, p. 304   MARY BRYAN, widow of Granville Co., to EDWARD
18 & 19 Feb. 1750   FENWICKE, ESQ., of Charleston, for Ł 1500 cur-
L & R   rency the S part of lot #197 in Charlston,
                          bounding E 31 ft. on a Great Street leading
from Old Church Street, toward White Point on Ashley River; W & S on JOHN
RIVERS; N 230 ft. on ALBERT DARTMAR. Whereas on 12 June 1694, the Earl
of Craven, Palatine, & the Lords Proprs., by Gov. THOMAS SMITH, granted
WILLIAM BAYLEY a half a. lot in Charleston known as #197, bounding E on
the great street leading from Ashley River to the Market Place; & whereas
by sundry mesne conveyances MARY BRYAN became owner of the S part, 31 x
230 ft., English measure; which, with the several buildings, she had
agreed to sell to FENWICKE; now the conveyance is made. Witnesses: JOHN
SMITH, WILLIAM BOWER WILLIAMSON. Before JOHN CLELAND, J.P. WILLIAM HOP-
TON, Register.

Book H-H, p. 309   HUGH HEXT, gentleman, son of JOHN HEXT of
28 Mar. 1751   Charleston, to ALEXANDER PERONNEAU, gentleman,
Sale   of Charleston, for Ł 700 currency, part of a
                          lot on the Bay of Charleston. Whereas EDWARD
HEXT, gentleman of Charleston, (Uncle of HUGH HEXT, party hereto), owned
a piece of land on the Bay of Charleston with a dwelling house & other
houses thereon; & whereas by his will dated 6 Oct. 1739 bequeathed to
HUGH HEXT, son of his brother JOHN HEXT, on reaching 21 years, the house
in which he lived on the Bay & the ground belonging to said house (as now
divided from the brick house & ground fronting Union Street), otherwise
the Bay house to _____ HEXT, son of his brother THOMAS HEXT; & whereas
said EDWARD HEXT by codicil dated 22 Apr. 1740 devised to his kinswoman,
ELIZABETH ETHERIDGE, free use of the house & grounds where he lived on
the Bay for as long as she saw fit to live there after his death, free of
rent or other charges; then his will to be carried out; & whereas EDWARD
HEXT by another codicil dated 28 Apr. 1740 devised to his kinswoman,
ELIZABETH ETHRIDGE, free & undisturbed use & liberty of the house &
grounds where he lived during her natural life, whether she lived in the
Province or not, & after her death his will to be carried out; & whereas
EDWARD HEXT died soon after, leaving the will & codicils in full force; &
whereas said ELIZABETH is still alive & has the premises (now occupied by
ROBERT AUSTIN) during her lifetime; & whereas HUGH HEXT, party hereto, is
heir expectant; now he conveys the reversion to PERONNEAU. Witnesses:
SAMUEL PERKINS, JOHN TROUP. Before JOHN DART, J.P. WILLIAM HOPTON, Reg-
ister.

Book H-H, p. 314   HUGH HEXT, gentleman, son of JOHN HEXT, to
28 Mar. 1751   ALEXANDER PERONNEAU, gentleman, both of
Bond   Charleston, in penal sum of Ł 3000 currency,
                          to keep agreements in above release (p. 309).
Witnesses: SAMUEL PERKINS, JOHN TROUP. Before JOHN DART, J.P. WILLIAM
HOPTON, Register.

Book H-H, p. 315   COL. GEORGE PAWLEY, ESQ., of Prince George
29 & 30 Nov. 1750   Parish, Craven Co., (in order to render the
L & R   will of JOHN ALLSTON, father of JOSIAS ALLSTON,
                          valied & effectual so far as relates to his
having devised 490 a. to his son JOSIAS, party hereto) releases & con-
forms JOHN ALLSTON in his title to the 490 a. called Unesaw on Waccamaw
Neck in Prince George Parish, on SW side of lands formerly belonging to
PERCIVAL PAWLEY. Whereas Gov. ROBERT GIBBES & the Lords Proprs. on 18
June 1711 granted ROBERT DANIEL 24,000 a., of which a tract of 1490 a.
was situated on Waccamaw Neck in Prince George Parish, Craven Co., bounding E on marsh of the seashore; W on Waccamaw River; N on ARCHIBALD JOHN-
STON; S on SAMUEL ALLSTON, son of JOHN ALLSTON; & whereas ROBERT DANIEL
on 19 June 1711 sold the lands to THOMAS SMITH, who on 10 Sept. following
conveyed the 1490 a. to MAJ. PERCIVAL PAWLEY, father of GEORGE PAWLEY; &
whereas PERCIVAL PAWLEY by will dated 5 June 1722 gave his brother JO-
SEPH'S daughters (named SUSANNAH & ANN) 490 a. (part of the 1490 a.) on
SW side of his son PERCIVAL'S land at Unesaw, implying only an estate

therein to them for life; & whereas JOSEPH ALLEN, of Waccamaw Neck, married SUSANNAH, 1 of JOSEPH PAWLEY'S daughters, & conceiving himself intitled to said 490 a. by his marriage with SUSANNAH & the death of ANN, & L & R dated 11 & 12 Mar. 1736/7 sold to JOHN ALLSTON, the father; & whereas SUSANNAH is dead, & for want of fee simple & inheritance being devised to anyone by PERCIVAL PAWLEY the 490 a. have descended to GEORGE PAWLEY, eldest son & heir of PERCIVAL; now GEORGE PAWLEY, releases his claim & confirms JOSIAS ALLSTON'S title to the 490 a. Witnesses: ZACHARIAH BRAZIER, ISAAC MARION, GABRIEL MARION. Before WILLIAM PINCKNEY, J.P. WILLIAM HOPTON, Register.

Book H-H, p. 321
23 July 1744
L & R

JOHN BLISS, & MARY his wife, of Craven Co., to GAWEN WITHERSPOON, of Williamsburgh, Craven Co., for Ł 80 SC money, 250 a. in Williamsburgh Township, Craven Co., bounding SE on ANDREW RUTLEDGE, ESQ., other sides on vacant land; also lot #111, containing 1/2 a., in Williamsburgh; MARY to renounce her dower upon request. Witnesses: WILLIAM FRIRSON (FRYARSON), JAMES GIBSON. Before WILLIAM FLEMING, J.P. WILLIAM HOPTON, Register.

Book H-H, p. 326
6 Apr. 1749
Judgment

CHARLES PRYEE against THOMAS SMITH, tailor, for Ł 692:16 SC money due on a bond & Ł 28: Ł 28:19:9-1/2 costs. JAMES WRIGHT, attorney for SMITH. Judgment signed by JAMES WEDDERBURN, clerk, C.P. Before BENJAMIN WHITAKER. WILLIAM HOPTON, Register.

Book H-H, p. 327
13 Apr. 1751
Mortgage

JOHN HUTCHINS, & ELIZABETH (her mark) his wife, of Berkeley Co., as security on 3 bonds dated 8 May 1749, given COL. ALEXANDER VANDERDUSSEN, in penal sum of Ł 4780 SC money, for payment of Ł 2390 currency, with interest, on 25 Apr. 1751; convey to VANDERDUSSEN lot #D according to plat of GEORGE ANSON'S lands in Ansonborough, containing 1 a. 2 roods, English measure, fronting 140 ft. on the Broad Path leading from Charleston, & 300 ft. on the "30 foot street"; also the brick tenement & other buildings thereon; also 6 Negroes. Witnesses: DELA CHAPPELL, CHARLES MURRINO. Before ROBERT AUSTIN, J.P. WILLIAM HOPTON, Register. On 26 Feb. 1752 for a valuable consideration paid to him by RICHARD WAINWRIGHT, butcher, of Charleston, ALEXANDER VANDERDUSSEN declared mortgage satisfied. Witness: WILLIAM HOPTON.

Book H-H, p. 329
9 Feb. 1750
Release

GEORGE HESKETT, wheelchair maker, eldest surviving brother & heir of JOSEPH HESKETT, of Berkeley Co., to MARY HESKETT, widow, of Charleston, for Ł 600 currency, 100 a. in St. Thomas Parish, lately belonging to JOSEPH HESKETT, planter, who died intestate, by whose death the land descended to GEORGE HESKETT; the 100 a. being part of 500 a. originally granted to WILLIAM NORTH; the 100 a. having been conveyed to JOSEPH HESKETT by ISAAC GUERIN; now bounding N on DANIEL LESESNE; E on STEPHEN MILLER; S & W on JOHN MILLER. Witnesses: JOSEPH MOODY, THOMAS BROUGHTON. Before JACOB MOTTE, J.P. WILLIAM HOPTON, Register.

Book H-H, p. 333
22 & 23 Apr. 1751
L & R

GEORGE SEAMAN, merchant, to GEORGE GABRIEL POWELL, ESQ., both of Charleston, for Ł 4700 currency, 800 a. in 2 tracts, in Craven Co., on N & S sides Peedee River, formerly belonging to HUGH SWINTON; 550 a. of which was part of 700 a., & 250 a. lying between N side Peedee River & the thoroughfare to Peedee. Whereas GEORGE II by Gov. ROBERT JOHNSON, on 16 Mar. 1732 granted STEPHEN PROCTER of Charleston, 700 a. in Craven Co., bounding SE on Peedee River; N on WILLIAM WATIES; SW on WILLIAM SWINTON; & whereas GEORGE II by Lt. Gov. THOMAS BROUGHTON, on 4 June 1735 granted HUGH SWINTON 250 a. in Craven Co., bounding NW on Peedee River; SE on a creek; SW on WILLIAM SWINTON; & whereas STEVEN PROCTOR by L & R dated 12 & 13 Apr. 1733 conveyed his 700 a. to HUGH SWINTON; & whereas HUGH SWINTON on 7 & 8 Jan. 1740 mortgated the 2 tracts of 700 & 250 a. to JAMES ABERCROMBIE for Ł 4270 currency (accept 70 a., part of the 700 a., previously sold by SWINTON to JAMES GORDON); for which SWINTON gave ABERCROMBIE 2 bonds for Ł 280 sterling & Ł 4270 currency; & whereas SWINTON did not pay ABERCROMBIE the sums of money & by release dated 26 Sept. 1746 confirmed to ABERCROMBIE

the 2 tracts, except the 70 a., & except 80 a. part of the 700 a. sold to
WILLIAM WATIES, adjoining the 70 a.; & whereas said JAMES ABERCROMBIE, of
the Parish of St. Martins in the Fields, City of Westminster, by letter
of attorney dated at London, 20 Feb. 1747, appointed JAMES WRIGHT, ROBERT
STIELL, & JOHN HUME, of SC, his attorneys to dispose of his lands in SC;
& whereas his attorneys by L & R dated 18 & 19 Sept. 1750 sold to GEORGE
SEAMAN the 800 a. on both sides Peedee River, formerly belonging to HUGH
SWINTON (i.e. 550 a. & part of the 700 a. granted to STEPHEN PROCTER);
now SEAMAN sells the 800 a. to POWELL. Witnesses: ANN PROCTER, ANDREW
MCMASTERS, JOHN SMITH. Before ROBERT BROWN, J.P. WILLIAM HOPTON, Reg-
ister. On 16 Aug. 1732 by order of JAMES ST. JOHN, Sur. Gen., WILLIAM
SWINTON, Dep. Sur., laid out to STEPHEN PROCTER 700 a. in Craven Co.,
bounding SE on Peedee River; N on WILLIAM WATIES; SW on WILLIAM SWINTON.
See surveyor's Book 1 fol. 294. Certified 1 Feb. 1750 by GEORGE HUNTER,
Sur. Gen. Plat laid off for 150 a. 94 chains resurveyed 10 Apr. 1751 by
THOMAS HASELL.

Book H-H, p. 344   The Rev. MR. FRANCIS GUICHARD, & BENJAMIN
3 July 1749   D'HARRIETTE, merchant, executors of will of
L & R   JAMES VOULOUX, gentleman, to JOHN MARTINI, sur-
                          geon; all of Charleston, at public auction,
for Ł 1001 currency; part of lot #104 in Charleston, bounding N 19 ft.
2 in. on Broad Street; S on the lot of the French trustees; E 208 ft. on
PAUL SMICHER, (SMYSER); W on PETER BOCQUETT; which lot, with other adjoining lands, JAMES VOULOUX purchased from ANTHONY MATHEWS & ANNE his
wife; & by will dated 11 Nov. 1748 directed his exeucotrs to sell the
above lot. Witnesses: JOSEPH WARD, CHARLES JACOB PICHARD, JOHN TIMOTHY.
Before JACOB MOTTE, J.P. WILLIAM HOPTON, Register.

Book H-H, p, 349   JOHN MARTINI, chirurgeon, & MARY his wife, to
20 Sept. 1749   DEBORAH FISHER, soap boiler; all of Charles-
L & R   ton; for Ł 1300 SC money, lot #104 bounding N
                          19 ft. 2 in. on Broad Street; S on lot of
French trustees; E 208 ft. on PAUL SMICHER (SMYSER); W on PETER BOCQUETT.
Witnesses: SAMUEL FAYRWEATHER, DANIEL BOURGET, JOHN TIMOTHY, JAMES FISHER.
Before JACOB MOTTE, J.P. WILLIAM HOPTON, Register.

Book H-H, p. 353   DEBORAH FISHER, widow, to DANIEL BOURGETT,
15 & 16 Apr. 1751   baker, both of Charleston, as security on bond
L & R by Mortgage   of even date in penal sum of Ł 1780 for pay-
                          ment of Ł 890 SC money, with interest, on 15
Apr. 1752, for the use of MARY HENRIETTA GAULTIER & CHARLOTTE GAULTIER;
part of lot #104 in Charleston, bounding N 19 ft. 2 in. on Broad Street;
S on lot of the French trustees; E 208 ft. on PAUL SMYSER; W on PETER
BOCQUETT; also 7 Negro slaves. Witnesses: SUSANNA BOURGETT, JOHN REMING-
TON. Before JACOB MOTTE, J.P. WILLIAM HOPTON, Register. On 12 Oct.
1752 BOURGETTE acknowledged receipt of Ł 445 currency & released the 7
slaves; on 30 July 1754 he acknowledged receipt of balance & declared
mortgage satisfied in full. Witness: WILLIAM HOPTON.

                          DEEDS BOOK "I-I"
                          MAY 1751 - JAN. 1752

Book I-I, p. 1   ANNE TUBB, spinster, lately of Hampstead Mar-
2 & 3 Mar. 1743   shall, Co. of Berks; JOHN WORTLEY, gentleman,
L & R   late of Parish of St. George, Hanover Square,
                          Co. of Middlesex & ELIZABETH his wife (former-
ly ELIZABETH TUBB); of the 1st part, by their attorney WILLIAM STONE,
merchant, of Charleston; to MARY HEXT, widow, of Charleston; for Ł 710 SC
money, lot #279 in Charleston, on Charles Town Green; bounding E on the
great street leading from the Market Place; W on VERTUE BAKER, widow
(formerly CHARLES BASDEN); N on MARGARET STANBURY (formerly CHARLES BAS-
DEN) & Moore Street, (a private street); S on estate of THOMAS HENNING
(formerly BARNARD SCHENCKINGH. Whereas the Lords Proprs. by grant dated
14 June 1694, signed by Gov. THOMAS SMITH in presence of PAUL GRIMBALL &
RICHARD CONANT, granted lot #279 containing half an a., on Charles Town
Green to CHARLES BASDEN; who dying intestate in 1700, leaving 3 daughters,
SARAH, REBECCA, & MARY, to whom the lot descended as daughters &

co-heiresses; & whereas they (broken, see p. 13) & their husbands (JONA-THAN COLLINGS, WILLIAM GUY) sold the lot to JONATHAN TUBB; who bequeathed the lot equally to his beloved sister, ANN TUBB, & to his beloved niece, ELIZABETH TUBB (daughter of his brother BENJAMIN TUBB), dwelling in Old England, in Parish of Hampstead Marshall, Co. of Berks; the plat & grant with the title then being in possession of THOMAS FLEMING of Johns Island, SC; whom JONATHAN TUBB appointed 1 of his executors; & whereas JONATHAN TUBB died in 1742; & whereas (broken) on 30 Sept. 1742, before SAMUEL MARTYN, Notary in London, ANN TUBB, spinster, sister of JONATHAN; & JOHN WORTLEY, gentleman & ELIZABETH his wife (daughter of BENJAMIN TUBB); appointed WILLIAM STONE, merchant, of Charleston, then in London, their attorney, with full power; now he conveys the lot to MARY HEXT. Witnesses: DAVID HEXT, JOHN LEA. Before JOHN DART, J.P. WILLIAM HOPTON, Register.

Book I-I, p. 13
21 & 22 Apr. 1746
L & R

MARY HEXT, widow, to ALEXANDER PERONNEAU, gentleman, both of Charleston, for Ⱡ 3400 currency, lot #279 on Charles Town Green. Whereas the Lords Proprs. on 14 June 1694 granted to CHARLES BASDEN, gentlemen, of Berkeley Co., lot #279 containing half an a., English measure, (see p. 1) & whereas CHARLES BASDEN died intestate at Charleston in 1700 & his 3 daughters, SARAH, REBECCA & MARY, inherited; & whereas JONATHAN COLLINGS & said SARAH his wife; WILLIAM GUY & said REBECCA his wife; & MARY BASDEN; on 27 Apr. 1721 sold the lot to JONATHAN TUBB, mariner, who, dying in 1742, bequeathed the lot equally to his sister, ANNE TUBB, & his niece, ELIZABETH TUBB, daughter of his brother BENJAMIN TUBB; & whereas ELIZABETH married JOHN WORTLEY, gentleman, of Parish of St. George, Hanover Square, Middlesex; & they (page 1) on 30 Sept. 1742 appointed WILLIAM STONE, merchant, of Charleston, their attorney; & he by L & R dated 2 & 3 Mar. 1743, sold the lot to MARY HEXT; now she sells it to ALEXANDER PERONNEAU. Witnesses: CHARLES PINCKNEY, CATHERINE DUNN. Before WILLIAM PINCKNEY, J.P. WILLIAM HOPTON, Register.

Book I-I, p. 21
2 & 3 May 1751
L & R

JOHN TOOMER, gentleman, of St. Andrew's Parish, to ALEXANDER RANTOWLE, storekeeper, of Stono, for Ⱡ 3000 currency, 557 a. of land & marsh, being the W half of 2 tracts of land & 1 tract of marsh, near Stono River, formerly belonging to HENRY TOOMER; bounding S & W on Stono River; N on JOHN HENRY BONNEAU; E on other half belonging to JOSHUA TOOMER. Whereas HENRY TOOMER, father of said JOHN, by will dated 17 Dec. 1737 devised to his 2 sons, JOSHUA & JOHN, 2 tracts of land & a tract of marsh fronting the 2 tracts, where he lived, being 961 a., to be divided 2 years after the death of said father; JOSHUA to have the E half on which the dwelling house stood; & whereas MARY TOOMER, widow of testator, & SAMUEL WEST, acting executrix & executor by deed of partition dated 27 May 1746, according to a plat made by JOSEPH ELLIOTT, Dep. Sur. & certified 9 May 1746 by THOMAS WITTER, Dep. Sur. allotted to JOHN TOOMER, party hereto, 557 a. of land & marsh, being the W half now he sells to RANTOWLE. Witnesses: ANDREW RUTLEDGE, THOMAS NETHERCOAT. Before ALEXANDER STEWART, J.P. WILLIAM HOPTON, Register. Witnesses to deed of partition: GERTRUDE RANTOWLE, ALEXANDER RANTOWLE, FREDERICK MERCKLEY.

Book I-I, p. 26
2 & 4 June 1750
L & R

JOHN (his mark) BLACK, yeoman, & UNITY his wife, of Fredericksburg Township, Craven Co., to JOHN PAIN, JR., blacksmith, of same place, for Ⱡ 200 currency, 269 a. in Fredericksburg Township, being part of 400 a. granted by Gov. JAMES GLEN on 4 Oct. 1749 to JOHN BLACK, bounding NE & NW on vacant land; SW on JOHN BLACK; SE on WILLIAM GREY (formerly JOHN BLACK). Witnesses: WILLIAM (his mark) BREWER, JOHN LEE, THOMAS WATERHOUSE LEEDOM. Before ROGER GIBSON, J.P. WILLIAM HOPTON, Register. Plat certified 16 Feb. 1749 by JOHN PEARSON, D.S.

Book I-I, p. 33
6 & 7 May 1751
L & R

ANDREW SLANN, planter, of St. George's Parish, Dorchester, Berkeley Co., & ANNE his wife, only daughter & heir of ANNE WARING, wife of the Hon. THOMAS WARING, ESQ.; to MARY DRAKE, widow of JOHN DRAKE, planter, of same Parish; for Ⱡ 1500 currency, 300 a., part of 2800 a., conveyed by L & R dated 29 & 30 June 1740 to ANDREW & ANNE SLANN by THOMAS WARING, planter, oldest son & heir of THOMAS WARING, ESQ.; bounding W on MRS. FRANCES DOWNING; N on other part 2800 a.; E on

231

THOMAS & JOHN DRAYTON (formerly ANDREW SLANN); S on MARY DRAKE. Witnesses: JOSEPH ARDEN, WILLIAM FULLER, ROBERT DYMES. Before RALPH IZARD, J.P. WILLIAM HOPTON, Register. Plat by JOHN STEVENS, Dep. Sur. dated 22 Apr. 1751.

Book I-I, p. 39
5 & 7 Jan. 1750
L & R by Mortgage

ISAAC CARR, planter, to DANIEL LAROCHE, ESQ., both of Prince George Parish, Craven Co., as security on 3 bonds dated 4 Jan. 1750, total Ł 700 currency, with interest, to be paid in certain amounts on certain dates; 500 a. in Prince Frederick Parish, Craven Co., bounding NE on Black River; NW & SW on JOHN WHITE; SE on WILLIAM CRIPSS & Green's Creek. Witnesses: JOHN HENTIE, ALLEN WELLS. Before ROBERT AUSTIN, J.P. WILLIAM HOPTON, Register.

Book I-I, p. 44
16 & 17 May 1751
L & R

JAMES CHAMBERS, tailor, now of Wadmalaw Island, Colleton Co., & BATHSHEBA (her mark) his wife, daughter of JOHN SAMS, planter, of same place, to ALEXANDER RANTOWLE, storekeeper, of Stono, for Ł 428 currency, 214 a., called Sams's Bluff, on Wadmalaw Island. Whereas JOHN SAMS owned 2 adjoining tracts, 1 of 200 a. formerly granted to JOHN FREER, the other of 14 a., part of a tract formerly belonging to WILLIAM GREEN, which 2 tracts, granted by the Lords Proprs.; after several mesne conveyances came to JOHN SAMS; making 1 tract of 214 a., bounding E on BONUM SAMS (now FRANCES VARAMBOUT); S on WILLIAM MC-GILVERY; W on WILLIAM GREEN; N on Wadmalaw River; & whereas JOHN SAMS died intestate, leaving his wife, HANNAH, & 4 daughters, MARTHA, ELIZABETH, BATHSHEBA, & ANN, his joint heirs; & whereas HANNAH, ELIZABETH, & ANN died before the estate was divided & MARTHA & BATHSHEBA inherited; & whereas JOHN HONEHAN, by marring MARTHA, became owner of half the 214 a.; & JAMES CHAMBERS, by marrying BATHSHEBA, became owner of the other half; & whereas by L & R dated 1 & 2 Mar. 1748 JOHN & MARTHA HONEHAN conveyed their 107 a. to JAMES CHAMBERS; now he sells the whole 214 a. to RANTOWLE, free from BATHSHEBA'S claim of dower. Witnesses: WILLIAM HOPTON, FREDERICK MERCKLEY. Before ALEXANDER STEWART, J.P. WILLIAM HOPTON, Register.

Book I-I, p. 52
11 & 12 May 1744
L & R

GEORGE HUNTER, gentleman, to ROBERT ROPER, gentleman, both of Charleston, for Ł 350 currency, paid to ANNE ELLERY & 10 shillings to GEORGE HUNTER, that part of lot #80 marked B in the general plat, fronting E 50 ft. 11 in. on the street laid out to the N from end of Bay near CRAVENS BASTION; bounding S 226 ft. on another street of lot #80, W on another street of lot #80; N 216 ft. on lot C part of lot #80 belonging to CHARLES PINCKNEY. Whereas the Lords Proprs. on 5 May. 1680 granted SIR PETER COLLETON a lot in Charleston known as #80 containing 9 a., 2 roods, 21 perches, English measure, of dry land & marsh land, with a small creek in the marsh land, bounding E on Cooper River & THOMAS COLLETON & Landgrave JAMES COLLETON; W on a small unnamed street; S on CAPT. WILLIAM WALLEY & 2 lots belonging to CAPT. JAMES ADIE; N on THOMAS COLLETON & another small unnamed street; & whereas lot #80 by various mesne conveyances became vested in JOHN COLLETON, of Fairlawn Barony, St. John's Parish, Berkeley Co., & he & SUSANNAH, his wife, by L & R dated 13 & 14 July 1736, for Ł 5000 currency sold the lot to GEORGE HUNTER; & whereas lot #80 by an agreement entered in by GEORGE HUNTER, CHARLES PINCKNEY, ESQ., & MRS. ANNE ELLERY, widow, has been laid out into several small lots, streets & lanes, according to a general plat; now HUNTER sells 1 of ANNE ELLERY'S lots to ROPER. Witnesses: SAMUEL PRIOLEAU, JR., CHARLES CALDER, JR. Before HECTOR BARRINGER DE BEAUFAIN, J.P. WILLIAM HOPTON, Register. Plat of lot B.

Book I-I, p. 60
1 & 2 Jan. 1745
L & R

DANIEL LESESNE, ESQ., to FRANCIS LESESNE, both of Winyaw, Craven Co., for Ł 50 SC money, 500 a. in Craven Co., at head of Georgetown Creek, bounding E on ISAAC LESESNE; N on MR. SIMONS; S & W on vacant land; as by plat attached to original grant dated 13 June 1733. Witnesses: JOSEPH DUTARQUE, JOHN CUTHBERT. Before WILLIAM PINCKNEY, J.P. WILLIAM HOPTON, Register.

Book I-I, p. 65
29 & 30 Apr. 1751
L & R

EDWARD PLOWDEN, ESQ., to FRANCIS LESESNE, both of Williamsburg Township, Winyaw, Craven Co., for Ł 300 SC money, 350 a. on N side Black

River, on Boggey Swamp, in Williamsburg Township, bounding W on JOHN
FLEMING; N on ROGER GORDON; E & S on vacant land; as by plat of original
grant dated Apr. 1736. Witnesses: ESTHER CUTHBERT, JOHN CUTHBERT. Before WILLIAM PINCKNEY, J.P. WILLIAM HOPTON, Register.

Book I-I, p. 71 RICHARD LAMBTON, ESQ., & ANNE his wife, of
17 & 18 May 1751 Charleston, to NATHANIEL BARNWELL, ESQ., of
L & R Port Royal Island, Granville Co., formerly
granted THOMAS BRINAN & then bounding S & SE
on vacant land & on ARTHUR DICK; W on Great Port Royal River; other sides
on vacant land. Whereas Gov. NATHANIEL JOHNSON on 14 May 1707 granted
THOMAS BRINAN 400 a. on Port Royal Island which he, by deed of feoffment
dated 5 Feb. 1710, he conveyed to the use of his wife LYDIA; & whereas
she after BRINAN'S death, married ROSS REYNOLDS, & by L & R dated 13 & 14
Nov. 1712 they conveyed to WILLIAM HYDE; after whose death the general
assembly on 15 Feb. 1714 turned his estate over to certain trustees to be
sold & the money used to pay HYDE'S debts & to support his widow & child,
by which act ELIZABETH WIGFALL ALLEN, as administratrix, by L & R dated
27 & 28 Jan. 1722 sold the 400 a. to JACOB BOND, mariner; & whereas BOND
by L & R dated 9 & 10 Mar. 1735 sold the land to RICHARD LAMBTON & ROW-
LAND VAUGHAN, not as jointenants but as tenants in common, each becoming
owner of 200 a., & VAUGHAN, by will dated 3 Aug. 1736 devised his share
to LAMBTON, who became owner of the 400 a., now he, with his wife, conveys to BARNWELL. Witness: ALEXANDER GORDON, JR. Before ALEXANDER GOR-
DON, J.P. WILLIAM HOPTON, Register.

Book I-I, p. 79 Lt. Gov. WILLIAM BULL, to NATHANIEL BARNWELL,
6 & 7 Mar. 1749 ESQ., of Granville Co., for Ł 1333:11:1 SC
L & R money, 418 a. on Port Royal Island, Granville
Co., bounding NW on vacant land; NE on ROBERT
WILKINSON; S on EVAN LEWIS & DAVID DUVAL; W on ARTHUR DICKS & MR. HYDE;
which land was granted by the Lords Proprs. on 17 Dec. 1714 to HENRY
QUINTYNE, ESQ. Witnesses: JOHN GIBBES, JOSEPH JENKINS. Before THOMAS
DRAYTON, J.P. WILLIAM HOPTON, Register.

Book I-I, p. 85 BENJAMIN HARVEY, planter, of Stono, to Gov.
4 Mar. 1750 JAMES GLEN, in penal sum of Ł 5000 currency,
Bond as security for payment of Ł 2500 currency,
with interest, on 4 Mar. 1751. Witnesses:
JAMES WRIGHT, HUGH ANDERSON, JAMES MOULTRIE. Before JAMES MICHIE, J.P.
WILLIAM HOPTON, Register.

Book I-I, p. 86 BENJAMIN HARVEY, planter, & ELIZABETH his wife,
4 & 5 Mar. 1750 of Stono, to Gov. JAMES GLEN, as security for
L & R by Mortgage payment of bond of even date in penal sum of
Ł 5000 for payment of Ł 2500 currency, with
interest on Mar. 4, 1751; part of a lot in Charleston, bounding S 154 ft.
on Broad Street; N 154 ft. on JOHN DRAYTON; E 104 ft. on ELIZABETH QUINCY;
W 104 ft. on JOHN HARVEY. Whereas WILLIAM HARVEY, gentleman, of Charleston, owned the above lot & by will bequeathed to his wife, SARAH, & to
his son, BENJAMIN, his brick house with its grounds where he lived, or-
daining that SARAH should during her lifetime pay all taxes & repairs &
pay 20 shillings currency, yearly rent to BENJAMIN; & whereas SARAH died
& BENJAMIN became sole owner; now he mortgages the premises to Gov. GLEN.
Witnesses: JAMES WRIGHT, JAMES MOULTRIE, JAMES GRINDLAY, JOHN THOMAS.
MOULTRIE appeared before JAMES MICHIE, J.P. WILLIAM HOPTON, Register.
GRINDLAY appeared before DANIEL CRAWFORD, J.P. ELIZABETH'S execution &
probate recorded 4 Sept. 1753 by WILLIAM HOPTON, Register.

Book I-I, p. 96 JOHN ALEXANDER PARRIS, planter, of Christ
____ Nov. 1750 Church Parish, grandson & legatee of ALEXANDER
Grant of a Pew PARRIS, ESQ., of Charleston, also devisee &
heir of JOHN ALEXANDER PARRIS, ESQ., for Ł 250
SC money; to GEORGE SEAMAN, merchant, of Charleston, that pew #1 at each
end of S aisle, of St. Philip's Church, Charleston, which pew SEAMAN has
occupied for several years past; which pew was formerly owned by ALEXAN-
DER PARRIS, who by will dated 6 Feb. 1735 bequeathed the bulk of his real
& personal estate to his son JOHN PARRIS; who by will dated 6 May 1736
devised the bulk of his real & personal estate to his son JOHN ALEXANDER
PARRIS with the proviso that should son JOHN ALEXANDER die before

233

reaching 18 years of age, the property should go to nephew JOHN ALEXANDER
PARRIS; & whereas the son died before reaching 18, the estate including
pew #1 was inherited by nephew JOHN ALEXANDER PARRIS, who now grants the
pew to SEAMAN. Witnesses: ALEXANDER MCDOUALL, LEONARD OUTERBRIDGE,
THOMAS LYNCH. Before PAUL TRAPIER, J.P. WILLIAM HOPTON, Register.

Book I-I, p. 98   Whereas WILLIAM LIVINGSTONE obtained his Ma-
23 June 1749 at London   jesty's order of Council dated 24 June 1742
Declaration of Trust   for 200,000 a. in SC, with a limit of 18
                         months for surveying & taking up the tract; &
whereas elapsed before any part of the land was taken up & the order became void; & whereas JOHN HAMILTON, ESQ., of St. George Parish, Hanover
Square, Middlesex Co. intends to petition his Majesty to renew the order
for LIVINGSTONE & HAMILTON'S use & has requested the use of LIVINGSTONE'S
name which request LIVINGSTONE grants, & declare that the order is applied for in his name solely for HAMILTON'S use & at the expense & trouble of HAMILTON, & obliges himself & his heirs to assign or convey such
lands to HAMILTON. Witness: DANIEL MACKERCHER. ALEXANDER GORDAN, clerk
of H.M. Council, recognized MACKERCHER'S signature before WILLIAM PINCK-
NEY, J.P. WILLIAM HOPTON, Register.

Book I-I, p. 100   WILLIAM LIVINGSTONE, ESQ., of Parish of St.
13 Dec. 1749   Martins, in the Fields, Co. of Middlesex, ac-
Assignment   cording to agreement (p. 98) assigns to JOHN
                         HAMILTON, ESQ., of Parish of St. George, Han-
over Square, Co. of Middlesex, all his title to 200,000 a. in SC & appoints JOHN HAMILTON his attorney in this matter by agreement dated 23
June 1749 (p. 98) LIVINGSTONE agreed to let HAMILTON use his name in a
petition to his Majesty's Council to renew an order dated 24 June 1742
for 200,000 a. in SC; which order Council renewed & ordered the Sur. Gen.
of SC to lay out the 200,000 a. for LIVINGSTONE & his associates in 4
parcels of 50,000 a. each, the 4 parcels to be as contiguous as possible,
but none more than 10 miles from another; & ordered the Gov. of SC to
pass grants to LIVINGSTONE & his associates of not less than 12,000 a.,
the whole to be taken up & surveyed & grants made within 3 years; LIVING-
STONE to pay usual fees & to settle 1000 Protestants on the lands within
10 years from date of grants, etc., etc. Witnesses: JAMES BERNARD, MOSES
SCHOMBERG. ISAAC DECOSTE recognized witnesses handwriting before ALEXAN-
DER GORDON, J.P. WILLIAM HOPTON, Register.

Book I-I, p. 106   CHARLES PINCKNEY, ESQ., & ELIZABETH his wife,
21 & 22 Dec. 1749   of Charleston, to BURREL MASSENBURGH HEYRNE,
L & R   ESQ., of Colleton Co., for Ł 2500 SC money,
                         the W half of 2223 a., (1100 a.) divided from
PINCKNEY'S E half by a line running a NW course 21 deg. W from Ashepoo
River to the head or upper line of 2 500 a. tracts. Whereas the Lords
Proprs. on 15 Sept. 1705 granted RICHARD WOODWARD 500 a. at head of W
branch of Ashepoo River in Colleton Co., bounding S & W branch said River;
NE on a creek; other sides on vacant land; & whereas the Lords Proprs.
granted WOODWARD another 500 a. at head of Ashepoo River; bounding NE on
Capt. JOHN WOODWARD the elder; SE on above 500 a.; SW on JOHN WOODWARD;
NW on vacant land; & whereas RICHARD WOODWARD by deed poll dated 22 July
1716, for Ł 900 currency, sold the 2 tracts to CAPT. JOHN WOODWARD; &
whereas, JOHN WOODWARD the elder by will dated 6 Dec. 1726 bequeathed the
2 tracts to his 3 sons, JOHN, RICHARD & THOMAS; & whereas THOMAS died in
infancy & JOHN & RICHARD inherited; & whereas JOHN & RICHARD, with ELIZA-
BETH (RICHARD'S wife) by L & R dated 4 & 5 Mar. 1741 sold the 1000 a. of
high land, river & swamp land, & surplus land, to CHARLES PINCKNEY, who
applied for a re-survey to ascertain the amount of surplus land, which
being granted & survey made the surplus land was found to measure 1223 a.
over & above the 1000 a., which surplus land was granted to PINCKNEY; now
PINCKNEY sells the W half to HEYRNE. Witnesses: THOMAS BURRINGTON,
CHARLES PINCKNEY, JR. Before WILLIAM PINCKNEY, J.P. WILLIAM HOPTON,
Register. Broken plat.

Book I-I, p. 116   JOHN ABBOT, merchant, by his attorney DANIEL
1 Apr. 1751   LAROCHE, merchant, (appointed 20 Mar. 1737);
Feoffment   to MARY WILLSON, widow; all of Georgetown; for
                         Ł 150 SC money, lot #85 in Georgetown, bound-
ing SW 100 ft. on Prince Street; NW 217.9 on Broad Street; NE on lot #109;

SE on lot #86. Witnesses: DAVID MONTAIGUT, CLAUDIUS PEGUES. Before PAUL
TRAPIER, J.P. WILLIAM HOPTON, Register.

Book I-I, p. 119   ROBERT REID, planter, of Colleton Co., to JER-
10 May 1751   MYN WRIGHT, CHARLES WRIGHT, & JOHN LAIRD, as
Mortgage   security on bond of even date in penal sum of
                          Ł 771:0:8 for payment of Ł 385:10:4 currency,
with interest, on 10 Mar. 1752; 435 a. in St. Bartholomews Parish, Colleton Co., bounding SE on SAMUEL SLIGH; NE on LAURENCE SANDERS. Witnesses:
DANIEL CAMPBELL, JAMES WILLIAMSON. Before JAMES BULLOCK, J.P. WILLIAM
HOPTON, Register.

Book I-I, p. 122   ROBERT ELLIS, merchant, formerly of Philadel-
12 July 1750   phia, Pennsylvania, now residing in London, &
Release   CATHERINE his wife, to his son, ROBERT ELLIS,
                          JR., merchant, of Philadelphia, for Ł 500
Pennsylvania money, natural love & affection & other considerations,
500 a. in Craven Co., SC, also 22 a. in Craven Co., also lot #13 in New
Town, NC on NE branch of Cape Fear River, & any other of his lands in SC
or NC whereas by L & R dated 29 & 30 July 1735 MOREAU SARAZIN, silversmith, of Charleston, SC & ELIZABETH his wife, sold to ROBERT ELLIS, the
father, 500 a. in Craven Co., on S side Black River, lately granted by
the King to SARAZIN, bounding S on MR. LLOYD; N on JOHN GREEN; W on MER-
EDITH HUGHES; & whereas ANTHONY WHITE, planter, of Craven Co., by deed
poll dated 14 July 1736 sold to ROBERT ELLIS, the father, 22 a. in Craven
Co., bounding SE on ELISHA SCREVEN; other sides on ANTHONY WHITE; & whereas JOHN WATSON, planter, of Hanover Precinct, Bath Co., NC, by deed poll
dated 8 Sept. 1737 (recorded in Register's office at Hanover in Book A.
fol. 260) sold to ROBERT ELLIS the father, lot #13 (according to plan by
MATHEW HIGINBOTHAM) in New Town on NE branch of Cape Fear River, in NC
having then & now a house thereon & being a water lot; & whereas MICHAEL
HIGGINS by deed poll dated 25 Feb. 1741 (Book B. fol. 398) quitclaimed
said lot #13 to ELLIS, the father; now ELLIS & his wife convey all their
possessions in NC & SC to their son ROBERT. Witnesses to father's signature: STEPHEN MESNARD, JAMES SHIRLEY, WILLIAM MCKNIGHT. Witnesses to
CATHERINE'S signature: MAGDALIN SWIF, ROBERT BALLANTINE. Before WILLIAM
PLUMSTED, Mayor of Philadelphia.

Book I-I, p. 128   JAMES HAMILTON, Lt. Gov. of Province of Penn-
                          sylvania & Counties of New Castle, Kent & Sus-
sec upon Delaware, testitied on 19 Apr. 1751 that WILLIAM PLUMSTED, was
Mayor & J.P. of Philadelphia & his certificates entitled to credit; which
certificate should have been recorded after following power of attorney.

Book I-I, p. 129   ROBERT ELLIS, merchant, formerly of Philadel-
18 Aug. 1750   phia, Pennsylvania, now of Parish of St. Mar-
Letter of Attorney   tins in the Fields, Co. of Middlesex, England,
                          appointed his son ROBERT ELLIS, merchant, of
Philadelphia, his attorney in NC & SC. Witnesses: STEPHEN MESNARD, JAMES
SHIRLEY, WILLIAM MCKNIGHT. Before WILLIAM PLUMSTED, Mayor of Philadel-
phia. WILLIAM HOPTON, Register.

Book I-I, p. 130   ROGER MOORE, ESQ., of Orton, on Cape Fear Riv-
1 Dec. 1747   er, NC, to his son, THOMAS SMITH, the younger,
Gift   merchant of Charleston, for love & affection
                          & other considerations, 200 a. on Hilton Head
Island, Granville Co., SC, bounding W on the River May; S on a creek; N &
E on vacant land; which tract was granted by the Lords Proprs. on 1 Sept.
1706 to JOHN BARNWELL, ESQ., Arrdshill, Granville Co., SC, who on 26 Apr.
1709 sold to JOHN PIGHT, gentleman, of SC & conveyed by PIGHT on 6 June
1719 to JOHN BAYLEY, surveyor, of Goose Creek, Berkeley Co., SC & sold by
said BAYLEY to said ROGER MOORE; also 700 a., called GIBBES'S Plantation,
in Berkeley Co., SC, bounding S on Goose Creek; W on COL. JOHN HERBERT; E
on heirs of COL. HUGH GRANGE; which 700 a. were conveyed by L & R dated 5
& 6 Mar. 1743 by PHILIP GIBBES, gentleman, of the Island of Barbadoes, to
said ROGER MOORE. Witnesses: HENRY LAURENS, WILLIAM MOORE. Before JACOB
MOTTE, J.P. WILLIAM HOPTON, Register.

Book I-I, p. 133   JOHN WATSONE, merchant, & ABIGAIL his wife, to
18 & 19 Jan. 1750   ALEXANDER PETRIE, goldsmith, both of

Charleston for Ł 3000 currency, that part of lot #13 in Charleston, bounding E on the Bay 21 ft. 6 in. from the house belonging to MR. COLLETON,
(occupied by ALEXANDER LIVIE) to the middle of the wall which divides the
tenement in which ALEXANDER PETRIE now lives from the tenement in which
JOHN WATSONE lives; W 18 ft. 7 in. from the outside of the wall next to
MR. COLLETON, to the middle of the wall of JOHN WATSONE'S yard; & 61 ft.
6 in. on the side from the Bay to the middle of the kitchen wall which
divides PETRIE'S kitchen from WATSONE'S kitchen; with use of drain, pump
& well formerly made by WATSONE; PETRIE to pay half the expense of keeping them in order. Whereas ANNE LEBRASSEUR, widow owned lot #13 in
Charleston, bounding E 56 ft. on the Bay; S 100 ft. on Elliott's Alley; W
71 ft. on another lot belonging to ANNE LEBRASSEUR; N 112 ft. on JOHN COL-
LETON; & by L & R dated 22 & 23 Dec. 1740 sold that part of lot #13 to
JOHN WATSONE; now he sells part of his lot to PETRIE. Witnesses: ISAAC
FOSTER, JOHN WAGNER. Before JAMES WRIGHT, J.P. WILLIAM HOPTON, Register.

Book I-I, p. 141   CHARLES CARROLL, peruke-maker, & EASTER his
21 & 22 Feb. 1750   wife, to WILLIAM GLEN, hatter, both of Charles-
L & R   ton, for Ł 1050 SC money, the W part of lot
                        #26, bounding S 23 ft. 2 in. on Prince Street,
(sometimes called Elliott Street, or Poinsett Street); W 90 ft. on WIL-
LIAM GLEN; (formerly MARY GAULTIER); N on JOHN RAVEN; E on CHARLES CAR-
ROLL; being part of a lot which WILLIAM STEWART, ESQ. & ANN his wife, by
L & R dated 17 & 18 Apr. 1750 sold to CHARLES CARROLL. Witnesses: MOREAU
SARRAZIN, JOHN REMINGTON. Before WILLIAM PINCKNEY, J.P. WILLIAM HOPTON,
Register.

Book I-I, p. 147   JOHN COLLETON, ESQ., of New Bond Street, Par-
13 Mar. 1750   ish of St. George, Hanover Square, Middlesex
Power of Attorney   Co., appoints JOHN HARLESTON, & ZACHARIAH VIL-
                        LEPONTEAUX, of SC, & JOSEPH BAIRD, gentleman,
now of Gosport in Hamphire but intending to go & reside in SC, forthwith,
his attorneys to look after his plantations, Negroes, cattle, etc., in SC,
subject to an agreement of even date with JOSEPH BAIRD as overseer of his
SC plantations. Witnesses: WILLIAM WHITE, ALEXANDER PEARSON. WHITE appeared before ROBERT AUSTIN, J.P. WILLIAM HOPTON, Register.

Book I-I, p. 148   RICHARD SPENCER, planter, of Craven Co., to
14 & 15 July 1751   JAMES MICHIE, ESQ., of Charleston, as security
L & R by Mortgage   on bond of (signed also by FRANCIS SPENCER) of
                        even date in penal sum of Ł 420 for payment of
Ł 210 SC money, with interest, on 24 July 1752; 150 a. in Craven Co.,
bounding N on FRANCIS SPENCER; E & S on heirs of MARTIN GLAZE BROOK
(GLAZEBROOK); W on Wambaw Creek, which tract was granted 8 Nov. 1740 by
Lt. Gov. WILLIAM BULL to RICHARD SPENCER. Witnesses: TIMOTHY MORGRIDGE,
JOHN TROUPE. Before HECTOR BERINGER DE BEAUFAIN, J.P. WILLIAM HOPTON,
Register.

Book I-I, p. 154   JOHN BRUNSON, planter, & ABIGAIL, his wife;
1 Mar. 1743   ISAAC BRADWELL, planter & REBECCA (her mark)
Release   his wife; all of St. George Parish, Berkeley
                        Co.; EBENEZER BRUNSON, planter; JOHN PENNY
(PHINNEY ?), planter, & HANNAH his wife, all of Colleton Co., of the 1st
part; to BURNABY BRANFORD, planter, of St. George Parish; for Ł 1000 currency; 200 a. in St. George Parish, bounding N on ROBERT MILLER; W on
ROBERT MILLER & MARY WALTOR; S on MATHEW BEARD; E on BURNABY BRANFORD; to
which land parties of first part were entitled by will of JOSEPH BRUNSON,
of St. George Parish. Witnesses: WILLIAM OSBORN, MORGAN (his mark) GRIF-
FIS, PHILLIP (his mark) SPULAR. Before RICHARD WARING, J.P. Memorial
registered in Auditor's office 25 July 1751 in Book #3, fol. 270, by
JAMES WEDDERBURN, Dep. Aud. WILLIAM HOPTON, Register.

Book I-I, p. 157   ALLARD BELIN, planter, of Prince George Parish,
9 & 10 Jan. 1749   Craven Co., to PAUL TRAPIER, ESQ., of George-
L & R   town, for Ł 100 currency; 1000 a. on N side
                        Santee River, in Prince George Parish, bound-
ing N on Landgrave THOMAS SMITH; S on THOMAS LYNCH; W on FINEAS (PHINEAS)
SPRY. Whereas COL. THOMAS LYNCH on 14 Aug. 1733 conveyed said 1000 a. to
JAMES BELIN, planter, & SARAH his wife, & to ALLARD BELIN & JAMES BELIN,
JR., (sons of said JAMES BELIN), for the lifetime of JAMES, the father;

died, & SARAH surrendered her interest to ALLARD (who had children); now
he sells to PAUL TRAPIER. Witnesses: WILLIAM POOLE, ISAAC TRAPIER. Before WILLIAM FLEMING, J.P. WILLIAM HOPTON, Register.

Book I-I, p. 161   PAUL TRAPIER, ESQ., of Georgetown, to ALLARD
12 & 13 Jan. 1749   BELIN, planter, of Prince George Parish, Cra-
L & R   ven Co., for ₺ 100 currency, 1000 a. on N side
                           Santee River, Prince George Parish, Craven Co.,
bounding N on estate of Landgrave THOMAS SMITH; S on THOMAS LYNCH; W on
FINEAS (PHINEAS) SPRY. Whereas COL. THOMAS LYNCH by L & R dated 3 Jan.
1733 conveyed to JAMES BELIN, the father, & SARAH his wife, & to ALLARD
BELIN & JAMES BELIN, JR., (sons of said JAMES) the said plantation during
the father's life; then to SARAH, ALLARD & JAMES, in succession; but in
case of default the tract to revert to donor's heir; & whereas JAMES, the
father died; & SARAH surrendered her interest to ALLARD (who had children,
male & female); & he by L & R dated 9 & 10 Jan. 1749 conveyed the land to
TRAPIER; now TRAPIER re-conveys the land to ALLARD BELIN. Witnesses: WIL-
LIAM SHACKELFORD, LEONARD OUTERBRIDGE. Before WILLIAM FLEMING, J.P. WIL-
LIAM HOPTON, Register.

Book I-I, p. 166   PAUL TOWNSEND, merchant, to PETER BENOIST, mer-
6 & 7 May 1751   chant, both of Charleston, as security on sev-
L & R by Mortgage   eral bonds; part of 2 lots in Charleston, 30
                           ft. x 125 ft., English measure, bounding N on
PETER LEGARE, cooper; S on ISAAC MAZYCK; W on STOREY & CHAMPMAN; E on
Bedons Alley. Whereas PAUL TOWNSEND gave PETER BENOIST a bond of even
date in penal sum of ₺ 2270 currency, reciting that whereas PETER BENOIST
went on TOWNSEND'S bond, to THOMAS LAMBOLL, dated 27 Feb. 1750 in penal
sum of ₺ 1270 for payment of ₺ 635 SC money, with interest, on 27 Feb.
1751; & whereas PETER BENOIST also signed another of TOWNSEND'S bonds to
LAMBOLL, dated 28 Feb. 1750 in penal sum of ₺ 400 for payment of ₺ 200,
with interest, on 28 Feb. 1751; & whereas BENOIST signed another bond
from TOWNSEND to THOMAS GLEN, dated 13 Apr. 1751 in penal sum of ₺ 600
for payment of ₺ 300 currency, with interest, on 1 Aug. 1751, now TOWN-
SEND conveys part of 2 lots to BENOIST as security. Witnesses: CHARLES
STEVENSON, WILLIAM BUCHANAN, JR. Before OTHNIEL BEALE, J.P. WILLIAM
HOPTON, Register. On 19 May 1763 EDWARD NEUFVILLE, executor of PETER
BENOIST, declared mortgage paid. Witness: WILLIAM HOPTON, Register.

Book I-I, p. 173   WILLIAM CATTELL, SR., planter, of St. Andrews
26 & 26 July 1751   Parish, Berkeley Co., to ISAAC NICHOLES, plant-
L & R   er, of St. Pauls Parish, Colleton Co., for
                           ₺ 1400 SC money, 210 a. at lower end of Horse
Savannah, bounding NE on HENRY MIDDLETON (formerly JOHN WILLIAMS); W on
THOMAS FULLER (formerly CARLILE'S, lately ANN DRAYTON'S); the 210 a. being partly in Berkeley Co., & Partly in Colleton Co. Apparently on 19
Aug. 1729 CATTELL purchased 168 a. from ALEXANDER TRENCH; 85 a. of which,
in Colleton Co., later formed part of the 210 a.; & on 14 Aug. 1726 had
purchased 322 a. from TRENCH, 125 a. of which, in Berkeley Co., formed
the other part of said 210 a. Witnesses: JOHN CATTELL, M. CATTELL, AN-
DREW LETCH. Before ROBERT AUSTIN, J.P. WILLIAM HOPTON, Register. Plat
of 210 a. dated 2 July 1751 by JOHN STEVENS, Dep. Sur.

Book I-I, p. 180   THOMAS LLOYD, gentleman, of Charleston, in
23 & 24 Mar. 1749   consideration of his marriage, already solem-
L & R in Trust   nized, with MARY, daughter of JAMES MATHEWS,
                           merchant, for the natural love & affection he
has for MARY; & for ₺ 5000 currency, or value thereof, received by THOMAS
as part of MARY'S marriage portion; & for other considerations; & in
order to settle certain lands, Negro slaves, etc., conveys to ANTHONY
MATTHEWS, ESQ., of Charleston; in trust for MARY; 260 a. in Colleton Co.,
bounding N on MAJ. BOON; S on a marsh of Caiwau River; W on WILLIAM WHIP-
PEY; E on Stono River; which tract OBADIAH WILKINS, planter, of John's
Island, & ELIZABETH his wife, by L & R dated 8 & 9 Feb. last, conveyed to
THOMAS LLOYD; also 22 Negro slaves. Witnesses: WILLIAM DUTHY, WILLIAM
BOON, JR., CHARLES PRYCE. Before JACOB MOTTE, J.P. WILLIAM HOPTON, Reg-
ister.

Book I-I, p. 186   JAMES AKIN, ESQ., gentleman, of Berkeley Co.,
23 & 24 Mar. 1750/51   to GEORGE MONTGOMERY, planter, of Williamsburg

L & R   Township, Craven Co., for Ł 750 SC money,
                               1000 a. in Craven Co., bounding SW on heirs of
NATHANIEL DREW (formerly THOMAS DIAL); NE on JAMES MCNEALEY & WILLIAM
GRIMES; SE partly on GEORGE MONTGOMERY; other sides on vacant land.
Whereas Lt. Gov. THOMAS BROUGHTON on 9 Apr. 1736 granted JAMES AKIN 500 a.
in Craven Co., bounding SW on CHARLES CODNER; other sides on vacant land;
on same date granted CHARLES CODNER 500 a. in Craven Co., bounding NE on
JAMES AKIN; other sides on vacant land; which land CODNER sold to AKIN by
L & R dated 1 & 2 May 1736; & whereas AKIN, by deed poll endorsed on said
grants, on 15 Dec. 1736, surrendered the 2 grants of 500 a. each to his
majesty, & whereas GEORGE II by Lt. Gov. BROUGHTON, on 18 Dec. 1736 granted AKIN the 1000 a. (granted in 2 tracts to AKIN & CODNER & surrendered
by AKIN) in Williamsburg Township; now AKIN sells the tract to MONTGOM-
ERY. Witnesses: ALEXANDER MCCREE, EDWARD HOWARD. Before ROBERT AUSTIN,
J.P. WILLIAM HOPTON, Register.

Book I-I, p. 192   MATHEW BEAIRD, planter, of St. John's Parish,
15 & 16 July 1751   Berkeley Co., to MARGARET O'NEAL, widow, vint-
L & R by Mortgage   ner, as security on bond dated 15 inst. July
                           in penal sum of Ł 473 for payment of Ł 236:14
currency, with interest, on 15 July 1752; 1500 a. in Granville Co.,
granted by Gov. ROBERT JOHNSON to MATTHEW BEAIRD, SR., bounding NE on
Saltcatcher River; SE on JOHN CARMICHAEL; S on vacant land; SW on MR.
FERGUSON. Witnesses: JAMES MCKELVEY, JR., SARAH CASYTY. Before NATHAN-
IEL BROUGHTON, J.P. WILLIAM HOPTON, Register. On 20 June 1771 JAMES MC-
KELVEY declared mortgage satisfied. L. POYNTELL.

Book I-I, p. 197   NEWEL EDWARDS, son & heir of EDWARD & MARY his
28 & 29 Apr. 1750   wife (formerly MARY SEARS, 1 of the grand-
L & R   daughters of GRACE BUCKLEY, to JOSEPH ORAM,
                           joiner, of Charleston, for love & affection &
Ł 50 currency; 300 a., part of 365 a. on N side Cooper River, in Berkeley
Co., bounding SE on Ittewan Creek; SW on NATHANIEL WILLIAMS; NW on a
branch of Cloters Creek & on RICHARD HARRIS; NE on said HARRIS; which
365 a. had been granted to GRACE BUCKLEY & by several mesne conveyances
became vested in NEWEL EDWARDS as son & heir of EDWARD & MARY EDWARDS;
the 65 a. having been sold by NEWEL EDWARDS to JOHN SCOTT, shipwright, of
Charleston. Witnesses: JORDAN ROCHE, WILLIAM LIVINGSTONE, BENJAMIN HAR-
VEY. Before JAMES WEDDERBURN, J.P. WILLIAM HOPTON, Register.

Book I-I, p. 203   JOSEPH ORAM, joiner, & FRANCES his wife, of
14 & 15 Aug. 1751   Charleston, to JOHN MOORE, planter, of St.
L & R   Thomas Parish, Berkeley Co., for Ł 800 curren-
                           cy, 200 a., being the N part of 300 a.; bound-
ing N on the 65 a. belonging to JOHN SCOTT & on GEORGE LOGAN (CLOWTERS);
S on the 100 a. (part of 365 a.) belonging to JOSEPH ORAM; E on marsh of
Etiwan Creek; W on marsh of Clowters Creek; as by plat of 200 a. signed
by PRINGLE HAMILTON. Whereas the Lords Proprs. on 23 July 1712 granted
GRACE BUCKLEY, widow, 365 a. on NE side Cooper River, in Berkeley Co.,
bounding SE on Etiwan Creek; S on NATHANIEL WILLIAMS; NW on a branch of
Clowters Creek & on RICHARD HARRIS; NE on RICHARD HARRIS; & whereas GRACE
BUCKLEY by will dated 14 Feb. 1721 bequeathed the 365 a. equally to her 2
granddaughters, CATHERINE LEA & MARY SEARS; & whereas CATHERINE LEA & her
husband JOSEPH LEA, shipwright, (now dead), had 2 children JOSEPH & ROB-
ERT, who died in infancy & CATHERINE died intestate & her half of the
tract descended to MARY SEARS, her only sister & heir, so that MARY SEARS
became owner of the whole tract, & whereas she married EDWARD EDWARDS,
planter; & after the death of said MARY & EDWARD, their eldest son, NEWEL
EDWARDS, inherited & sold the 65 a. in the N part to JOHN SCOTT, shipwright, of Charleston; & by L & R dated 28 & 29 Apr. 1750 conveyed the
300 a. to JOSEPH ORAM, party hereto; now ORAM sells part of the 300 a.
(that is 200 a.) to MOORE. Witnesses: EDWARD NEUFVILLE, BENJAMIN WAIN-
WRIGHT. Before WILLIAM PINCKNEY, J.P. WILLIAM HOPTON, Register.

Book I-I, p. 210   ROBERT TAYLOR, planter, & CATHERINE his wife,
5 & 6 Dec. 1737   to JAMES MAXWELL, both of Berkeley Co., for
L & R   Ł 1500 currency, 2 tracts, 206 a. & 100 a.,
                           total 306 a., at Wampee, Berkeley Co., bound-
ing N on WILLIAM GREENLAND; E on JAMES MAXWELL; S on RENE MARCHANT; W on
WILLIAM GREENLAND & JOHN PAMOR (later written PALMER). Witnesses: JOHN

SUMMERS, JOHN AUSTIN, DAVID LAFONS. Before THOMAS FERGUSON, J.P. WIL-LIAM HOPTON, Register.

Book I-I, p. 215   BARNARD ELLIOTT & BENJAMIN ELLIOTT, of St.
10 Oct. 1749   Andrews Parish, Berkeley Co., to WILLIAM
Sale   ELLIOTT, SR., for Ł 175 paid to each, each of
their quarter parts of the 10 a. that old MR.
ELLIOTT, father of BARNARD & grand-father of BENJAMIN, bought from MR.
WRIGHT, C.J., lying near Bacon's Bridge at head of Ashley River; with the
houses, improvements, etc. Witnesses: JOHN MCQUEEN, JOHN COCKFIELD, JO-
SEPH PERRY. Delivery by turf & twig. Before JOHN DART, J.P. WILLIAM
HOPTON, Register.

Book I-I, p. 216   WILLIAM LOGAN, merchant, of Charleston, to
16 Oct. 1750   RICHARD BAKER, planter, of Ashley River, in
Bond   penal sum of Ł 1628 for payment of Ł 814 currency, with interest, on 16 Oct. 1754. Wit-
nesses: ALEXANDER GOODBE, NOAH DUTARQUE. Before ALEANCDER CRAMAHE, J.P.
WILLIAM HOPTON, Register.

Book I-I, p. 217   WILLIAM LOGAN, merchant, of Charleston, to
1 & 2 July 1751   RICHARD BAKER, planter, of Ashley River, as
L & R by Mortgage   security on above land (p. 216); 10 a., formerly belonging to ROBERT WRIGHT, ESQ., who
conveyed to LOGAN; on Ashley River in Berkeley Co., bounding NW on the
high road leading to Stevens Bridge; NE on Ashley River & ROBERT WRIGHT.
Witnesses: ALEXANDER GOODBE, NOAH DUTARQUE. Before ALEXANDER CRAMAHE,
J.P. WILLIAM HOPTON, Register.

Book I-I, p. 223   JOSHUA TOOMER, planter, formerly of Stono, SC,
15 & 16 May 1751   now of NC, & SOPHIA his wife, to JOHN WATSONE,
L & R   merchant, of Charleston, for Ł 500 SC money,
400 a. in Colleton Co., bounding E on JAMES
HARTLEY; N on THOMAS ELLIOTT; W on THOMAS SANDERS; S on ROBERT MCKEWN.
Witnesses: EDWARD BULLARD, THOMAS FLEMING. Before JAMES WRIGHT, J.P.
WILLIAM HOPTON, Register.

Book I-I, p. 228   SOPHIA TOOMER, wife of JOSHUA TOOMER, before
16 May 1751   JAMES HASELL, C.J. of NC, declared she volun-
Renunciation of Dower tarily joined her husband in above conveyance
(p. 223). WILLIAM HOPTON, Register.

Book I-I, p. 230   NATHANIEL BURT & REBECCA (her mark) his wife,
30 & 31 Aug. 1751   of Charleston, to JOHN WESTFIELD, planter, of
L & R   Craven Co., for Ł 150 SC money, 150 a. in the
Welch tract Craven Co., granted 29 Nov. 1750
by Gov. JAMES GLEN to said NATHANIEL BURT, bounding W on Peedee River; N
on NATHANIEL BURT; E & S on vacant land; also 250 a. in the Welch tract,
granted same date by Gov. GLEN to NATHANIEL BURT, bounding NE on Peedee
River; NW on 3 creeks; the other sides on vacant land. Before WILLIAM
PINCKNEY, J.P. WILLIAM HOPTON, Register.

Book I-I, p. 235   NATHANIEL BURT, shoe-maker, & REBECCA (her
31 Aug. & 1 Sept. 1751 mark) his wife, of Charleston, to JOHN WEST-
L & R   FIELD, blacksmith, of Craven Co., for Ł 150 SC
money, 150 a. in the Welch tract, Craven Co.,
granted 1 June 1750 by Gov. JAMES GLEN to said NATHANIEL BURT, bounding N
on vacant land & on WILLIAM EVANS; S on NATHANIEL BURT; E on vacant land;
W on Peedee River. Witnesses: GEORGE MATHEWS, NATHANIEL BURT, JR. WIL-
LIAM PINCKNEY, J.P. WILLIAM HOPTON, Register.

Book I-I, p. 240   See Book F.F. fols. 193, 194. ANN ELLERY, wid-
11 & 12 Mar. 1747   ow, of THOMAS ELLERY, gentleman, of St. Johns
Release by Agreement   Parish, Berkeley Co., to CHARLES PINCKNEY,
ESQ., of Charleston, for Ł 120 currency, paid
by PINCKNEY to CAPT. EDWARD LIGHTWOOD on ANNE ELLERY'S account; for her
marsh land or low lot on SE side of the canal in the marsh of Colleton
Square in Charleston, shown on plat by letter (g), bounding E on the
bridge from N end of Bay Street over said marsh; S on lot #34 belonging
to Landgrave DANIEL; W on a marsh lot in the square belonging to CHARLES

PINCKNEY; N on said canal running to the W through said marsh. Witnesses: THOMAS CROSTHWAITE, JOSEPH BROWN (gentleman). Before WILLIAM PINCK-NEY, J.P. WILLIAM HOPTON, Register.

Book I-I, p. 244
12 Feb. 1750
Release of Dower

SARAH MANNING, widow, of JAMES MANNING, shoemaker, of St. Andrews Parish, to ELIZABETH BELLINGER ELLIOTT, widow & executrix of will of EDWARD BELLINGER Landgrave, the 2nd Landgrave, her title to the 100 a. conveyed by JAMES MANNING, by L & R dated 3 & 4 Aug. 1747, to said MRS. BELLINGER; the 100 a. being part of 150 a. of land. Witnesses: ISAAC LADSON, GEORGE BELLINGER. Before JOHN DRAYTON, J.P. WILLIAM HOPTON, Register.

Book I-I, p. 246
2 & 3 Apr. 1751
L & R

ELIZABETH ELLIOTT, wife of THOMAS ELLIOTT, planter, of Stono, Colleton Co., of 1st part; RICHARD LAKE, ESQ., of Lakefarm, St. Andrew Parish, Berkeley Co., of 2nd part; CHARLES PINCKNEY, ESQ., & JOHN WATSON, merchant, of Charleston, truestees, of 3rd part. Whereas by marriage settlement dated 10 Apr. 1745 between THOMAS ELLIOTT & his wife ELIZABETH (formerly widow & devisee of Landgrave EDMUND BELLINGER) of 1st part & PINCKNEY & WATSON of 2nd part, all the lands, tenements, plantations, slaves, stock, debts, goods & chattels, whatsoever belonging to ELIZABETH at the time of her marriage with ELLIOTT were assigned to PINCKNEY & WATSONE in trust for ELIZABETH'S sole use; & whereas among the debts so settled on ELIZABETH, was one owing to said ELIZABETH, as executrix; from 1 JAMES MANNING, shoemaker, of St. Andrews Parish, which on 4 Aug. 1747 amounted to Ł 613 currency; & whereas MANNING by L & R dated 3 & 4 Aug. 1747 conveyed to ELIZABETH ELLIOTT 100 a., part of 250 a., in St. Andrews Parish, Berkeley Co., bounding N on FRANCIS LADSON; E on CHARLES WEST; S & W on STEPHEN DRAYTON; & whereas ELIZABETH has occasion to raise a sum of money for her use & support, she appoints PINCKNEY & WATSONE to sell MANNINGS land to the highest bidder; now they sell to RICHARD LAKE for Ł 500 currency. Witnesses: THOMAS BURRINGTON, J.P., CHARLES PINCKNEY, JR., WILLIAM BELLINGER, SAMUEL WADE, ISAAC FOSTER. BELLINGER appeared before THOMAS DRAYTON, J.P. CHARLES PINCKNEY testified before WILLIAM PINCKNEY, J.P. WILLIAM HOPTON, Register.

Book I-I, p. 253
24 & 25 Feb. 1730
L & R

BENJAMIN WHITAKER, ESQ., & SARAH his wife, of Charleston, to BENJAMIN GODFREY, planter, of Berkeley Co., for Ł 5000 currency, 160 a., English measure, on Ashley River, bounding E on BENJAMIN GODFREY; W & S on BENJAMIN WHITAKER (formerly CAPT. JOHN WOODWARD); N on a marsh of Ashley River; which tract by deed of exchange was conveyed by JOHN GODFREY, gentleman, to BENJAMIN WHITAKER; also 86 a. in Berkeley Co., bounding NE on CHARLES HILL; NW on BENJAMIN GODFREY; SW on JOHN WOODWARD; SE on said 160 a.; which 86 a. WHITAKER purchased from JOHN WOODWARD; also the vacant land between said plantations which WHITAKER lately purchased from ALEXANDER TRENCH. Witnesses: ANDREW DEVEAUX, JS. DEVEAUX. Before THOMAS LAMBOLL, J.P. WILLIAM HOPTON, Register.

Book I-I, p. 261
3 & 4 Oct. 1751
L & R

JOHN HARVEY, gentleman, & CATHERINE his wife, to FREDERICK GRIMKÉ, gentleman, both of Charleston, for Ł 1200 currency, that piece of land lately purchased by HARVEY from JORDAN ROCHE, gentleman, & REBECCA, his wife of Charleston; being part of 2 lots #162 & #169 or 1 of them in Charleston; bounding S 51 ft. on Broad Street; E 200 ft. on WILLIAM HARVEY; W on ANTHONY MATHEWS; N on OTHNIEL BEALE. Witnesses: RICHARD LAMBTON, JOHN BEEKMAN. Before THOMAS LAMBOLL, J.P. WILLIAM HOPTON, Register.

Book I-I, p. 268
1 Sept. 1750
Release & Confirmation

MARTIN CAMPBELL, PATRICK BROWN & ALEXANDER WOOD, merchant traders, of New Windsor, Granville Co., to CHARLES PINCKNEY, ESQ., OF Charleston, for 10 shillings each, confirm PINCKNEY'S title to 500 a. in Granville Co. Whereas WILLIAM BULL on 10 Apr. 1738 granted WILLIAM TRUEMAN 500 a. in Granville Co., near Silver Bluff on Savannah River, bounding NW on JOHN FRAISER; SW & S on the River; SE & NE on vacant land; & whereas WILLIAM TRUEMAN by L & R dated 30 & 31 Oct. 1738 conveyed the tract to WOOD, BROWN & CAMPBELL; who on 15 Oct.

1744 conveyed to WILLIAM GASCOIGNE, of Silver Bluff; who on 15 Apr. 1745
transferred the land to CHARLES RICHMOND GASCOIGNE, his eldest son; who
by L & R dated 3 & 4 Aug. 1750 conveyed the 500 a. to CHARLES PINCKNEY; &
whereas there is some doubt regarding the title of CHARLES RICHMOND GAS-
COIGNE from WOOD, BROWN & CAMPBELL, CHARLES RICHMOND GASCOIGNE by said L
& R authorized PINCKNEY to receive good & sufficient conveyances from
WOOD, BROWN & CAMPBELL; now they confirm PINCKNEY'S title. Witnesses:
WILLIAM PINCKNEY, CHARLES PINCKNEY, JR., WILLIAM GLEN, ALEXANDER WYLLY.
Before WILLIAM PINCKNEY, J.P.   WILLIAM HOPTON, Register.

Book I-I, p. 272   JOACHIM (his mark) PALTHASER, bricklayer &
27 Mar. 1751   plasterer, to JOHN DUTARQUE, planter, both of
Mortgage   St. James Santee Parish, Craven Co., as secur-
                       ity on bond of even date for payment of Ł 741
currency, with interest, on 27 Mar. 1752; 112 a. at Echaw in said Parish,
bounding SE on PETER DUMAY; NE on CAPT. MICHEAU; NW on Echaw Creek. Witnesses: ANTHONY BONNEAU, DAVID FOGARTIE, JOHN DUTARQUE, JR. Before ROB-
ERT AUSTIN, J.P. WILLIAM HOPTON, Register.

Book I-I, p. 275   Landgrave EDMUND BELLINGER & MARY LUCIA his
5 & 6 Apr. 1750   wife, to MRS. MARGARET TOBIAS, of Prince Wil-
L & R   liam Parish, Granville Co., for Ł 849 curren,
                       cy, 548 a., being the SW part of 1000 a. on
head of Pocotaligo River, bounding NE on marsh & W branch of said river;
& on the Rev. MR. WILLIAM HUTSON; S on the high road leading up from said
river towards Chulyfinna Creek; SW on estate of Landgrave EDMUND BELLING-
ER, the father; NW on ELIZABETH BELLINGER. Whereas Landgrave EDMUND BEL-
LINGER, the father, under his patent for 48,000 a., had a tract of 13,000
a. laid out for him at head of Pocotaligo River, in Granville Co., bounding E on COL. WILLIAM BULL; other sides on vacant land; & by will dated
21 Feb. 1739 bequeathed to his son, EDMUND, party hereto, 1000 a. to be
assigned to him by his mother, ELIZABETH, testator's wife; & ELIZABETH
assigned him 1000 a. out of the 13,000 a., bounding S & SW on the High
Road, & other part of the 13,000 belonging to said ELIZABETH BELLINGER; N
on JOHN BULL; E on the other part of the 13,000 a.; now EDMUND, the son,
the second Landgrave, sells a part of his 1000 a. to MARGARET TOBIAS.
Witnesses: JONATHAN BRYAN, ELIZABETH BULL, EDMUND PALMER. Before WILLIAM
PINCKNEY, ESQ., J.P. WILLIAM HOPTON, Register. Plat dated 30 Mar. 1750
by HUGH BRYAN, Dep. Sur.

Book I-I, p. 282   GEORGE SATCHWELL (SACHEVERELL?), planter, of
25 & 26 June 1751   Craven Co., to ROBERT STIELL, gentleman, for
L & R   Ł 400 currency, 200 a. in Craven Co., bounding
                       W on Santee River, opposite Saxegotha Town-
ship; N on RICHARD JACKSON; S on MARY HYDE & ELIZABETH VERDETTY; E on
ELIZABETH VERDETTY. Whereas King GEORGE II on 12 Apr. 1744, by Gov.
JAMES GLEN, granted NICHOLAS HAYNES, victualer, of Charleston, 200 a. in
Craven Co., bounding W on Santee River; other sides on vacant land; &
whereas HAYNES by L & R dated 7 & 8 May 1744 conveyed the 200 a. to
GEORGE SATCHWELL; now he sells to STIELL. Witnesses: EDWARD CUSICK,
JAMES LESSLY. Before STEPHEN CRELLE, J.P. WILLIAM HOPTON, Register.

Book I-I, p. 289   ELIZABETH SATCHWELL, wife of GEORGE SATCHWELL,
25 June 1751   planter, of Craven Co., renounces all claim to
Renunciation of Dower the 200 a. conveyed by her husband to ROBERT
                       STIELL this date, for Ł 400. See p. 282.
Witnesses: EDWARD CUSICK, JAMES LESSLY. Before STEPHEN CRELLE, J.P.
WILLIAM HOPTON, Register.

Book I-I, p. 291   GABRIEL GUIGNARD, cooper, & FRANCES his wife,
16 & 17 Sept. 1751   of Charleston, to JOHN DUTARQUE, planter, of
L & R   Berkeley Co., for Ł 280 currency, part of lot
                       #80 in Charleston, bounding N 40 ft. on Pinck-
ney Street; W 75 ft. on TIMOTHY CROSBY; S on GABRIEL GUIGNARD (formerly
JOHN RICHMOND GASCOIGNE); E on MRS. MIMECH. Witnesses: MARGARET REMING-
TON, JOHN REMINGTON. Before DANIEL CRAWFORD, J.P. WILLIAM HOPTON, Register. On 31 Aug. 1744 CHARLES PINCKNEY, ESQ., granted GABRIEL GUIGNARD
a large part of lot #80, of which the within is a part. The whole lot
#80 contained 9 a., 2 roods, 21 perches of dry land & marsh.

241

Book I-I, p. 297   RICHARD JACKSON, planter, of Craven Co., for
1 Oct. 1751   the fatherly love & care he bears his 4 young-
Gift for Uses   est children, JOHN, RICHARD, MILES, & MARY
                          (having provided for his oldest children) &
for the singular confidence & trust he reposes in his well beloved son-
in-law, HENRY SNELLING, planter, conveys to SNELLING, for the use of said
4 children, 200 a. in Amelia Township, Berkeley Co., bounding NW on vacant land & on JOHN JOYNER; also lot #317 in Amelia Town, containing half
an a.; also 133 a. at the Congarees, opposite Saxegotha Township, purchased from GEORGE HAIG, bounding E on EDWARD BROWN, (formerly ELIZABETH
VERDETY); S on GEORGE STACHWELL (formerly NICHOLAS HAYNES); W on Santee
River; also 150 a. in Craven Co., opposite Saxegotha Township bounding W
on JACOB PENNINGTON, originally granted to JOHN BLEWER; that is; the 200
a. & lot in Amelia Township for the us of son JOHN JACKSON; should he die
under age then to son RICHARD JACKSON; should he die under age then to
son MILES JACKSON; to 150 a. opposite Saxegotha Township to use of son
RICHARD; should he die under age then to MILES; the 133 a. on Santee to
son MILES; should he die under age, then to survivors; he delivers to
SNELLING 1 riffled gun, 1 bed & 1 iron pot to son JOHN; 1 riffled gun, 1
bed & 1 iron pot to son RICHARD; 1 riffled gun, 1 bed, & 1 iron pot to
son MILES; 1 bed & 1 iron pot to daughter MARY; the plows, carts, & all
plantation tools equally to RICHARD, MILES, & MARY; he delivers to SNELL-
ING all horses & cattle branded JI, the cattle marked with a bolt in 1
ear & crop & under keel in the other, & all hogs marked with same earmark, for use of JOHN; all horses & cattle branded RI; the cattle marked
with a crop in right ear & a swallowfork & nick under it in the left; all
hogs marked with same earmark to the joint & equally use of RICHARD,
MILES, & MARY. Witnesses: NICHOLAS VAN SANT, WILLIAM (his mark) LLOYD,
JOHANNA CRELL. Before STEPHEN CRELL, J.P. WILLIAM HOPTON, Register.

Book I-I, p. 303   ROBERT AUSTIN, merchant, & MARY his wife, of
21 & 22 Nov. 1748   Charleston, to RENE PEYRE, planter, of Santee,
L & R   in Craven Co., for Ł 1200 currency, 400 a. in
                          St. James Santee which RICHARD ALLEIN by deed
of feoffment dated 29 Sept. 1737 conveyed to AUSTIN (see book R. fol.
420-421); bounding N on Santee River Swamp; E on EDWARD THOMAS; W on
RICHARD ALLEIN; S on vacant land; also 400 a. on S side Santee River,
which THOMAS CORDES by L & R dated 11 & 12 Dec. 1741 sold to AUSTIN, (see
Bk. W. fol. 172-177); bounding SE on THOMAS CORDES; NW & S on said 400 a.
NE on SAMUEL THOMAS; other side on vacant land. Witnesses: JACOB MOTTE,
JOHN REMINGTON. Before JOHN DART, J.P. WILLIAM HOPTON, Register.

Book I-I, p. 310   JAMES ROGERS, cordwainer, of Berkeley Co., to
10 & 11 Oct. 1746   DANIEL MCDANIEL, planter, of Craven Co., for
L & R   Ł 150 currency; 50 a. on great Peedee River in
                          the Welch tract, Craven Co., which Gov. JAMES
GLEN on 2 Mar. 1743 granted JAMES ROGERS, bounding according to grant.
Witnesses: STEPHEN TOUSSIGER, HERCULES (his mark) COYTE, DANIEL DEVONALD.
Before WILLIAM JAMES, J.P. WILLIAM HOPTON, Register.

Book I-I, p. 316   JOHN GEORGE DALLABACH, bricklayer, & JOANNA
6 Nov. 1751   his wife, to THOMAS PEACOCK, gunsmith, both of
L & R by Mortgage   Charleston, as security on bond of even date
                          in penal sum of Ł 350 currency, for payment of
Ł 175 currency, with interest, on 6 Nov. 1753; that portion of land on
Charleston Neck, bounding NE 25 ft. on the Broad Path leading to Charles-
ton; SW on the parsonage or land belonging to the Free School; NW 416 ft.
on JAMES VOULOUX (formerly JOHN GEORGE DALLABACH); SE on JOSEPH WRAGG,
ESQ., being part of the land sold by JOSEPH WRAGG to DALLABACH. Witness-
es: MARON FOUCPIET, CHARLES PINCKNEY, JR. Before WILLIAM PINCKNEY, J.P.
WILLIAM HOPTON, Register.

Book I-I, p. 322   SARAH FULLER, of Charleston, widow & sole ex-
5 & 6 Nov. 1751   ecutrix of will of NATHANIEL FULLER the elder,
L & R   planter, of Berkeley Co., of 1st part; JOSEPH
                          FULLER, planter, sole executor of will of BEN-
JAMIN FULLER, planter, of Berkeley Co., of 2nd part; NATHANIEL FULLER, an
infant, only surviving son & child of said NATHANIEL FULLER, & nephew &
universal devisee of will of said BENJAMIN FULLER, of 3rd part. Whereas
WILLIAM FULLER the elder, planter, of St. Andrew's Parish, owned a tract

land commonly called the back land, containing 745 a., on the S end of
land that belonged to his late son RICHARD, & by will dated 30 Aug. 1731,
after several other bequests, bequeathed to his son NATHANIEL FULLER,
since deceased, on reaching age of 21 years, 445 a., the remainder of
Back Land, to be laid out & allotted to him as his executors should think
fit (he having therein before given to his son RICHARD 50 a., & to son
BENJAMIN 250 a. of said Back Land); appointing his kinsman WILLIAM CAT-
TELL & his son RICHARD FULLER, his executors; & whereas when NATHANIEL
reached 21 years the executors allotted to him the 445 a.; & whereas he,
NATHANIEL FULLER the elder, by will dated 23 Dec. 1749 desired all his
estate sold by his executrix, his wife SARAH FULLER, party hereto; &
whereas she agreed to sell said BENJAMIN FULLER, as highest bidder, the
445 a. for Ł 3100 currency, but he died before execution of conveyance; &
by his will dated 19 Feb. 1750 bequeathed all his real & personal estate
to his nephew, NATHANIEL, an infant; but should said NATHANIEL die before
reaching 21 then to BENJAMIN FULLER, son of his brother, WILLIAM FULLER;
& in case of his dying without issue then to his nephew WILLIAM FULLER; &
appointed his brother, JOSEPH FULLER, sole executor; now to carry out the
agreement, SARAH FULLER, executrix, for Ł 3100 currency paid her by JO-
SEPH FULLER, conveys to NATHANIEL FULLER, the infant, the 445 a., bounding E on WILLIAM LADSON; S on SARAH BUTLER, widow; W on the High Road; N
on NATHANIEL FULLER & on JOHN ANGEL; should NATHANIEL die before 21 then
to BENJAMIN (son of WILLIAM the elder brother of testator BENJAMIN); in
case of default then to WILLIAM, (son of WILLIAM elder brother of testator BENJAMIN). Witnesses: JOHN PRUE, RICHARD FENDIN. Before THOMAS LAM-
BOLL, J.P. WILLIAM HOPTON, Register.

Book I-I, p. 334   BARNARD ELLIOTT, planter, & ELIZABETH his wife,
9 & 10 Nov. 1750   to JOSEPH FULLER, planter, both of Berkeley
L & R   Co., for Ł 3250 currency, 340 a., an inland
                          plantation, given him by his father, WILLIAM
ELLIOTT, on NE side Stono River, bounding N on THOMAS DRAYTON, E on ____
ELLIOTT; W on JOHN BONNEAU; S on a 22-3/4 a. tract belonging to BARNARD
ELLIOTT & on MATTHEW GUERIN; also the 22-3/4 a. sold to BARNARD ELLIOTT
by JOSHUA TOOMER, bounding S & E on MATTHEW GUERIN; W on JOHN BONNEAU; N
on said 340 a. Witnesses: FRANCIS GUICHARD, JOSEPH GREENLAND. Before
THOMAS LAMBOLL, J.P. WILLIAM HOPTON, Register.

Book I-I, p. 343   TIMOTHY CROSBY, bricklayer & planter, to ISAAC
15 & 16 July 1751   J HOLMES, ESQ., both of Charleston, as security
L & R by Mortgage   on bond of even date in penal sum of Ł 812 for
                          payment of Ł 406 currency, with interest, on
16 July 1752; part of lot in Charleston bounding N 30 ft. on Pinckney
Street; E 75 ft. on estate of JOHN LEE; S on GABRIEL GUIGNARD; W on JO-
SEPH BLACK. Witnesses: JOSIAH SMITH, JR., JAMES FISHER. Before JOHN
LINING, J.P. WILLIAM HOPTON, Register.

Book I-I, p. 350   PAUL SMYSER shopkeeper, & RACHEL (her mark)
22 & 23 Oct. 1751   his wife, to PETER BOCKETT (BOCQUET), baker,
L & R by Mortgage   both of Charleston, as security on bond of
                          even date whereby SMYSER & BOCKETT jointly be-
came bound to HENRY PERONNEAU, ESQ., of Charleston, in penal sum of
Ł 1000 for payment of Ł 500 currency, with interest, on 23 Oct. 1752, the
bond being given solely for SMYSER'S debt; that part of a lot in Charleston bounding N 25 ft. 10 in. on Broad Street; W 200 ft. on MRS. FISHER
(formerly JAMES VOULOUX); S on land belonging to the French Church; E on
MATHURIN GUERIN. Witnesses: CHARLES RICHMOND GASCOIGN, ROBERT RAWLINS.
Before ALEXANDER STEWART, J.P. WILLIAM HOPTON, Register. On 11 Nov.
1756 PETER BOCKETT declared mortgage satisfied & PERONNEAU fully paid.
Witnesses: WILLIAM HOPTON, Register.

Book I-I, p. 358   CAPT. JOHN WOODWARD, planter, of Berkeley Co.,
3 & 4 Dec. 1722   to BENJAMIN WHITAKER, ESQ., of Charleston, for
L & R   Ł 301 currency, 86 a. in Berkeley Co., bound-
                          ing NE on CHARLES HILL, ESQ.; NW on BENJAMIN
GODFREY; SW of JOHN WOODWARD; SE on BENJAMIN WHITAKER; free from all
claims except mortgage dated 6 & 7 Dec. 1720 given by WOODWARD to BENJA-
MIN GODIN & BENJAMIN DELA CONSEILLERE to secure payment of Ł 5893:13:8 &
interest. Witnesses: JOHN GIBBES, CHARLES HILL. Before JACOB MOTTE, J.P.
WILLIAM HOPTON, Register. Plat of 86 a. dated 6 July 1722 by CHAMPERNOWN

ELLIOTT.

Book I-I, p. 364   BENJAMIN GODIN & BENJAMIN DE LA CONSELLERE,
28 Jan. 1722/3   ESQ., of Charleston, SC, to BENJAMIN WHITAKER,
Release   for Ł 301 currency, secured to paid, release
                        their claim to 86 a. (p. 358). Whereas JOHN
WOODWARD, planter, of Berkeley Co., by L & R dated 4 & 5 Dec. 1722, WOOD-
WARD conveyed to WHITAKER 86 a. in Berkeley Co.; & whereas WOODWARD by L
& R dated 6 & 7 Dec. 1720, as security for payment of Ł 5893:13:8 on the
date mentioned, conveyed to GODIN & DELA CONSEILLERE 350 a., part of
500 a. granted him by JOHN GODFREY, planter, bounding according to plat
attached to grant dated 9 Nov. 1717 of said lands to, JOHN GODFREY, ESQ.,
father of JOHN GODFREY, planter; & whereas the 86 a. conveyed to WHITAKER
by WOODWARD is part of said 350 a.; now GODIN & DELA CONSEILLE release
their claim to the 86 a. to WHITAKER. Witnesses: CHARLES HILL, MILES (?)
BREWTON. On 23 Sept. 1751 JOHN GUERARD appeared before WILLIAM PINCKNEY,
J.P. to recognize signatures of GODIN, DELA CONSEILLERE, HILL, & BREWTON.
WILLIAM HOPTON, Register.

Book I-I, p. 368   BENJAMIN GODIN & BENJAMIN DELA CONSEILLERE,
Release   ESQ., of Charleston, to RICHARD WOODWARD, for
                        Ł 1200 secured to be paid, release their claim
to 193-1/2 a. Whereas JOHN WOODWARD, planter of Berkeley Co., by L & R
dated 10 & 11 May (?) conveyed to RICHARD WOODWARD, planter, 193-1/2 a.
in Berkeley Co., bounding E on Mill Creek & on lands belonging to BENJA-
MIN WHITAKER & JOHN BENJAMIN GODFREY; W & N on GEORGE LUCAS; S on Wappoe
Creek; & whereas JOHN WOODWARD by L & R dated 6 & 7 Dec. 1720 mortgaged a
tract of 350 a. (part of 500 a. conveyed to him by JOHN GODFREY) to GODIN
& DELA CONSEILLERE to secure payment of Ł 5893:13:8, the 500 a. bounding
according to plat of said lands conveyed to JOHN GODFREY by his father,
JOHN GODFREY, planter, dated 9 Nov. 1717; & whereas the 193-1/2 a. is a
part of the 350 a.; now GODIN & DELA CONSEILLERE release their claim to
that tract. Witnesses: LAWRENCE COULLIETTE, JOHN GUERARD. Recorded 25
Nov. 1751 by WILLIAM HOPTON, Register.

Book I-I, p. 372   WILLIAM POOLE, ESQ., of Georgetown & GEORGE
1749   STARRAT, planter, of Kingstown Township agree
Agreement   as follows: POOLE binds himself to sell to
                        STARRAT on 1 Mar. next, the 2000 a. tract call-
ed POOLE'S Plantation, bounding E on the sea; W on Wacamaw River; S on
PERCIVAL PAWLEY; N on GEORGE PAWLEY, JR., & WILLIAM ALLSTON; also 100 a.
opposite the above 2000 a., on W side Wacamaw River; & agrees to deliver
the premises in same condition they are in on this date; should STARRAT
have occasion to enter upon the plantation before 1st Mar., POOLE to furnish him with suitable accommodation & Negroes until 1st Mar.; STARRAT
agrees to pay POOLE Ł 4725 currency either in cash or bonds. PAUL TRAP-
IER testified concerning handwriting before ROBERT AUSTIN 9 Aug. 1741.
WILLIAM HOPTON, Register.

Book I-I, p. 374   ANN SMITH, spinster; CHARLES FAUCHEREAUD,
20 & 21 Nov. 1751   painter, & JANE his wife; & SARAH HILL, widow,
L & R   all of Berkeley Co., of 1st part (ANN, JANE, &
                        SARAH being daughters & coheiresses of GEORGE
SMITH, gentleman, of St. Andrews Parish; said GEORGE SMITH being 1 of the
sons of Landgrave THOMAS SMITH, of Berkeley Co.), to the Hon. EDWARD FEN-
WICKE, ESQ., of Charleston, for Ł 825 SC money; lot #146 on White Point,
Charleston, bounding 132 ft. on Meeting House Street; & extending east-
ward 314 ft.; being about 60 ft. eastward from the E side of the street
that leads to BROUGHTON'S Battery; N on EDWARD FENWICKE; which lot #146
Landgrave THOMAS SMITH & MARY his wife on 1 Sept. 1718 conveyed to GEORGE
SMITH (Book D. fol. 136-139). Witnesses: JOHN PAUL GRIMKE, JOHN REMING-
TON. Before ROBERT AUSTIN, J.P. WILLIAM HOPTON, Register.

Book I-I, p. 385   ANN SMITH, spinster; CHARLES FAUCHEREAUD,
21 Nov. 1750   planter, & JANE his wife; & SARAH HILL, widow,
Bond of Performance all of Berkeley Co., give bond to the Hon. ED-
                        WARD FENWICKE, ESQ., of Charleston, in penal
sum of Ł 1650 currency, for keeping agreements in above conveyance. Witnesses: JOHN PAUL GRIMKE, JOHN REMINGTON. Before ROBERT AUSTIN, J.P.
WILLIAM HOPTON, Register.

Book I-I, p. 387   HENRY KENNAN, merchant, of Charleston; to DOU-
1 & 2 Mar. 1750   GAL CAMPBELL, merchant, of Winyaw, & THOMAS
L & R   LYNCH, ESQ., of Santee, for Ł 12,000 currency,
                          lot #306 in Charleston, containing half an a.,
English measure. Whereas by L & R dated 29 & 30 Nov. 1748, between SARAH
CLIFFORD, widow, of Charleston (formerly called SARAH SMITH, daughter of
WILLIAM SMITH, gentleman, of Berkeley Co.) of 1st part, & HENRY KENNAN,
merchant, of 2nd part, reciting that: Whereas the Lords Proprs. on 19
Mar. 1694/5 granted WILLIAM SMITH a half a. lot, #306 in Charleston,
bounding N on the great street leading from Cooper River by the Market
Place (Broad Street); SW on a marsh; E on MARTIN COCK'S (afterwards JAMES
GREEME) lot (deed registered 19 Apr. 1695); & further reciting that:
Whereas said WILLIAM SMITH the elder by deed of feoffment dated 30 July
1712 gave said SARAH, his daughter, the lot #306; which she conveyed to
KENNAN (Book F.F.); now KENNAN sells to CAMPBELL & LYNCH. Witnesses: ED-
WARD NEUVILLE, PAUL VILLEPONTOUX. Before JACOB MOTTE, J.P.

Book I-I, p. 398   JAMES SKIRVING, ESQ., & JOHN LAIRD, executors
28 & 29 Mar. 1750   of will of GEORGE MITCHELL, practitioner in
L & R   physic; to THOMAS SACHEVEREL, planter; all of
                          St. Bartholomews Parish, Colleton Co., for
Ł 1500 currency, 250 a. Whereas the Lords Proprs. on 25 Feb. 1714 granted JAMES FULTON the elder 250 a. E of the freshes of Edisto, within land,
in Colleton Co., bounding NE on THOMAS SACHEVEREL; S on ELIZABETH DIDCOTT;
W on MR. BELLINGER; which land descended to his eldest son & heir, JAMES
FULTON, of Charleston; who by L & R dated 13 & 14 June 1737, for Ł 1200
currency, sold the tract to GEORGE MITCHELL; who, on 20 Apr. 1749, agreed
to convey to THOMAS SACHEVEREL for Ł 1500 currency, but died before execution of deed; & by will directed his executors to convey to SACHEVEREL;
now the executors carry out the agreement. Witnesses: GEORGE LIVINGSTON,
ABRAHAM SNELLING. Before JAMES BULLOCK, J.P. WILLIAM HOPTON, Register.

Book I-I, p. 409   JAMES BULLOCH (BULLOCK) of St. Pauls Parish,
17 Oct. 1751   gives bond to THOMAS SACHEVEREL of same place,
Born   in sum of Ł 780 SC money, that he will on 25 .
                          Mar. 1759 convey to SACHEVEREL, 65 a. in St.
Pauls Parish, on S side of the road leading from Charleston to PonPon
Bridge, being part of 400 a. granted by the Lords Proprs. to JOHN BEE;
who conveyed to MATHEW BEE; & conveyed by JOHN ARNOLD & MARTHA his wife
(1 of MATHEW BEE'S daughters) to JAMES BULLOCH. Witnesses: THOMAS CLIF-
FORD, SAMUEL WALLACE. Before ALEXANDER STEWART, J.P. WILLIAM HOPTON,
Register.

Book I-I, p. 411   CHARLES WRIGHT, merchant, of Charleston, to
22 & 23 Apr. 1751   JAMES WILLIAMSON, tailor, of St. Bartholomews
L & R   Parish, Colleton Co., for Ł 200 currency, lot
                          #27 in Jacksonburgh, bounding 100 ft. on Mar-
ket Street; 218 ft. deep; which lot was conveyed to ELIZABETH BRABANT by
JOHN ANDREW by L & R 1 & 2 Feb. 1744/5 (see Book A.A. fol. 413-417); &
conveyed by BRABANT to CHARLES WRIGHT, party hereto, on 26 & 27 Apr. 1748.
Witnesses: ROBERT REID, JOHN LAIRD. Before JAMES BULLOCK, J.P. WILLIAM
HOPTON, Register.

Book I-I, p. 418   JOHN PENNY, of St. Bartholomews Parish, Colle-
22 Apr. 1745   ton Co., for valuable considerations; conveys
Gift   to THOMAS PAGE, 50 a. in St. Pauls Parish,
                          bounding NW on WILLIAM FARGUSON; SE on JOHN
PETER; SW on estate of JOHN EDWARD; being half a tract of 100 a. Witness-
es: ROBERT HIETT, WILLIAM SANDERS. Before JAMES SKIRVING, J.P. WILLIAM
HOPTON, Register.

Book I-I, p. 419   THOMAS PAGE, planter, of St. Bartholomews Par-
13 & 14 Dec. 1747   ish, Colleton Co., to HENRY LIVINGSTON, plant-
L & R   of St. Pauls Parish, for Ł 225 currency, 50 a.
                          on E side PonPon River, in St. Pauls Parish,
bounding N on WILLIAM FARGUSON; SE on JOHN PETERS; S on estate of JOHN
EDWARDS. Witnesses: JONATHAN WITTED, EDWARD FERGUSON. Before JAMES BUL-
LOCK, J.P. WILLIAM HOPTON, Register.

Book I-I, p. 427   HENRY LIVINGSTONE, planter, & AGNES his wife,

245

10 & 11 Oct. 1749   of St. Pauls Parish, Colleton Co., to WILLIAM
L & R   DONNOM, planter, of St. Bartholomews Parish,
                         for Ł 250 currency, 50 a. on E side PonPon Riv-
er, in St. Pauls Parish, bounding N on WILLIAM FARGUSON; SE on JOHN PE-
TERS; S on estate of JOHN EDWARDS. Witnesses: EDWARD FERGUSON, SAMUEL
SPRY, WILLIAM JEFFERYES. Before JAMES BULLOCK, J.P. WILLIAM HOPTON, Reg-
ister.

Book I-I, p. 435   WILLIAM DONNOM, planter, to JOSEPH FABIAN,
23 & 24 Oct. 1751   planter, both of St. Pauls Parish, Colleton
L & R   Co., for Ł 500 currency, 156 a. on E side Pon-
                         Pon River, in St. Pauls Parish, bounding E on
ELIZABETH DEDCOTT; S on estate of JOHN PETER; W on estate of DR. GEORGE
MITCHELL; N on WILLIAM FERGUSON; being part of a tract granted by the
Lords Proprs. to JOHN PENNY; 50 a., part of 150 a., having been given by
JOHN PENNY (grandson of above named JOHN PENNY) to THOMAS PAGE, 22 Apr.
1745, & conveyed by him to HENRY LIVINGSTON by L & R dated 14 Dec. 1747;
& conveyed by him to WILLIAM DONNOM by L & R dated 11 Oct. 1749; another
50 a. of said 156 a. having been sold to DONNOM by JOHN PENNY by L & R
dated 24 Jan. 1749/50. MARY DONNOM, wife of WILLIAM, renounces her dower.
Witnesses: JAMES HENDRICK, THOMAS KNIGHT, JOHN BARKLEY. Before JAMES
BULLOCK, J.P. WILLIAM HOPTON, Register.

Book I-I, p. 444   JOHN ABERLY, carpenter, to HENRY BROWN, tanner,
11 & 12 Feb. 1750   of Berkeley Co., for Ł 140 currency, 250 a.
L & R   granted by Gov. JAMES GLEN on 4 June 1749 to
                         JOHN ABERLY, on NE side of Santee or Congaree
River, opposite Saxagotha Township, bounding W & S on vacant land; E on
JAMES MAZYCK & JOHN GEORGE SHELEPPY. Witnesses: HANNAH BARBARA (her
mark) HOUX, FREDERICK MERCKLEY. Before STEPHEN CRELL, J.P. WILLIAM HOP-
TON, Register.

Book I-I, p. 450   DOUGAL CAMPBELL, merchant, formerly of Winyaw,
19 & 20 Nov. 1751   now of Charleston, & THOMAS LYNCH, planter, of
L & R   Santee, Craven Co., to HENRY KENNAN, merchant,
                         of Charleston, for Ł 3400 currency, 1 full un-
divided third part of lot #306 in Charleston, containing half an a., Eng-
ligh measure, with a third part of the houses, etc.; also 1 full third
part of all the materials, copper furnaces & utensils used for refining
sugar. Whereas the Lords Proprs. on 19 Mar. 1694/5 granted WILLIAM SMITH,
gentleman, then of Berkeley Co., lot #306 in Charleston, containing half
an a., English measure, bounding N on Broad Street; W & S on a marsh; E
on MARTIN COCK (now JAMES GREEME); which deed was registered in Charleston 19 Apr. 1695; & whereas said WILLIAM SMITH the elder by deed of feoffment dated 30 July 1712 gave the lot to his daughter SARAH; who, by L & R
dated 29 & 30 Nov. 1748, under the name of SARAH CLIFFORD, widow, sold
the lot to HENRY KENNAN, merchant, of Charleston; who, by L & R dated 1 &
2 Mar. 1750, for Ł 12,000 currency, sold the lot & its appurtenances to
CAMPBELL & LYNCH; now they sell 1 share to KENNAN. Witnesses: CHARLES
PINCKNEY, DR. THOMAS GLEN. Before JOHN LINING, J.P. WILLIAM HOPTON,
Register. List of sundry materials belonging to the Sugar House under
date of 10 Oct. 1751 annexed to above deed.

DEEDS BOOK "K-K"
JAN. 1752 - MAY 1752

Book K-K, p. 1   DOUGAL CAMPBELL, merchant, formerly of Winyaw,
19 & 20 Nov. 1750   now Charleston, & THOMAS LYNCH, planter, of
L & R   Santee, Craven Co., to THOMAS GLEN, ESQ., of
                         Charleston, for Ł 3400 currency, 1 full undi-
vided third part of lot #306 in Charleston, with 1/3 of the houses, etc.,
also 1/3 of all the materials, copper furnaces, & utensils for refining
of sugar. Whereas the Lords Proprs. on 19 Mar. 1694/5 granted WILLIAM
SMITH, gentleman, of Berkeley, (Registered 19 Apr. 1695), lot #306 in
Charleston, containing half an a., bounding N on the Great Street leading
from Cooper River by the Market Place, (Broad Street), S & W on a marsh;
E on JAMES GRAME (formerly MARTIN COCK); & whereas WILLIAM SMITH, the
elder, by deed of feoffment dated 30 July 1712 for natural love &

affection conveyed the lot to his daughter, SARAH SMITH, spinster; & whereas by L & R dated 29 & 30 Nov. 1748 SARAH, now SARAH CLIFFORD, widow, conveyed lot #306 to HENRY KENNAN, merchant, of Charleston, who, by L & R dated 1 & 2 Mar. 1750 conveyed to DOUGAL CAMPBELL & THOMAS LYNCH for ₺ 12,000; now they sell to GLEN 1 full undivided third part of the lot, buildings & utensils for refining sugar. List of equipment given. Witnesses: HENRY KENNAN, CHARLES PINCKNEY. Before JOHN LINING, J.P. WILLIAM HOPTON, Register.

Book K-K, p. 12
1 & 2 Apr. 1748
L & R

JOSEPH DUBOURDIEU, executor of will of COL. ANTHONY WHITE of Craven Co., to ELIAS FOISSIN, ESQ., gentleman, of Craven Co., for ₺ 200 SC money, 6-1/2 lots in Georgetown, bounding as follows: lots 5 & 6, half of lot #3, & lots 7 & 8 bounding SW 50 ft. each on Front Street each 217.9 ft. deep, lot #17 fronting SW 50 ft. on Front Street, 217.9 ft. deep; bounding NW on Orange Street, lots #50, 51 & 52 fronting NE 100 ft. each on Prince Street, & each 217.9 ft. deep. Witnesses: WILLIAM SHACKELFORD, GABRIEL GEORGE POWELL. Before PAUL TRAPIER, J.P. WILLIAM HOPTON, Register.

Book K-K, p. 20
23 Apr. 1737
Sale

SAMUEL STOCK, planter, & ELIZABETH his wife, to WILLIAM HOLMAN, planter, both of Colleton Co., for ₺ 500 SC money, 500 a., bounding W on ISAAC ____ DETT; E on Chehaw River; S on SAMUEL STOCK; SW on SILAS WELLS. Witnesses: ROBERT FOULIS, THOMAS STOCK, SARAH FENDIN. On 7 Nov. 1752 SARAH KING (formerly SARAH FENDIN) testified before JAMES SKIRVING, J.P. WILLIAM HOPTON, Register.

Book K-K, p. 22
27 & 28 Aug. 1751
L & R

WILLIAM HOLMAN, planter, & RACHEL his wife, of Colleton Co., to FRANCIS SMITH, planter, of Wannels Neck, Colleton Co., for ₺ 600 SC money; 960 a. in Colleton Co., formerly granted said HOLMAN; bounding E on JOHN PALMER; W on MR. SHEPPARD & ELIAS FISHER; N on marsh of Cheehaw River; S on SAMUEL TURNER. Witnesses: WILLIAM DALTON, WILLIAM GRAY. Before HENRY HYRNE, J.P. WILLIAM HOPTON, Register.

Book K-K, p. 29
15 & 16 May 1749
L & R

WILLIAM DALTON, planter, & HANNAH his wife, to FRANCIS SMITH, planter, both of Colleton Co., for 5 shillings (₺ 420?) currency, 210 a. called Round Island, being 1 of the 2 islands called Shittin Sams, in Colleton Co. HANNAH DALTON to renounce her dower. Witnesses: WILLIAM GRAY, WILLIAM SMYES, WILLIAM REDDER. Before HENRY HYRNE, J.P. WILLIAM HOPTON, Register.

Book K-K, p. 36
17 Aug. 1739
Feoffment

ULRICK (his mark) REBER, planter, of Berkeley Co., & ANGLE (her mark) REBER, to PETER ROHTE, carpenter, for ₺ 75 currency, 150 a. in Orangeburg Township, Berkeley Co. Witnesses: WALTER GORING, ADIN FROGATT, JOHN PEARSON. Before CHRISTIAN MOTE, J.P. at Orangeburg. WILLIAM HOPTON, Register.

Book K-K, p. 40
8 Jan. 1752
Bond & Release

MARTHA BONEY, spinster, to WILLIAM HULL, planter, of St. Bartholomews Parish, Colleton Co. in penal sum of ₺ 2000 currency, in releasing her title to certain lands. Whereas by will of WILLIAM WATIES of Winyaw, dated 19 Dec. 1749, he bequeathed to his wife certain tracts of land on great PeeDee River known as Uhaney & containing 650 a.; & whereas on HANNAH'S death her sister ANN HULL & MARTHA BONEY inherited; now, for ₺ 750 SC money, MARTHA conveys her share to WILLIAM HULL, giving bond for performance. Witnesses: JOSEPH ANDREW, JOSEPH HULL, JOHN (his mark) BURLEY. Before JAMES SKIRVING, J.P. WILLIAM HOPTON, Register.

Book K-K, p. 42
29 Jan. 1752
Mortgage

ARCHIBALD (his mark) MCGHIE (MCGHEI, MCKEE), planter, of Winyaw, Craven Co., to SIR ALEXANDER NISBETT, of Dean Baronet (Barony) as security for payment of ₺ 280 currency, on 28 Jan. 1762; 280 a. in Craven Co., according to grant dated 12 Jan. 1737. Witnesses: DAVID CRAWFORD, ROBERT RAWLINS. Before JAMES WEDDERBURN, J.P. WILLIAM HOPTON, Register.

Book K-K, p. 45   JAMES EDES, shopkeeper, to JOHN DART, OTHNIEL
2 July 1750   BEALE, JOHN GUERARD & HENRY LAURENS, merchants,
Mortgage   all of Charleston, in trust, as security on
                         bond of even date in penal sum of Ł 11,007 for
payment of various bonds, with interest, at various times; the N part of
the half part of 3 lots (lately belonging to ANTHONY BONNEAU, heretofore
of JOHN LAURENS) known as #101, #___, & #59, fronting W 63 ft. on Old
Church Street; 132 ft. deep; bounding N on ROBERT HUME & SUSANNA WIGING-
TON; S on JOHN LAUREN'S other half; with the houses thereon. Whereas
EDES gave bond to JOHN MARTINI, physician, for Ł 1000, which sum DART,
BEALE, GUERARD, & LAURENS, have agreed to pay; & whereas EDES had also
given other bonds to several other persons, total Ł 4503:8:2 currency; &
whereas EDES has agreed to pay the interest & part of the principal annually, the whole to be paid within 3 years; now as security EDES conveys
his half of 3 lots in Charleston. Witnesses: TIMOTHY PHILLIPS, JOSIAH
SMITH, JR. Before ROBERT AUSTIN, J.P. WILLIAM HOPTON, Register. This
mortgage was assigned by DART & others to JAMES HUNTER who bought the
premises; as recorded Book H.H. fols. 446, 447. Conveyance from EDES &
wife recorded Book H.H. fols. 451, 458.

Book K-K, p. 52   AMOS SHAW, to WILLIAM TURNER, both of Berkeley
30 & 31 Oct. 1751   Co., for Ł 1000 currency, 850 a. in Prince
L & R   Frederick Parish, Craven Co., bounding SW on
                         Black River; SE on Black River & DANIEL LA-
ROCHE; NW on the Rev. MR. LEWIS JONES; NE on vacant land. Witnesses: DUR-
HAM HANDCOCK, ISSACHAR WILLCOCKS. Before JAMES FRANCIS, J.P. WILLIAM
HOPTON, Register.

Book K-K, p. 57   CHARLES CANTEY, & HERRIETT his wife, to PAT-
1 Oct. 1746   RICK BRINOUN, both of Craven Co., for Ł 100
L & R   currency, 100 a., part of 1000 a. granted WIL-
                         LIAM DRAKE in 1726, & part of 48,000 a. grant-
ed Landgrave THOMAS SMITH on 13 May 1691 by JOHN, Earl of Bath, Palatine,
& the Lords Proprs; the 100 a. being in St. James Santee, Craven Co., on
S side Santee River, bounding W on JOHN DRAKE; other sides on CHARLES
CANTEY. Witnesses: DANIEL SWILVANT, PETER SINKLER, MICHAEL BRINOUN. Be-
fore SAMUEL THOMAS, J.P. WILLIAM HOPTON, Register. Plat by JOHN GOUGH,
Dep. Sur. dated 24 July 1746.

Book K-K, p. 63   DANIEL LAROCHE, ESQ., of Prince George Parish,
17 Jan. 1752   Craven Co., & THOMAS LANDER, leather-dresser,
Feoffment   of Georgetown; to MARY ELIZABETH MILLER, wid-
                         ow, of Parish of St. Thomas, Berkeley Co.,
for Ł 500 currency, lot #61 in Georgetown, bounding NW 217.9 ft. on Broad
Street; NE 100 ft. on Prince Street; SE on lot #62; SW on lots #25 & 26;
subject to an equity of redemption in THOMAS LANDEN which he hereby releases, which is the reason why he joins in this release. Witnesses:
DAVID MONTAIGUT, THOMAS HASELL. Before PAUL TRAPIER, J.P. Seizin delivered to MARY ELIZABETH MILLER, by ELIAS FOISSIN, ESQ., her attorney.
WILLIAM HOPTON, Register.

Book K-K, p. 67   The Hon. JOHN CLELAND, ESQ., & MARY his wife
3 & 4 July 1745   to their nephew, ARCHIBALD BAIRD, ESQ., of
L & R   Georgetown, for love & affection & for Ł 5 cur-
                         rency; lot in Georgetown, marked E on the plat,
bounding SW 50 ft. on the low water mark of Georgetown River; SE 217.9 ft.
on Cannon Street; NW on lot marked D on plat; NE 50 ft. on Front Street.
Witnesses: MARY CROW, WILLIAM HOPTON. Before JACOB MOTTE, J.P. WILLIAM
HOPTON, Register.

Book K-K, p. 74   DANIEL LAROCHE, ESQ., of Georgetown, Craven
23 & 24 Jan. 1752   Co., to GEORGE SAXBY, ESQ., of Charleston, as
L & R by Mortgage   security on bond dated 22 Jan. 1752 in penal
                         sum of Ł 47,113 currency (because SAXBY stood
security on several bonds given by LAROCHE to various people, & on account of other matters mentioned in said bond; lots #37, 40, 151, 152,
204, 205, 145, & 146 in Georgetown; also 550 a. where he (LAROCHE) lives,
bounding SE on Peedee River; SW on ELIAS FOISSIN, ESQ.; NW on JOHN GREEN;
NE on estate of WILLIAM SWINTON; also 200 a. of swampland on an island in
Peedee River opposite said 550 a., bounding NE on estate of WILLIAM

SWINTON; SE on a thoroughfare leading from Peedee River to Waccamaw River; also 1000 a. in 2 tracts of 500 a., each in Prince George Parish, Craven Co., bounding S on LUKE STOUTENBURGH, ESQ.; W on vacant land; E on Peedee River; NW on JOHN OULDFIELD, ESQ.; also 300 a. on an island in Peedee River, opposite said 2 tracts, bounding E on WILLIAM ALLSTON; S on LUKE STOUTENBURGH; W on Peedee River; N on JOHN OULDFIELD; also 850 a. of pineland on SW side Peedee River, bounding E on JOSEPH LABRUCE & JOHN OULD-FIELD; N on JOHN ALLSTON; W on vacant land, also his half of 1800 a. on Cat Island, Winyaw Bay, Craven Co., held by him & ELIAS FOISSIN as tenants in common; also his half of 2100 a. on Cat Island held by him & ELIAS FOISSIN as tenants in common; also his half of 1100 a. on Cat Island held by him & ELIAS FOISSIN in joint tenancy & his right of survivorship therein; also 110 a. called the Tanyard, in Prince George Parish, Craven Co., bounding S on Black River; E on JOHN HADDRELL; W on JOHN BOGGS; N on vacant land; also an island in Winyaw Bay near the sea, containing 854 a., called North Island; also 1940 a. called Hickory Grove in Prince Frederick Parish, commonly said to be in Craven Co., also 2 tracts of 250 a. each, 1 on N side the other on S side Great Peedee River, both purchased from SAMUEL BAKER; also 543 a. in Craven Co., purchased from GEORGE SAUDNERS, bounding SW on DANIEL LAROCHE & Great Peedee River; NW on MR. GIBBES; NE & SE on vacant land; also 500 a. in Craven Co., purchased from WILLIAM ANDREE; bounding NW on ALEXANDER STEWART; SE on DAVID MCCLELAND; SW on vacant land; NE on Peedee River; also 3 tracts at Bear Bluff, on NE side Waccamaw River, containing 4600 a., also 2 tracts of 300 a. each on opposite side Waccamaw River, being opposite the upper part of said 4600 a.; also 292 a. below Bears Bluff, on Waccamaw River, bounding NW on the River; SW on CAPT. TAYLOR; NE on MR. WATIES; SE on BENJAMIN DELA CONSEILLERE; also 460 a. at Potatoe Ferry, in Prince Frederick Parish, bounding NE on Black River; NW on PETER JOHNSON; SE on ISAAC DAVIS. Witnesses: THOMAS BLYTHE, JOHN HENTIE. Before WILLIAM PINCKNEY, J.P. WILLIAM HOPTON, Register.

Book K-K, p. 85   DANIEL LAROCHE, merchant, of Georgetown, to
27 & 28 Jan. 1752   ELIAS FOISSIN, ESQ., of Prince George Parish,
L & R by Mortgage   Craven Co., as security on bond dated 24 Jan.
                         1752 in penal sum of ₺ 3500 sterling British
because FOISSIN stood security on several of LAROCHE'S bonds to various people; also as security on a bond from LAROCHE to FOISSIN dated 1 Dec. 1751 in penal sum of ₺ 10,000 SC money for payment of ₺ 5000, with interest, on 1 Feb. 1752; & on a bond from LAROCHE to ANDREW DELA (CONSEILLERE?) & DAVID MONTAIGUT, merchants, of Georgetown, dated 1 Jan. 1752 in penal sum of ₺ 6200 for payment of ₺ 3100 SC money on 1 May 1752; lots #37, 40, 151, 152, 204, 205, 145, & 146; also 550 a. where LAROCHE lives, bounding SE on Peedee River; SW on ELIAS FOISSIN; NW on JOHN GREEN; NE on estate of WILLIAM SWINTON; also 200 a. of swamp land on an island in Peedee River opposite the 550 a., bounding NE on estate of WILLIAM SWINTON; SE on a thoroughfare leading from Peedee River to Waccamaw River; also 1000 a. in 2 tracts of 500 a. each, in Prince George Parish, bounding S on LUKE STOUTENBURGH; W on vacant land; NW on JOHN OULDFIELD; also 300 a. on an island opposite the 2 tracts of 500 a. each, bounding E on WILLIAM ALLSTON; SE on LUKE STOUTENBURGH; W on Peedee River; N on JOHN OULDFIELD; also 850 a. of pineland bounding E on JOSEPH LABRUCE & JOHN OULDFIELD, N on JOHN ALLSTON; W on vacant land, also his half of, 3 tracts on Cat Island, in Winyaw Bay, held by LAROCHE & FOISSIN as tenants in common, 1 of 1800 a.; 1 of 2100 a., & 1 of 11 a.; also 110 a., called the Tanyard, in Pringe George Parish, bounding S on Black River; E on JOHN HADDRELL; W on JOHN BOGGS; N on vacant land; also 854 a. called North Island in Winyaw Bay near the sea; also 1940 a. called Hickory Grove in Prince Frederick Parish; also 2 tracts of 250 a. each, 1 on each side great Peedee River, both purchased from SAMUEL BAKER; also 543 a. in Craven Co., purchased from GEORGE SANDERS, bounding SW on DANIEL LAROCHE & Great Peedee River; NW on MRS. GIBBES; NE & SE on vacant land; also 500 a. purchased from WILLIAM ANDREE, bounding NW on ALEXANDER STEWART; SE on DAVID MCCLELAND; SW on vacant land; NE on Peedee River; also 3 tracts at Bear Bluff on N side Waccamaw River, total 4600 a.; also 2 tracts of 300 a. each, on opposite side Waccamaw River, also 292 a., on Waccamaw River below Bear Bluff, bounding NW on the river; SW on CAPT. TAYLOR; NE on MR. WATIES; SE on BENJAMIN DELA CONSEILLERS; also 460 a. called Potatoe Ferry in Prince Frederick Parish, bounding NE on Black River; NW on PETER JOHNSTONE; SE on ISAAC DAVIS. Witnesses: WILLIAM BLYTHE, THOMAS BLYTHE. Before PAUL

TRAPIER, J.P. WILLIAM HOPTON, Register. On 21 May 1753 ELIAS FOISSIN declared mortgage satisfied. Witness: WILLIAM HOPTON.

Book K-K, p. 95
14 & 15 Dec. 1750
L & R Tripartite

SAMUEL WEST, & MARY His wife, of Charleston, of 1st part; CHARLES WEST, planter, & SARAH his wife, formerly of SC, now of Colony of Georgia, of 2nd part; JOHN AINGER, planter, of 3rd part. Whereas SAMUEL WEST bought 250 a. in Berkeley Co., from FRANCIS LADSON, bound E on RICHARD BUTLER; W on WILLOUGHBY WEST; N on FRANCIS LADSON; & whereas WEST died intestate & his eldest son & heir, SAMUEL, party hereto, inherited; & he by deed of feoffment dated 8 Apr. 1734 assigned 100 a., part of the 250 a., to his brother CHARLES WEST, party hereto; the 100 a. bounding E on RICHARD BUTLER; W on WILLOUGHBY WEST; S on part of the 250 a. owned by WILLOUGHBY WEST; N on FRANCIS LADSON; & whereas SAMUEL WEST party hereto, conveyed 50 a. of the 250 a. to his mother, SARAH WEST; who, by will dated 24 Oct. o735 bequeathed 25 a., part of the 50 a., to her son CHARLES WEST; which will was never proved or recorded, so that the 25 a. became the property of SAMUEL, as heir to his mother; & whereas CHARLES WEST, by L & R by mortgage, dated 9 & 10 Apr. 1747; in consideration of his debt to JOHN DRAYTON in the amount of Ł 527:13:6, conveyed to DRAYTON all the 100 a. (part of said 250 a.); & whereas DRAYTON on 10 Sept. 1748 by indorsement on back of release assigned his interest to JOHN AINGER; & whereas by L & R by mortgage, dated 10 & 11 Apr. 1747 CHARLES WEST conveyed to JOHN GUERARD, surviving partner of RICHARD HILL as security on a debt of Ł 1692:17:8 the 100 a. given him by his brother SAMUEL, also the 25 a. bequeathed him by his mother; & whereas AINGER wants to make an absolute purchase of the 2 tracts, by agreement between GUERARD & AINGER, dated 27 July 1750, reciting that AINGER has an assignment from JOHN DRAYTON of a mortgage of 100 a. on Long Savannah, belonging to CHARLES WEST; on which 100 a. & 25 a. more GUERARD has a second mortgage from CHARLES & SAMUEL WEST; now GUERARD agrees to sell to AVINGER the 125 a. at Ł 7 currency per a.; & AINGER agrees to give GUERARD a bond for the surplus purchase money & interest, payable 1 Jan. 1750; now SAMUEL & MARY, CHARLES & SARAH, release to JOHN AINGER the 125 a. (100 & 25) bounding E on RICHARD BUTLER; W & S on WILLOUGHBY WEST; N & FRANCIS LADSON. Witnesses: JOHN HARON, LEWIS MELLEAIR, WILLOUGHBY WEST, JOHN GUERARD, ADAM DANIELL. Before THOMAS LAMBOLL, J.P. & JACOB MOTTE, J.P. WILLIAM HOPTON, Register.

Book K-K, p. 106
25 Nov. 1751
Feoffment

LYDIA CLARK (CLARKE), (heretofore LYDIA VIART) widow, & JACOB VIART, bookbinder, to RICHARD WAINWRIGHT, butcher; all of Charleston; for Ł 550 currency, that lot in Charleston bounding N 25 ft. on Dock (alias Queen) Street; S on MR. MOORE; E 150 ft. on ELIZABETH BAMPFIELD; W on WILLIAM COOPER; being the same land which JOHN BRAND, gentleman, by L & R dated 13 & 14 Oct. 1735 sold to LYDIA VIART. Witnesses: RICHARD WATERS, JOHN REMINGTON, WILLIAM GREENLAND, THOMAS ROSE. Before OTHNIEL BEALE, J.P. WILLIAM HOPTON, Register.

Book K-K, p. 110
25 & 26 Feb. 1752
L & R by Mortgage

RICHARD WAINWRIGHT, butcher, to ALEXANDER VANDERDUSSEN, ESQ., both of Charleston, as security on bond of even date in penal sum of Ł 430 for payment of Ł 215 currency, with interest, on 26 May 1752; that lot in Charleston bounding N 25 ft. on Dock (alias Queen) Street; S on MR. MOORE; E 150 ft. on ELIZABETH BAMPFIELD; W on WILLIAM COOPER; being the lot which JOHN BRAND, gentleman, by L & R dated 13 & 14 Oct. 1735 sold to LYDIA VIART (now LYDIA CLARK) & which she & her son, JACOB VIART, bookbinder, on 25 Nov. 1751 conveyed to WAINWRIGHT. Witnesses: JOHN ROSE, WILLIAM MOUAT. Before JACOB MOTTE, J.P. WILLIAM HOPTON, Register. On 22 June 1752, ALEXANDER VANDERDUSSEN declared mortgage satisfied. Witness: WILLIAM HOPTON.

Book K-K, p. 119
11 & 12 Mar. 1750
L & R

CHARLES PINCKNEY, ESQ., & ELIZABETH his wife, to GEORGE EVELEIGH, merchant, both of Charleston, for Ł 1500 currency; the N part of front lot #327 in Charleston, bounding W 32 ft. on the wharf line & same width at low water mark of Cooper River; S on part of lot #327 sold by CHARLES PINCKNEY to JOHN FENWICKE, ESQ.; N on the front or shole lot opposite lot #4 now in possession of GEORGE EVELEIGH. Whereas the Lords Proprs. on 14 Dec. 1698 (see book A.A. p. 469) granted

THOMAS PINCKNEY, merchant, of Charleston, father of said CHARLES, all the shole or low water lot #327 lying opposite lot #3 lately belonging to said THOMAS PINCKNEY, fronting W on the warfline, E on Cooper River down to low water mark; bounding N on the front or shole land opposite lot #4 laid out to WILLIAM WILLIAMS; S on the front or shole lot opposite lot #2 lately in possession of WILLIAM NEWALL; & whereas the low water lot #327 by several wills & mesne conveyances became the property of CHARLES PINCK- NEY; now he sells to EVELEIGH. Witnesses: THOMAS BURRINGTON, CHARLES PINCKNEY, JR. Before WILLIAM PINCKNEY, J.P. WILLIAM HOPTON, Register.

Book K-K, p. 127
10 & 11 May 1749
L & R

JOHN PAYNE, gentleman, of Kentish Town, Pan- cras Parish, Co. of Middlesex, England (form- erly Lt. of H.M.S. Thetis) by his attorneys BENJAMIN SAVAGE, the elder & GABRIEL MANIGAULT, merchants, of Charleston, SC, of 1st part; to GEORGE EVELEIGH, merchant, of Charleston, for ₺ 2000 SC money, the best price obtainable, 303 a. on John's Island, Colleton Co., bounding W on Benjamin D'HARRIETTE; E & S on Stono River; N & NW on JOHN SEABROOK. Whereas JOHN SEABROOK, planter, of Colleton Co., through various mesne conveyances & other legal assignments became owner of a certain tract of 303 a. which he & MARY his wife by L & R dated 24 & 25 Apr. 1745 sold to LT. JOHN PAYNE of H.M.S. The Rose, then in Charleston Harbor; & whereas JOHN PAYNE, on 29 Dec. 1748 appointed BEN- JAMIN SAVAGE, the elder & GABRIEL MANIGAULT, his attorneys, with authori- ty to sell his lands, slaves, etc., in John's Island, SC; now they sell the 303 a. to GEORGE EVELEIGH. Witnesses: JOHN SAVAGE, JOHN SCOTT. Be- fore THOMAS DALE, J.P. WILLIAM HOPTON, Register.

Book K-K, p. 130
29 Dec. 1748
Letter of Attorney

JOHN PAYNE, gentleman, of Kentish Town, Pan- cras Parish, Middlesex Co., England, late Lt. of H.M.S. The Thetis, appoints BENJAMIN SAV- AGE the elder, & GABRIEL MANIGAULT, merchants, of Charleston, SC, his attorneys, with authority to sell the land on John's Island, SC, which he purchased from JOHN SEABROOK. Witnesses: HENRY BOYTON, THOMAS RICHARDS. BOYTON appeared before ROBERT AUSTIN, J. P. WILLIAM HOPTON, Register.

Book K-K, p. 139
28 & 29 Mar. 1743
L & R

JOHN HODSDEN, gentleman, to GEORGE EVELEIGH, gentleman, both of Charleston, for ₺ 1000 SC money, part of lot #298 in Charleston, bound- ing W 56 ft. on the great street leading from Ashley River by the old Churchyard, Market Place & Meeting Houses; N 276 ft. on ARNOLDUS VANDERHORST; E part (16 ft.) on ARNOLDUS VANDERHORST & part (40 ft. S) on a new street leading from Broughton's Battery North- ward to the great Broad Bridge over the marsh or creek into New Church Street, S 274 ft. on ELIAS VANDERHORST. Whereas JOHN VANDERHORST, plant- er, only son of JOHN VANDERHORST, planter, owned (among other lands, messuages, etc.) part of lot #298 in Charlston & by will dated 13 Sept. 1743 (stating that he owned several lots & parcels of lots at White Point in Charleston with houses, & improvements, etc., thereon) bequeathed his real estate equally to such of his sons as may be living at the time of his death, his executors to divide the property equally as soon as pos- sible, & appointed HENRY PERONNEAU, JR., ALEXANDER PERONNEAU & his sons JOSEPH VANDERHORST & JOHN VANDERHORST his executors; & whereas JOHN VAN- DERHORST, JR., became entitled to 1 part of the land & buildings at White Point, & by will dated 13 Sept. 1740 devised to his wife MARY, 1/2 of his real & personal estate, the other half to their children; & whereas MARY died intestate & without issue, 1/2 the property at White Point became vested in JOHN HODSDEN, as her only brother & heir; & whereas the execu- tors, divided the property into 5 equal parts, & the part of lot #298 became the property of JOHN HODSDEN; now he sells to GEORGE EVELEIGH. Witnesses: JOSEPH HESKETT, THOMAS ELLIS. Before ALEXANDER CRAMAHE, J.P. WILLIAM HOPTON, Register.

Book K-K, p. 152
24 & 25 Feb. 1752
L & R

JOHN MAYRANT, ESQ., of St. James Santee Parish, Craven Co., to DAVID CAW, practitioner in Physick, of Charleston, for ₺ 515 currency, 139 a. in St. James Santee, part of 500 a. granted by the Lords Proprs. to DANIEL HUGER; who conveyed to JOHN MAY- RANT, planter; who died intestate; & inherited by his eldest son & heir, JOHN MAYRANT, party hereto; the 139 a. bounding SE on JOHN MAYRANT; NE on

Manigault Creek; SW on DAVID CAW, (formerly JACOB JEANNERET). Witnesses: CHARLES PINCKNEY, CHARLES PINCKNEY, JR. Before WILLIAM PINCKNEY, J.P. WILLIAM HOPTON, Register. Plat by JOHN HENTIE dated 1752.

Book K-K, p. 158
26 & 27 Feb. 1752
L & R

JOHN HUTCHINS, warden of the workhouse, Charleston, & ELIZABETH (her mark) his wife, to RICHARD WAINWRIGHT, butcher, for Ł 1200 currency, that lot in Ansonborough near Charleston, containing 1 a., 2 roods, English measure, bounding W 165 ft. on the Broad Path leading to Charleston, S 400 ft. deep, on a street called the 30 ft. street; E on LUKE STOUTENBURGH; N on GEORGE HUNTER; which lot (marked D on plan of ANSON'S land), HUTCHINS purchased from BENJAMIN WHITAKER, attorney for GEORGE ANSON, now Lord ANSON. Witnesses: ROBERT BALDWIN, WILLIAM MOUAT, PATIENCE CHAPPELLE. Before JOHN DART, J.P. WILLIAM HOPTON, Register.

Book K-K, p. 166
27 & 28 Feb. 1752
L & R by Mortgage

RICHARD WAINWRIGHT, butcher, to SAMUEL WRAGG, merchant, both of Charleston, as security on bond of even date in penal sum of Ł 1035 for payment of Ł 517:10 currency, with interest, on 28 Feb. 1753; that lot marked D on the plan of Ansonborough, near Charleston, containing 1 a., 2 roods, English measure, bounding W 165 ft. on the Broad Path leading to Charleston; S 400 ft. on a 30 ft. street; E on LUKE STOUTENBURGH; N on GEORGE HUNTER, which lot was formerly the property of GEORGE ANSON, now Lord ANSON, who, through his attorney, BENJAMIN WHITAKER sold to JOHN HUTCHINS, warden of the workhouse, of Charleston, who by L & R dated 26 & 27 Feb. 1752 conveyed to WAINWRIGHT. Witnesses: JOSEPH CROFT, WILLIAM MOUAT. Before JOHN DART, J.P. WILLIAM HOPTON, Register. On 2 Sept. 1756 SAMUEL WRAGG declared mortgage satisfied. Witness: WILLIAM HOPTON.

Book K-K, p. 173
3 & 4 Mar. 1752
L & R

ALEXANDER MITCHELL, laborer, of the Waterees, to ISAAC DA COSTA, shop-keeper, of Charleston, for Ł 75 currency, 150 a. opposite Fredericksburg Township, Craven Co., bounding SE by LUKE GIBSON; NE on Wateree River; NW & SW on vacant land; according to grant from Gov. JAMES GLEN dated 3 Sept. 1751. Witnesses: JOHN HAMILTON, ROGER GIBSON, JOHN PATIENT. Before WILLIAM PINCKNEY, J.P. WILLIAM HOPTON, Register.

Book K-K, p. 178
21 & 22 Nov. 1751
L & R by Mortgage

HENRY KENNAN, merchant, & SUSANNA his wife, to THOMAS GLEN, ESQ., both of Charleston, as security on bond of even date in the penal sum of Ł 1400 British for payment of Ł 700 British, with interest, on 1 Oct. 1752; 1 full undivided third part of lot #306 in Charelston, containing 1/2 a., English measure, bounding N on Broad Street; W & S on a marsh; E on JAMES GRAME, ESQ. Whereas DOUGAL CAMPBELL, merchant, formerly of Winyaw, now of Charleston, & THOMAS LYNCH, planter, of Santee, Craven Co., by various mesne conveyances became owners of said lot #306 & various materials, cooper furnaces, & utensils for refining sugar on said premises; also of a large brick house erected thereon, called the Sugar House; & whereas CAMPBELL & LYNCH by L & R dated 19 & 20 Nov. last past, for Ł 3400 currency, sold KENNAN an undivided third part of the whole lot, equipment, premises, etc.; now KENNAN mortgages his share to GLEN. Witnesses: CHARLES PINCKNEY, CHARLES PINCKNEY, JR. Before WILLIAM PINCKNEY, J.P. WILLIAM HOPTON, Register.

Book K-K, p. 186
23 Sept. 1751
Lease

GABRIEL MANIGAULT, merchant, & ANNE his wife, of Berkeley Co., to ANDREW HALL (?) (incomplete) pages 187, 197 missing.

Book K-K, p. 197

Indenture signed by JAMES COACHMAN. Witnesses: ELIZABETH PINCKNEY, CHARLES PINCKNEY, JR. Before WILLIAM PINCKNEY, J.P. on 14 Mar. 1752. WILLIAM HOPTON, Register.

Book K-K, p. 197
13 Mar. 1752 (N.S.)
Released

JAMES COACHMAN, planter, & _____ hiw wife, of St. George Parish, Berkeley Co., to ABRAHAM DUPONT, planter, of same Parish, for Ł 3000 currency, several plantations in Berkeley Co., 500 a. on Sandy Run, near Wassamsaw, bounding on all sides on vacant land;

also 150 (?) a. on Four Hole Swamp, bounding N on JOB HOWES; & other sides on vacant land; also 400 a., part of 710 a. lying across the Indian Field Swamp, bounding NW on ELIZABETH MOORE, widow; & on vacant land; SE on SAMUEL MILLER & vacant land; SW on vacant land; 160 a. bounding NW & NE on RICHARD SINGLETON; NE & SE on vacant land; SW & NE (?) on a pond; NW on vacant land; also 125 a. on S side Fosters Creek in St. James Goose Creek Parish, bounding W on JOHN GOODBEE, which 125 a. COACHMAN purchased from HANNAH GOODBEE, widow. Witnesses: ELIZABETH PINCKNEY, CHARLES PINCKNEY, JR. (Note: COACHMAN'S wife died before execution of deed). Before WILLIAM PINCKNEY, J.P. WILLIAM HOPTON, Register.

Book K-K, p. 201
25 & 26 Apr. 1751
L & R

LEONARD OUTERBRIDGE, mariner, & MARY his wife, of Craven Co., to JOHN MCCALL, merchant, of Charleston, for Ł 2000 currency, lot #19 in Charleston, bounding SW 50 ft. on Front Street; NW 217.9 ft. on lot #18; NE on lot #58; SE on lot #20. Witnesses: GEORGE MILLIGAN, ROBERT COLLINS, ROBERT JOHNSTON. Before OTHNIEL BEALE, J.P. WILLIAM HOPTON, Register.

Book K-K, p. 206
11 Dec. 1751
Mortgage

THOMAS GLEN, ESQ., of Charleston, to the Hon. WILLIAM MIDDLETON, attorney, for the Society for the Propagation of the Gospel in Foreign Parts; as security for payment of bond of even date given by THOMAS GLEN & HENRY KENNAN to said MIDDLETON as attorney for said Society, jointly or severally, in penal sum of Ł 3600 for payment of Ł 1800 currency, with interest, on 11 Dec. 1752; part of lot #93 in Charleston on King Street, & premises; for the remainder of the term of 50 years. Whereas the Rev. MR. FRANCIS GUICHARD, pastor of the Church of French Protestants in Charleston, GABRIEL MANIGAULT, ISAAC MAZYCK, PAUL MAZYCK, JACOB MARTIN, JOHN NEUFVILLE, & BENJAMIN D'HARRIETTE, elders of said church, on 1 Oct. 1742, leased for 50 years to DAVID MONGINE, watchmaker, of Charleston for Ł 3:5 sterling a year; part of lot #93 bounding W 30 ft. 6 in. on King Street, S on JOHN VAUGHAN; E on WILLIAM MCKENZIE; N on MAY POSTAL & others; on which MONGINE agreed to erect a substantial brick house; & whereas MONGINE on 8 Aug. last, for (approximately) Ł 1100 assigned the premises to GLEN for the unexpired term. Witnesses: CHARLES PINCKNEY, CHARLES PINCKNEY, JR. Before CHARLES PINCKNEY, J.P. WILLIAM HOPTON, Register. On 7 Dec. 1752 WILLIAM MIDDLETON, as attorney for the Society declared mortgage satisfied. Witness: WILLIAM HOPTON, Register.

Book K-K, p. 212
5 & 6 Aug. 1745
L & R by Mortgage

WILLIAM BROWN, planter, of Craven Co., to JOHN MCCALL, merchant, of Charleston, as security on bond dated 2 July 1744 covering Ł 699:11:7 currency, with interest, payable 6 Oct. next; also on a mortgage of Negroes; 500 a. in Craven Co., on N branch Black River granted to WILLIAM WHITESIDES; bounding S on WILLIAM SWINTON; other sides on vacant land. Witnesses: JORDAN ROCHE, THOMAS CORKER, JONATHAN FITCH. Before JOHN DART, J.P. WILLIAM HOPTON, Register.

Book K-K, p. 219
8 & 9 May 1748
L & R

JOHN ALLEN, merchant, to THOMAS BENNETT, carpenter, both of Charleston, for Ł 400 currency, part of 2 lots, #268 & #270 bounding E on HENRY CHRISTIE; W 140-1/2 ft. on CAPT. WILLIAM PINCKNEY; S 36 ft. on Broad Street, N on an alley belonging to JAMES ST. JOHN & ROBERT THORPE. Witnesses: RICHARD FOWLER, ALBERT DETMAR, WILLIAM SMITH. Before ROBERT AUSTIN, J.P. WILLIAM HOPTON, Register.

Book K-K, p. 225
23 Apr. 1745
Release

ANNE BENNETT, widow, of THOMAS BENNETT, carpenter, & THOMAS BENNETT, their only son, to HENRY CHRISTIE, carpenter; all of Charleston; for Ł 350 SC money, part of 2 lots in Charleston, #268 & #270; bounding E on HENRY CHRISTIE; W 140-1/2 ft. on CAPT. WILLIAM PINCKNEY; S 36 ft. on Broad Street; N on an alley belonging to JAMES ST. JOHN & ROBERT THORP. Witnesses: ALEXANDER MAINE, JOHN REMINGTON. Before ROBERT AUSTIN, J.P. WILLIAM HOPTON, Register.

Book K-K, p. 228
20 Mar. 1752
Sale

RAWLINS LOWNDES, Provost Marshal of SC, to THOMAS FERGUSON, planter, of St. Paul's Parish, Colleton Co., for Ł 600 currency, several

tracts of land, total 1150 a. in Colleton Co.; whereas EDWARD NORTH of
St. Paul's Parish, by grant dated 6 Dec. 1733, owned 400 a. in Colleton
Co., bounding NW on Ponpon River; W on COL. BUTT; E on BENJAMIN PERRY; N
on EDWARD NORTH; as by plat dated 11 Jan. 1731/2; & whereas on 20 June
1728 he obtained from JAMES BOND, planter, of Colleton Co., 450 a. which
BOND had purchased from ALGERNON ASH, bounding S on COL. WILLIAM BULL; N
on 300 a. belonging to EDWARD NORTH; W on Ponpon River; & whereas on 20
(?) June, 1728 purchased from RICHARD ASH, planter, 300 a., bounding S on
450 a.; N on 750 a. belonging to SAMUEL ASH; W on Ponpon River; the last
2 (450 & 300) being part of 1750 a. on E side of freshes of Edisto River
conveyed by the Rev. MR. WILLIAM LIVINGSTONE, of Charleston, to THOMAS
SMITH, JR. in trust for the use of said THOMAS SMITH, JR. & the children
of JOHN ASH, viz: JOHN, RICHARD, ALGERNON, SAMUEL, ISABELLA (wife of BEN-
JAMIN PERRY) & THEODORA (wife of JOSEPH LAW); to be divided equally
amongst them; by which partition ALGERNON received the 450 a. & RICHARD
received the 300 a., which by several mesne conveyances came to said ED-
WARD NORTH; & whereas, upon the death of NORTH, WILLIAM STONE, merchant,
of Charleston, obtained a judgment against JOHN NORTH, executor of ED-
WARD NORTH'S will; to recover a debt of Ł 435:10 7 Ł 31:6:5-1/2 damages;
& whereas Asst. Judge JOHN LINING on 7 Oct. 1746 issued a writ of fieri
facias ordering the Provost Marshall to sell EDWARD'S estate; & whereas
ISAAC HOLMES by judgment, recovered a debt of Ł 490 & Ł 31:6:5-1/2 damages against JOHN NORTH, executor, & THOMAS DALE, Asst. Judge, on Oct.
1746 issued a writ of fieri facias commanding the P.M. to obtain the sums
from the estate of EDWARD NORTH; & whereas parliment had issued an act
for the recovery of debts in the Provinces; & whereas LOWNDES seized the
3 tracts of 400, 450 & 300 a., total 1150 a.; now he sells at public auction to FERGUSON, the highest bidder. Witnesses: MICHAEL YONGE, WILLIAM
READ. Before ALEXANDER STEWART, J.P.

Book K-K, p. 235   Broken Pages. JOHN PINNEY, planter, & MARY
L & R   his wife, of St. Bartholomews Parish, to WIL-
                          LIAM DONNON, for Ł 100 currency, 50 a. on E
side _____ River, St. Paul's Parish, being half of 100 a.; bounding on
WILLIAM F___ G; estate of JOHN F____, JOHN EDWARDS. Witnesses: JOHN
LITTLE, SAMUEL ELMES, JOSEPH HOGER. Before JACOB MOTTE, J.P.

Book K-K, p. 242   Broken Pages. JOSIAH CANTEY, & SUSANNAH his
21 Feb. 1752   wife, to THOMAS MELL, for Ł 300 (?) currency,
Sale   287-1/4 a. in St. Andrews Parish, bounding on
                          estate of THOMAS ELMES; _____ ORAM; JOSIAH
PENDARVIS; BENJAMIN CHILDS. Witnesses: SIMON GALE, SAMUEL (his mark)
WILLIAMS, JOSIAH EVANS. Before RICHARD RIC____. Memorial entered in
Auditor's Office 2 Apr. 1752 in Bk. #3 fol. 306 by JAMES WEDDERBURN, Dep.
Aud. WILLIAM HOPTON, Register.

Book K-K, p. 246   (Broken Pages). SINDINIAH BOSWOOD, & SAMUEL
15 May 1735   BOSWOOD, executrix & executor of JAMES BOSWOOD,
Feoffment   of Berkeley Co., for Ł 150 currency, to THOMAS
                          MELL, 107 (?) a. on N side Ashley River, bound-
ing E on CAPT. JOHN GRANT; W on BENJAMIN WOOD; S on THOMAS MELL; N on
SINDINIAH BOSWOOD. Witnesses: JAMES BOSWOOD, HENRY WOOD, JR., WILLIAM
FULLER. Before RALPH IZARD, J.P. Memorial entered in Auditor's Office 2
Apr. 1752 in Bk. #3, fol. 306, by JAMES WEDDERBURN, Dep. Aud. WILLIAM
HOPTON, Register.

Book K-K, p. 249   ELIAS FOISSIN, planter, of Craven Co., to HEN-
1 & 2 Apr. 1752   RY PERONNEAU & ALEXANDER PERONNEAU, surviving
L & R by Mortgage   executors of will of CAPT. JOHN VANDERHORST,
                          planter, as security on bond of even date in
penal sum of Ł 3600 for payment of Ł 1800 currency, with interest, on 2
Apr. 1753; 1125 a. in Christ Church Parish, bounding N on ALEXANDER FRI-
ZELL & ANTHONY BONNEAU; SW on GEORGE BENSON & MRS. SUSANNAH DUBOSE; SE on
JOHN HUGGANS; which 1125 a. by L & R dated 5 & 6 Jan. 1731 JONAS BONHOSTE
& ELIZABETH his wife sold to FOISSIN (see Bk. N. fol. 156-161). Witness-
es: TIMOTHY MORGRIDGE, JOHN TROUP. Before JAMES MICHIC, J.P. WILLIAM
HOPTON, Register.

Book K-K, p. 258   WILLIAM GLEN, vendue master, & ANN his wife,
8 & 9 Apr. 1752   of Charleston, to JOHN DELAGAYE, merchant, of

254

L & R   Beaufort, for Ł 700 currency, lot #301 in
                             Beaufort, Port Royal, Granville Co., bounding
S on the Bay; E on COL. JOHN BARNWELL; W on RANDOLPH EVANS; N on MORGAN
ELLIS; which lot CHARLES PINCKNEY & GABRIEL MANIGAULT by L & R dated 11 &
12 Feb. last sold to WILLIAM GLEN. Witnesses: WILLIAM MICKIE, JOHN REM-
INGTON. Before JAMES GRAME, J.P. WILLIAM HOPTON, Register.

Book K-K, p. 263   ARNOLD HARVEY, planter, of Berkeley Co., 1 of
8 & 9 Apr. 1752   the sons & devisees of WILLIAM HARVEY, gentle-
L & R by Mortgage   man, of Charleston, to ALEXANDER PERONNEAU,
(lease on P. 307)   gentleman, of Charleston, as security on bond
                            of even date in penal sum of Ł 4000 for pay-
ment of Ł 2000 currency, with interest, on 9 Apr. 1753; lot #47 near
White Point in Charleston 155 ft. on E side of King Street & 245 ft. on S
side of 16 ft. lane called Rivers Street running from King to Old Church
Street, (Meeting Street), bounding E on SAMUEL PERONNEAU; S on JAMES
COCHMAN & ARTHUR HALL; also 200 a., English measure, near Wappoe, St. Andrews Parish, Berkeley Co., bounding E on marsh of Ashley River; N on
JOHN HARVEY; W on Mill Creek; S on BENJAMIN HARVEY & Wappoe Creek.
Whereas WILLIAM HARVEY owned part (or all) of lot #47 in Charleston, also
200 a. in Berkeley Co., & by will dated 21 Sept. 1749 (59?) & codicil
attached, bequeathed to his son ARNOLD the 200 a. at Wappoe, which he had
purchased from MR. GIBBES & others, lying W of a tract of (214 ?) a. before devised to BENJAMIN HARVEY; also 2 parcels of land, E of King Street
which he had purchased from JOHN RIVERS; now ARNOLD mortgages his property to PERONNEAU. Witnesses: WILLIAM HARVEY, THOMAS HAUGHTON. Before
THOMAS LAMBOLL, J.P. WILLIAM HOPTON, Register. On 12 Dec. 1755 ALEXAN-
DER PERONNEAU declared mortgage satisfied. Witness: WILLIAM HOPTON.

Book K-K, p. 273   Broken Pages. ANDREW DELAVILLETTE, gentleman,
30 & 31 Jan. 1743   of Craven Co., to ISAAC MAZYCK, ESQ., of
L & R by Mortgage   Charleston, as security on bond of even date
                            in penal sum of Ł 4150 for payment of Ł 2075
currency, with interest, on 1 Jan. next; 3 tracts of land in Craven Co.;
total 900 a.; 500 a. on N side Santee River, bounding SW on Wadbaccan
Creek; NE on DANIEL JAUDON (formerly RALPH IZARD); NE on NOAH SERRÉ; SE
on ANDREW DELAVILLETTE; 200 a., bounding S & W on NOAH SERRÉ; E on RALPH
IZARD; N on Wadbaccan Creek; also 200 a. bounding NE on NOAH SERRÉ; NW &
SE on RALPH IZARD; SW on Wadbaccan Creek. Witnesses: JOHN GIGNILLIAT,
PAUL MAZYCK, JOHN GUERARD. Before THOMAS MIDDLETON, J.P.

Book K-K, p. 281   WILLIAM WILLIAMS, tailor, to WILLIAM ARNOLD
Broken Pages   for Ł 500 currency, 200 a. on Stono Island,
Dates Missing   part of a tract of 300 a. formerly granted to
L & R   MICHAEL REYNOLDS bounding NE on MR. FLOYD;
                            other sides on JAMES WILLIAMS, JR., ANTHONY
MATHEWS. Witnesses: GEORGE RIVERS, CHARLES MELLICHAMP. Before JACOB
MOTTE, J.P.

Book K-K, p. 287   EDWARD FENWICKE, son & heir of JOHN FENWICKE,
Broken Pages   to GEORGE EVELEIGH, for Ł 1000 currency, part
Dates Missing   of a low water front lot #137 (?) formerly be-
(17 Apr. 1752) L & R   longing to THOMAS PINCKNEY, measuring 1 rod
                            32 ft., bounding N on another low water lot
opposite lot #4. Names & facts mentioned. Whereas MARY ____ widow, by
L & R ____ Sept. 1726, to JOHN FENWICKE, father of EDWARD; part of low
____ formerly belonging to THOMAS PINCKNEY ____ whole rod 32 ____
bounding ____ water lot ____ opposite #4 ____ WILLIAM WILLIAMS; W on
lot #2 ____; ____ THOMAS PINCKNEY in his ____ GEORGE SMITH ____ which
was afterwards ____ LOYD ____ part of lot #3 ____ said premises descended ____ party hereto as only son & heir ____ now EDWARD FENWICKE,
for Ł 1000 currency, ____ releases to GEORGE EVELEIGH ____. Witnesses: JOHN MCCALL, ALEXANDER GORDON, JR. Before JACOB MOTTE, J.P. WIL-
LIAM HOPTON, Register.

Book K-K, p. 293   JOHN ELLIOTT, planter, of Colleton Co., only
24 & 25 Mar. 1752   son of WILLIAM ELLIOTT, planter, who was only
L & R   brother which left issue surviving him of
                            THOMAS (JOHN ELLIOTT), planter, & cousin-ger-
man by the father's side & heir-at-law to AMARENTIA ELLIOTT (afterwards

255

AMARENTIA LOWNDES) only surviving child of said THOMAS (JOHN) ELLIOTT, who was only sister & heir-at-law of "JOHN PENDARVIS ELLIOTT & EDMUND ELLIOTT, the 2 only sons & devisees of said THOMAS (JOHN) ELLIOTT, who both died in their infancy without issue; as did also said AMARENTIA LOWNDES"; & ELIZABETH his wife, of the 1 part; & JOHN SMITH, planter, of Colleton Co., of the other part. Whereas the Lords Proprs. & Gov. ROBERT GIBBES, by 2 separate deeds granted THOMAS ELLIOTT, (great-uncle of JOHN ELLIOTT) planter, 2 adjoining tracts of land at head of NW branch of Stono River in a place called Morris's Nook, 1 of 410 a., the other 390 a.; & whereas THOMAS ELLIOTT by deed poll dated 8 May 1723, reciting as herin before in part recited, & having a parchment plat of 60 a., part of the 2 tracts of 410 & 390 a., dated 8 May 1723, surveyed & certified by WILLIAM BULL, Dep. Sur. Gen., conveyed to his nephew, said THOMAS (JOHN) ELLIOTT, by name of THOMAS ELLIOTT, son of his brother JOHN ELLIOTT, 60 a., bounding according to said plat; & whereas the Lords Proprs. on 7 May 1698 appointed EDMUND BELLINGER, the elder, 1 of the Landgraves of SC, granting him 48,000 a., which title & land descended to his son, EDMUND, the younger; & whereas WILLIAM BULL, at the request of EDMUND the younger, on 9 May 1723, an island plantation 403 a., near head of NW branch of Stono River, as part of the 48,000 a.; & whereas said EDMUND BELLINGER, the younger, by L & R dated 1 & 2 May 1730 sold THOMAS JOHN ELLIOTT, shipwright, of Colleton Co., the 403 a.; & whereas by will devised all his lands equally to his 2 sons, JOHN PENDARVIS ELLIOTT & EDMUND ELLIOTT; both of them dying in their infancy shortly after the death of their father; & the 2 tracts of 50 a. & 403 a. descended to their only sister & surviving child of THOMAS JOHN ELLIOTT, AMARENTIA, who as heir to her 2 brothers & to her father, took possession of the 2 tracts & afterwards married RAWLINS LOWNDES, ESQ., & died under 21 years & without issue, whereby the 2 plantations became vested in JOHN ELLIOTT, as heir-at-law & next of kin of the whole blood to AMARENTIA; now he, & ELIZABETH his wife, for ₤ 2800 currency, convey to JOHN SMITH the 2 tracts of 60 a. & 403 a.; the 60 a., at Morris's Nook, now bounding N & W on land formerly belonging to THOMAS JOHN ELLIOTT; E on said THOMAS ELLIOTT, deceased; S on MR. TUCKER; the 403 a. near head of NW branch of Stono River; now bounding E on the 60 a. & another tract; S on the 60 a. & on TUCKER & on HUGH HEXT; W on HUGH HEXT. Witnesses: MARY HEAPE, THOMAS LAMBOLL. Before JACOB MOTTE, Register.

Book K-K, p. 311
16 & 17 Apr. 1752
L & R

BENJAMIN ELLIOTT, planter, & MARY his wife, to THOMAS ELLIOTT, planter, both of St. Andrews Parish, Berkeley Co., for ₤ 975 currency, 125 a. (part of 325 a.) bounding N on other part said 325 a.; E on THOMAS HOLMAN; S on THOMAS ELLIOTT; W on SAMUEL ELLIOTT. Whereas THOMAS ELLIOTT, planter, by will dated 23 Oct. 1738 gave to his 3 sons, THOMAS (party hereto), BENJAMIN & SAMUEL, equally the rest of his real & personal estate not otherwise devised, to be divided as the majority saw fit, appointing his 3 brothers WILLIAM ELLIOTT, BARNARD ELLIOTT, & JOSEPH ELLIOTT, executors; & whereas brother JOSEPH ELLIOTT, executor, died soon afterwards & by deed poll dated 10 Oct. 1749; WILLIAM & BARNARD, executors; divided the land & allotted to BENJAMIN, party hereto, 325 a. in St. Andrews Parish, bounding E on THOMAS HOLMAN; S on THOMAS ELLIOTT; W on SAMUEL ELLIOTT; N on MR. RIVERS; now BENJAMIN sells part of the tract to THOMAS ELLIOTT. Witnesses: MARY LARDENT, CHARLES PINCKNEY, JR. Before WILLIAM PINCKNEY, J.P. WILLIAM HOPTON, Register.

Book K-K, p. 317
1 & 2 Jan. 1752 (N.S.)
L & R

GEORGE LOGAN, JR., planter, of Christ Church Parish, & ELIZABETH his wife, lately called ELIZABETH BAKER, grand-daughter & devisee of RICHARD HARRIS, planter, of Berkeley Co., to RICHARD BERESFORD, ESQ., of St. Thomas Parish; for ₤ 1600 currency, 420 a. in Berkeley Co., commonly called Clowters. Whereas the Lords Proprs on 14 Aug. 1710 granted THOMAS LAKE, gentleman, 420 a. called Clowter's in Berkeley Co., bounding N on HENRY QUINTON; E partly on Ittewan Creek leading to the plantation of RICHARD BERESFORD, ESQ., & partly on MRS. GRACE BUCKLEY; S on marsh of Clowters Creek & on said GRACE BUCKLEY; W on Clowters Creek & marsh; & whereas THOMAS LAKE by deed of feoffment dated 13 Oct. 1710, for ₤ 200, sold the 420 a. to RICHARD HARRIS, of Berkeley Co.; who, by will dated 10 Jan. 1731 bequeathed the tract to his granddaughter ELIZABETH BAKER, who afterwards married GEORGE LOGAN; now they

sell the land to RICHARD BERESFORD. Witnesses: ANN WATSON, CHARLES
PINCKNEY, JR. Before WILLIAM PINCKNEY, J.P. WILLIAM HOPTON, Register.

Book K-K, p. 325   JOHN HAMILTON, ESQ., of Charleston, to JOHN
17 & 18 Apr. 1752   MARTINI, practitioner in physick, formerly of
L & R by Mortgage   Charleston, now of South Hampton, England (or
                          his attorneys JOHN STANYARNE, BENJAMIN D'HAR-
RIETTE, & JAMES MICHIE) as security on bond dated 26 Mar. 1751 in penal
sum of Ł 140:5:6 British which is equal to Ł 981:18:6 currency, for payment of Ł 70:2:10 British, or value, with interest, on 26 Mar. 1752; & as
security on another bond to MARTINI, of even date; in penal sum of
Ł 666:13:4 for payment of Ł 333:6:8 currency, with interest, on 27 Apr.
1752; 2900 a. on the branches of Stephen's Creek, out of Savannah River,
bounding SE on JOHN HAMILTON & on vacant land; other sides on vacant
land; which 2900 a. were granted 6 Nov. 1751 by Gov. JAMES GLEN to JOHN
HAMILTON. Witnesses: TIMOTHY MORGRIDGE, JOHN TROUP. Before JAMES MICH-
IE, J.P. WILLIAM HOPTON, Register.

Book K-K, p. 333   JOSIAH WARING, planter, of Berkeley Co., to
7 Feb. 1749   JOSEPH BLAKE & GEORGE SUMMERS, church-wardens,
Sale   of Dorchester, St. George Parish, in trust, &
                          to be annexed to the cemetery of the Parish
Church of Dorchester, a piece of ground 40 ft. on the NE end of lots 50 &
51; bounding to the Ne on the church yard 8 rods in length; to the SW on
said lots; NW on lot #49; SE on lot #54. Witnesses: WILLIAM FULLER, JOHN
IOOR, SAMUEL POSTELL. Before RALPH IZARD, J.P. WILLIAM HOPTON, Register.

Book K-K, p. 335   At Bermuda, alias Somer Island. ROBER BREW-
7 Feb. 1752   TON, JR., gentleman, of Town of St. George,
Release   Bermuda, quit claims to DANIEL BADGER, plant-
                          er, of Charleston, SC, all his title to 38 ft.
of land, part of a lot on N side Tradd Street, sold by COL. ROBERT BREW-
TON & said ROBERT BREWTON, JR., to said DANIEL BADGER. Witnesses: JOHN
QUILL, ROBERT HAWKES. HAWKES appeared before ROBERT AUSTIN, J.P. WIL-
LIAM HOPTON, Register.

Book K-K, p. 337   MARY ELIZABETH MILLER, widow, of St. Thomas
18 Jan. 1752   Parish, Berkeley Co., appoints her brother,
Power of Attorney   ELIAS FOISSIN, ESQ., of Georgetown, her at-
                          torney to receive livery & seizin of lot #61
in Georgetown, to be conveyed to her by DANIEL LAROCHE, ESQ., & THOMAS
LANDON of Georgetown. Witnesses: SAMUEL WIGFALL, JAMES BOURDEAUX. Before JAMES AKIN, J.P. WILLIAM HOPTON, Register.

Book K-K, p. 338   HENRY SHERIFF, planter, & MARGARET his wife,
6 & 7 Mar. 1751   to ARCHIBALD SCOTT, both of St. Andrews Par-
L & R   ish, Berkeley Co., for Ł 65:17:6 currency,
                          7-3/4 a. in Berkeley Co., bounding NE on the
Broad Road; SE on MR. SCOTT; W on ROBERT SCRIVEN; which 7-3/4 a. had be-
longed to WILLIAM LANCHESTER & JAMES HAMILTON. Witnesses: PRINGLE HAMIL-
TON, CORNELIUS COOK, MARTHA REMINGTON. Before DANIEL PEPPER, J.P. WIL-
LIAM HOPTON, Register.

                         DEEDS BOOK "L-L"
                       MAY 1752 - SEPT. 1752

Book L-L, p. 3   JOHN HODSDEN, merchant, to GEORGE EVELEIGH,
23 & 24 Apr. 1752   merchant, both of Charleston, for Ł 500 cur-
L & R on Condition   rency, that piece of shoal land E of the cur-
                          tain line of East Bay, opposite the S part of
lot #4, bounding W 27 ft. on East Bay; N & S on GEORGE EVELEIGH'S wharf;
which land was sold to HODSDEN by MARY ELLIS, widow, of Charleston, but
EVELEIGH not to have the privilege of filling up or raising the height of
the ground above the level of East Bay Street, or to build any house,
shed, hut, or other building thereon. Should EVELEIGH disregard these
provisoes then this conveyance to be void. Witnesses: CHARLES JONES,
THOMAS LAMBOLL. Before JACOB MOTTE, J.P. WILLIAM HOPTON, Register.

Book L-L, p. 11   GEORGE EVELEIGH, gentleman, to EDWARD FEN-
23 & 24 Mar. 1751   WICKE, ESQ., both of Charleston, for Ł 500
L & R   currency, part of lot #179 in Charleston,
                         bounding E 17 ft. on Old Church Street; N on
GABRIEL ESCOTT; W on JOHN RIVERS; S on EDWARD FENWICKE (formerly MARY
BRYAN). Witnesses: JOHN MCCALL, ALEXANDER GORDON, JR. Before ALEXANDER
GORDON, SR., J.P. WILLIAM HOPTON, Register.

Book L-L, p. 15   THOMAS FARR, JR., planter, of St. Pauls Par-
5 May 1752   ish, Colleton Co., to THOMAS ELLIOTT, ESQ., of
L & R   Charleston, for Ł 551:0:10 currency, 350 a.,
                         bounding E on HENRY WILLIAMSON; N on COL. JOHN
SMITH; W on JOSEPH FULLER; S on DAVID CRAWFORD; which 350 a. were granted
by the Lords Proprs. to THOMAS FARR, SR., who bequeathed to THOMAS FARR,
JR., who now conveys to THOMAS ELLIOTT. Witnesses: ROBERT MACKEWN, JR.,
JEHU ELLIOTT. Before OTHNIEL BEALE, J.P. WILLIAM HOPTON, Register.

Book L-L, p. 21   DANIEL LAROCHE, ESQ., of Georgetown, who sur-
30 Apr. 1752   vived THOMAS LAROCHE, to JAMES WRIGHT, ESQ.,
Assignment of Mortgage   of Charleston. Whereas by L & R dated 6 & 7
                         Oct. 1737, JOHN THOMPSON, JR., planter, of
Winyaw, & WILLIAM THOMPSON, JR., (for JOHN'S debt) gave bond dated 1 May
1737 to DANIEL & THOMAS LAROCHE, merchants, of Georgetown in the penal
sum of Ł 4419 for payment of Ł 2209:16:7 currency, with interest, on 1
Jan. next; & on 20 July 1737 gave them (for JOHN'S debt) another bond in
penal sum of Ł 4060 for payment of Ł 2029:13:4-1/2 currency, with interest, on 1 Sept. next; & whereas DANIEL & THOMAS LAROCHE became security
on these bonds to several persons; & whereas JOHN THOMPSON, as security,
conveyed to DANIEL & THOMAS LAROCHE the 200 a. in Craven Co. on which he
lived, on N branch of Black River, bounding on all sides on JOHN THOMPSON,
JR.; also 1500 a. in Craven Co., part of 2000 a. granted by the Lords
Proprs. to COL. WILLIAM RHETT & purchased by ROGER MOORE (there being 4
plats thereof); bounding on Black River; SW on SAMUEL HUNTER; N on AN-
THONY WHITE; N on JOHN THOMPSON, JR.; also 250 a. on N side N branch of
Black River, bounding N on JOHN THOMPSON, SR.; SE on WILLIAM SWINTON;
also 975 a. on S side of N branch of Black River, bounding NW on WILLIAM
THOMPSON, SR.; SE on JOHN THOMPSON, JR.; & whereas THOMAS LAROCHE died &
the several sums & interest have not been paid by JOHN THOMPSON, nor by
anyone since his death, to either LAROCHE; & there is a considerable sum
due DANIEL LAROCHE from the estate of JOHN THOMPSON; & whereas DANIEL LA-
ROCHE gave 1 bond dated 2 May 1748 to JAMES WRIGHT in penal sum of Ł 1442
for payment of Ł 721 currency on 2 May then next; & another bond dated 2
May 1751 in penal sum of Ł 1058:3:9 for payment of Ł 579:1:10-1/2 currency on 2 May then next; which sums are due & unpaid; now DANIEL LAROCHE,
as security, conveys to WRIGHT the 4 several tracts of 200 a., 1500 a.,
250 a., & 975 a. mortgaged to him by JOHN THOMPSON. Witnesses: ISAAC
SECARE, JOHN CHEESBOROUGH. Before ELIAS FOISSIN, J.P. WILLIAM HOPTON,
Register.

Book L-L, p. 31   JOHN COOPER, HENRY KENNAN, & ROBERT WILLIAMS,
8 & 9 May 1752   merchants, of Charleston, to the Hon. WILLIAM
L & R by Mortgage   MIDDLETON, attorney for the Society for the
                         Propagation of the Gospel in Foreign Parts; as
security on bond of even date in penal sum of Ł 256:5:0 British for payment of Ł 178:2:0 British, with interest, on 9 May 1753; 4 tracts of 440
a., 90 a., 100 a., & 170 a. in Christ Church Parish, Berkeley Co., total
800 a., bounding S on Shimee Creek, now Parris's Creek; according to
plats; also 200 a. adjoining, formerly belonging to JOHN RUBERY; making
1000 a.; as formerly occupied by JOHN ALEXANDER PARRIS & now held by JOHN
COOPER, HENRY KENNAN, & ROBERT WILLIAMS. Witnesses: CHARLES PINCKNEY,
JR., DANIEL BAYNE. Before WILLIAM PINCKNEY, J.P. WILLIAM HOPTON, Register.

Book L-L, p. 39   PETER SANDERS, saddler, & ELIZABETH his wife,
11 & 12 Feb. 1752   of Charleston, to STEPHEN CLYATT, planter, of
L & R   Craven Co., for Ł 125 currency, 250 a., the
                         back half of 500 a., in Craven Co., bounding N
on vacant land; E on WRAGG'S Barony; W on JOHN EVANT (AVANT?). Whereas
PETER SANDERS, planter, of Craven Co., owned 500 a. & by will dated 30
Aug. 1727 bequeathed the land equally to his 2 sons ZACHARIAH & PETER;

258

now PETER sells his share to CLYATT. Witnesses: FRANCIS AVANT, JOHN
TROUP. Before PAUL TRAPIER, J.P. WILLIAM HOPTON, Register.

Book L-L, p. 46   PETER LANE, planter, & SARAH his wife, to SAM-
27 & 28 Mar. 1743   UEL CLYATT, carpenter, both of Craven Co., for
L & R   Ƚ 450 currency, 618 a., English measure, on N
                         side Georgetown River, in Craven Co., bounding
NE on CAPT. ANTHONY WHITE & CAPT. SOUTHERLAND & JOHN LANE; N on MR. MAY-
LONE; SW on JOHN SUMMER & CAPT. THOMAS BENNY & CAPT. CRITCHLOW; SE on
Three-mile Creek; free from SARAH'S claim of dower; which 618 a. were
part of 918 a. granted MRS. MARY SMITH, of Craven Co., on 8 May by Lt.
Gov. THOMAS BROUGHTON; & conveyed by her by L & R dated 14 & 15 Oct. 1737
to DANIEL & THOMAS LAROCHE; who assigned 618 a. to PETER LANE by L & R
dated 1 & 2 Jan. 1738. Witnesses: JAMES LANE, JOHN WALKER. Before WIL-
LIAM FLEMING, J.P. WILLIAM HOPTON, Register.

Book L-L, p. 54   JAMES LESSLEY, yeoman, & SIBBLE (her mark) his
19 & 20 Mar. 1749   wife, to WILLIAM STROTHER, gentleman, both of
L & R   Craven Co., for Ƚ 300 currency, 300 a. at the
                         Congarees, opposite Saxegotha Township, grant-
ed by Gov. JAMES GLEN on 10 Feb. 1749, to JAMES LESSLEY; bounding S on
vacant land & on WILLIAM HOWELL; W on Santee (Congaree)River; N on THOMAS
MCPHERSON; E on vacant land. Witnesses: JOHN BRACKAU, JOHN (his mark)
WILSON, JOHN PEARSON. Before JAMES GILL, J.P. WILLIAM HOPTON, Register.

Book L-L, p. 62   WILLIAM HOWELL, planter, & MARTHA his wife, to
3 & 4 Apr. 1750   WILLIAM STROTHER, gentleman, both of Craven
L & R   Co., for Ƚ 250 currency, 200 a. on N side San-
                         tee River, in Craven Co., bounding on all
other sides on vacant land; as granted by Gov. JAMES GLEN on 8 Mar. 1743
to WILLIAM HOWELL. Witnesses: JOHN PETTINGER, JOHN PEARSON. Before
STEPHEN CRELL, J.P. WILLIAM HOPTON, Register.

Book L-L, p. 69   BENJAMIN ELLIOTT, planter, of St. Andrews Par-
30 Apr. 1752   ish, to his uncle, WILLIAM ELLIOTT, for Ƚ 75
Feoffment   currency, 25 a., being a quarter part of 100
                         a. which his grandfather, WILLIAM ELLIOTT,
purchased from JOSEPH LAW, which 25 a. were given to BENJAMIN as his
share of his father's estate. Delivery by Turf & Twig. Witnesses: JOHN
STONE, JR., THOMAS PEACOCK. Before ALEXANDER STEWART, J.P. WILLIAM HOP-
TON, Register.

Book L-L, p. 71   JOHN MCCULLOGH, blacksmith, of St. Johns Par-
28 Apr. 1752   ish, Wadmalaw Island, Colleton Co., to HANSE
Mortgage   MCCOLLOUGH, & ANDREW MCCULLOGH, of St. Pauls
                         Parish, Colleton Co., as security on bond of
even date in penal sum of Ƚ 1324 for payment of Ƚ 662 currency, with interest, on 1 Mar. next; 210 a. on Wadmalaw Island, in St. Johns Parish,
bounding N on Wadmalaw River; E on JAMES MICHIE; S on ROBERT TURNER; W on
HENRY LEVINGSTON; being part of a tract granted ROBERT SEABROOK by Gov.
JOSEPH BLAKE, on 16 Sept. 1698; also 4 Negroes, 2 mares, 2 horse colts
branded MG; a stock of cattle with same brand & marked with a crop in
left ear & slit with 2 halfpennies in right ear; also stock of sheep &
hogs; & all his household furniture. Witnesses: SAMUEL SPRY, NICHOLAS
(his mark) LEE. Before JAMES BULLOCK, J.P. WILLIAM HOPTON, Register.

Book L-L, p. 73   WILLIAM SHACKELFORD, SR., vintner, & HESTER
8 & 9 May 1752   his wife, to ROBERT WEAVER, carpenter, both of
L & R   Georgetown, for Ƚ 100 currency, 471 a. in Cra-
                         ven Co., bounding SE on JOHN GOODWIN; NW on
MR. SIMPSON; SW on vacant land; NE on Lynch's Creek. Witnesses: THOMAS
LEITH, JOHN MITCHELL. Before PAUL TRAPIER, J.P. WILLIAM HOPTON, Regis-
ter.

Book L-L, p. 80   DANIEL LAROCHE, merchant, of Prince George
30 Apr. & May 1, 1752   Parish, Craven Co., to EDWARD LIGHTWOOD, mer-
L & R   chant, of Charleston, for Ƚ 1000 currency, 600
                         a. in Craven Co., bounding SW & SE on MR. LAW;
NW & NE on JOHN GREEN & ELISHA SCREVEN. Witnesses: ISAAC SECARE, JOHN
CHEESBOROUGH. Before ELIAS FOISSIN, J.P. WILLIAM HOPTON, Register.

Book L-L, p. 85   PETER LEGER, cooper, of St. Philips Parish,
11 & 12 Feb. 1752   Charleston, to JACOB MOTTE, ESQ., as security
L & R by Mortgage   on bond of even date in penal sum of Ł 1776
                       for payment of Ł 888 currency, with interest,
on 12 Feb. 1753; that lot in Charleston, bounding E 32 ft. on Bedon
Street; N 215 ft. on THOMAS LEGARE; W on Church Street; S on house of
PAUL TOWNSEND; with all buildings thereon. Witnesses: JOSEPH PICKERING,
JOSEPH KERSHAW. Before OTHNIEL BEALE, J.P. WILLIAM HOPTON, Register.
On 9 Apr. 1753 JACOB MOTTE declared mortgage satisfied. Witness: PETER
JOHN MONCLAR.

Book L-L, p. 91   HENRY KENNAN, merchant, to SARAH STOUTENBURGH
23 & 24 Feb. 1749   (lately SARAH MACKENZIE, executrix of will of
L & R by Mortgage   WILLIAM MACKENZIE, merchant, of Charleston),
                       as security on bond of even date in penal sum
of Ł 2120 for payment of Ł 1060 currency, with interest, on 24 Feb. 1750;
that lot in Charleston conveyed by JOHN RATTRAY, gentleman, of Charleston, & HESTER his wife, by L & R dated 9 & 10 Mar. 1747, to HENRY KENNAN.
Witnesses: LUKE STOUTENBURGH, JOHN TROUP. Before JAMES MICKIE, J.P.
WILLIAM HOPTON, Register.

Book L-L, p. 98   ELISHA BUTLER, planter, & ELIZABETH his wife,
27 Oct. 1738   of Colleton Co., to their son WILLIAM ELLIOTT
Feoffment   (BUTLER?) for love & affection & other consid-
                       erations, the 570 a. on which they live, in 4
tracts, at head of N branch of Stono River, in Colleton Co., bounding according to plats. In case of default the 570 a. to be equally divided
between their daughters ELIZABETH ELLIOTT (BUTLER?) & MARY ELLIOTT
(BUTLER?). Witnesses: THOMAS ROSE, ARTHUR MOWBRAY, JOSEPH ELLIOTT. Before ALEXANDER STEWART, J.P. WILLIAM HOPTON, Register. Recorded in Secretary's Book I.I. fol. 203, by WILLIAM PINCKNEY, Dep. Sec.

Book L-L, p. 100   ANN BRUCE, widow, of Parish of St. Margaret,
27 Feb. 1750   Westminster, Co. of Middlesex, Great Britain,
Letter of Attorney   appoints MRS. SARAH BLAKEWAY, widow, of SC,
                       her attorney, with power to sell her houses,
etc. Witness: ALEXANDER PEARSON. Before DAVID EWART, clerk to GYLES
LONE, Notary. PEARSON appeared before ALEXANDER CRAMAHE, J.P. WILLIAM
HOPTON, Register.

Book L-L, p. 102   ANN BRUCE, widow, of Parish of St. Margaret,
6 & 7 Feb. 1752   Westminster, by her attorney, SARAH BLAKEWAY,
L & R   to JOHN BARNWELL, gentleman, of Granville Co.,
                       for Ł 100 SC money, that corner lot #71 in the
old town of Beaufort Port Royal. Witnesses: JOHN TROUP, ALEXANDER GOR-
DON, JR. Before ROBERT AUSTIN, J.P. WILLIAM HOPTON, Register.

Book L-L, p. 106   CHARLES PINCKNEY, ESQ., of Charleston, Speaker
18 & 19 Sept. 1751   of Commons House of Assembly, & GABRIEL MANI-
L & R   GAULT, ESQ., Public Treasure & Receiver of SC,
                       to COL. NATHANIEL BARNWELL, ESQ., of Beaufort
Port Royal, Granville Co., for Ł 2041 currency, to be used in discharging
"Appropriation Orders"' the SE half of Archers Island, about 1500 a.,
with all contiguous broken islands next to the entrance of Port Royal
Harbor. Whereas by L & R dated 23 & 24 Mar. 1737 between JOHN PARRIS,
ESQ., of Charleston, eldest son & heir of ALEXANDER PARRIS, (late Public
Treasurer & Receiver), & executor of his father's will, of 1st part, &
said CHARLES PINCKNEY & GABRIEL MANIGAULT of 2nd part; reciting that
whereas certain commissioners had been appointed to settle said ALEXANDER
PARRIS'S accounts & their final report was made to the Commons House of
Assembly on 2 Mar. 1737, & it was resolved that the estate of ALEXANDER
PARRIS was indebted Ł 22,931 on account of outstanding Appropriation
Orders & also Ł 800 allowed in said accouts for crossing & filing of orders, which appeared·not ot have been duly performed, therefore then due
the Township Fund; also Ł 1930:18:8:3 balance of tax accounts for 1727,
1731, 1732, & 1733; & Ł 1509:5:8-1/2 on Fortifications Account; total
Ł 27,171:4:5:1; & any further debt over & above this amount to be chargeable to said estate; & whereas Ł 8587:3:9 had been put in commissioners
account on 23 Jan. then last for which no voucher had been produced, the
vouchers being in the hands of persons with accounts, & the public should

be indemnified against all demands; & in order to raise the sum of
L 27,171:4:5:1, JOHN PARRIS conveyed to PINCKNEY & MANIGAULT that part of
a lot in Charleston on which stood the dwelling house fronting the Bay
(since burned down), then in possession of SEAMAN & CROKATT; also 3 Pine
Island, behing JOHNSON'S Fort; also 552 a. in Craven Co.; bounding W on
NOAH SERRÉ; N on then vacant land; also 500 a. on Winyaw River in Craven
Co., bounding E on Peedee River; S on MR. DILLON; W & N on vacant land;
also 9 lots in Beaufort, Granville Co., Nos. 5, 27, 30, 63, 64, 66, 82,
86, & 301; also half of Archers Island in Granville Co., near Port Royall
Island, & adjoining the half belonging to JOHN DELABERE, ESQ.; all of
which pieces of real estate formerly belonged to ALEXANDER PARRIS, then
to JOHN PARRIS; JOHN PARRIS to hold the property for 12 months; then
within 18 months the trustees to sell as much of the property as necessary to raise required amount; now said trustees sell half of Archers Island to BARNWELL. Witnesses: JACOB MOTTE, CHARLES PINCKNEY, JR. Before
ROBERT AUSTIN, J.P. WILLIAM HOPTON, Register.

Book L-L, p. 117   JOHN ALEXANDER PARRIS, eldest son & heir of
26 Nov. 1751   ALEXANDER PARRIS, JR., also now heir of COL.
Release & Confirmation   ALEXANDER PARRIS, Public Treasure & Receiver
                          of SC, confirms NATHANIEL BARNWELL'S title to
half of Archers Island. Whereas by L & R dated 23 & 24 Mar. 1737 JOHN
PARRIS, then eldest son & heir of said ALEXANDER PARRIS, Public Treasurer
& also his devisee & executor, conveyed to CHARLES PINCKNEY & GABRIEL
MANIGAULT, trustee (see p. 106), sundry houses & lands, including half of
Archers Island; & whereas by Act of Assembly dated 25 Mar. 1738 it was
enacted that the estate of ALEXANDER PARRIS should be vested in PINCKNEY
& MANIGAULT for the purposes mentioned therein, with authority to sell
the property; & whereas by L & R dated 18 & 19 Sept. 1751 they sold the S
half of Archers Island to COL. NATHANIEL BARNWELL, of Beaufort, Granville
Co., for L 2041 currency; & whereas some claim may appear to belong to
JOHN ALEXANDER PARRIS, party hereto, because of his being eldest son &
heir of ALEXANDER PARRIS, JR., now for 10 shillings & other considerations he releases his claim to half of Archers Island to BARNWELL. Witnesses: JACOB MOTTE, JOSEPH KERSHAW. Before OTHNIEL BEALE, J.P. WILLIAM
HOPTON, Register.

Book L-L, p. 121   Declaration on release recorded in Book G.G.
31 Dec. 1751   pages 141-146 after his coming of age of his
Confirmation   consent to & confirmation of that deed. JOHN
                          CATTELL, JR., having reached 21 years of age
on 5 Sept. 1751 now conveys to ARCHIBALD SCOTT, for L 343:10:0 currency,
the 1/4 part of the consideration money, his 1/4 part of 2 tracts of
99-1/2 a. & 15 a. mentioned in said release. Witnesses: JOHN REMINGTON,
JR., JOHN REMINGTON. Before JOHN LINING, J.P. WILLIAM HOPTON, Register.

Book L-L, p. 123   JOSEPH DUBOURDIEU, executor of will of COL.
1 & 2 Apr. 1748   ANTHONY WHITE, to DANIEL LAROCHE, gentleman,
L & R   both of Craven Co., for L 100 currency, 950 a.
                          in 2 tracts; 600 a. in Craven Co., on S side
Black River, bounding NW on the Hon. JOHN CLELAND or ELISHA SCREVEN &
JOHN GREEN; SW & SE on BENJAMIN LAW; 350 a. on S side Black River, part
of 1150 a. granted by Gov. ROBERT JOHNSON to BENJAMIN LAW, bounding S on
BENJAMIN LAW; E on ELISHA SCREVEN of JOHN CLELAND; N on ANTHONY WHITE.
Whereas ANTHONY WHITE by will dated 8 Feb. 1746 ordered all his real &
personal estate sold by his executors to pay his debts, now his executor
DUBOURDIEU sells 2 tracts to LAROCHE. Witnesses: JAMES CROKATT, JOHN
DEXTER. Before ELIAS FOISSIN, J.P. WILLIAM HOPTON, Register.

Book L-L, p. 129   JAMES (his mark) SCOTT, planter, & FRANCES
17 & 18 Feb. 1752   (her mark) his wife, to JOHN TUCKER, planter,
L & R   both of Berkeley Co., for L 50 currency, 600
                          a. in Berkeley Co., bounding E on WILLIAM TIN-
KEN'S land on S prong of Broad River & on vacant land. Witnesses: SAMUEL
LYNES, JOHN (his mark) STEEL, JOHN (his mark) GIBSON. Before JAMES FRAN-
CIS, J.P. WILLIAM HOPTON, Register.

Book L-L, p. 134   WILLIAM RANDALL, merchant, of Charleston, to
1 & 2 Nov. 1751   JAMES CROKATT, ESQ., ALEXANDER WATSON, & RICH-
L & R by Mortgage   ARD GRUBB, merchants, of London, England, as

security on bond of even date in penal sum of Ⱡ 5522 British for payment of Ⱡ 2761:5:0 British, with interest, on 1 Nov. next; the N half of lot #210 in Charleston, bounding S 207 ft. on JOHN TIPPER; N on CAPT. WILLIAM PRIVIT; E 50 ft. on a street leading from Ashley River to the Broad Path; W on heirs of WILLIAM LIVINGSTON. Witnesses: RICE PRICE, ROBERT RAPER. Before H. BERINGER DE BEAUFAIN. WILLIAM HOPTON, Register.

Book L-L, p. 141   WILLIAM HEXT, gentleman, of Johns Island, to
21 & 22 Sept. 1751   EDWARD FENWICKE, ESQ., of Charleston, as se-
L & R by Mortgage   curity on bond of even date in penal sum of
                          Ⱡ 2414 for payment of Ⱡ 1207 currency, with
interest, on 1 May 1752; 300 a. on Johns Island known as the Indian
Graves, bounding S on WILLIAM STEPHENS; W on ABRAHAM WAIGHT; E & N on
ALEXANDER HEXT, brother of said WILLIAM HEXT; also 8 Negro slaves. Witnesses: ANDREW RUTLEDGE, ALEXANDER GORDON, JR. Note: The above premises
to also stand security for another bond for payment of Ⱡ 200 & interest.
Before WILLIAM PINCKNEY, J.P. Recorded in Secretary's Book V.V. fol.
218-220 on 15 Oct. 1751 by WILLIAM PINCKNEY, Dep. Sec. WILLIAM HOPTON,
Register.

Book L-L, p. 147   ANDREW RUTLEDGE, ESQ., of Charleston, to HAN-
5 & 6 June 1752   NAH MILLER, (MILNER?), widow, of Christ Church
L & R   Parish, for Ⱡ 1339 currency, 446-1/2 a. in
                          Christ Church Parish, Berkeley Co., bounding
according to plat certified 4 June 1752 by WILLIAM WILKINS, Dep. Sur.;
the N part of which is part of a larger tract granted to JOHN SAVERANCE
of said Parish & later belonging to his son, JOSEPH SAVERANCE, & by several mesne conveyances came to ANDREW RUTLEDGE; the S part being part of
500 a. granted to THOMAS BARTON. Witnesses: CHARLES BARKSDALE, ALEXANDER
GORDON, JR. Before ALEXANDER GORDON, ESQ. WILLIAM HOPTON, Register.
Plat of 446-1/2 a. bounding N on heirs of DR. RUTLEDGE, on parsonage
land & on heirs of MR. SAVERANCE; E on said SAVERANCE & on MR. PHILIP &
on CAPT. BENSON; S on CAPT. BENSON & on marsh of MRS. BOONE; W on MRS.
BOON & ANDREW RUTLEDGE & heirs of DR. RUTLEDGE.

Book L-L, p. 152   ELEANOR COBLEY (lately ELEANOR WRIGHT); JOHN
18 & 19 Nov. 1751   GORDON & ELIZABETH his wife (lately ELIZABETH
L & R   WRIGHT); of 1st part; to GEORGE SEAMAN, mer-
                          chant, of Charleston, for Ⱡ 3000 currency,
part of lot #8 in Charleston fronting 30 ft. on the Bay. Whereas the Rt.
Hon. WILLIAM, Earl of Craven, & the Lords Proprs. on 20 Apr. 1681 granted
EDWARD MUSSON lot #8 in Charleston; & he, on 29 Nov. 1681, sold the S
half of the lot, containing 1/4 a., to THOMAS GREATCASH, cordwainer, of
Charleston, the half lot then bounding E on Cooper River; W on PHILLIP
BUCKLEY; S on RICHARD TRADD; & whereas THOMAS GREATCASH on 4 Oct. 1692
sold the half lot to WILLIAM WALESBY (reserving 50 ft. sq. at lower end
or W part said half lot for himself); & whereas WALESBY by letter of
attorney dated 2 Sept. 1696 authorized GEORGE RAYNER, of Colleton Co., to
sell his estate in SC; & GEORGE RAYER & CATHERINE WALESBY (wife of WIL-
LIAM WALESBY) on 20 Mar. 1697 sold the half lot (except 50 ft. sq.) to
JOSEPH KEYS, of Charleston; & he, by will dated 15 Nov. 1716, bequeathed
the N part, on which was a tenement in which KEYS lived, to his daughter,
JANE KEYS; & whereas JANE KEYS married JOHN WRIGHT, merchant, of Charleston, & they had 2 children; ELEANOR & ELIZABETH, parties hereto; & whereas both JOHN & JANE WRIGHT died without making disposition of the property & said 2 daughters inherited; & whereas ELEANOR married JEMMET COBLEY,
merchant, of Charleston, since deceased, & ELIZABETH married JOHN GORDON;
now ELEANOR & ELIZABETH & JOHN GORDON sell that part of lot #8 as shown
on plat certified 20 Jan. 1752; bounding E 30 ft. on E Bay; S on part of
lot #8 belonging to heirs of JAMES OSMOND; W 24-3/4 ft. on JOHN RAVEN; N
on other half of lot belonging to GEORGE SEAMAN. Witnesses: NATHANIEL
BARNWELL, JOHN SMITH. Before JACOB MOTTE, J.P. WILLIAM HOPTON, Register. Plat given.

Book L-L, p. 163   SUSANNAH BILBEAU, widow, of St. Thomas & St.
11 June 1752   Dennis Parish, Berkeley Co., to her son PHILIP
Gift   NORMAND, for love & affection & other consid-
                          erations, 550 a. in St. Thomas & St. Dennis
Parish, formerly belonging to her husband JAMES BILBEAU, who bequeathed
the land to their son, JAMES BILBEAU, upon whose death SUSANNAH became

owner; the 550 a. being on E side Cooper River, within land, bounding NE
on SOLOMON BREMAR; SW on NICHOLAS BOSCKET & DANIEL TREZEVANT; NW on JAMES
AUMONIER & ANTHONY POITEVIN; SE on DANIEL GOBBLE. Witnesses: FRANCIS
DESCHAMPS, PETER BROCKET, SAMUEL BOCKET. Before THOMAS MIDDLETON, J.P.
WILLIAM HOPTON, Register.

Book L-L, p. 165   MAGDALEN DELIESSELINE, JOHN DELIESSELINE, &
5 & 6 Sept. 1750   DOROTHY his wife, of 1st part; to PHILIP NOR-
L & R   MAND; all of Craven Co., for L 213 currency,
                          213 a. surveyed 7 June 1750 by JOHN HENTIE,
Dep. Sur., & taken out of several tracts belonging to MAGDALEN DELIESSE-
LINE, in St. James Santee, Craven Co., bounding on 1 side on Itshaw Creek.
Whereas MAGDALEN DELIESSELINE, by will of her uncle, JAMES LANGLOIS, be-
came possessed of several tracts of land, with the proviso that after her
death they should go to her first wife; & whereas she has delivered the
land to her son JOHN; now she & JOHN & his wife DOROTHY, sell a part to
NORMAND. Plat given. Witnesses: WILLIAM THOMAS, ALEXANDER CHAUVINT
(CHOUIN), ISAAC CHAUVINT (CHOUIN). Before JOHN GENDRON, J.P. WILLIAM
HOPTON, Register.

Book L-L, p. 173   WILLIAM OSBORN, planter, of Colleton Co., to
26 & 27 Mar. 1750   RICHARD HAINSWORTH, planter, of Craven Co.,
L & R   for L 150 currency, 300 a. in Craven Co., on
                          NW side Santee River near FIBBIN's land,
bounding NE on WILLIAM OSBORN; other sides on vacant land. Witnesses:
SIMON GALE, JOHN CARGILL, PETER (his mark) WILSON. Before RICHARD RICH-
ARDSON, J.P. WILLIAM HOPTON, Register.

Book L-L, p. 179   ROBERT PRINGLE, merchant, & JUDITH his wife,
23 & 24 Sept. 1751   of Charleston, to JOHN BARNWELL, gentleman, of
L & R   Granville Co., for L 540 currency, lots #5 &
                          #30 in Beaufort Port Royal, Granville Co.
Whereas ALEXANDER PARRIS, ESQ., Public Treasurer & Receiver of SC, owned
sundry houses, lands, town lots, etc., including 3 lots, 5, 7, & 30, in
Beaufort; & whereas JOHN PARRIS, as eldest son & heir & devisee became
owner of his father's real estate; & whereas the father (ALEXANDER) at
his death was considerably indebted to the Public & his estate became
liable for said debts & whereas JOHN by L & R dated 23 & 24 Mar. 1737
conveyed to CHARLES PINCKNEY & GABRIEL MANIGAULT, as trustees, his father's estate to be sold to satisfy said debts (see p. 106); & they, by
L & R dated 18 & 19 this Sept. 1751 sold said 3 lots in Beaufort for
L 435 currency to ROBERT PRINGLE; now PRINGLE sells 2 of the lots to JOHN
BARNWELL. Witnesses: THOMAS NETHERCOAT, JOHN RUTLEDGE. Before ALEXANDER
GORDON, J.P. WILLIAM HOPTON, Register.

Book L-L, p. 186   ELISHA BUTLER, planter, of Colleton Co., &
28 Oct. 1738   ELIZABETH his wife, equally to their 2 sons,
Gift   STEPHEN ELLIOTT & WILLIAM ELLIOTT, for natural
                          love & affection & other considerations, 200
a. in Colleton Co., bounding E on JOHN GODFREY; S & W on THOMAS ELLIOTT.
Witnesses: THOMAS ELLIOTT, RICHARD GODFREY. Before HENRY HYRNE, J.P.
WILLIAM HOPTON, D. Nav. Officer.

Book L-L, p. 187   THOMAS BARKSDALE, JR., planter, to JOHN JEF-
17 & 18 June 1752   FORDS, planter, both of Berkeley Co., for
L & R   L 1510 currency, 500 a. granted 1 May 1706 by
                          Gov. NATHANIEL JOHNSON to JOHN ABRAHAM MOTTE;
on NW side Seawee Bay, bounding S on JOHN ABRAHAM MOTTE; other sides on
vacant land; which land JOHN JEFFORDS, & MARY his wife, by L & R dated 9
& 10 June 1752 sold to THOMAS BARKSDALE, JR. Witnesses: HENRY CORNISH,
CHRISTOPHER GILLYARD, GEORGE BARKSDALE. Before THOMAS LAMBOLL, J.P.
WILLIAM HOPTON, Register.

Book L-L, p. 194   FRANCIS DESCHAMPS, & MARIANN his wife, of
13 & 14 July 1750   Christ Church Parish, Berkeley Co., to CATHER-
L & R   INE WIGFALL, widow, of same Parish, for L 900
                          currency, 2 tracts, total 695 a.; 404 a.
granted by Gov. ROBERT GIBBS to JOHN CARRIERE; who conveyed to JOHN HODG-
SON; who conveyed to FRANCIS DESCHAMPS; in St. Thomas & St. Dennis Parish; bounding NE on THOMAS COOK; SE on JOHN BEEN; SW & NW on vacant land;

& 291 a. purchased by FRANCIS DESCHAMPS under a King's warrant in same Parish, bounding NW on SINGALTERY; NE on FRANCIS DESCHAMPS; S on HENRY BONNEAU; other sides on vacant land. Witnesses: RICHARD BLAKE, MARY MILLER, SARAH WIGFALL. Before SAMUEL THOMAS, J.P. See Auditor's Book No. 3, fol. 311 on 11 May 1752 by JAMES WEDDERBURN, Dep. Aud. WILLIAM HOPTON, Register.

Book L-L, p. 201   ANDREW REMBERT, & HESTER his wife, to ISAAC
25 May 1750   LEGRAND, both of St. James Santee, Craven Co.,
Release   for Ƚ 900 currency, 483 a. in St. James Santee
                          Parish, which REMBERT purchased from PAUL BRU-
NEAU; bounding SE on Wambaw Creek; E & S on ABRAHAM PERDRIAU; W & S on
PAUL BRUNEAU. Witnesses: PETER DUMAY, MICHAEL BOINEAU, STEPHEN GUERRY.
Before JOHN GENDRON, J.P. Entered in Auditor's Book No. 3, fol. 306, on
17 Apr. 1752, by JAMES WEDDERBURN, Dep. Aud. WILLIAM HOPTON, Register.

Book L-L, p. 206   ELIZABETH JENYS, widow, of PAUL JENNYS, ESQ.,
23 Aug. 1743   of Berkeley Co., of 1st part; HENRY BEDON &
Marriage Settlement   BRAMFIELD EVANCE, merchants, of Charleston, of
Tripartite   2nd part; COL. JOHN GIBBES, of St. Johns Par-
                         ish, Colleton Co., of 3rd part. Whereas a
marriage is intended between JOHN GIBBES & ELIZABETH JENYS; & whereas she
owns considerable real & personal estate in SC consisting of plantations,
houses, wharves, etc., slaves, cattle, horses, chariots, chaises, furniture, jewels, ready money, bonds, mortgages, etc., etc.; & whereas it is
mutually agreed between them that ELIZABETH'S property shall be conveyed
to trustees for her sole use & disposal; now, to carry out this agreement,
she, with his consent, conveys to BEDON & EVANCE, as trustees, her 118
slaves (named); her cariot & horses; all her neat cattle at Johns Island
Beechhill & Jehosha, branded T.R.; her sheep; her carts, wagons, & "car-
riages as well by water as by land"; plows, plantation tools, etc.; her
household stuff, plate, & furniture; her watches, rings, jewels & other
personal ornaments; all rents & profits from plantations, houses, wharves,
cranes, etc.; the yearly rent of Ƚ 1000 currency payable to her out of
the estate during her life; all bonds, mortgages, etc.; for her sole use
& benefit; & whereas ELIZABETH is entitled to dower in various plantations, etc., which belonged to her first husband, JOHN RAVEN, of Colleton
Co.; & to Ƚ 1000 a year from PAUL JENYS'S estate; & to various commis-
sions, etc.; all of which are turned over to the trustees for her use.
Witnesses: STEPHEN BEDON, JR., JOHN RAVEN BEDON. Before ROBERT AUSTIN,
J.P. WILLIAM HOPTON, Register.

Book L-L, p. 215   Whereas ELIZABETH GIBBES, now wife of COL.
2 July 1752   JOHN GIBBES, of St. Johns Parish, Colleton Co.,
Indemnification   (& formerly widow of PAUL JENYS, ESQ., of
                         Charleston), & her then intended husband (JOHN
GIBBES) on 23 Aug. 1743 (see page 206) conveyed all her real & personal
estate to HENRY BEDON & BRAMFIELD EVANCE (now deceased) as trustees, the
property & income to be for her special use & benefit; & whereas her
present husband, JOHN GIBBES, has at her request entered into several obligations for her benefit, in which he has no concern, & particularly on
this day joined with her (she being widow & surviving executrix of PAUL
JENYS, merchant, of Charleston, surviving partner of JOHN BAKER) in conveying to THOMAS LAMBOLL, ESQ., of Charleston, surviving executor (for
American affairs) of will of said JOHN BAKER by way of settling all disputes & differences between ELIZABETH GIBBES & THOMAS LAMBOLL touching
the estates of PAUL JENYS & JOHN BAKER, & to indemnify LAMBOLL & all executors of JOHN BAKER from suits, etc.; & whereas her husband may hereafter enter into other obligations on her account & to protect him & his
estate; now ELIZABETH directs her trustee, HENRY BEDON, to transfer to
her husband such slaves, goods, & chattles & estates as shall amount to
the value of all such debts of his incurred for her sake. Witnesses:
CHARLES PINCKNEY, JR., JOHN BASSNETT. Before THOMAS LAMBOLL, J.P. WIL-
LIAM HOPTON, Register.

Book L-L, p. 223   ELIZABETH ELLIOTT, wife of THOMAS ELLIOTT,
9 & 10 July 1752   planter, of Stono, Colleton Co., (formerly
L & R   ELIZABETH BELLINGER, widow & executrix of will
                         of Landgrave EDMUND BELLINGER, 1st) by her
attorneys (her sons EDMUND & GEORGE BELLINGER); of 1st part; to Lt. Gov.

WILLIAM BULL, for L 350 currency, 254 a., part of 300 a. allotted to said
ELIZABETH ELLIOTT. Whereas Landgrave EDMUND BELLINGER, the father, under
his patent for 48,000 a., had a plantation of 13,000 a. surveyed in Granville Co., & by will dated 21 Feb. 1739 directed all his lands, not
otherwise disposed of, sold by his wife; & in case of her death by his
son EDMUND; the money to be used in paying his debts & the remainder divided equally amongst his wife 7 children; & whereas ELIZABETH proved the
will & after selling some of the land & paying testator's debts some land
remained, which were divided on 16 Jan. 1747 & allotted to her & her
children, & she received 300 a. & whereas on 30 Apr. 1752 she appointed
her 2 sons, EDMUND & GEORGE BELLINGER, her attorneys to sell her tract
containing between 200 & 300 a., adjoining the church land & DR. ROSE'S
land, near Lt. Gov. BULL'S land in Granville Co.; now she, ELIZABETH
ELLIOTT, by her attorneys, sells a part of her 300 a. to Lt. Gov. WILLIAM
BULL. Witnesses: CHARLES PINCKNEY, JR., JOHN BEALE. Before WILLIAM
BULL, JR., J.P. WILLIAM HOPTON, Register. Plat of 254 a. in Prince William Parish certified 9 June 1752 by STEPHEN BULL, Dep. Sur.; bounding SW
on the parsonage; SE on Lt. Gov. WILLIAM BULL; NE on DR. WILLIAM ROSE; NW
on WILLIAM BOWER WILLIAMSON.

Book L-L, p. 231   JAMES CROKATT, ESQ., formerly of Charleston,
25 July 1749   SC, now of London, & ESTHER his wife, to THOM-
Release   AS SMITH, JR., merchant, of SC, for L 250
                         British, the piece of land described in plat
dated 8 Mar. 1745 by GEORGE HUNTER, Sur. Gen.; being part of lots 38 & 81
occupying 33 ft. on N side of Broad Street; bounding W on part of lot #38
belonging to MATHEW ROCHE & part of lot #29 belonging to MRS. ELIZABETH
GIBBES; E on JAMES CORKATT; part of lot #81 bounding N on HENRY SHERIFF;
W on MRS. ELIZABETH GIBBES; S partly on MATTHEW ROCHE; except that CRO-
KATT reserves 8 in. of land for eavesdroppings of the kitchen & for the
watercourse of the kitchen; which premises, with the larger part of the 2
lots were conveyed by L & R dated 8 & 9 Feb. 1731 by JOSEPH WRAGG, & JU-
DITH his wife, to JAMES CROKATT; the property to be free from ESTHER CRO-
KATT'S claim of dower. Witnesses: ISAAC HOLMES, RICHARD WARING, JR. Be-
fore PETER TAYLOR, J.P. WILLIAM HOPTON, Register.

Book L-L, p. 238   GEORGE MOORE, gentleman, of New Hanover Co.,
29 July 1751   NC, eldest son & heir of ROGER MOORE, ESQ., of
Release & Confirmation   said Co., & WILLIAM MOORE, second son of said
                         ROGER MOORE, release to THOMAS SMITH, their
claim to certain lands. Whereas ROGER MOORE on 1 Dec. 1747 sold to his
son-in-law, THOMAS SMITH, merchant, of Charleston, 200 a. on Hilton Head
Island, Granville Co., bounding W on the River May; S on a creek; N & E
on vacant land, also 700 a. called Gibbes's Plantation, in Berkeley Co.,
bounding S on Goose Creek; W on COL. JOHN HERBERT; E on heirs of COL.
HUGH GRANTE; & whereas ROGER MOORE, by will dated 7 Mar. 1747 bequeathed
to his 2 sons, GEORGE & WILLIAM, equally, the residue of his real & personal estate; & whereas doubts may arise regarding the validity of the
conveyance to THOMAS SMITH, especially as there is no endorsement on said
deed of any livery & seizin of the premises having been made & given;
now, to remove all doubts, & for L 100 NC money, GEORGE & WILLIAM release
the lands & confirm THOMAS SMITH in his title. Witnesses: JOHN RUSSELL,
MAURICE MOORE, SR. Before PETER TAYLOR, J.P. WILLIAM HOPTON, Register.

Book L-L, p. 243   HENRY SIMMONS (SIMMONDS), gentleman, of Bladen
10 June 1748   Co., NC, by his attorney, PETER SIMMONS, of
Release   of same place but at present in Charleston,
                         SC, to THOMAS SMITH, merchant, of Charleston,
for L 300 SC money, lot #207 in Charleston. Whereas the Lords Proprs. on
17 May 1694 granted PETER GIRARD, merchant, of Charleston, lot #207 in
Charleston, 66 ft. x 330 ft.; bounding N on lot #123 belonging to heirs
of SARAH TROTT; E on Colleton Square; S on lot #206; W on Meeting House
Street; & whereas PETER GIRARD (GUERARD) by will dated 30 Aug. 1707 bequeathed the residue of his estate including said lot to his executors
(his friends HENRY NOBLE, PETER DE ST. JULIEN, & LEWIS PASQUERDAU) in
trust for his daughter JUDITH, to be delivered to her either in specie or
full value thereof when 21 years or on day of her marriage; & whereas she
attained 21 years & married HENRY SIMONDS, of Charleston, & the lot a-
mongst other things, was delivered to her; & whereas they owned the lot
until some time in 1734 when JUDITH died, & HENRY SIMMONDS, the father,

265

died in 1742; & HENRY SIMMONDS, the son, inherited; & whereas on 2 May 1748 he appointed PETER SIMMONDS his attorney with authority to sell the lot; now PETER as attorney, sells the lot to THOMAS SMITH. Witnesses: WILLIAM PLAYTERS, WILLIAM BAMPFIELD. Before JAMES WRIGHT, J.P. WILLIAM HOPTON, Register.

Book L-L, p. 250
14 & 15 July 1752
L & R by Mortgage

ANN WATSON, widow, to JACOB MARTIN, practitioner of physic, both of Charleston, as security on bond of even date in penal sum of Ł 6000 for payment of Ł 3000 currency, with interest, on 15 July 1753; lot #28 in Charleston, with its tenements; bounding S 54 ft. on Broad Street; W 100 ft. on the house of JOHN CROKATT (formerly DR. JOHN DELAUNE); N on heirs of MR. JENYS (formerly Madam BRETELL); E on HENRY KENNAN (formerly MATTHEW ROCHE, afterwards JOHN RATTRAY). Witnesses: JAMES GRINDLAY, MARK ANTHONY BESSELLEU. Before JAMES MICKIE, J.P. WILLIAM HOPTON, Register. On 17 Feb. 1758 JACOB MARTIN declared mortgage satisfied. Witness: WILLIAM HOPTON.

Book L-L, p. 256
11 & 12 Mar. 1752
L & R

ROBERT SCREVEN, planter, & SARAH his wife, of James Island, to JOHN CROFT, planter, of Craven Co., for Ł 1900 currency, 450 a., in Craven Co., bounding NW, NNE, & SE on Sampit Creek. Whereas Gov. NATHANIEL JOHNSON & the Lords Proprs. on 14 Sept. 1705 granted JOHN ABRAHAM MOTTE 100 a. in Craven Co., bounding E on Winyaw; N, S, & W on vacant land; & whereas Gov. ROBERT GIBBES on 20 Mar. 1712 granted ROBERT SCREVEN, father of ROBERT, party hereto, 500 a. in Craven Co., bounding E on Winyaw River; S & W on vacant land; N on Sandpit Creek; & whereas JOHN ABRAHAM MOTTE on 13 Apr. 1709 sold the 100 a. to WILLIAM SCREVEN, of Craven Co., who, by will dated 14 Oct. 1711 bequeathed the tract to his son, ROBER, (father of ROBERT, party hereto), who thus owned both tracts of 100 a. & 500 a., & dying intestate, about 1732, ROBERT the son inherited; & whereas a resurvey showed the tracts to be adjoining & to contain only 490 a.; now ROBERT SCREVEN sells a part of it, 450 a., to JOHN CROFT. Witnesses: MARGARET REMINGTON, JOHN REMINGTON. Before WILLIAM PINCKNEY, J.P. WILLIAM HOPTON, Register. Plat given, showing MR. TRAPIER'S house; MR. CLELAND'S house; 40 a. belonging to GEORGE HUNTER; land claimed by heirs of NATHANIEL WICKHAM.

Book L-L, p. 265
29 & 30 June 1752
L & R by Mortgage

HENRY KENNAN, merchant, of JOHN CROKATT, merchant; both of Charleston; as security on bond of even date in penal sum of Ł 7000 for payment of Ł 3500 currency, with interest, on 7 July 1752; a lot in Charleston, bounding S on Broad Street; E & N on THOMAS SMITH, JR.; W on MRS. ANN WATSON, widow. Witnesses: JAMES MICKIE, JOHN TROUP. Before ALEXANDER VANDERDUSSEN, J.P. WILLIAM HOPTON, Register.

Book L-L, p. 271
3 & 4 Apr. 1752
L & R by Mortgage

HENRY CHRISTIE, carpenter, & CATHERINE his wife, to JACOB MARTIN, gentleman; both of Charleston; as security on bond of even date in penal sum of Ł 800 for payment of Ł 400 currency, with interest, on 15 Apr. 1753; part of 2 lots, #268 & #270, in Charleston, bounding W on WILLIAM PINCKNEY; S 36 ft. on Broad Street; N on an alley formerly belonging to JAMES ST. JOHN & ROBERT THORPE; E 140-1/2 ft. on HENRY CHRISTIE. Witnesses: JOHN CLIFFORD, ANN LLOYD. Before JAMES MICKIE, J.P. WILLIAM HOPTON, Register. On 31 July 1758 JACOB MARTIN declared mortgage satisfied. Witness: WILLIAM HOPTON.

Book L-L, p. 278
16 & 17 May 1751
L & R

WILLIAM GRAY, planter, & ANNE his wife, to WILLIAM DALTON, planter, both of Colleton Co., for Ł 496 currency, 248 a. in Colleton Co., formerly granted to WILLIAM DALTON; bounding NW on WILLIAM DALTON; NE on HUGH BRYAN; other sides on head of Wannells Creek. Witnesses: FRANCIS (his mark) SMITH, JOHN WARING, WILLIAM DALTON. Before HENRY HYRNE, J.P. WILLIAM HOPTON, Register.

Book L-L, p.283
14 & 16 Nov. 1751
L & R

JOHN (his mark) TODD, SR., planter, & SARAH, (her mark) his wife, to TIMOTHY KELLY, gentleman, both of Craven Co., for Ł 247 currency, 300 a. in Craven Co., on S side Wateree River, granted by Gov. JAMES GLEN to JOHN TODD, SR.; bounding SE on JAMES OUSELY; other sides on vacant land. Witnesses: JOHN MARTIN, JOHN KELLY. Before ROGER GIBSON, J.P. WILLIAM HOPTON, Register.

Book L-L, p. 289   CHARLES CANTEY, planter, of Santee to JAMES
27 & 28 Mar. 1752   BAKER, planter, of St. George Parish, for
L & R   ₺ 1500 currency, 298 a., part of 400 a., in
                         St. George Parish; except 1/4 a. reserved as a
burying ground; bounding N & SW on PAUL JENYS; NE on WALTER IZARD, ESQ.;
S on vacant land. Witnesses: JOHN BLAMYER, JOHN IOOR, WILLIAM MAINE.
Before J. SKENE, J.P. WILLIAM HOPTON, Register.

Book L-L, p. 296   PAUL BRUNEAU, planter, to GEORGE SIMONS, plant-
26 & 27 Apr. 1751   er, both of St. James Santee, Craven Co., for
L & R   ₺ 573 currency, 145 a. as Wambaw in Craven Co.,
                         bounding E & NE on ISAAC LEGRAND; N on GEORGE
SIMONS; E on GEORGE SIMONS & vacant land; S & SE on PAUL BRUNEAU. Wit-
nesses: AUGUSTUS LAURENS, JAMES BOISSEAU. Before JOHN GENDRON, J.P.
WILLIAM HOPTON, Register. Plat of 145 a. dated 24 Apr. 1751 by JOHN HEN-
TIE.

Book L-L, p. 302   LAWRENCE SANDERS & JOSEPH JACKSON, executors
22 & 23 June 1749   of will of MALACHI GLAZE, planter, & WILLIAM
L & R   GLAZE (1 of the sons & devisees of MALACHI
                         GLAZE, planter, of Berkeley Co.) to JOHN GLAZE,
another son of MALACHI GLAZE, for ₺ 1800 currency, 410-1/4 a. 3 undivided
fourth parts of 547 a. Whereas MALACHI GLAZE owned various plantations
in SC, including 1 tract of 547 a. in St. George Parish, Berkeley Co.,
bounding NE on RICHARD SPENCER; SE on CHARLES BAKER; SW on estate of MAL-
ACHI GLAZE; NW on estate of HENRY IZARD; & whereas by will dated 3 May
1740 MALACHI GLAZE bequeathed all his real estate equally to his 5 sons,
JOHN, WILLIAM, MALACHI, LAURENCE, & JAMES, to be delivered to them as
they came of age; & authorized his executors to dispose of his real &
personal estate for the advantage of said children; & appointed SARAH,
his wife, executrix, & LAWRENCE SANDERS & JOSEPH JACKSON, executors; &
whereas SARAH died some time after; & whereas WILLIAM GLAZE is entitled
to 1/4 undivided part of said 547 a.; now the executors (thinking it for
the advantage of said children) & WILLIAM GLAZE sell 3/4 parts to JOHN
GLAZE. Witnesses: GEORGE JACKSON, JOHN ELCOCK, DANIEL DONOVAN. Before
JACOB MOTTE, J.P. WILLIAM HOPTON, Register. Plat dated 1749 by JOHN
STEPHENS.

Book L-L, p. 310   GEORGE SNOW, planter, of Charleston Neck, &
18 & 19 Aug. 1752   ANGEL (her mark) his wife (formerly ANGEL HAR-
L & R by Mortgage   DEN, widow of THOMAS HARDEN, mariner, of
                         Charleston), to RAWLINS LOWNDES, ESQ., of
Charleston, as security on bond of even date in penal sum of ₺ 2000 for
payment of ₺ 1000 currency, with interest, on 19 Aug. 1753; parts of lots
#18 & #92 in Charleston. Whereas THOMAS HARDIN owned part of lot #18 in
Charleston, bounding W 43 ft. on Union Street; S on ELIZABETH HAWKINS
(widow of EDMOND HAWKINS); E on RICE PRICE & JAMES WITHERS; N 136 ft. on
Queen Street; also a brick house & ground part of lot #92; bounding W
25 ft. on King Street; S on EDWARD SCULL; E on DANIEL BOURGETT; N on ROB-
ERT HARVEY; which BENJAMIN D'HARRIETTE & other elders of the French Protestant Church, in Charleston, leased to THOMAS HARDEN for 50 years from 1
Oct. 1742; & whereas by will dated 6 July 1742 THOMAS HARDEN bequeathed
all his real & personal estate to his wife, ANGEL, who, after his death,
married GEORGE SNOW; now they mortgage the part of lot #18 now occupied
by 1 GUNTER, & the brick house on lot #92, to RAWLINS LOWNDES. Witnesses: MICHAEL TONGE (YONGE?), WILLIAM READ. Before JAMES MICHIE, J.P.
WILLIAM HOPTON, Register.

Book L-L, p. 319   JOHN DELIESSELINE, planter, & DOROTHY his wife,
11 & 12 Apr. 1750   to ALEXANDER CHOVINE, planter, both of St.
L & R   James Santee, Craven Co., for ₺ 500 currency,
                         240 a. in St. James Santee, part of the land
bequeathed to JOHN DELIESSELINE by JAMES LEGRAND DE LOMBOY; bounding N on
Santee River; E & S on JOHN DELIESSELINE; W on JONATHAN DUBOSE. Witnesses: JOHN BARNETT, JACOB JEANERETT, WILLIAM THOMAS. Before JOHN GENDRON,
J.P. Plat given.

Book L-L, p. 324   JOHN DELIESSELINE, planter, & DOROTHY his wife,
1 & 2 May 1751   to ALEXANDER CHOVINE, planter, both of St.
L & R   James Santee, Craven Co., for ₺ 250 currency,
                          140 a. in St. James Santee, part of the land
bequeathed to JOHN DELIESSELINE by JAMES LEGRAND DELOMBOY; bounding NE on
Santee River; SW & SE on JOHN DELIESSELINE; NW on ALEXANDER CHOVINE.
Witnesses: PAUL LAPIERE, JOHN BARNETT. Before JOHN GENDRON, J.P. WIL-
LIAM HOPTON, Register. Plat dated 27 Apr. 1751 by JOHN HENTIE.

Book L-L, p. 328   ELIAS JAUDON, planter, & ELIZABETH his wife,
2 & 3 July 1739   to ISAAC CHOVIN (CHAUVIN), planter, both of
L & R   Craven Co., for ₺ 600 currency, 200 a., part
                          of 500 a. purchased by SAMUEL PRIOLEAU, gold-
smith, of Charleston, & by several deeds came to ELIAS JAUDON; the 200 a.
taken from W part of the 500 a. by a direct line from S to N on each side
Daho Lake including 25 chains front on each side said lake, as the plat
runs, & 80 chains in length, making just 200 a.; bounding W on Santee
Parish Glebe land; N on JOHN DUBOSE (formerly purchased by SAMUEL PRIO-
LEAU); E on remaining 300 a. where the dwelling house & other buildings
of ELIAS JAUDON now lie; S on vacant land. Witnesses: DANIEL JAUDON,
DAVID BALDY, RALPH BUGNION. Before JOHN GENDRON, J.P. WILLIAM HOPTON,
Register.

Book L-L, p. 334   ISAAC CHAUVIN, planter, to ALEXANDER CHOVIN
3 & 4 Apr. 1745   (CHAUVIN), planter, both of Craven Co., for
L & R   ₺ 300 currency, 200 a. on Daho Lake, in Prince
                          Frederick Parish, Craven Co., purchased by
ISAAC CHOVIN by L & R dated 2 & 3 July 1739 from ELIAS JAUDON; bounding W
on Parish Glebe land; N on JOHN DUBOSE; E on THOMAS BOONE, JR.; S on vacant land. Witnesses: ELIAS JAUDON, JAMES ROBERTS. Before PAUL TRAPIER,
J.P. WILLIAM HOPTON, Register.

Book L-L, p. 339   ROBERT HANCOCK, planter, of Colleton Co., only
14 Aug. 1750   surviving child, & devisee of will of ELIAS
Confirmation   HANCOCK, the elder, victualler, of Charleston,
                          confirms SAMUEL WAINWRIGHT'S title to half of
lot #92 in Charleston. Whereas ELIAS HANCOCK owned divers lands, tenements, etc., including part of a lot in Charleston, & by will dated 20
Nov. 1729 bequeathed to his 3rd son, when 21, ROBERT, the N half of lot
#92 in Charleston with all houses thereon; but should ROBERT die without
issue the fortune to be divided equally amongst the other surviving
children; & whereas by L & R dated 1 & 2 June 1747 between ROBERT HANCOCK
(& others) of 1st part; & SAMUEL WAINWRIGHT, butcher, of Charleston, of
2nd part; ROBERT & others, for ₺ 1000 currency, sold WAINWRIGHT the said
half of lot #92 in Charleston, bounding W 100 ft. on King Street; S
61-1/2 ft. on Tradd Street; E on part said lot; N on HESTER SIMMONS
(formerly CORNELIUS BATOON); but because ROBERT at that time had no
children but since then he & his wife, MARY, have had a son named ELIAS,
now ROBERT confirms WAINWRIGHT'S title to the property. Witnesses: SU-
SANNA BUTLER, JOHN FRYER. Before THOMAS LAMBOLL, J.P. WILLIAM HOPTON,
Register.

Book L-L, p. 344   ABRAHAM (his mark) HUSENHOOD, laborer, & MARY
10 & 11 May 1751   (her mark) his wife, to HENRY FELDER, cord-
L & R   wainer, both of Berkeley Co., for ₺ 60 curren-
                          cy, 200 a. in Orangeburgh Township, Berkeley
Co., granted JOHN HUSENHOOD, uncle of ABRAHAM; bounding NE on ULRICH
SPIES; NW on JOHN FUSTER; SW on PonPon River; SE on PETER FAURE & vacant
land; also lot #265 in Orangeburgh. MARY renounces her claim. Witness-
es: JACOB RUMPH, ALEXANDER (his mark) MAXWELL. Before MOSES THOMSON,
J.P. Entered in Auditor's Book #3, fol. 291, on 17 Mar. 1752, by JAMES
WEDDERBURN, Dep. Aud. WILLIAM HOPTON, Register.

Book L-L, p. 351   HENRY WURSTER, planter, & VERENA (her mark)
13 & 14 July 1752   his wife, to JOHN INDERABNET, both of Berkeley
L & R   Co., for ₺ 500 currency, 150 a. in Orangeburg
                          Township, Berkeley Co., bounding NE on vacant
land; NW on JOHN STRUTZENAKER & JOHN PRUDER; SW on PonPon River; SE on
ULRICK TOBLER. BERENS renounces her claim. Witnesses: HENRY FELDER,
JOHN GIESSENDANNER. Before JAMES TILLY, J.P. WILLIAM HOPTON, Register.

Book L-L, p. 358   DEBORAH FISHER, tallow chandler, to JOSEPH
20 & 21 Jan. 1752   MOODY, merchant, both of Charleston, as secu-
L & R by Mortgage   rity on 2 bonds dated 5 Sept. 1744 & 19 June
                          1748, in penal sum of Ł 1700 currency (recit-
ing that whereas MOODY at DEBORAH'S request on 5 Sept. 1744 gave bond
with DEBORAH to SUSANNAH LANSAC in penal sum of Ł 700 for payment of
Ł 350 currency, with interest, on 5 Sept. 1745, & another on 19 June 1748
to PETER HEARN in penal sum of Ł 1000 for payment of Ł 500, with interest,
on 19 June 1749) on condition that DEBORAH pay the said bonds; now DEB-
ORAH conveys to MOODY, part of lot #104 in Charleston, bounding N 19 ft.
2 in. on Broad Street; S on lot of French trustees; E 208 ft. on PAUL
SMYSER; W on PETER BOCQUETT; free except for mortgage to DANIEL BOURGETT
for Ł 900 currency. Witnesses: PAUL SMYSER, JAMES FISHER. Before WIL-
LIAM PINCKNEY, J.P. WILLIAM HOPTON, Register.

Book L-L, p. 365   WILLIAM PALMER & EVANS PALMER, to THOMAS RIG-
27 May 1752   DON SMITH, in penal sum of Ł 1000 sterling
Bond   British. Whereas COL. JOHN PALMER bequeathed
                          to his son RICHARD, a plantation in 4 plats
called Green Point, on Combee River; but in case RICHARD should die then
his sons EDMOND & EVANS to inherit; & whereas RICHARD died & WILLIAM &
EVANS, (only male survivors of JOHN PALMER'S sons) inherited, & have
agreed to sell the plantation to SMITH for Ł 600; now they give bond that
they will, on 11 July 1753, give SMITH the necessary deeds to the land.
Witness: NATHAN SMITH. Before JAMES BULLOCK, J.P. WILLIAM HOPTON, Register.

DEEDS BOOK "M-M"
1752 to 1753

Book M-M, p. 1   JOHN CLELAND & wife   1st part
30 June 1737   ELISHA SCREVEN & others,   2nd part
Conveyance of Georgetown GEORGE PAWLEY & others   3rd part

                          JOHN CLELAND, merchant, of Charleston, & MARY
                          his wife, daughter & devisee of JOHN PERRY,
                          merchant, formerly of Island of Antigua, now
                          of Parish of St. James Westminster, Co. of
                          Middlesex, of 1st part.

                          ELISHA SCREVEN, gentleman, of Prince George
                          Parish, Winyaw, Craven Co., SC, WILLIAM SCRE-
                          VEN, gentleman, of James Island; ROBERT SCRE-
                          VEN, gentleman, of Berkeley Co., ROBERT WRIGHT,
                          C.J.; ALEXANDER SKENE, ESQ.; NICHOLAS TROTT,
                          ESQ., & SARAH his wife; JAMES ABERCROMBY, ROB-
                          ERT JOHNSTON, THOMAS GADSDEN, WILLIAM WATIES,
                          OTHNIEL BEALE, NATHANIEL BROUGHTON, ANDREW
                          BROUGHTON, WILLIAM SWINTON, ELIAS FOISSIN, JR.,
                          JOHN OULDFIELD, ALEXANDER NISBETT, JOHN WALLIS,
                          MEREDITH HUGHES, DANIEL LAROCHE, THOMAS LA-
                          ROCHE, ISAAC CHARDON, JOHN BERESFORD, RICHARD
                          ALLEIN, BENJAMIN WHITAKER, CHARLES PINCKNEY,
                          ESQRS.; MARY LAROCHE, widow; WILLIAM ALSTON,
                          JOHN ALLSTON, ANTHONY ATKINSON; JOHN ARTHUR,
                          JAMES ATKINS, JOHN ABBOTT, JOSEPH ALLEN, WIL-
                          LIAM ANDERSON, JOHN ATCHISON, STEPHEN BEAU-
                          CHAMP, THOMAS BOLEM, ABRAHAM BOND, THOMAS
                          BLYTH, DANIEL BOURGETT, WILLIAM BORLEN, THOMAS
                          BLUNDELL, THOMAS BURTON, JAMES BAXTER, DANIEL
                          CRAWFORD, CHRISTOPHER CANE, WILLIAM COLT,
                          THOMAS CHARNOCK, WILLIAM CRIPPS, JOHN COMMAN-
                          DER, JOSEPH COMMANDER, JOHN COACHMAN, JONATHAN
                          COLKIN, DANIEL DWIGHT, ROBERT ELLIS, ARTHUR
                          FORSTER, JOSEPH GOUDE, THOMAS HENNING, THOMAS
                          HURST, JOHN HARD, DENNIS, HAUKINS, EDMUND HAW-
                          KINS, WILLIAM HINCKLEY, STEPHEN HEARTLEY,
                          CHARLES HOPE, JOHN JORDAN, SAMUEL JENNINGS,

JOHN LANE, JOHN LAWRANCE, ISAAC LEGRAND DON-
NERVILLE, THOMAS LANDEN, JOHN MCKIEVER, GEORGE
PAWLEY, PIERCE PAWLEY, JOSHUA PEART, ALEXANDER
ROBERTSON, WILLIAM ROMSEY, JOHN RICHARDS, PE-
TER & JAMES CLEOPAS SIMONDS, GEORGE SMITH, JO-
SIAH SMITH, ROBERT STEWART, MARY SMITH, JAMES
STEWART, JOHN SANDIFORD, CHRISTOPHER SEAMOUR,
JOHN SULLENS, JOHN, THOMPSON, JR., WILLIAM
THOMAS, HENRY TOOMER, WILLIAM TILLEY, ANTHONY
WHITE, JOHN WHITE, WILLIAM WALLIS, gentlemen,
of 2nd part.

GEORGE PAWLEY, WILLIAM SWINTON & DANIEL LA-
ROCHE, of Craven Co., of 3rd. part.

Whereas by L & R dated 14 & 15 Jan. 1734, ELI-
SHA SCREVEN, gentleman, & HANNAH his wife, of Prince George WINYAW, Craven Co., conveyed to parties of 3rd part in trust, 74-1/2 a. at Sampit,
Prince George Winyaw Parish, bounding SW on the Town River; other sides
on ELISHA SCREVENS; 174-1/2 a. for a town to be called George Town, to be
laid out in lots according to plan by SCREVEN, PAWLEY, SWINTON, & LA-
ROCHE to sell the lots to persons desireing to become inhabitants of said
town; the 100 a. residue to be a common for the town; & whereas PAWLEY,
SWINTON, & LEGARE conveyed lots as follows: To WILLIAM SCREVEN (3), 28,
135, 136; ROBERT SCREVEN (1) 27; ROBERT WRIGHT, C.J. (2) 79 & 80; ALEXAN-
DER SKENE (1) 104; NICHOLAS TROTT & SARAH his wife (4) 178, 179, 190,
215; JAMES ABERCROMBY (1) 206; ROBERT JOHNSTON (1) 221; THOMAS GADSDEN
(1) 22; WILLIAM WATIES (9) 41, 42, 69, 1 (?), 139, 141, 142, 161, 164;
OTHNIEL BEALE (4) 13, 106, 107, 83; NATHANIEL BROUGHTON (1) 162; ANDREW
BROUGHTON (1) 163; WILLIAM SWINTON (7) 18, 57, 177, 277, 201, 176, 200;
ELIAS FOISSIN, JR. (1) 148; JOHN OULDFIELD (1) 147; ALEXANDER NISBETT (1)
210; JOHN WALLIS (2) 25, 150; MEREDITH HUGHES (8) 98, 218, 219, 73, 169,
170 (?), 132, 154; WILLIAM ROMSEY & CO., (3) 35, 36, 26; DANIEL LAROCHE &
THOMAS LAROCHE in Co. (5) 151, 152, 204, 205, 59; DANIEL LAROCHE, alone
(1) 145; THOMAS LAROCHE, alone (1) 146; ISAAC CHARDON, alone (2) 89, 90;
JOHN BERESFORD (3) 43, 44, 70; RICHARD ALLEIN (1) D; BENJAMIN WHITAKER
(1) C; CHARLES PINCKNEY (1) B; MARY LAROCHE (1) 38; WILLIAM ALLSTON (5)
165, 131, 189, 213, 47; JOHN _____ (1) 94; ANTHONY ATKINSON (2) 129, 130;
JOHN ARTHUR (1) 58; JAMES ATKINS (2) 197, 198; JOHN ABBOTT (3) 82, 85,
88; JOSEPH ALLEIN (1) 114; WILLIAM ANDERSON (1) 63; JOHN ATCHISON (2)
187, 188; STEPHEN BEAUCHAMP (2) 195, 209; THOMAS BOLEM (4) 109, 155, 156,
62; ABRAHAM BOND (2) 157, 158; THOMAS BLYTH (1) 116; DANIEL BOURGETT (3)
111,112, 91; WILLIAM BORLEN (1) 180; THOMAS BLUNDELL (1) 21; THOMAS BUR-
TON (1) 39; JAMES BAXTER (1) 78; DANIEL CRAWFORD (3) 23, 101, 102; CHRIS-
TOPHER CANE (2) 54, 55; WILLIAM COLT (2) 211, 212; THOMAS CHARNOCK (1)
110; WILLIAM CRIPPS (2) 67, 140; JOHN COMMANDER (1) 105; JOSEPH COMMANDER
(1) 81; JOHN COACHMAN (1) 216; JOSEPH COLKIN (1) 12; _____ EL DWIGHT (1)
182; ROBERT ELLIS (2) 75, 76; ARTHUR FORSTER (3) 15, 16, 56; JOSEPH GOUDE
(1) 181; THOMAS HENNING (1) 30; THOMAS HURST (3) 92, 99, 100; JOHN HERD
(1) 108; DENNIS HAUKINS (1) 143; EDMUND HAWKINS (2) 40, 77; WILLIAM HIN-
CKLEY (1) 160; STEPHEN HEARTLEY (1) 171; CHARLES HOPE (1) 172; JOHN JOR-
DAN (3) 115, 168, 192; SAMUEL JENNINGS (1) 207; JOHN LANE (3) 9, 10, 53;
JOHN LAWRENCE (1) 60; ISAAC LEGRAND DONNERVILLE (3) 45, 46, 71, also A;
THOMAS LANDEN (2) 127, 61; JOHN MCKIEVER (1) 86; GEORGE PAWLEY (7) 31,
32, 96, 120, 119, 144, 95; PIERCE PAWLEY (4) 64, 184, 208, 103; JOSHUA
PEART (2) 137, 138; ALEXANDER ROBERTSON (4) 125, 126, 173, 174; DANIEL
LAROCHE & Co. (1) 37; WILLIAM ROMSEY, alone (1) 193; JOHN RICHARDS (2)
74, 97; PETER & JAMES CLEOPAS SIMONDS (3) 217, 14, 68; GEORGE SMITH (2)
223, 224; JOSIAH SMITH (1) 222; ROBERT STEWART (1) 220 & half #4; MARY
SMITH (1) 113; JAMES STEWART (1) 128; JOHN SANDIFORD (2) 133, 134; CHRIS-
TOPHER SEAMOUR (1) 118; JOHN SULLENS (1) 29; JOHN THOMPSON, JR. (1) 175;
WILLIAM THOMAS (1) 87; HENRY TOOMER (1) 72; WILLIAM TILLEY (1) 153; AN-
THONY WHITE (13) 1, 2, 5, 6, 7, 8, 49, 50, 51, 52, 17, 20, 84, & half of
3; JOHN WHITE (2) 19, 93; WILLIAM WALLIS (1) 24; reserving for ELISHA
SCRIVEN (7) 33, 34, 65, 66, 185, 186, 199 free from all provisoes & con-
ditions except for building of brick chimneys; & whereas some doubts &
disputes have arisen in regard to validity of ELISHA SCREVENS'S title to
the land laid out for the town & his conveyance to PAWLEY, SWINTON & LA-
ROCHE; now to avoid such doubts & to confirm the rights of all parties,
for Ł 18 SC money agreed to be paid by each & every of the said parties

to JOHN CLELAND for each of said town lots; JOHN CLELAND & MARY his wife
have confirmed to ELISHA SCREVEN & other parties of 2nd part the lots
claimed by each of them; & whereas all parties have agreed that it should
be lawful for JOHN CLELAND to enlarge the town, enlarging the common in
proportion, which he has done according to present plan, now it is agreed
that the 88 lots added to the old plan of the town, vizt: 230, 231, 232,
233, 234, 235, 236, 238, 239, 240, 241, 242, 243, 244, 245, 246, 247,
248, 249, 250, 251, 252, 253, 524, 255, 256, 257, 258, 260, 261, 262,
263, 264, 265, 266, 267, 268, 269, 270, 271, 272, 273, 274, 275, 276,
277, 278, 279, 280, 281, 282, 283, 284, 285, 286, 287, 288, 289, 290,
291, 292, 293, 294, 295, 296, 297, 298, 299, 300, 301, 302, 303, 304,
305, 306, 307, 308, 309, 310, 311, 312, 313, 314, 315, 316, & 317, are
vested in JOHN CLELAND to be disposed of for the most money he can rea-
sonably get; also that JOHN CLELAND shall have right of common for said
88 lots & all other lots in the new common containing 130 a.; which common has been set apart as a common appurtenant to said town; CLELAND
agrees to cause his wife MARY to renounce her right of inheritance before
ROBERT WRIGHT, C.J.; lots 227, 226, 228, 225, 149, 150, & 229 to be set
apart & vested in PAWLEY, SWINTON, & LAROCHE, trustees, for public use as
follows: lot 227, containing 2 a., set apart for a church & churchyard
for worship according to Church of England, the rector to be nominated
only by such inhabitants as belong to the Church of England; lot 226, 1
a., set apart for a Presbyterian Meeting House for divine worship according to Doctrine & Discipline of Church of Scotland, or what is now used
amongst English Presbyterians, as such English or Scottish Presbyterian
inhabitants agree, also a burial place; lot #228, 1 a., for a Meeting
house for the Antipedo Baptists & a burial place; lot #225, 1 a., for a
grammar school wherein to teach grammar & other literature, the master to
be licensed by the Bishop of London & approved by the majority of the inhabitants, said Bishop of London, or his Commissary in SC; lots 149 & 150,
total 1 a., for a tholsel or townhouse, courthouse & prison when the town
is incorporated by charter from his majesty; the market place for the
"uttering & vending" of wholesome provisions to continue in the Broad
Street as represented in plan; lot 229 at head of Queen Street, 1 a., for
a house of correction; all the streets, passages, lanes, alleys, market
place, & all public streets, lots & places set apart for public use to
remain to same public uses; but lot #48 to remain to JOHN CLELAND & his
heirs; lots 202 & 203 to be for a parsonage & glebe for the rector of the
town & whereas in said L & R dated 15 Jan. 1734 it was agreed that all
lots & vacant land lying between Front Street, (or Bay Street) & low water mark should remain to ELISHA SCREVEN & that no building or storehouses should be built thereon to obstruct the prospect of said front
lots or buildings on the Bay, except that owners of front lots might
build bridges or wharves fronting their lots for landing goods & merchandise, the owners to have the profits; now all parties agree that all the
lots & lands lying between Front or Bay Street, & low water mark shall be
vested in ELISHA SCREVEN in trust for the respective owners; that is, in
front of lots 217 & 13 for PETER SIMONDS & JAMES CLEOPAS SIMONDS; in
front of 218 & 219 for MEREDITH HUGHES; in front of 220 for ROBERT STE-
WART; in front of 221 for ROBERT JOHNSTON (eldest son of late Gov. ROBERT
JOHNSTON); 222 for JOSIAH SMITH; 223 & 224 for GEORGE SMITH; 9 & 10 for
JOHN LANE; 12 for JONATHAN COLKIN; 13 for OTHNIEL BEALE; 15 & 16 for AR-
THUR FORSTER; 17 & 2 for ANTHONY WHITE; 18 for WILLIAM SWINTON; 19 for
JOHN WHITE; 21 for THOMAS BLUNDELL; 22 for THOMAS GADSDEN; 23 for DANIEL
CRAWFORD; 25 for JOHN WALLIS; 37 for DANIEL LAROCHE & Co.; 27 for ROBERT
SCREVEN; 28 for WILLIAM SCREVEN; 29 for JOHN SULLENS; 30 for THOMAS HEN-
NING; 31 & 32 for GEORGE PAWLEY; 33 & 34 for ELISHA SCREVEN; 35, 36, & 26
for WILLIAM ROMSEY & Co.; 38 for MARY LAROCHE; 39 for THOMAS BURTON; 40
for EDMUND HAWKINS; 41 & 42 for WILLIAM WATIES; 24 for WILLIAM WALLIS; no
buildings to be erected except storehouses whose roofs shall not exceed
15 ft. from low water mark; all such low water lots being vested in ELI-
SHA SCREVEN in trust for the several owners, the lots having the same
breadth & number of feet as their respective lots on Front or Bay Street;
MARY CLELAND to renounce her right to said low water lots; further agreed
that lots 11, 121, 122, 123, 124, 183, 166, 167, 191, 174, 196, & 214 to
be vested in JOHN CLELAND free from all provisoes & conditions; & for the
better preservation of the health of the inhabitants & "for the conveniency of the air" no private buildings to be erected at the extremities
of the streets or on the vacancies or openings at SW end of streets towards the river or on openings at NW end of streets towards the common,

or openings on NE & SE ends of streets, or at ends of any street; except
such public buildings as already agreed upon; & whereas since 15 Jan.
1734, 5 other lots have, by the consent of all parties, been added at SE
end of Front or Bay Street, lettered A, B, C, D, & E to be sold with low
water lots as follows: E to JOHN CLELAND; D to RICHARD ALLEIN; C to BEN-
JAMIN WHITAKER; B to CHARLES PINCKNEY; A to ISAAC LEGRAND DONNERVILLE;
such lots to be exempted from provisoes of building & improving same, but
the low water lots to be subject to building restrictions; lots of ALLEIN,
WHITAKER & PINCKNEY (D, C, & B) for Ł 15 SC money for each lot payable to
CLELAND; E & A being exempted; further agreed that all lots not built on
or improved upon within 3 years, according to dimensions given, & with
brick chimneys, shall become forfeited to CLELAND; each of parties of 2nd
part to pay CLELAND Ł 18 SC money at his house in Charleston, or at house
of DANIEL LAROCHE in Georgetown within 12 months; those not paying to be
excluded from this agreement; the flats or low water lots & the lots for
public buildings being exempted; & whereas lots 1, 2, 3, 4, 5, 6, 7, & 8
were front lots but are now become back lots by adding other lots in
front, it is agreed that lots 1 & 2 shall be deemed 1 lot; 3 & 4 1 lot; 5
& 6 1 lot; 7 & 8 1 lot; total 4 lots; Ł 18 to be paid for each of the 4;
& whereas pending the present agreement between said parties, JOHN CLE-
LAND has requested liberty to alter the old common on NE side of the town
in consideration of his appropriating for a common 130 a. on NW part of
the town; now CLELAND turns over to the trustees 130 a. at Sampit bounding SE on said town; W on JOHN FORBES; other sides of JOHN CLELAND; to
prevent the common from being surcharged, agreed that freeholders only
shall have a right of common & that only for 1 horse & 1 cow & no more
for each lot, & not for oxen, sheep, goats or swine; lots from #8 exclusive to #48 inclusive (even though but 1/4 a.) shall be deemed as a whole
lot to entitle them to commonage; agreed that Ł 3 out of the Ł 18 paid to
be used by trustees to pay costs of deeds & other expenses. Witnesses to
JOHN CLELAND'S signature: RICHARD ALLEN, JAMES WEDDERBURNE, CHARLES HOPE,
GEORGE DICK. On 30 June 1737 CLELAND appoints DANIEL LAROCHE his attor-
ney to receive the payments for lots & give receipt. Witnesses: ELIAS
FOISSIN, JR., JAMES WEDDERBURN. Also on 11 June 1739 as witnessed by
WILLIAM WHITESIDE, JAMES CRADDOCK, ARCHIBALD BAIRD, ALEXANDER MCDOUAL.
Other witnesses to various signatures of owners of lots: JOHN DEXTER,
ELIZABETH HUST, PAUL TRAPIER, MARY THOMAS, JOSEPH ROUS, JOHN OULDFIELD,
JR., JOHN BLAKE, WILLIAM CROOK, EDWARD DAVIS, GEORGE PAWLEY, WILLIAM
POOLE, JOSEPH COMMANDER, JOHN COMMANDER, THOMAS JEWNING, JAMES FOORD,
ANTHONY ATKINSON, ANTHONY WHITE, JOHN SEAMAN, WILLIAM GREEN. WILLIAM
HOPTON, Public Register.

Book M-M, p. 29   RICHARD GODFREY, planter, & REBECCA his wife,
18 & 19 Sept. 1752   of St. Andrews Parish, Berkeley Co., to JOHN
L & R   LINING, ESQ., of Charleston, for Ł 2448 cur-
                         rency, 200 a. in St. Andrews Parish, part of
lot #3 originally containing 224 a., bounding N on ANDREW DEVEAUX (formerly MR. LESADE) & BENJAMIN GODFREY; S on COL. GEORGE LUCAS; E on MRS.
QUINCY (formerly MRS. ELIZABETH HILL) & on BENJAMIN GODFREY; W on JOHN
RIVERS & on said 106 a.; also 106 a. in St. Andrews, part of lot #4 on
the plan, bounding E on the 24 a. sold to BENJAMIN GODFREY by JOHN GOD-
FREY & lot #3; N on NATHANIEL BROWN; W on lot #6 now belonging to JOHN
GODFREY; S on JOHN RIVERS; said tracts of 200 & 106 a. being all that remain of lots 3 & 4 in possession of RICHARD GODFREY, party hereto. Whereas the Lords Proprs. on 11 May 1699 granted CAPT. JOHN GODFREY 974 a. in
Berkeley Co., according to plat certified by JOSEPH MARTIN, Sur. Gen. on
13 Apr. 1698; & whereas JOHN GODFREY owned several other tracts adjoining
the 974 a., according to a general plat of all; & by will directed that
all the residue of his real & personal estate (should his wife marry or
die) not before given should be equally divided to his surviving children;
but his will not having been executed or perfected, said CAPT. JOHN GOD-
FREY died intestate as to his real estate & his lands descended to his
eldest son, JOHN 2nd, as heir-at-law; & whereas son JOHN 2nd to carry out
his father's intentions, on 9 Nov. 1717 caused the several tracts of land
to be resurveyed & divided into 7 equal shares to be divided amongst his
brothers & sisters, as by general plat certified by CHAMPERNOON ELLIOTT,
Dep. Sur. on 9 Nov. last; & whereas lot #3 fell to said JOHN 2nd eldest
son; & whereas son JOHN GODFREY 2nd, also owned considerable real estate
& died intestate & his lands descended to his eldest son, JOHN GODFREY
3rd as heir at law; & whereas said JOHN GODFREY 3rd (grandson of CAPT.

JOHN) having sold 24 a. out of lot #3 to BENJAMIN GODFREY, butcher, &
died intestate, so that the remainder of lot #3 (200 a.) descended to
RICHARD GODFREY, party hereto, as eldest brother's son & heir to last
mentioned JOHN GODFREY, & whereas lot #4 by allotment fell to JANE, wife
of JAMES STANYARNE (sister of JOHN GODFREY, 2nd); & whereas by Act of
General Assembly to confirm RICHARD'S title to said 200 a., lately belonging JAMES STANYARNE, deceased (reciting that whereas JAMES STANYARNE
on 10 Mar. 1712, for Ł 50 currency, paid by RICHARD GODFREY, assigned to
RICHARD the 200 a., bounding E & S on said RICHARD GODFREY; W on CAPT.
WILLIAM BULL & SARAH GODFREY; N on JOHN BROWN; which 200 a. by will of
JOHN GODFREY, gentleman, dated 20 June 1705 bequeathed to his daughter
JANE, widow of said JAMES STANYARNE, who gave bond to RICHARD GODFREY to
deliver the 200 a. to RICHARD, which conveyance was not executed by STAN-
YARNE because STANYARNE died before division of the lands; & whereas
JANE, before a committee, gave her consent to the sale of the 200 a. when
STANYARNE assigned the tract to RICHARD & was still willing to assign the
land to RICHARD) it was enacted on 9 June 1717 by JOHN, Loard Carteret,
Palatine, & the Lords Proprs. that the title to the 200 a. should be vested in RICHARD, free from JANE'S claim of dower; & whereas RICHARD GODFREY
died intestate & lot #4 & his other real estate descended to his eldest
son & heir, RICHARD, party hereto; now he sells the 200 a. & a tract of
106 a. to JOHN LINING. Witnesses: TIMOTHY MORGRIDGE, JOHN TROUP. Before
JAMES MICHIE, J.P. WILLIAM HOPTON, Register. Plat given.

Book M-M, p. 38   RAWLINS LOWNDES, Provost Marshal, to THOMAS
25 Apr. 1751   WARING, storekeeper, of Dorchester, for Ł 325
Sale   currency, lot #15 in town of Dorchester, con-
                         taining half an a. Whereas WILLIAM WEBB, mer-
chant, of Charleston, surviving copartner of HOUSTON & WEBB, owned lot
#15 in Dorchester, bounding E on the High Street; S on DR. WILLIAM WHITE;
W on undivided lands; N on MRS. BOONE; with the buildings thereon; &
whereas WEBB gave bond dated 12 Sept. 1748 to MESSRS. THOMAS ROGERS, &
ELY DYSON, merchants, of London, in penal sum of Ł 3000 British for payment of Ł 1474:2:11 British or value, on 25 Dec. 1748, which bond WEBB
did pay & ROGERS & DYSON obtained a judgment against him for amount of
bond & Ł 28:7:3-1/2 SC money costs; & whereas a writ of fieri facias was
issued by BENJAMIN WHITAKER, C.J., on 3 Jan. 1748 directing RAWLINS LOWN-
DES, P.M., to levy the 2 sums on the good & chattels, lands, etc., of
WILLIAM WEBB; whereby LOWNDES seized lot #15 in town of Dorchester; now
he sells the lot at public auction to WARING as highest bidder. Witnesses: CHARLES PINCKNEY, JR., GOERGE DAY. Before WILLIAM PINCKNEY, J.P.
WILLIAM HOPTON, Register.

Book M-M, p. 42   DAVID BROWN, shipwright, to JAMES WRIGHT, gen-
31 Aug. & 1 Sept. 1752   tleman, both of Charleston, as security on
L & R by Mortgage   bond dated Sept. 1, 1749 in penal sum of
                            Ł 1002 for payment of Ł 501 currency, with in-
terest, on 1 Sept. then next; part of Colleton Square in Charleston marked D in the general plan, bounding S on CHARLES PINCKNEY'S lot C; W 50 ft.
on GEORGE HUNTERS lot D; N on lot #51 belonging to heirs of GEORGE LEA; E
on Cooper River. Witnesses: DANIEL DWIGHT, JOHN MENZIES. Before JAMES
MICHIE, J.P. WILLIAM HOPTON, Register.

Book M-M, p. 47   NATHANIEL BROUGHTON, JR., gentleman, & MARY
12 & 13 Aug. 1752   his wife, to ALEXANDER BROUGHTON, gentleman;
L & R   both of St. John's Parish, Berkeley Co., for
                            Ł 1500 currency, 1107 a. known as Kiblesworth.
Whereas Lt. Gov. THOMAS BROUGHTON owned 1107 a. called Keblesworth, in
St. Johns Parish, Berkeley Co., which by will dated 22 July 1725 he bequeathed to his grandson, THOMAS BROUGHTON, son of CAPT. NATHANIEL BROUGH-
TON, "from & after the time that testators son, ANDREW BROUGHTON, should
enter upon a plantation called Seaton", given ANDREW by said will; but in
case grandson THOMAS should die before that time, the plantation should
go to grandson NATHANIEL BROUGHTON; & whereas THOMAS lived until after
ANDREW entered upon Seaton, & then THOMAS took possession of Kiblesworth
& sometime afterwards died intestate, leaving NATHANIEL, party hereto,
his next brother & heir-at-law; now NATHANIEL sells to ALEXANDER BROUGH-
TON. Witnesses: NATHANIEL BROUGHTON, ESQ., THOMAS DWIGHT, JOHN BRYEN.
Before FRANCIS LEJAU, J.P. WILLIAM HOPTON, Register. Play by ISAAC POR-
CHER, Dep. Sur. certified 9 June 1752, of 1107 a., part of the MULBERY'S

land, on W branch Cooper River, bounding N on MRS. GIBBS; E on MRS. BROUGHTON.

Book M-M, p. 52
26 Aug. 1751
Sale

BRAND PENDARVIS, planter, & URSULA (her mark) his wife, to LUKE PATRICK, planter, both of Colleton Co., for Ł 100 currency, 400 a. in Colleton Co., bounding E on PonPon River; other sides on vacant land; according to plat & grant dated 4 June 1735 to WILLIAM COOPER; who with his wife, SARAH, on 26 Feb. 1744 conveyed the 400 a. to BRAND PENDARVIS. See Bk. C.C. p. 142. Witness: JAMES HOME, Register. Witnesses: JOHN PENDARVIS, ABRAHAM BOYD, JOHN (his mark) JENNINGS, WILLIAM PENDARVIS. Before CHRISTIAN MINNICK, J.P. WILLIAM HOPTON, Register.

Book M-M, p. 54
23 July 1752
Feoffment

ABRAHAM WALCUTT, cordwainer, to DAVID CRAWFORD, storekeeper, both of Colleton Co., for Ł 350 currency, 2 tracts, total 250 a., in Colleton Co., bounding N on Tobedoo Creek; S & W on CAPT. WILLIAM EDIN; E on SAMUEL DAVISON (formerly JAMES BATT). Whereas the Lords Proprs. on 2 Jan. 1697 granted ALEXANDER CLARKE 50 a. in Colleton Co., which CLARKE sold to JOSEPH TOWNSEND; & whereas the Lords Proprs. on 12 Jan. 1705 granted JOSEPH TOWNSEND 200 adjoining a., bounding N on Tobedo Creek; S & W on CAPT. WILLIAM EDINS; E on land laid out; & whereas the 2 tracts of 250 a. at the death of TOWNSEND descend to his only daughter & heir, ELIZABETH, afterwards known as ELIZABETH WALCUTT; at whose death her oldest son & heir, ABRAHAM WALCUTT inherited; now he sells to CRAWFORD. Witnesses: NATHANIEL DEAN, JOHN (his mark) GARROT, SAMUEL DAVISON. Delivery by turf & twig. Before JAMES STOBO, J.P. WILLIAM HOPTON, Register.

Book M-M, p. 57
17 & 18 Aug. 1752
L & R

BENJAMIN DE ST. JULIEN, gentleman, to WILLIAM MOULTRIE, ESQ., both of St. Johns Parish, Berkeley Co., for Ł 3000 currency, 1020 a. called Northampton Plantation, part of 3 tracts in St. John's Parish, lately belonging to JAMES DE ST. JULIEN; bounding S on the Indian fields belonging to BENJAMIN DE ST. JULIEN; N on Clowter's Plantation (formerly RENE RAVENEL, JR.); E on Pooshee Plantation belonging to RENE RAVENEL; W on Brunswick Plantation belonging to heirs of JOSEPH DE ST. JULIEN; which plantation, called Northampton, was bequeathed by will of JAMES DE ST. JULIEN to his nephew JAMES DE ST. JULIEN, JR: & who bequeathed to PETER & BENJAMIN DE ST. JULIEN; PETER dying intestate, BENJAMIN inherited. Witnesses: HENRY RAVENEL, DANIEL RAVENEL, JR., JAMES RAVENEL. Before JACOB MOTTE, J.P. WILLIAM HOPTON, Register.

Book M-M, p. 61
18 & 19 Sept. 1751
L & R

WILLIAM BRAGGINS, tailor, to WILLIAM BUCHANAN, planter, of Granville Co., for Ł 1000 SC money, 550 a. in 2 tracts; 400 a. bounding N on Broad Road leading from Combee to Ashepoo; W on marsh; S on WILLIAM FULLER; 150 a. bounding S on swamp & marsh; W on marsh; NE on the 400 a. Whereas JOHN, Lord Granville, & the Lords Proprs. on 15 Sept. 1705, by grant signed by Gov. NATHANIEL JOHNSON, gave WILLIAM FULLER 150 a. in Colleton Co., on 1 Feb. 1706 gave him another tract of 500 a., bounding N on vacant land; E on a swamp; W on a swamp & marsh of Combee River; which 2 tracts WILLIAM FULLER & his wife, ELIZABETH on 2 Oct. 1707 sold to JOHN JACKSON; upon whose death his widow, GRACE JACKSON, was appointed administratrix by Lt. Gov. ROBERT DANIEL on 28 Feb. 1717; & whereas GRACE JACKSON bequeathed the 650 a. to her grandson, WILLIAM BRAGGINS, who sold 100 a. to ROBERT HILL, now he sells the remaining 550 a. to BUCHANAN. Witnesses: CATHERINE WELSHUYSEN, DANIEL WELSHUYSEN, JOHN VAN MARJENHOFF. Before ROBERT AUSTIN, J.P. WILLIAM HOPTON, Register.

Book M-M, p. 66
2 Nov. 1752
Sale

JAMES (his mark) GORDON, of Amelia Township, Berkeley Co., to MICHAEL YONGE (TONGE ?) of Charleston, for Ł 25 currency, 100 a. in Amelia Township, on a branch of Ox Swamp originally granted by Gov. JAMES GLEN to said JAMES GORDON; bounding SW on THOMAS BARKER; NW on vacant land & on WILLIAM CAMPBELL; NE & SE on vacant land. Witnesses: HUGH ANDERSON, WILLIAM READ. Before JAMES MICHIE, J.P. WILLIAM HOPTON, Register.

Book M-M, p. 69   WILLIAM HOPTON, merchant, of Charleston, to
24 & 25 Sept. 1751   DANIEL HUNT, gentleman, of St. Philip's Parish
L & R in Trust   in trust, half of lot #30 in W part of Charles-
                       ton, bounding S on 53 ft. on Broad Street; E
187 ft. on part same lot formerly belonging to ISAAC MAZYCK, then occupied by PAUL MAZYCK; & now belonging to his heirs; W on vacant land intended for a market & now called New Market; & on _____; N? on _____ HUNT
to let the premises to best tenants & highest rents, pay taxes & repairs,
etc., paying the profits to SARAH HOPTON during her lifetime, the money
to be used by SARAH for the support of herself & her children; SARAH to
mortgage, sell or dispose of the property as she sees fit. Whereas WIL-
LIAM HOPTON on 3 Apr. 1744 married SARAH, widow of GILSON CLAPP, merchant,
of Charleston & received with his wife sundry household goods & plate of
considerable value, & more than ₤ 3500 SC money left her by will of GIL-
SON CLAPP; & whereas JOHN ROYER & ANNE his wife, by L & R dated 14 & 15
Apr. 1747, sold WILLIAM HOPTON half of lot #30 in W part of Charleston;
whereas WILLIAM HOPTON & SARAH now have 1 son, JOHN & 2 daughters, MARY
CHRISTIANA & ALICIA; & whereas WILLIAM HOPTON has never made any settlement on SARAH, as recompense for the portion he received from her, for
the support of her & her children should she survive him; now he conveys
the half lot to DANIEL HUNT in trust for SARAH; SARAH to have full control of the property. Witnesses: MARY CROW, JOSEPH HOOLE. Before JOHN
CLELAND, J.P. WILLIAM HOPTON, Register.

Book M-M, p. 76   DAVID TOOMER, planter, of Stono, Colleton Co.,
26 & 27 June 1752   son of HENRY TOOMER, to JOSEPH STANYARNE,
L & R   planter, of Johns Island, for ₤ 1400 currency,
                       400 a. in Colleton Co., bounding at time of
original grant, E on MCCALET TOOMER; N on a cypress swamp at head of
Stono River; W on JOHN WILLIAMSON, ESQ.; S on vacant land, as by plat
certified by THOMAS BROUGHTON, Sur. Gen. Whereas Gov. ROBERT GIBBES &
the Lords Proprs. on 13 Jan. 1710 granted HENRY TOOMER, father of DAVID,
400 a. in Colleton Co., which by will dated 17 Dec. 1737 he devised to
his son DAVID; now he sells to STANYARNE. Witnesses: ROBERT WILLIAMS,
JR., DOUGAL CAMPBELL. Before JACOB MOTTE, J.P. WILLIAM HOPTON, Register.

Book M-M, p. 80   MARY ALBERGOTTI, spinster, of Beaufort, to
21 & 22 Aug. 1752   JOHN DELAGAYE, storekeeper, of Beaufort, for
L & R   ₤ 100 currency, the back part of lot #305 in
                       Beaufort, formerly belonging to ROWLAND SER-
JEANT & inherited by his only child, ELIZABETH, who married HILLERSDON
WIGG. They sold the lot to JOHN DELAGAYE; who with his wife, CATHERINE,
conveyed to ULYSSES ANTHONY ALBERGOTTI; who with PRUDENCE, his wife, conveyed the lot to their daughter, MARY, party hereto. The said part of
lot 305 measuring northerly 72-1/2 ft. from N end of E line of lots #300
& #301; from thence W 102 ft. & having 3 unequal sides; bounding N on
lots 303 & 304; E on part of lot 305; S on lot 301 & on small part of 302.
Witnesses: FRANCIS STUART, WILLIAM GOUGH. Before WILLIAM HARVEY, J.P. of
G. Co. WILLIAM HOPTON, Register.

Book M-M, p. 84   Whereas a marriage is intended between ANDREW
30 Nov. 1752   AGGNEW & MARY ALBERGOTTI & whereas MARY ALBER-
Release in Trust   GOTTI owns lot #305 in Beaufort, except that
                       part she sold by L & R on 21 & 21 Aug. 1752 to
JOHN DELAGAYE, storekeeper, of Beaufort, & also owns several slaves,
household goods & kitchen furniture; now to secure said possessions to
MARY, it is agreed to convey said possessions to JOHN DELAGAYE in trust
for MARY; ANDREW & MARY to live on the lot & have the use of slaves &
goods, etc. Witnesses: WILLIAM GOUGH, ANTHONY ALBERGOTTI. Before WIL-
LIAM HARVEY, J.C. of G. Co. WILLIAM HOPTON, Register.

Book M-M, p. 88   GEORGE MONTGOMERY, & JANET his wife, to ALEX-
16 & 17 Dec. 1751   ANDER MCCREE, both of Williamsburgh Township,
L & R   Craven Co., for ₤ 207:10 currency, 250 a. part
                       of 1000 a. formerly belonging to JAMES AKIN,
ESQ., in Craven Co., bounding SW on widow HOWARD; NE on GEORGE MONTGOMERY;
other sides on vacant land. Witnesses: JOHN LIVISTON, JOHN SCOTT. Before JAMES AKIN, J.P. WILLIAM HOPTON, Register. Plat by JOHN LIVISTON,
D.S., 4 Sept. 1751.

Book M-M, p. 91   LEWIS LAFONTAINE, cordwainer, & HANNAH MARIA
14 & 15 Sept. 1752   (her mark) his wife, of Colleton Co., to HENRY
L & R   GOLLMAN, planter, of Berkeley Co., for Ł 30
                         currency, 75 a., being the N part of 250 a.
within the limits of Saxegotha Township, on SW side Santee River, Berkeley Co., the whole tract bounding NE on Santee River; SE on JACOB REMEN-
SPERGER; SW on vacant land; NW on vacant land & JOSEPH CRELL; as by grant
of 250 a. to HANNAH MARIA STOLEA (?) by Gov. JAMES GLEN on 8 Dec. 1744;
also lot #52 in Saxegotha containing half an a. Witnesses: ANDREW LETCH,
JOHN FREYMOUTH, RACHEL LETCH. Before OTHNIEL BEALE, J.P. WILLIAM HOPTON,
Register.

Book M-M, p. 96   ANN SMITH, spinster; & CHARLES FAUCHERCAUD,
24 & 25 Apr. 1752   planter; & SARAH HILL, widow; co-parceners, of
L & R   Berkeley Co., of 1st part; to DANIEL HORRY,
                         planter, of Craven Co., for Ł 300 currency,
700 a. Whereas Gov. JOSEPH BLAKE & the Lords Proprs. on 5 Dec. 1696
granted ARNOUD BRUNO DECHABUSHEIR an island of 700 a. on N side Cape Ro-
mana, Craven Co., bounding E on entrance of Santee River; S on the sea; W
& N on marsh; & whereas by will ARNOUD BRUNO DEGHABUSHEIR gave the 700 a.
to his nephew & heir, PAUL BRUNO (BRUNEAU); who by will, named PAUL BRUNO
his executor & heir; & whereas PAUL BRUNEAU with MARIANNE BRUNEAU (his
wife) by deed poll dated 26 Sept. 1711 sold to EDWARD WEEKLY; who, with
ELIZABETH his wife, on 5 July 1725 sold to THOMAS SMITH, JR. [only brother of the whole blood to GEORGE SMITH, father of ANN SMITH & SARAH (formerly SARAH SMITH) & of JANE SMITH (lately JANE FAUCHERAUD, wife of
CHARLES FAUCHERAUD) which GEORGE SMITH afterwards died intestate, leaving
issue said ANN, JANE & SARAH, his 3 only children & co-heirs]; & whereas
by will of THOMAS SMITH, JR., the 700 a. descended to his only son & heir,
THOMAS SMITH, an infant who died in his minority; & the said GEORGE SMITH,
his only uncle of the whole blood, being also then dead, the land descended to his 3 children, ANN, JANE & SARAH; & whereas CHARLES FAUCHERAUD &
said JANE his wife, by L & R dated 18 & 19 June 1749, sold their undivided third part to GIDEON FAUCHERAUD, planter; & whereas GIDEON FAUCHERAUD
by L & R dated 17 & 18 Mar. 1752 sold said undivided third part to said
CHARLES FAUCHERAUD; now ANN SMITH, CHARLES FAUCHERAUD & SARAH HILL sell
their respective shares to HARRY. Witnesses: DR. FREDERICK HOLZENDORT,
ROSINA HOLZENDORF. Before J. SKENE, J.P. WILLIAM HOPTON, Register.

Book M-M, p. 103   ELISHA BUTLER, planter, & ELIZABETH his wife,
28 Oct. 1738   of Colleton Co., to their daughter, ELIZABETH
Gift   ELLIOTT, for natural love & affection & other
                         considerations, 150 a. in Colleton Co., near
the Horse Shoe, known as RALPH SAVANNAH, bounding 1 side on JOHN CHAMP-
NEYS, the other on ROGER SAUNDERS. Witnesses: THOMAS ELLIOTT, RICHARD
GODFREY. Before JAMES BULLOCK, J.P. WILLIAM BUTLER, Now husband of
ELIZABETH ELLIOTT, put in possession by delivery of turf & twig. Witness-
es: HUGH FERGUSON, CHARLES JONES. Before JAMES SKIRVING, J.B. WILLIAM
HOPTON, Register.

Book M-M, p. 104   PETER SANDERS, saddler, to WILLIAM WOODROP &
22 Nov. 1752   PAUL DOUXSAINT, merchants, all of Charleston,
Mortgage   as security on bond of even date in sum of
                         Ł 3000 currency (given WOODDROP & DOUXSAINT
because they stood as security on SANDER'S bond dated 22 this Nov. to
HENRY PERONNEAU, gentleman, of Charleston, in penal sum of Ł 3000 for
payment of Ł 1500 currency, with interest, on 22 Nov. 1753); part of lot
#80, in Charleston which PETER SANDERS purchased from GABRIEL GUIGNARD, &
known by the letter M in a division of the lot between GEORGE HUNTER &
CHARLES PINCKNEY, ESQRS.; & ANN ELLERY, widow & devisee of THOMAS ELLERY;
bounding N 25 ft. on a street 20 ft. wide called Guignard Street; W 45
ft. on a 12 ft. alley called Guignards Alley; S & E on other part of
division M belonging to said GUIGNARD; also that part of Colleton Square
which PETER SANDERS purchased from WILLIAM FISHBURNE, bounding N 75 ft.
on Guignard Street, W on GABRIEL GUIGNARD; S on THOMAS BURHAM; E 50 ft.
on a 12 ft. alley called French (?) Alley; with houses, etc. Witnesses:
WILLIAM STANYARNE, ANDREW CATHCART. Before WILLIAM PINCKNEY, J.P. WIL-
LIAM HOPTON, Register. On 16 Feb. 1756 PAUL DOUXSAINT declared mortgage
satisfied. Witness: WILLIAM HOPTON.

Book M-M, p. 107   PETER GIRARDEAU, planter, & ELIZABETH his wife,
9 & 10 May 1734   of Berkeley Co., to WILLIAM WEBB, planter, of
L & R   Colleton Co., for Ł 800 currency, 500 a. in
                      Colleton Co., bounding N on Ashepoo River, S &
W on CAPT. EDMUND BELLINGER; E on RICHARD BAKER. Witnesses: THOMAS BUT-
LER, JOHN GIRARDEAU. Before HENRY HYRNE, J.P. of Colleton Co. WILLIAM
HOPTON, Register.

Book M-M, p. 111   RICHARD BAKER, planter, of Berkeley Co., to
30 Dec. 1738   WILLIAM WEBB, planter, of Colleton Co., for
Sale   Ł 1500 currency, 500 a. Whereas Landgrave ED-
                      MUND BELLINGER owned 1000 a. at a place called
Ashepoe, in Colleton Co., & by will gave his daughter MARGARET (late wife
of NICHOLAS BOHUN, also deceased) the 1000 a.; & whereas she married
NICHOLAS BOHUN & they had 2 daughters, MARY the elder, (afterwards wife
of RICHARD BAKER, party hereto), & ELIZABETH (later wife of PETER GIRAR-
DEAU), who inherited the land on the death of their mother, MARGARET; &
whereas NICHOLAS BOHUN bequeathed to said 2 daughters, MARY & ELIZABETH,
the 1000 a.; & whereas sometime later the land was divided into 2 equal
parts & RICHARD BAKER & his wife MARY (she being the elder & having right
of 1st choice) having chosen the E half, bounding N on Ashepoo River, on
which NICHOLAS BOHUN'S dwelling house formerly stood; & whereas RICHARD &
MARY had several children & after the death of his wife MARY, RICHARD
BAKER by curtesie of England became tenant for life, the reversion being
in WILLIAM BAKER, an infant, the eldest son, now aged 12 years; & whereas
RICHARD BAKER for himself & eldest son WILLIAM, has agreed to sell the
500 a. to WILLIAM WEBB; now RICHARD conveys the land to WEBB; WILLIAM
BAKER to confirm the sale when he comes of age. Witnesses: JOSEPH ELL-
IOTT, JOSEPH ELLICOTT. Before RICHARD WRIGHT, J.P. WILLIAM HOPTON, Reg-
ister.

Book M-M, 115   DAVID MONGINE (MONGIN), watchmaker, to THOMAS
8 Aug. 1751   GLEN, ESQ., both of Charleston, for Ł 1195
Assignment of Lease   currency, part of a lot in Charleston for the
                      unexpired term of 50 years. Whereas the Rev.
MR. FRANCIS GUICHARD, pastor of the Church of French Protestants in
Charleston, & GABRIEL MANIGAULT, ISAAC MAZYCK, PAUL MAZYCK, JACOB MARTIN,
JOHN NEUFVILLE, & BENJAMIN D'HARRIETTE, elders of said church, on 1 Oct.
1742 leased to DAVID MONGINE, for 50 years, at a rental of Ł 3:5 shillings Sterling per annum, that part of lot #93, bounding W 30 ft. 6 in. on
King Street; S on JOHN VAUGHAN; E on MRS. MACKENZIE; N on MARY PORTAL &
others; MONGINE to build a substantial brick house on the lot according
to specifications given & keep it in good repair; now MONGINE assigns the
lease to GLEN.

Book M-M, p. 120   ROBERT (his mark) SEAWRIGHT, planter, & ANN
27 & 28 Aug. 1752   (her mark) his wife, of Craven Co., to JAMES
L & R   MICHIE, ESQ., of Charleston, for Ł 10 curren-
                      cy, 50 a. in Fredericksburg Township, Craven
Co., bounding NW on WILLIAM SEAWRIGHT; NE & SW on Wateree River; SE on
GEORGE SENIOR & WILLIAM NEWITT EDWARDS; which 50 a. was granted on 5
Sept. 1750 by Gov. JAMES GLEN to ROBERT SEAWRIGHT. Witnesses: SAMUEL
WYLY, JOHN SEAWRIGHT. Before JOHN LINING, J.P. WILLIAM HOPTON, Register.

Book M-M, p. 125   JOHN FLEMING, SR., planter, & MARTHA his wife
7 & 8 June 1752   of Prince Fredericks Parish, to JOHN FLEMING,
L & R   JR., carpenter, of Williamsburg Township, for
                      Ł 37:10 currency, 75 a. in Williamsburg Town-
ship, part of 450 a. formerly belonging to JOHN FLEMING, SR., by whose
will dated 2 June 1750 the 75 a. & as much more was bequeathed to JOHN
FLEMING, party hereto; bounding S on the part bequeathed to ELIZABETH
BLACKLY (alias FLEMING); N on the part bought by JAMES FLEMING from said
JOHN FLEMING, SR.; E on EDWARD PLOWDEN; W on vacant land; with shape as
appears by 2 pricked lines A, B, C, D on plat of original grant; MARTHA
to renounce her dower. Witnesses: JOHN HEWIT, ROBERT WRIGHT, JAMES FLEM-
ING. Before JOHN LIVISTON, J.P. WILLIAM HOPTON, Register.

Book M-M, p. 128   JOHN FLEMING, SR., planter, & MARTHA his wife
7 & 8 June 1752   of Prince Fredericks Parish, to JAMES FLEMING,
L & R   planter, of Williamsburg Township, for

Ł 37:10:0 currency, 75 a. in Williamsburg Township, part of 450 a. formerly belonging to JOHN FLEMING, by whose will, dated 2 June 1750, the
75 a. & as much more were bequeathed to JOHN FLEMING, party hereto; bounding S on the part of said 450 a. belonging to JOHN FLEMING, JR., carpenter; N on part bequeathed to JAMES FLEMING by said will; E on EDWARD PLOW-
DEN; W on vacant land; with shape as shown by 2 pricked lines C,D, E, F
on plat of original grant; MARTHA to renounce her dower. Witnesses: JOHN
HEWIT, ROBERT WRIGHT, JOHN FLEMING. Before JOHN LIVISTON, J.P. of Craven
Co. WILLIAM HOPTON, Register.

Book M-M, p. 132
26 Aug. 1752
Sale

MARGARET BRUNSON, widow to DAVID BRUNSON, both
of Craven Co., for Ł 20 currency, 300 a. in
Craven Co., bounding NW on Wateree River; SE
on CAPT. PETER PORCHER; other sides on vacant
land. Witnesses: ISAAC BRUNSON, SAMUEL NELSON, JR., MARY BRUNSON. Before JARED NELSON, J.P. WILLIAM HOPTON, Register.

Book M-M, p. 134
26 & 27 Oct. 1750
L & R

DAVID WITHERSPOON, planter, & ANN (her mark)
his wife, to MOSES GORDON, planter, both of
Craven Co., for Ł 5 currency, 100 a. in Wil-
liamsburg Township, Craven Co., on N side San-
tee, bounding NE on WILLIAM JAMES; NW on DAVID JOHNSON; SW on the town;
SE on vacant land. Witnesses: JOHN NEWMAN OGLETHORP, WILLIAM PRESSLY,
ELINOR THOMPSON (THOMSON). Before JOHN LIVISTON, J.P. WILLIAM HOPTON,
Register.

Book M-M, p. 138
26 & 27 Oct. 1752
L & R

DAVID WITHERSPOON, planter, & ANN (her mark)
his wife, to MOSES GORDON, planter, both of
Craven Co., for Ł 5 currency, 100 a. in Williamsburg Township, Craven Co., on N side San-
tee River, bounding N on JAMES ARMSTRONG; W on WILLIAM JAMES; S on EDWARD
PLOWDEN; E on vacant land. Witnesses: JOHN NEWMAN OGLETHORPE, WILLIAM
PRESSLY, SARAH PRESSLY. Before JOHN LIVISTON, Register.

Book M-M, p. 142
30 June 1752
Release

DR. WILLIAM KEITH, practitioner in physick, &
ANN his wife, of Keithfield, St. Johns Parish,
Berkeley Co., to NATHANIEL BROUGHTON, JR., gentleman, of same Parish, for Ł 2693 currency,
673-1/2 a., called Wampee Plantation, on Biggon Swamp, St. Johns Parish,
being half of 1346-3/4 a. consisting of smaller tracts lately belonging
to JAMES MAXWELL on which he lived, which was bought by WILLIAM KEITH
from JORDON ROCHE; the 673-1/2 a. bounding N on FRANCIS MURRALL & on estate of the Rev. MR. DANIEL DWIGHT; NE on estate of JOHN GIGNILLIAT; SE
on the part belonging to WILLIAM KEITH; W on MRS. KEITH & estate of DR.
JAMES REPAULT. Witnesses: ANDREW BROUGHTON, SAMUEL CORDES, SIMEON THEUS.
Before NATHANIEL BROUGHTON, J.P. WILLIAM HOPTON, Register.

Book M-M, p. 144
17 Aug. 1749
Release

MARY MONCK, widow devisee & executrix, of will,
of THOMAS MONCK, ESQ., of St. Johns Parish,
Berkeley Co., to WILLIAM KEITH, of Keithfield,
practitioner in physick, for Ł 800 currency,
400 a. adjoining the 600 a. which THOMAS MONCK settled upon his daughter,
JOANNA BROUGHTON MONCK; the 400 a. being in St. James Parish on W side
Biggin Creek; bounding E on JOHN COLLETON, ESQ., of London; N on JAMES
MAXWELL (formerly MAJ. HUGH BUTLER); W on RENE MERCHAND; S on JOANNA
MONCK. Whereas THOMAS MONCK owned divers lands, plantations, etc., in
Berkeley Co., & by will dated 22 Apr. 1746 directed that all his real estate not devised be sold; devised to his beloved wife, MARY MONCK, 400 a.
adjoining the 600 a. settled upon his daughter, JOANNA BROUGHTON MONCK,
together with all the lands purchased from GEORGE COLLETON; appointed his
wife MARY, & NATHANIEL BROUGHTON & THOMAS BROUGHTON, executrix & executors; now MARY MONCK sells the 400 a. tract to KEITH. Witnesses: JAMES
MAXWELL, NATHAN (his mark) JOYNER, JOHN (his mark) WILLIAMS. Before NA-
THANIEL BROUGHTON, J.P. WILLIAM HOPTON, Register.

Book M-M, p. 148
15 Aug. 1749
Release

ANNE LEBAS, widow & executrix; & THOMAS SABB,
exeuctor, of will of JAMES LEBAS, to WILLIAM
KEITH, of Keithfield, practitioner in physic,
all of Berkeley Co., for Ł 1000 currency, 91
a. Whereas JAMES LEBAS owned, with other lands, 91 a. in St. Johns

Parish, Berkeley Co., bounding N on MRS. ANNE LEBAS & on Watboo; E & S on
THOMAS MONCK; W on JOHN COLLETON; the 91 a. being part of 1500 a. granted
by the Lords Proprs. on 15 Nov. 1680 to Landgrave JOSEPH WEST & which by
various conveyances descended to JAMES LEBAS; & whereas because of various debts by will dated 3 Dec. 1737 JAMES LEBAS, bequeathed all his real
& personal estate to his executors to be sold, appointing his wife, ANNE,
& THOMAS SABB, executrix & executor; now they sell 91 a. to DR. KEITH.
Witnesses: THOMAS CORDES, JOHN SEARS, JAMES CORDES. Before NATHANIEL
BROUGHTON, J.P. WILLIAM HOPTON, Register.

Book M-M, p. 151   JORDAN ROCHE, ESQ., & REBECCA his wife, of
6 Dec. 1751   Charleston, to WILLIAM KEITH, practitioner in
Release   Physick, of Keithfield, St. Johns Parish,
                          Berkeley Co., for Ł 5327 currency, 1346-3/4 a.,
bounding according to lines shaded yellow in the plat. Whereas JAMES MAX-
WELL, planter, of St. Johns Parish, owned 1206 a. in St. Johns Parish,
made up of 4 adjacent tracts; that is, 500 a. called Compliment Hill, or
Bettison's Plantation; 400 a. called Mount Pleasant; both purchased by
JAMES MAXWELL from HUGH BUTLER, ESQ., by L & R dated 9 & 10 Feb. 1735;
206 a. & 100 a. purchased by MAXWELL from ROBERT TAYLOR, planter, of said
Parish; the 1206 a. bounding E on Watboo Barony; S on WILLIAM KEITH; W on
JOHN PALMER; NW on estate of the Rev. MR. DANIEL DWIGHT; N on JOHN GIG-
NILLIANT purchased from MR. DUBOURDIER; & whereas JAMES MAXWELL gave bond
dated 9 Feb. 1748 to MATHEW ROCHE, merchant, in penal sum of Ł 20,000
British for payment of Ł 10,000 British on 1 Apr. next; & whereas ROCHE
obtained adjugment against MAXWELL for this amount & costs; & whereas
JAMES GRAEME, C.J. on 2 Oct. 1750 commanded RAWLINS LOWNDES to levy the
sums of Ł 20,000 British & Ł 29:18:1-1/2 SC money against MAXWELL'S estate; & whereas at public auction held 22 Jan. JORDAN ROCHE was highest
bidder; for the 1206 a. therefore RAWLINS LOWNDES, P.M. sold the 1206 a.
to ROCHE for Ł 4700 currency; & whereas WILLIAM MAYNE, Dep. Sur., re-surveyed the land & found 1346-3/4 a. within the boundaries as shown by the
lines shaded yellow on the plat; now JORDAN ROCHE sells the tract to DR.
KEITH. Witnesses: FRANCIS ARTHUR, ALEXANDER BROUGHTON. Before NATHANIEL
BROUGHTON, J.P. WILLIAM HOPTON, Register.

Book M-M, p. 156   THOMAS LYNCH, to JOSEPH COX, title to, part of
16 Jan. 1753   lot #204 in Charleston. Whereas in 1750 THOM-
Confirmation   AS LYNCH, & ELIZABETH His wife, since deceased,
                          for Ł 215 currency, conveyed to JOSEPH COX,
mariner, of Charleston, that part of lot 204 in Charleston, bounding W
29 ft. on New Church Street, running to BROUGHTON'S Battery, at White
Point, sometimes called Broughton Street; being 25 ft. wide; N 75 ft. on
Lynch's Lane being 12 ft. wide; E 31 ft. on the part belonging to DANIEL
SMITH; S 34 ft. on RICHARD MORTIMER & 40 ft. on THOMAS LYNCH, total 74 ft.
on S side. Whereas in the "dreadful hurrican & inundation of water" on
15 Sept. last the dwelling house of said JOSEPH COX was blown down, destroyed & carried away & the L & R lost & destroyed; now, in order to
prevent all doubts as to the validity of COX'S title to the lot & premises, THOMAS LYNCH confirms the property to COX. Witnesses: DAVID DEAS,
JOHN DEAS. Before JACOB MOTTE, J.P. WILLIAM HOPTON, Register.

Book M-M, p. 159   ANTHONY BONNEAU, planter, & MARGARET HENRIETTE,
1 & 2 May 1751   his wife, of Berkeley Co., to AUGUSTUS LAWRENS,
L & R   planter, of Craven Co., for Ł 600 currency,
                          500 a. in Craven Co., bounding N & W on DANIEL
HORRY; S on MR. DELFE & vacant land; E on JOHN VANDERHORST & vacant land;
whereas Gov. NATHANIEL JOHNSON on 1 June 1709 granted to ELIAS HORRY, SR.,
(see book F., p. 201) 500 a. in Craven Co., & whereas said ELIAS HORRY,
by will dated 19 Sept. 1736, devised all his real estate of 750 a. to his
executors, DANIEL HUGER, ESQ., & his 2 sons DANIEL HORRY & ELIAS HORRY,
in trust, to sell the land to 1 or more of his children but to no other
person, the money to be equally divided among his children (vis. DANIEL,
ELIAS, JOHN, PETER, MARGARET HENRIETTE & MAGDELIN); & whereas ANTHONY
BONNEAU married MARGARET HENRIETTE & became co-heir; & the executors sold
500 a. to BONNEAU (see Book T, for 389-392); now BONNEAU sells the 500 a.
to LAWRENS. Witnesses: JOHN FREER, JACOBUS PEYN, JOHN SNOW. Before JOHN
GENDRON, J.P. WILLIAM HOPTON, Register.

Book M-M, p. 162   RAWLINS LOWNDES, P.M., to AUGUSTUS LAURENS,

20 Feb. 1752   for ₺ 200 currency, 454 a. Whereas JAMES AN-
Sale   DERSON obtained judgment against JOSEPH DELPH,
                      carpenter, for ₺ 58:6:10 currency & ₺ 49:19:2
costs, upon which judgment a writ of fieri facias dated 2 Oct. 1750 was
issued by JAMES GRAEME, C.J., commanding LOWNDES to seize a tract of 454
a. in Craven Co., conveyed by ELIAS HORRY, ESQ., to JOSEPH DELPH, bounding S on ELIAS HORRY; NW on vacant land; E on MR. STOUTENBURGH; now LOWN-
DES sells the land at public auction to LAURENS. Witnesses: LAMBERT
LANCE, FRANCIS BREMAR. Before OTHNIEL BEALE, J.P. WILLIAM HOPTON, Register.

Book M-M, p. 164   GEORGE LOGAN, planter, & MARTHA his wife, of
30 & 31 Aug. 1721   Berkeley Co., to JOSEPH WRAGG, merchant, of
L & R   Charleston, for ₺ 500 currency, that part of
                      lot #33 in on the Bay of Charleston, bounding
E 78 ft. on Cooper River; N 210 ft. (or more) on MRS. ANN DANIEL; S on
THOMAS DYMES; also that piece of land fronting said lot, from the wall or
fortification of said town to low water mark. Whereas the Lords Proprs.
on 13 Mar. 1693/4 sold JAMES MOORE lot #33 in Charleston, which on 16
Mar. 1693 MOORE sold to CAPT. WILLIAM HAWETT; who on 16 Oct. 1696 sold to
ROBERT DANIEL of Berkeley Co., who on 10 July 1704 appointed CHARLES BURN-
HAM, of Berkeley Co., his attorney, to assign to his son CAPT. ROBERT
DANIEL & his wife SARAH, for & during their natural lives & no longer, 2
lots in Charlest; & whereas BURNHAM therefore on 20 May 1705 turned 2
lots over to said CAPT. ROBERT DANIEL & his wife, SARAH; & whereas ROBERT
DANIEL, the father, by will dated 1 May 1718 bequeathed to his wife MAR-
THA (now MARTHA LOGAN) after the death of said SARAH, the said 2 lots #33
& #34; & whereas SARAH DANIEL, wife of ROBERT, on 16 Apr. 1719 surrendered her interest in the lots to MARTHA DANIEL; & whereas by L & R at the
marriage of MARTHA DANIEL & COL. GEORGE LOGAN, lot #33 was settled in
trust for the use of MARTHA DANIEL, JR., (now MARTHA LOGAN, wife of said
GEORGE LOGAN, JR.); now GEORGE LOGAN & MARTHA his wife sell lot #33 to
WRAGG. Witnesses: SARAH BLAKEWEY, THOMAS DYMES, ROBERT HUME. Before
ROBERT AUSTIN, J.P. WILLIAM HOPTON, Register.

Book M-M, p. 170   MARY BLAMYER, widow, of Charleston, to EDWARD
20 & 21 June 1749   RAWLINS, planter, for ₺ 55 currency, 450 a. in
L & R   Berkeley Co., bounding W on JOHN DEWREN; E on
                      BETHEL DEWS; S & N on vacant land. Witnesses:
MARY WRIGHT, WILLIAM MOUAT, JOHN FAIRCHILD. Before MOSES THOMSON, J.P.
on 26 Mar. 1750 EDWARD RAWLINGS released his release to WILLIAM VANTS.
WILLIAM HOPTON, Register.

Book M-M, p. 174   EDWARD RAWLINS, planter, to WILLIAM VANTS,
25 & 26 Mar. 1750   planter, for ₺ 75 currency, 450 a. in Berkeley
L & R   Co., bounding W on JOHN DEWREN; E on BETHEL
                      DEWS; S & N on vacant land. Witnesses: MOSES
THOMPSON, THOMAS CARTER, CHARLES COLLETON. Before ALEXANDER STEWART, J.P.
WILLIAM HOPTON, Register.

Book M-M, p. 177   WILLIAM BREDY (BREADY), planter, to SAMUEL
23 & 24 Aug. 1752   WYLY, planter, both of Craven Co., for ₺ 20
L & R   currency, 50 a. on N side Wateree River, in
                      Fredericksburg Township, Craven Co., bounding
SE on BRYAN ROCK; other sides on vacant land; which tract was granted to
BREDY by Gov. JAMES GLEN on 24 Apr. 1752. Witnesses: JOSIAH TOMLINSON
(A Quaker), T_OMAS CASITY. Before JARED NELSON, J.P. WILLIAM HOPTON,
Register.

Book M-M, p. 182   JAMES OUSLEY, planter, of Christ Church Parish,
25 & 27 Apr. 1752   to SAMUEL RUSSELL, planter, of the Wateree,
L & R   Fredericksburg, Craven Co., for ₺ 150 curren-
                      cy, 300 a. on S side Wateree River, in Craven
Co., bounding on vacant lands; which tract Gov. JAMES GLEN granted on 12
June 1751 to OUSLEY. Witnesses: JONATHAN SCOTT, SAMUEL WYLY (a Quaker).
Before JARED NELSON, J.P. WILLIAM HOPTON, Register.

Book M-M, p. 186   BRYAN (his mark) ROCK, planer, to SAMUEL WYLY,
17 & 18 Aug.   planter, both of Craven Co., for ₺ 100 curren-
L & R   cy, 140 a. in Fredericksburg Township, Craven

Co., on N side Wateree River, bounding SW on the river; SE on JOHN BEN-
NETT & vacant land; NE on vacant land; NW on WILLIAM BREDY & vacant land;
which tract on 24 Apr. 1752 was granted by Gov. JAMES GLEN to BRYAN ROCK.
Witnesses: SAMUEL MILHOUS, JOHN WILIEE (a Quaker). Before JARED NELSON,
J.P. WILLIAM HOPTON, Register.

Book M-M, p. 191   GAVIN WITHERSPOON, & JANE (her mark) his wife,
27 & 28 Mar. 1751   to DAVID WITHERSPOON, both of Craven Co., for
L & R   Ł 40 currency, 50 a. in Williamsburgh, Craven
                          Co., bounding NE on MR. JAMESON; SE on Black
River; JANE to renounce her dower upon request. Witnesses: JOHN LIVI-
STON, WILLIAM PRESSLY. Before PAUL TRAPIER, J.P. WILLIAM HOPTON, Reg-
ister.

Book M-M, p. 194   ROGER GORDON, & MARY (her mark) his wife, of
__ Jan. 1736   Williamsburgh, Craven Co., to DAVID WITHER-
Feoffment   SPOON, for Ł 200 currency, 200 a. in Williams-
                          burgh, bounding SW on vacant land; SE on Black
River. MARY, wife of ROGER GORDON, renounces her dower. Witnesses: DA-
VID ALLAN, JAMES MCCLELLAND, WILLIAM JAMES. Before JOHN EDWARDS, J.P.
WILLIAM HOPTON, Register.

Book M-M, p. 196   JOHN ATHOL (ATHON), carpenter, of Williams-
2 Mar. 1736   burgh, Craven Co., to DAVID WITHERSPOON, weav-
Sale   er, of same place, for Ł 50 currency, 50 a. in
                          Williamsburgh, Craven Co., bounding N on DAVID
WITHERSPOON; SW on JOHN JAMESON & GAVIN WITHERSPOON. Delivery by turf &
twig. Witnesses: ANTHONY WILLIAMS, WILLIAM JAMES, JAMES FLEMING. ATHOL
sells a town lot in Williamsburgh & above premises for said sum of Ł 50
currency. Before JOHN EDWARDS, J.P. WILLIAM HOPTON, Register.

Book M-M, p. 197   WILLIAM DRY, ESQ., of Cape Fear, NC & MARY
1 & 2 Dec. 1752   JANE, his wife (formerly MARY JANE RHETT, 1 of
L & R   the daughters & co-heiresses of WILLIAM RHETT,
                          the younger, gentleman, of Charleston) to
CHARLES MAYNE, merchant, of Charleston, for Ł 5500 currency, all their
undivided half part of the half part of lot #15 in Charleston, bounding E
on the Bay; W on Union Street; also their undivided half part of the
bridge & wharf & low water lot #333, bounding S on ____; W on the curtain line before the Bay; N on lot #16; & running E into Cooper River as
far as low water mark; also their undivided half part of the half part of
low water lot #16, bounding S on low water lot #333; W 50 ft. on the curtain before the Bay; N on other half of said lot; & running E into Cooper River as far as low water mark; also their undivided half part of the
bridge & wharf & low water lot #333; also their undivided half of the
half part of low water lot #16. Whereas the Lords Proprs. on 8 May 1683
granted PETER HEARN, gentleman, lot #15 in Charleston, & he, by will dated 18 Dec. 1688 bequeathed all his real & personal estate to his wife,
JANE, & to his 7 children, appointing his wife & 7 children executrix &
executors; & whereas on 17 Jan. 1694 the General Assembly authorized
JAMES WITTER & EDWARD DRAKE to sell said lot & on 18 Jan. 1694 they sold
the lot & premises to Landgrave JOSEPH BLAKE; who on 3 June 1695 conveyed
the lot & houses to WILLIAM DRY, planter; & whereas WILLIAM DRY on 6 Nov.
1696 sold to WILLIAM RHETT, merchant, of Charleston, father of WILLIAM
RHETT the younger, that half of lot #15 bounding E on the wharf on Cooper River; N on MARY CROSS, widow; S on the other half; W on a little
street; & whereas Gov. JOSEPH BLAKE & the Lords Proprs. on 13 Dec. 1698,
granted WILLIAM RHETT the elder, a front lot #333, bounding W on the
wharf line laid out by the commissioners, by Act of Assembly, lying opposite lot #15 & containing 36 perches, bounding N on front lot #16 belonging to MARY BADSDEN (formerly to MARY CROSS) & running E into Cooper
River as far as low water mark; & whereas WILLIAM RHETT the elder, &
SARAH his wife, by L & R dated 3 & 4 Aug. 1716 conveyed to WILLIAM RHETT
the younger, that half of lot #15 bounding E on the Bay; N on land formerly belonging to MARY CROSS, widow; S on the other half now belonging to
EDWARD CROFT; extending 134 ft. W & divided from the other half by a
brick wall; with the brick house thereon; also the bridge or wharf & low
water lot #333; & whereas WILLIAM RHETT the younger, by L & R dated 4 & 5
Oct. 1717, in consideration of his intended marriage with MARY TROTT,
daughter of NICHOLAS TROTT, ESQ., of Charleston, conveyed to WILLIAM

RHETT the elder, & to NICHOLAS TROTT, in trust for WILLIAM the younger,
the half of lot #15, with buildings, the bridge or wharf & lots #333 until his marriage & then to him & MARY & their heirs; & whereas the marriage took place & they had 2 daughters, SARAH & MARY JANE; & whereas
SARAH married THOMAS FRANKLAND, ESQ., of old Bond Street, St. George Parish, Middlesex Co., Great Britain, & MARY JANE married WILLIAM DRY (party
hereto) & WILLIAM DRY & MARY JANE now own 1 undivided half of the premises; & whereas WILLIAM RHETT the elder, by will dated 6 July 1722 authorized his wife SARAH to sell all his real estate except as excepted, & bequeathed the residue of his real & personal estate, except as excepted, &
the money from the sale of the estate, to his wife SARAH; so that after
his death SARAH became owner of the other or W half of lot #15, fronting
W 48 on Union Street, with 2 dwelling houses thereon & other buildings
now occupied by JOHN BONNETHEAU & JOHN COWDEN, & divided from the E part
by a brick wall, S on other half; N on JOHN MOORE; & whereas SARAH RHETT
afterwards married NICHOLAS TROTT & they owned half of front lot #16,
bounding S on low water lot #333; E on Cooper River; N on other half; W
50 ft. on the curtain line of the Bay; & whereas NICHOLAS TROTT & SARAH
his wife by L & R dated 12 & 13 Mar. 1734 conveyed to the Rev. MR. ALEX-
ANDER GARDEN, rector of Parish of St. Philips & to JOSEPH WRAGG, merchant,
of Charleston, in trust for their grand children (SARAH RHETT, now SARAH
FRANKLAND, & MARY JANE RHETT, now MARY JANE DRY) infant daughters of WIL-
LIAM RHETT the younger, & MARY his wife, the half of lot #15 with the 2
dwelling houses & other buildings & the half of low water lot #16; &
whereas JOSEPH WRAGG died, & ALEXANDER GARDEN released his trust to SARAH
FRANKLAND & MARY JANE DRY as tenants in common; now WILLIAM DRY & MARY
JANE convey their undivided shares in the various pieces of property to
CHARLES MAYNE. Witnesses: ALEXANDER MACCAULAY, JOHN MOORE, JOHN STEVEN-
SON. Before JAMES WRIGHT, J.P. WILLIAM HOPTON, Register.

Book M-M, p. 209   MARY SEAMAN, wife of GEORGE SEAMAN, merchant,
3 & 4 Oct. 1752   lately MARY ALLEN (mother & testamentary guard-
L & R   ian of ELIZABETH ALLEN, an infant daughter of
                      WILLIAM ALLEN, deceased & granddaughter of AN-
DREW ALLEN), to THOMAS CROSSTHWAITE, all of Charleston, for 5 shillings
part of lot #66; bounding S on JOHN LEWIS (formerly MILES DREWTON & SU-
SANNAH his wife); E on HUGH ANDERSON (formerly MARY MULLINS); W & N on
St. Philips Churchyard, the whole lot #66 being 84 ft. 4 in. from N to S
& 60 ft. from E to W; whereas MATHEW PORTER, sawyer, of Charleston,
agreed to purchase from JOHN MILNER, mariner & ELIZABETH his wife, that
part of lot #66 in Charleston, bounding W 200 ft. on a street leading to
St. Philips Church; S 60 ft. on the street leading by the French Church;
N on St. Philips Churchyard; E on part of said lot belonging to MRS. MARY
MULLINS; but PORTER died before conveyance was made, having first, by
will dated 15 Nov. 1717, bequeathed his real estate to his beloved wife
SUSANNAH PORTER during her lifetime; & all the residue to his mother,
MARY PORTER, & his brothers JOHN & JAMES & his sister HANNAH, share &
share alike; after the death of his wife the real estate to be sold & the
money divided amongst his mother, brothers & sister; appointing his wife,
executrix & ANDREW ALLEN & ROBERT TRADD, executors; & whereas the executors, as trustees, paid the MILNERS the money agreed upon for the lot,
the L & R being dated 7 & 8 Mar. 1717; & whereas ANDREW ALLEN & ROBERT
TRADD, by deed of trust dated 8 Mar. 1717, declared that the purchase
money belonged to the estate of MATHEW PORTER & used by them in trust; &
whereas ANDREW ALLEN survived ROBERT TRADD, & afterwards died, leaving 2
sons, JOHN ALLEN & WILLIAM ALLEN; JOHN dying without issue during lifetime of WILLIAM ALLEN; & whereas WILLIAM ALLEN died, leaving an infant
daughter, ELIZABETH ALLEN, legal owner; & whereas THOMAS CROSSTHWAITE has
purchased the several rights & claims of the several legatees & devisees
of MATTHEW PORTER & the representatives of such as have died, & CROSS-
THWAITE has agreed to sell the premises, or part thereof, to the church
wardens of St. Philip's Parish for a burial place & it is necessary that
ANDREW ALLEN'S heir-at-law should convey the premises to him in accordance with the deed of trust, but ELIZABETH being too young to convey the
premises; & whereas an act of the General Assembly on 17 Apr. 1724 authorized the commissioners of the new brick church to purchase lots for a
churchyard & should any owner be under 21 years of age that person's
guardian was authorized to execute a conveyance; now MARY SEAMAN, as
mother & guardian of ELIZABETH ALLEN, conveys the property to CROSS-
THWAITE. Witnesses: JOHN REMINGTON, JR., JOHN REMINGTON. Before JACOB

MOTTE, J.P. WILLIAM HOPTON, Register.

Book M-M, p. 216   THOMAS CROSSTHWAITE, merchant, & MARY his
4 & 5 Dec. 1752   wife, to DAVID DEAS & FRANCIS BREMAR, church
L & R   wardens of St. Philip's Parish, all of
                          Charleston; for Ŀ 337:6:3 SC money, to be used
as a burial place, part of lot #66, the lot being 84 ft. 4 in. from N to
S, & 60 ft. from E to W which part is bounding S on JOHN LEWIS (formerly
MILES BREWTON & SUSANNAH his wife); E on HUGH ANDERSON (formerly MARY
MULLINS); W & N on St. Philip's Churchyard (see P. 209 for details of
conveyance to CROSSTHWAITE). Witnesses: GABRIEL MANIGAULT, CHARLES GRIM-
BALL. Before JACOB MOTTE, J.P. WILLIAM HOPTON, Register.

Book M-M, p. 223   THOMAS CROSSTHWAITE, merchant, & MARY his
5 Dec. 1752   wife, give bond to DAVID DEAS & FRANCIS BRE-
Bond of Feoffment   MAR, church wardens of St. Philips Parish, in
                          sum of Ŀ 674:12:6 currency to keep agreements
in above conveyance (p. 216). Witnesses: GABRIEL MANIGAULT, CHARLES
GRIMBALL. Before JACOB MOTTE, J.P. WILLIAM HOPTON, Register.

Book M-M, p. 224   GEORGE LOGAN, of New Hanover Co., NC, appoints
22 Jan. 1742   MARTHA LOGAN, of Charleston, his attorney,
Power of Attorney   with authority to sell or mortgage his lands &
                          slaves in SC. Witnesses: JOSEPH COKE, CARTER
STEVENS. Before HENRY GIBBES, J.P. Recorded in Secretary's Book F.F.,
p. 113 by JOHN CHAMPNEYS, Dep. Sec. WILLIAM HOPTON, Register.

Book M-M, p. 225   PAUL TRAPIER, merchant, to WILLIAM SHACKEL-
5 & 6 July 1752   FORD, vintner, both of Georgetown, Craven Co.,
L & R   for Ŀ 80:5:0 currency; 75 a., part of 2 tracts,
                          1 purchased from WILLIAM FORBES; the other
from JOSEPH DUBOURDIEU, executor of will of ANTHONY WHITE; the 75 a.
bounding SE & NE on JOHN CLELAND, ESQ., other sides on PAUL TRAPIER.
Witnesses: THOMAS LEITH, JOSEPH DUBOURDIEU. Before ELIAS FOISSIN, J.P.
WILLIAM HOPTON, Register.

Book M-M, p. 228   WILLIAM SHACKELFORD, SR., vintner, to his son
1 & 2 Oct. 1752   WILLIAM SHACKELFORD, JR., both of Georgetown,
L & R   Craven Co., for Ŀ 80 currency, 75 a., part of
                          2 tracts purchased from PAUL TRAPIER on 6 July
1752; 1 tract purchased by TRAPIER from WILLIAM FORBES, the other from
JOSEPH DUBOURDIEU, executor of will of ANTHONY WHITE; the 75 a. in Craven
Co., bounding SE & NE on JOHN CLELAND, ESQ.; other sides on PAUL TRAPIER.
Witnesses: CLAUDIUS PEGUES, SAMUEL GROVE. Before THOMAS HASELL, J.P.
WILLIAM HOPTON, Register. Plat given.

Book M-M, p. 231   WILLIAM LENARD, planter, & LUCY (her mark) his
15 Apr. 1751   wife, to WILLIAM KIRLAY, both of Craven Co.,
Feoffment   for Ŀ 200 currency, 150 a. in Craven Co., on N
                          side Santee River, near the Cypress Swamp,
bounding SW on land granted to THOMAS MASSLES; other sides on vacant land.
Witnesses: JOSIAH EVANS, SAMUEL FLEY, ROBERT WHITE. Before RICHARD RICH-
ARDSON, J.P. WILLIAM HOPTON, Register.

Book M-M, p. 233   ALEXANDER WOOD, planter, of Goose Creek, to
5 & 6 Mar. 1753   the Rev. MR. ALEXANDER GARDEN, rector of St.
L & R by Mortgage   Philip's Parish, Charleston, as security on
                          bond of even date in penal sum of Ŀ 2000 for
payment of Ŀ 1000 currency, with interest, on 6 Mar. 1754; 200 a., Eng-
lish measure, in St. James Goose Creek, Berkeley Co., bounding SE & E on
Landgrave THOMAS SMITH; NW on heirs of RICHARD SPLATT (formerly EDWARD
CURRANT). Witnesses: FRANCIS PINCKNEY, CHARLES PINCKNEY, JR. Before
JACOB MOTTE, J.P. WILLIAM HOPTON, Register. On 22 July 1757 SAMPSON
NEYLE, executor of will of said ALEXANDER GARDEN, acknowledged receipt of
full payment of mortgage from WILLIAM PINCKNEY, executor of will of ALEX-
ANDER WOOD. Witness: WILLIAM HOPTON.

Book M-M, p. 237   JOHN BESWICKE, JOHN CROKATT & ALEXANDER LIVIE
25 & 26 Feb. 1753   & Co., merchants, of Charleston, to ALEXANDER
L & R   RANTOWLE, merchant, of Stono, Colleton Co.,

for ₺ 800 currency, 200 a. formerly owned by THOMAS WALLACE, near the middle bridge at Stono, in Colleton Co., also 53 a. of marsh & firm land formerly belonging to THOMAS WALLACE, bounding S on JOSEPH BARTON & THOMAS WALLACE; W on MRS. PHOEBE PETERS; E on THOMAS WALLACE; E on W branch of Stono River. Whereas THOMAS WALLACE, planter, of Colleton Co., owned 200 a., near the middle bridge at Stono which he had obtained from JOHN JACKSON, cordwainer; being a part of a larger tract granted by the Lords Proprs. to JAMES LAROCHE, SR.; & whereas WALLACE also owned 53 a. of marsh & firm land; & whereas WALLACE gave bond dated 1 May 1739 to WILLIAM CATTELL in penal sum of ₺ 400 currency; & whereas WALLACE died & WILLIAM WILLIAMS was made administrator; & whereas CATTELL obtained a judgment against WILLIAMS, as administrator; & the P.M., RAWLINS LOWNDES, sold the 2 tracts at public auction to BESWICKE, CROKATT & LIVIE for ₺ 760 currency on 25 Apr. 1750; now they sell the 2 tracts to RANTOWLE. Witnesses: WILLIAM BIRCH, ALEXANDER GORDON, JR. Before ALEXANDER GORDON, ESQ., J.P. WILLIAM HOPTON, Register.

Book M-M, p. 242
2 May 1748
Mortgage

PHILIP (his mark) POOLE, millwright, of Saxegotha Township, Berkeley Co., gave MARTIN FRIDAY & CONRAD MYRE, a bond this date in penal sum of ₺ 1000 SC money because they signed a bail bond for him this date, & as security conveyed to them 500 a. in Saxegotha Township, bounding NE on Santee River; SE on land formerly belonging to HANNAH MARIAH STOLLER (now HENRY GOLLMAN); NW on STEPHEN CREEL; also 20 head neat cattle, 2 horses, a mare, & all houses, mills & buildings on said land. Witnesses: RICHARD CLANCY, (shoemaker) WILLIAM MOUATT. Before WILLIAM PINCKNEY, J.P. WILLIAM HOPTON, Register.

Book M-M, p. 243
6 Feb. 1750
Release in Trust

The Hon. JOHN CLELAND, ESQ., & MARY his wife, of Georgetown, Craven Co., to ARCHIBALD BAIRD & RICHARD GOUGH, gentleman, in trust; 1818 a. Whereas JOHN PERRIE, merchant, of Island of Antigua, owned certain plantations & by will dated 24 June 1708 amongst other things bequeathed to his daughter MARY PERRIE, now MARY CLELAND, party hereto, his plantation in SC & whereas JOHN CLELAND & his then intended wife, MARY PERRY, by agreement dated 14 Nov. 1728, before their marriage, agreed with the trustees named therein, that the property in SC be sold & the money put out at interest in government securities or used to purchase land in England for the use of JOHN & MARY & their heirs; & whereas JOHN PERRIE did not reside in SC & in his absence ELISHA SCRIVEN & certain other persons had possessed themselves of certain lands near Georgetown, in Craven Co., part of the premises which belonged to PERRIE & which he had devised, SCRIVEN & others having possessed the same for upwards of 7 years during PERRIE'S absence & pretended to hold the same by virtue of the Limitation Act; & whereas JOHN CLELAND & MARY his wife, after their marriage, sold a tract called Younghall, part of the premises, for ₺ 5250 SC money, which money was applied by JOHN & MARY CLELAND towards purchasing other lands in SC in lieu of said plantation called Younghall & "as a composition with said ELISAH SCRIVEN & others" for buying out the pretended claim of SCRIVEN & others & to avoid a lawsuit; & whereas JOHN & MARY CLELAND have not sold the other part of the plantation; & whereas a marriage is intended between FRANCIS KINLOCH, ESQ., son of the Hon. JAMES KINLOCH, ESQ., of Goose Creek, & ANNE ISABELLA CLELAND, daughter of JOHN & MARY CLELAND; now for the love & affection they have for ANNE ISABELLA & the dowry she is entitled to out of the estate of FRANCIS KINLOCH, & in consideration of ₺ 600 British settled on ANNE ISABELLA by FRANCIS KINLOCH out of his own estate; now JOHN & MARY CLELAND convey to BAIRD & GOUGH, as trustees, 1818 a. on Wehaw Creek in Prince George Parish, Craven Co., bounding W on the heirs of ANTHONY WHITE; N on heirs of ANTHONY WHITE & WILLIAM POOLE (formerly WILLIAM SCRIVEN); E on Black River; S on Kingsington Plantation belonging to JOHN & MARY CLELAND; the 1818 a. being part of the land formerly owned by JOHN PERRIE & devised as aforesaid; in trust for JOHN & MARY CLELAND; with details in regard to inheritance. Witnesses: JAMES WRIGHT, JAMES MOULTRIE. Before JAMES MICHIE, J.P. WILLIAM HOPTON, Register.

Book M-M, p. 249
3 & 4 Sept. 1751
L & R

JAMES BULLOCH, planter, & ANNE his wife, of St. Pauls Parish, Colleton Co., to RICHARD JENKINS, planter, of St. Johns Parish, Colleton Co., for ₺ 1150 currency, 460 a. in

Colleton Co., granted by GEORGE II through Gov. JAMES GLEN on 4 Oct. 1749
to JAMES BULLOCH, bounding SW on JOHN FRAMPTON; other sides on a navig-
able salt water creek. Witnesses: RICHARD COCHRAN ASH, DANIEL TOWNSEND.
Before OTHNIEL BEALE, J.P. WILLIAM HOPTON, Register.

Book M-M, p. 253   GEORGE HUNTER, gentleman, of Charleston, to
9 & 10 Feb. 1746   ANNE ELLERY, of Berkeley Co., widow & execu-
L & R   trix of THOMAS ELLERY, of Charleston, for Ł 10
                          currency, that piece of ground, part of the
premises marked H in the general plat, 35 ft. x 150 ft., bounding N on a
street from Cooper River; E on lot G belonging to ANNE ELLERY & on lots
E & F belonging to GEORGE HUNTER; S on a street; W on lot I belonging to
GEORGE HUNTER; also that piece of ground marked K on the general plat,
35 ft. x 150 ft., bounding N & S on 2 streets; E on lot I belonging to
GEORGE HUNTER; W on another street laid out by consent of parties; also
that piece marked O on the general plat, fronting N & S 134-1/2 ft. on 2
streets, & 150 ft. deep, bounding E on lot P belonging to GEORGE HUNTER;
W on lot N belonging to THOMAS WALKER & the marsh lot fronting the same;
also the marsh lots marked b, o, & g. Whereas the Lords Proprs. on 5
Mar. 1680 granted SIR PETER COLLETON a lot in Charelston, known as #80,
containing 9 a., 2 roods, 21 perches, English measure, of dry land &
marsh, with a small creek in the marsh land; bounding E on Cooper River &
on lots of THOMAS COLLETON & Landgrave JAMES COLLETON; W on a small unnamed street; S on CAPT. WILLIAM WALLEY & 2 lots belonging to CAPT. JAMES
ADIE; N on another lot belonging to THOMAS COLLETON & on a small unnamed
street; & whereas lot #80 by various mesne conveyances became vested in
JOHN COLLETON, ESQ., of Fairlawn Barony, & St. Johns Parish, Berkeley Co.,
& whereas JOHN COLLETON & SUSANNAH his wife, by L & R dated 13 & 14 July
1736, for Ł 5000 currency, sold the lot & premises to GEORGE HUNTER: &
whereas the title was made out to GEORGE HUNTER alone, but the purchase
money was paid by GEORGE HUNTER, CHARLES PINCKNEY, & THOMAS ELLERY, jointly; & whereas THOMAS ELLERY by will dated 2 Oct. 1738 bequeathed the premises mentioned to ANNE ELLERY, party hereto; & whereas by agreement between GEORGE HUNTER, CHARLES PINCKNEY, & ANNE ELLERY (widow of THOMAS
ELLERY) the land has been laid out in small lots, with streets & lanes;
now ANNE receives certain portions as her share. Witness: JOHN OYSTON.
Before OTHNIEL BEALE, J.P. WILLIAM HOPTON, Register.

Book M-M, p. 260   FRANCIS KINLOCH, gentleman, of Craven Co., to
14 Mar. 1753   JOHN CLELAND, ESQ. Whereas by Indenture Tri-
Release & Confirmation   partite dated 1 June 1730 between RICHARD RIG-
                         BY, ESQ., of Misley Hall, Essex Co., & ANNE
his wife, 1 of the surviving daughters of JOHN PERRIE, formerly of Island
of Antigua, afterwards of St. James Parish, Westminster, Middlesex Co.,
of 1st part; GEORGE BAKER, merchant, of London, & DOROTHY his wife, another surviving daughter of JOHN PERRIE, of 2nd part; & the Hon. JOHN
CLELAND, gentleman, of the Parish of St. Peters Poor, London, & MARY his
wife, another surviving daughter of JOHN PERRIE, of 3rd part; the said
RICHARD & ANN RIGBY & the said GEORGE & DOROTHY BAKER, released to JOHN &
MARY CLELAND that plantation in SC devised to MARY by will of JOHN PERRIE;
& whereas by L & R dated 5 & 6 Feb. 1750, between the Hon. JOHN CLELAND,
of Georgetown, Craven Co., SC & MARY his wife, of the 1st part; & ARCHI-
BALD BAIRD & RICHARD GOUGH, gentlemen, of 2nd part, reciting that after
their marriage JOHN & MARY CLELAND had sold a plantation called Younghall,
part of the lands devised to MARY, to BAIRD & GOUGH for Ł 5250 currency,
which sum they applied to the purchasing of other lands in SC in lieu of
the plantation called Younghall & as a composition with ELISHA SCRIVEN &
others who had possessed themselves of certain lands near Georgetown, being part of said lands devised by JOHN PERRIE & who pretended to hold the
land by virtue of the Limitation Act; & also reciting that whereas a marriage was intended between FRANCIS KINLOCH & ANNE ISABELLA CLELAND,
daughter of JOHN & MARY CLELAND, they the said JOHN & MARY had conveyed
to BAIRD & GOUGH the tract of 1818 a. on Wehaw Creek, Prince George Parish, in trust for certain purposes; & whereas some doubts have arisen concerning the validity of the deed of confirmation & the right & property
in the said lands & in other large tracts near Georgetown in possession
of JOHN CLELAND on pretense that they belonged to JOHN PERRIE at the time
of his death & on pretense that KINLOCH & his heirs by virture of said
marriage will have a right to the reversion of the real estate mentioned
in the deed & said other lands near Georgetown after the death of JOHN &

MARY CLELAND, which may defeat the purpose of the deed & tend to prevent JOHN CLELAND from disposing of the other lands now in his possession; now, to confirm the rights of ELISHA SCRIVEN & other persons named in the deed of confirmation to the several lots of land, & of GEORGE PAWLEY & DANIEL LAROCHE as surviving trustees for the several trusts mentioned, as of the said JOHN & MARY CLELAND to so many parcels of land as reserved to them by the deed & plan of Georgetown, & for CLELAND & his heirs in their right to said other lands near Georgetown, & for Ł 20 paid by CLELAND to KINLOCH; KINLOCH now confirms the deed of confirmation & confirms to SCRIVEN, PAWLEY, LAROCHE, CLELAND & others, the lots mentioned & claimed by them. Witnesses: JAMES MICHIE, JAMES SIMPSON. Before JAMES BULLOCH, J.P. WILLIAM HOPTON, Register.

Book M-M, p. 265   JOHN DANIELL, gentleman, of New Hanover Co.,
27 & 28 Mar.   NC, & SARAH his wife, to GEORGE LOGAN & LIONEL
L & R   CHALMERS, of Berkeley Co., executors of estate of MARTHA LOGAN in trust for MARTHA LOGAN,
for Ł 300 SC money, that piece of low water mark land on Bay of Charleston, bounding E 78 ft. on Cooper River; N & S on other low water lots belonging to JOHN DANIEL; W on lot given to MARTHA my marriage settlement
from her mother MARTHA LOGAN, now deceased, now in possession of JOSEPH
WRAGG; which low water lands on 10 Dec. 1714 were granted by Gov. CHARLES
CRAVEN to COL. ROBERT DANIELL, who bequeathed them to his wife MARTHA,
who on 18 Feb. 1736 conveyed to JOHN DANIELL. Witnesses: HENRY SHAW,
WILLIAM (his mark) HANKINSON. Memo: It is hereby provided that JOHN
DANIELL grants no other right or title than he stands invested with by
deed dated 18 Feb. 1736 given him by his mother MARTHA LOGAN. Before
WILLIAM FORBES, J.P. of New Hanover Co., NC. WILLIAM HOPTON, Register.

Book M-M, p. 270   JOHN DANIELL to GEORGE LOGAN & LIONEL CHALMERS,
28 Mar. 1747   executors, in trust for MARTHA LOGAN, to es-
Discharge as Executors   tate of her mother, MARTHA LOGAN; a full discharge as executors. Witnesses: HENRY SHAW,
WILLIAM HOPTON. Before ROBERT AUSTIN, J.P. WILLIAM HOPTON, Register.

Book M-M, p. 270   JOHN TUCKER, & RUTH (her mark) his wife, of
5 Dec. 1723   Colleton Co., to BARNABY BULL, planter, of
Feoffment   Berkeley Co., for Ł 900 currency, 300 a. in
Colleton Co., bounding N on CAPT. HENRY
NICHOLS; E on JAMES & ROBERT MACKEWN; S on RALPH EMMS; W on HENRY NICHOLS.
Whereas WILLIAM, Earl of Craven, Palatine, & the Lords Proprs. by Gov.
JOHN ARCHDALE, on 9 Sept. 1696 granted RALPH EMMS 300 a. in Colleton Co.,
near the head of the N branch of Stono River, within land; which EMMS, by
will dated 16 Feb. 1711/2, bequeathed to his daughter, RUTH EMMS; now she
& her husband sell to BULL. Witnesses: THOMAS FARR, SR., THOMAS FARR,
JR. Before THOMAS FARR, SR. RUTH TUCKER renounced her dower before
THOMAS FARR, C.J. of Wilton Precinct Court, Colleton Co., on 5 Dec. 1723.
Memorial entered in Auditor's office 1 May 1733 in Book 4, fol. 53-54, by
JAMES ST. JOHN, Dep. Aud. WILLIAM HOPTON, Register.

Book M-M, p. 274   BURNABY BULL, ESQ., of Granville Co., to
18 & 19 Jan. 1749   ALGERNOON WILSON, planter, of Colleton Co.,
L & R   for Ł 1500 SC money, 300 a. in Colleton Co.,
bounding N & W on MR. NICHOLS; S on JOHN GOD-
FREY; E on ROBERT MACKEWN; which land was granted by the Lords Proprs. to
RALPH EMMS on 9 Sept. 1696. Witnesses: Lt. Gov. WILLIAM BULL, JR.,
STEPHEN BULL, JR. Before WILLIAM BULL, JR. WILLIAM HOPTON, Register.

Book M-M, p. 277   ROBERT STEVENS, planter, of Stono, devisee &
13 & 14 Sept. 1747   executor of will of HEZEKIAH EMMES, planter,
L & R   of St. Pauls Parish; & ANN (her mark) STEVENS
his wife; to WILLIAM BUTLER, storekeeper, of
same place; for Ł 1595 SC money, 693 a. in Colleton Co.; whereas the
Lords Proprs. on 9 Sept. 1696 by Gov. JOHN ARCHDALE, granted RALPH SPOAD
100 a. in Colleton Co., on S side of branch of Stono River; & he by deed
of feoffment dated 4 Nov. 1696 endorsed on said grant sold the 100 a. to
ALEXANDER WEDGBURY; & whereas JOHN WILLIAMSON, on 4 Aug. 1701, sold to
said WEDGBURY 100 a. on E side of the above 100 a.; & WEDGBURY on 1 July
1702 sold the 2 tracts to RALPH EMMS, SR., planter; & whereas the Lords
Proprs. on 8 Aug. 1704, by Gov. NATHANIEL JOHNSON, granted JOHN

WILLIAMSON 400 a. in Colleton Co., which WILLIAMSON, on 17 Nov. 1704 sold
to RALPH EMMS; & whereas the Lords Proprs. on 8 Feb. 1704, by Gov. NA-
THANIEL JOHNSON granted JOHN WILLIAMSON 1000 a. in Colleton Co., on E
side of the 100 a. tract sold by WILLIAMSON to WEDGBURY; & whereas WIL-
LIAMSON on 22 May 1706 sold RALPH EMMS 360 a., part of the 1000 a., according to plat in Grant Book A, fol. 253; so that RALPH EMMS became owner of 4 adjacent tracts, or 960 a., which he bequeathed to his son WIL-
LIAM EMMS; & he, by L & R dated 20 & 21 July 1730, sold to JOHN TUCKER
200 a. out of the W part of the 960 a., adjoining COL. JOHN SMITH'S land;
& whereas by a resurvey of the 400 a. it was found that 67 a. at the SW
corner was contained in a prior grant to HENRY WILLIAMSON & was accordingly pricked off the plat of WILLIAM EMM'S land, so that the 960 a. was
reduced to 693 a., because of 200 a. having been sold by WILLIAM EMMS to
JOHN TUCKER, & the 67 a. mentioned; the 693 a. bounding N on the marsh of
the middle branch of Stono River; E on BENJAMIN WILLIAMSON; S on estate
of HENRY WILLIAMSON; W on JOHN TUCKER'S 200 a.; & whereas WILLIAM EMMS
died intestate in 1730 & the premises descended to his brother & heir,
HEZEKIAH EMMS; who by will dated 24 Oct. 1739 bequeathed the 693 a. to
his loving friend, ROBERT STEVENS, planter; now he sells the land to WIL-
LIAM BUTLER. Witnesses: STEPHEN FITCH, DAVID STEVENS, JOHN WILLIAMS.
Before JAMES BULLOCK, J.P. WILLIAM HOPTON, Register.

Book M-M, p. 284   BENJAMIN LAW, planter, of Christ Church Par-
4 & 5 May 1738   ish, to JOHN ALLEN, merchant, of Charleston,
L & R   for Ł 3800 currency, 615 a. in Christ Church
                        Parish, bounding N on CAPT. THOMAS BOONE &
MRS. BRIDGET FRY; W on CAPT. JACOB BOND; S & E on JAMES PAYNE & THOMAS
BOONE. Witnesses: JAMES PAINE, ROBERT PAINE, BRYAN KYANADY. Before
THOMAS LAMBOLL, J.Q. WILLIAM HOPTON, Register. Plat of 615 a. in Christ
Church Parish exclusive of 100 a. belonging to DR. WHITE, dated 4 May
1738.

Book M-M, p. 288   SARAH LAW, widow of BENJAMIN LAW, planter, of
29 Sept. 1740   Christ Church Parish, for Ł 500 currency, re-
Renunciation of Dower   nounces all her claim to the 615 a. which her
                        husband, BENJAMIN LAW, sold on 4 & 5 May 1738
to JOHN ALLEN, merchant, of Charleston. (See p. 284). Witnesses: THOMAS
LAMBOLL, THOMAS BARKSDALE. Before JACOB MOTTE, J.P. WILLIAM HOPTON,
Register.

Book M-M, p. 290   JOHN BALLANTINE, gentleman, & ELIZABETH (her
5 & 6 June 1733   mark) his wife; & JAMES BALLANTINE, gentleman;
L & R   to SOLOMON MIDDLETON, pilot; all of Charles-
                        ton; for Ł 250 currency, that part of lot #297
in Charleston, bounding W 25 ft. on that broad street leading from the
late old church to White Point; N 113-1/2 ft. on the part belonging to
EDMUND HOLLAND, pilot; E on lots 297 & 298 belonging to JOHN VANDERHORST;
S on JOHN & JAMES BALLANTINE. Whereas WILLIAM, Earl of Crave, Palatine,
& the Lords Proprs., through Gov. THOMAS SMITH, Landgrave, on 12 Sept.
1692 granted SUSANNA VAREEN, widow, 2 lots in Charleston, containing 1 a.
English measure, known as #297 & 298; which she sold on 29 June 1695 to
JOHN VANDERHORST, of Charleston; & whereas on 8 Sept. 1696 he sold a part
of the 2 lots to JOHN STEWART, gentleman; who on 29 Oct. 1706, reconveyed
to JOHN VANDERHORST; & whereas VANDERHORST on 12 Jan. 1711 sold to PAT-
RICK BALLANTINE that part of lot #297 bounding W 144 ft. on the broad
street running from the late old church to the White Point; N & E on
parts of lots 297 & 298 belonging to JOHN VANDERHORST; S 144 ft. on a
neighborhood alley; making a square; & whereas BALLANTINE bequeathed that
part of lot #297 to his sons, JOHN & JAMES; now they sell a part of the
square to MIDDLETON. Witnesses: JOSEPH MASSEY, JOSHUA MORGAN, JOHN SAV-
AGE. It is further agreed that for Ł 20 currency paid 9 Apr. 1734 JOHN &
ELIZABETH BALLANTINE sell to SOLOMON MIDDLETON 2 feet more, adjoining
that purchased by MIDDLETON. Witnesses: EDWARD MORRIS, JOHN MILNER. Before JACOB MOTTE, J.P. WILLIAM HOPTON, Register.

Book M-M, p. 296   SOLOMON MIDDLETON, pilot, & ANNA his wife, to
2 & 3 May 1737   JOHN ALLEN, merchant, both of Charleston, for
L & R   Ł 1500 currency, that part of lot #297, with
                        the house thereon, bounding N 113-1/2 ft. on
the part belonging to EDMUND HOLLAND; E 27 ft. on JOHN VANDERHORST; S on

JOHN & JAMES BALLANTINE; W on the broad street running from the late old
church to White Point. Witnesses: JAMES GRAEME, KATHERINE (her mark)
MIDDLETON, THOMAS HUTCHINSON. Before ROBERT AUSTIN, J.P. WILLIAM HOP-
TON, Register.

Book M-M, p. 300   JOHN BALLANTINE, gentleman, of Charleston, &
23 & 24 Feb. 1740   ELIZABETH (her mark) his wife, to JOHN ALLEN,
L & R   gentleman, of Berkeley Co., for Ł 210 curren-
                          cy, that piece of land on E side the great
street leading from Ashley River N to the old churchyard & market place
at or near the White Point; bounding W 14 ft. on said street; N on JOHN
ALLEN (formerly SOLOMON MIDDLETON); bounding E on JOHN BROWNELL; S 112
ft. on JOHN BALLANTINE. Witnesses: JAMES PARKER, JOHN SAVAGE. Before
JACOB MOTTE, J.P. WILLIAM HOPTON, Register.

Book M-M, p. 304   MARY OLIVER, widow, of GEORGE OLIVER, releases
15 May 1744   & confirms to JAMES WHITE, his title to 1/2 a
Release & Confirmation   tract of 100 a. Whereas by L & R dated 26 &
                          27 Oct. 1737 GEORGE OLIVER, gentleman, of
Christ Church Parish, & MARY his then wife (1 of the daughters & co-heirs
of JOHN SIMES, gentleman, of Berkeley Co.), sold to JAMES WHITE, surgeon,
of Christ Church Parish, MARY OLIVER'S undivided half part of 100 a.
formerly the estate of JOHN SIMES which descended equally to MARY & her
sister SARAH, wife of said JAMES WHITE; which land, according to conveyance from ANN BEVILL, widow of TIMOTHY BEVILL, to JOHN SIMES, dated 1
June 1706 was specified as bounding NE & NW on RICHARD BUTLER; SE & SW on
FRANCIS JONES; & was part of a larger tract belonging to said FRANCIS
JONES; & whereas MARY was then under the coverture of GEORGE OLIVER, but
by his death, now legally qualified to perfect WHITE'S title; now she releases all her claim to half the 100 a. Witnesses: JOHN WINGOOD, THOMAS
LOREY. Before WILLIAM HENDRICK, J.P. WILLIAM HOPTON, Register.

Book M-M, p. 306   JAMES WHITE, chirurgeon, of Berkeley Co., &
28 & 29 June 1744   SARAH his wife, 1 of the daughters & co-heirs
L & R   of JOHN SIMES, to JOHN ALLEN, gentleman, of
                          Charleston, for Ł 800 currency, 100 a. now
bounding on all sides on lands of JOHN ALLEN. Whereas JOHN SIMES owned
100 a. in Christ Church Parish, which he had purchased from ANNE BEAVILL,
widow of TIMOTHY BEAVILL, on 1 June 1706, then bounding NE & NW on RICH-
ARD BUTLER; SE & SW on FRANCIS JONES; being part of a larger tract formerly belonging to FRANCIS JONES; & whereas the 100 a. descended to his 2
daughters, MARY (now widow of GEORGE OLIVER) & SARAH, wife of said JAMES
WHITE, as coheirs; & whereas by L & R dated 26 & 26 Oct. 1737 GEORGE &
MARY OLIVER sold to JAMES & SARAH WHITE the undivided half belonging to
MARY; & whereas, since the death of GEORGE OLIVER, MARY on 15 May last
perfected JAMES WHITE'S title to said MARY'S half; now JAMES & SARAH
WHITE sell the whole 100 a. to ALLEN. Witnesses: JOHN SMITH, JOSEPH HES-
KETT. Before ROBERT AUSTIN, J.P. WILLIAM HOPTON, Register.

Book M-M, p. 312   JOHN SAVAGE, merchant, & ANNE his wife, to
1 & 2 Feb. 1753   WILLIAM SCOTT, merchant, both of Charleston,
L & R   for Ł 5000 SC money, that part of lot #297 in
                          Charleston with the tenement thereon; also
715 a. in Christ Church Parish; also 2 adjacent plantations on Dawfauskie
Island, in Granville Co., 1 of 400 a., the other 600 a. Whereas JOHN
ALLEN, gentleman, of Charleston, owned part of a lot in Charleston known
as #297, with a tenement thereon, bounding W 41 ft. on a great street
leading N from Ashley River to Broad Street, N 113-1/2 ft. on DANIEL
CRAWFORD (formerly EDMUND HOLLAND); E on JOHN VANDERHORST; S on heirs of
JOHN BALLANTINE; also 615 a. in Christ Church Parish, bounding N on CAPT.
THOMAS BOONE & on MRS. FRY; W on CAPT. JACOB BOND; S & E on JAMES PAINE &
THOMAS BOONE; which 615 a. ALLEN purchased from BENJAMIN LAW on 4 & 5 May
1738; also 100 a. bounding on all sides on above 615 a., conveyed to
ALLEN by JAMES WHITE & SARAH his wife by L & R dated 28 & 29 June 1744;
also 2 adjoining plantations on Dawfauskie Island, Granville Co., 1 of
400 a., the other of 500 a., bounding N & NE on ELIZABETH VARNER & HUGH
EVANS; SE on HUGH EVANS & JOHN WRIGHT; SE & SW on Day's Creek, mouth of
New River, West River, & VARNERS land; & whereas by will dated 5 Mar.
1747 devised all his real estate to his beloved wife, ANN ALLEN (now ANN
SAVAGE, party hereto); now she & her present husband, JOHN SAVAGE, sell

the various tracts to SCOTT. Witnesses: JAMES MACKAY, JOHN REMINGTON.
Before JACOB MOTTE, J.P. WILLIAM HOPTON, Register.

Book M-M, p. 318   WILLIAM SCOTT, merchant, to JOHN SAVAGE, mer-
9 & 10 Feb. 1753   chant, both of Charleston, for Ł 5100 currency,
L & R   part of lot #297, with tenement, on E side of
a certain great street leading N from Ashely
River to Broad Street, bounding 41 ft. on said street; N 113-1/2 ft. on
DANIEL CRAWFORD (formerly EDMUND HOLLAND); E on JOHN VANDERHORST; S on
heirs of JO_N BALLANTINE; also 715 a. in Christ Church Parish, bounding N
on CAPT. THOMAS BOONE & MRS. FRY; W on CAPT. JACOB BOND; S & E on JAMES
PAINE & THOMAS BOONE; also 2 adjoining plantations on Dawfuskie Island,
in Granville Co., 1 of 400 a., the other of 500 a., bounding N & NE on
ELIZABETH VARNER & HUGH EVANS; SE on HUGH EVANS & JOHN WRIGHT; SE & SW on
Day's Creek, mouth of New River & West River, & VARNERS land. Witnesses:
JAMES MACKAY, JOHN REMINGTON. Before JACOB MOTTE, J.P. WILLIAM HOPTON,
Register.

Book M-M, p. 322   JOSEPH VANDERHORST, planter, of Christ Church
23 & 24 Nov. 1741   Parish (eldest brother & heir of ANDREW VAN-
L & R   DERHORST who was son & devisee of JOHN VANDER-
HORST, planter, of Berkeley Co.), & MARY his
wife, to ARNOLDUS VANDERHORST, another son of said JOHN VANDER-
HORST, for
Ł 500 currency, that part of a tract of 500 a. bequeathed by JOHN VANDER-
HORST, the father, to said ANDREW VANDERHORST, bounding S on the part bequeathed to said ARNOLDUS VANDERHORST; E on MRS. JOHN BAXTER; W on a
creek. Whereas JOHN VANDERHORST, the father, owned 500 a. in Christ
Church Parish, Berkeley Co., on which he lived, being half a tract of
1000 a. called The Four Men's Ramble; being the half bounding on NW Creek
out of Wando River; & by will dated 29 Nov. 1738 bequeathed the S part
(as divided on a plat lately surveyed & made by THOMAS WITTER by a line
drawn from a low cedar post to a small pine on the sands) to his son
ARNOLDUS, bounding S on ANDREW RUTLEDGE; E & W on COL. THOMAS LYNCH; N on
the part where he lived; & bequeathed to son ANDREW VANDERHORST the other
or N part with all the buildings & improvements, bounding S on ARNOLDUS
VANDERHORST; E on JOHN BAXTER; W on the creek; & whereas ANDREW, after
his fathers death, died a minor & his tract descended to JOSEPH VANDER-
HORST, his eldest brother & heir-at-law; now JOSEPH VANDERHORST sells his
tract to ARNOLDUS VANDERHORST. Witnesses: NATHANIEL NEWELL, JOHN ATCHI-
SON. Before WILLIAM HENDRICK, J.P. WILLIAM HOPTON, Register.

Book M-M, p. 327   THOMAS LYNCH, planter, & ELIZABETH his wife,
4 & 5 Jan. 1749   of Craven Co., to ARNOLDUS VANDERHORST, of
L & R   Berkeley Co., for Ł 1665 currency, 333 a.,
English measure, in Christ Church Parish,
bounding NW on ARNOLDUS VANDERHORST; NE on JOHN BAXTER; SE on JOHN ATCHI-
SON & a creek of Wando River; SW on JOHN RUTLEDGE; which tract the Lords
Proprs. on 8 Sept. 1697 granted EDMUND BELLINGER; who on 28 Apr. 1704,
for Ł 150 currency, sold to ALEXANDER PARRIS of Charleston; who on 22
Nov. 1710, for Ł 280 currency, conveyed to THOMAS LYNCH, of Berkeley Co.,
father of THOMAS LYNCH, party hereto. Witnesses: JOSEPH WHELDON, MARY
BONELL. Before ROBERT AUSTIN, J.P. WILLIAM HOPTON, Register.

DEEDS BOOK "N-N"
APR. 1753 -- NOV. 1753

Book N-N, p. 1   ARCHIBALD NEILL, planter, & SARAH his wife, of
2 & 3 Apr. 1753   Berkeley Co., to ANTHONY MATHEWES, ESQ., of
L & R   Charleston, for Ł 1020 currency, 100 a. in
Berkeley Co., bounding S on Newton Creek; W on
COL. ARTHUR HALL; E on JOHN WILKINS; N on LAMBRIGHT WILKINS & WILLIAM
WILKINS; which tract was granted by the Lords Proprs. in May 1699 to
CHRISTOPHER JARRARD & by several mesne conveyances became vested in NEILL.
Witnesses: JAMES SIMPSON, JOHN TROUP. Before JAMES MICHIE, J.P. WILLIAM
HOPTON, Register.

Book N-N, p. 8   HENRY HYRNE, ESQ., & ELIZABETH CLARKE HYRNE,
21 Oct. 1752   his wife, to SAMUEL BLINCOE, planter, both of

L & R   Colleton Co., for ₺ 500 currency, 348 a. in
                             Colleton Co., bounding N on HENRY HYRNE; E on
WILLIAM WILKINS; S on EDMUND BELLINGER; W on JOHN HILL; according to
Grant dated 27 Aug. 1751. Witnesses: ADAM CULLIATT, JR., HENRY HYRNE,
JR. Before JAMES SKIRVING, J.P. WILLIAM HOPTON, Register.

Book N-N, p. 13   The Rev. MR. LEVI DURAND, rector of Christ
8 & 9 Dec. 1748   Church Parish, & SUSANNAH, his wife, (lately
L & R   SUSANNAH HEXT, widow & devisee of HUGH HEXT,
                            planter, of Colleton Co., who was son & de-
visee of AMIAS HEXT, planter, of St. Pauls Parish), to ELIZABETH NICHOLS
(late widow of FRANCIS HEXT, JR., planter, of Johns Island) & ELIZABETH
HEXT, daughter of FRANCIS HEXT; for ₺ 2000 currency paid by FRANCIS HEXT
during his lifetime & ₺ 200 paid by ELIZABETH NICHOLS & ELIZABETH HEXT;
380 a. on Johns Island. Whereas AMIAS HEXT owned 380 a. on Johns Island,
bounding E on JOHN STANYARNE; S on the parsonage; W on ISAAC WAIGHT; N on
FRANCIS HEXT, JR., which he bequeathed to his son, HUGH HEXT; who by will
dated 9 Nov. 1744 bequeathed the tract to his wife SUSANNAH during her
lifetime, then to his son THOMAS HEXT; but in case THOMAS should die before reaching 21, then to SUSANNAH; & whereas THOMAS died soon after his
father, SUSANNAH his mother, inherited, later marrying LEVI DURAND, party
hereto; & whereas LEVI & SUSANNAH DURAND on 5 July 1745 agreed to sell
the 380 a. to FRANCIS HEXT for ₺ 2000 currency, & FRANCIS agreed to settle the tract on his wife ELIZABETH & his child, ELIZABETH (both parties
hereto), but FRANCIS died before the transfer of property; now the sale
is completed. Witnesses: ELIZABETH CORNISH, CHARLES PINCKNEY. Payment
made through JOHN STANYARNE. Before WILLIAM PINCKNEY, J.P. WILLIAM HOP-
TON, Register.

Book N-N, p. 21   RAWLINS LOWNDES, P.M., to JOHN STANYARNE, at
16 Apr. 1753   public auction, for ₺ 571:4:6 SC money, 380 a.
Sale   on Johns Island. Whereas FRANCIS HEXT, plant-
                           er, owned 380 a. on Johns Island, bounding E
on JOHN STANYARNE; S on the parsonage; W on ISAAC WAITE; N on FRANCIS
HEXT; which he had purchased from LEVI DURAND, rector of Christ Church
Parish, & SUSANNAH his wife (see p. 13) on 9 Dec. 1748; & whereas Lt.
JOHN PAYNE, of H.M.S. Rose, obtained a judgement against JOHN STANYARNE &
WILLIAM HEXT, executors of will of FRANCIS HEXT, JR., for ₺ 300 British &
costs, which sums the P.M. was commanded by CHARLES PINCKNEY, C.J. to
levy on the estate left by HEXT; now LOWNDES sells the 380 a. to STAN-
YARNE. Witnesses: ALEXANDER MCGREGOR, WILLIAM READ. Before ALEXANDER
STEWART, J.P. WILLIAM HOPTON, Register.

Book N-N, p. 24   DEBORAH FISHER, soapboiler, to JOSEPH MOODY,
22 & 23 Jan. 1753   merchant, both of Charleston, for ₺ 1000 cur-
L & R   rency, lot #104 in Charleston, bounding N 19
                           ft. 2 in. on Broad Street, S on lot belonging
to French trustees; E 208 ft. on PAUL SMICHER; W on PETER BOCQUETT. Witnesses: PETER LEGAR, JR., AGNES PARKER, JAMES FISHER. Before JOHN DART,
J.P. WILLIAM HOPTON, Register.

Book N-N, p. 29   JEREMIAH CUTTINOE, gunsmith, & ANN JUDITH, his
6 Apr. 1753   wife, of Georgetown, to HENRY BOSSARD, SR.,
L & R   planter, of Prince George Parish, for ₺ 460
                           currency, 1/2 of lot #88 in Georgetown with
tenement thereon, bounding SE 108-1/2 ft. on Screven Street; NE 100 ft.
on DANIEL BOURGET'S lot #112; NW on WILLIAM THOMAS'S lot #87; SW on
Princess Street. Witnesses: ZACHARIAH BRAZIER, HENRY LEWIS. Before
THOMAS HASELL, J.P. WILLIAM HOPTON, Register.

Book N-N, p. 34   OBADIAH WILKINS, planter, to THOMAS HANSCOMB,
29 & 30 Mar. 1753   planter, both of Colleton Co., for ₺ 1000 cur-
L & R   rency, 165 a. on Johns Island, Colleton Co.,
                           conveyed to OBADIAH WILKINS by ARCHIBALD WIL-
KINS, planter, bounding N on JOHN SPENCER; E on JONATHAN WILKINS; S on A.
B. Poolaw Creek; W on THOMAS FLEMING. Witnesses: CHARLES PINCKNEY, JR.,
PETER FREER. Before WILLIAM PINCKNEY, J.P. WILLIAM HOPTON, Register.

Book N-N, p. 40   THOMAS SMITH the younger, merchant, & SARAH
_____ 1752   his wife, of Charleston, to BENJAMIN COACHMAN,

gentleman, of Goose Creek, for £ 2000 currency, 700 a., the residue of
940 a., on E side of Goose Creek. Whereas the Lords Proprs. on 14 July
1680 granted BARNARD SCHENCKINGH 700 a. on Goose Creek, bounding S on
JONAH LYNCH & the creek; N on vacant land; W on JOHN MELL & the creek; E
on JONAH LYNCH & JOHN MAVERICK & vacant land; whereas the Lords Proprs.
on 28 Sept. 1702 granted BENJAMIN SCHENCKINGH, son of said BARNARD, 1040
a. (being the said 700 granted his father & 340 more); whereas he, on 1
Nov. 1703, sold to WILLOUGHBY GIBBES, widow, of Island of Barbados 940 a.,
part of the 1040 a., on E side of Goose Creek, & whereas MARGARET
SCHENCKINGH, wife of BENJAMIN, on 27 Jan. 1703 voluntarily renounced her
dower in the 940 a. to WILLOUGHBY GIBBES before NICHOLAS TROTT, C.J., &
whereas WILLOUGHBY GIBBES sold 200 a. & the 740 a. remaining were inherited by her son PHILIP GIBBES, gentleman, of Island of Barbados; & whereas he, on 5 & 6 Mar. 1743, sold the plantation to ROGER MOORE, ESQ., of
Cape Fear, NC & whereas ELIZABETH GIBBES, wife of PHILIP, on 12 Mar. 1746
voluntarily renounced her dower to MOORE before JAMES BRUCE, C.J. of St.
Michael's Precinct, Barbados; & whereas ROGER MOORE on 1 Dec. 1747 conveyed the tract to THOMAS SMITH; & whereas, in order to remove any doubt
regarding the validity of conveyance from ROGER MOORE (broken page) to
Hanover Co. _____ son & heir of ROGER _____ second son & heir of ROGER ___
which said GEORGE MOORE & WILLIAM MOORE, who are also residuary devisees
of ROGER MOORE, by their release & confirmation dated 29 July 1751 confirmed THOMAS SMITH'S title; now SMITH conveys to COACHMAN. Witnesses:
THOMAS AKIN, WILLIAM BAMPFIELD. Before JAMES WRIGHT, J.P. WILLIAM HOP-
TON, Register.

Book N-N, p. 48   GEORGE SNOW, cooper, of Parish of St. Thomas &
3 & 4 May 1753   St. Dennis, eldest son & heir of THOMAS SNOW,
L & R   joiner, to SIR ALEXANDER NISBETT of Dean Bar-
                         ony, for £ 500 currency, part of a lot in
Charleston, bounding N 30 ft. on a street leading westward from Cooper
River by the French Church; E on ROBERT HUME; S on THOMAS CARY; W on 113-
1/2 ft. on other part same lot. Witnesses: JOHN TROUP, JAMES SIMPSON.
Before JAMES MICHIE, J.P. WILLIAM HOPTON, Register.

Book N-N, p. 53   The Hon. JOHN CLELAND, & MARY his wife, to
20 & 21 Mar. 1753   THOMAS MITCHELL, planter, for £ 1000 currency,
L & R   105-1/3 a., part of a tract lately granted to
                         CLELAND, on S side Black River, near its mouth
in Craven Co. Witnesses: PETER MONCLAR, JOHN TROUP. Before JAMES MICHIE,
J.P. WILLIAM HOPTON, Register. Plat by T. HASELL dated 29 Nov. 1752.

Book N-N, p. 60   SAMUEL STOCKS, planter, eldest son & heir of
7 & 8 May 1753   SAMUEL STOCKS the elder, planter, to NATHANIEL
L & R   BROWN, planter, all of Berkeley Co., for
                         £ 1050 currency, 210 a. on S side Ashley River,
in St. Andrews Parish, Berkeley Co., bounding N on WILLIAM BULL, JR., E
on MR. SAMWAYS; S on MR. GODFREY (now JOHN LINING) & on MR. LESADE (now
MR. DEVEAUX); W on NATHANIEL BROWN (formerly ROBERT WILKINSON); which 210
a. is part of 1080 a. granted by the Lords Proprs. & Gov. NATHANIEL JOHN-
SON on 14 May 1707 to WILLIAM BULL, planter, father of said WILLIAM BULL,
JR., who, with MARY, his wife, conveyed 210 a. on 27 Aug. 1707 to JOHN
GIRARDEAU, who willed it to his only son PETER GIRARDEAU; who in 1736,
with his wife, ELIZABETH, sold to SAMUEL STOCKS the elder; who died in-
testate & his son SAMUEL inherited; now he conveys to BROWN. Witnesses:
JOHN RIVERS, RICHARD GODFREY, BENJAMIN GODFREY. Before WILLIAM PINCKNEY,
J.P. WILLIAM HOPTON, Register.

Book N-N, p. 70   JACOB MOTTE, ESQ., to the Hon. CHARLES PINCK-
29 & 30 Dec. 1752   NEY, HECTOR BERENGER DEBEAUFAIN, & WILLIAM
L & R   BULL, JR., members of H.M. Council, & DAVIS
                         CAW, GABRIEL MANIGAULT, THOMAS SMITH, JOHN
SAVAGE, & RAWLINS LOWNDES, ESQRS., all of Charleston. Whereas JACOB
MOTTE for several years past has been Public Treasure & Receiver of SC &
in that capacity received large sums of money (broken page) & has not
sufficient cash to make good the several payments but is willing to assign his real & personal estate to certain trustees, on behalf of the
public to raise money to be applied first towards exchanging outstanding
tax certificates issued by him as treasurer in 1746, 1747, 1748, 1749,
1750 & 1751; & whereas JACOB MOTTE computed to amount about £ 90,000

currency & said trustees out of friendship to him & their zeal for public
service are willing to act as trustees without compensation, MOTTE turns
over to them that part of lot #7 on N side of Tradd Street, which formerly belonged to ROBERT TRADD, gentleman, & conveyed by his executors,
MILES BREWTON & THOMAS LAMBOLL to JACOB MOTTE, with a store in front occupied by JOHN COOPER & ROBERT WILLIAMS, & 2 stores in the back occupied
by JAMES IRVINS, ESQ.; also MOTTE'S wharf on the Bay with the contiguous
shoal & low water lot, bounding N on heirs of JAMES OSMOND; W on the curtain line; E on Cooper River; S on the Public Market & lands & shoal lot
belonging to JAMES MATHEWS; also MOTTE'S half of the house & shop occupied by JAMES LAURENS & Co., also MOTTE'S half of the adjoining house &
store in Tradd Street near the Bay occupied by THOMAS BONNY, formerly the
estate of ROBERT TRADD & conveyed to MOTTE by THOMAS SHUBRICK & SARAH his
wife; also the W end of lot #60 formerly the estate of ROBERT TRADD,
bounding N 100 ft. 8 in. on Tradd Street; W _____ on old Church Street; E
on heirs of DANIEL TOWNSEND; also 56-1/3 a. In Christ Church Parish purchased by MOTTE from HENRY GRAY, bounding NW on part of same tract belonging to GRAY; NE on the Broad Road of the Parish & on GRAY & on PETER
VILLEPONTEAUX; SW on Hogg Island Creek; also 19 a. 3 roods in said Parish
sold to MOTTE by RAWLINS LOWNDES, P.M. of SC & formerly part of PETER
VILLEPONTEAUX'S plantation, bounding SE & NE on VILLEPONTEAUX; NW on JA-
COB MOTTE; also 1000 a. near Orangeburgh Township granted MOTTE by Lt.
Gov. THOMAS BROUGHTON on 2 June 1736 (?) then bounding on all sides on
vacant land also 29 Negro & other slaves, all cattle, horses, sheep,
plate, household furniture & other goods mentioned in schedule #1 also
all bonds, mortgages, etc., mentioned in schedule #2; & whereas MOTTE'S
wife is absent from the Province & a renunciation of dower cannot be obtained from her MOTTE agrees that should she come back & not renounce her
title within 1 month after arrival he will pay the trustees Ł 4000 currency. Witnesses: JAMES LAURENS, JOSEPH KERSHAW. Before ROBERT AUSTIN,
J.P. WILLIAM HOPTON, Register. Schedule 1 & 2 given. Names listed in
#2: ISAAC MOTTE; PETER LEGER; ROBERT MACMURDY; WILLIAM FLEMING; ANDREW
JOHNSTON; THOMAS DOUGHTY; HUGH CARTWRIGHT; ZACHARIAH VILLEPONTEAU; SAMUEL
WRAGG, JR.; JOB ROTHMAHLER; PAUL TRAPIER; HENRY HYRNE; BURREL HYRNE; WIL-
LIAM BUTLER; ELISHA BUTLER; THOMAS ROSE; CHRISTOPHER GADSDEN; JOSEPH
WRAGG; RICHARD LAMBTON; CHILDERMAS CROFT; RICHARD BAKER; JOHN JENKINS;
DAVID ADAMS; JOHN FRAMPTON; SAMUEL JONES; OBADIAH WILKINS; VINCENT LAY-
CROFT; JOHN HEARN; JOHN PARSONS; JOHN TUCKER; DANIEL SLADE; A. SCHERMER-
HORN; WILLIAM FULWOOD; JONATHAN BRYAN; EDWARD WILKINSON; JOHN RAVEN BE-
DON; WILLIAM FORBIS; JOSEPH PICKERING; RICHARD CAPERS; JOHN MCIVER; WIL-
LIAM STONE; JOHN WHITE; ELIAS FOISSIN; JOHN ROYER; THOMAS CHARNOCK; JO-
SEPH SHUTE; JOHN CROKATT; THOMAS SHUBRICK; MORGAN SABB; MILLER ST. JOHN.

Book N-N, p. 87   MATHEW BEAIRD, to MARGARET O'NEALE, widow, of
29 May & 1 June 1752   Berkeley Co., for Ł 200 currency, 500 a. in
L & R   Berkeley Co., bounding N on Santee River;
                         other sides on Landgrave TRENCH; which land
was granted 14 Nov. 1704 by NATHANIEL JOHNSON, JAMES MOORE, & JOB HOWES,
Lords Proprs. to JAMES BEAIRD. Witnesses: JAMES BLEAR, JAMES DEALE.
ROBERT BROWN, J.P. WILLIAM HOPTON, Register.

Book N-N, p. 93   PETER SANDERS, saddler, to WILLIAM HOPTON,
14 & 15 May 1753   merchant, both of Charleston, as security on
L & R by Mortgage   bond of even date in penal sum of Ł 494:11:0
                         for payment of Ł 247:5:6 currency, with in-
terest, on 15 May 1754; the E part of lot #207 in Charleston, bounding S
40 ft. on Guignard Street, E 56 ft. on another street also called Guignard Street; N 40 ft. on lot #123 belonging to heirs of SARAH TROTT; W
56 ft. on the part belonging to JOSEPH WARD. Whereas lot #207 was originally granted on 17 May 1694 to PETER GERARD; who devised the lot to his
daughter JUDITH who married HENRY SIMMONDS, & their son HENRY SIMMONDS,
gentleman, now of Bladen Co., NC, inherited; & he, by his attorney PETER
SIMMONDS, by L & R dated 9 & 10 June 1748 sold the lot to THOMAS SMITH,
JR., merchant, of Charleston; who by L & R dated 20 & 21 Jan. 1752 sold
the E half to JOSEPH WARD, merchant, & PETER SANDERS, as tenants in common & not as joint tenants; & whereas WARD & SANDERS by deed of partition
dated 31 Aug. 1752 divided their lot equally, & SANDERS was allotted the
eastern 40 ft. & the western 43-1/2 ft. as his share, & WARD received
83-1/2 ft. of the half lot, lying in the middle between the eastern 40
ft. & the western 43-1/2 ft. allotted to SANDERS as his share; now

292

SANDERS mortgaged his E lot to HOPTON. Witnesses: THOMAS LINTHWAITE, PETER JOHN MONCLAR. Before JOHN CLELAND, J.P. WILLIAM HOPTON, Register. On 14 Jan. 1755 HOPTON declared mortgage satisfied. Witness: PETER MON-CLAR.

Book N-N, p. 102   GEORGE SAXBY, ESQ., & ELIZABETH his wife, of
2 & 3 Feb. 1753   Charleston, to GEORGE CUSSINGS, planter, for
L & R   Ł 5500 currency, 5 adjacent tracts in Colleton
                       Co., 100 a. purchased by JOHN GODFREY, plant-
er, from THOMAS ELLIOTT, SR., the original grantee; 72 a.; & 340 a., both
purchased by GODFREY from ELLIOTT; which 3 tracts were conveyed by JOHN
GODFREY & MARY, his wife, to ALEXANDER HEXT, planter, of St. Johns Island;
whose executors sold to JOHN SEABROOK, planter; who conveyed to GEORGE
SAXBY; 58 a. purchased from MARTHA WILLIAMSON; & 210 a. lately purchased
by GEORGE SAXBY from THOMAS ELLIOTT, planter; total 780 a., bounding N on
THOMAS ELLIOTT; S on MRS. GREEN; E on THOMAS ELLIOTT & WILLIAM FAIRCHILDS;
W on RIVER STANYARNE & THOMAS ELLIOTT. Witnesses: JOHN RATTRAY, GEORGE
JACKSON. Before DANIEL CRAWFORD, J.P. WILLIAM HOPTON, Register. Plat
given.

Book N-N, p. 110   WILLIAM CHAPMAN, JR., planter, of James Is-
23 & 24 May 1753   land, to PETER PERRY, planter, of St. Pauls
L & R   Parish, for Ł 1892 currency, 473 a. on St.
                       Helena's Island, Granville Co., bounding W & S
on WILLIAM CHAPMAN; NW on Chapman's Creek; NE on RICHARD CAPERS; according to plat dated 12 May 1720. Witnesses: CHRISTOPHER GUY, ROBERT JOHN-
SON, JOHN MCCALL. Before JACOB MOTTE, J.P. WILLIAM HOPTON, Register.

Book N-N, p. 117   THOMAS JAMSON, planter, & ANNE his wife, to
18 Oct. 1748   PHILIP PEROT, cooper, both of Berkeley Co.,
Release   for Ł 350 currency, 400 a. in Berkeley Co.,
                       bounding S on ABRAHAM SANDERS; other sides on
vacant land; which tract was granted on 7 Aug. 1735 to THOMAS POWELL.
Witnesses: HENRY DE ST. JULIEN, JOHN CHOVENS, DAVID LAFONS. Before NA-
THANIEL BROUGHTON, J.P. A memorial entered in Auditor's Book D. #3, fol.
22 on 27 May 1753 by JAMES MICHIE, Dep. Aud. WILLIAM HOPTON, Register.

Book N-N, p. 120   FRANCIS YONGE, planter, & SARAH his wife, to
9 & 10 May 1753   SUSANNAH WEDDERBURN, widow, of Charleston, for
L & R   Ł 1600 currency, part of lot #42 in Charleston,
                       bounding N 44 ft. on Tradd Street; E 98 ft. on
JONATHAN BADGER; W on MRS. SUSANNAH BOSOMWORTH (formerly GEORGE CHICKEN);
S on MILES BREWTON. Witnesses: CHARLES LORIMER, ROBERT WILLIAMS, JR.,
THOMAS SACHEVEREL. Before DANIEL CRAWFORD, J.P. WILLIAM HOPTON, Regis-
ter.

Book N-N, p. 126   JOHN FRIPP, planter, of St. Helena Parish,
12 May 1753   Granville Co., confirms to JOHN FIELD, plant-
Confirmation   er, of Colleton Co., for Ł 200 currency, his
                       title to Bowers Point Plantation. Whereas
JOHN FIELD for some time past has been in possession of 450 a. in Colleton Co., called Bowers Point, bounding S & SW on Combahee River; E on
marsh & a creek out of Chehaw River; N on vacant land; which tract FIELD
had purchased from GEORGE SEAMAN, merchant, of Charleston, & which SEA-
MAN, by L & R dated 1 & 2 Aug. 1750 had purchased from WILLIAM STEWART &
ANNE, his wife, daughter & devisee of COL. HALL, & to which FRIPP had set
up a claim as heir-at-law to JAMES SEABROOK; now FRIPP sells his claim to
FIELD. Witnesses: CHARLES PINCKNEY, JR., JOHN TROUP. Before JAMES
MICHIE, J.P. WILLIAM HOPTON, Register. Note: L & R from SEAMAN to
FIELD recorded in this book pages 171-177.

Book N-N, p. 129   WILLIAM SWINTON, planter, & HANNAH his wife,
11 & 12 Apr. 1734   to DANIEL LAROCHE & THOMAS LAROCHE, merchants,
L & R   all of Craven Co., for Ł 550 currency, 550 a.
                       in Craven Co., bounding SE on Peedee River; SW
on ELIAS FOISSIN; NW on JOHN GREEN; NE on WILLIAM SWINTON. Whereas Gov.
ROBERT JOHNSON on 6 Apr. 1733 granted JAMES PAINE 900 a. in Craven Co.,
bounding SE on Peedee River; NW on JOHN GREEN; NE on STEPHEN PROCTOR; &
whereas JAMES PAINE & MARY, his wife, on 5 June 1733 conveyed the 900 a.
to WILLIAM SWINTON; now he sells a part of the tract to DANIEL & THOMAS

LAROCHE. Witnesses: HUGH SWINTON, ALEXANDER ROBERTSON, MARK GUTHRIE.
Before ELIAS FOISSIN, J.P. WILLIAM HOPTON, Register.

Book N-N, p. 133   WILLIAM SWINTON, planter, & HANNAH his wife,
11 & 12 Apr. 1734   of Winyaw, Craven Co., to DANIEL LAROCHE &
L & R   THOMAS LAROCHE, merchants, equally, as ten-
                       ants in common & not as joint tenants, for
Ł 200 currency, 200 a., part of 325 a., part of an island in Peedee Riv-
er in Craven Co., bounding NW on Peedee River, NE on WILLIAM SWINTON; SE
on a thoroughfare to Waccamaw River. Whereas Gov. ROBERT JOHNSON on 6
Dec. 1733 granted WILLIAM SWINTON 325 a. in Craven Co., bounding SE on a
thoroughfare leading to Waccamaw River; NE on HUGH SWINTON; NW on Peedee
River; now he sells a part to DANIEL & THOMAS LAROCHE. Witnesses: HUGH
SWINTON, ALEXANDER ROBERTSON, MARK GUTHRIE. Before ELIAS FOISSIN, J.P.
WILLIAM HOPTON, Register.

Book N-N, p. 139   GEORGE SAXBY, ESQ., & ELIZABETH his wife, to
4 & 5 June 1753   GEORGE AUSTIN, merchant, all of Charleston,
L & R   for Ł 5001 currency, 750 a. in Craven Co.,
                     bounding NW on JOHN GREEN; NE on WILLIAM SWIN-
TON; SE on Peedee River & Waccamaw thoroughfare; SW on ELIAS FOISSIN.
Witnesses: JOHN CROKATT, JOHN RATTRAY. Before DANIEL CRAWFORD, J.P.
WILLIAM HOPTON, Register. Plat of 750 a. showing Peedee River dividing
it into 2 sections, 550 & 200 a., unsigned, not dated.

Book N-N, p. 145   An Act of Assembly to Incorporate the SC Soc-
20 Dec. 1752   iety & Confirmation & Ratification in Council,
                     at Court of St. James, 20 Dec. 1752.

Present
The King's Most Excellent Majesty

Lord Chancellor	Earl of Jersey	Mr. Chan. of Exchequer
Archibishop of York	Earl of Hynford	Master of the Rolls
Lord President	Earl of Halifax	Horatio Walpole, Esq.
Duke of Devonshire	Earl Waldegrave	Sir John Rushout
Duke of Atholl	Lord Delawarr	George Doddington, Esq.
Duke of New Castle	Ld. Berkeley of Stra.	Sir Thomas Robinson
Duke of Dorset	Lord Edgcumbe	
Earl of Holdernesse	Mr. Vice Chamberlain	

Whereas on 17 May 1751 the Gov. & Council &
Assembly of SC passed an act to incorporate the SC Society, & whereas
ROBERT RAPER, JOHN MCCALL, BENJAMIN ADDISON, present wardens, & others
who have associated themselves together for pious & charitable purposes
for the past 13 years under the name of the SC Society have petitioned
the General Assembly setting forth that the Society now has a considerable sum of money which they desire to apply to charitable uses & towards
erecting, endowing & supporting schools & almshouses (for the poor?) &
pray to be incorporated as a body politic & be invested with powers &
authority to further the intentions of the association; praying Gov.
JAMES GLEN, the Countil & the Assembly, that said wardens & other officers & members be declared 1 body corporate & politic, with authority to
handle the money, etc., belonging to the Society, etc., etc. In Council
Chamber 17 May 1751, ANDREW RUTLEDGE, Speaker; assented to: JAMES GLEN.
And whereas the act was referred to a committee, & approved & act confirmed & ratified. Signed. W. SHARPE. WILLIAM HOPTON, Register.

Book N-N, p. 148   TACITUS GAILLARD, planter, & ANNE his wife, of
6 & 7 June 1753   Santee, to the vestry of the Parish of St.
L & R by Mortgage   Thomas, Berkeley Co., as security on bond of
                     even date in penal sum of Ł 2000 for payment
of Ł 1000 currency, with interest, on 7 June 1754; 192 a., part of 300 a.,
bounding SE on THEODORE GAILLARD; other sides on TACITUS GAILLARD; also
258 a., bounding NE & SE on THEODORE GAILLARD; SW on TACITUS GAILLARD; NW
on vacant land. Whereas BARTHOLOMEW GAILLARD, planter, owned sundry
plantations in SC, & by will, after devising some particular lands to his
eldest son, FREDERICK GAILLARD, devised his other lands equally to his 3
other sons, THEODORE, ALCIMUS, & TACITUS; & whereas after the fathers
death, on 1 Aug. 1741 THEODORE, ALCIMUS & TACITUS divided the land &

agreed that TICITUS should have, with other lands, the 300 a. on Wambaw Swamp, Craven Co., bounding SE on BARTHOLOMEW GAILLARD; other sides on lands vacant at time of grant; but by deed of partition said to be bounding E on THEODORE GAILLARD; W on heirs of ISAAC LEGRAND; & whereas Lt. Gov. WILLIAM BULL on 5 July 1740 granted LEWIS GOURDIN 620 a. in Craven Co., bounding S on the MESSRS. GAILLARD & ISAAC LEGRAND; NE on JAMES SAVINEAU; NW on an impassable swamp; & whereas LEWIS GOURDIN & MARY ANNE, his wife, by L & R dated 10 & 11 Aug. 1740 sold TACITUS GAILLARD 258 a. of the 620 a. on Wambaw Swamp, bounding NE on LEWIS GOURDIN; SE on THEODORE GAILLARD; SW on TACITUS GAILLARD & ISAAC LEGRAND; NW on vacant land; now TACITUS GAILLARD mortgages the 2 tracts of 192 a. & 258 a. to the vestry of St. Thomas Parish. Witnesses: JOHN MENZIES, DANIEL DWIGHT. Before JAMES WRIGHT, J.P. WILLIAM HOPTON, Register. On 17 July 1754 ALEXANDER GARDEN, rector of Parish of St. Thomas, declared mortgage paid in full. Witness: WILLIAM HOPTON.

Book N-N, p. 159
7 & 8 June 1753
L & R

JOHN MAYRANT, ESQ., of St. James Santee, Craven Co. to ROBERT PRINGLE, merchant, of Charleston, for Ł 1350 currency, 500 a. in Craven Co., granted by the Lords Proprs. to DANIEL HUGER, who conveyed to JAMES NICHOLAS MAYRANT, & inherited by his only son, JOHN; bounding W on land vacant at time of grant; N & E on JOHN MAYRANT; S on Wambaw Creek. Witnesses: JOHN HOLMES, JOEL HOLMES. Before ALEXANDER STEWART, J.P. WILLIAM HOPTON, Register. Plat.

Book N-N, p. 164
24 & 25 Oct. 1746
L & R

PETER TIMOTHY, printer, son & heir of LEWIS TIMOTHY, to ELIZABETH TIMOTHY, widow, both of Charleston, for Ł 1000 currency, part of lots #164 & #186 in Charleston, bounding E 50 ft. on King Street; W on ELIAS HANCOCK; S 200 ft. on other part of lot #186 belonging to PETER TIMOTHY; N on part of lot #164; with the house thereon. Witnesses: JOHN RATTRAY, HENRY COULTON. Before JACOB MOTTE, J.P. WILLIAM HOPTON, Register.

Book N-N, p. 171
1 & 2 Aug. 1750
L & R

GEORGE SEAMAN, merchant, of Charleston, to JOHN FIELD, planter, of Granville Co., for Ł 450 currency, 450 a. called Bowers Point, in Colleton Co., on N side Combee River; bounding S & SW on the river; E on marsh & a creek of Chehaw River; NW on vacant land. Witnesses: JOHN TROUP, THOMAS BONNY, JR. Before JAMES MICHIE, J.P. WILLIAM HOPTON, Register. See p. 126 for confirmation by JOHN FRIPP who claimed this land.

Book N-N, p. 177
2 & 3 Sept. 1751
L & R

WILLIAM NEWITT EDWARDS, planter, & ANN (her mark) his wife, of Craven Co., to JAMES MICHIE, ESQ., of Charleston, for Ł 290 currency, 290 a. in Fredericksborough Township, Craven Co., bounding NW on ROBERT SEAWRIGHT; NE on GEORGE SENIOR & JOHN WILLIAMS; other sides on Wateree River; which 290 a. Gov. JAMES GLEN granted on 15 May 1751 (?) to WILLIAM NEWITT EDWARDS, WILLIAM SCOTT, JAMES MCCULLY. Before ROGER GIBSON, J.P. WILLIAM HOPTON, Register.

Book N-N, p. 184
17 & 18 Aug. 1752
L & R

WILLIAM SEAWRIGHT, planter, & ESTHER his wife, of Craven Co., to JAMES MICHIE, ESQ., of Charleston, for Ł 200 currency, 250 a. in Fredericksborough Township, Craven Co., bounding SE on ROBERT SEAWRIGHT; other sides on Wateree River; which street was granted 5 Sept. 1750 by Gov. JAMES GLEN to WILLIAM SEAWRIGHT. Witnesses: JOHN SEAWRIGHT, HENRY HAMMOND, ROBERT STIELL. Before OTHNIEL BEALE, J.P. WILLIAM HOPTON, Register.

Book N-N, p. 192
22 & 23 June 1753
L & R by Mortgage

THOMAS BEAZLEY, mariner, of Charleston, to WILLIAM WOODROP & PAUL DOUXSAINT, merchants, of Charleston, as security on bond of even date in penal sum of Ł 1800 for payment of Ł 900 currency, with interest, on 23 Sept. next; 200 a. in Berkeley Co., bounding N on PETER CONLIES; E on ANN COOK, widow; S on PETER JOHNSON, JR.; W on Morrils Creek running into Cooper River; which 200 a. were purchased from HEZEKIAH RUSS by JOHN BRUCE, who conveyed to THOMAS BEAZLEY. Witnesses: WILLIAM STANYARNE, ANDREW CATHCART. WILLIAM PINCKNEY, J.P.

WILLIAM HOPTON, Register.

Book N-N, p. 197   CHARLES DEVON, gentleman, of London, son &
13 Dec. 1752   heir & executor of will of RICHARD DEVON of
Release   London; by his attorney ROBERT RAPER, gentleman, of Charleston; to JOHN MILES, WILLIAM
MILES, & JEREMIAH MILES, planters, of Colleton Co., for ₺ 700 SC money;
640 a. in Colleton Co., bounding according to plat. Whereas the Lords
Proprs. on the 28 June 1711 granted JOHN HILL 640 a. in Colleton Co.,
which HILL & ELIZABETH his wife on 5 Sept. 1716 sold to RICHARD DEVON; &
was inherited by his son CHARLES; & whereas CHARLES DEVON; on 20 May 1748,
appointed ROBERT RAPER his attorney with authority to sell the tract; now
he sells to JOHN, WILLIAM & JEREMIAH MILES. Witnesses: JOHN REMINGTON,
EDWARD SWAN. Before ROBERT AUSTIN, J.P. WILLIAM HOPTON, Register. Plat
of 640 a., an inland plantation in Colleton Co., known as Beech Hill, on
S side of Ashepoo River; bounding N on JOHN SEABROOK; other sides on vacant land, certified 5 July 1711 by THOMAS BROUGHTON, L on p. 288.

Book N-N, p. 201   WILLIAM BRANFORD, planter, (eldest son & heir
30 & 31 Oct. 1752   of WILLIAM BRANFORD the elder, planter) of
L & R in Trust   Berkeley Co., & ELIZABETH his wife, because of
WILLIAM'S love & affection for his eldest sis-
ter ELIZABETH (now ELIZABETH HOLMES wife of FRANCIS HOLMES, gentleman) &
for the support of her & her children, convey to ANTHONY MATTHEWES & JOHN
MATHEWES, in trust for ELIZABETH HOLMES, 280 a., English measure, on S
side of Ashley River in St. Andrews Parish, Berkeley Co., bounding SE on
Ashley Ferry Path & on WILLIAM MILES; SW on WILLIAM BRANFORD; NW on BEN-
JAMIN STANYARNE; NE on WILLIAM MILES. Whereas the Lords Proprs. & Gov.
NATHANIEL JOHNSON on 16 July 1703 granted SHEM BUTLER 1332 a., English
measure, on SW side Ashley River in Berkeley Co., which by will dated 9
Oct. 1718 he bequeathed equally to his wife ESTHER & 7 children, appointing RICHARD BUTLER & EDMUND BELLINGER his executors, & after his death on
1 May 1724 they divided & allotted the real & personal estate, the said
220 a. being allotted to said ESTHER BUTLER (afterwards ESTHER ELLIOTT),
widow of SHEM BUTLER; & whereas said ESTHER ELLIOTT, by L & R dated 8 & 9
Feb. 1741 sold her tract to WILLIAM BRANFORD; who died intestate; & the
tract was inherited by his eldest son, WILLIAM, party hereto; now he conveys to ANTHONY & JOHN MATHEWS, in trust for his sister ELIZABETH, wife
of FRANCIS HOLMES. Witnesses: JAMES BALLANTINE, JOHN BALLANTINE.

Book N-N, p. 211   BENEDICT BOURQUIN, planter, of Purysburg,
12 Feb. 1751   Granville Co., to WILLIAM ELBERT, planter, of
L & R   same Co., for ₺ 525 currency, 300 a. in Purysburg Township, which Lt. Gov. WILLIAM BULL had
granted 16 Sept. 1738 to ABRAHAM CHARDONELL, bounding S on May River; N &
W on vacant land; E & S on PETER MASON & JOHN HENRY DEROCHE; & sold by
CHARDONELL to BENEDICT BOURQUIN (recorded Book D.D. fol. 64-66 on 24 Feb.
1747). Witnesses: ABRAHAM JEANNERET, JOHN LOUIS BOURQUIN. Before ANDREW
VERDIER, J.P. WILLIAM HOPTON, Register. JANN JUDAH (her mark) BOURQUIN,
wife of BENEDICT BOURQUIN, released her title & dower on 12 Feb. 1750/1.

Book N-N, p. 217   ELISHA BUTLER, planter, & WILLIAM BUTLER,
22 & 23 June 1752   planter, both of Stono, in Colleton Co., ex-
L & R   ecutors of will of RICHARD BUTLER, planter, of
St. Andrews Parish, to RICHARD LAKE, ESQ., of
St. Andrews; for ₺ 1150 currency, 2 adjoining tracts; 220 a. & 54 a., at
Bare Swamp, in Berkeley Co., total 274 a., now occupied by SARAH BUTLER.
Whereas the Lords Proprs. on 15 Dec. 1705 granted HENRY NICHOLS 220 a. at
a place called Bare Swamp, in Berkeley Co., then bounding N on WILLIAM
FULLER (now NATHANIEL FULLER'S estate); E on NATHANIEL NICHOLS (now THOM-
AS LADSON, JR.); W on FRANCIS LADSON (now JOHN ANGER & FRANCIS LADSON); S
on THOMAS DRAYTON & whereas by assignment on back of said grant on 30
Dec. 1712, transferred the 220 a. to ISAAC REMMICK; who on 3 July 1713
conveyed to RALPH EMMES; who by deed of feoffment dated 18 Sept. 1717,
for ₺ 320 conveyed to RICHARD BUTLER; & whereas Landgrave THOMAS SMITH &
MARY his wife, on 23 Apr. 1723 sold 54 a., adjoining the 220 a., to RICH-
ARD BUTLER; who by will dated 8 Aug. 1735 directed that his real estate
be sold, & appointed his 2 sons, ELISHA & WILLIAM his executors; now they
sell both tracts to RICHARD LAKE. Witnesses: ELIZABETH PINCKNEY, CHARLES
PINCKNEY. Before WILLIAM BULL, JR., J.P. WILLIAM HOPTON, Register.

Book N-N, p. 224   COL. MOSES WILSON, & MARGARET his wife, of
29 Aug. 1735   Berkeley Co., to ISAAC HOLMES, gentleman, of
Release   Charleston, for Ł 1500 currency, part of lot
                           #31 in Charleston, bounding E 25-1/2 ft., Eng-
lish measure, on Church Street; (20 ft. of the 25-1/2 ft. being part of
lot #31 MOSES WILSON bought from JOHN BAYLEY, cordwainer, of Charleston;
the 5-1/2 ft. part of lot #31, he purchased from WILLIAM LOUGHTON, & MARY
his wife, of Charleston); N on WILLIAM WATSON; S the whole depth of lot
on ISAAC HOLMES; W on JONATHAN COLLINS. Witnesses: ROBERT WOOD, JOHN
FIDLING, JOHN FRYER. Before THOMAS LAMBOLL, J.P. WILLIAM HOPTON, Register.

Book N-N, p. 227   RAWLINS LOWNDES, P.M. of SC, to NATHANIEL
18 June 1753   BARNWELL, ESQ., of Beaufort, at public auc-
Sale   tion, for Ł 1000 currency, 500 a. on Port Roy-
                           al Island. Whereas TWEEDIE SOMERVILLE, mer-
chant, of Charleston, owned 500 a. on Port Royal Island, Granville Co.,
formerly granted to EVANS LEWIS & then bounding N & NE on THOMAS DEWES; E
on a small creek out of Port Royal River the Less; S on WILLIAM FORD; &
whereas SOMERVILLE on 1 May 1731 mortgaged the tract to SAMUEL WRAGG,
giving bond in penal sum of Ł 1860 Sterling for payment of Ł 933:17:1-1/2,
with interest, on 1 July then next; & whereas SOMERVILLE by will appointed his widow SARAH his executrix; & in her will she appointed EDWARD
CROFT, CHILDERMAS CROFT, & EDWARD WIGG, her executors; & whereas SAMUEL
WRAGG by will & codicil appointed WILLIAM WRAGG, ROBERT RENSHAW, his executors & MARY WRAGG & JUDITH WRAGG, his executrixes; & whereas they,
WRAGG'S executors, obtained a judgment against the executors of SARAH
SOMERVILLE for the penal sum & costs; & whereas CHARLES PINCKNEY, C.J.,
issued a writ of fieri facias on 13 Feb. 1753 ordering the P.M. to levy
these sums on the estate of TWEEDIE SOMERVILLE; now the P.M. sells the
500 a. to BARNWELL. Witnesses: FRANCIS MACARTEN, ALEXANDER GORDON, JR.
Before ALEXANDER GORDON, J.P. WILLIAM HOPTON, Register.

Book N-N, p. 231   RAWLINS LOWNDES, P.M. of SC, to FRANCIS MACAR-
18 June 1753   TAN, merchant, at public auction, for Ł 25,000,
Sale   part of lot #5 & the brick house thereon, in
                           Charleston. Whereas TWEEDIE SOMERVILLE, mer-
chant, of Charleston, owned part of lot #5 in Charleston, bounding E on
the Bay; S on the part occupied by THOMAS MIDDLETON, ESQ., N on the part
owned by COL. JOHN GIBBES; W on WILLIAM CHAPMAN; & had free use of the
2 alleys, 1 on N side other on S side; & whereas SOMERVILLE mortgaged the
said lot to SAMUEL WRAGG; giving bond in penal sum of Ł 1860 British; &
whereas SOMERVILLE by will appointed his widow, SARAH, his executrix; &
she, by her will appointed EDWARD CROFT, CHILDERMAS CROFT, & EDWARD WIGG
her executors; & whereas SAMUEL WRAGG died after the death of SARAH SOM-
ERVILLE, & by will & codicil appointed WILLIAM WRAGG, ROBERT HENSHAW,
MARY WRAGG, & JUDITH WRAGG, his executors & executrixes; & whereas
WRAGG'S executors obtained a judgment against SARAH SOMERVILLE'S executors in the full amount of the bond, with costs; & on 13 Feb. 1753,
CHARLES PINCKNEY, C.J., issued a writ of fieri facias, ordering the P.M.
to levy this amount of TWEEDIE SOMERVILLE'S estate; now the P.M. sells
above house & lot to MACARTAN, the highest bidder. Witnesses: JOHN
GIBBES, ALEXANDER GORDON, JR. Before ALEXANDER GORDON, J.P. WILLIAM
HOPTON, Register.

Book N-N, p. 235   The Hon. WILLIAM WRAGG, ESQ., of Charleston,
29 & 30 June 1753   to ELIZABETH GIBBES, wife of COL. JOHN GIBBES,
L & R   of Charleston, for Ł 2800 currency, part of
                           lot #5 in Charleston, bounding E on the Bay; S
on ELIZABETH GIBBES; W on WILLIAM CHAPMAN. Whereas RAWLINS LOWNDES, P.M.,
seized the estate of TWEEDIE SOMERVILLE to satisfy a judgment obtained by
the executors of SAMUEL WRAGG & on 18 June 1753 sold the above lot to
FRANCIS MACARTAN, merchant, who, by L & R dated 19 & 20 June 1753 sold
the lot to WILLIAM WRAGG, party hereto; who now sells the lot to ELIZA-
BETH GIBBES, with the use of the 2 alleys to the N & S of said lot. Witnesses: FRANCIS MACARTAN, ALEXANDER GORDON, JR. Before ALEXANDER GORDON,
J.P. WILLIAM HOPTON, Register.

Book N-N, p. 240   WILLIAM WHIPPY, planter, & MARY his wife, of
3 & 4 July 1753   Colleton Co., to RALPH BAILEY, planter, of

297

L & R   same Co., for Ł 1050 currency, 300 a., in Col-
          leton Co., according to original grant. Wit-
nesses: WILLIAM DAVIS, BAYNARD FRY, WILLIAM BAYNARD. Before JACOB MOTTE,
Register. WILLIAM HOPTON, Register.

Book N-N, p. 246   WILLIAM ROPER, merchant, & GRACE his wife, to
2 & 3 Apr. 1752   GEORGE EVELEIGH, gentleman, both of Charles-
L & R   ton, for Ł 1000 currency, the N half of the S
          part of lot #327 in Charleston, bounding W
17-1/2 ft. on the wharf line; S on part of same lot #327; N on GEORGE
EVELEIGH; E on Cooper River down to low water mark; as owned by WILLIAM
ROPER. Whereas JOHN LLOYD, ESQ., of Charleston, by various mesne conveyances became owner of all the S part of lot #327 in Charleston; fronting
35 ft. on the wharf line, & opposite lot #3; bounding N on land opposite
lot #4 formerly belonging to WILLIAM WILLIAMS; S on a front lot opposite
lot #2 formerly owned by WILLIAM NORVELL & others; E on Cooper River as
far as low water mark; & whereas JOHN LLOYD & MARY his wife, by L & R
dated 22 & 23 Jan. 1750, for Ł 2000 currency, sold to WILLIAM ROPER all
the aforesaid S part of lot #327 bounding 35 ft. on the wharf line; also
a bridge or wharf erected thereon, called Lloyd's Wharf; & whereas WIL-
LIAM ROPER, for Ł 1000 currency, agreed to sell the N half to GEORGE EVE-
LEIGH; now ROPER sells EVELEIGH half his lot, half the wharf & improvements, with all buildings thereon, fees, perquisites, etc., etc. Witnesses: WILLIAM EDINGS, THOMAS HUTCHINSON. Before THOMAS MIDDLETON, J.P.
WILLIAM HOPTON, Register.

Book N-N, p. 251   BENJAMIN ROMSEY, merchant, formerly of Bris-
1 & 2 May 1744   tol, Great Britain, now of SC (eldest son &
L & R   heir of BENJAMIN ROMSEY the elder, merchant,
          of Charleston, SC, & only brother of WILLIAM
ROMSEY, merchant, of Craven Co., who died intestate, & uncle & heir of
BENJAMIN ROMSEY his only child, an infant, also deceased) of 1st part; to
MARY ELLIS, widow of Charleston; for Ł 2582 currency; 2 parts of 2 adjacent lots in E part of Charleston, containing together in breadth at E
end 30-1/2 ft.; 30-1/2 ft. at W end; that is, 3-1/2 ft. in breadth out of
the N part of lot #3 sold by CHARLES PINCKNEY, ESQ., to MARTHA ROMSEY,
widow, the remaining part out of the w part of lot #4 formerly belonging
to DR. WILLIAM CROOK & devised by him to his wife MARTHA (afterwards MAR-
THA ROMSEY); bounding E on the Bay; S on said PINCKNEY; W on _____; N on
GEORGE EVELEIGH, merchant; according to a certain parchment plat made &
certified 13 Mar. last by THOMAS WITTER; also that piece of vacant ground
lately granted to BENJAMIN ROMSEY, party hereto, fronting 27 ft. on E
side of curtain line & extending E towards Cooper River, fronting the S
part of lot #4; as by grant from Gov. JAMES GLEN dated 12 Apr. 1744.
CHARLES PINCKNEY reserves the right to put windows in the sides or ends
of nay houses already built or to be built on the dividing property line
without interference from MARY ELLIS according to agreement dated 1 May
1721 executed between MARTHA ROMSEY & CHARLES PINCKNEY. Witnesses: ISAAC
HOLMES, WILLIAM ROPER, GEORGE INGLIS. Before HENRY GIBBES, J.P. WILLIAM
HOPTON, Register. Plat of a lot near the S part of the Bay in Charleston
formerly belonging to DR. CROOK but now to MR. ROMSEY, bounding E on the
Bay; S on the Hon. CHARLES PINCKNEY; N on GEORGE EVELEIGH; certified 13
Mar. 1743/4 by THOMAS WITTER.

Book N-N, p. 260   MARY ELLIS, widow, to JOHN HODSDEN, merchant,
2 & 3 Apr. 1750   both of Charleston, for Ł 4500 currency, a
L & R   brick house & piece of ground W of East Bay,
          consisting of parts of lots #3 & #4; 298 ft.
deep; 31 ft. at E end; 22-1/2 ft. at W end as the lot now stands enclosed; bounding E on the Bay; S on CHARLES PINCKNEY; W on BENJAMIN MATHEWES;
N on GEORGE EVELEIGH; also the shoal lot 27 ft. wide, E of the curtain
line of East Bay; extending towards Cooper River; lying opposite the S
part of lot #4. Witnesses: THOMAS SAMBROOKE, ISAAC LEGARE. Before THOM-
AS LAMBOLL, J.P. WILLIAM HOPTON, Register.

Book N-N, p. 266   JOHN MILNER, gunsmith, eldest son & 1 of the
3 & 4 Dec. 1750   residuary devisees & executors of will of JOHN
L & R   MILNER, SR., gunsmith, & BATHSHEBA his wife; &
          SOLOMON MILNER, merchant, the other son, re-
siduary devisee & executor of will of said JOHN MILNER, SR., & MARY his

wife; to JOHN HODSDEN, merchant, all of Charleston; for ₺ 4110 currency,
all the real estate in Charleston formerly belonging to JOHN MILNER, consisting of 1 house & lot, being the part of the S half of lot #53, on N
side Tradd Street, & on E side of Old Church Street, or Meeting House
Street, bounding E on DR. JOHN RUTLEDGE (formerly MARY MULLINS); S 56 ft.
on GEORGE DUCAT; W 46 ft. on other part lot #53 belonging to heirs of
JEREMIAH MILNER; N on an alley dividing lot #53; also the 3 story brick
house (or SE corner house) & part of lot #39 on N side Tradd Street, & W
side New Church Street, bounding N 17 ft. on ALEXANDER LONGUEMAR; W 33
ft. part of lot #39 belonging to JOHN REDMAN (formerly JOHN BULLOCK);
also part of lot #39 formerly belonging to ALEXANDER LONGUERMAR; on W
side New Church Street, bounding N on MR. HENDRICK; W 22 ft. on part of
lot #39 formerly belonging to JOHN BULLOCK; S 104 ft. on part of lot #39
now sold to JOHN HODSDEN & partly on another part of #39 formerly belonging to JOHN BULLOCK; the 2 parts sold HODSDEN being contiguous. Whereas
JOHN MILNER owned 3 parts of lots in Charleston & by will dated 27 Sept.
1749 bequeathed to his daughter SARAH MILNER ₺ 800 currency to be paid
within the 3 years after his death, in the meantime ₺ 70 to be paid her
yearly from the rents, etc.; & bequeathed to his daughter, MARY MILNER,
₺ 850 currency in same way, to his daughter, MARTHA MILNER, ₺ 1000 currency, in same way; to his wife, AGATHA MILNER, ₺ 500 currency, in same
way; to his 2 sons, JOHN & SOLOMON, equally, all his real estate, subject
to above payments; with authority to sell the real estate to meet the
payments; appointing said sons his executors; & whereas JOHN & SOLOMON
concluded to dispose of the real estate to the highest bidder, they now
sell to JOHN HODSDEN. Witnesses: HENRY BEDON, JOSIAH SMITH, JR. Before
JOHN DART, J.P. WILLIAM HOPTON, Register.

Book N-N, p. 280   SUSANNA BEE, of Charleston, widow & executrix
23 & 24 Oct. 1752   of will of JOHN BEE the younger, gentleman, of
L & R   Colleton Co.; & WILLIAM SIMMONS, planter, of
                          Granville Co., executor of will of said JOHN
BEE; to JOHN HODSDEN, merchant, of Charleston; for ₺ 7500 currency; the S
part of lot #2, with houses, buildings, etc., free from SUSANNAH'S claim
of dower. Whereas JOHN BEE by several mesme conveyances & by his father's, JOHN BEE the elder's, will, became possessed of that S part of
lot #2 near the S end of East Bay in Charleston, originally granted by
the Lords Proprs. on 7 Sept. 1681 to THEOPHILUS PATEY, bounding E 51 ft.
on East Bay; S on WILLIAM ROPER (formerly CAPT. GEORGE SMITH); W on marsh
belonging to Landgrave THOMAS SMITH; N on JOSEPH BOONE; according to plat
attached to a certain deed of feoffment dated 2 July 1717 from Landgrave
THOMAS SMITH & GEORGE SMITH (as attorneys for GEORGE SMITH of Bermuda &
DOROTHY his wife) to JOHN HUTCHINSON & ANNE his wife of Charleston; &
whereas JOHN BEE, the younger, by will dated 25 Feb. 1748 ordered that
his house or 2 tenements be sold as soon as convenient, & appointed his
wife SUSANNA, executrix, & his son; JOHN, his son-in-law, ISAAC HAYNE, &
his brother-in-law, THOMAS SIMMONS (all 3 since deceased) & said WILLIAM
SIMMONS, his executors; now SUSANNA BEE, executrix, & WILLIAM SIMMONS,
executor, sell to JOHN HODSDEN. Witnesses: SOLOMON LEGARE, JR., SARAH
FREER, JOHN EDWARDS. Before JOHN DART, J.P. WILLIAM HOPTON, Register.

Book N-N, p. 289   CHARLES DEVON, gentleman, of London, son &
12 Dec. 1752   heir, & executor of will of RICHARD DEVON, of
Lease   London; by his attorney, ROBERT RAPER, gentle-
                          man, of Charleston, to JOHN MILES, WILLIAM
MILES & JEREMIAH MILES. See release p. 197.

Book N-N, p. 291   LOIS MATHEWES, widow, to GEORGE EVELEIGH, gen-
8 May 1752   tleman, both of Charleston, for ₺ 100 curren-
Feoffment   cy, the E & N part of shoal or broken land,
                          part of lot #298 near White Point, in Charles-
ton, conveyed to LOIS MATHEWES by WILLIAM VANDERHORST, 1 of the sons &
devisees of JOHN VANDERHORST, the elder; the shoal land beginning at NW
corner of lot #298, on E side New Church Street, continued to Broughton's Battery at White Point; & from said street running SE 78 deg. for
206 ft., thence running NE 87-1/2 deg. for 215 ft. to the side of a certain canal there begun; thence along SW side said canal NW 68 deg. for
121 ft. 8 in.; from thence returning SW 87-1/2 deg. for 302 ft. to NW
corner lot #298; bounding W on said street; S on remaining part LOIS
MATHEWES'S part of lot #298; E on canal; N on shoal of GEORGE EVELEIGH &

on canal. Witnesses: WILLIAM DANDRIDGE, THOMAS LAMBOLL. Before JACOB
MOTTE, J.P. WILLIAM HOPTON, Register. Plat with part shaded yellow
showing part of lot #298 sold by LOIS MATHEWES to GEORGE EVELEIGH; certified 25 Apr. 17__ by WILLIAM WILKINS, Dep. Sur.

Book N-N, p. 295   WILLIAM VANDERHORST, planter, of Berkeley Co.,
1 & 2 May 1751   1 of the sons & devisees of will of JOHN VAN-
L & R   DERHORST the elder, planter, to GEORGE EVE-
                         LEIGH, gentleman, of Charleston, for Ł 450
currency, the NE part of lot #298 in Charleston, near White Point, fronting New Church Street, continued to a certain bridge southward to Broughton's Battery at White Point 35 ft.; 272 ft. long; on NW side said bridge
100 ft. on NE side from N corner to E corner near to an ESE course along
the SW side of a certain canal formerly called Vanderhorst's Creek 207
ft., bounding W on said street; S on other part of lot #298 lately sold
by VANDERHORST to LOIS MATHEWES; NW on said bridge or causeway; NE on the
canal; according to plat by WILLIAM VANDERHORST. Whereas JOHN VANDER-
HORST, the father, by will dated 29 Nov. 1738 stated he owned several
lots of land near White Point in Charleston, with several houses, buildings & improvements thereon, which he bequeathed to his surviving sons
when they came of age; to be divided by his executors into equal shares;
& appointed HENRY PERONNEAU, JR., & ALEXANDER PERONNEAU, merchant, & his
2 sons JOSEPH VANDERHORST & JOHN VANDERHORST, JR., (both since deceased)
his executors; & whereas the executors in May 1741 divided the real estate into 5 equal parts for the 5 then living sons, allotting to each his
share or fifth part; the shoal land mentioned herein being allotted to
WILLIAM VANDERHORST; now he sells his shoal lot to EVELEIGH. Witnesses:
SAMUEL EVELEIGH, THOMAS LAMBOLL. Before JACOB MOTTE, J.P. WILLIAM HOP-
TON, Register.

Book N-N, p. 304   WILLIAM VANDERHORST, planter, of Berkeley Co.,
1 May 1751   to GEORGE EVELEIGH, gentleman, in penal sum of
Bond   Ł 900 currency, to make sure that MARGARET,
                         wife of WILLIAM VANDERHORST, shall within 4
months after reaching age of 21, shall renounce her claim of dower in
above property (p. 295) conveyed to EVELEIGH. Witnesses: SAMUEL EVE-
LEIGH, THOMAS LAMBOLL. Before JACOB MOTTE, J.P. WILLIAM HOPTON, Register.

Book N-N, p. 306   PAUL TRAPIER, merchant, to SUSANNAH GIGNILLIAT,
12 & 13 July   both of Georgetown, for Ł 186 currency, lot
L & R   #54 in Georgetown, with its houses, & right of
                         commonage for 1 horse & 1 cow. Whereas by L &
R dated 14 & 15 Jan. 1734 ELISHA SCREVEN & HANNAH his wife, of Craven Co.,
conveyed to GEORGE PAWLEY, WILLIAM SWINTON, & DANIEL LAROCHE, in trust,
with authority to sell the town lots to such persons desiring to become
inhabitants; & whereas said trustees on 25 Feb. 1734 sold yOHN CAINS,
blacksmith, lot #54, bounding NE 100 ft. on Prince Street; SE 217.9 ft.
on lot #55; SW on lots #11 & #12; NW on lot #53; which lot CAINS by assignment on back of the release conveyed to CHRISTOPHER CAINS; & whereas
CHRISTOPHER CAINS, by another assignment on back of same deed sold to
JOHN ARTHUR; & he, by another assignment on back of same deed, conveyed
to MARY THOMAS, party hereto, who married WILLIAM TOPPING, & at his death
inherited his property, & on 4 Oct. 1752 sold the lot to PAUL TRAPIER;
now he sells to SUSANNAH GIGNILLIAT. Witnesses: THOMAS HASELL, JOSEPH
DUBOURDIER. Before GEORGE PAWLEY, J.P. WILLIAM HOPTON, Register

Book N-N, p. 311   MARY TOPPING, widow, to PAUL TRAPIER, merchant,
3 & 4 Oct. 1752   both of Georgetown, for Ł 175 currency, lot
L & R   #54 in Georgetown, with right of commonage for
                         1 horse & 1 cow. Whereas by L & R dated 14 &
15 Jan. 1734 ELISHA SCREVEN, & HANNAH his wife, conveyed to GEORGE PAWLEY;
WILLIAM SWINTON, & DANIEL LAROCHE, as trustees, certain lots in Georgetown to be sold to such people as desired to become inhabitants; & whereas said trustees on 25 Feb. 1734 sold lot #54 to JOHN CAINS, blacksmith,
bounding NE 100 ft. on Prince Street, SE 217.9 ft., on lot #55; SW on
lots 11 & 12; NW on lot #53, which lot CAINS, by an assignment on back of
said release, conveyed to CHRISTOPHER CAINS; who, by another assignment
on the back of same release, conveyed the lot to JOHN ARTHUR; who, by
another assignment on the back of same release, conveyed to MARY THOMAS,

party hereto, who married WILLIAM TOPPING, & after his death, inherited his property; now she conveys the lot to TRAPIER. Witnesses: JOHN SKRINE, DANIEL BROCKINGTON. Before THOMAS HASELL, J.P. WILLIAM HOPTON, Register.

Book N-N, p. 317   PAUL TRAPIER, ESQ., of Georgetown, appointed
19 & 20 Sept. 1751   in 1737 as attorney for JOHN ARTHUR, black-
L & R   smith, formerly of SC, now of NC; to FRANCES
                      STEWART, widow, for ₺ 300 currency, lot #58 in
Georgetown, bounding NE 100 ft. on Prince Street; NW 217.9 ft. on lot #57,
SE on lot #59; SW on lots #19 & #20. Witnesses: JOHN LESESNE, SAMUEL
PECK. Before THOMAS HASELL, J.P. WILLIAM HOPTON, Register.

Book N-N, p. 321   JOHN DURANT, to JAMES SUMMERS, both of Prince
31 Jan. & 1 Feb. 1747 George Winyaw, for ₺ 360 SC money, 180 a. in
L & R   Craven Co., bounding W on JOSHUA WILKS; N on
                      MR. WHITESIDES & JOHN GOUGH; E on WILLIAM
SHACKELFORD; SE & SW on JOSEPH PORT. Witnesses: THOMAS HASELL, ANN SUM-
MERS. Before PAUL TRAPIER, J.P. WILLIAM HOPTON, Register.

Book N-N, p. 324   PAUL TRAPIER, ESQ., of Georgetown, executor of
14 & 15 Mar. 1748   will of CHARLES BENOIST, planter, of Prince
L & R   George Parish, Craven Co., to JAMES SUMMERS,
                      planter, of same Parish, for ₺ 750 currency,
500 a. in Craven Co. Whereas Lt. Gov. THOMAS BROUGHTON on 6 Aug. 1735
granted JOHN GOUGH 500 a. in Craven Co., bounding N on JOHN LANE; W on
vacant land; S on WILLIAM SHACKELFORD (now ANDREW JOHNSTON); which land
GOUGH conveyed to RICHARD MALONE by L & R dated 18 & 19 Aug. 1735; &
whereas MALONE by L & R dated 29 & 30 Nov. 1737 conveyed to ALCIMUS GAIL-
LARD; who with SARAH his wife, by L & R dated 20 & 21 June, 1740 conveyed
to CHARLES BENOIST; & whereas BENOIST by will dated 13 Oct. 1744 ordered
his land sold & appointed PAUL TRAPIER & MOREAU SARRAZIN his executors,
but SARRAZIN refused to act; now TRAPIER sells the 500 a. to SUMMERS.
Witnesses: JOSEPH DUBOURDIEU, WILLIAM PARKER. Before GEORGE PAWLEY, J.P.
WILLIAM HOPTON, Register.

Book N-N, p. 329   THOMAS HASELL, gentleman, of Georgetown, to
9 Jan. 1751   JAMES SUMMERS, planter, of Prince George Par-
Feoffment   ish, Craven Co., for ₺ 2000 currency, the part
                      of lot #24 in Georgetown, bounding SW 38 ft.
on Front or Bay Street; NE on the part belonging to CROSTHWAITE, BROWN &
DRAKEFORD; SE 74 ft. on Broad Street; NW on remaining part of lot #24;
also the land in front, extending from Front Street, down to low water
mark. Witnesses: ALEXANDER MCDONALL, WILLIAM CROOK. Before GEORGE PAW-
LEY, J.P. WILLIAM HOPTON, Register.

Book N-N, p. 331   JOSEPH LAW, planter, of Christ Church Parish,
15 & 16 Feb. 1753   only son & heir of BENJAMIN LAW, planter, who
L & R   was eldest brother & heir of JOSEPH LAW,
                      planter, of same Parish; to DANIEL LEGARE,
planter, of Berkeley Co., for ₺ 2000 currency, 200 a. & 60 a., making
260 a. in Christ Church Parish, bounding N on EDMUND ATKIN, ESQ.; NE on
JOHN METHRINGHAM; E & S on RICHARD FOWLER; as occupied by RICHARD TOOKER-
MAN, & before him by MAJ. WILLIAM PINCKNEY, as undertenants of said JO-
SEPH LAW or his guardian. Whereas JOSEPH LAW owned 200 a. in Christ
Church Parish which he had purchased from WILLIAM JONES & REBECCA his
wife as 2 separate tracts of 100 a. each, the first deed dated 24 June
1722, the other 9 Dec. 1722; & also owned 60 a., English measure, adjoining the S & W part of the above tract, which he had purchased from AN-
THONY VARDILL by deed of feoffment dated 21 Aug. 1722; making 1 tract of
260 a. on which JOSEPH LAW lived; & which, he by will dated 17 July 1732,
he bequeathed to his beloved nephew, JOSEPH LAW, party hereto, after the
death of his wife; & whereas by a defect because said will was not executed or published in the presence of 3 or more creditable witnesses,
the land became vested in BENJAMIN LAW, father of JOSEPH, as eldest
brother & heir of JOSEPH LAW, deceased, who enjoyed the land until his
death & JOSEPH LAW (party hereto) inherited; now he sells to LEGARE.
Witnesses: CHARLES PINCKNEY, JR., ARCHIBALD HAMILTON, WILLIAM WRIGHT.
Before JOHN DART, J.P. WILLIAM HOPTON, Register.

Book N-N, p. 337   JOHN HAMMERTON, ESQ., of Charleston, to

6 July 1743   WILLIAM STEPHENS, ESQ., of Savannah, Ga., for
Bond   the use of the trustees of Georgia, in penal
                     sum of Ł 300 British for payment of Ł 114:16:6
British on 25 Dec. 1743. Witnesses: SARAH METHRINGHAM, WILLIAM HOPTON.
Before JAMES WRIGHT, J.P. WILLIAM HOPTON, Register.

Book N-N, p. 338   JOHN HAMMERTON, ESQ., of Charleston, to WIL-
5 May 1744   LIAM STEPHENS, ESQ., if Savannah, Ga., as se-
Mortgage   curity on above bond (p. 337) dated 6 July
                     1743 in penal sum of Ł 300 British for payment
of Ł 114:16:6 sterling to STEPHENS for the use of the Hon. Trustees for
establishing the Colony of Georgia; all HAMMERTON'S title & the interest
in the office of Secretary & Register in SC, with the fees, salary, ad-
vantages, etc., belonging thereto. Witnesses: THOMAS SMITH, HENRY LAU-
RENS. Before ANDREW RUTLEDGE, J.P. Recorded in Secretary's Book G.G.
fol. 508-509 by JOHN CHAMPNEYS, Dep. Sec. WILLIAM HOPTON, Register.

Book N-N, p. 340   The Hon. WILLIAM MIDDLETON, & SARAH his wife,
10 & 11 Aug. 1753   of Berkeley Co., to GEORGE SHEED, gentleman,
L & R   of Charleston, for Ł 1500 currency, the W part
                     of lot #199 fronting 30 ft. N size Queen
Street, in Charleston, bounding W 167 ft. on JOHN CART; N 22-1/2 ft. on
WILLIAM MIDDLETON; E 167 ft. on a house occupied by HENRY MIDDLETON, ESQ.
Witnesses: HENRY MIDDLETON, JOHN REMINGTON. Before WILLIAM PINCKNEY,
J.P. WILLIAM HOPTON, Register.

Book N-N, p. 346   JOHN DELAGAYE, merchant, & CATHERINE his wife,
16 & 17 Oct. 1752   to FRANCIS STUART, merchant, both of Beaufort,
L & R   Port Royal, for Ł 400 currency, part of lot
                     #301 in Beaufort, bounding S on Bay of Beau-
fort; E on COL. JOHN BARNWELL; W on RANDOLPH EVANS; N on MORGAN ELLIS;
which lot #301 CHARLES PINCKNEY & GABRIEL MANIGAULT by L & R dated 11 &
12 Feb. last conveyed to WILLIAM GLEN, vendue master, of Charleston, who,
with ANNE his wife, on 8 & 9 Apr. last, conveyed to JOHN DELAGAYE, of
Beaufort; & measuring 60 ft. in front of the Bay eastward from the SE
corner of lot belonging to RANDOLPH EVANS; & from the NE corner of
EVANS'S lot 70 ft. eastward, which by a line drawn S from the E point of
the 60 ft. in front, contain the boundaries of said lot; also, part of
lot #305, being part of a greater part of lot #305 which MARY ALBERGOTTI,
spinster, of Beaufort, by L & R dated 21 & 22 Aug. last conveyed to JOHN
DELAGAYE; lot #305 having formerly been purchased by MARY ALBERGOTTI from
said DELAGAYE; which part now sold runs N from the E point of the 70 ft.
or back front of part of lot #301 aforesaid 37 ft.; & from thence W 50
ft. & there joins the W end of said 70 ft.; being in the form of a tri-
angle whose longest side is the back front of said part of lot #301.
Witnesses: JOHN CHAMPMAN, GREY ELLIOTT. Before WILLIAM HARVEY, J.P.
WILLIAM HOPTON, Register.

Book N-N, p. 353   GEORGE CLARK, to PHILIP MARTINGALE, planter,
1 & 2 Aug. 1753   both of St. Helena Island, Granville Co., as
L & R by Mortgage   security on bond of even date in penal sum of
                     Ł 2000 currency for performing covenants in
release hereafter named: 400 a. on St. Helena Island, bounding W on a
creek of Port Royal River; N on WILLIAM ALLEN; SE on MR. REYNOLDS; SW on
MR. SEALY; being part of 600 a. granted by the Lords Proprs. on 15 May
1715 to ARTHUR DICKS, of Granville Co., whereas on 16 Mar. 1726, ARTHUR
DICKS assigned the 600 a. to JOHN JOHNSON of St. Helena Island; who died
11 May 1746; & whereas the 600 a. was inherited equally by his 4 daughters, who agreed to divide the land; & whereas MARGARET TOBIAS & ELIZA-
BETH PARMENTER, 2 of the daughters, by L & R dated 23 & 24 Oct. 1752 sold
their divisions & their half share of the premises to ISAAC EDWARDS, of
St. Helena; & whereas he died 24 Jan. 1753 & bequeathed the 400 (?) a. &
his other effects to his wife SOPHIA; who later married GEORGE CLARKE; &
the 400 a. & 4 Negroes became vested in him; now CLARKE conveys the land
& the Negroes to MARTINANGELE; but should CLARKE pay MASSINANGELE the unpaid money on account of the estate of ISAAC EDWARDS, within 3 years from
date, this mortgage to be void. Should the payments justly due from said
estate be paid by MARTINANGELE then MARTINANGELE to have peaceable possession. Witnesses: MAGDALENE GOUGH, WILLIAM GOUGH. Before WILLIAM HAR-
VEY, J.P. WILLIAM HOPTON, Register.

Book N-N, p. 358   SAMUEL EATON, planter, of Edisto Island, eld-
28 May 1750   est son & heir of JONAS EATON, planter, of
Deed of Gift   same Island; to his brother JOSHUA EATON, for
                          natural love & affection, the 100 a., being
the eastern part of 2 tracts of 140 & 100 a.; bounding S on HENRY BAILEY;
E on THOMAS RACK. Whereas the Lords Proprs. by 2 grants dated 29 Mar.
1700 granted JOHN BRAY 2 adjoining tracts of 140 & 100 a. in Colleton Co.,
as enrolled in the Auditor's Office 6 Apr. 1733 in Book #2 fol. 339-340;
which tracts by various mesne conveyances came to JONAS EATON, who died
intestate, & were inherited by his eldest son, SAMUEL; now SAMUEL gives
the 2 tracts to his brother JOSHUA. Witnesses: JONATHAN WILKINS, JOHN
COX, WILLIAM RUSSELL. Before OTHNIEL BEALE, J.P. WILLIAM HOPTON, Register.

Book N-N, p. 361   JOSHUA EATON, & SARAH (her mark) his wife, to
2 Apr. 1753   BAYNARD FRY, planter, both of Edisto Island,
Release   Colleton Co., for Ł 400 currency, 100 a. on
                          Edisto Island, bounding ____ on MR. RIPPIN; S
on RALPH BAILEY; W on SAMUEL EATON. Witnesses: JONATHAN WILKINS, SAMUEL
EATON, MARY (her mark) COX. Before OTHNIEL BEALE, J.P. WILLIAM HOPTON,
Register.

Book N-N, p. 365   GEORGE SHEED, JR., schoolmaster, of Charles-
21 & 22 Aug. 1753   ton, to the Rev. MR. ALEXANDER GARDEN, rector
L & R by Mortgage   of St. Philip's Parish, Charleston, as secur-
                          ity on bond dated 10 Aug. 1753, in penal sum
of Ł 3000 for payment of Ł 1500 currency, with interest, on 1 Mar. 1754;
part of lot #199 in Charleston, bounding S 30 ft. on Queen Street; W 167
ft. on JOHN CART; N 22-1/2 ft. on the Hon. WILLIAM MIDDLETON; E 167 ft.
on a house & lot occupied by HENRY MIDDLETON, ESQ. Witnesses: GABRIEL
MANIGAULT, CHARLES GRIMBALL. Before ROBERT AUSTIN, J.P. WILLIAM HOPTON,
Register. On 10 Dec. 1756 FRANCIS BREMAR, executor of will of ALEXANDER
GARDEN declared mortgage satisfied. Witness: WILLIAM HOPTON.

Book N-N, p. 372   THOMAS WALKER, gentleman, to ALEXANDER PER-
11 Sept. 1753   ONNEAU, gentleman, both of Charleston, as se-
Mortgage   curity on bond of even date in penal sum of
                          Ł 6000 for payment of Ł 3000 currency, with
interest, on 11 Sept. 1754; part of a lot in Colleton Square, Charleston,
bounding E 150 ft. on THOMAS ELLERY; S 70 ft. on Hunter's Street; W on
Charles Street; N on Ellery Street. Witnesses: THOMAS LAMBOLL, CHARLES
GRIMBALL. Before JOHN DART, J.P. WILLIAM HOPTON, Register. On 28 May
1762 ALEXANDER PERONNEAU declared mortgage satisfied. Witness: WILLIAM
HOPTON.

Book N-N, p. 376   HENRY WARNER, schoolmaster, of St. Bartholo-
20 Aug. 1753   mew's Parish, Colleton Co., to ABRAHAM HAYNE,
Mortgage   planter, of St. Paul's Parish, Colleton Co.,
                          as security on bond of even date in penal sum
                          of Ł 404:16:0 for payment of Ł 202:8:0 curren-
cy, with interest, on 20 Jan. 1754; a half a. lot, #48, in Jacksonsburgh;
also 3 a. adjoining said lot; bounding E on said lot & on JOHN LAIRD; N
on JOHN PETET (not DAVID HEXT); S on the High Road leading to the Horseshoe; W on JOHN PETER (now DAVID HEXT). Witnesses: ARCHIBALD HAMILTON,
WILLIAM GLAZE, BENJAMIN SPLATT. Before JAMES BULLOCK, J.P. WILLIAM HOP-
TON, Register.

Book N-N, p. 378   The Hon. JOHN CLELAND, & MARY his wife, to
24 & 25 Aug. 1753   MARY LAROCHE, gentlewoman, of Charleston, for
L & R   Ł 817:10:0 currency, 81 a. 88 chains, part of
                          a tract granted JOHN CLELAND, being in Prince
George Parish, Craven Co., on S side Black River, near its mouth, bounding S on THOMAS MITCHELL; SW & NW on Georgetown. Witnesses: ARCHIBALD
BAIRD, JAMES CROKATT. Before THOMAS HASELL, J.P. WILLIAM HOPTON, Register. Plat by THOMAS HASELL dated 11 Aug. 1753.

Book N-N, p. 384   JOHN MCCALL, merchant, to BENJAMIN D'HARRIETTE,
27 Sept. 1753   merchant, both of Charleston, as security on
Mortgage   bond of even date in penal sum of Ł 8000 for
                          payment of Ł 4000 currency, with interest, on

27 Sept. 1754; his brick house & part of lot #73 in which he lives, &
which he purchased from SARAH JOHNSTON, widow; bounding N 40 ft. on Tradd
Street; W 100 ft. on JOHN STONE; S on MR. GIBBES; E on MR. WARHAM (formerly MR. GREY); also the brick house & part of lot #6 where JAMES MARSH
lives, which MCCOLL purchased from DAVID HEXT, gentleman, & ANN his wife,
of Berkeley Co., bounding N 29 ft. on Tradd Street; W 51-1/2 ft. on part
lot #6 belonging to DAVID HEXT; S on ANTHONY MATHEWS; E on part of lot #6
belonging to ALEXANDER HEXT, & part to JAMES MATHEWES. Witnesses: MAU-
RICE ANDERSON, THOMAS LAMBOLL. Before JOHN DART, J.P. WILLIAM HOPTON,
Register.

Book N-N, p. 389   The Rev. MR. FRANCIS GUICHARD, pastor of
1 Oct. 1742   Church of French Protestants, GABRIEL MANI-
Lease for 50 years   GAULT, ISAAC MAZYCK, PAUL MAZYCK, JACOB MAR-
                          TIN, JOHN NEUFVILLE, BENJAMIN D'HARRIETTE, &
GIDEON FAUCHERAUD, of 1st part; to JOHN VANN, carpenter, of Charleston,
of 2nd part; for Ł 3:4:0 sterling a year, for 50 a., lot #93 bounding W
30 ft. on King Street; S on JAMES HILLIARD; E on MRS. BONGHAR; N on other
part lot #93. VANN agrees to build & keep in good repair a substantial
brick house on the lot, 15 ft. front, 27 ft. deep, with 2 chimneys, 1
story & attic. Witnesses: CHARLES PINCKNEY, J. BONNETHEAU. No probate
on deed. WILLIAM HOPTON, Register.

Book N-N, p. 394   JOHN VANN, to ROBERT RAWLINS, for Ł 650 SC
19 Aug. 1749   money, assigns the above lease, with lot &
Assignment of above   premises, for balance of term of 50 years.
lease   RAWLINS to pay the yearly rent of Ł 3:4:0
                          sterling payable to the Congregation of the
French Church. Witnesses: FREDERICK STRUBELL, JOHN WILLKYE. Before
JAMES WEDDERBURN, J.P. WILLIAM HOPTON, Register.

Book N-N, p. 395   FRANCIS GUICHARD, gentleman, & BENJAMIN D'HAR-
18 & 19 Sept. 1751   RIETTE, merchant, executors of will & codicil
L & R   of JAMES VOULOUX, of St. Philips Parish,
                          Charleston, to ROBERT RAWLINS, gentleman, for
Ł 380 currency, that house & land lately belonging to JAMES VOULOUX, on
SW side of High Road in St. Philips Parish leading NW from Charleston
into the Co., bounding NW on HUGH ANDERSON; SE on JOHN GEORGE DALLIBACH;
SW on the lands which by codicil JAMES VOULOUX bequeathed to his wife,
LYDIA, now LYDIA RAWLINS, wife of ROBERT RAWLINS; being 35 ft. from NW to
SE & 384 ft. from SW to NE. Whereas JAMES BOULOUX, besides other tenements & lands, owned the above house & lot, & by will dated 11 Nov. 1748
authorized his executors to sell his 2 houses & the rest of his real estate, appointing GUICHARD & D'HARRIETTE his executors; & afterwards on 26
Nov. 1748, by codicil confirmed his will except that he bequeathed to his
wife LYDIA, the land at the A end of Charleston Neck; fronting W on a
certain passageway, being 30 ft. from E to W & from S to N the whole
breadth of his land; & whereas ROBERT RAWLINS, as highest bidder, has
agreed to purchase the other house & land; now the executors complete the
sale. Witnesses: JAMES BALLANTINE, THOMAS LAMBOLL. Before JOHN LINING,
J.P. WILLIAM HOPTON, Register.

Book N-N, p. 404   ROBERT RAWLINS, scrivener, & LYDIA his wife,
2 & 3 Oct. 1753   of Charleston, to the Rev. MR. ALEXANDER GAR-
L & R by Mortgage   DEN, rector of St. Philip's Parish, Charles-
                          ton, as security on bond of even date, in the
penal sum of Ł 2200 for payment of Ł 1100 currency, with interest, on a
certain date in 1754; & whereas by lease dated 1 Oct. 1752 the Rev. MR.
FRANCIS GUICHARD, GABRIEL MANIGAULT, ISAAC MAZYCK, PAUL MAZYCK, JACOB
MARTIN, JOHN NEUFVILLE, BENJAMIN D'HARRIETTE & GIDEON FAUCHERAUD leased
to JOHN VANN, for 50 years, part of lot #93 bounding W 30 ft. on King
Street; S on JAMES HILLIARD (now JOHN BASSNETT); E on MR. MONSHAR; N on
other part lot #93; at a yearly rent of Ł 3:4:0 sterling; with certain
agreements in the lease; & whereas VANN by indorsement on back of said
lease, on 19 Aug. 1749, transferred the property to ROBERT RAWLINS for
the balance of the term of 50 years, subject to said yearly rent; now
RAWLINS conveys to GARDEN & others the above named lease; also the house
& land he purchased from the executors of JAMES VOULOUX (p. 395); 35 ft.
by 384 ft. on Charleston Neck; also the adjoining house & lot which JAMES
VOULOUX, by codicil bequeathed to his wife LYDIA, now wife of said ROBERT

RAWLINS. Witnesses: CHARLES PRYCE, JORDAN ROCHE, THOMAS YEOMANS. Before
WILLIAM BULL, JR., J.P. WILLIAM HOPTON, Register. On Jan. 12, 1758,
SAMPSON NEYLE, executor of the Rev. MR. ALEXANDER GARDEN declared, by
note to MR. HOPTON, that mortgage was satisfied by MR. RAWLINS.

Book N-N, p. 414   RAWLINS LOWNDES, P.M. to THOMAS BOLTON, mer-
2 Oct. 1753   chant, of Charleston, at public auction, for
Sale   Ł 2730 currency, 340 a. on SE side Wando Riv-
                          er. Whereas the Lords Proprs. on 11 May, 1709
granted BENJAMIN QUELCH 340 a., English measure, on SE side Wando River,
in Berkeley Co., bounding NE on Wackindaw Creek; E on DAVID MAYBANK; S on
Malassa Creek; which by will dated 17 July 1716 he bequeathed to his
wife ELIZABETH during her lifetime & afterwards to his son GEORGE QUELCH,
or by default to his son ANDREW, or his son BENJAMIN; & whereas after the
death of BENJAMIN, the father, GEORGE & BENJAMIN the sons died; & whereas
ELIZABETH QUELCH also died & son ANDREW inherited & has had possession
for over 20 years & has children, so that he now has an absolute estate
of inheritance; & whereas on 4 July 1748 ANDREW QUELCH gave bond to THOM-
AS BOLTON in penal sum of Ł 10,300 for payment of Ł 5150 currency, with
interest, on 4 July 1749, & as security conveyed to BOLTON, by L & R dated 11 & 12 July 1748, the said 340 a.; & whereas QUELCH failed to redeem
the property & BOLTON obtained a judgment against QUELCH for Ł 10,300 &
costs; & whereas WILLIAM BULL, JR., Ass't. J., in the absence of CHARLES
PINCKNEY, C.J., on 3 Apr. 1753 issued a writ of fieri facias to the P.M.
who seized the property; now he sells to the highest bidder, said THOMAS
BOLTON. Witnesses: DOUGAL CAMPBELL, WILLIAM READ. Before JAMES WRIGHT,
J.P. WILLIAM HOPTON, Register.

Book N-N, p. 422   PATRICK (his mark) MARCH, planter, to THOMAS
14 & 15 Jan. 1752   LLOYD, both of Granville Co., for Ł 200 cur-
L & R   rency, 350 a. on Stephens Creek, on NE side
                          Savannah River in Granville Co., granted by
Gov. JAMES GLEN on 6 Oct. 1752 to said PATRICK MARCH; bounding SW on
Stephen's Creek; other sides on vacant land. Witnesses: JOSEPH CHATWIN,
THOMAS MONEY. Before JOHN TOBLER, J.P. WILLIAM HOPTON, Register.

Book N-N, p. 426   THOMAS BOLTON, merchant, & ELIZABETH his wife,
3 & 4 Oct. 1753   to JOHN ROSE & JAMES STEWART, ship carpenters,
L & R   all of Charleston, for Ł 2900 currency, 340 a.
                          on SE side Wando River. Whereas the Lords
Proprs. on 11 May 1709 granted BENJAMIN QUELCH 340 a., English measure,
in Berkeley Co., bounding NW on Wando River; N on Wackindaw Creek; E on
DAVID MAYBANK; S on Malesse Creek; which by will dated 17 July 1716 he
bequeathed to his wife for her lifetime & afterwards to son GEORGE, or to
son ANDREW, or to son BENJAMIN in case of default; & whereas after the
death of BENJAMIN the father, GEORGE & BENJAMIN, the sons, died; & ELIZA-
BETH having also died, son ANDREW QUELCH inherited, & has had possession
for over 20 years; & whereas ANDREW had children & therefore had an absolute estate of inheritance; & whereas ANDREW mortgaged the land to THOMAS
BOLTON (see p. 414) & failed to pay the mortgage, so that the land was
sold at public auction & purchased by BOLTON, as highest bidder; now BOL-
TON sells the land to STEWART & ROSE. Witnesses: PETER DAVID, JAMES
MICHIE. Before OTHNIEL BEALE, J.P. WILLIAM HOPTON, Register.

Book N-N, p. 440   PETER GIRARDEAU, & ELIZABETH his wife, of Col-
13 & 14 June 1753   leton Co., to WILLIAM ROSE, practitioner of
L & R   physic, of Ashepoo, for Ł 1400 currency, 931
                          a. in Granville Co., bounding according to
plat. Witnesses: MARY GIRARDEAU, ELIZABETH GIRARDEAU, JOHN BILNEY. Before Lt. Gov. WILLIAM BULL. WILLIAM HOPTON, Register. Plat of 931 a.
which on being resurveyed were found to be 896 a., of irregular shape,
bounding NE on JOSEPH IZARD; E on STEPHEN BULL & on a MR. IZARD; S on
Gov. BULL; W on MRS. BRYAN, JAMES DEVEAUX & old MR. DEVEAUX (formerly
Landgrave EDMUND BELLINGER).

Book N-N, p. 446   JOHN (his mark) CHAVONS, planter, to JOHN
14 & 15 Apr. 1752   SCOTT, planter, of Craven Co., for Ł 600 cur-
L & R   rency, 600 a. in Granville Co., bounding SW on
                          Little River; other sides on vacant land;
which tract Gov. JAMES GLEN on 13 Mar. 1752 granted to JOHN CHAVONS.

Witnesses: ROGER ROBERTS, ANN (her mark) ROBERTS. Before JOHN TOBLER,
J.P. of Granville Co. WILLIAM HOPTON, Register.

Book N-N, p. 453   JOHN GOLDING (GOULDING), planter, & SARAH his
3 & 4 June 1753   wife, of St. George's Parish, Berkeley Co., to
L & R   JOHN MCQUEEN, storekeeper, of Charleston, for
                          Ŀ 1400 currency, 93 a. on Cow Savannah in St.
George's Parish, bounding NW on estate of JOSIAH BAKER & on RALPH IZARD;
NE on RALPH IZARD; SE on the public road leading from Bacons Bridge to
PonPon; SW on JOSIAH BAKER'S estate; which tract after several mesne con-
veyances came to PETER GOLDING (father of said JOHN GOLDING) who died in-
testate, & was inherited by JOHN GOLDING, who now sells to MCQUEEN. SAR-
AH (her mark) wife of JOHN GOLDING, voluntarily renounces her dower.
Witnesses: WILLIAM MAINE, WILLIAM HARRISON, JAMES SMITH. Before J. SKENE,
J.P. WILLIAM HOPTON, Register.

Book N-N, p. 461   JOHN GOULDING, planter, of St. George's Par-
4 June 1753   ish, Berkeley Co., to JOHN MCQUEEN, in penal
Bond   sum of Ŀ 2000 currency, as a guarantee that
                          his wife, SARAH GOULDING, will not claim her
dower to above mentioned 93 a. (p. 453). Witnesses: WILLIAM MAINE, WIL-
LIAM HARRISON, JAMES SMITH. Before J. SKENE, J.P. WILLIAM HOPTON, Register. On 12 July 1753 JOHN MCQUEEN assigned the bond to RALPH IZARD.
Witness: JAMES PARKER. Before JOHN DART, J.P. WILLIAM HOPTON, Register.

Book N-N, p. 464   JOHN MCQUEEN, merchant, & ANN his wife, of
10 & 11 July 1753   Charleston, to RALPH IZARD, ESQ., of St.
L & R   George's Parish, Berkeley Co., for Ŀ 1400 cur-
                          rency, 93 a. in St. George's Parish. Whereas
PETER GOULDING, blacksmith, owned 93 a. in St. George's Parish, being a
part of 2 tracts which he had purchased from GEORGE FLOOD; the 93 a.
bounding NW on the estate of JOSIAH BAKER & RALPH IZARD; NE on part of
Ashley Barony called Cow Savannah now belonging to RALPH IZARD; SE on the
public road leading from Bacon Bridge to PonPon; SE on estate of JOSIAH
BAKER; as by plat dated 14 May last certified by WILLIAM MAINE, Dep. Sur.
& annexed to release dated 4 June last from JOHN GOULDING & SARAH his
wife, to JOHN MCQUEEN; & whereas PETER GOULDING died intestate & his eldest son, JOHN, Inherited the 93 a. & the rest of his father's real estate, & on 4 June 1753, for Ŀ 1400 currency, sold the 93 a. to MCQUEEN;
now MCQUEEN sells to IZARD. ANN MCQUEEN voluntarily renounces her dower.
Witnesses: MARY YEOMANS, JOSEPH NICHOLSON, JAMES PARKER. Before JOHN
DART, J.P. WILLIAM HOPTON, Register.

Book N-N, p. 473   The Hon. JOHN CLELAND & MARY his wife, to THOM-
11 & 12 Sept. 1753   AS HASELL, of Georgetown, Winyaw, for
L & R   Ŀ 387:10:0 currency, 31 a. in Prince George
                          Parish, Winyaw, bounding SE on Wood Street, in
Georgetown; SW on the harbor in Sandpit Creek; NE on Sand Pit Road & a
line continuing the same course from the first angle thereof; NW on PAUL
TRAPIER; being part of 3996 a. granted JOHN CLELAND. Witnesses: ARCHI-
BALD BAIRD, JAMES SUMMERS. Before GEORGE PAWLEY, J.P. WILLIAM HOPTON,
Register. Plat of resurvey by THOMAS HASELL dated 7 Sept. 1753, & show-
ing 2 a. belonging to JOHN CRAWFORD.

Book N-N, p. 479   HUGH ROSS, carter, & SARAH (her mark) his wife,
10 & 11 Oct. 1753   to ROBERT RAWLINS, scrivener, both of Charles-
L & R   ton, for Ŀ 400 currency, a piece of land on
                          Charleston Neck being part of a tract sold by
JOSEPH WRAGG to JOHN GEORGE DALLABACH. Whereas by L & R dated 5 & 6 May
1752 JOHN GEORGE DALLABACH, bricklayer, & JOHANNA his wife, of Charleston
sold to HUGH ROSS, carter, that piece of land on Charleston Neck, in
Berkeley Co., bounding NE on the Broad Path or high road of St. Philip's
Parish leading to & from Charleston; SE on JOSEPH WRAGG; SW on Parish
lands to be used for a Glebe or Free School or both; NW on ROBERT RAWLINS
(formerly JOHN GEORGE DALLABACH, who sold to JAMES VOULOUX); breadth 25
ft. SE from ROBERT RAWLINS; length 416 ft. SW from High Road; now ROSS
sells to RAWLINS. Witnesses: WILLIAM SIMPSON, CHARLES BLUNDY. Before
ROBERT AUSTIN, J.P. WILLIAM HOPTON, Register.

Book N-N, p. 486   CHILDERMAS CROFT, gentleman, of Charleston, to

17 & 8 Oct. 1753   the Rev. MR. ALEXANDER GARDEN, rector of St.
L & R vy Mortgage   Philips Parish, Charleston, as security on
                           bond of even date in penal sum of Ł 5000 for
payment of Ł 2500 currency, with interest, on 18 Oct. 1754; a lot bound-
ing S 46 ft. on Broad Street; N on Queen Street; E 492 ft. on ANTHONY
MATHEWES; W on MRS. DEVEAUX & MRS. GRAME; also 81 a. on Charleston Neck,
bounding N on heirs of JOHN PENDARVIS; S on BRANVILLE EVANS; E on JAMES
MCLACLAN; W on a marsh. Witnesses: JOHN RATTRAY, JOHN HARVEY. Before
DANIEL CRAWFORD, J.P. WILLIAM HOPTON, Register. On 22 May 1754 SAMPSON
NEYLE, attorney, for ALEXANDER GARDEN, declared mortgage satisfied. Wit-
ness: WILLIAM HOPTON.

Book N-N, p. 491   ABRAHAM BOND, carpenter, of Georgetown, Prince
26 Jan. 1753   George Winyaw Parish, to JOSEPH BROWN, mer-
Release   chant of Georgetown, for Ł 300 currency, lots
                          #157 & #158 in Georgetown. Whereas GEORGE
PAWLEY, WILLIAM SWINTON, & DANIEL LAROCHE, on 8 Feb. 1734 sold BOND lot
157, bounding NE 100 ft. on Duke Street; SE 217.9 ft. on lot #158; SW
on lot #133; NW on Broad Street; & on 25 Apr. 1737 sold BOND lot #158,
bounding NE 100 ft. on Duke Street; SE on lot #159; SW on lot #134; NW
217.9 ft. on lot #157; with right of commonage for 1 horse & 1 cow for
each lot; now BOND sells the 2 lots to BROWN. Witnesses: JOHN SKRINE,
JAMES RICHARDS. Before WILLIAM PINCKNEY, J.P. WILLIAM HOPTON, Register.

Book N-N, p. 494   THOMAS FRANKLAND, ESQ., of Old Bond Street,
17 & 18 May 1753   St. George Parish, Middlesex Co., Great Brit-
L & R   ain, & SARAH his wife (formerly SARAH RHETT, 1
                          of the daughters & coheiresses of WILLIAM
RHETT the younger, gentleman, of Charleston, SC); to CHARLES MAYNE, merchant, of Charleston; for Ł 5500 SC money, their undivided half share of
the half part of lot #15 in Charleston, bounding E on the Bay; W on Union
Street; also their undivided half part of a bridge & wharf & low water
lot #333, bounding W on the curtain line of the Bay; N on lot #16; & running E to Cooper River; also their undivided half share of the half part
of low water lot #16; bounding S on low water lot #333; W 50 ft. on the
curtain line; N on the other half of the lot; running E as far as low
water mark. Whereas the Lords Proprs. on 8 May 1683 granted PETER HEARN,
gentleman, lot #15 in Charleston; & he, by will dated 18 Dec. 1688, bequeathed all his real & personal estate to his wife, JANE, & their 7
children named in the will, appointing his wife & 7 children executrix &
executors; & whereas by an Act of General Assembly ratified 17 Jan. 1694
JAMES WITTER & EDWARD DRAKE were authorized to sell lot #15 & on 18 Jan.
1694 sold the lot with its houses & buildings to Landgrave JOSEPH BLAKE;
who on 3 June 1695 sold the lot to WILLIAM DRY, planter; who on 6 Nov.
1696 sold to WILLIAM RHETT, merchant, of Charleston, father of WILLIAM
the younger, the N half of lot #15, bounding E on the wharf on Cooper
River; N on MARY CROSS, widow; W on a little street; & whereas the Lords
Proprs. on 13 Dec. 1698, by Gov. JOSEPH BLAKE, granted WILLIAM RHETT the
elder, a front lot in Charleston, #333, fronting W on the wharf line, lying opposite lot #15, & containing 36 perches, bounding N on front lot
#16 belonging to MARY BASDEN (formerly to MARY CROSS); & running E to low
water mark; so that WILLIAM RHETT the elder, owned half of lot #15, & all
of lot #333 & by L & R dated 3 & 4 Aug. 1716 he & his wife SARAH sold
WILLIAM RHETT the younger, the half of lot #15 the S half of which now
belongs to EDWARD CROFT); extending W 134 ft. & divided from S half by a
brick wall; also the wharf & low water lot #333; with the brick tenements
& other buildings on lot #15; & whereas WILLIAM RHETT the younger, by L &
R dated 4 & 5 Oct. 1717, for the consideration mentioned & in consideration of the intended marriage between WILLIAM RHETT the younger, & MARY
TROTT, daughter of NICHOLAS TROTT, ESQ., of Charleston, conveyed to
NICHOLAS TROTT & WILLIAM RHETT the elder, in trust for said WILLIAM &
MARY, the said half of lot #15, with its buildings, the wharf, & lot
#333; & whereas the marriage took place & they had 2 daughters SARAH &
MARY JANE, their only children; & whereas SARAH married THOMAS FRANKLAND,
party hereto, & MARY JANE married WILLIAM DRY, gentleman, of NC; & where-
as WILLIAM RHETT the elder, by will dated 6 July 1722 authorized his wife
SARAH, to sell all his real estate (except as excepted) leaving all his
estate to her & after his death she became owner of the other half of lot
#15 with its houses & buildings now occupied by JOHN BONNETHEAU & JOHN
COWDEN, the parts being divided by a brick wall; S on other half; W on

307

Union Street; N on JOHN MOORE; & whereas SARAH afterwards married NICHO-
LAS TROTT, & they owned half of lot #16, 15 ft. wide; & whereas NICHOLAS
& SARAH TROTT by L & R dated 12 & 13 Mar. 1734 conveyed to the Rev. MR.
ALEXANDER GARDEN, rector of St. Philip's Parish, & JOSEPH WRAGG, merchant, in trust for their grandchildren SARAH FRANKLAND & MARY JANE DRY,
infants, half of lot #15 with 2 dwelling houses & other buildings, also
half of lot #16; & whereas ALEXANDER GARDEN, sole surviving trustee, has
released his trust & has conveyed his estate to SARAH & MARY JANE, & they
& their husbands are now tenants in common; now THOMAS & SARAH FRANKLAND
sell their half share to CHARLES MAYNE. Witnesses: JOHN WATSONE, WILLIAM
WHITE, JOHN BROWNE. Before JACOB MOTTE, J.P. WILLIAM HOPTON, Register.

Book N-N, p. 513   THOMAS FRANKLAND, gives CHARLES MAYNE, a bond
18 May 1753   in penal sum of Ł 1100 currency, as a guaran-
Bond   tee of performance in above sale & as guaran-
                tee that his wife SARAH will not claim her
dower (p. 493). Witnesses: JOHN WATSONE, WILLIAM WHITE, JOHN BROWNE.
Before JACOB MOTTE, J.P. WILLIAM HOPTON, Register.

Book N-N, p. 516   JOHN ANDERSON, dealer, of Craven Co., to THOM-
31 Oct. 1753   AS CORKER, merchant, of Charleston, as securi-
Mortgage   ty on bond dated 28 Mar. 1752 in penal sum of
                Ł 532:15:0 for payment of Ł 266:7:6 currency
with interest, on 26 July 1754; the balance now due being Ł 189:7:6; 250
a. near the Congarees, on Santee River, granted by Gov. JAMES GLEN; bounding N on HENRY SNELLING (formerly RICHARD JACKSON) & MRS. ELIZABETH VER-
DITY; W on MRS VERDITY & vacant land; S & E on vacant land; also 170 a.
granted by Gov. JAMES GLEN to JOHN ANDERSON, bounding S on the Congaree
River; W on vacant land; N & E on Raiford's Creek. Witness: ROBERT MC-
DOUGALL. Before JOHN DART, J.P. WILLIAM HOPTON, Register.

Book N-N, p. 518   JAMES (his mark) BABER, planter, of the Welch
24 & 25 June 1752   tract, Craven Co., to ROBERT WILLIAMS, yeoman,
L & R   of Craven Co., for Ł 700 currency, 400 a. in
                said Welch tract, on SW side Peedee River,
bounding N on JACOB BUCKLE & EDWARD BOYKIN; NE on vacant land; SE on SAM-
UEL WIGGINS; E on HENRY ROACH; SE & SW on vacant land. Witnesses: HENRY
LEDBETTER, JAMES SMART. Before WILLIAM JAMES, J.P. No probate to lease.
Recorded in Secretary's book I.I. fol. 407 by WILLIAM PINCKNEY, Dep. Sec.
WILLIAM HOPTON, Register.

Book N-N, p. 524   CHRISTOPHER DAWSON (son & heir of RICHARD DAW-
1 & 2 Jan. 1753   SON, tailor, of Granville Co.), to PHILIP MAR-
L & R   TINANGEL, planter, for Ł 350 currency, 200 a.
                on Hilton Head, Granville Co., bounding E, N,
& S on ALEXANDER TRENCH; W on Scull Creek. Whereas JOHN, Earl of Bath,
& the Lords Proprs. on 16 Aug. 1698 created JOHN BAYLY the elder, of Bal-
linclough, in Co. of Tipperary, Ireland, a Landgrave of SC, & granted him
48,000 a.; & whereas his son & heir, JOHN BAYLY, on 9 Nov. 1722, appointed ALEXANDER TRENCH, merchant, of Charleston, his attorney, with authori-
ty to sell the land, reserving 8000 a. for BAYLY; & by L & R dated 1 & 2
Jan. 1725 sold RICHARD DAWSON 200 a. (out of the 48,000); now his son,
CHRISTOPHER, sells the 200 a. to MARTINANGEL. Witnesses: LAURENCE WOL-
FORSTON, JULIAN MARONSY, JAMES SCOTT. Before WILLIAM HARVEY, J.P. WIL-
LIAM HOPTON, Register.

Book N-N, p. 532   JOHN (his mark) GREADY, planter, & JANE his
6 & 7 Aug. 1752   wife, (1 of the 4 daughters & coheiresses of
L & R   JOHN JOHNSON, planter), of St. Helena, Gran-
                ville Co., to WILLIAM ALLEN, planter, of same
place, for Ł 500 currency, their 1/4 undivided part of 600 a. & premises.
Whereas the Lords Proprs. on 15 May 1715 granted ARTHUR DICK (DICKS), of
Granville Co., 600 a. on St. Helena Island, bounding W on a small creek
out of Port Royal River; N on JOSEPH PAGE; E on then vacant land; S on
DANIEL DICK; & whereas ARTHUR DICKS on 16 Mar. 1726 sold the 600 a. to
JOHN JOHNSON, planter, who died intestate 11 May 1746, leaving 4 daughters, MARGARET, SARAH, JANE & ELIZABETH, coheiresses; & whereas JANE mar-
ried JOHN GREADY; now they sell their share of the estate to ALLEN. Witnesses: THOMAS WIGG, PHILIP MARTINANGELE. Before WILLIAM HARVEY, J.P.
WILLIAM HOPTON, Register.

Book N-N, p. 539   HENRY CHRISTIE, carpenter, to the Rev. Mr. AL-
4 Nov. 1753   EXANDER GARDEN, rector of St. Philips Parish,
Release of Equity   Charleston, to satisfy a certain bond, releas-
                         es his claim to part of lot #268 part of Ha-
wett's Square (later GIBBONS & ALLENS Square). Whereas CHRISTIE gave
GARDEN a bond dated 23 July 1750 in penal sum of Ł 2000 for payment of
Ł 1000 currency, with interest, on 23 July 1751 & as security conveyed to
GARDEN that part of lot #268 in Charleston, bounding E 140-1/2 ft. on
Allen Street; W on THOMAS BENNETT; N 36 ft. on an alley belonging to
JAMES ST. JOHN & ROBERT THORPE; S on Broad Street; & whereas there is now
due of the bond Ł 1100:12:0 currency; now CHRISTIE releases his title to
GARDEN. Witnesses: JOHN RATTRAY, GEORGE JACKSON. Before DANIEL CRAWFORD,
J.P. WILLIAM HOPTON, Register.

Book N-N, p. 543   SARAH BLAKEWAY, widow & executrix of will of
1 & 2 May 1752   WILLIAM BLAKEWAY, ESQ., of Charleston, to
L & R   PHILIP MARTINANGELE, planter, of Granville Co.,
                         for Ł 200 currency, 200 a. on Hilton Head Is-
land (Trench's Island); bounding N on Scull Creek, NE & SE on ALEXANDER
TRENCH; S on CHRISTOPHER DAWSON. Whereas WILLIAM BLAKEWAY purchased from
ALEXANDER TRENCH, attorney, for Landgrave JOHN BAYLY (son & heir of JOHN
BAYLY, of Ballinaclough, Co. of Tipperary, Ireland) by L & R dated 5 & 6
Apr. 1726, 200 a. on Hilton Head Island, which by will dated 1 July 1727
he bequeathed to his wife, SARAH; now she sells to MARTINANGELE. Wit-
nesses: RICHARD BERISFORD, CHARLES PINCKNEY, JR. Before JACOB MOTTE, J.P.
WILLIAM HOPTON, Register.

Book N-N, p. 550   SARAH BLAKEWEY, widow, of Charleston, & GEORGE
2 May 1752   LOGAN, JR., of St. Thomas Parish, Berkeley Co.,
Bond   to PHILIP MARTINANGELE, in penal sum of Ł 400
                        currency, as a guarantee for keeping agree-
ments in above conveyance (p. 543). Witnesses: RICHARD BERISFORD,
CHARLES PINCKNEY, JR. Before JACOB MOTTE, J.P. WILLIAM HOPTON, Register.

Book N-N, p. 551   The Hon. JOHN CLELAND, & MARY his wife, to
28 & 29 Aug. 1753   JAMES SUMMERS, planter, both of Craven Co.,
L & R   for Ł 500 currency, 2 adjoining lots #233 &
                         #234 in Georgetown, bounding SE on Georgetown
River to low water mark; SE on lot #235; NW on lot #232; NE on Front
Street; each lot being 50 ft. from SE to NW; & 217.9 ft. from SW to NE.
Witnesses: ARCHIBALD BAIRD, DAVID DRENNAN. Before THOMAS HASELL, J.P.
WILLIAM HOPTON, Register.

Book N-N, p. 558   JOHN CLELAND, ESQ., & MARY his wife, to JAMES
8 & 9 Sept. 1753   SUMMERS, planter, both of Georgetown, Craven
L & R   Co., for Ł 1200 currency, 10 whole lots & half
                         a lot in Georgetown; Nos. 239, 240, 241, 242,
243, 244, 245, 246, 247, 248, & half of lot #249; lots 239 & half of 249
bounding NE on #238 & remaining half of #249; lots #247, 247, 248, & part
of 249 NE on Prince Street, #245 & 246 NW on Cannon Street; 239, 240,
241, 242, 243, 244, & 245, & an addition of 40 ft. taken from Front
Street added to the length of these 7 lots to SW on Front Street. Witnesses: ARCHIBALD BAIRD, DAVID DRENNAN. Before THOMAS HASELL, J.P. WIL-
LIAM HOPTON, Register.

                         DEEDS BOOK "O-O"
                         NOV. 1753 - OCT. 1754

Book O-O, p. 1   HANNAH HASELL, of St. Thomas Parish, Berkeley
8 & 9 Mar. 1753   Co., widow of JOHN HASELL, planter, to ROBERT
L & R   QUASH, planter, of same Parish, for Ł 2155
                         currency, several adjoining tracts, total 1004
a., in St. Thomas Parish, bounding S on HENRY VIDEAU; NW on HANNAH HASELL
& THOMAS ASHBY; SE on land called Cypress Pond belonging to PETER SIMMONS.
Whereas the Lords Proprs. on 12 June. 1709 granted SAMUEL KING 180 a. in
St. Thomas Parish; & on 24 Jan. 1716/7 granted him 324 a.; & on 4 Apr.
1717 granted him 500 a; both adjoining said 180 a.; & whereas SAMUEL KING
conveyed 100 a. to THOMAS VALLY of said Parish; & by deed of gift gave

his daughter ELIZABETH, wife of THOMAS VALLY, 100 a., & by will gave his
executors authority to dispose of the remainder of his land; & whereas
they sold 804 a., the residue, to JOHN HASELL, who had purchased from
THOMAS VALLY & his wife the other 200 a.; & whereas JOHN HASELL bequeathed to his wife, HANNAH HASELL, the 3 tracts; now she sells them to QUASH.
Witnesses: JOHN FARQUHARSON, DAVID ANDERSON. Before SAMUEL THOMAS, J.P.
WILLIAM HOPTON, Register.

Book O-O, p. 7   JOHN RIVERS, carpenter, & ELIZABETH his wife,
2 Apr. 1753   to JOHN FRYER, carpenter, & RACHAEL his wife;
Lease for Life   all of Charleston; for Ł 4 SC money a year;
                            that part of a lot in Charleston bounding N
40 ft. on ELIZABETH HUNT, widow; E 140 ft. on GABRIEL ESCOTT & EDWARD
FENWICK & COL. JOHN GIBBES; S on Rivers Street; W 140 ft. on other part
of JOHN RIVERS'S lot. Witnesses: HENRY FENDIN, THOMAS LAMBOLL. Before
WILLIAM PINCKNEY, J.P. Recorded in Secretary's Book I.I. fol. 549-551 on
12 Sept. 1753 by WILLIAM PINCKNEY for Dep. Sec. WILLIAM HOPTON, Register.

Book O-O, p. 11   The Hon. JOHN CLELAND, ESQ., & MARY his wife,
16 & 17 Nov. 1753   to BENJAMIN DARLING, shipwright, of George-
L & R   town, for Ł 750 currency, 3 lots in George-
                            town, Craven Co., Nos. 230, 231, & 232; bound-
ing SE on lot #233; NW on Cannon Street; NE on Front or Bay Street; SW to
low water on Georgetown River. Witnesses: ARCHIBALD BAIRD, THOMAS GOD-
FREY. Before THOMAS HASELL, J.P. WILLIAM HOPTON, Register.

Book O-O, p. 17   BENJAMIN DARLING, shipwright, of Georgetown,
21 & 22 Nov. 1753   to the Hon. JOHN CLELAND, as security on bond
L & R by Mortgage   dated 1 Nov. 1753 in penal sum of Ł 9425 for
                            payment of Ł 4712:11:4 currency, with inter-
est, on 1 Apr. 1754; 4 lots in Georgetown, containing 1 a., English measure, Nos. 48, 230, 231, 232. Witnesses: ARCHIBALD BAIRD, JOHN FRANCIS.
Before GEORGE PAWLEY, J.P. WILLIAM HOPTON, Register.

Book O-O, p. 22   THOMAS BOONE, ESQ., of Charleston, SC &
10 July 1753   CHARLES BOONE, ESQ., of Parish of St. George,
Feoffment   Hanover Square, Co. of Middlesex, by his at-
                            torney said THOMAS BOONE of Charleston; to
THOMAS SMITH, ESQ., of Charleston, for Ł 3600 SC money the N half of lot
#2 in Charleston, bounding E 50 ft. on the Bay; N 300 ft. on part of lot
#3 belonging to CAPT. GEORGE SMITH; S on COL. JAMES RISBEE; W on WILLIAM
CHAPMAN; with a large dwelling house lately occupied by ANNE BOONE.
Whereas ANNE BOONE, widow, owned (with divers other lands, tenements,
etc.) the N half of lot #2 on the Bay in Charleston; & by will dated 1
Dec. 1749 bequeathed said house & lot in which she lived, in Charleston,
to her 2 nephews, THOMAS & CHARLES, sons of her brother-in-law CHARLES
BOONE by his second wife; & whereas CHARLES BOONE by letter of attorney
dated 2 Sept. 1752 appointed THOMAS BOONE his attorney to rent or sell
any of his property in SC to which he was entitled jointly with THOMAS
FORD or under the will of JOSEPH BOONE, which letter of attorney was pr
proved 14 Sept. 1752 before ROBERT ALSOP, mayor of London, & recorded in
Secretary's office in SC in Book I.I. for 356; now THOMAS BOONE sells the
house & lot to SMITH. Witnesses: ROBERT WILLIAMS, JR., BENDIS WAAG, JOHN
RATTRAY. Before DANIEL CRAWFORD, J.P. WILLIAM HOPTON, Register.

Book O-O, p. 28   THOMAS SMITH, ESQ., & MARY his wife, to WIL-
14 Dec. 1753   LIAM ROPER, merchant, both of Charleston, for
Foeffment   Ł 4100 currency, the N half of lot #2 in
                            Charleston with the large dwelling house form-
erly belonging to ANNE BOONE, widow, which THOMAS BOONE of Charleston for
himself & as attorney for CHARLES BOONE, ESQ., of the Parish of St.
George, Hanover Square, Middlesex Co., Great Britain, (p. 22) sold on
July 10, 1753 to THOMAS SMITH; bounding E 50 ft. on the Bay; N on lot #3
belonging to CAPT. GEORGE SMITH, S 300 ft. on COL. JAMES RISBEE; W on
WILLIAM CHAPMAN. Witnesses: JOHN RATTRAY, ROBERT WILLIAMS, JR., BENJAMIN
STEAD. Before DANIEL CRAWFORD, J.P. WILLIAM HOPTON, Register.

Book O-O, p. 34   JAMES MICHIE, ESQ., & MARTHA his wife, of
30 Nov. & 1 Dec. 1744   Charleston, of 1st part; WILLIAM STUART, ESQ.,

L & R Tripartite of Island of New Providence, by his attorney, GEORGE SEAMAN, merchant, of Charleston, of 2nd part; HUGH CARTWRIGHT, bricklayer, of Charleston, of 3rd part. Whereas by L & R dated 7 & 8 May 1741 HENRY PERONNEAU, JR., & JAMES OSMOND, merchants, of Charleston, surviving devisees & executors of will of ARTHUR HALL, ESQ., of Berkeley Co., (reciting that whereas the Lords Proprs. on 13 July 1694 granted JAMES MARTEL, GOULARD DE VERVENT, ESQ., 1000 a. in Colleton Co., between Ashepoo River & South Edisto River, bounding N & S on Ahsepoo River & marsh; SE on marsh & vacant land; which he on 12 Sept. 1694 sold to ROBERT SEABROOK, planter, of Colleton Co., & whereas the Lords Proprs. on 9 Sept. 1696, by Gov. JOHN ARCHDALE, granted ROBERT SEABROOK 244 a. in Colleton Co., bounding N on marsh of S Edisto River; NW on JAMES MARTEL, GOULARD DE VERVANT; W on Ashepoo River; S & E on marsh of said river; & whereas the Lords Proprs. on 11 Jan. 1700, by Gov. JAMES MOORE, granted ROBERT SEABROOK 110 a. in Colleton Co., containing 3 islands on W side of S Edisto River; the 3 adjoining tracts making 1 tract of 1354 a. called Seabrooks Island which by will dated 20 Nov. 1710 ROBERT SEABROOK bequeathed to his son ROBERT & his heirs, & for want of heirs to JOSEPH & BENJAMIN SEABROOK; & whereas ROBERT, the son, died an infant before his father's death, & JOSEPH & BENJAMIN inherited in jointenancy; & whereas BENJAMIN died in SC & JOSEPH inherited the whole; & whereas he, by L & R dated 1 & 2 Nov. 1726 conveyed to ARTHUR HALL, ESQ., of Berkeley Co., & whereas by agreement dated 26 Nov. 1726 JOSEPH SEABROOK & ARTHUR HALL agreed that if SEABROOK should pay HALL Ł 4439 currency on 1 Feb. 1728 at the house of COL. MILES BREWTON in Charleston then HALL would, within 6 months after payment reconvey the premises to SEABROOK; & whereas the money was not paid to HALL so that became owner, & by will dated 27 June 1732 devised SEABROOKS Island to his executors in trust for his brother-in-law, said JOSEPH SEABROOK if SEABROOK should pay the money on 10 Mar. next, otherwise to sell the island, appointing HENRY PERONNEAU, JAMES OSMOND, JOHN RAVEN & MARTHA HALL his executors; & whereas on 20 Sept. 1732 ARTHUR HALL died; & to avoid suit, a judgment having been obtained before ROBERT WRIGHT, C.J. against JOSEPH SEABROOK, he on 19 Feb. 1734 released his claim to the executors; & (as above said, they) conveyed to WILLIAM STEWART & JAMES MICHIE, for Ł 4000 SC money, the 1354 a. in 3 tracts, half to STEWART & half to MICHIE; now JAMES MICHIE, & MARTHA his wife, for Ł 2500 SC money, sell to HUGH CARTWRIGHT their undivided half of the 1354 a.; & WILLIAM STEWART, by his attorney, GEORGE SEAMAN, also sells his half to CARTWRIGHT for Ł 2500 SC money; so that CARTWRIGHT becomes sole owner of the entire 1354 a. Witnesses: JOHN RATTRAY, DANIEL DUNNOVAN. Before DANIEL CRAWFORD, J.P. WILLIAM HOPTON, Register.

Book O-O, p. 54 BARRACK NORMAN, blacksmith, to SAMUEL STEVENS, 13 Oct. 1750 planter, both of St. George Parish, as security on bond of even date in penal sum of Ł 1082 for payment of Ł 541 currency, with interest, on 13 Oct. 1751; 3 Negroes, a horse branded SS; a horse branded T; 5 mares, 4 colts, & a young horse all branded 𝔞𝑉 ; all his cattle branded 𝔞𝑉 & marked a crop & a half crop in 1 ear & a slit & under keel in the other; 9 sheep, 5 featherbeds & furniture; 2 wool beds; all household & kitchen furniture; all smith & plantation tools & all his personal estate; also all his real estate, being 76 a. bounding N on the High Road; NE on Madam ANN BOON; SE on NATHAN WHITE; S & W on RALPH IZARD; also a 1/4 a. lot in Dorchester. Horse named Toby delivered for whole. Witnesses: MALACHI GLAZE, WILLIAM ANDERSON. Before J. SKENE, J.P. WILLIAM HOPTON, Register. On 1 Dec. 1758 SAMUEL STEVENS declared mortgage satisfied. Witness: WILLIAM HOPTON.

Book O-O, p. 57 JAMES TAYLOR, planter, & ESTHER his wife, of 9 & 10 July 1750 James Island, Berkeley Co., to their daughter, L & R wife of ROBERT FAIRCHILD, cabinetmaker & joiner, of James Island, for Ł 100 proclamation money, 40 a. on James Island, part of 100 a. bounding W on PAUL HAMBLETON'S 50 a. formerly a part of said 100 a.; E on JAMES TAYLOR; S on PAUL HAMBLETON; N on New Town Creek or marsh; the 100 a. having been granted 10 May 1694 by THOMAS SMITH, PAUL GRIMBALL & JOSEPH BLACK (BLAKE), Lords Proprs., to JOSEPH ELLICOTT & formerly laid out to ROBERT COLE, & lately in possession of WALTER FRANCIS. Witnesses: JAMES FICKLING, JOHN FAIRCHILD. Before WILLIAM PINCKNEY, J.P. Recorded in Secretary's Book

I.I. fol. 102-104 on 15 Nov. 1751 by WILLIAM PINCKNEY, Dep. Sec. WILLIAM
HOPTON, Register.

Book O-O, p. 63   BARNABY BRANFORD, planter, & executor of will
23 & 24 Aug. 1745   of SAMUEL WAY; to GIDEON DOWSE, practitioner
L & R   of physick, both of St. George Parish, Berke-
                         ley Co., for Ь 400 currency, 88-2/6 a. in St.
George Parish, part of WRAGG'S Barony, lately belonging to SAMUEL WAY who
authorized his executor, said BARNABY BRANFORD, to sell the tract; bound-
ing E on estate of JOSIAH OSGOOD; W on heirs of SAMUEL CLARK & on BENJA-
MIN BAKER; S on SAMUEL CLARK; N on JERMIN & CHARLES WRIGHT. Witnesses:
NATHANIEL CLARK, BENJAMIN BAKER, THOMAS WAY, JR. Before J. SKENE, J.P.
WILLIAM HOPTON, Register.

Book O-O, p. 69   HUGH DOWSE, planter, of St. George Parish,
11 & 12 Sept. 1751   Berkeley Co., executor of will of GIDEON
L & R   DOWSE; MARY DOWSE, widow of GIDEON DOWSE; &
                         ELIZABETH OSGOOD, daughter of JOSIAH OSGOOD, &
sister of MARY DOWSE; of 1st part; to DANIEL SLADE, planter, of same Parish; for Ь 340:8:4 currency, 132 a. in St. George Parish, bounding E on
JERMIN & CHARLES WRIGHT; S on SAMUEL CLARK; W on SAMUEL CLARK & BENJAMIN
BAKER; N on JERMIN (GERMAN) & CHARLES WRIGHT. Witnesses: JOHN SMITH,
SOLOMON DINGLE, SARAH DOWSE. Before J. SKENE, J.P. WILLIAM HOPTON, Register.

Book O-O, p. 74   DANIEL DONNOM, carpenter, of Colleton Co., &
23 & 24 Dec. 1753   ELIZABETH his wife, to DANIEL SLADE, carpen-
L & R   ter, of St. George Parish, Berkeley Co., for
                         Ь 57 currency, 22 a., being 1/6 part of 132 a.,
formerly belonging to JOSIAH OSGOOD, & originally a part of Ashley Barony, granted to the Rt. Hon. ANTHONY, Lord Ashley, Earl of Shaftsbury & by
various mesne conveyances became vested in JACOB SATUR, who conveyed to
JOSIAH OSGOOD on 28 Mar. 1721; the 22 a. bounding SW on SAMUEL CLARK; NW
on BENJAMIN BAKER; NE & SE on CHARLES WRIGHT. Whereas JOSIAH OSGOOD, father of ELIZABETH DONNOM owned said 132-1/2 a. & by will gave his son JO-
SIAH 2/3 of the land & the other 1/3 to another son, SOLOMON; & whereas
SOLOMON died in his infancy & his 1/3 descended to his 2 sisters, MARY &
ELIZABETH; & whereas MARY, jointly with HUGH DOWSE, her husband on 12
Sept. 1751 sold to DANIEL SLADE her title to the land, & the other half
of SOLOMON'S land remained vested in ELIZABETH, who married DANIEL DON-
NOM; now they sell their share to SLADE. Witnesses: EDWARD PERRY, JR.,
JONATHAN DONNOM. Before J. SKENE, J.P. WILLIAM HOPTON, Register.

Book O-O, p. 82   DANIEL SLADE, carpenter, & PERSIANA his wife,
26 & 27 Dec. 1753   of St. George Parish, Berkeley Co., to JOHN
L & R   REILY, planter, of St. Pauls Parish, Colleton
                         Co., for Ь 1100 currency, 149 a. in St. George
Parish, Berkeley Co., bounding SW on SAMUEL CLARK; NW on the public road
leading from Bacon's Bridge to Beach Hill, & on BENJAMIN BAKER (now DR.
SAMUEL STEVENS); NE & SE on CHARLES & JERMAN WRIGHT; according to plat
made & certified by WILLIAM MAINE, Dep. Sur. PERSIANA SLADE renounces
her dower. Whereas JACOB SATUR by various conveyances became owner of
132-1/2 a. in St. George Parish, being a part of Ashley Barony, originl-
ly granted to the Rt. Hon. ANTHONY, Lord Ashley, Earl of Shaftsbury; &
whereas SATUR for Ь 331:5:0 currency sold the tract on 28 Mar. 1721 to
JOSIAH OSGOOD, SR.; who bequeathed 2/3 of the plantation to his son, JO-
SIAH, & 1/3 to his younger son by a second wife, SOLOMON; & whereas SOL-
OMON died under age & his 1/3 descended to his 2 sisters by the same
mother, MARY & ELIZABETH; & whereas JOSIAH, JR., for Ь 528 currency, sold
his 2/3 (88-2/6 a.) to SAMUEL WAY by L & R dated 26 & 27 May 1744; &
whereas SAMUEL WAY authorized his executor BARNABY BRANFORD, to sell the
land, & he sold it by L & R dated 23 & 24 Aug. 1745 for Ь 400 currency to
GIDEON DOWSE; & whereas HUGH DOWSE; executor of will of GIDEON DOWSE;
MARY DOWSE, widow of GIDEON & proprietor of 1/2 of SOLOMON OSGOOD'S 1/3
part of 132-1/2 a.; & ELIZABETH OSGOOD, then a minor, by L & R dated 11 &
12 Sept. 1751, for Ь 340:8:4 currency, sold the 132-1/2 a. to DANIEL
SLADE; & whereas ELIZABETH OSGOOD being then a minor, her part was inva-
lid, & she having since married DANIEL DONNOM, to secure SLADE'S title to
her 1/6 part & to prevent any disputes DANIEL & ELIZABETH DONNOM by L & R
dated 23 & 24 Dec. 1753, for Ь 57 currency, sold their 1/6 part to SLADE;

so that SLADE became owner of the 132-1/2 a.; & whereas by a re-survey of
the land by WILLIAM MAINE, Dep. Sur., the tract was found to contain 149
a. including a small exchange between JOSIAH OSGOOD & THOMAS BAKER on the
N side, changing the shape from a quadrangle to a 7 sided figure; now
SLADE sells the tract to REILY. Witnesses: EDWARD PERRY, JR., JOHN MC-
QUEEN, WILLIAM MAINE. Before J. SKENE, J.P. WILLIAM HOPTON, Register.
Plat by MAINE showing original lines A.B.C.D. changed to A.B.C.E.F.G.D.

Book O-O, p. 92   GEORGE LOGAN, gentleman, formerly of SC, now
9 & 10 Nov. 1753   of Brunswick, NC, only surviving son of GEORGE
L & R   LOGAN, ESQ., of SC & surviving brother of PAT-
                         RICK LOGAN, another son of GEORGE LOGAN, ESQ.,
& also 1 of the devisees in will of GEORGE DEARSLEY, of SC; of the 1st
part; to JOHN HOPTON, gentleman, son of WILLIAM HOPTON, of SC; for Ł 400
currency, lot #155 in Charleston, containing 1/2 a., with all buildings.
Whereas the Lords Proprs. on 9 May 1695, by Gov. JOSEPH BLAKE of SC,
granted JOHN BARKSDALE lot #155 in Charleston, according to certificate
dated 18 Mar. 1694 in Sur. Gen. office, bounding S of lot #262; (JOHN
BRUSE) W on lot #157; N on lot #156; (old fortification) E on King Street,
& whereas BARKSDALE sold the lot to GEORGE DEARSLEY; who by will dated 20
June 1702 bequeathed to PATRICK LOGAN, son of GEORGE LOGAN, ESQ., the
southernmost 2 of the 4 lots he had purchased from JOHN BARKSDALE (#155
being the eastern lot of the 2), & in case of PATRICK'S death the 2 lots
to go to his brother GEORGE LOGAN, JR.; & whereas on the death of PATRICK
LOGAN, who was only tenant for life, lot #155 became the property of
GEORGE LOGAN, JR.; now he sells lot #155 to JOHN HOPTON. Witnesses:
RICHARD QUINCE, ROBERT JONES. Before JOHN HAMILTON, J.P. WILLIAM HOP-
TON, Register. Plat of S part of lot #155 in Charleston lying to southward or within the old fortifications, said lot being divided by the
fortifications & a 16 ft. street on the N side of the ditch running from
Archdale Street to King Street so that only 43 ft. fronting on King
Street remain of said lot within said fortification & 54 ft. front without said works & 16 ft. street, according to Act of Assembly passed 17
June 1746; the S part of which lot the surveyor (WILLIAM WILKINS) exactly
found from GEORGE HUNTER'S plat of resurvey of NW part of Charleston in
Secretary's office established by said act & by measuring from the corner
of Queen Street down King Street to the SE corner of lot #155 which S
part of said lot within the old fortifications is represented by lines
shaded yellow. Surveyed at request of WILLIAM HOPTON, father of JOHN
HOPTON, & certified 12 Nov. 1753 by WILLIAM WILKINS.

Book O-O, p. 101   JOHN RATTRAY & CHILDERMAS CROFT, gentlemen,
17 & 18 Oct. 1753   executors of will of HUGH CARTWRIGHT, brick-
L & R   layer, to the Hon. EDWARD FENWICKE, all of
                         Charleston, for Ł 5000 currency, 1354 a., form-
erly called Seabrooks Island, now Cartwright's Island, between Ashepoo &
S Edisto Rivers in Colleton Co. Whereas by tripartite indentures dated 1
Dec. 1744 between JAMES MICHIE & MARTHA his wife, of 1st part; WILLIAM
STEWART, of Island of Providence by his attorney GEORGE SEAMAN, merchant,
of Charleston, of 2nd part; & HUGH CARTWRIGHT of 3rd part; JAMES & MARTHA
MICHIE sold to HUGH CARTWRIGHT, 1 undivided half of 3 adjoining tracts of
1000 a., 244 a., & 110 a., total 1354 a. between Ashepoo & S Edisto Riv-
ers; & whereas WILLIAM STEWART, by his attorney GEORGE SEAMAN sold HUGH
CARTWRIGHT the other undivided half of the same 1354 a.; & whereas by
will dated 13 Aug. 1753 CARTWRIGHT authorized his executors to sell his
real & personal estate & pay his debts, appointing JOHN RATTRAY & CHILD-
ERMAS CROFT his executors; now they sell the land to EDWARD FENWICKE.
Witnesses: THOMAS ROSE, JAMES GRINDLEY. JACOB MOTTE, J.P. WILLIAM HOP-
TON, Register.

Book O-O, p. 110   JOHN LITTLE, planter, of Colleton Co., to JER-
26 Mar. 1752   MYN WRIGHT, CHARLES WRIGHT, & JOHN LAIRD, mer-
Mortgage   chants, as security on bond of even date in
                         penal sum of Ł 972 for payment of Ł 481 cur-
rency, with interest, on 1 Dec. next; 500 a. in Craven Co., in Williamsburg Township, bounding SW on Black River, other sides on vacant land;
also lot #366 in Williamsburg Township. Witnesses: THOMAS BUER, GEORGE
MITCHELL. Before JAMES BULLOCK, J.P. WILLIAM HOPTON, Register.

Book O-O, p. 112   WILLIAM WHIPPY, planter, to CHARLES WRIGHT,

2 & 3 Apr. 1747   merchant, both of Colleton Co., for ₺ 750 cur-
L & R   rency, 500 a. in Granville Co., bounding NW on
                         public land; E on Combee River; S on WILLIAM
BUCHANAN (formerly WILLIAM MCPHERSON); which 500 a. were granted by Gov.
ROBERT JOHNSON on 28 Apr. 1733 to ANN HARGRAVE, widow; who by L & R dated
23 & 24 Dec. 1736 sold to JERMYN WRIGHT; who, by L & R dated 3 & 4 Mar.
1743 conveyed to WILLIAM WHIPPY. Witnesses: MARY COSSINS, LYDIA MITCHELL,
JOHN LAIRD. Before JAMES BULLOCK, J.P. WILLIAM HOPTON, Register.

Book O-O, p. 120   JOHN BENNETT (BENNET), planter, & MARY (her
9 & 10 Jan. 1753   mark) his wife, to SAMUEL WYLY, planter, both
L & R   of Craven Co., for ₺ 120 currency, 100 a. in
                         Fredericksburg Township, Craven Co., on N side
of Wateree River, bounding NW on BRYAN ROCK; NE on vacant land; SE on
PATRICK MCCORMICK; which 100 a. were granted by JAMES GLEN on 6 Oct. 1752
to JOHN BENNETT. Witnesses: THOMAS MAPLES, MICHAEL BRENEN. Before JARED
NELSON, J.P. WILLIAM HOPTON, Register.

Book O-O, p. 126   DANIEL BREADY (BRADY), planter, to ANTHONY
19 & 20 Jan. 1752   DISTO, planter, both of Craven Co., for ₺ 100
L & R   currency, 100 a. in Fredericksburg Township,
                         Craven Co., on N side Wateree River, bounding
NW on JOHN HUDSON; NE on vacant land; SE on ANTHONY DISTO; which 100 a.
were granted by Gov. JAMES GLEN on 29 Nov. 1750 to DANIEL BRADY. Witnesses: SAMUEL WYLY, JOHN GIBSON. Before JARED NELSON, J.P. WILLIAM
HOPTON, Register.

Book O-O, p. 132   ELIZABETH VERDITTY, widow, of St. Johns Parish,
6 & 7 June 1750   to THOMAS MCPHERSON, planter, of Craven Co.,
L & R   for 10 shillings, 130 a. near the Congrees, in
                         Craven Co., granted ELIZABETH VERDITTY on 1
June 1750 by the Gov. & Council of SC, bounding NE & SE on Patricks Creek;
SW on heirs of DR. DANIEL GIBSON, THOMAS SITTSMITH & HENRY GIGNILLIAT; NW
on heirs of THOMAS STITTSMITH, as recorded in Secretary's Book M.M. fol.
89. Witnesses: MARY MONCK, PETER PORCHER, JR. Before ALEXANDER STEWART,
J.P. WILLIAM HOPTON, Register.

Book O-O, p. 138   The Hon. JOHN CLELAND, & MARY his wife, to
9 & 10 Nov. 1753   ARCHIBALD BAIRD, gentleman, for ₺ 3000 SC mon-
L & R   ey, 127 a. 35 chains on N side Winyaw Bay, in
                         Craven Co., bounding E & S on the Bay, W on
Sampit (Sand Pit) Creek on Georgetown River & on lots #236, 239, 249,
250, 257 in Georgetown including half the 3 last mentioned lots; N on the
High Road leading to the Bay; being part of a large tract granted JOHN
CLELAND. Witnesses: THOMAS HASELL, THOMAS GODFREY. Before PAUL TRAPIER,
J.P. WILLIAM HOPTON, Register. Plat certified 11 Nov. 1753 by THOMAS
HASELL.

Book O-O, p. 145   Letter of Attorney, or deputation for the of-
4 July 1753   of Clerk of the Council of SC. JOHN HAMMERTON
                         to WILLIAM SIMPSON. Whereas GEORGE II on 11
Feb. in 4th year of his reign granted EDWARD BERTIE & JOHN HAMMERTON,
ESQRS., the offices of Secretary & Register of SC & for their joint lives.
& the life of the longer liver of them all fees, etc., belonging to the
offices, with power & authority to be present at all meetings of the
Governor, Council, or Assembly, to keep an exact register of all their
proceedings, acts, & orders, etc., & whereas BERTIE died & the offices
became vested solely in HAMMERTON; now he appoints WILLIAM SIMPSON, gentleman, formerly of London, now of SC, to be Clerk of the Council in SC,
in place of ALEXANDER GORDON, with all fees, etc. Witnesses: WILLIAM
WOLTON, Bow Street, Convent Garden, No. 9; WILLIAM BATTERSON, tobacconist,
of James Street, Covent Garden, Co. of Middlesex. Before mayor CRISP
GASCOYNE, Guildhall, London. Entered in the Plantation Office Whitehall
12 July 1753 by SAMUEL GELLEBRAND, Dep. Sec. WILLIAM HOPTON, Register.

Book O-O, p. 147   HENRY SMITH, gentleman, of Goose Creek, only
13 & 14 July 1752   acting executor of will of ANNE BOONE, widow,
L & R   of Charleston, of 1st part; to HUMPHREY SOMERS,
                         bricklayer, of Charleston, for ₺ 2142 currency,
half of lot #7 in Charleston, bounding S 59-1/2 ft. on Tradd Street; W

94-3/4 ft. on Bedon's Alley; N 59-1/2 ft. on JOHN RAVEN; E 94-3/4 ft. on
EDWARD LIGHTWOOD. Whereas the Lords Proprs. on 24 Aug. 1688 granted
RICHARD TRADE lot #7 in Charleston, bounding S on Tradd Street; W on a
lot then belonging to CHARLES BUCKLEY (now on Bedon's Alley); N on EDWARD
MUSSON (now JOHN RAVEN); E on Cooper River; & whereas RICHARD TRADE on 12
June 1688 (?) sold half the lot to WILLIAM DUNLAP, ESQ., & JOHN ALEXAN-
DER, merchant, bounding W on CHARLES BUCKLEY; N on EDWARD MUSSON; E 100
ft. on part same lot; S 64-1/2 ft. on Tradd Street; & whereas WILLIAM
DUNLAP on 10 Oct. 1697 sold or assigned his share to JOHN ALEXANDER; who
by will dated 26 Sept. 1699 devised to his wife, ANNE ALEXANDER, half his
real & personal estate, & the other half to his daughter ANNE ALEXANDER;
& whereas ANNE, his widow, married JOSEPH BOONE, merchant, of Charleston,
& he purchased daughter ANNE'S half of said half lot, so that he & his
wife, ANNE, became sole owners of a full half of lot #7; that is, he owned half & ANNE half of the half lot; & whereas JOSEPH BOONE, by will dated 14 Mar. 1733 bequeathed his half to his wife ANNE; & she by will dated
1 Dec. 1749 directed her executors to sell the residue of her real & personal estate, except as excepted & bequeathed to her nephew, The Hon. JO-
SEPH BLAKE, in trust for the purposes named in the will, the half lot not
being excepted; now the executor sells the half lot to SOMERS. Witnesses: THOMAS SMITH, JR., JOSEPH SMITH. Before JACOB MOTTE, J.P. WILLIAM
HOPTON, Register.

Book O-O, p. 156   BENJAMIN HARVEY, planter, of Colleton Co., &
20 & 21 Dec. 1751   ELIZABETH his wife; & JOHN HARVEY, planter, of
L & R   Berkeley Co., & CATHERINE his wife; BENJAMIN &
                        JOHN being 2 of the sons & devisees of will of
WILLIAM HARVEY, gentleman; of 1st part; to HUMPHREY SOMMERS, bricklayer,
of Charleston; for Ł 4364 currency, their respective shares & interests
in certain lands; whereas WILLIAM HARVEY owned certain lands mentioned
herein as well as other lands, tenements, etc., & by will dated 21 Sept.
1739 gave his son, BENJAMIN HARVEY, when 21, half his land (between 1100
& 1200 a.) at Stono purchased from MANLEY WILLIAMSON & JOHN WILLIAMS,
that is, that half part on High Park side; & gave his son, JOHN HARVEY,
when 21, the other half (1100 or 1200 a.) at Stono; & whereas BENJAMIN &
JOHN both reached 21 years & took possession of their lands; now they &
their respective wives sell to SOMMERS 684-1/2 a. (part of the 2 half
parts) in Colleton Co., at Stono, bounding N on vacant land; E on THOMAS
KINGDON SMITH; S on the heirs of DANIEL GREEN & on BENJAMIN HARVEY; W on
WILLIAM HARVEY. BENJAMIN HARVEY gives SOMMERS an open roadway 20 ft.
wide leading S from present causeway through BENJAMIN'S swamp to the
High Road. Witnesses: THOMAS ELFE, GEORGE TEW. Before ALEXANDER STEW-
ART, J.P. WILLIAM HOPTON, Register. Plat of 684-1/2 a. in 2 tracts;
plat of 461-1/2 a., shaded red, taken from JOHN HARVEYS part, being part
of tract of 640 a. granted MANLY WILLIAMSON; 223 a., shaded yellow, being
part of BENJAMIN HARVEY'S tract; made & certified 16 Dec. 1751 by WILLIAM
WILKINS, Dep. Sur.

Book O-O, p. 167   JOHN HARVEY, planter, & CATHARINE his wife, to
21 & 22 Dec. 1753   HUMPHREY SOMMERS, bricklayer, of Charleston,
L & R   for Ł 1517:5:0 currency, 238 a. at Stono, in
                        Colleton Co., bounding W on WILLIAM HARVEY; S
on BENJAMIN HARVEY & on MR. GREEN; N & E on HUMPHREY SOMMERS. Whereas
WILLIAM HARVEY, father of JOHN HARVEY, by will dated 21 Sept. 1739 gave
his son BENJAMIN 1/2 (1100 or 1200 a.) his land at Stono which he had
purchased from MANLY WILLIAMSON, that is, half on the high side & the
other half adjoining; now JOHN HARVEY sells a part to SOMMERS. Witnesses: THOMAS HUTCHINSON, ROBERT HARVEY. Before JOHN LINING, J.P. WILLIAM
HOPTON, Register. Plat given.

Book O-O, p. 173   JOHN HARVEY, planter, of Berkeley Co., &
27 & 28 Jan. 1752   CATHERINE his wife, to HUMPHREY SOMMERS, brick-
L & R   layer, of Charleston, for Ł 880 currency, 138
                        a. in Colleton Co., granted 9 Jan. 1752 by Gov.
JAMES GLEN to JOHN HARVEY, bounding SE on JOHN HARVEY & BENJAMIN HARVEY;
W on WILLIAM HARVEY; NW on MRS. FITCH & on JAMES HARTLY; NE on JAMES HART-
LY. Witnesses: ALEXANDER FRASER, THOMAS FULLER. Before THOMAS LAMBOLL,
J.P. WILLIAM HOPTON, Register.

Book O-O, p. 182   JAMES KILPATRICK (KILLPATRICK; KIRKPATRICK),

315

27 June 1753   doctor in physic, formerly of SC, now of Lon-
Letter of Attorney   don, appointed SAMUEL EVELEIGH, ESQ., of
                      Charleston, SC, his attorney to dispose of all
his lands in SC. Witnesses: JOHN BROWNE, SAMUEL KYNASTON, ROBERT MAC-
KENZIE. Before ANTHONY WHITE, Not. Pub. in London. KYANSTON appeared
JACOB MOTTE, J.P. WILLIAM HOPTON, Register.

Book O-O, p. 184   GEORGE EVELEIGH, gentleman, of Southampton,
12 Jan. 1753   Great Britain, appoints SAMUEL EVELEIGH, BEN-
Power of Attorney   JAMIN STEAD & SOLOMON MILNER, merchants, of
                     Charleston, his attorneys, with authority to
sell his dwelling house at White Point, in Charleston, where he recently
lived; also his plantation on John's Island, with its buildings; his Ne-
groes & slaves, all live stock, plantation tools. Witnesses: A. WOOD,
SAMUEL TIGALL READE, MARK NOBLE, a Master Extraordinary in H.M. High
Court of Chancery & Not. Pub., BENJAMIN MATHEWES & MOSES AUDIBERT, of
Charleston, recognized GEORGE EVELEIGH before JOHN DART, J.P. WILLIAM
HOPTON, Register.

Book O-O, p. 187   ROBERT DANIEL, planter, to ANTHONY BONNEAU,
8 & 9 May 1749   planter, both of Berkeley Co., for Ł 900 SC
L & R   money, 590 a. in Berkeley Co., bounding S on
                     MESSRS. BERRISFORD, SAMUEL WELLS, JOSEPH WAR-
NOCK & ANTHONY BONNEAU; E on ISAAC GUERIN & ANTHONY BONNEAU; N on LEWIS
MOUZON, SR., & JOHN LESESNE; W on JOHN LESESNE & ALEXANDER PERONNEAU.
Whereas the Lords Proprs. granted JOHN RUSS, planter, of Berkeley Co.,
590 a. in Berkeley Co., which he bequeathed to his son THOMAS RUSS; who
sold to ROBERT DANIEL, father of ROBERT DANIEL, party hereto; who by will
dated 1 June 1732 bequeathed his real & personal estate, except as ex-
cepted, to his son ROBERT; now he sells the land to BONNEAU. Witnesses:
JOSEPH WARNOCK, SAMUEL DRAKE, DAVID FOGARTIE. Before FRANCIS LEJAU, J.P.
WILLIAM HOPTON, Register.

Book O-O, p. 193   JOSEPH WARNOCK, planter, & MARY his wife, to
29 & 30 Jan. 1752   ANTHONY BONNEAU, planter, both of Berkeley Co.,
L & R   for Ł 450 currency, 250 a. in Berkeley Co.,
                     bounding S on Wando River; W on SAMUEL WELLS;
N & E on ANTHONY BONNEAU. Whereas the Lords Proprs. granted ABRAHAM WAR-
NOCK, planter, 1000 a. in Berkeley Co., & after his death his son ABRAHAM
& his wife TAMMERRON on 3 Mar. 1725/6 sold the E part, 500 a., to JERE-
MIAH ROPER, bounding S on Wando River; W on ABRAHAM WARNOCK (now SAMUEL
WELLS) N on JOHN RUSS (now ANTHONY BONNEAU) E on JEREMIAH ROPER (now AN-
THONY BONNEAU) & whereas JEREMIAH ROPER on 30 Apr. 1745 sold 400 a. (part
of the 500) to JOSEPH WARNOCK, bounding S on the River; W on SAMUEL WELLS;
N on ANTHONY BONNEAU; E on part of the 500 a. now belonging to BONNEAU;
now WARNOCK sells a part of the 400 a. to BONNEAU. Witnesses: ELIZABETH
HAYES, MARGARET ASHBY, SAMUEL DRAKE. Before PAUL TRAPIER, J.P. WILLIAM
HOPTON, Register.

Book O-O, p. 200   WILLIAM (his mark) STEWART, cooper, to ALEX-
3 & 4 July 1752   ANDER STEWART, planter, both of Craven Co.,
L & R   for Ł 50 currency, 150 a. on N side Wateree
                     River (part of 450 a. granted in Mar. 1752 by
Gov. JAMES GLEN to said WILLIAM STEWART), bounding on the other sides on
vacant land. Witnesses: JOHN COOK, HENRY DONGWORTH, PATRICK (his mark)
MCCORMICK. Before JAMES MCGIRT, J.P. of C. Co. Note only 1 execution to
L & R. WILLIAM HOPTON, Register. Plat of 150 a. certified 1 July 1752
by JOHN HAMILTON, Dep. Sur.

Book O-O, p. 205   MARY YEOMANS, widow, to EASTER CARROLL, widow,
16 & 17 July 1753   both of Charleston, as security on bond of
L & R by Mortgage   even date in penal sum of Ł 1200 for payment
                     of Ł 600 currency, with interest, on 17 July
1754; that part of lot #37 in Charleston now occupied by GLEN & COOPER,
merchants; bounding N 37 ft. 10 in. on Elliott Street; W on part #37 belonging partly to CATHERINE LOGAN & partly to MARY YEOMANS; S on heirs of
WILLIAM SMITH; E 82 ft. on part of #37 belonging to WILLIAM CARWITHEN.
Witnesses: ALEXANDER MICHIE, JOHN REMINGTON. Before WILLIAM PINCKNEY,
J.P. WILLIAM HOPTON, Register.

Book O-O, p. 212   JOHN MCCALL, merchant, & MARTHA his wife, of
15 & 16 Feb. 1754   Charleston, to CATHARINE WIGFALL, widow, for
L & R   Ł 1000 currency, 472 a. in Berkeley Co., as
                          granted to ISAAC TRESVANT; bounding SW on
ISAAC GUERIN; NW on SOLOMON BREMMAR; NE on ROBERT JOHNSTON; SE on JOHN
RUBERRY. Witnesses: JOHN LLOYD, FRANCIS ROCHE, WILLIAM BOONE. Before
JACOB MOTTE, J.P. Lease had no probate. WILLIAM HOPTON, Register. Plat
of original grant & memos given. Memo showing COL. WALTER IZARD'S land
held on grants from Lords Proprs. 230 a.; THOMAS IZARD'S 493 a.; RALPH
IZARD'S 277 a.; Dec. 29, 1752 by HUGH BRYAN, Dep. Sur. at request of WAL-
TER, RALPH, THOMAS, & JOHN IZARD, HUGH BRYAN resurveyed & divided equally
among them the 5 adjoining tracts of land of 3509 a., English measure,
belonging to the estate of their father, WALTER IZARD, in Granville Co.,
bounding N on Combahee River & IZARD'S Creek; E on HOBUNNERS (HOBUNNEYS)
Creek & on said WALTER IZARD (formerly JOSEPH BRYAN); S & SW on DR. ROSE
(formerly Landgrave EDMUND BELLINGER), STEPHEN BULL, & estate of JOSEPH
IZARD (formerly CAPT. JOHN BULL); W & NW on STEPHEN BULL, DR. ROSE, &
estate of JOSEPH IZARD & on JOHN DEAS (formerly JAMES HARTLY); the black
lines representing division lines between lands of said parties whose
names are written on their respective tracts; the green lines representing 1000 a. formerly granted by the Lords Proprs. to JAMES COCHRAN &
therefore distinguished from the other lands held on grants on a differ-
ent quit rent. Certified 29 Dec. 1752 by HUGH BRYAN, Dep. Sur. Registered 27 Feb. 1754 by WILLIAM HOPTON, Register.

Book O-O, p. 218   MORGAN SABB, planter, of St. Helena Parish,
31 Sept. & 1 Oct. 1753   Colleton Co., to CAPT. ABRAHAM DUPONT, of Four
L & R   Holes, Berkeley Co., for Ł 695:12:6 currency,
                          795 a. in Granville Co., bounding E on DRURY
DUM & vacant land; N on vacant land; S on the 584 a. sold by SABB to HEN-
RY DESSAUSSURE. Whereas GEORGE II on 6 Oct. 1752 granted MORGAN SABB a
plantation on the head of Deas Creek Swamp in Granville Co., between
Coosa Hatchee & Savannah River, bounding NW on vacant land; S by the
grand line of Purysburgh; E on vacant land then begun to be surveyed for
DRURY DUM; & whereas SABB, after obtaining the grant, by L & R dated 24 &
25 Dec. 1752 sold HENRY DESSAUSSURE 584 a.; but upon resurveying the
lands, it appeared that the lands within the lines of the plat attached
to the original grant as marked by the Sur. Gen. contained 1379 a. without deducting the 584 a. conveyed to DESSAUSSURE, so that 795 a. still
remain to SABB; now he sells this residue to DUPONT; MARY ESTHER SABB,
wife of MORGAN SABB to renounce her dower on 23 Oct. inst. Since there
is a difference of 220 a. between the number of a. mentioned in original
grant (1159 a.) & the number of a. mentioned in the resurvey (1379), SABB
promises DUPONT that he will, within 3 months, obtain another grant of
the 220 surplus a. & convey them to DUPONT. Witnesses: THOMAS DOUGHTY,
DANIEL DWIGHT. Before JAMES WRIGHT, J.P. WILLIAM HOPTON, Register.

Book O-O, p. 227   HUGH BRYAN, planter, of Prince William Parish,
13 Aug. 1750   to BARNABY BULL & STEPHEN BULL, planters, of
Mortgage   same Parish, as security on a bond of perform-
                          ance of even date in penal sum of Ł 4600 for
payment of Ł 1700 currency, with interest, to BARNABY BULL within 18
months, & for payment of Ł 1000 currency (balance due on a bond dated 12
June 1745 payable, with interest, to GABRIEL MANIGAULT & BENJAMIN SAVAGE,
of Charleston, in which bond STEPHEN BULL was jointly bound & has paid
his part, the remainder being BRYAN'S debt) within 18 months; his plantation of 857 a. on which he (HUGH BRYAN) lives, in 2 tracts, on W side
Pocotaligo River, in Granville Co., bounding SE on the river & marsh; NE
& NW on CAPT. EDMUND BELLINGER'S Barony; SW on CAPT. BULL (now MR. MAT-
THEWS) & on JAMES ST. JOHN & on MR. BLAND. Witnesses: CONRADE HOBER,
BENJAMIN SEALY, SABINA WILSON. Before STEPHEN BULL, J.P. Delivery by
turf & twig. WILLIAM HOPTON, Register. According to another probate on
p. 259 of same mortgage SABINA WILSON, spinster, appeared before EDWARD
FENWICKE, J.P. WILLIAM HOPTON, Register.

Book O-O, p. 230   JOHN STONE, SR., tanner, of Berkeley Co., to
22 Apr. 1715   his eldest son, JOHN STONE, for Ł 1 currency,
Gift   1/2 his lands, 105 a., in Berkeley Co., on E
                          side Cooper River, bounding on JOHN MILLMAN,
THOMAS MONK & HUMPHREY FUNQUITT, & Near DR. BRABANT'S land, except 60 a.

in front on the marsh which he reserves for himself & his wife MARY
(mother of JOHN) during their lives. Witnesses: HANNAH CLYATT, MRS. MARY
MORANEY (later MARY BUTLER), DEBORAH STONE, ROBERT CLYATT. Before WIL-
LIAM CATTELL, J.P. WILLIAM HOPTON, Register. Plat of 195 a. shows 80 a.
belonging to HANNAH CLYATT, 64 a. of which were sold to her by JOHN STONE
& 16 a. by JONATHAN SINGLETARY; certified in Apr. 1715 by ROBERT CLYATT.

Book O-O, p. 232
20 May 1721
Feoffment

JOHN STONE, JR., shoemaker or cordwainer, of
St. Thomas Parish, Berkeley Co., & his wife
SUSANNAH, to his brother-in-law JONATHAN SIN-
GLETARY, planter, for ₺ 200 currency, all the
land given him on 2 Apr. 1715 by his father, JOHN STONE, 195 a. in St.
Thomas Parish, Berkeley Co., on E side Cooper River, bounding N on JOHN
MILLMAN (formerly ANDREW DROMANT) & S on his brother JOSEPH STONES land
being the other half of his fathers land; except the 64 a. to the E which
he sold to his sister HANNAH CLYATT on 10 Mar. 1718/19 as witnessed by
JOHN AIKINS, PAUL SIART, & MARY CARROLL. SUSANNAH renounces her claim.
Witnesses: JEREMIAH RUSSELL, JOSEPH STONE, HANNAH CLYATT, ROBERT CLYATT.
One room of the house delivered. A memorial for 115 a. entered in Aud-
itor's office 15 May 1733. Before MICHAEL DARBY, J.P. WILLIAM HOPTON,
Register.

Book O-O, p. 236
10 May 1725
Sale

JOSEPH ASHBY, ESQ., of Berkeley Co., grandson
& heir of JOHN ASHBY, 1 of the Cassiques of
SC, to JONATHAN SINGLETARY of same Parish, for
₺ 10 currency, 75 a. in Berkeley Co., bounding
N on JOHN STONE; W on marsh of Cooper River. Witnesses: ARCHIBALD HAM-
ILTON, HUGH CAMPBELL. Before ANTHONY BONNEAU, J.P. A memorial entered
in Auditor's office 15 May 1733. WILLIAM HOPTON, Register. By warrant
dated 6 Aug. 1718 from the Hon. ROBERT JOHNSTON 74 a. of marsh land were
laid out to JOHN STONE, JR., bounding N on dry land belonging to STONE; W
on marsh of Cooper River; S on vacant marsh; E on said STONE.

Book O-O, p. 239
14 & 15 Dec. 1753
L & R by Mortgage

JOSEPH BLACK, bricklayer, & ANN (her mark) his
wife, of Charleston, to ANNE PEACOCK, widow,
as security on bond of even date in penal sum
of ₺ 1200 for payment of ₺ 600 currency, with
interest, on 14 Dec. 1754; part of lot #80 in Charleston, bounding N 45
ft. on Pinckney Street; W & S on part same lot belonging to GABRIEL GUIG-
NARD; E 75 ft. on GRIFFITH TABBS. Witnesses: JOHN HAMPTON, JOHN REMING-
TON. Before JACOB MOTTE, J.P. WILLIAM HOPTON, Register. On 9 June 1758
ANN PEACOCK declared mortgage satisfied. Witnesses: ANN HUNDLEY, PETER
MONCLAR.

Book O-O, p. 245
6 Dec. 1740
Gift

ROBERT OSWELL & RACHEL, his wife, to their son
JAMES OSWELL, 100 a. in St. Bartholomews Parish, Colleton Co., granted by the Lords Proprs.
to SAMUEL FARLEY on 15 Sept. 1705 & conveyed
by FARLEY on 13 Jan. 1705/6 to GEORGE TUCKER; bounding according to plat
of grant. Witnesses: THOMAS SIMONS, WILLIAM OSWELL, ELIZABETH FARLEY.
Before JAMES WILKINSON, J.P. WILLIAM HOPTON, Register.

Book O-O, p. 246
23 & 24 Sept. 1753
L & R

WILLIAM BASFORD, planter, & SUSANNAH his wife,
of Granville Co., to ROBERT OSWALD, planter,
of Colleton Co., for ₺ 1155 currency, 165 a.
in Colleton Co., bounding N on SAMUEL FARLEY;
E on MRS. JACKSON; S on vacant land; W on Whitmarsh Neck; which 165 a.
were sold by STEPHEN MONK, ESQ., of Goose Creek, Berkeley Co., son & heir
of JOHN MONK, 1 of the Cassiques of SC, by L & R dated 12 & 13 May 1729
(see Book T. fols. 569-574 dated 20 & 21 May 1740) to JAMES BRASFORD,
planter, of Colleton Co., father of WILLIAM BASFORD, party hereto. Witnesses: WILLIAM REYNOLDS, JR., JAMES OSWALD, HENRY WARNER. Before JAMES
BULLOCK, J.P. WILLIAM HOPTON, Register.

Book O-O, p. 254
24 & 25 May 1753
L & R

JOHN SCOTT & SARAH, (her mark) his wife, to
JACOB SUMMARALL (SUMMERALL) both of Granville
Co., for ₺ 175 currency, 150 a. in Granville
Co., on 1 of the branches of Stephen's Creek &
bounding on all sides on vacant land; granted by Gov. JAMES GLEN on 13
Mar. 1752 to JOHN SCOTT. Witnesses: ROGER ROBERTS, JOHN (his mark) HULL.

Before JOHN TOBLER, J.P. WILLIAM HOPTON, Register.

Book O-O, p. 260   RAWLINS LOWNDES, P.M. to BARNABY BULL, gentle-
26 Mar. 1754   man, of Granville Co., at public auction, for
Sale   Ⱡ 2060:12:6 currency, 605 a., part of 5000 a.;
                                & 500 a., part of same tract in Prince William
Parish, Granville Co. Whereas ROBERT THORPE, merchant, of Port Royal,
owned said 5000 a. which he conveyed to EDWARD LOWRY, merchant, of London, as security on a bond dated 25 June 1743, in the penal sum of Ⱡ 1634
British (value Ⱡ 11,438 SC money) for payment of Ⱡ 817 British on 25 Feb.
1743/4; which sum was not paid; & whereas LOWRY obtained a judgment
against RICHARD THORPE, administrator of will of ROBERT THORPE in the
full penal sum & costs, & a writ of fieri facias was issued by CHARLES
PINCKNEY, C.J., on 27 Feb. 1753, directing the P.M. to raise these
amounts from the estate of ROBERT THORPE; & whereas RAWLINS LOWNDES, P.M.
seized a tract of 605 a., part of THORPE'S 5000 a., bounding NW on Lt.
Gov. WILLIAM BULL; SW, SE, & NE on other divisions of the 5000 a.; also a
tract of 500 a., part of said 5000, bounding NW on Lt. Gov. WILLIAM BULL;
SW on the 605 a.; SE & NE on other parts of said 5000 a.; now he sells
the 2 tracts to BARNABY BULL. Witnesses: SAMUEL BRAILSFORD, JOHN MEN-
ZIES. Before JAMES WRIGHT, J.P. WILLIAM HOPTON, Register.

Book O-O, p. 265   GEORGE GIESSENDANNER, planter, & SUSANNAH BAR-
18 Apr. 1753   BARA (her mark) his wife to JACOB HORGUER,
Release   both of Berkeley Co., for Ⱡ 50 currency, 300
                                a. in Orangeburg Township, Berkeley Co., being
part of 550 a. granted 19 Oct. 1748 to GEORGE GIESSENDANNER (see Secretary's Book E.E. fol. 302); bounding NE on GEORGE GIESSENDANNER; other
sides on vacant land. SUSANNAH BARBARA renounces her dower. Witnesses:
HENRY FELDER, JOHN (his mark) GIEGELMAN. Before JAMES TILLY, J.P. WIL-
LIAM HOPTON, Register. Plat of 300 a. resurveyed from original 6 Apr.
1753, by PETER FAINE, Dep. Sur.

Book O-O, p. 269   CHARLES CANTEY, & HARRIETT his wife, to WIL-
8 & 9 Jan. 1747   LIAM WRIGHT, JR., both of Craven Co., for
L & R   Ⱡ 135 currency, 300 a. in Craven Co., on N
                                side Santee River, part of 48,000 granted 7
May 1698 by JOHN, Earl of Bath, Palatine, & the Lords Proprs. to Landgrave EDMOND BELLINGER; the 300 a. bounding NW on CHARLES CANTEY; NE on
vacant land; SE on PETER SALLEY. Witnesses: DAVID DAVIS, SOLOMON JUNE,
MATTHEW (his mark) PATTISON. Before SAMUEL THOMAS, J.P. Memorial enter-
ed in Auditor's office 19 Dec. 1750 in Book 3 fol. 253 by JAMES WEDDER-
BURN, Dep. Aud. WILLIAM HOPTON, Register.

Book O-O, p. 274   ALLEN WELLS, planter, of New Town Winyaw, to
12 & 13 Mar. 1754   JONATHAN CALKINS, planter, of Georgetown, Win-
L & R   yaw, for Ⱡ 10 currency, lot #22 in Georgetown,
                                containing 1/4 a., bounding SW 50 ft. on the
Bay or Front Street; SE 217.9 ft. on lot #23; NE on lot #59; NW on lot
#21; which lot #22 was conveyed by ELISHA SCREVEN to ALLEN WELLS on 6
Oct. 1731. Witnesses: JAMES BROWN, WILLIAM NICHOLSON. Before THOMAS
HASELL, J.P. WILLIAM HOPTON, Register.

Book O-O, p. 279   NICHOLAS TROTT, ESQ., & SARAH his wife, of St.
16 & 17 Apr. 1734   Philips Parish, Charleston, to the Rev. MR.
L & R in Trust   ALEXANDER GARDEN, rector of St. Philips & JO-
                                SEPH WRAGG, merchant, of Charleston, in con-
sideration of an intended marriage between RICHARD WRIGHT, ESQ., of
Berkeley Co., & MARY RHETT, daughter of SARAH TROTT (formerly SARAH
RHETT) in trust for NICHOLAS & SARAH TROTT during their lives then to
RICHARD WRIGHT & MARY his wife, during their lives; for 5 shillings cur-
rency, 10 a., English measure, in Berkeley Co., bounding N on ISAAC MA-
ZYCK; S on the Charleston line; W on the Broad Path; E on JONATHAN AMORY;
which 10 a. were purchased by AMORY from ISAAC MAZYCK, merchant; also,
10 a., English measure, on Charleston Neck, near Charleston, bounding N &
W on JOHN COMING; E on Cooper River & several tracts sold by NICHOLAS &
SARAH TROTT to WILLIAM HENDRICK, planter (75 x 200 ft.); JOHN SCOTT.
shipwright (25 x 200); & EXPERIENCE HOWARD, carpenter (30 x 200 ft.); S
on town lots; which 10 a. were purchased by AMORY from JOB HOWES, gentleman; also lot #48 in Charleston, formerly belonging to JOHN COMING;

319

bounding E on Cooper River; W on vacant lots; which lot #48 AMORY purchased from JOB HOWES; also 4 town lots Nos. 302, 303, 304, & 305; which 4 lots AMORY purchased from DANIEL HUGER, merchant, of Charleston; also 4 town lots Nos. 121, 122, 123, & 209 formerly granted by the Lords Proprs. to AMORY, each of the 4 grants being dated 13 Aug. 1695; also lot #138; also lot #139; also 8 a. of marsh in Berkeley Co., bounding E on Cooper River; S & W on COL. WILLIAM RHETT; N on MR. MAZYCK'S marsh; all of which lots & parcels of land by several mesne conveyances became vested in SARAH RHETT (now SARAH TROTT) & known as Point Plantation, or Rhetts Berry; also a large brick mansion & other buildings on the plantation & lots. Witnesses: RICHARD LAMBTON, PETER HORRY, WILLIAM ROMSEY. Before JOHN LINING, J.P. WILLIAM HOPTON, Register.

Book O-O, p. 291
1 Apr. 1754
Satisfaction of
Mortgage

Whereas the Hon. JOHN CLELAND, & MARY his wife, by L & R dated 24 & 25 Jan. 1752 mortgaged to WILLIAM STONE, merchant, of Charleston, 1800 a. in Prince George Parish, Craven Co., part of 3996 a. granted to JOHN CLELAND; bounding E on Peedee & Black Rivers; S on Sampit Creek, Georgetown, the Common, & FORBE'S land; W on the creek Town Common, FORBES & estate of COL. ANTHONY WHITE; N on other part said 3996 a.; to secure payment of Ł 11,427 currency, with interest, on 1 June then next; & whereas JOHN & MARY CLELAND, by L & R dated 24 & 25 Aug. 1753, with STONE'S consent for Ł 817:10 currency, sold to MARY LAROCHE, gentlewoman, of Charleston, 81 a. 88 chains, part of the 1800 a., on W side Black River near its mouth, bounding S on THOMAS MITCHELL, N & S on Georgetown; as recorded in Book N.N. 378-384; the purchase having been paid to STONE as part of the mortgage & therefore STONE declares mortgage satisfied in regard to that portion of land. Witnesses: GEORGE AUSTIN, WILLIAM HOPTON. Before ANTHONY MATHEWES, J.P. WILLIAM HOPTON, Register. Mortgage not recorded.

Book O-O, p. 293
3 & 4 July 1749
L & R

WILLIAM HUGHES, planter, & SARAH his wife, to THOMAS WRIGHT, both of Prince Frederick Parish, Craven Co., for Ł 100 currency, 300 a. on S side Black River in Craven Co., bounding E on MEREDITH HUGHES; S on CAPT. ANTHONY WHITE; N on Green's Creek; W on CALEB AVANT; which 300 a. were granted to HUGHES on 8 Feb. 1736/7. Witnesses: THOMAS POTTS, MARY JOHNSTON. Before PAUL TRAPIER, J.P. WILLIAM HOPTON, Register.

Book O-O, p. 296
31 Jan. 1754
Feoffment

JOHN MAN, ESQ., of Prince Frederick Parish, to THOMAS WRIGHT, of Prince George, Winyaw, for Ł 5 currency, 365 a. in Craven Co., bounding S on Green's Creek & CALEB AVANT; NW on heirs of the Rev. MR. THOMAS MORRITT; NE on JOHN WHITE & JOHN MAN; originally granted to WILLIAM COLT. Signed by SUSANNA MAN & JOHN MAN. Witnesses: JOHN PYATT, WILLIAM PATMER. Before THOMAS HASELL, J.P. WILLIAM HOPTON, Register. Plat by THOMAS HASELL dated 26 Jan. 1754 showing he laid off to THOMAS WRIGHT 365 a., part of 900 a. formerly granted to WILLIAM COLT.

Book O-Q, p. 299
10 & 12 Nov. 1752
L & R

JOHN TODD, JR., laborer, & MARY (her mark) his wife, to WILLIAM HARRISON, both of Craven Co., for Ł 150 currency, 150 a. in Craven Co., on S side of Wateree River on the Dutchman's Creek, bounding NW on SAMUEL BACOT; other sides on vacant land; according to grant dated 12 June 1757 from Gov. JAMES GLEN to JOHN TODD, JR. Witnesses: RICHARD KIRKLAND, ROBERT HUMPHREYS, MOSES KIRKLAND. Before JAMES MCGIRT, J.P. WILLIAM HOPTON, Register.

Book O-O, p. 305
20 & 21 Mar. 1743
L & R

JAMES MICHIE, ESQ., & MARTHA his wife, of Charleston, to WILLIAM CHAMBERS, planter, of Wadmalaw Island, for Ł 100 currency, 92 a. in St. John's Parish, Colleton Co. granted by Lt. Gov. WILLIAM BULL on 6 Mar. 1741 to JAMES MICHIE, bounding N & E on ABRAHAM WAIGHT; S on JOHN LADSON; SW on JAMES MICHIE. Witnesses: JOHN TROUP, JAMES SIMPSON, JR. Before DANIEL CRAWFORD, J.P. WILLIAM HOPTON, Register.

Book O-O, p. 312
17 & 18 Apr. 1747

JOHN JONES, planter, of the Welch tract, in Craven Co., to JOHN EVANS, planter, of same

L & R   place, for Ł 100 currency, 100 a., part of
                               500 a. in the WELCH tract. Whereas Gov. JAMES
GLEN on 10 Mar. 1743 granted JOHN JONES 500 a. in the WELCH tract, bound-
ing SE on WILLIAM HUGHES; other sides on vacant land; now JONES sells to
EVANS 100 a. bounding 70 chains 71 links SE on WILLIAM HUGHES; SW on va-
cant land 6 chains to a small gum, thence N 35° 44 chains to a red oak,
thence N 12° 33 chains thence SE 45° 29 chains 80 links. Witnesses: BEN-
JAMIN (his mark) ROGERS, WILLIAM HUGHES. Before WILLIAM JAMES, J.P.
WILLIAM HOPTON, Register. Plat shows lands belonging to WILLIAM DELOATCH,
PHILIP EVANS, JOHN JONES, JOHN EVANS, WILLIAM HUGHES.

Book O-O, p. 318   ROBERT RAWLINS, & LYDIA his wife, to JAMES WED-
9 & 10 Oct. 1751   DERBURN, ESQ., both of Charleston, as security
L & R by Mortgage   on 2 bonds, 1 dated 4 Sept. 1749 given to the
                          Rev. MR. FRANCIS GUICHARD in penal sum of
Ł 800 for payment of Ł 400 currency, balance due being Ł 200 & interest;
1 date 13 Sept. 1749 given to HENRY PERONNEAU, gentleman, of Charleston,
in penal sum of Ł 1600 for payment of Ł 800; which with the Ł 200 makes
Ł 1000 currency, with interest, on which 2 bonds JAMES WEDDERBURN became
bound with RAWLINS; that piece of land on Charleston Neck in St. Philips
Parish, Berkeley Co., 30 ft. x 414 ft., bounding NE on the High Road; NW
on HUGH ANDERSON; SW on Glebe land & Free School land; SE on JOHN GEORGE
DALLIBACH being the NW part of a piece of land conveyed by JOSEPH WRAGG,
ESQ., of Charleston, to JOHN GEORGE DALLIBACH; who conveyed to JAMES VOU-
LOUX, of Charleston; whose executors conveyed to ROBERT RAWLINS. Wit-
nesses: JAMES BOX, WILLIAM BARRAN. Before ALEXANDER STEWART, J.P. WIL-
LIAM HOPTON, Register. Lease not proved. On 11 Apr. 1764 the Rev. MR.
CHARLES LORIMER, mortgagee through his marriage to the widow of JAMES WED-
DERBURN, declared mortgage satisfied. Witness: FENWICKE BULL.

Book O-O, p. 326   JOHN (his mark) THOMPSON, SR., planter, to
15 July 1749   JAMES MCREE, & DEBORAH his wife, daughter of
L & R   JOHN THOMPSON; both of Craven Co., for love &
                          affection & 15 shillings; 1/2 of 900 a. (450
a.), bounding NW on the Rev. MR. JOHN BAXTER & on JOHN LANE; N on vacant
land; SE on COL. ANTHONY WHITE; SW on CAPT. WILLIAM BROCKINGTON. Witnesses: JOSEPH ROPER, MARY EDGELL, JOHN THOMPSON, JR. Before WILLIAM
FLEMING, J.P. WILLIAM HOPTON, Register. Plat given.

Book O-O, p. 331   JAMES MCREE, planter, & DEBORAH his wife, to
16 & 17 Sept. 1753   the Rev. MR. JOHN BAXTER, both of Craven Co.,
L & R   for Ł 281:5:0 currency, 1/2 of 900 a. (450 a.),
                          in Craven Co., bounding NW on JOHN BAXTER,
where he now lives; formerly belonging to JOHN LANE; N on vacant land; SE
on COL. ANTHONY WHITE; SW on CAPT. WILLIAM BROCKINGTON. Witnesses: MAR-
GARET WELLS, SAMUEL THOMPSON, WILLIAM THOMPSON. Before JOHN LEVISTON,
J.P. WILLIAM HOPTON, Register. Plat given.

Book O-O, p. 337   FRANCIS FUTHY, planter, to ROBERT FUTHY, plant-
9 Oct. 1751   er, both of Craven Co., for Ł 800 currency, of
L & R   825 a., his half of 1650 a. Whereas ANTHONY
                          WHITE, by will, ordered his real estate sold &
his executor JOSEPH DUBOURDIEU on 2 Apr. 1748 sold 2 tracts in Craven Co.,
total 1650 a., to DANIEL LAROCHE & WILLIAM FLEMING; bounding S on a great
swamp; N on vacant land; E on JASPER KING; W on JOHN THOMPSON; & whereas
LAROCHE & FLEMING on 2 Apr. 1748 sold the 2 tracts to FRANCIS FUTHY & ROB-
ERT FUTHY; now FRANCIS FUTHY sells his half to ROBERT FUTHY. Witnesses:
ANTHONY M. WHITE, JOSEPH WHITE. Before ELIAS FOISSIN, J.P. WILLIAM HOP-
TON, Register.

Book O-O, p. 342   DANIEL HUGER, ESQ., of Berkeley Co., to DANIEL
26 & 29 July 1736   HORRY, planter, of Craven Co., for Ł 5 curren-
L & R   cy, 1000 a. in St. James Santee, Craven Co.,
                          granted 3 Sept. 1735 by Lt. Gov. THOMAS BROUGH-
TON to DANIEL HUGER; bounding N on RICHARD & FRANCIS SPENCER; E on DANIEL
& ELIAS HORRY; W & NW on PAUL MAZYCK & WAMBAW CREEK; S & SW on vacant
land & ELIAS HORRY. Witnesses: WILLIAM CHILD, ISAAC CHILD. Before FRAN-
CIS LEJAU, J.P. WILLIAM HOPTON, Register.

Book O-O, p. 347   JOHN HUME, merchant, & SUSANNA his wife, to

17 & 18 Apr. 1754   JOHN HODSDEN & WILLIAM ELLIS, merchants, all
L & R   of Charleston; for ₤ 1700 currency, 46 a. in
                       St. Philips Parish, Charleston, bounding E on
the Hon. JOSEPH BLAKE; S on THOMAS GADSDEN; W & N on DANIEL HUNT (formerly RICHARD CARTWRIGHT). Whereas JAMES CROKATT, merchant, of Charleston,
owned said 46 a. in St. Philips Parish, Charleston, & with ESTHER his
wife, by L & R dated 12 & 13 Sept. 1735 sold the tract to JOHN HAMMERTON;
who, with ELIZABETH his wife, by L & R dated 19 & 20 July 1737, sold to
ALEXANDER BENNETT, ESQ., of London; & whereas BENNETT, by his attorney,
BENJAMIN WHITAKER, in 1743 sold to JOHN HUME, now he sells to HODSDEN &
ELLIS as tenants in common, not as joint tenants. Witnesses: RICHARD
LAMBTON, WHITE OUTERBRIDGE. Before JAMES WRIGHT, J.P. WILLIAM HOPTON,
Register.

Book O-O, p. 350   EDWARD (his mark) JONES, of the Independent
28 & 29 Mar. 1754   Company belonging to CAPT. RAYMOND DEMAREE, to
L & R   MOSES PARMIENTO, sutler, of Charleston, for
                       ₤ 75 currency, 200 a. in Amelia Township,
bounding SE on MILES JACKSON & vacant land; other sides on vacant land;
according to grant dated 29 Nov. 1750 from Gov. JAMES GLEN, plat certified by GEORGE HUNTER, Sur. Gen., on 2 Jan. 1749. Witnesses: ALBERT MC-
ALLISTER, JOHN PATIENT. Before ALEXANDER STEWART, J.P. WILLIAM HOPTON,
Register.

Book O-O, p. 361   The Hon. WILLIAM MIDDLETON, ESQ., & SARAH his
4 & 5 Sept. 1753   wife, to the Rev. MR. LEVI DURAND, of St.
L & R   Johns Parish, Berkeley Co., for ₤ 3400 curren-
                       cy, the middle part of lot #199 in Charleston,
bounding S 55 ft. on Queen Street, W on a tenement belonging to GEORGE
SHEED & occupied by MR. COSSINS; N on WILLIAM MIDDLETON; E 167 ft. on a
house & lot belonging to JOHN REMINGTON. Witnesses: ALICE LEAKE, JOHN
RICE. Before PETER TAYLOR, J.P. WILLIAM HOPTON, Register.

Book O-O, p. 367   THOMAS ELLIOT, sole executor & only surviving
27 Apr. 1754   son of THOMAS ELLIOT, planter, of Berkeley
Certificate of   Co., in accordance with his father's will dat-
Partition   ed 9 June 1731 certifies that he has view all
                       his father's estate on S side of PonPon River
& has allotted the land to the several devisees as follows; for his own
third; lot marked No. 1, 500 a., shown by green lines on the plat; on
Horse Shoe Creek & Savannah, originally granted to THOMAS ELLIOT, the
father, by the Lords Proprs.; the third part allotted to the heirs of his
brother, JOSEPH ELLIOT, 2 parcels, total 672 a., shown with yellow lines
on the plat & marked No. 2, A & B; that is, lot A containing 500 a.,
granted the father by the Lords Proprs., bounding N on JOHN BARNET; W
partly on the E parcel (172 a.) of a certain tract of 300 a. sold by JOHN
WHITEMARSH to THOMAS ELLIOT, the father; E on MR. FARLEY; lot B, said 172
a., bounding E on A (500 a.); the other third equally to the heirs of his
nephew, STEPHEN ELLIOT, & heirs of his nephew WILLIAM ELLIOT, grandsons
of THOMAS ELLIOT, 526 a. in 4 parcels, 3 A, 3 B, 4 A, & 4 B; divisions
3 A & 3 B, shown by red lines allotted to heirs of STEPHEN ELLIOT, con-
formable to an award made by THOMAS LAMBOLL & JOHN BASNET on 7 Feb. 1754;
3 A being 135 a., the N part of a tract of 307 a. sold by WILLIAM WEST-
BURY to THOMAS ELLIOT, the father, 3 B being 128 a., the W part of 300 a.
sold by JOHN WHITEMARSH to said THOMAS ELLIOT, the father; to the heirs
of WILLIAM ELLIOT, 4 A & 4 B, lying separately but shown within blue
lines; 4 A being 91 a. on the Horse Shoe Creek adjacent to a MR. PETER;
4 B, 172 a., being the S part of a tract of 307 a. sold by WILLIAM WEST-
BURY to THOMAS ELLIOT, the father; bounding S on GEORGE MITCHELL. Witnesses: JOHN PRUE, PETER MONCLAR. Before the Hon. JOHN CLELAND, J.P.
WILLIAM HOPTON, Register. Plat given.

Book O-O, p. 370   REBECCA GRIMBALL, widow, of ISAAC GRIMBALL, of
5 & 6 Dec. 1753   Charleston; THOMAS GRIMBALL, planter, of Gran-
L & R   ville Co., & CHARLES GRIMBALL, gentleman, of
                       Berkeley Co., (REBECCA, THOMAS & CHARLES, be-
ing executrix & executors of will of ISAAC); of 1st part; to JOSEPH SEA-
LY, planter, of Granville Co.; for ₤ 801 currency; 500 a., English measure, on Burrows Neck, on the Indian Land in Granville Co., bounding E on
Youhaugh Creek & marsh; S on marsh; W & N on CHARLES ODINGSELLS & the SE

half part of 1000 a. granted to CHARLES ODINGSELLS the elder, father of above named CHARLES; who sold the above half (500 a.) to ISAAC GRIMBALL. Whereas ISAAC GRIMBALL, by will dated 4 Feb. 1752 authorized his executors to sell his 500 a. & use the money as directed, & appointed REBECCA his executrix as long as she remained his widow, & THOMAS & CHARLES GRIMBALL his executors; now they sell to SEALY. Witnesses: JAMES LOWRY, BENJAMIN D'HARRIETTE. Before JAMES MICHIE, J.P. WILLIAM HOPTON, Register.

Book O-O, p. 379
19 & 20 Dec. 1752
L & R

LEWIS MOUZON, planter, & SUSANNA ELIZABETH his wife, to JAMES MOUZON, planter, both of St. Thomas & St. Dennis Parish, Berkeley Co., for Ł 100 currency, his undivided share of the 500 a. on which LEWIS MOUZON, the father lived, in Berkeley Co., & devised to his sons, LEWIS, JAMES, PETER, SAMUEL & HENRY & the son to be born after his death. Whereas LEWIS MOUZON, SR., father of LEWIS & JAMES, parties hereto, by will dated 1745 bequeathed the 500 a. on which he lived equally to his sons JAMES, SAMUEL, PETER, & HENRY; JAMES the eldest, to have his choice (except the part on which are the houses, buildings, etc., which is to be for HENRY); but should they die before reaching their majority LEWIS to have the share of the 1 dying; should there be a posthumous son he to inherit equally; & whereas a son was born after testators death & died in infancy, so that LEWIS inherited that sons share as well as his own; now LEWIS sells his 2/6 to JAMES. Witnesses: PETER DUBOIS, ANTHONY BOCHET. Before JACOB MOTTE, J.P. WILLIAM HOPTON, Register.

Book O-O, p. 384
13 Apr. 1754
Annuity Bond

GEORGE SAXBY, ESQ., of Charleston, gave bond to ISABELLA GRAEME, widow, of JAMES GRAEME, C.J., in penal sum of Ł 2400 British, to secure his paying her, during her natural life, Ł 140 British every year on the Royal Exchange in London if she shall reside in Great Britain or at her dwelling house in Charleston if she shall reside in Charleston, in 2 half yearly payments. Witnesses: DAVID GRAEME, ALEXANDER GORDON, JR. GEORGE SAXBY agrees that a proportionable part of Ł 70 shall be paid to the executors or administrators of ISABELLA GRAEME as long as she shall live after the 13 Oct. next. Before JAMES MICHIE, J.P. WILLIAM HOPTON, Register.

Book O-O, p. 386
12 & 13 Apr. 1754
L & R by Mortgage

GEORGE SAXBY, ESQ., & ELIZABETH his wife, to ISABELLA GRAEME, widow of JAMES GRAEME, C.J.; both of Charleston; as security on above annuity bond (p. 384); that lot in Charleston bounding S 104 ft. on Broad Street; N on Queen Street; E 481 ft. on MRS. MAGDALEN DEVEAUX & on GEORGE SAXBY; W on Allen Street; also that lot bounding S 48 ft. on MRS. MAGDALEN DEAVEAUX; N on Queen Street; E 150 ft. on CHILDERMAS CROFT; W on 1st lot; also the W half of a half-a. lot #229; bounding E on the other half; W on proprietors of the Sugar House; S on marsh of Ashley River; N on Broad Street. Witnesses: DAVID GRAME, THOMAS YEOMANS. Before JAMES MICHIE, J.P. WILLIAM HOPTON, Register.

Book O-O, p. 394
27 & 28 1752
L & R

CHARLES ODINGSELLS, planter, & ESTHER his wife, of Will Town, Colleton, to JOSEPH SEALY, planter, of St. Helena Parish, Granville Co., for Ł 1000 currency, 500 a. half of 1000 a. in St. Helena Parish originally granted to CAPT. CHARLES ODINGSELLS 4 Jan. 1731 (see Book A.A. fol. 12); bounding W on JOSEPH SEALY & vacant land; N & E on marsh & creeks out of Youhaugh (Eupaugh) Creek; S on ISAAC GRIMBALL (part of said 1000 a.) & on marsh of a creek of Port Royal River. Witnesses: BENJAMIN D'HARRIETTE, JOHN JONES. Memorial entered in Auditor's Book D #4, fol. 62-63, on 2 May 1754, by JAMES MICHIE, Dep. Aud. Before JAMES MICHIE, J.P. WILLIAM HOPTON, Register. Plat of 500 a. in Granville Co., half of 1000 a. granted to CAPT. CHARLES ODINGSELLS & after his death inherited by CHARLES ODINSELLS, JR., who sold 500 a. to JOSEPH SEALY; certified 24 Apr. 1750 by WILLIAM WILKINS, Dep. Sur.

Book O-O, p. 400
8 & 9 Mar. 1753 (4)
L & R

JAMES ADAMSON, & ELEANOR (her mark) his wife, to ALEXANDER STEWART, weaver; both of Wateree River; for Ł 100 currency, 200 a. on Sauneys Creek, a branch of Wateree, granted by Gov. JAMES GLEN on 7 Mar. 1754 to JAMES ADAMSON, bounding SE & SW on said

creek; NW & NE on vacant land. Witnesses: BRYAN (his mark) TOWLAND, ROB-
ERT (his mark) STEWART. Before JAMES MCGIRT, J.P. WILLIAM HOPTON, Register. Lease not proved.

Book O-O, p. 405   ROBERT OSWALD, planter, & SUSANNA his wife, to
6 & 7 May 1754   WALTER IZARD, ESQ., both of PonPon for ₤ 3650
L & R   SC money, 3 tracts of land, 400 a., 165 a., &
                          100 a.; total 665 a. old measure which on re-
survey by WILLIAM MAINE, Dep. Sur., appear to be 840 a., in PonPon, Colleton Co., bounding E on land originally granted to WILLIAM PETERS; N & N
W on vacant land & on SAMUEL FARLEY; W on Whitmarsh Neck; S on JOHN JACK-
SON & on JOHN MATHEWES. Whereas the Lords Proprs. granted JOHN JACKSON
400 a. in Colleton Co. (resurvey showing 494-1/2 a.), bounding N on SAM-
UEL FARLEY & on vacant land; E on WILLIAM PETERS & on vacant land; S on
JOHN JACKSON; W on Tupelaw Swamp; & by will dated 20 Aug. 1723 bequeathed
200 a. to his 2 sons, THOMAS & JOSEPH, & 200 a. to his 2 sons PHILAMON &
GEORGE; & whereas the 4 sons by L & R dated 3 & 4 Aug. 1743 sold the 400
a. to JOHN LEARY; who by his will dated 4 Sept. 1745 directed that the
land be sold at public auction, & appointed GEORGE JACKSON & REGINALD
JACKSON, planters, his executors; & whereas they, by L & R dated 6 & 7
Dec. 1745, sold the 400 a. to ROBERT OSWALD; & whereas STEPHEN MONK, ESQ.,
of Goose Creek, son & heir of JOHN MONK, ESQ., Cassique, owned 165 a. (resurvey showing 226-1/2 a.) in Colleton Co., to the E of said 400 a.,
bounding NW on SAMUEL FARLEY; E on MR. JACKSON; S on vacant land; SW on
Whitmarsh Neck; & on JOHN MATTHEWS; which 165 a. were part of 24,000 a.
granted by the Lords Proprs. to the Cassaque; & by L & R dated 12 & 13
May 1729 sold the 165 a. to JAMES BASFORD, planter, of Colleton Co.;
after whose death his son, WILLIAM BASFORD, planter, of Granville Co.,
inherited; & whereas by L & R dated 23 & 24 Sept. 1753 WILLIAM BASFORD &
SUSANNA his wife, sold the 165 a. to ROBERT OSWALD; who not only becomes
owner of the 400 a. & 165 a. but also owns 100 a. (resurvey showing 119
a.), adjoining the 2 & originally granted to SAMUEL FARLEY & whereas the
inheritance being vested in JAMES OSWALD, son of ROBERT, an infant under
21 years, & he therefore cannot convey the 100 a. to WALTER IZARD; ROBERT
has agreed with IZARD to release the tract & within 6 months after JAMES
reaches 21 years to confirm the sale; now the transfer is made. Witnesses: JOHN RATTRAY, GEORGE JACKSON. Before BENJAMIN SMITH, J.P. WILLIAM
HOPTON, Register. Plat of various tracts certified 27 Apr. 1754 by WIL-
LIAM MAINE, Dep. Sur.

Book O-O, p. 416   SAMUEL BACOT, planter, & REBECCA his wife, to
27 & 28 Aug. 1753   RICHARD KIRKLAND, planter, both of Craven Co.,
L & R   for ₤ 100 currency, 567 a. in Craven Co., on S
                          side of Wateree River granted 6 Oct. 1752 by
Gov. JAMES GLEN to SAMUEL BACOT bounding SE on vacant land & JOHN TOD,
JR.; other sides on vacant land. Witnesses: JOSIAH CANTEY, WILLIAM CAN-
TEY, WILLIAM RANLEY. Before RICHARD RICHARDSON. WILLIAM HOPTON, Reg-
ister.

Book O-O, p. 423   LEWIS (LOUIS) MOUZON, the elder, to his grand-
9 May 1754   son, JAMES MOUZON, for natural love & affec-
Gift   tion, 2/5 of his plantation of 200 a. in
                          Berkeley Co. Whereas LOUIS MOUZON, the elder,
of St. Thomas & St. Dennis Parish, Berkeley Co., on 20 June 1728 gave his
son, LEWIS MOUZON, planter, 300 a., part of the 500 a. granted the father
on 1 Feb. 1708/9, then bounding W on ANTHONY BONNEAU; N on ANN LIVING;
STON; E on JOHN ALSTON; S on other part of 500 a.; & whereas LEWIS, the
son, by will dated 1745, bequeathed to 4 of his sons, JAMES, PETER, SAM-
UEL & HENRY, equally, the 500 a. on which he lived, being the same 500 a.
granted the father, the eldest to have his choice (except that the part
on which were the houses & buildings which part should be HENRY'S); but
should any son die before reaching 21 years then LEWIS to have that son's
share; & should any son be born after the death of LEWIS (2nd) he to have
his equal share; & whereas a son was born so lived to be christened, &
died, so that LEWIS (3rd) became entitled to a fifth of the land so devised; but inasmuch as LEWIS (2nd) was wrong in devising 500 a. because
he was entitled to no more than 300 a., the remaining 200 a. being still
the property of LEWIS the elder & in no wise conveyed; & whereas by L & R
dated 19 & 20 Dec. 1752 LEWIS MOUZON (3rd) the grandson, & SUSANNA ELIZ-
ABETH his wife sold to JAMES MOUZON (grandson) his undivided interest to

324

the 500 a. on which his father (LEWIS 2nd), lived; & whereas notwithstanding the devise of LEWIS (2nd) & L & R of grandson LEWIS (3rd) & his wife
to JAMES MOUZON, JAMES is not entitled to more than 2/5 of the 300 a.,
(that is 120 a.); but in order that JAMES may have the full quantity of
land he expected (that is, 200 a.), now LEWIS MOUZON the elder gives him
2/5 of 200 a., or 80 a. Witnesses: ISAAC GUERIN, SR., SAMUEL BOCHET,
ISAAC GUERIN, JR. Before SAMUEL THOMAS, J.P. WILLIAM HOPTON, Register.

Book O-O, p. 427   EDWARD PERRY, SR., planter, & ROSAMOND his
15 & 16 Apr. 1743   wife, of St. Pauls Parish, Colleton Co., to
L & R   ROBERT LADSON, THOMAS LADSON, & JAMES LADSON,
                      planters, of St. Andrews & St. Pauls Parishes,
for Ł 587 currency, 1/2 of 1174 a., or 587 a., English measure, in Colleton Co., bounding N on vacant land; E on JOHN GODFREY; S on ROBERT LAD-
SON; W on vacant land. Whereas Gov. ROBERT JOHNSON on 28 Apr. 1733 granted ROBERT LADSON, SR., h174 a., English measure, in Colleton Co., bounding N & W on vacant land; E on JOHN GODFREY; S on HENRY YOUNG; & whereas
by will dated 19 Dec. 1732 for good causes & considerations he bequeathed
to EDWARD PERRY, SR., half the plantation; now PERRY sells his half to
ROBERT, JR., THOMAS, & JAMES LADSON. Witnesses: ANDREW LETCH, EDWARD
PERRY, JR., SILAS MILES. Before ALEXANDER STEWART, J.P. WILLIAM HOPTON,
Register.

Book O-O, p. 436   ELISHA BUTLER, planter, & MARY his wife (form-
31 Oct. 1749   erly MARY WRIGHT, widow of RICHARD WRIGHT,
Release   planter), of Stono, Colleton Co., & THOMAS
                      WRIGHT & WILLIAM ROPER, merchants, of Charles-
ton, executors of will of RICHARD WRIGHT; of 1st part; to JAMES HARTLEY,
planter, of Colleton Co., for Ł 3000 currency, 587 a., called Buck Hall,
where RICHARD WRIGHT lived, on Cacaw Swamp, near head of NW branch of
Stono River, in St. Pauls Parish, Colleton Co., bounding E on RIVERS
STANYARNE; SE on MR. MESHEW; S on WILLIAM HARVEY; SW on JONATHAN FITCH; W
on THOMAS ELLIOT & FREDERICK GRIMKE. Whereas RICHARD WRIGHT owned the
above tract of 587 a., made up of several smaller tracts purchased by
said WRIGHT; that is, 350 a. which SARAH WOODWARD, widow, by L & R dated
20 & 21 Dec. 1730 sold to WRIGHT; the 350 a. being part of 1050 a. "off
of" French's patent land conveyed under the patent to JOHN GODFREY, planter, of Colleton Co., who conveyed to SARAH WOODWARD; then bounding N on
RALPH EMMS; S on MARTHA WILLIAMSON, & on GODFREY & on the Rev. MR. TRED-
WELL BULL; E on other part said 1050 a.; W on JONATHAN FITCH; also 100 a.
on said swamp on NW brand of Stono River, being part of 250 a. formerly
granted to RALPH EMMS; also 276 a. on said swamp, part of 470 a. granted
to RALPH EMMS; which 100 a. & 276 a. were sold by L & R dated 7 & 8 Apr.
1737 by MARTAH WILLIAMSON, widow, daughter of RALPH EMMS, to RICHARD
WRIGHT; & whereas RICHARD WRIGHT sold the E part of the 276 a. to COL.
ALEXANDER HEXT, reducing the 3 tracts to about 587 a., & by will dated 2
Jan. 1744 directed executors to sell the remainder of his real & personal
estate, & appointed his wife MARY (now MARY BUTLER) & his friend THOMAS
ELLIOT, SR., His brother THOMAS WRIGHT, ELISHA BUTLER, & WILLIAM ROPER,
his executrix & executors; who proved the will; & whereas ELISHA BUTLER
married said MARY WRIGHT; now they, the executrix & the executors, sell
the 587 a. to HARTLY. Witnesses: ROBERT ROPER, AUSTEN ROBERT LOCKTON,
CHARLES PINCKNEY. Before H. BERINGER DE BEAUFAIN, J.P. WILLIAM HOPTON,
Register.

Book O-O, p. 443   WILLIAM CLIFFORD, planter, & MARY his wife, of
11 Dec. 1743   St. James Goose Creek, Berkeley Co., to JAMES
Release   HARTLY, of St. Pauls Parish, Colleton Co., for
                      Ł 375 currency, 150 a. in St. Pauls Parish,
called High Park, adjoining the land in which HARTLY lives. Witnesses:
JAMES ELDERTON; ANDREW LETCH, planter, of St. Pauls Parish; THOMAS LAD-
SON, JOHN MILES. Before ALEXANDER STEWART, J.P. WILLIAM HOPTON, Register.

Book O-O, p. 447   THOMAS RIGDON SMITH, planter, to JAMES HARTLY,
22 Nov. 1751   planter, both of Colleton Co., for Ł 550 cur-
Release   rency, 109 a. in Colleton Co. Whereas Gov.
                      JAMES GLEN on 6 Nov. 1751 granted THOMAS RIG-
DON SMITH a tract said to contain 300 a., plat certified by THOMAS BROUGH-
TON, Sur. Gen. on 23 July 1711 & annexed to a grant to THOMAS ELLIOT, but

which was found to contain 109 surplus a., according to plat dated 26
Jan. last, by GEORGE HUNTER, Sur. Gen., showing the 109 a. bounding SW on
MANLY WILLIAMSON (later WILLIAM HARVEY); NW on JAMES HARTLY; NE on RIV-
ERS STANYARNE; SE on other part of 300 a.; now SMITH sells the 109 a. to
HARTLY. Witnesses: ALEXANDER GARDEN, JR., MICHAEL TONGE (?). Before
THOMAS LAMBOLL, J.P. WILLIAM HOPTON, Register.

Book O-O, p. 452　　　　　　THOMAS FITCH, planter, to JAMES HARTLEY,
6 June 1741　　　　　　　　 planter, both of Colleton Co., for Ł 1600 cur-
Release　　　　　　　　　　 rency, 350 a., part of 500 a. given FITCH by
　　　　　　　　　　　　　　 his grandfather, THOMAS ELLIOT'S will; the
350 a. being in St. Paul's Parish, Colleton Co., on Caucaw Swamp, bound-
N on WILLIAM CLIFFORD; S on CALEB TOOMER; W on the swamp; according to
grant of 1000 a., English measure, to RALPH EMMS, SR., by Gov. NATHANIEL
JOHNSON on 3 Sept. 1709. Whereas it appears that the 1000 a. were purchased by RALPH EMMS & THOMAS ELLIOT, SR., at an equal charge, for the
use of poor friends in England with the proviso that they come to SC
within 7 years, but they not coming within that time RALPH EMMS by will
authorized ELLIOT to dispose of the half of the 1000 a. as his own property; which 500 a. ELLIOT bequeathed as follows: to his son-in-law WIL-
LIAM CLIFFORD, 150 a. at High Park, adjoining MR. NICHOLS; to his grandson, THOMAS FITCH, the remaining 350 a.; now FITCH conveys the 350 a. to
HARTLY. Witnesses: ANDREW LETCH, JOHN MILES, JOSEPH LADSON. Before
ALEXANDER STEWART, J.P. WILLIAM HOPTON, Register.

Book O-O, p. 458　　　　　　MAJ. WILLIAM PALMER, planter, of Granville
17 Feb. 1753　　　　　　　　 Co., eldest son & heir of COL. JOHN PALMER,
Release　　　　　　　　　　 planter; & EVANS PALMER, youngest son & de-
　　　　　　　　　　　　　　 visee of said JOHN PALMER; of 1st part; to
JAMES HARTLY, planter, of Colleton Co., for Ł 2300 currency, 1225 a. in
several tracts, on SW side Combee River, called Green Point, as owned by
JOHN PALMER; whereas JOHN PALMER owned 1225 a. in several tracts; that
is, 200 a. granted by the Lords Proprs. to JAMES ATKINS; 200 a. granted
by the Lords Proprs. to RICHARD SMALLWOOD; & by several mesne conveyances
came down to JOHN PALMER; 300 a. granted by the Lords Proprs. to JOHN
PALMER; 2 tracts of 211 & 314 a., total 525 a.; making 1 plantation of
1225 called Green Point, on SW side Combee River, bounding W on ROBERT
THORPE; S on CAPT. JOHN BULL; N on Lt. Gov. COL. WILLIAM BULL; & whereas
JOHN PALMER bequeathed the plantation (as shown by 4 plats) to his son
RICHARD, except as excepted; but in case of default to his sons EDMOND &
EVANS, with the cypress trees reserved on son WILLIAM'S land; which cy-
press trees he bequeaths to son RICHARD except the use of so many as are
reserved; & whereas RICHARD survived his brother EDMOND & afterwards died
without male issue whereupon the reversion of the 525 a. on death of
RICHARD descended upon WILLIAM, party hereto, & the estate for life in
said EVANS PALMER as surviving devisee; now WILLIAM & EVANS PALMER sell
the 1225 a. to HARTLY. Witnesses: MARY FENDIN, JAMES WILLIAMS, THOMAS
RIGDON SMITH. Before GEORGE SAXBY, J.P. WILLIAM HOPTON, Register. Plat
of 314 & 211 a.

Book O-O, p. 463　　　　　　GEORGE SCOTT, surgeon, of Johns Island, to
15 & 16 May 1754　　　　　　 FRANCIS GOTTIER, silversmith, of Charleston,
L & R by Mortgage　　　　　 as security on bond of even date in penal sum
　　　　　　　　　　　　　　 of Ł 750 for payment of Ł 379:12:0 currency,
with interest, on 16 Sept. 1754; 200 a. on John's Island, in Colleton
Co., bounding SE on WILLIAM SPENCER; S on COL. HALL; W on DR. KILPATRICK;
N on CHARLES CALEB. Witnesses: JAMES ROBERTSON, WADE BLAIR. Before
LIONEL CHALMERS, J.P. WILLIAM HOPTON, Register.

Book O-O, p. 468　　　　　　RICHARD JENKINS, planter, & MARTHA his wife,
23 & 24 Nov. 1753　　　　　　to WILLIAM MAY, cordwainer, both of St. Johns
L & R　　　　　　　　　　　　Parish, Edisto Island, Colleton Co., for Ł 800
　　　　　　　　　　　　　　 currency, 300 a. on Edisto Island, bounding E
on DR. ARCHIBALD CALDERS; W on JONATHAN WILKINS; N on WILLIAM BOWER; S on
ANDREW TOWNSEND. Witnesses: ANDREW TOWNSEND, JOHN FRY, RICHARD RIPPIN.
Before JACOB MOTTE, J.P. WILLIAM HOPTON, Register.

Book O-O, p. 474　　　　　　JOSHUA SANDERS, & ELIZABETH CLARK SANDERS, his
9 & 10 Sept. 1745　　　　　　wife, to GEORGE JACKSON, both of St. Bartholo-
L & R　　　　　　　　　　　　mews Parish, Colleton Co., for Ł 3000 currency,

bounding S on THOMAS BUER; NE on JOSHUA GREEN; E on JOHN PARKER; SE on
JOHN HUNT; S on the Barony. Witnesses: JOSEPH PAGE, THOMAS DEANE, MARY
FLETCHER. Before JOHN RATTRAY, J.P. WILLIAM HOPTON, Register.

Book O-O, p. 478   GEORGE JACKSON, planter, & MARY his wife, of
26 & 27 Mar. 1754   St. Bartholomews Parish, Colleton Co., to WIL-
L & R   LIAM LADSON, ESQ., of St. Johns Parish, Colle-
                          ton Co., for £ 2750 currency, 464 a. in St.
Bartholomews Parish, bounding SW on THOMAS BUER; NE on heirs of JOSHUA
GREEN; E on JOHN PARKER; SE on JOHN HUNT; S on the Barony. Whereas the
Lords Proprs. on 24 Feb. 1708, by Gov. NATHANIEL JOHNSON, granted ALEXAN-
DER CLARK 300 a., English measure, in Colleton Co., on S side PonPon Riv-
er, bounding S on JOSEPH BOON; other sides on vacant land; & whereas
ALEXANDER CLARK by will dated 17 Mar. 1718 bequeathed the tract to his
daughter, ELIZABETH, who afterwards married JOSHUA SANDERS, planter, of
St. Bartholomews Parish; & whereas on 16 Mar. 1732, Gov. ROBERT JOHNSON
granted JOSHUA SANDERS 364 a. in Colleton Co.; the 2 tracts making 1
plantation of 664 a.; & whereas JOSHUA SANDERS sold 200 a. the N part of
the 364 a. to JAMES BOGGS; leaving 464 a.; which by L & R dated 9 & 10
Sept. 1745 SANDERS sold to GEORGE JACKSON; now JACKSON sells the 464 a.
to LADSON. Plat of 522 a. in 2 tracts granted JOSHUA SANDERS on 16 Mar.
1732.

Book O-O, p. 486   PHILEMON JACKSON, planter, of St. Bartholo-
28 Mar. 1754   mews Parish, grandson of ALEXANDER CLARK; &
Confirmation   JOSEPH HARLEY, planter, of same Parish, & JANE
                          his wife, grand-daughter of said ALEXANDER
CLARK; of 1st part; to WILLIAM LADSON, ESQ., of St. Johns Parish, Colleton Co. Whereas the Lords Proprs. on 24 Feb. 1708, by Gov. NATHANIEL
JOHNSON, granted ALEXANDER CLARK 300 a., English measure, in Colleton
Co., on S side PonPon River, bounding S on JOSEPH BOON; other sides on
vacant land; & whereas ALEXANDER CLARK by will dated 17 Mar. 1718 bequeathed the plantation to his daughter, ELIZABETH CLARK, who later married JOSHUA SANDERS, planter, of St. Bartholomews Parish; & whereas by L
& R dated 9 & 10 Sept. 1745 they sold to GEORGE JACKSON the 300 a. & also
164 a. adjoining (part of 364 a. granted said JOSHUA SANDERS on 16 Mar.
1732); total 464 a.; & whereas GEORGE JACKSON & MARY his wife, by L & R
dated 26 & 26 Mar. 1754 sold WILLIAM LADSON the 464 a. in St. Bartholomews Parish; & whereas in ALEXANDER CLARK'S will it is apprehended that
the 300 a. were given to his daughter ELIZABETH for her life, but PHILE-
MON JACKSON, JOSEPH HARLEY, & JANE his wife, are convinced that CLARK intended to bequeath it to her absolutely in fee; & it being also apprehended that PHILEMON JACKSON & JANE HARLEY, eldest son & only daughter of
JANE, daughter of ALEXANDER CLARK, or their heirs, may after the death of
ELIZABETH (other daughter of ALEXANDER CLARK) claim an interest in the
300 a.; therefore, for £ 10 currency, PHILEMON JACKSON & JOSEPH HARLEY
confirm WILLIAM LADSON in his possession (p. 478). Witnesses: JAMES
GRINDLEY, JOHN MCKENSIE. Before JOHN DART, J.P. WILLIAM HOPTON, Register.

Book O-O, p. 492   Satisfaction of Mortgage (not recorded).
4 Apr. 1754   Whereas the Hon. JOHN CLELAND, & MARY his wife,
                          by L & R dated 24 & 25 Jan. 1752 mortgaged to
WILLIAM STONE, merchant, of Charleston, 1800 a. in Prince George Parish,
Craven Co., part of 3996 a. granted to CLELAND; bounding E on Peedee &
Black Rivers; S on Sampit Creek, Georgetown, The Common & MR. FORBES; W
on said creek, town, common, FORBES, & estate of COL. ANTHONY WHITE; N on
another part of 3996 a. belonging to CLELAND; to secure payment of
£ 11,420 currency, with interest; & whereas JOHN CLELAND & MARY his wife,
with STONE'S consent, by L & R dated 11 & 12 Sept. 1753 sold to THOMAS
HASELL, gentleman, for £ 387:10:0 currency, 31 a. in Prince George Parish,
part of the 1800 a., bounding SE on Wood Street in Georgetown; S on the
harbour in Sampit Creek; NE on Sampit Road & a line continuing same
course from 1st angle thereof; NW on PAUL TRAPIER (see Book N.N. page
473-479); the purchase money being paid to STONE towards discharging the
mortgage; now STONE declares mortgage satisfied as far as the 31 a. are
concerned. Witnesses: JOHN WAGNER, EDWARD WEBLEY. Before JACOB MOTTE,
J.P. WILLIAM HOPTON, Register.

Book O-O, p. 494   GEORGE SAXBY, of Charleston, to JAMES HEART,

3 & 4 Apr. 1754   of Craven Co., for ₺ 150 currency, 110 a. in
L & R   Craven Co., bounding S on Black River; W on
                         JOHN BOGGS. Witnesses: MARY GREENE, WILLIAM
CHAMBERS. Before JOHN LINING, J.P. WILLIAM HOPTON, Register.

Book O-O, p. 500   ELIZABETH BONHOSTE, widow, & administratrix of
11 & 12 Oct. 1749   JONAS BONHOSTE; CATHERINE BONHOSTE, MARY BON-
L & R   HOSTE, SUSANNAH BONHOSTE, & GABRIEL CAPERS, of
                         Christ Church Parish, Berkeley Co., of 1st
part; to WILLIAM PORTER, nonconformist pastor & teacher; for ₺ 730:12:6
currency, 225 a. granted to JONAS BONHOSTE; bounding NW on WILLIAM
BOLLEUGH; SW on SAMUEL SEBLEY; SE on ANTHONY DARNELLS Creek; NE on JOHN
WHELDEN. Witnesses: FRANCIS DESCHAMPS, RICHARD CAPERS, ROBERT MURRELL.
Before JACOB MOTTE, J.P. WILLIAM HOPTON, Register.

Book O-O, p. 508   RAWLINS LOWNDES, P.M. of SC, to WILLIAM SMITH,
31 May 1754   at auction, for ₺ 600 SC money, 440 a. in Col-
Sale   leton Co., formerly belonging to JAMES BERRIE,
                         bounding N on CAPT. JOHN BULL; W on JAMES RIX-
ON; S on JOHN SPLATT; E on WILLIAM BUTLER. Whereas THOMAS SACHEVERAL,
SAMUEL SPRY, & HENRY SPRY, executors of will of ROYAL SPRY; recovered a
judgment against MILLER ST. JOHN as executor of JAMES BERRIE in the sum
of ₺ 276 currency & costs; upon which a writ of fieri facias was issued
by JAMES GRAHAM, C.J., on 2 Jan. 1749, commanding the P.M. to levy those
sums on BERRIE'S estate; & whereas LOWNDES took possession of said 440 a.;
now he sells the tract to the highest bidder, WILLIAM SMITH. Witnesses:
THOMAS FERGUSON, CHARLES LOWNDES. Before JACOB MOTTE, J.P. WILLIAM HOP-
TON, Register.

Book O-O, p. 510   CHARLES PINCKNEY, ESQ., to his nephew, THOMAS
28 & 29 Mar. 1753   PINCKNEY, gentleman, both of Charleston, to
L & R   fulfil certain covenants, & for natural love &
                         affection; the W part of 2 town lots, Nos. 20
& 73, intended for MARY PINCKNEY; bounding N on Queen Street; E on other
part said lots belonging to THOMAS PINCKNEY, heir to SARAH PINCKNEY, & on
MOSES MITCHELL; S on other parts said lots belonging to heirs or devisees
of ADAM BEAUCHAMP; W on NOAH SERRE. Whereas by deed of settlement dated
30 Sept. 1746 recorded in Book C.C.P. 188, between CHARLES PINCKNEY, ESQ.,
of 1st part; THOMAS PINCKNEY, eldest son of MAJ. WILLIAM PINCKNEY, of
Charleston, the youngest brother of said CHARLES PINCKNEY, of 2nd part;
MARY PINCKNEY, eldest daughter of WILLIAM PINCKNEY, of 3rd part; SARAH
PINCKNEY second daughter of WILLIAM PINCKNEY of 4th part; for settling
certain parts of lots 20 & 73 & the houses & buildings thereon, lately
belonging to MRS. MARY BETSON, widow, mother of CHARLES & WILLIAM, on
which she lived; & whereas she died intestate the parts of lots descended
to CHARLES as her eldest son & heir; & whereas he agreed with the others
(THOMAS, MARY, & SARAH) that he would hold the lots under certain provisoes; that is, the W part, marked B with its houses & buildings, fronting 62 ft. on Queen (Dock) Street; 137 ft. deep; for MARY PINCKNEY; but
in case she should die before 21, without heirs, then CHARLES to convey
the lot to some other child or children of WILLIAM PINCKNEY; & whereas
MARY died in Sept. 1749 at Charleston, under 21 & without issue; &
CHARLES wishing to convey the land to his nephew, THOMAS PINCKNEY; now he
carries out the intent of the covenant. Witnesses: WILLIAM PINCKNEY,
CHARLES PINCKNEY, JR., WILLIAM PINCKNEY, JR. Before JOHN DART, J.P.
WILLIAM HOPTON, Register.

Book O-O, p. 516   THOMAS PINCKNEY, gentleman, of 1st part; WIL-
30 & 31 Mar. 1753   LIAM PINCKNEY, ESQ., & RUTH his wife (father &
L & R   mother of said THOMAS PINCKNEY), of 2nd part;
                         ANNE PINCKNEY, spinster, (sister of THOMAS &
daughter of WILLIAM & RUTH), of 3rd part. Whereas by deed of settlement
dated 30 Sept. 1746 between CHARLES PINCKNEY, ESQ., of 1st part; THOMAS
PINCKNEY, eldest son of MAJ. WILLIAM PINCKNEY, younger brother of CHARLES,
of 2nd part; MARY PINCKNEY, eldest daughter of WILLIAM, of 3rd part;
SARAH PINCKNEY, second daughter of WILLIAM, of 4th part; for settling
certain parts of 2 lots #20 & #73, in Charleston, with the houses &
buildings thereon; lately belonging to MRS. MARY BETSON, widow, mother of
CHARLES & WILLIAM PINCKNEY, in which she lived; & which when she died intestate descended to CHARLES PINCKNEY, her eldest son; who agreed with

THOMAS, MARY & SARAH, that he would stand seized of the 2 lots with certain provisoes regarding W part of lot marked B on the plat, with its houses, fronting 62 ft. on Queen (or Dock) Street, 137 ft. deep, to the use of MARY, but should she die before 21 & without issue then CHARLES to have authority that part of the 2 lots to some child or children of WILLIAM, as CHARLES should think fit, (Book C.C. page 188); & whereas CHARLES PINCKNEY by deed of settlement dated 28 & 29 this Mar., further reciting that whereas MARY died in Sept. 1749 at Charleston under 21 & without issue & CHARLES conveyed to his nephew THOMAS the W part of lots 20 & 70 intended for MARY; & whereas WILLIAM has lived on said premises for some years & laid out considerable sums of money in buildings & improvements, & his son THOMAS is willing to convey the premises to his father & mother during their lives & afterwards to his sister, ANNE; now, in consideration of the sums spent by his father, & for natural love & affection for his father, mother, & sister, THOMAS conveys the premises to them. Witnesses: CHARLES PINCKNEY, CHARLES PINCKNEY, JR., WILLIAM PINCKNEY, JR. Before JOHN DART, J.P. WILLIAM HOPTON, Register.

Book O-O, p. 524   LEMUEL NESMITH, planter, & MARY his wife, to
27 & 28 May 1754   JOHN BROCKINGTON, planter, both of Craven Co.,
L & R   for £ 235 currency, 166 a. in Craven Co., part
                     of 500 a. granted on 23 Jan. 1726 to JOHN NE-
SMITH, SR.; who bequeathed said 166 a. to his son LEMUEL, party hereto; bounding NE on COL. ANTHONY WHITE; SE on part of said 500 a. belonging to LEMUEL NESMITH; SW on DOUGAL MCKEITHAN; NW on JOHN BROCKINGTON. Witnesses: MARGARET DRAW, SAMUEL NESMITH, SARAH (her mark) NESMITH. Before JOHN HAMILTON, J.P. WILLIAM HOPTON, Register.

Book O-O, p. 529   WILLIAM BACKSHELL, gentleman, of Charleston,
10 & 11 Aug. 1753   to AGNES LOVEKIN, widow of ROGER LOVEKIN, of
L & R   Coosa River, for £ 750 currency, 300 a. in
                     Granville Co., on N side Coosa River; bounding
W on THOMAS LLOYD; other sides on vacant land. Whereas MOSES BENJAMIN obtained a warrant for 300 a. from ROBERT DANIEL, Dep. Gov. on 18 Jan. 1716/17, as by plat certified by FRANCIS YONGE, Sur. Gen., on 2 Mar. following, for which the grant was passed 9 Apr. (recorded in Secretary's office fol. 402); & whereas MOSES BENJAMIN ON 23 Feb. 1710, or 12 Feb. 1720, for 10 pistols (pistoles?) sold the 300 a. to CAPT. JOHN HAM (by indorsement on back of deed); & whereas HAM, by will dated 19 Dec. 1721 (proved 30 said month at Providence) bequeathed to his daughter, JERUSHA KING, 100 a., & by said will gave his whole estate to his wife (JERUSHA), his sole executrix; & whereas JERUSHA KING (daughter) inherited the 300 a., & for £ 50 sold the tract to the Rev. MR. THOMAS SIMMONDS; who died intestate; & his daughter, HANNAH, his only surviving child, wife of THOMAS DALE, ESQ., became sole heir; & whereas THOMAS DALE on 9 Sept. 1749 leased (to ROGER LOVEKIN?) the 300 a., 100 of which were to be cultivated, for 20 shillings for each cultivated a. for 7 years & 5 years; & the land was in possession of AGNES LOVEKIN, widow of ROGER LOVEKIN; & whereas THOMAS DALE died, leaving his wife, HANNAH, his sole executrix; & whereas HANNAH died 10 Apr. 1751 & by her will (Book D. fol. 162) appointed the Hon. CHARLES PINCKNEY & WILLIAM BACKSHELL her executors with authority to sell her lands; now BACKSHELL sells to AGNES LOVEKIN. Witnesses: JONATHAN SCOTT, JOSEPH BROWN. Before ALEXANDER STEWART, J.P. WILLIAM HOPTON, Register.

Book O-O, p. 537   RICHARD HAMPTON, butcher, of Charleston, to
8 & 10 Dec. 1753   WILLIAM TURNER, of Berkeley Co., for £ 200 cur-
L & R   rency, 200 a. on which HAMPTON lived, on N
                     side of S branch of Santee River, bounding on
upper side by CORNELIUS COX; other sides on vacant land. Witnesses: PETER OLIVER, MCOLINEAR. Before ALEXANDER GARDEN, J.P. WILLIAM HOPTON, Register.

Book O-O, p. 543   MARY SMITH, planter, of St. Pauls Parish, to
19 June 1754   SMITH PRENTICE, cooper, of New England but now
Sale   living in SC, for 10 shillings & other con-
                     siderations, 344 a. in Beech Hill, St. Pauls
Parish willed to her by CAPT. JOSEPH SMITH; bounding N on WILLIAM & JOHN GRAVES; W on JOHN GRAVES; E on COL. RICHARD BEDON. Witnesses: JOHN STEWART, ANDREW WAY, WILLIAM (his mark) SMITH. Before J. SKENE, J.P.

Book O-O, p. 545
4 & 5 Apr. 1754
L & R

PETER TAYLOR, ESQ., surviving executor of will of WILLIAM SMITH, planter, of St. Philip's Parish, Charleston, who was eldest son & 1 of the devisees of will of WILLIAM SMITH, merchant of Charleston; of 1st part; ELIJAH PRIOLEAU, ANDREW SMITH, & JOSEPH SMITH, executors, & MARGARET SMITH, executrix, of will of JOHN SMITH, planter, of Colleton Co., another son & devisee of WILLIAM SMITH, merchant, of 2nd part; BARNARD ELLIOT, planter, of 3rd part. Whereas WILLIAM SMITH the elder owned 250 a. of land & marsh granted by the Lords Proprs. to JAMES MORTELL GOULARD DE VERVENT, on N side Ashley River, on Charleston Neck, with the mansion house thereon built by said WILLIAM SMITH, & by his will dated 30 Aug. 1710 bequeathed the plantation & houses equally to his 2 sons, WILLIAM & JOHN; & whereas WILLIAM the younger by his will dated 30 Dec. 1741 appointed his wife ELIZABETH SMITH, executrix; & his brothers, PETER TAYLOR & THOMAS DALE; his friends WILLIAM ELLIOT & JOHN STANYARNE, executors; & after several legacies to his wife & children authorized his executors to sell the half part of said plantation & the rest of his real & personal estate & divide the money among amongst his wife & childre; & whereas the will was proved by PETER TAYLOR & THOMAS DALE before Lt. Gov. WILLIAM BULL; & whereas DALE died & TAYLOR became sole executor; & whereas JOHN SMITH by his will dated 6 Sept. 1753 appointed his wife, MARGARET SMITH executrix, & his sons ANDREW & JOSEPH SMITH; & his son-in-law ELIJAH PRIOLEAU, executors, directing them to sell his half of said plantation & his real & personal estate & pay his debts; & whereas PETER TAYLOR, ELIJAH PRIOLEAU, ANDREW SMITH, JOSEPH SMITH, & MARY SMITH decided it would be better to sell the plantation in lots instead of as a whole & BERNARD ELLIOT being highest bidder for 23-1/2 a. at Ł 705 currency, they sell him the 23-1/2 a. bounding N on JOHN DRAYTON; E & W on other parts said 250 a.; S on land laid out on the Broad Path in lots to be sold. Witnesses: SARAH STOUTENBURGH, LUKE STOUTENBURGH, ARCHIBALD STANYARNE, JOSEPH STANYARNE, JR., THOMAS FARR, THOMAS SMITH, JR., THOMAS BAMPFIELD. Before JACOB MOTTE, J.P. WILLIAM HOPTON, Register.

Book O-O, p. 555
1 June 1748
Surrender

ELEANOR SANDWELL, widow, formerly widow of WILLIAM LINTHWAITE, brazier, of Charleston, in order to satisfy her former husband's (WILLIAM LINTHWAITE'S) debts, surrenders to the executrix & executors of LINTHWAITE'S will, all her claim to a town lot. Whereas WILLIAM LINTHWAITE by will dated 28 Apr. 1739 directed that his debts be paid & bequeathed to his wife ELINOR for her lifetime a certain part of lot #105 in Charleston, bounding E 80 ft. on JAMES PAINE (now DR. JOHN MARTINI); W on part same lot; N 60 ft. on same lot; S on Broad Street; & whereas his personal estate was not sufficient to pay his debts, ELINOR surrenders to SARAH HOPTON (formerly SARAH CLAPP) executrix, & JOHN MOULTRIE, executor of LINTHWAITE'S will, all her claim to said lot of land. Witnesses: ELIZABETH HAMMILL, WILLIAM BAMPFIELD, WILLIAM VANDERHORST. Before WILLIAM SIMPSON, J.P. WILLIAM HOPTON, Register.

Book O-O, p. 557
2 & 3 June 1748
L & R

SARAH HOPTON (lately SARAH CLAPP), executrix; & JOHN MOULTRIE, executor, of will of WILLIAM LINTHWAITE, brazier, of Charleston; to THOMAS JOHNSON, ESQ., for Ł 2500 currency, part of lot #105 in Charleston. Whereas WILLIAM LINTHWAITE owned a part of lot #105 in Charleston; bounding E 80 ft. on JAMES PAINE (now DR. JOHN MARTINI); N & W on other parts said lot; S 60 ft. on Broad Street, & by will dated 28 Apr. 1739 directed that his debts be paid & bequeathed said part of a lot to his wife ELINOR for her natural life & afterwards to be sold for certain uses; & whereas his personal estate was not sufficient to pay his debts & ELINOR on 1 this June surrendered to the executors her interest in the premises; now they sell to JOHNSON. Witnesses: ELIZABETH HAMMILL, WILLIAM BAMPFIELD, WILLIAM VANDERHORST. Before WILLIAM SIMPSON, J.P. WILLIAM HOPTON, Register.

Book O-O, p. 564
6 & 7 June 1748
L & R

THOMAS JOHNSON, ESQ., of Berkeley Co., to ELINOR SANDIVELL, widow, of Charleston, for Ł 2500 currency, the part of lot #105 in

Charleston mentioned above (p. 564). Witnesses: ELIZABETH HAMMILL, WIL-
LIAM BAMPFIELD, WILLIAM VANDERHORST. Before WILLIAM HOPTON, J.P. & Register.

Book O-O, p. 568   THOMAS LINTHWAITE, tanner, of Ashley River,
28 & 29 June 1754   son & 1 of the devisees of will of ELINOR
L & R   SANDWELL, widow, of Charleston; to WILLIAM
                          HOPTON, gentleman, of Charleston, for ₺ 1300
currency, his undivided half part of the SE part of lot #105 in Charleston, bounding E 80 ft. on DR. JOHN MARTINI; N on DR. THOMAS HALL (formerly REBECCA [RICHARD] FLAVELL); W on heirs of JOB ROTHMAHLER; S 60 ft. on
Broad Street; with the large wooden house thereon where ANNE MARIA HOY-
LAND, sole trader, now lives. Whereas ELINOR SANDWELL (formerly ELINOR
LINTHWAITE) owned the SE part of lot #105 with a large wooden house &
other buildings on it, & by will dated 8 Aug. 1749 bequeathed to her son,
THOMAS LINTHWAITE, when 21, half the residue of her estate, he to be
maintained meanwhile out of the rents & profits; & to include in said
half (besides the 3 Negro slaves named in the will) half the house, etc.,
on Broad Street in which she lived; appointing WILLIAM HOPTON, executor,
with full power to sell any or all her estate for the benefit of her
children; & whereas HOPTON proved the will & THOMAS attained 21 years &
took possession of his half; now he sells his half to HOPTON. Witnesses:
THOMAS GLEN, SARAH CLARKE, PETER MONCLAR. Before WILLIAM SIMPSON, J.P.
WILLIAM HOPTON, Register.

Book O-O, p. 577   THOMAS LINTHWAITE, tanner, & JAMES WITHERS,
29 June 1754   gentleman, both of Berkeley Co., to WILLIAM
Bond of Performance   HOPTON, gentleman, of Charleston, in penal sum
                          of ₺ 1300 currency, as security that ANNE,
wife of THOMAS LINTHWAITE, now between 18 & 19 years of age, shall, within 6 months after reaching 21 years, release to HOPTON her title of dower
in the half of the SE part of lot #105 & the house, etc., thereon (P.
568). Witnesses: PETER MONCLAR, MARTHA REES. Before WILLIAM SIMPSON,
J.P. WILLIAM HOPTON, Register.

Book O-O, p. 579   PATRICK CLARKE, planter, & JANE (her mark) his
19 Mar. 1754   wife, to ANNE ROBERTSON, vintner, both of
Mortgage   Berkeley Co., for ₺ 1200 currency, 40 a. with
                          its houses, commonly called the Quarter House,
bounding W & S on RALPH IZARD; E on JOHN BIRD; N on PAUL GRIMBALL; on
condition that CLARK will pay ANN ROBERTSON the sums ₺ 400 with interest,
on 1 Apr. 1754; 1755 & 1756. Witnesses: ROBERT RAWLINS, LYDIA RAWLINS,
FREDERICK MERCKLY. Before WILLIAM SIMPSON, J.P. WILLIAM HOPTON, Register. On Jan. 17, 1755 ANNE ROBERTSON acknowledged she received full satisfaction of mortgage from WILLIAM GLEN & JOHN COOPER. Witness: JOHN
REMINGTON. Before WILLIAM HOPTON. Recorded 22 Aug. 1755 by WILLIAM HOP-
TON, Register.

Book O-O, p. 583   JOSHUA TOOMER, gentleman, of Wilmington, New
17 Dec. 1753   Hanover, NC, appoints WILLIAM BACKSHELL, of SC,
Power of Attorney   his attorney, with authority to sell his 187 a.
                          on Stono River, Berkeley Co., SC, bounding W
on MATTHURINE GUERIN; N on BARNARD & JOSEPH ELLIOT; E on JOSEPH ELLIOT'S
marsh; S on Stono River. Witnesses: PHILIP SMITH, JOHN WILLIAMS, JR.
Before J. HAMILTON, JR. WILLIAM HOPTON, Register.

Book O-O, p. 586   JOSHUA TOOMER, ESQ., of Wilmington, NC, by his
15 Jan. 1754   attorney, WILLIAM BACKSHELL; to JOSEPH ELLIOT,
Release   planter, of Stono, SC, for ₺ 700 SC money, his
                          plantation & tan yard, being 152 a. of land &
marsh & all buildings thereon, in St. Andrews Parish, Berkeley Co., bounding W on MATHURIN GUERIN; N on JOSEPH FULLER (formerly BARNARD ELLIOTT) &
on JOSEPH ELLIOT; E on JOSEPH ELLIOT'S marsh; S on Stono River; the premises being free & clear, the mortgage having been paid, as by receipt on
back of deed. Whereas HENRY TOOMER, planter, of St. Andrews Parish,
Berkley Co., owned certain lands & by will dated 17 Dec. 1737 (recorded
13 Feb. 1739) gave his 2 sons, JOSHUA & JOHN TOOMER, certain lands &
marsh, containing 961 a., on Stono River, to be divided between them 2
years after testator's death & whereas JOSHUA TOOMER, on 29 Nov. 1746
mortgaged his 152 a. on which he lived to MATHURIN GUERIN, ELISHA &

WILLIAM BUTLER, trustees for the Baptist Church, at Stono, in the penal sum of Ⱡ 513:18:6 for payment of Ⱡ 256:19:3 with interest; the 152 a. then bounding NE on JOSEPH ELLIOT; W on MATHURIN GUERIN; S on Stono River; & whereas JOSHUA TOOMER in NC on Dec. 17, 1753 appointed WILLIAM BACKSHELL his attorney; now he sells the tract to JOSEPH ELLIOT. Witnesses: MATHURIN GUERIN, THOMAS TEW, tailor. Before JAMES PARSONS, J.P. WILLIAM HOPTON, Register.

Book O-O, p. 591   THOMAS ELIOT, SR., of St. Pauls Parish, Colle-
8 Oct. 1751   ton Co., to JOSEPH ELLIOT, of St. Andrews Par-
Sale   ish, for Ⱡ 10 currency, 500 a. in St. Andrews
                          Parish, on N side Stono River, bounding E & N
on WILLIAM ELLIOT; S on JOSEPH ELLIOT; W on JOSEPH FULLER. Witnesses:
HENRY HYRNE, THOMAS L. ELLIOT. Before JOHN DART, J.P. WILLIAM HOPTON,
Register.

Book O-O, p. 592   WILLIAM HOPTON, gentleman, of Charleston, sole
26 & 27 June 1754   executor of will of ELEANOR SANDWELL, widow; &
L & R   trustee for ANNA MARIA HOYLAND, daughter & 1
                          of the devisees of will of ELEANOR SANDWELL; &
ANNA MARIA HOYLAND, sole trader; of 1st part; to DANIEL HUNT, gentleman,
of St. Philips Parish, Berkeley Co., for Ⱡ 1700 currency, the undivided
half of a large wooden dwelling house & SE part of lot #105 in Charleston
(see pages 568, 577). Whereas ELEANOR SANDWELL owned said house & SE
part of lot #105 in Charleston where she lived, & by will dated 8 Aug.
1749 bequeathed half her real & personal estate, including the said house
& lot, to WILLIAM HOPTON upon the special trust that he would permit her
daughter, ANNA MARIA HOYLAND, wife of THOMAS HOYLANDj to use the same or
the rents & profits thereof during life (from which THOMAS HOYLAND was to
be excluded); her executor to have power to sell testatrix's estate, if
he thought it necessary, for the benefit of her children; nominating WIL-
LIAM HOPTON her executor; he after her death, proving the will; now HOP-
TON, with the consent of ANNA MARIA HOYLAND, sells ANNA'S undivided half
of said house & lot to DANIEL HUNT. Witnesses: SARAH CLARKE, PETER MON-
CLAR. Before WILLIAM SIMPSON, J.P. WILLIAM HOPTON, Register.

Book O-O, p. 600   DANIEL HUNT, gentleman, of St. Philips Parish,
28 & 29 June 1754   Berkeley Co., to WILLIAM HOPTON, gentleman, of
L & R   Charleston, for Ⱡ 1700 currency, his undivided
                          half part of a large wooden dwelling house &
the SE part of lot #105 in Charleston, where ANNA MARIA HOYLAND, sole
trader now lives, & lately sold by WILLIAM HOPTON, as executor of will of
ELINOR SANDWELL, widow, to DANIEL HUNT; bounding E 80 ft. on DR. JOHN
MARTINI; N on THOMAS HALL (formerly REBECCA FLAVEL); W on heirs of JOB
ROTHMAHLER; S 60 ft. on Broad Street. Witnesses: ELIZABETH BENFIELD,
PETER MONCLAR. Before WILLIAM SIMPSON, J.P. WILLIAM HOPTON, Register.

Book O-O, p. 606   Between WILLIAM HOPTON, gentleman, & SARAH his
29 June 1754   wife, & ANNA MARIA HOYLAND, sole trader, both
Declaration of Trust   of Charleston. Whereas ANNA MARIA HOYLAND
                          gave 3 separate bonds this date to WILLIAM &
SARAH HOPTON in penal sum of Ⱡ 2000 for payment of Ⱡ 1000 currency, with
interest on 29 June 1755; 1 for the sole use & benefit of MARY CHRISTIANA
HOPTON, an infant duaghter of WILLIAM & SARAH HOPTON; 1 for the sole use
& benefit of ALICIA HOPTON, another infant daughter of WILLIAM & SARAH
HOPTON; & 1 for the sole use & benefit of SARAH HOPTON; another infant
daughter of WILLIAM & SARAH HOPTON; & whereas THOMAS LINTHWAITE, tanner,
of Ashley River, son & devisee of ELEANOR SANDWELL, by L & R this date
for Ⱡ 1300 currency, sold to WILLIAM HOPTON his undivided half of a large
wooden dwelling & SE part of lot #105 in Charleston (p. 568); & whereas
DANIEL HUNT, gentleman, of St. Philip's Parish, this date, sold to WIL-
LIAM HOPTON, for Ⱡ 1700 currency, his undivided half of the same property
(p. 600); & whereas the property was purchased (p. 592) in trust for the
use of ANNA MARIA HOYLAND, sole trader, without the control of her husband THOMAS HOYLAND, but subject to certain intents & purposes, & the
purchase money Ⱡ 1300 & Ⱡ 1700 were paid to ANNA MARIA HOYLAND out of her
own money, that is to say, the Ⱡ 3000 she borrowed from WILLIAM & SARAH
HOPTON of money belonging to their 3 daughters (Ⱡ 1000 each) for which
she gave 3 bonds; & the 2 undivided half parts of the property on lot
#105 were conveyed to HOPTON as security on said 3 bonds, & accrued

interest, in the first place & afterwards in trust for ANNA MARIA HOYLAND; now it is mutually agreed that in case of default in paying the 3 bonds on 29 June 1755 then HOPTON may take possession of the property, but until default ANNA MARIA HOYLAND to have the use of the property. Witnesses: SARAH CLARKE, PETER MONCLAR. Before WILLIAM SIMPSON, J.P. WILLIAM HOPTON, Register.

Book O-O, p. 616
29 & 30 Apr. 1754
L & R
MOSES THOMPSON, planter, & JANE (her mark) his wife, to TIMOTHY DARGON, planter, both of Berkeley Co., for ₺ 200 currency, 500 a. in Amelia Township, Berkeley Co., on S side Santee River, part of 2000 a. granted to the Hon. ROBERT WRIGHT on 12 Nov. 1736 & conveyed on 19 Mar. 1742 by ISABELLA WRIGHT, his widow & sole executrix, to JAMES MAXWELL & by writ of fieri facias, at suit of MATTHEW ROCHE against JAMES MAXWELL sold (2000 a.) by RAWLINS LOWNDES, P.M., at public auction on 22 Jan. 1750, to MOSES THOMPSON; the 500 a. bounding S on vacant land & BENJAMIN NEWTON (adjoining ALEXANDER TATE); NW & SE on vacant land; SW on vacant land & on land joining TIMOTHY DARGAN; NE on other part of 2000 a., 500 of which are now in possession of ANN WATTS. Witnesses: JOHN FAIRCHILD, BENJAMIN WALKER, JOSEPH DARGAN. Before JOHN FOCQUET (FOQUET), J.P. WILLIAM HOPTON, Register. Plat of 500 a.

Book O-O, p. 623
29 & 30 Apr. 1754
L & R
MOSES THOMPSON, planter, & JANE his wife, to ANN (ANNA) WELLS, planter, both of Berkeley Co., for ₺ 200 currency, 500 a. in Amelia Township, Berkeley Co., on S side Santee River, part of 2000 a. originally granted on 12 Nov. 1736 to the Hon. PHILIP WRIGHT; see p. 616. Witnesses: JOHN FAIRCHILD, BENJAMIN WALKER, JOHN DARGAN. Before JOHN FOUQUET, J.P. WILLIAM HOPTON, Register. Plat given.

Book O-O, p. 629
22 & 23 May 1754
L & R by Mortgage
CHRISTIAN (his mark) RETHLESPERGER, planter, & ANN (her mark) his wife, to ABRAHAM DUPONT, planter, both of Berkeley Co., as security on bond of even date in penal sum of ₺ 1615:5:0 for payment of ₺ 807:12:6 currency, with interest, on 1 Feb. 1758; 4 adjoining tracts of 500 a., 100 a., 140 a., & 183 a., total 923 a., in Berkeley Co., also 100 a. within the limits of Saxagotha Township, Berkeley Co., bounding SE on WILLIAM BAKER & vacant land; SW on vacant land; NW on RICHARD MAZYCK; NE on Santee River; also 200 a. in Amelia Township, on SW side Santee River, bounding on all sides on vacant land. Witnesses: LUDWIG LINDER, WILLIAM YOUNG, DANIEL LINDER. Before JAMES MICHIE, J.P. WILLIAM HOPTON, Register.

Book O-O, p. 640
10 & 11 Oct. 1753
L & R
BENJAMIN DE ST. JULIEN, gentleman, brother & heir of PETER DE ST. JULIEN, gentleman; to ELIZABETH DE ST. JULIEN, widow of PETER DE ST. JULIEN; both of Berkeley Co., for ₺ 1000 currency; the E half of lot #56 in Charleston, bounding S 47-1/2 ft. on Broad Street; N & W on ISAAC MAZYCK'S lots; E on estate of JOSEPH DE ST. JULIEN. Whereas the Lords Proprs. on 24 Apr. 1683 granted JOHN PALMER, JR. lot #56 on N side Broad Street, & whereas the E half of the lot by various mesne conveyances became the property of PETER DE ST. JULIEN; who died intestate; & his brother BENJAMIN inherited; now BENJAMIN sells to ELIZABETH, widow of PETER. Witnesses: JOHN SIMONS, JOHN DAVIS, THOMAS MAXWELL. Before JACOB MOTTE, J.P. WILLIAM HOPTON, Register.

Book O-O, p. 648
14 & 15 Mar. 1754
L & R
ELIZABETH DE ST. JULIEN, widow of PETER DE ST. JULIEN, gentleman, of Berkeley Co., to BENJAMIN STEAD, merchant, of Charleston, for ₺ 1500 currency, the E half of lot #56 on Broad Street in Charleston (see p. 640). Witnesses: ISAAC MAZYCK, ISAAC MAZYCK, JR., DUGAL CAMPBELL. Before JAMES MICHIE, J.P. WILLIAM HOPTON, Register.

Book O-O, p. 656
2 Dec. 1754
Lease for 4 Years
JOSEPH HASFORT, planter, of Goose Creek, leases to CAPT. BENJAMIN COACHMAN, planter, of same place, for 4 years, for ₺ 150 currency, 146 a. on which HASFORT now lives, bounding S on THOMAS ELMES; E on SAMUEL ELMES; W on BENJAMIN CHILDS; N on JOHN PARKER. Witnesses: JAMES ROBERTSON, ALEXANDER MCGREGOR. On 2 Sept. 1754 COACHMAN paid HASFORT (HASFORD) ₺ 50 for the crops on the land & the

cattle & hogs. Before WILLIAM SIMPSON, J.P. WILLIAM HOPTON, Register.

Book O-O, p. 658   EPHRIAM (his mark) CLARK, & KATHERINE (her
21 Mar. 1753 (N.S.)   mark) his wife, to WILLIAM LEONARD, of Santee,
Release   Craven Co., for Ł 100 SC money, 200 a. on the
                          Cypress ponds on N side Santee River, bounding
SE on ANGEL HARDING; other sides on vacant land, as by plat dated 4 Aug.
1752. Witnesses: JOHN (his mark) ATHERTON, SAMUEL WILLIAMS, JOHN DAVIS.
Before JOHN TOBLER, J.P., Granville Co. WILLIAM HOPTON, Register.

Book O-O, p. 662   WILLIAM LEONARD, & LUCH (her mark) his wife,
18 Aug. 1753 (N.S.)   to FRANCIS JAMES, both of Craven Co., for
Release   Ł 150 currency, 200 a. on N side Santee River
                          on the Cypress Pond in Craven Co., bounding SE
on ANGEL HARDING; other sides on vacant land; as by plat dated 4 Aug.
1752; originally granted to EPHRAIM CLARK. Witnesses: ALEXANDER CAMPBELL,
JOHN EVANS, JOHN JAMES. Before RICHARD RICHARDSON, J.P. WILLIAM HOPTON,
Register.

Book O-O, p. 666   JAMES BULLOCK, planter, & ANN his wife, of St.
1 & 2 Aug. 1754   Pauls Parish, Colleton Co., to Gov. JAMES GLEN,
L & R by Mortgage   as security on bond of even date given by
                          JAMES BULLOCK & ISAAC NICHOLS, planter, same
place to Gov. JAMES GLEN, in the penal sum of Ł 3000 British for payment
of Ł 210 British annually to Gov. GLEN during his natural life; 400 a. in
Colleton Co., bounding W on JOHN PEACURN, & originally granted to JOHN
BEE by the Lords Proprs. on 6 May 1704; also 100 a. on PonPon River formerly granted on 23 July 1711 to MATTHEW BEE; also 200 a. in Colleton Co.,
formerly granted to MATTHEW BEE on 23 July 1711, bounding N on MATTHEW
BEE; also 866 a. in Granville Co., granted JAMES BULLOCK by WILLIAM BULL
on 16 Sept. 1738, bounding NW on vacant land; N on DANIEL CRAWFORD; E & N
on lands formerly laid out; SE on the Rev. MR. ARCHIBALD STOBO; SW on
branch of Savannah River. Witnesses: WILLIAM SIMPSON, EGERTON LEIGH.
Before WILLIAM BURROWS, J.P. WILLIAM HOPTON, Register.

Book O-O, p. 673   JOHN STEPHENS, to JOHN SAVAGE, merchant, both
24 & 25 June 1754   of Charleston, for Ł 500 currency, 500 a. on S
L & R in Trust   side Great Ogechee River in the Colony of
                          Georgia, bounding E on GRIFFITH WILLIAMS; N by
a line designed for the New Township; other side on vacant land; upon
trust for the use of ANN MCKAY, wife of CAPT. JAMES MCKAY, during her
natural life; & upon further trust that SAVAGE will execute such conveyances as ANN MCKAY shall direct. Witnesses: JEREMIAH SAVAGE, THOMAS SAV-
AGE. Before JACOB MOTTE, J.P. WILLIAM HOPTON, Register.

Book O-O, p. 681   WILLIAM GRAY, planter, & ELIZABETH (her mark)
15 & 16 Sept. 1754   his wife, of Craven Co., to WILLIAM LERUG,
L & R   planter, of Fredericksburg Township, Craven
                          Co., for Ł 275 currency, 350 a. in Fredericks-
burg Township, bounding SW on Wateree River; NW on JOHN BLACK & vacant
land; other sides on vacant land; which 350 a. were granted on 3 Apr.
1754 by Gov. JAMES GLEN to WILLIAM GRAY. Witnesses: ALEXANDER (JOHN)
RATTRAY, DANIEL MCDANIEL, THOMAS MOON. Before STEPHEN CRELL, J.P. WIL-
LIAM HOPTON, Register.

Book O-O, p. 687   JOHN SAVAGE, merchant, & ANNE his wife, to
16 & 17 Sept. 1754   CHARLES PINCKNEY, JR., attorney-at-law, both
L & R   of Charleston, for Ł 2700 SC money, 715 a. in
                          Christ Church Parish in 2 tracts of 615 a. &
100 a. Whereas JOHN ALLEN, gentleman, of Charleston, owned (among other
lands, tenements, town lots, plantations, etc.), 615 a. in Christ Church
Parish, bounding N on CAPT. THOMAS BOONE & CAPT. JACOB BOND (formerly
MRS. FRY); W on CAPT. BOND; S & E on JAMES PAINE & THOMAS BOONE; which
615 a. he purchased from BENJAMIN LAW by L & R dated 4 & 5 May 1738; also
100 a. surrounded on all sides by said 615 a.; which 100 a. he had purchased from DR. JAMES WHITE & SARAH his wife by L & R dated 28 & 29 June
1744; & whereas JOHN ALLEN by will dated 5 Mar. 1747 devised to his wife
ANN ALLEN (now ANN SAVAGE, party hereto) all his real & personal estate;
& whereas JOHN SAVAGE & ANN his wife (lately ANN ALLEN) by L & R dated 1
& 2 Feb. 1753 conveyed the 715 a. (with other property) to WILLIAM SCOTT,

merchant of Charleston (see Book M.M. pages 312-317); who, by L & R dated
9 & 10 Feb. 1753 reconveyed the said 715 a. (with other property) to JOHN
SAVAGE (see Book M.M. pages 318-321); now SAVAGE conveys to PINCKNEY.
Witnesses: JEREMIAH SAVAGE, THOMAS SAVAGE. Before JACOB MOTTE, J.P.
WILLIAM HOPTON, Register. Plat of 715 a.

Book O-O, p. 697   JAMES (his mark) WESTON, planter, & ELIZABETH
10 Jan. 1754   his wife, to THOMAS HOWELL, planter, both of
L & R   Craven Co., for Ŀ 200 currency, 100 a. on N
                         side Congaree River, bounding SW & NW on va-
cant land & on "old lines" & on VINSON SIMMONS; NE & SE on vacant land;
as by grant from Gov. JAMES GLEN in Council Chamber 8 Aug. 1753. Witnesses: JAMES DANIEL, CHARLES STROTHER, JOHN ALYNCK (MYRICK?). Before
STEPHEN CRELL, J.P. WILLIAM HOPTON, Register.

Book O-O, p. 701   WILLIAM HART, planter, & SARAH his wife, to
7 Mar. 1753   THOMAS HOWELL, planter, both of Craven Co.,
L & R   for Ŀ 200 currency, 100 a. on N side Congaree
                         River, bounding E on ARTHUR HOWELL & vacant
land; N on vacant land; W on HUGH BUTLER & THOMAS HOWELL; according to
grant from Gov. JAMES GLEN in Council Chamber, 15 May 1751. Witnesses:
DANIEL HOUGH, JOHN LESTER, JOHN MYRICK. Before STEPHEN CRELL, J.P.
Lease not proved. WILLIAM HOPTON, Register.

Book O-O, p. 707   ROBERT COUNSELL, planter, of the Welch tract
8 July 1754   in Craven Co., to SAMUEL WRAGG & JOB ROTHMAH-
L & R   LER, merchants, of Georgetown, for Ŀ 150 cur-
                         rency, 25 a. in the Welch tract, bounding E on
Peedee River & HARDY COUNCIL; S on WILLIAM GREEN; N on BENJAMIN WALL; W
on vacant land. Witnesses: THOMAS JAMES, JAMES CRAWFORD (CROFFORD). Before THOMAS HASELL, J.P. WILLIAM HOPTON, Register.

Book O-O, p. 713   ABRAHAM WALCOTT (WALCUTT), cordwainer, to SAM-
18 & 19 JULY 1749   UEL LOWLE, planter, both of Colleton Co., for
L & R   Ŀ 300 currency, 200 a. in St. Pauls Parish,
                         Colleton Co., bounding N on heirs of JOSEPH
PECOM; E on JOHN ARNOLD & CHRISTOPHER SMITH; S & W on a large creek of
Edisto River. Witnesses: JAMES DONNON, JOSEPH SEALY, JR. Before JAMES
BULLOCK, J.P. WILLIAM HOPTON, Register.

Book O-O, p. 720   THOMAS SACHEVEREL, planter, of Colleton Co.,
29 & 30 May 1751   (only surviving brother & heir of JOHN SACHE-
L & R   VEREL, who was heir to his AUNT SARAH HAYNES,
                         late wife of JOHN HAYNES, & 1 of the 3 daugh-
ters & heirs of MATTHEW BEE, planter; which JOHN SACHEVEREL died under
age of 21 & without issue), & MARY his wife; of 1st part; to SAMUEL LOWLE,
planter, of Colleton Co.; for Ŀ 1000 currency; 200 a. originally granted
to PATRICK MARTIN by Gov. JAMES MOORE on 5 Nov. 1701, on E side of a
fresh water creek of Edisto River, then called Bee's Creek; bounding N on
JONATHAN HAYNES & vacant land; E on vacant land; S on JAMES ROGERS; which
tract was sold by PATRICK MARTIN by deed of feoffment dated 6 Apr. 1709
to MATTHEW BEE; also 300 a. now belonging to THOMAS SACHEVEREL but originally granted on 23 July 1711 by Gov. ROBERT GIBBES to MATHEW BEE; also
on E side Bee's Creek, bounding N & W on said creek; E on vacant land; S
on MATTHEW BEE'S 200 a. mentioned above; both tracts free from MARY'S
claim of dower. Witnesses: JAMES REID, WILLIAM BEATTY. Before JAMES
BULLOCK, J.P. WILLIAM HOPTON, Register.

Book O-O, p. 729   WILLIAM GRAVES, planter, & MARY his wife, to
8 Oct. 1754   JOHN GRAVES, planter, of Colleton Co., for
Feoffment   Ŀ 450 currency, 100 a. in Beech Hill, St.
                       Pauls Parish, Colleton Co., bounding NE on es-
tate of SAMUEL STILES; SE & SW on RICHARD WARING & JOHN GRAVES (formerly
WILLIAM SIMMONS); NW on JOHN GRAVES (also lately purchased from WILLIAM
SIMMONS); the 100 a. being part of 500 a. granted 13 Jan. 1710 by the
Lords Proprs. to JOSEPH SUMNER with plat dated 16 Oct. 1710; being part
of a tract purchased from JOSEPH SUMNER by SAMUEL SUMNER, who by will
left it to be sold the 100 a. being purchased from REBECCA SUMNER, executrix, of will of SAMUEL SUMNER, by MOSES GRAVES, who devised the tract
to his son, WILLIAM GRAVES. Witnesses: THOMAS WEY, MARY HAYNE.

Possession & seizin taken by WILLIAM GRAVES & delivered by him to JOHN GRAVES by turf & twig. Before RALPH IZARD, J.P. WILLIAM HOPTON, Register.

Book O-O, p. 732   WILLIAM SIMMONS, planter, to JOHN GRAVES,
29 & 30 Apr. 1752   planter, both of Colleton lo., for Ŀ 2000 cur-
L & R   rency, 400 a. (except 1/8 a. called the bury-
ing ground including what is non-pailed in &
NW from said pails to make 1/8 a. which WILLIAM SIMMONS reserves as a
burying place throughout all generations) at Beech Hill, in St. Pauls
Parish, Colleton Co., bounding NE on estate of JOSEPH SMITH; SE on WIL-
LIAM GRAVES (formerly SAMUEL SUMNER) & on heirs of THOMAS QUARTERMAN; SW
& W on the part of 500 a. devised by JOHN SIMMONS to his son THOMAS SIM-
MONS, now the property of the heirs of SAMUEL STYLES; NW on heirs of ROB-
ERT WINN & heirs of WILLIAM HOLMES. Whereas JOHN SIMMONS owned 2 tracts
in Colleton Co., 1 of 500 a. granted by the Lords Proprs. on 30 Jan. 1710
with plat dated 6 Oct. 1709 by THOMAS BROUGHTON, Sur. Gen.; the other 100
a., purchased from ROGER SUMNER 4 June 1722; & whereas JOHN SIMMONS by
will dated 18 Jan. 1722 divided his lands into 3 parts, devising to his
wife REBECCA 1 part of 200 a.; to his sons JOHN & THOMAS SIMMONS, the
other 2 parts, each 200 a., with the proviso that should JOHN die without
issue his share to go to his 3rd son WILLIAM SIMMONS; which happened; &
whereas REBECCA, widow of JOHN the elder, later married _____ STILES, dying soon after, & by will dated July 1749 devised her 200 a. (among other
things) to her son WILLIAM SIMMONS; now he sells to JOHN GRAVES 400 a. in
2 adjoining tracts of 300 a. & 100 a.; the 300 a. being the E part of
said 500 a. granted to JOHN SIMMONS & willed to WILLIAM; the 100 a., NW
of the 300 a., having been purchased by JOHN SIMMONS from ROGER SUMNER &
willed to REBECCA who gave to WILLIAM. Witnesses: JOSEPH MASSEY, BENJA-
MIN CHAPPELL. Before JAMES SKIRVING, J.P. WILLIAM HOPTON, Register.

Book O-O, p. 739   WILLIAM BRISBANE, gentleman, & MARGARET his
28 May 1751   wife, of Charleston, to WILLIAM GRAVES, plant-
Release   er, for Ŀ 2000 currency, 421 a. Whereas ED-
WARD WAY, planter, of St. George Parish,
Berkeley Co., owned 371 a. part of 408 a. partly in Berkeley Co., partly
in Colleton Co., granted by the Lords Proprs. to WILLIAM WAY, father of
said EDWARD; bounding NW on RICHARD BEDON; SW & SE on THOMAS DISTON; (now
JOSEPH BLAKE); NE on ANN SACHEVEREL; & whereas EDWARD WAY, & ANNE his
wife, by L & R dated 23 & 24 Feb. 1745 sold the 371 a. to WILLIAM BRIS-
BANE; & whereas HENRY SALTERS, (SALTUS), planter, owned 55 a. adjoining
said 371 a., & after his death 50 a. of the 55 were taken on execution &
sold by RAWLINS LOWNDES, P.M., on 11 Aug. 1747 at public auction, for
Ŀ 131 currency to WILLIAM BRISBANE; now he sells the 2 tracts, total 421
a., to WILLIAM GRAVES. Witnesses: JOHN GRAVES, JAMES BAKER. Before J.
SKENE, J.P. WILLIAM HOPTON, Register.

Book O-O, p. 744   WILLIAM GRAVES, planter, & MARY his wife, of
28 Mar. 1752   St. Pauls Parish, Colleton Co., to JOHN ELLIOT,
Release   planter, of St. George Parish, Berkeley Co.,
for Ŀ 1600 currency, 421 a. partly in Berkley,
partly in Colleton Co.; bounding NW on RICHARD BEDON; SW & SE on THOMAS
DISTON (now belonging to heirs of JOSEPH BLAKE); NE on JOSEPH WAY. Witnesses: PARMENAS WAY, JOHN GRAVES. Before J. SKENE, J.P. WILLIAM HOP-
TON, Register.

DEEDS BOOK "P-P"
OCT. 1754 - SEPT. 1755

Book P-P, p. 1   Lt. Gov. WILLIAM BULL, OTHNIEL BEALE, DAVID
19 & 20 Mar. 1740   HEXT, ISAAC HOLMES, & ISAAC MAZYCK, ESQ., hav-
L & R   ing been appointed, by an act of the General
Assembly, passed 17 June 1746, trustees for
preserving the fortifications & for appropriating certain surplus lands
in Charleston, & whereas it was declared in said act that on a resurvey
it was found that certain surplus lands near Queen Street, in NW part of
Schenckinghs Square, as endorsed by yellow lines on a certain plat in the
Secretary's office, should be in the hands of said trustees, to be sold

within 18 months at public auction, & the money used to pay the owners of
lots 248 & 249 taken up by the ditch & rampart, the surplus money to be
placed in the hands of the public treasurer; now having divided the surplus land into 4 parcels, according to plat, they sell to WILLIAM WEBB,
merchant, of Charleston, the highest bidder, for Ⱡ 660 currency, the SE
parcel, #3, bounding E 49 ft. on Old Church or Meeting House Street; S
230 ft. on MRS. BOURGARD; W on part purchased by JOHN DANIEL; N on part
purchased by HENRY PERONNEAU. Witnesses: CHARLES PINCKNEY, SAMUEL PRIO-
LEAU, JR. Before JOHN DART, J.P. WILLIAM HOPTON, Register. Plat of
surplas land bounding E about 98-1/2 ft. on Old Church Street, W 132 ft.
on King Street; S about 460 ft. on MRS. BOGAR; N 460 ft. on DR. MARTIN;
lots #1 & #2 purchased by JOHN DANIEL; lot #3 by WILLIAM WEBB; lot #4 by
HENRY PERONNEAU.

Book P-P, p. 7   RAWLINS LOWNDES, P.M., to JAMES IRVING, mer-
14 July 1749   chant, of Charleston, for Ⱡ 920 SC money, part
Sale   of a lot in Charleston, bounding N on HENRY
                       PERONNEAU'S lot occupied by JAMES MICHIE; S
230 ft. on BARNARD ELLIOT'S land occupied by the Rev. MR. FRANCIS GUI-
CHARD; W on JOHN DANIEL; E 49 ft. on Meeting Street, which piece of
ground was purchased by WILLIAM WEBB from certain trustees (p. 1).
Whereas WILLIAM WEBB owned said part of a lot on Meeting Street (see p.
1) & on 12 Sept. 1748 gave bond to THOMAS ROGERS & ELY DYSON, merchants,
of London, in penal sum of Ⱡ 3000 British for payment of Ⱡ 1474:2:11
British; & whereas ROGERS & DYSON obtained a judgment against WEBB & a
writ of fieri facias was issued directing the P.M. to recover the debt &
costs from WEBB'S estate; now LOWNDES sells the above lot at public auction to IRVING. Witnesses: WILLIAM BISSET, RICHARD DOWNES. Memo: It
was agreed between said parties that while the deed refers to plat annexed to deed of conveyance (p. 1) from the commissioners to WILLIAM WEBB
yet the title held good for only so much of the land as was really within
WEBB'S fence on the day of the sale; this endorsement to be no bar or
hindrance to IRVING'S recovering the residue of land shown in plat from
BARNARD ELLIOT if he shall be minded to prosecute for the same. Before
JACOB MOTTE, J.P. WILLIAM HOPTON, Register.

Book P-P, p. 12   JAMES IRVING, merchant, & ELIZABETH his wife,
23 & 24 May 1754   to HENRY PERONNEAU, merchant, both of Charles-
L & R   ton, for Ⱡ 1100 currency, that part of a lot
                        on Meeting Street which WILLIAM WEBB purchased
from certain commissioners (see p. 1) & which was sold under execution to
IRVING (see p. 7). Witnesses: JAMES MCGHEE, ARTHUR FORBES. Memo: It is
agreed between the parties that while the deed refers to the plat annexed
to the deed of conveyance from the commissioners to WILLIAM WEBB yet the
titles are to hold good for only so much of the land as is within MR.
IRVING'S fence on day of the sale; this endorsement to be no hindrance to
PERONNEAU'S recovering the residue of the land from BARNARD ELLIOT if he
be minded to prosecute for the same. Before BENJAMIN SMITH, J.P. WIL-
LIAM HOPTON, Register.

Book P-P, p. 25   ULRICH STARACH, SR., planer, & MARGARET his
1 & 2 Dec. 1753   wife, of Wassamasaw, Colleton Co., to BRAND
L & R   PENDARVIS, planter, of the Fork of Edisto, for
                        Ⱡ 25 currency, 150 a. in the Fork of Edisto,
bounding NE on PonPon River; other sides on vacant land. Witnesses: ROG-
ER ADAM, JOHN MAY, DAVID RUMPH. Before RALPH IZARD, J.P. WILLIAM HOP-
TON, Register.

Book P-P, p. 30   WILLIAM GREEN, planter, & JANE his wife, eld-
21 & 22 Aug. 1754   est son & heir of JOHN GREEN, planter, to
L & R   JAMES COACHMAN, planter; all of Craven Co.,
                        for Ⱡ 1700 currency, 500 a. in Craven Co.,
granted 2 July 1718 by Gov. ROBERT JOHNSTON & the Lords Proprs. to JOHN
GREEN; who by bill of sale dated 7 Sept. 1741 sold or gave the land to
WILLIAM GREEN but did not deliver possession & seizin & died without be-
queathing the land; so that WILLIAM inherited; bounding NE on Black River; SW on vacant land; NW on a Barony; SE on JOHN GREEN; according to
plat certified by FRANCIS YONGE, Sur. Ge., on 5 Nov. 1717. Witnesses:
THOMAS LYNCH, ZACHARIAH BRAZIER, RICHARD GREEN, WILLIAM PALMER. Before
THOMAS HASELL, J.P. WILLIAM HOPTON, Register.

Book P-P, p. 38   WILLIAM GREEN, planter, & JOHN GREEN & RICHARD
1 & 2 Mar. 1754   GREEN, executors of will of JOHN GREEN, the
L & R   elder; to JAMES COACHMAN, gentleman, of George-
                         town, for ₺ 1250 currency, 500 a. in Craven
Co., bounding NE on Black River; SW on vacant land; NW on JOHN GREEN; SE
on SAMUEL SCREVEN & vacant land; which land Gov. ROBERT JOHNSTON on 2
July 1718 granted JOHN GREEN; & which, by will dated 8 Jan. 1749, JOHN
GREEN ordered sold by his executors. Witnesses: THOMAS HASELL, JOSEPH
DUBOURDIER. Before GEORGE PAWLEY, J.P. WILLIAM HOPTON, Register.

Book P-P, p. 43   STEPHEN HOLSTON, planter, & JUDITH (her mark)
27 & 28 Oct. 1752   his wife, to THOMAS KENNERLY, planter, both of
L & R   Berkeley Co., for ₺ 200 currency, 500 a. on
                         Turkey Creek, on S side Broad River, Berkeley
Co., bounding NE on the river; other sides on vacant land. Witnesses:
JOHANNA CRELL, CASPAR (his mark) GALLESER. Before STEPHEN CRELL, J.P.
WILLIAM HOPTON, Register.

Book P-P, p. 49   GEORGE (his mark) HINDALS HILES, planter, &
25 & 26 Feb. 1752   ELIZABETH (her mark) his wife, to THOMAS KEN-
L & R   KERLY, planter, both of Craven Co., for ₺ 150
                         currency, 300 a. in Craven Co., bounding SW on
Broad River; SE on GASPAR FAMT (?), other sides on vacant land. Witness-
es: PETER HENRY DORSIUS, JOHN ADAM SCHASHWELDER. Before STEPHEN CRELL,
J.P. WILLIAM HOPTON, Register.

Book P-P, p. 54   BENJAMIN MAZYCK, planter, son & devisee of
5 & 6 July 1754   ISAAC MAZYCK, merchant, & DEMARIS, BENJAMIN'S
L & R   wife; STEPHEN MAZYCK, another son & devisee of
                         ISAAC, & SUSANNAH, STEPHEN'S wife; & ISAAC
MAZYCK, ESQ., eldest son & heir of said ISAAC; of the 1st part; to EDWARD
FENWICKE, ESQ., of Charleston; for ₺ 8000 SC money, 2 plantations, 1090
a. & 1181 a., total 2271 a., in Colleton Co., bounding N on 2 tracts of
517 & 69 a.; & on COL. JOHN GIBBES; W on COL. JOHN GIBBES; S on Ashepoo
River; E on the Horse Shoe & Chetsey Creeks, as by plat certified by WIL-
LIAM WILKINS, Sur. Whereas Gov. JAMES MOORE & the Lords Proprs. on 21
Feb. 1700 granted JAMES STANYARNE 1590 a. in Colleton Co.; & he bequeath-
ed to his son, JAMES STANYARNE, 1090 a., part of the 1590 a., marked A in
the center of a certain plat & enclosed by yellow lines; & whereas said
JAMES, the son, owned the 1090 a. & also 517 a. to the N of said 1090 a.,
& shown within red lines on the plat, & by will directed that the 2
tracts be sold for the payment of his debts, & appointed ALEXANDER SKENE,
JOHN WILLIAMS, WILLIAM CATTELL, & JOHN GODFREY his executors; & whereas
SKENE & WILLIAMS by L & R dated 16 & 17 Mar. 1721 sold to ISAAC MAZYCK
the 2 tracts; & whereas Gov. ROBERT JOHNSTON on 28 Apr. 1733 granted
ISAAC MAZYCK 1250 a. in Colleton Co., bounding N on said ISAAC MAZYCK; S
on Ashepoo River; E on Chelsy Creek; W on JOHN WOODWARD; which tract are
now divided into 2 parcels, 1 of 69 a. adjoining the 517 a. & shown within green lines on the map; the other, 1181 a., marked B, adjoining the
1090 a. marked A, & enclosed within blue lines on the plat; & whereas
ISAAC MAZYCK, by will dated 10 Jan. 1735, gave his 2 sons, BENJAMIN &
STEPHEN, parties hereto, the 1090 a. & the 1181 a., total 2271 a., which
lands BENJAMIN & STEPHEN have owned since their father's death; now they,
in conjunction with ISAAC (eldest son & heir) sell the 2 tracts to FEN-
WICKE. Witnesses: DAVID LAFONS, DANIEL RAVENEL. Before JOHN BASSINETT,
J.P. Memo: On 6 July 1754, WILLIAM WILKINS, Dep. Sur., states that upon examination of the plat he finds a mistake in number of a. within the
green lines & that, instead of 69 a., the lines contain 169 a. WILLIAM
HOPTON, Register. Play by WILKINS taken from survey made by JOHN HENTIE,
certified 10 Apr. 1733; pricked off 24 June 1754 by WILKINS plat shows
500 a. marked Old Field belonging to MR. WOODMAN.

Book P-P, p. 65   JOHN GREGG, planter, & JANET his wife, to the
13 & 14 Nov. 1754   Rev. MR. JOHN BAXTER, both of Prince Frederick
L & R   Parish, Craven Co., for ₺ 300 currency, 350 a.
                         on Sockee Swamp, near Peedee River, in Craven
Co., bounding SE & partly NE on WILLIAM HOLMES; SW on MR. BAXTER; other
sides on vacant land. Witnesses: GEORGE (his mark) BARROWS, ROBERT HAM-
ILTON. Before JOHN LEVISTON, J.P. WILLIAM HOPTON, Register.

Book P-P, p. 71   Whereas Landgrave EDMUND BELLINGER by will dat-
16 Jan. 1747   ed 21 Feb. 1739, reciting that whereas he was
Certificate & Plat   entitled to 48,000 a. of land by virtue of a
                         Landgrave's patent granted by the Lords Proprs.
to his father, Landgrave EDMUND BELLINGER, of which 6,000 a. were taken
up by testator's father in his lifetime & that the remainder of the
48,000 a. had been taken up by the testator himself, & bequeathed sundry
legacies, to be allotted out of such part of his patent land, not already
disposed of, by his wife, ELIZABETH; & whereas in pursuance of an agreement made in his lifetime with WILLIAM ELLIOT, ESQ., of St. Andrews, to
allot 500 a. to ELLIOT; now, at ELIZABETH'S order, WILLIAM MCPHERSON lays
out to ELLIOT 500 a. on marsh joining Port Royal River, in Granville Co.,
bounding N on MR. WRAGG; S on patent land; E on marsh; W on vacant land.
ELIZABETH BELLINGER ELLIOT (formerly ELIZABETH BELLINGER) certified that
the 500 a. were laid out to ELLIOT by MCPHERSON by her order. Witness:
WILLIAM BACKSHELL. Before JOHN HAMILTON, J.P. WILLIAM HOPTON, Register.

Book P-P, p. 73   ROBERT BREWTON, ESQ., to WILLIAM ELLIOT, ESQ.,
20 & 21 July 1753   both of Charleston, for ₺ 600 currency, the SE
L & R   corner part of lot #193 in Charleston. Where-
                         as COL. MILES BREWTON, father of said ROBERT,
for many years before his death owned the SE corner of lot #193, formerly
granted to JOHN HILL, bounding E 54 ft. 4 in. on King Street; S 99 ft. 4
in. on Tradd Street; W on part of said lot belonging to MARY BAKER, widow
of CAPT. FRANCIS BAKER; N on WILLIAM ELLIOT; & whereas MILES BREWTON by
will dated 11 Aug. 1743 bequeathed to his wife, MARY, the free use for
life of a quarter part of a lot he had obtained from JOHN HILL, & now occupied by JOHN OWENS, tailor; & by a residuary devise in the will bequeathed to his son ROBERT, the remainder of his lands, houses, Negroes,
plate gold, & all his real & personal estate; & whereas, after MARY'S
death, the reversion of said lot was devised to ROBERT; & MARY on 2 Oct.
1745 surrendered her interest in the lot, & other estate, to ROBERT; &
whereas the corner lot adjoins the part belonging to WILLIAM ELLIOT & he
desires to purchase it; now ROBERT BREWTON sells the corner lot to ELLIOT.
Witnesses: WILLIAM MASON, CHARLES PINCKNEY. Before WILLIAM BURROWS, J.P.
WILLIAM HOPTON, Register.

Book P-P, p. 80   EDWARD WAY, EDWARD SUMNER, THOMAS WAY, JR., &
25 & 26 April 1754   ANDREW WAY, executors of will of SAMUEL SUMNER
L & R   (eldest son & heir of REBECCA SUMNER, widow of
                         SAMUEL SUMNER, cooper of Berkeley Co.), to
RICHARD WARING, planter, of St. George Parish, for ₺ 1664 SC money, 256
a. at Beechhill, St. Pauls Parish, Colleton Co., bounding N on WILLIAM
GRAVES; E on DANIEL & DAVID SUMNER; S on JOHN SUMNER; W on MICHAEL BACON
being the N half of original tract of 500 a. Whereas the Lords Proprs.
on 13 Jan. 1710 granted JOSEPH SUMNER, planter, of Berkeley Co., 500 a.,
English measure, in Berkeley Co., bounding SW on head of Ashley River; &
whereas JOSEPH SUMNER & MARTHA his wife, by deed of feoffment dated 7
Aug. 1717 conveyed the N half of the 500 a. (250) a. to SAMUEL SUMNER,
cooper, of Berkeley Co., who, by will dated 24 Aug. 1730 bequeathed all
his real estate, including said 250 a., to his wife, REBECCA SUMNER, for
her lifetime & to her heirs, but in case of default to his sisters SU-
SANNAH MASON & ABIGAIL BRUNSON; & whereas, after his death, REBECCA married BENJAMIN SUMNER, planter, of Berkeley Co., & they had 2 sons, SAMUEL
& WILLIAM; & whereas REBECCA died, & her youngest son, WILLIAM, died in
infancy, & her elder son, SAMUEL, inherited; & whereas by his will, dated
17 Feb. last, he directed that all his real & personal estate be sold, &
appointed EDWARD WAY, EDWARD SUMNER, THOMAS WAY, JR., & ANDREW WAY, his
executors; & whereas they put his real & personal estate up for sale &
public auction, & RICHARD WARING was highest bidder for the 250 a. at
₺ 1664 currency; & whereas a resurvey showed that the tract actually contained 256 a. instead of 250 a., now they sell the 256 a. to WARING for
that price. Witnesses: SAMUEL STEVENS, JOHN JONLEE. Before RALPH IZARD,
J.P. WILLIAM HOPTON, Register. Plat certified 18 Jan. 1737 by JOHN DOR-
SEY, Dep. Sur.

Book P-P, p. 88   THOMAS WALKER, planter, to JOHN RATTRAY, at-
12 & 13 Sept. 1753   torney, of Charleston, as security on bond of
L & R by Mortgage   even date in penal sum of ₺ 4000 given the
                         Rev. MR. ALEXANDER GARDEN, rector of St.

Philip's, Charleston, (which bond RATTRAY signed at request of WALKER),
for payment of Ł 2000 currency, with interest, on 13 Sept. 1754; half of
2 tracts total 245 a., in St. Thomas Parish, Berkeley Co., purchased by
THOMAS WALKER & JOHN WALKER, his brother, from JACOB WOOLFORD; that is
105 a. (half of 210 a.) granted COL. ROBERT DANIEL, on Thomas Island,
bounding NW on Watcoe Creek; SW on JOHN DURHAM; SE on heirs of RICHARD
CODNER; NE on RICHARD CODNER being the other half of said 210 a.; also
140 a. (half another tract) on Thomas Island, bounding S on Wando River;
N on JOHN DURHAM; W on ISAAC LESESNE; E on heirs of RICHARD CODNER; also
530 a., English measure, in Berkeley Co., on E side Cooper River; bounding S on Simmons Creek; SE on land belonging to vestry of St. Thomas Parish for use of a free school; NE on PETER JOHNSON; NW on LEWIS DUTARQUE;
W on RICHARD GRIFFIN; which 530 a. were granted 27 June 1711 to JOHN WAL-
BANK, father of RUTH BONNY, & conveyed by THOMAS BONNY & RUTH his wife,
to THOMAS WALKER; also 70 a. in St. Thomas Parish, Berkeley Co., on W
side Cooper River, bounding SW on CAPT. JOHN VANDERHORST; NW & SW on
JAMES TAGGART; being part of 270 a. granted by the Lords Proprs. to JAMES
TAGGART on 8 Sept. 1690, & sold by him to SARAH MURREL; who sold to THOM-
AS WALKER. Witnesses: ROBERT WILLIAMS, JR., GEORGE JACKSON. Before DAN-
IEL CRAWFORD, J.P. WILLIAM HOPTON, Register. On 14 Jan. 1758 JOHN RAT-
TRAY declared mortgage satisfied. Witness: WILLIAM HOPTON.

Book P-P, p. 99   JOHN ATCHISON, planter, to THOMAS LYNCH, ESQ.,
15 & 16 July 1754   both of Craven Co., for Ł 2700 currency, sev-
L & R   eral contiguous tracts, total 997 a., bounding
                       NE on Lady BLAKE; NW on vacant land & on JOHN
ATCHISON; SW on Lady BLAKE & DR. JAMES WILLIAMS; SE on marsh & a creek of
Wadmalaw River; also 100 a. bounding SE on a tract of 617 a.; other sides
on COL. BLAKE; total 1097 a. Whereas the Lords Proprs. on 11 & 13 Jan.
1700 granted JAMES GILBERSON, planter, 3 tracts in Colleton Co., (150 a.,
617 a., 230 a.) making 1 tract of 997 a.; & whereas GILBERSON bequeathed
the tracts to his only daughter, NANCY (ANNE), who died without issue, &
the land descended to DAVID ATCHISON, eldest brother of said JOHN, as
heir-at-law; & whereas DAVID ATCHISON, by L & R dated 22 & 23 June 1727
conveyed the 3 tracts to GEORGE ATCHISON, another brother of JOHN; &
whereas GEORGE devised the land to JOHN, who also owned a tract SE of the
617 a., bounded on all other sides by COL. BLAKE'S land; now JOHN sells
the entire tract of 1097 a. to LYNCH. Witnesses: DAVID DEES, JOSEPH AN-
DERSON. Before DANIEL CRAWFORD, J.P. WILLIAM HOPTON, Register.

Book P-P, p. 107   THOMAS LYNCH, ESQ., of Craven Co., to THOMAS
12 & 13 July 1754   SMITH, SR., merchant, of Charleston, for
L & R   Ł 2700 currency, 1097 a. in Colleton Co.,
                       bounding NE on Lady BLAKE; NW on vacant land &
on COL. BLAKE; SW on Lady BLAKE & DR. JAMES WILLIAMS; SE on marsh & on a
creek of Wadmalaw River. Witnesses: JOHN RATTRAY, GEORGE JACKSON. Before DANIEL CRAWFORD, J.P. WILLIAM HOPTON, Register.

Book P-P, p. 113   JOHN ELLIOT, planter, of St. George Parish,
4 Feb. 1754   Berkeley Co., to JOHN MILES, of St. Pauls Par-
Sale   ish, Colleton Co., for 5 shillings & other
                       considerations; lot #1 at Bacons Bridge in St.
George's Parish, bounding N on the river; E 76 ft. on the road leading to
bridge; W on JOHN BAKER. Witnesses: THOMAS MILES, JR., JOHN WINN, MOSES
LINUS. Before J. SKENE, J.P. WILLIAM HOPTON, Register.

Book P-P, p. 114   JOHN ELLIOT, planter, & ELIZABETH his wife, of
4 Feb. 1754   St. George Parish, Berkeley Co., to JOHN MILES,
Sale   planter, of St. Pauls Parish, Colleton Co.,
                       for Ł 1800 currency, 421 a. (?). Whereas the
Lords Proprs., by Gov. ROBERT GIBBES, on 13 Jan. 1710 granted WILLIAM WAY
an inland plantation of 408 a. partly in Berkeley & partly in Colleton
Co., bounding NW on RICHARD BEDON; SW & SE on THOMAS DISTON (now to heirs
of JOSEPH BLAKE); NE on JOSEPH WAY; & whereas EDWARD WAY, son of WILLIAM
WAY, by his own right & by conveynaces from his brothers, WILLIAM WAY,
DANIEL WAY, & JOHN GIRARDEAU, became entitled to 371 of the 421 a.; &
whereas EDWARD WAY on 24 Feb. 1745 conveyed to WILLIAM BRISBANE; & BRIS-
BANE on 28 May 1751 sold the tract to WILLIAM GRAVES (also 50 a. more,
being the SE part of 100 a., adjoining the 371 a., sold by JOSEPH SMITH
on 6 Apr. 1737 to HENRY SALTERS, & seized by execution & sold by RAWLINS

LOWNDES, P.M., to WILLIAM BRISBANE on 11 Aug. 1747); & whereas WILLIAM
GRAVES on 28 Mar. 1752 sold the 421 a. to JOHN ELLIOT (who now owns the
tract except 37 a. of the NE side lately conveyed to JOSEPH WAY); now he
conveys to MILES. Witnesses: THOMAS MILES, JOHN WINN, MOSES LINUS. Before J. SKENE, J.P. WILLIAM HOPTON, Register.

Book P-P, p. 119   JAMES MCGIRT, ESQ., & PRISCILLA his wife, to
11 & 12 May 1753   ROBERT MILHOUS, both of Craven Co., for Ł 200
L & R   currency, 350 a. in Fredericksburg Township,
                     Craven Co., bounding SW on Wateree River & on
vacant land; other sides on vacant land; granted 14 May 1752 by Gov.
JAMES GLEN to JAMES MCGIRT. Witnesses: JOHN CANTEY, JOSEPH EVANS (a
Quaker). Before SAMUEL WYLY, J.P. WILLIAM HOPTON, Register.

Book P-P, p. 126   GEORGE SENIOR, planter, & ELIZABETH his wife,
4 & 5 June 1753   of Rowan Co., NC, to ROBERT MILLHOUS, planter,
L & R   of Craven Co., SC, for Ł 300 currency, 400 a.
                     in Fredericksburgh Township, Craven Co., SC,
on NE side Wateree River; bounding NW on JOHN COLLINS; SW on the Great
Neck; SE on land surveyed by JOHN WILLIAMS & since granted to JAMES MC-
GIRT, ESQ.; NE on vacant land; which tract was granted 6 Mar. 1750 by
Gov. JAMES GLEN to GEORGE SENIOR. Witnesses: JOHN COLLINS, JR., WILLIAM
SIMS,\ JOHN FURNAS (a Quaker). Before SAMUEL WYLY, J.P. WILLIAM HOPTON,
Register.

Book P-P, p. 133   RAWLINS LOWNDES, P.M., to WILLIAM BRISBANE, at
11 Aug. 1747   public auction, for Ł 131 currency, 50 a. at
Sale   Beech Hill, being the SE half of 100 a. which
                     HENRY SALTUS purchased from JOSEPH SMITH on 6
Apr. 1737. Whereas by writ of fieri facias dated 7 July last, issued by
JOHN LINING in the absence of BENJAMIN WHITAKER, C.J., the P.M. was commanded to seize & sell the property of HENRY SALTUS, planter, to satisfy
2 judgments; 1 of Ł 800, & costs, obtained by HENRY PERONNEAU & ALEXANDER
PERONNEAU, executors of will of HENRY PERONNEAU, gentleman, of Charleston,
against RICHARD BEDON, administrator & THOMAS PORTER & ELIZABETH his wife
(lately ELIZABETH SALTUS, administratrix of said HENRY SALTUS); the other
of Ł 234 currency, & costs, obtained by LAWRENCE SANDERS against said BE-
DON, PORTER & ELIZABETH PORTER; now LOWNDES sells 50 a. to BRISBANE.
Witnesses: CHARLES LOWNDES, LEOPOLD BOUDON. Before CHARLES PINCKNEY, J.P.
WILLIAM HOPTON, Register.

Book P-P, p. 135   JOHN HARVEY, planter, of Charleston, & CATHER-
18 & 19 Nov. 1754   INE his wife, to PETER TAYLOR, ESQ., & the
L & R by Mortgage   Rev. MR. THOMAS HARRISON, of St. James Goose
                     Creek, attorneys for the Society for the Prop-
agation of the Gospel in Foreign Parts; as security on bond of even date
in penal sum of Ł 3000 for payment of Ł 1500 currency, with interest, on
19 Nov. 1755; 414 a. in Berkeley Co., formerly 2 tracts of 214 & 200 a.;
commonly called Wappoo Plantation; the 214 a. having been conveyed by L &
R 26 & 27 Apr. 1744 to JOHN HARVEY by his brother, BENJAMIN, to whom it
had been bequeathed by his father, WILLIAM HARVEY; bounding E on Ashley
River; S & S on Wappoo Creek; N on ARNOLD HARVEY; according to grant to
COL. ROBERT GIBBES by the Lords Proprs. on 28 June 1711; the 200 a. having been devised to JOHN by will of his father, WILLIAM HARVEY; dated 23
Sept. 1739, formerly belonging to estate of BENJAMIN GODFREY; & described
as beginning at mouth of Oliver Jordan Creek, out of Wappoo Creek, being
N & W of Wappoo Creek, & bounding W of said creek running to head of said
creek, & from mouth of Mill Creek & to the E of said creek, running N to
the extent of ROBERT GIBES'S land to a stake pr. pine 3 x, thence running
E within the lines parting CAPT. JOHN GODFREY & said GIBBES, commonly
called the Long Fence, & taking an equal breadth within said GIBBES'S
land to a marsh on Ashley River to a hickory 3 x, bounding on land formerly of FENDAL until said breadth, together with said land between Mill
Creek & Oliver Jaudon's Creek, complete the 200 a. intended to be conveyed. Witnesses: CHARLES PINCKNEY, EDWARD MORTIMER. Before WILLIAM BUR-
ROWS, J.P. WILLIAM HOPTON, Register. On 21 May 1767 JAMES HARRISON
acknowledged receipt of full satisfaction of mortgage by the hands of
ROGER PINCKNEY, P.M. Witness: FENWICK BULL.

Book P-P, p. 144   ROGER PAGET, planter, to SAMUEL WYLY, planter,

5 & 6 Feb. 1754   both of Craven Co., for ₤ 500 currency, 200 a.
L & R   in Fredericksburgh Township, Craven Co., on N
                         side Wateree River, bounding NW on MARK CHAT-
TERTON; other sides on vacant land; granted 24 Apr. 1752 by Gov. JAMES
GLEN to ROGER PAGET. Witnesses: JOHN GORDON, BENJAMIN (his mark) GORDON,
JOHN PEARSON (D.S. of the Congarees). Before JAMES MCGIRT, J.P. WILLIAM
HOPTON, Register.

Book P-P, p. 152   ANTHONY WRIGHT, laborer, & MARY his wife, to
1 & 2 Apr. 1753   EDWARD KIRKLAND, laborer, both of Craven Co.,
L & R   for ₤ 181 currency, 162 a. in Craven Co., on S
                        side Wateree River, bounding SE on JAMES MICH-
IE; other sides on vacant land; granted by Gov. JAMES GLEN to ANTHONY
WHITE on 7 June 1751. Witnesses: WILLIAM HARRISON, MOSES KIRKLAND, ROB-
ERT KIRKLAND. Before JAMES MCGIRT, J.P. No probate to lease. WILLIAM
HOPTON, Register.

Book P-P, p. 159   RICHARD ASH & WILLIAM LIVINGSTON, of Colleton
9 & 10 Jan. 1737/8   Co., executors of will of SAMUEL ASH, to JOHN
L & R   ATCHISON, gentleman, for ₤ 800 currency, 440
                        a. in Craven Co., on S side of mouth of Santee
River, bounding NW on Washaw Creek; N on Santee River & marsh; E & S on
Alligator Marsh; W on JOHN BENNETT; which land was granted on 13 July
1737 by GEORGE II to ASH & LIVINGSTON, executors. Witnesses: JOHN ATCHI-
SON, GEORGE MITCHEL. Before ROBERT YONGE, J.P. WILLIAM HOPTON, Regis-
ter.

Book P-P, p. 165   JOHN LINING, practitioner in physic, & SARAH
30 & 31 Dec. 1754   his wife, to CHARLES MAYNE, merchant, both of
L & R   Charleston, for ₤ 300 currency, 440 a. in Cra-
                        ven Co., bounding NW on Washaw Creek; N on
Santee River & marsh; E & S on Alligator Marsh; W on JOHN BENNETT; which
tract was granted to RICHARD ASH & WILLIAM LIVINGSTON, executors of will
of SAMUEL ASH; & conveyed by them to JOHN ATCHISON; also 795 a. of marsh
land to the N of said 440 a., granted to ATCHISON, & bounding W on JOHN
ATCHISON; SE on Alligator Creek; the 2 tracts making 1 plantation of 1235
a. of land & marsh, which by L & R dated 14 & 15 Feb. 1739 were conveyed
by ATCHISON to JOHN LINING. Witnesses: DAVID OLIPHANT, JAMES SIMPSON.
Before WILLIAM SIMPSON, J.P. WILLIAM HOPTON, Register.

Book P-P, p. 171   RICHARD CAPERS, planter, to NATHANIEL ADAMS,
12 Mar. 1750   planter, both of Island of St. Helena, SC, for
Lease for Life   life for 10 shillings & a yearly rent of 1 In-
                       dian corn if demanded; 100 a. on said island,
bounding W on a creek; S on WILLIAM CHAPMAN; E on RICHARD CAPERS; N on a
path leading to the Kings High Road. Each gives bond of performance in
penal sum of ₤ 300 currency. Witnesses: WILLIAM GOUGH, ANTHONY ALBERGOT-
TIE. Before ROBERT WILLIAMS, J.P. WILLIAM HOPTON, Register.

Book P-P, p. 174   GREGORY (his mark) STEERLY & ADRY (her mark)
17 & 18 Dec. 1752   STEERLY, to JACOB STROUBART, both of Purys-
L & R   burgh, Granville Co., for ₤ 43 currency, 150
                       a. in Purysburgh Township, bounding N on RALPH
NETMEN & HENRY MYERHOUSE (MEYERHOVER ?); W on GEORGE MINGLESDORFF & AN-
DREW WINKLAR; S on DAVID VILLAR; E on GREGORY STEERLY. Witnesses: ISAAC
BRABANT, DAVID BOURGIN. Before JOHN BOURGIN, J.P. WILLIAM HOPTON, Reg-
ister.

Book P-P, p. 180   HENRY (his mark) MYERHOVER (MEYERHOUSE), gen-
26 & 27 Dec. 1752   tleman, to JACOB STROUBART, both of Purysburgh,
L & R   Granville Co., for ₤ 43 currency, 100 a. in
                       Purysburgh Township, bounding N on COL. PURY;
W on BENEDICT BOURGIN & ANDREW WINKLAR; S & E on vacant land. Witnesses:
DAVID BOURGIN, HENRY (his mark) MYERHOVER. Before JOHN BOURGIN. No pro-
bate to lease. WILLIAM HOPTON, Register.

Book P-P, p. 186   WILLIAM MOORE, planter, to TACITUS GAILLARD,
18 & 19 Sept. 1754   ESQ., both of Craven Co., for ₤ 700 currency,
L & R   400 a. in Berkeley Co., granted 9 Aug. 1737 to
                       JOHN MOULTRIE, surgeon, of Charleston, who by

342

L & R dated 19 & 20 Nov. 1747 sold to THOMAS CARTER, planter, of St.
Johns Parish, Berkeley Co., who with MARY his wife, by L & R dated 3 & 4
July 1753 conveyed to WILLIAM MOORE; bounding SW & SE on vacant land; NE
on JOHN NELSON; NW on PETER DE ST. JULIEN. Witnesses: JAMES RUSSELL,
STEPHEN TOUSSIGER, JR. Before JOHN GENDRON, J.P. WILLIAM HOPTON, Regis-
ter.

Book P-P, p. 193   THOMAS CARTER, planter, & MARY his wife, of
3 & 4 July 1753   Berkeley Co., to WILLIAM MOORE, planter, of
L & R   Craven Co., for Ł 450 currency, 400 a. in
                        Berkeley Co., bounding SW & SE on vacant land;
N on JOHN NELSON; NW on PETER DE ST. JULIEN. Witnesses: THOMAS PLATT,
EDWARD RAWLINS, ELIZABETH VANDERDUSIN. Before RICHARD RICHARDSON, J.P.
WILLIAM HOPTON, Register.

Book P-P, p. 199   ROBERT PRINGLE, merchant, of St. Philips Par-
2 Feb. 1754   ish, Charleston, to TACITUS GAILLARD, of Cra-
L & R   ven Co., for Ł 5 currency, 40 a. in St. James
                        Santee, Craven Co., bounding W on TACITUS GAIL-
LARD; N on ROBERT PRINGLE, other sides on Wambaw Creek; being part of 500
a. conveyed to ROBERT PRINGLE by JOHN MAYRANT by L & R dated 7 & 8 June
1753. Witnesses: JAMES ROBERT, JOEL HOLMES, PETER MAZYCK. Before ALEX-
ANDER STEWART, J.P. Sketch given. WILLIAM HOPTON, Register.

Book P-P, p. 206   JOHN MAYRANT, gentleman, & ANNE his wife, to
1 & 2 Feb. 1754   TACITUS GAILLARD, ESQ., both of St. James San-
L & R   tee Parish, Craven Co., for Ł 500 currency,
                        500 a. in Craven Co., bounding S on Wambaw
Creek & JOHN BARNET, formerly granted to COL. JOHN GENDRON; W & N on vacant land; E on land of ROBERT PRINGLE, ESQ., of Charleston. Witnesses:
WILLIAM STONE, JOHN WAGNER. Before ALEXANDER STEWART, J.P. Sketch giv-
en. WILLIAM HOPTON, Register.

Book P-P, p. 212   CHARLES LOWNDES, P.M., to EDMUND BARNES, at
19 Dec. 1754   public auction, for Ł 2000 currency, 2 tracts
Sale   of 500 a. each in Granville Co. Whereas ED-
                        WARD LOURRY obtained a judgment against RICH-
ARD LAMBTON, administrator of estate of ROBERT THORPE, merchant, of Port
Royal, for Ł 11, 438 currency, & costs, & a writ of fieri facias was issued on 27 Feb. 1753 by CHARLES PINCKNEY, then C.J., directing the P.M.
to levy that sum against said THORPE estate, & RAWLINS LOWNDES, the then
P.M. seized certain plantations belonging to the estate, 6323 a. of which
remained unsold, now the present P.M. (CHARLES LOWNDES) sells BARNES 500
a., bounding SE on THOMAS MIDDLETON; NE on JAMES HEARTLY; other sides on
ROBERT THORPE'S estate; also 500 a. bounding NE on JAMES HEARTLY; other
sides on ROBERT THORPE'S estate. Witnesses: JAMES WRIGHT, DANIEL HORRY,
JR. Before ALEXANDER STEWART, J.P. WILLIAM HOPTON, Register.

Book P-P, p. 215   ANN WARNOCK, wife of ABRAHAM WARNOCK, to HENRY
9 & 10 May 1744   WARNER, schoolmaster, both of Craven Co., for
L & R   Ł 1000 currency, 300 a. in St. Thomas Parish,
                        Berkeley Co., on E side Wando River, bounding
NW on DANIEL (DAVID?) EVANS; SW on JONATHAN RUSS; which tract was granted
by WILLIAM, Earl of Craven, Palatine on 14 Apr. 1710 to THOMAS MONK, who,
with MARTHA his wife, by deed of feoffment dated 12 Dec. 1712 conveyed to
MARY WARNOCK; who, by deed of feoffment dated 6 Aug. 1717 conveyed to
MICHAEL DARBY; who, with his wife MARY, by deed of feoffment dated 16
Mar. 1718/9 conveyed to PHILIP CHEEVERS, planter, of Berkeley Co.; after
whose death the land was inherited by his son, PHILIP CHEEVERS; & now in
possession of his daughter, ANNE, wife of ABRAHAM (ABRAM) WARNOCK; ABRA-
HAM releasing his claim. Witnesses: THOMAS PAGET, JOHN HITCHCOCK. Be-
fore WILLIAM WHITESIDES, J.P. WILLIAM HOPTON, Register.

Book P-P, p. 223   HENRY WARNER, schoolmaster, & JANE (her mark)
4 & 5 June 1745   his wife, to ABRAHAM WARNOCK, planter, both of
L & R   Craven Co., for Ł 1000 currency, the 300 a. in
                        St. Thomas Parish, Berkeley Co., (see p. 215)
purchased from ANN WARNOCK. Witnesses: JOHN DAVIS, BENJAMIN WEBB. Before WILLIAM WHITESIDES, J.P. WILLIAM HOPTON, Register.

Book P-P, p. 230   ARCHIBALD JOHNSTON, planter, & ESTHER his wife,
17 & 18 Jan. 1755   to JOSEPH ALLSTON, planter, both of Prince
L & R   George Parish, Craven Co., for ₤ 1500 curren-
                          cy, 640 a. in Craven Co., sold to JOHNSTON by
the executors of WILLIAM ALLSTON, father of said JOSEPH; bounding E on
salt marsh; S on JOSEPH ALLSTON; W on Waccamaw River; N on GABRIEL MARION
& JOHN WATIES. Witnesses: THOMAS WATIES, JOHN REMINGTON. Before WILLIAM
HOPTON, J.P. & Pub. Reg.

Book P-P, p. 236   GEORGE HUNTER, ESQ., Sur. Gen., to EGERTON
24 Jan. 1755   LEIGH, ESQ., both of Charleston, for ₤ 2000
Feoffment   currency, 2 lots in Colleton Square, Charles-
                          ton, marked E & F on the plat, b unding E on
Bay Street; N on lot G belonging to heirs of THOMAS ELLERY; W on lot H
belonging to JOHN MCKENSIE; S on Hunters Street; also right of passage
through most convenient streets. Plat given. Witnesses: JAMES SIMPSON,
SAMUEL MOUBRAY. Before WILLIAM SIMPSON, J.P. WILLIAM HOPTON, Register.

Book P-P, p. 238   LEWIS MIDDLETON, carpenter, only son & heir of
30 June 1753   SOLOMON MIDDLETON, mariner, who died intestate;
Mortgage   to ESAIE BRUNET, carpenter; both of Charleston;
                          as security on bond dated 29 June 1753, in pe-
nal sum of ₤ 1080 for payment of ₤ 540 currency, on 29 June 1754, the
house & part of lot #222 bounding E 28 ft. on a certain street; N on part
of lot #222 belonging to heirs of THOMAS HOLTON; W on MR. LEGARE; S on
FREDERIC GRIMKE. Witnesses: JOHN NEWBULL, THOMAS LAMBOLL. Before WIL-
LIAM HOPTON, J.P. & Pub. Reg. On 28 Feb. 1755 ESAIE BRUNET acknowledged
payment of mortgage by JOSEPH HUTCHINS to whom BRUNET sold the house &
lot after MIDDLETON had conveyed to him. Witness: WILLIAM HOPTON.

Book P-P, p. 244   EDWARD CROFT, planter, of Berkeley Co., to JA-
15 Aug. 1750   COB MARTIN, practitioner in physic, of Charles-
L & R by Mortgage   ton, as security on bond of even date in penal
                          sum of ₤ 2400 for payment of ₤ 1200 currency,
with interest, on 15 Aug. next; the S part of lot #15 in Charleston with
all buildings, now occupied by SAMUEL BAWMAN, bounding E on the Bay; N on
part same lot belonging to HENRY PERONNEAU; W on part same lot belonging
to heirs of RICHARD ROWE. Witness: JOHN ERNEST POYAS. Before JAMES
MICHIE, J.P. WILLIAM HOPTON, Register. On 22 Dec. 1758 JACOB MARTIN declared mortgage satisfied. Witness: WILLIAM DOCKWRAY.

Book P-P, p. 249   SAMUEL WEST, gentleman, of Charleston, to WIL-
15 & 16 Jan. 1755   LIAM NEILSON, planter, of Craven Co., for ₤ 50
L & R   currency, 160 a. in Craven Co., on N side of
                          Santee River, bounding W on RICHARD RATTON
(now JOSEPH MURNAY); other sides on vacant land; which land was granted 7
Aug. 1735 by Gov. THOMAS BROUGHTON to SARAH WEST. Witnesses: MARK AN-
THONY BESSELLUE, WILLIAM POWER. Before JACOB MOTTE, J.P. WILLIAM HOP-
TON, Register.

Book P-P, p. 256   JOHN PAGE, to WILLIAM TURNER, both of Berkeley
23 & 24 Sept. 1754   Co., for ₤ 350 currency, 300 a. on N side of S
L & R   branch of Santee River, bounding SW on WILLIAM
                          SINGLEFIELD; other sides on vacant land. Wit-
nesses: THOMAS ANDERSON, JAMES EDES, SARAH (her mark) CHAPPELL. Before
JAMES FRANCIS, J.P. WILLIAM HOPTON, Register.

Book P-P, p. 262   EDWARD BOYKIN, planter, of the WELCH tract in
27 & 28 Mar. 1754   Craven Co., to ROBERT WILLIAMS, yeoman, of
L & R   Craven Co., for ₤ 500 currency, 200 a. in the
                          WELCH tract, part of 250 a., on SW side Peedee
River, bounding SE on JOHN BABER; SW on JACOB BUCKLES; NE on SOLOMON TOWN-
SEND (the other part of said 250 a.); the 2 parts being separated by Cock
Run, a line agreed upon by all parties, including TOWNSEND. Witnesses:
JOSHUA HICKMAN, HENRY BOYKIN. Before JOHN CRAWFORD, J.P. WILLIAM HOP-
TON, Register.

Book P-P, p. 269   WILLIAM DELOATCH, planter, of the WELCH tract
27 & 28 Mar. 1754   in Craven Co., to ROBERT WILLIAMS, yeoman, of
L & R   Craven Co., for ₤ 500 currency, 200 a. in the

344

WELCH tract, on SW side Peedee River, bounding on other sides on vacant
land. Witnesses: ARTHUR BRYAN, JOSEPH (his mark) DOWNER. Before JOHN
CRAWFORD, J.P. WILLIAM HOPTON, Register.

Book P-P, p. 275   SOLOMON ADE, shoemaker, & MARGARET (her mark)
1 & 2 Aug. 1754   his wife, of Saluda, SC, to GODFREY DREYER,
L & R   wheelwright, of Saxe Gotha Township, for Ł 100
                        currency, 50 a. with the mill houses, etc.,
bounding SW on Saluda River; W on SOLOMON ADE; NE on vacant land; SE on
GODFREY DREHER; being the E part of 200 a. near the upper part of Saxe
Gotha Township granted 19 July 1748 by Gov. JAMES GLEN to SOLOMON ADE;
the 200 a. then bounding NW on HENRY METZ & vacant land; NE on vacant
land; SE on vacant land & Santee River (or Congaree); SW on the river &
on HENRY METZ. MARGARET ADE, sole trader, is willing for the present to
be subject to SC laws concerning femmes couvert. Witnesses: CHRISTIAN
DREPER (DREYER); FRTR CSSATH (?); JOHN PEARSON. Before JOHN HAMILTON,
J.P. WILLIAM HOPTON, Register. Plat certified 2 Aug. 1754 by JOHN PEAR-
SON, Dep. Sur.

Book P-P, p. 281   JOSEPH MOODY, merchant, & CATHERINE his wife,
5 & 6 Dec. 1754   to JOHN HODSDEN, merchant, both of Charleston,
L & R by Mortgage   as security on bond dated 27 July 1754 given
                        by MOODY to JOHN MOORE, planter, of St. Thomas
Parish, which bond HODSDEN signed at MOODY'S request, in penal sum of
Ł 2662 for payment of Ł 1331 currency, with interest, on 27 July 1755;
part of lot #104 measuring 19 ft. 2 in. on S side Broad Street, conveyed
to MOODY by DEBORAH FISHER, widow; bounding E 208 ft. on part same lot
occupied by PAUL SMYZER; S on lot held by trustees of the French Protes-
tant Society of Christians; W on PETER BOCQUET. Witnesses: JOHN EDWARDS,
EDWARD JONES. Before WILLIAM SIMPSON, J.P. WILLIAM HOPTON, Register.
On 28 July 1757 JOHN HODSDEN declared mortgage satisfied. Witness: PETER
MONCLAR.

Book P-P, p. 292   PHILIP (his mark) POOL, miller, of Saxe Gotha
1 Feb. 1755   Township, to WILLIAM SEAWRIGHT (SEWRIGHT), of
Bond & Mortgage   Beaver Creek, JOHN MYRICK & JAMES GERALD, gen-
                        tlemen, of Congaree, because they signed his
bond of even date given JAMES MICHIE of Charleston, in penal sum of Ł 796
for payment of Ł 398 currency to MICHIE, with interest, on 1 Feb. 1756;
the plantation on which he lives, in 2 tracts, total 500 a., in Saxe Gotha Township, bounding E on Santee River; N on STEPHEN CRELL; W on vacant
land; S on vacant land & HENRY GALLMAN; also a going flour mill on Thames
Creek on said plantation, & other buildings; also stock of cattle branded
FP; hogs; 6 horses; household stuff & plantation utensils. Witnesses:
JOHANNA FRIST, HENRY (his mark) SNELLING, GILBERT FOWLER. Before WILLIAM
HOPTON, J.P. & Pub. Reg.

Book P-P, p. 297   MICHAEL FINLAYSON, tailor, of Berkeley Co., to
11 & 12 Feb. 1755   WILLIAM GLEN (GLENN), feltmaker, of Charles-
L & R   ton, for Ł 500 SC money, 2 tenements on W side
                        Union Street, in Charleston now occupied by
DANIEL DA COSTA & CAPT. DRUMMOND, bounding S & W on MARGARET SHERIFF (now
MARGARET GLEN); N on store belonging to GABRIEL MANIGAULT. Whereas HENRY
SHERIFF of James Island, Berkeley Co., by will dated 28 Mar. 1750 be-
queathed to his nephew, MICHAEL FINLAYSON, the 2 tenements in Union
Street then rented to CATHERINE CROFTS & MR. LONG, barber, at the expira-
tion of 3-1/2 years after testator's death, during which term the rent to
be bequeathed to testator's wife, MARGARET SHERIFF, to enable her to pay
off his just debts & legacies; & whereas said HENRY SHERIFF died on 23
July 1751 & FINLAYSON took possession; now he sells to GLEN. Witnesses:
WILLIAM ROGERS, JOHN REMINGTON. Before WILLIAM HOPTON, J.P. & Pub. Reg.

Book P-P, p. 302   The Rev. MR. JOSIAH SMITH of St. Thomas Parish,
25 & 26 Oct. 1754   Berkeley Co., & ELIZABETH his wife, to THOMAS
L & R   RALPH, joiner, of Georgetown, Winyaw, for
                        Ł 100 currency, lot #222 in Georgetown, bound-
ing SW on the public ground along the river; NW on lot #221; NE 50 ft. on
Front Street; SE 217.9 ft. on lot #223. Witnesses: ELIAS BONNEAU, JACOB
REHEL, STEPHEN HARTLY. Before WILLIAM SIMPSON, J.P. WILLIAM HOPTON,
Register.

Book P-P, p. 309   JOSEPH SHUTE, merchant, of Charleston (now of
4 Dec. 1754   Philadelphia) & JOHN WITTER, planter, of James
Conveyance   Island, SC, of 1st part; SAMUEL WITTER, JAMES
                          VERREE, JOHN SINCLAIR, ROBERT MILLHOUSE, &
SAMUEL WYLY, all of SC; ISAAC PEMBERTON, JAMES PEMBERTON, WILLIAM LOGAN,
& JOHN SMITH, all of Philadelphia, metchants, of 2nd part. Whereas
THOMAS KIMBERLY, merchant, of Charleston, obtained from GEORGE II a grant,
signed by Gov. ROBERT JOHNSON on 3 Mar. 1731, of a tract containing 1
rood 29 perches in Charleston, commonly called the Quakers lot; & whereas
on 17 Feb. 1731 he sold the lot to JOHN WITTER, JOSEPH SHUTE, & THOMAS
FLEMING, merchants, of Charleston, for ₤ 100 currency, for the use of the
Quakers residing in Charleston or any part of SC, as a place on which a
Meeting House should be built for them; & whereas WITTER, SHUTE, & FLEM-
ING by a writing on the back of the deed agreed, among other things, that
KIMBERLY should be a trustee with them of the land & that upon the death
of any of said trustees the majority of the survivors should appoint his
successor (see Book A-1 pages 661-667); & whereas KIMBERLY & FLEMING are
dead, & JOHN WITTER & JOSEPH SHUTE have appointed SAMUEL WITTER, JAMES
VERREE, JOHN SINCLAIR, ROBERT MILLHOUSE, SAMUEL WYLY, ISRAEL PEMBERTON,
JAMES PEMBERTON, WILLIAM LOGAN, & JOHN SMITH trustees, with themselves,
to keep the trust estate; now WITTER & SHUTE, for 10 shillings British
paid them by the others, release to them as trustees, the Quakers lot,
with the Meeting House & other improvements, in trust for the Quakers.
Witnesses: SAMUEL FETHERGILL, CHARLESS ROSS, JAMES ABERCROMBIE. Before
LIONEL CHALMERS, J.P. WILLIAM HOPTON, Register.

Book P-P, p. 315   JACOB DESURRENCY, to WILLIAM GARDEN, both of
5 Feb. 1755   Craven Co., for ₤ 200 currency, 200 a., the
L & R   lower part of 367 a. in the WELCH tract in
                          Craven Co., granted by Gov. JAMES GLEN on 22
Jan. 1747 to SAMUEL DESURRENCY who bequeathed the land to his son & heir,
JACOB; the 367 a. bounding NW on WILLIAM KARY; NE on Peedee River & said
KARY (KARRY); SE on the river & on KARY'S land; SW on THOMAS BOWEN. Wit-
nesses: GEORGE HICKS, JR., THOMAS CRANFORD. Before GEORGE HICKS, J.P.
WILLIAM HOPTON, Register.

Book P-P, p. 320   JOHN HICKS, to GEORGE HICKS, both of Craven
4 June 1748   Co., for ₤ 800 currency, 350 a. in the WELCH
L & R   tract, Craven Co., bounding SW on Peedee Riv-
                          er; other sides on vacant land. Witnesses:
EDMUND IRBY, HENRY REDINGFIELD. Before J. GILLESPIE, J.P. WILLIAM HOP-
TON, Register.

Book P-P, p. 327   JOHN BOOTH, to GEORGE HICKS, both of Craven
26 & 27 May 1753   Co., for ₤ 80 VA. money, 200 a. in the WELCH
L & R   tract in Craven Co., bounded SW by Peedee Riv-
                          er; & other sides by vacant land; which tract
was granted by Gov. JAMES GLEN on 24 May 1745 to JOHN BOOTH. Witnesses:
RICHARD HUBBARD, GEORGE HICKS, JR. Before WILLIAM JAMES, J.P. WILLIAM
HOPTON, Register.

Book P-P, p. 331   LEWIS MIDDLETON, joiner, of Charleston, ap-
14 Feb. 1755   points his friend ESAIE BRUNET, carpenter, of
Letter of Attorney   Charleston, his attorney, to sell his house &
                          lot (part of lot #222) on W side of King
Street for not less than ₤ 650 currency; the property bounding E 28 ft.
on King Street; S on FREDERIC GRIMKE; N on MR. ROBERTS. Witnesses: TIM-
OTHY PHILLIPS, JOSEPH HUTCHINS. Before WILLIAM HOPTON, J.P. & Pub. Reg.

Book P-P, p. 333   LEWIS MIDDLETON, joiner, of Charleston, only
25 & 26 Feb. 1755   son & heir of SOLOMON MIDDLETON, mariner; by
L & R of Reversion   his attorney, ESAIE BRUNET; to JOSEPH HUTCHINS,
                          mariner of Charleston; for ₤ 650 SC money,
MIDDLETON'S house & part of lot #222 as now fenced in, bounding 28 ft. on
W side King Street; S on FREDERIC GRIMKE; W & N on MR. ROBERTS; which
house belonged to SOLOMON MIDDLETON who died intestate, & was inherited
by his son LEWIS, who on 14 Feb. 1755 appointed BRUNET his attorney with
authority to sell. Witnesses: LEWIS MIDDLETON, THOMAS LAMBOLL. Before
WILLIAM HOPTON, J.P. & Pub. Reg.

Book P-P, p. 340   ANDREW DEVEAUX, of Granville Co., son & heir
3 Jan. 1755   of ANDREW DEVEAUX, of St. Andrews Parish, of
Deed of Partition   1st part; JAMES DEVEAUX, of Granville Co., of
Tripartite   2nd part; JOHN DEVEAUX, of same place, of 3rd
                          part; JAMES & JOHN also being sons & devisees
of ANDREW, SR., & brothers of ANDREW, party hereto. Whereas ANDREW DE-
VEAUX, the father, owned 935 a. in Granville Co., called Jericho, which
he had purchased from WILLIAM PALMER; & by will dated 2 Feb. 1754 gave
his real & personal estate equally to his 3 sons; now ANDREW, JAMES &
JOHN have mutually agreed to divide the 935 a. as follows: JAMES to have
part, adjoining his plantation, running along the high road leading to
the SW part of the tract, then corner a NE course to intersect the other
side line of said tract adjoining DR. WILLIAM ROSE, including 311-1/2 a.
with all buildings thereon; ANDREW & JOHN to have the residue. Plat of
311 a. dated 3 Jan. 1755, by ANDREW DEVEAUX, Dep. Sur., bounding SE on
JAMES DEVEAUX; SW on WILLIAM SIMMONS; NE on ANDREW DEVEAUX; NE on DR.
WILLIAM ROSE. Witnesses: JEAN GARNIER, MAGDALENE GARNIER, ANDREW DEVEAUX,
JR. Before STEPHEN BULL, J.P. WILLIAM HOPTON, Register.

Book P-P, p. 345   PATRICK (his mark) CARDIFF, laborer, of Gran-
22 & 23 Mar. 1754   ville Co., SC, to PATRICK CLERK, planter, of
L & R   Augusta, Ga., for Ł 100 SC money; 350 a. in
                          Granville Co., which by deed of gift dated 2
Jan. 1754 Gov. JAMES GLEN gave to PATRICK CARDIFF, bounding SW on Savan-
nah River; other sides on vacant land. Witnesses: GEORGE BEDON, WILLIAM
SPENCER. Before JOHN HAMILTON, J.P. WILLIAM HOPTON, Register.

Book P-P, p. 350   JOHN CAIN, of Combee, to WILLIAM HARRISON, of
9 & 10 Sept. 1754   Wateree, Craven Co., for Ł 300 SC money, 450 a.
L & R   in Craven Co., granted 3 Sept. 1754 by Gov.
                          JAMES GLEN to JOHN CAIN; bounding NE on Wa-
teree River; SE on JAMES MICHIE; other sides on vacant land. Witnesses:
ABRAHAM (his mark) SUTTON, HENRY FOX, J. KIRKLAND. Before WILLIAM SIMP-
SON, J.P. WILLIAM HOPTON, Register.

Book P-P, p. 355   RICHARD CAPERS, WILLIAM BENNISON, & RICHARD
25 & 26 Jan. 1749   BENNISON, executors of will of GEORGE BENNISON,
L & R   gentleman, of Christ Church Parish, Berkeley
                          Co., to ROBERT DANIEL, of same Parish, for
Ł 600 currency, 400 a., called the White House, bounding W on RICHARD
CAPERS; S on JOHN HOLLYBUSH; N on salt marsh; E on RICHARD ROWSER (form-
erly as part of same tract). Whereas GEORGE BENNISON, by will dated 15
Sept. 1747, in order to settle his debts, desired his executors to sell
White House Plantation; which he had purchased from his son, GEORGE BEN-
NISON, & another tract of 492 a. known as the Swamp Plantation, & appoint-
ed as executors his brother RICHARD CAPERS, & his sons WILLIAM BENNISON &
RICHARD BENNISON; now the executors are obliged to sell White House Plan-
tation & apply the money towards payment of said debts. Witnesses: JONAH
BONHOSTE, CHARLES CAPERS, JOHN BENNETT. Before JOHN RUTLEDGE, J.P. WIL-
LIAM HOPTON, Register.

Book P-P, p. 363   JAMES DEVEAUX, planter, & ANNE his wife, of
24 & 25 Jan. 1755   Prince William Parish, Granville Co., to RALPH
L & R   IZARD, ESQ., of St. George Parish, Berkeley
                          Co., for Ł 8500 currency, 2 tracts of 906 a.
& 311-1/2 a., total 1217-1/2 a.; the 906 a. (part of 13,000 formerly belonging to Landgrave EDMUND BELLINGER, being part of his 48,000 a.) on
TIMOTHY SAVANNAH, in Granville Co., bounding SW on JOSEPH BRYAN; NW on
the part of the 13,000 a. belonging to COL. PALMER; NE on CAPT. JOHN BULL
& the High Road leading from the Haspa Neck to Saltketchers; NE on the
part of the 13,000 a. resurveyed under THOMAS BULLEN'S warrant; as by
plat certified by HUGH BRYAN, Dep. Sur., & attached to L & R dated 24 &
25 July 1744 from ELIZABETH BELLINGER, widow & executrix of will of said
Landgrave EDMUND BELLINGER, conveying said tract to JAMES DEVEAUX, party
hereto; & the 311-1/2 a. in Granville Co., bounding SE on said 906 a.; SW
on WILLIAM SIMMONS; NW on 2 undivided third parts formerly belonging to
ANDREW DEVEAUX, SR.; NE on WILLIAM ROSE; which 311-1/2 a. is JAMES 1/3
part of 935 a. purchased by ANDREW DEVEAUX, SR., from WILLIAM PALMER &
bequeathed equally to his 3 sons, ANDREW, JAMES & JOHN DEVEAUX (see p.
340). Witnesses: JEAN GARNIER, ANDREW DEVEAUX, ANDREW DEVEAUX, JR.

Before STEPHEN BULL, J.P. WILLIAM HOPTON, Register.

Book P-P, p. 372   BENJAMIN PERDRIAN, planter, & MARY (her mark)
3 & 4 Aug. 1749   his wife, of St. James Santee Parish, Craven
L & R   Co., to EDWARD JERMAN, planter, of same Par-
                          ish, for Ł 800 currency, 2 tracts at Wambaw,
St. James Santee Parish; 1 of 200 a. bounding SW on MR. SIMMONS; NW on
other tract; NE on BENJAMIN PERDRIAN; SE on said SIMMONS & BENJAMIN PER-
DRIAN; the other being 63 a., part of 289 a., bounding SW on MR. SIMMONS;
NW on vacant land; NE on the remaining part of said 289 a. belonging to
BENJAMIN PERDRIAN; SE on the 200 a.; also original plat & grant dated 23
May 1734 of said 200 a. to said BENJAMIN PERDRIAN. Witnesses: JOHN GEN-
DRON, JR., JOHN HENTIE. Before JOHN GENDRON, J.P. WILLIAM HOPTON, Reg-
ister.

Book P-P, p. 379   DANIEL GELZAR, planter, of Colleton Co., to
8 Mar. 1755   SAMUEL WAINWRIGHT, gentleman, of Charleston,
Release   for Ł 2160 SC money, 360 a. in Colleton Co.
                          Whereas Gov. CHARLES CRAVEN & the Lords
Proprs. on 18 Aug. 1714 granted JOHN GIRARDEAU, the elder, 360 a. near
Horse Savannah, in Colleton Co., then bounding NW & NE on WILLIAM ELLIOT;
S & E on THOMAS DRAYTON & HENRY NICHOLS; & whereas said GIRARDEAU by will
gave the plantation to 4 of his then sons, JOHN, JR., RICHARD, JAMES &
ISAAC, who took possession soon after their father's death; & whereas
RICHARD, JAMES, & ISAAC, by deed of foeffment dated 8 Mar. 1745 conveyed
their shares to their brother, JOHN, who died intestate & without issue &
the land became vested in PETER GIRARDEAU, planter, of Colleton Co., as
eldest brother & heir to said JOHN, JR., & whereas PETER GIRARDEAU, &
ELIZABETH his wife, by L & R dated 28 & 29 Dec. 1750, sold the 350 a. to
DANIEL GELZAR (KELSAR); now GELZAR sells to WAINWRIGHT. Witnesses: WIL-
LIAM SELBY, BENJAMIN SINGLETON, THOMAS LAMBOLL. Before WILLIAM HOPTON,
J.P. & Register.

Book P-P, p. 387   MATHEW WHITEFIELD, planter, to CHARLES COLLE-
7 Mar. 1755   TON, planter, for Ł 250 currency, 500 a. call-
Mortgage   ed Belau, bounding NE on Santee River; SE on
                          MAJ. COLLETON (now SAMUEL PEYRE); other sides
on vacant land. Date of redemption: 1 Dec. next. Witnesses: WILLIAM
PARTRIDGE, JOHN WITHERSPOON, THOMAS SILLIVANT. Before PETER TAYLOR, J.P.
WILLIAM HOPTON, Register.

Book P-P, p. 389   ROBERT SCREVEN, planter, of Berkeley Co.,
5 & 6 Sept. 1754   (only son & heir of ROBERT SCREVEN, the elder,
L & R   & HANNAH, widow, of ROBERT the elder) & ELIZA-
                          BETH his present wife, to SAMUEL SIMMONS, the
elder, planter, of Berkeley Co., for Ł 1200 SC money, 638-1/2 a. on NW
side of marsh of Seawee Bay, bounding N & NW on GEORGE HUGGINS & MR.
WEBB; W & SW on MR. WEBB & HUMPHREY HUGGINS & MR. STOON; S & SE on MR.
CAPERS, MR. STOON, marsh & ANTHONY SIMMONS; E & NE on marsh, ANTHONY SIM-
MONS, & heirs of DR. THOMPSON; according to plat by WILLIAM WILKINS, Sur.,
certified 4 Sept. 1754. Whereas ROBERT SCREVEN, party hereto, by various
conveyances became owner of 660-1/2 a., in 4 contiguous tracts, 300 a.,
120 a., 150 a., & 90-1/2 a.; that is, 300 a. granted by the Lords Proprs.
on 10 Oct. 1700 to ANDREW WARNOCK, 22 a. of which ROBERT SCREVEN, party
hereto, & MARTHA his then wife, sold to ANTHONY SIMMONS, a free Negro;
120 a. granted 16 Sept. 1702 to PETER PRESCOTT; 150 a. granted 19 Nov.
1702 to PETER PRESCOTT; 90-1/2 a., part of 175 a. originally granted to
JOSEPH WEBB; now he sells the balance, 638-1/2 a., to SAMUEL SIMMONS.
Witnesses: BENTLY STOCKS, THOMAS LAMBOLL. Before WILLIAM HOPTON, J.P. &
Pub. Reg. Plat of 655 a. in Berkeley Co., found by a resurvey within the
bounds of 4 plats held by ROBERT SCREVEN certified 4 Sept. 1754 by WIL-
LIAM WILKINS, Sur.

Book P-P, p. 398   MUMFORD MILNER, & ELIZABETH his wife, of
2 & 3 Feb. 1749   Christ Church Parish, to GABRIEL MANIGAULT,
L & R   ESQ., of Charleston, for Ł 2000 currency, part
                          of lot #6 in Charleston, bounding N 22 ft. on
Tradd Street; E 96 ft. on JOHN COLCOCK; S on ELIZABETH GIBBES; W on JO-
SEPH MOODY; which land was sold by OLIVER SPENCER, blacksmith by deed of
foeffment dated 5 Feb. 1694/5 to JEREMIAH MILNER, who by will dated 1 Aug.

348

1739 & codicil annexed, dated 6 Aug. 1741, devised it to his son, MUMFORD, party hereto. Witnesses: THOMAS CORBETT, PETER MANIGAULT. Before WILLIAM HOPTON, Register.

Book P-P, p. 405   EDWARD WAY, EDWARD SUMNER, ANDREW WAY, & THOM-
25 Apr. 1754   AS WAY, planters, of St. Pauls Parish, & ex-
Release   ecutors of will of SAMUEL SUMNER, of 1st part;
to BARNABY BRANFORD, planter, of St. George
Parish, for Ł 275 currency, 110 a. in St. George Parish, Berkeley Co.,
part of a larger tract granted to BENJAMIN SUMNER; bounding N on MR. BO-
SAM; E on AARON WAY; SW on ROGER SUMNER; W on Cypress Swamp running into
Ashley River; which 110 a. "descended to said SAMUEL SUMNER at the death
of MOSES WAY he the said SAMUEL being heir-at-law." Witnesses: MAURICE
C. HARVEY, ROBERT DYMES. Before J. SKENE, J.P. WILLIAM HOPTON, Register.

Book P-P, p. 408   MARY (her mark) EVANS, widow, of St. George
14 Nov. 1754   Parish, Colleton Co., to ELIZABETH SNIPES,
Release   widow of THOMAS SNIPES, planter, of St. Pauls
Parish, Colleton Co., for Ł 200 currency, the
W half of a tract of 130 a. in St. Andrews Parish, Berkeley Co., on W
side Ashley River at head of Guppain Creek, bounding NE on MANLY WILLIAM-
SON & SHEM BUTLER; NW on SHEM BUTLER & CHARLES JONES; SW on SAMUEL JONES;
SE on THOMAS RIVERS & vacant land. Whereas Gov. NATHANIEL JOHNSON & the
Lords Proprs. on 10 June 1704 granted 130 a. in Berkeley Co., to WILLIAM
CLAY, who, by will dated 29 Oct. 1719, bequeathed all his houses, lands,
goods & chattels to his wife, ELIZABETH, as long as she remained his widow, for the maintenance of his children, but should she marry, then to
his son, WILLIAM; & whereas, after the death of said ELIZABETH CLAY, the
land descended equally to MARY EVANS & ELIZABETH SNIPES, parties hereto,
the only surviving children of said WILLIAM CLAY, & the land was divided
according to a line pricked on the plat of the land; now MARY sells her
half to ELIZABETH. Witnesses: THOMAS RIGDON SMITH, MARTHA EVANS, ANN
SMITH. Before JAMES PARSONS, J.P. WILLIAM HOPTON, Register.

Book P-P, p. 413   THOMAS SHUBRICK, merchant, & SARAH his wife,
18 & 19 Mar. 1755   of Charleston, to DANIEL LESESNE, planter, for
L & R   Ł 2000 currency, 200 a. in St. Thoams Parish,
Berkeley Co., bounding SW on Wando River; E on
ALEXANDER PERONNEAU; granted by the Lords Proprs. on 16 July 1697 to
CLARKE KING & by various mesne conveyances descended to SHUBRICK. Wit-
nesses: THOMAS TUTTRIDGE, GEORGE JACKSON. Before WILLIAM SIMPSON, J.P.
WILLIAM SIMPSON, J.P. WILLIAM HOPTON, Register.

Book P-P, p. 419   JOHN WINGOOD, yeoman, son of JOHN WINGOOD, SR.,
10 & 11 Mar. 1755   to THOMAS PHILLIPS, planter, both of Christ
L & R   Church Parish, Berkeley Co., for Ł 240 curren-
cy, 100 a. in said Parish, bounding NE on
THOMAS HUTCHINSON (formerly WILLIAM HENDRICK); N on the parsonage & Glebe
land; SW on THOMAS PHILLIPS (formerly RICHARD CAPERS); S on JOHN BENNETT;
SE on a creek & marsh. Witnesses: J. OUSLEY, THOMAS WHITESIDES. Before
JAMES WHITE, J.P. Lease not proved. WILLIAM HOPTON, Register.

Book P-P, p. 424   JAMES BOSWOOD, & MARTHA his wife, of Berkeley
14 Feb. 1752   Co., to THOMAS MELL, for Ł 40 currency, 500 a.,
Sale   bounding E on JOHN GRANT; W on BENJAMIN WOOD;
N on BENJAMIN GODDIN; S on THOMAS MELL. Wit-
nesses: BRIDGET (her mark) GORDON, MARGARET BOSWOOD, JOHN MELL. Before
BENJAMIN SMITH, J.P. WILLIAM HOPTON, Register.

Book P-P, p. 426   JOHN COLLETON, ESQ., of Fairlawn Barony, St.
13 & 14 1736   John's Parish, Berkeley Co., & SUSANNAH his
L & R   wife, to GEORGE HUNTER, gentleman, of Charleston, for Ł 5000 SC money, lot #80 in Charles-
ton containing 9 a., 2 roods, 21 perches, English measure, of dry land &
marsh land, with a small creek in the marsh, bounding E on Cooper River &
lots of THOMAS COLLETON, ESQ., & Landgrave JAMES COLLETON; W on a small
unnamed street; S on CAPT. WILLIAM WALLEY & 2 lots of CAPT. JAMES ADIE;
N on THOMAS COLLETON & another small unnamed street; also lot #A with all
its marsh, bounding N on lot #1; S on a creek of Cooper River; E on

Cooper River; W on said creek. Whereas the Lords Proprs. on 5 Mar. 1680 granted PETER COLLETON, Baronet, said lot #80 in Charleston; & on same date granted SIR PETER COLLETON, Baronet; THOMAS COLLETON, ESQ., & Landgrave JAMES COLLETON the lot marked A, with its marsh land; which 2 lots descended to JOHN COLLETON; now he sells them to HUNTER. Witnesses: EBENEZER FOORD (overseer for JOHN COLLETON); PETER COLLETON. SARAH HOPTON testified in regard to handwriting & other details before WILLIAM HOPTON, Register.

Book P-P, p. 435   MARY YEOMANS, widow, to WILLIAM GLEN & JOHN
28 Feb. & 1 Mar. 1755   COOPER, merchants, of Charleston, as security
L & R by Mortgage   on bond of even date in penal sum of Ⱡ 2532
                          for payment of Ⱡ 1266 currency, with interest,
on 1 Mar. 1756; part of lot #37 in Charleston, bounding N 37 ft. 10 in.
on Elliott Street; W on CATHERINE LOYER & MARY YEOMANS; S on heirs of
WILLIAM SMITH; E 82 ft. on WILLIAM CARWITHEN. Witnesses: CHARLES STEVEN-
SON, WILLIAM MICHIE. Before ALEXANDER STEWART, J.P. WILLIAM HOPTON,
Register.

Book P-P, p. 442   JOHN RODOLPH PURY (PURRY), to HENRY CHIFFELLE,
10 & 11 Oct. 1739   of Purysburgh, for Ⱡ 182 currency, 300 a. in
L & R   Purysburgh Township, Granville Co., bounding
                          E & W & S on vacant land; N on MR. MONTAGUE &
vacant land; granted by WILLIAM BULL to said PURY on 10 Apr. 1738. Witnesses: JAMES RICHARD, ISAAC BONIFOT. Before FREDERICK DE JEAN, J.P.
WILLIAM HOPTON, Register.

Book P-P, p. 446   CHARLES JONES, planter, of St. Bartholomews
5 & 6 Mar. 1755   Parish, Colleton Co., to ELIZABETH FULLER,
L & R   widow, of St. Andrews Parish, Berkeley Co.,
                          for Ⱡ 250 currency, 25 a., part of 140 a.
granted by Gov. JAMES MOORE on 14 Aug. 1701 to FRANCES FIDLING, & conveyed by ABRAHAM WAIGHT on 22 July 1703 to CHARLES JONES; the 25 a. in
Berkeley Co., bounding NE on part same tract sold to JOSEPH WILLIAMS; SE
on the part given for a Glebe; SW on road leading to Wadmalaw; NW on a
street. Witnesses: ANN CLELAND, BENJAMIN FULLER. Before JOHN DRAYTON,
J.P. WILLIAM HOPTON, Register. Plat dated 27 July 1754 by NATHANIEL
DEAN, Sur.

Book P-P, p. 452   Between CHARLES PINCKNEY, ESQ., & GEORGE HUN-
31 July 1745   TER, ESQ., both of Charleston. Whereas PINCK-
Exchange   NEY owned lot "F" in Colleton Square, bounding
                          E on a street; S on lot E belonging to GEORGE
HUNTER; W on lot H; N on lot G belonging to MRS. ANN ELLERY; & whereas
HUNTER owned lot D in Colleton Square, bounding E on said street; S on
lot C belonging to said CHARLES PINCKNEY; W on a little street in said
square laid out by ELLERY, HUNTER, & PINCKNEY; N on another street laid
out by them; now PINCKNEY conveys lot F to HUNTER, & HUNTER conveys lot D
in exchange to PINCKNEY. Witness: CHARLES CALDER. On 22 Apr. 1755 JAMES
WRIGHT recognized PINCKNEYS & CALDER'S signatures before WILLIAM HOPTON,
J.P. & Pub. Reg.

Book P-P, p. 455   ALEXANDER GOODBEE, planter, of Berkeley Co.,
13 & 14 Dec. 1731   to JOHN DANIEL & GEORGE LOGAN, gentlemen, as
L & R in Trust   trustees, 380 a. in St. Thomas Parish. Where-
                          as on 8 & 9 Dec. 1725 a marriage was intended
between ALEXANDER GOODBEE & ANN DANIEL, 1 of the daughters of MARTHA LO-
GAN, widow of COL. ROBERT DANIEL, & in consideration of a marriage por-
tion given GOODBEE, & to settle a competent maintenance for ANN, & for
other considerations, GOODBEE by L & R dated 8 & 9 Dec. 1725 conveyed to
WILLIAM BLAKEWAY & JOHN DANIEL, as trustees, 340 a. in St. James Goose
Creek Parish, Berkeley Co., bounding NW on ROBERT HOW (now THOMAS CLIF-
FORD); SW on BENJAMIN GODIN & the Hon. ARCHIBALD MIDDLETON; W on COL.
JOHN HERBERT; in trust for the use of GOODBEE during his life & afterwards for ANN DANIEL; & whereas JOHN DANIEL, the surviving trustee, with
the consent of ALEXANDER & ANN GOODBEE, has agreed to reconvey the 340 a.
to GOODBEE; now ALEXANDER, in consideration of ANN'S consenting to reconvey said tract to him, & in consideration of the marriage portion he
received, & for her better support, oncveys to DANIEL & LOGAN, as trustees, 380 a. on E side Cooper River; in St. Thomas Parish, Berkeley Co.,

part of 2 tracts of 1005 a. granted by the Lords Proprs. to SOLOMON BRE-
MAR, & by several mesne conveyances being vested in GOODBEE; the 380 a.
bounding according to bill of sale dated 31 Jan. 1723 from PETER BREMAR
to DANIEL TREZVANT; GOODBEE to have the use of the property during his
lifetime; then ANN. Witnesses: MARTHA LOGAN, JR., ANDREW SHAPELY, LEWIS
DANIEL BREBANT. Before WILLIAM HOPTON, J.P. & Pub. Reg.

Book P-P, p. 464   JOHN CLELAND, ESQ., of Georgetown, to FRANCIS
26 Mar. 1755   KINLOCH, ESQ., of Charleston, for Ł 500 SC
Release   money, 100 a. in Prince George Parish, Craven
                         Co., bounding on all sides on JOHN CLELAND.
Witnesses: SAMUEL WRAGG, ARCHIBALD BAIRD. Before THOMAS LYNCH, J.P.
WILLIAM HOPTON, Register. Plat of 100 a. certified 20 Mar. 1755 by ZACH-
ARIAH BRAZIER, Dep. Sur.

Book P-P, p. 468   Between JOHN CLELAND of Craven Co., & FRANCIS
11 Apr. 1755   KINLOCH, of Charleston. Whereas by 2 deeds of
Agreement   settlement, both dated 6 Feb. 1750, between
                       JOHN CLELAND, & MARY his wife, of 1st part; &
ARCHIBALD BAIRD & RICHARD GOUGH, gentlemen, of 2nd part, reciting that
whereas a marriage was intended between FRANCIS KINLOCH & ANNE ISABELLA
CLELAND, daughter of said JOHN & MARY CLELAND, the CLELANDS conveyed to
BAIRD & GOUGH, as trustees, 1818 a. on Weehaw Creek in Prince George Par-
ish, Craven Co., bounding W on heris of ANTHONY WHITE; N on heirs of AN-
THONY WHITE & on WILLIAM SCREVEN (now WILLIAM POOLE); E on Black River; S
on Kensington Plantation belonging to JOHN & MARY CLELAND; which tract
was granted by Gov. JAMES GLEN on 17 Jan. 1750 to JOHN CLELAND; JOHN &
MARY to have the use of the land during their lives; then FRANCIS & ISA-
BELLA; & whereas the boundary line between said 1818 a. & the Kensington
tract has never been rightfully determined; now CLELAND & KINLOCH agree
that the line represented in annexed plat from stake 3 X on W side of the
broad road SE 90 chains to a tupelo 3 X on edge of the high land, thence
W & S on edge of high land belonging to KINLOCH to a stake 3 X being 3
chains 55 links to S of the causeway & parallel to causeway SW 55° 47
chains to stake 3 X per river shall be the boundary line between the 2
tracts. Witnesses: WILLIAM SIMPSON, JAMES SIMPSON. Memo: whereas JOHN &
MARY CLELAND on 3 Sept. 1753 assigned to WILLIAM STONE, merchant, of
Charleston, the land called Kensington Plantation, now, he agrees to said
boundary line. Witnesses: WILLIAM SIMPSON, SAMUEL MOWBRAY. Before WIL-
LIAM HOPTON, J.P. & Pub. Reg. Plat of 908 a. of high land & marsh, in
Prince George Parish, Craven Co., being the N half of 1818 a. near George-
town, belonging to JOHN CLELAND; bounding N on WILLIAM POOLE & heirs of
COL. ANTHONY WHITE; W on 100 a., belonging to heirs of FRANCIS KINLOCH; S
on said CLELAND; E on entrances of Peedee & Black Rivers & on WILLIAM
POOLE; surveyed by ZACHARIAH BRAZIER, Dep. Sur.; certified 9 Apr. 1755 by
GEORGE HUNTER, Sur. Gen.

Book P-P, p. 473   CHARLES WRIGHT, of Charleston, to JOSEPH SCOTT,
2 & 3 Apr. 1755   planter, for Ł 600 SC money, 300 a. in St.
L & R   Bartholomews Parish, Colleton Co., bounding NW
                        on JOHN PARKER; SW on JEAN SANDERS; SE on JER-
MYN WRIGHT; NE on PonPon River. Whereas ELIZABETH CLIFT of Charleston
owned 200 a. which on 30 Aug. 1742 she sold to JERMYN WRIGHT, then of SC;
& whereas on 14 Apr. 1742 JOSHUA SANDERS, planter, of Colleton Co., sold
said JERMYN WRIGHT another tract; now CHARLES WRIGHT, by virtue of a power granted him by said JERMYN WRIGHT, ESQ., of London, sells JOSEPH SCOTT
a part of the 2 tracts. Witnesses: JOHN HUME, CHARLES ROBERTSON. Before
ALEXANDER STEWART, J.P. WILLIAM HOPTON, Register.

Book P-P, p. 479   MOSES MILLER, & ANN His wife, of Parish of St.
13 & 14 Mar. 1755   Thomas & St. Dennis, Berkeley Co., to ROBERT
L & R   COLLINS, merchant, of same Parish, for Ł 600
                        SC money, 63 a. Whereas on 11 July 1733 Gov.
ROBERT JOHNSON granted MOMER (father of said MOSES MILLER MOMER being the
French equivolent for MILLER) 63 a. on E side of E branch of Cooper River,
according to the grant, which is an error, the true location being "on a
branch that makes out of the E branch of Cooper River" (that is, Lynch's
Creek, or Wishbone Creek) bounding NE & SE on DUTART; NE on heirs of PE-
TER BONNEAU (formerly PETER ROBERT); & whereas MOSES MOMER died intestate
on 4 Oct. 1740 & the tract descended to his eldest son & heir, MOSES

351

MILLER; now he sells to COLLINS. Witnesses: JOHN HOLMES, JOSEPH DILL. Before JACOB MOTTE, J.P. WILLIAM HOPTON, Register.

Book P-P, p. 487
24 & 25 Apr. 1750
L & R
DANIEL CONWAY, of Charleston, & ANN his wife (lately ANN GOODBEE), to ISAAC LESESNE (LESSENE), planter, for Ł 270 currency, 380 a. on E side Cooper River, in St. Thomas Parish, Berkeley Co., part of 2 tracts of 1005 a. originally granted by the Lords Proprs. to SOLOMON BREMAR & by several mesne conveyances vested in ALEXANDER GOODBEE, according to plat attached to bill of sale dated 30 Jan. 1723 from PETER BREMAR to DANIEL TREZVANT. Whereas by deed of settlement dated 14 Dec. 1731 ALEXANDER GOODBEE, planter, of Berkeley Co., conveyed the above tract to JOHN DANIEL & GOERGE LOGAN, gentlemen, in trust for said ALEXANDER GOODBEE during his lifetime, then in trust for said ANN; now she & her present husband, DANIEL CONWAY, sell to LESSENE. Witnesses: ROBERT WILLIAMS, JR., JAMES GRINDLAY. Before LIONEL CHALMERS, J.P. WILLIAM HOPTON, Register.

Book P-P, p. 494
24 Apr. 1755
Deed of Gift
ISAM YOUNG, of Craven Co., to EDWARD HOLMES (JONES), planter, for love & affection, 150 a. in Craven Co., bounding NE on Peedee River; N on EVAN VAUGHAN; S on FRANCIS YOUNG; SE on JOHN THOMPSON, JR.; also 100 a. adjoining the old field belonging to another tract. Possession given by delivery of 1 clasp knife. Witnesses: WILLIAM RHODES, JOHN WADE, JOHN LIDE. Before JOHN CRANFORD, J.P. WILLIAM HOPTON, Register.

Book P-P, p. 496
31 July 1746
Mortgage
GABRIEL GUIGNARD, cooper, to JOSEPH BLACK, bricklayer, as security on bond for payment of Ł 175 currency, with interest, on 1 July next; that piece of land bounding N 40 ft. on Pinckney Street; W & S on said GUIGNARD; E 75 ft. on GRIFFITH TUBBS. Witnesses: GEORGE HUNTER, JOHN LEA, GRIFFITH TUBBS. On 11 Nov. 1749 GABRIEL & FRANCES GUIGNARD acknowledged bond paid in full. Before WILLIAM HOPTON, J.P. & Pub. Reg.

Book P-P, p. 498
17 & 18 Mar. 1755
L & R
JEREMIAH CUTTINO, gunsmith, to GEORGE GABRIEL POWELL, ESQ., both of Georgetown, SC, for Ł 820 currency, half of lot #88 in Georgetown, on which a tenement is built, bounding SE 108.9 ft. on Screven Street; 100 ft. deep; NE on lot #112; NW on lot #87; SW on other half of #88 belonging to JEREMIAH CUTTINO. Whereas DANIEL LAROCHE & THOMAS LAROCHE, merchants, of Georgetown, as attorneys for JOHN ABBOT, merchant, by deed of feoffment dated 6 Apr. 1739 sold JEREMIAH CUTTINO lot #88 in Georgetown, bounding SW 100 ft. on Prince Street; 217.9 ft. deep; SE on Screven Street; NE on lot #112; NW on lot #87; now CUTTINO sells half the lot to POWELL. Witnesses: THOMAS HASELL, JOSEPH DUBORDIEU. Before PAUL TRAPIER, J.P. WILLIAM HOPTON, Register.

Book P-P, p. 504
11 & 12 Sept. 1754
L & R
HENRY FOX, to EDWARD KIRKLAND, both of Craven Co., for Ł 200 currency, 200 a. in Craven Co., granted by Gov. JAMES GLEN on 3 Sept. 1754 to HENRY FOX; bounding NW on JOHN GENDRON; NE on the Wateree River; other sides on vacant land. Witnesses: HENRY DOUGWORTH, HENRY MAREFILL, WILLIAM HARRISON. Before SAMUEL WYLY, J.P. WILLIAM HOPTON, Register.

Book P-P, p. 509
1 & 2 Jan. 1747
L & R
BENJAMIN SMITH, merchant, of Charleston, only acting executor of will of ADAM LEWIS, peddler, to MORGAN SABB, planter, for Ł 576 currency, 576 a. in Berkeley Co., bounding E on HENRY RUSSELL; other sides on vacant land. Whereas ABRAHAM SANDERS, planter, of Berkeley Co., owned said 576 a. & with his wife MARGARET, by L & R dated 20 & 21 Oct. 1740 sold the tract to ADAM LEWIS who by will dated 6 May 1741 appointed JAMES CROKATT, merchant, of London, & BENJAMIN SMITH his executors, & directed that his just debts be paid; & whereas at the time he was greatly in debt & it became necessary to sell the property; now SMITH sells the tract to SABB. Witnesses: JOHN JONES, MILES BREWTON. Before DAVID GRAME, J.P. WILLIAM HOPTON, Register.

Book P-P, p. 514   Between ELIZABETH JENKINS, of Charleston, &
1 Apr. 1755   DAVID ADAMS, planter, of Colleton Co., eldest
Covenant   son & heir of said ELIZABETH JENKINS. Whereas
                          ELIZABETH JENKINS owns part of lot #64 on E
side of New Church Street, bounding S on land formerly occupied by CAPT.
GEORGE SMITH & his wife; E on MARY DART; N on a 5 ft. alley, part of said
lot, laid off by said ELIZABETH to be always kept open; & whereas she
laid out the S part of the lot into 4 equal parts by 3 distinct lines
running N & S at proper distances from each other; the W parcel marked A
bounding W 15 ft. on a street; E on parcel B; S on land formerly occupied
by GEORGE SMITH & his wife; N on the alley; & whereas DAVID ADAMS has
built on lot A, at his own expense, a brick house & other improvements,
now in possession of ELIZABETH JENKINS who lives in said brick house; now
ELIZABETH in consideration of DAVID'S having built said house of lot A at
his own expense, & for natural love & affection, & to settle the house &
lot on DAVID, separately from the other 3 sections, they agree that ELIZ-
ABETH shall have the use of the house & lot A during her lifetime & then
DAVID to take possession. Witnesses: ROBERT BRISBANE, WILLIAM BRISBANE,
NATHANIEL BULLINE. Before JAMES SKIRVING, J.P. WILLIAM HOPTON, Regis-
ter.

Book P-P, p. 518   CORNELIUS OWEN, merchant, of Thames Street,
29 & 30 May 1755   London, by his attorney, ANDREW RUTLEDGE, ESQ.,
L & R   of Charleston, to JOHN DRAYTON, ESQ., of
                          Berkeley Co., for ₺ 600 British, 1/4 undivided
part of 12,000 a. called the southernmost Barony, on the Yamasee land, in
Granville Co., bounding E on JOHN BEE & a branch of Coosawhatchie Creek;
S & W on vacant land; N on other Barony of 12,000 a. belonging to JOHN
DAWSON. Whereas JOHN, Lord Cartaret, Palatine, the Lords Proprs. on 5
Dec. 1718 granted JOHN DAWSON, then 1 of the Lords Proprs. 2 Baronies,
each of 12,000 a., English measure, on the land called Yamasee land, 1/4
part only fronting the river where the land should lie & the rest in a
direct line backwards; & whereas the 2 Baronies were duly laid out; &
whereas by L & R dated 29 & 30 Aug. 1722 sold the 2 Baronies to WILLIAM
WRAGG, draper, a citizen of London; & whereas by several mesne conveyances from WRAGG said CORNELIUS OWEN obtained 1/4 undivided part of the
southernmost Barony, as by plat made & certified by JOHN TRIPP on 20 May
1730; & whereas OWEN has agreed to sell his undivided fourth part to
DRAYTON for ₺ 600 British; now the conveyance is completed. Witnesses:
ALEXANDER GORDON, JOHN RUTLEDGE. Before JACOB MOTTE, J.P. WILLIAM HOP-
TON, Register.

Book P-P, p. 524   SARAH RUTLEDGE, of Charleston, daughter & heir
2 & 3 June 1755   of HUGH HEXT, planter, of Berkeley Co., to
L & R   ALEXANDER ANDERSON, gentleman; for ₺ 450 cur-
                          rency, that part of a lot in Charleston lying
in the alley leading to New Church Street, bounding S 27-1/2 ft. on the
alley; E 54 ft. on RIPTON HUTCHINSON (formerly CAPT. LAURENCE DEMIS); W
on other part said lot belonging to JOHN BRETON (formerly occupied by
THOMAS BAKER); N 34 ft. on PAUL DOUXSAINT. Witnesses: MARY YEOMANS, SAM-
UEL MOWBRAY, JOHN RUTLEDGE. Before JACOB MOTTE, J.P. WILLIAM HOPTON,
Register.

Book P-P, p. 528   GEORGE (his mark) TAYLOR, & ELIZABETH (her
10 & 11 Jan. 1754   mark) his wife, to JOHN LEE, both of the Wat-
L & R   eree River, for ₺ 100 currency, 400 a. on a
                          branch of Wateree River, called Rocker Creek,
bounding on all sides on vacant land, which land was granted 2 Jan. 1754
by Gov. JAMES GLEN to GEORGE TAYLOR; & ELIZABETH, being sole trader,
promises to be subject to the act concerning Femmes Coverts. Witnesses:
FRANCIS LEE, ROBERT (his mark) LEE, JOHN (his mark) HALL. Before JOHN
HAMILTON, J.P. WILLIAM HOPTON, Register.

Book P-P, p. 534   TIMOTHY CROSBY, bricklayer, & SARAH his wife,
4 & 5 Mar. 1755   to DANIEL LEGARE & ARNOLDUS VANDERHORST,
L & R by Mortgage   planters, executors of will of WILLIAM HEND-
                          RICK, planter; all of Berkeley Co., for
₺ 527:17:0 currency, which CROSBY owes the estate of WILLIAM HENDRICK,
his house & lot near the N side of Charleston, being part of lot #80;
bounding N 30 ft. on Pinckney Street, E 75 ft. on part said lot belonging

to JOHN LEA; W on part said lot belonging JOSEPH BLACK; S on part said lot belonging to CHARLES RICHMOND GASCOIGNE; as staked out by GEORGE HUNTER, Sur. Gen., & conveyed by deed of feoffment dated 29 May 1747 by GABRIEL GUIGNARD, cooper, to said TIMOTHY CROSBY. Date of redemption: 4 Mar. 1756. Witnesses: ISAAC LEGARE, ANDREW LORREMORE. Before JAMES WHITE, J.P. WILLIAM HOPTON, Register. On 6 Mar. 1764 DANIEL LEGARE, 1 of the executors of WILLIAM HENDRICK, declared mortgage paid in full. Witness: WILLIAM HOPTON.

Book P-P, p. 542
10 & 11 June 1755
L & R

GABRIEL MANIGAULT & ROBERT JOHNSON (brother & heir of THOMAS JOHNSON), by his attorney, HECTOR BERINGER DE BEAUFAIN, of 1st part; to GEORGE HOGG, of Granville Co., for Ł 1240 currency, 620 a., part of 8073 a. formerly belonging to Gov. ROBERT JOHNSON; the 620 a. being on W side Port Royal River in Granville Co., bounding E on a marsh; S & SW on part said 8073 a.; N on RICHARD SHUBRICK & THOMAS SHUBRICK; as by plat dated 30 Jan. 1753 by JAMES MCPHERSON, Dep. Sur. Whereas said 8073 a. was laid out & held by Gov. ROBERT JOHNSON, who bequeathed the tract to his 2 younger sons, NATHANIEL & THOMAS, as tenants in common; & whereas NATHANIEL died intestate soon after his father's death & his half descended to ROBERT JOHNSON, his eldest brother & heir; who by L & R dated 7 & 8 May 1739 conveyed NATHANIEL'S undivided half to GABRIEL MANIGAULT, ESQ.; & whereas THOMAS JOHNSON died intestate & without issue & ROBERT inherited his share, so that ROBERT JOHNSON & GABRIEL MANIGAULT became owners, as tenants in common, of the 8073 a., & they have agreed to sell a part, or 620 a., to GEORGE HOGG; now the conveyance is complete. Witnesses: THOMAS STONE, SR., CHARLES GRIMBALL. Before WILLIAM HOPTON, J.P. & Pub. Reg. Plat given.

Book P-P, p. 548
27 & 28 May 1754
L & R

JAMES ROULAIN, SR., gentleman, in trust to JAMES ROULAIN, JR., of St. Thomas Parish, Berkeley Co., for natural love & affection, & Ł 10 currency, 200 a. in St. Thomas Parish, bounding W on Cooper River; other sides on RICHARD BERRESFORD, ESQ.; also 500 a. in Granville Co., on Saltketcher Fork; & all those lots near the market square in Charleston; also 2 Negro women slaves, MILLY & PHILLIS; also all real & personal estate of every nature; for the use of JAMES ROULAIN, SR., & MARY MAGDALEN his wife, during their lives; then MOLLY & her children to go to ABRAHAM ROULAIN, son of JAMES, SR.; PHILLIS & her children to belong to DANIEL ROULAIN, son of JAMES, SR.; & after the death of JAMES ROULAIN, SR., & MARY MAGDALEN his wife, then JAMES, JR., shall raise enough money by the sale of the real estate to pay the debts of JAMES, SR.; then JAMES, JR., to own the balance of the real & personal estate; should JAMES, JR., die without heris, then ABRAHAM & DANIEL to share the estate. Witnesses: JOHN MOORE, MARY COFING. Before WILLIAM SIMPSON, J.P. WILLIAM HOPTON, Register.

Book P-P, p. 552
1 & 2 May 1754
L & R

ALEXANDER SWINTON, planter, & ELIZABETH his wife, to ELISHA SCREVEN, planter, both of Craven Co., for Ł 370 SC money, 275 a. in Craven Co., on Pritchard's Creek; bounding SE partly on 2100 a. granted to THOMAS LYNCH, now belonging to ALEXANDER SWINTON, & partly on land sold by ALEXANDER SWINTON to JOSIAH GARNIER DUPRE; NE on said DUPRE & on WILLIAM BROWN; NW on WILLIAM BROWN, MARMADUKE BELL, & ELISHA SCREVEN; SW on vacant land. Whereas on 28 Apr. 1733 THOMAS LYNCH, ESQ., was granted 2100 a. in Craven Co., bounding S on JOHN PRITCHARD; W on MATTHEW BELL; E on JOHN BRUNSON; which, by L & R dated 10 & 11 May 1733, LYNCH conveyed to WILLIAM SWINTON; & by him bequeathed by will dated 20 Feb. 1741 to his son ALEXANDER SWINTON; now he sells a part, 275 a., to SCREVEN. Witnesses: JAMES THOMPSON, JOHN BROCKINGTON, WILLIAM SMITH. Before THOMAS HASELL, J.P. WILLIAM HOPTON, Register. Plat of 275 a. by JAMES THOMPSON, Dep. Sur. dated 30 Apr. 1754.

Book P-P, p. 558
5 Apr. 1755
Deed of Partition
Tripartite

PHILIP PRIOLEAU, merchant, of Island of Jamaica, of 1st part; SAMUEL PRIOLEAU, merchant, of Charleston, of 2nd part; ELIJAH PRIOLEAU, planter, of SC, of 3rd part. Whereas SAMUEL PRIOLEAU, ESQ., of Charleston, father of said PHILIP, SAMUEL & ELIJAH, owned lot #182 in Charleston, containing 1 a., 1 rood, 2 perches; bounding E on Friend Street; N on Broad Street; NW on

lot #307 belonging to heirs of JAMES ST. JOHN, ESQ.; W on marsh belonging
to JOHN CROKATT; S on part of a lot belonging to THOMAS ELLIOTT; also a
plantation of 3250 a. on the branches of Coosawatchie & Chula Phinny
Creeks in Granville Co., bounding NW on WILLIAM FISHBURN; SE on JONATHAN
RUSS; other sides on vacant land; which plantation was originally granted
to SAMUEL PRIOLEAU, the father; who, by will dated 25 Oct. 1751, directed
that said town lot be divided into 3 equal parts, 1/3 to go to each son,
PHILIP, SAMUEL & ELIJAH; & the plantation be divided into 3 equal parts,
each son to have 1/3; & whereas the 3 sons have by various plats divided
the town lot & the plantation into 3 equal parts each; they agree to cast
lots to decide the ownership of the sections marked A, B, & C; & whereas
Section A of the town lot, bounding N on Broad Street; & Section B of the
plantation, fell to the lot of PHILIP PRIOLEAU; & Section B of the town
lot & Section A of the plantation fell to the lot of SAMUEL PRIOLEAU; &
section C of the town lot, bounding S on THOMAS ELLIOTT, & the Section C
of the plantation fell by lot to ELIJAH PRIOLEAU; & whereas each is satisfied with his lot as drawn; now each confirms the other's title to the
portions drawn by him. Witnesses: SOLOMON MILNER, LAMBERT LANCE, JAMES
ADAM, HENRY LIVINGSTON, JOHN GORDON. Before JACOB MOTTE, J.P. WILLIAM
HOPTON, Register. Plat of lot #182 in Charleston certified 9 Jan. 1754
by GEORGE HUNTER, Sur. Gen. Plat of 3250 a. by JAMES ST. JOHN, Sur. Gen.
dated 24 July 1736; copy attested 22 Nov. 1754 by GEORGE HUNTER, Sur.
Gen.; divided by 2 pricked lines into 3 parts, A, B, & C, 22 Nov. 1754 by
GEORGE HUNTER, Sur. Gen.; lots drawn 25 Nov. 1754 by SAMUEL PHILIPS &
ELIJAH PRIOLEAU in presence of CHARLES WARHAM, ALEXANDER TAYLOR.

Book P-P, p. 569   PETER SANDERS, saddler, & ELIZABETH his wife,
6 & 7 Jan. 1755   to MARY ELLIS, sole trader, both of Charles-
L & R   ton, for ₤ 580 currency, part of the E half of
                          lot #207 in Charleston, bounding E 56 on Cross
Street; W on JOSEPH WARD; N 40 ft. on heirs of SARAH TROTT; S on Guignard
Street. Whereas by L & R dated 20 & 21 Jan. 1752 THOMAS SMITH, JR., merchant, of Charleston, sold to JOSEPH WARD, merchant, & PETER SANDERS,
saddler, of Charleston, that E half of lot #207 in Charleston bounding N
171 ft. on part of lot #123 belonging to the heirs of SARAH TROTT; E 56
ft. on Colleton Square; S on part of lot #206; W on the other half of lot
#207; which lot #207 was originally granted 17 May 1694 to PETER GERARD,
merchant, of Charleston, who devised the lot to his daughter JUDITH; who
married HENRY SIMONDS; & after the death of JUDITH & HENRY SIMONDS was
inherited by their son, HENRY SIMONDS, gentleman, now of Bladen Co., NC;
who, by his attorney PETER SIMONDS, by L & R dated 9 & 10 June 1748 sold
the lot to THOMAS SMITH; who sold the E half to WARD & SANDERS as tenants
in common & not as joint tenants; & whereas by deed of partition dated 1
Aug. 1752 WARD & SANDERS divided the lot into 2 equal shares & SANDERS
was allotted the E part of said half of lot #207, being 56 ft. x 83-1/2
ft.; now SANDERS sells a part of his piece to MARY ELLIS. Witnesses:
CHRISTOPHER FITZSIMONS, JOHN TROUP. Before WILLIAM HOPTON, J.P. & Pub.
Reg.

Book P-P, p. 578   SARAH FARROW, to JANE GREADY, ELIZABETH PAR-
24 Oct. 1752   MENTER, & ELIZABETH TOBIAS. JOHN GREADY &
Consent to Division   CHARLES FARROW, planter, of Granville Co.,
                          administrators of estate of JOHN JOHNSON,
planter, of Island of St. Helena, Granville Co., & with the consent &
agreement of MARGARET (her mark) TOBIAS, widow; SARAH, wife of said
CHARLES FARROW; JANE, wife of JOHN GREADY; & ELIZABETH PARMENTER, widow;
daughters & co-heiresses of said JOHN JOHNSON; have made 4 equal divisions of a tract of 600 a. on St. Helena, being part of JOHN JOHNSONS
estate; & allotted the shares to 4 daughters; now each being satisfied
with the share allotted her, confirms the title of the others to the
share allotted them. Witnesses: JOHN (his mark) GREADY, WILLIAM GOUGH,
JOHN FENDEN, JR. Before WILLIAM HARVEY, J.P. WILLIAM HOPTON, Register.

Book P-P, p. 579   MARGARET (her mark) TOBIAS, widow, of 1st
23 & 24 Oct. 1752   part; ELIZABETH PARMENTER, widow, of 2nd part;
L & R Tripartite   MARGARET & ELIZABETH being daughters & 2 of
                          the co-heiresses of JOHN JOHNSON, planter, of
Island of St. Helena; ISAAC EDWARDS, gentleman, formerly of Island of St.
Christopher, West Indies, now of St. Helena Island, SC, of 3rd part.
Whereas the Lords Proprs. on 15 May 1715 granted ARTHUR DICKS, of

Granville Co., 600 a. on St. Helena Island, bounding W on a small creek
out of Port Royal River; N on JOSEPH PAGE; E on vacant land; S on DANIEL
DICK; & whereas ARTHUR DICKS on 16 Mar. 1726 conveyed the land to JOHN
JOHNSON, planter; who died intestate on 11 May 1746; & his land descended
to his 4 daughters, MARGARET, SARAH, JANE & ELIZABETH, as co-heiresses; &
whereas they divided the 600 a. into 4 equal parts, each daughter being
allotted 1 part, being content therein; now MARGARET TOBIAS, for ₤ 500
currency, & ELIZABETH PARMENTER, for ₤ 500 currency, sell to ISAAC ED-
WARDS their 2 adjoining divisions or half the tract of 600 a., bounding W
on a creek of Port Royal River; N on part of said tract sold to WILLIAM
ALLEN; SE on REYNOLD'S land; SW on MR. SELY, according to plat dated 22
Oct. 1752 by JAMES MACPHERSON, Dep. Sur. [Note: Both L & R give 400 a.
as being half of 600 a., see p. 588, C.A.L.]. Witnesses: WILLIAM GOUGH,
JOHN FENDER, JR. Before WILLIAM HARVEY, J.P. WILLIAM HOPTON, Register.

Book P-P, p. 588   SARAH KENNEDY, widow, of Granville Co., to
21 & 22 Aug. 1754   Francis Stuart, merchant, of Beaufort, for
L & R   ₤ 500 currency, her quarter part of 600 a. on
                          St. Helena Island, being about 200 a., except
the place of burial. Whereas the Lords Proprs. on 15 May 1715 granted
ARTHUR DICKS 600 a. on St. Helena Island, Granville Co., (see p. 579)
which he, on 16 Mar. 1726 sold to JOHN JOHNSON, who died intestate 11 May
1746; & his 4 daughters inherited; & whereas they divided the tract, each
taking a fourth part; now SARAH KENNEDY, 1 of the daughters, sells her
share (about 200 a.) to STUART. Witnesses: WILLIAM GOUGH, BARNABAS GIL-
BERT. Before WILLIAM HARVEY, J.P. WILLIAM HOPTON, Register.

Book P-P, p. 596   FRANCIS STUART, merchant, of Beaufort, & ANN
26 & 27 Aug. 1754   his wife, to JOHN TOOMER, planter, of Island
L & R   of St. Helena, for ₤ 500 currency, 200 a. on
                          St. Helena Island, being 1/4 of a tract of
600 (?) a. (see p. 579 & 588) granted to ARTHUR DICKS; who sold to JOHN
JOHNSON; whose 4 daughters inherited equally; SARAH selling her quarter
part, (except the burial place) to FRANCIS STUART; who now sells to TOOM-
ER. Witnesses: WILLIAM GOUGH, PHILIP BOX. Before WILLIAM HARVEY, J.P.
WILLIAM HOPTON, Register.

Book P-P, p. 605   HANNAH MILLER, widow, to NATHAN TART, planter,
9 & 10 June 1755   both of Berkeley Co., for ₤ 900 currency, 400
L & R   a., being the SE, S & SW parts of 500 a. orig-
                          inally granted to WILLIAM NORTH, & lately be-
longing to JOHN MILLER, planter; in St. Thomas Parish, on the N side of
the NE branch of Wando River; bounding E on THOMAS BASKERFIELD & the remaining 100 a. belonging to MARY HESKETT, widow; N partly on ROBERT KING;
W on ROBERT KING & marsh. Witnesses: GEORGE BARKSDALE, WILLIAM SANDERS.
Before JACOB MOTTE, J.P. WILLIAM HOPTON, Register.

Book P-P, p. 611   HANNAH MILLER, widow, of Berkeley Co., & THOM-
10 June 1755   AS BARKSDALE, planter, give NATHAN TART a bond
Bond of Performance   in penal sum of ₤ 1800 currency, as security
                          that HANNAH will keep the covenants made in
previous conveyance (p. 605). Witnesses: GEORGE BARKSDALE, WILLIAM SAND-
ERS. Before JACOB MOTTE, J.P. WILLIAM HOPTON, Register.

Book P-P, p. 612   ABRAHAM MICHAU, planter, & LYDIA his wife, of
21 & 22 Feb. 1755   Craven Co., to MOSES MILLER, planter, of
L & R   Berkeley Co., for ₤ 300 currency, 300 a. in
                          Craven Co., originally granted in 2 tracts of
150 a. each on 12 Jan. 1737 to ALEXANDER CHOVIN & ISAAC CHOVIN; bounding
N on Black River; other sides on vacant land; see Secretary's Book I.I.
fol. 36-38; & by several mesne conveyances became vested in ABRAHAM MI-
CHAU in fee. Witnesses: ALBERT LENUD, SAMUEL CLEGG. Before JACOB MOTTE,
J.P. WILLIAM HOPTON, Register.

Book P-P, p. 618   MICHAU gives bond to MILLER that he will keep
22 Feb. 1755   covenants in above conveyance. Witnesses: AL-
Bond   BERT LENUD, SAMUEL CLEGG. Before JACOB MOTTE,
                          J.P. WILLIAM HOPTON, Register.

Book P-P, p. 619   ADAM DANIEL & JOHN DANIEL, sons of JOHN DANIEL

30 May 1755   of Charleston, of 1st part; & THOMAS SMITH,
Agreement   merchant, of Charleston, & MARY his wife, formerly widow of said JOHN DANIEL, executors of
will of said JOHN DANIEL, of 2nd part. Whereas JOHN DANIEL, by will dated 12 July 1747, amongst other things, bequeathed to his 3 children, ADAM,
JOHN, & MARY, all his real estate & a considerable part of his personal
estate, & ordered all his real estate divided by his executrix & executor
equally amongst said children when 21, & should 1 die before reaching 21
that childs portion to be equally divided between the others; & whereas
both ADAM & JOHN have reached 21 years & are willing to divide the real
estate at the discretion of THOMAS & MARY SMITH; & whereas MARY, the
daughter, has lately married JOHN PARKER, planter, but has not yet reached 21 years, but her brothers desire to place her 1/3 interest in the
hands of THOMAS & MARY SMITH, as trustees, now it is mutually agreed that
THOMAS & MARY SMITH MAY divide the residuary real & personal estate &
allot shares to ADAM, JOHN & MARY; & whereas for finishing & repairing
certain buildings & houses in Charleston, it became necessary for said
MARY SMITH, during her widowhood & for THOMAS & MARY SMITH since their
marriage, to pay out a considerable part of the estate & moneys of testator, so that an equal division of the real estate cannot be made with out
injury to 1 or more of the children & devisee; & it is expedient that all
parties should agree that division should be made with discretion, rather
than exactly ; & ADAM & JOHN agree that the allotments made by THOMAS &
MARY SMITH shall be final & binding; now they relinquish all claim to
MARY PARKER'S third part; with provisoes in case of her death. Witnesses: SOLOMON ISAACS, JOSEPH ALLSTON, DAVID BROWN, LAMBERT LANCE. Before
JAMES GRINDLEY, J.P. WILLIAM HOPTON, Register.

Book P-P, p. 625   THOMAS SMITH, merchant, of Charleston, & MARY
12 June 1755   his wife, formerly widow of JOHN DANIEL, ship
Deed of Partition   carpenter, & executrix of his will, of 1st
Quadripartite   part; ADAM DANIEL, planter, eldest son of said
JOHN DANIEL, of 2nd part; JOHN DANIEL, plant-
er, youngest son of JOHN DANIEL, of 3rd part; & JOHN PARKER, planter, &
MARY his wife, only daughter of said JOHN DANIEL, of 4th part. See above
agreement for details. In order to divide JOHN DANIELS residuary real &
personal estate with discretion rather than with exactitude, all being
agreed, the estate amounting to Ł 22,500 SC currency, & whereas ADAM in
consideration of his allotment has agreed to pay JOHN, his brother,
Ł 3480 currency, to cover inequality; now THOMAS & MARY SMITH, as executors, allot to ADAM the lands; tenements, etc., listed in schedule A, enclosed with a double black line, & valued at Ł 10,980 currency, out of
which he is entitled to receive Ł 7,500 currency; that is; lot #1 on S
end of the Bay, bounding E on the Bay; S on the brick wall that joins
GRANVILLE BASTION & on the spiles per small bridge; W on marsh; N on part
of lot #1 occupied by JOHN COOPER; also the part of lot #1 remaining unimproved & bounding N on heirs of GEORGE SMITH; also that part of a lot S
of lot #1, known as A in the plat at Charleston, bounding E on Cooper River; S on part said lot; W on a creek now filled up but represented in
plat attached to release of said land by GEORGE HUNTER to JOHN DANIEL;
also part of lot #115, bounding E 32 ft. on King Street; S 100 ft. on a
house formerly belonging to THOMAS HOLTON; N on part said lot belonging
to EDWARD VANVELSEN; W on part same lot; also part of lot #42 bounding S
31 ft. on Broad Street; W on MR. DE ST. JULIEN; N on MR. WATSON; E on
JOHN MCKENZIE; also the corner part of lot #14 bounding S 19 ft. 3 in. on
Broad Street; W 83 ft. on Union Street; E on part same lot formerly occupied by JOHN BESWICK; N on JOHN DANIEL'S estate allotted to MARY PARKER;
also half of an adjoining back piece of land as occupied by MR. MORAN,
which was granted by GEORGE HESKETT to JOHN DANIEL; also the piece of
ground bounding E 118 ft. on King Street; S 230 ft. on DR. MARTIN; W on
MR. WEBB & HENRY PERONNEAU; N on BARNARD ELLIOTT; with all houses, buildings, etc., on said parcels of ground, to the full value of Ł 10,980 currency; subject to the payment to JOHN of Ł 3480 currency for equality of
partition; & THOMAS & MARY SMITH allot to JOHN DANIEL, 837 a. on Wando
River, valued at Ł 2000 currency & composed of 3 tracts of 600 a., 170 a.,
& 67 a., formerly belonging to JOSHUA WILKS, who sold to JOHN DANIEL, the
father; also the Ł 3480 paid by ADAM; also Ł 2020 currency; total Ł 7500,
his full share; marked B in schedule & enclosed within double red lines
on plat; & THOMAS & MARY SMITH allot to MARY PARKER the N part of corner
lot #14 in Charleston, bounding W 37 ft. on Union Street; N on EDWARD

CROFT; S on ADAM DANIEL; E on CAPT. KING; which includes the other half
of the back piece conveyed by GEORGE HESKETT to JOHN DANIEL, the father;
with all houses, etc., to value of Ł 1200 currency; also Ł 6300 currency;
total Ł 7500; according to schedule marked C & enclosed by single black
line; each declares the division just & satisfactory. Witnesses: SOLOMON
ISAACS, THOMAS CROSSTHWAITE, WILLIAM SCOTT. Before JAMES GRINDLAY, J.P.
WILLIAM HOPTON, Register. Schedule given shows value of estate Ł 22,500
currency. "A" includes: part lot #1 occupied by JOHN COOPER, Ł 3000; N
part lot #1, unimproved, Ł 600; part low water lot adjoining the above
southward, Ł 300; part lot #115 on King Street, Ł 300; part lot #42 on
Broad Street, with 2 brick tenements, Ł 2365; part lot #14, including
part of back lot formerly belonging GEORGE HESKET, & including a brick
tenement on Union Street, adjoining northward, Ł 3385; part lot on King
Street, Ł 1030; total 10,980; cash to JOHN DANIEL, Ł 3480; balance Ł 7500;
schedule "B"; 837 a. on Wando River, Ł 2000; cash from ADAM DANIEL,
Ł 3480; from testator's personal estate, Ł 2020; total Ł 7500; schedule
"C"; N part of piece of lot #14 on Broad Street including other part of
back lot formerly belonging to GEORGE HESKET, Ł 1200; cash from personal
estate, Ł 6300; total Ł 7500.

Book P-P, p. 635   WILLIAM LLOYD, merchant, & MARTHA his wife, to
1 & 2 Jan. 1755   THOMAS SMITH, merchant, of Charleston, as se-
L & R by Mortgage   curity on bond of even date in penal sum of
                          Ł 5600 for payment of Ł 2800 currency, on 1
July next; 817 a. in Christ Church Parish, Berkeley Co., bounding W on
Wando River & GEORGE LOGAN; N on GEORGE LOGAN & vacant marsh; E on AR-
NULDUS VANDERHORST; S on JOHN RUTLEDGE; which 817 a. formerly belonged to
THOMAS LYNCH, & purchased by WILLIAM LLOYD from said THOMAS SMITH; re-
serving to THOMAS LYNCH the burying ground of his father as now railed in.
Witnesses: ROBERT WILLIAMS, JR., CHRISTOPHER SIMPSON. Before WILLIAM
MURRAY, J.P. WILLIAM HOPTON, Register. On 23 Apr. 1759 THOMAS SMITH de-
clared mortgage paid in full. Witness: WILLIAM HOPTON.

Book P-P, p. 640   BENJAMIN FARLY, planter, to WILLIAM SMITH,
26 & 27 Jan. 1755   planter, both of PonPon, for Ł 2900 currency,
L & R   612 a. in Colleton Co., in 5 adjoining tracts.
                          Witnesses: THOMAS FERGUSON, WILLIAM GLAZE,
JOHN BULLEN. Before JAMES BULLOCK, J.P. WILLIAM HOPTON, Register. No
plat.

Book P-P, p. 647   GEORGE SEAMAN, merchant, of Charleston, & MARY
16 & 17 June 1755   his wife, (formerly MARY KEATING 1 of the sis-
L & R   ters of MAURICE KEATING, gentleman, of Goose
                          Creek); & RACHEL GOUGH, formerly RACHEL KEAT-
ING, another sister of said MAURICE KEATING; of 1st part; to JAMES LEN-
NOX, merchant, of Charleston; for Ł 1400 currency; 2 undivided third
parts of 500 a. in Goose Creek, Berkeley Co., bounding E on MAURICE KEAT-
ING; S on DAVID CAW (formerly NOAH SERRE); W on JAMES BAGBY; N on JOSEPH
NORMAN. Whereas the Lords Proprs. on 5 May 1704, by SIR NATHANIEL JOHN-
SON, granted DANIEL DEANE 500 a. in Berkeley Co.; upon whose death the
land was inherited by his son & heir, DANIEL DEANE; who, by L & R dated
9 & 10 Dec. 1723, sold to JOB ROTHMAHLER, merchant; who, by will gave the
tract, after the death of his wife ANN, to his son JOB ROTHMAHLER; who,
by L & R dated 21 & 22 Feb. 1746 sold the land to MAURICE KEATING; who
died intestate & the 500 a. descended equally to his 3 sisters ANNE (wife
of BENJAMIN SIMMONS, planter, of St. Thomas Parish), MARY (wife of GEORGE
SEAMAN), & RACHAEL (widow of RICHARD GOUGH); now MARY & GEORGE SEAMAN, &
RACHAEL GOUGH sell shares to LENNOX. Witnesses: ROBERT BROWN, JOHN
CORDES. Before JACOB MOTTE, J.P. WILLIAM HOPTON, Register.

Book P-P, p. 657   BENJAMIN SIMMONS, planter, of St. Thomas Par-
17 June 1755   ish, Berkeley Co., to JAMES LENNOX, merchant,
Lease for Life   of Charleston, for 5 shillings a year, for the
                          term of BENJAMIN SIMMONS'S life; his undivided
third part of 500 a. (see p. 647) formerly belonging to his brother-in-
law, MAURICE KEATING. Witnesses: ROBERT BROWN, JOHN CORDES. Before JA-
COB MOTTE, J.P. WILLIAM HOPTON, Register.

Book P-P, p. 661   BENJAMIN SIMMONS, planter, of St. Thomas Par-
17 June 1755   ish, Berkeley Co., gives JAMES LENNOX,

Bond of Performance   merchant, of Charleston, bond in penal sum of
Ŀ 2000 that his infant son, BENJAMIN SIMMONS,
shall within 6 months after reaching 21 years of age, convey good title
to LENNOX to his undivided third part of 500 a. (see p. 647 for details).
Whereas GEORGE SEAMAN & MARY his wife, & RACHAEL GOUGH, sold their 2 undivided third parts of said 500 a. to JAMES LENNOX; & whereas ANNE, wife
of BENJAMIN SIMMONS is dead, & her third part descends to her infant son,
BENJAMIN; & whereas BENJAMIN SIMMONS, the father has conveyed ANNE'S
third part to JAMES LENNOX for Ŀ 700 currency for the use of infant BEN-
JAMIN; now BENJAMIN, the father, promises that the son shall give full
conveyance on coming of age. Witnesses: ROBERT BROWN, JOHN CORDES. Before JACOB MOTTE, J.P. WILLIAM HOPTON, Register.

Book P-P, p. 663   ADAM DANIEL, planter, to JOHN PAUL GRIMKE,
20 June 1755   jeweler, of Charleston, for Ŀ 5750 currency,
Feoffment   part of lot #42 in Charleston, bounding S 31
ft. on Broad Street; W 90 ft. on MR. DE ST.
JULIEN; N on MRS. WATSON; E on JOHN MCKENSIE; also the corner part of lot
#14 bounding S 19 ft. 3 in. on Broad Street; W 83 ft. 6 in. on Union
Street; N on MARY PARKER; E on CAPT. KING (now MRS. HESKETT); with all
houses, etc. Witnesses: JOHN RATTRAY, CHARLES PINCKNEY. Before JACOB
MOTTE, J.P. WILLIAM HOPTON, Register. Plat dated 13 June 1755 by ROBERT
MCMURDY.

Book P-P, p. 666   ADAM DANIEL, JOHN DANIEL, planters, & THOMAS
20 June 1755   SMITH, SR., merchant, of Charleston, give JOHN
Bond   PAUL GRIMKE, jeweler, of Charleston, bond in
penal sum of Ŀ 5750 currency, that he may
quietly enjoy the property conveyed to him (see p. 663). Witnesses: JOHN
RATTRAY, CHARLES PINCKNEY. Before JACOB MOTTE, J.P. WILLIAM HOPTON,
Register.

Book P-P, p. 669   DRURY DUNN, planter, to ABRAHAM DUPONT, plant-
5 June 1754   er, both of Granville Co., for Ŀ 400 currency,
Feoffment   400 a. in Granville Co., granted DUNN 13 Feb.
1753; bounding W on MORGAN SABB; other sides
on vacant land. Witnesses: PAUL PORCHER, JAMES HARTLY. Before WILLIAM
SIMPSON, J.P. WILLIAM HOPTON, Register.

Book P-P, p. 671   WILLIAM GRAY, planter, & ELIZABETH (her mark)
12 & 7 (?) Sept. 1754   his wife, of Craven Co., to JAMES MCGIRT,
L & R   planter, of Fredericksburgh Township, for
Ŀ 220 currency, 350 a. in Fredericksburgh
Township, bounding SW on Wateree River; NW on JOHN BLACK & vacant land;
other sides on vacant land; which 350 a. were granted by Gov. JAMES GLEN
on 3 Apr. 1754 to WILLIAM GRAY. Before JOHN COOK, WILLIAM COLLINS, JAMES
(his mark) WOOD. Before SAMUEL WYLY, J.P. WILLIAM HOPTON, Register.

Book P-P, p. 679   ADAM DANIEL, planter, son of JOHN DANIEL, to
31 July 1755   HENRY PERONNEAU, gentleman, for Ŀ 1030 curren-
Feoffment   cy, part of a lot in Charleston, bounding W
107 ft. on King Street; N 231 ft. on DR. MAR-
TIN; E on estate of HENRY PERONNEAU; S on BARNARD ELLIOT (see p. 625).
Witnesses: THOMAS RAVEN, GEORGE JACKSON. Before JAMES GRINDLAY, J.P.
WILLIAM HOPTON, Register. Plat certified 19 July 1755 by WILLIAM WILKINS,
Sur.

Book P-P, p. 681   JONATHAN WILKINS, planter, of Edisto Island, &
8 & 9 July 1755   MARY his wife, to SUSANNAH LORIMER, wife of
L & R   CHARLES LORIMER (LORIMORE), minister of the
gospel, at Johns Island, for love & affection
& Ŀ 900 currency, 162-1/2 a. on Johns Island, bounding E on Stono River;
S on Abpoola Creek; W on THOMAS HUNSCOMBE & JOHN SPENCER; N on JOHN
HOLMES. Whereas by deed of settlement tripartite dated 3 June 1755 be-
tween CHARLES LORIMER, of 1st part; SUSANNA WEDDERBURN, widow, of 2nd
part; & WILLIAM WOODDROP, merchant, of 3rd part; CHARLES LORIMER "secur-
ed" SUSANNA'S real & personal estate; now WILKINS conveys 400 a. to SUSAN-
NAH. Witnesses: WILLIAM KEAN, SAMUEL MOUBRAY. Before WILLIAM SIMPSON,
J.P. WILLIAM HOPTON, Register.

Book P-P, p. 688   PATRICK CLARK, planter, & JANE (her mark) his
25 & 26 Nov. 1754   wife, of Berkeley Co., to WILLIAM GLEN & JOHN
L & R by Mortgage   COOPER, merchants, of Charleston, as security
                          on bond of even date in penal sum of Ł 3312
for payment of Ł 1656 currency, with interest, on 26 Nov. 1755; 40 a. in
Berkeley Co., with tenement thereon, commonly called the Quarter House,
formerly belonging to JOSEPH HAWKINS, bounding W & S on RALPH IZARD; E on
JOHN BIRD; N on PAUL GRIMBALL; also 4 Negro slaves. Witnesses: WILLIAM
MICHIE, JOHN REMINGTON. Before WILLIAM MURRAY, J.P. & Dep. Sur. See
Secretary's Book W.W. p. 609. WILLIAM HOPTON, Register.

Book P-P, p. 696   JOHN METHRINGHAM, planter, of Christ Church
18 Aug. 1755   Parish, to JOSEPH TOBIAS, shopkeeper, of
Assignment   Charleston. Whereas JOHN METHRINGHAM owns a
                          house (2 tenements) on the alley leading from
Union Street to Church Street, now occupied by GEORGE VANN, silversmith,
& a MR. FICKLING, shoemaker; which house METHRINGHAM has held for some
years past as tenant for life, by deed from JOHN BRETON, & has constantly
received the rents & profits for his own use; & whereas METHRINGHAM gave
JOSEPH TOBIAS a bond in the penal sum of Ł 547:10:0 for payment of
Ł 273:15:0 SC money, with interest on 1 Jan. 1756, which sum he cannot
pay, except by assigning to TOBIAS his life interest in said tenements
for as long as it would take for TOBIAS to recover the amount in rents, &
to repay TOBIAS for any repairs, etc., now METHRINGHAM makes the assignment. Witnesses: CHARLES PINCKNEY, JOSEPH BRAMBLE. Before CHARLES
PINCKNEY, J.P. WILLIAM HOPTON, Register.

Book P-P, p. 700   RAWLINS LOWNDES, P.M., to JOHN RATTRAY, ESQ.,
20 June 1753   of Charleston, at public auction, for Ł 2660
Sale   currency, part of a lot on Broad Street, in
                          Charleston. Whereas HENRY KENNAN, merchant,
of Charleston, owned a house & lot on N side of Broad Street, then oc-
cupied by MESSRS. DEWAR & MARSHALL; bounding S 30 ft. on Broad Street; E
& N on THOMAS SMITH, JR. (formerly JOSEPH WRAGG); W 100 ft. on a house of
MRS. ANN WATSON; which house KENNAN had purchased from JOHN RATTRAY &
HELEN his wife, by L & R dated 9 & 10 Mar. 1747; & whereas HENRY KENNAN &
DOUGAL CAMPBELL gave bond dated 5 Oct. 1751 to ANN WATSON, as executrix
of estate of JOHN WATSON, in penal sum of Ł 10,168:5:10 for payment of
Ł 5084:2:11 currency, with interest, on 1 Nov. then next; & whereas ANN
WATSON brought suit & recovered judgment, with costs, as recorded 13 Nov.
1751; & whereas a writ of fieri facias was issued by JAMES GRAME, C.J. on
7 July 1752, directing the P.M. to seize the real estate, goods & chattels of KENNAN & CAMPBELL & sell them for said debt; now the P.M. sells
said house & lot to RATTRAY. Witnesses: ALEXANDER MCGREGOR, WILLIAM
READ. Before DANIEL CRAWFORD, J.P. WILLIAM HOPTON, Register.

Book P-P, p. 706   JOHN JONES, merchant, of Charleston, brother &
11 Aug. 1755   sole executor of will of CHARLES JONES, plant-
Feoffment   er, of Wadmalaw, St. Johns Parish, of 1st part,
                          at public auction, to DANIEL CRAWFORD, WILLIAM
WOODRUP, GEORGE MARSHALL, GEORGE INGLIS, & JOHN RATTRAY, gentlemen, of
Charleston, of 2nd part; for Ł 1830 currency, part of lot #241 in Charleston, bounding N 237 ft. on "Scots Meeting"; S on JOHN FRASER; E 50 ft. on
Meeting Street, which piece of ground formerly belonged to CHARLES JONES;
who by will dated 3 Mar. last ordered all his real & personal estate to
be sold by his executors within 12 months after his death & appointed his
brother JOHN sole executor. Witnesses: WILLIAM HARVEY, GEORGE JACKSON.
Before JAMES GRINDLAY, J.P. WILLIAM HOPTON, Register.

Book P-P, p. 709   JAMES POSTELL, planter, of Colleton Co., to
18 May 1753   JAMES SKIRVING, planter, for Ł 50 currency,
Feoffment   23 a. in Colleton Co., bounding W on JAMES
                          POSTELL; other sides on JAMES SKIRVING; grant-
ed to WILLIAM OSWELL & by various mesne conveyances descended to POSTELL.
Witnesses: ADAM OULLIAT, JOSEPH PRINCE. Delivery by turf & twig. Before
HENRY HYRNE, J.P. WILLIAM HOPTON, Register.

Book P-P, p. 712   GEORGE JACKSON, planter, to JAMES SKIRVING,
3 Mar. 1749   planter, both of Colleton Co., for Ł 200 cur-
Feoffment   rency, 350 a. in Colleton Co., bounding W on

Horse Shoe Creek; N on heirs of JAMES MARTIN; E on DANIEL MCEVANS; S on
JAMES POSTELL & JAMES SKIRVING; which 350 a. were granted to DAVID ALLEN;
who conveyed to ROYAL SPRY; who, with his wife JEAN, conveyed to GEORGE
JACKSON by L & R dated 9 & 10 July 1742. Witnesses: JOSHUA SANDERS, DAN-
IEL JORDON. Delivery by turf & twig. Before HENRY HYRNE, J.P. WILLIAM
HOPTON, Register.

Book P-P, p. 715   CHARLES COLLETON, & SUSANNA his wife, to JOHN
26 & 27 Apr. 1755   HAMILTON, planter, both of Berkeley Co., for
L & R   ₺ 250 currency, 408 a. in Berkeley Co., bound-
                           ing N on JOHN GREEN; SW on MAJ. CHARLES COLLE-
TON; which land was granted by the Lords Proprs. on 9 Oct. 1718 to MAJ.
CHARLES COLLETON. Witnesses: BENJAMIN SINGLETON, THOMAS HUTCHINSON, JON-
ATHAN DUNNAVANT. Before WILLIAM HOPTON, J.P. & Pub. Reg.

Book P-P, p. 721   HUMPHREY SOMMERS, bricklayer, & SUSANNA his
29 & 30 June 1755   wife, to GEORGE SOMMERS, ESQ., both of
L & R   Charleston, for ₺ 4268:1:3 currency, 699-1/2
                           a. in Colleton Co., bounding according to
plat; which tract is part of a tract HUMPHREY SOMMERS purchased from BEN-
JAMIN HARVEY & JOHN HARVEY by L & R dated 20 & 21 Dec. 1751. Witnesses:
CHARLES PINCKNEY, WILLIAM MCPHERSON, SIMON SERJEANT. Before JACOB MOTTE,
J.P. WILLIAM HOPTON, Register. Plat showing 699-1/2 a. in 2 divisions
of 217 a. & 482-1/2 a.; bounding N on HUMPHREY SOMMERS; E on THOMAS RIG-
DON SMITH; S on estate of DANIEL GREEN; W on WILLIAM HARVEY.

Book P-P, p. 728   WILLIAM GLEN, merchant, of Charleston, to JOHN
16 May 1755   COOPER & ROBERT WILLIAMS, proprietors of the
Assignment   distillery in Charleston. Whereas COOPER gave
                           GLEN a bond dated 12 May 1755 in penal sum of
₺ 60,000 for payment of ₺ 30,000 SC money on 19 May next; & whereas GLEN
recovered a judgment against COOPER for said ₺ 60,000 & costs before JOHN
LINING, Ass't. Judge; & whereas COOPER & WILLIAMS then owned, jointly,
200 a. in Christ Church Parish, Berkeley Co., bounding E on COL. PARRIS
(formerly ROBERT COLLINS); S on Shem Creek; W on JOHN WATKINS; N on CAPT.
HERBERT; & whereas COOPER'S undivided share is bound by said judgment,
but it is not GLEN'S design that this joint estate be applied towards the
payment of his private debts, & being willing to relinquish his right
under the judgment; now GLEN, for ₺ 5, paid by COOPER & WILLIAMS, surrenders his claim to COOPER & WILLIAMS. Witnesses: WILLIAM MICHIE, ROBERT
WILLIAMS, JR. Before JACOB MOTTE, J.P. WILLIAM HOPTON, Register.

Book P-P, p. 730   JOHN COOPER & ROBERT WILLIAMS, to GEORGE
10 July 1755   INGLIS & JOSEPH PICKERING, merchants; all of
L & R by Mortgage   Charleston; as security on bond of even date
                           in penal sum of ₺ 1526:19:2 for payment of
₺ 763:9:7 SC money, with interest, on 1 Jan. 1756; 200 a. in Christ
Church Parish, Berkeley Co., bounding E on COL. PARRIS (formerly ROBERT
COLLINS); S on Shem Creek; W on JOHN WATKINS; N on CAPT. HERBERT. Wit-
nesses: WILLIAM ANDRUM, GEORGE ABBOLD HALL. Before JACOB MOTTE, J.P.
WILLIAM HOPTON, Register.

Book P-P, p. 763   JOHN BRAND, gentleman, to HALLAM DELAMERE &
5 & 6 Apr. 1736   ELIZABETH BAMPFIELD, widow; all of Charleston;
L & R   for ₺ 1300 currency, that lot in Charleston
                           bounding N 100 ft. on Queen (Dock) Street; E
41 ft. on street leading from Ashley River to the broad path; W on LYDIA
WARE; S on JOHN BRAND. Witnesses: JAMES GRAME, THOMAS BECKETT. Before
BENJAMIN SMITH, J.P. WILLIAM HOPTON, Register.

BEALE, cont'd:
  Othniel cont'd: 240,248
   250,253,258,260,261,269
   270,271,276,280,285,295
   303,305,336
BEALLE, Othniel 199
BEAMOR, Jacob 148,207
  John 203
BEAN, John 98
BEARD, Elizabeth 159,160
  Mathew 236
  Matthew 159,160
BEATTY, John 183
  William 335
BEAUCHAMP, Adam 68,132,328
  Elizabeth 170
  Stephen 269,270
BEAVILL, Anne 288
  Timothy 288
BEAZLEY, Thomas 183,295
BECKET, Thomas 50
BECKETT, Thomas 361
BECKMAN, John 49,141
  Mr. 96,114
BEDON, George 3,166,347
  Henry 3,80,105,166,177
   185,186,264,299
  John Raven 264,292
  Magdalene 36
  Mary Ann 105,185
  Richard 34,57,154,177,
   193,329,336,340,341
  Richard, Sr. 105
  Stephen 27,62,156
   Stephen, Jr. 165,264
BEE, John 12,20,29,31,69,
  71,90,91,108,123,128,
  133,137,181,208,210,245
  299,334,353
  John, Jr. 69
  Joseph 97,98
  Martha 91,136,182
  Mathew 90,91,245,335
  Matthew 334,335
  Mrs. 117
  Susanna 299
  Thomas 90,91,219
  William 185
BEECH, Christopher 113,147
  Grace 147
  John 147
  Joseph 147
BEEKITT, Thomas 20
BEEKMAN, John 10,211,240
BEEN, John 263
BEESTON, William 79
BELIN, Allard 1,182,236,
  237
  James 1,182,206,236,237
  Sarah 182,206,237
  William 1,182
  William Danforth 171
BELL, Andrew 28,41,155
  Ann 81
  Daniel 55
  Duke 97,101
  George 55
  Jacob 177
  John 81,101,126,177
  Marmaduke 87,354
  Martha 87
  Mathew 354
BELLAMY, Ann 123
  Anne 56,92
  Catherine 73
  Mary 56,92,122,189
  Saray 56
  Thomas 73
  Timothy 56,92,122,189
   217
BELLINGER, E. 51
  Edmond 89,90,91,95,149
  178,193,319

BELLINIGER, cont'd:
  Edmund 10,11,18,19,33,
  39,47,56,69,72,74,75,91
  95,115,118,120,135,144
  150,154,170,174,198,204
  217,226,227,241,256,264
  265,277,289,290,296,305
  317,339,347
  Edward 51,240
  Elizabeth 33,39,69,72,
  89,90,91,92,95,120,150
  170,174,204,240,241,264
  339,347
  George 91,95,120,130,
  174,240,264,265
  John 204
  Margaret 277
  Mary Lucia 170,204,241
  Mr. 245
  William 240
BENFIELD, Elizabeth 332
BENISON, (Maj.) 144
  George, Jr. 43
  George, Sr. 43
  George 20,35,139,162,
  221,225
  Richard 225
BENJAMIN, Moses 329
BENNET, George 79
  John 144
  Thomas 214
BENNETT, Alexander 110,332
  Anne 253
  John 66,281,314,342,347
  349
  Mary 314
  Moses 177
  Thomas 253,309
BENNISON, George 127,199,
  225,347
  Richard 199,347
  William 199,225,347
BENNY, Thomas 259
BENOIST, Charles 1,60,301
  Daniel 52
  James 227
  John 227
  Peter 52,53,62,110,113
  151,180,187,237
  Samuel 227
BENSON, Capt. 262
  George 254
  Mary 38,99
BENSTONE, John 53,180
BENTLEY, George 42
BENYSON, Charles 225
BERENS, (?) 268
BERESFORD, John 173,269,
  270
  Mr. 153
  Richard 15,33,71,92,179
  193,194,217,256,257
BERISFORD, Richard 309
BERNALL, Jacob 177
BERNARD, James 234
BERNEAU, Paul 207
BERRESFORD, Richard 354
BERRIE, James 64,220,328
  Purchess 220
BERRINGER, John 62,152
BERRINGES, John 152
BERRISFORD, John 91
  Mr. 316
BERTIE, Edward 45,314
BESSELLEN, Mark Anthony
  150,159
BESSELLEU, Mark Anthony
  266
BESSELLUE, Anthony 344
BESWICK, John 114,357
BESWICKE, John 109,283
  Mr. 284
  Thomas 170

BETHAL, Slingsby 156
BETSON, Mary 132,328
BETTESON, Catherine 120
BETTISON, David 169,172
  Jonathan 221
  William 73
BEVILL, Ann 288
BEVILL, Timothy 288
BEZELEY, Thomas 122
BIGGS, Thomas 79
BILBEAU, James 262
  Susannah 262
BILBOA, James 160
BILLIALD, John 33
BILLING, Hester 139
  Zenobia 32
BILNEY, John 39,305
BINFORD, Thomas 177
BINO, Michael 44
BIRCH, Thomas 204
  William 284
BIRD, John 93,133,331,360
  Patrick 29,36
BIRMAN, Christopher 53
BISSET, William 337
BISSETT, Mary 210
BLACK, Ann 207
  Christopher 214
  David 49,129
  John 231,334,359
  Joseph 185,186,207,243,
  311,318,352,354
  Unity 231
BLAIR, David 144
  Wade 326
BLAKE, Col. 340
  John 147,150,272
  Joseph 10,24,33,35,36,
  46,57,86,89,110,111,139
  140,176,187,215,257,259
  276,281,307,311,313,315
  322,336,340
  Lady 340
  Richard 264
BLAKEWAY, Sarah 260,309
  William 309,350
BLAKEWEY, Ann 26
  Sarah 72,73,144,194,280
  309
  William 72
BLAMYER, John 123,162,267
  Mary 49,144
BLANCOES, Noah Hurt 198
BLAND, Mr. 317
BLEAR, James 292
BLEWER, John 242
BLINCOE, Samuel 289
BLISS, John 229
  Mary 229
BLUNDELL, John 30
  Thomas 10,269,270,271,
BLUNDY, Charles 306
BLYTH, Robert 73
  Thomas 269,270
BLYTHE, Joseph 139
  Thomas 40,52,70,77,125,
  185,220,249
  William 249
BOCHET, Anthony 323
  Nicholas 52
  Samuel 325
BOCHETT, Henry 160
  Peter 160
BOCKET, Samuel 263
BOCKETT (BOCQUET), Peter
  243
BOCKETT, Peter 243
BOCQUET, Peter 14,77,96,
  345
BOCQUETT, Peter 230,269,
  290
BODDICOT, Richard 157
BODDICOTT, Richard 37

BODDINGTON, George 127
BODETT, Mr. 195
BODICOT, Richard 157
BODICOTT, Richard 93
BOGAR, Mrs. 337
BOGGS, James 179,327
   John 39,49,107,249,320
   Thomas 101
BOHANNON, John 208
   William 202
BOHUN, Elizabeth 277
   Margaret 277
   Mary 277
   Nicholas 277
BOINEAU, Michael 264
BOISSAN, John 70
BOISSEAU, James 267
   John 80
BOLEM, Susanna 3
   Thomas 3,269,270
BOLLEUGH, William 328
BOLLOUGH, William 222
BOLLOW, John 175
BOLTON, Elizabeth 305
   James 109,189
   Mr. 124,170
   Thomas 45,93,123,142,
   167,169,188,189,191,200
   225,305
BOLTUS, Mr. 198
BOND, Abraham 269,270,307
   Capt., 20,45
   JCO. 100
   Jacob 27,43,47,79,81,
   221,233,287,288,289,334
   James 254
   Susannah 43
BONELL, Mary 217,289
BONEY, Martha 247
BONGHAR, Mrs. 304
BONHOISE, Jonas 199
BONHOIST, John 199
   Jonas 221
BONHOST, Jane 225
   Jonah 225
BONHOSTE, Catherine 328
   Elizabeth 254,328
   Jonah 347
   Jonas 116,254,328
   Mary 328
   Susannah 328
BONIFOT, Isaac 350
BONNEAHEAU, John 166
BONNEAU, Anthony, Jr. 29,
   52,76
   Anthony 3,10,14,15,17,
   42,43,50,52,55,59,85,
   113,133,158,194,199,205
   221,241,248,254,279,316
   318,324
   Elias 42,345
   Henry 89,205,264
   Jacob 52,55,158
   Jane Elizabeth 14,15
   Jane 52,55,158
   John Henry 231
   John 42,95,243
   Margaret Henrietta 85
   Mary 158
   Peter 144,351
BONNELL, John 17,60,155
BONNETHEAU, J. 304
   John 41,101,282,307
BONNIE, Capt. 100
BONNIT, John 55
BONNITHEAU, John 113
BONNOIT, Jean 16
   John 42,181
   Magdalene 181
BONNY, Ann 17
   Capt. 161
   Ruth 17,340
   Thomas, Jr. 199,295

BONNY, cont'd:
   Thomas 17,28,59,116,129
   292,340
BONOIST, Peter 48
BOON (BOONE), Mrs. 262
BOON, Ann 311
   Capers 227
   Joseph 17,24,85,327
   Maj. 195,237
   Mrs. 159
   William, Jr. 237
   William 163,227
BOONE, Ann 183
   Anne 310,314
   Capers 222
   Charles 310
   James 154,209
   Joseph 180,299,310,315
   Madam 133
   Mr. 90,172,225
   Mrs. 273
   Thomas, Jr. 268
   Thomas 18,20,222,287,
   288,289,310,334
   William, Jr. 171
   William 49,89,119,156,
   162,164,190,227,317
BOONEAU, Mr. 198
BOONS, Joseph 67
BOOTH, Connor 157,163,171,
   172
   John 346
   Katherine 21
   Martha 6,13,211
   Robert 6
BORDEAUX, James 223,257
BORLAND, William 16,131
BORLEN, William 269,270
BORNAU, Elie 54
BOSAM, Mr. 349
BOSCKET, Nicholas 263
BOSOMWORTH, Susannah 293
BOSSARD, Henry, Jr. 290
BOSWOOD, James 55,64,76,
   254,349
   Joseph 64
   Margaret 349
   Martha 76,349
   Samuel 254
   Sindiniah 254
   William 64
BOUDON, Leo Paul 39
   Leopold 130,133,145,151
   165,191,341
BOUGHAR, Mr. 101
BOUGUARD, Mr. 99
BOULD, William 122
BOULOUX, James 304
BOURGARD, Mr. 337
BOURGATT, Daniel 102
BOURGET, Daniel 15,107,146
   154,166,175,230,290
BOURGETT, Daniel 101,102,
   230,269,270
   Daniel 267
   Susanna 230
BOURGIN, Benedict 342
   David 342
   John 342
BOURQUIN, Benedict 154,296
   Jann Judah 296
   John Louis 296
BOUSHAR, Mrs. 87
BOWEN, Christian 98
BOWEN, Thomas 98,346
BOWER, Elizabeth 58
   Henry 58
   Sarah 214
   Thomas 214
   William 58,182,214,215,
   326
BOWERS, Giles 12,177
   Martha 12

BOWLARD, William 217
BOWMAN, Thomas 28,155,203
   William 54
BOWRY, Joseph 154
BOX, James 321
   Philip 185,186,356
BOYD, Abraham 274
BOYKIN, Edward 308,344
   Henry 344
BOYTON, Henry 251
BRABANT, Elizabeth 245
   Isaac 342
BRACKAU, John 259
BRACKAS, Sarah 163
   William 163
BRADDOCK, David Cutler
   137
BRADFORD, William 88
BRADLEY, Henry 181
   James 136
   William 80,81
BRADWELL, Isaac 236
   Jacob 55,65,66
   Rebecca 236
BRADY, Daniel 314
BRAGGINS, William 274
BRAILFORD, Edward, Jr.
   207
BRAILSFORD, Elizabeth 86
   Joseph 116
   Mr. 210
   Samuel 111,319
BRAMBLE, Joseph 360
BRAND, John 20,34,52,141,
   250,361
   Mr. 140
   Thomas 52
BRANFORD, Barnaby 35,36,39
   160,182,312,349
   Burnaby 186,202,206,236
   Elizabeth 296
   John 143
   MARTHA 182
   Mary 182,202
   William, Jr. 19,139,150
   182,201,202,206
   William, Sr. 179,201
   William 18,19,35,38,142
   154,155,160,182,201,202
   206,224,296
BRANNEAU, Paul 173
BRASFORD, James 318
BRAY, John 303
BRAYBANT, Dr. 317
BRAZIER, Zachariah 229,290
   337,351
BREADY (BRADY), Daniel 314
BREBANT, Daniel 84,223,351
   Elizah 102
BREDY (BREADY), William
   280
BREDY, William 281
BREMAN, Francis 15
BREMAR(?), Francis 43
BREMAR, Elizabeth 14,15,32
   43,193
   Francis 69,160,280,283,
   303
   James 14,33,52,,55,61,
   160,223
   Martha 29,160
   Mrs. 33
   Peter 15,160,200,223,
   351,352
   Sarah 223
   Solomon 160,200,223,263
   351,352
BREMER, James 158
BREMMAR, Solomon 317
BRENEAU, Paul 207
BRENEN, Michael 314
BRETALL, Madam 194
BRETELL, Madam 122,124,189

BRETELL, Madam cont'd:
196,266
BRETON, John 7,14,107,353,
360
BREWER, William 231
BREWINGTON, Col. 46
BREWTON, Col. 177,127
Mary 91,114,122,189,216
339
Miles 10,17,21,22,38,78
86,91,122,174,185,189,
227,244,283,292,293,311
339,352
Millicent 93
Robert, Jr. 9,10,29,30,
31,38,81,93,144,257
Robert, Sr. 81,93,144
Robert 20,28,51,114,186
215,339
Susannah 283
BRICKLES, Richard 172
Sarah 172
BRINAN, Lydia 233
Thomas 233
BRINOUN, Michael 248
Patrick 248
BRISBANE, Margaret 336
Robert 28,41,109,153,
353
William 29,166,207,336,
340,341,353
BRITTON, Francis 127
Sarah 146
BROCKENBURG, Charles   210
BROCKET, Peter 263
BROCKHAS, Sarah 172
William 172
BROCKINGTON, Capt.10,90
Daniel 301
Elizabeth 139
John 329,354
Mr. 153
Thomas 12
William 12,13,28,57,76,
87,155,321
BROCKINTON, William 38,207
BRODWELL, Jacob 55
BROOK, Martin Glaze 236
BROOKS, Mangus 213
BROUGHTON, Capt. 69
Alexander 273,279
Andrew 74,75,150,211,
269,270,273,278
Charlotte Henrietta
146
Edward 50
John 15
Mary 273
Mrs. 274
Nathaniel 68,69,74,75,
146,174,196,238,269,270
273,278,279,293
Thomas, Jr. 91,211
Thomas 1,2,6,8,10,11,15
18,26,27,35,40,49,57,60
69,74,75,76,77,87,89,96
103,107,108,109,116,126
127,128,130,133,139,155
156,161,164,168,181,183
189,194,199,200,205,209
214,215,217,221,225,227
229,238,259,273,275,278
292,296,301,321,325,336
344
BROWN, (Land) 25
Alexander 67,121
Ann 77
Christianna 61
David 273,357
Edward 242
Henry 246
James 319
John, Jr. 61

BROWN, cont'd:
John 2,25,61,62,87,117
176,197,219,273
Jonathan 197
Joseph 77,177,240,307,
329
Judith 61
Margaret 141,142,166
Mr. 191,301
Nathaniel 25,40,61,62,
129,142,180,202,206,
272,291
Patrick 210,240,241
Peter 119
Robert 42,44,53,217,
227,230,292,358,359
Talbert 114
Tolbot 141,142
Thomas 77,92,108,127
William 2,84,101,121,
166,215,253,354
BROWNE, Clement 81
John 53,308,316
Nathaniel 87
BROWNELL, John 288
BROZETT (BROZET), James
90
BRUCE, Ann 260
James 291
John 127,183,295
William 12,14,93,160,
210
BRUEAU, Marianne 276
BRUNEAU, Henry 43,55
Paul 3,36,67,68,103,
173,264,267
BRUNET, Esaie 140,174,177
344,346
Susanah Mary 140
BRUNNEAU, Paul 95,96,112,
222
BRUNO (BRUNEAU), Paul
276
BRUNSON, Abigail 236,339
Ann 78
David 278
Ebenezer 236
Isaac 278
John 160,236,354
Joseph, Jr. 206
Joseph 35,236
Margaret 278
Mary 278
BRUSE, John 313
BRYAN, Anne 184
Arthur 345
Hugh 12,13,19,23,24,28
58,95,134,137,138,140,
154,184,192,204,241,
266,317,347
James 155
Jonathan 92,99,120,154
174,184,192,221,241,
292
Joseph 6,23,24,38,39,
58,95,103,104,154,184,
317,347
Martha 182
Mary 14,104,138,154,
184,192,228,258
Mrs. 38,305
BRYEN, John 273
BRYON, Mary 14
BUCHANAN, William, Jr.
237
William 67,70,83,86,90
150,201,274,314
BUCHANON, William 201
BUCKLE, Jacob 308
BUCKLES, Jacob 344
BUCKLEY, (Widow) 186
Charles 315
Grace 200,238,256

BUCKLEY, cont'd:
John 7
Katherin 7
Phillip 262
Widow 218,219
BUER, James 11,77
Thomas 11,313,327
William Melvin 11
BUGNIAN, Ralph 60
BUGNION, Joseph 3
Ralph 204,268
BULL, Arthur 91,95
Barnaby 115,286,317,319
Burnaby 286
Elizabeth 24,154,170,
204,241
Fenwick 341
Fenwicke 13,70,118,179,
321
John, Jr. 88,142
John 7,18,55,57,64,65,
95,114,120,170,174,241,
317,326,328,347
Judith 161,164,165
Mary H. 136,146,197
Mary Henrietta 53
Mary 35,53,57,164,291
Mr. 130,136,225
Stephen, Jr. 103
Stephen 6,35,53,57,61,
62,103,104,118,142,146,
155,161,164,165,180,184
201,202,265,286,305,317
347,348
Tredwell 325
William, Jr. 6,25,33,38
39,47,53,56,62,103,104,
119,146,184,213,291
William Tredwell 137,
194
William 1,2,5,7,30,32,
35,37,39,40,41,45,47,52
53,54,55,57,58,60,61,62
65,67,74,75,87,88,95,
107,115,116,118,136,144
157,164,167,170,172,175
176,178,179,184,202,208
227,233,236,240,241,256
265,273,286,295,296,305
319,320,326,330,334,336
350
BULLARD, Edward 13,34,93,
94,211,239
Elizabeth 34
Griffith 157,162
BULLEN, John 358
Thomas 347
BULLINE, Nathaniel 353
Thomas, Sr. 162
Thomas 95,109
BULLOCH, Anne 284
James 23,55,245,284,285
286
John 93
Mary 93
BULLOCK, Ann   334
Anne 129
James 41,60,85,120,126,
129,162,175,179,220,235
245,246,259,269,276,287
303,313,314,318,334,335
358
John 51,299
Mary 51,93
Mr. 181
Stephen Pemil 222
BUR, Thomas 79
BURCHALL, Joseph 90
BURCHAM, Samuel 43
BURD, William 97
BURDELL, John 169
BURDOC, Mr. 103
BURETELL, Elizabeth 217

DUBOSE, cont'd:
    Mr. 44
    Peter 95
    Stephen 95
    Susannah 254
DUBOUDIEU, Anthony 84
DUBOURDIER, Joseph 300,338
    Mr. 279
DUBOURDIEU, Joseph 67,109,
    199,215,247,261,283,301
    321
    Mr. 191
    Peter 40
    Samuel 199,215
DUCAT, George 154,204,299
    Martha 90
DUCATT, George 98,105,128
    Robert 5
DUCKATT, Mr. 93
DUCKET, George 186
DUFFEY, Astis (Anties)
    116
    Hugh 59,116
DUGU, Mr. 184
DUM, Drury 317
DUMARY, Peter 173,241,264
DUMONS, Isaac 196
DUNBAR, Charles 131
    Jean 44,89
    Walter 44,89,178
DUNCAN, John 28
DUNHAM, John 15
DUNLAP, William 315
DUNLAPE, James 28
DUNN, Catherine 231
    Drury 359
DUNNAHO, James 55
DUNNAVANT, Jonathan 361
DUNNOVAN, Daniel 311
DUPLESSES, Andre 94
    Anne 94
    Elisha 94
    Elizabeth 94
    Lydia 94
    Margaret 94
    Peter 94
DUPONT, Abraham 45,130,164
    199,252,317,333,359
    Alexander 94,193
    Ann 130
    Gideon 45,199
    Jane 45
DUPRE, Josiah Gar. 75,76
    Josiah Garnier 354
    Josias Gar. 71
DUPREE, Cornelius 120
    Josias Gar. 19
    Samuel 214
DUPREY, Jane 187
DUPUY, Jane 142,209
DUPY, Andrew 90
DUQUE, Mr. 105
DURAND, Levi 27,290,322
    Susannah 290
DURANT, Henry 3
    John 301
DURARQUE, John 241
DURFFEY, Hugh 144
DURHAM, (?) 161
    John 340
    Lydia 65
DUTAQUE, John 241
DUTARQUE, John, Jr. 241
    John 10,29,136,153,182,
    205
    Lewis 17,29,32,136,193,
    340
    Mr. 241
    Noah 239
DUTART, Daniel 44
    Mary 44
    Mr. 351
DUTCH, Robert 48

DUVAL, Catherine 125
    David 35,57,233
    John 125
DUVOIS, Mr. 221
DWEICK, Henry 43
DWIGHT, __el 270
    Daniel 74,75,191,269,
    273,278,279,295,317
    Thomas 273
DYEL, Mary 56
    Thomas 56
DYER, Jeane 116
DYMES, Robert 232,349
    Thomas 11,47,280
DYSON, Ely 273,337

EADE, James 187
EADES, James 142
EASTON, Thomas 204,205
EATON, Jonas 303
    Joshua 303
    Samuel 94,303
    Sarah 303
EBBERSON, William 221
EBERSON, William 169
ECALLES, Robert 199
EDDINGS, Abraham 68
    Theodora 68
    William, Jr. 68
    William, Sr. 68
    William 55,97,137
EDDLESTONE, Susanna 7
EDEN, James 116
EDES, James 80,153,248,
    344
    Penelope 153
EDGAR, Edward 168
    Samuel 99,166,227
EDGELL, Mary 321
EDIN, William 274
EDINGS, Mr. 188
    William 1,28,43,82,114
    298
EDINS, William 274
EDWARD, John 245
EDWARDS, Ann 218,295
    Edward 186,238
    Isaac 302,355,356
    John 36,179,185,245,
    246,254,281,299,345
    Mary 238
    Newel 186,200,238
    Newell 199
    Richard 203
    Sophia 302
    William Newitt 277,295
    William 186
ELBERT, William 137,296
ELCOCK, John 267
ELDERS, John 113,217
ELDERTON, James 165,325
ELFE, Thomas 315
ELING, Thomas 73
ELIOT, Thomas, Sr. 332
ELJAU, Francis 206
ELLERY, Ann 172,210,211,
    239,276,350
    Anne 80,89,156,190,232
    285
    George 211
    Thomas 31,34,37,68,80,
    89,106,107,110,156,172
    239,276,285,303,344
ELLIAS, Mary 33
ELLICOT, Joseph 16
ELLICOTT, Joseph 30,31,48
    311
    William 31,80
ELLIIOTT, Mr. 188
ELLIOT, Barnard 330,331,
    337,359
    Beulah 13
    Elizabeth 63,339,340

ELLIOT, cont'd:
    John 336,340
    Joseph 62,322,331,332
    Stephen 322
    Thomas, L. 332
    Thomas, Sr. 326
    Thomas 13,322,325,326
    William 117,322,330,332
    339,348
ELLIOTT, Amarentia 255
    Ann 127
    Artemas 196
    Artimas 139
    Barnard 21,41,42,185,
    190,198,199,202,224,239
    243,256,357
    Benjamin 180,201,202,
    224,227,239,256,259
    Bernard 16,95
    Beulah 124
    Champernoon 18,272
    Edmund 256
    Elizabeth Bellinger
    118,150,155,240
    Elizabeth 120,213,240,
    243,256,260,264,265,276
    Esther 18,38,39,149,150
    296
    Frances 15,21
    Francis 150
    Grey 302
    Hester 91
    Humphrey 139
    Jehu 258
    John Pendarvis 256
    John 105,255,256
    Joseph 16,21,30,37,39,
    109,112,125,151,163,202
    224,231,256,260,277
    Katherine 19
    Mary 139,196,256,260
    Mr. 61,120
    Robert 196
    Samuel 21,190,202,224,
    256
    Stephen 161,263
    Susanna 46
    Thomas, Jr. 9,10,11,46
    Thomas, Sr. 137,194
    Thomas 6,11,19,25,31,37
    46,61,64,65,108,109,112
    117,118,120,124,125,127
    135,145,158,163,180,185
    197,201,202,210,224,227
    240,255,256,258,263,264
    276,293,355
    Umphrey 88
    William, Sr. 190,239
    William 6,15,19,21,30,
    39,42,80,91,95,115,124,
    125,129,139,150,164,176
    184,187,191,197,199,202
    206,210,220,224,227,243
    255,259,260,263
ELLIS, Catherine 235
    John, Jr. 203
    John, Sr. 156
    John 156
    Judith 156
    Mary 33,48,49,151,180,
    187,257,298,355
    Morgan 255,302
    Robert 119,235,269,270
    Thomas 142,251
    William 64,160,171,322
ELMES, Ann 170
    Benjamin 47
    Ralph 187
    Samuel 47,254,333
    Thomas 46,158,170,254,
    333
EMMES, Hezekiah 286
    Ralph 296

HUST, Elizabeth 272
HUTCHENS, Mr. 174
HUTCHENSON, James 226
HUTCHINS, Elizabeth 135,
    227,229,252
    John 106,135,136,146,
    158,213,227,229,252
    Joseph 344,346
    Juhn 135
    Sarah 158
HUTCHINSON, Ann 135
    Anne 299
    Edward 181
    James 37
    John 8,21,71,110,127,
    135,169,188,299
    Providence 148
    Ribton 41,72,134,148
    Ripton 353
    Thomas 135,288,298,315,
    349
HUTCHISON, Thomas 361
HUTNER, George 132
HUTSON, William 170,184,
    241
HYDE, Mary 241
    Mr. 155,233
    William 233
HYRNE, Burrel 292
    Elizabeth Clarke 289
    Henry 18,86,90,91,109,
    133,147,158,169,172,193
    194,204,247,263,266,277
    289,290,292,332,360,361

I'ON, Richard 199
IMDORFF, John 113
    Magdalene 113
INDERABNET, John 268
INGLIS, George 298,360,361
INNS, Thomas 6,7,53
IOOR, Catherine 42,177
    John 52,181,257,267
    Mary 52
IRBY, Edmund 346
IRVING, Elizabeth 337
    James 223,337
IRVINS, James 292
IRWIN, William 39
ISAACS, Solomon 357,358
ISARD, Ralph 22
IZARD, Benjamin 47
    Charles 74,75
    George 47
    Henry 11,74,75,115,147,
    148,149,151,152,176,183
    184,185,267
    John 317
    Joseph 174,305,317
    Magdalene Elizabeth
    146
    Magdelene Eliz. 74
    Ralph 18,46,47,74,75,80
    84,93,146,151,152,165,
    168,176,185,193,226,227
    232,254,255,257,306,311
    317,331,336,337,339,347
    360
    Thomas 317
    W. 10
    Walter, Jr. 185
    Walter 35,57,267,317,
    324

JACKSON, Ann 198
    George 41,44,78,85,102,
    126,177,203,208,267,293
    309,324,326,327,340,349
    359,360,361
    Grace 274
    Hannah 128
    Henry 36,183,198
    James 198

JACKSON, cont'd:
    Jane 44
    John 44,78,126,198,208,
    242,274,284,324
    Joseph 267,324
    Mary 127,128,203,242,
    327
    Miles 242,322
    Mr. 134
    Mrs. 318
    Philamon/Philemon 324,
    327
    Reginold 116,126,137,
    183,198,324
    Reginall 183
    Richard 127,128,241,242
    308
    Samuel 183
    Sarah 128
    Thomas 324
    William 183
JAMES, Francis 334
    John 334
    Thomas 177,335
    William 75,96,99,140,
    166,177,197,218,223,242
    278,281,308,321,346
JAMESON, John 281
JAMISON, John 162
JAMSON, Anne 293
    Thomas 293
JANEWAY, William 128
JARMAN, Edward 41
JARRARD, Christopher 289
JAUDON, Daniel, Jr. 35
    Daniel 14,96,120,152,
    255,268
    Elias 2,14,268
    Elizabeth 268
    Marian 14
    Mary Ann 14
JEAN, Michael 98
JEANERETT, Jacob 267
JEANES, Michael 37,56,211
JEANNERET, Abraham 296
    Henri 174
    Jacob 96,97,152,153,
    173,189,252
    Margaret/Margarett
    96,97,152,153,173
JEFFERDS (JEFFORDS), John
    25
JEFFERDS, Margaret 25
JEFFERYES, William 246
JEFFORDS, John 263
    Mary 263
JENINS, Thomas 84
JENKINS, Edward 82,125
    Elizabeth 50,125,353
    James 128
    Jane 85
    John 76,187,292
    Joseph 233
    Martha 326
    Mary 50
    Richard 284,326
    Thomas 39,60,143
    William 97,214
JENNER, John 143
JENNINGS, John 274
    Samuel 269,270
JENNYS, Paul 264
JENYS, (Mr.) 24
    (Mrs.) 27
    Elizabeth (Mrs.) 152
    Elizabeth 6,11,16,27,93
    264
    Mr. 122,124,189,194,
    196,207,266
    Paul 53,111,123,133,267
    Thomas 6,16,23,57,58
JERDON, Abraham 158
JERMAN, Edward 183,348

JERMAN, cont'd:
    Ralph 10,85,173
JEWING, Mary 143
    Thomas 143
JEWNING, Thomas 193,272
JINKS, Thomas 173,218
    Violet 218
JOACHIM, Palthaser 241
JOANS, Thomas 79
JOHNSON (JOHNSTON),
    Robert 69
JOHNSON, John 356
    (Gov) 90
    Andrew 107,143,192
    Claud 196
    David 278
    Elizabeth 308,356
    Gov. 25
    James 143
    Jane 308,356
    John 5,7,13,64,70,302,
    308,355,356
    Katherine 7
    Margaret 74,75,308,356
    Nathaniel 5,7,10,17,35
    39,53,57,58,60,61,81,
    111,168,172,197,233,
    263,266,274,279,286,
    287,291,292,296,326,
    327,349,354,358
    Peter, Sr. 223
    Peter 17,84,143,249,
    295,340
    Robert 4,8,18,26,37,47
    51,58,70,74,82,83,90,
    96,103,106,111,116,122
    123,140,146,194,212,
    213,221,226,229,238,
    261,293,294,314,327,
    346,351,354
    Sarah 69,87,122,308,
    356
    Thomas 15,100,210,330,
    354
    William 80
JOHNSTON, Andrew 69,107,
    121,175,192,193,202,
    207,292,301
    Archibald 107,121,214,
    225,228
    David 80
    Esther 344
    John 65,69
    Mary 320
    Robert 253,269,270,
    271,317,318,337,338
    Sarah 154,219,304
JOHNSTONE, Peter 249
JOHSTON, Archibald 344
JOLLIFF, James 119,120
JOLLITT, James 51
JONES, Ann 195
    Ansty 42
    Benjamin 199
    Charles 39,47,62,130,
    139,150,158,257,276,
    350
    Dorothy 37,87,179,180
    Edward 322,345
    Francis 288
    Hannah 179
    James 196
    John 38,56,140,167,174
    195,220,320,321,323,
    352,360
    Lewis 160,248
    Mary 179
    Mr. 20,34,38,119,144
    Philip 20,45
    Priscilla 62
    Rachel 47
    Rebecca 148,301
    Robert 313

www.ingramcontent.com/pod-product-compliance
Lightning Source LLC
Chambersburg PA
CBHW021844020426
42334CB00013B/180